2015
NOVEL & SHORT STORY WRITER'S MARKET

includes a 1-year online subscription to **Novel & Short Story Writer's Market** on

Where & How to Sell What You Write

THE ULTIMATE MARKET RESEARCH TOOL FOR WRITERS

To register your *2015 Novel & Short Story Writer's Market* book and **start your 1-year online genre-only subscription**, scratch off the block below to reveal your activation code, then go to www.WritersMarket.com. Find the box that says "Have an Activation Code?" then click on "Sign Up Now" and enter your contact information and activation code. It's that easy!

UPDATED MARKET LISTINGS FOR YOUR INTEREST AREA
EASY-TO-USE SEARCHABLE DATABASE • RECORD-KEEPING TOOLS
PROFESSIONAL TIPS & ADVICE • INDUSTRY NEWS

Your purchase of *Novel & Short Story Writer's Market* gives you access to updated listings related to this genre of writing (valid through 12/31/15). For just $9.99, you can upgrade your subscription and get access to listings from all of our best-selling Market Books. Visit **www.WritersMarket.com** for more information.

WritersMarket.com

Where & How to Sell What You Write

Activate your WritersMarket.com subscription to get instant access to:

- **UPDATED LISTINGS IN YOUR WRITING GENRE:** Find additional listings that didn't make it into the book, updated contact information, and more. WritersMarket.com provides the most comprehensive database of verified markets available anywhere.

- **EASY-TO-USE SEARCHABLE DATABASE:** Looking for a specific magazine or book publisher? Just type in its name. Or widen your prospects with the Advanced Search. You can also search for listings that have been recently updated!

- **PERSONALIZED TOOLS:** Store your best-bet markets, and use our popular recording-keeping tools to track your submissions. Plus, get new and updated market listings, query reminders, and more—every time you log in!

- **PROFESSIONAL TIPS & ADVICE:** From pay-rate charts to sample query letters, and from how-to articles to Q&A's with literary agents, we have the resources writers need.

YOU'LL GET ALL OF THIS WITH YOUR INCLUDED SUBSCRIPTION TO

WritersMarket.com

Where & How to Sell What You Write

2015

NOVEL & SHORT STORY WRITER'S MARKET

Rachel Randall, Editor

WRITER'S DIGEST
BOOKS

WritersDigest.com
Cincinnati, Ohio

Publisher: Phil Sexton

Writer's Market website: www.writersmarket.com

Writer's Digest website: www.writersdigest.com

Distributed in Canada by Fraser Direct
100 Armstrong Avenue
Georgetown, Ontario, Canada L7G 5S4
Tel: (905) 877-4411

Distributed in the U.K. and Europe by F&W Media International
Brunel House, Newton Abbot, Devon, TQ12 4PU, England
Tel: (+44) 1626-323200, Fax: (+44) 1626-323319
E-mail: postmaster@davidandcharles.co.uk

Distributed in Australia by Capricorn Link
P.O. Box 704, Windsor, NSW 2756 Australia
Tel: (02) 4577-3555

ISSN: 0897-9812
ISBN-13: 978-1-59963-841-6
ISBN-10: 1-59963-841-X

Attention Booksellers: This is an annual directory of F+W Media, Inc. Return deadline for this edition is December 31, 2015.

Edited by: Rachel Randall
Cover designed by: Claudean Wheeler
Designed by: Geoff Raker
Production coordinated by: Greg Nock and Debbie Thomas

CONTENTS

FROM THE EDITOR 1

HOW TO USE *NSSWM* 2

CRAFT & TECHNIQUE

ANATOMY OF A SUCCESSFUL SHORT STORY
by Jennifer D. Foster 6

WRITING STRONG SCENES
by Jack Smith 16

MAKING MAGIC
by Kristin Bair O'Keeffe 24

STUCK IN THE MIDDLE
by Larry Brooks 30

CAPTURING READERS' INTEREST
by Janice Gable Bashman 36

THE STUFF SERIES ARE MADE OF
by Karen S. Wiesner 41

PICTURE PERFECT
by Adrienne Crezo 47

GETTING PUBLISHED

THE BUSINESS OF FICTION WRITING 52

BREAKING IN
by Jennifer D. Foster 61

IT STARTED WITH A HASHTAG
by Diane Shipley 68

"IT HAS MERIT, BUT ..."
by Marie Lamba 74

WHAT LITERARY JOURNALS *REALLY* LOOK FOR
    by James Duncan 81

SIZING UP SMALL PRESSES
    by Robert Lee Brewer 89

BEST OF BOTH WORLDS
    by Chuck Wendig 93

EMERGING VOICES
    by Chuck Sambuchino 98

MARKETING & PROMOTION

GOING PUBLIC
    by Elizabeth Sims 104

BEST PRACTICES FOR BLOGGING
    by Jack Smith 110

10 TIPS FOR YOUR VIRTUAL BOOK TOUR
    by Erika Dreifus 117

MARKETS

LITERARY AGENTS 122

MAGAZINES 196

BOOK PUBLISHERS 329

CONTESTS & AWARDS 421

CONFERENCES & WORKSHOPS 457

RESOURCES

PUBLISHERS & THEIR IMPRINTS 478

GLOSSARY 484

GENRE GLOSSARY..*492*

PROFESSIONAL ORGANIZATIONS...*501*

INDEX

LITERARY AGENTS SPECIALITIES INDEX....................................*505*

CATEGORY INDEX..*525*

GENERAL INDEX...*551*

FROM THE EDITOR

When I started working as an editor, I found that it was increasingly difficult to make time for my fiction. I'd arrive home, my brain still buzzing from a day of analyzing content, organizing production schedules, and proofreading copy, and I'd feel … drained. When I finally managed to sit down at the keyboard, the blinking cursor on the page seemed to snicker at me. *You've used up all your mental energy*, it would say. *You don't have time to devote to your craft*.

Writers I've talked to have shared similar struggles. None of us, it seems, have enough *time*. We're so consumed with juggling the day-to-day tasks of our lives—work, school, kids, dinner, dentist appointments, groceries—that when 9:00 P.M. hits and we collapse into our office chairs, we can hardly form an original thought, much less a sentence or a scene or a *story*.

But writers who are serious about their craft—those of us who not only want to write fiction but *get it published*—do need to make the time. And so we start looking for solutions, ways to balance the demands of everyday life with a writing career.

And we start looking for tools that will help us save time. You're holding one in your hands right now. *Novel & Short Story Writer's Market* is designed to make your writing time more efficient by giving you instant access to a wealth of publishing resources: listings for literary agents, book publishers, magazines, contests, and conferences. You'll also find a variety of articles focusing on improving your fiction, getting it published, and marketing it to readers, and you'll gain access to an exclusive webinar from best-selling author Cheryl St. John that explores emotional high points in fiction (go to www.writersmarket.com/nsswm15-webinar). Ultimately, you'll spend less time researching your craft and more time *writing*.

I can't magically add more hours to your day or babysit your kids for the next few hours (unless you happen to live in the Greater Cincinnati area), but I can say with certainty that *NSSWM* will give you back some precious minutes that you can devote to your craft and your creativity.

The rest, as they say, is up to you.

Rachel Randall
Managing Editor, Writer's Market

HOW TO USE
NSSWM

To make the most of *Novel & Short Story Writer's Market*, you need to know how to use it. And with more than five hundred pages of fiction publishing markets and resources, a writer could easily get lost amid the information. This quick-start guide will help you navigate through the pages of *Novel & Short Story Writer's Market*—as well as the fiction publishing process—and accomplish your dream of seeing your work in print.

1. READ, READ, READ. Read numerous magazines, fiction collections, and novels to determine if your fiction compares favorably with work currently being published. If your fiction is at least the same caliber as what you're reading, then move on to step two. If not, postpone submitting your work and spend your time polishing your fiction. Reading the work of others is one of the best ways to improve your craft.

You'll find advice and inspiration from best-selling authors and seasoned writers in the articles found in the first few sections of this book (**Craft & Technique**, **Getting Published**, and **Marketing & Promotion**). *Novel & Short Story Writer's Market* also includes listings for **Literary Agents** who accept fiction submissions, **Book Publishers** and **Magazines** that publish fiction in a variety of genres, **Contests & Awards** to enter, and **Conferences & Workshops** where you can meet with fellow writers and attend instructive sessions to hone your skills.

2. ANALYZE YOUR FICTION. Determine the type of fiction you write to best target markets most suitable for your work. Do you write literary, genre, mainstream, or one of many other categories of fiction? For definitions and explanations of genres and subgenres, check out the **Glossary** and the **Genre Glossary** in the **Resources** section of the book. Many magazines and presses arc currently seeking specialized work in each of these areas as well as numerous others.

For editors and publishers with specialized interests, see the **Category Index** in the back of the book.

3. LEARN ABOUT THE MARKET. Read *Writer's Digest* magazine (F+W Media, Inc.); *Publishers Weekly*, the trade magazine of the publishing industry; and *Independent Publisher,* which contains information about small- to medium-sized independent presses. And don't forget the Internet. The number of sites for writers seems to grow daily, and among them you'll find www.writersmarket.com and www.writersdigest.com.

4. FIND MARKETS FOR YOUR WORK. There are a variety of ways to locate markets for fiction. The periodical section in bookstores and libraries is a great place to discover new journals and magazines that might be open to your type of short stories. Read writing-related magazines and newsletters for information about new markets and publications seeking fiction submissions. Also, frequently browse bookstore shelves to see what novels and short story collections are being published and by whom. Check acknowledgment pages for names of editors and agents, too. Online journals often have links to the websites of other journals that may publish fiction. And last but certainly not least, read the listings found here in *Novel & Short Story Writer's Market*.

5. SEND FOR GUIDELINES. In the listings in this book, we try to include as much submission information as we can get from editors and publishers. Over the course of the year, however, editors' expectations and needs may change. Therefore, it is best to request submission guidelines by sending a self-addressed stamped envelope (SASE). You can also check each magazine's and press's website—they usually contain a page with guideline information. For an even more comprehensive and continually updated online markets list, access your one-year subscription to the fiction-related listings on www.writersmarket.com; you'll find the access code on the first page of this book.

6. BEGIN YOUR PUBLISHING EFFORTS WITH JOURNALS AND CONTESTS OPEN TO BEGINNERS. If this is your first attempt at publishing your work, your best bet is to begin with local publications or those you know are open to beginning writers. After you have built a publication history, you can try submitting to the more prestigious and nationally distributed magazines. For markets most open to beginners, look for the ⦾ symbol preceding listing titles. Also, look for the ◕ symbol that identifies markets open to exceptional work from beginners as well as work from experienced, previously published writers.

7. SUBMIT YOUR FICTION IN A PROFESSIONAL MANNER. Take the time to show editors that you care about your work and are serious about publishing. By following a publication's or book publisher's submission guidelines and practicing standard submission etiquette, you

- ⊕ market new to this edition

- Ⓐ market accepts agented submissions only

- ⊘ market does not accept unsolicited submissions

- ◉ award-winning market

- ◌ Canadian market

- ◕ market located outside of the U.S. and Canada

- ⑂ market pays (in magazine sections)

- ◯ comment from the editor of *Novel & Short Story Writer's Market*

- ◯ actively seeking new writers

- ◐ seeks both new and established writers

- ● prefers working with established writers, mostly referrals

- ◉ market has a specialized focus

- ◐ imprint, subsidiary or division of larger book publishing house (in book publishers section)

- ☻ publisher of graphic novels or comics

can increase your chances that an editor will want to take the time to read your work and consider it for publication. Remember, first impressions last; a carelessly assembled submission packet can jeopardize your chances before your story or novel manuscript has had a chance to speak for itself.

8. KEEP TRACK OF YOUR SUBMISSIONS. Know when and where you have sent fiction and how long you need to wait before expecting a reply. If an editor does not respond in the time indicated in his or her market listing or guidelines, wait a few more months, and then follow up with a letter (and SASE) asking when the editor anticipates making a decision. If you still do not receive a reply from the editor within a month or two, send a letter withdrawing your work from consideration and move on to the next market on your list.

9. LEARN FROM REJECTION. Rejection is the hardest part of the publication process. Unfortunately rejection happens to every writer, and every writer needs to learn to deal with the negativity involved. On the other hand, rejection can be valuable when used as a teaching tool rather than a reason to doubt yourself and your work. If an editor offers suggestions with his or her rejection slip, take those comments into consideration. You don't have to agree with an editor's opinion of your work. It may be that the editor has a different perspective on the piece than you do. Or you may find that the editor's suggestions give you new insight into your work and help you improve your craft.

10. DON'T GIVE UP. The best advice for you as you try to get published is to be persistent and to always believe in yourself and your work. By continually reading other writers' work, constantly working on the craft of fiction writing, and relentlessly submitting your work, you will eventually find that magazine or book publisher that's the perfect match for your fiction. *Novel & Short Story Writer's Market* will be here to help you every step of the way.

Below is an example of the market listings contained in *Novel & Short Story Writer's Market* with callouts identifying the various format features of the listings. (For an explanation of the icons used, see the sidebar on the opposite page.)

EASY-TO-USE REFERENCE ICONS

E-MAIL AND WEBSITE INFORMATION

SPECIFIC CONTACT NAMES

DETAILED SUBMISSION GUIDELINES

EDITOR'S COMMENTS

THE SOUTHERN REVIEW

Old President's House, Louisiana State University, Baton Rouge, LA 70803-5001. (225)578-5108. Fax: (225)578-5098. E-mail: southernreview@lsu.edu (**Website:** www.lsu.edu/thesouthern review/.

Contact Cara Blue Adams, editor. Magazine: 6 ¼ × 10; 240 pages; 50 lb. Glatfelter paper; 65 lb. #1 grade cover stock. Quarterly. Circ. 3,000.

• Several stories published in The Southern Review were Pushcart Prize selections.

NEEDS Literary. "We select fiction that conveys a unique and compelling voice and vision." Receives approximately 300 unsolicited mss/month. Accepts 4-6 mss/issue. Reading period: September-June. Publishes ms 6 months after acceptance. Agented fiction 1%. Publishes 10-12 new writers/year. Recently published work by Jack Driscoll, Don Lee, Peter Levine, and Debbie Urbanski. Also publishes literary essays, literary criticism, poetry and book reviews.

HOW TO CONTACT Mail hard copy of ms with cover letter and SASE. No queries. ("Prefer brief letters giving author's professional information, including recent or notable publications. Biographical info not necessary." Responds within 10 weeks to mss. Sample copy for $8. Writer's guidelines online. Reviews fiction, poetry.

PAYMENT/TERMS Pays $30/page. Pays on publication for first North American serial rights. Sends page proof to author via e-mail. Sponsors awards/contests.

TIPS "Careful attention to craftsmanship and technique combined with a developed sense of the creation of story will always make us pay attention."

ANATOMY OF A SUCCESSFUL SHORT STORY

Jennifer D. Foster

Short stories are perhaps one of the best places for novice writers to start their careers. They're not too long and complicated, and they offer the writer a chance to intimately explore a plot, a character, and a theme. Short stories also offer writers the opportunity to hone their craft and actually finish a piece of fiction—a great confidence booster!

But don't be fooled by their length (many industry experts agree that short stories range from 1,000 to 7,500 words) or assumed simplicity. Short stories are not necessarily any easier to write than novels or novellas. It takes considerable skill, discipline, and practice to write an exceptional short story that both covers and condenses the essential elements of fiction into a significantly smaller space. But armed with practical how-tos from these best-selling short story authors, as well as key insights and sound advice from a selection of writing instructors, authors, editors, and publishers, you may be well on your way to becoming the next Alice Munro.

DEFINING THE SHORT STORY

Master storyteller Edgar Allan Poe described a short story as a piece that can be read in one sitting, allowing the reader to enjoy an uninterrupted, fully realized, indelible experience with fiction. Length may be the most obvious difference between a novel or novella and a short story, but it's not the only one. J. Madison Davis, author and Gaylord Family Endowed Chair of Professional Writing, Gaylord College of Journalism and Mass Communication, University of Oklahoma, puts it this way: "[Short stories are] more concentrated … and notable for what they leave out." He believes novels are rich and full of complex details and "tend to be fish-eye lenses, whereas short stories tend to be close-ups."

Susan Hesemeier, an instructor of English and communications at MacEwan University in Edmonton, Alberta, concurs. "Unlike novels, the story elaborates in detail one particular moment and its significances." She cites John Steinbeck's *The Chrysanthemums* as an example wherein the protagonist, Elisa, "during the course of a day undergoes a transformation from the liminal space between youth and old age to accepting a life after youth."

Halifax, Nova Scotia-based author Nina Munteanu agrees. The writing instructor and author of the short story collection *Natural Selection* and *The Fiction Writer: Get Published, Write Now!* says the short story is "a metaphoric event, a moment in time. It's a single place—a crossroad—compared with the landscape of a novel." She also believes short stories are "more about awareness … and have the potential to be far more memorable and disturbing, with the power to enlighten." Kevin Barry, Irish award-winning author of the short story collections *Dark Lies the Island* and *There are Little Kingdoms,* shares similar sentiments: "A novel can be a little looser and can go off on tangents; it can have a wildness and a looseness in the way that life can be wild and loose." In contrast, he says, "with a short story, you're working within a very limited frame, and every sentence has to do its work. I often think it's like a high-wire act—every sentence in a story is a step along the line, and it's so easy to lose your footing and trip onto the floor."

Terence M. Green, a novelist, short story author, and writing instructor at Western University in London, Ontario, explains the concept this way: "The short story has a specific focus. It should be tight, dense … read in one sitting, and the final impact should resonate fully upon completion. The novel can meander, digress, explore. Not so with the short story." And that's precisely why each and every sentence in a short story needs to either advance the plot or build character—or both.

Another main difference is the beginning of the story itself. Short stories are infamous for starting *in medias res* (in the middle of things), which, says Davis, "is crucial. The reader must be thrown into the water immediately." Why? "There isn't time or space to wind up. We must be thrust into the problem immediately," he stresses. And that's why, says Steve Woodward, associate editor of Graywolf Press in Minneapolis, Minnesota, "good first lines are so vital—they can tell you everything you need to know in an instant. Find that right first line, even if it means cutting several pages to get to it, and build outward from there." Kevin Watson, founder of Press 53 in Winston-Salem, North Carolina, concurs: "As [writer] Robert Morgan once told me, 'A short story is like a snake in that it strikes quick and draws blood.'" Barry adds to that, stressing that "the really difficult thing about a short story is that you have to get a believable world up and running very quickly." Mark Levene, a professor in the Department of English at the University of Toronto, Ontario, explains it this way: "Short stories tend to have openings markedly different from novels. They are at once a flash, a sudden emergence, and an announcement of a possibility chosen." He supports Nobel Prize-winning short story author Nadine Gordimer's "brilliant conception of short stories and their existential nature as 'the flash of fireflies, in and out, now here, now there, in darkness.'"

For Andrew J. Borkowski, a Toronto-based editor, writer, and author of the 2012 Toronto Book Award-winning short story collection *Copernicus Avenue*, another difference lies in their expansiveness and implied meaning. "Writing a short story is like skipping a stone across the water. You're setting off ripples, reverberations that suggest a feeling or a meaning far deeper than the words themselves express. In a novel you spell things out. You have to in order to keep the reader with you." And for award-winning, best-selling Canadian author Andrew Pyper, who penned the short story collection *Kiss Me*, "it's a distinction of conception. A novel is the result of lengthy mulling, while a short story is the rising of an event out of the subconscious."

THE ELEMENTS OF FICTION: HOW THEY PERTAIN TO SHORT STORIES

Theme

The message—or theme—of the short story is its *raison d'être*. In *How to Write Short Stories, 4th Edition*, Sharon Sorenson succinctly states, "If you have no message, you have no story." And while theme is broad, says Sorenson, remember that your short story "is a *specific* example of the theme." In other words, theme is, she says, what children would call the "moral of the story." And how do writers convey their themes? "By putting characters in conflict with one another. What happens as a result of that conflict reveals the writer's message." Sorenson also stresses that theme is closely related to the outcome of the conflict. And, she says, "theme can be stated, but it is most often implied," providing "insight into life or human nature."

Munteanu concurs. "Every good story explores a theme. In a short story, it is a single theme told as a 'statement' rather than a novel's 'argument.' It's a 'close-up' rather than a novel's landscape. All story elements reflect the theme." Hesemeier adds that the theme must be "limited to one subject or overall message rather than [the] multiple, interconnected themes [found] in a novel." In her book *How to Write Short Stories that Sell*, Louise Boggess states that "by knowing the theme, you can move your major character forward and backward toward the solution of the problem." She also states that "a theme summarizes in one brief sentence what the major character learned from the events of the story. This sentence usually comes near the end." And, she explains, "a strong theme will linger indefinitely in the reader's memory long after he has forgotten the events. Strive to give your theme this kind of power." But that's not necessarily easy. For author Margot Livesey, fiction editor of Emerson College's *Ploughshares* magazine in Boston, Massachusetts, "theme is probably the hardest element to define, but we recognize its absence when we call something an anecdote."

Conflict

Conflict, according to Boggess, "is the heartbeat of a story." Conflict usually begins when the protagonist (main character) faces an obstacle or dilemma. There are two main types of conflict: inner (or internal) conflict, such as guilt, sorrow, indecision, and depression, and outer (or external), such as the environment (floods, drought, fire) or another person, referred to as the antagonist. For Boggess, internal conflict is the struggle for dominance between the positive and negative traits of the main character, while outer conflict occurs when "the major character expresses this inner turmoil by agreeing or disagreeing with the other characters." She adds that writers should "make the problem so vital ... that [the character] must act at once or find himself engulfed by disaster." Regardless of the type of conflict a writer chooses, "believable conflict holds the reader's attention," says Boggess.

And what's the difference between conflict in a short story versus a novel? For Hesemeier, in a short story "there are fewer conflicts that lead to one climax; in a novel, a series of smaller conflicts and climaxes lead to or connect with a larger overall conflict and climax."

Plot

Sorenson describes plot as "what happens as a result of the main conflict. ... The plot develops as the protagonist struggles with the problem, finds a solution, and accepts the changes which result." She breaks plot into six succinct categories or phases:

1. **EXPOSITION:** introduces characters and setting, establishes point of view, and provides background information
2. **OPENING INCIDENT:** leads the main character to a conflict and begins the plot
3. **RISING ACTION:** builds the conflict and adds new, more complicated incidents, leading to the climax
4. **CLIMAX:** intense conflict, which changes the course of events or the way the reader understands the story, either through an event or an insight
5. **FALLING ACTION:** though not always used, it reduces conflict, preparing the reader for the resolution
6. **RESOLUTION:** ends the conflict and leaves the reader satisfied

Watson has a slightly different take on plot. He suggests a great short story, much like a novel, "is presented to the reader in layers, delivered using setting, character, conflict, and dialogue." And, he says, at the center of those layers lie the plot, the theme, and the heart of everything that's been presented. He cites Hemingway's "Hills Like White Elephants" and Kurt Vonnegut's "More Stately Mansions" as key examples of short stories that appear simple until "you begin peeling back the layers of what's been said, how the characters move or don't move, and even the surrounding landscape."

Livesey says her most-admired short stories have a "subplot, where there are two storylines working together to reveal the heart of the story." She also believes that "stories divide into plot-driven and voice-driven. Voice-driven stories tend to have less plot. And highly plotted stories tend to have less intrusive narrators."

Barry has an entirely different take, stating that "one of the greatest story writers, William Trevor, said once that a short story doesn't need a plot, it just needs a point; this is strong evidence to keep in mind." Borkowski wholeheartedly agrees: "Plot is less vital to the short story than longer forms, which is one of the reasons I love stories. Where plot is a factor, it's usually a matter of a single word, gesture, or incident and a handful of actions leading up to it."

Character(s)

In almost every short story, you'll encounter major and minor characters. The former are often also called "round characters," as the reader comes to know them well, while the latter are referred to as "flat," with little or no personal development. Livesey stresses that a "short story takes the character(s) through a smaller psychological arc" than a novel, while still allowing us to "see briefly and incisively into the character's psyche." As Sorenson states in her book, "Believable, motivated characters make or break a story. If readers cannot understand or accept them, nothing else you do matters. Why? The actions of your characters convey theme."

Green agrees. "Character is most important. Make the long chord of understanding and involvement with a character the goal. This is the emotional resonance, the epiphany that is the goal of the best long-lasting fiction." Alice Munro's stories operate this way for Green. "Her characters change by the story's end, and the reader cares about them." And, adds Hesemeier, "[Munro] is able to share her insight into the human experience in a way that can be universally understood, no matter where a reader is from." Green also believes that both Munro (recipient of the 2013 Nobel Prize for Literature) and author Margaret Atwood "have penetrating insights into the lives of their characters. All their stories 'ring true.'"

How else do you know if you've nailed a character? A well-written character "allows us to feel what it's like to be someone else, in a specific set of circumstances, who reacts a certain way. To step into the skin of another and live their life, for a time, as if it were your own," says Woodward. And how many characters do you include? Just one or two, or more? Borkowski advises to "select one character as your focus, [and put him] in conflict with another character." Hesemeier adds, "Usually only the protagonist is developed in enough detail to be a round character, with other characters flat or stock to support the protagonist's development." Regardless of the types of characters included, "the most important part of portraying effective characterization is showing, not telling about, your subject," says Sorenson. And, she stresses, "avoid stereotypes. Readers find no suspense if they know exactly how a character will behave."

Setting

Setting is another vital element; it immediately helps provide context and establish atmosphere, ideally defined or inferred within the first paragraph or two. Sorenson describes setting as "the time and place, or series of times and places, where the protagonist and antagonist meet. Characters and action should interact with the setting." Borkowski describes its role this way: "Setting is important as a conveyor of mood or atmosphere, and it has to be rendered succinctly, poetically almost." Says Hesemeier, "Setting is usually limited to essentials that are necessary to describe the particular moment or that have symbolic significance for the reader's understanding of the story."

Boggess expands on setting further. "The setting may dominate the action of the story, help the reader to identify with the major character, or merely form the background. If possible, choose a setting that will provide or help intensify the character conflict in the story." She believes that "setting can help establish the dominant emotional tone, suggest the type of characters who will appear, create the social atmosphere, and indicate the time of day." Munteanu helps further clarify: "A short story's plot, setting, and character are often portrayed through strong metaphor, the short story writer's major tool. Metaphor conveys so much more than the surface narrative might suggest; this is because metaphor by its very nature resonates with deeper truths, interpreted individually by members of a culture."

Point of View

Boggess defines point of view as "the emotional focus from which you project the action of the story." If your story focuses on a single character's personal odyssey, first-person point of view allows for an intimate perspective on the character's feelings and thoughts, "offering easy characterization, strong emotion, and fast reader identification," she says.

Third person is another common point of view used in short stories. Third-person omniscient allows the story to be told via an outsider: The writer provides exclusive access to all aspects of a character's (or characters') motives, thoughts, and feelings, as well as to the events and experiences that surround not only them, but also often the broader world and the era in which the story occurs. And the third-person limited point of view uses a third-person narrator who "is not part of the story and cannot read any character's minds," clarifies Sorenson.

Regardless of the perspective chosen, Livesey says "point of view lies at the heart of the short story. … The choice of point of view determines the story to be told." For Borkowski, it's all about picking a side and sticking with it. "Once you start wanting to explore the inner lives of multiple characters, you're on your way to something bigger than a short story."

Woodward believes that "once you have established voice, everything else follows." And he prefers a solo voice. "Stories are wonderful when concise and focused, often confined to a single narrative voice and to a single moment in time."

Tone and Style

According to Livesey, tone and style "govern meaning and thus are intricately connected to theme." Says Sorenson, "Tone results from the narrator's attitude … and point of view. From the story's tone, readers can make inferences about characters and plot." Borkowski adds that "tone and style are what the short story is all about. These are your most important tools in suggesting themes and levels of meaning that can't be spelled out within the parameters of the short story." Hesemeier agrees: "An author may have to imply more details in a short story or leave them for readers to fill in, which may impact aspects of the author's style such as the amount of dialogue used in interactions between characters. It may also impact tone by having more of the perspective from one character rather than other characters or an editorializing narrator." For Boggess, "style is your signature." It allows the reader to recognize your work even without a byline. Sorenson says the story's tone and mood must be consistent throughout, thereby helping readers identify with the main character. "Let the tone help reflect character, setting, and plot. The result will be a clearly established mood for readers."

EXCEPTIONAL SHORT STORIES

So what makes a short story exceptional? Myriad elements, according to these sources. For Borkowski, it's the intensity of emotion felt by the reader that really hits home: "A great short story leaves you feeling you've experienced ten times more than what's actually described on the page." Munteanu shares a similar view: "The best short story is an elegant thing. It draws you into a singular experience that resonates at a visceral level, like an arrow through the heart; no time to think—just feel. A bad short story misses the heart … and this is why writers who master the short story form are some of the very best authors in the world." Davis says that because almost no original plots exist, "the real issue becomes the authenticity of the characters [and] setting, and the pleasure of the words themselves." Barry agrees: "If the characters are talking to each other on the page, very believably, and if the reader starts to wonder about what's not being said, then you may be onto a good one."

Watson says, "Everything is energy, even the words on the page. The story has to flow through and connect with the reader. I want to experience the story, to be drawn into the story and leave it only after the last word is read." Watson also believes the writer must "*tell* the story by *showing* [it] to the reader, by allowing the reader to enter the world of the characters and walk beside them and witness the story as it unfolds." He believes it's like "magic in that the words on the page quite literally become images in the reader's mind and transport the reader to wherever the story is taking place … staying with the reader long after the last page is read and leaving the reader asking questions, wondering why a character did this or why the character said that, and even why the story took place at a given time or place." Pyper couldn't agree more: "It's about the capacity of the story to transport or fail to lift off. And you never know which one your story is until it's too late."

In a similar vein, Livesey looks for "sentences that make me see the world in a new way, details that convince me this author has a story to tell that I haven't heard before." And tied directly to the sentence is voice. As Woodward explains, "What I want in a short story is an arresting narrative voice. If the voice is right, the rest will often fall into place: a clearly defined style, an economy of language, and fresh subject matter."

For Levene, "exceptional" is defined by "the inventiveness of many recent stories that hits like a wave. The result is a startling sense, very often, as [Irish writer] Frank O'Connor said years ago, of the particular 'intensity' of 'human loneliness' so many stories are honed to create." Adds Green: "In his Nobel Prize acceptance speech, William Faulkner said 'the human heart in conflict with itself' is alone worth writing about, 'worth the agony and the sweat.'"

MISSING THE MARK

What makes a short story fall flat? Again, the list is varied. Watson knows a story hasn't hit the target when he finds himself "drifting because of speed bumps or pot holes" caused by anything from "typos to improper punctuation to a character acting out of character." For him, word arrangement can stifle the "flow of energy, which might cause me to stumble on a word or phrase and have to go back and read it again." Livesey says "bad, predictable prose, clichéd characterization, and an implausible plot" spell short story disaster for her. Borkowski believes "a failed short story leaves you feeling you've read ten times more than what the author actually experienced in its genesis." Woodward stresses that "nothing kills a story faster than a bland narrative voice. Slack language, well-worn subject matter, and lack of conflict are also common pitfalls."

Hesemeier stresses the importance of singularity. "Trying to take on too many themes, characters, subplots, and so forth will not satisfy the reader as much as developing one main theme, character, or plot really well. Don't attempt to create a 'mini-novel' in a short story." For Green, it's a lack of depth that breaks a story. "Life is not simple. People are not simple. Your short story should not be simple." Also, for him, the story's end is crucial. "The ending should be both convincing and believable, and should not be cheap or easy: 'Then I woke up. … It was all a dream!'"

BEST TIPS OF THE TRADE

Looking for some writerly inspiration and advice on nailing a short story? Our experts weigh in.

"Focus on one main question. Know *exactly* what your story is about. Know its theme. Name it in one word. Then write just to it." —**Nina Munteanu**

"[Start] with a character, a place, or an incident that fascinates you. Throw everything at it, then rewrite, rewrite, rewrite, and rewrite. Then rewrite some more until every word is undeniable." —**Andrew J. Borkowski**

"Outline, even if it's the most rudimentary way. It leads to inspired deviations. … [Don't] think too hard about ticking off [your] boxes in advance. A good story— long or short—will provide them by virtue of its being good." —**Andrew Pyper**

"If you're disciplined and hit the desk at a regular time on a very regular basis, your work will start to improve very, very quickly. Also, read your work aloud— the ear will pick out the false notes much quicker than the eye will catch them on the page." —**Kevin Barry**

"Knock the gremlin of self-doubt from your shoulder and believe in yourself. Soon you will get the 'hang' of writing, and technique becomes an automatic reflex that makes writing a joy." —**Louise Boggess**

"[Break] the story into sections by using fewer large paragraphs and instead using short sentences, short paragraphs, and dialogue that will make it easier for a contemporary reader to stay engaged. And trim anything that is not essential to the conflict and climax of the story." —**Susan Hesemeier**

"Read. Read voluminously all the short stories you can; otherwise, you're operating in a vacuum." —**Terence M. Green**

"[Learn] from the best by reading your favorite writers. What impresses you about their work? How do they do it? Read and reread, then take what you've learned and apply it to your own work. Be sure to read recently published work in your genre to make sure you know what else is out there right now. Other than that, all bets are off. Learn the rules, then learn to break them. Anything is fair game in a short story." —**Steve Woodward**

Jennifer D. Foster is a Toronto, Canada-based freelance editor and writer, and her company is Planet Word. She's been freelancing since 2003 and has been in the business nineteen years. Her clients are from the publishing, magazine, corporate communication, and arts and culture fields and include HarperCollins Canada, the Art Gallery of Ontario, *The Globe and Mail*, Scholastic Canada, and *Quill & Quire*. She has two university degrees, an honors bachelor of arts in sociology and mass communication from Toronto's York University and a bachelor of applied arts in journalism from Ryerson University in Toronto, specializing in magazines, and is a mentor to novice editors and writers. To learn more about her freelance skills and experience, visit her website lifeonplanetword.wordpress.com or her LinkedIn profile.

WRITING STRONG SCENES

....

Jack Smith

The mainstay of strong fiction is scene. Scenes bring readers up close, involving them in dramatic action and making them feel like life is happening right *before* them—and *to* them—as they identify with the character or characters.

Strong scenes often include both the external and internal, both observed action and character thought and reflection. We tend to think of scenes as focused primarily on dialogue, but not all scenes are—some are narrative. But whether they are narrative- or dialogue-driven, they must *move* with energy and vitality. The strong scene is a complex mix of character, conflict, language—and more. To learn how to master this alchemy and craft strong moments that pull readers in, read on.

NARRATIVE SCENES

Consider the following narrative scene from Flannery O'Connor's classic story "A Good Man Is Hard to Find":

> *"It's not much farther," the grandmother said and just as she said it, a horrible thought came to her. The thought was so embarrassing that she turned red in the face and her eyes dilated and her feet jumped up, upsetting her valise in the corner. The instant the valise moved, the newspaper top she had over the basket under it rose with a snarl and Pitty Sing, the cat, sprang onto Bailey's shoulder.*

This sudden landing of the cat on his shoulder causes Bailey to lose control of the car, pitching the passengers about and flipping the car over so that it—fortunately—lands "right-side-up" in a ditch. What energizes this narrative scene is the way the action results from the grandmother's "horrible thought," her sudden realization that she has caused her son Bailey to go the wrong direction—way, way wrong. The image of the cat on Bailey's shoulder is delightfully comic and becomes more so when O'Connor describes it as "clinging to his neck like a caterpillar." The scene's finely compressed action, told with dark humor, gives it verve and movement.

Robert Garner McBrearty, winner of the Sherwood Anderson Foundation Fiction Award for his collection *Episode*, is struck by O'Connor's carefully chosen words to create the dark humor in this passage: "It's comical, and yet O'Connor uses tension-evoking words such as 'horrible,' 'red in the face,' 'eyes dilated,' and 'snarl.' These word choices create an uneasiness in us. Do we laugh or recoil in horror? In this accident scene—and in the whole story—we can't help but do both."

O'Connor's adept handling of humor in this accident scene demonstrates that action alone may not be all that enlivens the best of scenes.

In fact, a narrative scene need not be action-oriented at all. Consider the opening scene from Russell Banks's *Continental Drift*. Notice how it grabs the reader's attention right away:

> *Robert Raymond Dubois (pronounced locally as "Doo-boys"), an oil burner repairman for the Abenaki Oil Company, walks slowly from the squat, dark brick garage where he has parked the company truck, walks hunched over with careful effort, like a man in a blizzard, though snow is falling lightly and there is no wind. He wears a dark blue trooper coat with a fur collar, and a black watchcap. In one hand he carries a black lunchbox, in the other an envelope containing his weekly paycheck, one hundred thirty-seven dollars and forty-four cents.*
>
> *Dubois thinks, A man reaches thirty, and he works at a trade for eight years for the same company, even goes to oil burner school nights for a year, and he stays honest, he doesn't sneak copper tubing or tools into his car at night, he doesn't put in for time he didn't work, he doesn't drink on the job—a man does his work, does it for eight long years, and for that he gets to take home to his wife and two kids a weekly paycheck for one hundred thirty-seven dollars and forty-four cents. Dirt money. Chump change. Money gone before it's got. No money at all.*

Banks's protagonist, Bob Dubois, is on his way home from work and about to stop in at a bar. He's disgusted with his job, with his life, with the little he can contribute to his family. He feels he's surely worth more as a worker and as a human being. The scene is mostly internal, empowered by the wintery darkness played out dramatically in Bob's soul.

Physical description helps fuel this scene, as McBrearty points out: "Notice the way concrete details of setting and character help convey his sense of gloom and despair. Notice that 'squat, dark brick garage' where he parks the company truck. He carries a black lunchbox on a winter day. Notice how he walks ('hunched over with careful effort') and what he wears ('dark blue trooper coat' and 'black watchcap'). The mood this scene creates resonates with many readers. Haven't we all from time to time felt that terrible gloom, the world pressing on us, not much to show for our efforts, just sort of trudging along?"

We connect with Bob Dubois. We get caught up in Bob's outrage as he makes his dismal walk from work. We're physically *there*. The scene moves.

When narrative scenes do *not* move, they fail for one or more reasons. They may lack substance, for one thing. The nature of the conflict doesn't seem important enough to warrant interest. Not that this conflict can't be *made* important enough—it might if we understand *why* it's so important to the character. A second reason is that the conflict lacks sufficient detail or development. It's sketchy. A third is the language itself. If it's dull and cumbersome, impeding the flow of the prose, then the reader will surely lose interest.

This matter of language takes us to a crucial element of all good narrative scenes—a strong persona or voice. Dennis Must is the author of two short story collections and two recent novels, *The World's Smallest Bible* and *Hush Now, Don't Explain*. Must states, "[To be successful,] narrative scenes without dialogue … should channel an author's persona, the quality which makes one's writing inimitable. It is her or his attitude and personality that invest any narration with an authentic identity. Readers familiar with Flannery O'Connor's work immediately recognize her voice just as if they were in her presence. Whether I'm recalling writers as diverse … as Raymond Chandler, Roberto Bolaño, Alice Munro, or Nathanael West, it's each author's voice initially greeting me, followed by any particular work."

SCENES WITH DIALOGUE

When we think of scene, we tend to think of dialogue. Indeed, a strong scene often results from strong dialogue. Consider the following excerpt from Tim O'Brien's *Going After Cacciato*, winner of the National Book Award for Fiction. Notice how it moves from narrative to dialogue as we see Cacciato making his exhibitionist farewell from the Vietnam War.

> Paul Berlin watched through the glasses as Cacciato's mouth opened and closed and opened, but there was only more thunder. And the arms kept flapping, faster now and less deliberate, wide spanning winging motions—flying, Paul Berlin suddenly realized. Awkward, unpracticed, but still flying.
>
> "A chicken!" Stink squealed. He pointed up the mountain. "Look it! See him?"
>
> "Mother of Children."
>
> "Look it!"
>
> "A squawking chicken, you see that? A chicken!"
>
> The thunder came again, and Lieutenant Corson clutched himself and rocked.
>
> "Just tell me," he moaned. "Just tell me, what's he saying?"
>
> Paul Berlin could not hear. But he saw the wide wings, and the big smile, and the movement of the boy's lips.
>
> "Tell me."
>
> So Paul Berlin, watching Cacciato fly, repeated it: "Good-bye."

A mix of things produces this fine scene. First, the point of view is compelling. These soldiers are trying to decipher just what Cacciato is up to. And what he's up to is, in a word, provocative. Here, Cacciato is leaving the war and imitating a chicken. Isn't that what a soldier who rejects a war is sometimes disparaged as being—a *chicken*? And yet Cacciato is making this very gesture as he bids farewell to his fellow soldiers. The description is vivid and vibrant. We can picture Cacciato enthusiastically flapping his bird wings. The dialogue itself is short and crisp and creates an impact through repetition of key words and phrases: "chicken," "tell me," "look it." And note how the scene ends with one word—with sharp impact: "Good-bye." Overall, it's a tightly written dramatic passage.

DeWitt Henry is founder of *Ploughshares* and author of *The Marriage of Anna Maye Potts*, winner of the inaugural Peter Taylor Prize for the Novel. For Henry, "The larger point for me is O'Brien's signature style, where he captures the reductive immediacy of in group idiom, and where the group is one of soldiers facing combat and of teenage boys of the 1970s. He plays with this ironic idiomizing and specialized slang in 'How to Tell a True War Story' and elsewhere. I love the pantomime here as it is viewed through binoculars as well as through mixed attitudes towards Cacciato, the deserter."

Now consider a quite different scene from Raymond Carver's "A Small, Good Thing," from *Cathedral*. Howard and Ann's young son, Scotty, is in the hospital in a coma, and they're worried about him not waking up. They conference with the doctor, and the dialogue becomes charged with emotion:

> *The doctor was a handsome, big-shouldered man with a tanned face. He wore a three-piece suit, a striped tie, and ivory cufflinks. His gray hair was combed along the sides of his head, and he looked as if he had just come from a concert. "He's all right," the doctor said. "Nothing to shout about, he could be better, I think. But he's all right. Still, I wish he'd wake up. He should wake up pretty soon."*

When the doctor takes another look at the boy, he tells the parents that more test results are due back in a few hours, and then they'll "know some more." Still, says the doctor, the boy is "all right, believe me, except for the hairline fracture of the skull. He does have that." Ann's response is: "Oh, no."

This scene can't help but grab our attention. First, a young child is in the hospital, in a coma, and this conflict creates immediate reader sympathy for the parents. But Carver doesn't depend on this alone. He masterfully balances the seriousness of the event with dark comedy. The doctor's physical appearance and general bearing, suggesting he's "just come from a concert," is quite incongruous with the sober nature of the young boy's medical condition in this hospital setting. The doctor also engages in an unintentional interplay of hope and despair. What he gives, he quickly takes away—or at least calls into question. The boy will be okay, and *yet*. … The colloquial expression "nothing to shout about" is hardly what we would expect of a medical diagnosis, and it creates tension in the listeners. And so the parents surely come away with less hope than fear, as we see in Ann's final abbreviated comment.

Gary Fincke, winner of the Flannery O'Connor Award for Short Fiction, has authored five collections of stories, his most recent being *The Proper Words for Sin*. Fincke states, "It calls up our collective fear of anything but certainty from doctors who are treating our children. The reader begins to listen like a parent, fastening on to every ambivalent phrase of assurance, but especially upon the one undeniable medical fact of hairline skull fracture. For us as well as the parents, it's not far from that admission to the beginning of panic, and Carver's doctor, in his 'concert outfit,' cannot sustain even two consecutive sentences of assurance."

Here's a much different scene, from "Starving," which appears in Elizabeth Strout's Pulitzer Prize-winning novel-in-stories, *Olive Kitteridge*:

> When he got home, Bonnie said, "What took you so long? I need you to climb up and fix those gutters like you've been promising to do."
>
> He handed her the bag with her doughnut.
>
> "And the pipe under the sink has been dripping into that bucket for weeks. Ironic you should own a hardware store."
>
> Unexpectedly, a ripple of terror went through him. He sat down in his La-Z-Boy. In a moment he said, "Hey, Bonnie, would you ever want to move?"
>
> "Move?"
>
> "Say to Florida or somewhere."
>
> "Are you crazy? Or are you kidding?"
>
> "Where there's sun all year long. Where the house isn't so big and empty."
>
> "I'm not even going to answer such a ludicrous thing." She peered into the bag with the doughnut. "Cinnamon? You know I hate cinnamon."
>
> "It's all they had." He picked up a magazine, so as not to look at her. But in a moment, he said, "Has it ever bothered you, Bonnie, that none of the boys want to take over the store?"
>
> Bonnie frowned. "We've talked about that, Harmon. Why in the world should it bother us? They're free to do what they like."
>
> "Of course they are. But it would've been nice. Have at least one of them around."
>
> "This negativity of yours. It's driving me nuts."
>
> "Negativity?"
>
> "I just wish you'd perk up." She crumpled the doughnut bag closed. "And clean out those gutters. It isn't pleasant, Harmon, having to feel like a nag."

Note the lively interchange representing the marital conflict between these two. Bonnie accuses Harmon of neglecting household chores he's promised to do. He ignores her accusations and proposes a move to a sunny climate and a house not "so big and empty." She says she won't even respond to such a "ludicrous" idea. Harmon wishes at least one of their sons would take over the family hardware business. Bonnie states she's tired of his "negativity."

The irony is that Bonnie is the negative one. We see she isn't very happy in her marriage. But neither is Harmon; before this scene we learn he's having an affair, though it's not clear that Bonnie knows about it. Bonnie's responses to Harmon, sometimes quite crisp, energize the dialogue, giving the scene substantial forward thrust. Note another technique—how Strout introduces the bag with the doughnut earlier on, but Bonnie doesn't react to it right away. And then she rejects it. The cinnamon doughnut focuses the conflict on something concrete, something we can picture. It's little things like this—ordinary, even trivial—that can add punch to a scene. The final flourish is, of course, when Bonnie regrets being a "nag." The directness of her complaint, her frank self-revelation, makes us rethink everything in the scene.

Ronna Wineberg is author of the prize-winning story collection *Second Language* and the novel *On Bittersweet Place* (Relegation Books, September 2014). Wineberg is interested in the scene's considerable dependence on dialogue: "Strout doesn't use adjectives or adverbs. In dialogue tags, she uses a simple *said* instead of more descriptive verbs such as *declared* or *snapped* or *shouted*—or she leaves the verbs out altogether. She relies on the words the characters speak to carry the emotion of the scene. She adds just a few gestures and minimal description to help the reader visualize characters and setting: Harmon hands Bonnie the bag; he sits in the recliner; Bonnie frowns. The characters reveal themselves through their words. Strout chooses those words with care. Harmon asks Bonnie if she's bothered that the boys didn't take over the store. The reader understands that he's really saying he's melancholy, upset; the boys are grown-up and life is passing by. Bonnie lets the reader know at the end that she understands Harmon's mood, and she has for awhile, and is frustrated by it."

As we've seen, rich dialogue can animate and drive a scene. But good dialogue doesn't act in isolation. The point of view of the stakeholders in the matter at hand must be provocative or interesting in some way. There must be conflict—conflict important enough to make the reader care. And then, driven by this conflict, the characters must come alive, revealing their needs, desires, flaws—their basic humanity. The dialogue itself must be distinctive and original. When it's not working, it tends to sound clunky and artificial.

Mark Wisniewski is a book doctor and author of several works of fiction, including a recent novel, *Show Up, Look Good*. Wisniewski states: "One problem with dialogue I see in rough manuscripts is clunkiness. Pedestrian or not, people in the real world tend not to speak in complete sentences. Often, then, the most interesting dialogue can occur when characters blurt sentence fragments or whatever words reflect an idiosyncratic personality being as blunt or honest or assertive as possible."

Two additional problems can result in handling dialogue, says Wisniewski. First, even if the dialogue is good, too much dialogue might, in certain cases, rob a scene of suspense. Wisniewski explains: "One problem I notice when I book-doctor novels and freelance-edit short stories is that sometimes writers have characters talk when it might be best if instead the characters did something without talking—or did something while the point-of-view character mulled over some significant problem or fear." It might seem counterintuitive, but Wisniewski says that "this choice to shut characters' mouths can add tension and suspense to a story." Yet there's an important qualification to keep in mind: "Of course the trick is to find something *interesting* for the characters to do while one or both or several of them are mulling over something significant, and if this thing they did could be an activity or physical engagement which as well carried subtle metaphoric weight in the overall story being narrated, all the better."

Second, dialogue sometimes lays things out so clearly that nothing is left to the reader to figure out on his own. But there's a way around this, says Wisniewski. "Sometimes it doesn't hurt to give your reader a little credit intelligence-wise: As long as your dialogue doesn't risk confusing your reader, it's not a bad idea to write a line in which one character is pulling another's leg, or joking, or 'testing' that character about something valuable or crucial in the story. If you can get the reader to feel privileged to be 'in' on what a character is actually saying but not saying literally, you, as a story's author, are clicking."

As Wisniewski shows here, writing a scene with dialogue calls for judgment. If the scene works great with mostly dialogue, go for it—but make sure it sizzles. If action works better in places, substitute action for dialogue. And don't let dialogue explain too much. Involve your reader as much as possible in the playing out of the scene.

THE FUNCTION OF SCENES

It's important to keep in mind that a scene must not only be strong dramatically, but it must also function in one or more ways in the story or novel: to develop or reflect character, to advance plot, or to help develop theme.

The accident scene from "A Good Man Is Hard to Find" reflects character and also develops plot. O'Connor reveals something about the grandmother's character in her realization of her silly and terrible mistake, but the scene also serves an important function plot-wise. Robert Garner McBrearty comments, "I'm struck by how well the scene serves to set up the upcoming scene—the arrival of the Misfit with all the ensuing terror. This is a good example of how scenes build. In another type of story, maybe the story would end with the accident. In this case, the horror is just starting. The family survives the accident, but not for long. O'Connor takes us into the most terrible of worlds and shakes us to the core."

Due to its tight compression, a short story has much less room than a novel to include scenes that develop character only. Midge Raymond is the author of *Forgetting English*, winner of the Spokane Prize for Short Fiction, as well as two books for writers: *Everyday Writing* and *Everyday Book Marketing*. Raymond explains the tightness of short story construction: "In a short story, every scene has to do so much work—the short story writer simply doesn't have the luxury to write scenes that don't multitask." Raymond keeps this in mind in her own writing: "When I'm writing a story, I'm always thinking of character above all else—

but it's amazing how closely connected character can be to plot and theme in a story; due to the nature of the genre, everything needs to be tightly woven together. So, for example, a good scene in a short story might be a flashback that reveals something about a character, and, at the same time, it may also include a little foreshadowing—that is, a glimpse into a character's past might give readers insight about how he or she may act in the future, in which case we get a peek at what might unfold in the plot of the story."

Even in a novel, though it's much longer, it's best for most scenes to develop both character and plot—and be tied in some way to theme. In *Continental Drift*, Russell Banks deals with the failure of the American Dream for a working-class man like Bob Dubois. The opening scene establishes Dubois's chagrin, but what Dubois doesn't know yet is that no matter what he does, no matter how hard he tries to beat the odds, the dream will remain beyond his reach, as it is for so many working-class people of Dubois's ilk.

SUMMING UP

Strong scenes don't just happen. Writers must combine several elements—character, circumstance, and language—and layer them in such a way that each scene is seamless. Scenes pull readers in when they can identify with the concerns of characters and when the language itself is interesting. But not every interesting event should be a scene. Keep in mind that scenes must play an important part in the story or novel as a whole—every scene should have a purpose.

Jack Smith has published two dozen articles in *Novel & Short Story Writer's Market*. His creative writing book, *Write and Revise for Publication: A 6-Month Plan for Crafting an Exceptional Novel and Other Works of Fiction*, was published in 2013 by Writer's Digest Books. His novel *Hog to Hog* won the 2007 George Garrett Fiction Prize and was published by Texas Review Press in 2008. He has published stories in a number of literary magazines, including *Southern Review*, *North American Review*, *Texas Review*, *X-Connect*, *In Posse Review*, and *Night Train*. His reviews have appeared widely in such publications as *Ploughshares*, *Georgia Review*, *American Book Review*, *Prairie Schooner*, *Mid-American Review*, *Pleiades*, the *Missouri Review*, and *Environment* magazine. His co-authored nonfiction environmental book titled *Killing Me Softly* was published by Monthly Review Press in 2002. Besides his writing, Smith co-edits the *Green Hills Literary Lantern*, an online literary magazine published by Truman State University. His novel *Icon* was published by Serving House Books in June 2014.

MAKING MAGIC

Exploring the Realm of Magic Realism

Kristin Bair O'Keeffe

Ever since I started writing as a kid, unusual things have happened in my well-grounded stories. A man named Harold sprouted a flower on his head. A line of seemingly nonsensical text became a secret code ("Tulips are on sale in Kanagawa—the place."). A tree sprouted in a girl's innards after her father fed her a cherry stone. A rabble of butterflies inspired a lusty softening of the heart. And in my latest novel, *The Art of Floating*, it's not quite clear whether a mysterious man who just walked out of the sea is alien, fish, or lost soul.

Early on, friends and family dubbed my work "the odd stuff Kristin writes," and it wasn't until a literature class in college that I realized there was a name for it—magic realism—and that an honorable lineage of writers had been writing such "odd stuff" for years. Brilliant authors like Gabriel García Márquez, whose *One Hundred Years of Solitude* introduced the world to the fictional town of Macondo and generations of the Buendía family whose lives are touched again and again by unusual and magical occurrences; Audrey Niffenegger, whose much more recent *The Time Traveler's Wife* makes you believe in the possibility of tumbling through time, as well as extraordinary love; the venerable Toni Morrison, who summoned the ghost of Sethe's child in *Beloved*; and Japanese author Haruki Murakami, whose *1Q84* commingles two representations of the same world so adeptly that you end up saying, "Wait, wait, back up! What is real here?" for more than 1,000 pages.

ORIGIN

According to history, German art critic Franz Roh coined the term *magical realism* in a 1925 essay and subsequent art book *Nach Expressionismus: Magischer Realismus: Probleme der neuesten europäischen Malerei* (*After Expressionism: Magical Realism: Problems of the newest European painting*). While he initially used the term to describe an artistic shift from abstraction to figural representation, the meaning grew muddy and controversial, and, soon after, the term fell out of fashion in the art world—as things tend to do. Sometime in the 1960s, when literary folks needed an appropriate descriptor for *One Hundred Years of Solitude*, the term *magic realism* was resurrected and reshaped by the literary community. "How else," they likely argued over whiskey and beer, "can we describe a novel that so stunningly straddles the magical and the realistic—a novel in which Remedios the Beauty ascends into the sky while folding a sheet, and Melquíades, the gypsy, dies not once, but twice?"

In this case, the term stuck. But what *magic realism* really is, what defines the genre, and just who the heck's work gets to be categorized as *magically realistic* has become one of the hottest debates in the literary community. Highbrow purists with fists in the air argue that only Latin American authors write authentic literature in this genre. Hybrids argue that magic realism crosses all borders and boundaries, and that it's more about the characteristics of the story than the place from which the author hails.

Because this debate tends to get bloody depending on the parties involved, I advise writers drawn to this magnificent genre to steer clear of the whole damn conversation and accept that, while magic realism may (or may not) have been birthed in Latin America, it has evolved and migrated. Stick to the writing and the ongoing development of your craft. After all, while the debate rages on, writers continue to create intoxicating stories that fall into the magically realistic genre. Just take a look at Sarah Addison Allen's *The Girl Who Chased the Moon* and Eowyn Ivey's *The Snow Child*.

MAGIC REALISM: WHAT IT IS (AND ISN'T)

Once again, a magically realistic story is one that is deeply grounded in a realistic place and situation but in which odd, unusual, and magical events occur. While reading such a tale, you may never be 100 percent sure what is real and what is not. It's a bit like looking at one of those images that occasionally trends on Facebook in which the first time you glance at the image you see a sheep, but if you stare and let your eyes go soft, you see an alien.

Glance: sheep.

Stare and soften: alien.

The complete image is made up of the two smaller images, but they're so artistically blended that you're never truly sure what you "should" see. And, in fact, there is no image that you "should" see because the story—if well crafted—is a perfectly balanced combination of the two.

One thing that writers do need to keep in mind—and one thing over which critics do not draw blood—is that magic realism is not the same as science fiction or fantasy. While these three genres share certain qualities, they differ greatly. In science fiction and fantasy, the line between what is real and what is magical or mystical is clear and distinct; in magic realism, it's fuzzy. In science fiction and fantasy, new worlds are often created; in magic realism, it's the same old world with interesting nuances. Science fiction and fantasy are often escapist; magic realism rarely is. And in science fiction and fantasy, rational explanations are provided for unusual occurrences. Do not expect an explanation in a magically realistic story. Things just *are*.

NUTS AND BOLTS

Before you set out to write your magically realistic tale, consider the nuts and bolts of the genre.

- **PLACE:** A realistic sense of place will help to move your story forward and facilitate magical occurrences. In the first chapter of *The Time Traveler's Wife*, Niffenegger introduces us to the unique features of Chicago's Newberry Library. Eventually, we learn that Henry is petrified of landing in the library's "cage" when tumbling through time because it has no exit. It's the perfect setup.

- **FANTASTICAL ELEMENTS:** In a magically realistic story, characters can levitate, implode, move objects with their minds, travel through time, speak languages they never were taught to speak, and much more. As long as you weave your carefully chosen fantastical elements into the realistic fabric of your story, anything goes.

- **HABITS, BELIEFS, AND QUIRKS:** Use your characters' habits, beliefs, and quirks to instigate or heighten the magical elements in your story. The fact that Clare Abshire, in *The Time Traveler's Wife*, is a paper artist becomes more integrated with Henry's time travel as the story progresses. In *1Q84*, Aomame's antisocial, über-efficient ways play right into the development of the plot. Keep in mind that figuring out which habits, beliefs, and quirks best lend themselves to your story takes time and many drafts. Don't rush it.

- **TONE:** Magically realistic stories are told without astonishment. Narrators don't run around yelling, "Oh, my god! I can't believe a ghost just sat down to dinner with us!" If a woman drifts away or a man travels through time or a woman climbs down a staircase from a highway and enters a different reality, the narrator shares that information in the same tone she'd use to inform you she was out of ketchup.

- **NARRATOR'S AUTHORITY AND RETICENCE:** Your narrator is the big boss who isn't interested in explaining things to readers. If a ghost sits down for dinner or a mysterious taxi driver points someone to a questionable stairwell, the narrator is not going to lean forward, give a wink, and whisper, "Here's how it works …" This would shatter readers' trust in the characters'—and the world's—credibility.

- **TIME:** In many magically realistic stories, time is fluid and cyclical, not rigid and linear. Now, then, the distant future, the distant past, yesterday, today, tomorrow— it's all good. *One Hundred Years of Solitude*, for example, opens with a flashback that stretches all the way back to a time when "[t]he world was so recent that many things lacked names, and in order to indicate them it was necessary to point." But in some stories, like Aimee Bender's *The Particular Sadness of Lemon Cake*, time is persistent and unidirectional. Make good use of this great flexibility with time. Decide which is best for your story, and then run with it.

- **RULES AND REGULATIONS:** Every establishment is governed by specific rules and regulations—towns, churches, governments, parks, schools, sales forces, families, friendships, marriages, genders, etc. In a magically realistic story, you can manipulate those rules. For example, in Japan during rush hour on a highway, a woman would never get out of a car, take off her shoes, and walk to a staircase reserved for emergency workers. In *1Q84*, Aomame does just that. As the writer, you must know the rules of the reality you present; only then can you allow characters to break those rules and see what gets stirred up.

- **HYBRIDITY:** Multiple planes of reality are common in magically realistic stories. In *1Q84*, two "versions" of the realistic world exist at the same time, and in *The Time Traveler's Wife*, present-day Henry often time travels to a period in which a younger or older Henry exists. Thus, often there are two Henrys present. Such hybridity allows you, the writer, an opportunity to reveal a deeper truth about the world that you wouldn't by simply representing one reality.

MAGIC REALISM: A READING LIST

- *One Hundred Years of Solitude* by Gabriel García Márquez
- *The Time Traveler's Wife* by Audrey Niffenegger
- *Beloved* by Toni Morrison
- *1Q84* by Haruki Murakami
- *The Girl Who Chased the Moon* by Sarah Addison Allen
- *The Particular Sadness of Lemon Cake* by Aimee Bender
- *The Snow Child* by Eowyn Ivey
- *Life of Pi* by Yann Martel
- *Song of Solomon* by Toni Morrison
- *The House of the Spirits* by Isabel Allende
- *Like Water for Chocolate* by Laura Esquivel
- *The Master and Margarita* by Mikhail Bulgakov
- *The Tiger's Wife* by Téa Obreht
- *The Museum of Extraordinary Things* by Alice Hoffman
- *The Ocean at the End of the Lane* by Neil Gaiman
- *Swamplandia!* by Karen Russell
- *Life After Life* by Kate Atkinson
- *The Night Circus* by Erin Morgenstern

MAGICAL IDEAS

Ever since I began writing, I've been a collector. Not of things—shells, stamps, figurines, stuffed monkeys, autographs, etc.—but of possibilities. Odd happenings and images from around the world and in my dreams that could—and often do—make their way into my writing. While many might be considered mundane observances, paired with the right character in the right situation, I know they'll make terrifically fantastic occurrences.

In recent years, these possibilities have included a giant eyeball that washed up on a beach in Florida; thousands of rotten pigs floating down the Huangpu River in Shanghai; an Arctic flower that was regenerated after 32,000 years of dormancy in a squirrel's burrow; 7,700 people who were sterilized against their will between 1933 and 1977 as an experiment in genetic engineering; a man who sells the moon; the death of the world's tallest woman in China's Anhui province; a house with ladders between floors that I dream about every few months; and many more.

Although sometimes I'm tempted to save every odd, quirky bit that comes my way, I've trained myself to save only those that cause a thump somewhere in my soul. Those are the bits that stick … the pieces that resonate with me as an artist.

If collecting possibilities doesn't come naturally to you, here are three surefire ways to happen upon interesting stuff:

1. Mine your dreams, and if you don't remember your own, mine your spouse's, child's, or friend's dreams. I'm lucky enough to have, and have always had, intense, detailed dreams that feed directly into my writing, but I'm not above poaching those my daughter or a good friend tell me about.
2. Follow headlines. Newspaper, Internet, and magazine headlines feature all kinds of kooky things happening in the world. Use them. And don't stick closely to the publications you read all the time. Check out publications you never read, including grocery store tabloids.
3. Listen in on conversations—to the two women gossiping in the fitting room next to you, to the father and son at the dentist's office, to the taxi driver talking to his dispatcher on the radio, to the endless number of phone conversations going on at airports, and so on.

When something does resonate with you, be sure to record and store it. If you don't, you'll lose track and forget all about it. How and where you record and store your possibilities will depend on your organizational style. As an Evernote devotee, I save everything that piques my interest to a folder in my Evernote account labeled "Possibilities." I've also been journaling since I was eight and blogging since 2006. When I'm deep into a novel, I'm constantly pulling out old journals, rereading past blog entries, and, yes, accessing my "Possibilities" folder.

WORLDBUILDING

Your first hurdle will likely be figuring out how to let your readers know that they're reading a magically realistic story. Different authors handle this in different ways. In the first pages of *1Q84*, the taxi driver tells Aomame, "[P]lease remember: things are not what they seem." And while he is talking directly to her, he's also talking to readers. In *The Time Traveler's Wife*, Clare and Henry simply talk about Henry's time travel capability as if it's the most normal thing on earth.

Once you've handled that hurdle, resist the urge to plunk in fantastical elements. Instead, imbue. The less you jar readers from the streamline of the story, the more trust they will place in you. The last thing you want as a writer is for your reader to get to a fantastical element, feel like it's a fake, and say, "No way. That could never happen."

As you set off on this journey to write a magically realistic story, the most important question you must ask yourself is not "How do I introduce magic into this story?" or "Can my setting support surrealistic elements?" but instead "What is possible in this world?" You must be able to imagine something happening in the world beyond what most people see. To this end, I encourage you to look under the rug, listen beneath the sound of the wave, peer beyond the solid figure that blots out the sun, and ask yourself again and again, "What is possible in this world?"

Then pick up your pen.

Kristin Bair O'Keeffe is the author of the novels *The Art of Floating* and *Thirsty*. Her work has appeared in numerous publications, including *Poets & Writers*, *The Gettysburg Review*, and *Hypertext Magazine*. Follow her on Twitter @kbairokeeffe.

STUCK IN THE MIDDLE

Larry Brooks

Nobody ever said writing a good novel was going to be easy. It's highly likely that at some point you'll find yourself thoroughly stuck, and when it happens in the middle it can make you crazy because it all started out so well. But the news isn't exclusively bad. Because once identified, a mid-story hiccup can become an opportunity to make your narrative even better, from start to finish.

A mid-draft slump is a *symptom*, which calls for a diagnosis before you can effectively treat it. Believing you can write your way out of this mess, that you can rescue the middle with a strong closing act, is a seductive trap, because your reader may never make it that far. When that reader is an agent or an editor, this assumption becomes a fatal one.

There are four common maladies that can result in a miserable middle. While you may find overlap in terms of these symptoms, sometimes all it takes is some simple care administered to any one to get the story ticking again.

1. IS YOUR PREMISE, WHILE THEMATIC AND A GREAT STAGE FOR YOUR CHARACTER, DRAMATICALLY WEAK?

The truth is, not all premises are created equal. "It seemed like a good idea at the time" is the lament of many missteps in life, and launching a story without the requisite dramatic chops is as stark an example as any. There's a reason Clive Cussler's breakout novel was titled *Raise the Titanic!* instead of *Raise the Aktiengesellschaft Barge!* Like most bestsellers that rocket careers to dizzying heights, Cussler's story had something conceptual behind its dramatic premise. Basically, he had us at *Titanic*.

DOES YOUR PREMISE HAVE SOMETHING CONCEPTUAL ENERGIZING IT? Premises grounded in rich historical or thematic settings can lead to wonderful stories. The problem comes when the setting *becomes* the story (take note, historical writers), rather than the *context* for a dramatic arc set *within* it. If your narrative is composed primarily of a series of moments and happenings showcasing place, time, setting, culture, politics, or a specific chapter in history, then your middle pages may already be asleep as a result.

DOES YOUR READER HAVE SOMETHING TO ROOT FOR IN YOUR MIDDLE CHAPTERS? If you can't immediately identify what they should be rooting for, the reason may connect to your premise. The role of a premise is to give the hero something to *do* rather than something to *exist within*, and good ones always ask the reader to *care about the hero* rather than just his surroundings or the issues he's facing.

When a story comes off as more diary-like than dramatic, when the narrative reads like a series of one-act plays rather than a larger, singular dramatic arc, the middle takes the hit. Because when readers get there, they're not going to be content to passively observe the events as they unfold. They'll be looking for something specific to root for.

2. CAN YOUR CORE STORY BE CLEARLY AND SUCCINCTLY STATED?

A workable premise almost always poses a compelling *dramatic question* that entices readers to stick around to see what happens. It keeps readers reading because there is something at stake, something you've made them care about. The dramatic question is the dramatization of the core story you are telling.

CAN YOU DEFINE YOUR CORE STORY AS A DRAMATIC ARC AND LIFT A COMPELLING DRAMATIC QUESTION, ONE THAT FRAMES YOUR CORE STORY, FROM YOUR PREMISE? *Will the hero rescue the kidnapped child?* is a dramatic question with huge stakes arising from this premise: *A bank manager is forced to rob his own bank in order to pay the ransom to get his daughter back.* Notice how they are different, how the dramatic question arises *from* the core story. Your middle chapters *must* further define the core story through the pursuit of an answer to the dramatic question.

WILL THE READER CARE ENOUGH ABOUT THE ANSWER TO THE DRAMATIC QUESTION? Causing your reader to care begins in the opening chapters, where you set up the premise, but you take it to another level when the hero is put under pressure or threat, which is the job of your middle chapters. Here is where the reader is swept vicariously away with the hero into the jaws of a dilemma of some kind. That dilemma is your core story.

IS YOUR MIDDLE WHOLLY ENGAGED IN ADVANCING YOUR CORE STORY? The real juice of storytelling is showing *how* the answer to the dramatic question will be revealed, thus rendering the question as context for the vicarious journey itself. If you don't have that question in play by the time you approach the middle chapters, if the narrative is still internal and experiential (as in, hero goes to Venice and does this and that to get over his divorce,

CORE SUPPORT: 9 FUNDAMENTALS

Middles don't stand alone. They depend on entry and egress, built from weight-bearing contexts that hold the pieces together as the story is propelled forward. Execute well, and the story will be built from the right structural stuff, allowing the whole to reach its highest dramatic potential without crumbling under the weight of its own thematic intentions.

Here are the nine major parts of a strong story, each with its own succinct contextual mission contributing to the whole. Numbers 4 though 6 comprise your middle, accommodating about 50 percent of your manuscript.

SET-UP SCENES

Opening chapters have much to accomplish: They introduce the hero and a pre-plot life and circumstance; foreshadow forthcoming drama by putting necessary pieces into play, often without context; launch both subplot and context; and insert the mechanics leading to the First Plot Point into the narrative.

HERO RESPONSE SCENES

The hero responds to this new situation. The antagonistic force rattles its sword and exposes its own goals, as the hero discovers more about the situation and makes seemingly necessary moves, which usually make things worse or more urgent.

HOOK

An early moment snags reader interest, relative to either plot or character. Often without explanation or context, something happens (be it subtle or large) that demands attention, clarity and resolution. The hook opens a dramatic door that invites the reader to come inside.

FIRST PLOT POINT (STORY BEAT)

New, story-changing information enters the narrative, defining an immediate situation, need, problem, goal or threat that causes the hero's life and priorities to shift and escalate urgently. This key story beat defines the hero's quest, and thus the core story itself. The plot is fully in motion, with antagonistic forces and stakes exerting pressure.

HERO PROBLEM ATTACK SCENES

The hero moves forward in context to more fully understanding the stakes and obstacles, with hands-on confrontation, strategy and cleverness. But the antagonistic force is ramping up its game, too, escalating drama and tension. Things usually get worse before they get better.

SCENES RAMPING TO CLIMAX

These scenes set up and execute the path toward a showdown as the hero takes action, as the issues and elements converge. The hero should be the primary catalyst, if not the architect, of the forthcoming resolution of the problem.

5 6 7 8 9

MIDPOINT (STORY BEAT)

New information enters the story and shifts the hero's context from that of a responder to that of a proactive attacker of the problem. This new information empowers and emboldens the hero on the quest. (For example, if a mysterious person has been chasing the hero up to now, this is where the identity of that person or thing might be revealed.)

SECOND PLOT POINT (STORY BEAT)

New information again arises, often as a result of the hero's efforts, that will lead the hero down a path toward resolution, calling for even more courage and ingenuity in the face of an even more energized antagonistic force. Stakes are at an all-time high.

RESOLUTION (STORY BEAT OR EPILOGUE)

What's been at stake in the story is achieved, and often the hero's immediate future is glimpsed, with everything changed because of the experience that has led to this point.

then goes home), you miss both boats: the readers' desire for an outcome, and their vicarious ride in getting to it.

When you're still in first gear by the time you hit the middle chapters, you risk stalling out altogether. If you're still in tour-guide mode without giving your hero a compelling problem to solve or a worthy goal to pursue, with threat and/or risk lurking and something of value hanging in the balance (stakes), if you're still revealing backstory and showing us the sights … that's your middle management miscue right there.

3. HAVE YOU LAUNCHED THE CORE STORY WITH A PIVOTAL FIRST PLOT POINT THAT IS WELL-PLACED AND FULLY REALIZED?

Defining a conceptually rich premise and then *executing* it are as different as taking a picture of a house and actually building one. Even if your core story is solid, how and *where* you launch it—story structure—is what defines the efficacy of your middle.

The moment of that launch is when the story shifts from set-up mode to full speed ahead. This is called the *First Plot Point*. It is a major story beat, the big twist that rocks the hero's world, commencing something urgent to do about a new situation or calling, with obstacles and stakes in play.

Mess this up, ignite this in the wrong place or leapfrog it entirely, and your middle will instantly be in trouble. Because your middle is entirely *about* the core story itself.

DOES YOUR FIRST PLOT POINT COMPEL YOUR HERO TO SHIFT INTO RESPONSE MODE? What new information changes the story in a way that accomplishes this? This should be a clear and succinct moment, a bolt of awareness, a calling, even an epiphany. It is often the moment when the hero is suddenly threatened and for better or worse decides what's next, be it avoidance or fleeing or simply pursuing more information. Whatever that response may be, it shifts the story into a higher gear. Stakes are involved, and the hero is now focused on a need and/or a goal. Nothing drums up emotion (for your hero *or* for your reader) quite like conflict, which is precisely what the First Plot Point imbues in the story.

DOES THIS FIRST PLOT POINT APPEAR AT THE PROPER PLACE IN THE STORY? Given that your opening chapters are tasked with setting up the context of the story, the First Plot Point should occur with the full benefit of that setup in place. Which means your opening hook is an ill-advised place to address the mission of the First Plot Point. Conversely, if you position it too late, you risk losing the reader in the process.

Your First Plot Point commences the whole of the middle arc of your story, a full 50 percent of the total, give or take. So this point is best situated at about the 20 to 25 percent mark.

4. HAVE THE NATURE AND CONTEXT OF YOUR HERO'S MISSION, FOCUS, PRIORITIES, NEEDS, AND DECISIONS/ACTIONS SHIFTED BECAUSE OF THE IMPLICATIONS OF THE FIRST PLOT POINT TURN?

An effective middle depends so heavily on a viable, potent, and clear First Plot Point because *it defines what the middle is about*: your hero's response to the newly minted quest.

IS YOUR HERO FULLY ENGAGED IN THE PURSUIT OF THE ANSWER TO THE STORY'S DRAMATIC QUESTION BY THE MIDPOINT? Your middle chapters should continue to elevate, escalate, and surprise. Within them, at some point, the hero is going to undergo another important transition: from responding to the problem to *attacking* the problem. There is a prescribed moment in classic story architecture for this shift: the *Midpoint* story beat, which resides squarely in the middle of your middle, if you will.

DOES YOUR HERO TURN A CORNER AT THE MIDPOINT? The events of your story should drive your hero to attack the core goal or problem more aggressively at approximately the middle of the story, turning a corner from responder to warrior (proactive and bold) based on new information offered at the middle. If the Midpoint doesn't transition the story from hero-response mode into proactive problem-attack mode, your whole middle will get stuck in second gear.

THE ENDGAME OF MIDDLE STORY MANAGEMENT

Change is the name of the game in the core of your story: from setup to hero as responder, from responder to warrior, and then, in the final quarter, from warrior to heroic problem-solver. Which won't work unless those middle chapters are solid.

This is where all of the key structural elements—conceptual premise, core story, dramatic question, First Plot Point, and Midpoint—become prerequisites to getting your middle right. If you find your story on weak ground, accurate diagnostics at each of these points are key, because an undetected broken link deflates each and every story beat that follows it.

You are the architect of that assembly—which, when it works, becomes a moving dramatic vehicle, sweeping readers along toward a destination. It's what they signed up for, so don't leave them waiting in the middle. Keep the story on track as you move it forward, and take thrilling twists and turns along the way.

When you do, readers will come back for more. And it'll be your middle, as much as your premise and your prose, that makes it happen.

Larry Brooks is the author of *Story Physics: Harnessing the Underlying Forces of Storytelling* (Writer's Digest Books). His latest novel is *Deadly Faux*. Visit his website at storyfix.com.

CAPTURING READERS' INTEREST

An Interview with J.T. Ellison

....

Janice Gable Bashman

J.T. Ellison knows how to hook readers from the very first pages of a novel. "A sharp, strong voice, an engaging style, and starting the action and story immediately are what it takes," she says. "Kick-start your story, set the tone, and assure your readers that you aren't going to waste their time making them wonder what this book is going to be about." Ellison's ability to engage readers' attention and draw them quickly into the story is one of the many reasons for her blockbuster success.

Ellison is the *New York Times* best-selling author of eleven novels, two novellas, and numerous short stories, and her fiction has been published in more than twenty countries. Her novels in the Lieutenant Taylor Jackson series include *Where All the Dead Lie*, *So Close the Hand of Death*, *The Immortals,* and four others. Her Samantha Owens series includes *When Shadows Fall*, *Edge of Black*, and *A Deeper Darkness*. She also co-wrote *The Final Cut* with Catherine Coulter. Ellison's novel *The Cold Room* won the ITW Thriller Award for Best Paperback Original, and *Where All The Dead Lie* was a RITA Nominee for Best Romantic Suspense. Here, she shares her advice for earning—and keeping—your readers' attention.

Point of view and voice are important factors in engaging readers. How can writers discover their voice and determine which point of view is appropriate for the story and will effectively engage readers?

Practice makes perfect, and the best way to practice is by writing short stories. Flash fiction (telling a full story in 1,000 words or less) is a great training tool. Every story needs to have a beginning, a middle, and an end. Every chapter needs a beginning, a middle, and an end. Most of my chapters run about 1,000 words, so it helps with pace, but it also allows for moving between points of view. POV is tough—every writer is different. If you try a few different styles in [short stories], you'll find the voice you're comfortable with for a full-length novel.

And once you decide on a point of view, stick to it. Head hopping, switching from first to third, [and] writing in present tense are all minefields for less-experienced writers. I'd suggest writing multiple short stories in every point of view, trying omniscient, close third, first person, and seeing what the story needs and what you're most comfortable doing. Remember, each story has its own requirements for POV. Something written in first person might not work, but switch it to close third, and *voilá*—magic.

What are the important points to remember when kick-starting the story and setting the tone?

You must grab the readers' attention immediately. Clean, straightforward prose, in the style of your genre, is vital. If you're writing a thriller, you start with a scene that establishes a question. (And at the end of the book, you must answer that question.) In a mystery, what is missing, what are the stakes? If it's a romance, what's the conflict? And whatever you do, don't interrupt the forward progress of the story to tell the reader the backstory. A good storyteller captures the imagination of the reader immediately and uses action and reaction to tell the story as the book progresses.

How do you accomplish this quickly in your thrillers?

By focusing the story *in medias res*. Begin in the middle. We so often start the story in the wrong place—much too early. I like to begin with the antagonist so the reader immediately sees what's at stake, or [sees] my hero up against a wall. This immediate action is like tossing a fishing lure in the middle of a waking pond in the early evening—the reader, like the fish, will strike and set on the hook and be hungry for more, and then you have them. And increase the stakes as quickly as possible. You don't want to start with a bang, then slip into a sedate voice.

For example, this is the opening of *The Cold Room*:

> *Gavin Adler jumped when a small chime sounded on his computer. He looked at the clock in surprise; it was already 6:00 p.m. During the winter months, darkness descended and reminded him to close up shop, but the Daylight Savings time change necessitated an alarm clock to let him know when it was time to leave. Otherwise, he'd get lost in his computer and never find his way home.*
>
> *He rose from his chair, stretched, turned off the computer and reached for his messenger bag. What a day. What a long and glorious day.*

Immediately we know something has happened this day. But what? There is no backstory, no explanation of who Gavin is and why we should care. The story continues, but the reader has the idea in the back of her mind: Why is it such a glorious day?

We follow Gavin home, through his workout, to the store, feeding his cat, and making a solitary dinner. It seems so innocuous, so innocent, so banal. And then we turn the page and find out why the day has been so glorious. Gavin has a terrible secret. He's been waiting to give himself a reward, one weeks in the making.

> *The padlock on the door to the basement was shiny with promise and lubricant. He inserted the key, twisting his wrist to keep it from jangling. He took the lock with him, holding it gingerly so he didn't get oil on his clothes. Oil was nearly impossible to get out. He made sure Art wasn't around, he didn't like the cat to get into the basement. He saw him sitting on the kitchen table, looking mournfully at the empty spot where Gavin's plate had rested.*
>
> *Inside the door, the stairs led to blackness. He flipped a switch and light flooded the stairwell. He slipped the end of the lock in the inside latch, then clicked it home. No sense taking chances.*
>
> *She was asleep. He was quiet, so he wouldn't wake her. He just wanted to look, anyway.*
>
> *The Plexiglas cage was the shape of a coffin with a long clear divider down the length—creating two perfectly sized compartments—with small drainage holes in the bottom and air holes along the top. It stood on a reinforced platform he had built himself. The concrete floor had a drain; all he needed to do was sluice water across the opening and presto, clean. He ran the water for a few minutes, clearing out the debris, then looked back to his love.*

Gavin, a mild-mannered computer expert who is having a seemingly normal evening suddenly turns into a frightening deviant with a kidnapped woman slowly dying in a glass coffin in his basement. The reader knows right away that Gavin isn't who he seems and that they are in for an unexpected ride.

And if you notice, there are *two* perfectly sized compartments, but only one woman. Why? Has another been there? Or is he planning to take one? Questions, conflict, and unexpected turns, all in the first three pages.

If the writer is not dropping a body on the first few pages, what other ways can he capture readers' attention?

Life is conflict. Anything that shows the main characters in conflict will draw the reader in. It can be as simple as a dinner between lovers—why are they there? What are they discussing? Is this a date? A breakup? Is she going to tell him she has cancer? Or that she's pregnant? Is he going to admit to an affair? Or are they recollecting the years behind them and planning for the future? Is their child sick and this is the first time they've been alone in weeks? You see where I'm going—even the simplest situation is loaded with intrigue in the right hands.

Is it more important to focus on plot or character, or both, in those first few pages? Why?

Plot is great and necessary, but it's characters that bring the readers back, time after time. If your reader cares about your protagonist and is afraid of or angry with your antagonist, you've done your job. It's important to remember to keep the writing clean, clear, and succinct. Finding the balance between story and character is vital, but always remember, the story is happening to the characters. Stay in their heads, not in yours.

How do you avoid wasting your readers' time and establish the premise of the book from the start?

By making the stakes clear immediately and establishing who's in charge. By that I mean making it clear up front whose book it is. If your protagonist doesn't appear until Chapter 13, then you've got a problem. If there are fifteen named characters introduced in the first chapter, you're going to lose the reader. Start where the story begins—not before and not after. This takes a bit of practice, but you'll get the hang of it quickly. Be clean, be focused, and make the reader gasp.

For example, the opening line of my novella *Whiteout* (from Storm Season) is in first person, and the stakes are clear immediately:

My father's screams echo in the small car.

It's not hard to imagine what a daughter might be feeling in this situation. And you'd be right.

Here is the whole scene. We immediately see the terror of the situation, the visceral reaction of this small girl, who, incidentally, grows up to become an assassin, visiting the same fear and horror she experienced as a child on others.

My father's screams echo in the small car.

"Monte, vite, vite. Angelie, baisse-toi! Baisse-toi!"

My head hits the floor just as the window shatters. Blood, thick and hot, sprays my bare legs. I wedge myself under my mother's skirts, her thighs heavy against my shoulders, somehow knowing she is already dead. We are all dead.

Flashes of black.

Their voices, two distinctly male, one female. Another, a stranger's call, silenced abruptly with a short fusillade of bullets. His bicycle smashes into the side of our aging Peugeot, his body catapults across the hood onto the pavement beyond. The crack sounds like the opening of a cantaloupe, ripe and hard.

My father, his life leaving him, slides down in the seat like a puppet cut from his strings. He's whispering words over and over, faintly, and with the cacophony in the background I can barely hear him. I risk a glance, wishing I'd not. The image shall never leave me. Red, pulpy and viscous. He is missing half his face, but his full lips are moving.

"Si toi survivras, cherché ton Oncle Pierre. On aime quelqu'un de tout son cœur."

I hear nothing but the first words. Panic fills me. Though I recognize what is happening, the reality has just crept in.

Si toi survivras. If you survive.

I want to take his hand, to comfort him, to tell him I am there, that I too love him with all my heart. I reach for him as he dies, shaking his head, trying to implore me to stay hidden, not to move. He isn't even speaking now, but I can hear the words in my head, like he has transferred his soul from his body to mine for these last fluttering moments, has given himself up early to crowd into my body and try to save me.

Undeterred, my hand steals across the gearshift. I touch the cold skin of his thumb.

A roaring in my ears. There is pain beyond anything I've ever felt, and I go blank.

You stated on your website that you "build the story with words, toss in the spices, and season it to taste. [You] can't necessarily explain *how* that happens, but [you] know when it's ready to be read, just as a master chef knows when it's time to turn off the heat and serve the dish." How can a writer who is not yet a "master chef" know when his story is ready to be read?

Deciding a story is finished is possibly the most difficult thing about writing. It's one of those innate skills all writers need to hone. Once you've answered the question you established in Chapter 1, the story is finished. Stop too soon and you'll shortchange the reader. Go on too long and they'll get bored. Use exactly the amount of words it takes to tell the story—no more, no less.

There is a natural rhythm to a story. Some call it the Hero's Journey, some break the story into three acts, some follow a "beginning, middle, end" structure, some just know when the story is done. It takes practice. Reading and deconstructing the books you like is a great way to figure out their innate rhythm.

Once you've finished, the real work begins. Editing, revising, making sure everything works—the story unfolds properly; the conflicts have been resolved; threads are pulled through; red herrings are well placed; time frames are correct; the language is clear; the manuscript is free of typos and spelling, grammar, and technical errors; and your research is spot on—these are the hallmarks of a true writer.

Janice Gable Bashman is the Bram Stoker-nominated author of *Wanted Undead or Alive* and *Predator* (young adult thriller, October 2014). She is the editor of *The Big Thrill*, the International Thriller Writers' magazine. Visit Janice at janicegablebashman.com.

THE STUFF SERIES ARE MADE OF

....

Karen S. Wiesner

"The disease of writing is dangerous and contagious," Abelard famously said to Heloise. So, too, can a book series become a relentless obsession: It's why readers follow series devotedly to the last, why writers write them for years on end, and why publishers contract them in spades. In our trend-driven world, series are hotter than ever.

But if writing a novel can seem overwhelming, the idea of creating a whole series of them can be exponentially more so. Whether you've been pondering starting a series from Page 1, or you've finished a book and don't want to let the characters go, there are plenty of simple things you can implement now to lay a strong foundation for what's to come.

TIES

If a series doesn't have a "tie" that connects each book, it can hardly be called a series. Ties can be any (or even all) of the following:

- A recurring character or couple (think Aloysius Pendergast in Douglas Preston and Lincoln Child's Pendergast series, or J.D. Robb's Eve and Roarke from the In Death series)
- A central group of characters (George R.R. Martin's A Song of Ice and Fire, Kate Jacobs's Friday Night Knitting Club)
- A plot or premise (Robin Cook's Jack Stapleton medical mysteries, Dan Brown's treasure hunts starring Robert Langdon)
- A setting (Twilight's Forks, Washington, Harry Potter's Hogwarts School of Witch-craft and Wizardry)

Series can be open-ended—in which each book stands on its own, and the series could continue indefinitely (Langdon)—or closed, in which an underlying plot continues in each book and resolves in the last (Harry Potter).

What connects the books in a series should be evident from Book 1. Ensuring this kind of continuity requires advance planning, starting as early as possible.

STORY ARCS AND SERIES ARCS

Every work of fiction, series or otherwise, has a contained story line. That story arc is introduced, developed, and concluded within each individual book. Series books often have a series arc as well: a long-term plot thread that is introduced in the first book; developed, expanded, and/or alluded to in some way in each subsequent book; and resolved only in the final installment of the series.

Series arcs can be prominent or can be more subtly defined. The series arc is generally separate from each individual story arc, though they must fit together seamlessly in each book to provide logical progression throughout the series. For example, in *Harry Potter and the Sorcerer's Stone,* the story arc is the Sorcerer's Stone plotline. The series arc, in the most simplified terms, is good overcoming evil among this set group of characters in the fantasy world of the series. The series arc runs progressively and cohesively beneath the individual story arcs in all the successive books.

Unless a series is completely open-ended, it is imperative that you pay off promises made early in your series arc in the concluding book. You've presented a nagging situation in the first book that *must* be settled satisfactorily in the last. Without that, readers who have invested time, money, and passion will feel cheated. If, in the course of Brandon Mull's Fablehaven Series, Kendra and Seth didn't defeat the evil threatening the Fablehaven preserve and stop the plague that could have led to a hoard of imprisoned demons escaping into the world, Mull would have left his fans crying foul because he broke the pledge of a satisfactory resolution implied in the first book.

Take the time to map out your series arc as much as you can up front, so you can work through that premise from the start and ensure you'll reward readers at the finish.

C-S-P SERIES POTENTIAL

Readers fall in love with characters, settings, and plots. They want conflict but don't want you to hurt their heroes. They want something different but don't want things to change. But a character, setting, or plot that doesn't evolve doesn't remain lifelike and eventually becomes boring.

Series characters, settings, and plots should have longevity and intriguing potential that continues to grow, never stagnating or waning, throughout the course of a series. While none of these should ever have a radical transplant from one book to the next, it's crucial they're affected by changes. Consider the three *P*s that make characters (and just as certainly settings and plots) three-dimensional:

1. **PERSONALITY:** always multifaceted, with strengths and weaknesses, and capable of growing—being molded, deeply delved, and stretched
2. **PROBLEMS:** combining light and dark, good and evil, simple and complex—not necessarily in equal parts
3. **PURPOSE:** evolving goals and motivations broad enough to introduce new and unpredictable themes throughout the series, but narrow enough to maintain focus in each individual story

If you don't introduce something new for series characters, settings, and plots in each book, your readers will lose motivation to read all the way to the end.

To plant seeds for future growth in your series, nurture your C-S-P (Character-Setting-Plot) potential by establishing "plants" in early books that can be cultivated at any time during the life of the series to expand on one or all three of these components. Naturally, the sooner you incorporate these, the more believable they'll be when it's time to fully develop them.

In Dan Brown's novels, for example, Robert Langdon frequently mentions the Mickey Mouse watch he wears—not something most grown men would be caught dead in. It was a gift from his parents on his ninth birthday, and it's rife with sentimental value. Considering that his plots involve racing against the clock, the significance of this object is heightened.

The watch becomes pivotal when Langdon is thrust in a tank of breathable oxygenated liquid in *The Lost Symbol* (Book 3). If that were the first time it was mentioned, the story's believability would have been drowned as a consequence. But Brown planted the item early enough in Book 1—during an appropriate time for passive reflection—that its later role in life-or-death action scenes doesn't feel contrived or overly convenient to the plot.

Most authors include numerous "plants" in the first book in a series without even realizing it. That's good news for you if your first book is already well under way. But that doesn't mean you shouldn't deliberately insert them. When developing your C-S-P series potential, do free-form summaries for the following questions. Don't worry if you can't come up with much right away; simply use these as a jumping-off point as the series progresses, assuming that these seeds may be planted (and left mostly unexplored) in the early books for development in later titles:

- How can you outfit *all* series characters, even minor ones, with heroic traits and habits in addition to flaws and vices that can lead to natural growth as well as interesting plots and subplots?
- How can you give them occupations, hobbies, interests, and idiosyncrasies that might be gradually developed?

- What relationships and potential enemies/villains can you add to expand the potential for subplots, characters, or ongoing conflicts or rivalries that might play a bigger role in a later book?
- What lessons, backstory, or experiences can be hinted at for later revelation and development that may lead to suspenseful plots or emotional crises?
- What life conditions, challenges, trials, grudges, grief, betrayals, threats, heartaches, or obsessions can characters face that may lead to compelling situations throughout the series? (Think romance, marriage, divorce, parents/children, illness, medical ailment, or death.)
- What locations can you set the series and individual books in to expand characters and plots?
- What world, regional, or local events, holidays, important dates, or disasters (natural or man-made) can provide a catalyst?
- What quest—fortuitous, cursed, or anywhere in between—can be undertaken?
- What item or object might become the basis for plot, setting, or character development?

Always leave plenty of plants unexplored to give your series longevity and your characters and story lines flexibility. In the early books in the Pendergast series, it was revealed that the protagonist's wife had been killed years earlier. Superficial details about this death were alluded to but kept sparse and flexible enough that, when the authors moved into their Helen Trilogy quite a few books later, they could easily mold this event any way they needed to and maintain believability. Had they locked down specific details early on, the trilogy might never have seen the light of day.

Hints and allusions are essential when implementing C-S-P potential. In real life, no one walks around with a list to show others of the people they know, the places they've been, or the things they've done. These are shared a little at a time. In the same way, from one book to the next, explore the facets of C-S-P slowly. If you give too much detail too soon, you may find it hard to change or adapt when the time comes to use a plant.

Remember: If no one wants to see more of these characters, settings, and plots over the long haul, the series is doomed. Always spin established facts on their axis so the reader will have a new, emotional, and unexpected journey in each story. Every offering must be *at least* as exciting as the one before. These are the ingredients that bring readers back for more.

ORGANIZATION OF DETAILS

The best way to learn how *not* to write a series is to do so with no organization whatsoever. You'll likely miss countless opportunities to plant and grow seeds for C-S-P series potential, be forced to backtrack to clear up issues that arise, and maybe even write yourself into a corner.

While some authors may be capable of outlining every book in a series before writing a word, that's not possible for everyone. Maybe the only way for you to figure out where you're going with your series is to complete the first book, then set it aside while you think about what might lie ahead: Which characters will take the lead? What story will be told, and which conflicts will arise? What seeds can you go back and plant in the first manuscript to prepare readers for the next installments? Even if you're not much of a planner, try answering the C-S-P potential questions (on the previous page) as much as you can. Never underestimate the value of the key story (and series!) questions percolating in your mind.

How much preplanning you do is up to you, but at minimum, I recommend you at least attempt to build on your C-S-P potential by writing summary blurbs for the series and its individual books. Just see how far you can get. Play with them and don't expect perfection the first time. You can work with them more as your series progresses.

For a series blurb, you're not focusing on individual stories but on the gist of what the series *as a whole* is about. If the series blurb is done well enough, it'll accurately reflect what every book in the series is about in a concise, intriguing summary. Remember your series ties while you're working; they'll help you figure out what your series arc should be. In no more than four sentences, define your series arc by using "leads to" logic (note that the components don't have to be in order, nor is a resolution required since you may not want to defuse the intrigue or tension):

Introduction → Change → Conflicts → Choices → Crisis → Resolutions

Here's an example from my Incognito series:

> *The Network is the world's most covert organization. Having unchallenged authority and skill to disable criminals, the Network takes over where regular law enforcement leaves off in the mission for absolute justice (**Introduction**). The price: men and women who have sacrificed their personal identities (**Choices**) to live in the shadows (**Change**) and uphold justice for all (**Conflicts**)—no matter the cost (**Crisis**).*

Next, try blurbing the individual stories you foresee comprising the series. It's all right if you've only gotten as far as brainstorming one or two books. Start with what you have and add later, as more comes to you. Even if you don't think you know enough to get started planning this way, you'll likely find that the process of putting your ideas into words helps your concepts multiply.

Focus on which characters will take the lead in individual stories and what each story arc (conflict) will be. Write free-form summaries covering the who, what, where, when, and why of each story. Then try creating a more compelling blurb using this equation (if you have more than one main character, do this for each):

(Name of Character) wants **(Goal to be Achieved)** because **(Motivation for Acting)**, but faces **(Conflict Standing in the Way)**.

As before, you can mix up the order of the components. Here's the story blurb from *Dark Approach*, the twelfth book in my Incognito series:

> *Network operatives and lovers Lucy Carlton and Vic Leventhal (Names of Characters) have spent years living in the shadows, the property of the covert organization they gave their loyalty to in the lofty pursuit of justice for all (Motivation for Acting). Disillusioned, they're now determined to live their lives on their own terms. When the Network's archenemy secretly approaches the two about defecting—freedom for information that will disable the Network (Goal to be Achieved)—the couple must choose between love and loyalty. In the process, they jeopardize the Network's anonymity … and its very existence (Conflict Standing in the Way).*

Blurbing in this way will help you develop your series—and get you excited about writing it.

The appeal of writing a series is obvious: You don't have to leave characters, places, or premises you've grown to love behind when you finish a single book. While each story should stand on its own, remember that no series book should feel quite complete without the others since readers will be emotionally invested in your story even more than they would with a stand-alone novel. Keep the above factors at the forefront as you work, and you'll keep your series satisfying for your fans—and for you.

Karen Wiesner is a multigenre author with 105 titles published, including five trilogies and twelve series, ranging from three to twelve books each—which have been nominated for and/or won 126 awards. Her latest is *Writing the Fiction Series: The Complete Guide for Novels and Novellas* (Writer's Digest Books). Visit Karen's website at www.karenwiesner.com and sign up for her free newsletter to qualify for her monthly book giveaways.

PICTURE PERFECT

An Interview with Ransom Riggs

Adrienne Crezo

Like most first conversations and bad first drafts, my interview with Ransom Riggs begins with a discussion about the weather. And not just *any* weather, either, but peculiar versions of standard precipitation: dust storms, cloudbursts, thundersnow, and tornadoes. Of course, Riggs is experiencing none of those phenomena as he sits in the warmth of the never-ending summer of Los Angeles. "I hate to tell you what it's like here right now," he says. "No, I don't. It's gorgeous. Just perfect."

That kind of easygoing humor is familiar to Riggs's fans. Readers of his *New York Times* best-selling young adult novel *Miss Peregrine's Home for Peculiar Children* and its sequel, *Hollow City,* convene on Twitter (@ransomriggs) and Instagram (instagram.com/ransomriggs) to follow the seemingly unshakable optimism of a guy who really enjoys what he does. Life is uncomplicated for Riggs, as is his approach to work and writing. "[I never] set out to be a writer," he tells me. "I took a fiction class [in college], but … I just thought, *That'd be a fun thing to do for a semester*, not, *This is my future*."

Whatever dreams Riggs may have had about his future, he couldn't have predicted the wild success of *Miss Peregrine's Home for Peculiar Children*, a tale of time travel and magic set against the eerie backdrop of unnerving black-and-white photos of levitating girls and creepy twin clowns. Before *Peculiar Children*'s release in 2011, the film rights had already been snapped up by 20th Century Fox, and the movie, directed by none other than Tim Burton, is slated for release in summer 2015. *Hollow City*, second of the three planned Peculiar Children books, was released in January 2014. And in the midst of all this, Riggs also released *Talking Pictures*, a coffee-table book of found photographs, in 2012.

It's easy to see why Riggs is enjoying the ride, but what appears to have happened overnight actually evolved over many years. It started with a love of film and photography, which led him to collecting old secondhand photographs. In 2009, Riggs was encouraged by an editor at Quirk Books to use the found pictures as the basis of a novel. At the time, Riggs was writing daily for mentalfloss.com, a popular general-interest trivia website, editing and filming short documentaries, and shooting photo essays as he traveled. He laughs to himself as he recalls his initial reaction to the conversation: "OK, Quirk. No one's going to read that. Let me go back to blogging."

Luckily, Riggs decided to take the editor's advice. He compiled his found photos and wound a weird, twisting tale around them—and, in return, an eager YA audience turned the Peculiar Children series into an unlikely hit. Here, Riggs talks about his writing and social media habits, why he doesn't follow rules, and why it's important to take time off.

Your photo collection plays a huge role in the Peculiar Children books. Can you tell us how you started collecting people's cast-off snapshots?

I was at this swap meet in Pasadena [in 2009] called the Rose Bowl. I knew people sold old photographs, sort of in the corner of my mind, but I was never very interested in them … because they all looked like junk. But then I found a booth at this particular swap meet that was operated by a fellow named Leonard, who had clearly gone through many, many, many bins of photos and chosen his favorite 200 and put them in little plastic sleeves. I started looking at them and I [thought], *Wow, there's something really special here. This guy has the eye of a curator, and every [photo] is like a little piece of lost, orphaned folk art. That's really cool!* As someone who grew up loving photography in every way I could, I would have loved to have had a photo collection of my own, but I couldn't afford to buy prints. … So I thought, *Here is a way I could start my own little museum of photographs.* You get to be your own curator; you're rescuing them from the trash and saying, "I decide this is art, and I'm going to keep it."

It occurred to me, as I collected more and more, that my taste in these photos ran in very specific directions. One was a sort of Edward Gorey-esque Victorian creepiness, and the other was photos with writing on them. I always felt like these were completely anonymous photos. … If they've written a little bit on the picture, especially if it's more than just a label, if it's a thought or a feeling or something revelatory, there's a window into this lost world that suddenly has context where it did not before. That's interesting.

Do you collect photos now solely for book material, or is it still a thing you just enjoy doing?

It's still partly just a hobby. Maybe one day they'll find their way into something I do, but maybe not. I just like owning them.

I started without anything in particular in mind to do with [the photos]; I just sort of wanted to have them. … And they're not all creepy. There are so many I have that I love that are just sort of evocative in some simple way—the look on someone's face, or a cool angle or interesting subject or something. I have a lot that I don't even necessarily know that I'll use—they don't fit in the Peculiar Children books and they don't fit in [*Talking Pictures*]. I just like them.

In *Peculiar Children* and its sequel, *Hollow City*, your protagonist, Jacob, has some pretty interesting magical powers, but he's also a teenager with all the typical teenager woes. You've called Jacob your "fantasy self." How much of you is in Jacob, really?

You'd have to be a literary critic or a psychiatrist to pick the writer out of his work. Every fictional story goes through this sort of blender process where you take some real experience … you know what's real or true when you put it into the blender with fiction, and then it gets all mixed up with something that didn't really happen, but there's still a little of you in there. I think the writer is in there no matter what you do. You can't really remove yourself from it.

Did you set out to be a novelist or did you have other plans?

No, I wanted to make movies. When I was a kid I wanted to be a novelist … but then around the eighth grade I discovered movies and I became completely obsessed and lost myself in this dream of making movies. My friends and I had a video camera, and we would make movies all the time.

I knew I wanted to go to film school, but I also knew I wanted to learn things first. I wanted to learn about the important ideas and read the great books, so I went to Kenyon [College], but always with the understanding that I would go to film school afterward.

[I] was chasing the white pony of having a film career [and] doing whatever I could do: making short films and editing things and freelance writing. The writing thing came about completely by accident. … I never really wanted [it] or looked for it. I feel like the opposite might be true, instead, where if I'd tried really hard to be a writer, maybe someone would've [asked], "Do you want to be a filmmaker instead?" And I would've [said], "OK"—the theory of inverse effort.

I think [filmmaking] was a way for me to get into novel writing, which is not something I might have done on my own. Now that I'm doing it, I find that with each Peculiar Children book I have to work harder to include photos. The story has all this momentum of its own now.

Will that momentum carry the Peculiar Children series beyond the three books you have planned?

This story that I'm telling now will conclude in book three, but I think I'll leave the door open to that world. I'm going to do something else next, but I will probably come back and write more [books for the series] one day.

Do you follow any specific writing rules?

I always distrust overly specific writing advice. I don't agree with it, necessarily. When you're thinking about what to write or how to write something, it's too easy to make a lot of arbitrary rules for yourself. I think the difficult thing with learning how to write is not learning the style or rules, but figuring out what story you want to tell.

I spent a lot of time telling the wrong stories, especially when … I was in college or when I was a kid trying to imitate C.S. Lewis or Stephen King. I never understood why my writing didn't take off. I would think, *Well, the sentences are correct, and the characters are talking and everything looks right, and it seems like a story. I did exactly what [they] told me to do, but there's no blood in it and I don't know why.* It's something you have to learn, how to tell the right stories *for you*, and it's this completely ineffable thing.

What about schedules? Do you wake up some days and think, *I'm not going to write; I'm not going to edit.* Do you take days off?

Oh, all the time! Sometimes I say, "Today, I'm going to clean my house and go to the movies." Or, "Today, [my wife] Tahereh and I are going to ride our bikes and go and eat too much Persian food." That happens a lot. That's a lot of our days, actually.

I spent the last three months plotting book three [of the Peculiar Children series]. So just in the last couple of days I've transitioned into writing actual sentences on pages of the book, and now that I have that momentum, I *do* want to write every day—at least a little, just to keep the thread. A lot, preferably, but between books I'll go months and months without writing. It's exhausting. I'm just like, "I can't."

That's a long break between projects! It's a wonder that you fall back into the groove at all. Is writer's block ever a problem for you?

I don't really believe in that whole "wait for the muse to strike" thing. I'm more of a "sit your ass in a chair and start typing" guy. … People treat writer's block like it's this kind of mythical, mystical ailment. It's actually a very specific problem, and that is that something is wrong with your story, or wrong with your scene, and you're trying to do something that is not motivated by your characters. If your writer's block is so complete that you don't even know where to start, it's probably that you're not spending enough time at the keyboard. It's all part of the process.

I also think that writer's block comes from judging yourself too much, and [thinking], *I only wrote one sentence today! I'm terrible!*

How do you keep yourself in a chair and working when you're so active on social media?

I find myself retreating from social media when I need to work. I realize that I'm becoming too dependent on talking to everyone on Twitter. It's too distracting. I'm constantly reaching for it, like a drug or something.

You can spend a whole day clicking and scrolling and feeling like you've gotten something done—*Oh man, that was a really funny tweet*—but then at the end of the day you're like, *I did nothing. All day, I've done nothing at all. I have nothing to show for it.* Except that funny tweet, of course.

So you live in Los Angeles with your wife, best-selling YA author Tahereh Mafi. And you two work together. Do you share a desk?

Yes. It's a very long desk, very wide. So there's space enough for our things and our laptops and all our books, and we put on our noise-canceling headphones and [work]. That's the thing about being married to another writer—we know all of the ways in which the other person is weird and quirky, because all writers are a little weird and quirky. So we [know we] need our quiet, broody time, but then we need to run around and go have fun when writing time is over—when work is over—because we've been kind of cooped up inside of our own brains all day. It works. Somehow it works.

You share a lot of your social media time with Tahereh, too, which your fans seem to love. But it seems as if it could become overwhelming at a certain point. Do you ever try to hold back?

I think we're pretty knee-deep in it all, we read a lot of it. And it's largely positive, which I think is pretty rare. I've been waiting for negative weirdness to start to surface, but it hasn't yet.

I wouldn't keep posting pictures of Tahereh on Instagram if people didn't keep going, "Yay! Give us more," you know? I feel like we both have been waiting for the Internet to collectively be like, "OK, gag me, it's enough already!" But, bafflingly, it hasn't happened yet, so we just keep going.

How about some parting advice for writers?

Just unclench, live your life, and spend less time berating yourself. Anxiety and stress are the enemies of creativity.

Adrienne Crezo is the managing editor of *Writer's Digest* magazine.

THE BUSINESS OF FICTION WRITING

It's true there are no substitutes for talent and hard work. A writer's first concern must always be attention to craft. No matter how well presented, a poorly written story or novel has little chance of being published. On the other hand, a well-written piece may be equally hard to sell in today's competitive publishing market. Talent alone is just not enough.

To be successful, writers need to study the field and pay careful attention to finding the right market. While the hours spent perfecting your writing are usually hours spent alone, you're not alone when it comes to developing your marketing plan. *Novel & Short Story Writer's Market* provides you with detailed listings containing the essential information you'll need to locate and contact the markets most suitable for your work.

Once you've determined where to send your work, you must turn your attention to presentation. We can help here, too. We've included the basics of manuscript preparation, along with information on submission procedures and how to approach markets. We also include tips on promoting your work. No matter where you're from or what level of experience you have, you'll find useful information here on everything from presentation to mailing to selling rights to promoting your work—the "business" of fiction.

APPROACHING MAGAZINE MARKETS

A query letter by itself is usually not required by most magazine fiction editors. If you are approaching a magazine to find out if fiction is accepted, a query is fine, but editors looking for short fiction want to see the actual piece. A cover letter can be useful as a letter of introduction, but the key here is brevity. A successful cover letter is no more than one page (20-lb. bond paper). It should be single-spaced with a double space between paragraphs, proofread carefully, and neatly typed in a standard typeface (not script or italic). The writer's name, address, phone number, and e-mail address must appear at the top, and the letter should be addressed, ideally, to a specific editor. (If the editor's name is unavailable, use "Fiction Editor.")

The body of a successful cover letter contains the name and word count of the story, a brief list of previous publications, if you have any, and the reason you are submitting to this particular publication. Mention that you have enclosed a self-addressed, stamped envelope for reply. Also, let the editor know if you are sending a disposable manuscript (not to be returned; more and more editors prefer disposable manuscripts that save them time and save you postage). Finally, don't forget to thank the editor for considering your story.

Note that more and more publications prefer to receive electronic submissions, both as e-mail attachments and through online submission forms. See individual listings for specific information on electronic submission requirements, and always visit magazines' websites for up-to-date guidelines.

APPROACHING BOOK PUBLISHERS

Some book publishers do ask for queries first, but most want a query plus sample chapters or an outline or, occasionally, the complete manuscript. Again, make your letter brief. Include the essentials about yourself: name, address, phone number, e-mail address, and publishing experience. Include a three- or four-sentence "pitch" and only the personal information related to your story. Show that you have researched the market with a few sentences about why you chose this publisher.

BOOK PROPOSALS

A book proposal is a package sent to a publisher that includes a cover letter and one or more of the following: sample chapters, outline, synopsis, author bio, publications list. When asked to send sample chapters, send up to three consecutive chapters. An outline covers the highlights of your book chapter by chapter. Be sure to include details on main characters, the plot, and subplots. Outlines can run up to thirty pages, depending on the length of your novel. The object is to tell what happens in a concise but clear manner. A synopsis is a shorter summary of your novel, written in a way that expresses the emotion of the story in addition to just explaining the essential points. Evan Marshall, literary agent and author of *The Marshall Plan for Getting Your Novel Published* (Writer's Digest Books), suggests you aim for a page of synopsis for every twenty-five pages of manuscript. Marshall also advises you write the synopsis as one unified narrative, without section heads, subheads, or chapters to break up the text. The terms *synopsis* and *outline* are sometimes used interchangeably, so be sure to find out exactly what each publisher wants.

A FEW WORDS ABOUT AGENTS

Agents are not usually needed for short fiction and most do not handle it unless they already have a working relationship with you. For novels, you may want to consider working with an agent, especially if you intend to market your book to publishers who do not look at unsolicited submissions. For more on approaching agents and to read listings of agents willing to work with beginning and established writers, see our **Literary Agents** section. You can also refer to this year's edition of *Guide to Literary Agents*, edited by Chuck Sambuchino.

MANUSCRIPT MECHANICS

A professionally presented manuscript will not guarantee publication. But a sloppy, hard-to-read manuscript will not be read—publishers simply do not have the time. Here's a list of suggested submission techniques for polished manuscript presentation:

- For a short story manuscript, your first page should include your name, address, phone number, and e-mail address (single spaced) in the upper left corner. In the upper right, indicate an approximate word count. Center the name of your story about one-third of the way down the page, skip a line, and center your byline (the byline is optional). Skip four lines and begin your story. On subsequent pages, put your last name and page number in the upper right corner.

- For book manuscripts, use a separate title page. Put your name, address, phone number, and e-mail address in the lower right corner and word count in the upper right. If you have representation, list your agent's name and address in the lower right. (This bumps your name and contact information to the upper left corner.) Center your title and byline about halfway down the page. Start your first chapter on the next page. Center the chapter number and title (if there is one) one-third of the way down the page. Include your last name and the novel's title in all caps in the upper left header, and put the page number in the upper right header of this page and each page to follow. Start each chapter with a new page.

- Proofread carefully. Keep a dictionary, thesaurus, and stylebook handy and use the spell-check function on your computer.

- Include a word count. Your word processing program can likely give you a word count.

- Suggest art where applicable. Most publishers do not expect you to provide artwork and some insist on selecting their own illustrators, but if you have suggestions, let them know. Magazine publishers work in a very visual field and are usually open to ideas.

- Keep accurate records. This can be done in a number of ways, but be sure to keep track of where your stories are and when you sent them out. Write down submission dates. If you do not hear about your submission for a long time—about one to two months longer than the reporting time stated in the listing—you may want to contact the publisher. When you do, you will need an accurate record for reference.

Electronic Submissions

- If sending electronic submissions via e-mail or online submission form, check the publisher's website first for specific information and follow the directions carefully.

Hard-Copy Submissions

- Use white 8½" × 11" bond paper, preferably 16- or 20-lb. weight. The paper must be heavy enough not to show pages underneath and strong enough to take handling by several people.

- Type your manuscript on a computer and print it out using a laser or ink-jet printer (or, if you must, use a typewriter with a new ribbon).

- An occasional spot of white-out is okay, but don't send a marked-up manuscript with many typos.

- Always double-space and leave a 1" margin on all sides of the page.

- Don't forget word count. If you are using a typewriter, there are several ways to count the number of words in your piece. One way is to count the words in five lines and divide that number by five to find an average. Then count the number of lines and multiply to find the total words. For long pieces, you may want to count the words in the first three pages, divide by three, and multiply by the number of pages you have.

- Always keep a copy. Manuscripts do get lost. To avoid expensive mailing costs, send only what is required. If you are including artwork or photos but you are not positive they will be used, send photocopies. Artwork is hard to replace.

- Enclose a self-addressed, stamped envelope (SASE) if you want a reply or if you want your manuscript returned. For most letters, a business-size (#10) envelope will do. Avoid using any envelope too small for an 8½" × 11" sheet of paper. For manuscripts, be sure to include enough postage and an envelope large enough to contain it. If you are requesting a sample copy of a magazine or a book publisher's catalog, send an appropriately sized envelope.

- Consider sending a disposable manuscript that saves editors time (this will also save you money).

ABOUT OUR POLICIES

We occasionally receive letters asking why a certain magazine, publisher, or contest is not in the book. Sometimes when we contact listings, the editors do not want to be listed because they:

- do not use very much fiction.
- are overwhelmed with submissions.
- are having financial difficulty or have been recently sold.
- use only solicited material.
- accept work from a select group of writers only.
- do not have the staff or time for the many unsolicited submissions a listing may bring.

Some of the listings do not appear because we have chosen not to list them. We investigate complaints of unprofessional conduct in editors' dealings with writers and misrepresentation of information provided to us by editors and publishers. If we find these reports to be true, after a thorough investigation we will delete the listing from future editions.

There is no charge to the companies that list in this book. Listings appearing in *Novel & Short Story Writer's Market* are compiled from detailed questionnaires, phone interviews, and information provided by editors, publishers, and directors of awards and conferences. The publishing industry is volatile, and changes of address, editor, policies, and needs happen frequently. To keep up with the changes between editions of the book, we suggest you check the market information on the Writer's Market website at www. writersmarket.com. Many magazine and book publishers offer updated information for writers on their websites. Check individual listings for those website addresses.

Organization newsletters and small magazines devoted to helping writers also list market information. Several offer online bulletin boards, message centers, and chat lines with up-to-the-minute changes and happenings in the writing community.

We rely on our readers, as well, for new markets and information about market conditions. E-mail us if you have any new information or if you have suggestions on how to improve our listings to better suit your writing needs.

The Copyright Law states that writers are selling one-time rights (in almost all cases) unless they and the publisher have agreed otherwise. A list of various rights follows. Be sure you know exactly what rights you are selling before you agree to the sale.

Copyright is the legal right to exclusive publication, sale, or distribution of a literary work. As the writer or creator of a written work, you need simply to include your name, date, and the copyright symbol © on your piece in order to copyright it. Be aware, however, that most editors today consider placing the copyright symbol on your work the sign of an amateur and many are even offended by it.

Some people are under the mistaken impression that copyright is something they have to send away for.

To get specific answers to questions about copyright (but not legal advice), you can call the Copyright Public Information Office at (202)707-3000 weekdays between 8:30 A.M. and 5 P.M. EST. Publications listed in *Novel & Short Story Writer's Market* are copyrighted unless otherwise stated. In the case of magazines that are not copyrighted, be sure to keep a copy of your manuscript with your notice printed on it. For more information on copyrighting your work, see *The Copyright Handbook: What Every Writer Needs to Know, 11th edition*, by Stephen Fishman (Nolo Press, 2011).

Some people are under the mistaken impression that copyright is something they have to send away for and that their writing is not properly protected until they have "received" their copyright from the government. The fact is, you don't have to register your work with the Copyright Office in order for your work to be copyrighted; all writing is copyrighted the moment it is put to paper.

Although it is generally unnecessary, registration is a matter of filling out an application form (for writers, that's Form TX). The Copyright Office now recommends filing an online claim at www.copyright.gov/forms. The online service carries a basic claim fee of $35. If you opt for snail mail, send the completed form, a nonreturnable copy of the work in question, and a check for $65 to the Library of Congress, Copyright Office-TX, 101 Independence Ave. SE, Washington, DC 20559-6000. If the thought of paying $65 each to register every piece you write does not appeal to you, you can cut costs by registering a group of your works with one form, under one title, for one $65 fee.

Most magazines are registered with the Copyright Office as single collective entities themselves; that is, the individual works that make up the magazine are not copyrighted individually in the names of the authors. You'll need to register your article yourself if you wish to have the additional protection of copyright registration.

For more information, visit the U.S. Copyright Office online at www.copyright.gov.

First Serial Rights

This means the writer offers a newspaper or magazine the right to publish the article, story, or poem for the first time in a particular periodical. All other rights to the material remain with the writer. The qualifier "North American" is often added to this phrase to specify a geographical limit to the license.

When material is excerpted from a book scheduled to be published and it appears in a magazine or newspaper prior to book publication, this is also called first serial rights.

One-Time Rights

A periodical that licenses one-time rights to a work (also known as simultaneous rights) buys the nonexclusive right to publish the work once. That is, there is nothing to stop the author from selling the work to other publications at the same time. Simultaneous sales would typically be to periodicals with different audiences.

Second Serial (Reprint) Rights

This gives a newspaper or magazine the opportunity to print an article, poem, or story after it has already appeared in another newspaper or magazine. Second serial rights are nonexclusive; that is, they can be licensed to more than one market.

All Rights

This is just what it sounds like. All rights means a publisher may use the manuscript anywhere and in any form, including movie and book club sales, without further payment to the writer (although such a transfer, or assignment, of rights will terminate after thirty-five years). If you think you'll want to use the material more than once, you must avoid submitting to such markets or refuse payment and withdraw your material. Ask the editor whether he is willing to buy first rights instead of all rights before you agree to an assignment or sale. Some editors will reassign rights to a writer after a given period, such as one year. It's worth an inquiry in writing.

Subsidiary Rights

These are the rights, other than book publication rights, that should be covered in a book contract. These may include various serial rights; movie, television, audiotape, and other electronic rights; translation rights, etc. The book contract should specify who controls these rights (author or publisher) and what percentage of sales from the licensing of these subrights goes to the author.

Dramatic, Television, and Motion Picture Rights

This means the writer is selling his material for use on the stage, in television, or in the movies. Often a one-year option to buy such rights is offered (generally for 10 percent of the total price). The interested party then tries to sell the idea to actors, directors, studios, or television networks. Some properties are optioned over and over again, but most fail to become dramatic productions. In such cases, the writer can sell his rights again and again—as long as there is interest in the material.

Electronic Rights

These rights cover usage in a broad range of electronic media, from online magazines and databases to interactive games. The editor should state in writing the specific electronic rights he is requesting. The presumption is that the writer keeps unspecified rights.

Compensation for electronic rights is a major source of conflict between writers and publishers, as many book publishers seek control of them and many magazines routinely include electronic rights in the purchase of print rights, often with no additional payment. Writers can suggest an alternative way of handling this issue by asking for an additional 15 percent to purchase first rights and a royalty system based on the number of times an article is accessed from an electronic database.

MARKETING AND PROMOTION

Everyone agrees writing is hard work whether you are published or not. Yet once you achieve publication, the work changes. Now not only do you continue writing and revising your next project, you must also concern yourself with getting your book into the hands of readers. It's time to switch hats from artist to salesperson.

While even best-selling authors whose publishers have committed big bucks to marketing are asked to help promote their books, new authors may have to take it upon themselves to plan and initiate some of their own promotion, usually dipping into their own pockets. While this does not mean that every author is expected to go on tour, sometimes at their own expense, it does mean authors should be prepared to offer suggestions for promoting their books.

Depending on the time, money, and personal preferences of the author and publisher, a promotional campaign could mean anything from mailing out press releases to setting up book signings to hitting the talk-show circuit. Most writers can contribute to their own promotion by providing contact names—reviewers, hometown newspapers, civic groups, organizations—that might have a special interest in the book or the writer.

Above all, when it comes to promotion, be creative. What is your book about? Try to capitalize on it. Focus on your potential audiences and how you can help them connect with your book.

IMPORTANT LISTING INFORMATION

- Listings are not advertisements. Although the information here is as accurate as possible, the listings are not endorsed or guaranteed by the editors of *Novel & Short Story Writer's Market*.
- *Novel & Short Story Writer's Market* reserves the right to exclude any listing that does not meet its requirements.

BREAKING IN

An Author Roundtable

....

Jennifer D. Foster

Ever wonder how some of the world's best-selling authors broke into the big leagues? You're not alone. In this roundtable, five award-winning novelists shed light on their paths to published prose. For some the journey was filled with luck and remarkably smooth, while others battled the dreaded self-doubt, slush piles, and "Thanks, but … " letters that many newbie authors encounter. Eventually, each of these authors landed their breakout book. Regardless of the journey, their stories are uniquely insightful, chock-full of writerly tips, well-earned advice, and motivation galore.

What were you doing before you were a published author?

ELIZABETH BERG: I was a really clumsy waitress, a receptionist at a law firm, an actress in an improvisational company, and a "girl singer" in the rock band The Blue Fox. My longest job was working as a nurse for ten years, and that was my school of writing. Being ill means that people drop a lot of their defenses and pretenses; their vulnerabilities are revealed, their true selves … and you're given a lifetime of material to write about.

CORA CARMACK: I was working as a high school theater teacher and getting my master's in creative writing for children and young adults at Vermont College of Fine Arts (VCFA). I was working remotely for a literary agency and for a small independent publisher and was running a successful book review blog and writing.

MARY LAWSON: I was a full-time mum. Prior to that I worked in the behavioral science unit of a research lab. I studied psychology at university.

LINDEN MACINTYRE: I had been a journalist for many years (I was and still am co-host of CBC television's *the fifth estate*) when my first novel was published, having worked

THE AUTHORS

ELIZABETH BERG

Breakout novel: *Durable Goods*, 1993, American Library Association Best Book of the Year selection

CORA CARMACK

Breakout novel: *Losing It*, 2012, *New York Times* and *USA Today* bestseller

MARY LAWSON

Breakout novel: *Crow Lake*, 2002, *New York Times* notable book selection, *Today Show* book club selection

LINDEN MACINTYRE

Breakout novel: *The Long Stretch*, 1999, shortlisted for the Dartmouth Book Award and the Canadian Booksellers Association Libris Award

ANDREW PYPER

Breakout novel: *Lost Girls*, 1999, *New York Times* notable book selection

in newspapers, radio, and television where I gathered much of the insight and material that informed my first and subsequent novels.

ANDREW PYPER: I was a student, first of literature, then of law. Fortunately, since that time, I've made good use of the former studies and no use of the latter.

How did you get into writing?

BERG: Like many writers, I always wrote. I submitted my first poem when I was nine years old. When I was a teenager, I filled notebooks with all my angst and weighty sorrow. But the real springboard was that I loved reading. If you don't love reading, I have doubts you'll be much of a writer.

CARMACK: My mother was an English teacher, so I've been drawn to stories all my life. In high school and college, I explored that love of stories through acting. I seriously thought about a career as an author in my junior year of college. I was an avid reader, studying abroad in the Netherlands. When my grandmother passed away, I needed to funnel that grief; I started writing. I finished that book and got an agent, but it wasn't meant to be. By then, I knew I wanted to tell stories; I never looked back.

LAWSON: I wanted to earn some money, but also wanted to be at home with my children, so I decided to try writing short stories for women's magazines. I did that, moderately successfully, for a number of years but didn't enjoy it much because of the formulaic nature of the stories the market required. Also, my biggest problem as a writer was coming up with ideas, and if you're trying to earn a living out of short stories, you need lots of them!

MACINTYRE: I grew up in the very small Port Hastings, Cape Breton. I developed a love of reading and stories early in life and, because the local culture valued musicians and storytellers, [I] nurtured an early ambition to tell/write stories. The necessity of earning a living led me toward journalism, and many years would pass before I'd seriously explore fiction as a medium for stories. The catalyst was an acquaintance with a background in publishing who persuaded me that I "had a book in me." He was obviously thinking of nonfiction, but I opted to try fiction.

PYPER: I always loved writing, telling stories, and making stuff up. Nevertheless, outside of the indulgence of daydreamed fantasy, I never thought of it in potentially professional terms. Making your living writing books? That was like playing hockey in the NHL—it just wasn't going to happen.

Tell me about your path to getting your first novel published.

BERG: I'd written articles for magazines for ten years before I attempted a novel. I began a book about a married couple in trouble, then switched abruptly to *Durable Goods*, which got done in two months. I'd acquired an agent because I was ready to try a book, and she had taken me on because of the first novel I was writing. When I got into *Du-*

rable Goods, I sent her around 100 pages and she loved it. She sent a partial manuscript to two publishers on a Friday; the next Monday, they both called her wanting to buy it. Talent is a big part of being published, but so is luck. And timing.

CARMACK: As a book blogger, I knew what people were reading. In June 2012, I wrote *Losing It* in about three weeks. Though I wasn't happy with my current agent, I sent her the manuscript. The first "new adult" books were catching the attention of traditional publishers. My agent was finally getting ready to submit *Losing It*, but her list consisted of mainly e-publishers who were open to new adult. In mid-September, I pulled *Losing It* from the few publishers who had it and got ready to self-publish in a month. My mother was my editor; my book-blogger sister was my proofreader. I made my own cover. I had about thirty blogs reveal the cover and blurb. I was using a pen name and rushed to create an entirely new online identity through social media. Soon, over one thousand readers had added the book to their "to read" shelf on goodreads.com. I sent out advance reading copies to bloggers, and [in] mid-October I self-published. I formatted the e-book myself for Barnes & Noble and Amazon. I hit the market at exactly the right time; it filled a hole in the market, and one day after I hit "publish," it hit number one on Barnes & Noble's e-book bestseller list. Within three days, I was getting interest from agents, publishers, foreign publishers, and film studios. Ten days after publishing, I signed with New Leaf Literary. That was also the day I found out *Losing It* debuted on *The New York Times* and *USA Today* bestseller lists! *Losing It* was submitted to traditional publishers, and I happily went with William Morrow/HarperCollins.

LAWSON: In England, where I live, you don't send manuscripts straight to publishers; very few of them will read a manuscript that doesn't come through a literary agency. *Crow Lake* was rejected by one agency after another for almost four years. All of them said much the same thing: The novel was well written, but "in the present commercial climate" no publisher would touch it. Had I not had such a supportive family I would certainly have given up. Then all at once three agencies wanted it, and when the one I chose sent it out to the publishers, there was a bidding war!

MACINTYRE: It was pure happenstance. A friend who was in the process of becoming a literary agent persuaded me to draft a proposal for a nonfiction book. He found out I had an unpublished fiction manuscript and used it with the nonfiction proposal to persuade a publisher that a television reporter could actually write something longer than a tweet. The publisher liked the story and shortly thereafter published it. He rejected the nonfiction idea.

PYPER: After [my short story collection] *Kiss Me* … was published by a small press in 1996, I was approached by Anne McDermid, an agent who'd recently returned to Toronto from London looking to build her client list. She liked my stories, but I had nothing for her to sell. "You will," she said. A couple of years later, after I finished law school,

I wrote *Lost Girls*. I gave it to Anne, expecting her to say, "What the hell do you expect me to do with *this*?" Instead, she sold it to a major publisher in Canada one week, and to big houses in the U.S. and U.K., in two book deals, the next.

What did you learn about yourself and the industry from having your first novel published?

BERG: I learned the best part is always in the writing. It's wonderful to be published. I was thrilled, of course, but nothing matches that original heat, that feeling that you're getting on the page what you want to, that it's *right*.

CARMACK: You never know what's going to lead to your break. If I hadn't had that poor agent relationship, if I weren't killing myself trying to learn about publishing, if I weren't such an avid reader, it's entirely possible none of this would have happened. It was such a perfect-storm kind of scenario.

LAWSON: Nobody knows whether or not a book will sell, and that includes agents and publishers. None of the agents who rejected *Crow Lake* were simply being unkind; if they'd thought it was publishable, they would have seized it with both hands.

MACINTYRE: I had a great deal to learn about fiction writing; the publishing business was perilous (my publisher went out of business before I could complete a second manuscript); and that, perhaps, I should stick to what I knew: journalism.

PYPER: Nothing changes about yourself from having a book published. It's still you staring back at you in the mirror, glassy-eyed and in need of some sun. [It's] still you when you sit at the desk and the blank screen laughs back. I probably made a couple of "mistakes" in being too candid or too ironic in interviews, but I wouldn't take any of it back. The last thing I want to be is cautious.

What advice do you have for new writers struggling with/working on their first manuscript?

BERG: Try NOT to struggle. Try to only have fun. Be fully in the art, and worry about the publication when you've finished your book. Learn what works best for you: Are you a slow writer or a fast one? Do you make your work better with multiple drafts, or do you drain it of its charm and originality? Do you need to write from a place of knowing or not knowing? Read for comfort. For inspiration. For guidance. A writer's job is to notice and feel, and, perhaps, above all, to be curious, to wonder *What if?*

CARMACK: My character's actions, words, and beliefs all tie back to the one thing they want out of life more than anything, and the heart of the story has to be about their attempts to achieve that objective and [overcome] the things in their way. Know your characters so well that they're leading your story, rather than being your puppets. Tell the story you would want to read. Writing and publishing are hard. Immerse yourself in the industry; the most successful authors are knowledgeable about craft and business.

LAWSON: I was fifty-five by the time *Crow Lake* was published, but I spent more than twenty years struggling. So much depends on luck in this business, and the odds against being able to make a career of writing fiction are so high that the only sensible reason to write is that you love writing so much that you can't help yourself. Write what you want; don't write for the market. And don't send out anything that is less than as good as you can make it; rejection is hard enough without courting it.

MACINTYRE: Develop a writing discipline; focus on the idea and on the page in front of you; do not allow yourself to dream of glory. The process is of necessity lonely—you must live, while writing, deep within your soul, which is not always a pleasant place to be. Be cautious and selective when you think it's time to get an outside view of what you're writing. My preference is to keep it to myself until I've "finished," knowing that when someone else has read it, I'll probably be back to square one. Fight vanity, be prepared for criticism, and get an agent.

PYPER: Don't submit too early. Get others to read your work; hire an editor; read the whole thing out loud to yourself. Hang on to it as long as you can, [until] you can honestly say it is the best thing you can possibly do. Only then should you hit SEND.

Any tips for writers aiming to get their first manuscript published?

BERG: Try to find the best agent you can, and make sure you feel comfortable with her. Read magazines about writing—*Writer's Digest*, for example, or *Poets & Writers*—for advice about agents and publication.

PYPER: Ask yourself if this is your story. Not the story of your life, necessarily, but *yours*. If the answer is "no" or "maybe," it's not the right book to send out into the world.

Any tips for dealing with rejection or negativity in the industry?

BERG: I wrote one magazine piece that was rejected [by] thirteen places. When I finally sold it, my rates were three times what they were when I started out! But publication, praise, and money do not give the real worth to your work. You do that. Even if you never get anything accepted after many, many tries, if you're a real writer, you will still write. Remember that Harry Potter was rejected a *lot*!

CARMACK: Brush it off. Remember, there are people in this world who don't like chocolate or pizza or Harry Potter. Rejection does not mean your work is inferior, and just by putting yourself out there, you're already halfway there.

LAWSON: No one knows whether or not a book is publishable, including whoever just sent you that rejection slip! As soon as you've sent out your manuscript, start writing another book. If you're a writer, your job is not sending out books or even dealing with rejection. Your job is writing. The rest is trivia and out of your hands. Ignore it. Keep reading great books, which are almost certainly what inspired you to write in the first place, and they'll inspire you to keep writing.

MACINTYRE: It's wise to anticipate negativity and possibly rejection. There are a lot of people writing. The imperatives that drive decisions by agents and publishers are established by global factors. Rejection is not always a reflection of the value of what you've written. So keep working at it, or start something new. Suppress feelings of defeat. Defeat only happens within your ego when you've acknowledged it.

PYPER: Eat it up and ask for more—because there's always more on its way.

What is your secret to staying positive and motivated?

BERG: I'm *not* always positive and motivated. Being a nurse taught me a lot about what really matters in life; it has more to do with relationships and the natural world than with word counts, awards for writing, big advances, and book tours. I write to find some deeper truth and meaning.

CARMACK: There have been moments when I was worn out. But I try to fall in love with storytelling again. I read, watch movies or television, see a play. I just refill the creative well and remember why I wanted to tell stories in the first place.

LAWSON: I am by no means always positive and motivated. It's very hard to drive yourself to write when you can't get something to work, and I'm frequently in that position. But having a routine helps. I sit down at my desk about 8:30 every morning, five days a week, and work for roughly seven hours. I just keep plugging away, hoping that in the end it will work out.

MACINTYRE: This is the hardest question. You can't stay positive and motivated all the time. Treat fatigue and even despair as situational and transient.

PYPER: Remember the pleasure in making stuff up. Never mind the business, the tactics, the search for the secret publishing handshake. Remember how making a story come to life makes you happy.

IT STARTED WITH A HASHTAG

How a Twitter Pitch Party Could Snag You an Agent (and More)

Diane Shipley

If you approach an agent or editor on Twitter about your book, you'll usually be given the brush-off—submission guidelines exist for a reason, after all. But there is an increasingly popular way to use social media to get your novel noticed without alienating the gatekeepers in the process: pitch parties.

Twitter pitch parties (sometimes called "pitch contests") are pre-arranged times when unpublished writers can tweet about their manuscripts using a specific hashtag on the understanding that publishing professionals will be reading. Depending on the event, an agent or editor will reply to your pitch or mark it as a "favorite" if they would like you to submit. Either way, they're not just being charitable: Writers are landing agents, signing deals, and having books published as a direct result of pitch parties.

Each one has its own rules, but in order to participate you usually need to be previously unpublished, and you can't already have an agent. Some parties are for a specific genre or reading age, and some advertise in advance which agents and editors will show up, while others are more speculative. Tweeting too often is frowned upon—twice an hour is often a suggested maximum—as is being self-absorbed. Encouraging other writers during the party is part of the fun.

Brenda Drake thinks she's the first person to have organized a Twitter pitch party, and she had no idea what a success it would be. She hosted a contest on her blog in March 2012, inviting aspiring authors to submit a short summary and the first 250 words of their book so that interested agents could compete for the right to request more pages. As a consolation, Drake asked writers who weren't picked to share their summaries on Twitter on a specific day, tagging them #PitMad, and invited agents to check it out. It was a hit, trending on

Twitter all day, and is now at least a twice-yearly occurrence. According to blogger David Oarr (davidoarr.com), who crunched the numbers, 16,914 tweets were sent during the September 2013 #PitMad, almost double the number of the previous event. Those tweets had a total reach of 24.4 million impressions (the number of people who potentially read one).

As informal as social media can be, Drake emphasizes that writers need to treat pitch parties as professionally as any other submission. "Your manuscript should be completely polished. It has to have been through your beta readers and critique partners, and you should have revised it a few times," she says. That same attention to detail needs to go into crafting a pitch, given the challenges of pitching in this format. In just 140 characters, you have to include protagonist, plot, genre, possibly tone, and definitely the relevant hashtag. Writers routinely workshop their tweets in advance of pitch parties in writing groups and online forums like CPSeek.com. Drake recommends readying at least ten different critiqued and tweaked pitches, as you never know which one will resonate.

ETIQUETTE ESSENTIALS

- Make sure your manuscript is ready to submit before you take part.
- Each pitch party is different, so read the rules (usually posted via tweet at the start of the event or on the organizer's website) and stick to them, especially regarding how many times an hour you're allowed to tweet. Follow the organizer(s) on Twitter to stay apprised of any changes.
- Encourage other writers by retweeting them or replying to pitches you like. But make sure not to favorite their tweets or you'll be mistaken for an agent (or a spammer).
- Don't tweet at an agent or editor unless they message you first, and as tempting as it might be, never direct message any publishing pros who follow you asking for advice, contacts, or their help hitting *The New York Times* Best Seller list.

Sarah J. Clift tried her successful pitch offline first. At a writing conference, she was offered the chance to sell an agent on her middle-grade novel, *Under the Midnight Sun*, in around thirty seconds. After getting positive feedback, she edited that summary to Twitter length and entered the following in #PitchMAS, another twice-yearly pitch party, in July 2013:

> *MG contemp Secret Garden retelling set in Barrow, Alaska where an 11yo Southern belle looks for hope in a forbidden greenhouse. #PitchMAS*

The Twitter pitch led to four requests for full manuscripts, and by the end of August Clift had signed with the Lippincott Massie McQuilkin agency. Although she had also sent out more traditional queries, Clift says that pitch parties brought her the most success. "With the pitch parties I entered, I got fourteen requests. By comparison, I sent out twenty-eight queries but got only four requests." She thinks that the book's strong hook (retelling a childhood classic in an unusual location) made it easy to sum up for Twitter but says a key reason for her success is that this type of event offers the chance to connect with a wider range of publishing professionals. "The best thing about Twitter pitch parties is being able to get your pitches out to agents that you wouldn't have thought to query."

When Kristine Carlson Asselin entered #PitMad in May 2013, she was attracted by the potential for immediate feedback. "I started doing Twitter pitch parties to find an agent; I wasn't really looking for a book deal. It was more trying to figure out another way besides sending a query and not really seeing any response." But instead of attracting an agent's interest, one of her tweets was favorited by editor Meredith Rich from digital imprint Bloomsbury Spark. That led to an offer, which gave Asselin the leverage to sign with an agent. Her debut young adult novel *Any Way You Slice It* will be released in fall 2014.

Interestingly, the tweet that impressed Rich was about a different manuscript, Asselin's sports-themed YA *The Sweet Spot*:

> *A near-miss kiss from Scott, Dad hires a hot new Brit & SOMEONE torches the 8th green. How can Kate focus on her golf game? #YA #pitmad*

Rich says that pitch parties aren't necessarily about acquiring a particular project as much as about gauging an author's sensibility. This pitch appealed to her because it included so much information and demonstrated an awareness of the potential audience. "From one sentence, we get a sense of the genre, romance, family aspect, potential conflict, mystery, and the main character's favorite sport. More than that, it showed me that she had a good sense of what makes a great contemporary YA—most of these elements—and the character's voice came across, too." She recommends that writers stay away from clichés like "he shook her to the core" or "how will she survive?" and be as specific about their characters and what makes them unique as possible. Unlike a more standard synopsis, you don't want to give the ending away; just include enough to provoke curiosity. "It should be a little bit suspenseful," says Rich. While pitch parties aren't an official part of her editorial strategy, she plans to continue monitoring them, as around one in four of the books she's acquired has come to her this way.

But not everyone who works in publishing is convinced of the value of pitch parties. Agent Eric Ruben has participated in a few but says he prefers to meet authors at conferences so he can tell if someone meshes with his personality. He also points out that it's easy to make a story sound exciting on Twitter, but that doesn't tell him enough about the quality of the writing. However, he does look at a potential client's social media profiles and says it pays to be aware of the image you're conveying. "Don't be a wiseass, and if you're not funny, don't be funny." Meredith Rich says that because her imprint is focused on digital publishing, she's looking for authors who have a presence on and understanding of social media. Ideally, these authors are already connecting with potential readers rather than just signing up in order to pitch their book.

As exciting as the instant validation of having a pitch favorited can be, don't let it distract you. You still need to research any agents or editors who invite you to submit and follow their guidelines. There's no obligation to send pages to everyone who requests them, but Kristine Carlson Asselin says she decided from the beginning that she would. "I had the idea that if it's not the right fit, I can always decline. But how do I know it's not the right fit if I've never talked to the person?"

HOW TWITTER CLIENTS CAN HELP

Twitter clients are websites (and in some cases, apps) from which you can access your Twitter feed. They offer functions beyond the basic features of Twitter.com, including the ability to customize how you view your feed, making it easier to follow specific topics or discussions. Sign up for various clients using your existing Twitter username and password.

TRACK THE CONVERSATION
The volume of tweets can be overwhelming, and you can't follow everyone who's taking part. That means you might overlook not only other people's pitches but also announcements by the organizer or participating agents and editors. You can use the search tool on twitter.com to monitor a specific hashtag, but switching between that and the homepage is a hassle. That's where Twitter clients come in.

Free to use, they allow you to create columns for key words (including hashtags) so you can see all those messages alongside your usual feed. (You can make columns for replies, direct messages, and sent tweets, too.) Some of the most popular:

- TweetDeck (about.twitter.com/products/tweetdeck)
- SocialOomph (www.socialoomph.com)
- HootSuite (hootsuite.com)—also works on iPads, iPhones, and Android devices

SCHEDULE TWEETS
Spread out your pitches by scheduling tweets throughout the day using HootSuite, TweetDeck, or Buffer (bufferapp.com).

SAVE YOUR FAVES
TweetDeck's custom time lines function lets you click and drag your favorite messages (e.g. replies from agents, pitches that impressed you) into a new column for your own reference, to share with friends, or even to add to a blog post.

A LITTLE LIGHT STALKING

Find out when agents or editors who are already following you are most likely to take notice of your pitch(es) with Tweriod (www.tweriod.com) which analyzes your Twitter usage and theirs to tell you the best time to tweet.

It's hard to know exactly how many authors have succeeded as a result of Twitter pitch parties—Drake says writers don't always let organizers know. But they're enough of a phenomenon that agents and publishers are not only taking part but also taking inspiration from them. In June 2013, Entangled Publishing ran a contest on the books website NA Alley (www.naalley.com), inviting writers to pitch their manuscript in the comments section in three sentences or less. Agents also run similar contests, often on writers' blogs—S.R. Johannes (www.srjohannes.com) has hosted several. And when the Lisa Ekus Group agency was looking for a new cookbook author, they held a Twitter pitch contest with multiple rounds.

While pitch parties offer unprecedented access to publishing pros and the chance to fast-track your career, there are downsides. Their popularity has brought an increase in spammers trying to hijack the hashtag or favorite tweets as a joke. It's also nerve-racking for people used to being rejected in private to post their ideas in a public forum. Neither Asselin nor Clift got any requests the first time they tried. "It's not for the faint of heart," Asselin admits. Drake says that agents and editors notice manuscripts that have done the rounds and recommends limiting yourself to two pitch parties or contests per book. "I think writers need to pick their contests and not [overdo it], and I think they need to query at the same time, and query widely."

Submitting the old-fashioned way is still how most writers find an agent, and none of the people I spoke to recommended pitch parties to the exclusion of other approaches. But they can offer benefits even if you don't get any requests: Summarizing your book in so few words forces you to confront any holes in your plot and assess how unique your idea or voice really is. "When you do a Twitter pitch you really narrow into what makes your book special," says Drake. It also means you learn how to talk about your book in a way that excites potential readers (an essential skill for any author). Besides learning what agents are responding to, you can also see what other writers are doing and feel the camaraderie of being part of a community. Drake says, "I'll see writers that are on the hashtag but they're not active in the community, and I feel sad for them because I think, *You're missing out, you could be making so many connections.*"

It's still too soon to tell whether Twitter pitch parties will become an established part of the querying process. But it's clear that social media and publishing are only becoming more integrated, and smart authors will use all the tools at their disposal to get noticed. If your book isn't snapped up on the back of a short summary, don't be disheartened. "If you don't get a request it's not a rejection. It just means that you got lost in the feed or the particular people who were participating that day weren't interested in your genre," says Asselin. It could also mean that your marketing skills need work, says Drake. "It's a tough, tough thing to do, and to get it right there has to be that special glitter in your Twitter pitch." Of course, having a manuscript worth raving about in the first place is the most important thing, whether it's snapped up via social media or not. "There's no magic answer," says Ruben. "Just write a really great book."

FIND OUT MORE

New events are taking place all the time—searching "pitch party" on Twitter (or creating a column for these key words on TweetDeck or HootSuite) will help you stay in the loop.

#PITMAD
Any genre or age range (be sure to state in the tweet) (www.brenda-drake.com)

#PITCHMAS
Any genre; three-day event (pitchmas.blogspot.com)

#ADPIT
For adult or new adult fiction (heidinorrod.wordpress.com)

CARISSA-TAYLOR.BLOGSPOT.COM
Carissa Taylor often posts about upcoming pitch parties, and her website includes a fun "pitch generator."

Diane Shipley is a freelance journalist based in the U.K. She's written for a variety of publications on both sides of the pond, including *The London Times*, the *Los Angeles Times*, *The Guardian*, *Writer's Digest*, and *Mental Health Today*. She's also an all-too-regular contributor to Twitter (@dianeshipley).

"IT HAS MERIT, BUT ..."

Why Your Full Manuscript Might Have Been Rejected

Marie Lamba

A number of years ago, before I became a published novelist and later stepped into my current role as an associate literary agent, I was an unknown writer sending out queries for my first novel, *The Time Passage*. And I was getting a ton of rejections.

But we writers are a persistent bunch. So I kept refining my query, polishing my opening pages, and submitting. Finally agents started requesting that I send my full manuscript for their review. Surely it was only a matter of time before I got an offer for representation, right?

What I got instead were rejections that basically read: "While your novel has merit, I'm afraid I'm going to pass. ..." Why were they declining to represent my work? The agents offered few details. And just like that, I'd hit a wall. Because I couldn't pinpoint what was wrong with *The Time Passage*, I ultimately placed that manuscript on my shelf, where it still sits today, and moved on to other stories that, fortunately, proved to be more successful.

These days, *I'm* the agent sending out the "It has merit, but ..." rejections. Unfortunately, I send out a lot of them. The query sounded great, the opening pages were clean and promising, yet in the end it was a no from me. Why?

When it comes to requested full manuscripts, I always make an effort to spell out why I passed—after all, I know firsthand how important that information is to a writer. And I think it's useful for *all* writers to know that there are common—and avoidable—flaws holding back the majority of the manuscripts agents see. The following are my own top ten reasons for rejecting a requested full, along with some possible fixes. If you think you're ready to start submitting, see if your manuscript passes this pressure test; if you're already engrossed in submissions but your manuscript isn't getting the results you want, perhaps one of these will strike a chord with you.

REASON #1: IT'S NOT WHAT WAS PROMISED.

When you query an agent, you're drawing her in with a promise of what's to come. But sometimes what I get is *very* different. I've requested what was described as a deep women's fiction story, only to find that it turns into an erotic romance—a category I don't represent. And a touching young adult novel I've been pitched is revealed to be a gory horror tale, another genre I'm not interested in. When I get a manuscript that's completely different from what I was expecting, I'm disappointed. Queries that aren't true representations of the story are a waste of my time *and* the author's (especially when I end up with genres I simply don't represent). Mislead me with your pitch, and you can bet I'll pass.

The Fix?

Give your query a closer look. Does it accurately describe your novel?

Sometimes writers fudge their novel's description just to fit what an agent says she wants, thinking that once they have the agent's attention, the manuscript will win her over. Or the author plays up what he thinks is a more marketable element of the story, even though it's a very minor part. And sometimes a query is inaccurate because the author simply doesn't have a solid grip on the book's true slant.

So make your query accurate. Believe me, it matters. Then agents who request your book will truly be interested in what you're sending.

REASON #2: IT'S WRONG FOR THE GENRE/AUDIENCE.

Works that are clearly not a fit for the intended readership get a swift rejection. Like when a novel intended for ages 8–12 ends up dealing with a serious romance. Or when a work of women's fiction has a misogynistic point of view. Or when two-thirds into a contemporary YA novel, it suddenly becomes a paranormal.

In each case, the writer didn't understand the need to meet certain genre conventions or audience expectations, and because of this has set herself up for failure by creating a novel the agent won't be able to sell.

The Fix?

Carefully identify your readership and genre, and study up to know what the marketplace standards are for manuscript content and length. Even writers who have done this up front can lose direction somewhere along the way without realizing it. Make sure your compass is steady. Work within those reader and genre expectations, and you'll help your novel succeed.

So, did your novel turn out to be much longer than what's typical of its category? (Word counts should be revealed in a query letter, but once in a while I'll have the full manuscript in hand before I realize the author failed to mention the "light and fluffy" romance is 175,000 words long.) Is the book's content too mature for its audience? Perhaps your middle-reader novel should actually be a young adult novel, which would require your main character to be a few years older. If you see a reason your book might be outside industry standards and you correct that, it could mean the difference between a no and a yes.

REASON #3: THE STORY LACKS AUTHENTICITY.

Not only must a novel be appropriate for its readership, it also must be smart and authentic enough to appeal strongly to that audience. Errors, false notes, and lazy writing will only make agents roll their eyes.

That means if there is humor, it must be memorable and witty. If the book is a medical thriller, then it demands startling twists and mind-blowing science that even a doctor will be impressed with. If a manuscript is set in England, you need real and fresh setting details, not info you could pull out of any guidebook. If the manuscript is YA, then you'd better be up on how teens think and what they do—otherwise, you'll seem out of touch.

The Fix?

Get smart. Read widely, and be a huge media consumer in all that is related to your topic so your point of view will be on target.

Also, why not go to the source and test out your material to get your details just right? When I was creating Raina, an Indian teen character for my novel *Over My Head*, I sought out real teenagers living in India who were willing to look over my dialogue and answer my questions. They helped me make Raina convincing and credible. So show your YA manuscript to a plugged-in teen for a fact check. Find a scientist to review your details and "what ifs." Pull together beta readers who read deeply within your intended genre to make sure your point of view is on target. Challenge yourself to strive for authenticity in even the smallest telling details.

REASON #4: THE MANUSCRIPT FALLS TO PIECES.

Writers spend so much time polishing their opening pages and trying to hook the reader that often they overlook the fact that the rest of the book is messy by comparison. There are typos, dropped plot threads, rambling story lines, and tense slips. Even character names start changing. It doesn't take long before agents will lose patience and simply stop reading.

The Fix?

You may have spit-shined your opening pages, but have you done this for the rest of the book? Don't be so impatient to start submitting that you cut corners. Obviously your entire manuscript should be free of spelling and grammatical errors. But polishing shouldn't stop there. Track your story elements for consistency and continuity. Chart each character's qualities and details so you don't suddenly change their eye color or hometown. And look closely for leftover story fragments that no longer belong—for instance, a dialogue where characters reference a fight that you've cut from the earlier chapters.

REASON #5: IT TAKES YOU TOO LONG TO GET ON WITH IT.

These novels had opening pages that drew me in with lovely imagery, a literary feel, a hint of intrigue, or an interesting voice. But when I got the rest of the manuscript, the story never took off and nothing seemed to ever happen—at least, not up to the point where my interest waned and I stopped reading. Lovely elements can hold an agent's interest for only so long.

The Fix?

First, ask yourself (and beta readers or critique partners, if possible) if you are starting the novel in the right spot. Many manuscripts begin too early in the tale instead of near the story's inciting incident. Telltale signs are when a character is traveling to where the real story will begin, or waking up and then going through the motions of getting ready.

Next, look closely at your structure. If you don't already have an outline, take the time to make one now, listing what happens scene by scene in each chapter. Is there something plot-related in every scene? Is the tension sustained? Are your characters taking action? Do the challenges grow? If you can find scenes where those answers are no, it's probably time to either cut them or make something happen.

REASON #6: THE WRITING LACKS CONFIDENCE.

When a writer doesn't trust the reader or trust himself, he starts tossing in more and more description, just in case we didn't understand what we were seeing. He tells us what just happened or how a character is feeling, even though we could have guessed from the context (and should have been allowed to). Instead of letting the main plotline do the job, he adds more and more elements. There's suddenly a murder, a heist, a romance, an elf, a ship from outer space, and nonstop action. Overwriting can alienate the reader and destroy what promised to be an engrossing tale.

The Fix?

Look for large blocks of prose that might harbor over-telling, and pare these sections down. Especially avoid stating emotions, which are best revealed through actions and reactions. One way to find these culprits is to search for the words *feel* and *felt*. When you spot places where you feed readers things like "She felt so angry she wanted to hit him," demonstrate more confidence in your abilities—and give your readers more credit—by instead writing something along the lines of "She glared at him and clenched her fists. Her sharp nails cut into her palms."

Also look at your plotlines—are they more complicated than necessary? How many issues does your main character really need to face? If you find you're resorting to gimmicks just to hold the reader's interest, less really can be more.

REASON #7: IT'S TOO FAMILIAR.

I'm seeking fresh and original books, so predictability is a killer. If I see your twist coming well in advance, then you haven't chosen a fresh option. Also not so fresh? Manuscripts that are thinly veiled versions of popular series such as Harry Potter or novels such as *Fight Club*. Relocating the story, renaming the characters, or changing the gender does not an original novel make.

Another side to this "too familiar" coin are the plots that everyone seems to be writing a version of. Example: The woman who is divorced/wronged who starts anew in a ramshackle home by the sea/in the mountains/in a European village and finds love/friendship/her "groove." Here's another: The kid who moves in with a strange older relative in a new town and discovers a huge secret.

The Fix?

Follow your own ideas, not knockoffs, and don't create in a void—know what's already out there and make sure your own novel stands apart. To avoid obvious plotting, ask yourself if you chose the first idea that came into your head. If so, can you push yourself further and pick perhaps the fourth idea, or even the eighth? Dig deep and you will probably find a new take on something that was just too obvious before.

REASON #8: YOU HAVEN'T MADE ME CARE.

If my attention starts to wander and I'm skimming pages, that's a bad sign. Another bad sign? If I can put the manuscript down and not feel a nagging urge to pick it up again. When agents aren't invested in the character or intrigued by the stakes, they're definitely passing, even if the manuscript is clean and the plot holds together.

The Fix?

Analyze your character's development. Why do we care about her or at least find her interesting? Do these feelings about her deepen as we learn more? Is what's happening throughout the novel significant enough? Or is it too trivial, like when a YA novel centers on a teen whose main goal in life is to be on the prom court? While you're trying to get character and plot details right in your final draft, it's possible to lose sight of the big picture. Take a step back now and make sure you're doing all you can to keep your reader plugged in. If not, it's time to revise before you submit again.

REASON #9: THE PAYOFF WAS DISAPPOINTING.

If the payoff in the book doesn't justify the read, then I'm going to feel cheated. If I'm flying through the pages of a thriller, you bet I want it to culminate in breathless action and a shocking twist. If I'm engrossed in a heartfelt coming-of-age story, of course I'm expecting deep emotion, perhaps pain, followed by satisfying triumph. If someone has been searching for her mother her whole life, then when that mother finally appears, it should definitely be handled in more than one paragraph! If I finish your manuscript thinking, *That's it? Really?*—even if you had me up to that point—it's ultimately a no from me.

The Fix?

Determine what is fueling your story's engine—what most keeps your reader engaged. Now look closely at the climactic moments. Do you answer the book's big question in a satisfying way? For example, if the book is about a guy and girl falling in love but being kept apart, then, when they finally get together, is this moment surprising and so wonderful it's nearly heartbreaking? Do you let readers linger a bit in that heartfelt moment? Or do you rush right past the scene to a quick resolution? Ask yourself if you're rewarding your reader for sticking with your story. If you realize you could do better, you've still got work to do.

REASON #10: IT'S JUST NOT STRONG ENOUGH.

This is the hardest book for me to reject. The author has done so many things correctly, including creating a plot that kept me reading until the end. Yet for reasons I have a hard time qualifying, I'm not jumping out of my chair and dashing to the phone to call with an offer for representation. The problem is, I'm not looking for a good book. I'm looking for an *amazing* book—something that challenges me or astonishes me with its brilliance. Agents go to bat for their clients' projects with big commercial publishers and well-established smaller presses, both of which are extremely competitive markets. If we don't feel dazzled by your novel, then we won't feel confident that a top editor will be motivated enough by it to offer a deal.

The Fix?

If the feedback you're getting gives you the sense that your story is good, but might not be *great*, it's time to do some soul-searching. What is your novel's strength? See if you can find a way for that strength to be heightened to make readers sit up and take notice. If it's plot-driven, can you imagine ways your plot could be even more innovative, more engaging? If it's character-driven, could you make the character more memorable? If it's an emotional read, are you hitting all the high *and* low notes in a remarkable way? If the novel is literary, are your images and language and observations as outstanding as you can make them?

Whatever your novel's special element may be, strive to make the element even stronger as the book progresses. Do this, and you'll be much more likely to finish as strong as you started.

In my experience, these are generally the most common reasons a full manuscript doesn't secure an offer. Remember, though, that another agent might see a novel I just rejected and find it perfect. So don't overreact to each rejection and immediately start revising your work. However, if you continue to have your requested full manuscript rejected again and again, do consider these ten points.

You might even find that more than one of these reasons applies to your work. That happened to me. Looking back to my old manuscript *The Time Passage*, I can now see it was a bit overwritten (No. 6) and that it wasn't quite a standout novel yet (No. 10). Perhaps if I'd applied the suggested fixes, that manuscript would be in bookstores instead of just sitting on my shelf gathering dust. Hmm … perhaps it's time to get busy and dust it off!

Keep these ten common flaws in mind, and instead of getting those "It has merit, but …" emails, just maybe you'll have agents diving for their phones, eager to make "the call" and offer you representation. And who knows? Maybe one of those agents will be me.

Marie Lamba (marielamba.com) is an associate literary agent at the Jennifer De Chiara Literary Agency (jdlit.com) and author of the YA novels *What I Meant …*, *Over My Head*, and *Drawn*.

WHAT LITERARY JOURNALS *REALLY* LOOK FOR

....

James Duncan

Literary magazines publish only famous authors. Or friends of the editor. Or people with a Master of Fine Arts writing program in their bio. Those are the rumors, especially among writers who may have had a hard time breaking in. But like most stereotypes, those misconceptions of the modern literary journal are not only untrue but shortsighted.

If anything, literary magazines now offer writers more opportunities than ever before. Their editors today are busy not just compiling their next issues but building a community online and off—branching out into Web editions, book imprints, workshops, conferences, and podcasts. And those editors have seen proof that agents and publishers are paying close attention to writers who make the cut.

Yes, there is a high standard of quality, and names like Munro, Saunders, Eggers, Shepard, and Lethem do appear with regularity. But it has become less and less surprising to find a newcomer's byline next to that of an author recently shortlisted for the National Book Award. So the question is, then, how can yours be among them?

Here, five editors from top journals—all of them welcoming to new writers—discuss how literary magazines are evolving, their role in the publishing world, and their best advice to writers looking to catch their eye when submitting short stories, poetry, and essays.

THE EDITORS

DAVE HOUSLEY is one of the founding editors of *Barrel-house*, a literary magazine that bridges the gap between serious art and pop culture. A writer, Web person and self-described normal dude, he is the author of *Ryan Seacrest Is Famous* and has been published in *Mid-American Review*, *Nerve*, *Quarterly West*, *Wigleaf*, and elsewhere.

DAVID H. LYNN has been the editor of *The Kenyon Review* since 1994. He is the author of *Year of Fire*, *Wrestling with Gabriel*, *Fortune Telling*, and *The Hero's Tale: Narrators in the Early Modern Novel*, a critical study. Lynn is also a professor of English at Kenyon College.

EMILY NEMENS is co-editor and prose editor of *The Southern Review*. Her first book of stories, *Scrub*, was published in 2007, and her writing has appeared in *The Gettysburg Review*, *Alimentum*, and on Esquire.com. As an illustrator she has collaborated with Harvey Pekar and has a painting blog with ninety thousand followers.

TODD SIMMONS is the publisher and editor of Wolverine Farm Publishing Co. and *Matter Journal*. He lives with his wife and their two children within arm's reach of Fort Collins, Colorado. On their farm, chickens outnumber cats, but cats outweigh chickens. It's a topsy-turvy world, and things are always resurfacing, especially when the children can find their shovels.

ROB SPILLMAN is editor of *Tin House* magazine and editorial advisor of Tin House Books. He has written for *The Baltimore Sun*, *British GQ*, *Connoisseur*, *The New York Times Book Review*, *Rolling Stone*, *Spin*, *Sports Illustrated*, *Vanity Fair*, *Vogue*, and *Worth*, among other publications.

In terms of quantity, quality, and competitiveness, what trends are you seeing in submissions? Are there stylistic or topical areas writers are leaving unexplored?

DAVID H. LYNN (*The Kenyon Review*): Each generation has its fashions, its tastes. I think we are seeing stories set more in the present tense and first person, engaged with the immediate, rather than with larger historical or political overviews. We are also seeing more work from different communities, especially involving the experience of immigrants, whether Chinese or Korean, African or Caribbean. This leads to great freshness.

ROB SPILLMAN (*Tin House*): Encouraging trends include more international submissions, and the overall competence has increased in the fifteen years since we started *Tin House*. But I do see a lack of humor, and most of the "humorous" pieces we do see are slapstick and go for the easy laughs. I also find a lack of engagement with real-world issues. There's a stunning amount of navel-gazing with tiny emotional epiphanies.

EMILY NEMENS (*The Southern Review*): I've only seen the quality and quantity of submissions increase—which means that the competitiveness has also gone up. In terms of trends, *The Southern Review* hasn't been exclusively "Southern" for decades, but it's exciting to see how global we've become. In a recent issue we featured Canadian writer Tamas Dobozy and his story about the Eastern Bloc; another piece is a translation about Argentinian soccer that [coincided] with the 2014 World Cup. I could always read more ambitious nonfiction pieces.

TODD SIMMONS (*Matter Journal*): I see a lack of place-based and informed writing—short stories or creative nonfiction that really gets a landscape, an ecosystem, or a skilled way of working in the world. Writing that goes beyond what we have now, where the characters exude a place.

DAVE HOUSLEY (*Barrelhouse*): There's no shortage of people writing short fiction, essays, and poetry, that's for sure. As for trends, I think we're through the part where a lot of short fiction writers were imitating George Saunders. You could certainly do worse in choosing somebody to imitate, but that particular imitation is extremely hard to pull off (I know, because I also spent a few years trying).

What really impresses you in a submission, aside from someone following the guidelines and reading a few issues?

SIMMONS: I'm impressed by a writer who takes our theme, shakes it around, and throws it back at us in a way we were not expecting. Catching us off guard with good writing is rewarding. We all know what we want, but when we come across something we didn't expect, something that cuts in a new and exciting way, that is a great way to attract attention.

SPILLMAN: … I'd much rather read an ambitious failure than a perfect little story of no consequence.

LYNN: Great writing is always unpredictable. I believe that successful stories, poems, and essays must offer hearty dashes of *surprise* and *delight*. Surprise, because one needs tension to keep reading. Delight—a deliberately capacious term—because stories and poems must always involve the emotions in some way. The emotion can be fear or sadness or rage or indignation—which can all delight us as readers. I'm also always looking for *mastery* over the craft, over the diction and sentences and rhythms of prose, over the lines and images of poetry.

HOUSLEY: Good stories just have an authority about them—you have a feeling that you're in good hands, that the author knows what they're doing and this is a story that could work. It's hard to pin down exactly what that means, but you know it when it's there, and you feel the absence immediately when it's not. And for me, humor really helps. I'm thinking of humor the way somebody like Steve Almond or Stacey Richter uses it—stories that aren't funny just to be funny, but humor is one of the things the author is working with, a color in his or her palette. I also tend to like stories that engage with the world we live in, which means their characters watch TV, listen to music, play games, do all the things people do in real life that sometimes writers back off of because they don't seem high-minded enough.

NEMENS: A nuanced character is one of the toughest things in the world to describe, especially in short fiction. … When I'm still thinking about a character a few days later, then I know it's a good piece.

On the flip side, what are the most common mistakes that keep writers out of quality literary journals?

HOUSLEY: On the writing side: Stories that take too long to get started, stories where nothing really happens or where most of the action is presented as backstory or flashback, stories that don't trust the reader to understand or figure out what's going on (usually this means the story halts at a certain point so a character can sum up what's happened and/or what it all means). I generally have a pile of stories in front of me, and if yours doesn't *really* start until page 3 or 5, the odds are very strong that I'm going to reject that story and pick up the next in the pile.

On the submitting side: Writers really shouldn't worry too much about cover letters. The work is the thing. If your work is amazing, I don't care what your cover letter says.

LYNN: Too many sloppy mistakes of grammar or diction. Stories or poems that are predictable or too familiar. More profoundly, while beginnings are the most important part of any story or poem … endings are always the hardest. So often I'm halfway through a story and just in love with the characters and situation, am moved by the drama, and then the writer will paint herself into a corner, with no way out.

NEMENS: Many people send work that's not really *done*—stories with plot holes, unresolved conflicts, underdeveloped concepts, or unbelievable dialogue. I can't fix every story, but when I see a promising piece that needs more work, I try to write an encouraging note back to the author.

SIMMONS: Disrespect for the medium. We don't need another piece of literature that tries to keep up with television, the movies, or the Internet. I've seen a marked increase in submissions that seem too loud and aggressive—almost as if the writing were shouting at me, and all I want to do is turn it off. Not that literature shouldn't be loud or aggressive, because there is a lot of interplay between all the different forms of media and expression, but when I read literature that feels like it belongs somewhere else, I'm less inclined to keep reading.

What do you feel writers of all levels have to gain by remaining active in the literary magazine arena? Do you know for a fact that agents, editors, and publishers read literary magazines with an eye open for new talent?

LYNN: I hear it all the time from many agents and editors: They do read literary journals, looking for new talent. It's also true that, more than ever before, there's a sense of a national community of writers who read and correspond (or e-mail or Facebook) with each other. They're a big audience for literary magazines because they want to see where their friends are publishing.

HOUSLEY: If you're a writer, this is the conversation you're hoping to join, so I think you'd be crazy to not be active in the literary magazine world. This is one of the very few places where people are doing what they're doing because they love writing and they want to support it and get it out into the world. I can't imagine not wanting to be a part of that community.

We get contacted by agents every now and then. I can't speak for large-market editors and publishers, but I know the independents are all reading literary magazines, and I think there are some people whose trajectories you can track pretty well by reviewing the literary magazines over a certain period of time.

NEMENS: Christine Sneed is a great example of this—her first story publications were in literary journals, including *The Southern Review*, and she says that her agent and editor were much more willing to take on her manuscripts because of those journal publications. A few years later, she's on the cover of *The New York Times Book Review*!

SPILLMAN: Literary magazines act as a giant filtration system for the publishing industry. We are very actively reading through the fifteen thousand submissions we receive each year (each piece is read by at least three readers). We get calls from agents as soon as every issue comes out asking if our new voices have representation. It is also a good place to see what is on the cutting edge, what the masters of the form—Jim Shepard, Karen Russell, Kelly Link, Alice Munro, et al—are doing in real time.

What are some common misconceptions about literary journals and editors? What are some stereotypes that are actually true?

SIMMONS: That literary culture doesn't exist outside of bookstores and college campuses. That we all come from MFA programs. That we don't know how to wield an axe or a hammer. That we can't sew. That we would be stimulating dinner guests.

NEMENS: True: We want to get excited about your writing. It helps that we, as editors, have lives outside the office (another misconception is that we don't). My co-editor, Jessica, is a mom who has written song lyrics for critically acclaimed albums. I'm an accomplished illustrator and have toured the world playing baritone sax. We know what it means to be engaged with a subject, and I think it helps us recognize that kind of energy when it comes across our desks in a poem, an essay, or a story.

LYNN: That we only publish our friends, or that we only publish writers who are already famous. I can't speak for other editors—though I suspect they will affirm the same truth—but we read every single submission that arrives at *The Kenyon Review* because we are always looking for exciting new voices. The single best part of editing is coming across a piece by an unknown writer that just knocks my socks off.

HOUSLEY: One misconception is that the whole process of evaluating somebody's writing could be anything other than wildly subjective. Every so often, somebody does that thing where they submit a story from *The New Yorker* or something to a bunch of literary magazines, and it gets rejected by all of them, and the conclusion is something along the lines of "gotcha!" But the idea of judging the merit of a story or poem is totally subjective. The editor who accepted that story at *The New Yorker* originally is probably not the same person rejecting it now. The idea that those two people would necessarily share an opinion about a particular piece of writing, or that they absolutely *have* to, just doesn't make sense to me.

How does the online literary scene fare against print journals in terms of quality? Is there still a gap, or is literary excellence in online and print magazines more symbiotic than people realize?

HOUSLEY: I don't know that there ever was a gap. There may have been a perceived gap, but I think that was mostly a transitional thing—people who were used to print, who really love print objects, getting used to the idea that something online wasn't necessarily inferior. If anything, we're seeing the lines blur, with print mags going online and online mags putting out physical books. (I'm thinking of *FiveChapters*, which [recently released] Ian Stansel's excellent collection of short fiction, *Everybody's Irish*.)

At the *Barrelhouse* writers' conference, I was talking with a very accomplished writer who told me that he tries to place things online lately, because he knows so many more people will see them and they'll have a longer shelf life than something in a print journal.

SIMMONS: … The online community seems much stronger in terms of interpersonal relations than that of print. They read and support each other much more. The medium makes this so. I see a lot of good in this, but the transitional period we are still in makes it difficult for much to stick. Things online don't last very long; they burn up like meteors entering the atmosphere, and it always seems to leave me either hungry for more, more, more, or ready to pull a good book off the shelf.

LYNN: I'm very excited about online publishing. In fact, we publish two entirely separate but complementary literary journals, the print *The Kenyon Review* and the electronic *KROnline*. I'd argue that the work we publish in KRO is every bit as good as in *The Kenyon Review*. There's a lot of very good work indeed being published online.

SPILLMAN: There are a few online ventures that are doing really quality work, notably *Electric Literature* and their offshoot *Recommended Reading*. I think there is still an overall gap mainly due to money—most online venues haven't figured out how to pay contributors.

What is the role of the modern literary magazine? Do you see it as a breeding ground for new talent, or perhaps as the last print market standing for established writers looking to keep their names out there between book publications? Or something else entirely?

NEMENS: Something else! Sure, it's both a breeding ground and a place for established writers working between bigger projects, but journals are also their own literary creature. It's fascinating to follow the narrative of a journal itself—how pieces are arranged in each issue and how themes interplay, how writers' relationships with the journal grow over time, the editorial voices that emerge over years. Obviously, following those kinds of developments takes more commitment from readers, writers, and editors alike, but it's an investment that pays dividends.

LYNN: I'd argue that the modern literary magazine remains a vital, vibrant part of the literary community and marketplace. We feature new talent, as I said [earlier], but I'm tickled when we can publish exciting new work by writers I've long admired, too. One dual example: In our fall 2013 issue, we published a marvelous story by the distinguished and talented T.C. Boyle. Side-by-side with him is a dazzling story by a very young writer named Austin Smith. His is called "Cicadas" and is miraculously good.

SPILLMAN: It is a combination of a proving ground for new talent, a showcase for the avant-garde, and a showcase for the masters of the essay, story, and poetry forms. There are many, many writers who are masters of the short story form and rarely, if ever, write novels. Look at Nobel winner Alice Munro … or Jim Shepard, Antonya Nelson, Amy Hempel, et al.

SIMMONS: The role of the modern literary magazine is still to find the unconventional or the writer lacking confidence, take a chance on them, and thrust them into the hands of readers. I also think the literary magazine has a lot of potential for improvement, both online and in print. In print, our design and intent need to be more stimulating and involved with the text—these things are objects, and we might as well make them interesting to look at! Online is more dangerous and exciting territory—it's such a hybridized landscape that anything is possible.

HOUSLEY: I also think it's the place where the most interesting work is being published. We're just smaller and more agile, and our meager economic structure plays to our advantage in that it allows us to take more risks. I also think there's a movement—and I hope *Barrelhouse* is a part of this—toward not just thinking about the literary magazine as a print object, but as a larger organization that promotes and supports writers in any number of different ways and places. At *Barrelhouse*, we do the print magazine, and books, and also the writers conference, a podcast, online writing workshops, and events, and we're kicking around a few other ideas. We're not the only ones: *PANK* does a lot of the same things, and *One Story*. More and more, I think the literary magazine is becoming a platform for all kinds of exciting things to happen.

James Duncan (www.jameshduncan.com) is an editor with Writer's Digest Books, the founding editor of the *Hobo Camp Review* literary magazine, and the self-published author of *The Cards We Keep: Ten Stories*.

SIZING UP SMALL PRESSES

Robert Lee Brewer

As the editor of *Writer's Market*, I'm often quizzed by writers about which is the better option: self-publishing, or getting an agent and trying to land a deal with a big book publisher.

While many professionals seem to acknowledge only these two paths to publication as well, there's a third route that should not be overlooked: the small press. There's a whole field of reputable publishers outside of New York's "Big Five" that can offer the support of the traditional publishing model on a smaller scale—and most accept unagented submissions.

So what are the pros and cons of publishing with a small press, and what should you expect if you decide to give it a go?

THE SUBMISSIONS PROCESS

There are some crucial differences in what small press editors look for in a submission, in contrast to the "Big Five." When I speak with writers at conferences, they often voice frustration over the importance of writing commercially marketable stories in today's publishing environment—and the lack of true risk-taking in the business. That's what they hear emphasized by editors at big houses, because those professionals have aggressive sales goals. Small presses obviously have sales goals, too, but they're typically more willing to take risks on projects they believe have artistic merit.

Jen Michalski, who in 2013 published a novel, a novella, and a short story collection with three different small presses (Black Lawrence Press, Dzanc Books, and Aqueous Books, respectively), says, "The most important draw about these presses was their willingness to publish work that was risky, a difficult read, and therefore inherently commercially unsuccessful."

Part of this mind-set is formed by how small presses view publishing and sales. "With a small press, there is no 90-day window to make your book a bestseller," Press 53 Publisher Kevin Morgan Watson says. "We continue to market and support our books and authors years after the book is released. It's a marathon, not a sprint."

Michalski says she didn't even discuss sales targets with the publisher of her novella. "Dzanc really loved what I was trying to do, and we never talked about whether or how it was going to sell, only that they were going to publish it," she says. "Because that's what they do—they publish challenging, boundary-pushing fiction. And they've achieved a formidable reputation by sticking to their principles."

If you think a small press might be a good fit for your work, what should you know about vetting your options? Whether the books are made available as print, digital, or both (formats and contract terms vary widely, which may give you room to negotiate), authors earn their money primarily through royalties—roughly 10 percent on print sales and up to 25 percent per digital purchase. On average, advances tend to be small—$1,000–2,000 is a common range—or even nonexistent. (At a larger publisher, you'd likely receive a bigger check upon signing—but remember that all advances are paid *against royalties*, meaning you aren't paid royalties until you "earn out" your advance. At a small press, you'd likely receive less payment up front, but earn royalties sooner.)

Of course, how many copies you can expect to sell will depend on the nature of your book, as well as the distribution and marketing support the press can offer. Don't hesitate to ask lots of questions along these lines, as well as what the expected print run would be, before you sign a contract—especially if you're doing so without agent representation.

Many small presses solicit manuscripts through a mix of open submission periods and book contests. I secured a contract for my poetry collection, *Solving the World's Problems,* by submitting directly to Press 53 during its open submission period. But like many other small publishers, Press 53 also offers book contests that award a lump sum and other prizes (in Press 53's case, a $1,000 advance and a launch party). Keep in mind that such contests are very competitive, and most require reading fees between $10 and $30 per entry. When deciding which are worth the investment, consider giving preference to those that offer all entrants a premium, such as a copy of the winning book, so you get something for your entry fee, even if it's not publication.

THE PUBLISHING PROCESS

When asked about the top advantage small presses offer to authors, Erika Goldman, publisher and editorial director of Bellevue Literary Press, says, "Tender, loving care."

Small press authors can expect to receive a lot of attention from the editor, designer, and even owner. That can translate into a more rewarding writer-editor relationship, as well as more involvement with the publicity department.

"We take the time to make sustaining connections for authors in the world of literature, scheduling author tours, and creating a thoughtful list of prizes to nominate their work," says Megan Bowden, director of operations and outreach for Sarabande Books.

In my case, I discussed distribution and marketing ideas directly with the owner of Press 53. I spent time on the phone with my editor during the day, in the evening, and even on weekends. And I had input on my book's cover, even being able to give a thumbs-up or thumbs-down on the suggested design. This type of artistic involvement is not available to most authors at larger houses—but in the small press world, my own experience was not an anomaly.

"I work directly on each book, designing it along with the author to produce something that a reader will want to purchase, as well as an object that best fits how the author wants their writings to be displayed," says Geoffrey Gatza, founder, editor, and publisher of BlazeVOX [books].

Of course, while book design and editorial input are important considerations for any author, that doesn't mean you should expect complete creative control. (Otherwise, why not self-publish?)

"We try to do what's best for the book in the end," Bowden says. "We want to hear the desires of the author, but we've also been publishing books for almost twenty years and hope that when an author agrees to publish their work with us, they trust that we're going to work hard and do all that we can to create a smart, bold cover that works with the overall theme of the book, edit the work to the best of our ability without compromising well-executed poetry or prose, all the while understanding the retail side of the publishing world enough to know how a book should look and feel to the reader."

CAREER BUILDING

Small presses offer unknown and emerging authors a place to get a foothold in their pursuit of success by publishing those early works upon which a career is built.

"The advantage of being a published author is what most of us want, and a small press can do that tremendously well," Gatza says. "A small press is the stepping-stone to bigger and better things, and not an end for a book—it is a wondrous beginning."

Unlike with self-publishing, this beginning is endorsed by an objective gatekeeper who believes in your work enough to invest time and energy in the project—and pay you for the effort.

Of course, small press authors are expected to do their part.

"We expect our authors to be actively publishing nationally and promoting through local and regional events and activities," Watson says. "You can't sit back and wait for readers to find you. Creativity does not end with writing the book."

HOW TO PICK A SMALL PRESS

EVALUATE CONTENT

If a small press is consistently putting out quality writing, chances are it has a solid editorial team. The amount of time it's been in existence and its general reputation are helpful indicators, too.

LOOK AT COVERS

You can't read every book, and neither can a book buyer. That's why covers are crucial. Consider presses that care about design.

CHOOSE WINNERS

Find lists of books honored by both national and regional awards. Small presses often appear on both. Award-winning presses tend to get better media coverage—and sales to match.

CONSIDER DISTRIBUTION AND FORMAT

Some small presses distribute to chains, but many rely on smaller, more specialized outlets. Some presses publish only chapbooks; some publish only in print; some publish digital first; others a mix.

FIND OUT WHAT AUTHORS THINK

If you have access to authors at small presses, ask them about their experiences. Or, follow them on social media and look for clues about how they feel about their publishers.

STUDY YOUR CONTRACT CAREFULLY

Before you sign, be sure you understand and accept all terms and expectations, and have gotten answers to all of your questions. If you have doubts about anything, have a legal professional look it over.

Robert Lee Brewer is senior content editor of the *Writer's Digest* community and author of the collection *Solving the World's Problems*.

BEST OF BOTH WORLDS

Traditional + Self-Publishing = Hybrid Author

Chuck Wendig

At our last house, the lawn died. One day it was green and lush. A week later a brown circle appeared in the grass. Another week went by and the whole yard suffered a withering demise, as if we'd angered the lawn goddesses and grass gods, as if our garden gnomes and lawn mower hymns were not enough.

At our current home, the lawn isn't so much a *lawn* as it is a *mighty gathering of weeds.* Hardly a blade of grass in the bunch. It's hearty and hale. Drought doesn't bother it. Disease can't kill it. It's so green, you might call it "emerald." Mow it over, it looks like any other lawn.

A lesson in the power of polyculture over monoculture.

Monocultures don't exist on their own. We create them. And they don't work well. Plant one thing over a single field—corn, soy, whatever—and it becomes vulnerable to disease and pests. Diversify planting across a single field, however, and resistance to pests and diseases rises sharply.

Diversity means survival. That's true in agriculture. It's true in our stock portfolios. It's true on our dinner plates.

And it's true in publishing. Survival as a writer means embracing diversity from the beginning. And that means thinking of yourself as a "hybrid" author.

PUBLISHING OPTIONS: PROS AND CONS

A "hybrid" author sounds like one that was grown in a lab. Some mutant of Stephen King and E.L. James breaking free of its enclosure, terrorizing Manhattan with deviant prose.

Thankfully, it's a whole lot nicer than that.

A hybrid author is one who refuses to accept that there exists One True Way up the Publishing Mountain and who embraces *all* available methods of getting their work out there.

The hybrid author takes a varied approach, utilizing the traditional system of publishing *and* acting as an *author-publisher* (a term I prefer to *self-publisher* because it signals the dual nature of the role you now inhabit).

Any form of publishing comes with benefits and disadvantages, and it's important to know these ahead of time.

For the traditional system of publishing, the pluses include: money earned up front (advance); professional quality control (editing, design); theoretical access to big marketing efforts; likelier access to ancillary rights (film, TV, foreign); better chance of being reviewed in mainstream media; better chance of being distributed to bookstores; money flows *to* the author (you don't pay production costs).

Minuses: It can be difficult to get projects that lack measurable commercial appeal through the gatekeepers (editors, agents); publishing is glacially slow; sometimes the marketing support never materializes and is left largely to the author; physical space on bookstore shelves is dwindling; it's a risk-averse environment; the system does not adapt quickly to change; contracts can occasionally be restrictive.

Being an author-publisher has its own panoply of ups and downs. Pluses: Creative control; a greater percentage of money earned (about 50–70 percent) remains with you; you become part of a strong community full of resources; some genres do gangbusters in this space (romance, military, sci-fi); it's faster than traditional; new options and distribution platforms are appearing all the time; you retain all rights; you can adapt faster to change; you can take greater calculated risks; you can potentially explore formats (digital shorts, etc.) and/or reach audiences deemed too niche by big publishing.

Minuses: There's an investment up front (typically $500–5,000 to get the book "out there" in a professional fashion) and no guarantee of return on that investment; you have reduced access to ancillary rights (film, TV, foreign), mainstream book reviewers, and physical book retailers; some genres are weak in this arena (literary, YA); self-publishing is easy to do poorly; authors often find that all their eggs are in the Amazon basket.

YOUR NEW MANTRA: "DO BOTH!"

You look over those lists of pluses and minuses and think, *Jeez, which one should I choose?* Forget that. Jump up, freeze-frame heel kick, and yell: "I want to do all the publishing!"

Because you can. That's what being a hybrid author is all about: It's about leveraging the advantages of each publishing form against the other. That diversity maximizes the benefits and mitigates the disadvantages.

Step 1: Write something great.

The first step to being a hybrid author is to write something amazing. Put your heart on the page. Bleed into the story. Practice your craft. Exercise your awesomeness. Write the best book (or novella, or short story, or comic book, or *whatever*) you can.

A great story is your first step and is also the best first defense against any problems that pop up on *either side* of the publishing fence. Anything less and you're doing yourself—and your future readership—a grave disservice.

Step 2: Write something else that's also great.

Being a hybrid author means making multiple works available across a variety of platforms … and that means you can't just write one thing and nest on it like a bird.

You're a writer. So you're going to have to write.

Write two things. Three things! *Write all the things.* Write one story, then as you work to edit it, write another. To be creative means to *create*.

Step 3: Share—one for me, one for you.

A lot of today's most celebrated hybrid authors began in one publishing arena, found success there, and moved into the other when it made sense. Hugh Howey began as an author-publisher before his bestseller status garnered offers from agents and big publishers. Lawrence Block had decades of experience (and success, and acclaim) in the traditional space before deciding to see what he could do on his own. Both now utilize both options simultaneously.

Finding success in one arena is of course a viable pathway to success in another. Maybe you're too busy right now to run your own small business (and be assured, self-publishing is exactly that) and so you'd rather leave your work to the vagaries of the traditional system. Or maybe you don't feel like waiting two years for your book to be on shelves and so you want to grab the reins and ride the horse instead of sitting in the cart. You can pick the style of publishing that seems to suit you up front and go that way, diversifying once you're more established.

Or, you can form a plan for attempting both. Reserve one of your works to be published yourself. Assign a second work to have a go at the traditional system.

How to choose the project best suited for each model? This requires a bit of educational guesswork mixed with polling your intestinal flora (aka "gut feelings"), and at the end it's important to note that neither path offers a guarantee at success. The trick is trying to suss out which of your works will gain the most success in each space. This isn't math, where you can plug in variables and calculate an answer with certainty, but you *can* look to strategies other authors have employed that make good sense.

A strong foot forward is to reserve your riskier work to publish yourself and to designate the more, well, *traditional* work for the traditional space. If this seems counterintuitive, remember that riskier works are much more difficult to get past the publishing gatekeepers. Publishers are more comfortable publishing known quantities. They like the kinds of books that they know will sell. (And frankly, if you have the means to reach a niche audience on your own—say, through your participation in specialized online communities—you might be better equipped to do so than a publisher would be, so why not retain more of the profits from your efforts?) They like certain genres and formats and manuscripts of certain lengths. A publisher might not be likely to accept these things from a first-time author, for instance:

- a novella (note also that new platforms available to self-publishers, such as digital shorts and e-singles, have no real counterparts in the traditional space)
- a short story collection
- a nonfiction work by an author without a big platform
- an epic fantasy of inordinate length (200,000+ words)
- a novel that is not easily labeled with a genre

So if you determine, "I think my chances of this particular story passing through the traditional gatekeepers—and then performing well—are low," then you'd likely be better served by self-publishing that work while sending another, less risky story out into the traditional channels.

For instance, you might note that YA fiction does not do particularly well in the digital self-publishing space because teens have been slow to embrace e-readers. Further, YA is really big right now in the traditional space and the advances reflect that. So, you might reserve an adult work to publish yourself while submitting the YA book to publishers.

KEYS TO YOUR SUCCESS

Sounds simple enough, right? But as with everything, to be truly successful, there are some caveats to be aware of.

Caveat #1: Hybrid authors benefit from having agent representation.

You want an agent. First, you'll need one to get your work in front of most major publishers in the traditional space. Second, an agent can also help you carry your self-published work into other spaces later on—you have a greater chance of selling alternate rights (including print!) for *all* of your works with an active agent.

Note also that some publishers have certain contract terms—particularly noncompete and right-of-first-refusal clauses—that can be unfriendly to hybrid authors. Thus, it's important for you, an agent, or a lawyer to negotiate those, along with any other restrictive language that grants them unnecessary rights to your work (particularly in digital).

The way to secure an agent is to pitch him a single project for which you are seeking traditional publication. But once you have an agent's interest, you need to discuss *up front* that you intend to be a hybrid author. That means seeking out agents who are not only comfortable with that, but savvy in that arena. An agent interested only in the traditional space and unaware of the options available to author-publishers will not be the best representative for you. And a bad agent can do more harm to your career than no agent at all.

Caveat #2: Hybrid authors need to self-publish well.

Self-publishing is easy to do, but difficult to do well. Still, you're going to need to do it well. Fortunately, there are myriad resources at your disposal to help you. Use them. Here's a preview of what you'll learn: Self-publishing well probably means putting some money on the table. It means professional editing. It means a great cover artist. It means putting out a book (or e-book) that looks as good as—no, *better* than—what you'd find on the shelf at Barnes & Noble. A poorly done effort will harm your chances in the traditional space, which means: No hybrid author for you.

Self-publishing well also means developing an author platform that you can rely upon to increase the visibility of your work. This often starts with a strong social media presence—not one devoted to marketing, but one devoted to you being the best version of yourself and engaging authentically with your potential audience.

For hybrid authors, it's *vital* that all of your social media outreach and other platform-related efforts lead to a central online space (a professional author website or blog) that showcases your other work. If your books are going to be coming from multiple sources, the one place interested readers can visit to learn about all of your offerings begins and ends with you.

DOWN THE ROAD

The hybridization of your writing career isn't just to get you going: This is a long game, not a short stint.

Should you be able to get a series of book releases in the traditional space, you could use the gaps between them to release other material yourself to strengthen the loyalty of that readership. Or, should you get a positive response to your self-published works, you could leverage that to gain more support from the publisher(s) for your traditional titles. The energy and marketing of your releases feed off one another. Meanwhile, with hope you'll be banking small-but-steady (and ideally growing) income from a variety of sources.

Note that diversity as an author can also mean working with a variety of publishers big and small. And experimentation (Kickstarter! Kindle Worlds! Serialized fiction!).

Of course, to do this, you need a healthy crop of stories. Which takes us back to step one: Write. Finish what you start. Make it great. Then do it all again.

Chuck Wendig is the author of *The Kick-Ass Writer: 1001 Ways to Write Great Fiction, Get Published & Earn Your Audience* (Writer's Digest Books). He blogs about life as a hybrid author at terribleminds.com.

EMERGING VOICES

Debut Authors Discuss Their Paths to Publication

....

Chuck Sambuchino

ROMILY BERNARD

Find Me
(young adult thriller, HarperTeen, September 2013)
"A teenage hacker trying to get out of the game gets blackmailed into finding a classmate's rapist."

How did *Find Me* come about?

I'd written women's fiction, chick lit, and historical romance. Almost every agent I submitted to said, "Wow, like your voice, but, um, the heroine is kind of … grouchy." Then, in 2010, I decided to try writing YA. Suddenly, my heroines weren't grouchy. They were spunky.

What was the time frame for the book?

I wrote *Find Me* in about nine months. After I was agented, we spent another four months rewriting it.

How did you meet your agent?

I'm repped by the amazing Sarah Davies of Greenhouse Literary. I found her online [and] then cross-referenced her information with *Publishers Weekly* deals, and supplemented that by researching her current authors.

What did you learn along the way?

For an industry that trades in dreams, publishing is still about product. That sounds heartless, but it's not. It means we have to make hard decisions about what's right for the book, but also what's right for the market.

Would you do anything differently?

I would have found YA sooner. But I think, for me, going through all those failed novels was part of the process. At [the 2013 BookExpo America], someone told me I was an overnight success. I told her 246 agent rejections over four years begged to differ.

Tell us a little about your platform.

I blog with the DoomsDaises, [a group of YA writers, at doomsdaisies.com].

Do you have any advice for aspiring writers?

Learn to separate constructive criticism from negative criticism. There are going to be people who are never going to like your writing. Ignore those people.

Romily Bernard writes from Atlanta. Visit her website at romilybernard.com.

MARLEN SUYAPA BODDEN

The Wedding Gift

(historical fiction, St. Martin's, September 2013)

"When plantation owner Cornelius Allen marries off his daughter, he presents her with a wedding gift: his other daughter, a young slave named Sarah."

How did *The Wedding Gift* come about?

I majored in history in college and loved to read nonfiction about history. … In 1999, I was reading a book on runaway slaves and came across, in a footnote, a summary of a court case in Alabama, in the 1840s, where a slave owner sued his wife for divorce because he claimed the child she gave birth to was not his. The court granted him all the property his wife brought into the marriage, including a young slave woman. I thought that would make for an interesting novel.

How did you meet your agent?

My book was first self-published (2009) because I could not find an agent. It sold 140,000 e-books and made *The Wall Street Journal* bestseller list. When that happened, a friend of mine introduced me to my agent, Victoria Sanders of Victoria Sanders & Associates [who sold the book to St. Martin's].

What was your biggest surprise?

I was told that a book about slavery would not sell, and I'm glad I ignored that.

What did you do right?

The single most important thing I did in the beginning was to invest in editing. … I knew that the stigma against self-published books mainly has to do with poor or no editing.

Tell us a little about your platform.

[Originally] I made a list of everyone who could help me spread the word. I asked everyone who was in a book club to recommend my book. … [Now I have] a PR and publicity firm to help. There also is my focused social networking campaign, including book clubs and Goodreads, and e-mail campaigns to women's fiction readers.

Marlen Suyapa Bodden writes from Stamford, Connecticut. Visit her website at marlenbodden.com.

SUSAN RIEGER

The Divorce Papers

(romantic comedy/mainstream fiction, Crown, March 2014)

"The story of a very messy, contentious, high-profile divorce, and the smart, funny, and sometimes prickly young female lawyer dragooned into handling it, told through e-mails, memos, letters, invitations, interviews, and laws."

How did *The Divorce Papers* come about?

As a new lawyer, I had taught a moot court course, which required me to make up a case for my students to brief and argue. I thought then that writing a novel using real documents might be an interesting way of telling a story. Years later, after my own divorce, I decided to follow up on the idea. I also spent years freelancing by writing articles on law and the way it intersects with daily life.

What was the time frame for the book?

The total was about twelve years, but mainly I wrote the book in two chunks, 1999–2001 and 2009–2011.

How did you meet your agent?

I asked a young novelist acquaintance if she would read the book and tell me if she thought it might be publishable. She liked the book a lot, and that gave me the confidence to look for an agent. My [second] husband, who's a journalist, approached his agent, Kathy Robbins of The Robbins Office, for her advice. After reading it, she said she'd like to be my agent—so long as my husband and I didn't see problems in sharing an agent. We didn't.

What did you learn along the way?

I had to learn to take criticism and figure out from my agent and my editor's suggestions how to rethink characters and situations I had known so long.

Do you have any advice for aspiring writers?

Remember TIC: tush in chair. It's crucial.

Susan Rieger writes from New York City.

M.L. ROWLAND

Zero-Degree Murder

(mystery, Berkley, January 2014)

"Search and rescue expert Gracie Kinkaid and movie star Rob Christian fight for their lives when they're stranded in the mountains by an early-season blizzard with an unknown killer closing in."

How did *Zero-Degree Murder* come about?

I spent years as a volunteer on a very active search and rescue team in the mountains of Southern California, so I wrote about what I know.

What was the time frame for the book?

[Around] six or seven years. Since this was my first attempt at fiction, it went through numerous manifestations.

How did you get your book deal?

I wrote countless query letters, receiving lots of rejections. Finally, I was introduced to a script manager, Anne McDermott of AM Management, by some screenwriter friends who thought my book would make a great movie. Anne put me in touch with an editor at Penguin Random House, who offered me a deal for three books.

What did you do right?

I wrote about a subject about which I have experience, expertise, and a lot of great stories. I read prodigiously—different genres as well as mysteries. I tried to never stop learning. And, while so many times I wanted to give up, I never did.

Tell us a little about your platform.

Both Gracie Kinkaid and I have Facebook pages. I have a website featuring segments on search and rescue, writing, and other things.

Do you have any advice for aspiring writers?

> Never stop living your life. It provides perspective, as well as great character and plot ideas.

. . . .

M.L. Rowland writes from Colorado. Visit her website at mlrowland.com.

. . . .

ADAM STERNBERGH

Shovel Ready

(futuristic noir thriller, Crown, January 2014)

"Spademan, a former garbage man turned hitman who's living in a post-dirty-bomb New York, is hired to kill the daughter of America's most famous evangelist."

What were you doing prior to writing *Shovel Ready*?

> I've been a journalist for fifteen years, the last three at *The New York Times Magazine*. *Shovel Ready* is my first published novel, but not my first novel. My first novel, which was not hardboiled, dystopian, or thrilling, now lives in quiet retirement in a very comfortable desk drawer.

What was the time frame for the book?

> The first draft was finished very quickly after just a few months of writing. Then came an extensive editing process, with notes first from my wife (who's a playwright) and then, later, from my editor.

How did you meet your agent?

> My agent is David McCormick of McCormick & Williams. He approached me about [representation] back in 2006, actually, because he'd been interested in some of my nonfiction journalism work.

What did you learn along the way?

> Just how many people are involved in making a single book. It's humbling and gratifying to have such a large team of talented people, from the cover designer to the copy editors to the sales force, all working together on something that sprang out of your brain.

What did you do right?

> For starters, I had to stop worrying, or even thinking, about getting published. My first novel (shelved) and second one (abandoned) were both strangulated, to some degree, by my inability to let go of notions I had about how each novel might eventually be received.

Do you have any advice for aspiring writers?

Write the book you want to read. It's the only way you'll write anything that's any good.

Adam Sternbergh writes from Brooklyn, New York. Visit his website at adamsternbergh.com.

CHRIS WILLRICH

Photo: Richard McCowen

The Scroll of Years

(fantasy, Pyr, September 2013)

"Persimmon Gaunt and Imago Bone, adventurers and lovers, are on the verge of giving up their roguish ways and starting a family when they must flee assassins all the way to the distant east of their continent, a realm with many dangers of its own."

What were you doing prior to writing *The Scroll of Years*?

For many years I've written short stories for science fiction and fantasy genre publications, including several stories featuring Gaunt and Bone, these mainly [appearing] in *Fantasy & Science Fiction*. …

What was the time frame for the book?

Originally this was going to be a novella titled *Empire of Walls*, and I started it in 2007. I put the work aside and actually forgot about it for a while, returning to it in 2010 and finishing the first solid draft in 2011. By then it was book-length.

How did you meet your agent?

I kept in touch with John Joseph Adams, formerly assistant editor at *Fantasy & Science Fiction*. When I asked him about breaking into novels, he put me in touch with his agent, Joe Monti of Barry Goldblatt Literary. As luck would have it, Joe thought the novel had potential and agreed to represent me.

Would you do anything differently?

I would have written more book-length material earlier.

Do you have any advice for aspiring writers?

Hang in there. You never know when things might work out. I first mailed a story to a magazine in 1985 (it didn't sell). But along with that, make sure you're writing what you love, because that's what it takes to stay with it year after year.

Chris Willrich writes from Mountain View, California. Visit his website at chriswillrich.com.

GOING PUBLIC

How to Ace Readings, Signings, Interviews, and More

....

Elizabeth Sims

It was a dark and stormy night in Northern California. I was in a large bookstore to read from my debut novel, *Holy Hell*, and this was my very first author event. Only four people had shown up, but I felt triumphant that it wasn't zero.

In honor of the occasion, I'd brought a box of fine chocolates to share. My small audience sat comfortably and paid attention as I spoke. At the end there were no questions, but everybody came up for an extra chocolate.

One person told me she'd enjoyed my reading. I tried to hand her a book, desperate to make at least one sale, saying, "Wouldn't you like to get one? I'd be glad to sign it for you."

"Oh, no," she said. The others were drifting away. "Goodnight, Ed!" she called. "Goodnight, Jerome!" The woman turned back to me. "See, we're all homeless, and we come in here to warm up. We can't buy anything."

"Oh," I said, then stammered the only thing I could think of: "Well, would you like to take the rest of the chocolates?"

"Yes, thank you." She took the box and left.

A low point to start from? Perhaps.

Since then, I've given a book *and* bus fare to a guy who attended one of my readings; showed up for an appearance in 104-degree heat to find that the air conditioning had broken (zero attendance there); and been snubbed by store clerks who perceived my mystery series as beneath them.

Fortunately, I've also enjoyed well-attended events and built lasting relationships with many booksellers and readers who appreciate my work—and tell their friends.

Having worked as both a bookstore manager and a media spokesperson before becoming an author, I've experienced the business from several angles. The main lesson: Your public persona as an author is not about you. Really. It's about your work and your audience. And all you need is a little preparation to serve them both well. Let's look at the most common scenarios you'll face.

BOOKSTORE APPEARANCES

The standard venue for a public appearance by an author is still the bookstore. Here's how to ensure each event you do is a successful one:

• **KNOW THAT YOU'LL BE JUDGED BY YOUR OWN COVER.** It might not be fair, but people accord greater respect to those who dress in good clothes. Show up in an outfit you'd wear to accept a literary prize. Be fastidious about your grooming (and breath). Look sharp, and you'll feel sharp.

• **ARRIVE EARLY.** Introduce yourself to the manager, and get squared away. You will have phoned or e-mailed weeks in advance to make sure they've stocked your books. (Always double-check all logistics—date and time, book inventory—even if you're published by a traditional house with someone assigned to make arrangements for you.) Check out the physical space and set up your stuff (a good pen for signing, bookmarks or other giveaways, sign-up sheet to join your e-mail list, water bottle, throat lozenges). Find out where the bathroom is.

Typically, you won't have much room to work with. It's reasonable to expect—and nicely ask for, if need be—eight to ten chairs, a table, and a little space for them. If nothing's set up, say, "OK if I just pitch in and help?" Then drag chairs over, hunt down your books, and make a good time of it.

Avoid demanding more from the bookstore unless you're a major or especially charismatic author. I remember one big-name author telling me quite frankly on the phone before his event, "I'm an alcoholic, and I'm going to need a bottle of scotch and a glass within easy reach, or things won't go well." Given that we expected to sell several hundred copies of his books, I gladly ran to the liquor store.

Unless you're that guy, bring your own liquor. Better still, unless you're that guy, show up sober and tidy.

• **BE CHARMING NO MATTER WHAT HAPPENS.** Realize that you are an entertainer and will be judged by how well you amuse and accommodate. When introduced to bookstore staff, look them in the eye, say their name twice, and then call them by name evermore. (It helps to picture a person's name engraved across her forehead.) Most mortals get upset when things go wrong; you can elevate yourself to special status by reacting with good humor to any mishap, such as a fire alarm getting pulled or the coffee machine breaking down.

• **TAKE COMMAND OF THE CLOCK.** Here is a good way to manage your time for a one-hour appearance:

5 minutes: Introduction, thank everyone for coming, thank the host, invite to sign up for your e-mail list. (Note: Be prepared to introduce yourself if no one is on hand to do it.)

10–15 minutes: Read, with intro/commentary.

10–15 minutes: Talk about your book and yourself.

10–15 minutes: Q&A, thank the audience and host.

10–15 minutes: Sign books, kibitz, wrap up, and go.

• **READ WELL, LIVELY, AND LITTLE.** Audiences like to hear, before you read, a short anecdote as to how your book came about. Then, a couple of passages totaling 10–15 minutes work well as an appetizer to entice your listeners to buy the book.

For fiction, avoid passages with long descriptions and/or lots of dialogue (imagine the task of trying to alter your tone or pitch for each different voice). An effective reading shows your protagonist engaged in some action and reveals a bit of his personality or motivation at the same time. Unless you're starting at the very beginning, provide some context: "OK, Officer Rodriguez has just gotten dumped by his girlfriend, but he doesn't know how his luck is about to change. We pick up with him as he's called to investigate a suspicious smell coming from the apartment next door."

Ideally, do a practice run in front of someone (or someones) who can provide constructive criticism. Vary your voice tones, put your emphasis in different places, vary your loudness and softness, use gestures. Also, it's OK to pause for effect. (This is a good time to look up and make eye contact with someone in the audience.)

It has become the fashion for authors reading aloud to laugh, or barely suppress laughter, at the witty places. Do not stoop to this. If your work is funny, reading it with straight earnestness will make them laugh. A well-timed pause can make all the difference. Take my word for it.

• **KEEP THEM LISTENING.** When you finish reading, it's OK to say a few things about your writing process and how you came to be an author, but mostly your attendees want to hear why they should spend their hard-earned money on your book.

Based on that, a good way to give a successful little talk is simply to tell anecdotes. How did you come up with the characters and their foibles? Audiences also love to hear stories about the research you did for your book. I've held rooms spellbound as I relayed how my friend, a surgeon, educated me in how it feels and sounds to set a broken bone.

• **ALWAYS TAKE QUESTIONS AT THE END.** Do this *before* you offer to sign books. Be generous in answering, and let one question lead to another.

If things are slow, I might jump-start the situation by pulling out a few cards and saying brightly, "As it happens, I brought a few questions from the old mailbag just in case!" Of course these are of my own devising, the crazier the better: I've "asked" myself about rabbits, golf, revenge, theatrical makeup, arson, and more, all of it relevant in some way to one of my books.

Enjoy your audience; let them see you having fun. If someone starts to monopolize the Q&A, just smile and say, "Let's you and I get together after I've wrapped up, OK?"

• **ADAPT YOUR TALK TO YOUR AUDIENCE.** All these tips work great whether you've got an audience of twelve or 120. But the No. 1 question I'm asked about bookstore appearances is this: What if nobody (or almost nobody) comes? It's a valid concern—we've all been there. But knowing how to handle it can set you apart.

If your census is between one and four, I suggest you forsake the lecture format, make a circle of the chairs, and just have a conversation. Forgo the awkwardness of standing in front of the room, and put your audience at ease. Often other customers will be drawn in. Still talk about your book and even read, but keep it loose and informal. The point is to bond with your listeners. Ask them what they're reading, what they're hungry for, whether they love only happy endings, even what they like to drink while reading.

If the worst happens and nobody turns out, chat up the staff. If they're busy, stay out of their way, but if there's downtime, ask them things. Booksellers are a fount of information. "Which book/author has most affected you?" "What books are getting your customers excited these days?" "Do you see any trends in the (fill-in-the-blank) genre?"

You can also sell books by roaming the store. Hold a copy of your book, walk around, smile, and introduce yourself as "today's author." Tell them something nice a reviewer has said, then say, "Here, take a look!"

• **SIGN PROPERLY.** When it's time to sign books, say, "Now I'll be glad to personalize a book for—well, everybody!" Take your position behind your table, make eye contact with one and all, get the spelling of each name right, and sign the title page (not inside the cover or on a flyleaf).

CONFERENCES/EVENTS

Writers tend to be horrible at schmoozing. That's because of a mistaken idea that they're supposed to "get something" out of other people, which feels awkward and uncomfortable. In fact, good schmoozing is about *engaging* with people.

You can get comfortable by realizing that everybody wants to be liked. It's magic when you take the initiative to make a friendly comment, smile, ask people about themselves, and pay attention to what they say. *Enjoy* people. Try to put everyone at ease, but stop short of being totally ingratiating. Do this by not hogging the spotlight. Listen with alert kindness. One of the best schmoozers I've ever seen made a point of introducing people to one another at events, always with some little connecting comment: "Do you know Dmitri? He teaches at the college!" She flitted around throwing people together all over the place, and everybody loved her.

When doing an event with multiple authors (always a great idea), be hearty, be happy to see them. A golden open-ended question is, "What are you working on now?"

It's a good rule of thumb to follow etiquette rules you might have been taught about polite conversation at dinner parties. Just as you wouldn't assume everybody around you shares your religion, do not assume they share your political slant. Don't be afraid to be yourself, but keep conversation topics in the neutral zone (unless, of course, your book/platform itself is related to a specific position or opinion).

MEDIA INTERVIEWS

Writers sometimes get featured in print, on the Web, on TV, and on radio. A useful and efficient way to prepare for these opportunities—while simultaneously creating an effective promotional tool you'll use again and again—is to start by interviewing yourself, in writing. Think of the things you're most likely to be asked, and write your answers out in basic Q&A form: *What led you to write this book? Why is your book important?* Etc.

You can then post this in a Q&A section on your website and even use choice responses in press releases and other promo materials.

And, having thought through these questions and more in advance, you'll find that you're now prepared for most any interview. Having a microphone in front of your face makes most people's adrenaline spike, so knowing what you want to say will help you keep calm. Speak slowly, and you'll sound normal.

The key to nailing an interview is to realize that the interviewer, who is usually at best vaguely familiar with you or your book, will be glad if you take his questions and run with them. Tell what *you* would like the world to know about your book, using the anecdotes you've worked up already. That way, the outcome of the interview is in your control, regardless of how lackluster the questions may be. It's not unusual for an author who is featured in a local newspaper to get a call from a radio producer who spotted the article. Or for a writer who gives an entertaining talk on a popular podcast to be invited to appear on TV. Taking the time to prepare and grant a good interview will likely pay off tenfold as one opportunity leads to another.

GUEST BLOGGING/BLOG TOURS

Whether you're invited to contribute to an existing blog, or you're actively organizing a promotional "blog tour" of your own (or just looking to expand your online platform), writing guest posts is a fun way to engage with potential readers. Ask the blog host what she's looking for, and accommodate as best you can. If the content is all up to you, consider your target audience's point of view: What might they find interesting, amusing, even salacious? (A little gossip goes a long way—remember my bit about the writer and the scotch?) You might include a short excerpt from your book or write up anecdotes just as you'd tell them in an interview.

Let your social network know when your post goes live, making sure to appreciatively acknowledge your host. Then, it's good form to check back on your post, especially the day of and the day after. Reply graciously to all comments, keeping the conversation going.

FOLLOW-THROUGH

Write a thank-you note for every appearance. For physical events, handwrite a note, address it to "The Management and Staff of XYZ Bookstore (or Library)," and let them know how much you appreciated their time and trouble. If you were a guest for an interview or blog, write an e-mail saying the same. Aside from the fact that it's the decent thing to do, a thank-you might help you get invited back.

Every chance for a writer to interact with the public is a special opportunity. By understanding the bigger picture, and by preparing yourself to maximize your impact and handle whatever happens with grace, you will stand the best chance of making a terrific impression, selling books, and creating good karma.

Elizabeth Sims (elizabethsims.com) is a prize-winning novelist and author of the bestseller *You've Got a Book in You: A Stress-Free Guide to Writing the Book of Your Dreams* (Writer's Digest Books).

BEST PRACTICES FOR BLOGGING

....

Jack Smith

The blogosphere is hot and heavy with lively conversations on innumerable topics. It's become a meeting ground for sharing thoughts, feelings, and experiences. For writers it serves as a cyber conference to meet new people and to gain attention for one's work. Sure, successful bloggers blog on their own sites, but they also guest blog on other sites and do blog tours when their new books are released. What's the payoff for all of this blogging? And how much time should a writer devote to it? Here, several blogging authors weigh in on the dos and don'ts of this essential platform booster.

BLOGGING AND BOOK SALES

In today's tough fiction market, blogging can serve as a key marketing tool. For Anne R. Allen, publishing industry blogger and comic mystery author, it's the center of her platform. "Without my blog, I'd have no career. My current publisher approached me because he liked my blog, and so did the two *NYT* bestsellers who have collaborated with me: Ruth Harris (now my blog partner and collaborator on our best-selling *Chanel and Gatsby* boxed set) and Catherine Ryan Hyde (my co-author for *How to Be a Writer in the E-Age*)." Elizabeth Spann Craig, who writes two mystery series for Penguin and self-publishes another, also sees her blog as vital to her platform. "Although I have not been able to measure a direct correlation between my own blogging and my book sales, my blog gives me a platform that provides both me and my books better exposure in web searches." Roz Morris is author of *My Memories of a Future Life*, *Lifeform Three*, and the Nail Your Novel series of writing books. Morris's blog is her prime marketing method. "It's certainly been my primary means of selling my books, because I don't do any paid-for advertising. A blog—or website—is an online base for readers to find you."

Blogging creates valuable PR for both author and work. "Word of mouth is the number one way books are sold," says Suzy Vitello, author of *The Moment Before* and *The Empress Chronicles*. "Blogging expands an author's reach and facilitates word of mouth, so it can help quite a bit. It can also be an extension of your book." According to Rachael Herron, author of *Pack up the Moon* and writer of the popular blog Yarnagogo.com, blogging connects you to the reading public, helps with sales of past work, and lays the groundwork for future sales: "Blogging is invaluable. You already have readers—fans—invested in *you*. They not only want to buy the last book, they've watched you go through the process of writing this new one, and they're going to want that, too."

A blog tour serves as a great PR tool. Stephanie Cowell, author of several novels including *Claude & Camille: A Novel of Monet*, states, "A blog tour is critical in PR. I don't blog much on my own website, but I guest blog a lot. I think my blog tour was critical to the PR in the beginning." Elizabeth Searle, author of four works of fiction, including *Girl Held in Home*, also values the blog tour for creating exposure for a book: "The smart young writers I know these days all seem to be going on a 'Blog Tour' rather than a 'Book Tour.' Blogging always has the potential of reaching large numbers of readers while you sit at home in your pajamas."

But if your sole purpose in blogging is book sales, you may want to rethink this strategy. Cari Luna, author of *The Revolution of Every Day*, sees this as a wrongheaded approach and one that might not be successful: "Blogging helps in selling a book to the extent that it helps you build an audience before you have a book to sell. Readers find you, they like your voice and stick with the blog, and when it comes time to promote a book, they're invested in it and excited to help support it. But I don't think this works if [you approach it] purely as a marketing vehicle. If you are only moved to blog because you think you need to do it to sell books, don't do it." According to Luna, a strictly self-promotional agenda will most likely reveal itself and lead to undesirable results: "I think the most important thing in blogging—as well as Twitter, Facebook, or any other form of social media—is community. If you don't genuinely want to be part of a community and its ongoing conversations, it shows. That's where you end up with blog posts that feel like assigned articles—no warmth or personal connection to them." And so if you blog with book sales only in mind, do reconsider this objective, suggests Luna: "Blog because you want to connect with people and want to do so with your writing in the informal, conversational manner that blogging implies. Reply to comments. Get to know your readers. The sales will follow naturally from that." Man Martin, two-time winner of Georgia Author of the Year for *Days of the Endless Corvette* and *Paradise Dogs*, also discourages an exclusive monetary motive in blogging: "I think bloggers whose motivation is to sell books are apt to fail and alienate readers besides."

DRIVING TRAFFIC TO YOUR BLOG

Let's assume you have your own blog. How can you drive traffic to it? Active writer-bloggers offer several suggestions, key among them strong content. Janice Hardy, author of the YA fantasy trilogy *The Healing Wars* notes, "Writing great content is the first step; that way you'll get links, and readers will send others your way." But what counts as strong content? For Hardy, it means "a solid stock of evergreen posts (posts that are always helpful, not constrained by current events)." Craig also emphasizes "helpful information," the kind that adds true value for readers. Allen encourages originality, which can mean either "original content" or "an original approach to something being discussed in the blogosphere."

Strong content can also mean blogs that capture the personality, character, and voice of the author. According to Morris, "You put your personality into it—with the subjects you like to talk about, your approach to writing, the pictures you choose. A good blog gives a sense of the person behind the writing and can be a very effective way for readers to get to know you. Once they do, they're more likely to be curious about your books." Herron agrees: "My most popular posts are the ones in which I reveal myself, flaws and all. They're the ones people most respond to and share with friends." Martin puts it this way: "I think the thing most readers want is a glimpse into the actual life and inner mental workings of an author. It sounds trite, but the advice for writing a good blog is probably the same for writing a good anything: Be yourself, write what you know, [and] develop your own voice."

If strong content can drive traffic to your blog, strong presentation values naturally attract readers and other bloggers. Be sure, says Vitello, to "make the physical space appealing," and, of crucial importance, make it "easy to navigate." Readability is a strong value, and it includes several different aspects, among them, says Allen, "No white fonts on black backgrounds. Not too busy. Lots of white space."

The posts themselves should be "pithy," says Christine Sneed, author of *Little Known Facts* and *Portraits of a Few of the People I've Made Cry*. Sneed recommends limiting posts to "1,500 words, often between 500–1000 words." Beyond this brevity issue, Craig adds that a good blog post "features copyright-free images to illustrate the post, content that is broken up into easy-to-skim paragraphs (potentially with bullet-points or a series of tips), and a byline, preferably with a Twitter handle included."

Once you've solved the problem of strong content and presentation, avoid being too insular—get fully connected with bloggers at other sites. "Go to other blogs and find posts you want to comment on," advises Morris. "Bloggers love to get into a conversation, and you can build great relationships with the owners of other blogs. When you leave a comment, the blog owner and all their readers can see where you came from, so if you look interesting they might check you out. They might even interview you, invite you to [do a] guest post, or reference one of your posts." And be sure to do guest posts, says Hardy. "Guest posts on other blogs are a good way to tell potential readers about your blog."

Fourth, be sure not to engage in too much self-promotion. Since this will put readers off, Morris advises against a "hard sell": "There's a theory that on social media you should spend 80 percent of the time *not* talking about your own work." Instead of promoting yourself, promote others, says Vitello: "If you think about blogging as an aspect of the readers'/writers' community, then you might liken increasing traffic to getting a reputation for throwing good parties. Be generous. Introduce people to one another. Facilitate interaction."

Finally, in order to drive traffic to your blog, you should participate as much as possible in the wide range of social media. "Running a blog isn't enough on its own to get readers," states Morris. "The blog is like your online home, but you also need to get out where people mingle online—the other social networks." Allen looks for distinctive advantages and disadvantages of each social media venue: "Right now, I think the essential site is Google+, because popular Google+ posts will move you up in the search rankings. I also get a lot of traffic through Twitter. Facebook is a distant third [for me] because Facebook discourages you from posting links to your own blog or website and will even put you in Facebook 'jail' (freeze your account) if you post too many blog links. Other authors say Pinterest is a great way to get traffic."

GUEST BLOGGING

Guest blogging can be an important activity in expanding your reach. If you intend to guest blog, how can you pick the blogs that will help you get your name and/or your book the greatest exposure possible?

Begin by searching for blogs that relate to your subject and also ones that appeal to you in terms of the overall tone and message. And a critical question to consider: Is the content updated regularly?

First, as to subject matter, "Is it a good fit for your kind of book?" asks Morris. "For instance, my book on writing (*Nail Your Novel*) is very practical and upbeat, and I'd look for blogs where the readers appreciated that approach." If you're a novelist, what kind of fiction do you write? Does it fit a certain genre? Are there sites that relate to your subject area? "If you write historical novels set in the Civil War," says Hardy, "blog on Civil War sites. If you write for children, parenting sites are possibilities." But don't overlook review sites and library sites, says Hardy. Beyond the question of subject matter, be sure to consider tone and message. "Nose around various blogs," Vitello advises. "Read through the comments. Is this your tribe? Could it be? It's all about reaching your audience. Growing your audience. Readers have the ever-increasing expectation that they'll be able to access authors whose books they love." Finally, subject matter-wise, there's the matter of regular updating of content. "Look for frequency of posts," says Morris. "Google sends search engine traffic to sites that post more frequently, so look for a blog that has a regular supply of good, fresh content that seems to please its readers."

As a potential guest blogger, you should also check out the reputation of the blog. Morris suggests asking these key questions: "Would it be beneficial for you to be associated with that blog? Does the presentation and artwork fit with the image you want to project? Are the articles well written and proofed so they would reflect well on you?" Also, consider the site's Alexa ranking (Alexa is the most popular website ranking tool), but, cautions Allen, "Don't judge a blog by its analytics alone. A blog with less traffic that appeals to *your* readers is much more important than just a high rating. On one blog tour I sold more books the day I visited a cozy little 'Boomer nostalgia blog' than I did visiting some of the highest-profile blogs in the business."

Be sure to keep blogging etiquette in mind, too. Before you make a final decision on the best blogs to guest post on, be sure to attend to three very important things, says Allen: "Pick blogs you actually *read*. Nothing annoys me more than requests to guest blog from people who have obviously never visited the blog. Every new writer-blogger should be reading a number of high-profile writing blogs and commenting regularly." Second, urges Allen, "*Read the guidelines* before you approach. This is the most ignored rule in the blogosphere, and it's the number one reason 99 percent of guest blog requests get denied or deleted." Third, be sensitive to the needs of the host bloggers: "Approach them in a friendly, conversational way," says Allen, "and propose a post on a particular topic you know to be of interest to their readers."

BEING AN "ACTIVE" BLOGGER

To be considered an "active" blogger, the general consensus is that you should blog at least once a week. According to Craig, "There are currently many proponents of so-called 'slow blogging,' the method of a weekly post. This keeps your blog active [and] retains [your] SEO (Search Engine Optimization) ranking but still allows you the luxury of more time to plan posts while maintaining your schedule for your non-blog-related writing. This works best when your blogging schedule is posted in your sidebar." Even though Hardy blogs daily, she recommends that you "blog at a schedule that you're comfortable with—something that allows you to keep up with your blog and engage your readers, but not at a pace that will burn you out or make you hate blogging." When calculating how active you are, Hardy believes you can also count "conversations in the comments" you make on your own as well as others' blogs; after all, "you're engaging with readers even if it's not in a post."

Searle finds she's able to structure her schedule just right to manage a once-a-week blog commitment: "For me, I find if I change the lead post at least once a week and check in every couple of days to reply to comments, then that seems to help sustain the blog. … I wouldn't want to do [more than that] because it would take up too much of my writerly energy." Herron sometimes does less herself. And for those struggling to maintain the weekly blogging goal, she cautions, "Don't just write to fill space." Luna also recommends blogging at least once a week, but she admits, "I don't always manage to do that these days. There's only so much time and energy to go around, and I find I'm preferring Twitter for connecting with people and getting the word out about the latest reviews of my novel, or upcoming readings, etc."

While Allen agrees that "the ideal blog is updated weekly to a set schedule," she also believes "you can consider your blog active if you blog once a month." And for Vitello, whether you update your blog once a week or once a month, the important thing is a "semi-consistent schedule."

LEARN BY EXAMPLE

Engaging, well-written blogs are the best teaching tools for starting your own. The blogs of the authors who contributed to this article are a great place to begin.

- **ANNE R. ALLEN:** annerallen.blogspot.com
- **STEPHANIE COWELL:** www.stephaniecowell.com/blog.htm
- **ELIZABETH SPANN CRAIG:** elizabethspanncraig.com/blog
- **JANICE HARDY:** www.janicehardy.com
- **RACHAEL HERRON:** www.yarnagogo.com
- **CARI LUNA:** cariluna.com/blog
- **MAN MARTIN:** manmartin.blogspot.com
- **ROZ MORRIS:** nailyournovel.wordpress.com
- **ELIZABETH SEARLE:** www.celebritiesindisgrace.wordpress.com
- **CHRISTINE SNEED:** www.christinesneed.com/blog
- **SUZY VITELLO:** www.suzyvitello.com/suzys-blog

THE NUMBER OF BLOGS TO BE ACTIVE ON

How many blogs should you maintain? How many other blogs should you be active on? Certainly you want as much exposure as possible for yourself as author, and for your fiction, but you don't want to overdo it. You don't want to exhaust yourself, nor do you want to take too much time away from your regular writing. So where do you draw the line?

If it's your own blog, one blog is enough, says Allen. "No more. You're supposed to be writing books, remember. I've seen so many writers start dozens of blogs—one for each book, or one for each aspect of their personality. Bad idea." And not bad just because it takes too much time away from your writing—but for another compelling reason as well: "You can't keep up," says Allen, "and you'll have lots of dead blogs hanging around the Interwebz. When somebody Googles you, the earliest blog will probably come up. A reader/agent/publisher visits and sees you haven't updated in three years and your career is as dead as the blog. I strongly urge authors *not* to start a bunch of blogs. If you have done so, go back to the first one and revive it. Then delete all the others."

Being active on too many group blogs can also be taxing, as Craig discovered. "I've been on as many as five group blogs, as well as my own individual blog … and I felt frantic as a result." But there is a way to avoid such intensity, one which will give you the opportunity to group blog and yet lighten the load. Seek out a group blog, says Craig, "where many writers are on the rotation in order to minimize your involvement … but make sure your contributions to the blog are attributed with a byline and headshot or book cover, if possible."

Ideas vary on the total number of blogs to be active on—and the nature of the commitment. Vitello suggests one or two of your own; beyond that, "choose a half-dozen or a dozen other blogs to visit and comment on frequently. Remember: It's about community." Sneed suggests posting on no more than three to four blogs at a time. "One or two is probably best for one's sanity and other writing obligations. It's hard to maintain freshness and to post regularly if you stretch yourself past two or three, I think." Cowell urges bloggers to be as active as possible, taking on as "many as you can without taking creativity from your new book. I was really active on four for a time, but I am not too active now; when the next book is in production, I intend to pick it up again."

Hardy believes one need not focus on an arbitrary number of blogs to be active on—or feel bound by some prescribed form of commitment. Be active, she says, on "as many as you enjoy and have time for. I read a lot of blogs, but I rarely make comments. But I do tweet links and share posts I find helpful, and invite bloggers I admire to [be guests] on my blog. Being genuine and building a community is more important than hitting an arbitrary number. Good blogging is about connecting with people, and there are so many ways of doing that these days."

SUMMING UP

As with any activity, types and levels of commitment naturally vary with blogging. As a writer-blogger, you need to decide what works best for you, given the constraints on your time and what you believe will be conducive to building community with other writers. While this shared community is certainly rewarding in itself, the exposure you gain for yourself as author, and for your work, is a second payoff.

10 TIPS FOR YOUR VIRTUAL BOOK TOUR

....

Erika Dreifus

No matter how you plan to publish your novel or short story collection—traditionally through a large or small press, or via self-publishing—promoting your book and generating buzz will be part of the work ahead for you. If you're fortunate enough to be affiliated with a well-resourced press, you're more likely to receive ample and expert assistance in publicity, promotion, and marketing efforts. Or, if you're able to (a) relinquish control and (b) spend your own money to fund such efforts, you can hire an independent publicist to do much of this work for you. But these days, many writers are assuming the lion's share of promotion and marketing responsibilities—which may explain the popularity of virtual book tours.

The basic idea behind virtual book touring is this: Instead of journeying in person from one physical location (often a bookstore) to another, a "touring" writer follows an online itinerary, essentially traveling from one URL to another, making authorial visits on various blogs or websites. In return, the hosts of each blog receive a complementary advance copy of the book being promoted. Ideally, each host commits to a date within the time span of the author's "tour," which normally lasts between two weeks and one month.

I discovered virtual tours several years ago when, as a blogger, I began to receive requests to host "stops" on other authors' online itineraries. But I approached these tours in a different way when a brand-new (and very small) publisher offered to release my short story collection to the world. At that point, I became my own tour planner and guide.

There was no budget for a traditional tour—or time, for that matter. I'm a writer with a year-round Monday-to-Friday day job that pays my bills. I'm not a professor blessed with lengthy winter vacations or summer breaks. I'm no longer a full-time freelancer with control over my schedule. A virtual tour seemed ideal for me.

If you're contemplating a tour of your own, consider these suggestions to enhance your chances for success.

1. START EARLY.

Even if you'll be touring from the comfort of home, you need to plan just as carefully as you would for any big adventure. And as the rest of this article will show, there's plenty of work to be done.

It's possible that I allowed myself more planning time than was absolutely necessary. I began lining up hosts three to four months ahead of the tour; at that point, I'd already completed some essential preliminaries. (For more about those, please keep reading!)

2. BE PREPARED.

Before you begin contacting your would-be hosts, be sure that you have these items on hand:

- review copies of your book (you can offer digital files, but don't be surprised if your hosts prefer to receive print copies)
- high-resolution author photo
- high-resolution image of your book cover
- short author bio

You may find it helpful to assemble an "online media kit," a section of your website where you can provide photos and other relevant information, such as a video trailer and press release, in one location. This way, you can give your hosts a single link instead of inundating them with attachments (which you'd never do in an initial e-mail anyway, right?).

This raises another point: If you don't yet have an author website, you need one. If you do have a site, you need to make sure it's up to date before you begin your outreach efforts. Similarly, if you plan to incorporate social media platforms such as Goodreads, Facebook, or Twitter into your tour—Twitter chats or Goodreads discussions are two possibilities—be sure that your accounts are established and active.

3. TAP YOUR NETWORK.

Wondering where to find hosts for your tour? Start with your own network of friends, family members, and colleagues. Explain what you're planning, and ask if they have any favorite blogs or other online venues to recommend. (Offer bonus points to anyone who provides contact information and a personal introduction or referral.)

Next, think more expansively about the meaning of "network." For example: Are you publishing a short story collection that features pieces previously published in literary journals? Check with those publications' editors—they've already supported your writing and might be happy to promote your book on their journals' blogs or podcasts. Don't forget your alumni newsletters or magazines, most of which now feature complementary online content as well. And your hometown media may be quite interested in the local author in their midst.

4. GO BEYOND YOUR NETWORK.

Don't limit yourself to those initial connections and ideas. Even if your friends, family, and colleagues aren't as helpful as you had hoped, you'll be able to locate some itinerary possibilities by doing a bit of extra work.

One way to discover potential tour hosts is to approach book bloggers where they congregate. For example, a book bloggers' conference takes place each year during the major BookExpo America (BEA) trade event. Don't worry: I'm not about to suggest that you travel to the conference to pitch these bloggers face-to-face. All you need to do is visit the BEA website (www.bookexpoamerica.com) and check under the "conferences" tab. There, you'll find more information for the BEA Bloggers Conference—including a list of bloggers who attended the previous year's gathering. Even better: That list includes each blogger's name, blog title, and book interests.

It's also fairly easy to discover sites where other authors have toured successfully. You needn't hire one of the companies that organizes virtual tours in order to benefit from its expertise. Most of these businesses—you can find them easily by using a search term like "virtual book tour"—publicize the tours they arrange for their own client-authors. Often, you can find sample itineraries posted on the companies' websites. Explore them. You're more than likely to discover venues that may be hospitable to your book, too.

Finally, think beyond the book blogs. Let's say that your book is an historical novel set during the First World War and features a British protagonist. In addition to the general book blogs, you might look for those that focus on historical fiction. You might search for places online where Anglophiles congregate. You might investigate popular blogs and websites where people discuss military history. Did you travel to Britain to research your book? Perhaps pitch a travel blog or podcast, too.

5. DO YOUR HOMEWORK.

Be sure that you've visited and become *thoroughly* familiar with each of your target sites or hosts before you reach out. In particular, look for the following:

- statements regarding review and guest-post policies, including information about the blogger's mission and/or reading interests
- contact preferences/directions
- quality of the writing/professionalism of the site (is this a site you'd be proud to promote as part of your virtual tour?)

- quantity and quality of the comments on the site. But don't automatically discount a site based on a lack of comments—readers may be opting to remark on the post when it's linked or shared on Twitter, Facebook, or elsewhere.

6. BE FLEXIBLE.

A book review penned by your host is one tried-and-true possibility for a tour stop, especially if it's accompanied by an offer to give away another signed copy of your book to a commenter on the review post. But be sure to make your flexibility known. Explain in your introductory message that you're equally willing to participate in a precompleted Q&A or live chat, write a guest post on a topic targeted to the blogger's readership, or consider other possibilities that the host may suggest.

Also, as much as you may want to pin down the dates of every blog tour, be patient! Follow up, but don't nag. If your request is declined, be gracious and move on. Which brings us to the next suggestion ...

7. BE PROFESSIONAL.

Take it from me: Some bloggers receive *many* requests. It's easy for them to become disillusioned when authors reach out via unpersonalized mass e-mails. Or misspell the blogger's name. Or send e-mails filled with spelling and/or grammar mistakes. *Don't be one of those authors.*

Remember that each and every one of your hosts will be doing you a great service. Be courteous, professional, and appreciative.

8. FOLLOW UP.

Once a blogger agrees to participate in your tour, follow up immediately. Thank the host, and send the promised review copy without delay.

Reconfirm the plan. Let's say that a blogger has agreed to post a review of your book and offer a signed giveaway copy to one lucky commenter. You might write something like this: "Per our exchange, I'm writing to confirm that [blog title] will post a review of [book title] on [date]. You will also select a giveaway winner from among those folks who comment on the post."

It's perfectly acceptable—and advisable—to check in with each host once or twice to make sure that review copies have been received and to ensure, closer to the actual tour date, that everything is in order. But don't overdo it or attempt to micromanage—you'll only succeed in annoying your host.

Keep track of your tour stops and begin publicizing the tour the same way you'd promote the book itself. Alert your own social media followers about the tour and keep them posted on where to find you along the way. (Trust me: Making other people's blogs the focus of your status updates provides a refreshing change from a drumbeat of "please buy my book!" posts.) You might consider creating a tour page on your website to highlight the stops ahead of time, updating each entry as the host's content goes live. See how I managed this over on my own website: www.erikadreifus.com/?p=7148.

9. CHECK IN AND ENGAGE.

Ideally, you've scheduled your tour to unfold at a time when you aren't overwhelmed by other responsibilities. Sure, life is full of surprises, but it doesn't make sense to plan any tour—virtual or not—during a season or cycle when you are typically busier than usual with family or professional responsibilities.

This is important because your engagement matters. Let's say that a blogger is posting an interview she conducted with you via e-mail. You'll want to stop by her blog when the interview is posted to respond to any additional questions or comments that her readers may leave.

And if a book giveaway is part of the deal, you'll need to check in to learn the winner's name and address, and to mail the promised copy.

10. SAY "THANK YOU."

Finally, remember to thank each host after your visit. This might seem like a no-brainer, but a little gratitude goes a long way—and it might earn you a repeat host for your next book!

You can do this in a number of ways. Send a handwritten thank-you note. Send an individualized e-mail message. Continue to visit your hosts' blogs and support *their* work. Like most marketing and promotion tasks, when you give a little, you receive a little in return.

Virtual book tours can be a useful and cost-efficient way to promote your book to a wide gamut of readers. As the online world adds platforms and innovations, the options for virtual tours expand. Be creative, stay organized, and above all—enjoy your trip!

Erika Dreifus is a New York City-based writer and publisher of *The Practicing Writer*, a free and popular e-newsletter on the craft and business of writing designed for fictionists, poets, and writers of creative nonfiction. She is the author of *Quiet Americans: Stories* (Last Light Studio), which was named an American Library Association Sophie Brody Medal Honor Title (for outstanding achievement in Jewish literature). Visit Erika online at www.erikadreifus.com.

LITERARY AGENTS

///

Many publishers are willing to look at unsolicited submissions, but most feel having an agent is in the writer's best interest. In this section, we include agents who specialize in or represent fiction.

The commercial fiction field is intensely competitive. Many publishers have small staffs and little time. For that reason, many book publishers rely on agents for new talent. Some publishers even rely on agents as "first readers" who must wade through the deluge of submissions from writers to find the very best. For writers, a good agent can be a foot in the door—someone willing to do the necessary work to put your manuscript in the right editor's hands.

It would seem today that finding a good agent is as hard as finding a good publisher. Yet those writers who have agents say they are invaluable. Not only can a good agent help you make your work more marketable, an agent also acts as your business manager and adviser, protecting your interests during and after contract negotiations.

Still, finding an agent can be very difficult for a new writer. If you are already published in magazines, you have a better chance than someone with no publishing credits. (Some agents read periodicals searching for new writers.) Although many agents do read queries and manuscripts from unpublished authors without introduction, referrals from their writer clients can be a big help. If you don't know any published authors with agents, attending a conference is a good way to meet agents. Some agents even set aside time at conferences to meet new writers.

Almost all the agents listed here have said they are open to working with new, previously unpublished writers as well as published writers. They do not charge a fee to cover the time and effort involved in reviewing a manuscript or a synopsis and chapters, but their time is still extremely valuable. Only send an agent your work when you feel it is as complete and polished as possible.

USING THE LISTINGS

It is especially important that you read individual listings carefully before contacting these busy agents. The first information after the company name includes the address and phone, fax, e-mail address (when available), and website. **Member Agents** gives the names of individual agents working at that company. (Specific types of fiction an agent handles are indicated in parentheses after that agent's name). The **Represents** section lists the types of fiction the agency works with. Reading the **Recent Sales** gives you the names of writers an agent is currently working with and, very important, publishers the agent has placed manuscripts with. **Tips** presents advice directly from the agent to authors.

Also, look closely at the openness to submissions icon that precedes most listings. It indicates how willing an agency is to take on new writers.

THE AHEARN AGENCY, INC.

2021 Pine St., New Orleans LA 70118. (504)861-8395. **Fax:** (504)866-6434. **E-mail:** pahearn@aol.com. **Website:** www.ahearnagency.com. **Contact:** Pamela G. Ahearn. Other memberships include MWA, RWA, ITW. Represents 35 clients. 20% of clients are new/unpublished writers.

- Prior to opening her agency, Ms. Ahearn was an agent for 8 years and an editor with Bantam Books.

REPRESENTS Considers these fiction areas: romance, suspense, thriller, women's.

- Handles women's fiction and suspense fiction only. Does not want to receive category romance, science fiction, or fantasy.

HOW TO CONTACT Query with SASE or via e-mail. Please send a one-page query letter stating the type of book you're writing, word length, where you feel your book fits into the current market, and any writing credentials you may possess. Please do not send ms pages or synopses if they haven't been previously requested. If you're querying via e-mail, send no attachments. Accepts simultaneous submissions. Responds in 2-3 months to queries and mss. Obtains most new clients through recommendations from others, solicitations, conferences.

TERMS Agent receives 15% commission on domestic sales. Agent receives 20% commission on foreign sales. Offers written contract, binding for 1 year; renewable by mutual consent.

RECENT SALES *To the Grave*, by Carlene Thompson; *The Spanish Revenge*, by Allan Topol, *Final Crossing*, by Carter Wilson; *The Incense Game*, by Laura Joh Rowland.

TIPS "Be professional! Always send in exactly what an agent/editor asks for—no more, no less. Keep query letters brief and to the point, giving your writing credentials and a very brief summary of your book. If 1 agent rejects you, keep trying—there are a lot of us out there!"

ALIVE COMMUNICATIONS, INC.

7680 Goddard St., Suite 200, Colorado Springs CO 80920. (719)260-7080. **Fax:** (719)260-8223. **E-mail:** submissions@alivecom.com. **Website:** www.alivecom.com. **Contact:** Rick Christian. Member of AAR. Other memberships include Authors Guild. Represents 100+ clients. 5% of clients are new/unpublished writers. Currently handles nonfiction books (50%), novels (40%), juvenile books (10%).

MEMBER AGENTS Rick Christian, president (blockbusters, bestsellers); Lee Hough (popular/commercial nonfiction and fiction, thoughtful spirituality, children's); Andrea Heinecke (thoughtful/inspirational nonfiction, women's fiction/nonfiction, popular/commercial nonfiction and fiction); Joel Kneedler (popular/commercial nonfiction and fiction, thoughtful spirituality, children's); Bryan Norman.

REPRESENTS nonfiction books, novels, short story collections, novellas. **Considers these fiction areas:** adventure, contemporary issues, crime, family saga, historical, humor, inspirational, literary, mainstream, mystery, police, religious, satire, suspense, thriller.

- This agency specializes in fiction, Christian living, how-to, and commercial nonfiction. Actively seeking inspirational, literary and mainstream fiction, and work from authors with established track records and platforms. Does not want to receive poetry, scripts, or dark themes.

HOW TO CONTACT "Because all our agents have full client loads, they are only considering queries from authors referred by clients and close contacts." New clients come through recommendations from others.

TERMS Agent receives 15% commission on domestic sales. Offers written contract; two-month notice must be given to terminate contract.

TIPS Rewrite and polish until the words on the page shine. Endorsements and great connections may help, provided you can write with power and passion. Network with publishing professionals by making contacts, joining critique groups, and attending writers conferences in order to make personal connections and to get feedback. Alive Communications, Inc., has established itself as a premiere literary agency. We serve an elite group of authors who are critically acclaimed and commercially successful in both Christian and general markets.

AMBASSADOR LITERARY AGENCY & SPEAKERS BUREAU

P.O. Box 50358, Nashville TN 37205. (615)370-4700. **Website:** www.ambassadoragency.com. **Contact:** Wes Yoder. Represents 25-30 clients. 10% of clients are new/unpublished writers. Currently handles nonfiction books (95%), novels (5%).

Prior to becoming an agent, Mr. Yoder founded a music artist agency in 1973; he established a speakers bureau division of the company in 1984.

REPRESENTS nonfiction books, novels.

"This agency specializes in religious market publishing dealing primarily with A-level publishers." Actively seeking popular nonfiction themes, including the following: practical living; Christian spirituality; literary fiction. Does not want to receive short stories, children's books, screenplays, or poetry.

HOW TO CONTACT Authors should e-mail a short description of their ms with a request to submit their work for review. Official submission guidelines will be sent if we agree to review a ms. Speakers should submit a bio, headshot, and speaking demo. Direct all inquiries and submissions to info@ambassador speakers.com. Accepts simultaneous submissions. Obtains most new clients through recommendations from others.

TERMS Agent receives 15% commission on domestic sales. Agent receives 20% commission on foreign sales. Offers written contract.

BETSY AMSTER LITERARY ENTERPRISES

6312 SW Capitol Hwy #503, Portland OR 97239. **Website:** www.amsterlit.com. **Contact:** Betsy Amster (adult); Mary Cummings (children's and YA). Estab. 1992. Member of AAR. Represents more than 65 clients. 35% of clients are new/unpublished writers. Currently handles nonfiction books (65%), novels (35%).

Prior to opening her agency, Ms. Amster was an editor at Pantheon and Vintage for 10 years and served as editorial director for the Globe Pequot Press for 2 years.

REPRESENTS nonfiction books, novels. **Considers these fiction areas:** ethnic, literary, women's, high quality.

"Actively seeking strong narrative nonfiction, particularly by journalists; outstanding literary fiction (the next Jennifer Haigh or Jess Walter); witty, intelligent commerical women's fiction (the next Elinor Lipman); mysteries that open new worlds to us; and high-profile self-help and psychology, preferably research based." Does not want to receive poetry, children's books, romances, western, science fiction, action/adventure, screenplays, fantasy, techno-thrillers, spy capers, apocalyptic scenarios, or political or religious arguments.

HOW TO CONTACT For adult titles: b.amster. assistant@gmail.com. "For fiction or memoirs, please embed the first 3 pages in the body of your e-mail. For nonfiction, please embed your proposal." For children's and YA: b.amster.kidsbooks@gmail.com. See submission requirements online at website. "For picture books, please embed the entire text in the body of your e-mail. For novels, please embed the first 3 pages." Accepts simultaneous submissions. Responds in 1 month to queries. Responds in 2 months to mss. Obtains most new clients through recommendations from others, solicitations, conferences.

TERMS Agent receives 15% commission on domestic sales. Agent receives 20% commission on foreign sales. Offers written contract, binding for 1 year; 3-month notice must be given to terminate contract. Charges for photocopying, postage, messengers, galleys/books used in submissions to foreign and film agents and to magazines for first serial rights.

WRITERS CONFERENCES Los Angeles Times Festival of Books; USC Masters in Professional Writing; San Diego State University Writers Conference; UCLA Extension Writers Program; The Loft Literary Center; Willamette Writers Conference.

MARCIA AMSTERDAM AGENCY

41 W. 82nd St., Suite 9A, New York NY 10024-5613. (212)873-4945. **Contact:** Marcia Amsterdam. Signatory of WGA. Currently handles nonfiction books (15%), novels (70%), movie scripts (5%), TV scripts (10%).

Prior to opening her agency, Ms. Amsterdam was an editor.

REPRESENTS novels, movie scripts, feature film, sitcom. **Considers these fiction areas:** adventure, detective, horror, mainstream, mystery, romance (contemporary, historical), science, thriller, young adult.

HOW TO CONTACT Query with SASE. Responds in 1 month to queries.

TERMS Agent receives 15% commission on domestic sales. Agent receives 20% commission on foreign sales. Agent receives 10% commission on film sales. Offers written contract, binding for 1 year. Charges clients for extra office expenses, foreign postage, copying, legal fees (when agreed upon).

RECENT SALES *Hidden Child* by Isaac Millman (FSG); *Lucky Leonardo*, by Jonathan Canter (Sourcebooks).

TIPS "We are always looking for interesting literary voices."

THE AXELROD AGENCY

55 Main St., P.O. Box 357, Chatham NY 12037. (518)392-2100. **E-mail:** steve@axelrodagency.com. **Website:** www.axelrodagency.com. **Contact:** Steven Axelrod. Member of AAR. Represents 15-20 clients. Currently handles novels (95%).

Prior to becoming an agent, Mr. Axelrod was a book club editor.

REPRESENTS novels. **Considers these fiction areas:** crime, mystery, new adult, romance, women's.

This agency specializes in women's fiction and romance.

HOW TO CONTACT Query. Accepts simultaneous submissions. Obtains most new clients through recommendations from others.

TERMS Agent receives 15% commission on domestic sales. Agent receives 20% commission on foreign sales. No written contract.

WRITERS CONFERENCES RWA National Conference.

JENNIFER AZANTIAN LITERARY AGENCY

E-mail: queries@azantianlitagency.com. **Website:** www.azantianlitagency.com. Estab. 2013.

Prior to her current position, Ms. Azantian was with Sandra Dijkstra Literary Agency.

REPRESENTS Considers these fiction areas: fantasy, horror, middle-grade, new adult, science fiction, young adult. She seeks all subgenres of fantasy and science fiction. She particularly likes horror, and it is horror submissions she wants to see in young adult, middle-grade and new adult submissions.

Horror. Does not want picture books.

HOW TO CONTACT To submit, send your query letter and one- to two-page synopsis, and first 10-15 pages all pasted in an e-mail (no attachments). Please note in the e-mail subject line if your work was requested at a conference, is an exclusive submission, or if your work was referred from a current client. Accepts simultaneous submissions. Responds within 6 weeks. Feel free to follow up if you have heard nothing by then.

BARER LITERARY, LLC

20 W. 20th St., Suite 601, New York NY 10011. (212)691-3513. **E-mail:** submissions@barerliterary. com. **Website:** www.barerliterary.com. **Contact:** Julie Barer. Estab. 2004. Member of AAR.

Before becoming an agent, Julie worked at Shakespeare & Co. Booksellers in New York. She is a graduate of Vassar College.

MEMBER AGENTS Julie Barer, Anna Geller, William Boggess (literary fiction and narrative nonfiction).

REPRESENTS nonfiction books, novels, short story collections. Julie Barer is especially interested in working with emerging writers and developing long-term relationships with new clients. **Considers these fiction areas:** contemporary issues, ethnic, historical, literary, mainstream.

This agency actively seeks most genres of fiction and nonfiction. This agency no longer accepts young adult submissions. No health/fitness, business/investing/finance, sports, mind/body/spirit, reference, thrillers/suspense, military, romance, children's books/picture books, screenplays.

HOW TO CONTACT Query; no attachments if query by e-mail. "We do not respond to queries via phone or fax."

TERMS Agent receives 15% commission on domestic sales. Agent receives 20% commission on foreign sales. Offers written contract. Charges for photocopying and books ordered.

RECENT SALES *The Unnamed*, by Joshua Ferris (Reagan Arthur Books); *Tunneling to the Center of the Earth*, by Kevin Wilson (Ecco Press); *A Disobedient Girl*, by Ru Freeman (Atria Books); *A Friend of the Family*, by Lauren Grodstein (Algonquin); *City of Veils*, by Zoe Ferraris (Little, Brown).

LORETTA BARRETT BOOKS, INC.

220 E. 23rd St., 11th Floor, New York NY 10010. (212)242-3420. **E-mail:** query@lorettabarrettbooks .com. **Website:** www.lorettabarrettbooks.com. **Contact:** Loretta A. Barrett; Nick Mullendore; Gabriel Davis. Estab. 1990. Member of AAR. Currently handles nonfiction books (50%), novels (50%).

Prior to opening her agency, Ms. Barrett was vice president and executive editor at Doubleday and editor-in-chief of Anchor Books.

MEMBER AGENTS Loretta A. Barrett; Nick Mullendore.

REPRESENTS nonfiction books, novels. **Considers these fiction areas:** commercial, literary, mainstream, metaphysical, mystery, romance, thriller, women's.

8—🔑 "Loretta Barrett Books, Inc., represents a wide variety of fiction and nonfiction for general audiences."

HOW TO CONTACT Query via snail mail or e-mail. No e-mail attachments. Paste all materials into the e-mail. "For hard-copy fiction queries, please send a one- to two-page query letter and a synopsis or chapter outline for your project. For hard-copy nonfiction queries, please send a one- to two-page query letter and a brief overview or chapter outline for your project." Accepts simultaneous submissions. Responds in 3-6 weeks to queries.

TERMS Agent receives 15% commission on domestic sales. Agent receives 20% commission on foreign sales. Offers written contract. Charges clients for shipping and photocopying.

○ BARRON'S LITERARY MANAGEMENT

4615 Rockland Dr., Arlington TX 76016. **E-mail:** barronsliterary@sbcglobal.net. **Contact:** Adele Brooks, president.

REPRESENTS Considers these fiction areas: crime, detective, historical, horror, mystery, paranormal, police, romance, suspense, thriller.

8—🔑 Barron's Literary Management is a small Dallas/Fort Worth–based agency with good publishing contacts. Seeks tightly written, fast-moving fiction, and nonfiction authors with a significant platform or subject area expertise.

HOW TO CONTACT Contact by e-mail initially. Send bio and a brief synopsis of story (fiction) or a nonfiction book proposal. Obtains most new clients through e-mail submissions.

TIPS "Have your book tightly edited, polished, and ready to be seen before contacting agents. I respond quickly and if interested may request an electronic or hard-copy mailing."

◎ FAYE BENDER LITERARY AGENCY

19 Cheever Place, Brooklyn NY 11231. **E-mail:** info@fbliterary.com. **Website:** www.fbliterary.com. **Contact:** Faye Bender. Estab. 2004. Member of AAR.

MEMBER AGENTS Faye Bender.

REPRESENTS nonfiction books, novels, juvenile. **Considers these fiction areas:** commercial, literary, middle-grade, women's, young adult.

8—🔑 "I choose books based on the narrative voice and strength of writing. I work with previously published and first-time authors." Faye does not represent picture books, genre fiction for adults (western, romance, horror, science fiction, fantasy), business books, spirituality, or screenplays.

HOW TO CONTACT Please submit a query letter and 10 sample pages to info@fbliterary.com (no attachments). "Due to the volume of e-mails, we can't respond to everything. If we are interested, we will be in touch as soon as we possibly can. Otherwise, please consider it a pass."

RECENT SALES Liane Moriarty's *The Husband's Secret* (Amy Einhorn Books); Rebecca Stead's *Liar & Spy* (Wendy Lamb Books); Kristin Cashore's *Bitterblue* (Dial); Dayna Lorentz's No Safety in Numbers series (Dial).

TIPS "Please keep your letters to the point, include all relevant information, and have a bit of patience."

THE BENT AGENCY

Bent Agency, The, 159 20th St., #2B, Brooklyn NY 11232. **E-mail:** info@thebentagency.com. **Website:** www.thebentagency.com. **Contact:** Jenny Bent; Susan Hawk; Molly Ker Hawn; Gemma Cooper; Louise Fury; Brooks Sherman; Beth Phelan; Victoria Lowes. Estab. 2009.

○ Prior to forming her own agency, Ms. Bent was an agent and vice president at Trident Media.

MEMBER AGENTS Member Agents: Jenny Bent (adult fiction including women's fiction, romance, and crime/suspense, she particularly likes novels with magical or fantasy elements that fall outside of genre fiction; young adult and middle-grade fiction; memoir; humor); Susan Hawk (young adult and middle-grade and picture books; within the realm of kids stories, she likes contemporary, mystery fantasy, science fiction, and historical fiction); Molly Ker Hawn (young adult and middle-grade books, including contemporary, historical science fiction, fantasy, thrillers, mystery); Gemma Cooper (all ages of children's and young adult books, including picture books, likes historical, contemporary, thrillers, mystery, humor, and science fiction); Louise Fury (picture books, literary middle-grade, all young adult, speculative fiction, suspense/thriller, commercial fiction, all subgenres of romance including erotic, nonfiction: cookbooks, pop culture); Brooks Sherman (speculative and literary adult fiction, select narrative nonfiction; all ages of children's and young adult books, including picture books; likes historical, contemporary, thrillers, humor, fantasy, and horror); Beth Phelan (young adult, thrillers, suspense and mystery, romance and women's fiction, literary and general fiction, cookbooks, lifestyle and pets/animals); Victoria Lowes (romance and women's fiction, thrillers and mystery, and young adult).

REPRESENTS Considers these fiction areas: commercial, crime, fantasy, historical, horror, literary, mystery, picture books, romance, suspense, thriller, women's, young adult.

HOW TO CONTACT For Jenny Bent, e-mail: queries@thebentagency.com; for Susan Hawk, e-mail: kidsqueries@thebentagency.com; for Molly Ker Hawn, e-mail: hawnqueries@thebentagency.com; for Gemma Cooper, e-mail: cooperqueries@thebentagency.com; for Louise Fury, e-mail: furyqueries@thebentagency.com; for Brooks Sherman, e-mail: shermanqueries@thebentagency.com; for Beth Phelan, e-mail: phelanagencies@thebentagency.com; for Victoria Lowes, e-mail: lowesqueries@thebentagency.com. "Tell us briefly who you are, what your book is, and why you're the one to write it. Then include the first 10 pages of your material in the body of your e-mail. We respond to all queries; please resend your query if you haven't had a response within 4 weeks." Accepts simultaneous submissions.

RECENT SALES *The Pocket Wife*, by Susan Crawford (Morrow); *The Smell of Other Peoples Houses*, by Bonnie-Sue Hitchcock (Wendy Lamb Books); *The Graham Cracker Plot*, by Shelley Tougas (Roaring Brook); *Murder Is Bad Manners*, by Robin Stevens (Simon & Schuster); *The Inside Out Series*, by Lisa Renee Jones (Simon & Schuster); *True North*, by Liora Blake (Pocket Star)

⊘ BLEECKER STREET ASSOCIATES, INC.

217 Thompson St., #519, New York NY 10012. (212)677-4492. **Fax:** (212)388-0001. **E-mail:** bleeckerst@hotmail.com. **Contact:** Agnes Birnbaum. Member of AAR. Other memberships include RWA, MWA. Represents 60 clients. 20% of clients are new/unpublished writers. Currently handles nonfiction books (75%), novels (25%).

○ Prior to becoming an agent, Ms. Birnbaum was a senior editor at Simon & Schuster, Dutton/Signet, and other publishing houses.

⌖ Does not want to receive science fiction, westerns, poetry, children's books, academic/scholarly/professional books, plays, scripts, or short stories.

HOW TO CONTACT Query by referral only. Accepts simultaneous submissions. Responds in 2 weeks to queries. Responds in 1 month to mss. "Obtains most new clients through recommendations from others, solicitations, conferences."

TERMS Agent receives 15% commission on domestic sales. Agent receives 25% commission on foreign sales. Offers written contract; one-month notice must be given to terminate contract. Charges for postage, long distance, fax, messengers, photocopies (not to exceed $200).

RECENT SALES Sold 14 titles in the last year. *Following Sarah*, by Daniel Brown (Morrow); *Biology of the Brain*, by Paul Swingle (Rutgers University Press); *Santa Miracles*, by Brad and Sherry Steiger (Adams); *Surviving the College Search*, by Jennifer Delahunt (St. Martin's).

TIPS "Keep query letters short and to the point; include only information pertaining to the book or background as a writer. Try to avoid superlatives in description. Work needs to stand on its own, so how much editing it may have received has no place in a query letter."

◎ BOOKENDS, LLC

136 Long Hill Rd., Gillette NJ 07933. **Website:** www.bookends-inc.com. **Contact:** Kim Lionetti, Jessica Alvarez, Beth Campbell. Member of AAR. RWA, MWA Represents 50+ clients. 10% of clients are new/unpublished writers. Currently handles nonfiction books (50%), novels (50%).

MEMBER AGENTS Jessica Faust (**no longer accepting unsolicited material**) (fiction: romance, women's fiction, mysteries and suspense; nonfiction: business, finance, career, parenting); Kim Lionetti (only currently considering romance, women's fiction, cozies, and contemporary young adult queries. "If your book is in any of these 3 categories, please be sure to specify 'Romance,' 'Women's Fiction,' or 'Young Adult' in your e-mail subject line. Any queries that do not follow these guidelines will not be considered."); Jessica Alvarez (romance, cozies, women's fiction, erotica, romantic suspense); Beth Campbell.

REPRESENTS nonfiction books, novels. **Considers these fiction areas:** detective, cozies, mainstream, mystery, romance, thrillers, women's.

> "BookEnds is currently accepting queries from published and unpublished writers in the areas of romance (and all its subgenres), erotica, mystery, suspense, women's fiction, and literary fiction." BookEnds does not want to receive children's books, screenplays, science fiction, poetry, or technical/military thrillers.

HOW TO CONTACT Review website for guidelines, as they change. BookEnds is no longer accepting unsolicited proposal packages or snail mail queries. Send query in the body of e-mail to only 1 agent.

BOOKS & SUCH LITERARY AGENCY

52 Mission Circle, Suite 122, PMB 170, Santa Rosa CA 95409. **E-mail:** representation@booksandsuch.com. **Website:** www.booksandsuch.biz. **Contact:** Janet Kobobel Grant, Wendy Lawton, Rachel Kent, Mary Keeley, Rachelle Gardner. Member of AAR. Member of CBA (associate), American Christian Fiction Writers. Represents 150 clients. 5% of clients are new/unpublished writers. Currently handles nonfiction books (50%), novels (50%).

> Prior to becoming an agent, Ms. Grant was an editor for Zondervan and managing editor for *Focus on the Family*; Ms. Lawton was an author, sculptor, and designer of porcelain dolls. Ms. Keeley accepts both nonfiction and adult fiction. She previously was an acquisition editor for Tyndale publishers.

REPRESENTS nonfiction books, novels. **Considers these fiction areas:** historical, literary, mainstream, new adult, religious, romance, young adult.

> This agency specializes in general and inspirational fiction, romance, and in the Christian booksellers market. Actively seeking well-crafted material that presents Judeo-Christian values, if only subtly.

HOW TO CONTACT Query via e-mail only; no attachments. Accepts simultaneous submissions. Responds in 1 month to queries. "If you don't hear from us asking to see more of your writing within 30 days after you have sent your e-mail, please know that we have read and considered your submission but determined that it would not be a good fit for us." Obtains

most new clients through recommendations from others, conferences.

TERMS Agent receives 15% commission on domestic sales. Agent receives 20% commission on foreign sales. Offers written contract; two-month notice must be given to terminate contract. No additional charges.

RECENT SALES *One Perfect Gift*, by Debbie Macomber (Howard Books); *Greetings from the Flipside*, by Rene Gutteridge and Cheryl Mckay (B&H Publishing); *Key on the Quilt*, by Stephanie Grace Whitson (Barbour Publishing); *Annotated Screwtape Letters, Annotations*, by Paul McCusker, (Harper One). Other clients include: Lauraine Snelling, Lori Copeland, Rene Gutteridge, Dale Cramer, BJ Hoff, Diann Mills. A full list of this agency's clients (and the awards they have won) is on the agency website.

WRITERS CONFERENCES Mount Hermon Christian Writers Conference; Writing for the Soul; American Christian Fiction Writers Conference; San Francisco Writers Conference.

TIPS "The heart of our agency's motivation is to develop relationships with the authors we serve, to do what we can to shine the light of success on them, and to help be a caretaker of their gifts and time."

THE BARBARA BOVA LITERARY AGENCY

3951 Gulf Shore Blvd. N., Unit PH 1-B, Naples FL 34103. (239)649-7263. **Fax:** (239)649-7263. **E-mail:** michaelburke@barbarabovaliteraryagency.com. **Website:** www.barbarabovaliteraryagency.com. **Contact:** Ken Bova, Michael Burke. Represents 30 clients. Currently handles nonfiction books (20%), fiction (80%).

REPRESENTS nonfiction books, novels. **Considers these fiction areas:** adventure, crime, detective, mystery, police, science fiction, suspense, thriller, women's, young adult teen lit.

> This agency specializes in fiction and nonfiction, hard and soft science. "We also handle foreign, movie, television, and audio rights." No scripts, poetry, or children's books.

HOW TO CONTACT Query through website. No attachments. "We accept short (3-5 pages) e-mail queries. All queries should have the word 'Query' in the subject line. Include all information as you would in a standard, snail mail query letter, such as pertinent credentials, publishing history, and an overview of the book. Include a word count of your project. You may include a short synopsis. We're looking for quality fiction and nonfiction." Obtains most new clients through recommendations from others.

TERMS Agent receives 15% commission on domestic sales. Agent receives 20% commission on foreign sales. Charges clients for overseas postage, overseas calls, photocopying, shipping.

◐ BRADFORD LITERARY AGENCY

5694 Mission Center Rd., #347, San Diego CA 92108. (619)521-1201. **E-mail:** queries@bradfordlit.com. **Website:** www.bradfordlit.com. **Contact:** Laura Bradford, Natalie Lakosil, Sarah LaPolla. Estab. 2001. Member of AAR. RWA, SCBWI, ALA Represents 50 clients. 20% of clients are new/unpublished writers. Currently handles nonfiction books (5%), novels (95%).

REPRESENTS Considers these fiction areas: erotica, middle-grade, mystery, paranormal, picture books, romance, thriller, women's, young adult.

8—➤ Actively seeking many types of romance (historical, romantic suspense, paranormal, category, contemporary, erotic). Does not want to receive poetry, screenplays, short stories, westerns, horror, new age, religion, crafts, cookbooks, gift books.

HOW TO CONTACT Accepts e-mail queries only; send to queries@bradfordlit.com (or sarah@bradfordlit if contacting Sarah LaPolla). The entire submission must appear in the body of the e-mail and not as an attachment. The subject line should begin as follows: QUERY: (the title of the ms or any short message that is important should follow). For fiction: e-mail a query letter along with the first chapter of ms and a synopsis. Include the genre and word count in cover letter. Nonfiction: e-mail full nonfiction proposal including a query letter and a sample chapter. Accepts simultaneous submissions. Responds in 2-4 weeks to queries. Responds in 10 weeks to mss. Obtains most new clients through solicitations.

TERMS Agent receives 15% commission on domestic sales. Agent receives 20% commission on foreign sales. Offers written contract, nonbinding for 2 years; 45-day notice must be given to terminate contract. Charges for extra copies of books for foreign submissions.

RECENT SALES Sold 68 titles in the last year. *All Fall Down,* by Megan Hart (Mira Books); *Body and Soul,* by Stacey Kade (Hyperion Children's); *All Things*

Wicked, by Karina Cooper (Avon); *Circle Eight: Matthew,* by Emma Lang (Kensington Brava); *Midnight Enchantment,* by Anya Bast (Berkley Sensation); *Outpost,* by Ann Aguirre (Feiwel and Friends); *The One That I Want,* by Jennifer Echols (Simon Pulse); *Catch Me a Cowboy,* by Katie Lane (Grand Central); *Back in a Soldier's Arms,* by Soraya Lane (Harlequin); *Enraptured,* by Elisabeth Naughton (Sourcebooks); *Wicked Road to Hell,* by Juliana Stone (Avon); *Master of Sin,* by Maggie Robinson (Kensington Brava); *Chaos Burning,* by Lauren Dane (Berkley Sensation); *If I Lie,* by Corrine Jackson (Simon Pulse); *Renegade,* by J.A. Souders (Tor).

WRITERS CONFERENCES RWA National Conference; Romantic Times Booklovers Convention.

◐ ANDREA BROWN LITERARY AGENCY, INC.

1076 Eagle Dr., Salinas CA 93905. (831)422-5925. **E-mail:** andrea@andreabrownlit.com; caryn@andreabrownlit.com; lauraqueries@gmail.com; jennifer@andreabrownlit.com; kelly@andreabrownlit.com; jennL@andreabrownlit.com; jamie@andreabrownlit.com; jmatt@andreabrownlit.com; lara@andreabrownlit.com. **Website:** www.andreabrownlit.com. **Contact:** Andrea Brown, president. Member of AAR. 10% of clients are new/unpublished writers.

◒ Prior to opening her agency, Ms. Brown served as an editorial assistant at Random House and Dell Publishing and as an editor with Knopf.

MEMBER AGENTS Andrea Brown (President); Laura Rennert (Senior Agent); Caryn Wiseman (Senior Agent); Kelly Sonnack (Agent); Jennifer Rofé (Agent); Jennifer Laughran (Agent); Jamie Weiss Chilton (Agent); Jennifer Mattson (Associate Agent); Lara Perkins (Associate Agent, Digital Manager).

REPRESENTS nonfiction, fiction, juvenile books. **Considers these fiction areas:** juvenile, literary, picture books, women's, young adult middle-grade, all juvenile genres.

8—➤ Specializes in "all kinds of children's books—illustrators and authors." 98% juvenile books. Considers: nonfiction, fiction, picture books, young adult.

HOW TO CONTACT For picture books, submit complete ms. For fiction, submit query letter, first 10 pages. For nonfiction, submit proposal, first 10 pages. Illustrators: submit a query letter and 2-3 illustration samples (in jpeg format), link to online portfolio, and text of picture book, if applicable. "We only accept queries via e-mail. No attachments, with the exception of jpeg illustrations from illustrators. Visit the agents' bios on our website and choose only 1 agent to whom you will submit your e-query. Send a short e-mail query letter to that agent with QUERY in the subject field. Accepts simultaneous submissions. "If we are interested in your work, we will certainly follow up by e-mail or by phone. However, if you haven't heard from us within 6 to 8 weeks, please assume that we are passing on your project." Obtains most new clients through referrals from editors, clients and agents. Check website for guidelines and information.

TERMS Agent receives 15% commission on domestic sales. Agent receives 25% commission on foreign sales. Offers written contract.

RECENT SALES *The Scorpio Races*, by Maggie Stiefvater (Scholastic); *The Raven Boys*, by Maggie Stiefvater (Scholastic); Wolves of Mercy Falls series, by Maggie Stiefvater (Scholastic); *The Future of Us*, by Jay Asher; *Triangles*, by Ellen Hopkins (Atria); *Crank*, by Ellen Hopkins (McElderry/S&S); *Burned*, by Ellen Hopkins (McElderry/S&S); *Impulse*, by Ellen Hopkins (McElderry/S&S); *Glass*, by Ellen Hopkins (McElderry/S&S); *Tricks*, by Ellen Hopkins (McElderry/S&S); *Fallout*, by Ellen Hopkins (McElderry/S&S); *Perfect*, by Ellen Hopkins (McElderry/S&S); *The Strange Case of Origami Yoda*, by Tom Angleberger (Amulet/Abrams); *Darth Paper Strikes Back*, by Tom Angleberger (Amulet/Abrams); *Becoming Chloe*, by Catherine Ryan Hyde (Knopf); *Sasha Cohen* autobiography (HarperCollins); *The Five Ancestors*, by Jeff Stone (Random House); *Thirteen Reasons Why*, by Jay Asher (Penguin); *Identical*, by Ellen Hopkins (S&S).

WRITERS CONFERENCES SCBWI; Asilomar; Maui Writers Conference; Southwest Writers Conference; San Diego State University Writers Conference; Big Sur Children's Writing Workshop; William Saroyan Writers Conference; Columbus Writers Conference; Willamette Writers Conference; La Jolla Writers Conference; San Francisco Writers Conference; Hilton Head Writers Conference; Pacific Northwest Conference; Pikes Peak Conference.

TIPS "ABLA is consistently ranked No. 1 in juvenile sales in Publishers Marketplace. Several clients have placed in the top 10 of the NY Times Bestseller List in the last year, including Tom Angleberger, Jay Asher, Ellen Hopkins, and Maggie Stiefvater. Awards recently won by ABLA clients include the Michael L. Printz Honor, the APALA Asian/Pacific Award and Honor, Charlotte Zolotow Honor, Cybils Award, EB White Read Aloud Award and Honor, Edgar Award Nominee, Indies Choice Honor Award, Jack Ezra Keats New Writer Award, Odyssey Honor Audiobook, Orbis Pictus Honor, Pura Belpré Illustrator Honor Book; SCBWI Golden Kite Award; Stonewall Honor; Texas Bluebonnet Award; Theodore Seuss Geisel Honor; William C. Morris YA Debut Award."

CURTIS BROWN, LTD.

10 Astor Place, New York NY 10003-6935. (212)473-5400. **E-mail:** gknowlton@cbltd.com. **Website:** www.curtisbrown.com. **Contact:** Ginger Knowlton. **Alternate address:** Peter Ginsberg, president at CBSF, 1750 Montgomery St., San Francisco CA 94111. (415)954-8566. Member of AAR. Signatory of WGA.

MEMBER AGENTS Ginger Clark (science fiction, fantasy, paranormal romance, literary horror, and young adult and middle-grade fiction); Katherine Fausset (adult fiction and nonfiction, including literary and commercial fiction, journalism, memoir, lifestyle, prescriptive and narrative nonfiction); Holly Frederick; Peter Ginsberg, president; Elizabeth Harding, vice president (represents authors and illustrators of juvenile, middle-grade and young adult fiction); Steve Kasdin (commercial fiction, including mysteries/thrillers, romantic suspense—emphasis on the suspense, and historical fiction; narrative nonfiction, including biography, history and current affairs; and young adult fiction, particularly if it has adult crossover appeal); Ginger Knowlton, executive vice president (authors and illustrators of children's books in all genres); Timothy Knowlton, chief executive officer; Jonathan Lyons (biographies, history, science, pop culture, sports, general narrative nonfiction, mysteries, thrillers, science fiction and fantasy, and young adult fiction); Laura Blake Peterson, vice president (memoir and biography, natural history, literary fiction, mystery, suspense, women's fiction, health and fitness, children's and young adult, faith issues and popular culture); Maureen Walters, senior vice president (working primarily in women's fiction and nonfiction projects on subjects as eclectic as parenting and child care, popular psychology, inspirational/motivational volumes as well as a few medical/nutritional book); Mitchell Waters (literary and commercial fiction and nonfiction, including mystery, history, biography, memoir, young adult, cookbooks, self-help and popular culture).

REPRESENTS nonfiction books, novels, short story collections, juvenile. **Considers these fiction areas:** adventure, confession, detective, erotica, ethnic, experimental, fantasy, feminist, gay, historical, horror, humor, juvenile, literary, mainstream, middle-grade, military, multicultural, multimedia, mystery, New Age, occult, picture books, regional, religious, romance, spiritual, sports, thriller, translation, women's, young adult.

HOW TO CONTACT "Send us a query letter, a synopsis of the work, a sample chapter and a brief résumé. Illustrators should send 1-2 samples of published work, along with 6-8 color copies (no original art). Please send all book queries to our address, Attn: Query Department. Please enclose a stamped, self-addressed envelope for our response and return postage if you wish to have your materials returned to you. We typically respond to queries within 6-8 weeks." Note that some agents list their e-mail on the agency website and are fine with e-mail submissions. Note if the submission/query is being considered elsewhere. Responds in 3 weeks to queries; 5 weeks to mss. Obtains most new clients through recommendations from others, solicitations, conferences.

TERMS Agent receives 15% commission on domestic sales; 20% on foreign sales. Offers written contract. 75-day notice must be given to terminate contract. Offers written contract. Charges for some postage (overseas, etc.).

RECENT SALES This agency prefers not to share information on specific sales.

◐ TRACY BROWN LITERARY AGENCY

P.O. Box 88, Scarsdale NY 10583. (914)400-4147. **Fax:** (914)931-1746. **E-mail:** tracy@brownlit.com. **Contact:** Tracy Brown. Represents 35 clients. Currently handles nonfiction books (90%), novels (10%).

○ Prior to becoming an agent, Mr. Brown was a book editor for 25 years.

REPRESENTS Considers these fiction areas: literary.

⚷ Specializes in thorough involvement with clients' books at every stage of the process, from writing to proposals to publication. Actively seeking serious nonfiction and fiction. Does not want to receive young adult, science fiction, or romance.

HOW TO CONTACT Submit outline/proposal, synopsis, author bio. Accepts simultaneous submissions.

Responds in 2 weeks to queries. Obtains most new clients through referrals.

TERMS Agent receives 15% commission on domestic sales. Agent receives 20% commission on foreign sales. Offers written contract.

RECENT SALES *Why Have Kids?* by Jessica Valenti (HarperCollins); *Tapdancing to Work*, by Carol J. Loomis (Portfolio); *Mating in Captivity*, by Esther Perel (HarperCollins).

◐ KIMBERLEY CAMERON & ASSOCIATES

1550 Tiburon Blvd., #704, Tiburon CA 94920. **Fax:** (415)789-9191. **E-mail:** info@kimberleycameron .com. **Website:** www.kimberleycameron.com. **Contact:** Kimberley Cameron. Member of AAR. 30% of clients are new/unpublished writers.

○ Kimberley Cameron & Associates (formerly The Reece Halsey Agency) has had an illustrious client list of established writers, including the estate of Aldous Huxley, and has represented Upton Sinclair, William Faulkner, and Henry Miller.

MEMBER AGENTS Kimberley Cameron; Elizabeth Kracht, liz@kimberleycameron.com (literary, commercial, women's, thrillers, mysteries, and young adult with crossover appeal); Pooja Menon, pooja@ kimberleycameron.com (international stories, literary, historical, commercial, fantasy and high-end women's fiction; in nonfiction, she's looking for adventure and travel memoirs, journalism, and human-interest stories, and self-help books addressing relationships and the human psychology from a fresh perspective); Amy Cloughley, amyc@kimberleycameron. com (literary and upmarket fiction, women's, mystery, narrative nonfiction); Mary C. Moore (literary fiction; she also loves a good commercial book; commercially she is looking for unusual fantasy, grounded science fiction, and atypical romance; strong female characters and unique cultures especially catch her eye); Ethan Vaughan (no submissions).

REPRESENTS Considers these fiction areas: commercial, fantasy, historical, literary, mystery, romance, science fiction, thriller, women's, young adult.

⚷ "We are looking for a unique and heartfelt voice that conveys a universal truth."

HOW TO CONTACT We accept e-mail queries only. Please address all queries to 1 agent only. Please send a query letter in the body of the e-mail, written in a professional manner and clearly addressed to the agent of your choice. Attach a one-page synopsis and the first 50 pages of your ms as separate Word or PDF documents. We have difficulties opening other file formats. Include "Author Submission" in the subject line. If submitting nonfiction, attach a nonfiction proposal. Obtains new clients through recommendations from others, solicitations.

TERMS Agent receives 15% on domestic sales; 10% on film sales. Offers written contract, binding for 1 year.

WRITERS CONFERENCES Texas Writing Retreat; Pacific Northwest Writers Association Conference; Women's Fiction Festival in Matera, Italy; Willamette Writers Conference; San Francisco Writers Conference; Book Passage Mystery and Travel Writers Con ferences; Chuckanut Writers Conference; many others.

TIPS "Please consult our submission guidelines and send a polite, well-written query to our e-mail address."

MARIA CARVAINIS AGENCY, INC.

Rockefeller Center, 1270 Avenue of the Americas, Suite 2320, New York NY 10020. (212)245-6365. **Fax:** (212)245-7196. **E-mail:** mca@mariacarvainisagency .com. **Website:** mariacarvainisagency.com. **Contact:** Maria Carvainis, Chelsea Gilmore. Estab. 1977. Member of AAR. Signatory of WGA. Other memberships include Authors Guild, Women's Media Group, ABA, MWA, RWA. Represents 75 clients.

○ Prior to opening her agency, Ms. Carvainis spent more than 10 years in the publishing industry as a senior editor with Macmillan Publishing, Basic Books, Avon Books, and Crown Publishers. Ms. Carvainis has served as a member of the AAR board of directors and AAR Treasurer, as well as serving as chair of the AAR Contracts Committee. She presently serves on the AAR Royalty Committee. Ms. Gilmore started her publishing career at Oxford University Press, in the Higher Education Group. She then worked at Avalon Books as associate editor. She is most interested in women's fiction, literary fiction, young adult, pop culture, and mystery/suspense.

MEMBER AGENTS Maria Carvainis, president/literary agent; Chelsea Gilmore, literary agent.

REPRESENTS nonfiction books, novels. **Considers these fiction areas:** historical, literary, mainstream, middle-grade, mystery, suspense, thriller, women's, young adult.

⊶ The agency does not represent screenplays, children's picture books, science fiction, or poetry.

HOW TO CONTACT You can query via e-mail or snail mail. If by snail mail, send your submission "ATTN: Query Department." Please send a query letter, a synopsis of the work, 2 sample chapters, and note any writing credentials. Obtains most new clients through recommendations from others, conferences, query letters.

TERMS Agent receives 15% commission on domestic sales. Agent receives 20% commission on foreign sales. Offers written contract. Charges clients for foreign postage and bulk copying.

RECENT SALES *A Secret Affair*, by Mary Balogh (Delacorte); *Tough Customer*, by Sandra Brown (Simon & Schuster); *A Lady Never Tells*, by Candace Camp (Pocket Books); *The King James Conspiracy*, by Phillip Depoy (St. Martin's Press).

WRITERS CONFERENCES BookExpo America; Frankfurt Book Fair; London Book Fair; Mystery Writers of America; Thrillerfest; Romance Writers of America.

CASTIGLIA LITERARY AGENCY

1155 Camino Del Mar, Suite 510, Del Mar CA 92014. **E-mail:** castigliaagency-query@yahoo.com. **Website:** www.castigliaagency.com. Member of AAR. Other memberships include PEN. Represents 65 clients. Currently handles nonfiction books (55%), novels (45%).

MEMBER AGENTS Julie Castiglia (not accepting queries at this time); Win Golden (fiction: thrillers, mystery, crime, science fiction, young adult, commercial/literary fiction; nonfiction: narrative nonfiction, current events, science, journalism).

REPRESENTS nonfiction books, novels. **Considers these fiction areas:** commercial, crime, literary, mystery, science fiction, thriller, young adult.

⊶ "We'd particularly like to hear from you if you are a journalist or published writer in magazines and newspapers, have expertise on the subject you're writing, together with media exposure and/or a speaking schedule. We'd like to hear from anyone who has had success with a previous novel. We do look at debut novels and it helps if you've been published in literary anthologies or magazines, if you have studied under well-known authors, or have an MFA. It's all about the writing, of course, but if great writing is accompanied by a marketing hook, that's a seductive combination." Does not want to receive horror, screenplays, poetry, or academic nonfiction.

HOW TO CONTACT Query via e-mail to Castiglia Agency-query@yahoo.com. Send no materials via first contact besides a one-page query. No snail-mail submissions accepted. Obtains most new clients through recommendations from others, solicitations, conferences.

TERMS Agent receives 15% commission on domestic sales. Agent receives 25% commission on foreign sales. Offers written contract; 6-week notice must be given to terminate contract.

RECENT SALES *Germs Gone Wild*, by Kenneth King (Pegasus); *The Insider* by Reece Hirsch (Berkley/Penguin); *The Leisure Seeker*, by Michael Zadoorian (Morrow/HarperCollins); *Beautiful: The Life of Hedy Lamarr*, by Stephen Shearer (St. Martin's Press); *American Libre*, by Raul Ramos y Sanchez (Grand Central); *The Two Krishnas*, by Ghalib Shiraz Dhalla (Alyson Books).

WRITERS CONFERENCES Santa Barbara Writers Conference; Southern California Writers Conference; Surrey International Writers Conference; San Diego State University Writers Conference; Willamette Writers Conference.

TIPS "Be professional with submissions. Attend workshops and conferences before you approach an agent."

JANE CHELIUS LITERARY AGENCY

548 Second St., Brooklyn NY 11215. (718)499-0236. **Fax:** (718)832-7335. **E-mail:** queries@janechelius.com. **Website:** www.janechelius.com. Member of AAR.
MEMBER AGENTS Jane Chelius, Mark Chelius.
REPRESENTS nonfiction books, novels. **Considers these fiction areas:** literary, mystery, suspense, women's.

Does not want to receive children's books, fantasy, science fiction, stage plays, screenplays, or poetry.

HOW TO CONTACT E-query. Does not consider e-mail queries with attachments. No unsolicited sample chapters or mss. Responds if interested. Responds in 3-4-weeks usually.

ELYSE CHENEY LITERARY ASSOCIATES, LLC

78 Fifth Avenue, 3rd Floor, New York NY 10011. (212)277-8007. **Fax:** (212)614-0728. **E-mail:** submissions@cheneyliterary.com. **Website:** www.cheneyliterary.com. **Contact:** Elyse Cheney; Adam Eaglin; Alex Jacobs.

Prior to her current position, Ms. Cheney was an agent with Sanford J. Greenburger Associates.

REPRESENTS nonfiction, novels. **Considers these fiction areas:** commercial, family saga, historical, literary, short story collections, suspense, women's.
HOW TO CONTACT Query by e-mail or snail mail. For a snail mail responses, include an SASE. If e-query, feel free to paste up to 25 pages of your work in the e-mail below your query.
RECENT SALES *Moonwalking with Einstein: The Art and Science of Remembering Everything*, by Joshua Foer; *The Possessed: Adventures with Russian Books and the People Who Read Them*, by Elif Batuman (Farrar, Strauss & Giroux); *The Coldest Winter Ever*, by Sister Souljah (Atria); *A Heartbreaking Work of Staggering Genius*, by Dave Eggers (Simon and Schuster); *No Easy Day*, by Mark Owen; *Malcom X: A Life of Reinvention*, by Manning Marable.

COMPASS TALENT

6 East 32nd Street, 6th Floor, New York NY 10016. (646)376-7718. **E-mail:** query@compasstalent.com. **Website:** www.compasstalent.com. **Contact:** Heather Schroder.
REPRESENTS **Considers these fiction areas:** commercial, juvenile, literary, mainstream.
HOW TO CONTACT Please send a query describing your project, along with a sample chapter and some information about yourself to query@compasstalent.com. Allow 8 weeks for a response. Please do not send your material to us through the mail.
RECENT SALES A full list of agency clients is available on the website.

DON CONGDON ASSOCIATES INC.

110 William St., Suite 2202, New York NY 10038. (212)645-1229. **Fax:** (212)727-2688. **E-mail:** dca@doncongdon.com. **Website:** doncongdon.com. **Contact:** Michael Congdon, Susan Ramer, Cristina Concepcion, Maura Kye Casella, Katie Kotchman, Katie Grimm. Member of AAR. Represents 100 clients.

REPRESENTS Considers these fiction areas: action, adventure, contemporary issues, crime, detective, literary, mainstream, middle-grade, mystery, police, short story collections, suspense, thriller, women's, young adult.

⚓ Especially interested in narrative nonfiction and literary fiction.

HOW TO CONTACT "For queries via e-mail, you must include the word *Query* and the agent's full name in your subject heading. Please also include your query and sample chapter in the body of the e-mail, as we do not open attachments for security reasons. Please query only 1 agent within the agency at a time." Responds in 3 weeks to queries. Responds in 1 month to mss. Obtains most new clients through recommendations from other authors.

TERMS Agent receives 15% commission on domestic sales. Agent receives 19% commission on foreign sales. Charges client for extra shipping costs, photocopying, copyright fees, book purchases.

RECENT SALES This agency represents many bestselling clients such as David Sedaris and Kathryn Stockett.

TIPS "Writing a query letter with an SASE is a must. We cannot guarantee replies to foreign queries via standard mail. No phone calls. We never download attachments to e-mail queries for security reasons, so please copy and paste material into your e-mail."

◉ **THE DOE COOVER AGENCY**

P.O. Box 668, Winchester MA 01890. (781)721-6000. **E-mail:** info@doecooveragency.com. **Website:** www.doecooveragency.com. Represents 150+ clients. Currently handles nonfiction books (80%), novels (20%).

MEMBER AGENTS Doe Coover (general nonfiction, including business, cooking/food writing, health, and science); Colleen Mohyde (literary and commercial fiction, general nonfiction); Associate: Frances Kennedy.

REPRESENTS Considers these fiction areas: commercial, literary.

⚓ The agency specializes in narrative nonfiction, particularly biography, business, cooking and food writing, health, history, popular science, social issues, gardening, and humor; literary and commercial fiction. The agency does not represent poetry, screenplays, romance, fantasy, science fiction, or unsolicited children's books.

HOW TO CONTACT Accepts queries by e-mail only. Check website for submission guidelines. No unsolicited mss. Accepts simultaneous submissions. Responds within 4-6 weeks, only if additional material is required. Obtains most new clients through solicitation and recommendation.

TERMS Agent receives 15% commission on domestic sales, 10% of original advance commission on foreign sales. No reading fees.

RECENT SALES *Vegetable Literacy*, by Deborah Madison (Ten Speed Press); *L.A. Son: My Life, My City, My Food*, by Roy Choi (Anthony Bourdain/Ecco); *The Big-Flavor Grill*, by Chris Schlesinger and John Willoughby (Ten Speed Press); *The Shape of the Eye: A Memoir*, by George Estreich (Tarcher). *Frontera: Margaritas, Guacamoles, and Snacks*, by Rick Bayless and Deann Groen Bayless (W.W. Norton); *The Essay*, by Robin Yocum (Arcade Publishing); *The Flower of Empire*, by Tatiana Holway (Oxford University Press); Dulcie Schwartz mystery series, by Clea Simon (Severn House U.K.). Other clients include: WGBH, New England Aquarium, Duke University, Cheryl and Bill Jamison, Blue Balliett, David Allen, Jacques Pepin, Cindy Pawlcyn, Joann Weir, Suzanne Berne, Paula Poundstone, Anita Silvey, Marjorie Sandor, Tracy Daugherty, Carl Rollyson, and Joel Magnuson.

◯ **CORVISIERO LITERARY AGENCY**

275 Madison Ave., 14th Floor, New York NY 10016. (646)942-8396. **Fax:** (646)217-3758. **E-mail:** contact@corvisieroagency.com. **E-mail:** query@corvisieroagency.com. **Website:** www.corvisieroagency.com. **Contact:** Marisa A. Corvisiero, senior agent and literary attorney.

MEMBER AGENTS Marisa A. Corvisiero, senior agent and literary attorney; Saritza Hernandez, senior agent; Sarah Negovetich, junior agent; Doreen McDonald, junior agent; Rebecca Simas, junior agent; Cate Hart, junior agent; Brittany Howard (Best Selling Author writing as Cora Carmack), literary consultant.

HOW TO CONTACT Accepts submissions via e-mail only. Include 5 pages of complete and polished ms pasted into the body of an e-mail, and a one- to two-page synopsis. For nonfiction, include a proposal instead of the synopsis. All sample pages must be properly formatted into 1-inch margins, double-spaced lines, Times New Roman black font size 12.

TIPS "For tips and discussions on what we look for in query letters and submissions, please take a look at Marisa A. Corvisiero's blog: Thoughts From a Literary Agent."

CRICHTON & ASSOCIATES

6940 Carroll Ave., Takoma Park MD 20912. (301)495-9663. **Fax:** (202)318-0050. **E-mail:** query@crichton-associates.com. **Website:** www.crichton-associates.com. **Contact:** Sha-Shana Crichton. 90% of clients are new/unpublished writers. Currently handles nonfiction books 50%, fiction 50%.

○ Prior to becoming an agent, Ms. Crichton did commercial litigation for a major law firm.

REPRESENTS nonfiction books, novels. **Considers these fiction areas:** ethnic, feminist, inspirational, literary, mainstream, mystery, religious, romance, suspense, chick lit.

⚡ Actively seeking women's fiction, romance, and chick lit. Looking also for multicultural fiction and nonfiction. Does not want to receive poetry, children's, young adult, science fiction, or screenplays.

HOW TO CONTACT "In the subject line of e-mail, please indicate whether your project is fiction or nonfiction. Please do not send attachments. Your query letter should include a description of the project and your biography. If you wish to send your query via snail mail, please include your telephone number and e-mail address. We will respond to you via e-mail. For fiction, include a short synopsis and the first 3 chapters with query. For nonfiction, send a book proposal." Responds in 3-5 weeks to queries.

TERMS Agent receives 15% commission on domestic sales. Agent receives 20% commission on foreign sales. Offers written contract, binding for 45 days. Only charges fees for postage and photocopying.

RECENT SALES *The African American Entrepreneur*, by W. Sherman Rogers (Praeger); *The Diversity Code*, by Michelle Johnson (Amacom); *Secret & Lies*, by Rhonda McKnight (Urban Books); *Love on the Rocks*, by Pamela Yaye (Harlequin). Other clients include Kimberley White, Beverley Long, Jessica Trap, Altonya Washington, Cheris Hodges.

WRITERS CONFERENCES Silicon Valley RWA; BookExpo America.

D4EO LITERARY AGENCY

7 Indian Valley Rd., Weston CT 06883. (203)544-7180. **Fax:** (203)544-7160. **Website:** www.d4eoliterary agency.com. **Contact:** Bob Diforio. Represents 100+ clients. 50% of clients are new/unpublished writers. Currently handles nonfiction books (70%), novels (25%), juvenile books (5%).

○ Prior to opening his agency, Mr. Diforio was a publisher.

MEMBER AGENTS Bob Diforio (referrals only); Mandy Hubbard (middle-grade, young adult, and genre romance); Kristin Miller-Vincent (closed to queries); Bree Odgen (children's, young adult, juvenile nonfiction, graphic novels, pop culture, art books, genre horror, noir, genre romance, historical, hard science fiction); Samantha Dighton (closed to queries); Joyce Holland (currently closed to submissions).

REPRESENTS nonfiction books, novels. **Considers these fiction areas:** adventure, detective, erotica, historical, horror, humor, juvenile, literary, mainstream, middle-grade, mystery, picture books, romance, sports, thriller.

HOW TO CONTACT Each of these agents has a different submission e-mail and different tastes regarding how they review material. See their individual agent pages on the agency website. Responds in 1 week to queries. Obtains most new clients through recommendations from others.

TERMS Agent receives 15% commission on domestic sales. Agent receives 25% commission on foreign sales. Offers written contract, binding for 2 years; 60-day notice must be given to terminate contract. Charges for photocopying and submission postage.

DANIEL LITERARY GROUP

1701 Kingsbury Dr., Suite 100, Nashville TN 37215. (615)730-8207. **E-mail:** submissions@danielliter arygroup.com. **Website:** www.danielliterarygroup.com. **Contact:** Greg Daniel. Represents 45 clients. 30% of clients are new/unpublished writers.

○ Prior to becoming an agent, Mr. Daniel spent 10 years in publishing—6 at the executive level at Thomas Nelson Publishers.

REPRESENTS nonfiction.

⚡ "We take pride in our ability to come alongside our authors and help strategize about where they want their writing to take them in both the near and long term. Forging close relationships with our authors, we help them with such critical factors as editorial refinement, branding, audience, and marketing." The agency is open to submissions in almost every popular category of nonfiction, especially if authors are recognized experts in their fields. No fiction, screenplays, poetry, science fiction/fantasy, romance, children's, or short stories.

HOW TO CONTACT Query via e-mail only. Submit publishing history, author bio, key selling points; no attachments. Check Submissions Guidelines before querying or submitting. Please do not query via telephone. Responds in 2-3 weeks to queries.

DARHANSOFF & VERRILL LITERARY AGENTS

236 W. 26th St., Suite 802, New York NY 10001. (917)305-1300. **Fax:** (917)305-1400. **E-mail:** submissions@dvagency.com. **Website:** www.dvagency.com. Member of AAR. Represents 120 clients. 10% of clients are new/unpublished writers. Currently handles nonfiction books (25%), novels (60%), story collections (15%).

MEMBER AGENTS Liz Darhansoff; Chuck Verrill; Michele Mortimer; Catherine Luttinger (science fiction, fantasy, historical fiction, young adult, thrillers, mysteries).

REPRESENTS Considers these fiction areas: fantasy, historical, literary, mystery, science fiction, suspense, thriller, young adult.

HOW TO CONTACT Send queries via e-mail (submissions@dvagency.com) or by snail mail with SASE. Obtains most new clients through recommendations from others.

RECENT SALES A full list of clients is available on their website.

JOELLE DELBOURGO ASSOCIATES, INC.

101 Park St., 3rd Floor, Montclair NJ 07042. (973)773-0836. **Fax:** (973)783-6802. **E-mail:** submissions@delbourgo.com. **Website:** www.delbourgo.com. Represents more than 100 clients. Currently handles nonfiction books (75%), novels (25%).

Prior to becoming an agent, Ms. Delbourgo was an editor and senior publishing executive at HarperCollins and Random House.

MEMBER AGENTS Joelle Delbourgo, joelle@delbourgo.com (broad range of adult nonfiction and fiction, as well as a select and growing list of young adult and middle-grade fiction and nonfiction); Jacqueline Flynn, jacqueline@delbourgo.com (thought-provoking nonfiction in business, history, self-help, memoir, current events, science, and more as well as

very select fiction and children's titles); **Carrie Cantor**, carrie@delbourgo.com (current events, politics, history, popular science and psychology, memoir, and narrative nonfiction).

REPRESENTS nonfiction books, novels. **Considers these fiction areas:** literary, mainstream, middle-grade, young adult.

"We are former publishers and editors with deep knowledge and an insider perspective. We have a reputation for individualized attention to clients, strategic management of authors' careers, and creating strong partnerships with publishers for our clients."

HOW TO CONTACT It's preferable if you submit via e-mail to a specific agent. Query 1 agent only. No attachments. More submission tips on agency website. Accepts simultaneous submissions.

TERMS Agent receives 15% commission on domestic sales. Agent receives 20% commission on foreign sales. Offers written contract. Charges clients for postage and photocopying.

RECENT SALES *Alexander the Great*, by Philip Freeman; *The Big Book of Parenting Solutions*, by Dr. Michele Borba; *The Secret Life of Ms. Finkelman*, by Ben H. Wintners; *Not Quite Adults*, by Richard Settersten, Jr., and Barbara Ray; *Tabloid Medicine*, by Robert Goldberg, PhD; *Table of Contents*, by Judy Gerlman and Vicky Levi Krupp.

TIPS "Do your homework. Do not cold call. Read and follow submission guidelines before contacting us. Do not call to find out if we received your material. No e-mail queries. Treat agents with respect, as you would any other professional, such as a doctor, lawyer, or financial advisor."

THE JENNIFER DECHIARA LITERARY AGENCY

31 East 32nd St., Suite 300, New York NY 10016. (212)481-8484. **Fax:** (212)481-9582. **Website:** www.jdlit.com.

MEMBER AGENTS Jennifer DeChiara, jenndec@aol.com (literary, commercial, women's fiction [no bodice-rippers, please], chick lit, mysteries, suspense, thrillers; for nonfiction: GLBTQ, memoirs, books about the arts and performing arts, behind-the-scenes-type books, and books about popular culture); Stephen Fraser, stephenafraser@verizon.net (one-of-a-kind picture books; strong chapter book series; whimsical, dramatic, or humorous middle-grade; dramatic or high-concept young adult; powerful and unusual nonfiction; nonfiction with a broad audience on topics as far reaching as art history, theater, film, literature, and travel); Marie Lamba, marie.jdlit@gmail.com (young adult and middle-grade fiction, along with general and women's fiction and some memoir); Linda Epstein, linda.p.epstein@gmail.com (young adult, middle-grade, literary fiction, quality upscale commercial fiction, vibrant narrative nonfiction, compelling memoirs, health and parenting books, cookbooks); Roseanne Wells, queryroseanne@gmail.com (literary fiction, young adult, middle-grade, narrative nonfiction, select memoir, science (popular or trade, not academic), history, religion (not inspirational), travel, humor, food/cooking, and similar subjects).

REPRESENTS nonfiction books, novels, juvenile. **Considers these fiction areas:** commercial, literary, middle-grade, mystery, picture books, suspense, thriller, women's, young adult.

HOW TO CONTACT Each agent has their own e-mail submission address and submission instructions. Accepts simultaneous submissions. Obtains most new clients through recommendations from others, conferences, query letters.

TERMS Agent receives 15% commission on domestic sales. Agent receives 20% commission on foreign sales. Offers written contract.

◐ DEFIORE & CO.

47 E. 19th St., 3rd Floor, New York NY 10003. (212)925-7744. **Fax:** (212)925-9803. **E-mail:** info@defioreandco.com; submissions@defioreandco.com. **Website:** www.defioreandco.com. Member of AAR.

○   Prior to becoming an agent, Mr. DeFiore was publisher of Villard Books (1997-1998), editor-in-chief of Hyperion (1992-1997), and editorial director of Delacorte Press (1988-1992).

MEMBER AGENTS Brian DeFiore (popular nonfiction, business, pop culture, parenting, commercial fiction); Laurie Abkemeier (memoir, parenting, business, how-to/self-help, popular science); Kate Garrick (literary fiction, memoir, popular nonfiction); Matthew Elblonk (young adult, popular culture, narrative nonfiction); Caryn Karmatz-Rudy (popular fiction, self-help, narrative nonfiction); Adam Schear (commercial fiction, humor, young adult, smart thrillers, historical fiction, and quirky debut literary novels. For nonfiction: popular science, politics, popular culture, and current events); Meredith Kaffel (smart upmarket women's fiction, literary fiction [especially debut] and literary thrillers, narrative nonfiction, nonfiction about science and tech, sophisticated pop culture/humor books); Rebecca Strauss (literary and commercial fiction, women's fiction, urban fantasy, romance, mystery, young adult, memoir, pop culture, and select nonfiction); Debra Goldstein (nonfiction books on how to live better).

REPRESENTS nonfiction books, novels. **Considers these fiction areas:** ethnic, literary, mainstream, middle-grade, mystery, paranormal, romance, short story collections, suspense, thriller, women's, young adult.

○━☜ "Please be advised that we are not considering children's picture books, poetry, adult science fiction and fantasy, romance, or dramatic projects at this time."

HOW TO CONTACT Query with SASE or e-mail to submissions@defioreandco.com. "Please include the word *Query* in the subject line. All attachments will be deleted; please insert all text in the body of the e-mail. For more information about our agents, their individual interests, and their query guidelines, please visit our About Us page on our website." There is more information (details, sales) for each agent on the agency website. Accepts simultaneous submissions. Obtains most new clients through recommendations from others.

TERMS Agent receives 15% commission on domestic sales. Agent receives 20% commission on foreign sales. Offers written contract; 10-day notice must be given to terminate contract. Charges clients for photocopying and overnight delivery (deducted only after a sale is made).

WRITERS CONFERENCES Maui Writers Conference; Pacific Northwest Writers Conference; North Carolina Writers Network Fall Conference.

◐ SANDRA DIJKSTRA LITERARY AGENCY

1155 Camino del Mar, PMB 515, Del Mar CA 92014. (858)755-3115. **Fax:** (858)794-2822. **E-mail:** elise@dijkstraagency.com. **Website:** www.dijkstraagency.com. Member of AAR. Other memberships include Authors Guild, PEN West, PEN USA, Organization of American Historians, Poets and Editors, MWA. Represents 100+ clients. 30% of clients are new/unpublished writers.

MEMBER AGENTS Sandra Dijkstra, president (adult only). Acquiring sub-agents: Elise Capron (adult only), Jill Marr (adult only), Thao Le (adult and young adult), Roz Foster (adult and young adult), Jessica Watterson (adult and young adult).

REPRESENTS nonfiction books, novels. **Considers these fiction areas:** commercial, horror, literary, middle-grade, science fiction, suspense, thriller, women's, young adult.

HOW TO CONTACT "Please see guidelines on our website, and note that we only accept e-mail submissions. Due to the large number of unsolicited submissions we receive, we are only able to respond to those submissions in which we are interested." Accepts simultaneous submissions. Responds to queries of interest within 6 weeks.

TERMS Works in conjunction with foreign and film agents. Agent receives 15% commission on domestic sales and 20% commission on foreign sales. Offers written contract. No reading fee.

TIPS "Remember that publishing is a business. Do your research and present your project in as professional a way as possible. Only submit your work when you are confident that it is polished and ready for prime time. Make yourself a part of the active writing community by getting stories and articles published, networking with other writers, and getting a good sense of where your work fits in the market."

JIM DONOVAN LITERARY

5635 SMU Blvd., Suite 201, Dallas TX 75206. **E-mail:** jdliterary@sbcglobal.net. **Contact:** Melissa Shultz, agent. Represents 30 clients. 10% of clients are new/unpublished writers. Currently handles nonfiction books (75%), novels (25%).

MEMBER AGENTS Jim Donovan (history: particularly American, military and Western; biography; sports; popular reference; popular culture; fiction: literary, thrillers and mystery); Melissa Shultz (parenting, women's issues, memoir).

This agency specializes in commercial fiction and nonfiction. "Does not want to receive poetry, children's, science fiction, fantasy, short stories, inspirational, or anything else not listed above."

HOW TO CONTACT "For nonfiction, I need a well-thought-out query letter telling me about the book: What it does, how it does it, why it's needed now, why it's better or different than what's out there on the subject, and why the author is the perfect writer for it. For fiction, the novel has to be finished, of course; a short (2- to 5-page) synopsis—not a teaser, but a summary of all the action, from first page to last—and the first 30-50 pages is enough. This material should be polished to as close to perfection as possible." Accepts simultaneous submissions. Responds in 2 weeks to queries. Responds in 1 month to mss. Obtains most new clients through recommendations from others.

TERMS Agent receives 15% commission on domestic sales. Agent receives 20% commission on foreign sales. Offers written contract, binding for 1 year; 30-day notice must be given to terminate contract. This agency charges for things such as overnight delivery and ms copying. Charges are discussed beforehand.

RECENT SALES *Below*, by Ryan Lockwood (Kensington); *The Dead Lands*, by Joe McKinney (Kensington); *Perfect: Don Larsen's Miraculous World Series Game and the Men Who Made It Happen*, by Lew Paper (NAL); *Untouchable: The Life and Times of Elliott Ness, America's Greatest Crime Fighter* (Viking); *Last Stand at Khe Sanh*, by Gregg Jones (DaCapo); *Soldier of Misfortune*, by Richard Bak; *Powerless* by Tim Washburn.

TIPS "Get published in short form—magazine reviews, journals, etc.—first. This will increase your credibility considerably and make it much easier to sell a full-length book."

DOYEN LITERARY SERVICES, INC.

1931 660th St., Newell IA 50568-7613. **Website:** www.barbaradoyen.com. **Contact:** (Ms.) B.J. Doyen, president. Represents over 100 clients. 20% of clients are new/unpublished writers. Currently handles nonfiction books (100%).

Prior to opening her agency, Ms. Doyen worked as a published author, teacher, guest speaker, and wrote and appeared in her own weekly TV show airing in 7 states. She is also the co-author of *The Everything Guide to Writing a Book Proposal* (Adams 2005) and *The Everything Guide to Getting Published* (Adams 2006).

REPRESENTS nonfiction for adults, no children's.

This agency specializes in nonfiction. Actively seeking business, health, science, how-to, self-help—all kinds of adult nonfiction suitable for the major trade publishers. Does not want to receive pornography, screenplays, children's books, fiction, or poetry.

HOW TO CONTACT Send a query letter initially. "Do not send us any attachments. Your text must be in the body of the e-mail. Please read the website before submitting a query. Include your background information in a bio. Send no unsolicited attachments." Reach this agency through its current e-mail, which is posted on the agency website. Accepts simultaneous submissions. Responds immediately to queries. Responds in 3 weeks to mss.

TERMS Agent receives 15% commission on domestic sales. Agent receives 20% commission on foreign sales. Offers written contract, binding for 2 years.

RECENT SALES *Stem Cells For Dummies*, by Lawrence S.B. Goldstein and Meg Schneider; *The Complete Idiot's Guide to Country Living*, by Kimberly Willis; *The Complete Illustrated Pregnancy Companion* by Robin Elise Weiss; *The Complete Idiot's Guide to Playing the Fiddle*, by Ellery Klein; *Healthy Aging for Dummies*, by Brent Agin, MD and Sharon Perkins, RN.

TIPS "Our authors receive personalized attention. We market aggressively, undeterred by rejection. We get the best possible publishing contracts. We are very interested in nonfiction book ideas at this time and will consider most topics. Many writers come to us from referrals, but we also get quite a few who initially approach us with query letters. Do not call us regarding queries. It is best if you do not collect editorial rejections prior to seeking an agent, but if you do, be upfront and honest about it. Do not submit your ms to more than 1 agent at a time—querying first can save you (and us) much time. We're open to established or beginning writers—just send us a terrific letter!"

◑ DUNHAM LITERARY, INC.

110 William St., Suite 2202, New York NY 10038. (212)929-0994. **E-mail:** dunhamlit@yahoo.com. **E-mail:** query@dunhamlit.com. **Website:** www.dunhamlit.com. **Contact:** Jennie Dunham. Member of AAR. SCBWI Represents 50 clients. 15% of clients are new/unpublished writers. Currently handles nonfiction books (25%), novels (25%), juvenile books (50%).

○ Prior to opening her agency, Ms. Dunham worked as a literary agent for Russell &

Volkening. The Rhoda Weyr Agency is now a division of Dunham Literary, Inc.

REPRESENTS nonfiction, fiction, novels, juvenile books. **Considers these fiction areas:** ethnic, juvenile, literary, mainstream, picture books, young adult.

HOW TO CONTACT Query with SASE. Responds in 3 weeks to queries; 2 months to mss. Obtains most new clients through recommendations from others, solicitations.

TERMS Agent receives 15% commission on domestic sales. Agent receives 20% commission on foreign sales.

RECENT SALES Sales include The Bad Kitty series, by Nick Bruel (Macmillan); *The Little Mermaid*, by Robert Sabuda (Simon & Schuster); *Transformers*, by Matthew Reinhart (Little, Brown); *The Gollywhopper Games* and Sequels, by Jody Feldman (Harper-Collins); *Learning Not To Drown*, by Anna Shinoda (Simon & Schuster); *The Things You Kiss Goodbye*, by Leslie Connor (HarperCollins); *Gangsterland*, by Tod Goldberg (Counterpoint); *Ancestors and Others*, by Fred Chappell (Macmillan), *Forward From Here*, by Reeve Lindbergh (Simon & Schuster).

○ DUNOW, CARLSON, & LERNER AGENCY

27 W. 20th St., Suite 1107, New York NY 10011. (212)645-7606. **E-mail:** mail@dclagency.com. **Website:** www.dclagency.com. Member of AAR.

MEMBER AGENTS Jennifer Carlson (narrative nonfiction writers and journalists covering current events and ideas and cultural history, as well as literary and upmarket commercial novelists); Henry Dunow (quality fiction—literary, historical, strongly written commercial—and with voice-driven nonfiction across a range of areas—narrative history, biography, memoir, current affairs, cultural trends and criticism, science, sports); Erin Hosier (nonfiction: popular culture, music, sociology and memoir); Betsy Lerner (nonfiction writers in the areas of psychology, history, cultural studies, biography, current events, business; fiction: literary, dark, funny, voice driven); Yishai Seidman (broad range of fiction: literary, postmodern, and thrillers; nonfiction: sports, music, and pop culture); Amy Hughes (nonfiction in the areas of history, cultural studies, memoir, current events, wellness, health, food, pop culture, and biography; also literary fiction); Eleanor Jackson (literary, commercial, memoir, art, food, science, and history); Julia Kenny (fiction—adult, middle-grade and young adult—and is especially interested in dark, literary thrillers and suspense).

REPRESENTS nonfiction books, novels, juvenile. **Considers these fiction areas:** commercial, literary, mainstream, middle-grade, mystery, picture books, thriller, young adult.

HOW TO CONTACT Query via snail mail with SASE or by e-mail. No attachments. Responds if interested.

RECENT SALES A full list of agency clients is on the website.

● EAST/WEST LITERARY AGENCY, LLC

1158 26th St., Suite 462, Santa Monica CA 90403. (310)573-9303. **Fax:** (310)453-9008. **E-mail:** dwarren@eastwestliteraryagency.com. **Contact:** Deborah Warren. Estab. 2000. Currently handles juvenile books (90%), adult books 10%.

MEMBER AGENTS Deborah Warren, founder.

REPRESENTS Considers these fiction areas: middle-grade, picture books, young adult.

HOW TO CONTACT By referral only. Submit proposal and first 3 sample chapters, table of contents (2 pages or fewer), synopsis (1 page). For picture books, submit entire ms. Requested submissions should be sent by mail as a Word document in Courier, 12-pt., double-spaced with 1.20-inch margin on left, ragged right text, 25 lines per page, continuously paginated, with all your contact info on the first page. Only responds if interested, no need for SASE. Responds in 60 days. Obtains new clients through recommendations from others.

TERMS Agent receives 15% commission on domestic sales. Agent receives 25% commission on foreign sales. Offers written contract; 30-day notice must be given to terminate contract. Charges for out-of-pocket expenses, such as postage and copying.

● ANNE EDELSTEIN LITERARY AGENCY

404 Riverside Dr., #12D, New York NY 10025. (212)414-4923. **Fax:** (212)414-2930. **E-mail:** submissions@aeliterary.com. **Website:** www.aeliterary.com. Member of AAR.

MEMBER AGENTS Anne Edelstein.

REPRESENTS nonfiction, fiction. **Considers these fiction areas:** commercial, literary.

This agency specializes in fiction and narrative nonfiction.

HOW TO CONTACT E-mail queries only; consult website for submission guidelines.

RECENT SALES *Amsterdam*, by Russell Shorto (Doubleday); *The Story of Beautiful Girl*, by Rachel Simon (Grand Central).

● ETHAN ELLENBERG LITERARY AGENCY

548 Broadway, #5-E, New York NY 10012. (212)431-4554. **Fax:** (212)941-4652. **E-mail:** agent@ethanellenberg.com. **Website:** ethanellenberg.com. **Contact:** Ethan Ellenberg. Estab. 1984. Represents 80 clients. 10% of clients are new/unpublished writers. Currently handles nonfiction books (25%), novels (75%).

Prior to opening his agency, Mr. Ellenberg was contracts manager of Berkley/Jove and associate contracts manager for Bantam.

MEMBER AGENTS Denise Little: deniselitt@aol.com. (accepts romance, paranormal, young adult, science fiction, fantasy, Christian fiction, and commercial nonfiction. Send a short query letter telling about your writing history and including the first 15 pages of the work you want her to represent. If she is interested in your work, she'll reply to you within 4 weeks); Evan Gregory (accepting clients).

REPRESENTS nonfiction books, novels children's books. **Considers these fiction areas:** commercial, fantasy, literary, mystery, romance, science fiction, suspense, thriller, women's, young adult, children's (all types).

"This agency specializes in commercial fiction—especially thrillers, romance/women's, and specialized nonfiction. We also do a lot of children's books. Actively seeking commercial fiction as noted above—romance/fiction for women, science fiction and fantasy, thrillers, suspense and mysteries. Our other 2 main areas of interest are children's books and narrative nonfiction. We are actively seeking clients; follow the directions on our website." Does not want to receive poetry, short stories, or screenplays.

HOW TO CONTACT Query by e-mail. Paste the query, synopsis, and first 50 pages into the e-mail. For nonfiction, paste the proposal. For picture books, paste the entire text. Accepts simultaneous submissions. Responds in 2 weeks to queries (no attachments); 4-6 weeks to mss.

TERMS Agent receives 15% commission on domestic sales. Agent receives 10% commission on foreign sales. Offers written contract. Charges clients (with their consent) for direct expenses limited to photocopying and postage.

WRITERS CONFERENCES RWA National Conference; Novelists, Inc.; and other regional conferences.

TIPS We do consider new material from unsolicited authors. Write a good, clear letter with a succinct description of your book. We prefer the first 3 chapters when we consider fiction. For all submissions, you must include an SASE or the material will be discarded. It's always hard to break in, but talent will find a home. Check our website for complete submission guidelines. We continue to see natural storytellers and nonfiction writers with important books.

⊘ THE ELAINE P. ENGLISH LITERARY AGENCY

4710 41st St. NW, Suite D, Washington DC 20016. (202)362-5190. **Fax:** (202)362-5192. **E-mail:** queries@elaineenglish.com. **E-mail:** elaine@elaineenglish.com. **Website:** www.elaineenglish.com/literary.php. **Contact:** Elaine English, Lindsey Skouras. Member of AAR. Represents 20 clients. 25% of clients are new/unpublished writers. Currently handles novels (100%).

○ Ms. English has been working in publishing for more than 20 years. She is also an attorney specializing in media and publishing law.

MEMBER AGENTS Elaine English (novels).

REPRESENTS novels. **Considers these fiction areas:** historical, multicultural, mystery, suspense, thriller, women's romance (single title, historical, contemporary, romantic, suspense, chick lit, erotic), general women's fiction. The agency is slowly but steadily acquiring in all mentioned areas.

⌐ Actively seeking women's fiction, including single-title romances. Does not want to receive any science fiction, time travel, or picture books.

HOW TO CONTACT Not accepting queries as of 2014. Keep checking the website for further information and updates. Responds in 4-8 weeks to queries; 3 months to requested submissions. Obtains most new clients through recommendations from others, conferences, submissions.

TERMS Agent receives 15% commission on domestic sales. Agent receives 20% commission on foreign sales. Offers written contract; 30-day notice must be given to terminate contract. Charges only for shipping expenses; generally taken from proceeds.

RECENT SALES Titles purchased by Sourcebooks, Tor, Harlequin.

WRITERS CONFERENCES RWA National Conference; Novelists, Inc.; Malice Domestic; Washington Romance Writers Retreat, among others.

◉ JUDITH EHRLICH LITERARY MANAGEMENT, LLC

880 Third Ave., 8th Floor, New York NY 10022. (646)505-1570. **Fax:** (646)505-1570. **E-mail:** jehrlich@judithehrlichliterary.com. **Website:** www.judithehrlichliterary.com. Member of the Author's Guild and the American Society of Journalists and Authors.

○ Prior to her current position, Ms. Ehrlich was a senior associate at the Linda Chester Agency and is an award-winning journalist; she is the co-author of *The New Crowd: The Changing of the Jewish Guard on Wall Street* (Little, Brown).

MEMBER AGENTS Judith Ehrlich; Sophia Seidner: sseidner@judithehrlichliterary.com (strong literary fiction and nonfiction including self-help, narrative nonfiction, memoir, and biography. Areas of special interest include medical and health-related topics, science [popular, political and social], animal welfare, current events, politics, law, history, ethics, parody and humor, sports, art, and business self-help).

REPRESENTS **Considers these fiction areas:** commercial, literary Also seeks prescriptive books offering fresh information and advice.

⌐ Does not want to receive novellas, poetry, textbooks, plays, or screenplays.

HOW TO CONTACT Queries should include a synopsis and some sample pages. Send e-queries to jehrlich@judithehrlichliterary.com. The agency will respond only if interested.

RECENT SALES *Power Branding: Leveraging the Success of the World's Best Brands*, by Steve McKee (Palgrave Macmillan); *What was the Underground Railroad?*, by Yona Zeldis McDonough (Grosset & Dunlap); *Confessions of a Sociopath: A Life Spent Hiding in Plain Sight*, by M.E. Thomas (Crown); *The Last Kiss*, by Leslie Brody (TitleTown); *Love, Loss, and Laughter: Seeing Alzheimer's Differently*, (Lyons Press); *Luck and Circumstance: A Coming of Age in New York, Hollywood, and Points Beyond*, by Michael Lindsay-Hogg (Knopf); *Paris Under Water: How the City of Light Survived the Great Flood of 1910*, by Jeffrey H. Jackson (Palgrave Macmillan). Fiction titles: *Two of a Kind*, by Yona Zeldis McDonough (NAL, September 2013);

Once We Were, by Kat Zhang (HarperCollins, September 2013).

◉ FAIRBANK LITERARY REPRESENTATION

P.O. Box 6, Hudson NY 12534-0006. (617)576-0030. **Fax:** (617)576-0030. **E-mail:** queries@fairbankliterary.com. **Website:** www.fairbankliterary.com. **Contact:** Sorche Fairbank. Member of AAR. Represents 45 clients. 20% of clients are new/unpublished writers. Currently handles nonfiction books (60%), novels (22%), story collections (3%), other (15% illustrated).

MEMBER AGENTS Sorche Fairbank (narrative nonfiction, commercial and literary fiction, memoir, food and wine); Matthew Frederick, matt@fairbankliterary.com (scout for sports nonfiction, architecture, design).

REPRESENTS nonfiction books, novels, short story collections. **Considers these fiction areas:** action, adventure, feminist, gay, lesbian, literary, mainstream, mystery, sports, suspense, thriller, women's Southern voices.

⊶ "I have a small agency in Harvard Square, where I tend to gravitate toward literary fiction and narrative nonfiction, with a strong interest in women's issues and women's voices, international voices, class and race issues, and projects that simply teach me something new about the greater world and society around us. We have a good reputation for working closely and developmentally with our authors, and we love what we do." Actively seeking literary fiction, international and culturally diverse voices, narrative nonfiction, topical subjects (politics, current affairs), history, sports, architecture/design and pop culture. Does not want to receive romance, poetry, science fiction, pirates, vampire, young adult, or children's works.

HOW TO CONTACT Query with SASE. Submit author bio. Accepts simultaneous submissions. Responds in 6 weeks to queries. Responds in 10 weeks to mss. Obtains most new clients through recommendations from others, solicitations, conferences, ideas generated in-house.

TERMS Agent receives 15% commission on domestic sales. Agent receives 20% commission on foreign sales. Offers written contract, binding for 12 months; 45-day notice must be given to terminate contract.

RECENT SALES *Red Dog/Blue Dog: When Pooches Get Political*, by Chuck Sambuchino (Running Press); 101 Things I Learned in School series, by Matthew Fredericks; all recent sales available on website.

WRITERS CONFERENCES San Francisco Writers Conference, Muse and the Marketplace/Grub Street Conference, Washington Independent Writers Conference, Murder in the Grove, Surrey International Writers Conference.

TIPS "Be professional from the very first contact. There shouldn't be a single typo or grammatical flub in your query. Have a reason for contacting me about your project other than I was the next name listed on some website. Please do not use form query software! Believe me, we can get a dozen or so a day that look identical—we know when you are using a form. Show me that you know your audience—and your competition. Have the writing and/or proposal at the very, very best it can be before starting the querying process. Don't assume that if someone likes it enough they'll 'fix' it. The biggest mistake new writers make is starting the querying process before they—and the work—are ready. Take your time and do it right."

◉ FELICIA ETH LITERARY REPRESENTATION

555 Bryant St., Suite 350, Palo Alto CA 94301-1700. (650)375-1276. **E-mail:** feliciaeth.literary@gmail.com. **Website:** ethliterary.com. **Contact:** Felicia Eth. Member of AAR. Represents 25-35 clients. Currently handles nonfiction books (75%), novels (25% adult).

REPRESENTS nonfiction books, novels. **Considers these fiction areas:** literary, mainstream.

⊶ This agency specializes in high-quality fiction (preferably mainstream/contemporary) and provocative, intelligent, and thoughtful nonfiction on a wide array of commercial subjects.

HOW TO CONTACT Query with SASE. Accepts simultaneous submissions. Responds in 3 weeks to queries. Responds in 4-6 weeks to mss.

TERMS Agent receives 15% commission on domestic sales. Agent receives 20% commission on foreign sales. Agent receives 20% commission on film sales. Charges clients for photocopying and express mail service.

RECENT SALES *Bumper Sticker Philosophy*, by Jack Bowen (Random House); *Boys Adrift* by Leonard Sax (Basic Books; *The Memory Thief*, by Emily Colin (Ballantine Books); *The World is a Carpet*, by Anna Badkhen (Riverhead).

WRITERS CONFERENCES "Wide array—from Squaw Valley to Mills College."

TIPS "For nonfiction, established expertise is certainly a plus—as is magazine publication—though not a prerequisite. I am highly dedicated to those projects I represent but highly selective in what I choose."

◍ DIANA FINCH LITERARY AGENCY

116 W. 23rd St., Suite 500, New York NY 10011. (917)544-4470. **E-mail:** diana.finch@verizon.net. **Website:** dianafinchliteraryagency.blogspot.com. **Contact:** Diana Finch. Member of AAR. Represents 40 clients. 20% of clients are new/unpublished writers. Currently handles nonfiction books (85%), novels (15%), juvenile books (5%), multimedia (5%).

○ Seeking to represent books that change lives. Prior to opening her agency in 2003, Ms. Finch worked at Ellen Levine Literary Agency for 18 years.

REPRESENTS nonfiction books, novels, scholarly. **Considers these fiction areas:** action, adventure, crime, detective, ethnic, historical, literary, mainstream, police, thriller, young adult.

⚬━ "Does not want romance, mysteries, or children's picture books."

HOW TO CONTACT This agency prefers submissions via its online form: https://dianafinchliterary agency.submittable.com/submit. Accepts simultaneous submissions. Obtains most new clients through recommendations from others.

TERMS Agent receives 15% commission on domestic sales. Agent receives 20% commission on foreign sales. Offers written contract. "I charge for photocopying, overseas postage, galleys, and books purchased, and try to recoup these costs from earnings received for a client, rather than charging outright."

RECENT SALES *Heidegger's Glasses*, by Thaisa Frank; *Genetic Rounds*, by Robert Marion, MD (Kaplan); *Honeymoon in Tehran*, by Azadeh Moaveni (Random House); *Darwin Slept Here* by Eric Simons (Overlook); *Black Tide,* by Antonia Juhasz (HarperCollins); *Stalin's Children,* by Owen Matthews (Bloomsbury); *Radiant Days,* by Michael Fitzgerald (Shoemaker & Hoard); *The Queen's Soprano,* by Carol Dines (Harcourt Young Adult); *What to Say to a Porcupine,* by Richard Gallagher (Amacom); *The Language of Trust,* by Michael Maslansky et al.

TIPS "Do as much research as you can on agents before you query. Have someone critique your query letter before you send it. It should be only 1 page and describe your book clearly—and why you are writing it—but also demonstrate creativity and a sense of your writing style."

FINEPRINT LITERARY MANAGEMENT

115 W. 29th, 3rd Floor, New York NY 10001. (212)279-1282. **E-mail:** stephany@fineprintlit.com. **Website:** www.fineprintlit.com. Member of AAR.

MEMBER AGENTS Peter Rubie, CEO (nonfiction: narrative nonfiction, popular science, spirituality, history, biography, pop culture, business, technology, parenting, health, self-help, music, and food; fiction: literate thrillers, crime fiction, science fiction and fantasy, military fiction, literary fiction, middle-grade and young adult fiction, and nonfiction for boys); Stephany Evans (nonfiction: health and wellness, especially women's health; spirituality, environment/sustainability, food and wine, memoir, and narrative nonfiction; fiction: stories with a strong and interesting female protagonist, both literary and upmarket commercial/book club fiction, romance—all subgenres; mysteries); Janet Reid (nonfiction: narrative nonfiction, history and biography; fiction: thrillers); Laura Wood (nonfiction: business, dance, economics, history, humor, law, science, narrative nonfiction, popular science; fiction: fantasy, science fiction, suspense); June Clark (see juneclark.com); Rachel Coyne (young adult novels of all stripes: historical, fantasy, romance, contemporary, literary, humorous, as well as middle-grade novels, especially with a humorous voice; she's also looking for adult historical, fantasy, urban fantasy, and science fiction).

REPRESENTS Considers these fiction areas: commercial, crime, fantasy, middle-grade, military, mystery, romance, science fiction, suspense, thriller, women's, young adult.

HOW TO CONTACT Query with SASE. Submit synopsis and first 3-5 pages of ms embedded in an e-mail proposal for nonfiction. Do not send attachments or mss without a request. See contact page online at website for e-mails. Obtains most new clients through recommendations from others, solicitations.

TERMS Agent receives 15% commission on domestic sales. Agent receives 20% commission on foreign sales.

◍ FLANNERY LITERARY

1140 Wickfield Ct., Naperville IL 60563. (630)428-2682. **Fax:** (630)428-2683. **E-mail:** jennifer@flannery-literary.com. **Contact:** Jennifer Flannery. Represents

40 clients. 50% of clients are new/unpublished writers. Currently handles juvenile books (100%).

REPRESENTS Considers these fiction areas: juvenile, middle-grade, young adult.

8—➤ This agency specializes in children's and young adult fiction and nonfiction. It also accepts picture books. 100% juvenile books.

HOW TO CONTACT Query by mail with SASE. "Multiple queries are fine, but please inform us. Mail that requires a signature will be returned to sender, as we are not always available to sign for mail." Responds in 2 weeks to queries; 1 month to mss. Obtains new clients through referrals and queries.

TERMS Agent receives 15% commission on domestic sales. Agent receives 20% commission on foreign sales. Offers written contract, binding for life of book in print; one-month notice must be given to terminate contract.

TIPS "Write an engrossing, succinct query describing your work. We are always looking for a fresh new voice."

FOLIO LITERARY MANAGEMENT, LLC

The Film Center Building, 630 Ninth Ave., Suite 1101, New York NY 10036. (212)400-1494. **Fax:** (212)967-0977. **Website:** www.foliolit.com. Member of AAR. Represents 100+ clients.

Prior to creating Folio Literary Management, Mr. Hoffman worked for several years at another agency; Mr. Kleinman was an agent at Graybill & English; Ms. Wheeler was an agent at Creative Media Agency.

MEMBER AGENTS Scott Hoffman; Jeff Kleinman; Paige Wheeler; Frank Weimann; Michelle Brower; Claudia Cross; Jita Fumich; Michael Harriot; Molly Jaffa; Erin Harris; Erin Niumata; Katherine Latshaw; Ruth Pomerance; Marcy Posner; Steve Troha; Emily van Beek; Melissa Sarver White; Maura Teitelbaum.

REPRESENTS nonfiction books, novels, short story collections. **Considers these fiction areas:** commercial, erotica, fantasy, horror, literary, middle-grade, mystery, picture books, religious, romance, thriller, women's, young adult.

8—➤ No poetry, stage plays, or screenplays.

HOW TO CONTACT Query via e-mail only (no attachments). Read agent bios online for specific submission guidelines and e-mail addresses. Responds in 1 month to queries.

TIPS "Please do not submit simultaneously to more than 1 agent at Folio. If you're not sure which of us is exactly right for your book, don't worry. We work closely as a team, and if one of our agents gets a query that might be more appropriate for someone else, we'll always pass it along. It's important that you check each agent's bio page for clear directions as to how to submit, as well as when to expect feedback."

FOREWORD LITERARY

E-mail: info@forewordliterary.com. **Website:** forewordliterary.com/. **Contact:** Laurie McLean.

MEMBER AGENTS Laurie McLean (referrals only); Gordon Warnock, querygordon@forewordliterary.com (nonfiction: memoir [adult, new adult, young adult, graphic], cookbooks and food studies, political and current events, pop-science, pop-culture [also punk culture and geek culture], self-help, how-to, humor, pets, business and career; Fiction: high-concept commercial fiction, literary fiction, new adult, contemporary young adult, graphic novels); Pam van Hylckama Vlieg, querypam@forewordliterary.com (young adult, middle-grade, romance, genre fiction [urban fantasy, paranormal, and epic/high fantasy], pop culture nonfiction and adult picture books); Connor Goldsmith, queryconnor@forewordliterary.com (science fiction, fantasy, horror, thrillers, upmarket commercial, literary, LGBT, many nonfiction categories); Jen Karsbaek, queryjen@forewordliterary.com (women's fiction, upmarket commercial fiction, historical fiction, and literary fiction); Emily Keyes, queryemily@forewordliterary.com (mostly young adult and middle-grade, but also commercial fiction which includes fantasy and science fiction, women's fiction, new adult fiction, along with pop culture and humor titles); Sara Sciuto (juvenile books, picture books).

REPRESENTS Considers these fiction areas: commercial, fantasy, gay, horror, lesbian, literary, mainstream, middle-grade, mystery, new adult, paranormal, picture books, romance, science fiction, suspense, thriller, women's, young adult.

HOW TO CONTACT E-query. Each agent has a different query e-mail and style. Check their individual pages on the website for the latest updated info. Accepts simultaneous submissions.

RECENT SALES *Hollow World*, by Michael J. Sullivan; *Looking For Home: Hope Springs*, by Sarah M. Eden; *Free Agent*, by J.C. Nelson.

WRITERS CONFERENCES San Diego State University Writers Conference, San Francisco Writers Conference, WNBA Pitch-O-Rama, LDS Storymakers Conference, SFWA Nebula Awards, Book Expo America, Ellen Hopkins' Ventana Sierra, Romance Writers of America Conference, Central Coast Writers Conference, World Fantasy Con, and many more. The agency website lists all.

◑ FOUNDRY LITERARY + MEDIA

33 West 17th St., PH, New York NY 10011. (212)929-5064. **Fax:** (212)929-5471. **Website:** www.foundry media.com.

MEMBER AGENTS Peter McGuigan, pmsubmissions@foundrymedia.com; Yfat Reiss Gendell, yrgsubmissions@foundrymedia.com (practical nonfiction projects in the areas of health and wellness, diet, lifestyle, how-to, and parenting and a broad range of narrative nonfiction that includes humor, memoir, history, science, pop culture, psychology, and adventure/travel stories); Stéphanie Abou, sasubmissions@foundrymedia.com; Mollie Glick, mgsubmissions@foundrymedia.com (literary fiction, young adult fiction, narrative nonfiction, and a bit of practical nonfiction in the areas of popular science, medicine, psychology, cultural history, memoir and current events); Stephen Barbara, sbsubmissions@foundrymedia.com (books for young readers, and adult fiction and nonfiction); David Patterson, dpsubmissions@foundrymedia.com (narrative and idea-driven nonfiction, with an emphasis on journalists, public figures, and scholars); Chris Park, cpsubmissions@foundrymedia.com (memoirs, narrative nonfiction, sports books, Christian nonfiction and character-driven fiction); Hannah Brown Gordon, hbgsubmissions@foundrymedia.com (stories and narratives that blend genres, including thriller, suspense, historical, literary, speculative, memoir, popscience, psychology, humor, and pop culture); Brandi Bowles, bbsubmissions@foundrymedia.com (literary and commercial fiction, especially high-concept novels that feature strong female bonds and psychological or scientific themes); Kirsten Neuhaus, knsubmissions@foundrymedia.com (platform-driven narrative nonfiction, in the areas of lifestyle (beauty/fashion/relationships), memoir, business, current events, history and stories with strong female voices, as well as smart, upmarket, and commercial fiction); Jessica Regel, jrsubmissions@foundrymedia.com (young adult and middle-grade books, as well as a select list of adult general fiction, women's fiction, and adult nonfiction); Anthony Mattero, amsubmissions@foundrymedia.com (smart, platform-driven nonfiction particularly in the genres of pop culture, humor, music, sports, and pop business).

REPRESENTS Considers these fiction areas: commercial, historical, humor, literary, middle-grade, suspense, thriller, women's, young adult.

HOW TO CONTACT Target 1 agent only. Send queries to the specific submission e-mail of the agent. For fiction: send query, synopsis, author bio, first 3 chapters—all pasted in the e-mail. For nonfiction, send query, sample chapters, table of contents, author bio—all pasted in the e-mail.

RECENT SALES *Tell the Wolves I'm Home*, by Carol Rifka Blunt; *The Rathbones*, by Janice Clark; *This Is Your Captain Speaking*, by Jon Methven; *The War Against the Assholes* and *The November Criminals*, by Sam Munson; *Ready Player One*, by Ernest Cline.

TIPS "Consult website for each agent's submission instructions."

FOX LITERARY

110 W. 40th St., Suite 410, New York NY 10018. **E-mail:** submissions@foxliterary.com. **Website:** www.publishersmarketplace.com/members/fox/.

REPRESENTS Considers these fiction areas: fantasy, historical, literary, mainstream, romance, science fiction, thriller, young adult graphic novels.

➤ "I am actively seeking the following: young adult fiction (all genres), science fiction/fantasy, romance, historical fiction, thrillers, and graphic novels. I'm always interested in books that cross genres and reinvent popular concepts with an engaging new twist (especially when there's a historical and/or speculative element involved). On the nonfiction side I'm interested in memoirs, biography, and smart narrative nonfiction; I particularly enjoy memoirs and other nonfiction about sex work, addiction and recovery, and pop culture." Does not want to receive screenplays, poetry, category westerns, horror, Christian/inspirational, or children's picture books.

HOW TO CONTACT E-mail query and first 5 pages in body of e-mail. E-mail queries preferred. For snail mail queries, must include an e-mail address for response and no response means No. Do not send SASE.

RECENT SALES *Black Ships* by Jo Graham (Orbit); *Evernight* series by Claudia Gray (HarperCollins); *October Daye* series by Seanan McGuire (DAW); *Salt and Silver* by Anna Katherine (Tor); *Alcestis* by Katharine Beutner (Soho Press); *Shadows Cast by Stars* by Catherine Knutsson (Atheneum); *Saving June* and *Speechless* by Hannah Harrington (Harlequin Teen); *Spellcaster* trilogy by Claudia Gray (HarperCollins).

LYNN C. FRANKLIN ASSOCIATES, LTD.

1350 Broadway, Suite 2015, New York NY 10018. (212)868-6311. **Fax:** (212)868-6312. **E-mail:** agency@fsainc.com. **E-mail:** agency@franklinandsiegal.com. **Contact:** Lynn Franklin, president; Claudia Nys, foreign rights. Other memberships include PEN America.

REPRESENTS nonfiction books, novels.

☛ "This agency specializes in general nonfiction with a special interest in self-help, biography/memoir, alternative health, and spirituality."

HOW TO CONTACT Query via e-mail to agency@franklinandsiegal.com. No unsolicited mss. No attachments. For nonfiction, query letter with short outline and synopsis. For fiction, query letter with short synopsis and a maximum of 10 sample pages (in the body of the e-mail). Please indicate "query adult" or "query children's" in the subject line. Accepts simultaneous submissions. Obtains most new clients through recommendations from others, solicitations.

TERMS Agent receives 15% commission on domestic sales. Agent receives 20% commission on foreign sales. Offers written contract.

RECENT SALES *The Wahls Protocol: How I Beat Progressive MS Using Paleo Principles and Functional Medicine* by Terry Wahls, M.D. (Avery/Penguin); *The Book of Forgiving: The Four-Fold Path to Healing for Ourselves and Our World* by Archbishop Desmond Tutu and Reverend Mpho Tutu (U.S.: HarperOne, U.K.: Collins); *The Customer Rules: 39 Essential Practices for Delivering Sensational Service* by Lee Cockerell (Crown Business/Random House); *My Name Is Jody Williams* by Jody Williams (University of California Press-Berkeley); *Everybody Matters: A Memoir* by Mary Robinson (U.S.: Bloomsbury, U.K. and Ireland: Hodder).

SARAH JANE FREYMANN LITERARY AGENCY

59 W. 71st St., Suite 9B, New York NY 10023. (212)362-9277. **E-mail:** sarah@sarahjanefreymann.com; submissions@SarahJaneFreymann.com. **Website:** www.sarahjanefreymann.com. **Contact:** Sarah Jane Freymann, Steve Schwartz. Represents 100 clients. 20% of clients are new/unpublished writers. Currently handles nonfiction books (75%), novels (23%), juvenile books (2%).

MEMBER AGENTS Sarah Jane Freymann; (nonfiction books, novels, illustrated books); Jessica Sinsheimer, Jessica@sarahjanefreymann.com (young adult fiction); Steven Schwartz, steve@sarahjanefreymann.com; Katharine Sands.

REPRESENTS Considers these fiction areas: ethnic, literary, mainstream, young adult.

HOW TO CONTACT Query with SASE. Responds in 2 weeks to queries. Responds in 6 weeks to mss. Obtains most new clients through recommendations from others.

TERMS Agent receives 15% commission on domestic sales. Agent receives 20% commission on foreign sales. Offers written contract. Charges clients for long distance, overseas postage, photocopying. 100% of business is derived from commissions on ms sales.

RECENT SALES *How to Make Love to a Plastic Cup: And Other Things I Learned While Trying to Knock Up My Wife*, by Greg Wolfe (Harper Collins); *I Want to Be Left Behind: Rapture Here on Earth*, by Brenda Peterson (a Merloyd Lawrence Book); *That Bird Has My Name: The Autobiography of an Innocent Man on Death Row*, by Jarvis Jay Masters with an Introduction by Pema Chodrun (HarperOne); *Perfect One-Dish Meals*, by Pam Anderson (Houghton Mifflin); *Birdology*, by Sy Montgomery (Simon & Schuster); *Emptying the Nest: Launching Your Reluctant Young Adult*, by Dr. Brad Sachs (Macmillan); *Tossed & Found*, by Linda and John Meyers (Stewart, Tabori & Chang); *32 Candles*, by Ernessa Carter; *God and Dog*, by Wendy Francisco.

TIPS "I love fresh, new, passionate works by authors who love what they are doing and have both natural talent and carefully honed skill."

FREDRICA S. FRIEDMAN AND CO., INC.

136 E. 57th St., 14th Floor, New York NY 10022. (212)829-9600. **Fax:** (212)829-9669. **E-mail:** info@fredricafriedman.com; submissions@fredricafriedman.com. **Website:** www.fredricafriedman.com. **Contact:** Ms. Chandler Smith.

Prior to establishing her own literary management firm, Ms. Friedman was the editorial director, associate publisher, and vice president of Little, Brown & Co., a division of Time Warner, and the first woman to hold those positions.

REPRESENTS nonfiction books, novels anthologies. **Considers these fiction areas:** literary.

🔑 "We represent a select group of outstanding nonfiction and fiction writers. We are particularly interested in helping writers expand their readership and develop their careers." Does not want poetry, plays, screenplays, children's books, science fiction/fantasy, or horror.

HOW TO CONTACT "Submit e-query, synopsis; be concise, and include any pertinent author information, including relevant writing history. If you are a fiction writer, we also request a one-page sample from your ms to provide its voice. We ask that you put all material in the body of the e-mail." Accepts simultaneous submissions. Responds in 4-6 weeks to queries. Responds in 4-6 weeks to mss. Obtains most new clients through recommendations from others.

TERMS Agent receives 15% commission on domestic sales. Agent receives 25% commission on foreign sales. Offers written contract. Charges for photocopying and messenger/shipping fees for proposals.

RECENT SALES *A World of Lies: The Crime and Consequences of Bernie Madoff*, by Diana B. Henriques (Times Books/Holt); *Polemic and Memoir: The Nixon Years* by Patrick J. Buchanan (St. Martin's Press); *Angry Fat Girls: Five Women, Five Hundred Pounds, and a Year of Losing It ... Again*, by Frances Kuffel (Berkley/Penguin); *Life with My Sister Madonna*, by Christopher Ciccone with Wendy Leigh (Simon & Schuster Spotlight); *The World Is Curved: Hidden Dangers to the Global Economy*, by David Smick (Portfolio/Penguin); *Going to See the Elephant*, by Rodes Fishburne (Delacorte/Random House); *Seducing the Boys Club: Uncensored Tactics from a Woman at the Top*, by Nina DiSesa (Ballantine/Random House); *The Girl from Foreign: A Search for Shipwrecked Ancestors, Forgotten Histories, and a Sense of Home*, by Sadia Shepard (Penguin Press).

TIPS "Spell the agent's name correctly on your query letter."

◑ FULL CIRCLE LITERARY, LLC

7676 Hazard Center Dr., Suite 500, San Diego CA 92108. **E-mail:** submissions@fullcircleliterary.com. **Website:** www.fullcircleliterary.com. **Contact:** Lilly Ghahremani, Stefanie Von Borstel. Represents 55 clients. 60% of clients are new/unpublished writers. Currently handles nonfiction books (70%), novels (10%), juvenile books (20%).

◑ Before forming Full Circle, Ms. Von Borstel worked in both marketing and editorial capacities at Penguin and Harcourt; Ms. Ghahremani received her law degree from UCLA and has experience in representing authors on legal affairs.

MEMBER AGENTS Lilly Ghahremani; Stefanie Von Borstel; Adriana Dominguez; Taylor Martindale (multicultural voices).

REPRESENTS nonfiction books, juvenile. **Considers these fiction areas:** literary, middle-grade, picture books, women's, young adult.

🔑 "Our full-service boutique agency, representing a range of nonfiction and children's books (limited fiction), provides a one-stop resource for authors. Our extensive experience in the realms of law and marketing provide Full Circle clients with a unique edge. Actively seeking nonfiction by authors with a unique and strong platform, projects that offer new and diverse viewpoints, and literature with a global or multicultural perspective. We are particularly interested in books with a Latino or Middle Eastern angle and books related to pop culture." Does not want to receive screenplays, poetry, commercial fiction or genre fiction (horror, thriller, mystery, western, science fiction, fantasy, romance, historical fiction).

HOW TO CONTACT Agency accepts e-queries. Put "Query for [Agent]" in the subject line. Send a one-page query letter (in the body of the e-mail) including a description of your book, writing credentials and author highlights. Following your query, please include the first 10 pages or complete picture book ms text within the body of the e-mail. For nonfiction, include a proposal with 1 sample chapter. Accepts simultaneous submissions. Obtains most new clients through recommendations from others, solicitations, conferences.

TERMS Agent receives 15% commission on domestic sales. Agent receives 20% commission on foreign sales. Offers written contract; up to 30-day notice must be given to terminate contract. Charges for copying and postage.

TIPS "Put your best foot forward. Contact us when you simply can't make your project any better on your own, and please be sure your work fits with what the agent you're approaching represents. Little things count, so copyedit your work. Join a writing group and attend conferences to get objective and constructive feedback before submitting. Be active about building your platform as an author before, during, and after publication. Remember this is a business and your agent is a business partner."

NANCY GALLT LITERARY AGENCY

273 Charlton Ave., South Orange NJ 07079. (973)761-6358. **Fax:** (973)761-6318. **E-mail:** submissions@nancygallt.com. **Website:** www.nancygallt.com. **Contact:** Nancy Gallt, Marietta Zacker. Represents 40 clients. 30% of clients are new/unpublished writers. Currently handles juvenile books (100%).

○ Prior to opening her agency, Ms. Gallt was subsidiary rights director of the children's book division at Morrow, Harper, and Viking.

MEMBER AGENTS Nancy Gallt; Marietta Zacker.

REPRESENTS juvenile. **Considers these fiction areas:** juvenile, middle-grade, picture books, young adult.

⚬— "We only handle children's books." Actively seeking picture books, middle-grade, and young adult novels. Does not want to receive rhyming picture book texts.

HOW TO CONTACT Submit through online submission for on agency website. Accepts simultaneous submissions. Obtains most new clients through recommendations from others, solicitations.

TERMS Agent receives 15% commission on domestic sales. Agent receives 20% commission on foreign sales. Offers written contract; 30-day notice must be given to terminate contract.

RECENT SALES Rick Riordan's Books (Hyperion); *Something Extraordinary*, by Ben Clanton (Simon & Schuster); *The Baby Tree*, by Sophie Blackall (Nancy Paulsen Books/Penguin); *Fenway and Hattie*, by Victoria J. Coe (Putnam/Penguin); *The Meaning of Maggie*, by Megan Jean Sovern (Chronicle); *The Misadventures of the Family Fletcher*, by Dana Alison Levy (Random House); *Abrakapow!*, by Isaiah Campbell (Simon & Schuster); *Subway Love*, by Nora Raleigh Baskin (Candlewick)]

TIPS "Writing and illustrations stand on their own, so submissions should tell the most compelling stories possible—whether visually, in words, or both."

GELFMAN SCHNEIDER / ICM PARTNERS

850 7th Ave., Suite 903, New York NY 10019. (212)245-1993. **Fax:** (212)245-8678. **E-mail:** mail@gelfmanschneider.com. **Website:** www.gelfmanschneider.com. **Contact:** Jane Gelfman, Deborah Schneider. Member of AAR. Represents 300+ clients. 10% of clients are new/unpublished writers.

MEMBER AGENTS Jane Gelfman, Victoria Marini, Heather Mitchell.

REPRESENTS fiction and nonfiction books. **Considers these fiction areas:** historical, literary, mainstream, middle-grade, mystery, suspense, women's, young adult.

⚬— Does not want to receive romance, science fiction, westerns, or illustrated children's books.

HOW TO CONTACT Query. Send queries via snail mail only. No unsolicited mss. Please send a query letter, a synopsis, and a *sample chapter only*. Consult website for each agent's submission requirements. Responds in 1 month to queries. Responds in 2 months to mss.

TERMS Agent receives 15% commission on domestic sales. Agent receives 20% commission on foreign sales. Agent receives 15% commission on film sales. Offers written contract. Charges clients for photocopying and messengers/couriers.

THE SUSAN GOLOMB LITERARY AGENCY

540 President St., 3rd Floor, Brooklyn NY 11215. **Fax:** (212)239-9503. **E-mail:** susan@sgolombagency.com; krista@sgolombagency.com. **Contact:** Susan Golomb; Krista Ingebretson. Currently handles nonfiction books (50%), novels (40%), story collections (10%).

MEMBER AGENTS Susan Golomb (accepts queries); Krista Ingebretson (accepts queries).

REPRESENTS novels, short story collections. **Considers these fiction areas:** ethnic, historical, humor, literary, mainstream, satire, thriller, women's, young adult, chick lit.

⚬— "We specialize in literary and upmarket fiction and nonfiction that is original, vibrant and of excellent quality and craft. Nonfiction should be edifying, paradigm-shifting, fresh and entertaining." Actively seeking writers with strong voices. Does not want to receive genre fiction.

HOW TO CONTACT Query via mail with SASE or by e-mail. Will respond if interested. Submit outline/proposal, synopsis, 1 sample chapter, author bio. Obtains most new clients through recommendations from others, solicitations, and unsolicited queries.

TERMS Offers written contract.

RECENT SALES *The Kraus Project*, by Jonathan Franzen (FSG); *The Word Exchange*, by Alena Graedon (Doubleday); *The Flamethrowers*, by Rachel Kushner (Scribner); *The Book of Jonah*, by Joshua Feldman (Holt); *Last Stories* and *Other Stories* and *The Dying Grass*, by William T. Vollmann (Viking)

◖ IRENE GOODMAN LITERARY AGENCY

27 W. 24th St., Suite 700B, New York NY 10010. **E-mail:** irene.queries@irenegoodman.com. **Website:** www.irenegoodman.com. **Contact:** Irene Goodman, Miriam Kriss. Member of AAR.

MEMBER AGENTS Irene Goodman; Beth Vesel; Miriam Kriss; Barbara Poelle; Rachel Ekstrom.

REPRESENTS nonfiction, novels. **Considers these fiction areas:** crime, detective, historical, mystery, romance, thriller, women's, young adult.

⊶ "Specializes in the finest in commercial fiction and nonfiction. We have a strong background in women's voices, including mysteries, romance, women's fiction, thrillers, suspense. Historical fiction is one of Irene's particular passions and Miriam is fanatical about modern urban fantasies. In nonfiction, Irene is looking for topics on narrative history, social issues and trends, education, Judaica, Francophilia, Anglophilia, other cultures, animals, food, crafts, and memoir. Barbara is looking for commercial thrillers with strong female protagonists; Miriam is looking for urban fantasy and edgy science fiction/young adult. No children's picture books, screenplays, poetry, or inspirational fiction.

HOW TO CONTACT Query. Submit synopsis, first 10 pages. E-mail queries only! See the website submission page. No e-mail attachments. Responds in 2 months to queries. Consult website for each agent's submission guidelines.

RECENT SALES *The Ark*, by Boyd Morrison; *Isolation*, by C.J. Lyons; *The Sleepwalkers*, by Paul Grossman; *Dead Man's Moon*, by Devon Monk; *Becoming Marie Antoinette*, by Juliet Grey; *What's Up Down There*, by Lissa Rankin; *Beg for Mercy*, by Toni Andrews; *The Devil Inside*, by Jenna Black.

TIPS "We are receiving an unprecedented amount of e-mail queries. If you find that the mailbox is full, please try again in 2 weeks. E-mail queries to our personal addresses will not be answered. E-mails to our personal inboxes will be deleted."

◔ GOUMEN & SMIRNOVA LITERARY AGENCY

Nauki pr., 19/2 fl. 293, St. Petersburg 195220 Russia. **E-mail:** info@gs-agency.com. **Website:** www.gs-agency.com. **Contact:** Julia Goumen, Natalia Smirnova. Represents 20 clients. 10% of clients are new/unpublished writers. Currently handles nonfiction books (10%), novels (80%), story collections (5%), juvenile books (5%).

◔ Prior to becoming agents, both Ms. Goumen and Ms. Smirnova worked as foreign rights managers with an established Russian publisher selling translation rights for literary fiction.

MEMBER AGENTS Julia Goumen (translation rights, Russian language rights, film rights); Natalia Smirnova (translation rights, Russian language rights, film rights).

REPRESENTS nonfiction books, novels, short story collections, novellas, movie, TV, TV movie, sitcom. **Considers these fiction areas:** adventure, experimental, family, historical, horror, literary, mainstream, mystery, romance, thriller, young adult, women's.

⊶ "We are the first full-service agency in Russia, representing our authors in book publishing, film, television, and other areas. We are also the first agency, representing Russian authors worldwide, based in Russia. The agency also represents international authors, agents, and publishers in Russia. Our philosophy is to provide an individual approach to each author, finding the right publisher both at home and across international cultural and linguistic borders, developing original marketing and promotional strategies for each title." Actively seeking mss written in Russian, both literary and commercial; and foreign publishers and agents with the high-profile fiction and general nonfiction lists to represent in Russia. Does not want to receive unpublished mss in languages other than Russian, or any information irrelevant to our activity.

HOW TO CONTACT Submit synopsis, author bio. Accepts simultaneous submissions. Responds in 14 days to mss. Obtains most new clients through recommendations from others, solicitations.

TERMS Agent receives 20% commission on domestic sales. Agent receives 20% commission on foreign sales. Offers written contract, binding for 1 year; 2-months notice must be given to terminate contract.

○ ASHLEY GRAYSON LITERARY AGENCY

1342 W. 18th St., San Pedro CA 90732. **E-mail:** graysonagent@earthlink.net. **Website:** www.publishers marketplace.com/members/CGrayson/. Estab. 1976. Member of AAR. Represents 100 clients. 5% of clients are new/unpublished writers. Currently handles nonfiction books (20%), novels (50%), juvenile books (30%).

MEMBER AGENTS Ashley Grayson (fantasy, mystery, thrillers, young adult); Carolyn Grayson (chick lit, mystery, children's, nonfiction, women's fiction, romance, thrillers); Lois Winston (women's fiction, chick lit, mystery).

REPRESENTS nonfiction books, novels. **Considers these fiction areas:** fantasy, juvenile, middle-grade, multicultural, mystery, romance, science fiction, suspense, women's, young adult.

8—¬ "We represent literary and commercial fiction, as well as nonfiction for adults (self-help, parenting, pop culture, mind/body/spirit, true crime, business, science). We also represent fiction for younger readers (chapter books through young adult). We are seeking more mysteries and thrillers." Actively seeking previously published fiction authors.

HOW TO CONTACT The agency is temporarily closed to queries from *fiction* writers who are not published at book length (self-published or print-on-demand do not count). There are only 3 exceptions to this policy: (1) Unpublished authors who have received an offer from a reputable publisher, who need an agent before beginning contract negotiations; (2) Authors who are recommended by a published author, editor, or agent who has read the work in question; (3) Authors whom we have met at conferences and from whom we have requested submissions. Nonfiction authors who are recognized within their field or area may still query with proposals. Note: We cannot review self-published, subsidy-published, and POD-published works to evaluate moving them to mainstream publishers.

TERMS Agent receives 15% commission on domestic sales. Agent receives 20% commission on foreign sales.

RECENT SALES *Juliet Dove, Queen of Love*, by Bruce Coville (Harcourt); *Alosha*, by Christopher Pike (TOR); *Sleeping Freshmen Never Lie*, by David Lubar (Dutton); *Ball Don't Lie*, by Matt de la Peña (Delacorte); *Wiley & Grampa's Creature Features*, by Kirk Scroggs (10-book series, Little Brown); *Snitch*, by Allison van Diepen (Simon Pulse). Also represents: J.B. Cheaney (Knopf), Bruce Wetter (Atheneum).

TIPS "We do request revisions as they are required. We are longtime agents, professional and known in the business. We perform professionally for our clients and we ask the same of them."

○ SANFORD J. GREENBURGER ASSOCIATES, INC.

55 Fifth Ave., New York NY 10003. (212)206-5600. **Fax:** (212)463-8718. **Website:** www.greenburger.com. Member of AAR. Represents 500 clients.

MEMBER AGENTS Matt Bialer, LRibar@sjga.com (fantasy, science fiction, thrillers, and mysteries as well as a select group of literary writers; he also loves smart narrative nonfiction including books about current events, popular culture, biography, history, music, race, and sports); Brenda Bowen, queryBB@ sjga.com (literary fiction, writers and illustrators of picture books, chapter books, and middle-grade and teen fiction); Lisa Gallagher, lgsubmissions@sjga .com (accessible literary fiction, quality commercial women's fiction, crime fiction, lively narrative nonfiction); Faith Hamlin, fhamlin@sjga.com (receives submissions by referral); Heide Lange, queryHL@ sjga.com; Daniel Mandel, querydm@sjga.com (literary and commercial fiction, as well as memoirs and nonfiction about business, art, history, politics, sports, and popular culture); Courtney Miller-Callihan, cmiller@sjga.com (young adult, middle-grade, women's fiction, romance, and historical novels, as well as nonfiction projects on unusual topics, humor, pop culture, and lifestyle books); Nicholas Ellison, nellison@sjga.com; Chelsea Lindman, clindman@sjga.com (playful literary fiction, upmarket crime fiction, and forward-thinking or boundary-pushing nonfiction); Rachael Dillon Fried, rfried@ sjga.com (both fiction and nonfiction authors, with a keen interest in unique literary voices, women's fiction, narrative nonfiction, memoir, and comedy);

Lindsay Ribar, co-agents with Matt Bailer (young adult and middle-grade fiction).

REPRESENTS nonfiction books and novels. **Considers these fiction areas:** crime, fantasy, historical, literary, middle-grade, mystery, picture books, romance, science fiction, thriller, women's, young adult.

☞ No westerns. No screenplays.

HOW TO CONTACT E-query. "Please look at each agent's profile page for current information about what each agent is looking for and for the correct e-mail address to use for queries to that agent. Please be sure to use the correct query e-mail address for each agent." Accepts simultaneous submissions. Responds in 2 months to queries and mss. Obtains most new clients through recommendations from others.

TERMS Agent receives 15% commission on domestic sales. Agent receives 20% commission on foreign sales. Charges for photocopying and books for foreign and subsidiary rights submissions.

RECENT SALES *Inferno*, by Dan Brown; *Hidden Order*, by Brad Thor; *The Chalice*, by Nancy Bilveau; *Horns*, by Joe Hill.

THE GREENHOUSE LITERARY AGENCY

11308 Lapham Dr., Oakton VA 22124. **E-mail:** submissions@greenhouseliterary.com. **Website:** www.greenhouseliterary.com. Member of AAR. Other memberships include SCBWI. Represents 20 clients. 100% of clients are new/unpublished writers. Currently handles juvenile books (100%).

Sarah Davies has had an editorial and management career in children's publishing spanning 25 years; for 5 years prior to launching the Greenhouse she was publishing director of Macmillan Children's Books in London and publishing leading authors from both sides of the Atlantic.

MEMBER AGENTS Sarah Davies, vice president (middle-grade and young adult); **John M. Cusick**, agent (picture books, middle-grade, young adult, and boy books for kids); **Polly Nolan**, agent (fiction by United Kingdom, Irish, Commonwealth—including Australia, New Zealand, and India—authors, from picture books to young fiction series, through middle-grade and young adult).

REPRESENTS juvenile. **Considers these fiction areas:** juvenile, middle-grade, picture books, young adult.

☞ "We exclusively represent authors writing fiction for children and teens. The agency has offices in both the United States and United Kingdom, and Sarah Davies (who is British) personally represents authors to both markets. The agency's commission structure reflects this—taking 15% for sales to both U.S. and U.K., thus treating both as 'domestic' market.'" All genres of children's and young adult fiction—ages 5+. Does not want to receive nonfiction, poetry, picture books (text or illustration), or work aimed at adults; short stories, educational, or religious/inspirational work, preschool/novelty material, or screenplays.

HOW TO CONTACT Query 1 agent only. Put the target agent's name in the subject line. Paste the first 5 pages of your story (or your complete picture book) after the query. Obtains most new clients through recommendations from others, solicitations, conferences.

TERMS Agent receives 15% commission on domestic sales. Agent receives 25% commission on foreign sales. Offers written contract. This agency occasionally charges for submission copies to film agents or foreign publishers.

RECENT SALES *Fracture*, by Megan Miranda (Walker); *Paper Valentine*, by Brenna Yovanff (Razorbill); *Uses for Boys*, by Erica L. Scheidt (St Martin's); *Dark Inside*, by Jeyn Roberts (Simon & Schuster); *Breathe*, by Sarah Crossan (HarperCollins); *After the Snow*, by SD Crockett (Feiwel/Macmillan); *Sean Griswold's Head*, by Lindsey Leavitt (Hyperion).

WRITERS CONFERENCES Bologna Children's Book Fair, ALA and SCBWI conferences, BookExpo America.

TIPS "Before submitting material, authors should read the Greenhouse's 'Top 10 Tips for Authors of Children's Fiction' and carefully follow our submission guidelines which can be found on the website."

KATHRYN GREEN LITERARY AGENCY, LLC

250 West 57th St., Suite 2302, New York NY 10107. (212)245-4225. **Fax:** (212)245-4042. **E-mail:** query@kgreenagency.com. **Contact:** Kathy Green. Other memberships include Women's Media Group. Represents approximately 20 clients. 50% of clients are new/unpublished writers. Currently handles nonfiction books (50%), novels (25%), juvenile books (25%).

Prior to becoming an agent, Ms. Green was a book and magazine editor.

REPRESENTS nonfiction books, novels, short story collections, juvenile, middle-grade and young adult only. **Considers these fiction areas:** crime, detective, family saga, historical, humor, juvenile, literary, mainstream, middle-grade, mystery, police, romance, satire, suspense, thriller, women's, young adult.

Keeping the client list small means that writers receive my full attention throughout the process of getting their project published. Does not want to receive science fiction or fantasy.

HOW TO CONTACT Query to query@kgreenagency.com. Send no samples unless requested. Accepts simultaneous submissions. Responds in 1-2 months to mss. Obtains most new clients through recommendations from others, solicitations, conferences.

TERMS Agent receives 15% commission on domestic sales. Agent receives 20% commission on foreign sales. No written contract.

RECENT SALES *Welcome to the Dark House*; *Extinct for a Reason*; *The Arnifour Affair*; *The Civil War in Color*; *The Racecar Book*.

TIPS "This agency offers a written agreement."

JILL GRINBERG LITERARY AGENCY

16 Court St., Suite 3306, Brooklyn NY 11241. (212)620-5883. **Fax:** (212)627-4725. **E-mail:** info@grinbergliterary.com. **Website:** www.jillgrinbergliterary.com. Estab. 1999.

Prior to her current position, Ms. Grinberg was at Anderson Grinberg Literary Management.

MEMBER AGENTS Jill Grinberg, jill@jillgrinbergliterary.com; Cheryl Pientka, cheryl@jillgrinbergliterary.com; Katelyn Detweiler, katelyn@jillgrinbergliterary.com.

REPRESENTS nonfiction books, novels. **Considers these fiction areas:** fantasy, juvenile, literary, mainstream, romance, science fiction, young adult.

HOW TO CONTACT Please send your query letter to info@jillgrinbergliterary.com and attach the first 50 pages (fiction) or proposal (nonfiction) as a Word doc file. All submissions will be read, but electronic mail is preferred.

RECENT SALES *Cinder*, by Marissa Meyer; *The Hero's Guide to Saving Your Kingdom*, by Christopher Healy; *Kiss and Make Up*, by Katie Anderson; *i*, by T.J. Stiles; *Eon* and *Eona*, by Alison Goodman; *American Nations*, by Colin Woodard; HALO Trilogy, by Alex-andra Adornetto; *Babymouse*, by Jennifer and Matthew Holm; Uglies/Leviathan Trilogy, by Scott Westerfeld; *Liar*, by Justine Larbalestier; *Turtle in Paradise*, by Jennifer Holm; *Wisdom's Kiss* and *Dairy Queen*, by Catherine Gilbert Murdock.

TIPS "We prefer submissions by mail."

JILL GROSJEAN LITERARY AGENCY

1390 Millstone Rd., Sag Harbor NY 11963. (631)725-7419. **E-mail:** JillLit310@aol.com. **Contact:** Jill Grosjean. Estab. 1999.

Prior to becoming an agent, Ms. Grosjean managed an independent bookstore. She also worked in publishing and advertising.

REPRESENTS Considers these fiction areas: literary, mainstream, mystery.

Actively seeking literary novels and mysteries.

HOW TO CONTACT E-mail queries preferred, no attachments. No cold calls, please. Accepts simultaneous submissions, though when ms requested, requires exclusive reading time. Accepts simultaneous submissions. Responds in 1 week to queries; 1 month to mss. Obtains most new clients through recommendations and solicitations.

TERMS Agent receives 15% commission on domestic sales; 20% commission on foreign and film sales.

RECENT SALES *A Spark of Death*, *Fatal Induction*, and *Capacity for Murder*, by Bernadette Pajer (Poison Pen Press); *Neutral Ground*, by Greg Garrett (Bondfire Books); *Threading the Needle*, by Marie Bostwick (Kensington Publishing); *Tim Cratchit's Christmas Carol: A Novel of Scrooge's Legacy*, by Jim Piecuch (Simon & Schuster).

WRITERS CONFERENCES Thrillerfest; Texas Writer's League; Book Passage Mystery's Writer's Conference.

LAURA GROSS LITERARY AGENCY

P.O. Box 610326, Newton Highlands MA 02461. (617)964-2977. **Fax:** (617)964-3023. **E-mail:** query@lg-la.com. **Website:** www.lg-la.com. **Contact:** Laura Gross. Estab. 1988. Represents 30 clients. Currently handles nonfiction books (40%), novels (50%), scholarly books (10%).

Prior to becoming an agent, Ms. Gross was an editor.

REPRESENTS nonfiction books, novels. **Considers these fiction areas:** historical, literary, mainstream, mystery, suspense, thriller.

HOW TO CONTACT Queries accepted online via online form on LGLA website. Responds in several days to queries. Obtains most new clients through recommendations from others.

TERMS Agent receives 15% commission on domestic sales. Agent receives 20% commission on foreign sales. Offers written contract.

THE MITCHELL J. HAMILBURG AGENCY

149 S. Barrington Ave., #732, Los Angeles CA 90049. (310)471-4024. **Fax:** (310)471-9588. **Contact:** Michael Hamilburg. Estab. 1937. Signatory of WGA. Represents 70 clients. Currently handles nonfiction books (70%), novels (30%).

REPRESENTS nonfiction books, novels. **Considers these fiction areas:** glitz, New Age, adventure, experimental, feminist, humor, military, mystery, occult, regional, religious, romance, sports, thriller crime, mainstream, psychic.

HOW TO CONTACT Query with outline, 2 sample chapters, SASE. Responds in 1 month to mss. Obtains most new clients through recommendations from others, conferences, personal search.

TERMS Agent receives 10-15% commission on domestic sales.

HARTLINE LITERARY AGENCY

123 Queenston Dr., Pittsburgh PA 15235-5429. (412)829-2483. **Fax:** (412)829-2432. **E-mail:** joyce@hartlineliterary.com. **Website:** www.hartlineliterary.com. **Contact:** Joyce A. Hart. Represents 40 clients. 20% of clients are new/unpublished writers. Currently handles nonfiction books (40%), novels (60%).

MEMBER AGENTS Joyce A. Hart, principal agent (no unsolicited queries); Jim Hart; Terry Burns: terry@hartlineliterary.com (some young adult and middle-grade along with his other interests); Diana Flegal: diana@hartlineliterary.com; Linda Glaz, linda@hartlineliterary.com; Andy Scheer, andy@hartlineliterary.com.

REPRESENTS nonfiction books, novels.

⌐ "This agency specializes in the Christian bookseller market." Actively seeking adult fiction, self-help, nutritional books, devotional, and business. Does not want to receive erotica, gay/lesbian, fantasy, horror, etc.

HOW TO CONTACT E-query only. Target 1 agent only. "All e-mail submissions sent to Hartline Agents should be sent as a MS Word doc (or in rich text file format from another word processing program) at-tached to an e-mail with 'submission: title, authors name and word count' in the subject line. A proposal is a single document, not a collection of files. Place the query letter in the e-mail itself. Do not send the entire proposal in the body of the e-mail, and do not send PDF files." Further guidelines online. Accepts simultaneous submissions. Responds in 2 months to queries. Responds in 3 months to mss. Obtains most new clients through recommendations from others.

TERMS Agent receives 15% commission on domestic sales. Offers written contract.

RECENT SALES *Aurora, An American Experience in Quilt, Community and Craft*, and *A Flickering Light*, by Jane Kirkpatrick (Waterbrook Multnomah); *Oprah Doesn't Know My Name*, by Jane Kirkpatric (Zondervan); *Paper Roses, Scattered Petals, and Summer Rains*, by Amanda Cabot (Revell Books); *Blood Ransom*, by Lisa Harris (Zondervan); *I Don't Want a Divorce*, by David Clark (Revell Books); *Love Finds You in Hope, Kansas*, by Pamela Griffin (Summerside Press); *Journey to the Well*, by Diana Wallis Taylor (Revell Books); *Paper Bag Christmas, The Nine Lessons*, by Kevin Milne (Center Street); *When Your Aging Parent Needs Care*, by Arrington & Atchley (Harvest House); *Katie at Sixteen*, by Kim Vogel Sawyer (Zondervan); *A Promise of Spring*, by Kim Vogel Sawyer (Bethany House); *The Big 5-OH!*, by Sandra Bricker (Abingdon Press); *A Silent Terror & A Silent Stalker*, by Lynette Eason (Steeple Hill); Extreme Devotion series, by Kathi Macias (New Hope Publishers); *On the Wings of the Storm*, by Tamira Barley (Whitaker House); *Tribute*, by Graham Garrison (Kregel Publications); *The Birth to Five Book*, by Brenda Nixon (Revell Books); *Fat to Skinny Fast and Easy*, by Doug Varrieur (Sterling Publishers).

JOHN HAWKINS & ASSOCIATES, INC.

71 W. 23rd St., Suite 1600, New York NY 10010. (212)807-7040. **Fax:** (212)807-9555. **E-mail:** jha@jhalit.com. **Website:** www.jhalit.com. **Contact:** Moses Cardona (rights and translations); Liz Free (permissions); Warren Frazier, literary agent; Anne Hawkins, literary agent. Member of AAR. Represents 100+ clients. 5-10% of clients are new/unpublished writers. Currently handles nonfiction books (40%), novels (40%), juvenile books (20%).

MEMBER AGENTS Moses Cardona, moses@jhalit.com (commercial fiction, suspense, business, science, and multicultural fiction); William Reiss, reiss@

jhalit.com (historical narratives, biography, slightly off-beat fiction, suspense fiction and children's books); Warren Frazier, frazier@jhalit.com (nonfiction—technology, history, world affairs and foreign policy); Anne Hawkins ahawkins@jhalit.com (thrillers to literary fiction to serious nonfiction; she also has particular interests in science, history, public policy, medicine, and women's issues).

REPRESENTS nonfiction books, novels. **Considers these fiction areas:** commercial, historical, literary, multicultural, suspense, thriller.

HOW TO CONTACT Query. Include the word *Query* in the subject line. For fiction, include 1-3 chapters of your book as a single Word attachment. For nonfiction, include your proposal as a single attachment. E-mail a particular agent directly if you are targeting one. Accepts simultaneous submissions. Responds in 1 month to queries. Obtains most new clients through recommendations from others.

TERMS Agent receives 15% commission on domestic sales. Agent receives 20% commission on foreign sales. Charges clients for photocopying.

RECENT SALES *The Doll*, by Taylor Stevens; *Flora*, by Gail Godwin; *The Affairs of Others*, by Amy Loyd.

○ HEACOCK HILL LITERARY AGENCY, INC.

West Coast Office, 1020 Hollywood Way, #439, Burbank CA 91505. (818)951-6788. **E-mail:** agent@heacockhill.com. **Website:** www.heacockhill.com. **Contact:** Catt LeBaigue or Tom Dark. Estab. 2009. Member of AAR. Other memberships include SCBWI.

○ Prior to becoming an agent, Ms. LeBaigue spent 18 years with Sony Pictures and Warner Bros.

MEMBER AGENTS Tom Dark (adult fiction, nonfiction); Catt LeBaigue (juvenile fiction, adult nonfiction including arts, crafts, anthropology, astronomy, nature studies, ecology, body/mind/spirit, humanities, self-help).

REPRESENTS nonfiction, fiction. **Considers these fiction areas:** juvenile, middle-grade, picture books, young adult.

✂ Not presently accepting new clients for adult fiction. Please check the website for updates.

HOW TO CONTACT E-mail queries only. No unsolicited mss. No e-mail attachments. Responds in 1 week to queries. Obtains most new clients through recommendations from others, solicitations.

TERMS Offers written contract.

TIPS "Write an informative original e-query expressing your book idea, your qualifications, and short excerpts of the work. No unfinished work, please."

◐ RICHARD HENSHAW GROUP

145 W. 28th St., 12th Floor, New York NY 10001. (212)414-1172. **E-mail:** submissions@henshaw.com. **Website:** www.richardhenshawgroup.com. **Contact:** Rich Henshaw. Member of AAR. Other memberships include SinC, MWA, HWA, SFWA, RWA. 20% of clients are new/unpublished writers. Currently handles nonfiction books (35%), novels (65%).

○ Prior to opening his agency, Mr. Henshaw served as an agent with Richard Curtis Associates, Inc.

REPRESENTS nonfiction books, novels. **Considers these fiction areas:** crime, detective, fantasy, historical, horror, literary, mainstream, mystery, police, science fiction, supernatural, suspense, thriller, young adult.

✂ This agency specializes in thrillers, mysteries, science fiction, fantasy, and horror. "We only consider works between 65,000-150,000 words." We do not represent children's books, screenplays, short fiction, poetry, textbooks, scholarly works, or coffee-table books.

HOW TO CONTACT "Please feel free to submit a query letter in the form of an e-mail of fewer than 250 words to submissions@henshaw.com address. As of December 1, 2013, we will no longer accept letters or partials at our physical address unless we have agreed in advance to make an exception." Responds in 3 weeks to queries. Responds in 6 weeks to mss. Obtains most new clients through recommendations from others, solicitations, conferences.

TERMS Agent receives 15% commission on domestic sales. Agent receives 20% commission on foreign sales. No written contract. Charges clients for photocopying and book orders.

RECENT SALES *Though Not Dead*, by Dana Stabenow; *The Perfect Suspect*, by Margaret Coel; *City of Ruins*, by Kristine Kathryn Rusch; *A Dead Man's Tale*, by James D. Doss; *Wickedly Charming*, by Kristine Grayson; History of the World series by Susan Wise Bauer; *Notorious Pleasures*, by Elizabeth Hoyt.

TIPS "While we do not have any reason to believe that our submission guidelines will change in the near future, writers can find up-to-date submission policy information on our website. Always include an SASE with correct return postage."

ⓘ HIDDEN VALUE GROUP

27758 Santa Margarita Pkwy #361, Mission Viejo CA 92691. **E-mail:** bookquery@hiddenvaluegroup.com. **Website:** www.hiddenvaluegroup.com. **Contact:** Nancy Jernigan. Represents 55 clients. 10% of clients are new/unpublished writers.

MEMBER AGENTS Jeff Jernigan, jjernigan@hiddenvaluegroup.com (men's nonfiction, fiction, Bible studies/curriculum, marriage and family); Nancy Jernigan, njernigan@hiddenvaluegroup.com (nonfiction, women's issues, inspiration, marriage and family, fiction).

REPRESENTS nonfiction books and adult fiction; no poetry.

⊱— We are currently interested in receiving proposals in a variety of genres such as family/parenting/marriage, inspirational, self-help, men's and women's issues, business and fiction. No poetry or short stories. Actively seeking established fiction authors, and authors who are focusing on women's issues.

HOW TO CONTACT Query with SASE. Submit synopsis, 2 sample chapters, author bio, and marketing and speaking summary. Accepts queries to bookquery@hiddenvaluegroup.com. No fax queries. Responds in 1 month to queries. Responds in 1 month to mss. Obtains most new clients through recommendations from others, solicitations.

TERMS Agent receives 15% commission on domestic sales. Agent receives 15% commission on foreign sales. Offers written contract.

WRITERS CONFERENCES Glorieta Christian Writers Conference; CLASS Publishing Conference.

HOPKINS LITERARY ASSOCIATES

2117 Buffalo Rd., Suite 327, Rochester NY 14624-1507. (585)352-6268. **Contact:** Pam Hopkins. Member of AAR. Other memberships include RWA. Represents 30 clients. 5% of clients are new/unpublished writers. Currently handles novels (100%).

REPRESENTS novels. **Considers these fiction areas:** romance, women's.

⊱— This agency specializes in women's fiction, particularly historical, contemporary, and category romance, as well as mainstream work.

HOW TO CONTACT Regular mail with synopsis, 3 sample chapters (or first 50 pages), SASE. Accepts simultaneous submissions. Obtains most new clients

through recommendations from others, solicitations, conferences.

TERMS Agent receives 15% commission on domestic sales. Agent receives 20% commission on foreign sales. No written contract.

RECENT SALES The Wilting Bloom series, by Madeline Hunter (Berkley); *The Dead Travel Fast*, by Deanna Raybourn; *Baggage Claim*, by Tanya Michna (NAL).

WRITERS CONFERENCES RWA National Conference.

ⓘ ANDREA HURST LITERARY MANAGEMENT

P.O. Box 1467, Coupeville WA 98239. **E-mail:** andrea@andreahurst.com. **Website:** www.andreahurst.com. **Contact:** Andrea Hurst. Represents 100+ clients. 50% of clients are new/unpublished writers. Currently handles nonfiction books (50%), novels (50%).

ⓞ Prior to becoming an agent, Ms. Hurst was an acquisitions editor as well as a freelance editor and published writer.

MEMBER AGENTS Andrea Hurst, andrea@andreahurst.com (adult fiction, women's fiction, nonfiction, including personal growth, health and wellness, science, business, parenting, relationships, women's issues, animals, spirituality, metaphysical, psychological, cookbooks, and self-help); kate@andreahurst.com, represents young adult fiction and nonfiction and adult nonfiction.

REPRESENTS nonfiction, novels, juvenile books. **Considers these fiction areas:** fantasy, inspirational, juvenile, literary, mainstream, psychic, religious, romance, science fiction, supernatural, suspense, thriller, women's, young adult.

⊱— "We work directly with our signed authors to help them polish their work and their platform for optimum marketability. Our staff is always available to answer phone calls and e-mails from our authors, and we stay with a project until we have exhausted all publishing avenues." Actively seeking "well-written nonfiction by authors with a strong platform; superbly crafted fiction with depth that touches the mind and heart and all of our listed subjects." Does not want to receive science fiction, horror, western, poetry, or screenplays.

HOW TO CONTACT E-mail query with SASE. Submit outline/proposal, synopsis, 2 sample chapters, author bio. Query a specific agent after reviewing website. Use (agentfirstname)@andreahurst.com. Accepts simultaneous submissions. Obtains most new clients through recommendations from others, solicitations, conferences.

TERMS Agent receives 15% commission on domestic sales. Agent receives 20% commission on foreign sales. Offers written contract, binding for 6 to 12 months; 30-day notice must be given to terminate contract. This agency charges for postage. No reading fees.

RECENT SALES *Art of Healing*, by Bernie Siegel; *Truly, Madly, Deadly*, by Hannah Jayne; *Ultimate Poultry Cookbook*, by Chef John Ash; *The Guestbook*, by Andrea Hurst; *No Buddy Left Behind*, by Terrir Crisp and Cindy Hurn, Lyons Press; *A Year of Miracles*, by Dr. Bernie Siegel, NWL; *Selling Your Crafts on Etsy* (St. Martin's); *The Underground Detective Agency* (Kensington); *Alaskan Seafood Cookbook* (Globe Pequot); *Faith, Hope and Healing*, by Dr. Bernie Siegel (Rodale); *Code Name: Polar Ice*, by Jean-Michel Cousteau and James Fraioli (Gibbs Smith); *How to Host a Killer Party*, by Penny Warner (Berkley/Penguin).

WRITERS CONFERENCES San Francisco Writers Conference; Willamette Writers Conference; PNWA; Whidbey Island Writers Conference.

TIPS "Do your homework and submit a professional package. Get to know the agent you are submitting to by researching their website or meeting them at a conference. Perfect your craft: Write well and edit ruthlessly over and over again before submitting to an agent. Be realistic: Understand that publishing is a business and be prepared to prove why your book is marketable and how you will market it on your own. Be persistent! Andrea Hurst is no longer accepting unsolicited query letters. Unless you have been referred by one of our authors, an agent or publisher, please check our website for another appropriate agent. www.andreahurst.com."

⬤ INKWELL MANAGEMENT, LLC

521 Fifth Ave., 26th Floor, New York NY 10175. (212)922-3500. **Fax:** (212)922-0535. **E-mail:** submissions@inkwellmanagement.com. **Website:** www.inkwellmanagement.com. Represents 500 clients.

MEMBER AGENTS Monika Woods (literary and commercial fiction, young adult, memoir, and compelling nonfiction in popular culture, science, and current affairs); Lauren Smythe (smart narrative nonfiction: narrative journalism, modern history, biography, cultural criticism, personal essay, humor; personality-driven practical nonfiction: cookbooks, fashion and style; and contemporary literary fiction); David Hale Smith; Hannah Schwartz; Eliza Rothstein (literary and commercial fiction, narrative nonfiction, memoir, popular science, and food writing); Charlie Olsen (fiction, children's books, graphic novels and illustrated works, and compelling narrative nonfiction); Jacqueline Murphy; Alyssa Mozdzen; Nathaniel Jacks (memoir, narrative nonfiction, social sciences, health, current affairs, business, religion, and popular history, as well as fiction: literary and commercial, women's, young adult, historical, short story, among others); Alexis Hurley (literary and commercial fiction, memoir, narrative nonfiction and more); Allison Hunter (literary and commercial fiction [including romance], memoir, narrative nonfiction, cultural studies, pop culture and prescriptive titles, including cookbooks); David Forrer (literary, commercial, historical and crime fiction to suspense/thriller, humorous nonfiction and popular history); Catherine Drayton (best-selling authors of books for children, young adults, and women readers); William Callahan (nonfiction of all stripes, especially American history and memoir, pop culture and illustrated books, as well as voice-driven fiction that stands out from the crowd); Lizz Blaise (literary fiction, women's and young adult fiction, suspense, and psychological thriller); Kimberly Witherspoon; Michael V Carlisle; Richard Pine.

REPRESENTS nonfiction books, novels. **Considers these fiction areas:** commercial, crime, historical, literary, middle-grade, picture books, romance, short story collections, suspense, thriller, women's, young adult.

HOW TO CONTACT In the body of your e-mail, please include a query letter and a short writing sample (1-2 chapters). We currently accept submissions in all genres except screenplays. Due to the volume of queries we receive, our response time may take up to 2 months. Feel free to put "Query for [Agent Name]: [Your Book Title]" in the e-mail subject line. Obtains most new clients through recommendations from others.

TERMS Agent receives 15% commission on domestic sales. Agent receives 20% commission on foreign sales. Offers written contract.

TIPS "We will not read mss before receiving a letter of inquiry."

⊘ ⊚ ICM PARTNERS

730 Fifth Ave., New York NY 10019. (212)556-5600. **Website:** www.icmtalent.com. **Contact:** Literary Department. Member of AAR. Signatory of WGA.
REPRESENTS nonfiction, fiction, novels, juvenile books.

✂—∞ *We do not accept unsolicited submissions.*

HOW TO CONTACT This agency is generally not open to unsolicited submissions. However, some agents do attend conferences and meet writers then. The agents take referrals, as well. Obtains most new clients through recommendations from others.
TERMS Agent receives 15% commission on domestic sales. Agent receives 20% commission on foreign sales.

◐ JABBERWOCKY LITERARY AGENCY

49 West 45th St., New York NY 10036. (718)392-5985. **Website:** www.awfulagent.com. **Contact:** Joshua Bilmes. Other memberships include SFWA. Represents 40 clients. 15% of clients are new/unpublished writers. Currently handles nonfiction books (15%), novels (75%), scholarly books (5%), other (5% other).
MEMBER AGENTS Joshua Bilmes; Eddie Schneider; Lisa Rodgers; Sam Morgan.
REPRESENTS novels. **Considers these fiction areas:** action, adventure, contemporary issues, crime, detective, ethnic, family saga, fantasy, gay, glitz, historical, horror, humor, lesbian, literary, mainstream, middle-grade, police, psychic, regional, satire, science fiction, sports, supernatural, thriller, young adult.

✂—∞ This agency represents quite a lot of genre fiction and is actively seeking to increase the amount of nonfiction projects. It does not handle children's or picture books. Book-length material only—no poetry, articles, or short fiction.

HOW TO CONTACT "We are currently open to unsolicited queries. No e-mail, phone, or fax queries, please. Query with SASE. Please check our website, as there may be times during the year when we are not accepting queries. Query letter only; no ms material unless requested." Accepts simultaneous submissions. Responds in 3 weeks to queries. Obtains most new clients through solicitations, recommendation by current clients.
TERMS Agent receives 15% commission on domestic sales. Agent receives 20% commission on foreign sales. Offers written contract, binding for 1 year. Charges

clients for book purchases, photocopying, international book/ms mailing.
RECENT SALES Sold 30 U.S. and 100 foreign titles in the last year. *Dead Ever After*, by Charlaine Harris; *Words of Radiance*, by Brandon Sanderson; *The Daylight War*, by Peter V. Brett; *Limits of Power*, by Elizabeth Moon. Other clients include Tanya Huff, Simon Green, Jack Campbell, Myke Cole, William C. Dietz, and Marie Brennan.
TIPS "In approaching with a query, the most important things to us are your credits and your biographical background to the extent it's relevant to your work. I (and most agents) will ignore the adjectives you may choose to describe your own work."

J DE S ASSOCIATES, INC.

9 Shagbark Road, Wilson Point, South Norwalk CT 06854. (203)838-7571. **E-mail:** Jdespoel@aol.com. **Website:** www.jdesassociates.com. **Contact:** Jacques de Spoelberch. Represents 50 clients. Currently handles nonfiction books (50%), novels (50%).

◒ Prior to opening his agency, Mr. de Spoelberch was an editor with Houghton Mifflin.

REPRESENTS nonfiction books, novels. **Considers these fiction areas:** crime, detective, frontier, historical, juvenile, literary, mainstream, mystery, New Age, police, suspense, westerns, young adult.
HOW TO CONTACT Brief queries by regular mail and e-mail are welcomed for fiction and nonfiction, but kindly do not include sample proposals or other material unless specifically requested to do so. Responds in 2 months to queries. Obtains most new clients through recommendations from authors and other clients.
TERMS Agent receives 15% commission on domestic sales. Agent receives 20% commission on foreign sales. Charges clients for foreign postage and photocopying.
RECENT SALES Joshilyn Jackson's new novel *A Grown-Up Kind of Pretty* (Grand Central), Margaret George's final Tudor historical *Elizabeth I* (Penguin), the fifth in Leighton Gage's series of Brazilian thrillers *A Vine in the Blood* (Soho), Genevieve Graham's romance *Under the Same Sky* (Berkley Sensation), Hilary Holladay's biography of the early Beat Herbert Huncke, *American Hipster* (Magnus), Ron Rozelle's *My Boys and Girls Are in There: The 1937 New London School Explosion* (Texas A&M), the concluding novel in Dom Testa's young adult science fiction series, *The Galahad Legacy* (Tor), and Bruce Coston's

new collection of animal stories *The Gift of Pets* (St. Martin's Press).

JET LITERARY ASSOCIATES

941 Calle Mejia, #507, Santa Fe NM 87501. (505)780-0721. **E-mail:** etp@jetliterary.com. **Website:** www.jetliterary.com. **Contact:** Liz Trupin-Pulli. Represents 75 clients. 35% of clients are new/unpublished writers.
MEMBER AGENTS Liz Trupin-Pulli (adult and young adult fiction/nonfiction; romance, mysteries, parenting); Jim Trupin (adult fiction/nonfiction, military history, pop culture); Jessica Trupin, associate agent based in Seattle (adult fiction and nonfiction, children's and young adult, memoir, pop culture).
REPRESENTS nonfiction books, novels, short story collections. **Considers these fiction areas:** action, adventure, crime, detective, erotica, ethnic, gay, glitz, historical, humor, lesbian, literary, mainstream, mystery, police, romance, suspense, thriller, women's, young adult.

"JET was founded in New York in 1975, so we bring a wealth of knowledge and contacts, as well as quite a bit of expertise to our representation of writers." Actively seeking women's fiction, mysteries and narrative nonfiction. JET represents the full range of adult and young adult fiction and nonfiction, including humor and cookbooks. Does not want to receive science fiction, fantasy, horror, poetry, children's, or religious.

HOW TO CONTACT Query via e-mail. Responds in 1 week to queries. Responds in 8 weeks to mss. Obtains most new clients through recommendations from others, solicitations, conferences.
TERMS Agent receives 15% commission on domestic sales. Agent receives 10% commission on foreign sales. Offers written contract, binding for 3 years. This agency charges for reimbursement of mailing and any photocopying.
RECENT SALES Sold 22 books in 2009 including several ghostwriting contracts. *Mom-in-chief*, by Jamie Woolf (Wiley, 2009); *Dangerous Games* by Charlotte Mede (Kensington, 2009); *So You Think You Can Spell!* by David Grambs and Ellen Levine (Perigee, 2009); *Cut, Drop & Die*, by Joanna Campbell Slan (Midnight Ink, 2009).
WRITERS CONFERENCES Women Writing the West; Southwest Writers Conference; Florida Writers Association Conference.

TIPS Do not write cute queries—stick to a straightforward message that includes the title and what your book is about, why you are suited to write this particular book, and what you have written in the past (if anything), along with a bit of a bio.

VIRGINIA KIDD LITERARY AGENCY, INC.

P.O. Box 278, Milford PA 18337. (570)296-6205. **Fax:** (570)296-7266. **Website:** www.vk-agency.com. Other memberships include SFWA, SFRA. Represents 80 clients.
REPRESENTS novels. **Considers these fiction areas:** fantasy, science fiction speculative.

This agency specializes in science fiction and fantasy. "The Virginia Kidd Literary Agency is one of the longest established, science fiction specialized literary agencies in the world—with almost half a century of rich experience in the science fiction and fantasy genres. Our client list reads like a top-notch who's who of science fiction: Beth Bernobich, Gene Wolfe, Anne McCaffrey, Ted Chiang, Alan Dean Foster, and others set the bar very high indeed. Our authors have won Hugos, Nebulas, World Fantasy, Tiptree, National Book Award, PEN Malamud, SFWA Grandmaster, Gandalf, Locus Award, Margaret Edwards Award, IAMTW Lifetime Achievement Award (Grand Master), Rhysling Award, Author Emeritus SFWA, BSFA Award—and more. The point is, we represent the best of the best. We welcome queries from prospective and published authors."

HOW TO CONTACT Snail mail queries only.
TERMS Agent receives 15% commission on domestic sales. Agent receives 20-25% commission on foreign sales. Agent receives 20% commission on film sales. Offers written contract; 2-months notice must be given to terminate contract. Charges clients occasionally for extraordinary expenses.
RECENT SALES *Sagramanda*, by Alan Dean Foster (Pyr); *Incredible Good Fortune*, by Ursula K. Le Guin (Shambhala); *The Wizard and Soldier of Sidon*, by Gene Wolfe (Tor); *Voices and Powers*, by Ursula K. Le Guin (Harcourt); *Galileo's Children*, by Gardner Dozois (Pyr); *The Light Years Beneath My Feet* and *Running From the Deity*, by Alan Dean Foster (Del Ray); *Chasing Fire*, by Michelle Welch. Other clients

include Eleanor Arnason, Ted Chiang, Jack Skilling-stead, Daryl Gregory, Patricia Briggs, and the estates for James Tiptree, Jr., Murray Leinster, E.E. "Doc" Smith, R.A. Lafferty.

TIPS "If you have a completed novel that is of extraordinary quality, please send us a query."

HARVEY KLINGER, INC.

300 W. 55th St., Suite 11V, New York NY 10019. (212)581-7068. **Website:** www.harveyklinger.com. **Contact:** Harvey Klinger. Member of AAR. Represents 100 clients. 25% of clients are new/unpublished writers. Currently handles nonfiction books (50%), novels (50%).

MEMBER AGENTS Harvey Klinger; David Dunton (popular culture, music-related books, literary fiction, young adult, fiction, and memoirs); Sara Crowe (children's and young adult authors, adult fiction and non-fiction, foreign rights sales); Andrea Somberg (literary fiction, commercial fiction, romance, science fiction/fantasy, mysteries/thrillers, young adult, middle-grade, quality narrative nonfiction, popular culture, how-to, self-help, humor, interior design, cookbooks, health/fitness).

REPRESENTS nonfiction books, novels. **Considers these fiction areas:** action, adventure, crime, detective, family saga, glitz, literary, mainstream, mystery, police, suspense, thriller.

⌐ This agency specializes in big, mainstream, contemporary fiction and nonfiction.

HOW TO CONTACT Use online e-mail submission form on the website, or query with SASE via snail mail. No phone or fax queries. Don't send unsolicited mss or e-mail attachments. Responds in 2 months to queries and mss. Obtains most new clients through recommendations from others.

TERMS Agent receives 15% commission on domestic sales. Agent receives 25% commission on foreign sales. Offers written contract. Charges for photocopying mss and overseas postage for mss.

RECENT SALES *Woman of a Thousand Secrets*, by Barbara Wood; *I Am Not a Serial Killer*, by Dan Wells; untitled memoir, by Bob Mould; *Children of the Mist*, by Paula Quinn; *Tutored*, by Allison Whittenberg; *Will You Take Me As I Am*, by Michelle Mercer. Other clients include: George Taber, Terry Kay, Scott Mebus, Jacqueline Kolosov, Jonathan Maberry, Tara Altebrando, Alex McAuley, Eva Nagorski, Greg Kot, Jus-tine Musk, Alex McAuley, Nick Tasler, Ashley Kahn, Barbara De Angelis.

KNEERIM, WILLIAMS & BLOOM

90 Canal St., Boston MA 02114. **E-mail:** submissions@kwlit.com. **Website:** www.kwlit.com. Also located in New York and Washington D.C. Estab. 1990.

Prior to becoming an agent, Mr. Williams was a lawyer; Ms. Kneerim was a publisher and editor; Mr. Wasserman was an editor and journalist; Ms. Bloom worked in magazines; Ms. Flynn in academia.

MEMBER AGENTS Brettne Bloom, bloom@kwblit.com (memoir, history, current events, biography, travel, adventure, science, parenting, popular culture, cooking and food narratives, personal growth and women's issues, adult commercial and literary fiction and young adult fiction); Hope Denekamp; Katherine Flynn, flynn@kwblit.com (history, biography, politics, current affairs, adventure, nature, pop culture, science, and psychology for nonfiction and particularly loves exciting narrative nonfiction; she also represents both literary and commercial fiction, and is fond of urban or foreign locales, crime novels, insight into women's lives, biting wit, and historical settings); Jill Kneerim; Ike Williams; Carol Franco; Gerald Gross.

⌐ Actively seeking distinguished authors, experts, professionals, intellectuals, and serious writers.

HOW TO CONTACT E-query an individual agent. Send no attachments. Put *Query* in the subject line. Accepts simultaneous submissions. Obtains most new clients through recommendations from others.

KRAAS LITERARY AGENCY

E-mail: irenekraas@sbcglobal.net. **Website:** www.kraasliteraryagency.com. **Contact:** Irene Kraas. Represents 35 clients. 75% of clients are new/unpublished writers. Currently handles novels 100%.

MEMBER AGENTS Irene Kraas, principal.

REPRESENTS novels. **Considers these fiction areas:** literary, thriller, young adult.

⌐ This agency is interested in working with published writers, but that does not mean self-published writers. "The agency is ONLY accepting new mss in the genre of adult thrillers and mysteries. Submissions should be the first 10 pages of a completed ms embedded in an e-mail. I do not open attachments or go to websites." Does not want to receive short stories, plays, or poetry. This agency no longer represents adult fantasy or science fiction.

HOW TO CONTACT Query and e-mail the first 10 pages of a completed ms. Requires exclusive read on mss. Attachments aren't accepted. Accepts simultaneous submissions.

TERMS Offers written contract.

TIPS "I am interested in material—in any genre—that is truly, truly unique."

● STUART KRICHEVSKY LITERARY AGENCY, INC.

381 Park Ave. S., Suite 428, New York NY 10016. (212)725-5288. **Fax:** (212)725-5275. **Website:** www.skagency.com. Member of AAR.

MEMBER AGENTS Stuart Krichevsky (query@skagency.com); Shana Cohen (SCquery@skagency.com); Ross Harris (RHquery@skagency.com; voice-driven humor and memoir, books on popular culture and our society, narrative nonfiction and select contemporary fiction).

REPRESENTS nonfiction books, novels. **Considers these fiction areas:** contemporary issues.

⊶ "Areas of interest include history, adventure, politics, and current affairs, biography, science and natural history, technology and culture, business and memoir. Our fiction list includes authors of literary and commercial fiction, science fiction and fantasy, and young adult fiction."

HOW TO CONTACT "Please send a query letter and the first few (up to 10) pages of your ms or proposal in the body of an e-mail (not an attachment) to one of the addresses below. For security reasons, we do not open attachments." Responds if interested. Obtains most new clients through recommendations from others, solicitations.

EDITE KROLL LITERARY AGENCY, INC.

20 Cross St., Saco ME 04072. (207)283-8797. **Fax:** (207)283-8799. **E-mail:** ekroll@maine.rr.com. **Contact:** Edite Kroll. Represents 45 clients. 20% of clients are new/unpublished writers. Currently handles nonfiction books (40%), novels (5%), juvenile books (40%), scholarly books (5%), other.

○ Prior to opening her agency, Ms. Kroll served as a book editor and translator.

REPRESENTS nonfiction books, novels, very selective, juvenile, scholarly. **Considers these fiction areas:**

juvenile, literary, picture books, young adult, middle-grade, adult.

⊶ "We represent writers and writer-artists of both adult and children's books. We have a special focus on international feminist writers, women writers, and artists who write their own books (including children's and humor books)." Actively seeking artists who write their own books and international feminists who write in English. Does not want to receive genre (mysteries, thrillers, diet, cookery, etc.), photography books, coffee-table books, romance, or commercial fiction.

HOW TO CONTACT Query with SASE. Submit outline/proposal, synopsis, 1-2 sample chapters, author bio, entire ms if sending picture book. No phone queries. Responds in 2-4 weeks to queries. Responds in 4-8 weeks to mss. Obtains most new clients through recommendations from others.

TERMS Agent receives 15% commission on domestic sales. Agent receives 20% commission on foreign sales. Offers written contract; 30-day notice must be given to terminate contract. Charges clients for photocopying and legal fees with prior approval from writer.

RECENT SALES Sold 12 domestic/30 foreign titles in the last year. This agency prefers not to share information on specific sales. Clients include Shel Silverstein estate, Suzy Becker, Geoffrey Hayes, Henrik Drescher, Charlotte Kasl, Gloria Skurzynski, Fatema Mernissa.

TIPS "Please do your research so you won't send me books/proposals I specifically excluded."

● KT LITERARY, LLC

9249 S. Broadway, #200-543, Highlands Ranch CO 80129. (720)344-4728. **Fax:** (720)344-4728. **E-mail:** queries@ktliterary.com. **Website:** ktliterary.com. **Contact:** Kate Schafer Testerman. Member of AAR. Other memberships include SCBWI. Represents 20 clients. 60% of clients are new/unpublished writers.

○ Prior to her current position, Ms. Schafer was an agent with Janklow & Nesbit.

REPRESENTS Considers these fiction areas: middle-grade, young adult.

⊶ "I'm bringing my years of experience in the New York publishing scene, as well as my lifelong love of reading, to a vibrant area for writers, proving that great work can be found, and sold, from anywhere. We're thrilled to be actively seeking new clients writing brilliant, funny, original middle-grade and young adult fiction, both literary and commercial." Does not want picture books, serious nonfiction, and adult literary fiction.

HOW TO CONTACT "To submit to kt literary, please e-mail us a query letter with the first 3 pages of your ms in the body of the e-mail. The subject line of your e-mail should include the word *Query* along with the title of your ms. Queries should not contain attachments. Attachments will not be read, and queries containing attachments will be deleted unread. We aim to reply to all queries within 2 weeks of receipt. No snail mail queries." Responds in 2 weeks to queries. Responds in 2 months to mss. Obtains most new clients through recommendations from others, solicitations, conferences.

TERMS Agent receives 15% commission on domestic sales. Agent receives 20% commission on foreign sales. Offers written contract; 30-day notice must be given to terminate contract.

RECENT SALES *Albatross*, by Julie Bloss; *The Last Good Place of Lily Odilon*, by Sara Beitia; *Texting the Underworld*, by Ellen Booraem. A full list of clients is available on the agency website.

WRITERS CONFERENCES Various SCBWI conferences, BookExpo.

TIPS "If we like your query, we'll ask for more. Continuing advice is offered regularly on my blog 'Ask Daphne,' which can be accessed from my website."

THE LA LITERARY AGENCY

P.O. Box 46370, Los Angeles CA 90046. (323)654-5288. **E-mail:** ann@laliteraryagency.com; mail@laliteraryagency.com. **Website:** www.laliteraryagency.com. **Contact:** Ann Cashman.

Prior to becoming an agent, Eric Lasher worked in broadcasting and publishing in New York and Los Angeles. Prior to opening the agency, Maureen Lasher worked in New York at Prentice-Hall, Liveright, and Random House.

MEMBER AGENTS Ann Cashman, Eric Lasher, Maureen Lasher.

REPRESENTS nonfiction books, novels. **Considers these fiction areas:** commercial, literary.

HOW TO CONTACT Prefers submissions by mail, but welcomes e-mail submissions as well. Nonfiction: query letter and book proposal. Fiction: Query with outline and first 50 pages as an attachment, 1 sample chapter. Accepts simultaneous submissions.

RECENT SALES *The Fourth Trimester*, by Susan Brink (University of California Press); *Rebels in Paradise*, by Hunter Drohojowska-Philp (Holt); *La Cucina Mexicana*, by Marilyn Tausend (UC Press); *Degas, Renoir and the Orpheus Clock*, by Simon Goodman (Scribner); *Cake Balls*, by DeDe Wilson (Harvard Common Press); *Michael Jackson: Before He Was King*, by Todd Gray (Chronicle).

PETER LAMPACK AGENCY, INC.

The Empire State Building, 350 Fifth Ave., Suite 5300, New York NY 10118. (212)687-9106. **Fax:** (212)687-9109. **E-mail:** andrew@peterlampackagency.com. **Website:** www.peterlampackagency.com. **Contact:** Andrew Lampack.

REPRESENTS nonfiction books, novels. **Considers these fiction areas:** adventure, commercial, crime, detective, family saga, literary, mainstream, mystery, police, suspense, thriller.

"This agency specializes in commercial fiction, and nonfiction by recognized experts." Actively seeking literary and commercial fiction, thrillers, mysteries, suspense, and psychological thrillers. Does not want to receive horror, romance, science fiction, westerns, historical literary fiction, or academic material.

HOW TO CONTACT The Peter Lampack Agency no longer accepts material through conventional mail. E-queries only. When submitting, you should include a cover letter, author biography, and a one- or two-page synopsis. Please do not send more than 1 sample chapter of your ms at a time. Due to the extremely high volume of submissions, we ask that you allow 4-6 weeks for a response. Accepts simultaneous submissions. Obtains most new clients through referrals made by clients.

TERMS Agent receives 15% commission on domestic sales. Agent receives 20% commission on foreign sales.

RECENT SALES *Spartan Gold*, by Clive Cussler with Grant Blackwood; *The Wrecker*, by Clive Cussler with Justin Scott; *Medusa*, by Clive Cussler and Paul Kemprecos; *Silent Sea* by Clive Cussler with Jack Dubrul; *Summertime*, by J.M. Coetzee; *Dreaming in French*, by Megan McAndrew; *Time Pirate*, by Ted Bell.

WRITERS CONFERENCES BookExpo America; Mystery Writers of America.

TIPS "Submit only your best work for consideration. Have a very specific agenda of goals you wish your prospective agent to accomplish for you. Provide the agent with a comprehensive statement of your credentials—educational and professional accomplishments."

◐ LAURA LANGLIE, LITERARY AGENT

147-149 Green St., Hudson NY 12534. (518)828-4708. **Fax:** (518)828-4787. **E-mail:** laura@lauralanglie.com. **Contact:** Laura Langlie. Represents 25 clients. 50% of clients are new/unpublished writers. Currently handles nonfiction books (15%), novels (58%), story collections (2%), juvenile books (25%).

○ Prior to opening her agency, Ms. Langlie worked in publishing for 7 years and as an agent at Kidde, Hoyt & Picard for 6 years.

REPRESENTS Considers these fiction areas: crime, detective, ethnic, feminist, historical, humor, juvenile, literary, mainstream, mystery, police, suspense, thriller, young adult, mainstream.

⚷ "I'm very involved with and committed to my clients. Most of my clients come to me via recommendations from other agents, clients, and editors. I've met very few at conferences. I've often sought out writers for projects, and I still find new clients via the traditional query letter." Does not want to receive how-to, children's picture books, hardcore science fiction, poetry, men's adventure, or erotica.

HOW TO CONTACT Query with SASE. Accepts queries via fax. Accepts simultaneous submissions. Responds in 1 week to queries. Responds in 1 month to mss. Obtains most new clients through recommendations, submissions.

TERMS Agent receives 15% commission on domestic sales. Agent receives 20% commission on foreign and dramatic sales. No written contract.

RECENT SALES Sold 15 titles in the last year. *As Close As Hands and Feet*, by Emily Arsenault (William Morrow); *The Aviator's Wife*, by Melanie Benjamin (Delacorte Press); *Free Verse* and *Ashes to Asheville*, by Sarah Dooley (G.P. Putnam's Son's/Penguin Young Reader's Group); *Miss Dimple Suspects*, by Mignon F. Ballard (St. Martin's Press); *Awaken*, by Meg Cabot (Scholastic, Inc.); *Size 12 and Ready to Rock*, by Meg Cabot (William Morrow); *Adaptation* and *Inheritance*, by Malinda Lo (Little, Brown & Co Books for Young Readers); *One Tough Chick*, by Les-

lie Margolis (Bloomsbury); *The Elite Gymnasts*, by Dominique Moceanu and Alicia Thompson (Disney/Hyperion); *The Lighthouse Road*, by Peter Geye (Unbridled Books); *The Nazi and the Psychiatrist*, by Jack El-Hai (Public Affairs Books); *The Last Animal*, by Abby Geni (Counterpoint Press); *Something Resembling Love*, by Mary Hogan (William Morrow); *Little Wolves*, by Thomas Maltman (Soho Press).

TIPS "Be complete, forthright, and clear in your communications. Do your research and know what a particular agent represents."

◐ MICHAEL LARSEN/ELIZABETH POMADA, LITERARY AGENTS

1029 Jones St., San Francisco CA 94109. (415)673-0939. **E-mail:** larsenpoma@aol.com. **Website:** www.larsenpomada.com. **Contact:** Mike Larsen, Elizabeth Pomada. Member of AAR. Other memberships include Authors Guild, ASJA, PEN, WNBA, California Writers Club, National Speakers Association. Represents 100 clients. 40-45% of clients are new/unpublished writers. Currently handles nonfiction books (70%), novels (30%).

○ Prior to opening their agency, Mr. Larsen and Ms. Pomada were promotion executives for major publishing houses. Mr. Larsen worked for Morrow, Bantam, and Pyramid (now part of Berkley); Ms. Pomada worked at Holt, David McKay, and Dial Press. Mr. Larsen is the author of the 4th edition of *How to Write a Book Proposal* and *How to Get a Literary Agent*, as well as the co-author of *Guerilla Marketing for Writers: 100 Weapons for Selling Your Work*, which was republished in September 2009.

MEMBER AGENTS Michael Larsen (nonfiction); Elizabeth Pomada (fiction and narrative nonfiction); Lynn Brown (associate agent, new in 2014).

REPRESENTS Considers these fiction areas: action, adventure, contemporary issues, crime, detective, ethnic, experimental, family saga, feminist, gay, glitz, historical, humor, inspirational, lesbian, literary, mainstream, mystery, police, religious, romance, satire, suspense.

⚷ We have diverse tastes. We look for fresh voices and new ideas. We handle literary, commercial, and genre fiction, and the full range of nonfiction books. Does not want to receive children's books, plays, short stories, screenplays, pornography, poetry, or stories of abuse.

HOW TO CONTACT Query with SASE. **Elizabeth Pomada** handles literary and commercial fiction, romance, thrillers, mysteries, narrative nonfiction, and mainstream women's fiction. If you have completed a novel, **please e-mail the first 10 pages and a 2-page synopsis to larsenpoma@aol.com.** Use 14-point typeface, double-space, and send as an e-mail letter with no attachments. For nonfiction, please read Michael's *How to Write a Book Proposal* book—available through your library or bookstore, and through our website—so you will know exactly what editors need. Then, before you start writing, send him the title, subtitle, and your promotion plan via conventional mail (with SASE) or e-mail. If sent as e-mail, please include the information in the body of your e-mail with no attachments. Please allow up to 2 weeks for a response. See each agent's page on the website for contact and submission information. Responds in 8 weeks to pages or submissions.

TERMS Agent receives 15% commission on domestic sales. Agent receives 20% (30% for Asia) commission on foreign sales. May charge for printing, postage for multiple submissions, foreign mail, foreign phone calls, galleys, books, legal fees.

RECENT SALES Sold at least 15 titles in the last year. *Secrets of the Tudor Court*, by D. Bogden (Kensington); *Zen & the Art of Horse Training*, by Allan Hamilton, MD (Storey Pub.); *The Solemn Lantern Maker* by Merlinda Bobis (Delta); *Bite Marks*, the fifth book in an urban fantasy series by J.D. Rardin (Orbit/Grand Central); *The Iron King*, by Julie Karawa (Harlequin Teen).

WRITERS CONFERENCES This agency organizes the annual San Francisco Writers Conference (www.sfwriters.org).

TIPS "We love helping writers get the rewards and recognition they deserve. If you can write books that meet the needs of the marketplace and you can promote your books, now is the best time ever to be a writer. We must find new writers to make a living, so we are very eager to hear from new writers whose work will interest large houses, and nonfiction writers who can promote their books. For a list of recent sales, helpful info, and 3 ways to make yourself irresistible to any publisher, please visit our website."

◎ THE STEVE LAUBE AGENCY

5025 N. Central Ave., #635, Phoenix AZ 85012. (602)336-8910. **E-mail:** krichards@stevelaube.com.

Website: www.stevelaube.com. **Contact:** Steve Laube, president, Tamela Hancock Murray, Karen Ball, or Dan Balow. Other memberships include CBA. Represents 60+ clients. 5% of clients are new/unpublished writers.

○ Prior to becoming an agent, Mr. Laube worked 11 years as a Christian bookseller and 11 years as editorial director of nonfiction with Bethany House Publishers. Mrs. Murray was an accomplished novelist and agent. Mrs. Ball was an executive editor with Tyndale, Multnomah, Zondervan, and B&H. Mr. Balow was marketing director for the Left Behind series at Tyndale.

REPRESENTS nonfiction books, novels. **Considers these fiction areas:** inspirational, religious.

⮕ Primarily serves the Christian market (CBA). Actively seeking Christian fiction and religious nonfiction. Does not want to receive children's picture books, poetry, or cookbooks.

HOW TO CONTACT Submit proposal package, outline, 3 sample chapters, SASE. For e-mail submissions, attach as Word doc or PDF. Consult website for guidelines. Accepts simultaneous submissions. Responds in 6-8 weeks to queries. Obtains most new clients through recommendations from others, solicitations, conferences.

TERMS Agent receives 15% commission on domestic sales. Agent receives 20% commission on foreign sales. Offers written contract; 30-day notice must be given to terminate contract.

RECENT SALES Sold 200 titles in the last year. Clients include Deborah Raney, Allison Bottke, H. Norman Wright, Ellie Kay, Jack Cavanaugh, Karen Ball, Susan May Warren, Lisa Bergren, Cindy Woodsmall, Karol Ladd, Judith Pella, Margaret Daley, William Lane Craig, Ginny Aiken, Kim Vogel Sawyer, Mesu Andrews, Mary Hunt, Hugh Ross, Bill and Pam Farrel, Ronie Kendig.

WRITERS CONFERENCES Mount Hermon Christian Writers Conference; American Christian Fiction Writers Conference; ACFW.

LEVINE GREENBERG LITERARY AGENCY, INC.

307 Seventh Ave., Suite 2407, New York NY 10001. (212)337-0934. **Fax:** (212)337-0948. **E-mail:** submit@levinegreenberg.com. **Website:** www.levinegreenberg.com. Member of AAR. Represents 250 clients. 33% of

clients are new/unpublished writers. Currently handles nonfiction books (70%), novels (30%).

○ Prior to opening his agency, Mr. Levine served as vice president of the Bank Street College of Education.

MEMBER AGENTS Jim Levine; Stephanie Rostan (adult fiction, nonfiction, young adult); Melissa Rowland; Daniel Greenberg (literary fiction; nonfiction: popular culture, narrative nonfiction, memoir, and humor); Victoria Skurnick; Danielle Svetcov; Elizabeth Fisher; Lindsay Edgecombe (narrative nonfiction, memoir, lifestyle and health, illustrated books, as well as literary fiction); Monika Verma (nonfiction: humor, pop culture, memoir, narrative nonfiction and style and fashion titles); Kerry Sparks (young adult and middle-grade); Tim Wojcik; Jamie Maurer; Miek Coccia; Arielle Eckstut; Kirsten Wolf.

REPRESENTS nonfiction books, novels. **Considers these fiction areas:** literary, mainstream, middle-grade, mystery, thriller, women's, young adult.

➣ This agency specializes in business, psychology, parenting, health/medicine, narrative nonfiction, spirituality, religion, women's issues, and commercial fiction.

HOW TO CONTACT See website for full submission procedure at "How to Submit." Or use our e-mail address (submit@levinegreenberg.com) if you prefer, or online submission form. Do not submit directly to agents. Prefers electronic submissions. Cannot respond to submissions by mail. Do not attach more than 50 pages. Obtains most new clients through recommendations from others.

TERMS Agent receives 15% commission on domestic sales. Agent receives 20% commission on foreign sales. Offers written contract. Charges clients for out-of-pocket expenses—telephone, fax, postage, photocopying—directly connected to the project.

RECENT SALES *Gone Girl*, by Gillian Flynn; *Hyperbole and a Half*, by Allie Brosh; *Our Dumb Century*, by editors of the The Onion; *Predictably Irrational*, by Dan Ariely.

WRITERS CONFERENCES ASJA Writers Conference.

TIPS "We focus on editorial development, business representation, and publicity and marketing strategy."

◐ **PAUL S. LEVINE LITERARY AGENCY**
1054 Superba Ave., Venice CA 90291. (310)450-6711. **Fax:** (310)450-0181. **E-mail:** paul@paulslevinelit.com.

Website: www.paulslevinelit.com. **Contact:** Paul S. Levine. Other memberships include the State Bar of California. Represents over 100 clients. 75% of clients are new/unpublished writers. Currently handles nonfiction books (60%), novels (10%), movie scripts (10%), TV scripts (5%), juvenile books (5%).

MEMBER AGENTS Paul S. Levine (children's and young adult fiction and nonfiction, adult fiction and nonfiction except science fiction, fantasy, and horror); Loren R. Grossman (archaeology, art/photography/architecture, gardening, education, health, medicine, science).

REPRESENTS nonfiction books, novels, episodic drama, movie, TV, movie scripts, feature film, TV movie of the week, sitcom, animation, documentary, miniseries syndicated material, reality show. **Considers these fiction areas:** action, adventure, comic books, confession, crime, detective, erotica, ethnic, experimental, family saga, feminist, frontier, gay, glitz, historical, humor, inspirational, lesbian, literary, mainstream, mystery, police, regional, religious, romance, satire, sports, suspense, thriller, westerns.

➣ Does not want to receive science fiction, fantasy, or horror.

HOW TO CONTACT Query with SASE. Accepts simultaneous submissions. Responds in 1 day to queries. Responds in 6-8 weeks to mss. Obtains most new clients through conferences, referrals, listings on various websites, and in directories.

TERMS Agent receives 15% commission on domestic sales. Offers written contract. Charges for postage and actual, out-of-pocket costs only.

RECENT SALES Sold 8 books in the last year.

WRITERS CONFERENCES Willamette Writers Conference; San Francisco Writers Conference; Santa Barbara Writers Conference and many others.

TIPS "Write good, sellable books."

◐ **LIPPINCOTT MASSIE MCQUILKIN**
27 West 20th Street, Suite 305, New York NY 10011. **Fax:** (212)352-2059. **E-mail:** info@lmqlit.com. **Website:** www.lmqlit.com.

MEMBER AGENTS Shannon O'Neill (writing that informs, intrigues, or inspires: special interests include narrative nonfiction, popular science, current affairs, the history of ideas, and literary and upmarket fiction); **Laney Katz Becker**; **Kent Wolf** (literary fiction, upmarket women's fiction, memoir, pop culture, all types of narrative nonfiction, and select young adult); **Ethan Bassoff** (emerging and established writers of literary and crime fiction and narrative nonfiction including history, science, humor, and sports writing); **Jason Anthony** (specializes in young adult and commercial fiction and most areas of nonfiction, including pop culture, memoir, true crime, and general psychology); **Will Lippincott** (politics, current events, narrative nonfiction, and history); **Maria Massie** (literary fiction, memoir, and cultural history); **Rob McQuilkin** (fiction, memoir, history, sociology, psychology, and graphic works).

REPRESENTS nonfiction books, novels, short story collections, scholarly graphic novels. **Considers these fiction areas:** action, adventure, cartoon, comic books, confession, family saga, feminist, gay, historical, humor, lesbian, literary, mainstream, regional, satire.

8—⚓ "LMQ focuses on bringing new voices in literary and commercial fiction to the market, as well as popularizing the ideas and arguments of scholars in the fields of history, psychology, sociology, political science, and current affairs. Actively seeking fiction writers who already have credits in magazines and quarterlies, as well as nonfiction writers who already have a media platform or some kind of a university affiliation." Does not want to receive romance, genre fiction, or children's material.

HOW TO CONTACT E-query. "Include the word *Query* as well as the agent you are querying in the subject line of your e-mail (i.e., 'Query for Maria Massie'). If your project is fiction, please also include the first 5-10 pages pasted into the body of your e-mail. We look forward to reviewing your work." Accepts simultaneous submissions. Obtains most new clients through recommendations from others, solicitations, conferences.

TERMS Agent receives 15% commission on domestic sales. Agent receives 20% commission on foreign sales. Offers written contract; 30-day notice must be given to terminate contract. Only charges for reasonable business expenses upon successful sale.

RECENT SALES Clients include: Peter Ho Davies, Kim Addonizio, Natasha Trethewey, Anne Carson, David Sirota, Katie Crouch, Uwen Akpan, Lydia Millet, Tom Perrotta, Jonathan Lopez, Chris Hayes, Caroline Weber.

◐ THE LITERARY GROUP INTERNATIONAL

1357 Broadway,, Suite 316, New York NY 10018. (212)400-1494, ext. 380. **Website:** www.theliterarygroup.com. **Contact:** Frank Weimann. 1900 Ave. of the Stars, 25 Fl., Los Angeles, CA 90067. (310)282-8961; **Fax:** (310) 282-8903. 65% of clients are new/unpublished writers. Currently handles nonfiction (50%), fiction (50%).

MEMBER AGENTS Frank Weimann.

REPRESENTS nonfiction books, novels graphic novels. **Considers these fiction areas:** adventure, contemporary issues, detective, ethnic, experimental, family saga, fantasy, feminist, historical, horror, humor, literary, multicultural, mystery, psychic, regional, romance, sports, thriller, young adult, graphic novels.

8—⚓ This agency specializes in nonfiction (memoir, military, history, biography, sports, how-to).

HOW TO CONTACT Query. Prefers to read materials exclusively. Only responds if interested. Obtains most new clients through referrals, writers conferences, query letters.

TERMS Agent receives 15% commission on domestic sales. Agent receives 20% commission on foreign sales. Offers written contract; 30-day notice must be given to terminate contract.

RECENT SALES *Living With Honor,* by Sal Giunta (Simon and Schuster); *Siempre,* by JR Darhower (Pocket Books), *Wear Your Dreams: My Life in Tattoos,* by Ed Hardy (St. Martin's Press); *The New Jewish Table: Modern Seasonal Recipes for Traditional Dishes,* by Todd Gray and Ellen Kassoff Gray (St. Martin's Press); *Grace, Gold, and Glory: My Leap of Faith,* by Gabby Douglas (HarperCollins).

WRITERS CONFERENCES San Diego State University Writers Conference; Agents and Editors Conference; NAHJ Convention in Puerto Rico, others.

◑ LIZA DAWSON ASSOCIATES

350 Seventh Ave., Suite 2003, New York NY 10001. (212)465-9071. **Website:** www.lizadawsonassociates.com. **Contact:** Anna Olswanger. Member of AAR. Other memberships include MWA, Women's Media Group. Represents 50+ clients. 30% of clients are new/unpublished writers.

◗ Prior to becoming an agent, Ms. Dawson was an editor for 20 years, spending 11 years at William Morrow as vice president and 2 years at Putnam as executive editor. Ms. Blasdell was a senior editor at HarperCollins and Avon. Ms. Olswanger is an author.

MEMBER AGENTS Liza Dawson (plot-driven literary fiction, historicals, thrillers, suspense, parenting books, history, psychology [both popular and clinical], politics, narrative nonfiction and memoirs); Caitlin Blasdell (science fiction, fantasy [both adult and young adult], parenting, business, thrillers, and women's fiction); Anna Olswanger (gift books for adults, young adult fiction and nonfiction, children's illustrated books, and Judaica); Havis Dawson (business books, how-to and practical books, spirituality, fantasy, Southern-culture fiction, and military memoirs); Hannah Bowman (commercial fiction, especially science fiction and fantasy; women's fiction; cozy mysteries; romance; young adult; also nonfiction in the areas of mathematics, science, and spirituality); Monica Odom (literary fiction, women's fiction, voice-driven memoir, nonfiction in the areas of pop culture, food and cooking, history, politics, and current affairs).

REPRESENTS nonfiction books, novels, and gift books (Olswanger only). **Considers these fiction areas:** commercial, fantasy, historical, literary, mystery, regional, romance, science fiction, suspense, thriller, women's, young adult fantasy and science fiction (Blasdell only).

☛ This agency specializes in readable literary fiction, thrillers, mainstream historicals, women's fiction, academics, historians, business, journalists, and psychology.

HOW TO CONTACT Query by e-mail only. No phone calls. Each of these agents has their own specific submission requirements, which you can find online at their website. querymonica@LizaDawsonAssociates.com; queryHannah@LizaDawsonAssociates.com; queryhavis@LizaDawsonAssociates.com; queryanna@LizaDawsonAssociates.com; queryCaitlin@LizaDawsonAssociates.com; queryliza@LizaDawsonAssociates.com. Responds in 4 weeks to queries; 8 weeks to mss. Obtains most new clients through recommendations from others, conferences.

TERMS Agent receives 15% commission on domestic sales. Agent receives 20% commission on foreign sales. Offers written contract.

○ LOWENSTEIN ASSOCIATES INC.

121 W. 27th St., Suite 501, New York NY 10001. (212)206-1630. **Fax:** (212)727-0280. **E-mail:** assistant@bookhaven.com. **Website:** www.lowensteinas

sociates.com. **Contact:** Barbara Lowenstein. Member of AAR. Represents 150 clients.

MEMBER AGENTS Barbara Lowenstein, president (nonfiction interests include narrative nonfiction, health, money, finance, travel, multicultural, popular culture, and memoir; fiction interests include literary fiction and women's fiction); **Emily Gref** (young adult, middle-grade, fantasy, science fiction, literary, commercial, various nonfiction).

REPRESENTS nonfiction books, novels. **Considers these fiction areas:** commercial, fantasy, literary, middle-grade, science fiction, women's, young adult.

☛ Barbara Lowenstein is currently looking for writers who have a platform and are leading experts in their field, including business, women's issues, psychology, health, science and social issues, and is particularly interested in strong new voices in fiction and narrative nonfiction. Does not want westerns, textbooks, children's picture books and books in need of translation.

HOW TO CONTACT "For fiction, please send us a one-page query letter, along with the first 10 pages pasted in the body of the message by e-mail to assistant@bookhaven.com. If nonfiction, please send a one-page query letter, a table of contents, and, if available, a proposal pasted into the body of the e-mail to assistant@bookhaven.com Please put the word *Query* and the title of your project in the subject field of your e-mail and address it to the agent of your choice. Please do not send an attachment as the message will be deleted without being read and no reply will be sent." Accepts simultaneous submissions. Responds in 6 weeks to queries. Obtains most new clients through recommendations from others, solicitations, conferences.

TERMS Agent receives 15% commission on domestic sales. Agent receives 20% commission on foreign sales. Offers written contract. Charges for large photocopy batches, messenger service, international postage.

WRITERS CONFERENCES Malice Domestic

TIPS "Know the genre you are working in, and read! Also, please see our website for details on which agent to query for your project."

○ DONALD MAASS LITERARY AGENCY

121 W. 27th St., Suite 801, New York NY 10001. (212)727-8383. **E-mail:** info@maassagency.com. **Website:** www.maassagency.com. Estab. 1980. Member

of AAR. Other memberships include SFWA, MWA, RWA. Represents more than 100 clients. 5% of clients are new/unpublished writers. Currently handles novels (100%).

○ Prior to opening his agency, Mr. Maass served as an editor at Dell Publishing (New York) and as a reader at Gollancz (London). He also served as the president of AAR.

MEMBER AGENTS Donald Maass (mainstream, literary, mystery/suspense, science fiction, romance); **Jennifer Jackson** (commercial fiction, romance, science fiction, fantasy, mystery/suspense); **Cameron McClure** (literary, mystery/suspense, urban, fantasy, narrative nonfiction and projects with multicultural, international, and environmental themes, gay/lesbian); **Stacia Decker** (fiction, memoir, narrative nonfiction, pop-culture [cooking, fashion, style, music, art], smart humor, upscale erotica/erotic memoir and multicultural fiction/nonfiction); **Amy Boggs** (fantasy and science fiction, especially urban fantasy, paranormal romance, steampunk, young adult/children's, and alternate history. historical fiction, multicultural fiction, westerns); **Katie Shea Boutillier** (women's fiction/book club; edgy/dark, realistic/contemporary young adult; commercial-scale literary fiction; and celebrity memoir); **Jennifer Udden** (speculative fiction [both science fiction and fantasy], urban fantasy, and mysteries, as well as historical, erotic, contemporary, and paranormal romance).

REPRESENTS nonfiction, novels. **Considers these fiction areas:** crime, detective, fantasy, historical, horror, literary, mainstream, multicultural, mystery, paranormal, police, psychic, romance, science fiction, supernatural, suspense, thriller, westerns, women's, young adult.

⌖ This agency specializes in commercial fiction, especially science fiction, fantasy, mystery and suspense. Actively seeking to expand in literary fiction and women's fiction. We are fiction specialists. All genres are welcome.

HOW TO CONTACT E-query. All the agents have different submission addresses and instructions. See the website and each agent's online profile for exact submission instruction. Accepts simultaneous submissions.

TERMS Agent receives 15% commission on domestic sales. Agent receives 20% commission on foreign sales.

RECENT SALES *Codex Alera 5: Princep's Fury*, by Jim Butcher (Ace); *Fonseca 6: Bright Futures*, by Stu-

art Kaimsky (Forge): *Fathom*, by Cherie Priest (Tor); *Gospel Grrls 3: Be Strong and Curvaceous*, by Shelly Adina (Faith Words); *Ariane 1: Peacekeeper*, by Laura Reeve (Roc); *Execution Dock*, by Anne Perry (Random House).

WRITERS CONFERENCES Donald Maass: World Science Fiction Convention; Frankfurt Book Fair; Pacific Northwest Writers Conference; Bouchercon. Jennifer Jackson: World Science Fiction Convention; RWA National Conference.

TIPS We are fiction specialists, also noted for our innovative approach to career planning. Few new clients are accepted, but interested authors should query with an SASE. Works with subagents in all principle foreign countries and Hollywood. No prescriptive nonfiction, picture books, or poetry will be considered.

⊘◎ **MACGREGOR LITERARY INC.**
2373 N.W. 185th Ave., Suite 165, Hillsboro OR 97124. (503)277-8308. **Website:** www.macgregorliterary.com. **Contact:** Chip MacGregor. Signatory of WGA. Represents 40 clients. 10% of clients are new/unpublished writers. Currently handles nonfiction books (40%), novels (60%).

○ Prior to his current position, Mr. MacGregor was the senior agent with Alive Communications. Most recently, he was associate publisher for Time-Warner Book Group's Faith Division and helped put together their Center Street imprint.

MEMBER AGENTS Chip MacGregor, Sandra Bishop, Amanda Luedeke, Holly Lorincz, Erin Buterbaugh.

REPRESENTS nonfiction books, novels. **Considers these fiction areas:** crime, detective, historical, inspirational, mainstream, mystery, police, religious, romance, suspense, thriller, women's, chick lit.

⌖ "My specialty has been in career planning with authors—finding commercial ideas, then helping authors bring them to market—and in the midst of that, assisting the authors as they get firmly established in their writing careers. I'm probably best known for my work with Christian books over the years, but I've done a fair amount of general market projects as well." Actively seeking authors with a Christian worldview and a growing platform. Does not want to receive fantasy, sci-fi, children's books, poetry, or screenplays.

HOW TO CONTACT Do not query this agency without an invitation or referral. Accepts simultaneous submissions. Responds in 3 weeks to queries. Obtains most new clients through recommendations from others. Not looking to add unpublished authors except through referrals from current clients.

TERMS Agent receives 15% commission on domestic sales. Agent receives 15% commission on foreign sales. Offers written contract; 30-day notice must be given to terminate contract. Charges for exceptional fees after receiving authors' permission.

WRITERS CONFERENCES Blue Ridge Christian Writers Conference; Write to Publish.

TIPS "Seriously consider attending a good writers conference. It will give you the chance to be face-to-face with people in the industry. Also, if you're a novelist, consider joining one of the national writers organizations. The American Christian Fiction Writers (ACFW) is a wonderful group for new as well as established writers. And if you're a Christian writer of any kind, check into The Writers View, an online writing group. All of these have proven helpful to writers."

CAROL MANN AGENCY

55 Fifth Ave., New York NY 10003. (212)206-5635. **Fax:** (212)675-4809. **E-mail:** submissions@carol mannagency.com. **Website:** www.carolmannagency .com. **Contact:** Lydia Blyfield. Member of AAR, Represents roughly 200 clients. 15% of clients are new/unpublished writers.

MEMBER AGENTS Carol Mann (health/medical, religion, spirituality, self-help, parenting, narrative nonfiction, current affairs); **Laura Yorke**; **Gareth Esersky**; **Myrsini Stephanides** (nonfiction: pop culture and music, humor, narrative nonfiction and memoir, cookbooks; fiction: offbeat literary fiction, graphic works, and edgy young adult); **Joanne Wyckoff** (nonfiction: memoir, narrative nonfiction, personal narrative, psychology, women's issues, education, health and wellness, parenting, serious self-help, natural history; also accepts fiction).

REPRESENTS nonfiction books, novels. **Considers these fiction areas:** commercial, literary, young adult graphic works.

Does not want to receive genre fiction (romance, mystery, etc.).

HOW TO CONTACT Please see website for submission guidelines. Responds in 4 weeks to queries.

TERMS Agent receives 15% commission on domestic sales. Agent receives 20% commission on foreign sales. Offers written contract.

MANSION STREET LITERARY MANAGEMENT

E-mail: mansionstreet@gmail.com. **E-mail:** query mansionstreet@gmail.com (Jean); querymichelle@ mansionstreet.com (Michelle). **Website:** mansion street.com. **Contact:** Jean Sagendorph; Michelle Witte.

MEMBER AGENTS Jean Sagendorph (pop culture, gift books, cookbooks, general nonfiction, lifestyle, design, brand extensions), **Michelle Witte** (young adult, middle-grade, juvenile nonfiction).

REPRESENTS **Considers these fiction areas:** juvenile, middle-grade, young adult.

HOW TO CONTACT Send a query letter and no more than the first 10 pages of your ms in the body of an e-mail. Query 1 specific agent at this agency. No attachments. You must list the genre in the subject line. If the genre is not in the subject line, your query will be deleted. Responds in up to 6 weeks.

RECENT SALES Clients include: Paul Thurlby, Steve Ouch, Steve Seabury, Gina Hyams, Sam Pocker, Kim Siebold, Jean Sagendorph, Heidi Antman, Shannon O'Malley, Meg Bartholomy, Dawn Sokol, Hollister Hovey, Porter Hovey, Robb Pearlman.

MANUS & ASSOCIATES LITERARY AGENCY, INC.

425 Sherman Ave., Suite 200, Palo Alto CA 94306. (650)470-5151. **Fax:** (650)470-5159. **E-mail:** manuslit@manuslit.com. **Website:** www.manuslit .com. **Contact:** Jillian Manus, Jandy Nelson, Penny Nelson. **NYC address:** 444 Madison Ave., 29th Floor, New York, NY 10022. Member of AAR. Represents 75 clients. 30% of clients are new/unpublished writers.

Prior to becoming an agent, Ms. Manus was associate publisher of 2 national magazines and director of development at Warner Bros., and Universal Studios; she has been a literary agent for 20 years.

MEMBER AGENTS Jandy Nelson (currently not taking new clients); Jillian Manus, jillian@manuslit .com (political, memoirs, self-help, history, sports, women's issues, thrillers); Penny Nelson, penny@ manuslit.com (memoirs, self-help, sports, nonfiction); Janet Wilkens Manus (narrative fact-based crime books, religion, pop psychology, inspiration, memoirs, cookbooks).

REPRESENTS nonfiction books, novels. **Considers these fiction areas:** thriller.

8—¬ "Our agency is unique in the way that we not only sell the material, but we edit, develop concepts, and participate in the marketing effort. We specialize in large, conceptual fiction and nonfiction, and always value a project that can be sold in the TV/feature film market." Actively seeking high-concept thrillers, commercial literary fiction, women's fiction, celebrity biographies, memoirs, multicultural fiction, popular health, women's empowerment, and mysteries. No horror, romance, science fiction, fantasy, western, young adult, children's, poetry, cookbooks, or magazine articles.

HOW TO CONTACT Query via snail mail. Include proper SASE for a reply. Send print queries to the California address. Accepts simultaneous submissions. Responds in 3 months to queries. Responds in 3 months to mss. Obtains most new clients through recommendations from others, solicitations, conferences.

TERMS Agent receives 15% commission on domestic sales. Agent receives 20-25% commission on foreign sales. Offers written contract, binding for 2 years; 60-day notice must be given to terminate contract. Charges for photocopying and postage/UPS.

RECENT SALES *Nothing Down for the 2000s* and *Multiple Streams of Income for the 2000s*, by Robert Allen; *Missed Fortune 101*, by Doug Andrew; *Cracking the Millionaire Code*, by Mark Victor Hansen and Robert Allen; *Stress Free for Good*, by Dr. Fred Luskin and Dr. Ken Pelletier; *The Mercy of Thin Air*, by Ronlyn Domangue; *The Fine Art of Small Talk*, by Debra Fine; *Bone Men of Bonares*, by Terry Tamoff.

WRITERS CONFERENCES Maui Writers Conference; San Diego State University Writers Conference; Willamette Writers Conference; BookExpo America; MEGA Book Marketing University.

TIPS "Research agents using a variety of sources."

◯ THE EVAN MARSHALL AGENCY

6 Tristam Place, Pine Brook NJ 07058-9445. (973)882-1122. **E-mail:** evanmarshall@optonline. net. **Contact:** Evan Marshall. Member of AAR.

Other memberships include MWA, Sisters in Crime. Currently handles novels (100%).

REPRESENTS novels. **Considers these fiction areas:** action, adventure, erotica, ethnic, frontier, historical, horror, humor, inspirational, literary, mainstream, mystery, religious, satire, science fiction, suspense, western romance (contemporary, gothic, historical, regency).

HOW TO CONTACT Do not query. Currently accepting clients only by referal from editors and our own clients. Responds in 1 week to queries. Responds in 1 month to mss. Obtains most new clients through recommendations from others.

TERMS Agent receives 15% commission on domestic sales. Agent receives 20% commission on foreign sales. Offers written contract.

RECENT SALES *If You Could See What I See*, by Cathy Lamb (Kensington); *Rebecca's Christmas Gift*, by Emma Miller (Love Inspired); *If He's Wicked*, by Hannah Howell (Kensington); *Amanda Weds a Good Man*, by Naomi King (NAL); *Born in Blood*, by Alexandra Ivy (Kensington).

◯ THE MARTELL AGENCY

1350 Avenue of the Americas, Suite 1205, New York NY 10019. **Fax:** (212)317-2676. **E-mail:** submissions@ themartellagency.com. **Website:** www.themartella gency.com. **Contact:** Alice Martell.

REPRESENTS nonfiction, novels. **Considers these fiction areas:** commercial, mystery, suspense, thriller.

HOW TO CONTACT E-query. Please send a query first to Alice Martell, by mail or e-mail. This should include a summary of the project and a short biography and any information, if appropriate, as to why you are qualified to write on the subject of your book, including any publishing credits. submissions@themar tellagency.com.

RECENT SALES *Peddling Peril: The Secret Nuclear Arms Trade* by David Albright and Joel Wit (Five Press); *America's Women: Four Hundred Years of Dolls, Drudges, Helpmates, and Heroines*, by Gail Collins (William Morrow). Other clients include Serena Bass, Janice Erlbaum, David Cay Johnston, Mark Derr, Barbara Rolls, PhD.

◗ MARGRET MCBRIDE LITERARY AGENCY

P.O. Box 9128, La Jolla CA 92038. (858)454-1550. **Fax:** (858)454-2156. **E-mail:** staff@mcbridelit.com. **Website:** www.mcbrideliterary.com. **Contact:** Michael

Daley, submissions manager. Member of AAR. Other memberships include Authors Guild.

○ Prior to opening her agency, Ms. McBride worked at Random House, Ballantine Books, and Warner Books.

REPRESENTS nonfiction books, novels. **Considers these fiction areas:** action, adventure, crime, detective, historical, humor, literary, mainstream, mystery, police, satire, suspense, thriller.

⚷ This agency specializes in mainstream fiction and nonfiction. Actively seeking commercial fiction and nonfiction, business, health, self-help. Please do not send: screenplays, romance, poetry, or children's.

HOW TO CONTACT Query via snail mail with SASE. Send a query and one- to two-page synopsis (for fiction). Accepts simultaneous submissions. Responds in 8 weeks to queries. Responds in 6-8 weeks to mss.

TERMS Agent receives 15% commission on domestic sales. Agent receives 25% commission on foreign sales. Charges for overnight delivery and photocopying.

RECENT SALES *Value Tales Treasure: Stories for Growing Good People,* by Spencer Johnson, MD (Simon & Schuster Children's); *The 6 Reasons You'll Get the Job: What Employers Really Want—Whether They Know it or Not,* by Debra MacDougall and Elisabeth Harney Sanders-Park (Tarcher); *The Solution: Conquer Your Fear, Control Your Future,* by Lucinda Bassett (Sterling).

TIPS "Our office does not accept e-mail queries!"

THE MCCARTHY AGENCY, LLC

7 Allen St., Rumson NJ 07660. Phone/**Fax:** (732)741-3065. **E-mail:** McCarthylit@aol.com; ntfrost@hotmail.com. **Contact:** Shawna McCarthy. Member of AAR. Currently handles nonfiction books (25%), novels (75%).

MEMBER AGENTS Shawna McCarthy, Nahvae Frost.

REPRESENTS nonfiction books, novels. **Considers these fiction areas:** fantasy, juvenile, mystery, romance, women's.

HOW TO CONTACT Query via e-mail or regular mail to The McCarthy Agency, c/o Nahvae Frost, 101 Clinton Ave., Apt. #2, Brooklyn, NY 11205 Accepts simultaneous submissions.

THE MCGILL AGENCY, INC.

10000 N. Central Expressway, Suite 400, Dallas TX 75231. (214)390-5970. **E-mail:** info.mcgillagency@ gmail.com. **Contact:** Jack Bollinger. Estab. 2009. Represents 10 clients. 50% of clients are new/unpublished writers.

MEMBER AGENTS Jack Bollinger (eclectic tastes in nonfiction and fiction); Amy Cohn (nonfiction: women's issues, gay/lesbian, ethnic/cultural, memoirs, true crime; fiction: mystery, suspense, and thriller).

REPRESENTS Considers these fiction areas: historical, mainstream, mystery, romance, thriller.

HOW TO CONTACT Query via e-mail. Responds in 2 weeks to queries and 6 weeks to mss. Obtains new clients through conferences.

TERMS Agent receives 15% commission.

MENDEL MEDIA GROUP, LLC

115 W. 30th St., Suite 800, New York NY 10001. (646)239-9896. **Fax:** (212)685-4717. **E-mail:** scott@ mendelmedia.com. **Website:** www.mendelmedia .com. Member of AAR. Represents 40-60 clients.

○ Prior to becoming an agent, Mr. Mendel was an academic. "I taught American literature, Yiddish, Jewish studies, and literary theory at the University of Chicago and the University of Illinois at Chicago while working on my PhD in English. I also worked as a freelance technical writer and as the managing editor of a healthcare magazine. In 1998, I began working for the late Jane Jordan Browne, a longtime agent in the book publishing world."

REPRESENTS nonfiction books, novels, scholarly, with potential for broad/popular appeal. **Considers these fiction areas:** action, adventure, contemporary issues, crime, detective, erotica, ethnic, feminist, gay, glitz, historical, humor, inspirational, juvenile, lesbian, literary, mainstream, mystery, picture books, police, religious, romance, satire, sports, thriller, young adult, Jewish fiction.

⚷ "I am interested in major works of history, current affairs, biography, business, politics, economics, science, major memoirs, narrative nonfiction, and other sorts of general nonfiction." Actively seeking new, major, or definitive work on a subject of broad interest, or a controversial, but authoritative, new book on a subject that affects many people's lives. I also represent more lighthearted nonfiction projects, such as gift or novelty books, when they suit the market particularly well." Does not want "queries about projects written years ago that were unsuccessfully shopped to a long list of trade publishers by either the author or another agent. I am specifically not interested in reading short category romances (regency, time travel, paranormal, etc.), horror novels, supernatural stories, poetry, original plays, or film scripts."

HOW TO CONTACT Query with SASE. Do not e-mail or fax queries. For nonfiction, include a complete, fully edited book proposal with sample chapters. For fiction, include a complete synopsis and no more than 20 pages of sample text. Responds in 2 weeks to queries. Responds in 4-6 weeks to mss. Obtains most new clients through recommendations from others.

TERMS Agent receives 15% commission on domestic sales. Agent receives 20% commission on foreign sales.

WRITERS CONFERENCES BookExpo America; Frankfurt Book Fair; London Book Fair; RWA National Conference; Modern Language Association Convention; Jerusalem Book Fair.

TIPS "While I am not interested in being flattered by a prospective client, it does matter to me that she knows why she is writing to me in the first place. Is one of my clients a colleague of hers? Has she read a book by one of my clients that led her to believe I might be interested in her work? Authors of descriptive nonfiction should have real credentials and expertise in their subject areas, either as academics, journalists, or policy experts, and authors of prescriptive nonfiction should have legitimate expertise and considerable experience communicating their ideas in seminars and workshops, in a successful business, through the media, etc."

◑ MOVEABLE TYPE MANAGEMENT

244 Madison Ave., Suite 334, New York NY 10016. (646)431-6134. **Website:** www.mtmgmt.net.

MEMBER AGENTS Adam Chromy.

REPRESENTS Considers these fiction areas: commercial, literary, mainstream, romance, women's, young adult.

⊶ Mr. Chromy is a generalist, meaning that he accepts fiction submissions of virtually any kind (except juvenile books aimed for middle-grade and younger) as well as nonfiction. He has sold books in the following categories: new adult, women's, romance, memoir, pop culture, young adult, lifestyle, horror, how-to, general fiction, and more.

RECENT SALES *The Gin Lovers*, by Jamie Brenner (St. Martin's Press); *Miss Chatterley*, by Logan Belle (Pocket/S&S); *Sons Of Zeus*, by Noble Smith (Thomas Dunne Books); *World Made By Hand* and *Too Much Magic*, by James Howard Kunstler (Grove/Atlantic Press); *Dirty Rocker Boys*, by Bobbie Brown (Gallery/S&S).

◑ DEE MURA LITERARY

P.O. Box 131, Massapequa NY 11762. (516)795-1616. **Fax:** (516)795-8797. **E-mail:** query@deemuraliterary.com. **Website:** www.deemuraliterary.com. **Contact:** Dee Mura. 50% of clients are new/unpublished writers.

◌ Prior to opening her agency, Ms. Mura was a public relations executive with a roster of film and entertainment clients. She is the president and CEO of both Dee Mura Literary and Dee Mura Entertainment.

MEMBER AGENTS Dee Mura, Kimiko Nakamura, Kaylee Davis.

REPRESENTS Considers these fiction areas: adventure, commercial, contemporary issues, crime, erotica, family saga, fantasy, historical, literary, middle-grade, mystery, new adult, paranormal, romance, satire, science fiction, suspense, thriller, women's, young adult, espionage, magical realism, speculative fiction.

⊶ Fiction with crossover film potential. No screenplays, poetry, or children's picture books.

HOW TO CONTACT Query with SASE or e-mail query@deemuraliterary.com (e-mail queries are preferred). Please include the first 25 pages in the body of the e-mail as well as a short author bio and synopsis of the work. Responds to queries in 3-4 weeks. Responds to mss in 8 weeks. Obtains new clients through recommendations, solicitation, and conferences. Accepts simultaneous submissions. Obtains new clients through recommendations, solicitation, and conferences.

TERMS Agent receives 15% commission on domestic sales. Agent receives 20% commission on foreign sales. Offers written contract.

WRITERS CONFERENCES Alaska Writers Guild Conference, BookExpo America, Hampton Roads Writers Conference, NESCBWI Regional Conference, San Francisco Writers Conference, Books Alive! Conference, Writer's Digest Conference East, LVW's Writers Meet Agents Conference

◯ JEAN V. NAGGAR LITERARY AGENCY, INC.

216 E. 75th St., Suite 1E, New York NY 10021. (212)794-1082. **E-mail:** jweltz@jvnla.com; atasman@jvnla.com. **Website:** www.jvnla.com. **Contact:** Jean Naggar. Member of AAR. Other memberships include PEN, Women's Media Group, Women's Forum, SCBWI. Represents 450 clients. 20% of clients are new/unpublished writers.

Ms. Naggar has served as president of AAR.

MEMBER AGENTS Jennifer Weltz (well-researched and original historicals, thrillers with a unique voice, wry dark humor, and magical realism; enthralling narrative nonfiction; young adult, middle-grade); Jean Naggar (taking no new clients); Alice Tasman (literary, commercial, young adult, middle-grade, and nonfiction in the categories of narrative, biography, music, or pop culture); Elizabeth Evans (narrative nonfiction, memoir, current affairs, pop science, journalism, health and wellness, psychology, history, pop culture, and humor); Laura Biagi (literary fiction, magical realism, young adult novels, middle-grade novels, and picture books).

REPRESENTS nonfiction books, novels. **Considers these fiction areas:** commercial, fantasy, literary, middle-grade, picture books, thriller, young adult.

➤ This agency specializes in mainstream fiction and nonfiction and literary fiction with commercial potential.

HOW TO CONTACT This agency now has an online submission form on its website. Accepts simultaneous submissions. Obtains most new clients through recommendations from others.

TERMS Agent receives 15% commission on domestic sales. Agent receives 20% commission on foreign sales. Offers written contract. Charges for overseas mailing, messenger services, book purchases, long-distance telephone, photocopying—all deductible from royalties received.

RECENT SALES *Night Navigation*, by Ginnah Howard; *After Hours at the Almost Home*, by Tara Yelen; *An Entirely Synthetic Fish: A Biography of Rainbow Trout*, by Anders Halverson; *The Patron Saint of Butterflies*, by Cecilia Galante; *Wondrous Strange*, by Lesley Livingston; *6 Sick Hipsters*, by Rayo Casablanca; *The Last Bridge*, by Teri Coyne; *Gypsy Goodbye*, by Nancy Springer; *Commuters*, by Emily Tedrowe; *The Language of Secrets*, by Dianne Dixon; *Smiling to Freedom*, by Martin Benoit Stiles; *The Tale of Halcyon Crane*, by Wendy Webb; *Fugitive*, by Phillip Margolin; *BlackBerry Girl*, by Aidan Donnelley Rowley; *Wild Girls*, by Pat Murphy.

WRITERS CONFERENCES Willamette Writers Conference; Pacific Northwest Writers Conference; Bread Loaf Writers Conference; Marymount Manhattan Writers Conference; SEAK Medical & Legal Fiction Writing Conference.

TIPS "Use a professional presentation. Because of the avalanche of unsolicited queries that flood the agency every week, we have had to modify our policy. We will now only guarantee to read and respond to queries from writers who come recommended by someone we know. Our areas are general fiction and nonfiction—no children's books by unpublished writers, no multimedia, no screenplays, no formula fiction, and no mysteries by unpublished writers. We recommend patience and fortitude: the courage to be true to your own vision, the fortitude to finish a novel and polish it again and again before sending it out, and the patience to accept rejection gracefully and to wait for the stars to align themselves appropriately for success."

◑ NELSON LITERARY AGENCY

1732 Wazee St., Suite 207, Denver CO 80202. (303)292-2805. **E-mail:** query@nelsonagency.com. **Website:** www.nelsonagency.com. **Contact:** Kristin Nelson, president and senior literary agent; Sara Megibow, associate literary agent. Estab. 2002. Member of AAR. RWA, SCBWI, SFWA.

Prior to opening her own agency, Ms. Nelson worked as a literary scout and subrights agent for agent Jody Rein.

MEMBER AGENTS Kristin Nelson; Sara Megibow.

REPRESENTS Considers these fiction areas: commercial, fantasy, literary, mainstream, middle-grade, new adult, romance, science fiction, women's, young adult.

➤ NLA specializes in representing commercial fiction and high-caliber literary fiction. They represent many pop genre categories, including things like historical romance, steampunk, and all subgenres of young adult. Does not want short story collections, mysteries, thrillers, Christian, horror, children's picture books, or screenplays.

HOW TO CONTACT Query by e-mail. Put the word *Query* in the e-mail subject line. No attachments. Address your query to Sara or Kristin. Responds within 1 month.

RECENT SALES *Champion*, by Marie Lu (young adult); *Wool*, by Hugh Howey (science fiction); *The Whatnot*, by Stefan Bachmann (middle-grade); *Catching Jordan*, by Miranda Kenneally (young adult); *Broken Like This*, by Monica Trasandes (debut literary fiction); *The Darwin Elevator*, by Jason Hough (debut science fiction). A full list of clients is available online.

✚ ◑ NEW LEAF LITERARY & MEDIA, INC.

110 W. 40th St., Suite 410, New York NY 10018. (646)248-7989. **Fax:** (646)861-4654. **E-mail:** query@newleafliterary.com. **Contact:** Joanna Volpe, Kathleen Ortiz, Suzie Townsend, Pouya Shahbazian. Member of AAR.

MEMBER AGENTS Joanna Volpe (women's fiction, thriller, horror, speculative fiction, literary fiction and historical fiction, young adult, middle-grade, art-focused picture books); **Kathleen Ortiz**, director of subsidiary rights (new voices in young adult, and animator/illustrator talent); **Suzie Townsend** (new adult, young adult, middle-grade, romance [all subgenres], fantasy [urban fantasy, science fiction, steampunk, epic fantasy] and crime fiction [mysteries, thrillers]; **Pouya Shahbazian**, film and television agent.

REPRESENTS Considers these fiction areas: crime, fantasy, historical, horror, literary, mainstream, middle-grade, mystery, new adult, paranormal, picture books, romance, thriller, women's, young adult.

HOW TO CONTACT E-mail queries only. "Put the word *Query* in subject line, plus the agent's name." No attachments. Responds only if interested.

RECENT SALES *Allegiant*, by Veronica Roth; *The Sharpest Blade*, by Sandy Williams (Ace); *Siege and Storm*, by Leigh Bardugo (Henry Holt); *Erased*, by Jennifer Rush (Little Brown Books for Young Readers).

◑ PARK LITERARY GROUP, LLC

270 Lafayette St., Suite 1504, New York NY 10012. (212)691-3500. **Fax:** (212)691-3540. **E-mail:** queries@parkliterary. **Website:** www.parkliterary.com. Estab. 2005.

MEMBER AGENTS Theresa Park (plot-driven fiction and serious nonfiction); **Abigail Koons** (popular science, history, politics, current affairs and art, and women's fiction); **Peter Knapp** (middle-grade and young adult fiction, as well as suspense and thrillers for all ages).

REPRESENTS nonfiction books, novels. **Considers these fiction areas:** middle-grade, suspense, thriller, women's, young adult.

☛ The Park Literary Group represents fiction and nonfiction with a boutique approach: an emphasis on servicing a relatively small number of clients, with the highest professional standards and focused personal attention. Does not want to receive poetry or screenplays.

HOW TO CONTACT Please specify the first and last name of the agent to whom you are submitting in the subject line of the e-mail, and send your query letter and accompanying material to queries@parkliterary.com. All materials must be in the body of the e-mail. Responds if interested. For fiction submissions to Abigail Koons or Theresa Park, please include a query letter with short synopsis and the first 3 chapters of your work. For middle-grade and young adult submissions to Peter Knapp, please include a query letter and the first 3 chapters or up to 10,000 words of your novel (no synopsis necessary). For nonfiction submissions, please send a query letter, proposal, and sample chapter(s).

RECENT SALES This agency's client list is on their website. It includes bestsellers Nicholas Sparks and Debbie Macomber.

◑ KATHI J. PATON LITERARY AGENCY

P.O. Box 2236 Radio City Station, New York NY 10101. (212)265-6586. **E-mail:** KJPLitBiz@optonline.net. **Website:** www.PatonLiterary.com. **Contact:** Kathi Paton.

REPRESENTS Considers these fiction areas: literary.

☛ This agency specializes in adult nonfiction. No science fiction, fantasy, horror, category romance, juvenile, young adult, or self-published books

HOW TO CONTACT E-mail queries only. Please include a brief description. If interested, we'll ask for the nonfiction proposal or fiction synopsis and sample chapter. Do not send attachments or referrals to websites, they will not be opened or visited. Responds if interested. Accepts simultaneous submissions. Accepts new clients through recommendations from current clients.

TERMS Agent receives 15% commission on domestic sales. Agent receives 20% commission on foreign sales. Offers written contract. Charges clients for photocopying.

RECENT SALES Byron Acohido, Jon Swartz: *Zero Day Threat: The Shocking Truth of How Banks and Credit Bureaus Help Cyber Crooks*; Mary Collins: *American Idle: A Journey Through Our Sedentary Culture*; Raphael Ezekiel: *The Racist Mind: Portraits of American Neo-Nazis and Klansmen*.

WRITERS CONFERENCES Attends major regional panels, seminars, and conferences.

L. PERKINS AGENCY

5800 Arlington Ave., Riverdale NY 10471. (718)543-5344. **Fax:** (718)543-5354. **E-mail:** submissions@lperkinsagency.com. **Website:** lperkinsagency.com. Member of AAR. Represents 90 clients. 10% of clients are new/unpublished writers.

Ms. Perkins has been an agent for 20 years. She is the author of *The Insider's Guide to Getting an Agent* (Writer's Digest Books), as well as 3 other nonfiction books. She has edited 12 erotic anthologies and is also the editorial director of Ravenousromance.com, an e-publisher.

MEMBER AGENTS Tish Beaty, ePub agent (erotic romance including paranormal, historical, gay/lesbian/bisexual, and light-BDSM fiction; also, she seeks new adult and young adult); Sandy Lu, sandy@lperkinsagency.com (fiction: she is looking for dark literary and commercial fiction, mystery, thriller, psychological horror, paranormal/urban fantasy, historical fiction, young adult, historical thrillers or mysteries set in Victorian times; nonfiction: narrative nonfiction, history, biography, pop science, pop psychology, pop culture [music/theatre/film], humor, and food writing); Lori Perkins (not currently taking new clients).

REPRESENTS nonfiction books, novels. **Considers these fiction areas:** commercial, erotica, gay, historical, horror, lesbian, mystery, new adult, paranormal, thriller, urban fantasy, young adult.

"Most of my clients write both fiction and nonfiction. This combination keeps my clients publishing for years. I am also a published author, so I know what it takes to write a good book." Does not want to receive anything outside of the above categories (westerns, romance, etc.).

HOW TO CONTACT E-queries only. Include your query, a one-page synopsis, and the first 5 pages from your novel pasted into the e-mail. No attachments. Submit to only 1 agent at the agency. No smail mail queries. Accepts simultaneous submissions. Responds in 12 weeks to queries. Responds in 3-6 months to mss. Obtains most new clients through recommendations from others, solicitations, conferences.

TERMS Agent receives 15% commission on domestic sales. Agent receives 20% commission on foreign sales. No written contract. Charges clients for photocopying.

WRITERS CONFERENCES NECON, Killercon, BookExpo America, World Fantasy Convention, RWA, Romantic Times.

TIPS "Research your field and contact professional writers organizations to see who is looking for what. Finish your novel before querying agents. Read my book, *An Insider's Guide to Getting an Agent*, to get a sense of how agents operate. Read agent blogs (agentinthemiddle.blogspot.com and ravenousromance.blogspot.com)."

LINN PRENTIS LITERARY

155 East 116th St., #2F, New York NY 10029. **Fax:** (212)875-5565. **E-mail:** ahayden@linnprentis.com; linn@linnprentis.com. **Website:** www.linnprentis.com. **Contact:** Amy Hayden, acquisitions; Linn Prentis, agent. Represents 18-20 clients. 25% of clients are new/unpublished writers. Currently handles nonfiction books (5%), novels (65%), story collections (7%), novella (10%), juvenile books (10%), scholarly books (3%).

Prior to becoming an agent, Ms. Prentis was a nonfiction writer and editor, primarily in magazines. She also worked in book promotion in New York. Ms. Prentis then worked for, and later ran, the Virginia Kidd Agency. She is known particularly for her assistance with ms development.

REPRESENTS **Considers these fiction areas:** adventure, ethnic, fantasy, gay, glitz, historical, horror, humor, lesbian, literary, mainstream, thriller.

"Because of the Virginia Kidd connection and the clients I brought with me at the start, I have a special interest in science fiction and fantasy, but, really, fiction is what interests me. As for nonfiction projects, they are books I just couldn't resist." Actively seeking hard science fiction, family saga, mystery, memoir, mainstream, literary, women's. Does not want "books for little kids."

HOW TO CONTACT Query. No phone or fax queries. No snail mail. E-mail queries to ahayden@linnprentis

.com. Include first 10 pages and synopsis as either attachment or as text in the e-mail. Accepts simultaneous submissions. Obtains most new clients through recommendations from others, solicitations.

TERMS Agent receives 15% commission on domestic sales. Agent and partners take 20% commission on foreign sales. Offers written contract; 60-day notice must be given to terminate contract.

RECENT SALES Sales include *Vienna* for new author William Kirby; *Hunting Ground, Frost Burned* and *Night Broken* titles in 2 series for *New York Times* best-selling author Patricia Briggs (as well as a graphic novel *Homecoming*) and a story collection; a duology of novels for A.M. Dellamonica whose first book, *Indigo Springs*, won Canada's annual award for best fantasy, as well as several books abroad for client Tachyon Publications.

TIPS "Consider query letters and synopses as writing assignments. Spell names correctly."

☺ P.S LITERARY AGENCY

20033 - 520 Kerr St., Oakville ON L6K 3C7 Canada. **E-mail:** query@psliterary.com. **Website:** www.psliterary.com. **Contact:** Curtis Russell, principal agent; Carly Watters, agent; Maria Vincente, associate agent. Estab. 2005. Currently handles nonfiction books (50%), novels (50%).

REPRESENTS nonfiction, novels, juvenile books. **Considers these fiction areas:** action, adventure, detective, erotica, ethnic, family saga, historical, horror, humor, juvenile, literary, mainstream, middle-grade, mystery, new adult, picture books, romance, sports, thriller, women's, young adult biography/autobiography, business, child guidance/parenting, cooking/food/nutrition, current affairs, government/politics/law, health/medicine, history, how-to, humor, memoirs, military/war, money/finance/economics, nature/environment, popular culture, science/technology, self-help/personal improvement, sports, true crime/investigative, women's issues/women's studies.

8—⚷ "What makes our agency distinct: We take on a small number of clients per year in order to provide focused, hands-on representation. We pride ourselves in providing industry-leading client service." Actively seeking both fiction and nonfiction. Seeking both new and established writers. Does not want to receive poetry or screenplays.

HOW TO CONTACT Queries by e-mail only. Submit query, and bio. "Please limit your query to 1 page." Accepts simultaneous submissions. Responds in 4-6 weeks to queries/proposals; mss 4-8 weeks. Obtains most new clients through solicitations.

TERMS Agent receives 15% commission on domestic sales. Agent receives 25% commission on foreign sales. We offer a written contract; 30-days notice to terminate. "This agency charges for postage/messenger services only if a project is sold."

TIPS "Please review our website for the most up-to-date submission guidelines. We do not charge reading fees. We do not offer a critique service."

⊕ REBECCA FRIEDMAN LITERARY AGENCY

E-mail: Abby@rfliterary.com. **Website:** www.rfliterary.com. Estab. 2013.

◔ Prior to opening her own agency in 2013, Ms. Friedman was with Sterling Lord Literistic and then with Frederick Hill Bonnie Nadell.

REPRESENTS **Considers these fiction areas:** commercial, literary, romance, suspense, women's, young adult.

8—⚷ The agency is interested in commercial and literary fiction with a focus on literary novels of suspense, women's fiction, contemporary romance, and young adult, as well as journalistic nonfiction and memoir. Most of all, we are looking for great stories told in strong voices.

HOW TO CONTACT Please submit your query letter and first chapter (no more than 15 pages, double-spaced) to Abby@rfliterary.com.

RECENT SALES *So Much Pretty*, by Cara Hoffman; *The Black Nile*, by Dan Morrison; *Maybe One Day*, by Melissa Kantor; *Devoured*, by Emily Snow. A complete list of agency authors is available online.

◑ HELEN REES LITERARY AGENCY

14 Beacon St., Suite 710, Boston MA 02108. (617)227-9014. **Fax:** (617)227-8762. **E-mail:** reesagency@reesagency.com. **Website:** reesagency.com. **Contact:** Joan Mazmanian, Ann Collette, Helen Rees, Lorin Rees. Estab. 1983. Member of AAR. Other memberships include PEN. Represents more than 100 clients. 50% of clients are new/unpublished writers. Currently handles nonfiction books (60%), novels (40%).

MEMBER AGENTS Ann Collette (fiction: literary, mystery, thrillers, suspense, vampire, and women's fiction; nonfiction: true crime, narrative nonfiction, military and war, work to do with race and class, and work set in or about Southeast Asia; Agent10702@aol.com). **Lorin Rees** (literary fiction, memoirs, business books, self-help, science, history, psychology, and narrative nonfiction; lorin@reesagency.com); **Nicole LaBombard** (historical fiction, upscale commercial fiction, compelling literary fiction, young adult, narrative nonfiction, health/fitness, and business; nicole@reesagency.com); **Rebecca Podos** (young adult fiction of all kinds, including contemporary, emotionally driven stories, mystery, romance, urban and historical fantasy, horror and sci-fi; occasionally, literary and commercial adult fiction, new adult, and narrative nonfiction; rebecca@reesagency.com).

REPRESENTS nonfiction books, novels. **Considers these fiction areas:** commercial, historical, horror, literary, mystery, new adult, romance, science fiction, suspense, thriller, urban fantasy, women's, young adult.

HOW TO CONTACT Consult website for each agent's submission guidelines, as they differ. Responds in 3-4 weeks to queries. Obtains most new clients through recommendations from others, conferences, submissions.

TERMS Agent receives 15% commission on domestic sales. Agent receives 20% commission on foreign sales.

RECENT SALES Recent titles include: *The Art Forger*, by B.A. Shapiro; *Busy Monsters*, by William Giraldi; *Pitch Dark*, by Steven Sidor; *You Know When the Men Are Gone*, by Siobhan Fallon; and *Death Drops*, by Chrystle Fiedler. Other titles include: *Get Your Ship Together*, by Capt. D. Michael Abrashoff; *Overpromise and Overdeliver*, by Rick Berrara; *Opacity*, by Joel Kurtzman; *America the Broke*, by Gerald Swanson; *Murder at the B-School*, by Jeffrey Cruikshank; *Bone Factory*, by Steven Sidor; *Father Said*, by Hal Sirowitz; *Winning*, by Jack Welch; *The Case for Israel*, by Alan Dershowitz; *As the Future Catches You*, by Juan Enriquez; *Blood Makes the Grass Grow Green*, by Johnny Rico; *DVD Movie Guide*, by Mick Martin and Marsha Porter; *Words That Work*, by Frank Luntz; *Stirring It Up*, by Gary Hirshberg; *Hot Spots*, by Martin Fletcher; *Andy Grove: The Life and Times of an American*, by Richard Tedlow; *Girls Most Likely To*, by Poonam Sharma.

ⓘ REGAL LITERARY AGENCY

236 W. 26th St., #801, New York NY 10001. (212)684-7900. **Fax:** (212)684-7906. **E-mail:** info@regal-literary.com. **E-mail:** submissions@regal-literary.com. **Website:** www.regal-literary.com. London Office: 36 Gloucester Ave., Primrose Hill, London NW1 7BB, United Kingdom, uk@regal-literary.com Estab. 2002. Member of AAR. Represents 70 clients. 20% of clients are new/unpublished writers.

MEMBER AGENTS Michelle Andelman; Claire Anderson-Wheeler; Markus Hoffmann; Leigh Huffine; Lauren Pearson; Joseph Regal.

REPRESENTS Considers these fiction areas: literary, middle-grade, picture books, thriller, women's, young adult.

➤ Actively seeking literary fiction and narrative nonfiction. "We do not consider romance, science fiction, poetry, or screenplays."

HOW TO CONTACT "Query with SASE or via e-mail. No phone calls. Submissions should consist of a one-page query letter detailing the book in question, as well as the qualifications of the author. For fiction, submissions may also include the first 10 pages of the novel or 1 short story from a collection." Responds if interested. Accepts simultaneous submissions. Responds in 4-8 weeks.

TERMS Agent receives 15% commission on domestic sales. Agent receives 20% commission on foreign sales. "We charge no reading fees."

RECENT SALES Audrey Niffenegger's *The Time Traveler's Wife* (Mariner) and *Her Fearful Symmetry* (Scribner); Gregory David Roberts' *Shantaram* (St. Martin's); Josh Bazell's *Beat the Reaper* (Little, Brown); John Twelve Hawks' The Fourth Realm Trilogy (Doubleday); James Reston, Jr.'s *The Conviction of Richard Nixon* (Three Rivers) and *Defenders of the Faith* (Penguin); Michael Psilakis' *How to Roast a Lamb: New Greek Classic Cooking* (Little, Brown); Colman Andrews' *Country Cooking of Ireland* (Chronicle) and *Reinventing Food: Ferran Adria and How He Changed the Way We Eat* (Phaidon).

TIPS "We are deeply committed to every aspect of our clients' careers and are engaged in everything from the editorial work of developing a great book proposal or line editing a fiction ms to negotiating state-of-the-art book deals and working to promote and publicize the book when it's published. We are at the forefront of the effort to increase authors' rights in publishing contracts in a rapidly changing commercial environment. We deal directly with co-agents and publishers in every foreign territory and also work directly and with co-agents for feature film and television rights, with extraordinary success in both arenas. Many of our clients' works have sold in dozens of translation markets, and a high proportion of our books have been sold in Hollywood. We have strong relationships with speaking agents, who can assist in arranging author tours and other corporate and college speaking opportunities when appropriate. We also have a staff publicist and marketer to help promote our clients and their work."

○ ANN RITTENBERG LITERARY AGENCY, INC.

15 Maiden Lane, Suite 206, New York NY 10038. **Website:** www.rittlit.com. **Contact:** Ann Rittenberg, president; Penn Whaling, associate. Member of AAR. Currently handles fiction 75%, nonfiction (25%).

REPRESENTS Considers these fiction areas: literary, mainstream, thriller, upmarket fiction.

⌐ This agent specializes in upmarket thrillers, literary fiction, and literary nonfiction. Does not want to receive screenplays, straight genre fiction, poetry, self-help.

HOW TO CONTACT Query with SASE. Submit outline, 3 sample chapters, SASE. Query via postal mail or e-mail to info@rittlit.com. Accepts simultaneous submissions. Responds in 6 weeks to queries. Responds in 2 months to mss. Obtains most new clients through referrals from established writers and editors.

TERMS Agent receives 15% commission on domestic sales. Agent receives 20% commission on foreign sales. Offers written contract. This agency charges clients for photocopying only.

RECENT SALES *Live By Night*, by Dennis Lehane; *Leaving Haven*, by Kathleen McCleary; *Massacre Pond*, by Paul Doiron; *The Highway*, by C.J. Box; *This Is Not a Writing Manual*, by Kerri Majors; *The Land of Dreams*, by Vidar Sundstol; *Behemoth*, by Ronald Tobias; and *Billboard Man*, by Jim Fusilli.

◐ RLR ASSOCIATES, LTD.

Literary Department, 7 W. 51st St., New York NY 10019. (212)541-8641. **Fax:** (212)262-7084. **E-mail:** sgould@rlrassociates.net. **Website:** www.rlrassociates.net. **Contact:** Scott Gould. Member of AAR. Represents 50 clients. 25% of clients are new/unpublished writers. Currently handles nonfiction books (70%), novels (25%), story collections (5%).

REPRESENTS nonfiction books, novels, short story collections, scholarly. **Considers these fiction areas:**

commercial, literary, mainstream, middle-grade, picture books, romance, women's, young adult.

⌐ "We provide a lot of editorial assistance to our clients, and we have connections." Actively seeking fiction, current affairs, history, art, popular culture, health, and business. Does not want to receive screenplays.

HOW TO CONTACT Query by either e-mail or snail mail. For fiction, send a query and 1-3 chapters (pasted). For nonfiction, send query or proposal. Accepts simultaneous submissions. "If you do not hear from us within 3 months, please assume that your work is out of active consideration." Obtains most new clients through recommendations from others.

TERMS Agent receives 15% commission on domestic sales. Agent receives 20% commission on foreign sales. Offers written contract.

RECENT SALES Clients include Shelby Foote, The Grief Recovery Institute, Don Wade, Don Zimmer, The Knot.com, David Plowden, PGA of America, Danny Peary, George Kalinsky, Peter Hyman, Daniel Parker, Lee Miller, Elise Miller, Nina Planck, Karyn Bosnak, Christopher Pike, Gerald Carbone, Jason Lethcoe, Andy Crouch.

TIPS "Please check out our website for more details on our agency."

◑ B.J. ROBBINS LITERARY AGENCY

5130 Bellaire Ave., North Hollywood CA 91607-2908. **E-mail:** Robbinsliterary@gmail.com. **E-mail:** angeline.bjrobbinsliterary@gmail.com. **Contact:** (Ms.) B.J. Robbins, or Amy Maldonado. Member of AAR. Represents 40 clients. 50% of clients are new/unpublished writers. Currently handles nonfiction books (50%), novels (50%).

REPRESENTS nonfiction books, novels. **Considers these fiction areas:** crime, detective, ethnic, literary, mainstream, mystery, police, sports, suspense, thriller.

HOW TO CONTACT Query with SASE. Submit outline/proposal, 3 sample chapters, SASE. Accepts e-mail queries (no attachments). Accepts simultaneous submissions. Responds in 2-6 weeks to queries. Responds in 6-8 weeks to mss. Obtains most new clients through conferences, referrals.

TERMS Agent receives 15% commission on domestic sales. Agent receives 20% commission on foreign sales. Offers written contract; 3-month notice must be given to terminate contract. This agency charges clients for postage and photocopying (only after sale of ms).

RECENT SALES *Shake Down the Stars* and *A Pinch of Ooh La La*, by Renee Swindle (NAL); *Headhunters On My Doorstep*, by J. Maarten Troost (Gotham); *The Sinatra Club*, by Sal Polisi and Steve Dougherty (Gallery Books); *Blood of Heroes*, by James Donovan (Little, Brown); *Little Bighorn*, by John Hough Jr. (Arcade); *The Paris Deadline*, by Max Byrd (Turner); *Blood Brothers*, by Deanne Stillman (Simon & Schuster).

WRITERS CONFERENCES Squaw Valley Writers Workshop; San Diego State University Writers Conference.

THE ROSENBERG GROUP

23 Lincoln Ave., Marblehead MA 01945. (781)990-1341. **Fax:** (781)990-1344. **Website:** www.rosenberggroup.com. **Contact:** Barbara Collins Rosenberg. Estab. 1998. Member of AAR. Recognized agent of the RWA. Represents 25 clients. 15% of clients are new/unpublished writers. Currently handles nonfiction books (30%), novels (30%), scholarly books (10%), college textbooks (30%).

Prior to becoming an agent, Ms. Rosenberg was a senior editor for Harcourt.

REPRESENTS nonfiction books, novels, textbooks, college textbooks only. **Considers these fiction areas:** romance, women's, chick lit.

Ms. Rosenberg is well versed in the romance market (both category and single title). She is a frequent speaker at romance conferences. The Rosenberg Group is accepting new clients working in romance fiction (please see my Areas of Interest for specific romance subgenres); women's fiction and chick lit. Does not want to receive inspirational, time travel, futuristic, or paranormal.

HOW TO CONTACT Query via snail mail. Your query letter should not exceed 1 page in length. It should include the title of your work, the genre and/or subgenre; the ms word count; and a brief description of the work. If you are writing category romance, please be certain to let her know the line for which your work is intended. Responds in 2 weeks to queries. Responds in 4-6 weeks to mss. Obtains most new clients through recommendations from others, solicitations, conferences.

TERMS Agent receives 15% commission on domestic sales. Agent receives 15% commission on foreign

sales. Offers written contract; one-month notice must be given to terminate contract. Charges maximum of $350/year for postage and photocopying.

RECENT SALES Sold 27 titles in the last year.

WRITERS CONFERENCES RWA National Conference; BookExpo America.

JANE ROTROSEN AGENCY LLC

318 E. 51st St., New York NY 10022. (212)593-4330. **Fax:** (212)935-6985. **Website:** www.janerotrosen.com. Estab. 1974. Member of AAR. Other memberships include Authors Guild. Represents more than 100 clients.

MEMBER AGENTS Jane Rotosen Berkey (not taking on clients); Andrea Cirillo, acirillo@janerotrosen.com (suspense and women's fiction); Annelise Robey, arobey@janerotrosen.com (women's fiction, suspense, mystery, literary fiction, and the occasional nonfiction project); Meg Ruley, mruley@janerotrosen.com (women's fiction as well as suspense, thrillers, and mystery); Christina Hogrebe, chogrebe@janerotrosen.com; Amy Tannenbaum, atannenbaum@janerotrosen.com (contemporary romance, new adult, women's fiction that falls into that sweet spot between literary and commercial).

REPRESENTS nonfiction books, novels. **Considers these fiction areas:** literary, mystery, new adult, romance, suspense, thriller, women's.

HOW TO CONTACT Agent submission e-mail addresses are different. Send a query letter, a brief synopsis, and up to 3 chapters of your novel or the proposal for nonfiction. No attachments. Responds in 2 weeks to writers who have been referred by a client or colleague. Responds in 2 months to mss. Obtains most new clients through recommendations from others.

TERMS Agent receives 15% commission on domestic sales. Agent receives 20% commission on foreign sales. Offers written contract, binding for 3 years; 2-month notice must be given to terminate contract. Charges clients for photocopying, express mail, overseas postage, book purchase.

VICTORIA SANDERS & ASSOCIATES

241 Avenue of the Americas, Suite 11 H, New York NY 10014. (212)633-8811. **Fax:** (212)633-0525. **E-mail:** queriesvsa@gmail.com. **Website:** www.victoriasanders.com. **Contact:** Victoria Sanders. Estab. 1992. Member of AAR. Signatory of WGA. Represents 135 clients. 25% of clients are new/unpublished writers.

MEMBER AGENTS Tanya McKinnon, Victoria Sanders, Chris Kepner, Bernadette Baker-Baughman. **REPRESENTS** nonfiction books, novels. **Considers these fiction areas:** action, adventure, contemporary issues, crime, ethnic, family saga, feminist, lesbian, literary, mainstream, mystery, new adult, picture books, thriller, young adult.

HOW TO CONTACT Query by e-mail only. "We will not respond to e-mails with attachments or attached files."

TERMS Agent receives 15% commission on domestic sales. Agent receives 20% commission on foreign/film sales. Offers written contract. Charges for photocopying, messenger, express mail. If in excess of $100, client approval is required.

RECENT SALES Sold 20+ titles in the last year.

TIPS "Limit query to letter (no calls) and give it your best shot. A good query is going to get a good response."

○ SCHIAVONE LITERARY AGENCY, INC.

236 Trails End, West Palm Beach FL 33413-2135. (561)966-9294. **Fax:** (561)966-9294. **E-mail:** jendu77@aol.com; francinedelman@aol.com. **Website:** www.publishersmarketplace.com/members/profschia; blog site: www.schiavoneliteraryagencyinc.blogspot.com. **Contact:** Dr. James Schiavone, CEO, corporate offices in Florida; Jennifer DuVall, president, New York office; Francine Edelman, senior executive VP. Other memberships include National Education Association. Represents 60+ clients. 2% of clients are new/unpublished writers. Currently handles nonfiction books (50%), novels (49%), textbooks (1%).

○ Prior to opening his agency, Dr. Schiavone was a full professor of developmental skills at the City University of New York and author of 5 trade books and 3 textbooks. Jennifer DuVall has many years of combined experience in office management and agenting.

REPRESENTS nonfiction books, novels, juvenile, scholarly, textbooks. **Considers these fiction areas:** ethnic, family saga, historical, horror, humor, juvenile, literary, mainstream, science fiction, young adult.

⌗ This agency specializes in celebrity biography, autobiography, and memoirs. Does not want to receive poetry.

HOW TO CONTACT Query with SASE. Do not send unsolicited materials or parcels requiring a signature. Send no e-attachments. Accepts simultaneous submissions. Responds in 2 weeks to queries. Responds in 6 weeks to mss. Obtains most new clients through recommendations from others, solicitations, conferences.

TERMS Agent receives 15% commission on domestic sales. Agent receives 20% commission on foreign sales. Offers written contract. Charges clients for postage only.

WRITERS CONFERENCES Key West Literary Seminar; South Florida Writers Conference; Tallahassee Writers Conference, Million Dollar Writers Conference; Alaska Writers Conference.

TIPS "We prefer to work with established authors published by major houses in New York. We will consider marketable proposals from new/previously unpublished writers."

◐◉ SUSAN SCHULMAN LITERARY AGENCY

454 W. 44th St., New York NY 10036. (212)713-1633. **Fax:** (212)581-8830. **E-mail:** schulmanqueries@yahoo.com. **Website:** www.publishersmarketplace.com/members/Schulman/. **Contact:** Susan Schulman. Estab. 1980. Member of AAR. Signatory of WGA. Other memberships include Dramatists Guild. 10% of clients are new/unpublished writers. Currently handles nonfiction books (50%), novels (25%), juvenile books (15%), stage plays (10%).

REPRESENTS Considers these fiction areas: juvenile, literary, mainstream, women's.

⌗ "We specialize in books for, by, and about women and women's issues, including nonfiction self-help books, fiction, and theater projects. We also handle the film, television, and allied rights for several agencies as well as foreign rights for several publishing houses." Actively seeking new nonfiction. Considers plays. Does not want to receive poetry, television scripts, or concepts for television.

HOW TO CONTACT For fiction: Query Letter with outline and 3 sample chapters, résumé, and SASE. For nonfiction: Query Letter with complete description of subject, at least 1 chapter, résumé, and SASE. Queries may be sent via regular mail or e-mail. Please do not submit queries via UPS or Federal Express. Please do not send attachments with e-mail queries. Accepts simultaneous submissions. Responds in 6 weeks to queries/mss. Obtains most new clients through recommendations from others, solicitations, conferences.

TERMS Agent receives 15% commission on domestic sales. Agent receives 20% commission on foreign sales. Offers written contract; 30-day notice must be given to terminate contract.

RECENT SALES Sold 50 titles in the last year; hundreds of subsidiary rights deals.

WRITERS CONFERENCES Geneva Writers Conference (Switzerland); Columbus Writers Conference; Skidmore Conference of the Independent Women's Writers Group.

TIPS "Keep writing!" Schulman describes her agency as "professional boutique, long-standing, eclectic."

○ SCRIBBLERS HOUSE, LLC LITERARY AGENCY

P.O. Box 1007, Cooper Station, New York NY 10276-1007. (212)714-7744. **E-mail:** query@scribblershouse.net. **Website:** www.scribblershouse.net. **Contact:** Stedman Mays, Garrett Gambino. 25% of clients are new/unpublished writers.

MEMBER AGENTS Stedman Mays, Garrett Gambino.

REPRESENTS nonfiction books, occasionally novels. **Considers these fiction areas:** crime, historical, literary, suspense, thriller, women's.

HOW TO CONTACT "Query via e-mail. Put 'nonfiction query' or 'fiction query' in the subject line followed by the title of your project (send to our submissions e-mail on our website). Do not send attachments or downloadable materials of any kind with query. We will request more materials if we are interested. Usually respond in 2 weeks to 2 months to e-mail queries, if we are interested (if we are not interested, we will not respond due to the overwhelming amount of queries we receive). We are only accepting e-mail queries at the present time." Accepts simultaneous submissions.

TERMS Agent receives 15% commission on domestic sales. Charges clients for postage, shipping, and copying.

TIPS "If you must send by snail mail, we will return material or respond to a U.S. Postal Service-accepted SASE. (No international coupons or outdated mail strips, please.) Presentation means a lot. A well-written query letter with a brief author bio and your credentials is important. For query letter models, look at the cover copy and flap copy on other books in your general area of interest. Emulate what's best. Have an idea of other notable books that will be perceived as being in the same vein as yours. Know what's fresh about your project and articulate it in as few words as possible. Consult our website for the most up-to-date information on submitting."

◑ SCRIBE AGENCY, LLC

5508 Joylynne Dr., Madison WI 53716. **E-mail:** whattheshizzle@scribeagency.com. **E-mail:** submissions@scribeagency.com. **Website:** www.scribeagency.com. **Contact:** Kristopher O'Higgins. Represents 11 clients. 18% of clients are new/unpublished writers. Currently handles novels (98%), story collections (2%).

○ "With more than 15 years experience in publishing, with time spent on both the agency and editorial sides, with marketing experience to boot, Scribe Agency is a full-service literary agency, working hands-on with its authors on their projects. Check the website (scribeagency.com) to make sure your work matches the Scribe aesthetic."

MEMBER AGENTS Kristopher O'Higgins.

REPRESENTS novels anthologies. **Considers these fiction areas:** experimental, fantasy, feminist, horror, literary, mainstream, science fiction, thriller.

☛ Actively seeking excellent writers with ideas and stories to tell.

HOW TO CONTACT E-queries only: submissions@scribeagency.com. See the website for submission info, as it may change. Responds in 3-4 weeks to queries. Responds in 5 months to mss.

TERMS Agent receives 15% commission on domestic sales. Agent receives 20% commission on foreign sales. Offers written contract. Charges for postage and photocopying.

RECENT SALES Sold 3 titles in the last year.

WRITERS CONFERENCES BookExpo America; WisCon; Wisconsin Book Festival; World Fantasy Convention; WorldCon.

SECRET AGENT MAN

P.O. Box 1078, Lake Forest CA 92609. (949)698-6987. **E-mail:** query@secretagentman.net. **Website:** www.secretagentman.net. **Contact:** Scott Mortenson.

☛ Selective mystery, thriller, suspense, and detective fiction. Does not want to receive scripts or screenplays.

HOW TO CONTACT Query via e-mail only; include sample chapter(s), synopsis and/or outline. Prefers to read the real thing rather than a description of it.

Obtains most new clients through recommendations from others.

LYNN SELIGMAN, LITERARY AGENT

400 Highland Ave., Upper Montclair NJ 07043. (973)783-3631. **Contact:** Lynn Seligman. Other memberships include Women's Media Group. Represents 32 clients. 15% of clients are new/unpublished writers. Currently handles nonfiction books (60%), novels (40%).

○ Prior to opening her agency, Ms. Seligman worked in the subsidiary rights department of Doubleday and Simon & Schuster, and served as an agent with Julian Bach Literary Agency (which became IMG Literary Agency). Foreign rights are represented by Books Crossing Borders, Inc.

REPRESENTS nonfiction books, novels. **Considers these fiction areas:** detective, ethnic, fantasy, feminist, historical, horror, humor, literary, mainstream, mystery, romance, contemporary, gothic, historical, regency, science fiction.

☞ "This agency specializes in general nonfiction and fiction. I also do illustrated and photography books, and have represented several photographers for books."

HOW TO CONTACT Query with SASE. Prefers to read materials exclusively. Accepts simultaneous submissions. Responds in 2 weeks to queries. Responds in 2 months to mss. Obtains most new clients through referrals from other writers and editors.

TERMS Agent receives 15% commission on domestic sales. Agent receives 25% commission on foreign sales. Charges clients for photocopying, unusual postage, express mail, telephone expenses (checks with author first).

RECENT SALES Sold 15 titles in the last year. Lords of Vice series, by Barbara Pierce; Untitled series, by Deborah Leblanc.

○ SERENDIPITY LITERARY AGENCY, LLC

305 Gates Ave., Brooklyn NY 11216. (718)230-7689. **Fax:** (718)230-7829. **E-mail:** rbrooks@serendipitylit.com; info@serendipitylit.com. **Website:** www.serendipitylit.com; facebook.com/serendipitylit. **Contact:** Regina Brooks. Represents 50 clients. 50% of clients are new/unpublished writers. Currently handles nonfiction books (50%), other (50% fiction).

○ Prior to becoming an agent, Ms. Brooks was an acquisitions editor for John Wiley & Sons, Inc., and McGraw-Hill Companies.

MEMBER AGENTS Regina Brooks; Dawn Michelle Hardy (sports, pop culture, blog and trend, music, lifestyle, and social science), **Karen Thomas** (narrative nonfiction; celebrity; pop culture; memoir; general fiction; women's fiction; romance; mystery; self-help; inspirational; Christian-based fiction and nonfiction, including Evangelical), **John Weber** (unique young adult and middle-grade); **Folade Bell** (literary and commercial women's fiction, young adult, literary mysteries and thrillers, historical fiction, African-American issues, gay/lesbian, Christian fiction, humor, and books that deeply explore other cultures); **Nadeen Gayle** (romance, memoir, pop culture, inspirational/religious, women's fiction, parenting, young adult, mystery, and political thrillers, and all forms of nonfiction); **Chelcee Johns** (narrative nonfiction, investigative journalism, memoir, inspirational self-help, religion/spirituality, international, popular culture, and current affairs as well as literary and commercial fiction).

REPRESENTS nonfiction books, novels, juvenile, scholarly, children's books. **Considers these fiction areas:** commercial, gay, historical, humor, lesbian, literary, middle-grade, mystery, romance, thriller, women's, young adult.

☞ African-American nonfiction, commercial fiction, young adult novels with an urban flair and juvenile books. No stage plays, screenplays or poetry.

HOW TO CONTACT Check the website, as there are online submission forms for fiction, nonfiction and juvenile. Accepts simultaneous submissions. Obtains most new clients through conferences, referrals.

TERMS Agent receives 15% commission on domestic sales. Agent receives 20% commission on foreign sales. Offers written contract; 2-month notice must be given to terminate contract. Charges clients for office fees, which are taken from any advance.

RECENT SALES Putting Makeup on the Fat Boy, by Bil Wright; You Should Really Write a Book: How to Write Sell, and Market Your Memoir, by Regina Brooks; Living Color, by Nina Jablonski; Swirling, by Christelyn D. Kazarin and Janice R. Littlejohn; Red Thread Sisters, by Carol Peacock; Nicki Minaj: Hop Pop Moments 4 Life, by Isoul Harris; Forgotten Burial, by Jodi Foster.

TIPS "See the book *Writing Great Books for Young Adults*. Looking for high-concept ideas with big hooks. If you get writer's block try the site possibiliteas.co; it's a muse in a cup."

THE SEYMOUR AGENCY

475 Miner St., Canton NY 13617. (315)386-1831. E-mail: marysue@twcny.rr.com; nicole@theseymouragency.com. **Website:** www.theseymouragency.com. **Contact:** Mary Sue Seymour, Nicole Resciniti. Member of AAR. Signatory of WGA. Other memberships include RWA, Authors Guild. Represents 50 clients. 5% of clients are new/unpublished writers. Currently handles nonfiction books (50%), other (50% fiction).

Ms. Seymour is a retired New York State certified teacher. Ms. Resciniti was recently named "Agent of the Year" by the ACFW.

MEMBER AGENTS Mary Sue Seymour (accepts queries in Christian, inspirational, romance, and nonfiction); Nicole Resciniti (accepts all genres of romance, young adult, middle-grade, new adult, suspense, thriller, mystery, science fiction, fantasy).

REPRESENTS nonfiction books, novels. **Considers these fiction areas:** action, fantasy, middle-grade, mystery, new adult, religious, romance, science fiction, suspense, thriller, young adult.

HOW TO CONTACT For Mary Sue: E-query with synopsis, first 50 pages for romance. Accepts e-mail queries. For Nicole: E-mail the query plus first 5 pages of the ms. Accepts simultaneous submissions. Responds in 1 month to queries. Responds in 3 months to mss.

TERMS Agent receives 12-15% commission on domestic sales.

RECENT SALES Sales include: *New York Times* best-selling author Shelley Shepard Gray (8-book deal to HarperCollins); Jen Turano (3-book deal to Bethany House); Pat Trainum (4-book deal to Revell); Jennifer Beckstrand (6-book deal to Kensington Publishing); Amy Lillard (3-book deal to Kensington Publishing); Vannetta Chapman (multibook deal to Zondervan); Jerry Eicher (3-book deal to Harvest House); Mary Ellis (3-book deal to Harvest House); *New York Times* best-selling author Julie Ann Walker (the next 4 books in her Black Knights Inc series); Melissa Lander (young adult science fiction novel, *Alienated,* to Disney/Hyperion); and Kate Meader (new contemporary romance series to Pocket/Gallery).

SHEREE BYKOFSKY ASSOCIATES, INC.

PO Box 706, Brigantine NJ 08203. **E-mail:** shereebee@aol.com. **E-mail:** submitbee@aol.com. **Website:** www.shereebee.com. **Contact:** Sheree Bykofsky. Member of AAR. Memberships include Author's Guild, Atlantic City Chamber of Commerce, WNBA. Currently handles nonfiction books (80%), novels (20%).

Prior to opening her agency, Ms. Bykofsky served as executive editor of the Stonesong Press and managing editor of Chiron Press. She is also the author or co-author of more than 20 books, including *The Complete Idiot's Guide to Getting Published.* As an adjunct professor, Ms. Bykofsky teaches publishing at Rosemont College, NYU, and SEAK, Inc.

MEMBER AGENTS Janet Rosen, associate; Thomas V. Hartmann, associate.

REPRESENTS nonfiction, novels. **Considers these fiction areas:** contemporary issues, literary, mainstream, mystery, suspense.

This agency specializes in popular reference nonfiction, commercial fiction with a literary quality, and mysteries. "I have wide-ranging interests, but it really depends on quality of writing, originality, and how a particular project appeals to me (or not). I take on fiction when I completely love it—it doesn't matter what area or genre." Does not want to receive poetry, material for children, screenplays, westerns, horror, science fiction, or fantasy.

HOW TO CONTACT "We only accept e-queries now and will only respond to those in which we are interested. E-mail short queries to submitbee@aol.com. Please, no attachments, snail mail, or phone calls. One-page query, one-page synopsis, and first page of ms in the body of the e-mail. Nonfiction: One-page query in the body of the e-mail. We cannot open attached Word files or any other types of attached files. These will be deleted." Accepts simultaneous submissions. Responds in 1 month to requested mss. Obtains most new clients through recommendations from others.

TERMS Agent receives 15% commission on domestic sales. Agent receives 20% commission on foreign sales. Offers written contract, binding for 1 year. Charges for postage, photocopying, fax.

RECENT SALES *ADHD Does Not Exist*, by Dr. Richard Saul (Harper Collins); *Be Bold and Win the Sale*, by Jeff Shore (McGraw-Hill); *Idea to Invention*, by Patricia Nolan-Brown (Amacom); *The Hour of Lead*, by Bruce Holbert (Counterpoint); *Slimed! An Oral History of Nickelodeon's Golden Age*, by Matthew Klickstein (Plume); *Bang the Keys: Four Steps to a Lifelong Writing Practice*, by Jill Dearman (Alpha, Penguin); *Signed, Your Student: Celebrities on the Teachers Who Made Them Who They Are Today*, by Holly Holbert (Kaplan); *The Five Ways We Grieve*, by Susan Berger (Trumpeter/Shambhala).

WRITERS CONFERENCES Truckee Meadow Community College, Keynote; ASJA Writers Conference; Asilomar; Florida Suncoast Writers Conference; Whidbey Island Writers Conference; Florida First Coast Writers Festival; Agents and Editors Conference; Columbus Writers Conference; Southwest Writers Conference; Willamette Writers Conference; Dorothy Canfield Fisher Conference; Maui Writers Conference; Pacific Northwest Writers Conference; IWWG.

TIPS "Read the agent listing carefully and comply with guidelines."

○ KEN SHERMAN & ASSOCIATES

1275 N. Hayworth, Suite 103, Los Angeles CA 90046. (310)273-8840. **Fax:** (310)271-2875. **E-mail:** kensher manassociates@gmail.com. **Website:** www.kensher manassociates.com/. **Contact:** Ken Sherman. Other memberships include BAFTA, PEN International, signatory of WGA. Represents approximately 35 clients. clients. 10% of clients are new/unpublished writers.

○ Prior to opening his agency, Mr. Sherman was with The William Morris Agency, The Lantz Office, and Paul Kohner, Inc. He has taught The Business of Writing for Film and Television and The Book Worlds at UCLA and USC. He also lectures extensively at writers conferences and film festivals around the U.S. He is currently a commissioner of arts and cultural affairs in the City of West Hollywood and is on the International Advisory Board of the Christopher Isherwood Foundation.

REPRESENTS nonfiction books, novels, movie, TV, (not episodic drama teleplays). **Considers these fiction areas:** glitz, New Age, psychic, adventure, comic, confession, detective, erotica, ethnic, experimental, family, fantasy, feminist, gay, gothic, hi lo, historical, horror, humor, literary, mainstream, military, multicultural, multimedia, mystery, occult, picture books, plays, poetry, poetry translation, regional, religious, romance, science, short, spiritual, sports, thriller, translation, western, young adult.

HOW TO CONTACT Contact by referral only. Reports in approximately 1 month to mss. Obtains most new clients through recommendations from others.

TERMS Agent receives 15% commission on domestic sales. Agent receives 15% commission on foreign sales. Agent receives 10-15% commission on film sales. Offers written contract. Charges clients for reasonable office expenses (postage, photocopying, etc.)

RECENT SALES Sold more than 20 scripts in the last year. *Back Roads*, by Tawni O'Dell with Adrian Lyne set to direct; *Priscilla Salyers Story*, produced by Andrea Baynes (ABC); *Toys of Glass*, by Martin Booth (ABC/Saban Entertainment); *Brazil*, by John Updike (film rights to Glaucia Carmagos); *Fifth Sacred Thing*, by Starhawk (Bantam), with Starhawk adapting her book into a screenplay; *Questions From Dad*, by Dwight Twilly (Tuttle); *Snow Falling on Cedars* by David Guterson (Universal Pictures); *The Witches of Eastwick—The Musical*, by John Updike (Cameron Macintosh, Ltd.); *Rabbit*, by John Updike (HBO one-hour series).

WRITERS CONFERENCES Maui Writers Conference; Squaw Valley Writers Workshop; Santa Barbara Writers Conference; Screenwriting Conference in Santa Fe; Aspen Summer Words Literary Festival (The Aspen Institute and the San Francisco Writer's Conference). San Francisco Writers Conference, Chautaq UA Writers Conference.

◉ WENDY SHERMAN ASSOCIATES, INC.

27 W. 24th St., Suite 700B, New York NY 10010. (212)279-9027. **E-mail:** wendy@wsherman.com. **E-mail:** submissions@wsherman.com. **Website:** www .wsherman.com. **Contact:** Wendy Sherman; Kim Perel. Member of AAR. Represents 50 clients.

○ Prior to opening the agency, Ms. Sherman served as vice president, executive director, associate publisher, subsidiary rights director, and sales and marketing director for major publishers.

MEMBER AGENTS Wendy Sherman (board member of AAR), Kim Perel.

REPRESENTS Considers these fiction areas: mainstream fiction that hits the sweet spot between literary and commercial.

⚷ "We specialize in developing new writers, as well as working with more established writers.

My experience as a publisher has proven to be a great asset to my clients."

HOW TO CONTACT Query via e-mail only. "We ask that you include your last name, title, and the name of the agent you are submitting to in the subject line. For fiction, please include a query letter and your first 10 pages copied and pasted in the body of the e-mail. We will not open attachments unless they have been requested. For nonfiction, please include your query letter and author bio. Due to the large number of e-mail submissions that we receive, we can only reply to e-mail queries in the affirmative. We respectfully ask that you do not send queries to our individual e-mail addresses." Accepts simultaneous submissions. Responds in 1 month to queries. Obtains most new clients through recommendations from other writers.

TERMS Agent receives standard 15% commission. Offers written contract.

RECENT SALES *Z, A Novel of Zelda Fitzgerald*, by Therese Anne Fowler; *The Silence of Bonaventure Arrow*, by Rita Leganski; *Together Tea*, by Marjan Kamali; *A Long Long Time Ago and Essentially True*, by Brigid Pasulka; *Illuminations*, by Mary Sharratt; *The Accounting*, by William Lashner; *Lunch in Paris*, by Elizabeth Bard; *The Rules of Inheritance*, by Claire Bidwell Smith; *Love in Ninety Days*, by Dr. Diana Kirschner; *The Wow Factor*, by Jacqui Stafford; *Humor Memoirs*, by Wade Rouse.

TIPS "The bottom line is: Do your homework. Be as well prepared as possible. Read the books that will help you present yourself and your work with polish. You want your submission to stand out."

JEFFREY SIMMONS LITERARY AGENCY

15 Penn House, Mallory St., London NW8 8SX England. (44)(207)224-8917. **E-mail:** jasimmons@ unicombox.co.uk. **Contact:** Jeffrey Simmons. Represents 43 clients. 40% of clients are new/unpublished writers. Currently handles nonfiction books (65%), novels (35%).

Prior to becoming an agent, Mr. Simmons was a publisher. He is also an author.

REPRESENTS nonfiction books, novels. **Considers these fiction areas:** action, adventure, confession, crime, detective, family saga, literary, mainstream, mystery, police, suspense, thriller.

"This agency seeks to handle good books and promising young writers. My long experience in publishing and as an author and ghost-writer means I can offer an excellent service all around, especially in terms of editorial experience where appropriate." Actively seeking quality fiction, biography, autobiography, showbiz, personality books, law, crime, politics, and world affairs. Does not want to receive science fiction, horror, fantasy, juvenile, academic books, or specialist subjects (e.g., cooking, gardening, religious).

HOW TO CONTACT Submit sample chapter, outline/proposal, SASE (IRCs if necessary). Prefers to read materials exclusively. Responds in 1 week to queries. Responds in 1 month to mss. Obtains most new clients through recommendations from others, solicitations.

TERMS Agent receives 10-15% commission on domestic sales. Agent receives 15% commission on foreign sales. Offers written contract, binding for lifetime of book in question or until it becomes out of print.

TIPS "When contacting us with an outline/proposal, include a brief biographical note (listing any previous publications with publishers and dates). Please tell us if the book has already been offered elsewhere."

BEVERLEY SLOPEN LITERARY AGENCY

131 Bloor St. W., Suite 711, Toronto ON M5S 1S3 Canada. (416)964-9598. **E-mail:** beverly@slopenagency.ca. **Website:** www.slopenagency.ca. **Contact:** Beverley Slopen. Represents 70 clients. 20% of clients are new/unpublished writers.

Prior to opening her agency, Ms. Slopen worked in publishing and as a journalist.

REPRESENTS nonfiction books, novels, scholarly. **Considers these fiction areas:** commercial, literary, mystery, suspense.

"This agency has a strong bent toward Canadian writers." Actively seeking serious nonfiction that is accessible and appealing to the general reader. Does not want to receive fantasy, science fiction, or children's books.

HOW TO CONTACT Query by e-mail. Returns materials only with SASE (Canadian postage only). To submit a work for consideration, e-mail a short query letter and a few sample pages. Submit only 1 work at a time. If we want to see more, we will contact the writer by phone or e-mail. Accepts simultaneous submissions. Responds in 2 months to queries.

TERMS Agent receives 15% commission on domestic sales. Agent receives 10% commission on foreign sales. Offers written contract, binding for 2 years; 3-months notice must be given to terminate contract.

RECENT SALES *Solar Dance*, by Modris Eksteins (Knopf Canada, Harvard University Press. U.S.); *The Novels*, by Terry Fallis; *God's Brain*, by Lionel Tiger and Michael McGuire (Prometheus Books); *What They Wanted*, by Donna Morrissey (Penguin Canada, Premium/DTV Germany); *The Age of Persuasion*, by Terry O'Reilly and Mike Tennant (Knopf Canada, Counterpoint U.S.); *Prisoner of Tehran*, by Marina Nemat (Penguin Canada, Free Press U.S., John Murray U.K.); *Race to the Polar Sea*, by Ken McGoogan (HarperCollins Canada, Counterpoint U.S.); *Transgression*, by James Nichol (HarperCollins U.S., McArthur Canada, Goldmann Germany); *Midwife of Venice* and *The Harem Midwife*, by Roberta Rich; *Vermeer's Hat*, by Timothy Brook (HarperCollins Canada, Bloomsbury U.S.); *Distantly Related to Freud*, by Ann Charney (Cormorant).

TIPS "Please, no unsolicited mss."

◑ SPECTRUM LITERARY AGENCY

320 Central Park W., Suite 1-D, New York NY 10025. **Fax:** (212)362-4562. **Website:** www.spectrumliteraryagency.com. **Contact:** Eleanor Wood, president. Estab. 1976. Member of SFWA. Represents 90 clients. Currently handles nonfiction books (10%), novels (90%).

MEMBER AGENTS Eleanor Wood (referrals only), Justin Bell (science fiction, mysteries, nonfiction).

REPRESENTS nonfiction books, novels. **Considers these fiction areas:** mystery, science fiction.

HOW TO CONTACT Snail mail query with SASE. Submit author bio, publishing credits. No unsolicited mss will be read. Responds in 1-3 months to queries. Obtains most new clients through recommendations from authors.

TERMS Agent receives 15% commission on domestic sales. Deducts for photocopying and book orders.

TIPS "Spectrum's policy is to read only book-length mss that we have specifically asked to see. Unsolicited mss are not accepted. The letter should describe your book briefly and include publishing credits and background information or qualifications relating to your work, if any."

◑ SPENCERHILL ASSOCIATES

P.O. Box 374, Chatham NY 12037. (518)392-9293. **Fax:** (518)392-9554. **E-mail:** submissions@spencer

hillassociates.com. **Website:** www.spencerhillassociates.com. **Contact:** Karen Solem or Nalini Akolekar. Member of AAR. Represents 96 clients. 10% of clients are new/unpublished writers.

◯   Prior to becoming an agent, Ms. Solem was editor-in-chief at HarperCollins and an associate publisher.

MEMBER AGENTS Karen Solem; Nalini Akolekar.

REPRESENTS novels. **Considers these fiction areas:** commercial, erotica, literary, mainstream, mystery, paranormal, romance, thriller.

☛   "We handle mostly commercial women's fiction, historical novels, romance (historical, contemporary, paranormal, urban fantasy), thrillers, and mysteries. We also represent Christian fiction only—no nonfiction, poetry, science fiction, children's picture books, or scripts.

HOW TO CONTACT "We accept electronic submissions and are no longer accepting paper queries. Please send us a query letter in the body of an e-mail, pitch us your project and tell us about yourself: Do you have prior publishing credits? Attach the first 3 chapters and synopsis preferably in .doc, .rtf, or .txt format to your e-mail. Send all queries to submission@spencerhillassociates.com. We do not have a preference for exclusive submissions but do appreciate knowing if the submission is simultaneous. We receive thousands of submissions a year and each query receives our attention. Unfortunately we are unable to respond to each query individually. If we are interested in your work, we will contact you within 8 weeks." Accepts simultaneous submissions.

TERMS Agent receives 15% commission on domestic sales. Agent receives 20% commission on foreign sales. Offers written contract; 3-month notice must be given to terminate contract.

RECENT SALES A full list of sales and clients is available on the agency website.

◑ THE SPIELER AGENCY

27 W. 20 St., Suite 305, New York NY 10011. **E-mail:** thespieleragency@gmail.com. **Contact:** Joe Spieler. Represents 160 clients. 2% of clients are new/unpublished writers.

◯   Prior to opening his agency, Mr. Spieler was a magazine editor.

MEMBER AGENTS Eric Myers, eric@TheSpieler Agency.com (pop culture, memoir, history, thrillers, young adult, middle-grade, new adult, and picture books [text only]); Victoria Shoemaker, victoria@ TheSpielerAgency.com (environment and natural history, popular culture, memoir, photography and film, literary fiction and poetry, and books on food and cooking); John Thornton, john@TheSpielerAgency .com (nonfiction); Joe Spieler, joe@TheSpielerAgency .com (nonfiction and fiction and books for children and young adults.).

REPRESENTS novels, juvenile books. **Considers these fiction areas:** literary, middle-grade, New Age, picture books, thriller, young adult.

HOW TO CONTACT Before submitting projects to the Spieler Agency, check the listings of our individual agents and see if any particular agent shows a general interest in your subject (e.g., history, memoir, young adult, etc.). Please send all queries either by e-mail or regular mail. If you query us by regular mail, we can only reply to you if you include a self-addressed, stamped envelope. Accepts simultaneous submissions. Cannot guarantee a personal response to all queries. Obtains most new clients through recommendations, and through the listing in *Guide to Literary Agents.*

TERMS Agent receives 15% commission on domestic sales. Charges clients for messenger bills, photocopying, postage.

WRITERS CONFERENCES London Book Fair.

TIPS "Check www.publishersmarketplace.com/ members/spielerlit/."

NANCY STAUFFER ASSOCIATES

P.O. Box 1203, Darien CT 06820. (203)202-2500. E-mail: nancy@staufferliterary.com. **Website:** publish ersmarketplace.com/members/nstauffer. **Contact:** Nancy Stauffer Cahoon. Other memberships include Authors Guild. Currently handles nonfiction books (10%), novels (90%).

> "Over the course of my more than 20-year career, I've held positions in the editorial, marketing, business, and rights departments of *The New York Times*, McGraw-Hill, and Doubleday. Before founding Nancy Stauffer Associates, I was director of foreign and performing rights, then director, subsidiary rights, for Doubleday, where I was honored to have worked with a diverse range of internationally known and best-selling authors of all genres."

HOW TO CONTACT Accepts simultaneous submissions. Obtains most new clients through referrals from existing clients.

TERMS Agent receives 15% commission on domestic sales. Agent receives 20% commission on foreign sales.

RECENT SALES *Blasphemy*, by Sherman Alexie; *Benediction*, by Kent Haruf; *Bone Fire*, by Mark Spragg; *The Carry Home*, by Gary Ferguson.

STEELE-PERKINS LITERARY AGENCY

26 Island Ln., Canandaigua NY 14424. (585)396-9290. **Fax:** (585)396-3579. **E-mail:** pattiesp@aol.com. **Contact:** Pattie Steele-Perkins. Member of AAR. Other memberships include RWA. Currently handles novels (100%).

REPRESENTS novels. **Considers these fiction areas:** romance, women's category romance, romantic suspense, historical, contemporary, multicultural, and inspirational.

HOW TO CONTACT Submit query along with synopsis and 1 chapter via e-mail (no attachments) or snail mail. Snail mail submissions require SASE. Accepts simultaneous submissions. Obtains most new clients through recommendations from others, queries/solicitations.

TERMS Agent receives 15% commission on domestic sales. Offers written contract, binding for 1 year; one-month notice must be given to terminate contract.

RECENT SALES Sold 130 titles last year. This agency prefers not to share specific sales information.

TIPS "Be patient. E-mail rather than call. Make sure what you are sending is the best it can be."

STERNIG & BYRNE LITERARY AGENCY

2370 S. 107th St., Apt. #4, Milwaukee WI 53227. (414)328-8034. **Fax:** (414)328-8034. **E-mail:** jack byrne@hotmail.com. **Website:** www.sff.net/people/ jackbyrne. **Contact:** Jack Byrne. Other memberships include SFWA, MWA. Represents 30 clients. 10% of clients are new/unpublished writers. Currently handles nonfiction books (5%), novels (90%), juvenile books (5%).

REPRESENTS nonfiction books, novels, juvenile. **Considers these fiction areas:** fantasy, horror, mystery, science fiction, suspense.

> "Our client list is comfortably full, and our current needs are therefore quite limited." Actively seeking science fiction/fantasy and mystery by established writers. Does not want to receive romance, poetry, textbooks, or highly specialized nonfiction.

HOW TO CONTACT Query with SASE. Prefers e-mail queries (no attachments); hard copy queries also acceptable. Responds in 3 weeks to queries. Responds in 3 months to mss.

TERMS Agent receives 15% commission on domestic sales. Agent receives 20% commission on foreign sales. Offers written contract; 2-month notice must be given to terminate contract.

TIPS "Don't send first drafts, have a professional presentation (including cover letter), and know your field. Read what's been done—good and bad."

◯ THE STROTHMAN AGENCY, LLC

P.O. Box 231132, Boston MA 02123. **E-mail:** info@strothmanagency.com. **Website:** www.strothmanagency.com. **Contact:** Wendy Strothman, Lauren MacLeod. Member of AAR. Other memberships include Authors' Guild. Represents 50 clients.

Prior to becoming an agent, Ms. Strothman was head of Beacon Press (1983-1995) and executive vice president of Houghton Mifflin's Trade & Reference Division (1996-2002).

MEMBER AGENTS Wendy Strothman; Lauren MacLeod.

REPRESENTS novels, juvenile books. **Considers these fiction areas:** literary, middle-grade, young adult.

"Because we are highly selective in the clients we represent, we increase the value publishers place on our properties. We specialize in narrative nonfiction, memoir, history, science and nature, arts and culture, literary travel, current affairs, and some business. We have a highly selective practice in literary fiction, young adult, and middle-grade fiction, and nonfiction. We are now opening our doors to more commercial fiction, but only from authors who have a platform. If you have a platform, please mention it in your query letter. The Strothman Agency seeks out scholars, journalists, and other acknowledged and emerging experts in their fields. We are now actively looking for authors of well-written young adult fiction and nonfiction. Browse the Latest News to get an idea of the types of books that we represent. For more about what we're looking for, read Pitching an Agent: The Strothman Agency on the publishing website www.strothmanagency.com." Does not want to receive commercial fiction, romance, science fiction, or self-help.

HOW TO CONTACT Accepts queries only via e-mail at strothmanagency@gmail.com. See submission guidelines online. Accepts simultaneous submissions. Responds in 4 weeks to queries. Responds in 6 weeks to mss. Obtains most new clients through recommendations from others.

TERMS Agent receives 15% commission on domestic sales. Agent receives 20% commission on foreign sales. Offers written contract; 30-day notice must be given to terminate contract.

◑ EMMA SWEENEY AGENCY, LLC

245 E 80th St., Suite 7E, New York NY 10075. **E-mail:** queries@emmasweeneyagency.com. **Website:** www.emmasweeneyagency.com. Member of AAR. Other memberships include Women's Media Group. Represents 80 clients. 5% of clients are new/unpublished writers. Currently handles nonfiction books (50%), novels (50%).

Prior to becoming an agent, Ms. Sweeney was director of subsidiary rights at Grove Press. Since 1990, she has been a literary agent.

MEMBER AGENTS Emma Sweeney, president; Noah Ballard, rights manager and agent.

REPRESENTS nonfiction books, novels. **Considers these fiction areas:** literary, mainstream, mystery.

Does not want to receive romance, Westerns or screenplays.

HOW TO CONTACT "We accept only electronic queries, and ask that all queries be sent to queries@emmasweeneyagency.com rather than to any agent directly. Please begin your query with a succinct (and hopefully catchy) description of your plot or proposal. Always include a brief cover letter telling us how you heard about ESA, your previous writing credits, and a few lines about yourself. We cannot open any attachments unless they were specifically requested, and ask that you paste the first 10 pages of your proposal or novel into the text of your e-mail."

TERMS Agent receives 15% commission on domestic sales. Agent receives 10% commission on foreign sales.

RECENT SALES *Equal of the Sun*, by Anita Amirrezvani (Scriber); *The Cottage at Glass Beach*, by Heather Barbieri (HarperCollins); *The Thinking Woman's Guide to Real Magic*, by Emily Croy Barker (Pam Dorman Books); *Where Rivers Run Sand,* by Julene Bair (Viking); *My First Coup D'etat*, by John Dramani Mahama (Bloomsbury); *The Day My Brain Exploded*, by Ashok Rajamani (Algonquin).

TALCOTT NOTCH LITERARY

2 Broad St., Second Floor, Suite 10, Milford CT 06460. (203)876-4959. **Fax:** (203)876-9517. **E-mail:** editorial@talcottnotch.net. **Website:** www.talcottnotch.net. **Contact:** Gina Panettieri, president. Represents 35 clients. 25% of clients are new/unpublished writers.

○ Prior to becoming an agent, Ms. Panettieri was a freelance writer and editor.

MEMBER AGENTS Gina Panettieri, gpanettieri@talcottnotch.net (history, business, self-help, science, gardening, cookbooks, crafts, parenting, memoir, true crime, travel, women's fiction, paranormal, urban fantasy, horror, science fiction, historical, mystery, thrillers, and suspense); **Paula Munier**, pmunier@talcottnotch.net (mystery/thriller, science fiction/fantasy, romance, young adult, memoir, humor, pop culture, health and wellness, cooking, self-help, pop psych, New Age, inspirational, technology, science, and writing); **Rachael Dugas**, rdugas@talcottnotch.net (young adult, middle-grade, romance, and women's fiction); **Jessica Negron**, jnegron@talcottnotch.net (commercial fiction, science fiction and fantasy (and all its little subgenres), psychological thrillers, cozy mysteries, romance, erotic romance, young adult).

REPRESENTS Considers these fiction areas: commercial, fantasy, historical, horror, mainstream, middle-grade, mystery, New Age, paranormal, romance, science fiction, suspense, thriller, urban fantasy, women's, young adult.

HOW TO CONTACT Query via e-mail (preferred) with first 10 pages of the ms within the body of the e-mail, not as an attachment. Accepts simultaneous submissions. Responds in 1 week to queries. Responds in 4-6 weeks to mss.

TERMS Agent receives 15% commission on domestic sales. Agent receives 20% commission on foreign sales. Offers written contract, binding for 1 year.

RECENT SALES Sold 36 titles in the last year. *Delivered From Evil*, by Ron Franscell (Fairwinds) and *Sourtoe* (Globe Pequot Press); *Hellforged*, by Nancy Holzner (Berkley Ace Science Fiction); *Welcoming Kitchen; 200 Allergen- and Gluten-Free Vegan Recipes*, by Kim Lutz and Megan Hart (Sterling); *Dr. Seth's Love Prescription*, by Dr. Seth Meyers (Adams Media); *The Book of Ancient Bastards*, by Brian Thornton (Adams Media); *Hope in Courage*, by Beth Fehlbaum (Westside Books; and more.

TIPS "Know your market and how to reach it. A strong platform is essential in your book proposal. Can you effectively use social media? Are you a strong networker? Are you familiar with the book bloggers in your genre? Are you involved with the interest-specific groups that can help you? What can you do to break through the 'noise' and help present your book to your readers? Check our website for more tips and information on this topic."

PATRICIA TEAL LITERARY AGENCY

2036 Vista Del Rosa, Fullerton CA 92831-1336. Phone/Fax: (714)738-8333. **Contact:** Patricia Teal. Member of AAR. Other memberships include RWA, Authors Guild. Represents 20 clients. Currently handles nonfiction books (10%), fiction (90%).

REPRESENTS nonfiction books, novels. **Considers these fiction areas:** glitz, mainstream, mystery, romance, suspense, women's.

⚷ This agency specializes in women's fiction, commercial how-to, and self-help nonfiction. Does not want to receive poetry, short stories, articles, science fiction, fantasy, or regency romance.

HOW TO CONTACT Published authors only. Submit query with SASE. Accepts simultaneous submissions. Obtains most new clients through conferences, recommendations from authors and editors.

TERMS Agent receives 10-15% commission on domestic sales. Agent receives 20% commission on foreign sales. Offers written contract, binding for 1 year. Charges clients for ms copies.

RECENT SALES Sold 30 titles in the last year. *Texas Rose*, by Marie Ferrarella (Silhouette); *Watch Your Language*, by Sterling Johnson (St. Martin's Press); *The Black Sheep's Baby*, by Kathleen Creighton (Silhouette); *Man With a Message*, by Muriel Jensen (Harlequin).

WRITERS CONFERENCES RWA Conferences; Asilomar; BookExpo America; Bouchercon; Maui Writers Conference.

TIPS "Include SASE with all correspondence. I am taking on published authors only."

TRANSATLANTIC LITERARY AGENCY

2 Bloor St., Suite 3500, Toronto ON M4W 1A8 Canada. (416)488-9214. **E-mail:** info@transatlanticagency.com. **Website:** transatlanticagency.com. Represents 250 clients. 10% of clients are new/unpublished writers.

MEMBER AGENTS Trena White (nonfiction); Amy Tompkins (fiction, nonfiction, juvenile); Stephanie Sinclair (fiction, nonfiction); Patricia Ocampo (juvenile/illustrators); Fiona Kenshole (juvenile, illustrators); Samantha Haywood (fiction, nonfiction, graphic novels); Jesse Finkelstein (nonfiction); Marie Campbell (middle-grade fiction); Shaun Bradley (referrals only); Jennifer Starkman; Barb Miller; Lynn Bennett; David Bennett.

REPRESENTS nonfiction books, novels, juvenile. **Considers these fiction areas:** commercial, historical, juvenile, literary, middle-grade, new adult, picture books, romance, women's, young adult.

8—¶ "In both children's and adult literature, we market directly into the United States, the United Kingdom, and Canada." Actively seeking literary children's and adult fiction, nonfiction. Does not want to receive picture books, poetry, screenplays, or stage plays.

HOW TO CONTACT Always refer to the website, as guidelines will change, and only various agents are open to new clients at any given time. Obtains most new clients through recommendations from others.

TERMS Agent receives 15% commission on domestic sales. Agent receives 20% commission on foreign sales. Offers written contract; 45-day notice must be given to terminate contract. This agency charges for photocopying and postage when it exceeds $100.

RECENT SALES Sold 250 titles in the last year.

◐ TRIADA U.S. LITERARY AGENCY, INC.

P.O. Box 561, Sewickley PA 15143. (412)401-3376. **E-mail:** uwe@triadaus.com. **Website:** www.triadaus.com. **Contact:** Dr. Uwe Stender. Member of AAR. Represents 65 clients. 20% of clients are new/unpublished writers.

REPRESENTS fiction, nonfiction. **Considers these fiction areas:** action, adventure, crime, detective, ethnic, historical, horror, juvenile, literary, mainstream, mystery, occult, police, romance, women's, young adult, and mysteries.

8—¶ "We are looking for great writing and story platforms. Our response time is fairly unique. We recognize that neither we nor the authors have time to waste, so we guarantee a 5-day response time. We usually respond within 24 hours. " Actively looking for both fiction and nonfiction in all areas.

HOW TO CONTACT E-mail queries preferred; otherwise query with SASE. "We do not respond to postal submission that aren't accompanied by SASE." Accepts simultaneous submissions. Obtains most new clients through recommendations from others, conferences.

TERMS Agent receives 15% commission on domestic sales. Agent receives 20% commission on foreign sales. Offers written contract; 30-day notice must be given to terminate contract.

RECENT SALES *The Man Whisperer*, by Samantha Brett and Donna Sozio (Adams Media); *Whatever Happened to Pudding Pops*, by Gael Fashingbauer Cooper and Brian Bellmont (Penguin/Perigee); *86'd*, by Dan Fante (Harper Perennial); *Hating Olivia*, by Mark SaFranko (Harper Perennial); *Everything I'm Not Made Me Everything I Am*, by Jeff Johnson (Smiley Books).

TIPS "I comment on all requested mss that I reject."

◐ TRIDENT MEDIA GROUP

41 Madison Ave., 36th Floor, New York NY 10010. (212)333-1511. **E-mail:** press@tridentmediagroup .com; info@tridentmediagroup.com. **E-mail:** ellen .assistant@tridentmediagroup.com. **Website:** www .tridentmediagroup.com. **Contact:** Ellen Levine. Member of AAR.

MEMBER AGENTS Kimberly Whalen, ws.assistant@ tridentmediagroup (commercial fiction and nonfiction, women's fiction, suspense, paranormal, and pop culture); Scott Miller, smiller@trident mediagroup.com (thrillers, crime fiction, women's and book club fiction, and a wide variety of nonfiction, such as military, celebrity and pop culture, narrative, sports, prescriptive, and current events); Alex Glass aglass@tridentmediagroup (literary fiction, crime fiction, pop culture, sports, health and wellness, narrative nonfiction, and children's books); Melissa Flashman, mflashman@tridentmediagroup .com (pop culture, memoir, wellness, popular science, business and economics, and technology—also fiction in the genres of mystery, suspense or young adult); Alyssa Eisner Henkin, ahenkin@trident mediagroup.com (juvenile, children's, young adult); Don Fehr, dfehr@tridentmediagroup.com (literary and commercial fiction, narrative nonfiction, memoirs, travel, science, and health); John Silbersack, silbersack.assistant@tridentmediagroup.com (commercial and literary fiction, science fiction and fantasy, narrative nonfiction, young adult, thrillers); Erica Spellman-Silverman; Ellen Levine, levine .assistant@tridentmediagroup.com (popular commercial fiction and compelling nonfiction—memoir, popular culture, narrative nonfiction, history, politics, biography, science, and the odd quirky book); Mark Gottlieb, mgottlieb@tridentmediagroup.com; MacKenzie Fraser-Bub, MFraserBub@tridentmedia group.com (many genres of fiction—specializing in women's fiction).

REPRESENTS Considers these fiction areas: commercial, crime, fantasy, juvenile, literary, middlegrade, mystery, paranormal, science fiction, suspense, thriller, women's, young adult.

8—☛ Actively seeking new or established authors in a variety of fiction and nonfiction genres.

HOW TO CONTACT Preferred method of query is through the online submission form on the agency website. Query only 1 agent at a time.

RECENT SALES Recent sales include: *Sacred River*, by Syl Cheney-Coker; *Saving Quinton*, by Jessica Sorensen; *The Secret History of Las Vegas*, by Chris Abani; *The Summer Wind*, by Mary Alice Munroe.

TIPS "If you have any questions, please check FAQ page before e-mailing us."

◐ THE UNTER AGENCY

23 W. 73rd St., Suite 100, New York NY 10023. (212)401-4068. **E-mail:** Jennifer@theunteragency .com. **Website:** www.theunteragency.com. **Contact:** Jennifer Unter. Estab. 2008.

◒ Ms. Unter began her book publishing career in the editorial department at Henry Holt & Co. She later worked at the Karpfinger Agency while she attended law school. She then became an associate at the entertainment firm of Cowan, DeBaets, Abrahams & Sheppard LLP, where she practiced primarily in the areas of publishing and copyright law.

REPRESENTS Considers these fiction areas: commercial, mainstream, middle-grade, picture books, young adult.

8—☛ This agency specializes in children's and nonfiction, but also takes quality fiction.

HOW TO CONTACT Send an e-query. There is also an online submission form. If you do not hear back from this agency within 3 months, consider that a No.

RECENT SALES A full list of recent sales/titles is available on the agency website.

◐ UPSTART CROW LITERARY

244 Fifth Avenue, 11th Floor, New York NY 10001. **E-mail:** danielle.submission@gmail.com; alexan dra.submission@gmail.com. **Website:** www.upstart crowliterary.com. **Contact:** Danielle Chiotti, Alexandra Penfold. Estab. 2009.

MEMBER AGENTS Michael Stearns (not accepting submissions); Danielle Chiotti (books ranging from contemporary women's fiction to narrative nonfiction, from romance to relationship stories, humorous tales, and young adult fiction); Ted Malawer (accepting queries only through conference submissions and client referrals); Alexandra Penfold (children's: picture books, middle-grade, YA; illustrators and author/illustrators).

REPRESENTS Considers these fiction areas: middle-grade, picture books, women's, young adult.

HOW TO CONTACT Danielle Chiotti and Alexandra Penfold are currently accepting submissions.

◐ VENTURE LITERARY

2683 Via de la Valle, G-714, Del Mar CA 92014. (619)807-1887. **Fax:** (772)365-8321. **E-mail:** submis sions@ventureliterary.com. **Website:** www.venture literary.com. **Contact:** Frank R. Scatoni. Represents 50 clients. 40% of clients are new/unpublished writers. Currently handles nonfiction books (80%), novels (20%).

◒ Prior to becoming an agent, Mr. Scatoni worked as an editor at Simon & Schuster.

MEMBER AGENTS Frank R. Scatoni (general nonfiction, biography, memoir, narrative nonfiction, sports, serious nonfiction, graphic novels, narratives).

REPRESENTS nonfiction books, novels, graphic novels, narratives. **Considers these fiction areas:** action, adventure, crime, detective, literary, mainstream, mystery, police, sports, suspense, thriller, women's.

8—☛ Specializes in nonfiction, sports, biography, gambling, and nonfiction narratives. Actively seeking nonfiction, graphic novels, and narratives. Does not want fantasy, science fiction, romance, children's picture books, or westerns.

HOW TO CONTACT Considers e-mail queries only. *No unsolicited mss* and no snail mail whatsoever. See website for complete submission guidelines. Obtains most new clients through recommendations from others.

TERMS Agent receives 15% commission on domestic sales. Agent receives 20% commission on foreign sales. Offers written contract.

RECENT SALES *The 9/11 Report: A Graphic Adaptation*, by Sid Jacobson and Ernie Colon (FSG); *Having a Baby*, by Cindy Margolis (Perigee/Penguin); *Phil Gordon's Little Blue Book*, by Phil Gordon (Simon & Schuster); *Atomic America*, by Todd Tucker (Free Press); *War as They Knew It*, by Michael Rosenberg (Grand Central); *Game Day*, by Craig James (Wiley); *The Blueprint*, by Christopher Price (Thomas Dunne Books).

CHERRY WEINER LITERARY AGENCY

925 Oak Bluff Ct., Dacula GA 30019. (732)446-2096. **Fax:** (732)792-0506. **E-mail:** cherry8486@aol.com. **Contact:** Cherry Weiner. Represents 40 clients. 10% of clients are new/unpublished writers. Currently handles nonfiction books (10-20%), novels (80-90%).

REPRESENTS nonfiction books, novels. **Considers these fiction areas:** action, adventure, contemporary issues, crime, detective, family saga, fantasy, frontier, historical, mainstream, mystery, police, psychic, romance, science fiction, supernatural, thriller, westerns.

➤ *This agency is currently not accepting new clients, except by referral or by personal contact at writers conferences.* Specializes in fantasy, science fiction, westerns, mysteries (both contemporary and historical), historical novels, Native-American works, mainstream, and all genre romances.

HOW TO CONTACT Query with SASE. Prefers to read materials exclusively. Does not accept e-mail queries. Responds in 1 week to queries. Responds in 2 months to mss that I have asked for.

TERMS Agent receives 15% commission on domestic sales. Agent receives 15% commission on foreign sales. Offers written contract. Charges clients for extra copies of mss, first-class postage for author's copies of books, express mail for important documents/mss.

RECENT SALES Sold 70 titles in the last year. This agency prefers not to share information on specific sales.

TIPS "Meet agents and publishers at conferences. Establish a relationship, then get in touch with them and remind them of the meeting and conference."

THE WEINGEL-FIDEL AGENCY

310 E. 46th St., 21E, New York NY 10017. (212)599-2959. **Contact:** Loretta Weingel-Fidel. Currently handles nonfiction books (75%), novels (25%).

💬 Prior to opening her agency, Ms. Weingel-Fidel was a psychoeducational diagnostician.

REPRESENTS nonfiction books, novels. **Considers these fiction areas:** literary, mainstream.

➤ This agency specializes in commercial and literary fiction and nonfiction. Actively seeking investigative journalism. Does not want to receive genre fiction, self-help, science fiction, or fantasy.

HOW TO CONTACT Accepts writers by referral only. *No unsolicited mss.*

TERMS Agent receives 15% commission on domestic sales. Agent receives 20% commission on foreign sales. Offers written contract, binding for 1 year with automatic renewal. Bills sent back to clients are all reasonable expenses, such as UPS, express mail, photocopying, etc.

TIPS "A very small, selective list enables me to work very closely with my clients to develop and nurture talent. I only take on projects and writers about which I am extremely enthusiastic."

LARRY WEISSMAN LITERARY, LLC

526 8th St., #2R, Brooklyn NY 11215. **E-mail:** lwsubmissions@gmail.com. **Contact:** Larry Weissman. Represents 35 clients. Currently handles nonfiction books (80%), novels (10%), story collections (10%).

REPRESENTS nonfiction books, novels, short story collections. **Considers these fiction areas:** literary.

➤ "Very interested in established journalists with bold voices. Interested in anything to do with food. Fiction has to feel 'vital' and short stories are accepted, but only if you can sell us on an idea for a novel as well." Nonfiction, including food and lifestyle, politics, pop culture, narrative, cultural/social issues, journalism. No genre fiction, poetry, or children's.

HOW TO CONTACT "Send e-queries only. If you don't hear back, your project was not right for our list."

TERMS Agent receives 15% commission on domestic sales. Agent receives 20% commission on foreign sales.

WELLS ARMS LITERARY

E-mail: info@wellsarms.com. **Website:** www.wellsarms.com. **Contact:** Victoria Wells Arms. Estab. 2013.

Prior to opening her agency, Victoria was a children's book editor for Dial Books.

REPRESENTS Considers these fiction areas: juvenile, middle-grade, picture books, young adult.

We focus on books for readers of all ages, and we particularly love board books, picture books, readers, chapter books, middle-grade, and young adult fiction—both authors and illustrators. We do not represent to the textbook, magazine, adult romance, or fine art markets.

HOW TO CONTACT E-query. Put *Query* in your e-mail subject line. No attachments.

WHIMSY LITERARY AGENCY, LLC

49 North 8th St., G6, Brooklyn NY 11249. (212)674-7161. **E-mail:** whimsynyc@aol.com. **Website:** whimsyliteraryagency.com/. **Contact:** Jackie Meyer. Other memberships include Center for Independent Publishing Advisory Board. Represents 30 clients. 20% of clients are new/unpublished writers. Currently handles nonfiction books (100%).

Prior to becoming an agent, Ms. Meyer was with Warner Books for 19 years; Ms. Vezeris and Ms. Legette have 30 years' experience at various book publishers.

MEMBER AGENTS Jackie Meyer; Olga Vezeris (fiction and nonfiction); Nansci LeGette, senior associate in LA.

REPRESENTS nonfiction books. **Considers these fiction areas:** mainstream.

"Whimsy looks for projects that are concept- and platform-driven. We seek books that educate, inspire and entertain." Actively seeking experts in their field with good platforms.

HOW TO CONTACT Send a query letter via e-mail. Send a synopsis, bio, platform, and proposal. No snail mail submissions. Responds "quickly, but only if interested" to queries. *Does not accept unsolicited mss.* Obtains most new clients through recommendations from others, solicitations.

TERMS Agent receives 15% commission on domestic sales. Agent receives 20% commission on foreign sales. Offers written contract.

WM CLARK ASSOCIATES

186 Fifth Ave., Second Floor, New York NY 10010. (212)675-2784. **Fax:** (347)-649-9262. **E-mail:** general@wmclark.com. **Website:** www.wmclark.com. Estab. 1997. Member of AAR. 50% of clients are new/unpublished writers. Currently handles nonfiction books (50%), novels (50%).

Prior to opening WCA, Mr. Clark was an agent at the William Morris Agency.

REPRESENTS nonfiction books, novels. **Considers these fiction areas:** contemporary issues, ethnic, historical, literary, mainstream Southern fiction.

William Clark represents a wide range of titles across all formats to the publishing, motion picture, television, and new media fields on behalf of authors of first fiction and award-winning, best-selling narrative nonfiction, international authors in translation, chefs, musicians, and artists. Offering individual focus and a global presence, the agency undertakes to discover, develop, and market today's most interesting content and the talent that created it, and forge sophisticated and innovative plans for self-promotion, reliable revenue streams, and an enduring creative career. Referral partners are available to provide services including editorial consultation, media training, lecture booking, marketing support, and public relations. Agency does not respond to screenplays or screenplay pitches. It is advised that before querying you become familiar with the kinds of books we handle by browsing our Book List, which is available on our website.

HOW TO CONTACT Accepts queries via online form only at www.wmclark.com/query-form.html. We respond to all queries submitted via this form. Responds in 1-2 months to queries.

TERMS Agent receives 15% commission on domestic sales. Agent receives 20% commission on foreign sales. Offers written contract.

TIPS "WCA works on a reciprocal basis with Ed Victor, Ltd., (U.K.) in representing select properties to the U.S. market and vice versa. Translation rights are sold directly in the German, Italian, Spanish, Portuguese, Latin American, French, Dutch, and Scandinavian territories in association with Andrew Nurnberg Associates, Ltd., (U.K.); through offices in China, Bulgaria, Czech Republic, Latvia, Poland, Hungary, and Russia; and through corresponding agents in Japan, Greece, Israel, Turkey, Korea, Taiwan, and Thailand."

WOLF LITERARY SERVICES, LLC

Website: wolflit.com. Estab. 2008.

MEMBER AGENTS Kirsten Wolf (not accepting queries); Adrianna Ranta (all genres for all age groups with a penchant for edgy, dark, quirky voices, unique settings, and everyman stories told with a new spin; she loves gritty, realistic, true-to-life stories with conflicts based in the real world; women's fiction and nonfiction; accessible, pop nonfiction in science, history, and craft; and smart, fresh, genre-bending works for children); Kate Johnson (literary fiction, particularly character-driven stories, psychological investigations, modern-day fables, and the occasional high-concept plot; she also represents memoir, cultural history and narrative nonfiction, and loves working with journalists); Allison Devereux (magical realism, literary fiction, stories featuring picaresque characters, and books on art and design).

REPRESENTS Considers these fiction areas: literary, women's, young adult, magical realism.

HOW TO CONTACT To submit a project, please send a query letter along with a 50-page writing sample (for fiction) or a detailed proposal (for nonfiction) to queries@wolflit.com. Samples may be submitted as an attachment or embedded in the body of the e-mail. Responds if interested.

RECENT SALES *Hoodoo*, by Ronald Smith (Clarion); *Edible*, by Daniella Martin (Amazon Publishing); *Not a Drop to Drink*, by Mandy McGinnis (Katherine Tegen Books); *The Empire Striketh Back*, by Ian Doescher (Quirk Books).

WOLFSON LITERARY AGENCY

P.O. Box 266, New York NY 10276. **E-mail:** query@ wolfsonliterary.com. **Website:** www.wolfsonliterary .com. **Contact:** Michelle Wolfson. Estab. 2007. Adheres to AAR canon of ethics.

○ Prior to forming her own agency in December 2007, Ms. Wolfson spent 2 years with Artists & Artisans, Inc., and 2 years with Ralph Vicinanza, Ltd.

⚬━ Actively seeking commercial fiction: young adult, mainstream, mysteries, thrillers, suspense, women's fiction, romance, practical or narrative nonfiction (particularly of interest to women).

HOW TO CONTACT E-queries only! Accepts simultaneous submissions. Responds only if interested. Positive response is generally given within 2-4 weeks. Responds in 3 months to mss. Obtains most new clients through queries or recommendations from others.

TERMS Agent receives 15% commission on domestic sales. Agent receives 25% commission on foreign sales. Offers written contract; 30-day notice must be given to terminate contract.

WRITERS CONFERENCES SDSU Writers Conference; New Jersey Romance Writers of America Writers Conference; American Independent Writers Conference in Washington D.C.

TIPS "Be persistent."

WRITERS' REPRESENTATIVES, LLC

116 W. 14th St., 11th Floor, New York NY 10011-7305. **E-mail:** transom@writersreps.com. **Website:** www .writersreps.com. Represents 100 clients. Currently handles nonfiction books (90%), novels (10%).

○ Prior to becoming an agent, Ms. Chu was a lawyer; Mr. Hartley worked at Simon & Schuster, Harper & Row, and Cornell University Press.

MEMBER AGENTS Lynn Chu, Glen Hartley.

REPRESENTS nonfiction books, novels. **Considers these fiction areas:** literary.

⚬━ Serious nonfiction and quality fiction. No motion picture or television screenplays.

HOW TO CONTACT Query with SASE. Prefers to read materials exclusively. Considers simultaneous queries, but must be informed at time of submission. Consult the "FAQ" section of the website for detailed submission guidelines.

TERMS Agent receives 15% commission on domestic sales. Agent receives 20% commission on foreign sales.

TIPS "Always include an SASE; it will ensure a response from the agent and the return of your submitted material."

HELEN ZIMMERMANN LITERARY AGENCY

New Paltz NY 12561. **E-mail:** submit@ZimmAgency .com. **Website:** www.zimmermannliterary.com. **Contact:** Helen Zimmermann. Estab. 2003. Currently handles nonfiction books (80%), other (20% fiction).

○ Prior to opening her agency, Ms. Zimmermann was the director of advertising and promotion at Random House and the events coordinator at an independent bookstore.

REPRESENTS Considers these fiction areas: literary.

⚬━ "As an agent who has experience at both a publishing house and a bookstore, I have a keen insight for viable projects. This experience also helps me ensure every client gets published well, through the whole process." Actively seeking memoirs, pop culture, women's issues, and accessible literary fiction. Does not want to receive horror, science fiction, poetry, or romance.

HOW TO CONTACT Accepts e-mail queries only. E-mail should include a short description of project and bio, whether it be fiction or nonfiction. Accepts simultaneous submissions. Responds in 2 weeks to queries. Responds in 1 month to mss. Obtains most new clients through recommendations from others, solicitations.

TERMS Agent receives 15% commission on domestic sales. Offers written contract; 30-day notice must be given to terminate contract.

WRITERS CONFERENCES BEA/Writer's Digest Books Writers Conference; Portland, ME Writers Conference; Berkshire Writers and Readers Conference; La Jolla Writers Conference; The New School Writers Conference; Vermont Writers Conference; ASJA Conference; Books Alive! Conference; Southeast Writers Conference; Kansas Writers Conference.

MAGAZINES

//

This section contains magazine listings that fall into one of several categories: literary, consumer, small circulation, and online. Our decision to combine magazines under one section was two-fold: All of these magazines represent markets specifically for short fiction, and many magazines now publish both print and online versions, making them more difficult to subcategorize. Below, we outline specifics for literary, online, consumer, and small circulation magazines.

LITERARY MAGAZINES

Although definitions of what constitutes literary writing vary, editors of literary journals agree they want to publish the best fiction they can acquire. Qualities they look for in fiction include fully developed characters, strong and unique narrative voice, flawless mechanics, and careful attention to detail in content and manuscript preparation. Most of the authors writing such fiction are well read and well educated, and many are students and graduates of university creative writing programs.

Stepping Stones to Recognition

Some well-established literary journals pay several hundred or even several thousand dollars for a short story. Most, though, can only pay with contributor's copies or a subscription to their publication. However, being published in literary journals offers the important benefits of experience, exposure, and prestige. Agents and major book publishers regularly read literary magazines in search of new writers. Work from these journals is also selected for inclusion in annual prize anthologies.

You'll find most of the well-known prestigious literary journals listed here. Many, including *The Southern Review* and *Ploughshares*, are associated with universities, while others like *The Paris Review* are independently published.

Selecting the Right Literary Magazine

Once you have browsed through this section and have a list of journals you might like to submit to, read those listings again carefully. Remember, this is information editors provide to help you submit work that fits their needs. Note that you will find some magazines that do not read submissions all year long. Whether limited reading periods are tied to a university schedule or meant to accommodate the capabilities of a very small staff, those periods are noted within listings (when the editors notify us). The staffs of university journals are usually made up of student editors and a managing editor who is also a faculty member. These staffs often change every year. Whenever possible, we indicate this in listings and give the name of the current editor and the length of that editor's term. Also be aware that the schedule of a university journal usually coincides with that university's academic year, meaning that the editors of most university publications are difficult or impossible to reach during the summer.

Furthering Your Search

It cannot be stressed enough that reading the listings for literary journals is only the first part of developing your marketing plan. The second part, equally important, is to obtain fiction guidelines and to read with great care the actual journal you'd like to submit to. Reading copies of these journals helps you determine the fine points of each magazine's publishing style and sensibility. There is no substitute for this type of hands-on research.

Unlike commercial periodicals available at most newsstands and bookstores, it requires a little more effort to obtain some of the literary magazines listed. The super-chain bookstores are doing a better job these days of stocking literaries, and you can find some in independent and college bookstores, especially those published in your area. The Internet is an invaluable resource for submission guidelines, as more and more journals establish an online presence. You may, however, need to send for a sample copy. We include sample copy prices in the listings whenever possible. In addition to reading your sample copies, pay close attention to the **Tips** section of each listing. There you'll often find a very specific description of the style of fiction the editors at that publication prefer.

Another way to find out more about literary magazines is to check out the various prize anthologies and take note of journals whose fiction is being selected for publication in them. Studying prize anthologies not only lets you know which magazines are publishing award-winning work, but it also provides a valuable overview of what is considered to be the best fiction published today. Those anthologies include:

- *Best American Short Stories*, published by Houghton Mifflin
- *New Stories from the South: The Year's Best*, published by Algonquin Books of Chapel Hill
- *The O. Henry Prize Stories*, published by Doubleday/Anchor
- *Pushcart Prize: Best of the Small Presses,* published by Pushcart Press

CONSUMER MAGAZINES

Consumer magazines are publications that reach a broad readership. Many have circulations in the hundreds of thousands or millions. And among the oldest magazines listed in this section are ones not only familiar to us, but also to our parents, grandparents, and even great-grandparents: *The Atlantic Monthly* (1857), *Esquire* (1933), and *Ellery Queen's Mystery Magazine* (1941).

Consumer periodicals make excellent markets for fiction in terms of exposure, prestige, and payment. Because these magazines are well known, however, competition is great. Even the largest consumer publications buy only one or two stories an issue, yet thousands of writers submit to these popular magazines.

Despite the odds, it is possible for talented new writers to break into consumer magazines. Your keys to breaking into these markets include careful research, professional presentation, and, of course, top-quality fiction.

SMALL-CIRCULATION MAGAZINES

Small-circulation magazines include general interest, special interest, regional, and genre magazines with circulations under ten thousand. Although these magazines vary greatly in size, theme, format, and management, the editors are all looking for short stories. Their specific fiction needs present writers of all degrees of expertise and interests with an abundance of publishing opportunities. Among the diverse publications in this section are magazines devoted to almost every topic, every level of writing, and every type of writer. Some of these markets publish fiction about a particular geographic area or by authors who live in that locale.

Although not as high-paying as the large-circulation consumer magazines, you'll find some of the publications listed here do pay writers 1–5¢/word or more. Also, unlike the big consumer magazines, these markets are very open to new writers and relatively easy to break into. Their only criterion is that your story be well written, well presented, and suitable for their particular readership.

ONLINE MARKETS

As production and distribution costs go up and the number of subscribers falls, more and more magazines are giving up print publication and moving online. Relatively inexpensive to maintain and quicker to accept and post submissions, online fiction sites are growing fast in numbers and legitimacy. The benefit for writers is that your stories can get more attention in online journals than in small literary journals. Small journals have small print runs—five hundred to one thousand copies—so there's a limit on how many people will read your work. There is no limit when your work appears online.

There is also no limit to the types of online journals being published, offering outlets for a rich and diverse community of voices. These include genre sites, particular those for science fiction, fantasy, and horror, and mainstream short fiction markets. Online literary journals range from the traditional to those with a decidedly quirkier bent. Writers will also find online outlets for more highly experimental and multimedia work.

While the medium of online publication is different, the traditional rules of publishing apply to submissions. Writers should research the site and archives carefully, looking for a match in sensibility for their work. Follow submission guidelines exactly and submit courteously. True, these sites aren't bound by traditional print schedules, so your work theoretically may be published more quickly. But that doesn't mean online journals have larger staffs, so exercise patience with editors considering your manuscript.

A final note about online publication: Like literary journals, the majority of these markets are either nonpaying or very low paying. In addition, writers will not receive print copies of the publications because of the medium. So in most cases, do not expect to be paid for your exposure.

SELECTING THE RIGHT MARKET

First, zero in on those markets most likely to be interested in your work. Begin by looking at the Category Index. If your work is more general—or conversely, very specialized—you may wish to browse through the listings, perhaps looking up those magazines published in your state or region.

In addition to browsing through the listings and using the Category Index, check the openness icons at the beginning of listings to find those most likely to be receptive to your work. This is especially true for beginning writers, who should look for magazines that say they are especially open to new writers O and for those giving equal weight to both new and established writers ◑. For more explanation about these icons, see the inside back cover of this book.

Once you have a list of magazines you might like to try, read their listings carefully. Much of the material within each listing carries clues that tell you more about the magazine. "How to Use *NSSWM*" describes in detail the listing information common to all the markets in this book.

The physical description appearing near the beginning of the listings can give you clues about the size and financial commitment to the publication. This is not always an indication of quality, but chances are a publication with expensive paper and four-color artwork on the cover has more prestige than a photocopied publication featuring a clip-art cover.

FURTHERING YOUR SEARCH

Most of the magazines listed here are published in the U.S. You will also find some English-speaking markets from around the world. These foreign publications are denoted with a ☻ symbol at the beginning of listings. To make it easier to find Canadian markets, we include a ☼ symbol at the start of those listings.

5-TROPE

Website: www.5trope.com. **Contact:** Gunnar Benediktsson, editor. Estab. 1999. "Our intention is to seek out guest editors, who will solicit excellent experimental work from their colleagues, which we will then publish; and in this way each issue will become the fruit of a single editor's labour and guidance, a thematically-united work of Internet art in its own right. Let us call this *5_trope*'s overarching experiment: to discover what happens when editorship and authorship collide. We welcome applications for guest editorship, but please be aware that applications will not be considered from novice writers and that we may not be able to respond to every person we do not select. Applications may be sent to: editor.5trope@gmail.com. Give us your best pitch."

✚◐ 580 SPLIT, A JOURNAL OF ARTS AND LETTERS

Mills College P.O. Box 9982, Oakland CA 94613-0982. **Website:** www.mills.edu/academics/graduate/eng/about/580_split.php. Mills College, P.O. Box 9982, Oakland CA 94613-0982. **Website:** www.580split.com. **Contact:** Nina LaCour, prose editor. Literary magazine/journal: 6×10, 170 pages, matte cover. Contains illustrations. Includes photographs. "We publish innovative, risk-taking fiction, poetry, creative nonfiction and art." Annual. Estab. 1999. Circ. 600. Member of SPD. "*580 Split* is an annual journal of arts and literature published by graduate students of the English Department at Mills College. This national literary journal includes innovative and risk-taking fiction, creative nonfiction, poetry, and art and is one of the few literary journals carried by the Oakland Public Library. *580 Split* is also distributed in well-known Bay Area bookstores."

NEEDS Experimental, humor/satire, literary, translations. Receives 50-70 mss/month. Accepts 7-10 mss/issue. Does not read mss November 1-July 1. Ms published 3 months after acceptance. **Publishes 5 new writers/year.** Published Michelle Lee, Victor LaValle, Karina Fuentes, Lisa Jarnot. Length: 4,500 words (maximum). Average length: 3,000 words. Publishes short shorts. Average length of short shorts: 500 words. Also publishes poetry. Never comments on/critiques rejected mss.

HOW TO CONTACT Send complete ms with cover letter. Include brief bio. Responds to queries in 3 weeks. Send disposable copy of ms and #10 SASE for reply only. Considers simultaneous submissions. Sample copy available for $7.50. Guidelines available for SASE.

PAYMENT/TERMS Writers receive 2 contributors copies. Additional copies $5. Pays on publication. Acquires first rights. Sends galleys to author. Publication is copyrighted.

TIPS "Get a hold of a past issue, read through it, find out what we are about. Check the website for most recent information."

◑ ABLE MUSE

467 Saratoga Ave., #602, San Jose CA 95129-1326. **Website:** www.ablemuse.com. **Contact:** Alex Pepple, editor. Estab. 1999. "*Able Muse: A Review of Poetry, Prose & Art*, published twice/year, features predominantly metrical and formal poetry complemented by art and photography, fiction, and nonfiction including essays, book reviews, and interviews. We are looking for well-crafted poems of any length or subject that employ skillful and imaginative use of meter and rhyme, executed in a contemporary idiom, that reads as naturally as your free verse poems."

○ Considers poetry by teens. "High levels of craft still required even for teen writers." Has published poetry by Mark Jarman, A.E. Stallings, Annie Finch, Rhina P. Espaillat, Rachel Hadas, and R.S. Gwynn. Receives about 1,500 poems/year, accepts about 5%. Subscription: $24 for 1 year. Also sponsors 2 annual contests: The Able Muse Write Prize for Poetry & Fiction, and The Able Muse Book Award for Poetry (in collaboration with Able Muse Press at www.ablemusepress.com). See website for details.

◑ ACM (ANOTHER CHICAGO MAGAZINE)

P.O. Box 408439, Chicago IL 60640. **E-mail:** editors@anotherchicagomagazine.net. **Website:** www.anotherchicagomagazine.net. **Contact:** Jacob S. Knabb, editor-in-chief; Caroline Eick Kasner, managing editor. Estab. 1977. "*Another Chicago Magazine* is a biannual literary magazine that publishes work by both new and established writers. We look for work that goes beyond the artistic and academic to include and address the larger world. The editors read submissions in fiction, poetry, creative nonfiction, etc., year-round. We often publish special theme issues and sections. We will post upcoming themes on our website. Fiction: Short stories and novel excerpts of 15-20 pages or less. Poetry: Usually no more than 4 pages. Creative Nonfiction: Usually no more than 20 pages. Et Al: Work that doesn't quite fit into the other genres, such as Word and Image Texts, Satire, and Interviews."

○ Work published in *ACM* has been included frequently in *The Best American Poetry* and *The Pushcart Prize*.

NEEDS Short stories and novel excerpts of 15-20 pages or less.

HOW TO CONTACT "Please include the following contact information in your cover letter and on your ms: Byline (name as you want it to appear if published), mailing address, phone number, and e-mail. Include a self-addressed stamped envelope (SASE). If an SASE is not enclosed, you will hear from us only if we are interested in your work. Include the genre (e.g., fiction) of your work in the address."

PAYMENT/TERMS Pays small honorarium when possible, contributor's copies and 1 year subscription.

TIPS "Support literary publishing by subscribing to at least 1 literary journal—if not ours, another. Get used to rejection slips, and don't get discouraged. Keep introductory letters short. Make sure ms has name and address on every page, and that it is clean, neat, and proofread. We are looking for stories with freshness and originality in subject angle and style and work that encounters the world."

◑ THE ADIRONDACK REVIEW

Black Lawrence Press, 8405 Bay Parkway, Apt C8, Brooklyn NY 11214. **E-mail:** editors@theadirondack review.com. **Website:** www.adirondackreview.home stead.com. **Contact:** Angela Leroux-Lindsey, editor; Kara Christenson, senior fiction editor; Nicholas Samaras, poetry editor. Estab. 2000. *The Adirondack Review*, published quarterly online, is a literary journal dedicated to quality free verse poetry and short fiction, as well as book and film reviews, art, photography, and interviews. "Our only requirement is excellence. We would like to publish more French and German poetry translations as well as original poems in these languages. We publish an eclectic mix of voices and styles, but all poems should show attention to craft. We are open to beginners who demonstrate talent, as well as established voices. The work should speak for itself."

○ Uses online submissions manager.

NEEDS Length: 700-8,000 words.

HOW TO CONTACT Send complete ms with cover letter. Include estimated word count, brief bio, list of publications, and "how you learned about the magazine." Submit via online submissions manager.

TIPS "*The Adirondack Review* accepts submissions all year long, so send us your poetry, fiction, nonfiction, translation, reviews, interviews, and art and photography. Please note that we've recently shifted our submission management to Submittable."

◐ ADVOCATE, PKA'S PUBLICATION

1881 Little Westkill Rd., Prattsville NY 12468. (518)299-3103. **Website:** Advocatepka.weebly.com; www.facebook.com/Advocate/PKAPublications; www.facebook.com/GaitedHorseAssociation. **Contact:** Patricia Keller, publisher. Estab. 1987. *Advocate, PKA's Publication*, published bimonthly, is an advertiser-supported tabloid using "original, previously unpublished works, such as feature stories, essays, 'think' pieces, letters to the editor, profiles, humor, fiction, poetry, puzzles, cartoons, or line drawings. Advocates for good writers and quality writings. We publish art, fiction, photos, and poetry. *Advocate*'s submitters are talented people of all ages who do not earn their livings as writers."

○ "This publication has a strong horse orientation." Includes Gaited Horse Association newsletter. Horse-oriented stories, poetry, art, and photos are currently needed.

NEEDS "Nothing religious, pornographic, violent, erotic, pro-drug or anti-enviroment."

HOW TO CONTACT Send complete ms.

TIPS "Please, no simultaneous submissions, work that has appeared on the Internet, pornography, overt religiousity, anti-environmentalism, or gratuitous violence. Artists and photographers should keep in mind that we are a b&w paper. Please do not send postcards. Use envelope with SASE."

◑ AFRICAN VOICES

African Voices Communications, Inc., 270 W. 96th St., New York NY 10025. (212)865-2982. **Fax:** (212)316-3335. **E-mail:** africanvoicesmag@gmail.com. **Website:** www.africanvoices.com. Estab. 1992. *African Voices*, published quarterly, is an "art and literary magazine that highlights the work of people of color. We publish ethnic literature and poetry on any subject. We also consider all themes and styles: avant-garde, free verse, haiku, light verse, and traditional. We do not wish to limit the reader or author."

Considers poetry written by children. Has published poetry by Reg E. Gaines, Maya Angelou, Jessica Care Moore, Asha Bandele, Tony Medina, and Louis Reyes Rivera. *African Voices* is about 48 pages, magazine-sized, professionally printed, saddle-stapled, with paper cover. Receives about 100 submissions/year, accepts about 30%. Press run is 20,000. Single copy: $6; subscription: $20.

NEEDS Length: 500-2,500 words.

HOW TO CONTACT Send complete ms. Include short bio. Send SASE for return of ms. Responds in 3 months to queries.

PAYMENT/TERMS Pays $25-50. Pays on publication for first North American serial rights.

TIPS "A ms stands out if it is neatly typed with a well-written and interesting storyline or plot. Originality is encouraged. We are interested in more horror, erotic, and drama pieces. *AV* wants to highlight the diversity in our culture. Stories must touch the humanity in us all. We strongly encourage new writers/poets to send in their work. Accepted contributors are encouraged to subscribe."

A GATHERING OF THE TRIBES

P.O. Box 20693, Tompkins Square Station, New York NY 10009. (212)674-3778. **Fax:** (212)674-5576. **E-mail:** gatheringofthetribes@gmail.com. **Website:** www.tribes.org. **Contact:** Steve Cannon. Estab. 1992. *A Gathering of the Trees* is a multicultural and multigenerational publication featuring poetry, fiction, interviews, essays, visual art, and musical scores. Audience is anyone interested in the arts from a diverse perspective."

Magazine: 8½×10; 130 pages; glossy paper and cover; illustrations; photos. Receives 20 unsolicited mss/month. Publishes 40% new writers/year. Has published work by Carl Watson, Ishle Park, Wang Pang, and Hanif Kureishi. Sponsors awards/contests.

NEEDS "Would like to see more satire/humor. We are open to all; just no poor writing/grammar/syntax." Publishes short shorts. Length: 2,500-5,000 words.

HOW TO CONTACT Send complete ms. Send SASE for reply or return of ms, or send a disposable copy of ms. Accepts simultaneous and reprints submissions.

PAYMENT/TERMS Pays 1 contributor's copy; additional copies $12.50.

TIPS "Make sure your work has substance."

AGNI

Creative Writing Program, Boston University, 236 Bay State Rd., Boston MA 02215. (617)353-7135. **Fax:** (617)353-7134. **E-mail:** agni@bu.edu. **Website:** www.agnimagazine.org. **Contact:** Sven Birkerts, editor. Estab. 1972. "Eclectic literary magazine publishing first-rate poems, essays, translations, and stories."

Reading period is September 1-May 31 only. Online magazine carries original content not found in print edition. All submissions are considered for both. Founding editor Askold Melnyczuk won the 2001 Nora Magid Award for Magazine Editing. Work from *AGNI* has been included and cited regularly in *The Pushcart Prize* and *Best American* anthologies.

NEEDS Buys stories, prose poems. "No science fiction or romance."

HOW TO CONTACT Query by mail.

PAYMENT/TERMS Pays $10/page up to $150, a one-year subscription, and for print publication: 2 contributor's copies and 4 gift copies.

TIPS "We're also looking for extraordinary translations from little-translated languages. It is important to read work published in *AGNI* before submitting, to see if your own might be compatible."

AG WEEKLY

Lee Agri-Media, P.O. Box 918, Bismarck ND 58501. (701)255-4905. **Fax:** (701)255-2312. **E-mail:** mark.conlon@lee.net. **Website:** www.agweekly.com. **Contact:** Mark Conlon, editor. *Ag Weekly* is an agricultural publication covering production, markets, regulation, politics. Writers need to be familiar with Idaho agricultural commodities. No printed component; website with 6,000 monthly unique visitors; weekly e-mail newsletter with 3,000 subscribers.

ALASKA QUARTERLY REVIEW

University of Alaska-Anchorage, 3211 Providence Dr. (ESH 208), Anchorage AK 99508. (907)786-6916. **E-mail:** aqr@uaa.alaska.edu. **Website:** www.uaa.alaska.edu/aqr. **Contact:** Ronald Spatz, editor-in-chief. Estab. 1982. *"Alaska Quarterly Review* is a literary journal devoted to contemporary literary art, publishing fiction, short plays, poetry, photo essays, and literary nonfiction in traditional and experimental styles. The editors encourage new and emerging writers, while continuing to publish award-winning and established writers."

○ Magazine: 6×9; 232-300 pages; 60 lb. Glatfelter paper; 12 pt. C1S black ink or 4-color; varnish cover stock; photos on cover and photo essays

NEEDS Receives 500 unsolicited mss/month. Accepts 7-18 mss/issue; 15-30 mss/year. Reads unsolicited mss August 15-May 15. Publishes ms 6 months after acceptance. **Publishes 6 new writers/year.** Recently published work by Linda LeGarde Grover, Scott Bear Don't Walk, Don Lago, Mark Wisniewski, Bojan Louis, Kirstin Allio, Aurelie Sheehan, Victoria Patterson, Amy Hempel, Lily Tuck, Christopher Kennedy, Julia Salvin, Bernard Cooper, Edith Pearlman. Publishes short shorts. "Works in *AQR* have certain characteristics: freshness, honesty, and a compelling subject. The voice of the piece must be strong—idiosyncratic enough to create a unique persona. We look for craft, putting it in a form where it becomes emotionally and intellectually complex. Many pieces in *AQR* concern everyday life. We're not asking our writers to go outside themselves and their experiences to the absolute exotic to catch our interest. We look for the experiential and revelatory qualities of the work. We will champion a piece that may be less polished or stylistically sophisticated, if it engages me, surprises me, and resonates for me. The joy in reading such a work is in discovering something true. Moreover, in keeping with our mission to publish new writers, we are looking for voices our readers do not know, voices that may not always be reflected in the dominant culture and that, in all instances, have something important to convey." No romance, children's, or inspirational/religious. Length: 100 pages maximum.

PAYMENT/TERMS Pays $50-200 subject to funding; pays in contributor's copies and subscriptions when funding is limited. Honorariums on publication when funding permits.

TIPS "Although we respond to e-mail queries, we cannot review electronic submissions."

◑◐◉ ALBEDO ONE

8 Bachelor's Walk, Dublin 1 Ireland. (353)1 8730 177. **E-mail:** bobn@yellowbrickroad.ie. **Website:** www.albedo.com. **Contact:** Bob Nielson. Estab. 1993. "We hope to publish interesting and unusual fiction by new and established writers. We will consider anything, as long as it is well written and entertaining, though our definitions of both may not be exactly mainstream. We like stories with plot and characters that live on the page. Most of our audience are prob-

ably committed genre fans, but we try to appeal to a broad spectrum of readers."

NEEDS Length: 2,000-8,000 words.

PAYMENT/TERMS Pays €6 per 1,000 words, to a maximum of 8,000 words, and 1 contributor's copy.

TIPS "We look for good writing, good plot, good characters. Read the magazine, and don't give up."

⊕◐ THE ALEMBIC

Providence College, English Department, Attn: The Alembic Editors, 1 Cunningham Square, Providence RI 02918-0001. **Website:** www.providence.edu/english/creative-writing/Pages/alembic.aspx. **Contact:** Magazine has revolving editor. Editorial term: 1 year. Estab. 1940. "*The Alembic* is an international literary journal featuring the work of both established and student writers and photographers. It is published each April by Providence College in Providence, Rhode Island."

○ Magazine: 6×9, 80 pages. Contains illustrations, photographs.

NEEDS "We are open to all styles of fiction." Receives 200 mss/month. Accepts 5 mss/issue; 5 mss/year. Does not read December-July. Published Bruce Smith, Robin Behn, Rane Arroyo, Sharon Dolin, Jeff Friedman, Khalid Mattawa. Length: 6,000 words maximum.

HOW TO CONTACT Send complete ms with cover letter. Include brief bio. Send SASE (or IRC) for return of ms. Considers simultaneous submissions. Guidelines available for SASE, via e-mail.

PAYMENT/TERMS Writers receive 2 contributor's copies. Additional copies $15.

TIPS "We're looking for stories that are wise, memorable, grammatical, economical, poetic in the right places, and end strongly. Take Heraclitus' claim that 'character is fate' to heart and study the strategies, styles, and craft of such masters as Anton Chekov, J. Cheever, Flannery O'Connor, John Updike, Rick Bass, Phillip Roth, Joyce Carol Oates, William Treavor, Lorrie Moore, and Ethan Canin."

◐ ALIMENTUM, THE LITERATURE OF FOOD

P.O. Box 210028, Nashville TN 37221. **E-mail:** editor@alimentumjournal.com. **Website:** www.alimentumjournal.com. **Contact:** Peter Selgin, fiction and nonfiction editor; Cortney Davis, poetry editor. Estab. 2005. "*Alimentum* celebrates the literature and art of food. We welcome work from like-minded writers, musicians, and artists."

○ Semiannual. *Alimentum* is 128 pages, perfect-bound, with matte coated cover with 4-color art, interior b&w illustration includes ads. Contains illustrations. Essays appearing in *Alimentium* have appeared in *Best American Essays* and *Best Food Writing*.

NEEDS Published Mark Kurlansky, Oliver Sacks, Dick Allen, Ann Hood, Carly Sachs. Publishes short shorts. Also publishes literary essays, poetry, spot illustrations. Rarely comments on/critiques rejected mss. Length: 2,000 words (maximum). Average length: 1,000-2,000 words.

HOW TO CONTACT Send complete ms with cover letter (snail mail only). Send either SASE (or IRC) for return of ms or send disposable copy of ms and #10 SASE for reply only.

PAYMENT/TERMS Writers receive 1 contributor's copy. Additional contributor's copies $8.

TIPS "No e-mail submissions, only snail mail. Mark outside envelope to the attention of Poetry, Fiction, or Nonfiction Editor."

◑⊛ ALIVE NOW

1908 Grand Ave., P.O. Box 340004, Nashville TN 37203. (615)340-7254. **Fax:** (615)340-7267. **E-mail:** alivenow@upperroom.org. **Website:** www.alivenow.org; www.upperroom.org. **Contact:** Beth A. Richardson, editor. Estab. 1971. *Alive Now*, published bimonthly, is a devotional magazine that invites readers to enter an ever-deepening relationship with God. "*Alive Now* seeks to nourish people who are hungry for a sacred way of living. Submissions should invite readers to see God in the midst of daily life by exploring how contemporary issues impact their faith lives. Each word must be vivid and dynamic and contribute to the whole. We make selections based on a list of upcoming themes. Mss which do not fit a theme will be returned." *Alive Now* is 48 pages.

PAYMENT/TERMS Pays $35 or more on acceptance.

⊕ ALL DUE RESPECT

Full Dark City Press, 2976 W. 100 S., Greenfield IN 46140. **E-mail:** allduerespectcrimeblog@yahoo.com. **Website:** all-due-respect.blogspot.com. **Contact:** Chris Ratigan, editor; Mike Monson, managing editor. Estab. 2010. *All Due Respect* is a quarterly digital and hard copy magazine featuring fiction. Works with publisher Full Dark City Press.

NEEDS Length: 3,000-10,000 words.

HOW TO CONTACT Submit complete ms via e-mail. Before submission, format your story in the following manner: double-spaced; first line of paragraphs indented ¼"; use 3 asterisks, centered, to indicate scene breaks; and save the file as: last name_title of story.doc (or .docx or .rtf).

PAYMENT/TERMS Pays $25 for fiction.

◐ THE ALLEGHENY REVIEW

Allegheny College Box 32, Meadville PA 16335. **Website:** alleghenyreview.wordpress.com. **Contact:** Senior Editor. Estab. 1983. "*The Allegheny Review* is one of America's only nationwide literary magazines exclusively for undergraduate works of poetry, fiction, and nonfiction. Our intended audience is persons interested in quality literature."

○ Annual. Magazine: 6×9; 100 pages; illustrations; photos. Has published work by Dianne Page, Monica Stahl, and DJ Kinney.

NEEDS Receives 50 unsolicited mss/month. Accepts 3 mss/issue. Publishes ms 2 months after deadline. Publishes roughly 90% new writers/year. Also publishes short shorts (up to 20 pages), nonfiction, and poetry. "We accept nothing but fiction by currently enrolled undergraduate students. We consider anything catering to an intellectual audience." Length: up to 20 pages, double-spaced.

HOW TO CONTACT Send complete mss with a cover letter. Accepts submissions through online submission system only. "We no longer accept regular mail or e-mail submissions."

PAYMENT/TERMS Pays 1 contributor's copy; additional copies $3. Sponsors awards/contests; reading fee of $5.

TIPS "We look for quality work that has been thoroughly revised. Unique voice, interesting topic, and playfulness with the English language. Revise, revise, revise! And be careful how you send it—the cover letter says a lot. We definitely look for diversity in the pieces we publish."

◐◑⊛ ALLEGORY

P.O. Box 2714, Cherry Hill NJ 08034. **E-mail:** submissions@allegoryezine.com. **Website:** www.allegoryezine.com. **Contact:** Ty Drago, editor. Estab. 1998. "We are an e-zine by writers for writers. Our articles focus on the art, craft, and business of writing. Our links and editorial policy all focus on the needs of fiction authors."

Peridot Books won the Page One Award for Literary Contribution.

NEEDS Receives 150 unsolicited mss/month. Accepts 8 mss/issue; 24 mss/year. Agented fiction 5%. Publishes 10 new writers/year. Also publishes literary essays, literary criticism. Often comments on rejected mss. "No media tie-ins (*Star Trek*, *Star Wars*, etc., or space opera, vampires)." Length: 1,500-7,500 words; average length: 4,500 words.

HOW TO CONTACT "All submissions should be sent by e-mail (no letters or telephone calls) in either TXT or .rtf format. Please type 'Submission [Title]-[first and last name]' in the subject line. Include the following in both the body of the e-mail and the attachment: your name, name to use on the story (byline) if different, your preferred e-mail address, your mailing address, the story's title, and the story's word count."

PAYMENT/TERMS Pays $15/story-article.

TIPS "Give us something original, preferably with a twist. Avoid gratuitous sex or violence. Funny always scores points. Be clever, imaginative, but be able to tell a story with proper mood and characterization. Put your name and e-mail address in the body of the story. Read the site and get a feel for it before submitting."

◑ ALLIGATOR JUNIPER

Prescott College, 220 Grove Ave., Prescott AZ 86301. **Website:** alligatorjuniper.wordpress.com. "*Alligator Juniper* features contemporary poetry, fiction, creative nonfiction, and b&w photography. We encourage submissions from writers and photographers at all levels—emerging, early career, and established." Annual magazine comprised of the winners and finalists of national contests. "All entrants pay a $15 submission fee and receive a complementary copy of that year's issue in the spring. First-place winning writers in each genre recieve a $1,000 prize. The first-place winner in photography receives a $500 award. Finalists in writing and images are published and paid in contributor copies. There is currently no avenue for submissions other than the annual contest."

NEEDS "No children's literature or genre work." Length: up to 30 pages.

HOW TO CONTACT Accepts submissions only through annual contest. Submit via online submission form or regular mail. If submitting by regular mail, include $15 entry fee payable to *Alligator Juniper* for each story. Simultaneous submissions accepted, but "contact us if your work is selected elsewhere."

Include cover letter with name, address, phone number, and e-mail. Mss should be typed with numbered pages, double-spaced, 12-point font, and 1" margins. Include author's name on first page. "Double-sided submissions are encouraged." No e-mail submissions.

◐ AMERICAN LITERARY REVIEW

University of North Texas, P.O. Box 311307, Denton TX 76203-1307. (940)565-2755. **Fax:** (940)565-4355. **E-mail:** americanliteraryreview@gmail.com. **Website:** www.english.unt.edu/alr/index.html. Estab. 1990. "The *American Literary Review* publishes excellent poetry, fiction, and nonfiction by writers at all stages of their careers." Beginning in fall 2013, *ALR* became an online publication. Submit online through submission manager for a fee of $3. Does not accept submissions via e-mail or postal mail.

Reading period is from October 1-May 1.

NEEDS Receives 150-200 unsolicited mss/month. Accepts 5-6 mss/issue; 12-16 mss/year. Reading period: October 1-May 1. Recently published work by Marylee MacDonald, Michael Isaac Shokrian, Arthur Brown, Roy Bentley, Julie Marie Wade, and Karin Forfota Poklen. Also publishes creative nonfiction, poetry. Critiques or comments on rejected mss. "We would like to see more short shorts and stylistically innovative and risk-taking fiction. We like to see stories that illuminate the various layers of characters and their situations with great artistry. Give us distinctive character-driven stories that explore the complexities of human existence." Looks for "the small moments that contain more than at first possible, that surprise us with more truth than we thought we had a right to expect." "No genre works." Length: 8,000 words or less.

HOW TO CONTACT "Submit only 1 story at a time. *American Literary Review* seeks distinctive, character-driven stories. Short fiction should be double-spaced and have the author's name, address, and phone number on first page. We generally avoid novel excerpts unless they can stand alone as stories." Send complete ms with cover letter.

PAYMENT/TERMS Pays in contributor's copies. Acquires one-time rights.

TIPS "We encourage writers and artists to examine our journal."

THE AMERICAN POETRY REVIEW

1700 Sansom St., Suite 800, Philadelphia PA 19103. **E-mail:** sberg@aprweb.org. **Website:** www.aprweb

.org. **Contact:** Stephen Berg, editor. Estab. 1972. "*The American Poetry Review* is dedicated to reaching a worldwide audience with a diverse array of the best contemporary poetry and literary prose. *APR* also aims to expand the audience interested in poetry and literature, and to provide authors, especially poets, with a far-reaching forum in which to present their work."

○ *APR* has included the work of over 1,500 writers, among whom there are 9 Nobel Prize laureates and 33 Pulitzer Prize winners.

NEEDS Mss should be typewritten or computer-printed on white, 8½×11 paper.

◐❸ AMERICAN SHORT FICTION

Badgerdog Literary Publishing, P.O. Box 301209, Austin TX 78703. (512) 538-1305. **Fax:** (512) 538-1306. **E-mail:** editors@americanshortfiction.org. **Website:** www.americanshortfiction.org. **Contact:** Jess Stoner, managing editor. Estab. 1991. "Issued triannually, *American Short Fiction* publishes work by emerging and established voices: stories that dive into the wreck, that stretch the reader between recognition and surprise, that conjure a particular world with delicate expertise—stories that take a different way home."

○ Stories published by *American Short Fiction* are anthologized in *Best American Short Stories*, *Best American Non-Required Reading*, *The O. Henry Prize Stories*, and *The Pushcart Prize: Best of the Small Presses*, and elsewhere.

NEEDS "Open to publishing mystery or speculative fiction if we feel it has literary value." Does not want young adult or genre fiction. Length: open.

HOW TO CONTACT *American Short Fiction* seeks "short fiction by some of the finest writers working in contemporary literature, whether they are established, or new or lesser-known authors." Also publishes stories under 2,000 words online. Submit 1 story at a time via online submissions manager ($3 fee). No paper submissions. Accepts simultaneous submissions, but author must notify publication immediately if piece is accepted elsewhere.

PAYMENT/TERMS Writers receive $250-500, 2 contributor's copies, free subscription to the magazine. Additional copies $5.

TIPS "We publish fiction that speaks to us emotionally, uses evocative and precise language, and takes risks in subject matter and/or form. Try to read an issue or two of *American Short Fiction* to get a sense of what we like. Also, to be concise is a great virtue."

◐ AMOSKEAG, THE JOURNAL OF SOUTHERN NEW HAMPSHIRE UNIVERSITY

2500 N. River Rd., Manchester NH 03106. **E-mail:** m.brien@snhu.edu. **Website:** www.amoskeagjournal.com. **Contact:** Benjamin Nugent, editor. Estab. 1983; literary journal since 2005. "We select fiction, creative nonfiction, and poetry that appeals to general readers, writers, and academics alike. We accept work from writers nationwide but also try to include New England writers. We tend not to accept much experimental work, but the language of poetry or prose must nevertheless be dense, careful, and surprising." Annual.

○ Magazine has revolving editor and occasional themes (see website). Literary magazine/journal: 6×9, 105-130 pages. Contains photographs. Receives 200 mss/month. Accepts 10 prose mss and 20-25 poems/issue. Does not read December-July. Reading period is August-November. Ms published in late April. Published Ann Hood, Donald Hall, Allan Gurganus, Leslie Jamison, Ayana Mathis, Craig Childs, Diane Les Becquets, Maxine Kumin, Jonathan Blake, Philip Dacey, Charles Harper Webb.

TIPS "We're looking for quality and pizzazz. Stories need good pacing, believable characters and dialogue, as well as unusual subjects to stand out. Read the news, live an exciting life. Write about remarkable people."

◐❸ ANALOG SCIENCE FICTION & FACT

Dell Magazines, 267 Broadway, 4th Floor, New York NY 10007-2352. (212)686-7188. **Fax:** (212)686-7414. **E-mail:** analog@dellmagazines.com. **Website:** www.analogsf.com. **Contact:** Dr. Stanley Schmidt, editor. Estab. 1930. *Analog* seeks "solidly entertaining stories exploring solidly thought-out speculative ideas. But the ideas, and consequently the stories, are always new. Real science and technology have always been important in *ASF*, not only as the foundation of its fiction, but as the subject of articles about real research with big implications for the future."

○ Fiction published in *Analog* has won numerous Nebula and Hugo Awards.

NEEDS Wants science fiction stories. "That is, stories in which some aspect of future science or technology is so integral to the plot that, if that aspect were removed, the story would collapse. The science can be physical, sociological, or psychological. The technology can be anything from electronic engineering to biogenetic engineering. But the stories must be strong and realistic, with believable people doing believable things—no matter how fantastic the background might be."

HOW TO CONTACT Submit via online submissions manager (preferred) or postal mail. Does not accept e-mail submissions. No fantasy or stories in which the scientific background is implausible or plays no essential role. Prefers lengths between 2,000-7,000 words for shorts, 10,000-20,000 words for novelettes, and 40,000-80,000 for serials. Submit via online submissions manager.

PAYMENT/TERMS *Analog* pays 7-9¢/word for short stories up to 7,500 words, $525-675 for stories between 7,500 and 10,000 words, and 7-7.5¢/word for longer material.

TIPS "I'm looking for irresistibly entertaining stories that make me think about things in ways I've never thought before. Read several issues to get a broad feel for our tastes, but don't try to imitate what you read."

◐Ⓢ ANCIENT PATHS

P.O. Box 7505, Fairfax Station VA 22039. **E-mail:** sklyarburris@yahoo.com. **Website:** www.editor skylar.com/magazine/table.html. **Contact:** Skylar H. Burris, Editor. Estab. 1998. *Ancient Paths*, published biennially in odd-numbered years, provides "a forum for quality Christian poetry. All works should have a spiritual theme. The theme may be explicitly Christian or broadly religious. Works published in *Ancient Paths* explore themes such as redemption, sin, forgiveness, doubt, faith, gratitude for the ordinary blessings of life, spiritual struggle, and spiritual growth. Please, no overly didactic works. Subtlety is preferred."

NEEDS E-mail submissions only. Paste flash fiction directly in e-mail message. Use the subject heading "AP Online Submission (title of your work)." Include name and e-mail address at top of e-mail. Previously published works accepted, provided they are not currently available online. Please indicate if your work has been published elsewhere." Length: no more than 900 words.

PAYMENT/TERMS "Payment for online publication will be $1.25 for the first work and $0.75 for each additional work accepted."

TIPS "Read the great religious poets: John Donne, George Herbert, T.S. Eliot, Lord Tennyson. Remember not to preach. This is a literary magazine, not a pulpit. This does not mean you do not communicate morals or celebrate God. It means you are not overbearing or simplistic when you do so."

◐Ⓢ THE ANTIGONISH REVIEW

St. Francis Xavier University, P.O. Box 5000, Antigonish NS B2G 2W5 Canada. (902)867-3962. **Fax:** (902)867-5563. **E-mail:** tar@stfx.ca. **Website:** www .antigonishreview.com. **Contact:** Bonnie McIsaac, office manager. Estab. 1970. *The Antigonish Review*, published quarterly, tries "to produce the kind of literary and visual mosaic that the modern sensibility requires or would respond to."

NEEDS Send complete ms. Accepts submissions by fax. Accepts electronic (disk compatible with WordPerfect/IBM and Windows) submissions. Prefers hard copy. No erotica. Length: 500-5,000 words.

HOW TO CONTACT Send complete ms.

PAYMENT/TERMS Pays $50 and 2 contributor's copies for stories.

TIPS "Send for guidelines and/or sample copy. Send ms with cover letter and SASE with submission."

◐Ⓢ ANTIOCH REVIEW

P.O. Box 148, Yellow Springs OH 45387-0148. **E-mail:** mkeyes@antiochreview.org. **Website:** www.antio chreview.org. **Contact:** Robert S. Fogarty, editor; Judith Hall, poetry editor. Estab. 1941. Literary and cultural review of contemporary issues and literature for general readership. *The Antioch Review* "is an independent quarterly of critical and creative thought. For well over 70 years, creative authors, poets, and thinkers have found a friendly reception—regardless of formal reputation. We get far more poetry than we can possibly accept, and the competition is keen. Here, where form and content are so inseparable and reaction is so personal, it is difficult to state requirements or limitations. Studying recent issues of *The Antioch Review* should be helpful."

◯ Work published in *The Antioch Review* has been included frequently in *The Best American Stories, Best American Essays,* and *The Best American Poetry.* Finalist for National Magazine Award for essays in 2009 and 2011, and for fiction in 2010.

NEEDS Quality fiction only, distinctive in style with fresh insights into the human condition. No science fiction, fantasy, or confessions. Length: generally under 8,000 words.

HOW TO CONTACT Send complete ms with SASE, preferably mailed flat. Fiction submissions are not accepted between June 1-September 1.

PAYMENT/TERMS Pays $20/printed page, plus 2 contributor's copies.

◑ APALACHEE REVIEW

Apalachee Press, P.O. Box 10469, Tallahassee FL 32302. (850)644-9114. **E-mail:** arsubmissions@gmail.com (for queries outside of the U.S.). **Website:** apalacheereview.org. **Contact:** Michael Trammell, editor; Mary Jane Ryals, fiction editor. Estab. 1976. "At *Apalachee Review,* we are interested in outstanding literary fiction, but we especially like poetry, fiction, and nonfiction that addresses intercultural issues in a domestic or international setting/context." Annual.

○ *Apalachee Review* is 120 pages, digest-sized, professionally printed, perfect-bound, with card cover. Press run is 400-500. Subscription: $15 for 2 issues ($30 foreign). Includes photographs. Member CLMP.

NEEDS Receives 60-100 mss/month. Accepts 5-10 mss/issue. Agented fiction: 0.5%. Publishes 1-2 new writers/year. Sample: $5. Has published Lu Vickers, Joe Clark, Joe Taylor, Jane Arrowsmith Edwards, Vivian Lawry, Linda Frysh, Charles Harper Webb, Reno Raymond Gwaltney. Also publishes short shorts. Does not want cliché-filled, genre-oriented fiction. Length: 600-5,500 words; average length: 3,500 words. Average length of short shorts: 250 words.

HOW TO CONTACT Send complete ms with cover letter. Include brief bio, list of publications. Send either SASE (international authors should see website for "international" guidelines: no IRCs, please) for return of ms or disposable copy of ms and #10 SASE for reply only.

PAYMENT/TERMS Pays 2 contributor's copies.

◑⑤ APEX MAGAZINE

Apex Publications, LLC, P.O. Box 24323, Lexington KY 40524. (859)312-3974. **E-mail:** jason@apexbookcompany.com. **Website:** www.apexbookcompany.com. Estab. 2004. "An elite repository for new and seasoned authors with an otherworldly interest in the unquestioned and slightly bizarre parts of the universe."

○ "We want science fiction, fantasy, horror, and mash-ups of all 3 of the dark, weird stuff down at the bottom of your little literary heart."

Monthly e-zine publishing dark speculative fiction. Circulation: 10,000 unique visits per month.

NEEDS Buys 24 mss/year. Send complete ms. Length: 100-7,500 words.

HOW TO CONTACT Send complete ms.

PAYMENT/TERMS Pays 5¢/word.

◑ APPALACHIAN HERITAGE

CPO 2166, Berea KY 40404. (859)985-3699. **Fax:** (859)985-3903. **E-mail:** george_brosi@berea.edu; appalachianheritage@berea.edu. **Website:** community.berea.edu/appalachianheritage. **Contact:** George Brosi. Estab. 1973. "We are seeking poetry, short fiction, literary criticism, biography, book reviews, and creative nonfiction, including memoirs, opinion pieces, and historical sketches. Unless you request not to be considered, all poems, stories, and articles published in *Appalachian Heritage* are eligible for our annual Plattner Award. All honorees are rewarded with a sliding bookrack with an attached commemorative plaque from Berea College Crafts, and First Place winners receive an additional stipend of $200."

NEEDS "We do not want to see fiction that has no ties to Southern Appalachia." Length: up to 3,500 words.

HOW TO CONTACT Submit complete ms. Send SASE for reply, return of ms.

PAYMENT/TERMS Pays 3 contributor's copies.

TIPS "Sure, we are *Appalachian Heritage* and we do appreciate the past, but we are a forward-looking contemporary literary quarterly, and, frankly, we receive too many nostalgic submissions. Please spare us the 'Papaw Was Perfect' poetry and the 'Mamaw Moved Mountains' mss and give us some hard-hitting prose, some innovative poetry, some inventive photography, and some original art. Help us be the groundbreaking, stimulating kind of quarterly we aspire to be."

◒◑◐ APPLE VALLEY REVIEW: A JOURNAL OF CONTEMPORARY LITERATURE

88 South 3rd St., Suite 336, San Jose CA 95113. **E-mail:** editor@leahbrowning.net. **Website:** www.applevalleyreview.com. **Contact:** Leah Browning, editor. Estab. 2005. *Apple Valley Review: A Journal of Contemporary Literature*, published semiannually online, features "beautifully crafted poetry, short fiction, and essays."

NEEDS Receives 100+ mss/month. Accepts 1-4 mss/issue; 2-8 mss/year. Published Glen Pourciau, Robert

Radin, Jessica Rafalko, Thomas Andrew Green, and Lisa Robertson. Also publishes short shorts. Does not want strict genre fiction, erotica, work containing explicit language, or anything "extremely violent or depressing." Length: 100-4,000+ words. Average length: 2,000 words. Average length of short shorts: 800 words.

HOW TO CONTACT Send complete ms with cover letter.

⬤ ARIES: A JOURNAL OF CREATIVE EXPRESSION

c/o Dr. Price McMurray, General Editor, School of Aries and Letters, 1201 Wesleyan St., Fort Worth TX 76105. **E-mail:** aries@txwes.edu; ariesjournal1@gmail.com. **Website:** ariesjournal.wix.com/aries. **Contact:** Rolanda West, managing editor. Estab. 1985. *Aries: A Journal of Creative Expression*, is published annually by the Department of Languages and Literature at Texas Wesleyan University. Accepting poetry, short fiction, creative nonfiction, short plays, and b&w photography. Reads submissions August 15-December 15.

NEEDS Submit ms by mail or e-mail. Include cover letter and SASE. Do not include name or contact info on ms. Length: up to 4,000 words.

TIPS *"Aries* is open to a wide variety of perspectives, ideas, and theoretical approaches; however, at the heart of all editorial decisions is the overall quality of the work submitted."

⬤ ARKANSAS REVIEW: A JOURNAL OF DELTA STUDIES

Department of English and Philosophy, P.O. Box 1890, Office: Wilson Hall, State University AR 72467-1890. (870) 972-3043; (870)972-2210. **Fax:** (870)972-3045. **E-mail:** mtribbet@astate.edu. **E-mail:** jcollins@astate.edu; arkansasreview@astate.edu. **Website:** altweb.astate.edu/arkreview. **Contact:** Dr. Marcus Tribbett, general editor. Estab. 1998. "All material, creative and scholarly, published in the *Arkansas Review* must evoke or respond to the natural and/or cultural experience of the Mississippi River Delta region."

🖝 *Arkansas Review* is 92 pages, magazine-sized, photo offset-printed, saddle-stapled, with 4-color cover. Press run is 600; 50 distributed free to contributors. Subscription: $20. Make checks payable to ASU Foundation.

NEEDS Receives 30-50 unsolicited mss/month. Accepts 2-3 mss/issue; 5-7 mss/year. Agented fiction 1%.

Publishes 3-4 new writers/year. Has published work by Susan Henderson, George Singleton, Scott Ely, and Pia Erhart. "No genre fiction. Must have a Delta focus." 10,000 words maximum.

HOW TO CONTACT Send complete ms.

PAYMENT/TERMS Pays 3 contributor's copies.

TIPS "Submit via mail. E-mails are more likely to be overlooked or lost. Submit a cover letter, but don't try to impress us with credentials or explanations of the submission. Immerse yourself in the literature of the Delta, but provide us with a fresh and original take on its land, its people, its culture. Surprise us. Amuse us. Recognize what makes this region particular as well as universal, and take risks. Help us shape a new Delta literature."

ARTFUL DODGE

Department of English, College of Wooster, Wooster OH 44691. (330)263-2577. **E-mail:** artfuldodge@wooster.edu. **Website:** www.wooster.edu/artfuldodge. **Contact:** Daniel Bourne, editor-in-chief; Karin Lin-Greenberg, fiction editor; Marcy Campbell, associate fiction editor; Carolyne Wright, translation editor. Estab. 1979. *Artful Dodge* is an Ohio-based literary magazine that publishes "work with a strong sense of place and cultural landscape. Besides new American fiction, poetry, and narrative essay, we're also interested in contemporary translation—from all over the globe. There is no theme in this magazine, except literary power. We also have an ongoing interest in translations from Central/Eastern Europe and elsewhere."

NEEDS "We judge by literary quality, not by genre. We are especially interested in fine English translations of significant prose writers. Translations should be submitted with original texts."

PAYMENT/TERMS Pays at least 2 contributor's copies.

TIPS "Poets may send books for review consideration; however, there is no guarantee we can review them."

⬤⬤ ARTS & LETTERS

Georgia College & State University, College of Arts & Sciences, Campus Box 89, Milledgeville GA 31061. (478)445-1289. **E-mail:** al.journal@gcsu.edu. **Website:** al.gcsu.edu. Estab. 1999. *Arts & Letters Journal of Contemporary Culture*, published semiannually, is devoted to contemporary arts and literature, featuring ongoing series such as The World Poetry Translation Series and The Mentors Interview Series. Wants work that is of the highest literary and artistic quality.

Work published in *Arts & Letters Journal* has received the Pushcart Prize.

NEEDS No genre fiction. Length: up to 25 pages typed and double-spaced.

PAYMENT/TERMS Pays $10 per printed age (minimum payment: $50), 1 contributor's copy, and one-year subscription.

TIPS "All submissions will now be considered for publication in *Arts & Letters* print, and specific pieces (preferably shorter works) will be chosen for *Arts & Letters* PRIME, our electronic supplement journal. The pieces chosen for PRIME will include audio of the author reading his or her work."

ART TIMES

A Literary Journal and Resource for All the Arts, P.O. Box 730, Mount Marion NY 12456. (845)246-6944. **Fax:** (845)246-6944. **E-mail:** info@ArtTimesJournal .com. **Website:** www.arttimesjournal.com. **Contact:** Raymond J. Steiner, editor. Estab. 1984. *"Art Times* covers the art fields and is distributed in locations most frequented by those enjoying the arts. Our copies are distributed throughout the lower part of the northeast as well as the metropolitan New York area; locations include theaters, galleries, museums, schools, art clubs, cultural centers, and the like. Our readers are mostly over 40, affluent, art-conscious and sophisticated. Subscribers are located across U.S. and abroad (Italy, France, Germany, Greece, Russia, etc.)."

NEEDS Looks for quality short fiction that aspires to be literary. Publishes 1 story each issue. "Nothing violent, sexist, erotic, juvenile, racist, romantic, political, offbeat, or related to sports or juvenile fiction." Length: up to 1,500 words.

HOW TO CONTACT Send complete ms.

PAYMENT/TERMS Pays $25 and a one-year subscription.

TIPS "Competition is greater (more submissions received), but keep trying. We print new as well as published writers. Be advised that we are presently on an approximate 3-year lead for short stories, 2-year lead for poetry. We are now receiving 300-400 poems and 40-50 short stories per month. Be familiar with *Art Times* and its special audience."

ASCENT ASPIRATIONS

1560 Arbutus Dr., Nanoose Bay BC C9P 9C8 Canada. **E-mail:** ascentaspirations@shaw.ca. **Website:** www .ascentaspirations.ca. **Contact:** David Fraser, editor. Estab. 1997. *"Ascent Aspirations* magazine publishes monthly online and once in print. The print issues are operated as contests. Please refer to current guidelines before submitting. *Ascent Aspirations* is a quality electronic publication dedicated to the promotion and encouragement of aspiring writers of any genre. The focus, however, is toward interesting experimental writing in dark mainstream, literary, science fiction, fantasy, and horror. Poetry can be on any theme. Essays need to be unique, current and have social, philosophical commentary."

Magazine: 40 electronic pages; illustrations; photos. Receives 100-200 unsolicited mss/month. Accepts 40 mss/issue; 240 mss/year. Publishes ms 3 months after acceptance. Publishes 10-50 new writers/year. Has published work by Taylor Graham, Janet Buck, Jim Manton, Steve Cartwright, Don Stockard, Penn Kemp, Sam Vargo, Vernon Waring, Margaret Karmazin, Bill Hughes; and recently spoken-word artists Sheri-D Wilson, Missy Peters, Ian Ferrier, Cathy Petch, and Bob Holdman.

NEEDS Length: 1,000 words or less. Publishes short shorts.

HOW TO CONTACT Query by e-mail with Word attachment. Include estimated word count, brief bio, and list of publications. "If you have to submit by mail because it is your only avenue, provide an SASE with either International Coupons or Canadian stamps only."

PAYMENT/TERMS "No payment at this time."

TIPS "Short fiction should first of all tell a good story, take the reader to new and interesting imaginary or real places. Short fiction should use language lyrically and effectively, be experimental in either form or content, and take the reader into realms where they can analyze and think about the human condition. Write with passion for your material, be concise and economical, and let the reader work to unravel your story. In terms of editing, always proofread to the point that what you submit is the best it possibly can be. Never be discouraged if your work is not accepted; it may just not be the right fit for a current publication."

ASIMOV'S SCIENCE FICTION

Dell Magazine Fiction Group, 267 Broadway, 4th Floor, New York NY 10007. (212)686-7188. **Fax:** (212)686-7414. **E-mail:** asimovssf@dellmagazines .com. **Website:** www.asimovs.com. **Contact:** Sheila Williams, editor; Victoria Green, senior art director.

Estab. 1977. "Magazine consists of science fiction and fantasy stories for adults and young adults. Publishes the best short science fiction available."

⚪ Named for a science fiction "legend," *Asimov's* regularly receives Hugo and Nebula Awards. Editor Gardner Dozois has received several awards for editing, including Hugos and those from *Locus* magazine.

NEEDS Wants "science fiction primarily. Some fantasy and humor. It is best to read a great deal of material in the genre to avoid the use of some very old ideas." Submit ms via online submissions manager or postal mail; no e-mail submissions. No horror or psychic/supernatural, sword and sorcery, explicit sex or violence that isn't integral to the story. Would like to see more hard science fiction. Length: 750-15,000 words.

PAYMENT/TERMS Pays 7-9¢/word for short stories up to 7,500 words; 7-7.5¢/word for longer material. Works between 7,500-10,000 words by authors who make more than 7¢/word for short stories will receive a flat rate that will be no less than the payment would be for a shorter story.)

TIPS "In general, we're looking for 'character-oriented' stories, those in which the characters, rather than the science, provide the main focus for the reader's interest. Serious, thoughtful, yet accessible fiction will constitute the majority of our purchases, but there's always room for the humorous as well."

⚪⚪ ASININE POETRY

P.O. Box 1349, New York NY 10276. **E-mail:** editor@asininepoetry.com. **Website:** www.asininepoetry.com. **Contact:** Shay Tasaday, editor. Estab. 1998. Humorous poetry and prose, published quarterly online, "features 8-9 new works each issue. We specialize in poetry that does not take itself seriously." Wants "any form of poetry, but for us the poetry must be in a humorous, parodic, or satirical style. We prefer well-crafted poems that may contain serious elements or cover serious subjects—but which are also amusing, absurd, or hilarious."

⚪⚪ THE ATLANTIC MONTHLY

The Watergate, 600 New Hampshire Ave., NW, Washington DC 20037. (202)266-6000. **Website:** www.theatlantic.com. **Contact:** James Bennet, editor; C. Michael Curtis, fiction editor; David Barber, poetry editor. Estab. 1857. General magazine for an educated readership with broad cultural and public-affairs interests. "*The Atlantic* considers unsolicited mss, either fiction or nonfiction. A general familiarity with what we have published in the past is the best guide to our needs and preferences."

NEEDS "Seeks fiction that is clear, tightly written with strong sense of 'story' and well-defined characters." No longer publishes fiction in the regular magazine. Instead it will appear in a special newsstand-only fiction issue. Submit via e-mail with Word document attachment to submissions@theatlantic.com. Mss submitted via postal mail must be typewritten and double-spaced. Receipt of mss will be acknowledged if accompanied by a self-addressed stamped envelope. Mss will not be returned. TheAtlantic.com no longer accepts unsolicited submissions." Receives 1,000 unsolicited mss/month. Accepts 7-8 mss/year. **Publishes 3-4 new writers/year.** Preferred length: 2,000-6,000 words

HOW TO CONTACT Send complete mss. Responds in 2 months. Send complete ms.

PAYMENT/TERMS Pays $3,000.

TIPS "Writers should be aware that this is not a market for beginner's work (nonfiction and fiction), nor is it truly for intermediate work. Study this magazine before sending only your best, most professional work. When making first contact, cover letters are sometimes helpful, particularly if they cite prior publications or involvement in writing programs. Common mistakes: melodrama, inconclusiveness, lack of development, unpersuasive characters and/or dialogue."

AUTHORSHIP

National Writers Association, 10940 S. Parker Rd., #508, Parker CO 80134. (303)841-0246. **E-mail:** natlwritersassn@hotmail.com. **Website:** www.nationalwriters.com. Estab. 1950s. "Association magazine targeted to beginning and professional writers. Covers how-to, humor, marketing issues. Disk and e-mail submissions preferred."

TIPS "Members of National Writers Association are given preference."

THE AVALON LITERARY REVIEW

CCI Publishing, P.O. Box 780696, Orlando FL 32878. (407)574-7355. **E-mail:** submissions@avalonliteraryreview.com. **Website:** www.avalonliteraryreview.com. **Contact:** Valerie Rubino, managing editor. Estab. 2011. Quarterly magazine. "*The Avalon Literary Review* welcomes work from both published and unpublished writers and poets. We accept submissions of poetry, short fiction, and personal essays. The author's voice and point of view should be unique and clear. We seek pieces which spring from the author's life and experiences. Submissions which explore both the sweet and bitter of life, with a touch of humor, are a good fit for our *Review.* While we appreciate the genres of fantasy, historical romance, science fiction, and horror, our magazine is not the forum for such work."

NEEDS No erotica, science fiction, or horror. Length: 250-2,500.

HOW TO CONTACT Submit complete ms. Only accepts electronic submissions.

PAYMENT/TERMS Pays 5 contributor's copies.

TIPS "We seek work that is carefully structured. We like vivid descriptions, striking characters, and realistic dialogue. A humorous but not ridiculous point of view is a plus."

🌀 BABEL: THE MULTILINGUAL, MULTICULTURAL ONLINE JOURNAL AND COMMUNITY OF ARTS AND IDEAS

E-mail: submissions@towerofbabel.com. **Website:** towerofbabel.com. **Contact:** Malcolm Lawrence, editor-in-chief. Estab. 1996. *Babel* publishes regional reports from international stringers all over the planet, as well as features, round-table discussions, fiction, columns, poetry, erotica, travelogues, and reviews of all the arts and editorials. "Our bloggers include James Schwartz, the first out gay poet raised in the Old Order Amish community in Southwestern Michigan and author of the book *The Literary Party*; Susanna Zaraysky, author of the book *Language Is Music: Making People Multilingual*; James Rovira, assistant professor of English and program chair of humanities at Tiffin University and author of the book *Blake & Kierkegaard: Creation and Anxiety*; and Paul B. Miller, assistant professor department of French and Italian at Vanderbilt University. We're interested in fiction, nonfiction, and poetry from all over the world, including multicultural or multilingual work." Cover letter is required. Reviews books/chapbooks of poetry and other magazines, single- and multibook format. Open to unsolicited reviews. Send materials for review consideration.

💭 *Babel* is recognized by the United Nations as one of the most important social and human sciences online periodicals.

NEEDS "We are currently looking for WordPress bloggers in the following languages: Arabic, Bulgarian, Bengali, Catalan, Czech, Welsh, Danish, German, English, Esperanto, Spanish, Persian, Finnish, Faroese, French, Hebrew, Croatian, Indonesian, Italian, Japanese, Korean, Latvian, Malay, Dutch, Polish, Portuguese, Russian, Albanian, Serbian, Swedish, Tamil, Thai, Ukrainian, Urdu, Uzbek, Vietnamese, and Chinese."

HOW TO CONTACT Send queries/mss by e-mail. "Please send submissions with a résumé/cover letter or biography attached to the e-mail."

PAYMENT/TERMS Does not pay.

TIPS "We would like to see more fiction with first-person male characters written by female authors, as well as more fiction first-person female characters written by male authors. We would also like to see that dynamic in action when it comes to other languages, cultures, races, classes, sexual orientations, and ages. Know what you are writing about and write passionately about it."

🌀 BABYBUG

70 East Lake St., Suite 800, Chicago IL 60601. **E-mail:** babybug@babyhugmagkids.com. **Website:** www.cricketmag.com/babybug; www.babybug magkids.com. **Contact:** Submissions editor. Estab. 1994. *Babybug* is a look-and-listen magazine for babies and toddlers ages 6 months-3 years. Publishes 9 issues per year.

NEEDS Very short, clear fiction. Length: 6 sentences maximum.

PAYMENT/TERMS Up to 25¢/word. Payment after publication. Rights vary.

TIPS "Imagine having to read your story or poem—out loud—50 times or more! That's what parents will have to do. Babies and toddlers demand, 'Read it again!' Your material must hold up under repetition. And humor is much appreciated by all."

🌀 THE BALTIMORE REVIEW

6514 Maplewood Rd., Baltimore MD 21212. **E-mail:** editor@baltimorereview.org. **Website:** www.balti morereview.org. **Contact:** Barbara Westwood Diehl, senior editor; Kathleen Hellen, senior editor. Estab. 1996. *The Baltimore Review* publishes poetry, fiction, and creative nonfiction from Baltimore and beyond. Submission periods are August 1-November 30 and February 1-May 31.

💭 In 2012, *The Baltimore Review* began its new life as a quarterly, online literary. Also prints annual anthology.

NEEDS Length: 100-6,000 words.

HOW TO CONTACT Send complete ms using online submission form. Publishes 16-20 mss per online issue. Work published online also published in annual anthology.

PAYMENT/TERMS Pays in contributor's copies.

TIPS "See editor preferences on staff page of website."

THE BANGALORE REVIEW

The Purple Patch Foundation, No. 149, 2nd Floor, 4th Cross, Kasturi Nagar, Bangalore Karnataka India. **E-mail:** info@bangalorereview.com. **E-mail:** submissions@bangalorereview.com. **Website:** www.bangalorereview.com. **Contact:** Arvind Radhakrishnan, editor; Suhail Rasheed, managing editor. Estab. 2013. *The Bangalore Review* is a monthly online magazine aimed at promoting literature, arts, culture, criticism, and philosophy at a deeper level. Strives to inculcate the habit of not just reading, but the reading of good literature in the youth of today while also aspiring to be an unbiased, nonrestrictive platform for young and promising independent writers. The editorial team seeks to strike a balance between the old and the young, the published and the unpublished, the known and the unknown, and the mainstream and the unconventional, while curating the articles for each edition.

NEEDS Does not want erotica. Length: 250-5,000.

HOW TO CONTACT Query with complete ms.

PAYMENT/TERMS Does not offer payment.

BARBARIC YAWP

BoneWorld Publishing, 3700 County Rt. 24, Russell NY 13684-3198. (315)347-2609. **Website:** www.boneworldpublishing.com. Estab. 1997.

Barbaric Yawp, published quarterly, is digest-sized; 56 pages; matte cover stock.

NEEDS "We publish what we like. Fiction should include some bounce and surprise. Our publication is intended for the intelligent, open-minded reader. We don't want any pornography, gratuitous violence, or whining."

HOW TO CONTACT Send SASE for reply, return of ms or send a disposable copy of ms. Accepts simultaneous, multiple submissions and reprints.

PAYMENT/TERMS Pays 1 contributor's copy; additional copies $3.

TIPS "Don't give up. Read much, write much, submit much. Observe closely the world around you. Don't borrow ideas from TV or films. Revision is often necessary—grit your teeth and do it. Never fear rejection."

THE BARCELONA REVIEW

Correu Vell 12-2, Barcelona 08002 Spain. (00 34) 93 319 15 96. **E-mail:** editor@barcelonareview.com. **Website:** www.barcelonareview.com. **Contact:** Jill Adams, editor. Estab. 1997. *The Barcelona Review* is "the Web's first multilingual review of international, contemporary, cutting-edge fiction. TBR is actually 3 separate reviews—English, Spanish, and Catalan—with occasional translations from 1 language to another. Original texts of other languages are presented along with English and Spanish translations as available."

NEEDS Length: no more than 4,500 words.

HOW TO CONTACT Submit 1 story at a time. To submit via e-mail, send an attached document. Do not send in the body of an e-mail. Include "Submission/Author Name" in the subject box. Accepts hard copies, but they will not be returned. Double-space ms.

PAYMENT/TERMS "We cannot offer money to contributors, but in lieu of pay we can sometimes offer an excellent Spanish translation (worth quite a bit of money in itself). Work is showcased along with two or more known authors in a high-quality literary review with an international readership."

TIPS "Send top drawer material that has been drafted 2, 3, 4 times—whatever it takes. Then sit on it for a while and look at it afresh. Keep the text tight. Grab the reader in the first paragraph and don't let go. Keep in mind that a perfectly crafted story that lacks a punch of some sort won't cut it. Make it new, make it different. Surprise the reader in some way. Read the best of the short fiction available in your area of writing to see how yours measures up. Don't send anything off until you feel it's ready, and then familiarize yourself with the content of the review/magazine to which you are submitting."

BATEAU

P.O. Box 1584, Northampton MA 01061. (413)586-2494. **E-mail:** info@bateaupress.org. **Website:** www.bateaupress.org. **Contact:** James Grinwis, editor. Estab. 2007. "*Bateau*, published semiannually, subscribes to no trend but serves to represent as wide a cross section of contemporary writing as possible. For this reason, readers will most likely love and hate at least something in each issue. We consider this a good thing. To us, it means *Bateau* is eclectic, open-ended, and not mired in a particular strain." Has published poetry by Tomaz Salamun, John Olsen, Michael

Burkhardt, Joshua Marie Wilkinson, Allison Titus, Allan Peterson, Dean Young.

○ *Bateau* is around 80 pages, digest-sized, offset-printed, perfect-bound, with a 100% recycled letterpress cover. Receives about 5,000 poems/year, accepts about 60. Press run is 250.

HOW TO CONTACT Submit via online submission form. Cover letter not needed.

PAYMENT/TERMS Pays in contributor's copies.

◐ BAYOU

English Department University of New Orleans, 2000 Lakeshore Dr., New Orleans LA 70148. (504)280-5423. **E-mail:** bayou@uno.edu. **Website:** www.uno.edu/bayou. **Contact:** Joanna Leake, editor. Estab. 2002. "A non-profit journal for the arts, each issue of *Bayou* contains beautiful fiction, nonfiction, and poetry. From quirky shorts to more traditional stories, we are committed to publishing solid work. Regardless of style, *Bayou* is always interested first in a well-told tale. Our poetry and prose are filled with memorable characters observing their world, acknowledging both the mundane and the sublime, often at once, and always with an eye toward beauty. *Bayou* is packed with a range of material from established, award-winning authors as well as new voices on the rise. Recent contributors include Eric Trethewey, Virgil Suarez, Marilyn Hacker, Sean Beaudoin, Tom Whalen, Mark Doty, Philip Cioffari, Lyn Lifshin, Timothy Liu, and Gaylord Brewer. And in 1 issue every year, *Bayou* features the winner of the annual Tennessee Williams/New Orleans Literary Festival One-Act Play Competition."

○ Does not accept e-mail submissions. Reads submissions from September 1-June 1.

NEEDS "Flash fiction and short-shorts are welcome. No novel excerpts, please, unless they can stand alone as short stories." No horror, gothic, or juvenile fiction. Length: no more than 7,500 words.

HOW TO CONTACT Send complete ms via online submission system.

PAYMENT/TERMS Pays 2 contributor's copies.

TIPS "Do not submit in more than 1 genre at a time. Don't send a second submission until you receive a response to the first."

◐◐ THE BEAR DELUXE MAGAZINE

Orlo, 810 SE Belmont, Studio 5, Portland OR 97214. **E-mail:** bear@orlo.org. **Website:** www.orlo.org. **Contact:** Tom Webb, editor-in-chief; Kristin Rogers Brown, art director. Estab. 1993. "*The Bear Deluxe Magazine* is a national independent environmental arts magazine publishing significant works of reporting, creative nonfiction, literature, visual art and design. Based in the Pacific Northwest, it reaches across cultural and political divides to engage readers on vital issues effecting the environment. Published twice per year, *The Bear Deluxe* includes a wider array and a higher-percentage of visual artwork and design than many other publications. Artwork is included both as editorial support and as stand-alone or independent art. It has included nationally recognized artists as well as emerging artists. As with any publication, artists are encouraged to review a sample copy for a clearer understanding of the magazine's approach. Unsolicited submissions and samples are accepted and encouraged."

NEEDS "Stories must have some environmental context, but we view that in a broad sense." No detective, children's, or horror. Length: 750-4,500 words.

HOW TO CONTACT Query or send complete ms.

PAYMENT/TERMS Pays free subscription to the magazine, contributor's copies and $25-400, depending on piece; additional copies for postage

TIPS "Offer to be a stringer for future ideas. Get a copy of the magazine and guidelines, and query us with specific nonfiction ideas and clips. We're looking for original, magazine-style stories, not fluff or PR. Fiction, essay, and poetry writers should know we have an open and blind review policy and should keep sending their best work even if rejected once. Be as specific as possible in queries."

◐ BEGINNINGS PUBLISHING INC.

P.O. Box 214, Bayport NJ 11705. **Website:** www.literarybeginnings.org. Estab. 1999. "*Beginnings* serves as a forum exclusively for the new writer, as well as a launching pad for their literary creations. This is the e-zine in which struggling, talented writers can finally share their published work!"

NEEDS "No pornography, sex or obscenities (within reason) and no content that is racist or otherwise extremely offensive or abusive to others." Length: up to 3,500 words.

HOW TO CONTACT Send complete ms to beginnings2014@yahoo.com. "Please put *fiction* in the subject line." Include cover letter with short bio. Include submission in body of e-mail; no attachments.

◐◐ BELLEVUE LITERARY REVIEW

NYU Langone Medical Center, Department of Medicine, 550 First Ave., OBV-A612, New York NY 10016.

(212)263-3973. **E-mail:** info@BLReview.org. **E-mail:** stacy.bodziak@nyumc.org. **Website:** www.blreview.org. **Contact:** Stacy Bodziak, managing editor. Estab. 2001. *Bellevue Literary Review*, published semiannually, prints "works of fiction, nonfiction, and poetry that touch upon relationships to the human body, illness, health, and healing."

○ *Bellevue Literary Review* is 192 pages, digest-sized, perfect-bound. Press run is 3,000; distributed free to literary magazine conferences, promotions, and other contacts. Single copy: $9; subscription: $20/year, $35/2 years; $48/3 years (plus $5/year postage to Canada, $8/year postage foreign). Make checks payable to *Bellevue Literary Review*. Work published in *Bellevue Literary Review* has appeared in *The Pushcart Prize*. Recently published work by Rafael Campo, Paul Harding, and Tom Sleigh.

NEEDS Receives 100-200 unsolicited mss/month. Accepts 10-12 mss/issue; 24 mss/year. Agented fiction 1%. Publishes 3-6 new writers/year. Publishes short-shorts. Sometimes comments on rejected mss. No genre fiction. Length: 5,000 words. Average length: 2,500 words.

HOW TO CONTACT Submit online at www.blreview.org (preferred). Also accepts mss via regular mail. Send complete ms. Send SASE (or IRC) for return of ms or disposable copy of the ms and #10 SASE for reply only.

PAYMENT/TERMS Pays 2 contributor's copies, one-year subscription, and one-year gift subscription; additional copies $6.

◐ BELLINGHAM REVIEW

Mail Stop 9053, Western Washington University, Bellingham WA 98225. (360)650-4863. **E-mail:** bhreview@wwu.edu. **Website:** wwww.bhreview.org. **Contact:** Lee Olsen, managing editor. Estab. 1977. Annual nonprofit magazine published once a year in the spring. Seeks "literature of palpable quality: poems stories and essays so beguiling they invite us to touch their essence. *Bellingham Review* hungers for a kind of writing that nudges the limits of form, or executes traditional forms exquisitely."

○ The editors are actively seeking submissions of creative nonfiction, as well as stories that push the boundaries of the form. The Tobias Wolff Award in Fiction contest runs December 1-March 15; see website for guidelines.

NEEDS Experimental, humor/satire, literary, regional (Northwest). Does not want anything nonliterary. 6,000 words maximum.

HOW TO CONTACT Send complete ms.

PAYMENT/TERMS Pays as funds allow.

TIPS "Open submission period is from September 15-December 1. Mss arriving between December 2 and September 14 will be returned unread. The *Bellingham Review* holds 3 annual contests: the 49th Parallel Award for poetry, the Annie Dillard Award for Nonfiction, and the Tobias Wolff Award for Fiction. Submissions: December 1-March 15. See the individual listings for these contests under Contests & Awards for full details."

◐◑ BELOIT FICTION JOURNAL

Box 11, Beloit College, 700 College St., Beloit WI 53511. (608)363-2079. **E-mail:** bfj@beloit.edu. **Website:** beloitfictionjournal.wordpress.com. **Contact:** Chris Fink, editor-in-chief. Estab. 1985. "We are interested in publishing the best contemporary fiction and are open to all themes except those involving pornographic, religiously dogmatic, or politically propagandistic representations. Our magazine is for general readership, though most of our readers will probably have a specific interest in literary magazines."

○ Annual literary magazine: 6×9; 250 pages; 60 lb. paper; 10 pt. C1S cover stock; illustrations; photos on cover; ad-free. Work first appearing in *Beloit Fiction Journal* has been reprinted in award-winning collections, including the Flannery O'Connor and the Milkweed Fiction Prize collections, and has won the Iowa Short Fiction award. Has published work by Dennis Lehane, Silas House, and David Harris Ebenbach.

NEEDS Receives 200 unsolicited mss/month. Accepts 20 mss/year. Publishes ms 9 months after acceptance. **Publishes 3 new writers/year.** Sometimes comments on rejected mss. No pornography, religious dogma, science fiction, horror, political propaganda or genre fiction. Length: 250-10,000 words; average length: 5,000 words.

HOW TO CONTACT "Our reading period is August 1-December 1 only. " No fax, e-mail, or disk submissions. Accepts simultaneous submissions if identified as such. Please send 1 story at a time. Always include SASE.

PAYMENT/TERMS Payment in copies.

TIPS "Many of our contributors are writers whose work we had previously rejected. Don't let 1 rejection slip turn you away from our—or any—magazine."

◐ BERKELEY FICTION REVIEW

10B Eshleman Hall, University of California, Berkeley CA 94720. (510)642-2892. **E-mail:** bfictionreview@yahoo.com. **Website:** www.ocf.berkeley.edu/~bfr. Estab. 1981. "The *Berkeley Fiction Review* is a UC Berkeley undergraduate, student-run publication. We look for innovative short fiction that plays with form and content, as well as traditionally constructed stories with fresh voices and original ideas."

○   BFR nominates to O.Henry, *Best American Short Stories*, and Pushcart prizes. Sponsored by the ASUC.

NEEDS Length: no more than 25 pages.

HOW TO CONTACT Submit via e-mail with "Submission: Name, Title" in subject line. Include cover letter in body of e-mail, with story as an attachment.

PAYMENT/TERMS Pays 1 contributor's copy.

TIPS "Our criteria is fiction that resonates. Voices that are strong and move a reader. Clear, powerful prose (either voice or rendering of subject) with a point. Unique ways of telling stories—these capture the editors. Work hard, don't give up. Ask an honest person to point out your writing weaknesses, and then work on them. We look forward to reading fresh new voices."

○ ⊜ BEYOND CENTAURI

P.O. Box 782, Cedar Rapids IA 52406-0782. **Website:** www.samsdotpublishing.com; www.whitecatpublications.com/guidelines/beyond-centauri. Estab. 2003. *Beyond Centauri*, published quarterly, contains fantasy, science fiction, sword and sorcery, very mild horror short stories, poetry, and illustrations for readers ages 10 and up. Wants fantasy, science fiction, spooky horror, and speculative poetry for younger readers. Does not want horror with excessive blood and gore. Considers poetry by children and teens. Has published poetry by Bruce Boston, Bobbi Sinha-Morey, Debbie Feo, Dorothy Imm, Cythera, and Terrie Leigh Relf.

○   *Beyond Centauri* is 44 pages, magazine-sized, offset-printed, perfect-bound, with paper cover for color art, includes ads. Receives about 200 poems/year, accepts about 50 (25%). Press run is 100; 5 distributed free to reviewers. Single copy: $6; subscription: $20/year, $37 for 2 years.

Make checks payable to Tyree Campbell/Sam's Dot Publishing.

NEEDS Looks for themes of science fiction or fantasy. Length: 2,500 words maximum.

HOW TO CONTACT Submit in the body of an e-mail, or as an .rtf attachment.

PAYMENT/TERMS Pays $6/story, $3/reprints, and $2/flash fiction (under 1,000 words).

◐◑ BIG MUDDY: A JOURNAL OF THE MISSISSIPPI RIVER VALLEY

Southeast Missouri State University Press, One University Plaza, MS 2650, Cape Girardeau MO 63701. (573)651-2044. **Website:** www6.semo.edu/universitypress/bigmuddy. **Contact:** Susan Swartwout, publisher/editor. Estab. 2000. "*Big Muddy* explores multidisciplinary, multicultural issues, people, and events mainly concerning, but not limited to, the 10-state area that borders the Mississippi River. We publish fiction, poetry, historical essays, creative nonfiction, environmental essays, biography, regional events, photography, art, etc."

○   Magazine: 5½×8½ perfect-bound; 150 pages; acid-free paper; color cover stock; lay-flat lamination; illustrations; photos.

NEEDS No romance, fantasy, or children's.

HOW TO CONTACT Receives 50 unsolicited mss/month. Accepts 20-25 mss/issue. Accepts multiple submissions.

PAYMENT/TERMS Pays 2 contributor's copies; additional copies $5.

TIPS "We look for clear language, avoidance of clichés except in necessary dialogue, a fresh vision of the theme or issue. Find some excellent and honest readers to comment on your work-in-progress and final draft. Consider their viewpoints carefully. Revise if needed."

◐ BILINGUAL REVIEW

P.O. Box 875303, Tempe AZ 85287-5303. (480)965-3867. **Fax:** (480)965-0315. **Website:** www.asu.edu/brp/submit/. Estab. 1974. *Bilingual Review* is "committed to publishing high-quality writing by both established and emerging writers."

○   Magazine: 7×10; 96 pages; 55 lb. acid-free paper; coated cover stock.

NEEDS Receives 50 unsolicited mss/month. Accepts 3 mss/issue; 9 mss/year. Submit via postal mail. Send 2 copies of complete ms with SAE and loose stamps. Does not usually accept e-mail submissions except through special circumstance/prior arrangement. "We do not publish literature about tourists in Latin America and their perceptions of the 'native culture.' We do not publish fiction about Latin America unless there is a clear tie to the U.S.."

HOW TO CONTACT Accepts submissions by mail only. Accepts simultaneous submissions and high-quality photocopied submissions. Sample copy for $8. Reviews fiction.

PAYMENT/TERMS Pays 2 contributor's copies; 30% discount for extras. Acquires 50% of reprint permission fee given to author as matter of policy rights.

THE BINNACLE

University of Maine at Machias, 116 O'Brien Ave., Machias ME 04654. **E-mail:** ummbinnacle@maine .edu. **Website:** www.umm.maine.edu/binnacle. Estab. 1957. "Please see our website (www.umm.maine .edu/binnacle) for details on our Annual Ultra-Short Competition (Prize a minimum of $300)." Semiannual, fall edition is the Ultra-Short Competition editon. Publishes ms 3-9 months after acceptance. Sample copy for $7. Writer's guidelines online at website only. Acquires one-time rights. "We are interested in fresh voices, not Raymond Carver's, and not the Iowa Workshop's. We want the peculiar, and the idiosyncratic. We want playful and experimental, but understandable. Please see our website for details on our Annual Ultra-Short Competition." (Prize of a minimum of $300.) "We accept submissions for the Fall Ultra-Short Edition from December 1 to March 15 and report to writers in early June. We accept submissions for the spring edition from September 1 to November 30 and report to writers between February 1 and March 1."

◑ Does not accepted paper submissions. Electronic/E-mail submissions only.

NEEDS ethnic/multicultural, experimental, humor/ satire, mainstream, slice-of-life vignettes, but any genre attuned to a general audience can work. No extreme erotica, fantasy, horror, or religious. Length: 2,500 words maximum.

HOW TO CONTACT Submissions by e-mail only. Responds in 1 month to queries; 3 months to mss. Accepts simultaneous submissions. Send complete ms via e-mail only.

PAYMENT/TERMS Pays $300 in prizes for Ultra-Short. $50 per issue for 1 work of editor's choice.

TIPS "We want fiction, poetry, and images that speak to real people, people who have lives, people who have troubles, people who laugh, too."

THE BITTER OLEANDER

4983 Tall Oaks Dr., Fayetteville NY 13066. **Fax:** (315)637-5056. **E-mail:** info@bitteroleander.com. **Website:** www.bitteroleander.com. **Contact:** Paul B. Roth, editor and publisher. "We're reading to find a language uncommitted to the commonplace and more integrated with the natural world. A language that helps define the same particulars in nature that exist in us but have not been socialized out of us."

◑ *The Bitter Oleander* is 6×9; 128 pages; 55 lb. paper; 12 pt. CIS cover stock; photos. Biannual.

NEEDS Receives 300 unsolicited mss/month. Accepts 4-5 mss/issue; 8-10 mss/year. Does not read in July. Recently published work by Kristiina Ehin (Estonia), Norberto Luis Romero (Spain), Anders Benson, Martín Camps, and Jane Arnold. Max length: 2,500 words. Publishes short shorts. Also publishes literary essays, poetry. Always comments on rejected mss. Does not want family stories with moralistic plots, and no fantasy that involves hyperreality of any sort. Length: 300-2,500 words.

HOW TO CONTACT Query. Send mss by mail with SASE for response. "Whether you live in the U.S. or outside of it, we accept e-mail submissions or regular mail submissions if SASE is enclosed."

PAYMENT/TERMS Pays contributor's copies.

TIPS "If you are writing poems or short fiction in the tradition of 98% of all journals publishing in this country, then your work will usually not fit for us. If within the first 400 words my mind drifts, the rest rarely makes it. Be yourself, and listen to no one but yourself."

◐ BLACKBIRD

Virginia Commonwealth University Department of English, P.O. Box 843082, Richmond VA 23284. (804)827-4729. **E-mail:** blackbird@vcu.edu. **Website:** www.blackbird.vcu.edu. Estab. 2001. *Blackbird* is published twice a year.

NEEDS "We primarily look for short stories, but novel excerpts are acceptable if self-contained."

HOW TO CONTACT Submit using online submissions manager or by postal mail. Online submission is preferred.

TIPS "We like a story that invites us into its world, that engages our senses, soul, and mind. We are able to publish long works in all genres, but query *Blackbird* before you send a prose piece over 8,000 words or a poem exceeding 10 pages."

○ BLACK LACE

P.O. Box 83912, Los Angeles CA 90083. (310)410-0808. **Fax:** (310)410-9250. **E-mail:** newsroom@blk.com. **Website:** www.blacklace.org. Estab. 1991. "*Black Lace* seeks stories, articles, photography, models, illustration, and a very limited amount of poetry all related to black women unclothed or in erotic situations."

NEEDS Length: 2,000-4,000 words.

HOW TO CONTACT Submit via postal mail (include SASE if you want your work returned), fax, or e-mail.

TIPS "*Black Lace* seeks erotic material of the highest quality, but it need not be written by professional writers. The most important thing is that the work be erotic and that it feature black women in the life or ITL themes. We are not interested in stories that demean black women or place them in stereotypical situations."

○○○ BLACK WARRIOR REVIEW

P.O. Box 862936, Tuscaloosa AL 35486. (205)348-4518. **E-mail:** interns.bwr@gmail.com. **Website:** www.bwr.ua.edu. **Contact:** Kirby Johnson, editor. Estab. 1974. "We publish contemporary fiction, poetry, reviews, essays, and art for a literary audience. We publish the freshest work we can find."

○   Work that appeared in the *Black Warrior Review* has been included in the *Pushcart Prize* anthology, *Harper's Magazine, Best American Short Stories, Best American Poetry,* and *New Stories from the South.*

NEEDS "We are open to good experimental writing and short-short fiction. No genre fiction please. Publishes novel excerpts if author is under contract to be published." Length: no more than 7,000 words.

HOW TO CONTACT One story/chapter per envelope. Wants work that is conscious of form and well-crafted.

PAYMENT/TERMS "*BWR* pays a one-year subscription and a nominal lump-sum fee for all works published."

TIPS "We look for attention to language, freshness, honesty, a convincing and sharp voice. Send us a clean, well-printed, proofread ms. Become familiar with the magazine prior to submission."

○○ BLOOD LOTUS

Wales. **E-mail:** bloodlotusjournal@gmail.com; bloodlotusfiction@gmail.com. **Website:** www.bloodlotusjournal.com. *Blood Lotus*, published quarterly online, publishes "poetry, fiction, and anything in between!" Wants "fresh language, memorable characters, strong images, and vivid artwork." Will not open attachments. Reads submissions year-round.

NEEDS Send "1-3 polished, self-contained short shorts or flash fiction pieces, e-mailed to bloodlotusfiction@gmail.com." No attachments.

TIPS "Don't be boring."

○ BLUELINE

120 Morey Hall, Department of English and Communication, Postdam NY 13676. (315)267-2043. **E-mail:** blueline@potsdam.edu. **Website:** bluelinemagadk.com. **Contact:** Donald McNutt, editor; Caroline Downing, art editor. Estab. 1979. "*Blueline* seeks poems, stories, and essays relating to the Adirondacks and regions similar in geography and spirit, or focusing on the shaping influence of nature. Payment in copies. Submission period is July through November. *Blueline* welcomes electronic submissions as Word document (.doc or .docx) attachments. Please identify genre in subject line. Please avoid using compression software."

○   Magazine: 6×9; 200 pages; 70 lb. white stock paper; 65 lb. smooth cover stock; illustrations; photos. "Proofread all submissions. It is difficult for our editors to get excited about work containing typographical and syntactic errors."

NEEDS Receives 8-10 unsolicited mss/month. Accepts 6-8 mss/issue. Does not read January-August. Publishes 2 new writers/year. Recently published work by Jim Meirose, T. Stores, Gail Gilliland, and Lou Gaglia. No urban stories or erotica. Length: 500-3,000 words. Average length: 2,500 words.

PAYMENT/TERMS Pays 1 contributor's copy; charges $7 each for 3 or more copies.

TIPS "We look for concise, clear, concrete prose that tells a story and touches upon a universal theme or situation. We prefer realism to romanticism but will consider nostalgia if well done. Pay attention to grammar and syntax. Avoid murky language, sentimentality, cuteness, or folkiness. We would like to see more good, creative nonfiction centered on the literature and/or culture of the Adirondacks, Northern New York, New England, or Eastern Canada. If ms has potential, we work with author to improve and reconsider for publication. Our readers prefer fiction to poetry (in general) or reviews. Write from your own experience, be specific and factual (within the bounds of your story), and if you write about universal features such as love, death, change, etc., write about them in a fresh way. You'll catch our attention if your writing is interesting, vigorous, and polished."

BLUE MESA REVIEW

E-mail: bmreditr@unm.edu. **Website:** www.unm.edu/~bluemesa/index.htm. **Contact:** Ben Dolan, editor; Christina Glessner, managing editor. Estab. 1989. "Originally founded by Rudolfo Anaya, Gene Frumkin, David Johnson, Patricia Clark Smith, and Lee Bartlette in 1989, the *Blue Mesa Review* emerged as a source of innovative writing produced in the Southwest. Over the years the magazine's nuance has changed, sometimes shifting towards more craft-oriented work, other times realigning with its original roots."

- Open for submissions from September 30-March 31. Contest: June 1-August 31. Only accepts submissions through online submissions manager, available through website.

BLUESTEM

English Deptartment, Eastern Illinois University, **E-mail:** info@bluestemmagazine.com. **Website:** www.bluestemmagazine.com. **Contact:** Olga Abella, editor. Estab. 1966. "*Bluestem*, formerly known as *Karamu*, produces a quarterly online issue (December, March, June, September) and an annual print issue. Submissions are accepted year-round. There is no compensation for online contributors, but we will promote your work enthusiastically and widely. Past issues have included themes such as: The Humor Issue, The Music Issue, The Millennium."

- Only accepts submissions through online submissions manager.

NEEDS Length: no more than 5,000 words.

HOW TO CONTACT Submit only 1 short story at a time. Include bio (less than 100 words) with submission. Query if longer than 5,000 words.

PAYMENT/TERMS Pays 1 contributor's copy and discount for additional copies.

BOSTON REVIEW

PO Box 425786, Cambridge MA 02142. (617)324-1360. **Fax:** (617)452-3356. **E-mail:** review@boston review.net. **Website:** www.bostonreview.net. Estab. 1975. "The editors are committed to a society and culture that foster human diversity and a democracy in which we seek common grounds of principle amidst our many differences. In the hope of advancing these ideals, the *Review* acts as a forum that seeks to enrich the language of public debate."

- *Boston Review* is a recipient of the Pushcart Prize in Poetry.

NEEDS Looking for "stories that are emotionally and intellectually substantive and also interesting on the level of language. Things that are shocking, dark, lewd, comic, or even insane are fine so long as the fiction is *controlled* and purposeful in a masterly way. Subtlety, delicacy, and lyricism are attractive, too. Simultaneous submissions are fine as long as we are notified of the fact." No romance, erotica, genre fiction. Length: 1,200-5,000 words. Average length: 2,000 words.

HOW TO CONTACT Send complete ms.

PAYMENT/TERMS Pays $25-300 and contributor's copies.

TIPS "The best way to get a sense of the kind of material *Boston Review* is looking for is to read the magazine."

BOULEVARD

Opojaz, Inc., 6614 Clayton Rd., Box 325, Richmond Heights MO 63117. (314)324-3351. **Fax:** (314)862-2982. **E-mail:** richardburgin@netzero.com; jessicarogen@boulevardmagazine.org. **E-mail:** https://boulevard.submittable.com/submit. **Website:** www.boulevard magazine.org. **Contact:** Richard Burgin, editor; Jessica Rogen, managing editor. Estab. 1985. The Short Fiction Contest for Emerging Writers: $1,500 and publication in *Boulevard*. Postmarked deadline is December 31. Entry fee is $15 for each individual story, with no limit per author. Entry fee includes a one-year subscription to *Boulevard* (1 per author). Make check payable to *Boulevard*. For contests, make check payable to *Boulevard* or submit online at https://boulevard.submittable.com/submit. "*Boulevard* is a diverse literary magazine presenting original creative work by well-known authors, as well as by writers of exciting promise." Triannual magazine featuring fiction, poetry, and essays. *Boulevard* is 175-250 pages, digest-sized, flat-spined, with glossy card cover. Receives over 600 unsolicited mss/month. Accepts about 10 mss/issue. Publishes 10 new writers/year. Recently published work by Joyce Carol Oates, Floyd Skloot, John Barth, Stephen Dixon, David Guterson, Albert

Goldbarth, Molly Peacock, Bob Hicok, Alice Friman, Dick Allen, and Tom Disch. Sometimes comments on rejected mss.

○ "*Boulevard* has been called 'one of the half-dozen best literary journals' by Poet Laureate Daniel Hoffman in *The Philadelphia Inquirer*. We strive to publish the finest in poetry, fiction, and nonfiction. We frequently publish writers with previous credits, we are very interested in publishing less-experienced or unpublished writers with exceptional promise. We've published everything from John Ashbery to Donald Hall to a wide variety of styles from new or lesser-known poets. We're eclectic. We are interested in original, moving poetry written from the head as well as the heart. It can be about any topic."

NEEDS Confessions, experimental, literary, mainstream, novel excerpts. "We do not want erotica, science fiction, romance, western, or children's stories." Length: 8,000 words maximum.

PAYMENT/TERMS Pays $50-500 (sometimes higher) for accepted work.

TIPS "Read the magazine first. The work *Boulevard* publishes is generally recognized as among the finest in the country. We continue to seek more good literary or cultural essays. Send only your best work."

◐◑ THE BRIAR CLIFF REVIEW

3303 Rebecca St., Sioux City IA 51104. (712)279-5477. **E-mail:** tricia.currans-sheehan@briarcliff.edu (editor); jeanne.emmons@briarcliff.edu (poetry). **Website:** www.briarcliff.edu/bcreview. **Contact:** Tricia Currans-Sheehan, Jeanne Emmons, Phil Hey, Paul Weber, editors. Estab. 1989. *The Briar Cliff Review*, published annually in April, is "an attractive, eclectic literary/art magazine." It focuses on (but is not limited to) "Siouxland writers and subjects. We are happy to proclaim ourselves a regional publication. It doesn't diminish us; it enhances us."

○ Magazine: 8½×11; 125 pages; 70 lb. 100# Altima Satin Text; illustrations; photos; perfect-bound, with 4-color cover on dull stock. Member: CLMP; Humanities International Complete.

NEEDS Accepts 5 mss/year. Reads mss only between August 1 and November 1. **Publishes 10-14 new writers/year.** Publishes ms 3-4 months after acceptance. Recently published work by Leslie Barnard, Da-

ryl Murphy, Patrick Hicks, Siobhan Fallon, Shelley Scaletta, Jenna Blum, Brian Bedard, Rebecca Tuch, Scott H. Andrews, and Josip Novakovich. "No romance, horror, or alien stories." Length: 2,500-5,000 words; average length: 3,000 words.

HOW TO CONTACT Send SASE for return of ms. Does not accept electronic submissions (unless from overseas). Responds in 4-5 months to mss. Seldom comments on rejected mss. Accepts simultaneous submissions.

PAYMENT/TERMS Pays 2 contributor's copies; additional copies available for $12.

TIPS "So many stories are just telling. We want some action. It has to move. We prefer stories in which there is no gimmick, no mechanical turn of events, no moral except the one we would draw privately."

◑ BRILLIANT CORNERS: A JOURNAL OF JAZZ & LITERATURE

Lycoming College, 700 College Place, Williamsport PA 17701. **Website:** www.lycoming.edu/brilliant corners. **Contact:** Sascha Feinstein. Estab. 1996. "We publish jazz-related literature—fiction, poetry, and nonfiction. We are open as to length and form." Semi-annual.

○ Journal: 6×9; 90 pages; 70 lb. Cougar opaque, vellum, natural paper; photographs. Does not read mss May 15-September 1. Receives 10-15 unsolicited mss/month. Accepts 1-2 mss/issue; 2-3 mss/year.

TIPS "We look for clear, moving prose that demostrates a love of both writing and jazz. We primarily publish established writers, but we read all submissions carefully and welcome work by outstanding young writers."

THE BROADKILL REVIEW

Broadkill Publishing Associates c/o John Milton & Company, 104 Federal St., Milton DE 19968. **E-mail:** the_broadkill_review@earthlink.net. **Website:** www.thebroadkillreview.blogspot.com; https://sites.google.com/site/thebroadkillreview. **Contact:** Jamie Brown, editor; Scott Whitaker, Web editors. Estab. 2005.

○ "*The Broadkill Review* accepts the best fiction, poetry, and nonfiction by new and established writers. We have published Pushcart-nominated fiction and poetry."

NEEDS No erotica, fantasy, science fiction "unless these serve some functional, literary purpose; most do not." Length: 6,000 words/maximum.

HOW TO CONTACT Send complete ms with cover letter online at https://thebroadkillreview.submittable.com/submit. Include estimated word count, brief bio, list of publications.

PAYMENT/TERMS Pays contributor's copy.

TIPS "Query the editor first. Visit our website to familiarize yourself with the type of material we publish. Request and read a copy of the magazine first!"

BRYANT LITERARY REVIEW

Faculty Suite F, Bryant University, 1150 Douglas Pike, Smithfield RI 02917. **E-mail:** blr@bryant.edu. **Website:** bryantliteraryreview.org. **Contact:** Tom Chandler, editor; Kimberly Keyes, managing editor; Jeff Cabusao, fiction editor; Lucie Koretsky, associate editor. Estab. 2000. *Bryant Literary Review* is an international magazine of poetry and fiction published annually in May. Features poetry, fiction, photography, and art. "Our only standard is quality."

Bryant Literary Review is 125 pages, digest-sized, offset-printed, perfect-bound, with 4-color cover with art or photo. Has published poetry by Michael S. Harper, Mary Crow, Denise Duhamel, and Baron Wormser.

NEEDS Reads submissions September 1-December 31. Length: up to 5,000 words.

HOW TO CONTACT Submit 1 ms at a time; include SASE.

PAYMENT/TERMS Pays contributor's copies.

TIPS "We expect readers of the *Bryant Literary Review* to be sophisticated, educated, and familiar with the conventions of contemporary literature. We see our purpose to be the cultivation of an active and growing connection between our community and the larger literary culture. Our production values are of the highest caliber, and our roster of published authors includes major award and fellowship winners. The *BLR* provides a respected venue for creative writing of every kind from around the world. Our only standard is quality. No abstract expressionist poems, please. We prefer accessible work of depth and quality."

BURNSIDE REVIEW

P.O. Box 1782, Portland OR 97207. **Website:** www.burnsidereview.org. **Contact:** Dan Kaplan, managing editor. Estab. 2004. *Burnside Review,* published every 9 months, prints "the best poetry and short fiction we can get our hands on." Each issue includes 1 featured poet with an interview and new poems. "We tend to publish writing that finds beauty in truly unexpected places; that combines urban and natural imagery; that breaks the heart."

Burnside Review is 80 pages, 6x6, professionally printed, perfect-bound.

NEEDS "Send anything from a group of flash-fiction pieces to a traditional short story, so long as the word count doesn't exceed 5,000 words. We like story. We like character. We don't like hobgoblins. Barthelme, Munro, Carver, and Bender are some of the folks whose work we love."

HOW TO CONTACT Submit 1 short story at a time. Accepts submissions through online submission manager only.

PAYMENT/TERMS Pays $25 plus 1 contributor's copy.

TIPS "*Burnside Review* accepts submissions of poetry and fiction. If you have something else that you think would be a perfect fit for our journal, please query the editor before submitting. We like work that breaks the heart. That leaves us in a place that we don't expect to be. We like the lyric. We like the narrative. We like when the two merge. We like whiskey. We like hourglass figures. We like crying over past mistakes. We like to be surprised. Surprise us. Read a past issue and try to understand our tastes. At the least, please read the sample poems that we have linked from our prior issues."

BUTTON

P.O. Box 77, Westminster MA 01473. **E-mail:** sally@moonsigns.net. **Website:** www.moonsigns.net. Estab. 1993. "*Button* is New England's tiniest magazine of poetry, fiction, and gracious living, published once a year. As 'gracious living' is on the cover, we like wit, brevity, cleverly conceived essays, recipes, poetry that isn't sentimental, or song lyrics. I started *Button* so that a century from now, when people read it in landfills or, preferably, libraries, they'll say, 'Gee, what a great time to have lived. I wish I lived back then.'"

Receives 20-40 unsolicited mss/month. Accepts 3-6 mss/issue; 3-6 mss/year. *Button* is 16-24 pages, saddle-stapled, with cardstock offset cover with illustrations that incorporate 1 or more buttons. Has published poetry by Amanda Powell, Brendan Galvin, Jean Monahan, Mary Campbell, Kevin McGrath, and Ed Conti.

NEEDS Seeks quality fiction. No genre fiction, science fiction, techno-thriller. "Wants more of anything Herman Melville, Henry James, or Betty MacDonald would like to read." Length: 300-2,000 words.

HOW TO CONTACT Send complete ms with bio, list of publications, and explain how you found the magazine. Include SASE.

PAYMENT/TERMS Pays honorarium and subscriptions.

TIPS "*Button* writers have been widely published elsewhere, in virtually all the major national magazines. They include Ralph Lombreglia, Lawrence Millman, They Might Be Giants, Combustible Edison, Sven Birkerts, Stephen McCauley, Amanda Powell, Wayne Wilson, David Barber, Romayne Dawnay, Brendan Galvin, and Diana DerHovanessian. Follow the guidelines, make sure you read your work aloud, and don't inflate or deflate your publications and experience. We've published plenty of new folks, but on the merits of the work."

CADET QUEST MAGAZINE

1333 Alger St. SE, Grand Rapids MI 49507. (616)241-5616. **Fax:** (616)241-5558. **E-mail:** submissions@calvinistcadets.org. **Website:** www.calvinistcadets.org. **Contact:** G. Richard Broene, editor. Estab. 1958. *Cadet Quest Magazine* shows boys 9-14 how God is at work in their lives and in the world around them.

Accepts submissions by mail or by e-mail (must include ms in text of e-mail). Will not open attachments.

NEEDS Middle readers, boys/early teens: adventure, arts/craft, games/puzzles, hobbies, humorous, multicultural, religious, science, sports. Fast-moving stories that appeal to a boy's sense of adventure or sense of humor are welcome. Avoid preachiness. Avoid simplistic answers to complicated problems. Avoid long dialogue and little action. No fantasy, science fiction, fashion, horror, or erotica. Length: 900-1,500 words.

HOW TO CONTACT Send complete ms.

PAYMENT/TERMS Pays 4-6¢/word, and 1 contributor's copy.

TIPS "Best time to submit stories/articles is early in the year (January-April). Also, remember, readers are boys ages 9-14. Stories must reflect or add to the theme of the issue and be from a Christian perspective."

THE CAFE IRREAL

E-mail: editors@cafeirreal.com. **Website:** www.cafeirreal.com. **Contact:** G.S. Evans, Alice Whittenburg, co-editors. Estab. 1998. "Our audience is composed of people who read or write literary fiction with fantastic themes, similar to the work of Franz Kafka, Kobo Abe, or Clarice Lispector. This is a type of fiction (irreal) that has difficulty finding its way into print in the English-speaking world and defies many of the conventions of American literature especially. As a result ours is a fairly specialized literary publication, and we would strongly recommend that prospective writers look at our current issue and guidelines carefully."

Recently published work by Marcel Béalu, Jeff Friedman, Daniel Chacón, Zdravka Evtimova, Michal Ajvaz, and Norman Lock.

NEEDS Accepts 6-8 mss/issue; 24-32 mss/year. No horror or slice-of-life stories; no genre or mainstream science fiction or fantasy. Length: 2,000 words (maximum).

HOW TO CONTACT Accepts submissions by e-mail. No attachments; include submission in body of e-mail. Include estimated word count.

PAYMENT/TERMS Pays 1¢/word, $2 minimum.

TIPS "Forget formulas. Write about what you don't know, take me places I couldn't possibly go, don't try to make me care about the characters. Read short fiction by writers such as Franz Kafka, Jorge Luis Borges, Donald Barthelme, Magnus Mills, Ana Maria Shua and Stanislaw Lem. Also read our website and guidelines."

CAKETRAIN

P.O. Box 82588, Pittsburgh PA 15218. **E-mail:** editors@caketrain.org. **Website:** www.caketrain.org. **Contact:** Amanda Raczkowski and Joseph Reed, editors. Estab. 2003.

NEEDS Submit via e-mail; no postal submissions. Include cover letter with titles of pieces and brief bio. Please do not submit any additional work until a decision has been made regarding your current submission.

PAYMENT/TERMS Pays 1 contributor's copy.

CALLALOO: A JOURNAL OF AFRICAN DIASPORA ARTS & LETTERS

Department of English, Texas A&M University, 4212 TAMU, College Station TX 77843-4227. (979)458-3108. **Fax:** (979)458-3275. **E-mail:** callaloo@tamu.edu. **Website:** callaloo.tamu.edu. Estab. 1976. *Callaloo: A Journal of African Diaspora Arts & Letters*, published quarterly, is devoted to poetry dealing with the African Diaspora, including North America, Europe, Africa, Latin and Central America, South America, and the Caribbean. Has published poetry by Aimeé Ceésaire, Lucille Clifton, Rita Dove, Yusef Komunyakaa, Natasha Tretheway, and Carl Phillips. Features about

15-20 poems (all forms and styles) in each issue along with short fiction, interviews, literary criticism, and concise critical book reviews. Subscription: $39, $107 for institutions.

NEEDS Would like to see more experimental fiction, science fiction, and well-crafted literary fiction particularly dealing with the black middle class, immigrant communities, and/or the black South. Accepts 3-5 mss/issue; 10-20 mss/year. **Publishes 5-10 new writers/year.** Recently published work by Charles Johnson, Edwidge Danticat, Thomas Glave, Nallo Hopkinson, John Edgar Wideman, Jamaica Kincaid, Percival Everett, and Patricia Powell. Also publishes poetry. No romance, confessional.

TIPS "We look for freshness of both writing and plot, strength of characterization, plausibility of plot. Read what's being written and published, especially in journals such as *Callaloo*."

CALLIOPE

30 Grove St., Suite C, Peterborough NH 03458-1454. (603)924-7209. **Fax:** (603)924-7380. **E-mail:** customerservice@caruspub.com. **Website:** www.cobblestonepub.com. **Contact:** Rosalie Baker and Charles Baker, co-editors; Lou Waryncia, editorial director; Ann Dillon, art director. Estab. 1990. Articles must relate to the issue's theme. Lively, original approaches to the subject are the primary concerns of the editors in choosing material.

NEEDS Middle readers and young adults: adventure, folktales, plays, history, biographical fiction. Material must relate to forthcoming themes. Length: no more than 1,000 words.

PAYMENT/TERMS Pays 20-25¢/word.

CALYX

Calyx, Inc., P.O. Box B, Corvallis OR 97339. (541)753-9384. **Fax:** (541)753-0515. **E-mail:** info@calyxpress.org; editor@calyxpress.org. **Website:** www.calyxpress.org. **Contact:** Rebecca Olson, senior editor. Estab. 1976. "*CALYX* exists to publish fine literature and art by women and is committed to publishing the work of all women, including women of color, older women, working-class women, and other voices that need to be heard. We are committed to discovering and nurturing developing writers."

Annual open submission period is October 1-December 31.

NEEDS Length: no more than 5,000 words.

HOW TO CONTACT All submissions should include author's name on each page and be accompanied by a brief (50-word or less) biographical statement, phone number, and e-mail address. Submit using online submissions manager.

PAYMENT/TERMS Pays in contributor's copies and one-volume subscription.

TIPS "A forum for women's creative work—including work by women of color, lesbian and queer women, young women, old women—*CALYX* breaks new ground. Each issue is packed with new poetry, short stories, full-color artwork, photography, essays, and reviews."

CANADIAN WRITER'S JOURNAL

Box 1178, New Liskeard ON P0J 1P0 Canada. (705)647-5424. **Fax:** (705)647-8366. **E-mail:** editor@cwj.ca. **Website:** www.cwj.ca. **Contact:** Deborah Ranchuk, editor. Estab. 1984. Digest-size magazine for writers emphasizing short "how-to" articles, which convey easily understood information useful to both apprentice and professional writers. General policy and postal subsidies require that the magazine must carry a substantial Canadian content. We try for about 90% Canadian content but prefer good material over country of origin or how well you're known. Writers may query, but unsolicited mss are welcome.

NEEDS Fiction is published only through semi-annual short fiction contest with April 30 deadline. Send SASE for rules, or see guidelines on website. Does not want gratuitous violence or sex subject matters.

HOW TO CONTACT Accepts submissions by e-mail. Responds in 2 months to queries. Pays on publication for one-time rights.

TIPS "We prefer short, tightly written, informative how-to articles. U.S. writers: note that U.S. postage cannot be used to mail from Canada. Obtain Canadian stamps, use IRCs, or send small amounts in cash."

THE CAPILANO REVIEW

2055 Purcell Way, North Vancouver BC V7J 3H5 Canada. (604)984-1712. **E-mail:** tcr@capilanou.ca. **Website:** www.thecapilanoreview.ca. **Contact:** Tamara Lee, managing editor. Estab. 1972. Tri-annual visual and literary arts magazine that "publishes only what the editors consider to be the very best fiction, poetry, drama, or visual art being produced. *TCR* editors are interested in fresh, original work that stimulates and challenges readers. Over the years, the magazine has developed a reputation for pushing beyond the boundaries of traditional art and writing. We are interested in work that is new in concept and in execution."

NEEDS No traditional, conventional fiction. Wants to see more innovative, genre-blurring work. Length: up to 6,000 words

HOW TO CONTACT Send complete ms with SASE and Canadian postage or IRCs. Does not accept submissions through e-mail or on disks.

PAYMENT/TERMS Pays $50-300.

ORSON SCOTT CARD'S INTERGALACTIC MEDICINE SHOW

Hatrack River Publications, P.O. Box 18184, Greensboro NC 27419. **Website:** InterGalacticMedicineShow.com; oscIGMS.com. **Contact:** Edmund R. Schubert, editor. Estab. 2005. *"Orson Scott Card's InterGalactic Medicine Show* is an online fantasy and science fiction magazine. We are a bimonthly publication featuring content from both established and talented new authors. In addition to our bimonthly issues, we offer weekly columns and reviews on books, movies, video games, and writing advice."

NEEDS "We like to see well-developed milieus and believable, engaging characters. We also look for clear, unaffected writing." Length: up to 17,000 words.

HOW TO CONTACT Submit electronically using online submission form. Submit only 1 story at a time. Include estimated word count, e-mail address.

PAYMENT/TERMS Pays 6¢/word up to 7,500 words and 5¢/word thereafter.

TIPS "Please note: *IGMS* is a PG-13 magazine and website. That means that while stories can deal with intense and adult themes, we will not accept stories with explicit or detailed sex of the sort that would earn a movie rating more restrictive than PG-13; nor will there be language of the sort that earns an R rating."

CC&D: CHILDREN, CHURCHES & DADDIES: THE UNRELIGIOUS, NON-FAMILY-ORIENTED LITERARY AND ART MAGAZINE

Scars Publications and Design, 829 Brian Court, Gurnee IL 60031. (847)281-9070. **E-mail:** ccandd96@scars.tv. **Website:** scars.tv/ccd. **Contact:** Janet Kuypers. Estab. 1993. "Our biases are works that relate to issues such as politics, sexism, society, and the like, but we are definitely not limited to such. We publish good work that makes you think, that makes you feel like you've lived through a scene instead of merely reading it. If it relates to how the world fits into a person's life (political story, a day in the life, coping with issues people face), it will probably win us over faster. We have received comments from readers and other editors saying that they thought some of our stories really happened. They didn't, but it was nice to know they were so concrete, so believable that people thought they were nonfiction. Do that to our readers." Publishes every other month online and in print; issues sold via Amazon.com throughout the U.S., U.K., and continental Europe. Publishes short shorts, essays, and stories. Also publishes poetry. Always comments on/critiques rejected mss if asked.

Monthly literary magazine/journal: 6x9 (full-color, full-bleed cover), perfect-bound, 84- to 108-page book. Contains illustrations and photographs as well as short stories, essays, and poetry. Has published Mel Waldman, Kenneth DiMaggio, Linda Webb Aceto, Brian Looney, Joseph Hart, Fritz Hamilton, G.A. Scheinoha, and Ken Dean.

NEEDS Interested in many topics including adventure, ethnic/multicultural, experimental, feminist, gay, historical, lesbian, literary, mystery/suspense, New Age, psychic/supernatural/occult, science fiction. Does not want religious, rhyming, or family-oriented material. Average length: 1,000 words. "Contact us if you are interested in submitting very long stories or parts of a novel (if you are accepted, it would appear in parts in multiple issues)."

HOW TO CONTACT Send complete ms with cover letter or query with clips of published work. Prefers submissions by e-mail. "If you do not have electronic access, there is a strong chance your work will not be considered. We recommend you e-mail submissions to us, either as an attachment (.txt, .rtf, .doc, or .docx, but not .pdf) or by placing it directly in the e-mail letter)." Considers simultaneous submissions, previously published submissions, multiple submissions. Reviews fiction, essays, journals, editorials, short fiction.

CHA

Hong Kong **E-mail:** editors@asiancha.com; j@asiancha.com. **E-mail:** submissions@asiancha.com. **Website:** www.asiancha.com. **Contact:** Tammy Ho Lai-Ming, founding co-editor; Jeff Zroback, founding co-editor; Eddie Tay, reviews editor. Estab. 2007. *Cha* is the first Hong Kong-based English online literary journal; it is dedicated to publishing quality poetry, fiction, creative nonfiction, reviews, photography and art. *Cha* has a strong focus on Asian-themed creative work and work done by Asian writers and artists. It also publishes established and emerging writers/artists from around the world. *Cha* is an affiliated organisation of the Asia-Pacific Writing Partnership and it is catalogued in the School of Oriental and African Studies (SOAS) Library, among other universities. *Cha* was named Best New Online Magazine of 2008. "At this time, we can only accept work in English or translated into English. If you want to review a book for *Cha*, please also write for further information."

NEEDS Length: 100-5,000 words.

HOW TO CONTACT Submit via e-mail.

TIPS "Please read the guidelines on our website carefully before you submit work to us. Do not send attachments in your e-mail. Include all writing in the body of e-mail. Include a brief biography (100 words)."

CHAFFIN JOURNAL

English Department, Eastern Kentucky University, C, Richmond KY 40475-3102. (859)622-3080. **E-mail:** robert.witt@eku.edu. **Website:** www.english.eku.edu/chaffin_journal. **Contact:** Robert Witt, editor. Estab. 1998. *The Chaffin Journal*, published annually in December, prints quality short fiction and poetry by new and established writers/poets. "We publish fiction on any subject; our only consideration is the quality."

○ Receives 20 unsolicited mss/month. Accepts 6-8 mss/year. Does not read mss October 1-May 31. Publishes 2-3 new writers/year. Has published work by Meridith Sue Willis, Marie Manilla, Raymond Abbott, Marjorie Bixler, Chris Helvey.

NEEDS No erotica, fantasy. Length: 10,000 words per submission period; average length: 5,000 words.

PAYMENT/TERMS Pays 1 contributor's copy.

TIPS "All mss submitted are considered."

CHAPMAN

Chapman Publishing, 4 Broughton Place, Edinburgh EH1 3RX Scotland. (44)(131)557-2207. **E-mail:** chapman-pub@blueyonder.co.uk. **Website:** www.chapman-pub.co.uk. **Contact:** Joy Hendry, editor. Estab. 1970. "*Chapman*, Scotland's quality literary magazine, is a dynamic force in Scotland, publishing poetry, fiction, criticism, reviews, and articles on theater, politics, language, and the arts. Our philosophy

is to publish new work from known and unknown writers—mainly Scottish, but also worldwide."

○ Does not accept e-mail submissions.

NEEDS "Any length, any topic considered—the criterion is quality. Please do not send more than 1 item at a time. We are looking for fiction that is challenging, surprising, different—in some way." No horror or science fiction. Length: "Any length, but average is 3,000 words."

HOW TO CONTACT "Submissions should be presented as double-spaced typescript with indented paragraphs. Use double quotes for dialogue and quotations, indicate italics with underscore. Avoid using footnotes—we are not an academic journal."

PAYMENT/TERMS Negotiates payment individually.

TIPS "Keep your stories for 6 months and edit carefully. We seek challenging work that attempts to explore difficult/new territory in content and form, but lighter work, if original enough, is welcome. We have no plans at present to publish longer fiction or novels."

THE CHARITON REVIEW

Truman State University Press, 100 E Normal Ave., Kirksville MO 63501. (660)785-8336. **E-mail:** chariton@truman.edu. **Website:** tsup.truman.edu/aboutChariton.asp. **Contact:** James D'Agostino, editor. Estab. 1975. "*The Chariton Review* is an international literary journal publishing the best in short fiction, essays, poetry, and translations in 2 issues each year. "

○ James D'Agostino became editor in July 2010. He teaches at Truman State University and is the author of *Nude with Anything*.

TIPS "TSUP also publishes essay collections. Send mss to: TSUP; 100 E. Normal Ave., Kirksville, MO 63501."

THE CHATTAHOOCHEE REVIEW: EXPORTING THE SOUTH, IMPORTING THE WORLD

555 N. Indian Creek Dr., Clarkston GA 30021. **Website:** thechattahoocheereview.gpc.edu. **Contact:** Lydia Ship, managing editor. Estab. 1980. *The Chattahoochee Review*, published quarterly, prints poetry, short fiction, essays, reviews, and interviews. "We publish a number of Southern writers, but *The Chattahoochee Review* is not by design a regional magazine. All themes, forms, and styles are considered as long as they impact the whole person: heart, mind, intuition, and imagination."

Has recently published work by George Garrett, Jim Daniels, Jack Pendarvis, Ignacio Padilla, and Kevin Canty. *The Chattahoochee Review* is 160 pages, digest-sized, professionally printed, flat-spined, with 4-color silk-matte card cover. Press run is 1,250; 300 are complimentary copies sent to editors and "miscellaneous VIPs."

NEEDS Length: 500-1,000 words for short shorts; up to 6,000 words for short stories and novellas.

HOW TO CONTACT "*TCR* publishes high-quality literary fiction characterized by interest in language, development of distinctive settings, compelling conflict, and complex, unique characters. Submit only 1 story or up to 3 short-shorts.

PAYMENT/TERMS Pays 2 contributor's copies.

CHAUTAUQUA LITERARY JOURNAL

Department of Creative Writing, University of North Carolina at Wilmington, 601 S. College Rd., Wilmington NC 28403. **E-mail:** clj@uncw.edu. **Website:** www.ciweb.org/literary-journal. **Contact:** Jill Gerard, editor; Philip Gerard, editor. Estab. 2003. *Chautauquu,* published annually in June, prints poetry, short fiction, and creative nonfiction. The editors actively solicit writing that expresses the values of Chautauqua Institution broadly construed: A sense of inquiry into questions of personal, social, political, spiritual, and aesthetic importance, regardless of genre. Considers the work of any writer, whether or not affiliated with Chautauqua Institution. Looking for a mastery of craft, attention to vivid and accurate language, a true lyric "ear," an original and compelling vision, and strong narrative instinct. Above all, values work that is intensely personal, yet somehow implicitly comments on larger public concerns; also values work that answers every reader's most urgent question: Why are you telling me this?

Reads submissions February 15-April 15 and August 15-November 15.

NEEDS *Chautauqua* short stories, self-contained novel excerpts, or flash fiction demonstrate a sound storytelling instinct, using suspense in the best sense, creating a compulsion in the reader to continue reading. Wants to engage reader's deep interest in the characters and their actions, unsettled issues of action or theme, or in some cases simple delight at the language itself. A superior story will exhibit the writer's attention to language—both in style and content—and should reveal a masterful control of diction and syn-

tax. Length: maximum of 25 double-spaced pages. Considers any piece up to 7,000 words.

CHICAGO QUARTERLY REVIEW

517 Sherman Ave., Evanston IL 60202. **Website:** www.chicagoquarterlyreview.com. **Contact:** Syed Afzal Haider and Elizabeth McKenzie, editors. Estab. 1994. Literary. Receives 100 unsolicited mss/month. Accepts 10-15 mss/issue; 20-30 mss/year. Publishes ms 6 months-1 year after acceptance. Agented fiction 5%. **Publishes 8-10 new writers/year.** Also publishes literary essays, poetry. Sometimes comments on rejected mss.

Magazine: 6×9; 225 pages; illustrations; photos.

NEEDS 5,000 words; average length: 2,500 words.

TIPS "The writer's voice ought to be clear and unique, and should explain something of what it means to be human. We want well-written stories that reflect an appreciation for the rhythm and music of language, work that shows passion and commitment to the art of writing."

CHIRON REVIEW

522 E. South Ave., St. John KS 67576. **E-mail:** editor@chironreview.com. **Website:** chironreview.com. **Contact:** Michael Hathaway, editor. Estab. 1982 as *The Kindred Spirit. Chiron Review*, published quarterly, presents the widest possible range of contemporary creative writing—fiction and nonfiction, traditional and offbeat—in an attractive, professional tabloid format, including artwork and photographs of featured writers. No taboos. Has published poetry by Quentin Crisp, Felice Picano, Edward Field, Wanda Coleman, and Marge Piercy. Press run is about 1,000. Subscription: $20/year (4 issues). Single issue: $7.

TIPS "*Chiron Review* is in transition and currently closed to submissions. Please visit our website for updates."

CICADA MAGAZINE

Cricket Magazine Group, 70 E. Lake St., Suite 800, Chicago IL 60601. **E-mail:** cicada@cicadamag.com. **Website:** www.cricketmag.com/cicada. **Contact:** Submissions editor. Estab. 1998. Bimonthly literary magazine for ages 14 and up. Publishes 6 issues per year.

NEEDS Length: 9,000 words maximum

PAYMENT/TERMS Pays up to 25¢/word.

TIPS "Quality writing, good literary style, genuine teen sensibility, depth, humor, good character development, avoidance of stereotypes. Read several issues to familiarize yourself with our style."

CIMARRON REVIEW

205 Morrill Hall, English Department, Oklahoma State University, Stillwater OK 74078. **E-mail:** cimarronreview@okstate.edu. **Website:** cimarronreview.com. **Contact:** Toni Graham, editor. Estab. 1967. "We want strong literary writing. We are partial to fiction in the modern realist tradition and distinctive poetry—lyrical, narrative, etc."

Magazine: 6.5×8.5; 110 pages. Accepts 3-5 mss/issue; 12-15 mss/year. Publishes 2-4 new writers/year. Eager to receive mss from both established and less-experienced writers "who intrigue us with their unusual perspective, language, imagery, and character." Has published work by Molly Giles, Gary Fincke, David Galef, Nona Caspers, Robin Beeman, Edward J. Delaney, William Stafford, John Ashbery, Grace Schulman, Barbara Hamby, Patricia Fargnoli, Phillip Dacey, Holly Prado, and Kim Addonizio.

NEEDS No juvenile or genre fiction. Length: 25 pages maximum.

HOW TO CONTACT Send complete ms with SASE or submit online through submission manager; include cover letter. Accepts simultaneous submissions.

PAYMENT/TERMS Pays 2 contributor's copies.

TIPS "All postal submissions must come with SASE. A cover letter is encouraged. No e-mail submissions from authors living in North America. Query first and follow guidelines. In order to get a feel for the kind of work we publish, please read an issue or 2 before submitting."

THE CINCINNATI REVIEW

P.O. Box 210069, Cincinnati OH 45221-0069. (513)556-3954. **E-mail:** editors@cincinnatireview.com. **Website:** www.cincinnatireview.com. **Contact:** Nicola Mason. Estab. 2003. A journal devoted to publishing the best new literary fiction, creative nonfiction, and poetry, as well as book reviews, essays, and interviews.

Considers submissions by mail and through online submission manager at cincinnatireview.com/submissions. Reads submissions August 15-April 15; mss arriving outside that period will not be read. *The Cincinnati Review* is 180-200 pages, digest-sized, perfect-bound, with matte paperback cover with full-color art.

Press run is 1,000. Single copy: $9 (current issue); subscription: $15.

NEEDS Does not want genre fiction. Length: 125-10,000 words.

HOW TO CONTACT Send complete mss with SASE. Does not consider e-mail submissions; does accept electronic submissions through submission manager at cincinnatireview.com/submissions. Accepts simultaneous submissions with notice.

PAYMENT/TERMS Pays $25/page and 2 contributor's copies.

TIPS "Each issue includes a translation feature. For more information on translations, please see our website."

THE CLAREMONT REVIEW

Suite 101, 1581-H Hillside Ave., Victoria V8T 2C1 B.C. (250)658-5221. **E-mail:** claremontreview@gmail.com. **Website:** www.theclaremontreview.ca. **Contact:** Linda Moran, managing editor. "We publish anything from traditional to postmodern, but with a preference for works that reveal something of the human condition. By this, we mean stories that explore real characters in modern settings. Who are we, what are we doing to the planet, what is our relationship to one another, the earth, or God. Also, reading samples on the website or from past issues will give you a clearer indication of what we are looking for."

NEEDS Does not want science fiction, fantasy, or romance. Length: 5,000 maximum.

HOW TO CONTACT Send complete ms; should be double-spaced. Include SASE.

TIPS "Read guidelines before submitting."

CLARK STREET REVIEW

P.O. Box 1377, Berthoud CO 80513. **E-mail:** clarkreview@earthlink.net. **Contact:** Ray Foreman, editor. Estab. 1998. *Clark Street Review*, published 6 times/year, uses narrative poetry and short shorts. Tries "to give writers and poets cause to keep writing by publishing their best work." Wants "narrative poetry under 100 lines that reaches readers who are mostly published poets and writers. Subjects are open." Does not want "obscure or formalist work."

"Editor reads everything with a critical eye of 30 years of experience in writing and publishing small press work." *Clark Street Review* is 20 pages, digest-sized, photocopied, saddle-stapled, with paper cover. Receives about 1,000 poems/year, accepts about 10%. Press run is

200. Single copy: $2; subscription: $6 for 6 issues postpaid for writers only. Make checks payable to R. Foreman.

⊕ CLOUD RODEO

E-mail: editors@cloudrodeo.org. **E-mail:** submit@cloudrodeo.org. **Website:** cloudrodeo.org. "We want your problems deploying a term liek nonelen. We want your isolated photographs of immense locomotives slogged down by the delirium of drunken yet pristine jungles. We want the one eye you caught on fire doing alchemy. The world you collapsed playing architect. We want what you think is too. We want you to anesthetize this aesthetic. Your Enfer, your Ciel, your Qu'importe. We want all your to to sound out."
HOW TO CONTACT Submit 1 prose piece.
TIPS "Let's get weird."

○ COAL CITY REVIEW

Coal City Press, University of Kansas, English Department, Lawrence KS 66045. **E-mail:** coalcity@sunflower.com. **E-mail:** briandal@ku.edu. **Website:** www.coalcityreview.com. **Contact:** Editor, Brian Daldorph. "*Coal City Review*, published annually in the fall, prints poetry, short stories, reviews, and interviews—"the best material I can find. As Pound said, 'Make it new.'"

◑ Only accepts submissions by postal mail.
NEEDS "Accepts mostly mainstream, 'literary' fiction. Don't send 'experimental' work our way." Length: no more than 4,000 words.
PAYMENT/TERMS Pays in contributor's copies.

◑◐ C/OASIS

Sunoasis Publishing, **E-mail:** eide491@earthlink.net. **Website:** www.sunoasis.com/oasis.html. **Contact:** David Eide, Editor. Estab. 1998. "*C/Oasis* has been dedicated to bringing to the Internet the best short story writing and poetry writing available."
NEEDS "For short stories, interesting twists are more valuable than character analysis."
TIPS "NOTICE: PLEASE NOTE! Sunoasis.com has set up a new network called Sunoasis Writers Network. If you want to submit poetry or a story go to sunoasis.ning.com and sign up. It is free. Then you can do one of several things: Put your poem or story or essay in a blog and load it onto the network; join a group, submit it there, and let others read it; or put a notice on the Forum that you have stories and poems and then give a link. The network has over 850 members at this time and is growing so take advantage of it. It was set up to provide writing and career opportunities for the writing crowd, but there are plenty of fiction and poetry writers on it. I've always been impressed by the level of talent *C/Oasis* was able to draw to it and hope that talent hops on the network!"

COBBLESTONE

Carus Publishing, 30 Grove St., Suite C, Peterborough NH 03458. (800)821-0115. **Fax:** (603)924-7380. **E-mail:** customerservice@caruspub.com. **Website:** www.cobblestonepub.com. "We are interested in articles of historical accuracy and lively, original approaches to the subject at hand. Writers are encouraged to study recent *Cobblestone* back issues for content and style. All material must relate to the theme of a specific upcoming issue in order to be considered. To be considered, a query must accompany each individual idea (however, you can mail them all together) and must include the following: a brief cover letter stating the subject and word length of the proposed article, a detailed one-page outline explaining the information to be presented in the article, an extensive bibliography of materials the author intends to use in preparing the article, an SASE. Authors are urged to use primary resources and up-to-date scholarly resources in their bibliography. Writers new to *Cobblestone* should send a writing sample with the query. If you would like to know if your query has been received, please also include a stamped postcard that requests acknowledgment of receipt. In all correspondence, please include your complete address as well as a telephone number where you can be reached. A writer may send as many queries for 1 issue as he or she wishes, but each query must have a separate cover letter, outline, bibliography, and SASE. All queries must be typed. Please do not send unsolicited mss— queries only! Prefers to work with published/established writers. Each issue presents a particular theme, making it exciting as well as informative. Half of all subscriptions are for schools. All material must relate to monthly theme."

◑ "*Cobblestone* stands apart from other children's magazines by offering a solid look at 1 subject and stressing strong editorial content, color photographs throughout, and original illustrations." *Cobblestone* themes and deadline are available on website or with SASE.
NEEDS Length: 800 words maximum.
HOW TO CONTACT Query.

PAYMENT/TERMS Pays 20-25¢/word.

TIPS "Review theme lists and past issues to see what we're looking for."

COLD MOUNTAIN REVIEW

Department of English, Appalachian State University, ASU Box 32052, Boone NC 28608. **E-mail:** coldmountain@appstate.edu. **Website:** www.coldmountain.appstate.edu. **Contact:** Betty Miller Conway, managing editor. *Cold Mountain Review*, published twice/year (Spring and Fall), features poetry, interviews with poets, poetry book reviews, and b&w graphic art. Has published poetry by Sarah Kennedy, Robert Morgan, Susan Ludvigson, Aleida Rodriíguez, R.T. Smith, and Virgil Suaárez.

Cold Mountain Review is about 72 pages, digest-sized, neatly printed with 1 poem/page (or 2-page spread), perfect-bound, with light cardstock cover. Publishes only 10-12 poems/issue; "hence, we are extremely competitive: send only your best." Reading period is August-May.

NEEDS Considers novel excerpts if the submissions is "an exemplary stand-alone piece." Length: up to 6,000 words.

PAYMENT/TERMS Pays in contributor's copies.

COLORADO REVIEW

Center for Literary Publishing, Colorado State University, 9105 Campus Delivery, Fort Collins CO 80523. (970)491-5449. **E-mail:** creview@colostate.edu. **Website:** coloradoreview.colostate.edu. **Contact:** Stephanie G'Schwind, editor-in-chief and nonfiction editor. Literary magazine published 3 times/year.

Work published in *Colorado Review* has been included in *Best American Poetry, Best New American Voices, Best Travel Writing, Best Food Writing,* and the *Pushcart Prize Anthology*.

NEEDS No genre fiction. Length: under 30 ms pages.

HOW TO CONTACT Send complete ms. Fiction mss are read August 1-April 30. Mss received May 1-July 31 will be returned unread. Send no more than 1 story at a time.

PAYMENT/TERMS Pays $200 for short stories.

COLUMBIA: A JOURNAL OF LITERATURE AND ART

Columbia University, New York NY 10027. **Website:** columbiajournal.org. **Contact:** Laura Standley, managing editor. Estab. 1977. "*Columbia: A Journal of Literature and Art* is an annual publication that features the very best in poetry, fiction, nonfiction, and art. We were founded in 1977 and continue to be one of the few national literary journals entirely edited, designed, and produced by students. You'll find that our minds are open, our interests diverse. We solicit mss from writers we love and select the most exciting finds from our virtual submission box. Above all, our commitment is to our readers—to producing a collection that informs, surprises, challenges, and inspires."

Reads submissions March 1-October 31.

HOW TO CONTACT Submit using online submissions manager.

COMMON GROUND REVIEW

Western New England College, H-5132, Western New England College, 1215 Wilbraham Rd., Springfield MA 01119. **E-mail:** editors@cgreview.org. **Website:** cgreview.org. **Contact:** Janet Bowdan, editor. Estab. 1999. *Common Ground Review*, published semiannually (spring/summer, fall/winter), prints poetry and 1 short nonfiction piece in the fall issue, 1 short fiction piece in spring issue. Has published poetry by James Doyle, B.Z. Nidith, Ann Lauinger, Kathryn Howd Machan, and Sheryl L. Nelms. "We want poems with strong imagery, a love of language, a fresh message, that evoke a sense of wonder. This is the official literary journal of Western New England College."

NEEDS Length: up to 12 pages double-spaced.

HOW TO CONTACT Submit fiction to fiction editor@cgreview.org.

PAYMENT/TERMS Pays 1 contributor's copy.

TIPS "For poems, use a few good images to convey ideas. Poems should be condensed and concise, free from words that do not contribute. The subject matter should be worthy of the reader's time and appeal to a wide range of readers. Sometimes the editors may suggest possible revisions."

CONCEIT MAGAZINE

P.O. Box 884223, San Francisco CA 94188-4223. (510479-5408. **E-mail:** conceitmagazine2007@yahoo.com. **Website:** https://sites.google.com/site/conceitmagazine/; www.myspace.com/conceitmagazine. **Contact:** Perry Terrell, editor. Estab. 2007.

Magazine. 8½×5½, number of pages vary, copy paper.

NEEDS List of upcoming themes available for SASE and on website. Receives 40-50 mss/month. Accepts 20-22 mss/issue; up to 264 mss/year. Ms published 3-10 months after acceptance. Publishes 150 new writers/year. Published D. Neil Simmers, Tamara Fey Turner, Eve J. Blohm, Barbara Hantman, David Body, Milton Kerr, and Juanita Torrence-Thompson. Does not want profanity, porn, gruesomeness. Length: 100 words (minimum)-3,000 words (maximum). Average length: 1,500-2,000 words. Publishes short shorts. Average length of short shorts: 50-500 words.

HOW TO CONTACT Also publishes literary essays, literary criticism, book reviews, poetry. "Send review copies to Perry Terrell." Sometimes comments on/critiques rejected mss. Query first or send complete ms with cover letter. Accepts submissions by e-mail and snail mail. Include estimated word count, brief bio, list of publications.

PAYMENT/TERMS Writers receive 1 contributor copy. Additional copies $4.50 (send payment via PayPal to conceitmagazine@yahoo.com). Pays writers through contests. "Occasionally sponsors contests. Send SASE or check blog on website for details."

TIPS "Uniqueness and creativity make a ms stand out. Be brave and confident. Let me see what you created."

CONCHO RIVER REVIEW

Angelo State University, ASU Station #10894, San Angelo TX 76909. (325)486-6139. **E-mail:** crr@angelo .edu. **Website:** www.angelo.edu/dept/english_mod ern_languages/concho_river_review.php. **Contact:** Erin Ashworth-King, general editor. "*CRR* aims to provide its readers with escape, insight, laughter, and inspiration for many years to come. We urge authors to submit to the journal and readers to subscribe to our publication."

NEEDS "Editors tend to publish traditional stories with a strong sense of conflict, finely drawn characters, and crisp dialogue." Length: 1,500-5,000 words.

HOW TO CONTACT Submit only 1 mss at a time. Electronic submissions preferred. See website for appropriate section editor.

PAYMENT/TERMS Pays 1 contributor's copy.

CONFRONTATION

English Department, LIU Post, Brookville NY 11548. (516)299-2720. **E-mail:** confrontationmag@gmail .com. **Website:** www.confrontationmagazine.org. **Contact:** Jonna Semeiks, editor-in-chief. Estab. 1968. "*Confrontation* has been in continuous publication since 1968. Our taste and our magazine is eclectic, but we always look for excellence in style, an important theme, a memorable voice. We enjoy discovering and fostering new talent. Each issue contains work by both well-established and new writers. In addition, *Confrontation* often features a thematic special section that 'confronts' a topic. The ensuing confrontation is an attempt to see the many sides of an issue or theme, rather than to present a formed conclusion. We prefer single submissions. Clear copy. No e-mail submissions unless writer resides outside the U.S. Mail submissions with an SASE. We read August 16-May 15. Do not send mss or e-mail submissions between May 16 and August 15. We publish theme issues. Upcoming themes are announced on our website and Facebook and Twitter pages and in our magazine."

Confrontation has garnered a long list of awards and honors, including the Editor's Award for Distinguished Achievement from CLMP (given to Martin Tucker, the founding editor of the magazine) and NEA grants. Work from the magazine has appeared in numerous anthologies, including the *Pushcart Prize*, *Best Short Stories*, and *The O. Henry Prize Stories*.

NEEDS "We judge on quality of writing and thought or imagination, so we will accept genre fiction. However, it must have literary merit, or it must transcend or challenge genre." No "proselytizing" literature or conventional genre fiction. Length: Up to 7,200 words

HOW TO CONTACT Send complete ms.

PAYMENT/TERMS Pays $50-125; more for commissioned work.

TIPS "We look for literary merit. Keep honing your skills and keep trying."

CONTRARY

P.O. Box 806363, Chicago IL 60616-3299 (do not send submissions here). **E-mail:** chicago@contrarymaga zine.com (do not send submissions here). **Website:** www.contrarymagazine.com. **Contact:** Jeff McMahon, editor. Estab. 2003. *Contrary* publishes fiction, poetry, literary commentary, and prefers work that combines the virtues of all those categories. Founded at the University of Chicago, it now operates independently and not-for-profit on the South Side of Chicago. "We like work that is not only contrary in content, but contrary in its evasion of the expectations established by its genre. Our fiction defies traditional story form. For example, a story may bring us to closure without ever delivering an ending. We don't insist on the ending, but we do insist on the closure. And we value fiction as poetic as any poem." Quarterly. Member CLMP.

Online literary magazine/journal. Contains illustrations. Receives 650 mss/month. Accepts 6 mss/issue; 24 mss/year. Publishes 1 new writer/year. Has published Sherman Alexie, Andrew Coburn, Amy Reed, Clare Kirwan, Stephanie Johnson, Laurence Davies, and Edward Mc-Whinney.

NEEDS Length: 2,000 words (maximum); average length: 750 words. Publishes short shorts. Average length of short shorts: 750 words.

HOW TO CONTACT Accepts submissions through website only: www.contrarymagazine.com/Contrary/Submissions.html. Include estimated word count, brief bio, list of publications. Considers simultaneous submissions.

PAYMENT/TERMS Pays $20-60.

TIPS "Beautiful writing catches our eye first. If we realize we're in the presence of unanticipated meaning, that's what clinches the deal. Also, we're not fond of expository fiction. We prefer to be seduced by beauty, profundity, and mystery than to be presented with the obvious. We look for fiction that entrances, that stays the reader's finger above the mouse button. That is, in part, why we favor microfiction, flash fiction, and short shorts. Also, we hope writers will remember that most editors are looking for very particular species of work. We try to describe our particular species in our mission statement and our submission guidelines, but those descriptions don't always convey nuance. That's why many editors urge writers to read the publication itself, in the hope that they will intuit an understanding of its particularities. If you happen to write that particular species of work we favor, your submission may find a happy home with us. If you don't, it does not necessarily reflect on your quality or your ability. It usually just means that your work has a happier home somewhere else."

CONVERGENCE: AN ONLINE JOURNAL OF POETRY AND ART

An Online Journal of Poetry and Art, **E-mail:** clinville@csus.edu. **Website:** www.convergence-journal.com. **Contact:** Cynthia Linville, managing editor. Estab. 2003. *Convergence* seeks to unify the literary and visual arts and draw new interpretations of the written word by pairing poems and flash fiction with complementary art. Quarterly. Estab. 2003. Circ. 200. "We look for well-crafted work with fresh images and a strong voice. Work from a series or with a com-

mon theme has a greater chance of being accepted. Seasonally themed work is appreciated (spring and summer for the January deadline, fall and winter for the June deadline). Please include a 75-word bio with your work (bios may be edited for length and clarity). A cover letter is not needed. Absolutely no simultaneous or previously published submissions."

Deadlines are January 5 and June 5.

NEEDS Accepts 5 mss/issue. Publishes ms 1-6 months after acceptance. Recently published work by Oliver Rice, Simon Perchik, Mary Ocher. Publishes short shorts. Also publishes poetry.

HOW TO CONTACT Send complete ms. E-mail submissions only with "Convergence" in subject line. No simultaneous submissions. Responds in less than a week to queries; 6 months to mss. Writer's guidelines online. Submit no more than 5 fiction pieces, no longer than 1,000 words each.

PAYMENT/TERMS Acquires first rights.

TIPS "We look for freshness and originality and a mastery of the craft of flash fiction. Working with a common theme has a greater chance of being accepted."

COTTONWOOD

Room 400 Kansas Union, 1301 Jayhawk Blvd., University of Kansas, Lawrence KS 66045. **E-mail:** tlorenz@ku.edu. **Website:** www2.ku.edu/~englishmfa/cottonwood. **Contact:** Tom Lorenz, fiction editor. Estab. 1965. "Established in the 1960s, *Cottonwood* is the nationally circulated literary review of the University of Kansas. We publish high-quality literary work in poetry, fiction, and creative nonfiction. Over the years authors such as William Stafford, Rita Dove, Connie May Fowler, Virgil Suarez, and Cris Mazza have appeared in the pages of *Cottonwood*, and recent issues have featured the work of Kim Chinquee, Quinn Dalton, Carol Lee Lorenzo, Jesse Kercheval, Joanne Lowery, and Oliver Rice. We welcome submissions from new and established writers. New issues appear once yearly, in the fall."

NEEDS Length: no more than 8,500 words.

HOW TO CONTACT Submit with SASE.

PAYMENT/TERMS Pays in contributor's copies.

TIPS "We're looking for depth and/or originality of subject matter, engaging voice and style, emotional honesty, command of the material and the structure. *Cottonwood* publishes high-quality literary fiction, but we are very open to the work of talented new writers. Write something honest and that you care about, and write it as well as you can. Don't hesitate to keep trying us. We sometimes take a piece from a writer we've rejected a number of times. We generally don't like clever, gimmicky writing. The style should be engaging but not claim all the the attention itself."

○ THE COUNTRY DOG REVIEW

P.O. Box 1476, Oxford MS 38655. **E-mail:** country dogreview@gmail.com. **Website:** www.countrydo greview.org. **Contact:** Danielle Sellers, editor. *The Country Dog Review*, published semiannually online, publishes "poetry, book reviews, and interviews with poets.

NEEDS Wants poetry of the highest quality, not limited to style or region. Also accepts book reviews and interviews.

HOW TO CONTACT Query first. Does not want "translations, fiction, nonfiction." Receives about 400 poems/year, accepts about 10%.

⑤ CRAB ORCHARD REVIEW

Department of English, Southern Illinois University Carbondale, Faner Hall 2380, Mail Code 4503, 1000 Faner Dr., Carbondale IL 62901. (618)453-6833. **Fax:** (618)453-8224. **Website:** www.craborchardreview .siuc.edu. **Contact:** Jon Tribble, managing editor. Estab. 1995. "We are a general-interest literary journal published twice/year. We strive to be a journal that writers admire and readers enjoy. We publish fiction, poetry, creative nonfiction, fiction translations, interviews, and reviews."

○ Reads submissions February 15-April 30 (winter/spring issue) and August 27-November 3 (special summer/fall issue).

NEEDS No science fiction, romance, western, horror, gothic, or children's. Wants more novel excerpts that also stand alone as pieces. Length: up to 25 pages double-spaced.

HOW TO CONTACT Send SASE for reply, return of ms.

PAYMENT/TERMS Pays $25/published magazine page, $100 minimum, 2 contributor's copies and one-year subscription.

CRAZYHORSE

College of Charleston, Department of English, 66 George St., Charleston SC 29424. (843)953-4470. **E-mail:** crazyhorse@cofc.edu. **Website:** crazyhorse .cofc.edu. Estab. 1960. "We like to print a mix of writing regardless of its form, genre, school, or politics.

We're especially on the lookout for original writing that doesn't fit the categories and that engages in the work of honest communication."

○ Reads submissions September 1-May 31.

NEEDS Accepts all fiction of fine quality, including short shorts and literary essays. Length: 2,500-8,500 words.

PAYMENT/TERMS Pays 2 contributor's copies and $20 per page.

TIPS "Write to explore subjects you care about. The subject should be one in which something is at stake. Before sending, ask, 'What's reckoned with that's important for other people to read?'"

○ CREATIVE WITH WORDS PUBLICATIONS

P.O. Box 223226, Carmel CA 93922. **Fax:** (831)655-8627. **E-mail:** geltrich@mbay.net. **Website:** creative withwords.tripod.com. **Contact:** Brigitta Gisella Geltrich-Ludgate, publisher and editor. Estab. 1975. "Poetry, prose, illustrations, photos by all ages."

NEEDS No violence or erotica, overly religious fiction, or sensationalism.

TIPS "We offer a great variety of themes. We look for clean family-type fiction/poetry. Also, we ask the writer to look at the world from a different perspective, research topic thoroughly, be creative, apply brevity, tell the story from a character's viewpoint, tighten dialogue, be less descriptive, proofread before submitting, and be patient. We will not publish every ms we receive. It has to be in standard English, well written, proofread. We do not appreciate receiving mss where we have to do the proofreading and the correcting of grammar."

⑤ CRICKET

70 E. Lake St., Suite 800, Chicago IL 60601. **E-mail:** cricket@cricketmagkids.com. **Website:** www.cricketmagkids.com. **Contact:** Submissions editor. Estab. 1973. "*Cricket* is a monthly literary magazine for ages 9-14." Publishes 9 issues per year.

NEEDS No didactic, sex, religious, or horror stories. Length: 1,200-1,800 words.

HOW TO CONTACT Submit complete ms.

PAYMENT/TERMS Pays up to 25¢/word.

TIPS Writers: "Read copies of back issues and current issues. Adhere to specified word limits. *Please* do not query." Would currently like to see more fantasy and science fiction. Illustrators: "Send only your best work and be able to reproduce that quality in assignments.

Put name and address on *all* samples. Know a publication before you submit."

CRUCIBLE

Barton College, College Station, Wilson NC 27893. (252)399-6343. **E-mail:** crucible@barton.edu. **Website:** www.barton.edu/academics/english/crucible .htm. **Contact:** Terrence L. Grimes, editor. Estab. 1964. *Crucible*, published annually in the fall, uses "poetry that demonstrates originality and integrity of craftsmanship as well as thought. Traditional metrical and rhyming poems are difficult to bring off in modern poetry. The best poetry is written out of deeply felt experience which has been crafted into pleasing form." Wants "free verse with attention paid particularly to image, line, stanza, and voice." Does not want "very long narratives, poetry that is forced." Has published poetry by Robert Grey, R.T. Smith, and Anthony S. Abbott. All submissions are part of the Poetry and Fiction Contest run each year.

○ *Crucible* is under 100 pages, digest-sized, professionally printed on high-quality paper, with matte card cover. Press run is 500.

NEEDS Length: up to 8,000 words.

HOW TO CONTACT Submit ms by e-mail. Ms accepted only through May 1. Do not include name on ms. Include separate bio.

PAYMENT/TERMS Pays contributor's copies.

CURRENT ACCOUNTS

Current Accounts, Apt. 2D, Bradshaw Hall, Hardcastle Gardens, Bolton BL2 4NZ U.K.. **E-mail:** bswscribe@gmail.com. **E-mail:** fjameshartnell@aol.com. **Website:** sites.google.com/site/bankstreetwriters/. **Contact:** Rod Riesco. Estab. 1994. *Current Accounts*, published semiannually, prints poetry, fiction, and nonfiction by members of Bank Street Writers, and other contributors. Open to all types of poetry. No requirements, although some space is reserved for members. Considers poetry by children and teens. Has published poetry by Pat Winslow, M.R. Peacocke, and Gerald England.

○ *Current Accounts* is 52 pages, A5, photocopied, saddle-stapled, with card cover with b&w or color photo or artwork. Receives about 300 poems/year, accepts about 5%. Press run is 80; 8 distributed free to competition winners. Subscription: £6. Sample: £3. Make checks payable to Bank Street Writers (sterling checks only).

TIPS Bank Street Writers meets once/month and offers workshops, guest speakers, and other activities. Write for details."We like originality of ideas, images, and use of language. No inspirational or religious verse unless it's also good in poetic terms."

THE DALHOUSIE REVIEW

Dalhousie University, Halifax NS B3H 4R2 Canada. **E-mail:** dalhousie.review@dal.ca. **Website:** dalhousiereview.dal.ca. **Contact:** Carrie Dawson, editor. Estab. 1921. *Dalhousie Review*, published 3 times/year, is a journal of criticism publishing poetry and fiction. Considers poetry from both new and established writers. *Dalhousie Review* is 144 pages, digest-sized. Accepts about 5% of poems received. Press run is 500. Single copy: $15 CAD; subscription: $22.50 CAD, $28 USD. Make checks payable to *Dalhousie Review*.

NEEDS Length: up to 5,000 words.

HOW TO CONTACT Submit via postal mail only. Writers are encouraged "to follow whatever canons of usage might govern the particular work in question, and to be inventive with language, ideas, and form."

PAYMENT/TERMS Pays 2 contributor's copies and 10 offprints.

DARGONZINE

E-mail: dargon@dargonzine.org. **Website:** dargonzine.org. **Contact:** Jon Evans, editor. "*DargonZine* is an e-zine that prints original fantasy fiction by aspiring fantasy writers. The Dargon Project is a shared world anthology whose goal is to provide a way for aspiring fantasy writers to meet and improve their writing skills through mutual contact and collaboration, as well as contact with a live readership via the Internet. Our goal is to write fantasy fiction that is mature, emotionally compelling, and professional. Membership in the Dargon Project is a requirement for publication."

○ Publishes 1-3 new writers/year.

PAYMENT/TERMS "As a strictly noncommercial magazine, our writers' only compensation is their growth and membership in a lively writing community."

TIPS "The Readers and Writers FAQs on our website provide much more detailed information about our mission, writing philosophy, and the value of writing for *DargonZine*."

⊙⑤ THE DARK

311 Fairbanks Ave., Northfield NJ 08225. **E-mail:** thedarkmagazine@gmail.com. **Website:** www.the darkmagazine.com. **Contact:** Jack Fisher. Estab. 2013.

NEEDS Does not want blatant horror, fantasy, or science fiction. All fiction must have a dark and strange blend. Length: 1,000-5,000 words.

HOW TO CONTACT Send complete mss by e-mail attached in Microsoft Word doc only. Accepts electronic submissions at thedarkmagazine@gmail.com. Accepts simultaneous submissions with notice.

PAYMENT/TERMS Pays $50-250.

TIPS "All fiction must have a dark, surreal, fantastical bend to it. It should be out of the ordinary and/or experimental. Can also be contemporary."

⊙◑ THE DEAD MULE SCHOOL OF SOUTHERN LITERATURE

NC **E-mail:** deadmule@gmail.com. **E-mail:** submit .mule@gmail.com. **Website:** www.deadmule.com. **Contact:** Valerie MacEwan, publisher and editor; Robert MacEwan, technical and design. "No good southern fiction is complete without a dead mule." Celebrating over 17 years online means *The Dead Mule* is one of the oldest, if not *the* oldest continuously published online literary journals alive today. Publisher and editor Valerie MacEwan welcomes submissions. *The Dead Mule School of Southern Literature* wants flash fiction, visual poetry, essays, and creative nonfiction. We usually publish new work on the 1st and 15th of the month, depending on whims, obligations, and mule jumping contest dates."

⊙ "*The Dead Mule School of Southern Literature* Institutional Alumni Association recruits year-round. Want to join the freshman class of 2018? Submit today."

HOW TO CONTACT We welcome the ingenue and the established writer. It's mostly about you entertaining us and capturing our interest. Everyone is South of Somewhere, go ahead, check us out."

TIPS "Read the site to get a feel for what we're looking to publish. Read the guidelines. We look forward to hearing from you. We are nothing if not for our writers. *The Dead Mule* strives to deliver quality writing in every issue. It is in this way that we pay tribute to our authors. The *Mule* sponsors flash-fiction contests with no entry fees. See the site for specifics. All submissions must be accompanied by a "southern legitimacy statement," details of which can be seen within each page on *The Dead Mule* and within the Submishmash entry page. We've been around for over 15 years, send us something original. Chapbooks published by invitation, also short fiction compilations. Sporadic payment to writers whenever cafepress/deadmule sales reach an agreeable amount, and then we share!"

⊙⊕ DENVER QUARTERLY

University of Denver, 2000 E. Asbury, Denver CO 80208. (303)871-2892. **Website:** www.denverquarterly .com. **Contact:** Bill Ramke. Estab. 1996. "We publish fiction, articles, and poetry for a generally well-educated audience, primarily interested in literature and the literary experience. They read *DQ* to find something a little different from a stictly academic quarterly or a creative writing outlet." Quarterly. Reads between September 15 and May 15.

⊙ *Denver Quarterly* received an honorable mention for content from the American Literary Magazine Awards and selections have been anthologized in the *Pushcart Prize* anthologies.

NEEDS "We are interested in experimental fiction (minimalism, magic realism, etc.) as well as in realistic fiction and in writing about fiction. No sentimental, science fiction, romance, or spy thrillers." Length: up to 15 pages.

HOW TO CONTACT Submit ms by mail, include SASE.

PAYMENT/TERMS Pays $5/page for fiction and poetry and 2 contributor's copies.

TIPS "We look for serious, realistic, and experimental fiction; stories which appeal to intelligent, demanding readers who are not themselves fiction writers. Nothing so quickly disqualifies a ms as sloppy proofreading and mechanics. Read the magazine before submitting to it. We try to remain eclectic, but the odds for beginners are bound to be small considering the fact that we receive nearly 10,000 mss per year and publish only about 10 short stories."

⊙ DESCANT

P.O. Box 314, Station P, Toronto ON M5S 2S8 Canada. (416)593-2557. **Fax:** (416)593-9362. **E-mail:** info@ descant.ca. **E-mail:** submit@descant.ca. **Website:** www.descant.ca. Estab. 1970.

NEEDS Short stories or book excerpts. Maximum length 6,000 words; 3,000 words or less preferred. No erotica, fantasy, gothic, horror, religious, romance, beat.

HOW TO CONTACT Send complete ms with cover letter. Include estimated word count and brief bio.

PAYMENT/TERMS Pays $100 honorarium, plus one-year's subscription for accepted submissions of any kind.

TIPS "Familiarize yourself with our magazine before submitting."

◐◑ DESCANT: FORT WORTH'S JOURNAL OF POETRY AND FICTION

TCU Box 298300, Ft. Worth TX 76129. (817)257-5907. **Fax:** (817)257-6239. **E-mail:** descant@tcu.edu. **Website:** www.descant.tcu.edu. **Contact:** Dan Williams, editor. Estab. 1956. Magazine: 6×9; 120-150 pages; acid-free paper; paper cover. "*descant* seeks high-quality poems and stories in both traditional and innovative form." Member CLMP.

○ Offers 4 cash awards: The $500 Frank O'Connor Award for the best story in an issue; the $250 Gary Wilson Award for an outstanding story in an issue; the $500 Betsy Colquitt Award for the best poem in an issue; and the $250 Baskerville Publishers Award for outstanding poem in an issue. Several stories first published by *descant* have appeared in *Best American Short Stories*.

NEEDS Receives 20-30 unsolicited mss/month. Accepts 25-35 mss/year. Publishes ms 1 year after acceptance. Publishes 50% new writers/year. Recently published work by William Harrison, Annette Sanford, Miller Williams, Patricia Chao, Vonesca Stroud, and Walt McDonald. No horror, romance, fantasy, erotica. Length: 1,000-5,000 words; average length: 2,500 words.

HOW TO CONTACT Send complete ms with cover letter. Include estimated word count and brief bio.

TIPS "We look for character and quality of prose. Send your best short work."

◖ DIAGRAM

Department of English, University of Arizona, P.O. Box 210067, Tucson AZ 85721-0067. **E-mail:** editor@thediagram.com. **Website:** www.thediagram.com. "*DIAGRAM* is an electronic journal of text and art, found and created. We're interested in representations, naming, indicating, schematics, labeling and taxonomy of things; in poems that masquerade as stories; in stories that disguise themselves as indices or obituaries. We specialize in work that pushes the boundaries of traditional genre or work that is in some way schematic. We do publish traditional fiction and poetry, too, but hybrid forms (short stories, prose poems, indexes, tables of contents, etc.) are particularly welcome! We also publish diagrams and schematics (original and found)."

○ Publishes 6 new writers/year. Bimonthly. Member CLMP. "We sponsor yearly contests for unpublished hybrid essays and innovative fiction. Guidelines on website."

NEEDS Receives 100 unsolicited mss/month. Accepts 2-3 mss/issue; 15 mss/year. "We don't publish genre fiction unless it's exceptional and transcends the genre boundaries." Average length: 250-2,000 words.

HOW TO CONTACT Send complete ms. Accepts submissions by Web submissions manager; no e-mail. If sending by snail mail, send SASE for return of the ms, or send disposable copy of the ms and #10 SASE for reply only.

PAYMENT/TERMS Acquires first, serial, electronic rights.

TIPS "Submit interesting text, images, sound, and new media. We value the insides of things, vivisection, urgency, risk, elegance, flamboyance, work that moves us, language that does something new—or does something old—well. We like iteration and reiteration. Ruins and ghosts. Mechanical, moving parts, balloons, and frenzy. We want art and writing that demonstrates/interaction; the processes of things; how functions are accomplished; how things become or expire, move or stand. We'll consider anything. We do not consider e-mail submissions but encourage electronic submissions via our submissions manager software. Look at the journal and submissions guidelines before submitting."

◖ DISLOCATE

University of Minnesota, 1 Lind Hall, 207 Church St. SE, Minneapolis MN 55455. **E-mail:** dislocate.magazine@gmail.com. **Website:** dislocate.umn.edu. *dislocate* is a print and online literary journal dedicated to publishing Minnesota art that pushes the traditional boundaries of form and genre. "We like work that operates in the gray areas, that resists categorization, that ignores the limits; we like work that plays with the relationship between form and content. We publish fiction, nonfiction, poetry, and art, but we don't mind (or even prefer) that we can't tell which one we're dealing with."

NEEDS Length: no more than 5,000 words.

HOW TO CONTACT Submit using online submission form. Submission period is November 1-December 1.

TIPS "We are primarily looking for work from Minnesotan writers and artists, but submissions are also open to artists from (or with a connection to) Wisconsin, Michigan, Iowa, Illinois, Indiana, and North and South Dakota."

⭕ DOWN IN THE DIRT

829 Brian Court, Gurnee IL 60031-3155. (847)281-9070. **E-mail:** dirt@scars.tv. **Website:** www.scars .tv/dirt. **Contact:** Janet Kuypers, editor. Estab. 2000. *Down in the Dirt*, published every other month online and in print issues sold via Amazon.com throughout the U.S., U.K., and continental Europe, prints "good work that makes you think, that makes you feel like you've lived through a scene instead of merely read it." Also considers poems. *Down in the Dirt* is published "electronically as well as in print, either as printed magazines sold over the Internet, on the Web (Internet web pages), or through our printer."

Literary magazine/journal: 6×9 (full color, full-bleed covers), perfect-bound, 84- to 108-page book. Contains illustrations and photographs as well as short stories, essays, and poetry. Has published work by Mel Waldman, Ken Dean, Jon Brunette, John Ragusa, and Liam Spencer.

NEEDS No religious, rhyming, or family-oriented material. Average length: 1,000 words.

HOW TO CONTACT Query editor with e-mail submission. "99.5% of all submissions are via e-mail only, so if you do not have electronic access, there is a strong chance you will not be considered. We recommend you e-mail submissions to us, either as an attachment (.txt, .rtf, .doc, or .docx files, but not .pdf) or by placing it directly in the e-mail letter). For samples of what we've printed in the past, visit our website. Contact us if you are interested in submitting very long stories or parts of a novel (if accepted, it would appear in parts in multiple issues)." Accepts simultaneous, multiple submissions and reprints.

PAYMENT/TERMS No payment.

TIPS Scars Publications sponsors a contest "where accepted writing appears in a collection book. Write or e-mail (dirt@scars.tv) for information." Also able to publish electronic chapbooks. Write for more information.

DRAMATICS MAGAZINE

Educational Theatre Association, 2343 Auburn Ave., Cincinnati OH 45219. (513)421-3900. **E-mail:** dcorathers@schooltheatre.org. **Website:** school theatre.org. **Contact:** Don Corathers, editor. Estab. 1929. *Dramatics* is for students (mainly high school age) and teachers of theater. Mix includes how-to (tech theater, acting, directing, etc.), informational, interview, photo feature, humorous, profile, technical. *Dramatics* wants student readers to grow as theater artists and become a more discerning and appreciative audience. Material is directed to both theater students and their teachers, with a strong slant toward students. Tries to portray the theater community in all its diversity.

NEEDS Young adults: drama (one-act and full-length plays). "We prefer unpublished scripts that have been produced at least once." Does not want to see plays that show no understanding of the conventions of the theater. No plays for children, no Christmas or didactic "message" plays. Length: 750-3,000 words.

HOW TO CONTACT Submit complete ms. Buys 5-9 plays/year. Emerging playwrights have better chances with résumé of credits.

PAYMENT/TERMS Pays $100-500 for plays.

TIPS "Obtain our writer's guidelines and look at recent back issues. The best way to break in is to know our audience—drama students, teachers, and others interested in theater—and to write for them. Writers who have some practical experience in theater, especially in technical areas, have an advantage, but we'll work with anybody who has a good idea. Some freelancers have become regular contributors."

◑ DUCTS

P.O. Box 3203, Grand Central Station, New York NY 10163. **E-mail:** vents@ducts.org. **Website:** www.ducts .org. **Contact:** Jonathan Kravetz, editor-in-chief. Estab. 1999. *DUCTS* is a webzine of personal stories, fiction, essays, memoirs, poetry, humor, profiles, reviews and art. "*DUCTS* was founded in 1999 with the intent of giving emerging writers a venue to regularly publish their compelling, personal stories. The site has been expanded to include art and creative works of all genres. We believe that these genres must and do overlap. *DUCTS* publishes the best, most compelling stories, and we hope to attract readers who are drawn to work that rises above." Semiannual.

NEEDS "Humor word count maximum is 1,200 words and due to the large number of submissions we receive for this department, we are only able to respond to those submissions we accept for publication."

HOW TO CONTACT Submit to appropriate (by department) e-mail address. See website.

TIPS "We prefer writing that tells a compelling story with a strong narrative drive."

⑤ ECHO INK REVIEW

E.I. Publishing Services, Published by Sildona Creative, 5920 Nall Ave., Suite 301, Mission KS 66202. **E-mail:** editor@echoinkreview.com. **Website:** www .echoinkreview.com. **Contact:** Don Balch, managing editor. Estab. 1997. The mission of *Echo Ink Review* is to "promote compelling writing and to recognize talented writers ahead of their renown."

○ "Works selected for publication have later been included in Pulitzer Prize–nominated short story collections. Short works critiqued in our workshop have found homes in a variety of journals while novel-length mss have been published by national presses."

NEEDS "Ultimately, we select mss that work, meaning we look for those mss that achieve the highest degree of unity between elements. However, mss that involve some element of surprise, irony, or understatement catch our immediate attention. We are especially receptive to beginning writers or writers with few publication credits. Even if we can't use a ms, we have a history of offering in-depth critiques and otherwise encouraging feedback." Length: 250-2,500/words for flash fiction; 2,501-10,000 for short fiction.

HOW TO CONTACT Submit using online submission manager.

PAYMENT/TERMS One contributor's copy.

TIPS The online submission manager offers different options that allow writers to pay for faster response times. Five-day response times are $10/submission; 30-day response times are $7.50/submission for submissions under 1,500 words. Submissions with no fee have a 4-month response time.

ECLECTICA

No public address available, **E-mail:** editors@eclec tica.org. **Website:** www.eclectica.org. **Contact:** Tom Dooley, managing editor. Estab. 1996. "A sterling-quality literary magazine on the World Wide Web.

Not bound by formula or genre, harnessing technology to further the reading experience and dynamic and interesting in content. *Eclectica* is a quarterly online journal devoted to showcasing the best writing on the Web, regardless of genre. 'Literary' and 'genre' work appear side-by-side in each issue, along with pieces that blur the distinctions between such categories. Pushcart Prize, National Poetry Series, and Pulitzer Prize winners, as well as Nebula Award nominees, have shared issues with previously unpublished authors."

NEEDS Needs "high-quality work in any genre." Accepts short stories and novellas. Length: up to 20,000 words for short fiction; longer novella-length pieces accepted.

HOW TO CONTACT Submit via online submissions manager.

TIPS "We pride ourselves on giving everyone (high schoolers, convicts, movie executives, etc.) an equal shot at publication, based solely on the quality of their work. Because we like eclecticism, we tend to favor the varied perspectives that often characterize the work of international authors, people of color, women, alternative lifestylists—but others who don't fit into these categories often surprise us."

ECOTONE

Department of Creative Writing, University of North Carolina Wilmington, 601 S. College Rd., Wilmington NC 28403. (910)962-2547. **Fax:** (910)962-7461. **E-mail:** info@ecotonejournal.com. **Website:** www.eco tonejournal.com. **Contact:** Sally J. Johnson, managing editor. "*Ecotone* is a literary journal of place that seeks to publish creative works about the environment and the natural world while avoiding the hushed tones and clichés of much of so-called nature writing. Reading period is August 15-April 15."

NEEDS Length: up to 30 pages double-spaced.

HOW TO CONTACT Send complete ms via postal mail or online submission manager.

○ ◑ ⑤ ELLERY QUEEN'S MYSTERY MAGAZINE

Dell Magazines, 267 Broadway, 4th Floor, New York NY 10017. (212)686-7188. **Fax:** (212)686-7414. **E-mail:** elleryqueenmm@dellmagazines.com. **Website:** www .themysteryplace.com/eqmm. **Contact:** Jackie Sherbow, assistant editor. Estab. 1941. "*Ellery Queen's Mystery Magazine* welcomes submissions from both new and established writers. We publish every kind of mystery short story: the psychological suspense tale, the deductive puzzle, the private-eye case—the gamut of crime and detection from the realistic (including the policeman's lot and stories of police procedure) to the more imaginative (including 'locked rooms' and 'impossible crimes'). We look for strong writing, an original and exciting plot, and professional craftsmanship. We encourage writers whose work meets these general criteria to read an issue of *EQMM* before making a submission."

Ⓞ Magazine: 5⅞×8⅝, 112 pages with special 192-page combined March/April and September/October issues.

NEEDS Publishes ms 6-12 months after acceptance. Agented fiction 50%. **Publishes 10 new writers/year.** Recently published work by Jeffery Deaver, Joyce Carol Oates, and Margaret Maron. Sometimes comments on rejected mss. "We always need detective stories. Special consideration given to anything timely and original." No explicit sex or violence, no gore or horror. Seldom publishes parodies or pastiches. "We do not want true detective or crime stories." Length: 2,500-8,000 words, but occasionally accepts longer and shorter submissions—including minute mysteries of 250 words, stories up to 12,000 words, and novellas of up to 20,000 words from established authors.

HOW TO CONTACT *EQMM* uses an online submission system (eqmm.magazinesubmissions.com) that has been designed to streamline our process and improve communication with authors. We ask that all submissions be made electronically, using this system, rather than on paper. All stories should be in standard ms format and submitted in .doc format. We cannot accept .docx, .rtf, or .txt files at this time. For detailed submission instructions, see eqmm.magazine submissions.com or our writers guidelines page (www .themysteryplace.com/eqmm/guidelines).

PAYMENT/TERMS Pays 5-8¢/word; occasionally higher for established authors

TIPS "We have a Department of First Stories to encourage writers whose fiction has never before been in print. We publish an average of 10 first stories every year. Mark subject line Attn: Department of First Stories."

◯Ⓢ ELLIPSIS MAGAZINE

Westminster College of Salt Lake City, 1840 S. 1300 East, Salt Lake City UT 84105. (801)832-2321. **E-mail:** ellipsis@westminstercollege.edu. **Website:** www

.westminstercollege.edu/ellipsis. Estab. 1967. *Ellipsis*, published annually in April, needs good literary poetry, fiction, essays, plays, and visual art. Has published poetry by Allison Joseph, Molly McQuade, Virgil Suaárez, Maurice Kilwein Guevara, Richard Cecil, and Ron Carlson.

Ⓞ Reads submissions August 1-November 1. Staff changes from year to year. Check website for an updated list of editors. *Ellipsis* is 120 pages, digest-sized, perfect-bound, with color cover. Accepts about 5% of submissions received. Press run is 2,000; most distributed free through college.

NEEDS Receives 110 unsolicited mss/month. Accepts 4 mss/issue. Does not read mss November 1-July 31. Publishes ms 3 months after acceptance. **Publishes 2 new writers/year.** Length: 6,000 words; average length: 4,000 words. Also publishes poetry. Rarely comments on rejected mss. Needs good literary fiction and plays. Length: 6,000 words.

HOW TO CONTACT Send complete ms. Send SASE (or IRC) for return of ms or send disposable copy of the ms and #10 SASE for reply only. Responds in 6 months to mss. Accepts simultaneous submissions. Sample copy for $7.50. Writer's guidelines online. Send complete ms. Submit through Submittable.

PAYMENT/TERMS Pays $50 per story and 2 contributor's copy; additional copies $3.50. Pays on publication for first North American serial rights. Not copyrighted. Pays $50 per story and 1 contributor's copy; additional copies $3.50

EPIPHANY EPIPHMAG.COM-WHERE CREATIVITY AND INSPIRATION EVOLVE!

E-mail: contact@epiphmag.com. **E-mail:** submissions@epiphmag.com. **Website:** www.epiphmag.com. **Contact:** JW Smith, editor. Estab. 2010. *Epiphany* was started in 2010, solely to be an online venue in which writers and artists can display their works. "*Epiphany*'s dynamic formatting sets our publication apart from other online magazines. We strive to bring poetry, prose, fiction, nonfiction, artwork, and photography together to form a visually and creatively stimulating experience for our readers." 4 issues/year in February, May, August, and November.

Ⓞ "*Epiphany* is a nonpaying market at this time."

NEEDS Length: 500-4,000 words.

HOW TO CONTACT Accepts 40-70 mss/year. Send complete ms. "Please write 'Fiction' in the subject line of your e-mail."

TIPS "We are open to a variety of writing styles and content subject matter. Our audience includes writers, artists, students, teachers, and all who enjoy reading short fiction, poetry, and creative nonfiction. We will not publish any works which we feel have a derogatory nature. Please visit our submission guidelines page at www.epiphmag.com/guide.html for more details. Please write the type of submission you are sending in the subject line of your e-mail."

EPOCH

251 Goldwin Smith Hall, Cornell University, Ithaca NY 14853. (607)255-3385. **Fax:** (607)255-6661. **Website:** english.arts.cornell.edu/publications/epoch. Estab. 1947. Well-written literary fiction, poetry, personal essays. Newcomers welcome. Open to mainstream and avant-garde writing.

Magazine: 6×9; 128 pages; quality paper and cover stock. Receives 500 unsolicited mss/ month. Accepts 15-20 mss/issue. Reads submissions September 15-April 15. Publishes 3-4 new writers/year. Has published work by Antonya Nelson, Doris Betts, Heidi Jon Schmidt.

NEEDS No genre fiction. Would like to see more Southern fiction (Southern U.S.).

HOW TO CONTACT Send complete ms. Considers fiction in all forms, short short to novella length.

PAYMENT/TERMS Pays $5 and up/printed page.

TIPS "Tell your story, speak your poem, straight from the heart. We are attracted to language and to good writing, but we are most interested in what the good writing leads us to, or where."

ESQUIRE

300 W. 57th St., 21st Floor, New York NY 10019. (212)649-4020. **Website:** www.esquire.com. Estab. 1933. *Esquire* is geared toward smart, well-off men. General readership is college educated and sophisticated, between ages 30 and 45. Written mostly by contributing editors on contract. Rarely accepts unsolicited mss.

NEEDS "Literary excellence is our only criterion." No pornography, science fiction, or true romance stories.

HOW TO CONTACT Send complete ms. To submit a story, use online submission manager at esquire submissions.com.

TIPS "A writer has the best chance of breaking in at *Esquire* by querying with a specific idea that requires special contacts and expertise. Ideas must be timely and national in scope."

ESSAYS & FICTIONS

526 S. Albany St., Apt. 1N, Ithaca NY 14850. (914)572-7351. **E-mail:** essaysandfictions@gmail.com. **Website:** essaysandfictions.com. **Contact:** David Pollock and Danielle Winterton, co-founding editors. Estab. 2007. "*Essays & Fictions* publishes fictional essay, reflective essay, academic rhetorical essay, literary narrative essay, lyric essay, linear fiction, nonlinear fiction, essayistic fiction, fictionalized memoir, questionable histories, false historical accounts, botched accounts, cultural analysis, criticism or commentary, compositional analysis, criticism or commentary, or any blend thereof. We do not differentiate between essay and fiction in the table of contents because we consciously challenge the validity of genre boundaries and definitions. We believe language is not fixed and neither is truth. As art, forms of literature have varying degrees of truth value. Many writers have recently chosen to compose works that blend or subvert the genres of short fiction and essay. We are particularly interested in publishing these kinds of writers. We encourage writers to experiment with hybrid forms that lead to literary transcendence." Semiannual.

NEEDS Receives 10-20 mss/month, accepts approx 3/ month, 6/year. Reading periods are February 1-May 31 for October issue, and September 1-December 31 for May issue. **Publishes 3-4 new writers each year.** Authors published: Veronica Vela, Charles Lowe, John Taylor, Philippe Jaccottet, Myronn Hardy, Joseph Michaels, Paul Stubbs, Veroniki Dalakoura, Margot Berwin, William Luvaas, Greg Sanders, Danielle Winterton, David Pollock, Karl Parker, and Lee Matthew Goldberg. Does not want "genre writing, American realism, or straight, formulaic reflective memoir." Length: up to 10,000 words. Average length: 3,000 words.

HOW TO CONTACT Send complete ms with cover letter.

PAYMENT/TERMS Contributors get 1 free copy and 15% off additional copies of the issue in which they are published.

TIPS "We look for confident work that uses form/ structure and voice in interesting ways without sounding overly self-conscious or deliberate. We encourage rigorous excellence of complex craft in our submissions and discourage bland reproductions of reality. Read the journal. Be familiar with the *Essays & Fictions* aesthetic. We are particularly interested in writers who read theory and/or have multiple intellectual and artistic interests, and who set high intellectual standards for themselves and their work."

◉○ EUROPEAN JUDAISM

LBC, The Sternberg Centre, 80 East End Rd., London N3 2SY England. **E-mail:** european.judaism@lbc .ac.uk. **Website:** www.berghahnbooks.com/journals/ ej. **Contact:** Managing Editor. Estab. 1966. *European Judaism*, published twice/year, is a "glossy, elegant magazine with emphasis on European Jewish theology/philosophy/literature/history, with some poetry in every issue. Poems should (preferably) be short and have some relevance to matters of Jewish interest." Has published poetry by Linda Pastan, Elaine Feinstein, Daniel Weissbort, and Dannie Abse. *European Judaism* is 110 pages, digest-sized, flat-spined. Press run is 950 (about 500 subscribers, over 100 libraries). Subscription: $45 individual, $20 student, $162 institution.

HOW TO CONTACT Submit through postal mail. Any material submitted for publication should be supplied on disk, accompanied by 1 double-spaced hard copy, and a brief biographical note on the author.

◉◉ EVANGEL

Light and Life Communications, 770 N. High School Rd., Indianapolis IN 46214. (317)244-3660. **Contact:** Julie Innes, editor. Estab. 1897 by free Methodist denomination. *Evangel,* published quarterly, is an adult Sunday School paper. "Devotional in nature, it lifts up Christ as the source of salvation and hope. The mission of *Evangel* is to increase the reader's understanding of the nature and character of God and the nature of a life lived for Christ. Material that fits this mission and isn't longer than 1 page will be considered."

○   *Evangel* is 8 pages, 5.5×8.5, printed in 4-color, unbound, color and b&w photos. Weekly distribution. Press run is about 10,000. Subscription: $2.59/quarter (13 weeks).

NEEDS Fiction involves people coping with everyday crises, making decisions that show spiritual growth. Accepts 3-4 mss/issue; 156-200 mss/year. Publishes 7 new writers/year. "No fiction without any semblance of Christian message or where the message clobbers the reader. Looking for devotional-style short pieces, 500 words or less."

HOW TO CONTACT Send complete ms. Accepts multiple submissions.

PAYMENT/TERMS Pays 5¢/word and 2 contributor's copies.

TIPS Desires concise, tight writing that supports a solid thesis and fits the mission expressed in the guidelines.

◉ EVANSVILLE REVIEW

University of Evansville Creative Writing Deptartment, 1800 Lincoln Ave., Evansville IN 47722. (812)488-1402. **E-mail:** evansvillereview@evans ville.edu. **Website:** evansvillereview.evansville.edu. Estab. 1990. "*The Evansville Review* is an annual literary journal published at the University of Evansville. Past contributors include Arthur Miller, Joseph Brodsky, John Updike, Rita Dove, Willis Barnstone, W.D. Snodgrass, Edward Albee, Dana Gioia, and Marjorie Agosin."

NEEDS "We're open to all creativity. No discrimination. All fiction, screenplays, nonfiction, poetry, interviews, and anything in between." Does not want erotica, fantasy, experimental, or children's fiction. Length: no more than 10,000 words.

HOW TO CONTACT Submit through postal mail. Include a brief bio.

PAYMENT/TERMS Pays in contributor's copies.

TIPS "Because editorial staff rolls over every 1-2 years, the journal always has a new flavor."

◉ EVENING STREET REVIEW

Evening Street Press, Inc., 7652 Sawmill Rd. #352, Dublin OH 43016. **E-mail:** editor@eveningstreetpress .com. **Website:** www.eveningstreetpress.com. Estab. 2007. "Intended for a general audience, *Evening Street Press* is centered on Elizabeth Cady Stanton's 1848 revision of the Declaration of Independence: 'that all men—and women—are created equal,' with equal rights to 'life, liberty, and the pursuit of happiness.' It focuses on the realities of experience, personal and historical, from the most gritty to the most dreamlike, including awareness of the personal and social forces that block or develop the possibilities of this new culture."

HOW TO CONTACT Send complete ms. E-mail submissions preferred.

PAYMENT/TERMS Pays 1 contributor's copy.

TIPS Does not want works that contain aspects of male chauvinism. Mss are read year-round. See website for chapbook and book competitions.

◉ FACES MAGAZINE

Cobblestone Publishing, Editorial Department, 30 Grove St., Peterborough NH 03458. (603)924-7209. E-

mail: facesmag@yahoo.com. **E-mail:** ecarpentiere@caruspub.com. **Website:** www.cricketmag.com. *FACES Magazine*, published 9 times/year, features cultures from around the globe for children ages 9-14. "Readers learn how other kids live around the world and about the important inventions and ideas that a particular culture has given to the world. All material must relate to the theme of a specific upcoming issue in order to be considered." Wants "clear, objective imagery. Serious and light verse considered. Must relate to theme." Subscription: $33.95/year (9 issues). Sample: $6.95 plus $2 shipping and handling.

Publishes theme issues; visit website for details.

NEEDS Query first; include cover letter. Wants "retold legends, folktales, stories, and original plays from around the world, etc., relating to the theme."

FAILBETTER.COM

2022 Grove Ave., Richmond VA 23221. **E-mail:** submissions@failbetter.com. **Website:** www.failbetter.com. **Contact:** Thom Didato, editor. Estab. 2000. "We are a quarterly online magazine published in the spirit of a traditional literary journal—dedicated to publishing quality fiction, poetry, and artwork. While the Web plays host to hundreds, if not thousands, of genre-related sites (many of which have merit), we are not one of them." Quarterly. Member CLMP.

NEEDS "If you're sending a short story or novel excerpt, send only 1 at a time. Wait to hear from us before sending another."

HOW TO CONTACT Submit work by pasting it into the body of an e-mail. Must put *Submission* in e-mail's subject line. Do not send attachments.

TIPS "Read an issue. Read our guidelines! We place a high degree of importance on originality, believing that even in this age of trends it is still possible. We are not looking for what is current or momentary. We are not concerned with length: One good sentence may find a home here, as the bulk of mediocrity will not. Most important, know that what you are saying could only come from you. When you are sure of this, please feel free to submit."

THE FAIRCLOTH REVIEW

E-mail: fairclothreview@gmail.com. **Website:** www.fairclothreview.com. **Contact:** Allen Coin, editor-in-chief; Lisa Pepin, managing editor. Estab. 2012. "*The Faircloth Review*, a weekly publication, is a paperless, online literary and arts journal with a wide range of focus. We accept fiction, nonfiction, poetry, photog-

raphy, art, music, videos … anything creative. We are open-minded and social media–oriented, and we specialize in previously unpublished artists."

NEEDS "No zombies, vampires, wizards, or werewolves, please, unless it's satirical." Length: under 7,500 words for short stories; under 5,000 words for flash fiction.

HOW TO CONTACT Submit complete ms.

TIPS "Please follow the submission guidelines on the site (include in your submission your name, location, a short blurb about yourself, your headshot, and a link to your personal website, if you have one). For photos: Provide captions. For fiction/nonfiction: Use .doc or .docx file and provide a very short summary."

FAULTLINE

University of California at Irvine, Department of English, 435 Humanities Instructional Building, Irvine CA 92697. (949)824-1573. **E-mail:** faultline@uci.edu. **Website:** faultline.sites.uci.edu. Estab. 1992.

Reading period is August 15-January 15. Submissions sent at any other time will not be read.

NEEDS Editors change in September of each year. Length: up to 20 pages.

HOW TO CONTACT Send complete ms. "While simultaneous submissions are accepted, multiple submissions are not accepted. Please restrict your submissions to 1 story at a time, regardless of length."

PAYMENT/TERMS Pays in contributor copies.

TIPS "Our commitment is to publish the best work possible from well-known and emerging authors with vivid and varied voices."

FEMINIST STUDIES

0103 Taliaferro, University of Maryland, College Park MD 20742. (301)405-7415. **Fax:** (301)405-8395. **E-mail:** atambe@umd.edu. **E-mail:** kmantilla@feministstudies.org. **Website:** www.feministstudies.org. **Contact:** Ashwini Tambe, editorial director; Karla Mantilla, managing editor. Estab. 1974. Over the years, *Feminist Studies* has been a reliable source of significant writings on issues that are important to all classes and races of women. Those familiar with the literature on women's studies are well aware of the importance and vitality of the journal and the frequency with which articles first published in *Feminist Studies* are cited and/or reprinted elsewhere. Indeed no less than 4 anthologies have been created from articles originally published in *Feminist Studies*: *Clio's Consciousness Raised: New Perspectives on the His-*

tory of Women; *Sex and Class in Women's History*; *U.S. Women in Struggle: A Feminist Studies Anthology*; and *Lesbian Subjects: A Feminist Studies Reader*."

⬭ "*Feminist Studies* is committed to publishing an interdisciplinary body of feminist knowledge that sees intersections of gender with racial identity, sexual orientation, economic means, geographical location, and physical ability as the touchstone for our politics and our intellectual analysis. Whether work is drawn from the complex past or the shifting present, the articles and essays that appear in *Feminist Studies* address social and political issues that intimately and significantly affect women and men in the U.S. and around the world."

⬤ FICKLE MUSES

2820 Utah Street NE, Albuquerque NM 87110. **E-mail:** editor@ficklemuses.com. **Website:** www.fickl emuses.com. "*Fickle Muses* is an online journal of poetry and fiction engaged with myth and legend. A poet or fiction writer is featured each week, with new selections posted on Sundays. Art is updated monthly."
HOW TO CONTACT Submit complete ms through online submissions manager. Query via e-mail. Submissions are accepted year-round.

TIPS "Originality. An innovative look at an old story. I'm looking to be swept away. Get a feel from our website."

FICTION

Department of English, The City College of New York, 138th St. and Covenant Ave., New York NY 10031. **Website:** www.fictioninc.com. **Contact:** Mark J. Mirsky, editor. Estab. 1972. "As the name implies, we publish only fiction; we are looking for the best new writing available, leaning toward the unconventional. *Fiction* has traditionally attempted to make accessible the inaccessible, to bring the experimental to a broader audience." Reading period for unsolicited mss is September 15-May 15.

⬭ Stories first published in *Fiction* have been selected for the *Pushcart Prize: Best of the Small Presses*, *O. Henry Prize Stories*, and *Best American Short Stories*.

NEEDS No romance, science fiction, etc. Length: up to 5,000 words.

HOW TO CONTACT Submit complete ms via online submissions manager.

TIPS "The guiding principle of *Fiction* has always been to go to terra incognita in the writing of the imagination and to ask that modern fiction set up serious questions, if often in absurd and comedic voices, interrogating the nature of the real and the fantastic. It represents no particular school of fiction, except the innovative. Its pages have often been a harbor for writers at odds with each other. As a result of its willingness to publish the difficult, experimental, and unusual, while not excluding the well known, *Fiction* has a unique reputation in the U.S. and abroad as a journal of future directions."

⬤⬤⬤ THE FIDDLEHEAD

University of New Brunswick, Campus House, 11 Garland Court, Box 4400, Fredericton NB E3B 5A3 Canada. (506)453-3501. **Fax:** (506) 453-5069. **E-mail:** fiddlehd@unb.ca. **Website:** www.thefiddle head.ca. **Contact:** Kathryn Taglia, managing editor. Estab. 1945. "Canada's longest living literary journal, *The Fiddlehead* is published 4 times/year at the University of New Brunswick, with the generous assistance of the University of New Brunswick, the Canada Council for the Arts, and the Province of New Brunswick. It is experienced; wise enough to recognize excellence; always looking for freshness and surprise. *The Fiddlehead* publishes short stories, poems, book reviews, and a small number of personal essays. Our full-color covers have become collectors' items and feature work by New Brunswick artists and from New Brunswick museums and art galleries. *The Fiddlehead* also sponsors an annual writing contest. The journal is open to good writing in English from all over the world, looking always for freshness and surprise. Our editors are always happy to see new unsolicited works in fiction and poetry. Work is read on an ongoing basis; the acceptance rate is around 1-2%. Apart from our annual contest, we have no deadlines for submissions."

⬭ Magazine: 6×9; 128-180 pages; ink illustrations; photos. "No criteria for publication except quality. *The Fiddlehead* is for a general audience, including many poets and writers." Has published work by Marjorie Celona, Wasela Hiyate, Alexander MacLeod, and Erika Van Winden.

NEEDS Receives 100-150 unsolicited mss/month. Accepts 4-5 mss/issue; 20-40 mss/year. Agented fiction: small percentage. Publishes high percentage of new writers/year. Length: up to 6,000 words. Also publishes short shorts.

HOW TO CONTACT Send SASE and *Canadian* stamps or IRCs for return of mss. No e-mail, fax, or disc submissions. Simultaneous submissions only if stated on cover letter; must contact immediately if accepted elsewhere.

PAYMENT/TERMS Pays up to $40 (Canadian)/ published page and 2 contributor's copies.

TIPS "If you are serious about submitting to *The Fiddlehead*, you should subscribe or read an issue or 2 to get a sense of the journal. Contact us if you would to order sample back issues ($10-15 plus postage)."

FILLING STATION

P.O. Box 22135, Bankers Hall, Calgary AB T2P 4J5 Canada. **E-mail:** mgmt@fillingstation.ca; poetry@ fillingstation.ca; fiction@fillingstation.ca; nonfiction@fillingstation.ca. **Website:** www.fillingstation .ca. **Contact:** Paul Zits, managing editor. Estab. 1993. *filling Station*, published 3 times/year, prints contemporary poetry, fiction, visual art, interviews, reviews, and articles. "We are looking for all forms of contemporary writing, but especially that which is original and/or experimental."

Has published poetry by Fred Wah, Larissa Lai, Margaret Christakos, Robert Kroetsch, Ron Silliman, Susan Holbrook, and many more. *filling Station* is 64 pages, 8.5×11, perfect-bound, with card cover, includes photos and artwork. Receives about 100 submissions for each issue, accepts approximately 10%. Press run is 700. Subscription: $20/3 issues; $36 for 6 issues.

HOW TO CONTACT E-mail up to 10 pages to fiction@fillingstation.ca. "We receive any of the following fiction, or a combination thereof: flash fiction, postcard fiction, short fiction, experimental fiction, or a novel excerpt that can stand alone. A submission lacking mailing address and/or bio will be considered incomplete."

TIPS "*filling Station* accepts singular or simultaneous submissions of previously unpublished poetry, fiction, creative nonfiction, nonfiction, or art. We are always on the hunt for great writing!"

FIRST CLASS

P.O. Box 86, Friendship IN 47021. **E-mail:** christopherm@four-sep.com. **Website:** www.four-sep .com. **Contact:** Christopher M, editor. Estab. 1995. *First Class* features short fiction and poetics from the cream of the small press and killer unknowns—mingling before your very hungry eyes. I publish plays, too."

NEEDS "No religious or traditional stories, or 'boomer angst,' therapy-driven self-loathing." Length: 5,000-8,000 words.

HOW TO CONTACT Send ms with SASE.

PAYMENT/TERMS Pays in contributor's copies.

TIPS "Don't bore me with puppy dogs and the morose/sappy feeling you have about death. Belt out a good, thought-provoking, graphic, uncommon short piece."

THE FIRST LINE

Blue Cubicle Press, LLC, P.O. Box 250382, Plano TX 75025. (972)824-0646. **E-mail:** submission@thefirst line.com. **Website:** www.thefirstline.com. **Contact:** Robin LaBounty, ms coordinator. Estab. 1999. "*The First Line* is an exercise in creativity for writers and a chance for readers to see how many different directions we can take when we start from the same place. The purpose of *The First Line* is to jump-start the imagination—to help writers break through the block that is the blank page. Each issue contains short stories that stem from a common first line; it also provides a forum for discussing favorite first lines in literature."

NEEDS "We only publish stories that start with the first line provided. We are a collection of tales—of different directions writers can take when they start from the same place. " Length: 300-5,000 words.

HOW TO CONTACT Submit complete ms.

PAYMENT/TERMS Pays $30.

TIPS "Don't just write the first story that comes to mind after you read the sentence. If it is obvious, chances are other people are writing about the same thing. Don't try so hard. Be willing to accept criticism."

FIVE CHAPTERS

Five Chapters, Wales. **Website:** www.fivechapters .com. FiveChapters.com is the home of the most exciting original fiction on the web. A 5-part story will be published every week, serial-style, beginning on Monday and with a new installment every weekday.

HOW TO CONTACT Send complete ms.

FIVE POINTS

Georgia State University, P.O. Box 3999, Atlanta GA 30302-3999. **E-mail:** fivepoints@gsu.edu. **Website:** www.fivepoints.gsu.edu. **Contact:** Megan Sexton. Estab. 1996. *"Five Points* is committed to publishing work that compels the imagination through the use of fresh and convincing language."

○ Magazine: 6×9; 200 pages; cotton paper; glossy cover; photos. Has recently published Alice Hoffman, Natasha Trethewey, Pamela Painter, Billy Collins, Philip Levine, George Singleton, Hugh Sheehy.

NEEDS Receives 250 unsolicited mss/month. Accepts 4 mss/issue; 15-20 mss/year. Reads fiction January 1-April 1. Publishes 1 new writer/year. Sometimes comments on rejected mss. Sponsors awards/contests. Average length: 7,500 words.

HOW TO CONTACT Include cover letter.

PAYMENT/TERMS Pays $15/page minimum; $250 maximum, free subscription to magazine and 2 contributor's copies; additional copies $4.

TIPS "We place no limitations on style or content. Our only criteria is excellence. If your writing has an original voice, substance, and significance, send it to us. We will publish distinctive, intelligent writing that has something to say and says it in a way that captures and maintains our attention."

⓪ FLINT HILLS REVIEW

Department of English, Modern Languages, and Journalist (Box 4019), Emporia State University, 1200 Commercial Street, Emporia KS 66801. **Website:** www.emporia.edu/fhr/. **Contact:** Kevin Rabas. Estab. 1996. *Flint Hills Review,* published annually in late summer, is "a regionally focused journal presenting writers of national distinction alongside new authors. *FHR* seeks work informed by a strong sense of place or region, especially Kansas and the Great Plains region. We seek to provide a publishing venue for writers of the Great Plains and Kansas while also publishing authors whose work evidences a strong sense of place, writing of literary quality, and accomplished use of language and depth of character development."

○ Magazine: 9×6; 120-200 pages; 60 lb. paper; glossy cover; illustrations; photos. Recently published work by Elizabeth Dodds, Kim Stafford, and Brian Daldorph.

NEEDS "No religious, inspirational, children's." Want to see more "writing of literary quality with a strong sense of place." List of upcoming themes online. Receives 5-15 unsolicited mss/month. Accepts 2-5 mss/issue; 2-5 mss/year. Does not read mss April-December. Publishes short shorts. Also publishes literary essays, literary criticism, poetry. Length: 1-3 pages for short-short stories; 7-25 pages for short stories.

HOW TO CONTACT Send a disposable copy of ms and #10 SASE for reply only.

PAYMENT/TERMS Pays 1 contributor's copy; additional copies at discounted price.

TIPS Submit writing that has "strong imagery and voice, writing that is informed by place or region, writing of literary quality with depth of character development. Hone the language down to the most literary depiction that is possible in the shortest space that still provides depth of development without excess length."

⓪ THE FLORIDA REVIEW

Department of English, University of Central Florida, P.O. Box 161346, Orlando FL 32816. **E-mail:** flreview@mail.ucf.edu. **Website:** floridareview.cah.ucf.edu/. **Contact:** Jocelyn Bartkevicius, editor. Estab. 1972.

○ Magazine: 6×9; 185 pages; semigloss full-color cover, perfect-bound. "We publish fiction of high 'literary' quality—stories that delight, instruct, and take risks. Our audience consists of avid readers of fiction, poetry, and creative nonfiction." Recently published work by Gerald Vizenor, Billy Collins, Sherwin Bitsui, Kelly Clancy, Denise Duhamel, Tony Hoagland, Baron Wormser, Marcia Aldrich, and Patricia Foster.

NEEDS No genre fiction. Length: no limit. "We prefer prose that is between 3 and 25 ms pages."

HOW TO CONTACT Send complete ms through postal mail or electronically on website.

TIPS "We're looking for writers with fresh voices and original stories. We like risk."

FLOYD COUNTY MOONSHINE

720 Christiansburg Pike, Floyd VA 24091. (540)745-5150. **E-mail:** floydshine@gmail.com. **Website:** www.floydcountymoonshine.org. **Contact:** Aaron Lee

Moore, editor-in-chief. Estab. 2008. *Floyd County Moonshine*, published biannually, is a "literary and arts magazine in Floyd, Virginia, and the New River Valley. We accept poetry, short stories, and essays addressing all manner of themes; however, preference is given to those works of a rural or Appalachian nature. *Floyd County Moonshine* has been in production for over 5 years, publishing a variety of homegrown Appalachian writers in addition to writers from across the country. We have published 15 issues and over 140 authors and artists. The mission of *Floyd County Moonshine* is to publish thought-provoking, well-crafted, free-thinking, uncensored prose and poetry. Our literature explores the dark and Gothic as well as the bright and pleasant in order to give an honest portrayal of the human condition. We aspire to publish quality literature in the local color genre, specifically writing that relates to Floyd, Virginia, and the New River Valley. Floyd and local Appalachian authors are given priority consideration; however, to stay versatile we also aspire to publish some writers from all around the country in every issue. We publish both well-established and beginning writers."

Wants "literature addressing rural or Appalachian themes." Has published poetry by Steve Kistulentz, Louis Gallo, Ernie Wormwood, R.T. Smith, Chelsea Adams, and Justin Askins. Single copy: $10; subscription: $20/1 year, $38/2 years.

TIPS "If we favor your work, it may appear in several issues, so prior contributors are also encouraged to resubmit. Every year we choose at least 1 featured author for an issue. We also nominate for Pushcart Prizes, and we will do book reviews if you mail us the book."

◐ FLYWAY

Department of English, 206 Ross Hall, Iowa State University, Ames IA 50011-1201. **E-mail:** flywayjournal@gmail.com; flyway@iastate.edu. **Website:** www.flyway.org. **Contact:** Michelle Donahue, managing editor. Estab. 1995. Based out of Iowa State University, *Flyway: Journal of Writing and Environment* publishes poetry, fiction, nonfiction, and visual art exploring the many complicated facets of the word environment—at once rural, urban, and suburban—

and its social and political implications. Also open to all different interpretations of environment.

Reading period is September 1-May 1. Has published work by Rick Bass, Jacob M. Appel, Madison Smartt Bell, Jane Smiley. Also sponsors the annual fall "Notes from the Field" nonfiction contest and the spring "Sweet Corn Prize in Fiction" short story contest. Details on website.

NEEDS Length: up to 5,000 words. Average length: 3,000 words. Also publishes short shorts of up to 1,000 words. Average length: 500 words.

HOW TO CONTACT Submit mss only via online submission manager. Receives 50-100 mss monthly. Accepts 3-5 stories per issue; up to 10 per year. Also reviews novels and short story collections. Submit 1 short story or up to 3 short shorts.

PAYMENT/TERMS Pays one-year subscription to *Flyway*.

TIPS "For *Flyway*, there should be tension between the environment or setting of the story and the characters in it. A well-known place should appear new, even alien and strange through the eyes and actions of the characters. We want to see an active environment, too—a setting that influences actions, triggers its own events."

⊘⑤ FOGGED CLARITY

Fogged Clarity and Nicotine Heart Press, P.O. Box 1016, Muskegon MI 49443-1016. (231)670-7033. **E-mail:** editor@foggedclarity.com. **E-mail:** submissions@foggedclarity.com. **Website:** www.foggedclarity.com. **Contact:** Ben Evans, executive editor/managing editor. Estab. 2008. "*Fogged Clarity* is an arts review that accepts submissions of poetry, fiction, nonfiction, music, visual art, and reviews of work in all mediums. We seek art that is stabbingly eloquent. Our print edition is released once every year, while new issues of our online journal come out at the beginning of every month. Artists maintain the copyrights to their work until they are monetarily compensated for said work. If your work is selected for our print edition and you consent to its publication, you will be compensated."

"By incorporating music and the visual arts and releasing a new issue monthly, *Fogged Clarity* aims to transcend the conventions of a typical literary journal. Our network is extensive, and our scope is as broad as thought itself; we are, you are, unconstrained. With that spirit in mind, *Fogged Clarity* examines the work of authors, artists, scholars, and musicians, providing a home for exceptional art and thought that warrants exposure."

NEEDS Does not want genre, experimental, religious, etc. "We tend to only publish literary fiction."

HOW TO CONTACT Send complete ms.

TIPS "The editors appreciate artists communicating the intention of their submitted work and the influences behind it in a brief cover letter. Any artists with proposals for features or special projects should feel free to contact our editors directly at editor@foggedclarity.com."

FOLIATE OAK LITERARY MAGAZINE

University of Arkansas-Monticello, P.O. Box 3460, Monticello AR 71656. (870)460-1247. **E-mail:** folioteoak@uamont.edu. **Website:** www.foliateoak.com. **Contact:** Online submission manager. Estab. 1973. Magazine: 6×9; 80 pages. Monthly.

NEEDS Adventure, comics/graphic novels, ethnic/multicultural, experimental, family saga, feminist, gay, historical, humor/satire, lesbian, literary, mainstream, science fiction (soft/sociological). No religious, sexist or homophobic work. Receives 80 unsolicited mss/month. Accepts 20 mss/issue; 160 mss/year. Does not read mss May-August. Publishes ms 1 month after acceptance. Publishes 130 new writers/year. Recently published work by David Barringer, Thom Didato, Joe Taylor, Molly Giles, Patricia Shevlin, Tony Hoagland. Length: 50-2,500 words; average length: 1,500 words. Publishes short shorts. Also publishes literary essays, literary criticism, poetry. Rarely comments on rejected mss.

HOW TO CONTACT "Use our online submission manager to submit work. Postal submissions will not be read. Responds in 4 weeks. Only accepts submissions August-April. Accepts simultaneous submissions and multiple submissions. Please contact ASAP if work is accepted elsewhere." Sample copy with SASE and 6×8 envelope. Read writer's guidelines online. Reviews fiction.

PAYMENT/TERMS Pays contributor's copy if included in the annual print anthology. Acquires electronic rights. Sends galleys to author. Not copyrighted.

TIPS "We're open to honest, experimental, offbeat, realistic, and surprising writing, if it has been ed-

ited. Limit poems to 5 per submission, and 1 short story or creative nonfiction (less than 2,500 words. You may send up to 3 flash fictions. Please put your flash fiction in 1 attachment. Please don't send more writing until you hear from us regarding your first submission. We are also looking for artwork sent as.jpg or.gif files."

FOLIO, A LITERARY JOURNAL AT AMERICAN UNIVERSITY

Department of Literature, American University, Washington DC 20016. (202)885-2971. **Fax:** (202)885-2938. **E-mail:** folio.editors@gmail.com. **Website:** www.american.edu/cas/literature/folio. Estab. 1984. "*Folio* is a nationally recognized literary journal sponsored by the College of Arts and Sciences at American University in Washington, DC. Since 1984, we have published original creative work by both new and established authors. Past issues have included work by Michael Reid Busk, Billy Collins, William Stafford, and Bruce Weigl, and interviews with Michael Cunningham, Charles Baxter, Amy Bloom, Ann Beattie, and Walter Kirn. We look for well-crafted poetry and prose that is bold and memorable."

Poems and prose are reviewed by editorial staff and senior editors. *Folio* is 80 pages, digest-sized, with matte cover with graphic art. Receives about 1,000 poems/year, accepts about 25. Press run is 400; 50-60 distributed free to the American University community and contributors.

NEEDS Length: up to 5,000 words.

HOW TO CONTACT Submit via online submission form at https://foliolitjournal.submittable.com/submit. "Cover letters must contain all of the following: brief bio, e-mail address, snail mail address, phone number, and title(s) of work enclosed. SASE required for notification only; mss are not returned." Reads submissions September 1-March 1.

PAYMENT/TERMS Pays 2 contributor's copies.

FOLIO

10 Gate St., Lincoln's Inn Fields, London WCZA 3HP United Kingdom. +44 0207 242 9562. **Fax:** +44 0207 242 1816. **E-mail:** info@folioart.co.uk. **Website:** www.folioart.co.uk.

FOURTEEN HILLS

Department of Creative Writing, San Francisco State University, 1600 Holloway Ave., San Francisco CA 94132-1722. **E-mail:** hills@sfsu.edu. **Web-site:** www.14hills.net. Estab. 1994. *"Fourteen Hills* publishes the highest-quality innovative fiction and poetry for a literary audience." Editors change each year. Always sends prepublication galleys.

○ Magazine: 6×9; 200 pages; 60 lb. paper; 10-pt. C15 cover.

NEEDS Receives 300 unsolicited mss/month. Accepts 8-10 mss/issue; 16-20 mss/year. Does not usually read mss during the summer. Publishes ms 2-4 months after acceptance. Recently published work by Susan Straight, Yiyun Li, Alice LaPlante, Terese Svoboda, Peter Rock, Stephen Dixon, and Adam Johnson. Publishes short shorts. Also publishes literary essays, flash fiction, creative nonfiction, poetry, and art.

HOW TO CONTACT Send 1 prose ms, maximum of 25 pages; visual art, experimental, and cross-genre literature also accepted; see website for guidelines. Writers may submit once per submission period. The submission periods are: September 1-January 1 for inclusion in the spring issue (released in May); March 1-July 1 for inclusion in the winter issue (released in December). Response times vary from 4-9 months, "depending on where your submission falls in the reading period; we will usually respond within 5 months. Mss and artwork may be mailed and addressed to the proper genre editor and *must* be accompanied by an SASE for notification, in addition to an e-mail and telephone contact. Due to the volume of submissions, mss cannot be returned, so please, do not send any originals. We accept simultaneous submissions; however, please be sure to notify us immediately by e-mail should you need to withdraw submissions due to publication elsewhere. Please note that we accept electronic submissions at this time via our website: www.14hills.net. However, we do not accept submissions by e-mail. Please check website for changes in submission policies."

PAYMENT/TERMS Pays 2 contributor's copies.

TIPS "Please read an issue of *Fourteen Hills* before submitting."

◑◐ FREEFALL MAGAZINE

Freefall Literary Society of Calgary, 922 Ninth Ave. SE, Calgary AB T2G 0S4 Canada. **E-mail:** editors@ freefallmagazine.ca. **Website:** www.freefallmagazine .ca. **Contact:** Lynn C. Fraser, managing editor. Estab.

1990. Magazine published triannually containing fiction, poetry, creative nonfiction, essays on writing, interviews, and reviews. "We are looking for exquisite writing with a strong narrative."

NEEDS Length: no more than 4,000 words.

HOW TO CONTACT Submit via website form. Attach submission file (file name format is lastname_firstname_storytitle.doc or .docx or .pdf).

PAYMENT/TERMS Pays $10 per printed page in the magazine, to a maximum of $100, and 1 contributor's copy.

TIPS "Our mission is to encourage the voices of new, emerging, and experienced Canadian writers and to provide a platform for their quality work. Although we accept work from all over the world, we maintain a commitment to 85% Canadian content."

◑◐ FREEXPRESSION

P.O. Box 4, West Hoxton NSW 2171 Australia. **E-mail:** editor@freexpression.com.au. **Website:** www.free xpression.com.au. **Contact:** Peter F. Pike, managing editor. Estab. 1993. *FreeXpresSion*, published monthly, contains "creative writing, how-to articles, short stories, and poetry including cinquain, haiku, etc., and bush verse." Open to all forms. "Christian themes are OK. Humorous material is welcome. No gratuitous sex; bad language is OK. We don't want to see anything degrading." Has published poetry by many prizewinning poets like Ron Stevens, Ellis Campbell, Brenda Joy, David Campbell, Max and Jacqui Merckenschlager. *FreeXpresSion* is 32 pages, magazine-sized, offset printed, saddle-stapled, with colored paper cover. Receives about 3,500 poems/year, accepts about 30%. Subscription: $15 AUS/3 months, $32 AUS/6 months, $60 AUS/1 year.

○ *FreeXpresSion* also publishes books up to 200 pages through subsidy arrangements with authors. Some poems published throughout the year are used in *Yearbooks* (annual anthologies).

HOW TO CONTACT Submit prose via e-mail.

◑◐ THE FROGMORE PAPERS

21 Mildmay Rd., Lewes, East Sussex BN7 1PJ England. **Website:** www.frogmorepress.co.uk. **Contact:** Jeremy Page, editor. Estab. 1983. *The Frogmore Papers,* published semiannually, is a literary magazine with emphasis on new poetry and short stories. "Quality

is generally the only criterion, although pressure of space means very long work (over 100 lines) is unlikely to be published." Has published poetry by Marita Over, Brian Aldiss, Carole Satyamurti, John Mole, Linda France, and Tobias Hill. *The Frogmore Papers* is 46 pages, photocopied in photo-reduced typescript, saddle-stapled, with matte card cover. Accepts 2% of poetry received. Press run is 500. Subscription: £10/1 year (2 issues); £15/2 years (4 issues).

NEEDS Length: no more than 2,000 words.

☺ ◗ FRONT & CENTRE

573 Gainsborough Ave., Ottawa ON K2A 2Y6 Canada. (613)729-8973. **E-mail:** firth@istar.ca. **Website:** www.blackbilepress.com. **Contact:** Matthew Firth, editor. Estab. 1998. Each issue of *Front&Centre* contains new fiction, book reviews, and commentary. "We are looking for fiction set in a realist tone, that concerns the contemporary. We are strictly nongenre and do not publish science fiction, horror, fantasy, or fluff of any kind. We prefer dirty realism, urban angst, noir, and tales of ordinary woe. Otherwise, thematically, the magazine is wide open. Quality new fiction is what we want."

○   Magazine: half letter size; 40-50 pages; illustrations; photos.

NEEDS Receives 20 unsolicited mss/month. Accepts 6-7 mss/issue; 10-20 mss/year. Publishes ms 6 months after acceptance. Agented fiction 10%. **Publishes 8-9 new writers/year.** Recently published work by Len Gasparini, Katharine Coldiron, Salvatore Difalco, Gerald Locklin, Amanda Earl, Tom Johns. Publishes short shorts. Always comments on rejected mss. "We look for new fiction from Canadian and international writers—bold, aggressive work that does not compromise quality." Length: up to 4,000 words.

HOW TO CONTACT Submit via postal mail with SASE or IRCs.

PAYMENT/TERMS Pays in contributor's copies.

TIPS "We look for attention to detail, unique voice, not overtly derivative, bold writing, not pretentious. We should like to see more realism. Read the magazine first—simple as that!"

☺ ◗ ◗ FUGUE LITERARY MAGAZINE

200 Brink Hall, University of Idaho, P.O. Box 44110, Moscow ID 83844. **E-mail:** fugue@uidaho.edu. **Website:** www.fuguejournal.org. **Contact:** Alexandra

Teague, faculty advisor. Estab. 1990. Biannual literary magazine. "Submissions are accepted online only. Poetry, fiction, and nonfiction submissions are accepted September 1-April 1. All material received outside of this period will not be read." $2 submission fee per entry. See website for submission instructions.

○   Work published in *Fugue* has won the Pushcart Prize and has been cited in *Best American Essays*.

HOW TO CONTACT "Please send no more than 2 short shorts or 1 story at a time. Submissions in more than 1 genre should be submitted separately. All multiple submissions will be returned unread. Once you have submitted a piece to us, wait for a response on this piece before submitting again." Submit using online submissions manager.

PAYMENT/TERMS All contributors receive payment and 2 contributor's copies.

TIPS "The best way, of course, to determine what we're looking for is to read the journal. As the name *Fugue* indicates, our goal is to present a wide range of literary perspectives. We like stories that satisfy us both intellectually and emotionally, with fresh language and characters so captivating that they stick with us and invite a second reading. We are also seeking creative literary criticism which illuminates a piece of literature or a specific writer by examining that writer's personal experience."

FUNNY TIMES

Funny Times, Inc., P.O. Box 18530, Cleveland Heights OH 44118. (216)371-8600. **Fax:** (216)371-8696. **E-mail:** info@funnytimes.com. **Website:** www.funnytimes.com. **Contact:** Ray Lesser and Susan Wolpert, editors. Estab. 1985. "*Funny Times* is a monthly review of America's funniest cartoonists and writers. We are the *Reader's Digest* of modern American humor with a progressive/peace-oriented/environmental/politically activist slant."

NEEDS Wants anything funny. Length: 500-700 words.

HOW TO CONTACT Query with published clips.

PAYMENT/TERMS Pays $50-150.

TIPS "Send us a small packet (1-3 items) of only your very funniest stuff. If this makes us laugh, we'll be glad to ask for more. We particularly welcome previously published material that has been well received elsewhere."

🟢 GARBANZO LITERARY JOURNAL

Seraphemera Books, 211 Greenwood Ave., Suite 224, Bethel CT 06801. **E-mail:** storyteller@garbanzolit eraryjournal.org. **Website:** www.garbanzoliterary journal.org. **Contact:** Marc Moorash and Ava Dawn Heydt, co-editors. Estab. 2010. Limited-edition hand-made book, also available at iBookstore. "We are call-ing out to all who have placed word on page (and even those who still carry all their works in the mind). Stories of up to 1,172 words, poems of up to 43 lines, microfiction, macrofiction, limericks, villanelles, cinquains, couplets, couplings, creative nonfiction, noncreative fictions … and whatever form your mov-ing, thoughtful, memorable tale wishes to take (which means disregard the rules, punk-rock style). In our specific instance, there is always a light that shines through these works, always a redemption that hap-pens in the end. We're whimsical and full of light, even though some of the subject matter and form is dark. If your work is full of sarcasm and cynicism, if your cover letter is full of the same, we're probably not a good fit for you. We somewhat consider each issue of *Garbanzo* to be a moment in infinite space when a group of mostly disparate people wind up in the same room due to some strange space/time glitch. We're not all going to agree on everything, and we probably wouldn't all get along, but we're not going to waste that moment together in complaint … We're going to celebrate, each picking up a feather and causing this massive bird to fly …"

NEEDS Length: 1-29,318 words.

HOW TO CONTACT Submit complete ms.

PAYMENT/TERMS Pays copies.

TIPS "Read our website and the various suggestions therein. We're not much for rules—so surprise us. In that same regard, if you send us certain things, it will be immediately obvious if you haven't bothered to learn about us. Those who pay attention to detail are far more interesting to work with—as we're very in-teractive with our published authors. We want people who want to work and play with our style of publish-ing as much as we want good writing."

GARBLED TRANSMISSIONS MAGAZINE

5813 NW 20th St., Margate FL 33063. **E-mail:** james robertpayne@yahoo.com. **E-mail:** editor@gar bledtransmission.com. **Website:** www.garbledtrans mission.com. **Contact:** James Payne, editor-in-chief.

Estab. 2011. Daily online literary magazine featuring fiction and book, movie, and comic book reviews.

🗨 "Stories should have a dark/strange/twisted slant to them and should be original ideas, or have such a twist to them that they redefine the genre. We like authors with an original voice. That being said, we like Stephen King, Rich-ard Matheson, Neil Gaiman, A. Lee Martinez, Chuck Palahniuk, and Clive Barker. Movies and TV shows that inspire us include *Lost*, *The Matrix*, *Fight Club*, *3:10 to Yuma*, *Dark City*, *The Sixth Sense*, *The X-Files*, and *Super 8*."

NEEDS No romance. Length: 500-15,000 words.

HOW TO CONTACT Send complete ms. Submit via e-mail with subject line "Garbled Transmissions Sub-mission."

PAYMENT/TERMS Pays 1 contributor's copy. "We currently do not offer monetary payment, though we plan to in the future, if all goes well. This is a labor of love, and although we currently do not pay, we expect nothing but your best."

TIPS "The best way to see what we like is to visit our website and read some of the stories we've published."

🔵 GARGOYLE

Paycock Press, 3819 N. 13th St., Arlington VA 22201. (703)525-9296. **E-mail:** rchrdpeabody@gmail.com. **E-mail:** gargoyle@gargoylemagazine.com. **Website:** www.gargoylemagazine.com. **Contact:** Richard Pea-body, editor, Lucinda Ebersole, co-editor. Estab. 1976. "*Gargoyle* has always been a scallywag magazine, a maverick magazine, a bit too academic for the under-ground and way too underground for the academics. We are a writer's magazine in that we are read by other writers and have never worried about reaching the masses." Annual. Wants "edgy realism or experimen-tal works. We run both." Wants to see more Canadian, British, Australian, and Third World fiction. Receives 200 unsolicited mss/week during submission period. Accepts 20-50 mss/issue. Accepts submissions from June 1 until full; in 2013 that was by June 17. Agented fiction 5%. **Publishes 2-3 new writers/year**. Recently published work by Anya Achtenberg, Yesim Agaolu, Nin Andrews, Gary Blankenburg, C.L. Beldsoe, Ann Bogle, Rae Bryant, Patrick Chapman, Nina Corwin, Jim Daniels, Kristina Marie Darling, Sean Thomas Dougherty, Guillermo Fadanelli, Gary Fincke, Re-becca Foust, Stephen Gibson, Maria Gillan, Joe Hall, Michael Hemmingson, Nancy Hightower, David

MacLeavey, Kat Meads, Teresa Mibrodt, Leslie F. Miller, Donaji Olmedo, Catherine Owen, David Plumb, Doug Ramspeck, Doug Rice, Kim Roberts, Barry Silesky, Edgar Gabriel Silex, Curtis Smith, Barry Spacks, Susan Tepper, Sue Ellen Thompson, Meredith Trede, Meg Tuite, Sara Uribe, Julie Wakeman-Linn, Vallie Lynn Watson, Brandi Wells, Mary-Sherman Willis, and Bill Wolak.

○ Receives 150 queries/year; 50 mss/year. Publishes 10% material from first-time authors; 75% from unagented writers. Publishes 2 titles/year. Format: trade paperback originals.

NEEDS No romance, horror, science fiction. Length: 1,000-4,500 words.

TIPS "We have to fall in love with a particular fiction."

○ GEORGETOWN REVIEW

Box 227, 400 East College St., Georgetown KY 40324. (502)863-8308. **Fax:** (502)868-8888. **E-mail:** gtownreview@georgetowncollege.edu. **Website:** georgetownreview.georgetowncollege.edu. **Contact:** Steven Carter, editor. Estab. 1993. *Georgetown Review*, published annually in May, is a literary journal of poetry, fiction, and creative nonfiction. Does not want "work that is merely sentimental, political, or inspirational."

○ *Georgetown Review* is 192 pages, digest-sized, offset-printed, perfect-bound, with 60 lb. glossy 4-color cover with art/graphics, includes ads. Press run is 1,000. Single copy: $7. Make checks payable to *Georgetown Review*.

NEEDS "We publish the best fiction we receive, regardless of theme or genre." Receives 100-125 mss/month. Accepts 8-10 mss/issue; 15-20/year. No agented fiction. **Publishes 3-4 new writers/year.** Published Andrew Plattner, Sallie Bingham, and Alison Stine. Also publishes literary essays, poetry, short shorts. Sometimes comments on/critiques rejected mss. "Sponsors annual contest with $1,000 prize. Check website for guidelines." Does not want adventure, children's, fantasy, romance. Average length: 4,000 words. Average length of short shorts: 500-1,500 words.

HOW TO CONTACT Send complete ms with cover letter. Include brief bio, list of publications.

PAYMENT/TERMS Writers receive 2 contributor's copies, free 2-year subscription to the magazine. Additional copies for $5.

TIPS "We look for fiction that is well written and that has a story line that keeps our interest. Don't send a first draft, and even if we don't take your first, second, or third submission, keep trying."

THE GEORGIA REVIEW

The University of Georgia, Athens GA 30602. (706)542-3481. **Fax:** (706)542-0047. **E-mail:** garev@uga.edu. **Website:** thegeorgiareview.com. **Contact:** Stephen Corey, editor. Estab. 1947. "Our readers are educated, inquisitive people who read a lot of work in the areas we feature, so they expect only the best in our pages. All work submitted should show evidence that the writer is at least as well-educated and well-read as our readers. Essays should be authoritative but accessible to a range of readers."

○ No simultaneous submissions. Electronic submissions available for $3 fee.

NEEDS "We seek original, excellent writing not bound by type. Ordinarily we do not publish novel excerpts or works translated into English, and we strongly discourage authors from submitting these."

HOW TO CONTACT Send complete ms. "We do not consider unsolicited mss between May 15 and August 15. Submissions received during that period will be returned unread. Work previously published in any form or submitted simultaneously to other journals will not be considered."

PAYMENT/TERMS Pays $50/published page.

TIPS "Unsolicited mss will not be considered May 15-August 15 (annually); all such submissions received during that period will be returned unread. Check website for submission guidelines."

THE GETTYSBURG REVIEW

Gettysburg College, Gettysburg PA 17325. (717)337-6770. **Fax:** (717)337-6775. **Website:** www.gettysburgreview.com. **Contact:** Peter Stitt, editor. Estab. 1988. "Our concern is quality. Mss submitted here should be extremely well written. Reading period September 1-May 31."

NEEDS Wants high-quality literary fiction. "We require that fiction be intelligent and esthetically written." No genre fiction. Length: 2,000-7,000 words.

HOW TO CONTACT Send complete ms with SASE.

PAYMENT/TERMS Pays $30/page and 1 contributor's copy.

⊕ GHLL

The Green Hills Literary Lantern, Truman State University, Department of English, Truman State University, Kirksville MO 63501. **E-mail:** adavis@truman.edu. **Website:** ghll.truman.edu. **Contact:** Adam

Brooke Davis, managing editor. Estab. 1990. *GHLL* is published annually, in June, by Truman State University. Historically the print publication ran between 200-300 pages, consisting of poetry, fiction, reviews, and interviews. The digital magazine is of similar proportions and artistic standards. Open to the work of new writers, as well as more established writers.

NEEDS "We are interested in stories that demonstrate a strong working knowledge of the craft. Avoid genre fiction or mainstream religious fiction. Otherwise, we are open to short stories of various settings, character conflict, and styles, including experimental. Above all, we demand that work be 'striking.' Language should be complex, with depth, through analogy, metaphor, simile, understatement, irony, etc.—but all this must not be overwrought or self-consciously literary. If style is to be at center stage, it must be interesting and provocative enough for the reader to focus on style alone. 'Overdone' writing surely is not either." No word limit.

HOW TO CONTACT Submit complete ms.

PAYMENT/TERMS No payment provided.

GINOSKO

P.O. Box 246, Fairfax CA 94978. **E-mail:** ginoskoedi tor@aol.com. **Website:** www.ginoskoliteraryjournal .com. **Contact:** Robert Paul Cesaretti, editor. Estab. 2003. "The definition of *Ginosko* (ghin-océ-koe): To perceive, understand, realize, come to know; knowledge that has an inception, a progress, an attainment. The recognition of truth by experience." Accepting short fiction and poetry, creative nonfiction, interviews, social-justice concerns, and spiritual insights for the website www.GinoskoLiteraryJournal.com. Member CLMP.

Reads year-round. Length of articles flexible; accepts excerpts. Publishing as semiannual e-zine. Check downloadable issues on website for tone and style. Downloads free; accepts donations. Also looking for books, art, and music to post on website, and links to exchange.

NEEDS *Ginosko* Flash Fiction Contest: Deadline is March 1; $5 entry fee; $250 prize.

GLIMMER TRAIN STORIES

Glimmer Train Press, Inc., P.O. Box 80430, Portland OR 97280. **Fax:** (503)221-0837. **E-mail:** eds@glim mertrain.org. **Website:** www.glimmertrain.org. Estab. 1991. "We are interested in literary short stories, particularly by new and emerging writers."

Receives 36,000 unsolicited mss/year. Accepts 10 mss/issue; 40 mss/year. Agented fiction 5%. Publishes 20 new writers/year. Recently published work by Charles Baxter, Thisbe Nissen, Herman Carrillo, Andre Dubus III, William Trevor, Patricia Henley, Alberto Rios, Ann Beattie, and Yiyun Li.

NEEDS Length: 1,200-12,000 words.

HOW TO CONTACT Submit via the website. "In a pinch, send a hard copy and include SASE for response."

PAYMENT/TERMS Pays $700 for standard submissions, up to $2,500 for contest-winning stories.

TIPS "In the last 2 years, over half of the first-place stories have been their authors' very first publications. See our contest listings in contest and awards section."

GOTHIC CITY PRESS

Sacred City Productions, Ltd., 5781 Springwood Ct., Mentor on the Lake OH 44060. (440)290-9325. **E-mail:** info@gothiccitypress.com. **E-mail:** info@goth iccitypress.com. **Website:** gothiccitypress.com. **Contact:** Erin and Colleen Garlock, editors/owners. Estab. 2013. *Gothic City Press* is a print and online imprint dedicated to creative endeavors using the back drop of all things Gothic or urban as inspiration.

NEEDS Gothic City Press's fiction focus is on dark fiction for publication in short story anthologies. "We tend to favor stories that have dark overtones, though this is not a requirement." Looking for 500-8,000 word stories.

HOW TO CONTACT Send completed story through online submission form.

PAYMENT/TERMS Pays $10 for stories over 500 words, $20 for stories over 2,000 words. Once royalties earned by the publication equal the total amount paid out to all contributors, the contributors will receive a 50/50 prorate share of the anthology's earnings, if any, will be paid as royalties at a ratio, to the aforementioned rates, relevant to the number of contributors. A royalty breakdown sheet will be supplied at the end of a project.

TIPS "We are very interested in submissions from first-time authors and authors with a very limited record."

⊙⊙$ GRAIN

P.O. Box 67, Saskatoon SK S7K 3K1 Canada. (306)244-2828. **Fax:** (306)244-0255. **E-mail:** grainmag@sasktel.net. **Website:** www.grainmagazine.ca. **Contact:** Rilla Friesen, editor. Estab. 1973. "*Grain, The Journal of Eclectic Writing*, is a literary quarterly that publishes engaging, diverse, and challenging writing, and art by some of the best Canadian and international writers and artists. Every issue features superb new writing from both developing and established writers. Each issue also highlights the unique artwork of a different visual artist. *Grain* has garnered national and international recognition for its distinctive, cutting-edge content and design."

◗ *Grain* is 112-128 pages, digest-sized, professionally printed. Press run is 1,100. Receives about 3,000 submissions/year. Subscription: $35 CAD/year, $55 CAD for 2 years. Sample: $13 CAD. (See website for U.S. and foreign postage fees.) Has published poetry by Lorna Crozier, Don Domanski, Cornelia Haeussler, Patrick Lane, Karen Solie, and Monty Reid.

NEEDS No romance, confession, science fiction, vignettes, mystery. Length: 5,000/words maximum; "stories at the longer end of the word count must be of exceptional quality."

HOW TO CONTACT "Submissions must be typed in readable font (ideally 12 point, Times Roman or Courier), free of typos, printed on 1 side only. No staples. Your name and address must be on every page. Pieces of more than 1 page must be numbered. Cover letter with all contact information, title(s), and genre of work is required."

TIPS "Submissions read September-May only. Mss postmarked between June 1 and August 31 will not be read. Only work of the highest literary quality is accepted. Read several back issues."

◗ GRASSLIMB

P.O. Box 420816, San Diego CA 92142. **E-mail:** editor@grasslimb.com. **Website:** www.grasslimb.com. **Contact:** Valerie Polichar, editor. Estab. 2002. "*Grasslimb* publishes literary prose, poetry, and art. Fiction is best when it is short and avant-garde or otherwise experimental." Semiannual.

◗ Magazine: 14×20; 8 pages; 60 lb. white paper; illustrations.

NEEDS Accepts 2-4 mss/issue; 4-8 mss/year. Publishes ms 3-6 months after acceptance. Publishes 4 new writers/year. Has published work by Kuzhali Manickavel, James Sallis. Publishes short shorts. Reviews fiction. Does not want romance, elder care/aging, children, or religious writings. Length: 500-2,000 words; average length: 1,500 words.

HOW TO CONTACT Send complete ms. Send SASE for return of ms or disposable copy of ms and #10 SASE for reply only. Accepts simultaneous and reprints, multiple submissions.

PAYMENT/TERMS Writers receive $10 minimum; $70 maximum, and 2 contributor's copies; additional copies $3.

TIPS "We publish brief fictional work that can be read in a single sitting over a cup of coffee. Work is generally literary in nature, rather than mainstream. Experimental work welcome. Remember to have your work proofread and to send short work. We cannot read over 2,500 and prefer under 2,000 words. Include word count."

◗◗ GREEN HILLS LITERARY LANTERN

McClain Hall, Truman State University, Kirksville MO 63501. (660)785-4513. **E-mail:** jbeneven@truman.edu. **Website:** ll.truman.edu/ghllweb/. **Contact:** Joe Benevento, poetry editor. Estab. 1990. "The mission of *GHLL* is to provide a literary market for quality fiction writers, both established and beginners, and to provide quality literature for readers from diverse backgrounds. We also see ourselves as a cultural resource for North Missouri. Our publication works to publish the highest-quality fiction—dense, layered, subtle—and, at the same time, fiction which grabs the ordinary reader. We tend to publish traditional short stories, but we are open to experimental forms." Annual. The *GHLL* is now an online, open-access journal.

NEEDS "Our main requirement is literary merit. We wants more quality fiction about rural culture." Receives 40 unsolicited mss/month. No adventure, crime, erotica, horror, inspirational, mystery/suspense, romance. Length: up to 7,000 words; average length: 3,000 words. Also publishes short shorts.

HOW TO CONTACT Strongly prefers postal mail submissions. Include SASE if you want ms returned.

GREEN MOUNTAINS REVIEW

Johnson State College, 337 College Hill, Johnson VT 05656. (802)635-1350. **E-mail:** gmr@jsc.edu. **Website:** greenmountainsreview.com/. **Contact:** Elizabeth Powell, editor. The editors are open to a wide rane of styles and subject matter.

"Mss received between March 1 and September 1 will not be read and will be returned."

NEEDS Adventure, experimental, humor/satire, literary, mainstream, serialized novels, translations. Recently published work by Tracy Daugherty, Terese Svoboda, Walter Wetherell, T.M. McNally, J. Robert Lennon, Louis B. Jones, and Tom Whalen. Publishes short shorts. Also publishes literary criticism, poetry. Sometimes comments on rejected mss. Length: up to 25 pages, double-spaced.

PAYMENT/TERMS Pays contributor's copies, one-year subscription and small honorarium, depending on grants.

TIPS "We encourage you to order some of our back issues to acquaint yourself with what has been accepted in the past."

THE GREENSBORO REVIEW

MFA Writing Program, 3302 HHRA Building, UNC-Greensboro, Greensboro NC 27402. (336)334-5459. E-mail: jlclark@uncg.edu. **Website:** www.greensbororeview.org. **Contact:** Jim Clark, editor. Estab. 1965. "A local lit mag with an international reputation. We've been 'old school' since 1965."

Stories for *the Greensboro Review* have been included in *Best American Short Stories, The O. Henry Awards Prize Stories, New Stories from The South,* and the *Pushcart Prize.* Does not accept e-mail submissions.

NEEDS Length: no more than 7,500 words.

HOW TO CONTACT Submit complete ms using online submission form or via postal mail. Include cover letter and estimated word count.

PAYMENT/TERMS Pays in contributor's copies.

TIPS "We want to see the best being written regardless of theme, subject, or style."

THE GRIFFIN

Gwynedd Mercy College, 1325 Sumneytown Pike, P.O. Box 901, Gwynedd Valley PA 19437-0901. (215)641-5518. **Fax:** (215)641-5552. **E-mail:** allego.d@GMUniversity.edu. **Website:** www.gmercyu.edu/about-gwynedd-mercy/publications/griffin. **Contact:** Dr. Donna M. Allego, editor. Estab. 1999.

NEEDS All genres considered. No slashers, graphic violence, or sex, however. Length: up to 2,500 words.

HOW TO CONTACT Submit complete ms via e-mail or on disk with a hard copy. Include short author bio.

TIPS "Pay attention to the word length requirements, the mission of the magazine, and how to submit ms

as set forth. These constitute the writer's guidelines listed online."

GUD MAGAZINE

Greatest Uncommon Denominator Publishing, P.O. Box 1537, Laconia NH 03247. **E-mail:** spiderbait1@gudmagazine.com. **Website:** www.gudmagazine.com. Estab. 2006. L *"GUD Magazine* transcends and encompasses the audiences of both genre and literary fiction by featuring fiction, art, poetry, essays and reports, comics, and short drama."

NEEDS Length: up to 15,000 words.

HOW TO CONTACT Submit via online submissions manager.

PAYMENT/TERMS Pays a minimum of $5/piece, or 3¢/word for longer pieces.

TIPS "We publish work in any genre, plus artwork, factual articles, and interviews. We'll publish something as short as 20 words or as long as 15,000, as long as it grabs us. Be warned: We read a lot. We've seen it all before. We are not easy to impress. Is your work original? Does it have something to say? Read it again. If you genuinely believe it to be so, send it. We do accept simultaneous submissions, as well as multiple submissions, but read the guidelines first."

GUERNICA MAGAZINE

112 W. 27th St., Suite 600, New York NY 10001. **E-mail:** editors@guernicamag.com; art@guernicamag.com; publisher@guernicamag.com. **Website:** www.guernicamag.com. **Contact:** Erica Wright, poetry; Dan Eckstein, art/photography. Estab. 2005. "*Guernica* is called a 'great online literary magazine' by *Esquire. Guernica* contributors come from dozens of countries and write in nearly as many languages."

Received Caine Prize for African Writing and Best of the Net."

NEEDS literary, preferably with an international approach. No genre fiction. No genre fiction. Length: 700-2500 words.

HOW TO CONTACT Submit complete ms with cover letter, attn: Meakin Armstrong to fiction@guernicamag.com. In subject line (please follow this format exactly): "fiction submission." Include bio and list of previous publications. Accepts 26 mss/year. Has published Jesse Ball, Elizabeth Crane, Josh Weil, Justo Arroyo, Sergio Ramírez Mercado, Matthew Derby, E.C. Osondu (Winner of the 2009 Caine Prize for African Writing).

TIPS "Please read the magazine before submitting. Most stories that are rejected simply do not fit our approach. Submission guidelines available online."

GULF COAST: A JOURNAL OF LITERATURE AND FINE ARTS

4800 Calhoun Road, Houston TX 77204-3013. (713)743-3223. **E-mail:** editors@gulfcoastmag.org. **Website:** www.gulfcoastmag.org. **Contact:** Zachary Martin, editor; Karyna McGlynn, managing editor; Michelle Oakes, Justine Post, Patrick James, poetry editors; Julia Brown, Laura Jok, Ashley Wurzbacher, fiction editors; Beth Lyons, Steve Sanders, nonfiction editors. Estab. 1986.

Magazine: 7x9; approximately 300 pages; stock paper, gloss cover; illustrations; photos. Receives 500 unsolicited mss/month. Accepts 6-8 mss/issue; 12-16 mss/year. Agented fiction: 5%. Publishes 2-8 new writers/year. Recently published work by Alan Heathcock, Anne Carson, Bret Anthony Johnston, John D'Agata, Lucie Brock-Broido, Clancy Martin, Steve Almond, Sam Lipsyte, Carl Phillips, Dean Young, and Eula Biss. Publishes short shorts.

NEEDS "Please do not send multiple submissions; we will read only 1 submission per author at a given time, except in the case of our annual contests." No children's, genre, religious/inspirational.

HOW TO CONTACT *Gulf Coast* reads general submissions, submitted by post or through the online submissions manager September 1-March 1. Submissions e-mailed directly to the editors or postmarked March 1-September 1 will not be read or responded to. "Please visit our contest page for contest submission guidelines."

PAYMENT/TERMS Pays $50/page.

TIPS "Submit only previously unpublished works. Include a cover letter. Online submissions are strongly preferred. Stories or essays should be typed, double-spaced, and paginated with your name, address, and phone number on the first page, title on subsequent pages. Poems should have your name, address, and phone number on the first page of each." The Annual Gulf Coast Prizes awards publication and $1,500 each in poetry, fiction, and nonfiction; opens in December of each year. Honorable mentions in each category will receive a $250 second prize. Postmark/online entry deadline: March 15 of each year. Winners and honorable mentions will be announced in May. **Entry fee:** $23 (includes one-year subscription). Make checks payable to *Gulf Coast.* Guidelines available on website.

GULF STREAM MAGAZINE

English Department, FIU, Biscayne Bay Campus, 3000 NE 151 St., North Miami FL 33181. **E-mail:** gulfstreamfiu@yahoo.com. **Website:** www.gulfstreamlitmag.com. **Contact:** Jason Jones, editor. Estab. 1989. "*Gulf Stream Magazine* has been publishing emerging and established writers of exceptional fiction, nonfiction, and poetry since 1989. We also publish interviews and book reviews. Past contributors include Sherman Alexie, Steve Almond, Jan Beatty, Lee Martin, Robert Wrigley, Dennis Lehane, Liz Robbins, Stuart Dybek, David Kirby, Ann Hood, Ha Jin, B.H. Fairchild, Naomi Shihab Nye, F. Daniel Rzicznek, and Connie May Fowler. *Gulf Stream Magazine* is supported by the Creative Writing Program at Florida International University in Miami, Florida. Each year we publish 2 online issues."

NEEDS Does not want romance, historical, juvenile, or religious work.

HOW TO CONTACT "Submit online only. Please read guidelines on website in full. Submissions that do not conform to our guidelines will be discarded. We do not accept e-mailed or mailed submissions. We read from September 1-November 1 and January 1-March 9."

PAYMENT/TERMS Pays contributor's copies.

TIPS "Looks for fresh, original writing—well-plotted stories with unforgettable characters, fresh poetry, and experimental writing. Usually longer stories do not get accepted. There are exceptions, however."

THE G.W. REVIEW

The George Washington University, 800 21st St. NW, Box 20, The Marvin Center, Washington DC 20052. (202)994-7779. **E-mail:** gwreview@gwu.edu; gwreview@gmail.com. **Website:** thegwreview.weebly.com. **Contact:** Linda Cui, editor-in-chief. Estab. 1980. *The G.W. Review* seeks to expose readers to new and emerging writers from both the U.S. and abroad. New, innovative writing—both in style and subject—is valued above the author's previous publishing history.

NEEDS Does not publish genre fiction (i.e., romance, mystery, crime, etc.). Length: No longer than 5,000 words.

HOW TO CONTACT Send complete ms, along with a cover letter, a short biography, and all necessary contact information. Submit between April and October for fall issue and November and March for spring issue.

PAYMENT/TERMS Pays with 2 contributor copies.

TIPS "We enjoy work that is thought-provoking and challenging in its subject matter and style."

HADASSAH MAGAZINE

50 W. 58th St., New York NY 10019. (212)688-0227. **Fax:** (212)446-9521. **E-mail:** magazine@hadassah .org. **Website:** www.hadassah.org/magazine. **Contact:** Elizabeth Goldberg. Zelda Shluker, managing editor. Jewish general-interest magazine: 7×10½; 64-80 pages; coated and uncoated paper; slick, medium-weight coated cover; drawings and photos. "*Hadassah* is a general interest Jewish feature and literary magazine. We speak to our readers on a vast array of subjects ranging from politics to parenting, to midlife crisis to Mideast crisis. Our readers want coverage on social and economic issues, Jewish women's (feminist) issues, the arts, travel, and health." Bi-monthly. Circ. 243,000.

NEEDS Ethnic/multicultural (Jewish). No personal memoirs, "schmaltzy" or shelter magazine fiction. Receives 20-25 unsolicited mss/month. Publishes some new writers/year. Recently published work by Jay Neugeboren and Curt Leviant. Short stories with strong plots and positive Jewish values. Length: 1,500-2,000 words.

HOW TO CONTACT Responds in 4 months to mss. Sample copy and writer's guidelines for 9×12 SASE. Stories can also be e-mailed to lbarnea@hadassah.org.

PAYMENT/TERMS Pays $700 minimum. Pays on acceptance for first North American serial, first rights. Pays $500 minimum.

TIPS "Stories on a Jewish theme should be neither self-hating nor schmaltzy."

◑ HAIGHT ASHBURY LITERARY JOURNAL

558 Joost Ave., San Francisco CA 94127. (415)584-8264. **E-mail:** haljeditor@gmail.com. **Website:** haightashburyliteraryjournal.wordpress.com; www .facebook.com/pages/Haight-Ashbury-Literary-Jour nal/365542018331. **Contact:** Alice Rogoff, Indigo Hotchkiss, and Cesar Love, editors. Estab. 1979. *Haight Ashbury Literary Journal*, publishes "well-written poetry and fiction. *HALJ*'s voices are often of people who have been marginalized, oppressed, or abused. *HALJ* strives to bring literary arts to the general public, to the San Francisco community of

writers, to the Haight Ashbury neighborhood, and to people of varying ages, genders, ethnicities, and sexual preferences. The Journal is produced as a tabloid to maintain an accessible price for low-income people."

◔ *Haight Ashbury* is 16 pages, includes ads. Includes fiction under 20 pages, 1 story/issue, and b&w drawings. Press run is 1,500. Subscription: $12/ 2 issues, $24 for 4 issues; $60 for back issues and future issues. Sample: $6. Has published poetry by Dan O'Connell, Diane Frank, Dancing Bear, Lee Herrick, Al Young, and Laura Beausoleil.

HARDBOILED

Gryphon Publications, P.O. Box 209, Brooklyn NY 11228. **Website:** www.gryphonbooks.com. Estab. 1988. "Hard-hitting crime fiction and private-eye stories—the newest and most cutting-edge work and classic reprints."

◔ Published 1-2 times/year, 100 pages with color cover.

NEEDS "No pastiches, violence for the sake of violence." Length: 500-3,000 words.

HOW TO CONTACT Query or send complete ms.

PAYMENT/TERMS Pays $5-50.

TIPS "Your best bet for breaking in is short hard-crime fiction filled with authenticity and brevity. Try a subscription to *Hardboiled* to get the perfect idea of what we are after."

HARPER'S MAGAZINE

666 Broadway, 11th Floor, New York NY 10012. (212)420-5720. **Fax:** (212)228-5889. **E-mail:** read ings@harpers.org; scg@harpers.org. **Website:** www .harpers.org. Estab. 1850. Magazine: 8×10¾; 80 pages; illustrations. "*Harper's Magazine* encourages national discussion on current and significant issues in a format that offers arresting facts and intelligent opinions. By means of its several shorter journalistic forms—Harper's Index, Readings, Forum, and Annotation—as well as with its acclaimed essays, fiction, and reporting, *Harper's* continues the tradition begun with its first issue in 1850: to inform readers across the whole spectrum of political, literary, cultural, and scientific affairs." Monthly. Estab. 1850. Circ. 230,000.

◔ *Harper's Magazine* will neither consider nor return unsolicited nonfiction mss that have not been preceded by a written query. *Harper's* will consider unsolicited fiction. Unsolicited poetry will not be considered or returned.

No queries or mss will be considered unless they are accompanied by an SASE. All submissions and written queries (with the exception of Readings submissions) must be sent by mail to above address.

NEEDS humor/satire. Stories on contemporary life and its problems. Receives 50 unsolicited mss/month. Accepts 12 mss/year. Publishes ms 3 months after acceptance. **Publishes some new writers/year.** Recently published work by Rebecca Curtis, George Saunders, Haruki Murakami, Margaret Atwood, Allan Gurganus, Evan Connell, and Dave Bezmosgis. Will consider unsolicited fiction. Length: 3,000-5,000 words.

HOW TO CONTACT Query by mail, except for submissions to the Readings section, which can be submitted via readings@harpers.org. Responds in 3 months to queries. Accepts reprints submissions. SASE required for all unsolicited material. Sample copy for $6.95. Query.

PAYMENT/TERMS Generally pays 50¢-$1/word. Pays on acceptance. Vary with author and material. Sends galleys to author. Generally pays 50¢-$1/word

TIPS Some readers expect their magazines to clothe them with opinions in the way that Bloomingdale's dresses them for the opera. The readers of *Harper's Magazine* belong to a different crowd. They strike me as the kind of people who would rather think in their own voices and come to their own conclusions.

HARPUR PALATE

English Department, P.O. Box 6000, Binghamton University, Binghamton NY 13902-6000. **E-mail:** harpur.palate@gmail.com. **Website:** harpurpalate .blogspot.com. **Contact:** Melanie Cordova and Trisha Cowen, editors. Estab. 2000. *Harpur Palate*, published biannually, is "dedicated to publishing the best poetry and prose, regardless of style, form, or genre. We have no restrictions on subject matter or form. Quite simply, send us your highest-quality fiction and poetry."

O Magazine: 6×9; 180-200 pages; coated or uncoated paper; 100 lb. coated cover; 4-color art portfolio insert.

NEEDS Receives 400 unsolicited mss/month. Accepts 5-10 mss/issue; 12-20 mss/year. Publishes ms 1-2 months after acceptance. Publishes 5 new writers/year. Has published work by Darryl Crawford and Tim Hedges, Jesse Goolsby, Ivan Faute, and Keith Meatto. Length: 250-6,000 words. Average length: 2,000-4,000 words.

HOW TO CONTACT Send complete ms with a cover letter. Include e-mail address on cover. Include estimated word count, brief bio, list of publications. Send a disposable copy of ms and #10 SASE for reply only. No more than 1 submission per envelope. Submission periods are September 1-November 15 for the winter issue, and January 1-April 15 for summer.

PAYMENT/TERMS Pays 2 contributor copies.

TIPS "We are interested in high-quality writing of all genres, but especially literary poetry and fiction. We also sponsor a fiction contest for the summer issue and a poetry and nonfiction contest for the winter issue with $500 prizes."

HAWAII REVIEW

University of Hawaii Board of Publications, 2445 Campus Rd., Hemenway Hall 107, Honolulu HI 96822. (808)956-3030. **Fax:** (808)956-3083. **E-mail:** hawaii review@gmail.com. **Website:** www.kaleo.org/hawaii_ review. Estab. 1973. *Hawaii Review* is a student-run biannual literary and visual arts print journal featuring national and international writing and visual art, as well as regional literature and visual art of Hawai'i and the Pacific.

O Accepts submissions online through Submittable only. Offers yearly award with $500 prizes in poetry and fiction.

HOW TO CONTACT Send complete ms.

TIPS "Make it new."

ⓄⓄⓈ HAYDEN'S FERRY REVIEW

c/o Department of English,, Arizona State University, P.O. Box 870302, Tempe AZ 85287. (480)965-1337. **E-mail:** HFR@asu.edu. **Website:** www.haydensferryre view.org. **Contact:** Sam Martone, editor. Estab. 1986. "*Hayden's Ferry Review* publishes the best-quality fiction, poetry, and creative nonfiction from new, emerging, and established writers."

O Work from *Hayden's Ferry Review* has been selected for inclusion in *Pushcart Prize* anthologies and *Best Creative Nonfiction*.

NEEDS Word length open.

HOW TO CONTACT Send complete ms.

⊝⊘ THE HELIX

Central Connecticut State University English Department, **E-mail:** helixmagazine@gmail.com. **Website:** helixmagazine.org. **Contact:** Collin Q. Glasow, editor-in-chief; Ashley Gravel, managing editor. "*The Helix* is a Central Connecticut State University publication, and it puts out an issue every semester. It accepts submissions from all over the globe. The magazine features writing from CCSU students, writing from the Hartford County community, and an array of submissions from all over the world. The magazine publishes multiple genres of literature and art including: poetry, fiction, drama, nonfiction, paintings, photography, watercolor, collage, stencil, and computer-generated artwork. It is a student-run publication, and is funded by the university. Payment for all accepted submissions is a copy of *The Helix*. Visit helixmagazine.org/submit for complete information about submitting to *The Helix*. If you do not submit according to our guidelines, we will not consider your piece but will instead ask you to resubmit your piece correctly. We only accept submissions through our submission manager, which can be found at the link above. For prose, the word limit is 3,000 words. We are not looking for any specific type of writing, but we still require quality work. To submit artwork, send all art to art helixmag@gmail.com"

TIPS "Please see our website for specific deadlines, as they change every semester, based on a variety of factors. We typically leave the submission manager open sometime starting in the summer to around the end of October for the fall issue, and during the winter to late February or mid-March for thespring issue. Contributions are invited from all members of the campus community, as well as the literary community at large."

HELLOHORROR

6609 Lindy Lane, Houston TX 77023. **E-mail:** info@hellohorror.com. **E-mail:** submissions@hellohorror.com. **Website:** www.hellohorror.com. **Contact:** Brent Armour, editor-in-chief. Estab. 2012. "*HelloHorror* is a recently created online literary magazine and blog. We are currently in search of literary pieces, photography, and visual art including film from writers and artists that have a special knack for inducing goose bumps and raised hairs. This genre has become, especially in film, noticeably saturated in gore and high shock-value aspects as a crutch to avoid the true challenge of bringing about real, psychological fear to an audience that's persistently more and more numb to its tactics. While we are not opposed to the extreme, we believe blood and guts need bones and cartilage. Otherwise it's just a sloppy mess."

NEEDS "We don't want fiction that can in no way be classified as horror. Some types of dark science fiction are acceptable, depending on the story." Length: 6-8 pages for short stories; up to 600 words for flash fiction.

HOW TO CONTACT Submit complete ms via e-mail.

TIPS "We like authors who show consideration for their readers. A great horror story leaves an impression on the reader long after it is finished. The motivation behind creating the site was the current saturation of gore and shock-value horror. A story that gives you goose bumps is a much greater achievement than a story that just grosses you out. We have television for that. Consider your reader and consider yourself. What really scares you as opposed to what's stereotypically supposed to scare you? Bring us and our readers into that place of fear with you."

HIGHLIGHTS FOR CHILDREN

803 Church St., Honesdale PA 18431. (570)253-1080. **Fax:** (570)251-7847. **Website:** www.highlights.com. **Contact:** Christine French Cully, editor-in-chief. Estab. 1946. "This book of wholesome fun is dedicated to helping children grow in basic skills and knowledge, in creativeness, in ability to think and reason, in sensitivity to others, in high ideals, and worthy ways of living—for children are the world's most important people. We publish stories for beginning and advanced readers. Up to 500 words for beginning readers, up to 800 words for advanced readers."

NEEDS Meaningful stories appealing to both girls and boys, up to age 12. Vivid, full of action. Engaging plot, strong characterization, lively language. Prefers stories in which a child protagonist solves a dilemma through his or her own resources. Seeks stories that the child ages 8-12 will eagerly read and the younger child will like to hear when read aloud (500-800 words). Stories require interesting plots and a number of illustration possiblities. Also need rebuses (picture stories 100 words), stories with urban settings, stories for beginning readers (100-500 words), sports and humorous stories, adventures, holiday stories, and mysteries. We also would like to see more material of one-page length (300 words), both fiction and factual. No stories glorifying war, crime, or violence.

HOW TO CONTACT Send complete ms.

PAYMENT/TERMS Pays $100 minimum plus 2 contributor's copies.

TIPS Know the magazine's style before submitting. Send for guidelines and sample issue if necessary. Writers: "At *Highlights* we're paying closer attention to acquiring more nonfiction for young readers than we have in the past." Illustrators: "Fresh, imaginative work encouraged. Flexibility in working relationships a plus. Illustrators presenting their work need not confine themselves to just children's illustrations as long as work can translate to our needs. We also use animal illustrations, real and imaginary. We need crafts, puzzles, and any activity that will stimulate children mentally and creatively. Familiarize yourself with our publication's standards and content by reading sample issues, not just the guidelines. Avoid tired themes, or put a fresh twist on an old theme so that its style is fun and lively. Write what inspires you, not what you think the market needs. We are pleased that many authors of children's literature report that their first published work was in the pages of *Highlights*. It is not our policy to consider fiction on the strength of the reputation of the author. We judge each submission on its own merits. Query with simple letter to establish whether the nonfiction subject is likely to be of interest. Expert reviews and complete bibliography required for nonfiction. A beginning writer should first become familiar with the type of material that *Highlights* publishes. Include special qualifications, if any, of author. Write for the child, not the editor. Write in a voice that children understand and relate to. Speak to today's kids, avoiding didactic, overt messages. Even though our general principles haven't changed over the years, we are contemporary in our approach to issues. Avoid worn themes."

◐◐ 〰 HOME PLANET NEWS

P.O. Box 455, High Falls NY 12440. (845)687-4084. **E-mail:** homeplanetnews@gmail.com. **Website:** www .homeplanetnews.org. **Contact:** Donald Lev, editor. Estab. 1979. Triannual. *Home Planet News* publishes mainly poetry along with some fiction, as well as reviews (books, theater, and art) and articles of literary interest.

○ *HPN* has received a small grant from the Puffin Foundation for its focus on AIDS issues. Tabloid: 11.5×16; 24 pages; newsprint; illustrations; photos. Receives 12 unsolicited mss/ month. Accepts 1 mss/issue; 3 mss/year. Has published work by Hugh Fox, Walter Jackman, Jim Story.

NEEDS No children's or genre stories (except rarely some science fiction). Length: 500-2,500 words; average length: 2,000 words.

HOW TO CONTACT Send complete ms. Send SASE for reply, return of ms, or send a disposable copy of the ms. Publishes special fiction issue or anthology.

PAYMENT/TERMS Pays 3 contributor's copies; additional copies $1.

TIPS "We use very little fiction, and a story we accept just has to grab us. We need short pieces of some complexity, stories about complex people facing situations which resist simple resolutions."

HORIZONS

100 Witherspoon St., Louisville KY 40202-1396. (502)569-5897. **Fax:** (502)569-8085. **E-mail:** yvonne .hileman@pcusa.org. **Website:** www.pcusa.org/ho rizons. **Contact:** Yvonne Hileman, assistant editor. Estab. 1988. "Magazine owned and operated by Presbyterian Women in the PC(USA), Inc., offering information and inspiration for Presbyterian women by addressing current issues facing the church and the world."

NEEDS Length: 600-1,800 words.

HOW TO CONTACT Submit queries and/or complete ms by mail, e-mail, or fax. Include contact information.

PAYMENT/TERMS Pays an honorarium of no less than $50 per page printed in the magazine—amount will vary depending on time and research required for writing the article.

◐ HOTEL AMERIKA

Columbia College, English Department, 600 S. Michigan Ave., Chicago IL 60605. (312)369-8175. **E-mail:** editors@hotelamerika.net. **Website:** www.ho telamerika.net. **Contact:** David Lazar, editor; Adam McOmber, managing editor. Estab. 2002. *Hotel Amerika* is a venue for both well-known and emerging writers. Publishes exceptional writing in all forms. Strives to house the most unique and provocative poetry, fiction, and nonfiction available.

○ Mss will be considered between September 1 and May 1. Materials received after May 1 and before September 1 will be returned unread. Send submissions only via mail, with SASE. Work published in *Hotel Amerika* has been included in *The Pushcart Prize* and *The Best American Poetry* and featured on *Poetry Daily*.

NEEDS Welcomes submissions in all genres of creative writing, generously defined. Does not publish book reviews as such, although considers review-like essays that transcend the specific objects of consideration.

THE HUDSON REVIEW

The Hudson Review, Inc., 684 Park Ave., New York NY 10065. **E-mail:** info@hudsonreview.com. **Website:** www.hudsonreview.com. **Contact:** Paula Deitz, editor. Estab. 1948.

○ Send with SASE. Mss sent outside accepted reading period will be returned unread if SASE contains sufficient postage.

NEEDS Reads between September 1-November 30 only. Length: up to 10,000 words.

TIPS "We do not specialize in publishing any particular 'type' of writing; our sole criterion for accepting unsolicited work is literary quality. The best way for you to get an idea of the range of work we publish is to read a current issue. We do not consider simultaneous submissions. Unsolicited mss submitted outside of specified reading times will be returned unread. Do not send submissions via e-mail."

○Ⓢ HUNGER MOUNTAIN

Vermont College of Fine Arts, 36 College St., Montpelier VT 05602. (802)828-8517. **E-mail:** hungermtn@vcfa.edu. **Website:** www.hungermtn.org. Estab. 2002. Accepts high-quality work from unknown, emerging, or successful writers. No genre fiction, drama, or academic articles, please.

○ *Hunger Mountain* is about 200 pages, 7×10, professionally printed, perfect-bound, with full-bleed color artwork on cover. Press run is 1,000; 10,000 visits online monthly. Single copy: $10; subscription: $12/year, $22 for 2 years. Make checks payable to Vermont College of Fine Arts. Member: CLMP. Uses online submissions manager.

NEEDS "We look for work that is beautifully crafted and tells a good story, with characters that are alive and kicking, story lines that stay with us long after we've finished reading, and sentences that slay us with their precision." No genre fiction, meaning science fiction, fantasy, horror, erotic, etc. Length: no more than 10,000 words.

HOW TO CONTACT Submit ms using online submissions manager.

PAYMENT/TERMS Pays $25-100.

TIPS "Mss must be typed, and prose double-spaced. Poets submit at least 3 poems. No multiple genre submissions. Fresh viewpoints and human interest are very important, as is originality. We are committed to publishing an outstanding journal of the arts. Do not send entire novels, mss, or short story collections. Do not send previously published work."

◍ⓒⓈ THE IDAHO REVIEW

Department of English, Boise State University, 1910 University Dr., Boise ID 83725. (208)426-1002. **Fax:** (208)426-4373. **E-mail:** idahoreview@boisestate.edu; mwieland@boisestate.edu. **Website:** idahoreview.org. **Contact:** Mitch Wieland, editor. Estab. 1998.

○ Recent stories reprinted in *The Best American Short Stories*, *The O. Henry Prize Stories*, *The Pushcart Prize*, and *New Stories from the South*.

NEEDS No genre fiction of any type.

HOW TO CONTACT Prefers submissions using online submissions manager but will accept submissions by postal mail.

PAYMENT/TERMS Pays in contributor's copies.

TIPS "We look for strongly crafted work that tells a story that needs to be told. We demand vision and intelligence and mystery in the fiction we publish."

◍ⓒⓈ IDEOMANCER

Canada. **E-mail:** publisher@ideomancer.com. **Website:** www.ideomancer.com. **Contact:** Leah Bobet, publisher. Estab. 2001. "*Ideomancer* publishes speculative fiction and poetry that explores the edges of ideas; stories that subvert, refute, and push the limits. We want unique pieces from authors willing to explore nontraditional narratives and take chances with tone, structure, and execution, balance ideas and character, emotion, and ruthlessness. We also have an eye for more traditional tales told with excellence."

○ Quarterly online magazine. Contains illustrations.

NEEDS Receives 160 mss/month. Accepts 3 mss/issue; 9-12 mss/year. Does not read February, May, August, and November. Ms published within 12 months of acceptance. **Publishes 1-2 new writers/year.** Published Sarah Monette, Ruth Nestvold, Christopher Barzak, Nicole Kornher-Stace, Tobias Buckell, Yoon Ha Lee, and David Kopaska-Merkel. Also publishes book reviews, poetry. *Requests only* to have a novel or collection reviewed should be sent to the reviews editor. Does not want fiction without a speculative element. Length: 7,000 words (maximum). Average length: 4,000 words. Publishes short shorts. Average length of short shorts: 1,000 words.

HOW TO CONTACT Send complete ms with cover letter. Accepts submissions by e-mail only. Include estimated word count.

PAYMENT/TERMS Writers receive 3¢ per word, maximum of $40.

TIPS "Beyond the basics of formatting the fiction as per our guidelines, good writing and intriguing characters and plot, in which the writer brings depth to the tale, make a ms stand out. We receive a number of submissions that showcase good writing but lack the details that make them spring to life for us. Visit our website and read some of our fiction to see if we're a good fit. Read our submission guidelines carefully and use .rtf formatting as requested. We're far more interested in your story than your cover letter, so spend your time polishing that."

⊜⊙ IDIOM 23

Central Queensland University, Idiom 23 Literary Magazine, Rockhampton QLD 4702 Australia. E-mail: idiom@cqu.edu.au. **Website:** www.cqu.edu .au/idiom23. **Contact:** *Idiom 23* editorial board. Estab. 1988. *Idiom 23*, published annually, is "named for the Tropic of Capricorn and is dedicated to developing the literary arts throughout the Central Queensland region. Submissions of original short stories, poems, articles, and b&w drawings and photographs are welcomed by the editorial collective. *Idiom 23* is not limited to a particular viewpoint but, on the contrary, hopes to encourage and publish a broad spectrum of writing. The collective seeks out creative work from community groups with as varied backgrounds as possible."

⊙ ILLYA'S HONEY

E-mail: dpcer09@gmail.com. **Website:** www.illyas honey.com. Estab. 1994. Illya's Honey is the online literary journal of the Dallas Poet's Community. Its main purpose has always been to publish well-crafted poetry using the best electronic means available.

    ⊙   Online magazine published in May and November.

⊙⊙⊛ INDIANA REVIEW

Ballantine Hall 465, 1020 E. Kirkwood, Indiana University, Bloomington IN 47405. (812)855-3439. **E-mail:** inreview@indiana.edu. **Website:** indianare view.org. **Contact:** Katie Moulton, editor. Estab. 1976. "*Indiana Review*, a nonprofit organization run by IU graduate students, is a journal of previously unpublished poetry and fiction. Literary interviews and essays are also considered. We publish innovative fiction, nonfiction, and poetry. We're interested in energy, originality, and careful attention to craft. While we publish many well-known writers, we also welcome new and emerging poets and fiction writers."

NEEDS "We look for daring stories which integrate theme, language, character, and form. We like polished writing, humor, and fiction which has consequence beyond the world of its narrator." No genre fiction. Length: up to 8,000 words.

HOW TO CONTACT Send complete ms. Cover letters should be *brief* and demonstrate specific familiarity with the content of a recent issue of *Indiana Review*. Include SASE.

PAYMENT/TERMS Pays $5/page ($10 minimum), plus 2 contributor's copies

TIPS "We're always looking for nonfiction essays that go beyond merely autobiographical revelation and that utilize sophisticated organization and slightly radical narrative strategies. We want essays that are both lyrical and analytical and in which confession does not mean nostalgia. Read us before you submit. Often reading time is slower in summer and holiday months. Submit work to journals you would proudly subscribe to, then subscribe to a few. Take care to read the latest 2 issues and specifically mention work you identify with and why. Submit work that 'stacks up' with the work we've published. Offers annual poetry, fiction, short short/prose poem prizes. See website for full guidelines."

⊜⊙ INTERPRETER'S HOUSE

Tryst Cottage, 16 Main Street, Monks Kirby, Nr Rugby Warwickshire Cv23 0QX England. **E-mail:** theinterpretershouse@aol.com. **Website:** www .theinterpreter'shouse.com. **Contact:** Martin Malone, editor. Estab. 1996. *The Interpreter's House*, published 3 times/year in February, June, and October, prints short stories and poetry.

NEEDS Length: no more than 2,000 words.

HOW TO CONTACT Submit up to 5 short stories via mail; include SASE.

⊙⊛ THE IOWA REVIEW

308 EPB, The University of Iowa, Iowa City IA 52242. (319)335-0462. **Website:** www.iowareview.org. **Contact:** Harilaos Stecopoulos. Estab. 1970. *The Iowa Review*, published 3 times/year, prints fiction, poetry, essays, reviews, and, occasionally, interviews.

The Iowa Review is 5½×8½, approximately 200 pages, professionally printed, flat-spined, first-grade offset paper, Carolina CS1 10-point cover stock. Receives about 5,000 submissions/year, accepts up to 100. Press run is 2,900; 1,500 distributed to stores. Subscription: $25. Stories, essays, and poems for a general readership interested in contemporary literature. "This magazine uses the help of colleagues and graduate assistants. Its reading period for unsolicited work is September 1-December 1. From January through April, we read entries to our annual Iowa Awards competition. Check our website for further information."

NEEDS "We are open to a range of styles and voices and always hope to be surprised by work we then feel we need." Receives 600 unsolicited mss/month. Accepts 4-6 mss/issue; 12-18 mss/year. Does not read mss January-August. Publishes ms an average of 12-18 months after acceptance. Agented fiction less than 2%. **Publishes some new writers/year.** Recently published work by Jen Fawkes, Chris Offutt, Chinelo Okparanta.

HOW TO CONTACT Send complete ms with cover letter. "Don't bother with queries." SASE for return of ms. SASE required. Responds in 4 months to mss. Accepts mss by snail mail and online submission form at https://iowareview.submittable.com/submit; no e-mail submissions. Simultaneous submissions accepted.

PAYMENT/TERMS Pays $.08 per word ($100 minimum), plus 2 contributor's copies.

TIPS "We publish essays, reviews, novel excerpts, stories, poems, and photography. We have no set guidelines as to content or length but strongly recommend that writers read a sample issue before submitting."

ISLAND

P.O. Box 210, Sandy Bay Tasmania 7006 Australia. (61)(3)6226-2325. **E-mail:** matthew@islandmag.com. **Website:** www.islandmag.com. **Contact:** Matthew Lamb, editor. Estab. 1979. *Island* seeks quality fiction, poetry, and essays. It is "one of Australia's leading literary magazines, tracing the contours of our national and international culture, while still retaining a uniquely Tasmanian perspective."

Only publishes the work of subscribers; you can submit if you are not currently a subscriber, but if your piece is chosen, the subscription will be taken from the fee paid for the piece.

HOW TO CONTACT Submit 1 piece at a time.

PAYMENT/TERMS Pay varies.

ITALIAN AMERICANA

University of Rhode Island, Alan Shawn Feinstein College of Continuing Education, 80 Washington St., Providence RI 02903. **E-mail:** it.americana@yahoo.com. **Website:** www.uri.edu/prov/research/italiana mericana/italianamericana.html. **Contact:** C.B. Albright, editor-in-chief. Estab. 1974. "A semiannual historical and cultural journal devoted to the Italian experience in America. *Italian Americana*, in cooperation with the American Italian Historical Association, is the first and only cultural as well as historical review dedicated to the Italian experience in the New World."

NEEDS Does not want nostalgia. Length: up to 20 pages double-spaced.

HOW TO CONTACT Send complete ms (in triplicate) with SASE and cover letter. Include 3-5 line bio, list of publications.

PAYMENT/TERMS Pays in contributor's copies.

JABBERWOCK REVIEW

Department of English, Mississippi State University, Drawer E, Mississippi State MS 39762. **E-mail:** jab berwockreview@english.msstate.edu. **Website:** www.msstate.edu/org/jabberwock. **Contact:** Becky Hagenston, editor. Estab. 1979. "*Jabberwock Review* is a literary journal published semiannually by students and faculty of Mississippi State University. The journal consists of art, poetry, fiction, and nonfiction from around the world. Funding is provided by the Office of the Provost, the College of Arts and Sciences, the Shackouls Honors College, the Department of English, fundraisers, and subscriptions."

Submissions will be accepted from August 15-October 20 and January 15-March 15.

NEEDS No science fiction, romance.

HOW TO CONTACT Submit no more than 1 story at a time.

PAYMENT/TERMS Pays in contributor's copies.

TIPS "It might take a few months to get a response from us, but your ms will be read with care. Our editors enjoy reading submissions (really!) and will remember writers who are persistent and committed to getting a story 'right' through revision."

⑤ JACK AND JILL

U.S. Kids, 1100 Waterway Blvd., Indianapolis IN 46206-0567. (317)634-1100. **E-mail:** editor@saturdayeveningpost.com. **Website:** www.jackandjillmag.org. Estab. 1938.

Ⓞ "Please do not send artwork. We prefer to work with professional illustrators of our own choosing."

NEEDS Submit complete ms via postal mail; no e-mail submissions. "The tone of the stories should be fun and engaging. Stories should hook readers right from the get-go and pull them through the story. Humor is very important! Dialogue should be witty instead of just furthering the plot. The story should convey some kind of positive message. Possible themes could include self-reliance, being kind to others, appreciating other cultures, and so on. There are a million positive messages, so get creative! Kids can see preachy coming from a mile away, though, so please focus on telling a good story over teaching a lesson. The message—if there is one—should come organically from the story and not feel tacked on." Length: 600-800 words.

PAYMENT/TERMS Pays 30¢/word.

TIPS "We are constantly looking for new writers who can tell good stories with interesting slants—stories that are not full of outdated and timeworn expressions. We like to see stories about kids who are smart and capable but not sarcastic or smug. Problem-solving skills, personal responsibility, and integrity are good topics for us. Obtain current issues of the magazine and study them to determine our present needs and editorial style."

Ⓞ JEWISH CURRENTS

P.O. Box 111, Accord NY 12404. (845)626-2427. **E-mail:** editor@jewishcurrents.org. **Website:** www.jewishcurrents.org. Estab. 1946. *Jewish Currents*, published 4 times/year, is a progressive Jewish bimonthly magazine that carries on the insurgent tradition of the Jewish left through independent journalism, political commentary, and a 'countercultural' approach to Jewish arts and literature.

Ⓞ *Jewish Currents* is 80 pages, magazine-sized, offset printed, saddle-stapled with a full-color arts section, "Jcultcha & Funny Pages."

HOW TO CONTACT Send complete ms with cover letter. "Writers should include brief biographical information, especially their publishing histories."

PAYMENT/TERMS Pays contributor's copies.

Ⓞ J JOURNAL: NEW WRITING ON JUSTICE

524 West 59th St., 7th Floor, New York NY 10019. (212) 327-8697. **E-mail:** jjournal@jjay.cuny.edu. **Website:** www.jjournal.org. **Contact:** Adam Berlin and Jeffrey Heiman, editors. Estab. 2008. "*J Journal* publishes literary fiction, creative nonfiction, and poetry on the justice theme. Subjects often include crime, criminal justice, law, law enforcement, and prison writing. While the theme is specific, it need not dominate the work. We're interested in questions of justice from all perspectives. Tangential connections to justice are often better than direct."

Ⓞ Literary magazine/journal: 6×9; 120 pages; 60 lb. paper; 80 lb. cover.

NEEDS Receives 100 mss/month. Accepts 20 mss/issue; 40 mss/year. Ms published 6 months after acceptance. Length: 750-6,000 words (maximum). Average length: 4,000 words.

HOW TO CONTACT Send complete ms with cover letter. Include estimated word count, brief bio, list of publications. Considers simultaneous submissions.

PAYMENT/TERMS Writers receive 2 contributor's copies. Additional copies $10.

TIPS "We're looking for literary fiction/memoir/personal narrative poetry with a connection, direct or tangential, to the theme of justice."

Ⓞ⑤ THE JOURNAL

The Ohio State University, 164 W. 17th Ave., Columbus OH 43210. (614)292-6065. **Fax:** (614)292-7816. **E-mail:** managingeditor@thejournalmag.org. **Website:** thejournalmag.org. Estab. 1973. "We are interested in quality fiction, poetry, nonfiction, art, and reviews of new books of poetry, fiction, and nonfiction. We impose no restrictions on category, type, or length of submission for fiction, poetry, and nonfiction. We are happy to consider long stories and self-contained excerpts of novels. Please double-space all prose submissions. Please send 3-5 poems in 1 submission. We accept online submissions only and will not respond to mailed submissions."

Ⓞ "We're open to all forms; we tend to favor work that gives evidence of a mature and sophisticated sense of the language."

NEEDS No romance, science fiction, or religious/devotional.

HOW TO CONTACT Does not accept queries. Send full ms via online submission system at thejournal.submittable.com.

TIPS "Mss are rejected because of lack of understanding of the short story form, shallow plots, undeveloped characters. Cure: Read as much well-written fiction as possible. Our readers prefer 'psychological' fiction rather than stories with intricate plots. Take care to present a clean, well-typed submission."

◯ KAIMANA: LITERARY ARTS HAWAI'I

Hawaii Literary Arts Council, P.O. Box 11213, Honolulu HI 96828. **E-mail:** reimersa001@hawaii.rr.com. **Website:** www.hawaii.edu/hlac. Estab. 1974. *Kaimana: Literary Arts Hawaii*, published annually, is the magazine of the Hawaii Literary Arts Council. Wants poems with "some Pacific reference—Asia, Polynesia, Hawaii—but not exclusively." Has published poetry by Kathryn Takara, Howard Nemerov, Anne Waldman, Reuel Denney, Haunani-Kay Trask, and Simon Perchik.

◖ *Kaimana* is 64-76 pages, 7.5×10, saddle-stapled, with high-quality printing. Press run is 1,000. "Poets published in Kaimana have received the Pushcart Prize, the Hawaii Award for Literature, the Stefan Baciu Award, the Cades Award, and the John Unterecker Award."

HOW TO CONTACT Submit ms with SASE. No e-mail submissions. Cover letter is preferred.

PAYMENT/TERMS Pays 2 contributor's copies.

TIPS "Hawaii gets a lot of 'travelling regionalists,' visiting writers with inevitably superficial observations. We also get superb visiting observers who are careful craftsmen. *Kaimana* is interested in the latter as a complement to our own best Hawaii writers."

◖◯◉ KALEIDOSCOPE

Kaleidoscope, 701 S. Main St., Akron OH 44311-1019. (330)762-9755. **Fax:** (330)762-0912. **E-mail:** kaleidoscope@udsakron.org. **Website:** www.kaleidoscopeonline.org. **Contact:** Gail Willmott, editor-in-chief. Estab. 1979. "*Kaleidoscope* magazine creatively focuses on the experiences of disability through literature and the fine arts. Unique to the field of disability studies, this award-winning publication expresses the diversity of the disablity experience from a variety of perspectives including: individuals, families, friends, caregivers, and health-care professionals, among others."

◖ *Kaleidoscope* has received awards from the Great Lakes Awards Competition and Ohio Public Images; received the Ohioana Award of Editorial Excellence.

NEEDS Short stories with a well-crafted plot and engaging characters. No fiction that is stereotypical, patronizing, sentimental, erotic, or maudlin. No romance, religious, or dogmatic fiction; no children's literature. Length: no more than 5,000 words. All rights revert to author upon publication.

HOW TO CONTACT Submit complete ms by website or e-mail. Include cover letter.

PAYMENT/TERMS Pays $10-100.

TIPS "The material chosen for *Kaleidoscope* challenges and overcomes stereotypical, patronizing, and sentimental attitudes about disability. We accept the work of writers with and without disabilities, however the work of a writer without a disability must focus on some aspect of disability. The criteria for good writing apply: effective technique, thought-provoking subject matter, and in general, a mature grasp of the art of storytelling. Writers should avoid using offensive language and always put the person before the disability."

◖◉ THE KELSEY REVIEW

Liberal Arts Division, Mercer County Community College, P.O. Box 17202, Trenton NJ 08690. **E-mail:** kelsey.review@mccc.edu. **Website:** www.mccc.edu/community_kelsey-review.shtml. **Contact:** Ed Carmien. Estab. 1988. *The Kelsey Review*, published annually in September by Mercer County Community College, serves as "an outlet for literary talent of people living and working in Mercer County, New Jersey only."

◖ *The Kelsey Review* is about 90 glossy pages, 7×11, with paper cover, b&w art. Receives 100+ submissions/year; accepts 10. Press run is 2,000; all distributed free to contributors, area libraries, bookstores, and schools. Has published poetry by Vida Chu, Carolyn Foote Edelmann, and Mary Mallery.

NEEDS Has no specifications as to form, subject matter, or style. Length: 4,000 word maximum.

HOW TO CONTACT Deadline is May 15. Submissions are limited to people who live, work, or give literary readings in Mercer County, New Jersey. Decisions on which material will be published are made by the 4-person editorial board in June and July. Contributors will be notified of submission acceptance determination(s) by the second week of August.

PAYMENT/TERMS Pays 3 contributor's copies.

TIPS "See *The Kelsey Review* website for current guidelines. Note: We accept submissions from the Mercer County, New Jersey, area only."

○$ KENTUCKY MONTHLY

P.O. Box 559, Frankfort KY 40602-0559. (502)227-0053; (888)329-0053. **Fax:** (502)227-5009. **E-mail:** kymonthly@kentuckymonthly.com; steve@kentuckymonthly.com. **Website:** www.kentuckymonthly.com. **Contact:** Stephen Vest, editor. Estab. 1998. "We publish stories about Kentucky and by Kentuckians, including stories written by those who live elsewhere."

NEEDS Adventure, historical, mainstream, novel excerpts. Publishes ms 4-10 months after acceptance. Length: 1,000-5,000 words.

HOW TO CONTACT Query with published clips. Accepts submissions by e-mail. Responds in 1-3 months to queries; 1 month to mss. Accepts simultaneous submissions. Writer's guidelines online. Query with published clips.

PAYMENT/TERMS Pays $50-100. Pays within 3 months of publication. Acquires first North American serial rights. Pays $50-100.

TIPS "Please read the magazine to get the flavor of what we're publishing each month. We accept articles via e-mail. Approximately 70% of articles are assigned."

○○$ THE KENYON REVIEW

Finn House, 102 W. Wiggin, Gambier OH 43022. (740)427-5208. **Fax:** (740)427-5417. **E-mail:** kenyonreview@kenyon.edu. **Website:** www.kenyonreview.org. **Contact:** Marlene Landefeld. Estab. 1939. "An international journal of literature, culture, and the arts, dedicated to an inclusive representation of the best in new writing (fiction, poetry, essays, interviews, criticism) from established and emerging writers."

○   *The Kenyon Review* is 180 pages, digest-sized, flat-spined. Receives about 7,000 submissions/ year. Also now publishes *KR Online*, a separate and complementary literary magazine.

NEEDS Receives 800 unsolicited mss/month. Unsolicited mss read September 15-January 15 only. Recently published work by Alice Hoffman, Beth Ann Fennelly, Romulus Linney, John Koethe, Albert Goldbarth, Erin McGraw. Length: 3-15 typeset pages preferred.

HOW TO CONTACT Only accepts mss via online submissions program; visit website for instructions. Do not submit via e-mail or snail mail.

PAYMENT/TERMS Pays $30/page.

TIPS "We no longer accept mailed or e-mailed submissions. Work will be read only if it is submitted through our online program on our website. Reading period is September 15-January 15. We look for strong voice, unusual perspective, and power in the writing."

○○$ LADYBUG

700 E. Lake St., Suite 800, Chicago IL 60601. **E-mail:** ladybug@ladybugmagkids.com. **Website:** www.cricketmag.com/ladybug; ladybugmagkids.com. **Contact:** Submissions editor. Estab. 1990. *LADYBUG Magazine* is an imaginative magazine with art and literature for young children (ages 3-6). Publishes 9 issues per year.

NEEDS Length: 800 words maximum.

HOW TO CONTACT Submit complete ms, include SASE.

PAYMENT/TERMS Pays up to 25¢/word.

○ LA KANCERKLINIKO

162 rue Paradis, P.O. Box 174, 13444 Marseille Cantini Cedex France. (33)2-48-61-81-98. **Fax:** (33)2-48-61-81-98. **E-mail:** lseptier@hotmail.com. **Contact:** Laurent Septier. An Esperanto magazine that appears 4 times annually. Each issue contains 32 pages. *La Kancerkliniko* is a political and cultural magazine. Accepts disk submissions.

○   Publishes 2-3 new writers/year. Has published work by Mao Zifu, Manuel de Seabra, Peter Brown, and Aldo de'Giorgi.

PAYMENT/TERMS Pays in contributor's copies.

○ LAKE EFFECT: A JOURNAL OF THE LITERARY ARTS

School of Humanities & Social Sciences, Penn State Erie, 4951 College Dr., Erie PA 16563-1501. (814)898-6281. **Fax:** (814)898-6032. **E-mail:** gol1@psu.edu. **Website:** www.pserie.psu.edu/lakeeffect. **Contact:** George Looney, editor-in-chief. Estab. 1978. *Lake Effect* is a publication of the School of Humanities and Social Sciences at Penn State Erie, The Behrend College.

NEEDS "*Lake Effect* is looking for stories that emerge from character and language as much as from plot. *Lake Effect* does not, in general, publish genre fiction, but literary fiction. *Lake Effect* seeks work from both established and new and emerging writers." Length: up to 15 pages, if longer, query first.

HOW TO CONTACT Submit complete ms with SASE.

⊖ LAKE SUPERIOR MAGAZINE

Lake Superior Port Cities, Inc., P.O. Box 16417, Duluth MN 55816-0417. (218)722-5002. **Fax:** (218)722-4096. **E-mail:** edit@lakesuperior.com. **Website:** www.lake superior.com. **Contact:** Konnie LeMay, editor. Estab. 1979.

NEEDS Ethnic, historic, humorous, mainstream, novel excerpts, slice-of-life vignettes, ghost stories. Must be targeted regionally. Wants stories that are Lake Superior related. Rarely uses fiction stories. Length: 300-2,500 words.

HOW TO CONTACT Query with published clips.

PAYMENT/TERMS Pays $50-125.

TIPS "Well-researched queries are attended to. We actively seek queries from writers in Lake Superior communities. We prefer mss to queries. Provide enough information on why the subject is important to the region and our readers, or why and how something is unique. We want details. The writer must have a thorough knowledge of the subject and how it relates to our region. We prefer a fresh, unused approach to the subject which provides the reader with an emotional involvement. Almost all of our articles feature quality photography, color or b&w. It is a prerequisite of all nonfiction. All submissions should include a *short* biography of author/photographer; mug shot sometimes used. Blanket submissions need not apply."

◐ LANDFALL: NEW ZEALAND ARTS AND LETTERS

Otago University Press, P.O. Box 56, Dunedin New Zealand. (64)(3)479-8807. **Fax:** (64)(3)479-8385. **E-mail:** landfall@otago.ac.nz. **Website:** www.otago .ac.nz/press/landfall. Estab. 1947. *Landfall: New Zealand Arts and Letters* contains literary fiction and essays, poetry, extracts from work in progress, commentary on New Zealand arts and culture, work by visual artists including photographers and reviews of local books. (*Landfall* does not accept unsolicited reviews.)

NEEDS Length: up to 5,000 words.

HOW TO CONTACT Submit up to 3 pieces at a time. Prefers e-mail submissions. Include cover letter with contact info and bio of about 30 words.

◐◑ LA PETITE ZINE

E-mail: lapetitezine@gmail.com. **Website:** www .lapetitezine.org. **Contact:** Melissa Broder, editor-in-chief; D.W. Lichtenberg, managing editor. Estab. 1999. *La Petite Zine* is an online literary magazine that cur-

rently publishes fierce poetry and petite prose pieces. *LPZ* is not affiliated with a particular literary school or movement; we like what we like. Above all else, *LPZ* seeks to be un-boring, a panacea for your emotional hangover. Has published work by Anne Boyer, Arielle Greenberg, Johannes Goransson, Joyelle McSweeney, Joshua Marie Wilkinson, and Jonah Winter. Receives about 3,000 poems/year, accepts about 150 (5%). *La Petite Zine*'s home page "indexes all authors for each specific issue and offers links to past issues, as well as information about the journal, its interests and editors, and links to other sites. Art and graphics are supplied by Web del Sol. Additionally we publish graphic poems, excerpts from graphic novels, and the like."

○ Work published in *La Petite Zine* has appeared in *The Best American Poetry*. "Any deviation from our guidelines will result in the disposal of your submission." Member: CLMP.

NEEDS Length: up to 1,000 words.

HOW TO CONTACT Only accepts submissions using submission manager on website. Cover letter is required. Include brief bio listing previous publications. Wait 4 months before submitting again. Reads year-round.

○ THE LAUREL REVIEW

Northwest Missouri State University, Department of English, Maryville MO 64468. (660)562-1739. **Website:** catpages.nwmissouri.edu/m/tlr. **Contact:** John Gallaher, Richard Sonnenmoser, or Luke Rolfes. Estab. 1960. "We publish poetry and fiction of high quality, from the traditional to the avant-garde. We are eclectic, open, and flexible. Good writing is all we seek."

○ Biannual magazine: 6×9; 124-128 pages; quality paper.

NEEDS Literary, contemporary. "No genre or politically polemical fiction." Receives 120 unsolicited mss/month. Accepts 3-5 mss/issue; 6-10 mss/year. Reading period: September 1-May 1. **Publishes 1-2 new writers/year.** Recently published work by Albert Goldbarth, Zachary Schomburg, Craig Morgan Teicher, and Ethan Paquin. Also publishes literary essays, poetry.

TIPS "Nothing really matters to us except our perception that the story presents something powerfully felt by the writer and communicated intensely to a serious reader. (We believe, incidentally, that comedy is just as serious a matter as tragedy, and we don't mind a bit if something makes us laugh out loud; we get too little that makes us laugh, in fact.) We try to reply promptly, though we don't always manage that. In short, we want good poems and good stories. We hope to be able to recognize them, and we print what we believe to the best work submitted."

⊚⊛ LEADING EDGE

4087 JKB, Provo UT 84602. **E-mail:** editor@lead ingedgemagazine.com; fiction@leadingedgemaga zine.com; art@leadingedgemagazine.com. **Website:** www.leadingedgemagazine.com. **Contact:** Diane Cardon, senior editor. Estab. 1981. "We strive to encourage developing and established talent and provide high-quality speculative fiction to our readers." Does not accept mss with sex, excessive violence, or profanity. "*Leading Edge* is a magazine dedicated to new and upcoming talent in the fields of science fiction and fantasy."

◐ Accepts unsolicited submissions.

NEEDS Length: 15,000 words maximum.

HOW TO CONTACT Send complete ms with cover letter and SASE. Include estimated word count.

PAYMENT/TERMS Pays 1¢/word; $10 minimum.

TIPS "Buy a sample issue to know what is currently selling in our magazine. Also, make sure to follow the writer's guidelines when submitting."

◑ THE LEDGE MAGAZINE

40 Maple Ave., Bellport NY 11713. (631)286-5252. **E-mail:** info@theledgemagazine.com. **Website:** www .theledgemagazine.com. **Contact:** Tim Monaghan, editor-in-chief and publisher. Estab. 1988. "*The Ledge Magazine* publishes cutting-edge contemporary fiction by emerging and established writers." Annual. Receives 120 mss/month. Accepts 9 mss/issue. Ms published 6 months after acceptance. Published Jacob M. Appel, Moira Egan, Rebecca Foust, Mary Makofske, and Cindy Hunter Morgan. Also publishes poetry. Rarely comments on/critiques rejected mss. Send complete ms with cover letter. Include estimated word count, brief bio. Send SASE (or IRC) for return of ms. Sample copy available for $10. Subscription: $22 (2 issues), $38 (4 issues). Guidelines available for SASE. Writers receive 1 contributor's copy. Additional copies $6. Sends galleys to author. Publication is copyrighted.

◑ Does not accept e-mail submissions.

NEEDS "We are open to all styles and schools of writing. Excellence is our only criterion." Length: 2,500-7,500 words.

HOW TO CONTACT Submit complete ms with SASE.

PAYMENT/TERMS Pays in contributor's copies.

TIPS "We seek compelling stories that employ innovative language and complex characterization. We especially enjoy poignant stories with a sense of purpose. We dislike careless or hackneyed writing."

◐ LE FORUM

University of Maine, Franco American Center, Orono ME 04469-5719. (207)581-3764. **Fax:** (207)581-1455. **E-mail:** lisa_michaud@umit.maine.edu. **Website:** Le Forum: umaine.edu/francoamerican/le-forum; Oral History: francoamericanarchives.org; Franco-American Library: francoamerican.org. **Contact:** Lisa Michaud, managing editor. Estab. 1972. "We will consider any type of short fiction, poetry, and critical essays having to do with Franco-American experience. They must be of good quality in French or English. We are also looking for Canadian writers with French-North American experiences."

HOW TO CONTACT Include SASE.

PAYMENT/TERMS Pays 3 contributor's copies.

TIPS "Write honestly. Start with a strongly felt personal Franco-American experience. If you make us feel what you have felt, we will publish it. We stress that this publication deals specifically with the Franco-American experience."

◐ LEFT CURVE

P.O. Box 472, Oakland CA 94604-0472. (510)763-7193. **E-mail:** editor@leftcurve.org. **Website:** www .leftcurve.org. **Contact:** Csaba Polony, editor. Estab. 1974. "*Left Curve* is an artist-produced journal addressing the problem(s) of cultural forms emerging from the crises of modernity that strive to be independent from the control of dominant institutions, based on the recognition of the destructiveness of commodity (capitalist) systems to all life." Published irregularly.

◐ Magazine: 8.5×11; 144 pages; 60 lb. paper; 100 pt. C1S gloss lay-flat lamination cover; illustrations; photos. Receives 50 unsolicited mss/month. Accepts 3-4 mss/issue. Has published work by Mike Standaert, Ilan Pappe, Terrence Cannon, John Gist.

NEEDS "No topical satire, religion-based pieces, melodrama. We publish critical, open, social/political-conscious writing." Length: 500-5,000 words; average length: 1,200 words. Also publishes short shorts.

HOW TO CONTACT Send complete ms with cover letter. Include "statement of writer's intent, brief bio, and reason for submitting to *Left Curve*. We accept electronic submissions and hard copy, though for accepted work we request e-mail copy, either in body of text or as attachments. For accepted longer work, we prefer submission of final draft in digital form via disk or e-mail."

PAYMENT/TERMS Pays in contributor's copies.

TIPS "We look for continuity, adequate descriptive passages, endings that are not simply abandoned (in both meanings). Dig deep; no superficial personalisms, no corny satire. Be honest, realistic, and gouge out the truth you wish to say. Understand yourself and the world. Have writing be a means to achieve or realize what is real."

○🌐💲 LIGUORIAN

One Liguori Dr., Liguori MO 63057. (636)223-1538. **Fax:** (636)223-1595. **E-mail:** liguorianeditor@liguori.org. **Website:** www.liguorian.org. **Contact:** Elizabeth Herzing, managing editor. Estab. 1913. "Our purpose is to lead our readers to a fuller Christian life by helping them better understand the teachings of the gospel and the church, and by illustrating how these teachings apply to life and the problems confronting them as members of families, the church, and society."

NEEDS Length: 1,500-2,200 words.

HOW TO CONTACT Send complete ms.

PAYMENT/TERMS Pays 12-15¢/word and 5 contributor's copies.

TIPS "First read several issues containing short stories. We look for originality and creative input in each story we read. Consideration requires the author studies the target market and presents a carefully polished ms. We publish 1 fiction story per issue. Compare this with the 25 or more we receive over the transom each month. We believe fiction is a highly effective mode for transmitting the Christian message; however, many fiction pieces are written without a specific goal or thrust—an interesting incident that goes nowhere is not a story."

LILITH MAGAZINE: INDEPENDENT, JEWISH & FRANKLY FEMINIST

250 W. 57th St., Suite 2432, New York NY 10107. (212)757-0818. **Fax:** (212)757-5705. **E-mail:** info@lilith.org; naomi@lilith.org. **Website:** www.lilith.org. **Contact:** Susan Weidman Schneider, editor-in-chief; Naomi Danis, managing editor. Estab. 1976. *Lilith Magazine: Independent, Jewish & Frankly Feminist*, published quarterly, has published poetry by Irena Klepfisz, Lyn Lifshin, Marcia Falk, Adrienne Rich, and Muriel Rukeyser.

○ *Lilith Magazine* is 48 pages, magazine-sized, with glossy color cover. Press run is about 10,000 (about 6,000 subscribers). Subscription: $26/year.

NEEDS Length: no more than 3,000 words.

HOW TO CONTACT Use online submissions manager or submit by postal mail. For all submissions: Make sure name and contact information appear on each page of mss. Include a short bio (1-2 sentences), written in third person.

TIPS "Read a copy of the publication before you submit your work. Please be patient."

◑ THE LISTENING EYE

Kent State University Geauga Campus, 14111 Claridon-Troy Rd., Burton OH 44021. (440)286-3840. **E-mail:** grace_butcher@msn.com. **Contact:** Grace Butcher, editor. Estab. 1970. "We look for powerful, unusual imagery, content, and plot in our short stories. In poetry, we look for tight lines that don't sound like prose; unexpected images or juxtapositions; the unusual use of language; noticeable relationships of sounds; a twist in viewpoint; an ordinary idea in extraordinary language; an amazing and complex idea simply stated; play on words and with words; an obvious love of language. Poets need to read the Big 3—Cummings, Thomas, Hopkins—to see the limits to which language can be taken. Then read the Big 2—Dickinson to see how simultaneously tight, terse, and universal a poem can be, and Whitman to see how sprawling, cosmic, and personal. Then read everything you can find that's being published in literary magazines today, and see how your work compares to all of the above."

○ Magazine: 5½×8½; 60 pages; photographs. "We publish the occasional very short stories (750 words/3 pages double-spaced) in any subject and any style, but the language must be strong, unusual, free from cliché and vagueness. We are a shoestring operation from a small campus, but we publish high-quality work."

NEEDS Literary fiction. "Pretty much anything will be considered except porn." Reads mss January 1-April 15 only. Publishes ms 3-4 months after acceptance. Recently published work by Elizabeth

Scott, Sam Ruddick, H.E. Wright. Publishes short shorts. Also publishes poetry. Sometimes comments on rejected mss.

◐◐ LITERAL LATTE

200 E. 10th St., Suite 240, New York NY 10003. (212)260-5532. **E-mail:** litlatte@aol.com. **Website:** www.literal-latte.com. **Contact:** Jenine Gordon Bockman. Estab. 1994. Bimonthly online publication with an annual print anthology featuring the best of the website. "We want great writing in all styles and subjects. A feast is made of a variety of flavors."

NEEDS Length: no more than 10,000 words.

HOW TO CONTACT Send complete ms.

PAYMENT/TERMS Pays minimum of anthology copies and maximum of $1,000.

TIPS "Keeping free thought free and challenging entertainment are 2 things that are not mutually exclusive. Words make a ms stand out—words beautifully woven together in striking and memorable patterns."

◐ LITERARY JUICE

Notre Dame IN 46545. **E-mail:** info@literaryjuice .com. **E-mail:** srajan@literaryjuice.com. **Website:** www.literaryjuice.com. **Contact:** Sara Rajan, editor-in-chief; Andrea O'Connor and Dinesh Rajan, managing editors. Bimonthly online literary magazine. "*Literary Juice* publishes original works of short fiction, flash fiction, and poetry. We do not publish nonfiction material, essays, or interviews, nor do we accept previously published works."

NEEDS "We do not publish works with intense sexual content." Length: 100-2,500 words.

HOW TO CONTACT Submit complete ms.

TIPS "It is crucial that writers read our submission guidelines, which can be found on our website. Most important, send us your very best writing. We are looking for works that are not only thought provoking but venture into unconventional territory as well. For instance, avoid sending mainstream stories and poems (stories about wizards or vampires fall into this category). Instead take the reader to a new realm that has yet to be explored."

◐◐◎ LITERARY MAMA

E-mail: lminfo@literarymama.com. **Website:** www. literarymama.com. **Contact:** Caroline M. Grant, editor-in-chief. Estab. 2003. Website offering writing about the complexities and many faces of motherhood in a variety of genres. "Departments include columns,

creative nonfiction, fiction, Literary Reflections, poetry, and Profiles & Reviews. We are interested in reading pieces that are long, complex, ambiguous, deep, raw, irreverent, ironic, andbody conscious."

TIPS "We seek top-notch creative writing. We also look for quality literary criticism about mother-centric literature and profiles of mother writers. We publish writing with fresh voices, superior craft, and vivid imagery. Please send submission (copied into e-mail) to appropriate departmental editors. Include a brief cover letter. We tend to like stark revelation (pathos, humor, and joy); clarity; concrete details; strong narrative development; ambiguity; thoughtfulness; delicacy; irreverence; lyricism; sincerity; the elegant. We need the submissions 3 months before the following months: October (Desiring Motherhood); May (Mother's Day Month); and June (Father's Day Month)."

◐◐ THE LITERARY REVIEW

285 Madison Ave., Madison NJ 07940. (973)443-8564. **Fax:** (973)443-8364. **E-mail:** info@theliteraryreview .org. **Website:** www.theliteraryreview.org. **Contact:** Minna Proctor, editor. Estab. 1957.

◐ Work published in *The Literary Review* has been included in *Editor's Choice, Best American Short Stories,* and *Pushcart Prize* anthologies. Uses online submissions manager.

NEEDS Wants works of high literary quality only. Does not want to see "overused subject matter or pat resolutions to conflicts."

HOW TO CONTACT Submit electronically only. Does not accept paper submissions.

PAYMENT/TERMS Pays 2 contributor's copies and a one-year subscription.

TIPS "We want original dramatic situations with complex moral and intellectual resonance and vivid prose. We don't want versions of familiar plots and relationships. Too much of what we are seeing today is openly derivative in subject, plot, and prose style. We pride ourselves on spotting new writers with fresh insight and approach."

◐◐ THE LONDON MAGAZINE

11 Queen's Gate, London SW7 5ELU England. +44 (0)20 7584 5977. **E-mail:** admin@thelondonmaga zine.org. **E-mail:** submissions@thelondonmagazine .org. **Website:** www.thelondonmagazine.org. **Contact:** Steven O'Brien, editor. Estab. 1732. "We publish literary writing of the highest quality. We look for po-

etry and short fiction that startles and entertains us. Reviews, essays, memoir pieces, and features should be erudite, lucid, and incisive. We are obviously interested in writing that has a London focus, but not exclusively so, since London is a world city with international concerns."

NEEDS "Short fiction should address mature and sophisticated themes. Moreover, it should have an elegance of style, structure and characterization. We do not normally publish science fiction or fantasy writing, or erotica." Length: no more than 4,000 words.

HOW TO CONTACT Send complete ms. Submit via e-mail, both as an attachment and in the body of the e-mail. Enclose SASE if submitting through postal mail.

TIPS "Please look at *The London Magazine* before you submit work, so that you can see the type of material we publish."

LONG LIFE

Longevity through Technology, The Immortalist Society, 1437 Pineapple Ave., Melbourne FL 32935. **E-mail:** porter@kih.net. **Website:** www.cryonics.org/resources/long-life-magazine. **Contact:** York Porter, executive editor. Estab. 1968. "*Long Life* magazine is a publication for people who are particularly interested in cryonic suspension: the theory, practice, legal problems, etc., associated with being frozen when you die in the hope of eventual restoration to life and health. Many people who receive the publication have relatives who have undergone cryonic preparation or have made such arrangements for themselves or are seriously considering this option. Readers are also interested in other aspects of life extension such as anti-aging research and food supplements that may slow aging. Articles we publish include speculation on what the future will be like; problems of living in a future world; and science in general, particularly as it may apply to cryonics and life extension."

NEEDS "We occasionally publish short fiction, but cryonics and life extension should be essential to the story. We are not interested in horror, in stories where the future is portrayed as gloom and doom, end-of-the-world stories, or those with an inspirational theme." Length: up to 2,500 words.

PAYMENT/TERMS Pays 1 contributor's copy.

TIPS "We are a small magazine but with a highly intelligent and educated readership which is socially and economically diverse. We currently don't pay for material but are seeking new authors and pro-vide contributors with copies of the magazine with the contributor's published works. Look over a copy of *Long Life*, or talk with the editor to get the tone of the publication. There is an excellent chance that your ms will be accepted if it is well written and 'on theme.' Pictures to accompany the article are always welcome, and we like to publish photos of the authors with their first ms."

◯ THE LONG STORY

18 Eaton St., Lawrence MA 01843. (978)686-7638. **E-mail:** rpburnham@mac.com. **Website:** www.longstorylitmag.com. **Contact:** R.P. Burnham. Estab. 1983. For serious, educated, literary people. We publish high literary quality of any kind but especially look for stories that have difficulty getting published elsewhere—committed fiction, working-class settings, left-wing themes, etc."

◖ Annual magazine: 5½×8½; 160 pages; 60 lb. cover stock; illustrations (b&w graphics). Receives 25-35 unsolicited mss/month. Accepts 6-7 mss/issue. Publishes 90% new writers/year.

NEEDS No science fiction, adventure, romance, etc. Length: 8,000-20,000 words; average length: 8,000-12,000 words.

HOW TO CONTACT Include SASE.

PAYMENT/TERMS Pays 2 contributor's copies; $5 charge for extras.

TIPS "Read us first and make sure submitted material is the kind we're interested in. Send clear, legible mss. We're not interested in commercial success; rather we want to provide a place for long stories, the most difficult literary form to publish in our country."

⊕ LOST LAKE FOLK OPERA

Shipwreckt Books Publishing Company, 309 W. Stevens Ave., Rushford MN 55971. **E-mail:** contact@shipwrecktbooks.com. **Website:** www.shipwrecktbooks.com. **Contact:** Tom Driscoll, managing editor. Estab. 2013. *Lost Lake Folk Opera* magazine is the arts heartbeat and journalistic pulse of rural Mid-America. Currently accepting submissions of critical journalism, short fiction, poetry, and graphic art. Published 3 times, annually.

NEEDS Length: 250-3,500 words.

HOW TO CONTACT Query with sample.

PAYMENT/TERMS Does not offer payment.

TIPS "Send clean copies of your work. When in doubt, edit and cut."

LOUISIANA LITERATURE

SLU Box 10792, Southeastern Louisiana University, Hammond LA 70402. **E-mail:** lalit@selu.edu. **Website:** www.louisianaliterature.org. **Contact:** Jack B. Bedell, editor. Estab. 1984. Semiannual. "Essays should be about Louisiana material; preference is given to fiction and poetry with Louisiana and Southern themes, but creative work can be set anywhere."

Magazine: 6×9; 150 pages; 70 lb. paper; card cover; illustrations. Receives 100 unsolicited mss/month. May not read mss June-July. Publishes 4 new writers/year. Publishes theme issues. Has published work by Anthony Bukowski, Aaron Gwyn, Robert Phillips, R.T. Smith.

NEEDS Reviews fiction. "No sloppy, ungrammatical mss." Length: 1,000-6,000 words; average length: 3,500 words.

HOW TO CONTACT Submit ms via online submissions manager.

PAYMENT/TERMS Pays 2 contributor's copies.

TIPS "Cut out everything that is not a functioning part of the story. Make sure your ms is professionally presented. Use relevant, specific detail in every scene. We love detail, local color, voice, and craft. Any professional ms stands out."

THE LOUISIANA REVIEW

Division of Liberal Arts, Louisiana State University Eunice, P.O. Box 1129, Eunice LA 70535. (337)550-1315. **E-mail:** bfonteno@lsue.edu. **Website:** web.lsue.edu/la-review. **Contact:** Dr. Billy Fontenot, fiction editor. Estab. 1999. *The Louisiana Review*, published annually during the fall or spring semester, offers "Louisiana poets, writers, and artists a place to showcase their most beautiful pieces. Others may submit Louisiana- or Southern-related poetry, stories, and b&w art, as well as interviews with Louisiana writers. We want to publish the highest-quality poetry, fiction, and art." Wants "strong imagery, metaphor, and evidence of craft."

The Louisiana Review is 100 pages, digest-sized, professionally printed, perfect-bound. Press run is 300-600. Single copy: $5

NEEDS Receives 25 unsolicited mss/month. Accepts 5-7 mss/issue. Reads year-round. Has published work by Ronald Frame, Tom Bonner, Laura Cario, Sheryl St. Germaine. Also publishes short shorts. Length: up to 9,000 words; average length: 2,000 words.

HOW TO CONTACT Send SASE for return of ms. Accepts multiple submissions.

PAYMENT/TERMS Pays 1 contributor's copy.

TIPS "We do like to have fiction play out visually as a film would, rather than static and undramatized. Louisiana or Gulf Coast settings and themes preferred."

LULLWATER REVIEW

Lullwater Review, P.O. Box 122036, Atlanta GA 30322. **E-mail:** lullwater@lullwaterreview.com. **Website:** www.lullwaterreview.com. **Contact:** Laura Kochman, editor-in-chief; Tonia Davis, managing editor. Estab. 1990. "We're a small, student-run literary magazine published out of Emory University in Atlanta, GA, with two issues yearly—once in the fall and once in the spring. You can find us in the *Index of American Periodical Verse*, the *American Humanities Index*, and as a member of the Council of Literary Magazines and Presses. We welcome work that brings a fresh perspective, whether through language or the visual arts."

NEEDS Recently published work by Greg Jenkins, Thomas Juvik, Jimmy Gleacher, Carla Vissers, and Judith Sudnolt. No romance or science fiction, please. 5,000 words maximum.

HOW TO CONTACT Send complete ms via e-mail. *Does not accept postal mail submissions.*

PAYMENT/TERMS Pays 3 contributor's copies.

TIPS "We at the *Lullwater Review* look for clear cogent writing, strong character development, and an engaging approach to the story in our fiction submissions. Stories with particularly strong voices and well-developed central themes are especially encouraged. Be sure that your ms is ready before mailing it off to us. Revise, revise, revise! Be original, honest, and of course, keep trying."

LUNGFULL!MAGAZINE

316 23rd St., Brooklyn NY 11215. **E-mail:** custom erservice@lungfull.org. **E-mail:** lungfull@rcn.com. **Website:** lungfull.org. **Contact:** Brendan Lorber, editor/publisher. Estab. 1994. "*LUNGFULL!* Magazine World Headquarters in Brooklyn is home to a team of daredevils who make it their job to bring you only the finest in typos, misspellings, and awkward phrases. That's because *LUNGFULL!magazine* is the only literary and art journal in America that prints the rough drafts of people's work so you can see the creative process as it happens."

○ *LUNGFULL!* was the recipient of a grant from the New York State Council for the Arts.

HOW TO CONTACT Submit up to 15 pages of prose. Include cover letter.

◑ THE MACGUFFIN

18600 Haggerty Rd., Livonia MI 48152. (734)462-4400, ext 5327. **E-mail:** macguffin@schoolcraft.edu. **Website:** www.macguffin.org. **Contact:** Steven A. Dolgin, editor; Gordon Krupsky, managing editor;. Estab. 1984. "Our purpose is to encourage, support, and enhance the literary arts in the Schoolcraft College community, the region, the state, and the nation. We also sponsor annual literary events and give voice to deserving new writers as well as established writers."

NEEDS Length: 5,000 words.

HOW TO CONTACT Submit 2 stories, maximum. Prose should be typed and double-spaced. Include word count. Send SASE or e-mail.

PAYMENT/TERMS Pays 2 contributor's copies.

◑ THE MADISON REVIEW

University of Wisconsin, 600 N, Park St., 6193 Helen C. White Hall, Madison WI 53706. **E-mail:** madisonrevw@gmail.com. **Website:** www.english.wisc.edu/madisonreview/. Estab. 1972. *The Madison Review* is a student-run literary magazine that looks to publish the best available fiction and poetry.

○ Does not publish unsolicited interviews or genre ficion. Send all submissions through online submissions manager.

NEEDS Well-crafted, compelling fiction featuring a wide range of styles and subjects. Does not read May-September. No genre: horror, fantasy, erotica, etc. Length: 500-30,000 words. No longer than 30 pages.

HOW TO CONTACT Send complete ms.

PAYMENT/TERMS Pays 2 contributor's copies, $5 charge for extras.

TIPS "Our editors have very ecclectic tastes, so don't specifically try to cater to us. Above all, we look for original, high-quality work."

◑◑◉◉ THE MAGAZINE OF FANTASY & SCIENCE FICTION

P.O. Box 3447, Hoboken NJ 07030. (201) 876-2551. **E-mail:** fandsf@aol.com. **Website:** www.fandsf.com. **Contact:** Gordon Van Gelder, editor. Estab. 1949. "*The Magazine of Fantasy and Science Fiction* publishes various types of science fiction and fantasy short stories and novellas, making up about 80% of each issue. The balance of each issue is devoted to articles about science fiction, a science column, book and film reviews, cartoons, and competitions." Bimonthly.

○ The *Magazine of Fantasy and Science Fiction* won a Nebula Award for Best Novelette for *What We Found* by Geoff Ryman in 2012. Also won the 2012 World Fantasy Award for Best Short Story for *The Paper Menagerie* by Ken Liu. Editor Van Gelder won the Hugo Award for Best Editor (short form) in 2007 and 2008.

NEEDS "Prefers character-oriented stories. We receive a lot of fantasy fiction but never enough science fiction." Length: up to 25,000 words

HOW TO CONTACT No electronic submissions. Send complete ms.

PAYMENT/TERMS Pays 7-10¢/word

TIPS "Good storytelling makes a submission stand out. Regarding mss, a well-prepared ms (i.e., one that follows the traditional format, like that described here: www.sfwa.org/writing/vonda/vonda.htm) stands out more than any gimmicks. Read an issue of the magazine before submitting. New writers should keep their submissions under 15,000 words—we rarely publish novellas by new writers."

◑ THE MAIN STREET RAG

P.O. Box 690100, Charlotte NC 28227-7001. (704)573-2516. **E-mail:** editor@mainstreetrag.com. **Website:** www.mainstreetrag.com. **Contact:** M. Scott Douglass, editor/publisher. Estab. 1996. *The Main Street Rag*, published quarterly, prints "poetry, short fiction, essays, interviews, reviews, photos, art. We like publishing good material from people who are interested in more than notching another publishing credit, people who support small independent publishers like ourselves." Will consider "almost anything," but prefers "writing with an edge—either gritty or bitingly humorous. Contributors are advised to visit our website prior to submission to confirm current needs."

○ *The Main Street Rag* is about 130 pages, digest-sized, perfect-bound, with 12-point laminated color cover. Receives about 5,000 submissions/year; publishes 50+ poems and 3-5 short stories per issue, a featured interview, photos, and an occasional nonfiction piece. Press run is about 500 (250 subscribers, 15 libraries). Single copy: $8; subscription: $24/year, $45 for 2 years.

THE MALAHAT REVIEW

The University of Victoria, P.O. Box 1700, STN CSC, Victoria BC V8W 2Y2 Canada. (250)721-8524. E-mail: malahat@uvic.ca (for queries only). **Website:** www.malahatreview.ca. **Contact:** John Barton, editor. Estab. 1967. "We try to achieve a balance of views and styles in each issue. We strive for a mix of the best writing by both established and new writers."

NEEDS Length: 8,000 words maximum.

HOW TO CONTACT Send complete ms.

PAYMENT/TERMS Pays $40/magazine page

TIPS "Please do not send more than 1 submission at a time: 4-8 poems, 1 piece of creative nonfiction, or 1 short story (do not mix poetry and prose in the same submission). See *The Malahat Review*'s Open Season Awards for poetry and short fiction, creative nonfiction, long poem, and novella contests in the Awards section of our website."

MANOA

English Department, University of Hawaii, Honolulu HI 96822. (808)956-3070. **Fax:** (808)956-3083. **E-mail:** mjournal-l@lists.hawaii.edu. **Website:** manoajournal.hawaii.edu. **Contact:** Frank Stewart, editor. Estab. 1989. *Manoa* is seeking "high-quality literary fiction, poetry, essays, personal narrative. In general, each issue is devoted to new work from Pacific and Asian nations. Our audience is international. U.S. writing need not be confined to Pacific settings or subjects. Please note that we seldom publish unsolicited work."

O   *Manoa* has received numerous awards, and work published in the magazine has been selected for prize anthologies. See website for recently published issues.

NEEDS Query first and/or see website. No Pacific exotica. Length: 1,000-7,500 words.

HOW TO CONTACT Send complete ms.

PAYMENT/TERMS Pays $100-500 normally ($25 per printed page).

TIPS "Not accepting unsolicited mss at this time because of commitments to special projects. Please query before sending mss as e-mail attachments."

THE MASSACHUSETTS REVIEW

South College, University of Massachusetts, Amherst MA 01003. (413)545-2689. **Fax:** (413)577-0740. **E-mail:** massrev@external.umass.edu. **Website:** www.massreview.org. **Contact:** Jim Hicks, editor. Estab. 1959. Seeks a balance between established writers and promising new ones. Interested in material of variety and vitality relevant to the intellectual and aesthetic questions of our time. Aspire to have a broad appeal.

O   Does not respond to mss without SASE.

NEEDS Wants short stories. Accepts 1 short story per submission. Include name and contact information on the first page. Encourages page numbers. Has published work by Ahdaf Soueif, Elizabeth Denton, Nicholas Montemarano. Length: a maximum of 30 pages or 8,000 words.

HOW TO CONTACT Send complete ms.

PAYMENT/TERMS Pays $50.

TIPS "No mss are considered May-September. Electronic submission process on website. No fax or e-mail submissions. No simultaneous submissions. Shorter rather than longer stories preferred (up to 28-30 pages)." Looks for works that "stop us in our tracks." Mss that stand out use "unexpected language, idiosyncrasy of outlook and are the opposite of ordinary."

MENSBOOK JOURNAL

CQS Media, Inc., P.O. Box 418, Sturbridge MA 01566. **Fax:** (508)347-8150. **E-mail:** features@mensbook.com. **Website:** www.mensbook.com. **Contact:** P.C. Carr, editor/publisher. Estab. 2008. "We target bright, inquisitive, discerning gay men who want more non-commercial substance from gay media. We seek primarily first-person autobiographical pieces—then: biographies, political and social analysis, cartoons, short fiction, commentary, travel, and humor."

NEEDS Length: 750-3,500 words.

HOW TO CONTACT Buys variable amounts of fiction mss/year. Send complete ms.

TIPS "Be a tight writer with a cogent, potent message. Structure your work with well-organized progressive sequencing. Edit everything down before you send it over so we know it is the best you can do, and we'll work together from there."

MERIDIAN

University of Virginia, P.O. Box 400145, Charlottesville VA 22904-4145. (434)982-5798. **Fax:** (434)924-1478. **E-mail:** MeridianUVA@gmail.com; meridianpoetry@gmail.com; meridianfiction@gmail.com. **Website:** www.readmeridian.org. Estab. 1998. *Meridian* Editors' Prize Contest offers annual $1,000 award. Submit online only; see website for formatting details. **Entry fee:** $8, includes one-year electronic subscription to *Meridian* for all U.S. entries or 1 copy of the prize issue for all international entries. **Deadline:** December or January; see website for current deadline.

Meridian, published semiannually, prints poetry, fiction, nonfiction, interviews, and reviews. "*Meridian* is interested in writing that is vibrant, moving, and alive, and welcomes contributions from a variety of aesthetic approaches. Has published such poets as Alexandra Teague, Gregory Pardlo, Sandra Meek, and Bob Hicok, and such fiction writers as Matt Bell, Kate Milliken, and Ron Carlson. Has recently interviewed C. Michael Curtis, Ann Beatty, and Claire Messud, among other luminaries. Also publishes a recurring feature called 'Lost Classic,' which resurrects previously unpublished work by celebrated writers and which has included illustrations from the mss of Jorge Luis Borges, letters written by Elizabeth Bishop, Stephen Crane's deleted chapter from *The Red Badge of Courage*, and a letter written by Flannery O'Connor about her novel *Wise Blood*."

○ *Meridian* is 130 pages, digest-sized, offset-printed, perfect-bound, with color cover. Receives about 2,500 poems/year, accepts about 40 (less than 1%). Press run is 1,000 (750 subscribers, 15 libraries, 200 shelf sales); 150 distributed free to writing programs. Work published in *Meridian* has appeared in *The Best American Poetry* and *The Pushcart Prize* anthology.

NEEDS No e-mail or disk submissions; accepts postal and online submissions ($2 upload fee; no fee for postal submissions). Cover letter is preferred. Reads submissions September-May primarily (do not send postal submissions April 15-August 15; accepts online submissions year-round). Reviews books of fiction.

PAYMENT/TERMS Pays 2 contributor's copies (additional copies available at discount).

○○$ MICHIGAN QUARTERLY REVIEW

0576 Rackham Bldg., 915 E. Washington, University of Michigan, Ann Arbor MI 48109-1070. (734)764-9265. **E-mail:** mqr@umich.edu. **Website:** www.michiganquarterlyreview.com. **Contact:** Jonathan Freedman, editor; Vicki Lawrence, managing editor. Estab. 1962. "*MQR* is an eclectic interdisciplinary journal of arts and culture that seeks to combine the best of poetry, fiction, and creative nonfiction with outstanding critical essays on literary, cultural, social, and political matters. The flagship journal of the University of Michigan, *MQR* draws on lively minds here and elsewhere, seeking to present accessible work of all varieties for sophisticated readers from within and without the academy."

○ The Laurence Goldstein Award is a $500 annual award to the best poem published in *MQR* during the previous year. The Lawrence Foundation Award is a $1,000 annual award to the best short story published in *MQR* during the previous year. The Page Davidson Clayton Award for Emerging Poets is a $500 annual award given to the best poet appearing in *MQR* during the previous year who has not yet published a book.

NEEDS "No restrictions on subject matter or language. We are very selective. We like stories that are unusual in tone and structure, and innovative in language. No genre fiction written for a market. Would like to see more fiction about social, political, cultural matters, not just centered on a love relationship or dysfunctional family." Receives 300 unsolicited mss/month. Accepts 3-4 mss/issue; 12-16 mss/year. Publishes 1-2 new writers/year. Has published work by Rebecca Makkai, Peter Ho Davies, Laura Kasischke, Gerald Shapiro, and Alan Cheuse. Length: 1,500-7,000 words; average length: 5,000 words.

HOW TO CONTACT Send complete ms.

PAYMENT/TERMS Pays $10/published page.

TIPS "Read the journal and assess the range of contents and the level of writing. We have no guidelines to offer or set expectations; every ms is judged on its unique qualities. On essays—query with a very thorough description of the argument and a copy of the first page. Watch for announcements of special issues, which are usually expanded issues and draw upon a lot of freelance writing. Be aware that this is a university quarterly that publishes a limited amount of fiction and poetry and that it is directed at an educated audience, one that has done a great deal of reading in all types of literature."

◐ MICROHORROR: SHORT STORIES. ENDLESS NIGHTMARES

P.O. Box 32259, Pikesville MD 21282-2259. (443) 670-6133. **E-mail:** microhorror@gmail.com. **Website:** www.microhorror.com. **Contact:** Nathan Rosen, editor. Estab. 2006. "*MicroHorror* is not a magazine in the traditional sense. Instead it is a free online archive for short-short horror fiction. With a strict limit of 666 words, *MicroHorror* showcases the power of the short-short horror to convey great emotional impact in only a few brief paragraphs."

○ Golden Horror Award from Horrorfind.com in 2007.

NEEDS Length: no more than 666 words.

HOW TO CONTACT Send all submissions through online submission form.

TIPS "This is horror. Scare me. Make shivers run down my spine. Make me afraid to look behind the shower curtain. Pack the biggest punch you can into a few well-chosen sentences. Read all the horror you can, and figure out what makes it scary. Trim away all the excess trappngs until you get right to the core, and use what you find."

◐◑ MID-AMERICAN REVIEW

Bowling Green State University, Department of English, Bowling Green OH 43403. (419)372-2725. **E-mail:** mar@bgsu.edu. **E-mail:** marsubmissions.bgsu .edu. **Website:** www.bgsu.edu/midamericanreview. **Contact:** Abigail Cloud, editor-in-chief. Estab. 1981. "We aim to put the best possible work in front of the biggest possible audience. We publish contemporary fiction, poetry, creative nonfiction, translations, and book reviews."

○ Magazine: 6×9; 208 pages; 60 lb. bond paper; coated cover stock. Contests: The Fineline Competition for Prose Poems, Short Shorts, and Everything In Between (June 1 deadline, $10 per 3 pieces, limit 500 words each); The Sherwood Anderson Fiction Award (November 1 deadline, $10 per piece); and the James Wright Poetry Award (November 1 deadline, $10 per 3 pieces).

NEEDS Publishes traditional, character-oriented, literary, experimental, prose poem, and short-short stories. No genre fiction. Length: 6,000 words maximum.

HOW TO CONTACT Submit ms by post with SASE or with online submission manager. Agented fiction 5%. Recently published work by Mollie Ficek and J. David Stevens.

TIPS "We are seeking translations of contemporary authors from all languages into English; submissions must include the original and proof of permission to translate. We would also like to see more creative nonfiction."

◑ MIDWAY JOURNAL

8 Durham Street #3, Somerville MA 02143. (763)516-7463. **E-mail:** editors@midwayjournal.com. **Web-**site: www.midwayjournal.com. **Contact:** Ralph Pennel, fiction editor. Estab. 2006. "Just off of I-94 and on the border between St. Paul and Minneapolis, the Midway, like any other state fairgrounds, is alive with a mix of energies and people. Its position as midway, as a place of boundary crossing, also reflects our vision for this journal. The work here complicates and questions the boundaries of genre, binary, and aesthetic. It offers surprises and ways of re-seeing, rethinking, and re-feeling: a veritable banquet of literary fare. Which is why, in each new issue, we are honored to present work by both new and established writers alike."

○ *Midway Journal* is a member of Council of Literary Magazines and Presses (CLMP).

HOW TO CONTACT Submit 1 piece of fiction or 2 pieces of flash/sudden fiction via online submissions manager.

TIPS "An interesting story with engaging writing, both in terms of style and voice, make a ms stand out. Round characters are a must. Writers who take chances either with content or with form grab an editor's immediate attention. Spend time with the words on the page. Spend time with the language. The language and voice are not vehicles; they, too, are tools."

○ MISSISSIPPI REVIEW

University of Southern Mississippi, 118 College Dr., #5144, Hattiesburg MS 39406-0001. (601)266-4321. **Fax:** (601)266-5757. **E-mail:** msreview@usm.edu. **Website:** www.usm.edu/mississippi-review. **Contact:** Andrew Malan Milward, editor-in-chief. Estab. 1972.

○ Publishes 25-30 new writers/year. Annual fiction and poetry competition: $1,000 awarded in each category, plus publication of all winners and finalists. Fiction entries: 8,000 words or less. Poetry entries: 1-5 poems; page limit is 10. $15 entry fee includes copy of prize issue. No limit on number of entries. Deadline: December 1. No mss returned.

NEEDS No juvenile or genre fiction. 30 pages maximum.

◐◑◉ THE MISSOURI REVIEW

357 McReynolds Hall, University of Missouri, Columbia MO 65211. (573)882-4474. **Fax:** (573)884-4671. **E-mail:** question@moreview.com. **Website:** www.missourireview.com. **Contact:** Speer Morgan, editor. Estab. 1978. Publishes contemporary fiction, poetry, interviews, personal essays, cartoons, special

features—such as History as Literature series and Found Text series—for the literary and the general reader interested in a wide range of subjects.

NEEDS No genre or flash fiction. Length: 9,000-12,000 words or flash fiction (2,000 words or less).

HOW TO CONTACT Send complete ms.

PAYMENT/TERMS Pays $40/printed page. Also, The William Peden Prize of $1,000 is awarded annually to the best piece of fiction to have appeared in the previous volume year. The winner is chosen by an outside judge from stories published in TMR. There is no separate application process.

TIPS "Send your best work."

MOBIUS

505 Christianson St., Madison WI 53714. (608)242-1009. **E-mail:** fmschep@charter.net. **Website:** www.mobiusmagazine.com. **Contact:** Fred Schepartz, publisher and executive editor. Estab. 1989. *Mobius: The Journal of Social Change* is an online-only journal, published quarterly in March, June, September, and December, in 2009.

NEEDS Wants fiction dealing with themes of social change. "We like social commentary, but mainly we like good writing. No porn, no racist, sexist or any other kind of -*ist*. No Christian or spirituality proselytizing fiction." Length: no more than 5,000 words.

HOW TO CONTACT Submit no more than 1 story at a time via e-mail (preferred). Paste story in body of e-mail or send as an attachment.

TIPS "We like high impact. We like plot- and character-driven stories that function like theater of the mind. We look first and foremost for good writing. Prose must be crisp and polished; the story must pique my interest and make me care due to a certain intellectual, emotional aspect. *Mobius* is about social change. We want stories that make some statement about the society we live in, either on a macro or micro level. Not that your story needs to preach from a soapbox (actually, we prefer that it doesn't), but your story needs to have something to say."

MORPHEUS TALES

116 Muriel St., London N1 9QU United Kingdom. **E-mail:** morpheustales@blueyonder.co.uk. **Website:** www.morpheustales.com. **Contact:** Adam Bradley, publisher. Estab. 2008. "We publish the best in horror, science fiction, and fantasy—both fiction and nonfiction."

NEEDS Length: 800-3,000 words.

HOW TO CONTACT Send complete ms.

MSLEXIA

Mslexia Publications Ltd., P.O. Box 656, Newcastle upon Tyne NE99 1PZ United Kingdom. (44)(191)204-8860. **E-mail:** submissions@mslexia.co.uk; postbag@mslexia.co.uk. **Website:** www.mslexia.co.uk. **Contact:** Debbie Taylor, editorial director. Estab. 1998. "*Mslexia* tells you all you need to know about exploring your creativity and getting into print. No other magazine provides *Mslexia*'s unique mix of advice and inspiration; news, reviews, interviews; competitions, events, grants; all served up with a challenging selection of new poetry and prose. *Mslexia* is read by authors and absolute beginners. A quarterly master class in the business and psychology of writing, it's the essential magazine for women who write."

This publication accepts e-mail submissions except from U.K. writers submitting to New Writing–themed writing.

NEEDS See guidelines on website. "Submissions not on 1 of our current themes will be returned (if submitted with an SASE) or destroyed." Length: 50-2,200 words.

HOW TO CONTACT Send complete ms.

PAYMENT/TERMS Pays £15 per 1,000 words prose plus contributor's copies.

TIPS "Read the magazine; subscribe if you can afford it. *Mslexia* has a particular style and relationship with its readers which is hard to assess at a quick glance. The majority of our readers live in the U.K., so feature pitches should be aware of this. We never commission work without seeing a written sample first. We rarely accept unsolicited mss but prefer a short letter suggesting a feature, plus a brief bio and writing sample."

MYTHIC DELIRIUM

3514 Signal Hill Ave. NW, Roanoke VA 24017-5148. **E-mail:** mythicdelirium@gmail.com. **Website:** www.mythicdelirium.com. **Contact:** Mike Allen, editor. Estab. 1998. "*Mythic Delirium* is an online and e-book venue for fiction and poetry that ranges through science fiction, fantasy, horror, interstitial, and cross-genre territory—we love blurred boundaries and tropes turned on their heads. We are interested in work that demonstrates ambition, that defies traditional approaches to genre, that introduces readers to the legends of other cultures, that re-evaluates the myths of old from a modern perspective, that twists reality in unexpected ways. We are committed to diversity and are open to and encourage submissions from people of every race, gender, nationality, sexual orientation, political affiliation, and religious belief. We publish 12 short stories and 24 poems a year. Our quarterly ebooks in PDF, EPUB, and MOBI formats, published in July, October, January, and April, will each contain 3 stories and 6 poems. We will also publish 1 story and 2 poems on our website each month." Reading period: August 1-October 1 annually.

○ Accepts electronic submissions only to mythicdelirium@gmail.com.

NEEDS "No unsolicited reprints or multiple submissions. Please use the words *fiction submission* in the e-mail subject line. Stories should be sent in standard ms format as .rtf or .doc attachments." Length: up to 4,000 words (firm).

PAYMENT/TERMS Pays 2¢/word.

TIPS "*Mythic Delirium* isn't easy to get into, but we publish newcomers in every issue. Show us how ambitious you can be, and don't give up."

○⑤ NA'AMAT WOMAN

505 Eighth Ave., Suite 2302, New York NY 10018. (212)563-5222. **Fax:** (212)563-5710. **E-mail:** naamat@naamat.org; judith@naamat.org. **Website:** www.naamat.org. **Contact:** Judith Sokoloff, editor. Estab. 1926. "Magazine covering a wide variety of subjects of interest to the Jewish community—including political and social issues, arts, profiles; many articles about Israel and women's issues. Fiction must have a Jewish theme. Readers are the American Jewish community." Circ. 15,000. "We cover issues and topics of interest to the Jewish community in the U.S., Israel, and the rest of the world with emphasis on Jewish women's issues."

NEEDS Ethnic/multicultural, historical, humor/satire, literary, novel excerpts, women-oriented. Receives 10 unsolicited mss/month. Accepts 3-5 mss/year. "We want serious fiction, with insight, reflection, and consciousness." "We do not want fiction that is mostly dialogue. No corny Jewish humor. No Holocaust fiction." Length: 2,000-3,000 words.

HOW TO CONTACT Query with published clips or send complete mss. Responds in 6 months to queries; 6 months to mss. Sample copy for 9×11½ SAE and $2 postage. Sample copy for $2. Writer's guidelines for #10 SASE, or by e-mail. Query with published clips or send complete ms.

PAYMENT/TERMS Pays 10¢/word and 2 contributor's copies. Pays on publication for first North American serial, first, one-time, second serial (reprint) rights, makes work-for-hire assignments. Pays 10-20¢/word for assigned articles and for unsolicited articles.

TIPS "No maudlin nostalgia or romance; no hackneyed Jewish humor."

○ NARRATIVE MAGAZINE

2443 Fillmore St. #214, San Francisco CA 94115. **Website:** www.narrativemagazine.com. Estab. 2003. *Narrative* publishes high-quality contemporary literature in a full range of styles, forms, and lengths. Submit poetry, fiction, and nonfiction, including stories, short shorts, novels, novel excerpts, novellas, personal essays, humor, sketches, memoirs, literary biographies, commentary, reportage, interviews, and short audio recordings of short-short stories and poems. "We welcome submissions of previously unpublished mss of all lengths, ranging from short-short stories to complete book-length works for serialization. In addition to submissions for issues of *Narrative* itself, we also encourage submissions for our Story of the Week, literary contests and Readers' Narratives. Please read our Submission Guidelines for all information on ms formatting, word lengths, author payment, and other policies. We accept submissions only through our electronic submission system. We do not accept submissions through postal services or e-mail. You may send us mss for the following submission categories: General Submissions, Narrative Prize, Story of the Week, Readers' Narrative, or a specific Contest. Your ms must be in one of the following file forms: .doc, .rtf, .pdf, .docx, .txt, .wpd, .odf, .mp3, .mp4, .mov, or .flv."

○ *Narrative* has received recognitions in *New Stories from the South*, *Best American Mystery Stories*, *O. Henry Prize Stories*, *Best American Short Stories*, *Best American Essays*, and the *Pushcart Prize Collection*. In their first quarterly issue of 2010, the National Endowment for the Arts featured an article on the business of books, with *Narrative*'s digital publishing model a key focus. Providing a behind-the-scenes look at the way in which *Narrative* functions and thrives, it is an essential read for anyone looking to learn more about the current state of publishing both in the print and digital arenas.

NEEDS Has published work by Amy Bloom, Tobias Wolff, Marvin Bell, Jane Smiley, Joyce Carol Oates,

E.L. Doctorow, Min Jin Lee, and Alice Munro. Publishes new and emerging writers.

HOW TO CONTACT Send complete ms.

PAYMENT/TERMS Pays on publication between $150-1,000, $1,000-5,000 for book length, plus annual prizes of more than $32,000 awarded.

TIPS "Log on and study our magazine online. Narrative fiction, graphic art, and multimedia are selected, first and foremost, for quality."

NASSAU REVIEW

Nassau Community College, State University of New York, English Department, 1 Education Dr., Garden City NY 11530. **E-mail:** nassaureview@ncc.edu. **Website:** www.ncc.edu/nassaureview. **Contact:** Christina Rau, editor. Estab. 1964. "*The Nassau Review* welcomes submissions of many genres via our online system only. Please read all guidelines and details on the website: www.ncc.edu/nassaureview. All open submissions are under consideration for the Writer Awards."

NATURAL BRIDGE

Department of English, University of Missouri-St. Louis, One University Blvd., St. Louis MO 63121. (314)516-7327. **E-mail:** natural@umsl.edu. **Website:** www.umsl.edu/~natural. Estab. 1999. *Natural Bridge*, published biannually, seeks "fresh, innovative poetry, both free and formal, on any subject. We want poems that work on first and subsequent readings—poems that entertain and resonate and challenge our readers. *Natural Bridge* also publishes fiction, essays, and translations." Has published poetry by Ross Gay, Beckian Fritz Goldberg, Joy Harjo, Bob Hicok, Sandra Kohler, and Timothy Liu.

No longer accepts submissions via e-mail. Accepts submissions through online submission form and postal mail only.

NEEDS Literary. Submit only July 1-August 31 and November 1-December 31. Recently published work by Tayari Jones, Steve Stern, Jamie Wriston Colbert, Lex Williford, and Mark Jay Mirsky. Also publishes literary essays, poetry. Sometimes comments on rejected mss.

HOW TO CONTACT Submit via postal mail or using online submission form. Send SASE for return of ms or send a disposable copy of ms and #10 SASE for reply only.

PAYMENT/TERMS Pays 2 contributor's copies and a one-year subscription; additional copies $5.

TIPS "The editors invite submissions of poetry, fiction, personal essays, and translations year-round. Because we are tied to the academic calendar, we will not read between May 1 and August 1."

NEBO

Arkansas Tech University, Department of English, Russellville AR 72801. (501)968-0256. **E-mail:** nebo@atu.edu. **Website:** www.atu.edu/worldlanguages/Nebo.php. **Contact:** Editor. Estab. 1983. "*Nebo* routinely publishes Arkansas Tech students and unpublished writers alongside nationally known writers."

Literary journal: 5×8; 50-60 pages. For general, academic audience. Receives 20-30 unsolicited mss per month. *Nebo* is published in the spring and fall. Subscriptions: $10.

NEEDS Accepts all genres. Theme changes by semester. Contact editor for specifics. Does not read April 1-August 15. "Submissions deadlines for all work are November 1 and March 1 of each year."

PAYMENT/TERMS Pays 1 contributor's copy.

TIPS "Avoid pretentiousness. Write something you genuinely care about. Please edit your work for spelling, grammar, cohesiveness, and overall purpose. The mss we receive should be publishable with a little polishing. Mss should never be submitted handwritten or on 'onion skin' or colored paper."

NECROLOGY SHORTS: TALES OF MACABRE AND HORROR

Isis International, P.O. Box 510232, St. Louis MO 63151. **E-mail:** editor@necrologyshorts.com; submit@necrologyshorts.com. **Website:** www.necrologyshorts.com. **Contact:** John Ferguson, editor. Estab. 2009. Consumer publication published online daily and through Amazon Kindle. Also offers an annual collection. "*Necrology Shorts* is an online publication which publishes fiction, articles, cartoons, artwork, and poetry daily. Embracing the Internet, e-book readers, and new technology, we aim to go beyond the long time standard of a regular publication to bringing our readers a daily flow of entertainment. We will also be publishing an annual collection for each year in print, e-book reader, and Adobe PDF format. Our main genre is suspense horror similar to H.P. Lovecraft and/or Robert E. Howard. We also publish science fiction and fantasy. We would love to see work continuing the Cthulhu Mythos, but we accept all horror. We also hold contests, judged by our readers, to select the top stories and artwork. Winners of contests receive various prizes, including cash."

NEEDS Length: 2,000 words minimum.

HOW TO CONTACT Send complete ms.

TIPS "*Necrology Shorts* is looking to break out of the traditional publication types to use the Internet, e-book readers, and other technology. We not only publish works of authors and artists, we let them use their published works to brand themselves and further their profits of their hard work. We love to see traditional short fiction and artwork, but we also look forward to those that go beyond that to create multimedia works. The best way to get to us is to let your creative side run wild and not send us the typical fare. Don't forget that we publish horror, sci-fi, and fantasy. We expect deranged, warped, twisted, strange, sadistic, and things that question sanity and reality."

NEON MAGAZINE

U.K.. **E-mail:** info@neonmagazine.co.uk. **Website:** www.neonmagazine.co.uk. **Contact:** Krishan Coupland. "Genre work is welcome. Experimentation is encouraged. We like stark poetry and weird prose. We seek work that is beautiful, shocking, intense, and memorable. Darker pieces are generally favored over humorous ones."

Note: *Neon* was previously published as *Four-Volts Magazine*.

NEEDS "No nonsensical prose; we are not appreciative of sentimentality." No word limit.

PAYMENT/TERMS Pays royalties.

TIPS "Send several poems, 1 or 2 pieces of prose, or several images via form e-mail. Include the word *submission* in your subject line. Include a short biographical note (up to 100 words). Read submission guidelines before submitting your work."

NEW ENGLAND REVIEW

Middlebury College, Middlebury VT 05753. (802)443-5075. **E-mail:** nereview@middlebury.edu. **E-mail:** Carolyn Kuebler, editor. **Website:** www.nereview.com. Estab. 1978. *New England Review* is a prestigious, nationally distributed literary journal. Reads September 1-May 31 (postmarked dates).

Literary only. *New England Review* is 200+ pages, 7×10, printed on heavy stock, flat-spined, with glossy cover with art. Receives 3,000-4,000 poetry submissions/year, accepts about 70-80 poems/year. Receives 550 unsolicited mss/month. Accepts 6 mss/issue; 24 fiction mss/year. Does not accept mss June-August. Agented fiction less than 5%. Publishes approximately 10 new writers/year. Subscription: $30. Overseas shipping fees add $25 for subscription, $12 for Canada; international shipping $5 for single issues. Has published work by Steve Almond, Christine Sneed, Roy Kesey, Thomas Gough, Norman Lock, Brock Clarke, Carl Phillips, Lucia Perillo, Linda Gregerson, and Natasha Trethewey.

NEEDS Send 1 story at a time, unless it is very short. Serious literary only, novel excerpts. Prose length: not strict on word count.

HOW TO CONTACT Send complete ms via online submission manager or postal mail (with SASE). No e-mail submissions. "Will consider simultaneous submissions, but must be stated as such, and you must notify us immediately if the ms accepted for publication elsewhere."

PAYMENT/TERMS Pays $10/page ($20 minimum), and 2 contributor's copies. "For the duration of 2014, *NER* will pay $20/page, courtesy of a year-long NEA grant."

TIPS "We consider short fiction, including short shorts, novellas, and self-contained extracts from novels in both traditional and experimental forms. In nonfiction, we consider a variety of general and literary, but not narrowly scholarly essays; we also publish long and short poems, screenplays, graphics, translations, critical reassessments, statements by artists working in various media, testimonies, and letters from abroad. We are committed to exploration of all forms of contemporary cultural expression in the U.S. and abroad. With few exceptions, we print only work not published previously elsewhere."

NEW LETTERS

University of Missouri-Kansas City, 5101 Rockhill Rd., Kansas City MO 64110. (816)235-1168. **Fax:** (816)235-2611. **E-mail:** newletters@umkc.edu. **Website:** www.newletters.org. **Contact:** Robert Stewart, editor-in-chief. Estab. 1934. "*New Letters* continues to seek the best new writing, whether from established writers or those ready and waiting to be discovered. In addition, it supports those writers, readers, and listeners who want to experience the joy of writing that can both surprise and inspire us all."

Submissions are not read between May 1 and October 1.

NEEDS No genre fiction. 5,000 words maximum.

HOW TO CONTACT Send complete ms.

PAYMENT/TERMS Pays $30-75.

TIPS "We prefer shorter stories and essays to longer ones (an average length is 3,500-4,000 words). We have no rigid preferences as to subject, style, or genre, although commercial efforts tend to put us off. Even so, our only fixed requirement is on good writing."

NEW MADRID

Murray State University, Department of English and Philosophy, 7C Faculty Hall, Murray KY 42071-3341. (270)809-4730. **E-mail:** msu.newmadrid@murray state.edu. **Website:** newmadridjournal.org. **Contact:** Ann Neelon, editor. "*New Madrid* is the national journal of the low-residency MFA program at Murray State University. It takes its name from the New Madrid seismic zone, which falls within the central Mississippi Valley and extends through western Kentucky."

See website for guidelines and upcoming themes. "We have 2 reading periods: one from August 15-October 15 and 1 from January 15-March 15." Also publishes poetry and creative nonfiction. Rarely comments on/critiques rejected mss.

HOW TO CONTACT Accepts submissions by online submissions manager only. Include brief bio, list of publications. Considers multiple submissions.

PAYMENT/TERMS Pays 2 contributor's copies on publication.

TIPS "Quality is the determining factor for breaking into *New Madrid*. We are looking for well-crafted, compelling writing in a range of genres, forms, and styles."

NEW MILLENNIUM WRITINGS

New Messenger Writing and Publishing, P.O. Box 2463, Knoxville TN 37901. (865)428-0389. **Website:** newmillenniumwritings.com. **Contact:** Elizabeth Petty, submissions editor. Estab. 1996. Only accepts general submissions January-April, but holds 4 contests twice each year for all types of fiction, nonfiction, short-short fiction, and poetry.

Annual anthology. 6×9, 204 pages, 50 lb. white paper, glossy 4-color cover. Contains illustrations. Includes photographs.

NEEDS Receives average of 200 mss/month. Accepts 60 mss/year. Agented fiction 0%. Publishes 10 new writers/year. Rarely comments on/critiques rejected mss. Has published work by Charles Wright, Ted Kooser, Pamela Uschuk, William Pitt Root, Allen Wier, Lucille Clifton, John Updike, and Don Williams. Length: 200-6,000 words. Average length: 4,000 words for fiction. Short-short fiction length: no more than 1,000 words.

HOW TO CONTACT Accepts fiction annually from January-April.

NEW OHIO REVIEW

English Department, 360 Ellis Hall, Ohio University, Athens OH 45701. (740)597-1360. **E-mail:** noredi tors@ohio.edu. **Website:** www.ohiou.edu/nor. **Contact:** Jill Allyn Rosser, editor. Estab. 2007. *NOR*, published biannually in spring and fall, publishes fiction, nonfiction, and poetry. Single: $9; Subscription: $16. Member: CLMP. Reading period is September 15-December 15 and January 15-April 1.

HOW TO CONTACT Send complete ms.

PAYMENT/TERMS Pays $30 minimum in addition to 2 contributor's copies and one-year subscription.

NEW ORLEANS REVIEW

Box 195, Loyola University, New Orleans LA 70118. (504)865-2295. **E-mail:** noreview@loyno.edu. **Website:** neworleansreview.org. **Contact:** Heidi Braden, managing editor. Estab. 1968. *New Orleans Review* is a biannual journal of contemporary literature and culture, publishing new poetry, fiction, nonfiction, art, photography, film and book reviews. The journal has published an eclectic variety of work by established and emerging writers including Walker Percy, Pablo Neruda, Ellen Gilchrist, Nelson Algren, Hunter S. Thompson, John Kennedy Toole, Richard Brautigan, Barry Spacks, James Sallis, Jack Gilbert, Paul Hoover, Rodney Jones, Annie Dillard, Everette Maddox, Julio Cortazar, Gordon Lish, Robert Walser, Mark Halliday, Jack Butler, Robert Olen Butler, Michael Harper, Angela Ball, Joyce Carol Oates, Diane Wakoski, Dermot Bolger, Roddy Doyle, William Kotzwinkle, Alain Robbe-Grillet, Arnost Lustig, Raymond Queneau, Yusef Komunyakaa, Michael Martone, Tess Gallagher, Matthea Harvey, D. A. Powell, Rikki Ducornet, and Ed Skoog.

NEEDS Length: up to 6,500 words.

HOW TO CONTACT "We are now using an online submission system and require a $3 fee." See website for details.

PAYMENT/TERMS Pays $25-50 and 2 copies.

TIPS "We're looking for dynamic writing that demonstrates attention to the language and a sense of the medium, writing that engages, surprises, moves us. We're not looking for genre fiction or academic articles. We subscribe to the belief that in order to truly write well, one must first master the rudiments: grammar and syntax, punctuation, the sentence, the paragraph, the line, the stanza. We receive about 3,000 mss a year and publish about 3% of them. Check out a recent issue, send us your best, proofread your work, be patient, be persistent."

NEW SOUTH

Campus Box 1894, Georgia State University, MSC 8R0322 Unit 8, Atlanta GA 30303-3083. (404)413-5874. **E-mail:** newsouth@gsu.edu; newsoutheditors@gmail.com. **Website:** www.newsouthjournal.com. Estab. 1980. Semiannual magazine dedicated to finding and publishing the best work from artists around the world. Wants original voices searching to rise above the ordinary. Seeks to publish high-quality work, regardless of genre, form, or regional ties. *New South* is 160+ pages. Press run is 2,000; 500 distributed free to students. Single copy: $5; subscription: $8/year; $14 for 2 years. Single issue: $5. Sample: $3 (back issue).

The *New South* Annual Writing Contest offers $1,000 for the best poem and $1,000 for the best story or essay; one-year subscription to all who submit. Submissions must be unpublished. Submit up to 3 poems, 1 story, or 1 essay on any subject or in any form. Specify *poetry* or *fiction* on outside envelope. Guidelines available by e-mail or on website. Deadline: March 4. Competition receives 300 entries. Past judges include Sharon Olds, Jane Hirschfield, Anthony Hecht, Phillip Levine, and Jake Adam York. Winner will be announced in the fall issue.

NEEDS Receives 200 unsolicited mss/month. Publishes and welcomes short shorts. Length: 9,000 words.

HOW TO CONTACT Send complete ms through Submittable.

PAYMENT/TERMS Pays 2 contributor's copies.

NEW WELSH REVIEW

P.O. Box 170, Aberystwyth, Ceredigion Wa SY23 1 WZ United Kingdom. 01970-626230. **E-mail:** editor@newwelshreview.com. **E-mail:** submissions@newwelshreview.com. **Website:** www.newwelshreview.com. **Contact:** Gwen Davies, editor. "*NWR*, a literary quarterly ranked in the top 5 of British literary magazines, publishes stories, poems, and critical essays. The best of Welsh writing in English, past and present, is celebrated, discussed, and debated. We seek poems, short stories, reviews, special features/articles, and commentary." Quarterly.

HOW TO CONTACT Send hard copy only with SASE or international money order for return. Outside the U.K., submission by e-mail only.

PAYMENT/TERMS Pays "cheque on publication and 1 free copy."

THE NEW WRITER

the new writer magazine, 1 Vicarage Lane, Stubbington Hampshire PO14 2JU United Kingdom. (44)(158)021-2626. **E-mail:** editor@thenewwriter.com. **Website:** www.thenewwriter.com. **Contact:** Madelaine Smith, editor. Estab. 1996. "Contemporary writing magazine which publishes the best in fact, fiction, and poetry."

NEEDS *No unsolicited mss.* Accepts fiction from subscribers only. "We will consider most categories apart from stories written for children. No horror, erotic, or cosy fiction." Length: 2,000-5,000 words.

HOW TO CONTACT Query with published clips.

TIPS "Hone it—always be prepared to improve the story. It's a competitive market."

THE NEW YORKER

4 Times Square, New York NY 10036. (212)286-5900. **Website:** www.newyorker.com. **Contact:** David Remnick, editor-in-chief. Estab. 1925. A quality weekly magazine of distinct news stories, articles, essays, and poems for a literate audience.

The New Yorker receives approximately 4,000 submissions per month. Subscription: $59.99/year (47 issues), $29.99 for 6 months (23 issues).

NEEDS Publishes 1 ms/issue.

HOW TO CONTACT Send complete ms. Fiction, poetry, Shouts & Murmurs, and newsbreaks should be sent as .pdf attachments.

PAYMENT/TERMS Payment varies.

TIPS "Be lively, original, not overly literary. Write what you want to write, not what you think the editor would like."

NINTH LETTER

Department of English, University of Illinois, 608 S. Wright St., Urbana IL 61801. (217)244-3145. **E-mail:** info@ninthletter.com; editor@ninthletter.com. **Website:** www.ninthletter.com. **Contact:** Jodee

Stanley, editor. "*Ninth Letter* accepts submissions of fiction, poetry, and essays from September 1-February 28 (postmark dates). *Ninth Letter* is published semiannually at the University of Illinois, Urbana-Champaign. We are interested in prose and poetry that experiment with form, narrative, and nontraditional subject matter, as well as more traditional literary work."

○ *Ninth Letter* won Best New Literary Journal 2005 from the Council of Editors of Learned Journals (CELJ) and has had poetry selected for *The Pushcart Prize*, *Best New Poets*, and *The Year's Best Fantasy and Horror*.

NEEDS Length: up to 8,000 words.

HOW TO CONTACT "Please send only 1 story at a time. All mailed submissions must include an SASE for reply."

PAYMENT/TERMS Pays $25 per printed page and 2 contributor's copies.

○ NITE-WRITER'S INTERNATIONAL LITERARY ARTS JOURNAL

158 Spencer Ave., Suite 100, Pittsburgh PA 15227. (412)668-0691. **E-mail:** nitewritersliteraryarts@gmail.com. **Website:** nitewritersinternational.webs.com. **Contact:** John Thompson. Estab. 1994. *Nite-Writer's International Literary Arts Journal* is an online literary arts journal. "We are 'dedicated to the emotional intellectual' with a creative perception of life." Wants strong imagery. Considers previously published poems and simultaneous submissions (let us know when and where your work has been published). Cover letter is preferred. "Give brief bio, state where you heard of us, state if material has been previously published and where." Does not want porn or violence.

○ Journal is open to beginners as well as professionals. Receives about 1,000 poems/year, accepts about 10-15%. Has published poetry by Lyn Lifshin, Rose Marie Hunold, Peter Vetrano, Carol Frances Brown, and Richard King Perkins II.

NEEDS Length: up to 1,200 words.

HOW TO CONTACT All literary works should be in MS Word at 12-point font.

TIPS "Read a lot of the genre you write in—study the market. Don't fear rejection, but use it as learning tool to strengthen your work before resubmitting."

⊕ ◐ NON + X: AN EXPERIMENTAL JOURNAL OF BUDDHIST THOUGHT

E-mail: admin@nonplusx.com. **E-mail:** wtompepper@att.net. **Website:** www.nonplusx.com. **Contact:** Tom Pepper, editor. Estab. 2012. "*non + x* is an experimental e-journal dedicated to the critique of Buddhist and other contemporary cultural materials. Our goal 'consists in wresting vital potentialities of humans from the artificial forms and static norms that subjugate them' (Marjorie Gracieuse)."

NEEDS Query.

TIPS "We welcome written work from anyone who wants to explore Buddhist materials along the lines suggested on the About page. We look for well-written, original pieces bearing on any aspect of contemporary Buddhism. If you have an idea about how the *non+x* critique may be applied to material other than Buddhist, we would love to hear from you as well. If you would like to write for us, please send whatever you have—a completed text, a well-developed idea, or merely the seed of one. Written contributions may be any length and take any form. Examples may include traditional genres, such as the essay, systematic argument, and textual analysis. But we especially welcome more creative approaches to criticism, such as genre-bending pieces, poetry, experimental writing, or schizoanalysis—whatever it takes to inject vitalizing language and thought into anemic Buddhist discourse. We accept only electronic submissions. Because of the limited scope of this new journal, we ask that you look at some issues (available online for free) and be sure what you are submitting fits our goals. If in doubt, query at wtompepper@att.net or admin@nonplusx.com"

THE NORMAL SCHOOL

The Press at the California State University Fresno, 5245 North Backer Ave., M/S PB 98, Fresno CA 93740-8001. **E-mail:** editors@thenormalschool.com. **E-mail:** submissions@thenormalschool.com. **Website:** thenormalschool.com. **Contact:** Steven Church, editor. Estab. 2008. Semiannual magazine that accepts outstanding work by beginning and established writers.

○ Mss are read from September 1-December 1 and from January 15-April 15. Address submissions to the appropriate editor.

NEEDS Also publishes short shorts (fewer than 1,500 words). Sponsor The Normal Prizes in Fiction Contest and Creative Nonfiction Contest. Does not want any genre writing. Length: 12,000 words maximum. **HOW TO CONTACT** Submit complete ms.

NORTH AMERICAN REVIEW

University of Northern Iowa, 1222 W. 27th St., Cedar Falls IA 50614. (319)273-6455. **Fax:** (319)273-4326. **E-mail:** nar@uni.edu. **Website:** northamericanreview .org. **Contact:** Kim Groninga, nonfiction editor. Estab. 1815.

"This is the oldest literary magazine in the country and one of the most prestigious. Also one of the most entertaining—and a tough market for the young writer. Though we have no prejudices about the subject matter of material sent to us, our first concern is quality."

NEEDS Open (literary). "No flat narrative stories where the inferiority of the character is the paramount concern." Wants to see more "well-crafted literary stories that emphasize family concerns. We'd also like to see more stories engaged with environmental concerns." Reads fiction mss all year. Publishes ms an average of 1 year after acceptance. **Publishes 2 new writers/year.** Recently published work by Lee Ann Roripaugh, Dick Allen, Rita Welty Bourke.

HOW TO CONTACT Accepts submissions by USPS mail only. Send complete ms with SASE. Responds in 3 months to queries; 4 months to mss. No simultaneous submissions. Sample copy for $7.

TIPS "We like stories that start quickly and have a strong narrative arc. Poems that are passionate about subject, language, and image are welcome, whether they are traditional or experimental, whether in formal or free verse (closed or open form). Nonfiction should combine art and fact with the finest writing. We do not accept simultaneous submissions; these will be returned unread. We read poetry, fiction, and nonfiction year-round."

NORTH CAROLINA LITERARY REVIEW

East Carolina University,, Mailstop 555 English, Greenville NC 27858-4353. (252)328-1537. **Fax:** (252)328-4889. **E-mail:** nclrsubmissions@ecu.edu. **Website:** www.nclr.ecu.edu. **Contact:** Gabrielle Freeman. Estab. 1992. "Articles should have a North Carolina slant. First consideration is always for quality of work. Although we treat academic and scholarly subjects, we do not wish to see jargon-laden prose; our readers, we hope, are found as often in bookstores and libraries as in academia. We seek to combine the best

elements of magazine for serious readers with best of scholarly journal."

Uses online submission form.

NEEDS "Fiction submissions accepted during Doris Betts Prize Competition; see our submission guidelines for detail." Length: no more than 5,000 words.

HOW TO CONTACT Query electronically using online submission form.

PAYMENT/TERMS Pays $50-100 honorarium, extra copies, back issues, or subscription (negotiable).

TIPS "By far the easiest way to break in is with special-issue sections. We are especially interested in reports on conferences, readings, meetings that involve North Carolina writers, and personal essays or short narratives with a strong sense of place. See back issues for other departments. Interviews are probably the second easiest place to break in; no discussions of poetics/theory, etc., except in reader-friendly (accessible) language; interviews should be personal, more like conversations, that explore connections between a writer's life and his/her work."

NORTH DAKOTA QUARTERLY

276 Centennial Dr. Stop 7209, Merrifield Hall Room 15, Grand Forks ND 58202. (701)777-3322. **E-mail:** und.ndq@email.und.edu. **Website:** www.und.nodak .edu/org/ndq. **Contact:** Sharon Carson, interim editor. Estab. 1911. "*North Dakota Quarterly* strives to publish the best fiction, poetry, and essays that in our estimation we can. Our tastes and interests are best reflected in what we have been recently publishing, and we suggest that you look at some current issues for guidance."

Only reads fiction and poetry between September 1-May 1. Work published in *North Dakota Quarterly* was selected for inclusion in *The O. Henry Prize Stories, The Pushcart Prize* anthologies, and *Best American Essays.*

HOW TO CONTACT Simultaneous submissions OK for fiction. Hard copies only.

NORTHWIND

Chain Bridge Press, LLC., 4201 Wilson Blvd., #110, Arlington VA 22203. **E-mail:** info@northwindmaga zine.com. **Website:** www.northwindmagazine.com. **Contact:** Tom Howard, managing editor. Estab. 2011. *Northwind* is an independent literary magazine published quarterly.

This publication is no longer taking submissions at this time. Query for future submission opportunities. Previous submission guidelines available online.

NEEDS "We want the best that you've got. We want crazy beautiful characters, unforced and unsentimental prose, unexpected plots, great opening lines, and edgy dialogue. But mostly we want great, honest stories that move us and leave us shaken through the sheer force of narrative will. Surprise us." Does not want flash fiction or microfiction. Length: 3,000-8,000 words.

HOW TO CONTACT Submit complete ms using online submission form only.

PAYMENT/TERMS "*Northwind* pays $150 for the issue's featured story only. All contributors, however, will be provided with a dedicated page on the site for biographical information (including photo), any relevant website links, and an optional feedback form for readers."

◐◑⊖ NOTRE DAME REVIEW

University of Notre Dame, 840 Flanner Hall, Notre Dame IN 46556. (574)631-6952. **Fax:** (574)631-4795. **E-mail:** english.ndreview.1@nd.edu. **Website:** ndreview.nd.edu. Estab. 1995. The *Notre Dame Review* is an indepenent, noncommercial magazine of contemporary American and international fiction, poetry, criticism, and art. Especially interested in work that takes on big issues by making the invisible seen, that gives voice to the voiceless. In addition to showcasing celebrated authors like Seamus Heaney and Czelaw Milosz, the *Notre Dame Review* introduces readers to authors they may have never encountered before, but who are doing innovative and important work. In conjunction with the *Notre Dame Review*, the online companion to the printed magazine, the *nd[re]view* engages readers as a community centered in literary rather than commercial concerns, a community we reach out to through critique and commentary as well as aesthetic experience.

◐ Does not accept e-mail submissions. Only reads hardcopy submissions from September-November and from January-March.

NEEDS "We're eclectic. Upcoming theme issues planned. List of upcoming themes or editorial calendar available for SASE. Does not read mss May-August." No genre fiction. Length: 3,000 words.

HOW TO CONTACT Send complete ms with cover letter. Include 4-sentence bio. Send SASE for response, return of ms, or send a disposable copy of ms.

PAYMENT/TERMS Pays $5-25.

TIPS "We're looking for high-quality work that takes on big issues in a literary way. Please read our back issues before submitting."

NOW & THEN; THE APPALACHIAN MAGAZINE

East Tennessee State University, Box 70556, Johnson City TN 37614-1707. (423)439-5348. **Fax:** (423)439-6340. **E-mail:** nowandthen@etsu.edu. **E-mail:** sandersr@etsu.edu. **Website:** www.etsu.edu/cass/nowandthen. **Contact:** Fred Sauceman, editor; Randy Sanders, managing editor; Marianne Worthington, poetry editor; Wayne Winkler, music editor; Charlie Warden, photo editor. Estab. 1984. Literary magazine published twice/year. "*Now & Then* accepts a variety of writing genres: fiction, poetry, nonfiction, essays, interviews, memoirs, and book reviews. All submissions must relate to Appalachia and to the issue's specific theme. Our readership is educated and interested in the region."

◐ Magazine: 8½×11; 72-80 pages; coated paper and cover stock; 4-color throughout; illustrations; photos. *Now & Then* tells the stories of Appalachia and presents a fresh, revealing picture of life in Appalachia, past and present, with engaging articles, personal essays, fiction, poetry, and photography.

NEEDS Accepts 1-2 mss/issue. Publishes ms 4 months after acceptance. Publishes some new writers/year. Length: 1,000-1,500 words.

HOW TO CONTACT Send complete ms. Accepts submissions by mail, e-mail, with a strong preference for e-mail. Include "information we can use for contributor's note." SASE (or IRC). Responds in 5 months to queries; 5 months to mss. Rarely accepts simultaneous submissions. Writer's guidelines online. Reviews fiction.

PAYMENT/TERMS Pays $50 each accepted article/$25 each accepted poem. Pays on publication.

TIPS "Keep in mind that *Now & Then* only publishes material related to the Appalachian region. Plus we only publish fiction that has some plausible connection to a specific issue's themes. We like to offer first-time publication to promising writers."

◑ NTH DEGREE

3502 Fernmoss Ct., Charlotte NC 28269. **E-mail:** submissions@nthzine.com. **Website:** www.nthzine.com. **Contact:** Michael Pederson. Estab. 2002. Free online

fanzine to promote up-and-coming new science fiction and fantasy authors and artists. Also supports the world of fandom and conventions.

🔾 No longer accepts hard-copy submissions.

NEEDS Length: no more than 7,500 words.

HOW TO CONTACT Submit complete ms via e-mail.

PAYMENT/TERMS Pays in contributor's copies.

TIPS "Don't submit anything that you may be ashamed of 10 years later."

🟤🟡🔵 NTHPOSITION

E-mail: val@nthposition.com; laura.a.bottomley@gmail.com. **Website:** www.nthposition.com. **Contact:** Laura Bottomley, poetry editor; Val Stevenson, managing editor. Estab. 2002. *nthposition*, published monthly online, is an eclectic, London-based journal with politics and opinion, travel writing, fiction and poetry, art reviews and interviews, and some high weirdness.

TIPS "Submit as text in the body of an e-mail, along with a brief bio note (2-3 sentences). If your work is accepted, it will be archived into the British Library's permanent collection."

OCEAN MAGAZINE

P.O. Box 84, Rodanthe NC 27968-0084. (252)256-2296. **E-mail:** diane@oceanmagazine.org. **Website:** www.oceanmagazine.org. Estab. 2004. *"OCEAN Magazine is a nature magazine. OCEAN publishes articles, stories, poems, essays, and photography related to the ocean."*

NEEDS Length: 100-2,000 words.

HOW TO CONTACT Query.

PAYMENT/TERMS Pays $75-150.

TIPS "Submit with a genuine love and concern for the ocean and its creatures."

🔵🟢 ON SPEC

P.O. Box 4727, Station South, Edmonton AB T6E 5G6 Canada. (780)628-7121. **E-mail:** onspec@onspec.ca. **E-mail:** onspecmag@gmail.com. **Website:** www.onspec.ca. Estab. 1989. "We publish speculative fiction and poetry by new and established writers, with a strong preference for Canadian-authored works."

🔾 See website guidelines for submission announcements. "Please refer to website for information regarding submissions, as we are not open year-round."

NEEDS No media tie-in or shaggy-alien stories. No condensed or excerpted novels, religious/inspirational stories, fairy tales. Length: 1,000-6,000 words.

HOW TO CONTACT Send complete ms. Electronic submissions preferred.

TIPS "We want to see stories with plausible characters, a well-constructed, consistent, and vividly described setting, a strong plot and believable emotions; characters must show us (not tell us) their emotional responses to each other and to the situation and/or challenge they face. Also: Don't send us stories written for television. We don't like media tie-ins, so don't watch TV for inspiration! Read instead! Strong preference given to submissions by Canadians."

🔵🟢 ON THE PREMISES: A GOOD PLACE TO START

On the Premises, LLC, 4323 Gingham Court, Alexandria VA 22310. **E-mail:** questions@onthepremises.com. **Website:** www.OnThePremises.com. **Contact:** Tarl Roger Kudrick or Bethany Granger, co-publishers. Estab. 2006. "Stories published in *On the Premises* are winning entries in contests that are held every 4 months. Each contest challenges writers to produce a great story based on a broad premise that our editors supply as part of the contest. *On the Premises* aims to promote newer and/or relatively unknown writers who can write what we feel are creative, compelling stories told in effective, uncluttered, and evocative prose. Entrants pay no fees, and winners receive cash prizes in addition to publication."

🔾 Does not read February, June, and October. Receives 50-125 mss/month. Accepts 3-6 mss/issue; 9-18 mss/year. Has published A'llyn Ettien, Cory Cramer, Mark Tullius, Michael Van Ornum, Ken Liu, and K. Stoddard Hayes. Member Small Press Promotions.

NEEDS Themes are announced the day each contest is launched. List of past and current premises available on website. "All genres considered. All stories must be based on the broad premise supplied as part of the contest. Sample premise, taken from the first issue: One or more characters are traveling in a vehicle and never reach their intended destination. Why not? What happens instead?" No young adult, children's, or "preachy" fiction. "In general, we don't like stories that were written solely to make a social or political point, especially if the story seems to assume that no intelligent person could possibly disagree with the author. Save the ideology for editorial and opinion pieces, please. But above all, we *never ever* want to see stories that do not use the contest premise! Use the

premise, and make it 'clear' and 'obvious' that you are using the premise." Length: 1,000-5,000 words. Average length: 3,500 words.

HOW TO CONTACT Send complete ms. "Submit stories only via submission form at onthepremises.sub mittable.com/submit. We no longer accept e-mailed submissions."

PAYMENT/TERMS Pays $40-180.

TIPS "Make sure you use the premise, not just interpret it. If the premise is 'must contain a real live dog,' then think of a creative, compelling way to use a real dog. Revise your draft, then revise again and again. Remember, we judge blindly, so craftmanship and creativity matter, not how well known you are."

OUTER ART

The University of New Mexico, 200 College Rd., Gallup NM 87301. **Website:** www.gallup.unm .edu/~smarandache/a/outer-art.htm. Estab. 2000. *"Outer-Art* is a movement set up as a protest against, or to ridicule, the random modern art which states that everything is… art! It was initiated by Florentin Smarandache in the 1990s, who ironically called for an upside-down artwork: to do art in a way it is not supposed to be done; i.e., to make art as ugly, as silly, as wrong as possible, and generally as impossible as possible."

OVERTIME

Blue Cubicle Press, LLC, P.O. Box 250382, Plano TX 75025. **E-mail:** overtime@workerswritejournal.com. **Website:** www.workerswritejournal.com/overtime .htm. **Contact:** David LaBounty, editor. Estab. 2006.

NEEDS 5,000-12,000

HOW TO CONTACT Query; send complete ms.

OXFORD MAGAZINE

356 Bachelor Hall, Miami University, Oxford OH 45056. **E-mail:** oxmag@muohio.edu. **Website:** www. oxfordmagazine.org. Estab. 1984. *Oxford Magazine,* published annually online in May, is open in terms of form, content, and subject matter. "Since our premiere in 1984, our magazine has received Pushcart Prizes for both fiction and poetry and has published authors such as Charles Baxter, William Stafford, Robert Pinsky, Stephen Dixon, Helena Maria Viramontes, Andre Dubus, and Stuart Dybek."

Work published in *Oxford Magazine* has been included in *The Pushcart Prize* anthology.

HOW TO CONTACT Submit using online submission form only.

OYEZ REVIEW

Roosevelt University, Department of Literature and Languages, 430 S. Michigan Ave., Chicago IL 60605-1394. (312)341-3500. **E-mail:** oyezreview@roosevelt .edu. **Website:** legacy.roosevelt.edu/roosevelt.edu/ oyezreview. Estab. 1965. Annual magazine of the Creative Writing Program at Roosevelt University, publishing fiction, creative nonfiction, poetry, and art. There are no restrictions on style, theme, or subject matter. Each issue has 104 pages: 92 pages of text and an 8-page spread of 1 artist's work (in color or b&w). Work by the issue's featured artist also appears on the front and back cover, totaling 10 pieces. The journal has featured work from such writers as Charles Bukowski, James McManus, Carla Panciera, Michael Onofrey, Tim Foley, John N. Miller, Gary Fincke, and Barry Silesky, and visual artists Vivian Nunley, C. Taylor, Jennifer Troyer, and Frank Spidale. with an e-book available. Accepts queries by e-mail. Sample copies availableby request, or using e-book retailers. Guidelines available online.

Reading period is August 1-October 1. Responds by mid-December.

NEEDS "Publishes short stories and flash fiction from established authors and newcomers. Literary excellence is our goal and our primary criterion. Send us your best work, and you will receive a thoughtful, thorough reading." Recently published J. Weintraub, Lori Rader Day, Joyce Goldenstern, Norman Lock, Peter Obourn, Jotham Burrello. We publish short stories and flash fiction on their merit as contemporary literature rather than the category within the genre. Length: 5,500 words maximum.

HOW TO CONTACT Strongly prefers submissions be sent via Submittable; e-mail for queries only. Sample copy available for $5. Guidelines available on website. Send complete ms.

PAYMENT/TERMS Writers receive 2 contributors copies. Acquires first North American serial rights.

OYSTER BOY REVIEW

P.O. Box 1483, Pacifica CA 94044. **E-mail:** email_2014@oysterboyreview.com. **Website:** www .oysterboyreview.com. **Contact:** Damon Suave, editor/ publisher. Estab. 1993. Electronic and print magazine. *Oyster Boy Review,* published annually, is interested in "the underrated, the ignored, the misunderstood, and the varietal. We'll make some mistakes."

NEEDS "Fiction that revolves around characters in conflict with themselves or each other; a plot that has a beginning, a middle, and an end; a narrative with a strong moral center (not necessarily 'moralistic'); a story with a satisfying resolution to the conflict; and an ethereal something that contributes to the mystery of a question, but does not necessarily seek or contrive to answer it." No genre fiction.

TIPS "Keep writing, keep submitting, keep revising."

⊕ PACIFICA LITERARY REVIEW

E-mail: pacificalitreview@gmail.com. **Website:** www.pacificareview.com. *Pacifica Literary Review* is a small literary arts magazine based in Seattle. Our print editions are published biannually in winter and summer. *PLR* is now accepting submissions of poetry, fiction, creative nonfiction, author interview, and b&w photography. Submission period: September 15-May 7.

NEEDS Looking for literary fiction up to 6,000 words or flash fiction of 300-1,000 words.

HOW TO CONTACT Submit complete ms.

◐☺ PACKINGTOWN REVIEW

111 S. Lincoln St., Batavia IL 60510. **E-mail:** editors@packingtownreview.com. **Website:** www.packingtownreview.com. Estab. 2008. *Packingtown Review* publishes imaginative and critical prose and poetry by emerging and established writers. Welcomes submissions of poetry, scholarly articles, drama, creative nonfiction, fiction, and literary translation, as well as genre-bending pieces.

○ Annual. Magazine has revolving editor. Editorial term: 2 years. Next term: 2014. Literary magazine/journal. 8½×11, 250 pages. Press run: 500.

NEEDS Does not want to see uninspired or unrevised work. Wants to avoid fantasy, science fiction, overtly religious, or romantic pieces. Length: 3,000-8,000 words.

HOW TO CONTACT Send complete ms with cover letter. Include estimated word count, brief bio.

PAYMENT/TERMS Pays 2 contributor's copies.

TIPS "We are looking for well-crafted prose. We are open to most styles and forms. We are also looking for prose that takes risks and does so successfully. We will consider articles about prose."

◐☺ PADDLEFISH

Mount Marty College, 1105 W. 8th St., Yankton SD 57078. (605) 688-1362. **E-mail:** james.reese@mtmc

.edu. **Website:** www.mtmc.edu/paddlefish. **Contact:** Dr. Jim Reese, Editor. Estab. 2007.

○ Literary magazine/journal. 6×9, 200 pages. Includes photographs. Does not accept e-mail submissions.

NEEDS "We publish unique and creative pieces." Annual. Receives 300 mss/month. Accepts 30 mss/year. Submission period is November 1-February 28. Published David Lee, William Kloefkorn, David Allen Evans, Jack Anderson, and Maria Mazziotti Gillan. Length: 2,500 words (maximum). Does not want excessive or gratuitous language, sex, or violence. Length: no more than 1,500 words.

HOW TO CONTACT Submit complete ms with SASE.

PAYMENT/TERMS Pays in contributor's copies.

◐◑☺ PAINTED BRIDE QUARTERLY

Drexel University, Department of English and Philosophy, 3141 Chestnut St., Philadelphia PA 19104. **E-mail:** pbq@drexel.edu. **Website:** www.webdelsol.com/pbq. Estab. 1973. *Painted Bride Quarterly* seeks literary fiction (experimental and traditional), poetry, and artwork and photographs.

NEEDS Publishes theme-related work, check website; holds annual fiction contests. Length: up to 5,000 words.

HOW TO CONTACT Send complete ms.

PAYMENT/TERMS Pays contributor's copy.

TIPS "We look for freshness of idea incorporated with high-quality writing. We receive an awful lot of nicely written work with worn-out plots. We want quality in whatever—we hold experimental work to as strict standards as anything else. Many of our readers write fiction; most of them enjoy a good reading. We hope to be an outlet for quality. A good story gives, first, enjoyment to the reader. We've seen a good many of them lately, and we've published the best of them."

☺◑ PAPERPLATES

19 Kenwood Ave., Toronto ON M6C 2R8 Canada. (416)651-2551. **E-mail:** magazine@paperplates.org. **Website:** www.paperplates.org. **Contact:** Bernard Kelly, publisher. Estab. 1990. *paperplates* is a literary quarterly published in Toronto. "We make no distinction between veterans and beginners. Some of our contributors have published several books; some have never before published a single line."

○ No longer accepts IRCs.

NEEDS Length: no more than 7,500 words.

HOW TO CONTACT "Do not send fiction as an e-mail attachment. Copy the first 300 words or so into the body of your message. If you prefer not to send a fragment, you have the option of using surface mail." Include short bio with submission.

THE PARIS REVIEW

544 West 27th St., New York NY 10001. (212)343-1333. **E-mail:** queries@theparisreview.org. **Website:** www.theparisreview.org. **Contact:** Lorin Stein, editor. "Fiction and poetry of superlative quality, whatever the genre, style, or mode. Our contributors include prominent, as well as less well-known and previously unpublished writers. Writers at Work interview series includes important contemporary writers discussing their own work and the craft of writing."

Address submissions to proper department. Do not make submissions via e-mail.

NEEDS Study the publication. Annual Plimpton Prize award of $10,000 given to a new voice published in the magazine. Recently published work by Ottessa Moshfegh, John Jeremiah Sullivan, and Lydia Davis. Length: no limit.

HOW TO CONTACT Send complete ms.

PAYMENT/TERMS Pays $1,000-3,000.

PASSAGES NORTH

English Department, Northern Michigan University, 1401 Presque Isle Ave., Marquette MI 49855. (906)227-1203. **E-mail:** passages@nmu.edu. **Website:** www.passagesnorth.com. **Contact:** Jennifer A. Howard, editor-in-chief. Estab. 1979. *Passages North*, published annually in spring, prints poetry, short fiction, creative nonfiction, essays, and interviews.

Magazine: 7×10; 200-300 pgs; 60 lb. paper. Publishes work by established and emerging writers. Has published poetry by Moira Egan, Frannie Lindsay, Ben Lerner, Bob Hicok, Gabe Gudding, John McNally, Steve Almond, Tracy Winn, and Midege Raymond. *Passages North* is 250 pages. Single copy: $13; subscription: $13/year, $23 for 2 years.

NEEDS "Don't be afraid to surprise us." No genre fiction, science fiction, "typical commercial-press work." Length: up to 7,000 words.

HOW TO CONTACT Send 1 short story or as many as 3 short-short stories (paste them all into 1 document).

TIPS "We look for voice, energetic prose, writers who take risks. We look for an engaging story in which the author evokes an emotional response from the reader through carefully rendered scenes, complex characters, and a smart, narrative design. Revise, revise. Read what we publish."

PASSION

Crescent Moon Publishing, P.O. Box 393, Maidstone Kent ME14 5XU United Kingdom. (44)(162)272-9593. **E-mail:** cresmopub@yahoo.co.uk. **Website:** www.crmoon.com. Estab. 1988. *Passion*, published quarterly, features poetry, fiction, reviews, and essays on feminism, art, philosophy, and the media.

Wants "thought-provoking, incisive, polemical, ironic, lyric, sensual, and hilarious work." Does not want "rubbish, trivia, party politics, sport, etc." Has published poetry by Jeremy Reed, Penelope Shuttle, Alan Bold, D.J. Enright, and Peter Redgrove. Single copy: £2.50 ($4 USD); subscription: £10 ($17 USD). Make checks payable to Crescent Moon Publishing.

THE PATERSON LITERARY REVIEW

Passaic County Community College, Cultural Affairs Department, One College Blvd., Paterson NJ 07505-1179. (973)684-6555. **Fax:** (973)523-6085. **E-mail:** mGillan@pccc.edu. **Website:** www.pccc.edu/poetry. **Contact:** Maria Mazziotti Gillan, editor/executive director. *Paterson Literary Review*, published annually, is produced by the The Poetry Center at Passaic County Community College. Wants poetry of "high quality; clear, direct, powerful work."

Paterson Literary Review is 300-400 pages, magazine-sized, professionally printed, perfect-bound, saddle-stapled, with glossy 4-color card cover. Press run is 2,500. Has published poetry and work by Diane di Prima, Ruth Stone, Marge Piercy, Laura Boss, Robert Mooney, and Abigail Stone. Work for *PLR* has been included in *The Pushcart Prize* anthology and *Best American Poetry*.

NEEDS "We are interested in quality short stories, with no taboos on subject matter." Receives 60 unsolicited mss/month. Publishes 5% new writers/year.

HOW TO CONTACT Send SASE for reply or return of ms. "Indicate whether you want your story returned."

PAYMENT/TERMS Pays in contributor's copies.

TIPS Looks for "clear, moving, and specific work."

THE PAUMANOK REVIEW

E-mail: editor@paumanokreview.com. **E-mail:** sub missions@paumanokreview.com. **Website:** www .paumanokreview.com. Estab. 2000. "*The Paumanok Review* is a quarterly Internet literary magazine dedicated to promoting and publishing the best in contemporary art, music, and literature. *TPR* is published exclusively on the Web and is available free of charge." **NEEDS** Short story length: 1,000-6,000+ words. Short-short story length: 200-1,000 words.

HOW TO CONTACT Submit complete ms by e-mail with cover letter.

TIPS "*TPR* does not accept multiple submissions. The best statement of *TPR*'s publishing preferences is the magazine itself. Please read at least 1 issue before submitting."

PEARL

3030 E. Second St., Long Beach CA 90803. (562)434-4523. **E-mail:** pearlmag@aol.com. **Website:** www .pearlmag.com. **Contact:** Joan Jobe Smith and Marilyn Johnson, poetry editors. Estab. 1974. "*Pearl* is an eclectic publication, a place for lively, readable poetry and prose that speaks to real people about real life in direct, living language, profane or sublime."

Submissions are accepted from January-June only. Mss. received between July and December will be returned unread. No e-mail submissions, except from countries outside the U.S. See guidelines.

NEEDS "Our annual fiction issue features the winner of our Pearl Short Story Prize contest as well as shorts shorts and some of the longer stories in our contest. Length: 1,200 words. No obscure, experimental fiction. The winner of the Pearl Short Story Prize receives $250 and 10 copies of the issue the story appears in. Entry fee is $15." Nothing sentimental, obscure, predictable, abstract, or cliché-ridden fiction. Length: 1,200 words.

PAYMENT/TERMS Short Story Prize of $250, 100 copies of the issue the story appears in.

TIPS "We look for vivid, *dramatized* situations and characters, stories written in an original 'voice,' that make sense and follow a clear narrative line. What makes a ms stand out is more elusive, though—more to do with feeling and imagination than anything else."

THE PEDESTAL MAGAZINE

6815 Honors Court, Charlotte NC 28210. (704)643-0244. **E-mail:** pedmagazine@carolina.rr.com. **Website:** www.thepedestalmagazine.com. **Contact:** John Amen, editor-in-chief. Estab. 2000. Committed to promoting diversity and celebrating the voice of the individual.

Submission period: April 1-May 31.

NEEDS "We are receptive to all sorts of high-quality literary fiction. Genre fiction is encouraged as long as it crosses or comments upon its genre and is both character-driven and psychologically acute. We encourage submissions of short fiction, no more than 3 flash fiction pieces at a time. There is no need to query prior to submitting; please submit via the submission form—no e-mail to the editor." Length: 4,000 words.

HOW TO CONTACT Query by e-mail.

PAYMENT/TERMS Pays $40/poem.

TIPS "If you send us your work, please wait for a response to your first submission before you submit again."

PENNSYLVANIA ENGLISH

Penn State DuBois, College Place, DuBois PA 15801-3199. (814)375-4785. **Fax:** (814)375-4785. **E-mail:** aval lone@psu.edu. **Website:** www.english.iup.edu/pcea/ publications.htm. **Contact:** Dr. Jess Haggerty, editor. Estab. 1985. *Pennsylvania English*, published annually, is "sponsored by the Pennsylvania College English Association. Our philosophy is quality. We publish literary fiction (and poetry and nonfiction). Our intended audience is literate, college-educated people."

Magazine: 5.25×8.25; up to 200 pages; perfect bound; full-color cover featuring the artwork of a Pennsylvania artist. Reads mss during the summer. Publishes 4-6 new writers/year. Has published work by Dave Kress, Dan Leone, Paul West, Liz Rosenberg, Walt MacDonald, Amy Pence, Jennifer Richter, and Jeff Schiff.

NEEDS No genre fiction or romance.

HOW TO CONTACT Submit via the online submission manager at https://paenglish.submittable.com/ submit. "For all submissions, please include a brief bio for the contributors' page. Be sure to include your name, address, phone number, e-mail address, institutional affiliation (if you have one), the title of your short story, and any other relevant information. We will edit if necessary for space."

PAYMENT/TERMS Pays 1 contributor's copy.

TIPS "Quality of the writing is our only measure. We're not impressed by long-winded cover letters detailing awards and publications we've never heard of. Beginners and professionals have the same chance with us. We receive stacks of competently written but boring fiction. For a story to rise out of the rejection pile, it takes more than the basic competence."

PENNSYLVANIA LITERARY JOURNAL

Anaphora Literary Press, 5755 E. River Rd., #2201, Tucson AZ 85750. (520)425-4266. **E-mail:** director@ anaphoraliterary.com. **Website:** anaphoraliterary .com. **Contact:** Anna Faktorovich, editor/director. Estab. 2009. Pennsylvania Literary Journal is a printed, peer-reviewed journal that publishes critical essays, book reviews, short stories, interviews, photographs, art, and poetry. Published tri-annually, most are special issues with room for random projects in a wide variety of different fields. These special issues can be used to present a set of conference papers, so feel free to apply on behalf of a conference you are in charge of, if you think attending writers might be interested in seeing their revised conference papers published.

NEEDS No word limit.

HOW TO CONTACT Send complete ms via e-mail

PAYMENT/TERMS Does not provide payment.

TIPS "We are just looking for great writing. Send your materials; if they are good, and you don't mind working for free, we'll take it."

PENTHOUSE VARIATIONS

FriendFinder Networks, 20 Broad Street, 14th Floor, New York NY 10005. **Website:** variations .com/?penthousevariations.com. Estab. 1978. A digest-sized print magazine publishing erotic short stories; prints 12 issues per year.

Send complete first-person, past tense, 3,000-3,500 word ms; no queries. Pays $400 for an accepted ms.

HOW TO CONTACT Send complete ms; no queries.

PAYMENT/TERMS True

TIPS "*Variations* publishes first person, sex-positive narratives in which the author fully describes sex scenes squarely focused within one of the magazine's usual categories, in highly explicit erotic detail. To submit material to *Variations* you must be 18 years of age or older."

PEREGRINE

Amherst Writers & Artists Press, P.O. Box 1076, Amherst MA 01004. (413)253-3307. **Fax:** (413)253-7764. **E-mail:** peregrine@amherstwriters.com. **Website:** www.amherstwriters.com. **Contact:** Jan Haag, editor. Estab. 1983. *Peregrine*, published annually, features poetry and fiction. "*Peregrine* has provided a forum for national and international writers since 1983 and is committed to finding excellent work by emerging as well as established writers. We welcome work reflecting diversity of voice. We like to be surprised. We look for writing that is honest, unpretentious, and memorable. All decisions are made by the editors."

Magazine: 6×9; 100 pages; 60 lb. white offset paper; glossy cover. Annual. Member CLMP. Only considers work submitted from March 15-May 15.

NEEDS Length: up to 750 words.

HOW TO CONTACT Submit via e-mail. Include word count on first page of submissions. "Shorter stories have a better chance."

PAYMENT/TERMS Pays in contributor's copies.

TIPS "Check guidelines before submitting your work. Familiarize yourself with *Peregrine*. We look for heart and soul as well as technical expertise. Trust your own voice."

PERMAFROST: A LITERARY JOURNAL

c/o English Department, University of Alaska Fairbanks, P.O. Box 755720, Fairbanks AK 99775. **Website:** permafrostmag.com. Estab. 1977. *Permafrost: A Literary Journal*, published in May/June, contains poems, short stories, creative nonfiction, b&w drawings, photographs, and prints. "We survive on both new and established writers, hoping and expecting to see the best work out there. We publish any style of poetry provided it is conceived, written, and revised with care. While we encourage submissions about Alaska and by Alaskans, we also welcome poems about anywhere, from anywhere. We have published work by E. Ethelbert Miller, W. Loran Smith, Peter Orlovsky, Jim Wayne Miller, Allen Ginsberg, and Andy Warhol."

Permafrost is about 200 pages, digest-sized, professionally printed, flat-spined. Also publishes summer online edition.

NEEDS Length: up to 8,000 words.

HOW TO CONTACT Type and double-space submissions; include name, address, phone, and e-mail at the top of page 1, with each page after numbered with name at top. Submit by mail (included SASE) or online submission manager at permafrostmag.sub mittable.com; "e-mail submissions will not be read." **PAYMENT/TERMS** Pays 1 contributor's copy. reduced contributor rate of $5 on additional copies.

PERSIMMON TREE: MAGAZINE OF THE ARTS BY WOMEN OVER SIXTY

1534 Campus Dr., Berkeley CA 94708. **E-mail:** editor@persimmontree.org; Submissions@persimmon tree.org. **Website:** www.persimmontree.org. **Contact:** Sue Leonard, editor. "*Persimmon Tree*, an online magazine, is a showcase for the creativity and talent of women over sixty. Too often older women's artistic work is ignored or disregarded, and only those few who are already established receive the attention they deserve. Yet many women are at the height of their creative abilities in their later decades and have a great deal to contribute. *Persimmon Tree* is committed to bringing this wealth of fiction, nonfiction, poetry, and art to a broader audience, for the benefit of all."

NEEDS Length: 1,200-3,000 words.

HOW TO CONTACT Submit complete ms via e-mail.

TIPS "High quality of writing, an interesting or unique point of view, make a ms stand out. Make it clear that you're familiar with the magazine. Tell us why the piece would work for our audience."

PHILADELPHIA STORIES

Fiction/Art/Poetry of the Delaware Valley, 93 Old York Rd., Suite 1/#1-753, Jenkintown PA 19046. (215) 551-5889. **E-mail:** christine@philadelphiastories.org; info@philadelphiastories.org. **Website:** www.phila delphiastories.org. **Contact:** Christine Weiser, executive director/co-publisher. Estab. 2004. *Philadelphia Stories*, published quarterly, publishes "fiction, poetry, essays, and art written by authors living in, or originally from, Pennsylvania, Delaware, or New Jersey. "*Philadelphia Stories* also hosts 2 national writing contests: The Marguerite McGlinn Short Story Contest ($2,000 first-place prize; $500 second-place prize; $250 third-place prize) and the Sandy Crimmins National Poetry Contest ($1,000 first-place prize, $250 second-place prize). Visit our website for details. "*Philadelphia Stories* also launched a 'junior' version in 2012 for Philadelphia-area writers ages 18 and younger. Visit www.philadelphiastories.org/ju nior for details.

Literary magazine/journal. 8.5×11; 24 pages; 70# matte text, all 4-color paper; 70# matte text cover. Contains illustrations, photographs. Subscription: "We offer $20 memberships that include home delivery." Make checks payable to *Philadelphia Stories*. Member: CLMP.

NEEDS Receives 45-80 mss/month. Accepts 3-4 mss/ issue for print, additional 1-2 online; 12-16 mss/year for print, 4-8 online. Publishes 50% new writers/year. Also publishes book reviews. Send review queries to: info@philadelphiastories.org. "We will consider anything that is well written but are most inclined to publish literary or mainstream fiction. We are *not* particularly interested in most genres (science fiction/ fantasy, romance, etc.)." Length: 5,000 words (maximum). Average length: 4,000 words. Also publishes short shorts; average length: 800 words.

PAYMENT/TERMS Pays 2+ contributor's copies.

TIPS "We look for exceptional, polished prose, a controlled voice, strong characters and place, and interesting subjects. Follow guidelines. We cannot stress this enough. Read every guideline carefully and thoroughly before sending anything out. Send out only polished material. We reject many quality pieces for various reasons; try not to take rejection personally. Just because your piece isn't right for one publication doesn't mean it's bad. Selection is an extremely subjective process."

PHOEBE: A JOURNAL OF LITERATURE AND ART

MSN 2C5, George Mason University, 400 University Dr., Fairfax VA 22030. **E-mail:** phoebe@gmu.edu. **Website:** www.phoebejournal.com. Estab. 1972. Publishes poetry, fiction, nonfiction, and visual art. "*Phoebe* prides itself on supporting up-and-coming writers, whose style, form, voice, and subject matter demonstrate a vigorous appeal to the senses, intellect, and emotions of our readers."

NEEDS "No romance or erotica." Length: up to 4,000 words.

HOW TO CONTACT Submit 1 fiction submission via online submission manager.

PAYMENT/TERMS Pays 2 contributor's copies.

PILGRIMAGE MAGAZINE

Colorado State University-Pueblo, Department of English, 2200 Bonforte Blvd., Pueblo CO 81001. **E-mail:** info@pilgrimagepress.org. **E-mail:** https://pil grimagemagazine.submittable.com/submit. **Website:** www.pilgrimagepress.org. **Contact:** Juan Moralez, editor. Estab. 1976. Serves an eclectic fellowship of readers, writers, artists, naturalists, contemplatives, activists, seekers, adventurers, and other kindred spirits.

NEEDS Length: up to 6,000 words. "Shorter works are easier to include, due to space constraints."

TIPS "Our interests include wildness in all its forms; inward and outward explorations; home ground, the open road, service, witness, peace, and justice; symbols, story, and myth in contemporary culture; struggle and resilience; insight and transformation; wisdom wherever it is found; and the great mystery of it all. We like good storytellers and a good sense of humor. No e-mail submissions, please."

◑ THE PINCH

English Department, University of Memphis, Memphis TN 38152. (901)678-4591. **E-mail:** editor@thepinchjournal.com. **Website:** www.thepinchjournal.com. **Contact:** Kristen Iverson, editor-in-chief; Ruth Baumann, managing editor. Estab. 1980. Semi-annual literary magazine. "We publish fiction, creative nonfiction, poetry, and art of literary quality by both established and emerging artists."

NEEDS Wants "character-based" fiction with a "fresh use of language." No genre fiction. Length: up to 5,000 words.

HOW TO CONTACT "We do not accept submissions via e-mail. Submissions sent via e-mail will not receive a response. To submit, see guidelines." Submit through mail or via online submissions manager.

TIPS "We have a new look and a new edge. We're soliciting work from writers with a national or international reputation as well as strong, interesting work from emerging writers. The Pinch Literary Award (previously River City Writing Award) in Fiction offers a $1,000 prize and publication. Check our website for details."

THE PINK CHAMELEON

E-mail: dpfreda@juno.com. **Website:** www.thepinkchameleon.com. **Contact:** Dorothy Paula Freda, editor/publisher. Estab. 2000. *The Pink Chameleon*, published annually online, contains "family-oriented, up-beat poetry, stories, essays, and articles, any genre in good taste that gives hope for the future."

◑ Receives 20 unsolicited mss/month. Publishes 50% new writers/year. Has published work by Deanne F. Purcell, Martin Green, Albert J. Manachino, James W. Collins, Ron Arnold, Sally Kosmalski, Susan Marie Davniero, and Glenn D. Hayes.

NEEDS Reading period is January 1-April 30 and September 1-October 31. "No violence for the sake of violence." No novels or novel excerpts. Length: 500-2,500 words; average length: 2,000 words.

HOW TO CONTACT Send complete ms in the body of the e-mail. No attachments. Accepts reprints. No simultaneous submissions.

PAYMENT/TERMS No payment.

TIPS Wants "simple, honest, evocative emotion, up-beat fiction and nonfiction submissions that give hope for the future; well-paced plots; stories, poetry, articles, essays that speak from the heart. Read guidelines carefully. Use a good, but not ostentatious, opening hook. Stories should have a beginning, middle, and end that make the reader feel the story was worth his or her time. This also applies to articles and essays. In the latter 2, wrap your comments and conclusions in a neatly packaged final paragraph. Turnoffs include violence and bad language. Simple, genuine, and sensitive work does not need to shock with vulgarity to be interesting and enjoyable."

◑ PINYON POETRY

Mesa State College, Languages, Literature, and Mass Communications, Mesa State College, 1100 North Ave., Grand Junction CO 81502. **E-mail:** rphillis@mesa5.mesa.colorado.edu. **Website:** myhome.coloradomesa.edu/~rphillis/. **Contact:** Randy Phillis, editor. Estab. 1995. *Pinyon*, published annually in June, prints "the best available contemporary American poetry. No restrictions other than excellence. We appreciate a strong voice."

◑ Literary magazine/journal: 8½×5½, 120 pages, heavy paper. Contains illustrations and photographs. Press run is 300; 100 distributed free to contributors, friends, etc.

TIPS "Ask yourself if the work is something you would like to read in a publication."

○ PISGAH REVIEW

Division of Humanities, Brevard College, 1 Brevard College Dr., Brevard NC 28712. (828)884-8349. **E-mail:** tinerjj@brevard.edu. **Website:** www.pisgahreview.com. **Contact:** Jubal Tiner, editor. Estab. 2005. "*Pisgah Review* publishes primarily literary short fiction, creative nonfiction, and poetry. Our only criteria is quality of work; we look for the best."

Literary magazine/journal: 5½×8½, 120 pages. Includes cover artwork. Published Ron Rash, Thomas Rain Crowe, Joan Conner, Gary Fincke, Steve Almond, and Fred Bahnson.

NEEDS Receives 85 mss/month. Accepts 6-8 mss/issue; 12-15 mss/year. Publishes 5 new writers/year. Does not want genre fiction or inspirational stories. Length: 2,000-7,500 words. Average length: 4,000 words. Average length of short shorts: 1,000 words.

HOW TO CONTACT "Send complete ms to our submission manager on our website."

PAYMENT/TERMS Writers receive 2 contributor's copies. Additional copies $7.

TIPS "We select work of only the highest quality. Grab us from the beginning and follow through. Engage us with your language and characters. A clean ms goes a long way toward acceptance. Stay true to the vision of your work, revise tirelessly, and submit persistently."

PLANET: THE WELSH INTERNATIONALIST

P.O. Box 44, Aberystwyth Ceredigion SY23 3ZZ United Kingdom. **E-mail:** emily.trahair@planetmagazine.org.uk. **Website:** www.planetmagazine.org.uk. **Contact:** Emily Trahair, associate editor. Estab. 1970. A literary/cultural/political journal centered on Welsh affairs but with a strong interest in minority cultures in Europe and elsewhere. *Planet: The Welsh Internationalist*, published quarterly, is a cultural magazine "centered on Wales, but with broader interests in arts, sociology, politics, history, and science."

Planet is 128 pages, A5, professionally printed, perfect-bound, with glossy color card cover. Receives about 500 submissions/year, accepts about 5%. Press run is 1,550 (1,500 subscribers, about 10% libraries, 200 shelf sales).

NEEDS Would like to see more inventive, imaginative fiction that pays attention to language and experiments with form. No magical realism, horror, science fiction. Length: 1,500-4,000 words.

HOW TO CONTACT Submit via mail or e-mail (with attachment). No submissions returned unless accompanied by an SASE. Writers submitting from abroad should send at least 3 IRCs for return of typescript; 1 IRC for reply only. E-mail queries accepted.

PAYMENT/TERMS Pays £50/1,000 words.

TIPS "We do not look for fiction which necessarily has a 'Welsh' connection, which some writers assume from our title. We try to publish a broad range of fic-tion, and our main criterion is quality. Try to read copies of any magazine you submit to. Don't write out of the blue to a magazine which might be completely inappropriate for your work. Recognize that you are likely to have a high rejection rate, as magazines tend to favor writers from their own countries."

PLEIADES

Pleiades Press, Department of English, University of Central Missouri, Martin 336, Warrensburg MO 64093. (660)543-8106. **E-mail:** pleiades@ucmo.edu. **Website:** www.ucmo.edu/englphil/pleiades. **Contact:** Kevin Prufer, editor-at-large. Estab. 1991. "We publish contemporary fiction, poetry, interviews, literary essays, special-interest personal essays, and reviews for a general and literary audience from authors from around the world." Reads August 15-May 15.

NEEDS Reads fiction year-round. No science fiction, fantasy, confession, erotica. Length: 2,000-6,000 words.

HOW TO CONTACT Send complete ms via online submission manager.

PAYMENT/TERMS Pays $10 and contributor's copies.

TIPS "Submit only 1 genre at a time to appropriate editors. Show care for your material and your readers—submit quality work in a professional format. Include cover letter with brief bio and list of publications. Include SASE. Cover art is solicited directly from artists. We accept queries for book reviews."

PLOUGHSHARES

Emerson College, Ploughshares, 120 Boylston St., Boston MA 02116. **Website:** www.pshares.org. **Contact:** Ladette Randolph, editor-in-chief/executive director; Andrea Martucci, managing editor. Estab. 1971. *Ploughshares*, published 3 times/year, is "a journal of new writing guest edited by prominent poets and writers to reflect different and contrasting points of view. Translations are welcome if permission has been granted. Our mission is to present dynamic, contrasting views on what is valid and important in contemporary literature and to discover and advance significant literary talent. We no longer structure issues around preconceived themes." Editors have included Carolyn Forché, Gerald Stern, Rita Dove, Chase Twichell, and Marilyn Hacker. Has published poetry by Donald Hall, Li-Young Lee, Robert Pinsky, Brenda Hillman, and Thylias Moss. Reads submissions June 1-January 15 (postmark); mss submitted January 16-May 31 will be returned unread. "We do accept electronic submissions—there is a $3 fee per submission, which is waived if you are a subscriber."

⊙ *Ploughshares* is 200 pages, digest-sized. Receives about 11,000 poetry, fiction, and essay submissions/year.

NEEDS Recently published work by ZZ Packer, Antonya Nelson, and Stuart Dybek. "No genre (science fiction, detective, gothic, adventure, etc.), popular formula or commerical fiction whose purpose is to entertain rather than to illuminate." Length: up to 6,000 words; prefers up to 5,000 words.

HOW TO CONTACT Submit online or by mail.

PAYMENT/TERMS Pays $25/printed page; $50 minimum, $250 maximum; 2 contributor's copies; and one-year subscription.

TIPS "We no longer structure issues around preconceived themes. If you believe your work is in keeping with our general standards of literary quality and value, submit at any time during our reading period."

⊙ PMS POEMMEMOIRSTORY

University of Alabama at Birmingham, HB 217, 1530 3rd Ave. S, Birmingham AL 35294. (205)934-2641. **Fax:** (205)975-8125. **E-mail:** poemmemoirstory@ gmail.com. **Website:** pms-journal.org. **Contact:** Kerry Madden, editor-in-chief. *PMSpoemmemoirstory* is a 140-page, perfect-bound, all-women's literary journal published annually by the University of Alabama at Birmingham. While we proudly publish the best work of the best women writers in the nation (i.e.,Maxine Chernoff, Elaine Equi, Amy Gerstler, Honorée Fanonne Jeffers, Molly Peacock, Lucia Perillo, Sonia Sanchez, Ruth Stone, and Natasha Trethewey, Dr.Alison Chapman, Masha Hamilton, and the Afghan Women's Writing Project, Mary JoBang, Heather Dundas, Donna Thomas, Jennifer Horne, Jeanie Thompson, and Nancy Rutland Glaub, among others) we also solicit a memoir for each issue written by a woman who may not be a writer, but who has experienced something of historic significance. Emily Lyons, the nurse who survived the 1998 New Woman All Women Birmingham clinic bombing by Eric Rudolph, wrote the first of these; women who experienced the World Trade Center on September 11th, the Civil Rights Movement in Birmingham, the war in Iraq, and Hurricane Katrina have also lent us their stories."

⊙ Work from *PMS* has been reprinted in a number of award anthologies: *New Stories from the South 2005, The Best Creative Nonfiction 2008, Best American Poetry 2003* and *2004*, and *Best American Essays 2005* and *2007*.

NEEDS Length: no more than 15 pages or 4,300 words.

HOW TO CONTACT "All submissions should be unpublished original work that we can recycle and should be accompanied by an SASE with sufficient postage for either return of your ms or notification. Or use online submission form." Include cover letter and short bio.

PAYMENT/TERMS Pays 2 contributor's copies and one-year subscription.

TIPS "We seek unpublished original work that we can recycle. Reading period runs January 1-March 31. Submissions received at other times of the year will be returned unread. Best way to make contact is through e-mail."

⊙ ⑤ POCKETS

The Upper Room, P.O. Box 340004, Nashville TN 37203. (615)340-7333. **Fax:** (615)340-7267. **E-mail:** pockets@upperroom.org. **Website:** pockets.upper room.org. **Contact:** Lynn W. Gilliam, editor. Estab. 1981. Magazine published 11 times/year. "*Pockets* is a Christian devotional magazine for children ages 8-12. All submissions should address the broad theme of the magazine. Each issue is built around 1 theme with material which can be used by children in a variety of ways. Scripture stories, fiction, poetry, prayers, art, graphics, puzzles, and activities are included. Submissions do not need to be overtly religious. They should help children experience a Christian lifestyle that is not always a neatly wrapped moral package but is open to the continuing revelation of God's will. Seasonal material, both secular and liturgical, is desired."

⊙ Does not accept e-mail or fax submissions.

TIPS "Theme stories, role models, and retold scripture stories are most open to freelancers. Poetry is also open. It is very helpful if writers read our writers' guidelines and themes on our website."

POETICA MAGAZINE, CONTEMPORARY JEWISH WRITING

P.O. Box 11014, Norfolk VA 23517. **E-mail:** michalpo etryeditor@poeticamagazine.com; jagodastoryedi tor@poeticamagazine.com. **Website:** www.poetica magazine.com. Estab. 2002. *Poetica Magazine, Reflections of Jewish Thought*, published in print 3 times/ year, offers "an outlet for the many writers who draw from their Jewish backgrounds and experiences to create poetry/prose/short stories, giving both emerging and recognized writers the opportunity to share their work with the larger community."

- *Poetica* is 70 pages, perfect-bound, full-color cover, includes some ads. Receives about 500 poems/year, accepts about 60%. Press run is 350. Single copy: $10; subscription: $21.50 individual; $24.95 libraries and Canada; $28.95 international.

TIPS "We publish original, unpublished works by Jewish and non-Jewish writers alike. We are interested in works that have the courage to acknowledge, challenge, and celebrate modern Jewish life beyond distinctions of secular and sacred. We like accessible works that find fresh meaning in old traditions that recognize the challenges of our generation. We evaluate works on several levels, including its skillful use of craft, its ability to hold interest, and layers of meaning."

POETRY INTERNATIONAL

San Diego State University, 5500 Campanile Dr., San Diego CA 92182-6020. (619)594-1522. **Fax:** (619)594-4998. **E-mail:** poetry.international@yahoo.com. **Website:** poetryinternational.sdsu.edu. **Contact:** Jenny Minniti-Shippey, managing editor. Estab. 1997. *Poetry International*, published annually in November, is "an eclectic poetry magazine intended to reflect a wide range of poetry being written today." Wants "a wide range of styles and subject matter. We're particularly interested in translations." Does not want "cliché-ridden, derivative, or obscure poetry." Has published poetry by Adrienne Rich, Robert Bly, Hayden Carruth, Kim Addonizio, Maxine Kumin, and Gary Soto. "We intend to continue to publish poetry that makes a difference in people's lives and startles us anew with the endless capacity of language to awaken our senses and expand our awareness."

- *Poetry International* is 200 pages, perfect-bound, with coated cardstock cover. Features the Poetry International Prize ($1,000) for best original poem. Submit up to 3 poems with a $10 entry fee.

HOW TO CONTACT Query.

TIPS "Seeks a wide range of styles and subject matter. We read unsolicited mss only between September 1-December 31 of each year. Mss received any other time will be returned unread."

POINTED CIRCLE

Portland Community College, Cascade Campus, SC 206, 705 N. Killingsworth Street, Portland OR 97217. **E-mail:** wendy.bourgeois@pcc.edu. **Website:** www.pcc.edu/about/literary-magazines/pointed-circle. **Contact:** Wendy Bourgeois, faculty advisor. Estab. 1980. Publishes "anything of interest to educationally/culturally mixed audience. We will read whatever is sent, but we encourage writers to remember we are a quality literary/arts magazine intended to promote the arts in the community. No pornography, nothing trite. Be mindful of deadlines and length limits." Accepts submissions by e-mail, mail; artwork in high-resolution digital form.

- Magazine: 80 pages; b&w illustrations; photos.

NEEDS Accepts submissions only October 1-March 1, for July 1 issue. Length: Up to 3,000 words.

HOW TO CONTACT Submitted materials will not be returned; SASE for notification only. Accepts multiple submissions.

PAYMENT/TERMS Pays 2 contributor's copies.

POLYPHONY H.S.

An International Student-Run Literary Magazine for High School Writers and Editors, Polyphony High School, 1514 Elmwood Ave., Suite 2, Evanston IL 60201. (847)910-3221. **E-mail:** info@polyphonyhs.com. **E-mail:** billy@polyphonyhs.com. **Website:** www.polyphonyhs.com. Estab. 2005. "Our mission is to create a high-quality literary magazine written, edited, and published by high school students. We believe that when young writers put precise and powerful language to their lives it helps them better understand their value as human beings. We believe the development of that creative voice depends upon close, careful, and compassionate attention. Helping young editors become proficient at providing thoughtful and informed attention to the work of their peers is essential to our mission. We believe this important exchange between young writers and editors provides each with a better understanding of craft, of the writing process, and of the value of putting words to their own lives while preparing them for participation in the broader literary community. We strive to build respectful, mutually beneficial, writer-editor relationships that form a community devoted to improving students' literary skills in the areas of poetry, fiction, and creative nonfiction."

- Does not accept hard-copy entries.

HOW TO CONTACT Submit with online submission process.

PAYMENT/TERMS Pays 2 contributor's copies.

PORTLAND MONTHLY

165 State St., Portland ME 04101. (207)775-4339. E-mail: staff@portlandmonthly.com. **Website:** www.portlandmagazine.com. **Contact:** Colin Sargent, editor. Estab. 1985. Monthly city lifestyle magazine: fiction, style, business, real estate, controversy, fashion, cuisine, interviews, and art relating to the Maine area.

NEEDS Length: up to 1,000 words.

HOW TO CONTACT Submit via online submission manager.

TIPS "Our target audience is our 100,000 readers ages 18 to 90. We write for our readers alone, and while in many cases we're delighted when our interview subjects enjoy our stories once they're in print, we are not writing for them but only for our readers. Interview subjects may not ever read or hear any portion of our stories before the stories are printed, and in the interest of objective distance, interview subjects are never to be promised complimentary copies of the magazine. It is the writer's responsibility to return all materials such as photos or illustrations to the interview subjects providing them."

PORTLAND REVIEW

Portland State University, P.O. Box 751, Portland OR 97207. (503)725-4533. **E-mail:** theportlandreview@gmail.com. **Website:** portlandreview.org. **Contact:** Brian Tibbetts, editor-in-chief. Estab. 1956. Press run is 1,000 for subscribers, libraries, and bookstores nationwide. Single copy: $12; subscription: $27/year, $54/2 years. Sample: $8.

NEEDS Length: 5,000 words maximum.

HOW TO CONTACT Send complete ms.

PAYMENT/TERMS Pays contributor's copies.

TIPS "View website for current guidelines."

POST ROAD

P.O. Box 600725, Newtown MA 02460. **E-mail:** postroad@bc.edu. **Website:** www.postroadmag.com. **Contact:** Chris Boucher, managing editor. *Post Road,* published twice yearly, accepts unsolicited poetry, fiction, nonfiction, short plays and monologues, and visual art submissions. Reads February 1-April 1 for the winter issue and June 1-August 1 for the spring issue.

Work from *Post Road* has received the following honors: honorable mention in the 2001 O. Henry Prize Issue guest edited by Michael Chabon, Mary Gordon, and Mona Simpson; the Pushcart Prize; honorable mention in *The Best American Nonfiction* series; and inclusion in the *Best American Short Stories* 2005.

HOW TO CONTACT Submit using online submission form.

PAYMENT/TERMS Pays 2 contributor's copies.

TIPS "Looking for interesting narrative, sharp dialogue, deft use of imagery and metaphor. Be persistent and be open to criticism."

POTOMAC REVIEW

Montgomery College, 51 Mannakee St., MT/212, Rockville MD 20850. (301)251-7417. **Fax:** (301)738-1745. **E-mail:** PotomacReviewEditor@montgomerycollege.edu. **Website:** www.montgomerycollege.edu/potomacreview. **Contact:** Julie Wakeman-Linn, editor-in-chief. Estab. 1994. Magazine: 5.5×8.5; 175 pages; 50 lb. paper; 65 lb. color cover. *Potomac Review* "reflects a view of our region looking out to the world, and in turn, seeks to hear how the world views the region." Biannual.

NEEDS Prose. Length: up to 5,000 words.

HOW TO CONTACT Submit via online submissions manager. Reading period September 1-May 1; only 1 submission per genre per reading period.

PAYMENT/TERMS Pays in contributor's copies.

TIPS "Send us interesting, well-crafted stories. Have something to say in an original, provocative voice. Read recent issue to get a sense of the journal's new direction."

POTOMAC REVIEW: A JOURNAL OF ARTS & HUMANITIES

Montgomery College, 51 Mannakee St., MT/212, Rockville MD 20850. (240)567-4100. **E-mail:** PotomacReviewEditor@montgomerycollege.edu. **Website:** www.montgomerycollege.edu/potomacreview. **Contact:** Julie Wakeman-Linn, editor-in-chief. Estab. 1994. *Potomac Review: A Journal of Arts & Humanities,* published semiannually in November and May, welcomes poetry, from across the spectrum, both traditional and nontraditional poetry, free verse and in-form (translations accepted). Essays, fiction, and creative nonfiction are also welcome. Has published work by David Wagoner, Elizabeth Spires, Ramola D, Amy Holman, and Luke Johnson.

Reading period: September 1-May1. *Potomac Review* is 150 pages, digest-sized, 50 lb paper; 65 lb cover stock. Receives about 2,500 poems/year, accepts 3%. Subscription: $18/year (includes 2 issues). Sample: $10.

NEEDS Submit up to 5,000 words.

HOW TO CONTACT Submit electronically through website.

◐◑⑨ THE PRAIRIE JOURNAL

P.O. Box 68073, 28 Crowfoot Terrace NW, Calgary AB Y3G 3N8 Canada. **E-mail:** editor@prairiejournal.org (queries only); prairiejournal@yahoo.com. **Website:** www.prairiejournal.org. **Contact:** A.E. Burke, literary editor. Estab. 1983. "The audience is literary, university, library, scholarly, and creative readers/writers."

◯ "Use our mailing address for submissions and queries with samples or for clippings."

NEEDS No genre (romance, horror, western—sagebrush or cowboys), erotic, science fiction, or mystery. Length: 100-3,000 words.

HOW TO CONTACT Send complete ms. No e-mail submissions.

PAYMENT/TERMS Pays $10-75.

TIPS "We publish many, many new writers and are always open to unsolicited submissions because we are 100% freelance. Do not send U.S. stamps, always use IRCs. We have poems, interviews, stories, and reviews online (query first)."

◑◯ PRAIRIE SCHOONER

The University of Nebraska Press, Prairie Schooner, 123 Andrews Hall, University of Nebraska, Lincoln NE 68588. (402)472-0911. **Fax:** (402)472-1817. **E-mail:** PrairieSchooner@unl.edu. **Website:** prairieschooner.unl.edu. **Contact:** Marianne Kunkel, managing editor. Estab. 1926. "We look for the best fiction, poetry, and nonfiction available to publish, and our readers expect to read stories, poems, and essays of extremely high quality. We try to publish a variety of styles, topics, themes, points of view, and writers with a variety of backgrounds in all stages of their careers. We like work that is compelling—intellectually or emotionally—either in form, language, or content."

◯ Submissions must be received between September 1 and May 1.

NEEDS "We try to remain open to a variety of styles, themes, and subject matter. We look for high-quality writing, 3D characters, well-wrought plots, setting, etc. We are open to realistic and/or experimental fiction."

HOW TO CONTACT Send complete ms with SASE and cover letter listing previous publications (where, when).

PAYMENT/TERMS Pays 3 copies of the issue in which the writer's work is published.

TIPS "Send us your best, most carefully crafted work, and be persistent. Submit again and again. Constantly work on improving your writing. Read widely in literary fiction, nonfiction, and poetry. Read *Prairie Schooner* to know what we publish."

PRAIRIE WINDS

Dakota Wesleyan University English Department, 1200 University Ave., Box 536, Mitchell SD 57301. (605)995-2633. **E-mail:** prairiewinds@dwu.edu. **Website:** www.dwu.edu/english/studentpublications/prairiewinds. **Contact:** Joe Ditta, faculty advisor. Estab. 1946. *Prairie Winds* is a literary annual interested in poetry, fiction, creative nonfiction, and essays of general interest. Selection of mss takes place in February, the magazine goes to press in March, and it is distributed in April of each year.

NEEDS No pornography. Length: 3,000 words maximum.

HOW TO CONTACT Submit complete ms by mail. Include SASE, short bio, and e-mail address.

PAYMENT/TERMS Pays contributor's copies.

TIPS *Prairie Winds* accepts only a small proportion of works submitted. There are no restrictions on subject matter, except pornography. There are no restrictions on style or form. Writers need to submit persuasively good work. Editors of *Prairie Winds* are eclectic and open-minded, and they like experimental as well as traditional work.

⑨◯ PREMONITIONS

13 Hazely Combe, Arrenton Isle of Wight PO30 3AJ United Kingdom. **E-mail:** mail@pigasuspress.co.uk. **Website:** www.pigasuspress.co.uk. **Contact:** Tony Lee, editor. "Science fiction and horror stories, plus genre poetry and fantastic artwork."

NEEDS Wants "original, high-quality science fiction/fantasy. Horror must have a science fiction element and be psychological or scary, rather than simply gory. Cutting-edge science fiction and experimental writing styles (cross-genre scenarios, slipstream, etc.) are always welcome." No supernatural fantasy-horror. Length: 500-6,000 words. Send 1 story at a time.

HOW TO CONTACT Submit via mail and include SAE or IRC if you want material returned. "Use a standard ms format: double-spaced text, no right-justify, no staples." Do not send submissions via e-mail, unless by special request from editor. Include personalized cover letter with brief bio and publication credits.

PAYMENT/TERMS Pays minimum $5 or £5 per 1,000 words, plus copy of magazine.

TIPS "Potential contributors are advised to study recent issues of the magazine."

⊙◍⊘◎⑤ PRISM INTERNATIONAL

Department of Creative Writing, Buch E462, 1866 Main Mall, University of British Columbia, Vancouver BC V6T 1Z1 Canada. (604)822-2514. **Fax:** (604)822-3616. **E-mail:** prismcirculation@gmail.com. **Website:** www.prismmagazine.ca. Estab. 1959. A quarterly international journal of contemporary writing—fiction, poetry, drama, creative nonfiction and translation. *PRISM international* is 80 pages, digest-sized, elegantly printed, flat-spined, with original color artwork on a glossy card cover. Readership: public and university libraries, individual subscriptions, bookstores—a worldwide audience concerned with the contemporary in literature. "We have no thematic or stylistic allegiances: Excellence is our main criterion for acceptance of mss." Receives 1,000 submissions/year, accepts about 80. Circulation is for 1,200 subscribers. Subscription: $35/year for Canadian subscriptions, $40/year for U.S. subscriptions, $45/year for international. Sample: $12.

NEEDS Experimental, traditional. New writing that is contemporary and literary. Short stories and self-contained novel excerpts (up to 25 double-spaced pages). Works of translation are eagerly sought and should be accompanied by a copy of the original. Would like to see more translations. "No gothic, confession, religious, romance, pornography, or science fiction." Also looking for creative nonfiction that is literary, not journalistic, in scope and tone. Receives over 100 unsolicited mss/month. Accepts 70 mss/year. "PRISM publishes both new and established writers; our contributors have included Franz Kafka, Gabriel Garcíía Maárquez, Michael Ondaatje, Margaret Laurence, Mark Anthony Jarman, Gail Anderson-Dargatz, and Eden Robinson." Publishes ms 4 months after acceptance. **Publishes 7 new writers/year.** Recently published work by Ibi Kaslik, Melanie Little, Mark Anthony Jarman. Publishes short shorts. Also publishes poetry. For Drama: one-acts/excerpts of no more than 1,500 words preferred. Also interested in seeing dramatic monologues. "New writing that is contemporary and literary. Short stories and self-contained novel excerpts. Works of translation are eagerly sought and should be accompanied by a copy of the original. Would like to see more translations. No gothic, confession, religious, romance, pornography, or science fiction." 25 pages maximum.

HOW TO CONTACT Send complete ms by mail: Department of Creative Writing, Buch E462, 1866 Main Mall, University of British Columbia, Vancouver BC V6T 1Z1 Canada; or submit online through prism-magazine.ca. "Keep it simple. U.S. contributors take note: Do not send SASEs with U.S. stamps, they are not valid in Canada. Send International Reply Coupons instead." Responds in 4 months to queries; 3-6 months to mss. Sample copy for $12 or on website. Writer's guidelines online. Send complete ms.

PAYMENT/TERMS Pays $20/printed page of prose, $40/printed page of poetry, and one-year subscription. Pays on publication for first North American serial rights. Selected authors are paid an additional $10/page for digital rights. Cover art pays $300 and 4 copies of issue. Sponsors awards/contests, including annual short fiction, poetry, and nonfiction contests. Pays $20/printed page, and one-year subscription

TIPS "We are looking for new and exciting fiction. Excellence is still our No. 1 criterion. In addition to poetry, imaginative nonfiction, and fiction, we are especially open to translations of all kinds, very short fiction pieces, and drama that works well on the page. Translations must come with a copy of the original language work. We pay an additional $10/printed page to selected authors whose work we place on our online version of *PRISM*."

◍⊘⑤ PSEUDOPOD

Escape Artists, Inc., P.O. Box 965609, Marietta GA 30066. **Fax:** (866)373-8739. **E-mail:** editor@pseudopod.org. **E-mail:** submit@pseudopod.org. **Website:** pseudopod.org. **Contact:** Shawn M. Garrett, editor. "*Pseudopod* is the premier horror podcast magazine. Every week we bring you chilling short stories from some of today's best horror authors, in convenient audio format for your computer or MP3 player."

NEEDS Length: 2,000-6,000 words (short fiction); 500-1,500 words (flash fiction).

HOW TO CONTACT Does not want multiple submissions. Paste submission in body of an e-mail you will use for correspondence. Include contact information, cover statement, and word count.

PAYMENT/TERMS Pays $100 for short fiction, $20 for flash fiction.

TIPS "Let the writing be guided by a strong sense of who the (hopefully somewhat interesting) protagonist is, even if zero time is spent developing any other characters. Preferably, tell the story using standard past tense, third-person, active voice."

O PUERTO DEL SOL

New Mexico State University, English Department, P.O.Box 30001, MSC 3E, Las Cruces NM 88003. (505)646-3931. **E-mail:** contact@puertodelsol.org. **Website:** www.puertodelsol.org. **Contact:** Carmen Giménez Smith, editor-in-chief. Estab. 1964. Publishes innovative work from emerging and established writers and artists. Poetry, fiction, nonfiction, drama, theory, artwork, interviews, reviews, and interesting combinations thereof.

Magazine: 7×9; 200 pages; 60 lb. paper; 70 lb. cover stock. *Puerto del Sol* is 150 pages, digest-sized, professionally printed, flat-spined, with matte card cover with art. Press run is 1,250 (300 subscribers, 25-30 libraries). Single copies: $10. Subscriptions: $20 for 1 year, $35 for 2 years, $45 for 3 years.

NEEDS Accepts 8-12 mss/issue; 16-24 mss/year. Reading period is September 15-March 31. Publishes several new writers/year. Recently published work by David Trinidad, Molly Gaudry, Ray Gonzalez, Cynthia Cruz, Steve Tomasula, Denise Leto, Rae Bryant, Joshua Cohen, Blake Butler, Trinie Dalton, and Rick Moody.

HOW TO CONTACT Send complete ms. Submit 1 short story or 2-4 short short stories at a time through online submission manager.

PAYMENT/TERMS Pays 2 contributor's copies.

TIPS "We are especially pleased to publish emerging writers who work to push their art form or field of study in new directions."

◐ QUARTER AFTER EIGHT

Ohio University, 360 Ellis Hall, Athens OH 45701. **Website:** www.quarteraftereight.org. **Contact:** Patrick Swaney and Brad Aaron, editors. "*Quarter After Eight* is an annual literary journal devoted to the exploration of innovative writing. We celebrate work that directly challenges the conventions of language, style, voice, or idea in literary forms. In its aesthetic commitment to diverse forms, *QAE* remains a unique publication among contemporary literary magazines."

Subscriptions: one-year subscription (1 volume): $10; 2-year subscription (2 volumes): $18; 3-year subscription (3 volumes): $25. Holds annual short prose contest with grand prize of $1,000. Deadline is November 30.

NEEDS Length: no more than 10,000 words.

PAYMENT/TERMS Pays 2 contributor's copies.

TIPS "We look for prose and poetry that is innovative, exploratory, and—most important—well written. Please subscribe to our journal and read what is published to get acquainted with the *QAE* aesthetic."

◐◑◉ QUARTERLY WEST

University of Utah, 255 S. Central Campus Dr., Room 3500, Salt Lake City UT 84112. **E-mail:** quarterlywest@gmail.com. **Website:** www.quarterlywest.com. **Contact:** Sadie Hoagland and Lillian Bertram, editors. Estab. 1976. "We publish fiction, poetry, and nonfiction in long and short formats, and will consider experimental as well as traditional works."

Quarterly West was awarded first place for editorial content from the American Literary Magazine Awards. Work published in the magazine has been selected for inclusion in *The Pushcart Prize* anthology and *The Best American Short Stories* anthology.

NEEDS No preferred lengths; interested in longer, fuller short stories and short shorts. No detective, science fiction, or romance.

HOW TO CONTACT Send complete ms using online submissions manager only.

TIPS "We publish a special section of short shorts every issue, and we also sponsor a biennial novella contest. We are open to experimental work—potential contributors should read the magazine! Don't send more than 1 story/submission. Biennial novella competition guidelines available upon request with SASE. We prefer work with interesting language and detail—plot or narrative are less important. We don't do Western themes or religious work."

◐◑◉ QUEEN'S QUARTERLY

144 Barrie St., Queen's University, Kingston ON K7L 3N6 Canada. (613)533-2667. **Fax:** (613)533-6822. **E-mail:** queens.quarterly@queensu.ca. **Website:** www .queensu.ca/quarterly. **Contact:** Joan Harcourt, edi-

tor. Estab. 1893. *Queen's Quarterly* is "a general interest intellectual review featuring articles on science, politics, humanities, arts and letters, extensive book reviews, some poetry and fiction."

○ Digest-sized, 224 pages. Press run is 3,500. Receives about 400 submissions of poetry/year, accepts 40. Has published work by Gail Anderson-Dargatz, Tim Bowling, Emma Donohue, Viktor Carr, Mark Jarman, Rick Bowers, and Dennis Bock. Subscription: $20 Canadian, $25 for U.S. and foreign subscribers. Sample: $6.50 U.S.

NEEDS Length: 2,500-3,000 words. "Submissions over 3,000 words shall not be accepted."

HOW TO CONTACT Send complete ms with SASE and/or IRC. No reply with insufficient postage. Accepts 2 mss/issue; 8 mss/year. Publishes 5 new writers/year.

PAYMENT/TERMS Pays on publication for first North American serial rights. Sends galleys to author.

THE RAG

11901 SW 34th Ave., Portland OR 97219. **E-mail:** raglitmag@gmail.com. **E-mail:** submissions@raglitmag.com. **Website:** raglitmag.com. **Contact:** Seth Porter, editor; Dan Reilly, editor. Estab. 2011. *The Rag* focuses on the grittier genres that tend to fall by the wayside at more traditional literary magazines. *The Rag*'s ultimate goal is to put the literary magazine magazine back into the entertainment market while rekindling the social and cultural value short fiction once held in North American literature.

○ Fee to submit online ($3) is waived if you subscribe or purchase a single issue.

NEEDS Accepts all styles and themes. Length: 2,000-10,000 words.

HOW TO CONTACT Send complete ms.

PAYMENT/TERMS Pays 5¢/word, the average being $250/story.

TIPS "We like gritty material; material that is psychologically believable and that has some humor in it, dark or otherwise. We like subtle themes, original characters, and sharp wit."

⑤ RAINBOW RUMPUS

P.O. Box 6881, Minneapolis MN 55406. (612)721-6442. **E-mail:** fictionandpoetry@rainbowrumpus.org; admin@rainbowrumpus.org. **Website:** www.rainbowrumpus.org. **Contact:** Beth Wallace, fiction editor. Estab. 2005. "*Rainbow Rumpus* is the world's only online literary magazine for children and youth with lesbian, gay, bisexual, and transgender (LGBT) parents. We are creating a new genre of children's and young adult fiction. Please carefully read and observe the guidelines on our website. All fiction and poetry submissions should be sent via our contact page. Be sure to select the 'Submissions' category. A staff member will be in touch with you shortly to obtain a copy of your ms."

NEEDS Length: "Stories for 4- to 12-year-old children should be approximately 800 to 2,500 words in length. Stories for 13- to 18-year-olds may be as long as 5,000 words."

HOW TO CONTACT "Stories should be written from the point of view of children or teens with lesbian, gay, bisexual, or transgender parents or other family members, or who are connected to the LGBT community. Stories featuring families of color, bisexual parents, transgender parents, family members with disabilities, and mixed-race families are particularly welcome."

PAYMENT/TERMS Pays $300/story.

TIPS "Emerging writers encouraged to submit. You do not need to be a member of the LGBT community to participate."

⊕◑ RALEIGH REVIEW LITERARY & ARTS MAGAZINE

P.O. Box 6725, Raleigh NC 27628-6725. **E-mail:** info@raleighreview.org. **Website:** www.raleighreview.org. **Contact:** Rob Greene, editor. Estab. 2010. "*Raleigh Review* is a national nonprofit magazine of poetry, short fiction (including flash), and art. We believe that great literature inspires empathy by allowing us to see the world through the eyes of our neighbors, whether across the street or across the globe. Our mission is to foster the creation and availability of accessible yet provocative contemporary literature. We look for work that is emotionally and intellectually complex without being unnecessarily 'difficult.'"

○ Semiannual literary magazine.

NEEDS "We are not looking for genre stories, though we are open to literary stories with genre elements. Anything cliché will be discarded immediately." Length: 250-7,500 words.

HOW TO CONTACT Submit complete ms.

PAYMENT/TERMS Pays $10 maximum.

TIPS "Please be sure to read the guidelines and look at sample work on our website. Send us writing we haven't seen before, preferably work that is physically grounded and accessible, though complex and rich in emotional or intellectual power. We delight in stories from unique voices and perspectives. Any fiction that is born from a relatively unknown place grabs our attention. We are not opposed to genre fiction, so long as it has real, human characters and is executed artfully. Every piece is read for its intrinsic value, so new/emerging voices are often published along nationally recognized, award-winning authors."

RATTAPALLAX

Rattapallax Press, 217 Thompson St., Suite 353, New York NY 10012. (212)560-7459. **E-mail:** info@rattapallax.com. **Website:** www.rattapallax.com. **Contact:** Flávia Rocha, editor-in-chief. Estab. 1999. *Rattapallax*, published semiannually, is named for "Wallace Stevens's word for the sound of thunder. The magazine includes a DVD featuring poetry films and audio files. *Rattapallax* is looking for the extraordinary in modern poetry and prose that reflect the diversity of world cultures. Our goals are to create international dialogue using literature and focus on what is relevant to our society."

○ *Rattapallax* is 112 pages, magazine-sized, offset printed, perfect-bound, with 12-pt. CS1 cover; some illustrations; photos. Press run is 2,000 (100 subscribers, 50 libraries, 1,200 shelf sales); 200 distributed free to contributors, reviews, and promos. Receives 15 unsolicited mss/month. Accepts 3 mss/issue; 6 mss/year. Agented fiction 15%. Receives about 5,000 poems/year; accepts 2%. Publishes 3 new writers/year. Has published work by Stuart Dybek, Howard Norman, Molly Giles, Rick Moody, Anthony Hecht, Sharon Olds, Lou Reed, Marilyn Hacker, Billy Collins, and Glyn Maxwell.

NEEDS Length: up to 2,000 words.

HOW TO CONTACT Submit via online submissions manager at rattapallax.submittable.com/submit.

PAYMENT/TERMS Pays 2 contributor's copies.

THE RAVEN CHRONICLES

A Journal of Art, Literature, and the Spoken Word, 12346 Sand Point Way N.E., Seattle WA 98125. (206)941-2955. **E-mail:** editors@ravenchronicles.org. **Website:** www.ravenchronicles.org. Estab. 1991. "*The Raven Chronicles* publishes work which reflects the cultural diversity of the Pacific Northwest, Canada, and other areas of America. We promote art, litera-

ture and the spoken word for an audience that is hip, literate, funny, informed, and lives in a society that has a multicultural sensibility. We publish fiction, talk art/spoken word, poetry, essays, reflective articles, reviews, interviews, and contemporary art. We look for work that reflects the author's experiences, perceptions, and insights."

NEEDS "Experimental work is always of interest." Length: 10-12 pages, 3,500-4,000 words. "Check with us for maximum length. We sometimes print longer pieces."

HOW TO CONTACT Submit complete ms via postal mail with SASE.

THE READER

The Reader Organisation, The Friary Centre, Bute St., Liverpool L5 3LA United Kingdom. **E-mail:** magazine@thereader.org.uk; info@thereader.org.uk. **Website:** www.thereader.org.uk. **Contact:** Philip Davis, editor. Estab. 1997. "*The Reader* is a quarterly literary magazine aimed at the intelligent 'common reader'—from those just beginning to explore serious literary reading to professional teachers, academics, and writers. As well as publishing short fiction and poetry by new writers and established names, the magazine features articles on all aspects of literature, language, and reading; regular features, including a literary quiz and a section on the Reading Revolution, reporting on The Reader Organisation's outreach work; reviews; and readers' recommendations of books that have made a difference to them. *The Reader* is unique among literary magazines in its focus on reading as a creative, important, and pleasurable activity, and in its combination of high-quality material and presentation with a genuine commitment to ordinary but dedicated readers." Also publishes literary essays, literary criticism, poetry.

NEEDS Has published work by Karen King Arbisala, Ray Tallis, Sasha Dugdale, Vicki Seal, David Constantine, Jonathan Meades, Ramesh Avadhani. Length: 1,000-3,000 words. Average length: 2,300 words. Publishes short shorts. Average length of short shorts: 1,500 words.

HOW TO CONTACT No e-mail submissions. Send complete ms with cover letter. Include estimated word count, brief bio, list of publications.

TIPS "The style or polish of the writing is less important than the deep structure of the story (though of course, it matters that it's well written). The main persuasive element is whether the story moves us—and that's quite hard to quantify—it's something to do with the force of the idea and the genuine nature of enquiry within the story. When fiction is the writer's natural means of thinking things through, that'll get us."

REDACTIONS: POETRY, POETICS, & PROSE

604 N. 31st Ave., Apt. D-2, Hattiesburg MS 39401. **E-mail:** redactionspoetry@yahoo.com (poetry); redactionsprose@yahoo.com (prose). **Website:** www.redactions.com. *Redactions*, released every 9 months, covers poems, reviews of new books of poems, translations, manifestos, interviews, essays concerning poetry, poetics, poetry movements, or concerning a specific poet or a group of poets; and anything dealing with poetry. "We now also publish fiction and creative nonfiction."

TIPS "We only accept submissions by e-mail. We read submissions throughout the year. E-mail us and attach submission into 1 Word, Wordpad, Notepad, .rtf, or .txt document, or place in the body of an e-mail. Include brief bio and your snai mail address. Query after 90 days if you haven't heard from us. See website for full guidelines for each genre, including artwork."

REDIVIDER

Department of Writing, Literature, and Publishing, Emerson College, 120 Boylston St., Boston MA 02116. **E-mail:** editor@redividerjournal.org. **Website:** www.redividerjournal.org. Estab. 1986. *Redivider*, a journal of literature and art, is published twice a year by students in the graduate writing, literature, and publishing department of Emerson College. Editors change each year. Prints high-quality poetry, art, fiction, and creative nonfiction. *Redivider* is 100+ pages, digest-sized, offset-printed, perfect-bound, with 4-color artwork on cover. Press run is 1,000. Single copy: $8; one-year subscription: $15; 2-year subscription: $25. Make checks payable to *Redivider* at Emerson College.

Every spring, *Redivider* hosts the Beacon Street Prize Writing Contest, awarding a cash prize and publication to the winning submission in fiction, poetry, and nonfiction categories. See www.redividerjournal.org for details.

NEEDS Length: no more than 10,000 words.

HOW TO CONTACT Submit electronically. Include cover letter.

PAYMENT/TERMS Pays 2 contributor's copies.

TIPS "Our deadlines are July 1 for the fall issue and December 1 for the spring issue."

RED ROCK REVIEW

College of Southern Nevada, CSN Department of English, J2A, 3200 E. Cheyenne Ave., North Las Vegas NV 89030. (702)651-4094. **Fax:** (702)651-4639. **E-mail:** redrockreview@csn.edu. **Website:** sites.csn.edu/english/redrockreview/. **Contact:** Todd Moffett, senior editor. Estab. 1994. Dedicated to the publication of fine contemporary literature. *Red Rock Review* is about 130 pages, magazine-sized, professionally printed, perfect-bound, with 10 pt. CS1 cover. Accepts about 15% of poems received/year. Press run is 2350. Subscriptions: $9.50/year. Sample: $5.50.

Does not accept submissions during June, July, August, or December. Any files sent at this time will be deleted.

NEEDS "We're looking for the very best literature. Stories need to be tightly crafted, strong in character development, built around conflict." Length: up to 5,000 words.

HOW TO CONTACT Submit with SASE.

PAYMENT/TERMS Pays 2 contributor's copies.

TIPS "Open to short fiction and poetry submissions from September 1-May 31. Include SASE and include brief bio. No general submissions between June 1 and August 31. See guidelines online."

REED MAGAZINE

San Jose State University, Department of English, One Washington Square, San Jose CA 95192. (408)924-4425. **E-mail:** reedmagazinesjsu@gmail.com. **Website:** www.reedmag.org/drupal. **Contact:** Cathleen Miller, faculty advisor. Estab. 1944. *Reed Magazine* publishes works of short fiction, nonfiction, poetry, and art.

Accepts electronic submissions only.

NEEDS Does not want children's, young adult, fantasy, or erotic. Length: no more than 5,000 words.

HOW TO CONTACT Include contact information on first page. Submit using online submissions manager.

PAYMENT/TERMS Writers receive free subscription to the magazine. Additional copies $5.

TIPS "Well-writen, original, clean grammatical prose is essential. Keep submitting! The readers are students and change every year."

REFORM JUDAISM

633 Third Ave., New York NY 10017-6778. (212)650-4240. **Fax:** (212)650-4249. **E-mail:** rjmagazine@urj

.org. **Website:** www.reformjudaismmag.org. **Contact:** Joy Weinberg, managing editor. Estab. 1972. *"Reform Judaism* is the official voice of the Union for Reform Judaism, linking the institutions and affiliates of Reform Judaism with every Reform Jew. *RJ* covers developments within the Movement while interpreting events and Jewish tradition from a Reform perspective."

◐   Magazine: 8×10⅞; 80-112 pages; illustrations; photos. Quarterly.

NEEDS Humor/satire, religious/inspirational, sophisticated, cutting-edge, superb writing. Receives 75 unsolicited mss/month. Accepts 3 mss/year. Publishes ms 3 months after acceptance. Recently published work by Published work by Frederick Fastow and Bob Sloan. Length: 600-2,500 words; average length: 1,500 words. Length: 600-2,500 words.

HOW TO CONTACT Send complete ms. SASE. Responds in 2 months to queries; 2 months to mss. Accepts simultaneous and reprints submissions. Sample copy for $3.50. Writer's guidelines online. Send complete ms.

PAYMENT/TERMS Pays 30¢/word. Pays on publication for first North American serial rights. Pays 30¢/published word.

TIPS "We prefer a stamped postcard including the following information/checklist: __Yes, we are interested in publishing; __No, unfortunately the submission doesn't meet our needs; __Maybe, we'd like to hold on to the article for now. Submissions sent this way will receive a faster response."

RHINO

The Poetry Forum, Inc., P.O. Box 591, Evanston IL 60204. **E-mail:** editors@rhinopoetry.org. **Website:** rhinopoetry.org. "This independent, eclectic annual journal of more than 35 years accepts poetry, flash fiction (750 words maximum), and poetry-in-translation from around the world that experiments, provokes, compels. More than 80 emerging and established poets are showcased." Accepts general submissions April 1-August 31 and Founders' Prize submissions September 1-October 31. Single copy: $12. Sample: $5 (back issue).

NEEDS Length: no more than 750 words.

PAYMENT/TERMS Pays in contributor's copies.

TIPS "Our diverse group of editors looks for the very best in contemporary writing, and we have created a dynamic process of soliciting and reading new work by local, national, and international writers. We are open to all styles and look for idiosyncratic, rigorous, well-crafted, lively, and passionate work."

◐⑤ RIVER STYX MAGAZINE

Big River Association, 3547 Olive St., Suite 107, St. Louis MO 63103. (314)533-4541. **E-mail:** bigriver@riverstyx.org. **Website:** www.riverstyx.org. **Contact:** Richard Newman, editor. Estab. 1975. *"River Styx* publishes the highest-quality fiction, poetry, interviews, essays, and visual art. We are an internationally distributed multicultural literary magazine. Mss read May-November."

◐   Triannual magazine. Work published in *River Styx* has been selected for inclusion in past volumes of *New Stories from the South, The Best American Poetry, Best New Poets,* and *The Pushcart Prize Anthology.*

NEEDS Recently published work by George Singleton, Philip Graham, Katherine Min, Richard Burgin, Nancy Zafris, Jacob Appel, and Eric Shade. No genre fiction, less thinly veiled autobiography. Length: no more than 23-30 ms pages.

HOW TO CONTACT Send complete ms with SASE.

PAYMENT/TERMS Pays 2 contributor copies, plus one-year subscription. Cash payment as funds permit.

◐ THE ROCKFORD REVIEW

The Rockford Writers Guild, P.O. Box 858, Rockford IL 61105. **E-mail:** rwg@rockfordwritersguild.com. **Website:** www.rockfordwritersguild.com. **Contact:** Connie Kluntz. Estab. 1947. "Published twice/year. Members only edition in summer-fall and winter-spring edition which is open to all writers. Open season to submit for the winter-spring edition of *The Rockford Review* is August. If pubished in the winter-spring edition of *The Rockford Review,* payment is 1 copy of magazine and $5 per published piece. Credit line given. Check website for frequent updates. We are also on Facebook under Rockford Writers' Guild."

◐   Poetry 50 lines or less, prose 1,300 words or less.

NEEDS "Prose should express fresh insights into the human condition." No sexist, pornographic, or supremacist content. Length: no more than 1,300 words.

TIPS "We're wide open to new and established writers alike—particularly short satire."

⊕ SACRED CITY PRODUCTIONS

Sacred City Productions, Ltd., 5781 Springwood Ct., Mentor on the Lake OH 44060. (440)290-9325.

E-mail: info@sacredcityproductions.com. **E-mail:** info@sacredcityproductions.com. **Website:** sacred cityproductions.com. **Contact:** Erin Garlock, editor/ owner. Estab. 2011. Sacred City Productions is dedicated to creative endeavors that promote the ideals of a positive faith life. "We ask people to think about what they believe and to take action on those beliefs. Our own actions reflect our Christian beliefs as we reach out in ministry to extend an uplifting hand to those around us."

NEEDS Sacred City Production's fiction focus is on speculative Christian fiction for publication in short story anthologies. Looking for stories between 500-8,000 words.

HOW TO CONTACT Submit completed story via online submission form.

PAYMENT/TERMS Pays $10 for stories over 500 words, $20 for stories over 2,000 words. Once royalties earned by the publication equal the total amount paid out to all contributors, the contributors will receive a 50/50 pro rate share of the anthology's earnings, if any, will be paid as royalties at a ratio, to the aforementioned rates, relevant to the number of contributors. A royalty breakdown sheet will be supplied at the end of a project.

TIPS "We are very interested in submissions from first-time authors and authors with a very limited record."

◐◑ SALMAGUNDI

Skidmore College, 815 North Broadway, Saratoga Springs NY 12866. **Fax:** (518)580-5188. **E-mail:** sal magun@skidmore.edu. **E-mail:** ssubmit@skidmore .edu. **Website:** cms.skidmore.edu/salmagundi. Estab. 1965. "*Salmagundi* publishes an eclectic variety of materials, ranging from short-short fiction to novellas from the surreal to the realistic. Authors include Nadine Gordimer, Russell Banks, Steven Millhauser, Gordon Lish, Clark Blaise, Mary Gordon, Joyce Carol Oates, and Cynthia Ozick. Our audience is a generally literate population of people who read for pleasure." Receives 300-500 unsolicited mss/month; "many sent, few accepted." Reads unsolicited mss February 1-April 15, "but from time to time we close the doors even during this period because the backlog tends to grow out of control." Agented fiction 10%. Pays 6-10 contributor's copies and 1-year free subscription to magazine.

Magazine: 8×5; illustrations; photos. *Salmagundi* authors are regularly represented in *Pushcart* collections and *Best American Short Story* collections.

TIPS "I look for excellence and a very unpredictable ability to appeal to the interests and tastes of the editors. Be brave. Don't be discouraged by rejection. Keep stories in circulation. Of course, it goes without saying: Work hard on the writing. Revise tirelessly. Study magazines and send only to those whose sensibility matches yours."

○ SANDY RIVER REVIEW

University of Maine at Farmington, 114 Prescott St., Farmington ME 04938. **E-mail:** srreview@gmail.com. **Website:** sandyriverreview.umf.maine.edu. **Contact:** Taylor McCafferty, editor. "The *Sandy River Review* seeks prose, poetry, and art submissions twice a year for our spring and fall issues. Prose submissions may be either fiction or creative nonfiction and should be 15 pages or fewer in length, 12-point, Times New Roman font, and double-spaced. Most of our art is published in b&w and must be submitted as 300 dpi quality, CMYK color mode, and saved as a TIFF file. We publish a wide variety of work from students as well as professional, established writers. Your submission should be polished and imaginative with strongly drawn characters and an interesting, original narrative. The review is the face of the University of Maine at Farmington's venerable BFA Creative Writing program, and we strive for the highest-quality prose and poetry standard."

NEEDS "The review is a literary journal—please, no horror, science fiction, romance." Length: 4,500-5,000 words.

HOW TO CONTACT Send complete ms.

PAYMENT/TERMS Pays 5 copies of the published issue.

TIPS "We recommend that you take time with your piece. As with all submissions to a literary journal, submissions should be fully completed, polished final drafts that require minimal to no revision once accepted. Double-check your prose pieces for basic grammatical errors before submitting."

◑ THE SARANAC REVIEW

CVH, Department of English, SUNY Plattsburgh, 101 Broad St., Plattsburgh NY 12901. (518)564-2414. **Fax:** (518)564-2140. **E-mail:** saranacreview@plattsburgh .edu. **Website:** http//www.saranacreview.com. **Con-**

tact: J.L. Torres, editor. Estab. 2004. "*The Saranac Review* is committed to dissolving boundaries of all kinds, seeking to publish a diverse array of emerging and established writers from Canada and the U.S. The Saranac Review aims to be a textual clearing in which a space is opened for cross-pollination between American and Canadian writers. In this way the magazine reflects the expansive bright spirit of the etymology of its name, Saranac, meaning 'cluster of stars.'" Published annually. "*The Saranac Review* is digest sized, with color photo or painting on cover, includes ads. Publishes both digital and print-on-demand versions. Check our website for subscriptions and submissions."

○ "Has published Lawrence Raab, Jacob M. Appel, Marilyn Nelson, Tom Wayman, Colette Inez, Louise Warren, Brian Campbell, Gregory Pardlo, Myfanwy Collins, William Giraldi, Xu Xi, Julia Alvarez, and other fine emerging and established writers."

NEEDS We only accept online submissions. Reads September 1-May 15 (firm). Cover letter is appreciated. Include phone and e-mail contact information (if possible) in cover letter. No e-mail or disk submissions. "No genre material or light verse please (fantasy, science fiction, etc.). Please look at specific genre guidelines on our website." Please send 1 story at a time. Maximum length: 7,000 words.

HOW TO CONTACT Send complete ms. Send SASE (or IRC) for return of ms or send disposable copy of the ms and #10 SASE for reply only. Reads submissions September 1-February 15 (firm). Cover letter is appreciated. Include phone and e-mail contact information (if possible) in cover letter. No e-mail or disk submissions.

PAYMENT/TERMS Pays 2 contributor's copies; discount on extras.

○ THE SAVAGE KICK LITERARY MAGAZINE

Murder Slim Press, 29 Alpha Rd., Gorleston Norfolk NR31 0EQ United Kingdom. **E-mail:** moonshine@murderslim.com. **Website:** www.murderslim.com. Estab. 2005. "*Savage Kick* primarily deals with viewpoints outside the mainstream: honest emotions told in a raw, simplistic way. It is recommended that you are very familiar with the *SK* style before submitting. We have only accepted 8 new writers in 4 years of the magazine. Ensure you have a distinctive voice and story to tell."

NEEDS "Real-life stories are preferred, unless the work is distinctively extreme within the crime genre. No poetry of any kind, no mainstream fiction, Oprah-style fiction, Internet/chat language, teen issues, excessive Shakespearean language, surrealism, overworked irony, or genre fiction (horror, fantasy, science fiction, western, erotica, etc.)." Length: 500-6,000 words.

HOW TO CONTACT Send complete ms.

PAYMENT/TERMS Pays $35.

⊕ SCREAMINMAMAS

Harmoni Productions, LLC, 1911 Cleveland St., Hollywood FL 33020. **E-mail:** screaminmamas@gmail.com. **Website:** www.screaminmamas.com. Estab. 2012. "We are the voice of everyday moms. We share their stories, revelations, humorous rants, photos, talent, children, ventures, etc."

NEEDS Does not want vulgar, obscene, derogatory, or negative fiction. Length: 800-3,000 words.

HOW TO CONTACT Send complete ms.

TIPS "Visit our submissions page and themes page on our website."

THE SEATTLE REVIEW

Box 354330, University of Washington, Seattle WA 98195. (206)543-2302. **E-mail:** seaview@uw.edu. **Website:** www.seattlereview.org. **Contact:** Andrew Feld, editor-in-chief. Estab. 1978. Includes poetry, fiction, and creative nonfiction. *The Seattle Review* is 8×10; 175-250 pages. Estab. 1978. Circ. 1,000. Receives 200 unsolicited mss/month. Accepts 10-15 mss/issue; 20-30 mss/year. Publishes ms 6 months-1 year after acceptance. Subscriptions: $20/3 issues, $32/5 issues. Back issue: $6.

○ *The Seattle Review* will only publish long works. Poetry must be 10 pages or longer and prose must be 40 pages or longer.

NEEDS "Currently, we do not consider, use, or have a place for genre fiction (science fiction, detective, etc.) or visual art." Length: 500-10,000 words.

HOW TO CONTACT Send complete ms.

TIPS "Know what we publish: no genre fiction. Look at our magazine and decide if your work might be appreciated. Beginners do well in our magazine if they send clean, well-written mss. We've published a lot of 'first stories' from all over the country and take pleasure in discovery."

◐ ⑤ SEEK

8805 Governor's Hill Dr., Suite 400, Cincinnati OH 45239. (513)931-4050, ext. 351. **E-mail:** seek@standardpub.com. **Website:** www.standardpub.com. Estab. 1970. "Inspirational stories of faith-in-action for Christian adults; a Sunday School take-home paper." Quarterly. Religious/inspirational, religious fiction and religiously slanted historical and humorous fiction. No poetry. List of upcoming themes available online. Accepts 150 mss/year. Send complete ms. Prefers submissions by e-mail. "*SEEK* corresponds to the topics of Standard Publishing's adult curriculum line and is designed to further apply these topics to everyday life. Unsolicited mss must be written to a theme list."

○ Magazine: 5.5×8.5; 8 pages; newsprint paper; art and photo in each issue.

HOW TO CONTACT Send complete ms. Prefers submissions by e-mail.

PAYMENT/TERMS Pays 7¢/word.

TIPS "Write a credible story with a Christian slant—no preachments; avoid overworked themes such as joy in suffering, generation gaps, etc. Most mss are rejected by us because of irrelevant topic or message, unrealistic story, or poor character and/or plot development. We use fiction stories that are believable."

THE SEWANEE REVIEW

University of the South, 735 University Ave., Sewanee TN 37383-1000. (931)598-1000. **Website:** www.sewanee.edu/sewanee_review. **Contact:** George Core, editor. Estab. 1892. The *Sewanee Review* is America's oldest continuously published literary quarterly. Publishes original fiction, poetry, essays on literary and related subjects, and book reviews for well-educated readers who appreciate good American and English literature. Only erudite work representing depth of knowledge and skill of expression is published.

○ Does not read mss June 1-August 31.

NEEDS Send complete ms via mail. No erotica, science fiction, fantasy or excessively violent or profane material. Length: 3,500-7,500 words. No short stories.

PAYMENT/TERMS Pays $10-12/printed page, plus 2 contributor's copies.

SHENANDOAH

Washington and Lee University, 17 Courthouse Square, Lexington VA 24450. (540)458-8908. **Fax:** (540)458-8461. **E-mail:** shenandoah@wlu.edu. **Website:** shenandoahliterary.org. **Contact:** R.T. Smith, editor. Estab. 1950. For over half a century, *Shenandoah* has been publishing splendid poems, stories, essays, and reviews which display passionate understanding, formal accomplishment and serious mischief.

○ Reads submissions September 1-May 15 only. Sponsors the annual James Boatwright III Prize for Poetry, a $1,000 prize awarded to the author of the best poem published in *Shenandoah* during a volume year.

NEEDS No sloppy, hasty, slight fiction.

HOW TO CONTACT Send complete ms.

PAYMENT/TERMS Pays $25/page ($250 maximum).

SHINE BRIGHTLY

GEMS Girls' Clubs, 1333 Alger St., SE, Grand Rapids MI 49507. (616)241-5616. **Fax:** (616)241-5558. **E-mail:** shinebrightly@gemsgc.org. **Website:** www.gemsgc.org. **Contact:** Kathryn Miller, executive director; Kelli Gilmore, managing editor. Estab. 1970. "Our purpose is to lead girls into a living relationship with Jesus Christ and to help them see how God is at work in their lives and the world around them. Puzzles, crafts, stories, and articles for girls ages 9-14."

NEEDS Does not want "unrealistic stories and those with trite, easy endings. We are interested in mss that show how girls can change the world." Believable only. Nothing too preachy. Length: 700-900 words.

HOW TO CONTACT Submit complete ms in body of e-mail. No attachments.

PAYMENT/TERMS Pays up to $35, plus 2 copies.

TIPS Writers: "Please check our website before submitting. We have a specific style and theme that deals with how girls can impact the world. The stories should be current, deal with preadolescent problems and joys, and help girls see God at work in their lives through humor as well as problem solving." Prefers not to see anything on the adult level, secular material, or violence. Writers frequently oversimplify the articles and often write with a Pollyanna attitude. An author should be able to see his/her writing style as exciting and appealing to girls ages 9-14. The style can be fun but also teach a truth. Subjects should be current and important to *SHINE brightly* readers. Use our theme update as a guide. We would like to receive material with a multicultural slant."

⊘ SHORT STUFF

Bowman Publications, 2001 I St., #5, Fairbury NE 68352. (402)587-5003. **E-mail:** shortstf89@aol.com. Estab. 1989. "We are perhaps an enigma in that we publish only clean stories in any genre. We'll tackle any subject but don't allow obscene language or pornographic description. Our magazine is for grown-ups, not X-rated 'adult' fare."

NEEDS Receives 500 unsolicited mss/month. Accepts 9-12 mss/issue; 76 mss/year. Has published work by Bill Hallstead, Dede Hammond, Skye Gibbons. "We want to see more humor—not essay format—real stories with humor; 1,000-word mysteries, modern lifestyles. The 1,000-word pieces have the best chance of publication. No erotica; nothing morbid or pornographic. Length: 500-1,500 words.

HOW TO CONTACT Send complete ms.

PAYMENT/TERMS Payment varies.

TIPS "We are holiday oriented; mark on outside of envelope if story is for Easter, Mother's Day, etc. We receive 500 mss each month. This is up about 200%. Because of this, I implore writers to send 1 ms at a time. I would not use stories from the same author more than once an issue and this means I might keep the others too long. Please don't e-mail your stories! If you have an e-mail address, please include that with cover letter so we can contact you. If SASE is not included, we destroy the ms."

◑ SIERRA NEVADA REVIEW

999 Tahoe Blvd., Incline Village NV 89451. **E-mail:** sncreview@sierranevada.edu. **Website:** www.sierranevada.edu/800. Estab. 1990. "*Sierra Nevada Review*, published annually in May, features poetry, short fiction, and literary nonfiction by new and established writers. Wants "image-oriented poems with a distinct, genuine voice. No limit on length, style, etc." Does not want "sentimental, clichéd, or obscure poetry."

HOW TO CONTACT Prose (fiction and nonfiction) submissions should be 4,000 words or less.

◑ SLOW TRAINS LITERARY JOURNAL

P.O. 4741, Denver CO 80155. **E-mail:** editor@slowtrains.com. **Website:** www.slowtrains.com. **Contact:** Susannah Grace Indigo, editor. Estab. 2000. Looking for fiction, essays, and poetry that reflect the spirit of adventure, the exploration of the soul, the energies of imagination, and the experience of Big Fun. Music, travel, sex, humor, love, loss, art, spirituality, childhood/coming of age, baseball, and dreams, but most of all *Slow Trains* wants to read about the things you are passionate about.

NEEDS Genre writing is not encouraged. No science fiction, erotica, horror, romance, though elements of

those may naturally be included. Length: less than 5,000 words.

HOW TO CONTACT Submit via e-mail only.

◑◉ SNOWY EGRET

The Fair Press, P.O. Box 9265, Terre Haute IN 47808. **Website:** www.snowyegret.net. Estab. 1922. *Snowy Egret*, published in spring and autumn, specializes in work that is nature oriented: poetry that celebrates the abundance and beauty of nature or explores the interconnections between nature and the human psyche. Has published poetry by Conrad Hilberry, Lyn Lifshin, Gayle Eleanor, James Armstrong, and Patricia Hooper.

○ All submissions accepted via mail. *Snowy Egret* is 60 pages, magazine-sized, offset-printed, saddle-stapled. Receives about 500 poems/year, accepts about 30. Press run is 400. Sample: $8; subscription: $15/year, $25 for 2 years. Semiannual.

NEEDS Publishes works which celebrate the abundance and beauty of nature and examine the variety of ways in which human beings interact with landscapes and living things. Nature writing from literary, artistic, psychological, philosophical, and historical perspectives. No genre fiction, e.g., horror, western, romance, etc.

HOW TO CONTACT Send complete ms with SASE. Cover letter optional: do not query. Responds in 2 months to mss. Accepts simultaneous submissions if noted.

PAYMENT/TERMS Pays $2/page plus 2 contributor's copies.

TIPS Looks for "honest, freshly detailed pieces with plenty of description and/or dialogue which will allow the reader to identify with the characters and step into the setting; fiction in which nature affects character development and the outcome of the story."

○ SNREVIEW

197 Fairchild Ave., Fairfield CT 06825-4856. (203)366-5991. **E-mail:** editor@snreview.org. **Website:** www.snreview.org. **Contact:** Joseph Conlin, editor. Estab. 1999. "We search for material that not only has strong characters and plot, but also a devotion to imagery." Quarterly.

○ Also publishes literary essays, literary criticism, poetry. Print and Kindle editions are now available from an on-demand printer.

NEEDS Receives 300 unsolicited mss/month. Accepts 40+ mss/issue; 150 mss/year. Publishes 75 new writers/year. Has published work by Frank X. Walker, Adrian Louis, Barbara Burkhardt, E. Lindsey Balkan, Marie Griffin, and Jonathan Lerner. Length: 1,000-7,000 words; average length: 4,000 words.

HOW TO CONTACT Accepts submissions by e-mail only. "Copy and paste work into the body of the e-mail. Don't send attachments." Include 100-word bio and list of publications.

SOLDIER OF FORTUNE

2135 11th St., Boulder CO 80302. (303)449-3750. **E-mail:** editorsof@aol.com. **Website:** www.sofmag.com. **Contact:** Lt. Col. Robert A. Brown, editor/publisher. Estab. 1975. "We are an action-oriented magazine; we cover combat hot spots around the world. We also provide timely features on state-of-the-art weapons and equipment; elite military and police units; and historical military operations. Readership is primarily active-duty military, veterans, and law enforcement."

TIPS "Submit a professionally prepared, complete package. All artwork with cutlines, double-spaced typed ms with 5.25 or 3.5 IBM-compatible disk, if available, cover letter including synopsis of article, supporting documentation where applicable, etc. Ms must be factual; writers have to do their homework and get all their facts straight. One error means rejection. Vietnam features, if carefully researched and art heavy, will always get a careful look. Combat reports, again, with good art, are No. 1 in our book and stand the best chance of being accepted. Military unit reports from around the world are well received, as are law-enforcement articles (units, police in action). If you write for us, be complete and factual; pros read *Soldier of Fortune*, and are very quick to let us know if we (and the author) err."

◑ SO TO SPEAK

George Mason University, 4400 University Dr., MSN 2C5, Fairfax VA 22030-4444. **E-mail:** sts@gmu.edu (inquiries only). **Website:** sotospeakjournal.org. **Contact:** Michele Johnson, editor-in-chief. Estab. 1993. *So to Speak*, published semiannually, prints "high-quality work relating to feminism, including poetry, fiction, nonfiction (including book reviews and interviews), photography, artwork, collaborations, lyrical essays, and other genre-questioning texts." Wants "work that addresses issues of significance to women's lives and movements for women's equality. Especially interested in pieces that explore issues of race, class,

and sexuality in relation to gender." Reads submissions August 1-October 15 for Spring issue and January 1-March 15 for Fall issue.

◑ *So to Speak* is 100-128 pages, digest-sized, photo-offset-printed, perfect-bound, with glossy cover; includes ads. Press run is 1,000 (75 subscribers, 100 shelf sales); 500 distributed free to students/contributors.

NEEDS Receives 100 unsolicited mss/month. Accepts 3-5 mss/issue; 6-10 mss/year. Publishes 7 new writers/year. Sponsors awards/contests. No science fiction, mystery, genre romance. Length: up to 5,000 words.

HOW TO CONTACT Accepts submissions only via submissions manager on website. Does not accept paper or e-mail submissions. "Fiction submitted during the January 1–March 15 reading period will be considered for our fall annual fiction contest and must be accompanied by a $15 reading fee. See contest guidelines. Contest entries will not be returned."

PAYMENT/TERMS Pays contributor copies.

TIPS "Every writer has something they do exceptionally well; do that and it will shine through in the work. We look for quality prose with a definite appeal to a feminist audience. We are trying to move away from strict genre lines. We want high-quality fiction, nonfiction, poetry, art, innovative and risk-taking work."

◑ SOUTH CAROLINA REVIEW

Clemson University, Strode Tower Room 611, Box 340522, Clemson SC 29634-0522. (864)656-5399. **Fax:** (864)656-1345. **E-mail:** cwayne@clemson.edu. **Website:** www.clemson.edu/cedp/cudp/scr/scrintro .htm. **Contact:** Wayne Chapman, editor. Estab. 1967. Magazine: 6×9; 200 pages; 60 lb. cream white vellum paper; 65 lb. color cover stock. Semiannual. Does not read mss June-August or December. Receives 50-60 unsolicited mss/month.

NEEDS Recently published work by Thomas E. Kennedy, Ronald Frame, Dennis McFadden, Dulane Upshaw Ponder, and Stephen Jones. Rarely comments on rejected mss.

◑ SOUTH DAKOTA REVIEW

University of South Dakota, 414 E. Clark St., Vermillion SD 57069. (605)677-5184. **E-mail:** sdreview@usd .edu. **Website:** www.usd.edu/sdreview. **Contact:** Brian Bedard and Lee Ann Roripaugh, editors. Estab. 1963. "*South Dakota Review*, published quarterly, is committed to cultural and aesthetic diversity. First and foremost, we seek to publish exciting and compelling work that reflects the full spectrum of the contemporary literary arts. Since its inception in 1963, *South Dakota Review* has maintained a tradition of supporting work by contemporary writers writing from or about the American West. We hope to retain this unique flavor through particularly welcoming works by American Indian writers, writers addressing the complexities and contradictions of the "New West," and writers exploring themes of landscape, place, and/or eco-criticism in surprising and innovative ways. At the same time, we'd like to set these ideas and themes in dialogue with and within the context of larger global literary communities. *South Dakota Review* publishes fiction, poetry, essays (and mixed/hybrid-genre work), as well as literary reviews, interviews, and translations. Press run is 500-600 (more than 500 subscribers, many of them libraries). Single copy: $12; subscription: $40/year, $65/2 years. Sample: $8.

O *Pushcart* and *Best American Essays* nominees.

NEEDS "Our aesthetic is eclectic, but we tend to favor deft use of language in both our poetry and prose selections, nuanced characterization in our fiction, and either elegantly or surprisingly executed formal strategies. As part of our unique flavor, a small handful works in each issue will typically engage with aspects of landscape, ecocritical issues, or place (oftentimes with respect to the American West)."

PAYMENT/TERMS Pays 2 contributor's copies.

O   THE SOUTHEAST REVIEW

Florida State University, Tallahassee FL 32306-1036. **Website:** southeastreview.org. **Contact:** Brandi George, editor-in-chief. Estab. 1979. "The mission of *The Southeast Review* is to present emerging writers on the same stage as well-established ones. In each semiannual issue, we publish literary fiction, creative nonfiction, poetry, interviews, book reviews, and art. With nearly 60 members on our editorial staff who come from throughout the country and the world, we strive to publish work that is representative of our diverse interests and aesthetics, and we celebrate the eclectic mix this produces. We receive approximately 400 submissions per month, and we accept less than 1-2% of them. We will comment briefly on rejected mss when time permits."

O   Magazine: 6×9; 160 pages; 70 lb. paper; 10 pt. Krome Kote cover; photos. Publishes 4-6 new writers/year. Has published work by Elizabeth

Hegwood, Anthony Varallo, B.J. Hollars, Tina Karelson, and John Dufresne.

NEEDS "We try to respond to submissions within 2-4 months. If after 4 months you have not heard back regarding your submission, you may query the appropriate section editor. *SER* accepts simultaneous submissions, but we request that you withdraw the submission by way of our online submission manager if your piece is accepted elsewhere." Length: 7,500 words maximum.

PAYMENT/TERMS Pays 2 contributor's copies.

TIPS "*The Southeast Review* accepts regular submissions for publication consideration year-round exclusively through the online submission manager. Except during contest season, paper submissions sent through regular postal mail will not be read or returned. Please note that during contest season entries to our World's Best Short Short Story, Poetry, and Creative Nonfiction competitions must still be sent through regular postal mail. Avoid trendy experimentation for its own sake (present-tense narration, observation that isn't also revelation). Fresh stories; moving, interesting characters; and a sensitivity to language are still fiction mainstays. We also publish the winner and runners-up of the World's Best Short Story Contest, Poetry Contest, and Creative Nonfiction Contest."

SOUTHERN HUMANITIES REVIEW

Auburn University, 9088 Haley Center, Auburn University AL 36849. (334)844-9088. **Fax:** (334)844-9027. **E-mail:** shrengl@auburn.edu. **E-mail:** shrsubmissions@auburn.edu. **Website:** www.cla.auburn.edu/shr. **Contact:** Karen Beckwith, managing editor. Estab. 1967. *Southern Humanities Review* publishes fiction, poetry, and critical essays on the arts, literature, philosophy, religion, and history for a well-read, scholarly audience.

NEEDS Length: 3,500-15,000 words.

HOW TO CONTACT Send complete ms. Send only 1 story per submission. "It is wise to submit no more than 4 times per year unless editors ask to see more of your work. Translations are encouraged, but please include .pdf scans of the original and written permission from the copyright holder."

PAYMENT/TERMS Pays 2 contributor copies

TIPS "Send us the ms with SASE. If we like it, we'll take it or we'll recommend changes. If we don't like it, we'll send it back as promptly as possible. Read the journal. Send typewritten, clean copy, carefully proofread. We also award the annual Hoepfner Prize of $100 for the best published essay or short story of the year. Let someone whose opinion you respect read your story and give you an honest appraisal. Rewrite, if necessary, to get the most from your story."

THE SOUTHERN REVIEW

3990 W. Lakeshore Dr., Baton Rouge LA 70808. (225)578-5108. **Fax:** (225)578-5098. **E-mail:** southernreview@lsu.edu. **Website:** thesouthernreview. org. **Contact:** Jessica Faust, co-editor and poetry editor; Emily Nemens, co-editor and prose editor. Estab. 1935. "*The Southern Review* is one of the nation's premiere literary journals. Hailed by *Time* as 'superior to any other journal in the English language,' we have made literary history since our founding in 1935. We publish a diverse array of fiction, nonfiction, and poetry by the country's—and the world's—most respected contemporary writers." Reading period: September 1-December 1. All mss submitted during outside the reading period will be recycled.

NEEDS Wants short stories of lasting literary merit, with emphasis on style and technique; novel excerpts. "We emphasize style and substantial content. No mystery, fantasy, or religious mss." Length: up to 8,000 words.

HOW TO CONTACT Submit 1 ms at a time by mail. "We rarely publish work that is longer than 8,000 words. We consider novel excerpts if they stand alone."

PAYMENT/TERMS Pays $25/printed page; maximum $200; 2 contributor's copies and one-year subscription.

TIPS "Careful attention to craftsmanship and technique combined with a developed sense of the creation of story will always make us pay attention."

SOUTHWESTERN AMERICAN LITERATURE

Center for the Study of the Southwest, Texas State University, Brazos Hall 212, 601 University Dr., San Marcos TX 78666. (512)245-2224. **Fax:** (512)245-7462. **E-mail:** swpublications@txstate.edu. **Website:** www .txstate.edu/cssw/publications/sal.html. **Contact:** William Jensen, editor. Estab. 1971.

NEEDS Wants "crisp language and an interesting approach to material; a regional approach is desired but not required. We seek stories that probe the relationship between the tradition of Southwestern American literature and the writer's own imagination in creative

ways—stories that move beyond stereotype." Length: no more than 6,000 words/25 pages.

HOW TO CONTACT Submit using online submissions manager. Include contact information and brief bio.

PAYMENT/TERMS Pays 2 contributor's copies.

TIPS "We look for crisp language, an interesting approach to material; a regional approach is desired but not required. Read widely, write often, revise carefully. We are looking for stories that probe the relationship between the tradition of Southwestern American literature and the writer's own imagination in creative ways. We seek stories that move beyond stereotype and approach the larger defining elements and also ones that, as William Faulkner noted in his Nobel Prize acceptance speech, treat subjects central to good literature—the old verities of the human heart, such as honor and courage and pity and suffering, fear and humor, love and sorrow."

SOUTHWEST REVIEW

P.O. Box 750374, Dallas TX 75275-0374. (214)768-1037. **Fax:** (214)768-1408. **E-mail:** swr@smu.edu. **Website:** www.smu.edu/southwestreview. **Contact:** Willard Spiegelman, editor-in-chief. Estab. 1915. The majority of readers are well-read adults who wish to stay abreast of the latest and best in contemporary fiction, poetry, and essays in all but the most specialized disciplines. Published quarterly.

Magazine: 6×9; 150 pages. Receives 200 unsolicited mss/month. Has published work by Alice Hoffman, Sabina Murray, Alix Ohlin. Publishes fiction, literary essays, poetry.

NEEDS Publishes fiction in widely varying styles. Prefers stories of character development, of psychological penetration, to those depending chiefly on plot. No specific requirements as to subject matter. Length: 3,500-7,000 words preferred.

HOW TO CONTACT Submissions accepted online for a $2 fee. No fee for submissions sent by mail. No simultaneous or previously published work accepted. Submit 1 story at a time. Reading period: September 1-May 31.

PAYMENT/TERMS Accepted pieces receive nominal payment upon publication and copies of the issue.

TIPS "Despite the title, we are not a regional magazine. Before you submit your work, it's a good idea to take a look at recent issues to familiarize yourself with the magazine. We strongly advise all writers to include a cover letter. Keep your cover letter professional and concise and don't include extraneous personal information, a story synopsis, or a résumé. When authors ask what we look for in a strong story submission the answer is simple regardless of graduate degrees in creative writing, workshops, or whom you know. We look for good writing, period."

⦿ SOU'WESTER

Department of English, Box 1438, Southern Illinois University Edwardsville, Edwardsville IL 62026. **Website:** souwester.org. Estab. 1960. *Sou'wester* appears biannually in spring and fall. Leans toward poetry with strong imagery, successful association of images, and skillful use of figurative language. Has published poetry by Robert Wrigley, Beckian Fritz Goldberg, Eric Pankey, Betsy Sholl, and Angie Estes.

○ Uses online submission form. Open to submissions in mid-August for fall and spring issues. Close submissions in winter and early spring. *Sou'wester* has 30-40 pages of poetry in each digest-sized, 100-page issue. *Sou'wester* is professionally printed, flat-spined, with textured matte card cover, press run is 300 for 500 subscribers of which 50 are libraries. Receives 3,000 poems (from 600 poets) each year, accepts 36-40, has a 6-month backlog. Subscription: $15/2 issues.

HOW TO CONTACT Submit 1 piece of prose at a time. Will consider a suite of 2 or 3 flash pieces.

PAYMENT/TERMS Pays 2 contributor's copies and a one-year subscription.

THE SPECULATIVE EDGE

E-mail: specedgeeditor@gmail.com. **Website:** https://sites.google.com/site/thespeculativeedge/home. **Contact:** Chloe Viner, editor; Shane R. Collins, managing editor. Estab. 2012. Biannual literary magazine. "Publishing stories and poems that are speculative is our primary goal, but ensuring they are also literary is a close second. Stories should balance characters with plot. They should be exciting but also written intelligently. Poetry should be insightful and imaginative, but also accessible. Our mission at *The Speculative Edge* is to extinguish the false pretense that 'genre' and 'literary' are mutually exclusive."

NEEDS Length: 500-15,000 words.

HOW TO CONTACT Submit complete ms.

TIPS "Send us your best work. Grammar mistakes are a huge turnoff for us. If we find a glaring a mistake in the first page of your ms—that might be it, depending on the editor's mood. Also, a professional, concise cover letter goes a long way. If you don't know how to write a cover letter, we have an explanation of what we want to see on the website. And finally, address your e-mail to the editor you're trying to contact. Our names are visible under the guidelines for all the submissions. Addressing us by name shows us that you've done your homework and are a serious writer."

⦿ SPITBALL: THE LITERARY BASEBALL MAGAZINE

5560 Fox Rd., Cincinnati OH 45239. **E-mail:** spitball5@hotmail.com. **Website:** www.spitballmag.com. **Contact:** Mike Shannon, editor-in-chief. Estab. 1981. *Spitball: The Literary Baseball Magazine*, published semiannually, is a unique magazine devoted to poetry, fiction, and book reviews exclusively about baseball. Newcomers are very welcome, but they must know the subject. "Perhaps a good place to start for beginners is one's personal reactions to the game, a game, a player, etc., and take it from there." Writers submitting to *Spitball* for the first time must buy a sample copy (waived for subscribers). "This is a one-time-only fee, which we regret, but economic reality dictates that we insist those who wish to be published in *Spitball* help support it, at least at this minimum level."

○ *Spitball* is 96 pages, digest-sized, computer typeset, perfect-bound. Receives about 1,000 submissions/year, accepts about 40. Press run is 1,000. Subscription: $12. Sample: $6.

NEEDS Length: 5-15 pages, double-spaced. Short stories longer than 20 pages must be exceptionally good.

HOW TO CONTACT Submit with a biography and SASE.

TIPS "Take the subject seriously. We do. In other words, get a clue (if you don't already have one) about the subject and about the poetry that has already been done and published about baseball. Learn from it—think about what you can add to the canon that is original and fresh—and don't assume that just anybody with the feeblest of efforts can write a baseball poem worthy of publication. And most important, stick with it. Genius seldom happens on the first try."

ST. ANTHONY MESSENGER

Franciscan Media, 28 W. Liberty St., Cincinnati OH 45202-6498. (513)241-5615. **Fax:** (513)241-0399. **E-mail:** mageditors@franciscanmedia.org. **Website:** www.stanthonymessenger.org. **Contact:** John Feister, editor. Estab. 1893. "*St. Anthony Messenger* is a Catholic family magazine which aims to help its readers lead more fully human and Christian lives. We publish articles that report on a changing church and world, opinion pieces written from the perspective of Christian faith and values, personality profiles, and fiction which entertains and informs."

NEEDS "We do not want mawkishly sentimental or preachy fiction. Stories are most often rejected for poor plotting and characterization, bad dialogue (listen to how people talk), and inadequate motivation. Many stories say nothing, are 'happenings' rather than stories. No fetal journals, no rewritten Bible stories." Length: 2,000-2,500 words.

HOW TO CONTACT Send complete ms.

PAYMENT/TERMS Pays 20¢/word maximum and 2 contributor's copies; $1 charge for extras.

STILL CRAZY

P.O. Box 777, Worthington OH 43085. (614)746-0859. **E-mail:** editor@crazylitmag.com. **Website:** www.crazylitmag.com. **Contact:** Barbara Kussow, editor. "*Still Crazy* publishes writing by people over age 50 and writing by people of any age if the topic is about people over 50 years old."

Accepts 3-4 mss/issue; 6-8/year. Occasionally considers previously published poems. "Do not submit material that has been published elsewhere online." Publication is not copyrighted. Reads submissions year-round.

NEEDS Publishes short shorts. Ms published 6-12 months after acceptance. Sometimes features a "First Story," a story by an author who has not been published before. Paper copies $10; subscriptions $18 (2 issues per year); downloads $4. Does not want material that is "too sentimental or inspirational, 'Geezer' humor, or anything too grim." Length: 3,500 words (maximum), but stories fewer than 3,000 words are more likely to be published.

HOW TO CONTACT Upload submissions via submissions manager on website. Include estimated word count, brief bio, age of writer or "Over 50."

PAYMENT/TERMS Pays 1 contributor's copy.

TIPS Looking for "interesting characters and interesting situations that might interest readers of all ages. Humor and lightness welcomed."

STIRRING: A LITERARY COLLECTION

c/o Erin Elizabeth Smith, Department of English, 301 McClung Tower, University of Tennessee, Knoxville TN 37996. **E-mail:** eesmith81@gmail.com. **Website:** www.sundresspublications.com/stirring. **Contact:** Erin Elizabeth Smith, managing and poetry editor. Estab. 1999.

"*Stirring* is one of the oldest continually published literary journals on the web. *Stirring* is a monthly literary magazine that publishes poetry, short fiction, creative nonfiction, and photography by established and emerging writers."

STONE SOUP

Children's Art Foundation, P.O. Box 83, Santa Cruz CA 95063-0083. (831)426-5557. **E-mail:** editor@stonesoup.com. **Website:** stonesoup.com. **Contact:** Ms. Gerry Mandel, editor. Estab. 1973.

Stone Soup is 48 pages, 7×10, professionally printed in color on heavy stock, saddle-stapled, with coated cover with full-color illustration. Receives 5,000 poetry submissions/year, accepts about 12. Press run is 15,000. Subscription: $37/year (U.S.). "We have a preference for writing and art based on real-life experiences; no formula stories or poems. We only publish writing by children ages 8 to 13. We do not publish writing by adults. Stories and poems from past issues are available online."

NEEDS "We do not like assignments or formula stories of any kind." Length: 150-2,500 words.

HOW TO CONTACT Send complete ms; no SASE.

PAYMENT/TERMS Pays $40 for stories, a certificate and 2 contributor's copies, plus discounts.

TIPS "All writing we publish is by young people ages 13 and under. We do not publish any writing by adults. We can't emphasize enough how important it is to read a couple of issues of the magazine. You can read stories and poems from past issues online. We have a strong preference for writing on subjects that mean a lot to the author. If you feel strongly about something that happened to you or something you observed, use that feeling as the basis for your story or poem. Stories should have good descriptions, realistic dialogue, and a point to make. In a poem, each word must be chosen carefully. Your poem should present a view of your subject, and a way of using words that are special and all your own."

STORY BYTES

E-mail: editor@storybytes.com. **Website:** www.storybytes.com. **Contact:** Mark Stanley Bubein. "A monthly e-zine and weekly electronic mailing list presenting the Internet's (and the world's) shortest stories—fiction ranging from 2 to 2,048 words. Just as eyes, art often provides a window to the soul. *Story Bytes'* very short stories offer a glimpse through this window into brief vignettes of life, often reflecting or revealing those things which make us human."

NEEDS "Story length must fall on a power of 2. That's 2, 4, 8, 16, 32, 64, 128, 256, 512, 1,024, and 2,048 words long. Stories must match 1 of these lengths exactly." See website for examples. No sexually explicit material. Length: 2-2,048 words.

HOW TO CONTACT Submit story as plain text via e-mail. "The easiest way to do so is to simply copy it from your word processor and paste it into an e-mail message. Specify the word count below the title."

TIPS "In *Story Bytes*, the very short stories themselves range in topic. Many explore a brief event—a vignette of something unusual, unique, and at times something even commonplace. Some stories can be bizarre, while others quite lucid. Some are based on actual events, while others are entirely fictional. Try to develop conflict early on (in the first sentence if possible!), and illustrate or resolve this conflict through action rather than description. I believe we'll find an audience for electronic published works primarily in the short story realm."

◐ STORYSOUTH

5603B W. Friendly Ave., Suite 282, Greensboro NC 27410. **E-mail:** terry@storysouth.com. **Website:** www.storysouth.com. **Contact:** Terry Kennedy, editor. Estab. 2001. "*storySouth* accepts unsolicited submissions of fiction, poetry, and creative nonfiction during 2 submission periods annually: March 15-June 15 and September 15-December 15. Long pieces are encouraged. Please make only 1 submission in a single genre per reading period."

NEEDS No word limit.

HOW TO CONTACT Submit 1 story via online submissions manager.

TIPS "What really makes a story stand out is a strong voice and a sense of urgency—a need for the reader to keep reading the story and not put it down until it is finished."

◐◑ THE STRAY BRANCH

E-mail: thestraybranchlitmag@yahoo.com. **Website:** www.thestraybranch.org. **Contact:** Debbie Berk, editor/publisher. Estab. 2008. *The Stray Branch* is "open to form and style; however free verse is pre-ferred. Shorter poems have a better chance of being published. Looking for edgy, darker material written from the gut, reflecting the heart and human condition known as 'existence.' Topics include depression, mental illness, loss, sorrow, addiction, recovery, abuse, survival, daily existence, self struggles, and discovery through words. Personal, confessional poems are welcomed and embraced here. Rhyming poems are OK. Does not want overschooled, arrogant, self-rigteous, religious, political, sentimental, or happy and light pretty poetry. No erotic or sexually explicit poetry."

◐ *The Stray Branch* does not accept work from children or teens, or work written for children or teens. E-mail submisssions only. Has published work by Andy Robertson, Keith Estes, Kate Sjostrand, Lena Vanelslander, Michael Grover, and Justin Blackburn. Issue price: $10; $7 for contributors with the use of a contributor discount code.

NEEDS "Please keep stories no longer than 2½ pages. Shorter pieces of fiction stand a better chance of being published."

HOW TO CONTACT Send submissions via e-mail; no more than 2 pieces of fiction per submission. "All fiction must be sent as attachments." No simultaneous submissions. Previously published fiction is OK. *The Stray Branch* also publishes flash fiction.

◐ STRAYLIGHT

UW-Parkside, English Department, University of Wisconsin-Parkside, 900 Wood Rd., Kenosha WI 53141. (262)595-2139. **Fax:** (262)595-2271. **Website:** www.straylightmag.com. Estab. 2005. *Straylight*, published biannually, seeks fiction and "poetry of almost any style as long as it's inventive."

◐ Literary magazine/journal: 6×9, 115 pages, quality paper, uncoated index stock cover. Contains illustrations. Includes photographs.

NEEDS Publishes short shorts and novellas. Accepts 3-5 mss/issue; 6-10 mss/year. Does not read May-August. Agented fiction 10%. Length: 1,000-5,000 words for short stories; under 1,000 words for flash fiction; 17,500-45,000 for novellas. Average length: 1,500-3,000 words.

HOW TO CONTACT Send complete ms with cover letter. Accepts submissions by mail, online submission manager. Include brief bio, list of publications. Send either SASE (or IRC) for return of ms or disposable copy of ms and #10 SASE for reply only.

PAYMENT/TERMS Writers receive 2 contributor's copies. Additional copies $3.

TIPS "We tend to publish character-based and inventive fiction with cutting-edge prose. We are unimpressed with works based on strict plot twists or novelties. Read a sample copy to get a feel for what we publish."

○ STRUGGLE: A MAGAZINE OF PROLETARIAN REVOLUTIONARY LITERATURE

P.O. Box 28536, Detroit MI 48228. (313)273-9039. **E-mail:** timhall11@yahoo.com. **Website:** www.struglemagazine.net. **Contact:** Tim Hall, editor. Estab. 1985. "A quarterly magazine featuring African-American, Latino, and other writers of color, prisoners, disgruntled workers, activists in the anti-war, anti-racist and other mass movements and many writers discontented with Obama and the Republicans, their austerity campaign against the workers and the poor, and their continuing aggressive wars and drone murders abroad. While we urge literature in the direction of revolutionary working-class politics and a vision of socialism as embodying a genuine workers' power, in distinction to the state-capitalist regimes of the former Soviet Union, present-day China, North Korea, Cuba, etc., we accept a broader range of rebellious viewpoints in order to encourage creativity and dialogue."

NEEDS "Readers would like fiction about anti-globalization, the fight against racism, prison conditions, neoconservatism and the Iraq and Afghanistan wars, the struggle of immigrants, and the disillusionment with the Obama Administration as it reveals its craven service to the rich billionaires. Would also like to see more fiction that depicts life, work, and struggle of the working class of every background; also the struggles of the 1930s and 1960s illustrated and brought to life." Length: 4,000 words; average length: 1,000-3,000 words.

HOW TO CONTACT Accepts submissions by e-mail, mail.

○◐◑◒◓ SUBTERRAIN

Strong Words for a Polite Nation, P.O. Box 3008, MPO, Vancouver BC V6B 3X5 Canada. (604)876-8710. **Fax:** (604)879-2667. **E-mail:** subter@portal.ca. **Website:** www.subterrain.ca. **Contact:** Brian Kaufman, editor-in-chief. Estab. 1988. "*subTerrain* magazine is published 3 times a year from modest offices just off of Main Street in Vancouver, BC. We strive to produce a stimulating fusion of fiction, poetry, photography, and graphic illustration from uprising Canadian, U.S., and international writers and artists."

○ Magazine: 8.25×10.75; 72 pages; gloss stock paper; color gloss cover stock; illustrations; photos. "Looking for unique work and perspectives from Canada and beyond."

NEEDS Receives 100 unsolicited mss/month. Accepts 4 mss/issue; 10-15 mss/year. Recently published work by Elaine McCluskey, Tammy Armstrong, and Peter Babiak. Does not want genre fiction or children's fiction.

HOW TO CONTACT Send complete ms. Include disposable copy of the ms and SASE for reply only. Accepts multiple submissions.

PAYMENT/TERMS Pays $50/page for prose.

TIPS "Read the magazine first. Get to know what kind of work we publish."

SUBTROPICS

University of Florida, P.O. Box 112075, 4008 Turlington Hall, Gainesville FL 32601. **E-mail:** subtropics@english.ufl.edu. **Website:** www.english.ufl.edu/subtropics. **Contact:** David Leavitt. Estab. 2005. Magazine published twice year through the University of Florida's English department. *Subtropics* seeks to publish the best literary fiction, essays, and poetry being written today, both by established and emerging authors. Will consider works of fiction of any length, from short shorts to novellas and self-contained novel excerpts. Gives the same latitude to essays. Appreciates work in translation and, from time to time, republish important and compelling stories, essays, and poems that have lapsed out of print by writers no longer living. Member CLMP.

○ Literary magazine/journal: 9×6, 160 pages. Includes photographs. Submissions accepted from September 1-April 15.

NEEDS Receives 1,000 mss/month. Accepts 5-6 mss/issue; 10-12 mss/year. Does not read May 1-August 31. Agented fiction 33%. Publishes 1-2 new writers/year. Has published John Barth, Ariel Dorfman, Tony D'Souza, Allan Gurganus, Frances Hwang, Kuzhali Manickavel, Eileen Pollack, Padgett Powell, Nancy Reisman, Jarret Rosenblatt, Joanna Scott, and Olga Slavnikova. No genre fiction. Average length: 5,000 words. Average length of short shorts: 400 words. No longer than 15,000 words.

HOW TO CONTACT Send complete ms with cover letter. Send disposable copy of ms. Replies via e-mail only. Do not include SASE. Considers simultaneous submissions.

PAYMENT/TERMS Pays $500 for short shorts; $1,000 for full stories; 2 contributor's copies.

TIPS "We publish longer works of fiction, including novellas and excerpts from forthcoming novels. Each issue will include a short-short story of about 250 words on the back cover. We are also interested in publishing works in translation for the magazine's English-speaking audience."

THE SUMMERSET REVIEW

25 Summerset Dr., Smithtown NY 11787. **E-mail:** editor@summersetreview.org. **Website:** www.summersetreview.org. **Contact:** Joseph Levens, editor. Estab. 2002. "Our goal is simply to publish the highest-quality literary fiction, nonfiction, and poetry intended for a general audience. This is a simple online literary journal of high-quality material, so simple you can call it unique."

Magazine: illustrations and photographs. Periodically releases print issues. Quarterly. Receives 150 unsolicited mss/month. Accepts 5 prose pieces and 5 sets of poetry/issue; 35 mss/year. Publishes 5-10 new writers/year. Also publishes literary essays.

NEEDS No science fiction, horror, or graphic erotica. Length: 8,000 words; average length: 3,000 words. Publishes short shorts.

HOW TO CONTACT Send complete ms. Accepts submissions by e-mail.

TIPS "Style counts. We prefer innovative or at least very smooth, convincing voices. Even the dullest premises or the complete lack of conflict make for an interesting story if it is told in the right voice and style. We like to find little, interesting facts and/or connections subtly sprinkled throughout the piece. Harsh language should be used only if/when necessary. If we are choosing between light and dark subjects, the light will usually win."

THE SUN

107 N. Roberson St., Chapel Hill NC 27516. (919)942-5282. **Fax:** (919)932-3101. **Website:** www.thesunmagazine.org. **Contact:** Sy Safransky, editor. Estab. 1974. "We are open to all kinds of writing, though we favor work of a personal nature."

Magazine: 8.5×11; 48 pages; offset paper; glossy cover stock; photos.

NEEDS Open to all fiction. Receives 800 unsolicited mss/month. Accepts 20 short stories/year. Recently published work by Sigrid Nunez, Susan Straight, Lydia Peelle, Stephen Elliott, David James Duncan, Linda McCullough Moore, Brenda Miller. No science fiction, horror, fantasy, or other genre fiction. "Read an issue before submitting." Length: 7,000 words maximum.

HOW TO CONTACT Send complete ms. Accepts reprint submissions.

PAYMENT/TERMS Pays $300-1,500.

TIPS "Do not send queries except for interviews. We're open to unusual work. Read the magazine to get a sense of what we're about. Our submission rate is extremely high. Please be patient after sending us your work and include return postage."

SUSPENSE MAGAZINE

JRSR Ventures, 26500 W. Agoura Rd., Suite 102-474, Calabasas CA 91302. **Fax:** (310)626-9670. **E-mail:** editor@suspensemagazine.com; john@suspensemagazine.com. **Website:** www.suspensemagazine.com. **Contact:** John Raab, publisher/CEO/editor-in-chief. Estab. 2007.

NEEDS No explicit scenes. Length: 500-5,000 words.

HOW TO CONTACT Query.

TIPS "Unpublished writers are welcome and encouraged to query. Our emphasis is on horror, suspense, thriller, and mystery."

SYCAMORE REVIEW

Purdue University Department of English, 500 Oval Dr., West Lafayette IN 47907. (765) 494-3783. **Fax:** (765) 494-3780. **E-mail:** sycamore@purdue.edu. **Website:** www.sycamorereview.com. **Contact:** Alisha Karabinus, managing editor; Jessica Jacobs, editor-in-chief. *Sycamore Review* is Purdue University's internationally acclaimed literary journal, affiliated with Purdue's College of Liberal Arts and the Department of English. Art should present politics in a language that can be felt. Strives to publish the best writing by new and established writers. Looks for well-crafted and engaging work, works that illuminate our lives in the collective human search for meaning. Would like to publish more work that takes a reflective look at national identity and how we are perceived by the world. Looks for diversity of voice, pluralistic worldviews, and political and social context.

HOW TO CONTACT All prose should be typed, double-spaced, with numbered pages and the author's name and title of the work easily visible on each page. Wait until you have received a response to submit again.

PAYMENT/TERMS Pays in contributor's copies and $50/short story.

TIPS "We look for originality, brevity, significance, strong dialogue, and vivid detail. We sponsor the Wabash Prize for Poetry (deadline: mid-October) and Fiction (deadline: March 1). $1,000 award for each. All contest submissions will be considered for regular inclusion in the *Sycamore Review*. No e-mail submissions—no exception. Include SASE."

✚○ TALENT DRIPS EROTIC LITERARY EZINE

Cleveland OH 44102. (216)799-9775. **E-mail:** talent dripseroticpublishing@yahoo.com. **Website:** eroti catalentdrips.wordpress.com. **Contact:** Kimberly Steele, founder. Estab. 2007. *Talent Drips*, published monthly online, focuses solely on showcasing new erotic fiction.

HOW TO CONTACT Submit short stories between 5,000 and 10,000 words by e-mail to talentdripserotic publishing@yahoo.com. Stories should be pasted into body of message. Reads submissions during publication months only.

PAYMENT/TERMS Pays $15 for each accepted short story.

TIPS "Please read our take on the difference between *erotica* and *pornography*; it's on the website. *Talent Drips* does not accept pornography. And please keep poetry 30 lines or less."

TALES OF THE TALISMAN

Hadrosaur Productions, P.O. Box 2194, Mesilla Park NM 88047-2194. **E-mail:** hadrosaur@zianet.com. **Website:** www.talesofthetalisman.com. **Contact:** David Lee Summers, editor. Estab. 1995. *"Tales of the Talisman* is a literary science fiction and fantasy magazine. We publish short stories, poetry, and articles with themes related to science fiction and fantasy. Above all, we are looking for thought-provoking ideas and good writing. Speculative fiction set in the past, present, and future is welcome. Likewise contemporary or historical fiction is welcome as long as it has a mythic or science fictional element. Our target audience includes adult fans of the science fiction and fantasy genres along with anyone else who enjoys thought-provoking and entertaining writing."

○ Fiction and poetry submissions are limited to reading periods of January 1-February 15 and July 1-August 15.

NEEDS "We do not want to see stories with graphic violence. Do not send mainstream fiction with no science fictional or fantastic elements. Do not send stories with copyrighted characters, unless you're the copyright holder." Length: 1,000-6,000 words.

HOW TO CONTACT Send complete ms.

PAYMENT/TERMS Pays $6-10.

TIPS "Let your imagination soar to its greatest heights and write down the results. Above all, we are looking for thought-provoking ideas and good writing. Our emphasis is on character-oriented science fiction and fantasy. If we don't believe in the people living the story, we generally won't believe in the story itself."

◑ TALKING RIVER

Division of Literature and Languages, 500 8th Ave., Lewiston ID 83501. (208)792-2189. **Fax:** (208)792-2324. **E-mail:** talkingriver@lcmail.lcsc.edu. **Website:** www.lcsc.edu/talkingriverreview. **Contact:** Kevin Goodan, editorial advisor. Estab. 1994. "We look for new voices with something to say to a discerning general audience." Wants more well-written, character-driven stories that surprise and delight the reader with fresh, arresting yet unselfconscious language, imagery, metaphor, revelation. Reads mss September 1-May 1 only. Recently published work by X.J. Kennedy and Gary Fincke. Length: 4,000 words; average length: 3,000 words. Also publishes literary essays, poetry. Sometimes comments on rejected mss.

NEEDS No stories that are sexist, racist, homophobic, erotic for shock value; no genre fiction. Length: 4,000 words; average length: 3,000 words.

TIPS "We look for the strong, the unique; we reject clichéd images and predictable climaxes."

TELLURIDE MAGAZINE

Big Earth Publishing, Inc., P.O. Box 3488, Telluride CO 81435. (970)728-4245. **Fax:** (866)936-8406. **E-mail:** deb@telluridemagazine.com. **Website:** www.telluridemagazine.com. **Contact:** Deb Dion Kees, editor-in-chief. Estab. 1982. *"Telluride Magazine* speaks specifically to Telluride and the surrounding mountain environment. Telluride is a resort town supported by the ski industry in winter, festivals in summer, outdoor recreation year-round, and the unique lifestyle all of that affords. As a National Historic Landmark District with a colorful mining history, it weaves a tale that readers seek out. The local/visitor interaction is key to Telluride's success in making profiles an important part of the content. Telluriders are an environmentally minded and progressive bunch who appreciate efforts toward sustainability and protecting the natural landscape and wilderness that are the region's No. 1 draw."

NEEDS "Please contact us; we are very specific about what we will accept." 800-1,200 words.

HOW TO CONTACT Query with published clips.

◑⊖ TERRAIN.ORG: A JOURNAL OF THE BUILT + NATURAL ENVIROMENTS

Terrain.org, P.O. Box 19161, Tucson AZ 19161. 520-241-7390. **Website:** www.terrain.org. **Contact:** Simmons Buntin, editor-in-chief. Terrain.org is based on and thus welcomes quality submissions from new and experienced authors and artists alike. Our online journal accepts only the finest poetry, essays, fiction, articles, artwork, and other contributions' material that reaches deep into the earth's fiery core, or humanity's incalculable core, and brings forth new insights and wisdom. Terrain.org is searching for that interface—the integration among the built and natural environments, that might be called the soul of place. The works contained within Terrain.org ultimately examine the physical realm around us, and how those environments influence us and each other physically, mentally, emotionally and spiritually." Sponsors Terrain.org Annual Contest in Poetry, Fiction, and Nonfiction. Submissions due by August 1. How to Submit: Go to Submission Manager online tool.

○ Beginning March 2014, publication schedule is rolling; we will no longer be issue based. Receives 25 mss/month. Accepts 12-15 mss/year. Agented fiction 5%. **Publishes 1-3 new writers/year.** Published Al Sim, Jacob MacAurthur Mooney, T.R. Healy, Deborah Fries, Andrew Wingfield, Braden Hepner, Chavawn Kelly, Tamara Kaye Sellman. Sometimes comments on/critiques rejected mss. Sends galleys to author. Publication is copyrighted.

NEEDS Does not want erotica. Length: 1,000-6,000 words. Average length: 5,000 words. Publishes short shorts. Average length of short shorts: 750 words.

HOW TO CONTACT Does not read August 1-September 30 and February 1-March 30.

TIPS "We have 3 primary criteria in reviewing fiction: 1) The story is compelling and well-crafted. 2) The story provides some element of surprise; i.e., whether in content, form, or delivery we are unexpectedly delighted in what we've read. 3) The story meets an upcoming theme, even if only peripherally. Read fiction in the current issue and perhaps some archived work, and if you like what you read—and our overall enviromental slant—then send us your best work. Make sure you follow our submission guidelines (including cover note with bio), and that your ms is as error-free as possible."

◑ TEXAS REVIEW

Texas Review Press, Department of English, Sam Houston State University, Box 2146, Huntsville TX 77341-2146. (936)294-1992. **Fax:** (936)294-3070. **E-mail:** eng_pdr@shsu.edu; cww006@shsu.edu. **Website:** www.shsu.edu/~www_trp/. **Contact:** Dr. Paul Ruffin, editor/director. Estab. 1976. "We publish top-quality poetry, fiction, articles, interviews, and reviews for a general audience." Semiannual.

○ Magazine: 6×9; 148-190 pages; best-quality paper; 70 lb. cover stock; illustrations; photos. Receives 40-60 unsolicited mss/month. Accepts 4 mss/issue; 6 mss/year. **Publishes some new writers/year.** Does not read mss May-September. A member of the Texas A&M University Press consortium.

NEEDS "We are eager enough to consider fiction of quality, no matter what its theme or subject matter. No juvenile fiction."

HOW TO CONTACT Send complete ms. No mss accepted via fax. Send disposable copy of ms and #10 SASE for reply only. Accepts multiple submissions.

PAYMENT/TERMS Pays contributor's copies and one-year subscription.

◑⊛ THEMA

Thema Literary Society, P.O. Box 8747, Metairie LA 70011-8747. **E-mail:** thema@cox.net. **Website:** the maliterarysociety.com. **Contact:** Gail Howard, poetry editor. Estab. 1988. "THEMA is designed to stimulate creative thinking by challenging writers with unusual themes, such as 'The Box Under the Bed' and 'Put It In Your Pocket, Lillian.' Appeals to writers, teachers of creative writing, and general reading audience."

THEMA is 100 pages, digest-sized professionally printed, with glossy card cover. Receives about 400 poems/year, accepts about 8%. Press run is 400 (230 subscribers, 30 libraries). Subscription: $20 U.S./$30 foreign. Has published poetry by Beverly Boyd, Elizabeth Creith, James Penha, and Matthew J. Spireng.

NEEDS No erotica.

HOW TO CONTACT Send complete ms with SASE, cover letter; include "name and address, brief introduction, specifying the intended target issue for the mss." SASE. Accepts simultaneous, multiple submissions, and reprints. Does not accept e-mailed submissions.

PAYMENT/TERMS Pays $10-25.

THIRD COAST

Western Michigan University, Department of English, Kalamazoo MI 49008-5331. **Website:** www.thirdcoastmagazine.com. **Contact:** Laurie Ann Cedilnik, editor. Estab. 1995. "*Third Coast* publishes poetry, fiction (including traditional and experimental fiction, shorts, and novel excerpts, but not genre fiction), creative nonfiction (including reportage, essay, memoir, and fragments), drama, and translations."

Third Coast is 176 pages, digest-sized, professionally printed, perfect-bound, with 4-color cover with art.

NEEDS Literary. Receives 600 unsolicited mss/month. Accepts 6-8 mss/issue; 15 mss/year. Recently published work by Bonnie Jo Campbell, Peter Ho Davies, Robin Romm, Lee Martin, Caitlin Horrocks, and Peter Orner. Also publishes literary essays, poetry, one-act plays. Sometimes comments on rejected mss. "While we don't want to see formulaic genre fiction, we will consider material that plays with or challenges generic forms." No genre fiction. Length: 600-9,000 words.

HOW TO CONTACT Send complete ms.

PAYMENT/TERMS Pays 2 contributor's copies as well as a one-year subscription to the publication; additional copies for $4.

TIPS "We will consider many different types of fiction and favor those exhibiting a freshness of vision and approach."

34TH PARALLEL

P.O. Box 4823, Irvine CA 92623. **E-mail:** 34thParallel@gmail.com. **Website:** www.34thparallel.net. **Contact:** Tracey Boone Swan, Martin Chipperfield, editors. *34th Parallel*, published quarterly in print and online, seeks "to promote and publish the exceptional writing of new and emerging writers overlooked by large commercial publishing houses and mainstream presses. Wants work that experiments with and tests boundaries. Anything that communicates a sense of wonder, reality, tragedy, fantasy, and/or brilliance. Does not want historical romance, erotica, Gothic horror, or book reviews."

"Submissions must be your own work and previously unpublished. Unpublished means not published in print or online in any way whatsoever, period."

NEEDS Length: 1,500-3,500 words.

PAYMENT/TERMS Pays 1 contributor's copy in PDF format.

TIPS "We want it all, but we don't want everything. Take a look at the mag to get a feel for our style."

THE THREEPENNY REVIEW

P.O. Box 9131, Berkeley CA 94709. (510)849-4545. **E-mail:** wlesser@threepennyreview.com. **Website:** www.threepennyreview.com. Estab. 1980. "We are a general-interest, national literary magazine with coverage of politics, the visual arts, and the performing arts." Reading period: January 1-June 30.

NEEDS No fragmentary, sentimental fiction. Length: 800-4,000 words.

HOW TO CONTACT Send complete ms.

PAYMENT/TERMS Pays $400 per poem or Table Talk piece

TIPS Nonfiction (political articles, memoirs, reviews) is most open to freelancers.

TIMBER JOURNAL

E-mail: timberjournal@gmail.com. **Website:** www.timberjournal.com. Timber is a literary journal, run by students in the MFA program at the University of Colorado-Boulder, dedicated to the promotion of innovative literature. Publishes work that explores the boundaries of poetry, fiction, creative nonfiction, and digital literatures. Produces both an online journal that explores the potentials of the digital medium, and a semiannual "book object," which is a venue for more traditional print-based work.

Reading period August-March (submit just once during this time). Include 30- to 50-word bio with submission. Staff changes regularly, see website for current staff members.

NEEDS Looking for innovative fiction. Length: up to 5,000 words.

PAYMENT/TERMS Pays 1 contributor copy.

TIPS "We are looking for innovative poetry, fiction, creative nonfiction, and digital lit (screenwriting, digital poetry, multimedia lit, etc.)."

TIN HOUSE

McCormack Communications, P.O. Box 10500, Portland OR 97210. (503)219-0622. **Fax:** (503)222-1154. **E-mail:** info@tinhouse.com. **Website:** www.tinhouse.com. **Contact:** Cheston Knapp, managing editor; Holly Macarthur, founding editor. Estab. 1998. "We are a general-interest literary quarterly. Our watchword is quality. Our audience includes people interested in literature in all its aspects, from the mundane to the exalted."

Send complete ms September 1-May 31 via regular mail or online submission form. No fax or e-mail submissions.

NEEDS Length up to 5,000 words.

HOW TO CONTACT Send complete ms September 1-May 31 via regular mail or online submission form No fax or e-mail submissions.

PAYMENT/TERMS Pays $200-800.

TIPS "Remember to send an SASE with your submission."

TOAD SUCK REVIEW

Department of Writing, University of Central Arkansas, Conway AR 72035. **E-mail:** toadsuckreview@gmail.com. **Website:** toadsuckreview.org. **Contact:** John Vanderslice, editor. Estab. 2011. "Born from the legendary *Exquisite Corpse Annual*, the innovative *Toad Suck Review* is a cutting-edge mixture of poetry, fiction, creative nonfiction, translations, reviews, and artwork with a provocative sense of humor and an interest in diverse cultures and politics. No previously published work. 'Previously published' work includes: poetry posted on a public website/blog/forum and poetry posted on a private, password-protected forum. Reads mss in the summer." Prefers submissions from skilled, experienced poets; will consider work from beginning poets.

The journal received a Library Journal award for being one of the 10 best lit mags published in 2012. *Toad Suck Review* is a 6×11 magazine, 200 pages, perfect-bound, flat spine. Lifetime subscription: $75. Has published work by Charles Bukowski, Lawrence Ferlinghetti, Edward Ab-

bey, Gary Snyder, Anne Waldman, Ed Sanders, Tyrone Jaeger, Jean Genet, Louis-Ferdinand Céline, Antler, David Gessner, C.D. Wright, and Amiri Baraka.

NEEDS No religious, straight-up realism, odes to dead dogs. Length: 200-10,000 words; average length: 5,000 words.

HOW TO CONTACT Send reviews of novels and short story collections to editor. Include cover letter with disposable copy of complete mss. Accepts 5 mss/year.

PAYMENT/TERMS Pays contributor's copies.

TIPS "Our guidelines are very open and ambiguous. Don't send us too much and don't make it too long. If you submit in an e-mail, use .rtf. We're easy. If it works, we'll be in touch. It's a brutal world—wear your helmet."

TOASTED CHEESE

E-mail: editors@toasted-cheese.com. **E-mail:** submit@toasted-cheese.com. **Website:** www.toasted-cheese.com. Estab. 2001. "*Toasted Cheese* accepts submissions of previously unpublished fiction, flash fiction, creative nonfiction, poetry, and book reviews. Our focus is on quality of work, not quantity. Some issues will therefore contain fewer/more pieces than previous issues. We don't restrict publication based on subject matter. We encourage submissions from innovative writers in all genres."

NEEDS Receives 150 unsolicited mss/month. Accepts 1-10 mss/issue; 5-30 mss/year. Publishes 15 new writers/year. Sponsors awards/contests. "No fan fiction. No chapters or excerpts unless they read as a stand-alone story. No first drafts."

HOW TO CONTACT Send complete ms in body of e-mail; no attachments. Accepts submissions by e-mail.

TIPS "We are looking for clean, professional writing from writers of any level. Accepted stories will be concise and compelling. We are looking for writers who are serious about the craft: tomorrow's literary stars before they're famous. Take your submission seriously, yet remember that levity is appreciated. You are submitting not to traditional 'editors' but to fellow writers who appreciate the efforts of those in the trenches. Follow online submission guidelines."

TORCH: POETRY, PROSE AND SHORT STORIES BY AFRICAN AMERICAN WOMEN

3720 Gattis School Rd., Suite 800, Round Rock TX 78664. **E-mail:** info@torchpoetry.org. **Website:** www.torchpoetry.org. **Contact:** Amanda Johnston, editor.

Estab. 2006. *TORCH: Poetry, Prose, and Short Stories by African American Women*, published semiannually online, provides "a place to publish contemporary poetry, prose, and short stories by experienced and emerging writers alike. We prefer our contributors to take risks, and we offer a diverse body of work that examines and challenges preconceived notions regarding race, ethnicity, gender roles, and identity." Has published poetry by Sharon Bridgforth, Patricia Smith, Crystal Wilkinson, Tayari Jones, and Natasha Trethewey. Reads submissions April 15-August 31 only. Sometimes comments on rejected poems. Always sends prepublication galleys. No payment. "Within *TORCH*, we offer a special section called "Flame" that features an interview, biography, and work sample by an established writer as well as an introduction to their Spark—an emerging writer who inspires them and adds to the boundless voice of creative writing by Black women." A free online newsletter is available; see website.

TRANSITION: AN INTERNATIONAL REVIEW

104 Mount Auburn St., 3R, Cambridge MA 02138. (617)496-2845. **Fax:** (617)496-2877. **E-mail:** transition@fas.harvard.edu. **Website:** hutchinscenter.fas.harvard.edu/transition. **Contact:** Sara Bruya, managing editor. Estab. 1961.

Essays first published in a recent issue of *Transition* were selected for inclusion in *Best American Essays 2008*, *Best American Nonrequired Reading 2008*, and *Best African American Writing 2009*. Four-time winner of the Alternative Press Award for international reporting (2001, 2000, 1999, 1995); finalist in the 2001 National Magazine Award in General Excellence category. Author Tope Folarin, winner of the 2013 Caine Prize for African Writing for story "Miracle," published in *Transition*.

HOW TO CONTACT "For all submissions, please include the following information in your e-mail or cover letter and in the top left corner of the first page of all documents: name, address, e-mail address, word count, date of submission. Please also include a title with each work."

PAYMENT/TERMS Pays 1 contributor's copy.

TIPS "We look for a nonwhite, alternative perspective, dealing with issues of race, ethnicity, and identity in an unpredictable, provocative way."

TRIQUARTERLY

School of Continuing Studies, Northwestern University, 339 E. Chicago Ave., Chicago IL 60611. **E-mail:** triquarterly@northwestern.edu. **Website:** www.triquarterly.org. Estab. 1964. *TriQuarterly* welcomes submissions of fiction, creative nonfiction, poetry, short drama, and hybrid work. "We also welcome short-short prose pieces." Reading period: October 16-July 15.

HOW TO CONTACT Submit complete ms up to 3,500 words.

PAYMENT/TERMS Pays honoraria.

TULANE REVIEW

122 Norman Mayer, New Orleans LA 70118. **E-mail:** tulane.review@gmail.com. **E-mail:** litsoc@tulane.edu. **Website:** www.tulane.edu/~litsoc/treview.html. Estab. 1988. *Tulane Review*, published biannually, is a national literary journal seeking quality submissions of prose, poetry, and art. Considers all types of poetry. Wants imaginative poems with bold, inventive images. Has published poetry by Tom Chandler, Ace Boggess, Carol Hamilton, and Brady Rhoades.

Tulane Review is the recipient of an AWP Literary Magazine Design Award. *Tulane Review* is 70 pages, 7×9, perfect-bound, with 100# cover with full-color artwork. Receives about 1,200 poems/year, accepts about 50 per issue. Single copy: $8; subscription: $15. Make checks payable to *Tulane Review*.

HOW TO CONTACT Limit prose to 1 piece, no longer than 4,000 words. Include a cover letter with a biography, an e-mail address, and a return address.

U.S. CATHOLIC

Claretian Publications, 205 W. Monroe St., Chicago IL 60606. (312)236-7782. **Fax:** (312)236-8207. **E-mail:** editors@uscatholic.org. **E-mail:** submissions@uscatholic.org. **Website:** www.uscatholic.org. Estab. 1935. "*U.S. Catholic* is dedicated to the belief that it makes a difference whether you're Catholic. We invite and help our readers explore the wisdom of their faith tradition and apply their faith to the challenges of the 21st century."

Please include SASE with written ms.

NEEDS Accepts short stories. "Topics vary, but unpublished fiction should be no longer than 1,800 words and should include strong characters and cause readers to stop for a moment and consider their relationships with others, the world, and/or God. Specifically religious themes are not required; subject matter is not restricted. E-mail submissions@uscatholic.org. Usually responds in 8-10 weeks. Minimum payment is $200." Length: 700-1,800 words.

HOW TO CONTACT Send complete ms.

◐○ VERANDAH LITERARY & ART JOURNAL

Faculty of Arts, Deakin University, 221 Burwood Hwy., Burwood, Victoria 3125 Australia. (61)(3)9251-7134. **E-mail:** verandah@deakin.edu.au. **Website:** www.deakin.edu.au/verandah. Estab. 1985. *Verandah*, published annually in September, is a high-quality literary journal edited by professional writing students. It aims to give voice to new and innovative writers and artists.

○ Submission period: February 1-June 10. Has published work by Christos Tsiolka, Dorothy Porter, Seamus Heaney, Les Murray, Ed Burger, and John Muk Muk Burke. *Verandah* is 120 pages, professionally printed on glossy stock, flat-spined, with full-color glossy card cover.

NEEDS Length: 350-2,000 words.

HOW TO CONTACT Submit by mail or e-mail. However, electronic version of work must be available if accepted by *Verandah*. Do not submit work without the required submission form (available for download on website). Reads submissions by June 1 deadline (postmark).

◑ VERSAL

Postbus 3865, Amsterdam 1054 EJ The Netherlands. **Website:** www.wordsinhere.com. **Contact:** Shayna Schapp, assistant art editor (artists); Megan Garr, editor (writers and designers). Estab. 2002. Literary magazine/journal: 20cm×20cm, 100 pages, offset, perfect-bound, acid-free color cover. Includes artwork. "*Versal* is the only English-language literary magazine in the Netherlands and publishes new poetry, prose, and art from around the world. We publish writers with an instinct for language and line break, content and form that is urgent, involved, and unexpected." Annual. Circ. 750. Annual print magazine. "*Versal*, published each May by *worsinhere*, is the only literary magazine of its kind in the Netherlands and publishes new poetry, prose, and art from around the world. *Versal* and the writers behind it are also at the forefront of a growing translocal European literary scene, which includes exciting communities in Amsterdam, Paris, and Berlin. *Versal* seeks work that is urgent, involved and unexpected."

NEEDS Experimental, literary. Receives 125 mss/month. Accepts 10 mss/year. Does not read mss January 16-September 14. Ms published 4-7 months after acceptance. Publishes 4 new writers/year. Published Derek White, Alissa Nutting, Russell Edson, Sawako Nakayasu. Length: 1,000 words (maximum). Publishes short shorts. Average length of short shorts: 1,500 words. Also publishes poetry. Sometimes comments on/critiques rejected mss.

HOW TO CONTACT Send complete ms with cover letter. Accepts submissions electronically only. Include brief bio. Responds to queries in 1 week. Responds to mss in 2 months. Considers simultaneous submissions. Guidelines available on website.

PAYMENT/TERMS Writers receive 1 contributor copy. Additional copies $15. Pays on publication. Acquires one-time rights. Sends galleys to author. Publication is copyrighted.

TIPS "We ask that all writers interested in submitting work first purchase a copy (available from our website) to get an idea of *Versal*'s personality. All unsolicited submissions must be submitted through our online submission system. The link to this system is live during the submission period, which is September 15–January 15 each year. We like to see that a story is really a story, or, regardless of your definition of story, that the text has a shape. Often we receive excellent ideas or anecdotes that have no real sense of development, evolution, or involution. Because we have a story limit of 3,000 words, the best stories have carefully considered their shape. A good shape for an 8,000 word story will rarely be successful in a 2,000- to 3,000-word story. We prefer the work of writers who have really thought through and utilized detail/imagery that is both vivid and can carry some symbolic/metaphoric weight. While we like stories that test or challenge language and syntax, we do publish plenty of amazing stories that imply traditional syntax. Even in these stories, however, it is clear that the writers have paid close attention to sound and language, which allows the stories to best display their power."

VESTAL REVIEW

127 Kilsyth Road, Apt. 3, Brighton MA 02135. **Website:** www.vestalreview.net. Semi-annual print magazine specializing in flash fiction. *Vestal Review*'s sto-

ries have been reprinted in the *Mammoth Book of Miniscule Fiction, Flash Writing, E2Ink Anthologies*, and in the *WW Norton Anthology Flash Fiction Forward*.

○ Does not read new submissions in January, June, July, and December. All submissions received during these months will be returned unopened.

NEEDS Length: 50-500 words.

HOW TO CONTACT "We accept submissions only through our submission manager."

PAYMENT/TERMS Pays 3-10¢/word and 1 contributor's copy; additional copies for $10 (plus postage).

TIPS "We like literary fiction, with a plot, that doesn't waste words. Don't send jokes masked as stories."

○Ⓢ THE VIRGINIA QUARTERLY REVIEW

P.O. Box 400223, Charlottesville VA 22904. **E-mail:** vqr@vqronline.org. **Website:** www.vqronline.org. Estab. 1925. *The Virginia Quarterly Review* is 256 pages, digest-sized, flat-spined. Press run is 7,000.

NEEDS "We are generally not interested in genre fiction (such as romance, science fiction, or fantasy)." Length: 2,000-10,000 words.

HOW TO CONTACT Accepts online submissions only at virginiaquarterlyreview.submittable.com/submit.

PAYMENT/TERMS Pays 25¢/word.

WEST BRANCH

Stadler Center for Poetry, Bucknell University, Lewisburg PA 17837-2029. (570)577-1853. **Fax:** (570)577-1885. **E-mail:** westbranch@bucknell.edu. **Website:** www.bucknell.edu/westbranch. *West Branch* publishes poetry, fiction, and nonfiction in both traditional and innovative styles.

○ Reading period: August 1-April 1. No more than 3 submissions from a single contributor in a given reading period.

NEEDS No genre fiction. Length: no more than 30 pages.

HOW TO CONTACT Send complete ms.

PAYMENT/TERMS Pays $10/page, with a maximum of $100.

TIPS "All submissions must be sent via our online submission manager. Please see website for guidelines. We recommend that you acquaint yourself with the magazine before submitting."

WESTERN HUMANITIES REVIEW

University of Utah, English Department, 255 S. Central Campus Dr., Salt Lake City UT 84112-0494.

(801)581-6070. **Fax:** (801)585-5167. **E-mail:** whr@mail.hum.utah.edu. **Website:** ourworld.info/whrweb/. **Contact:** Barry Weller, editor; Nate Liederbach, managing editor. Estab. 1947.

NEEDS Does not want genre (romance, science fiction, etc.). Length: 5,000 words.

HOW TO CONTACT Send complete ms.

PAYMENT/TERMS Pays $5/published page (when funds available).

TIPS "Because of changes in our editorial staff, we urge familiarity with recent issues of the magazine. We do not publish writer's guidelines because we think that the magazine itself conveys an accurate picture of our requirements. Please, no e-mail submissions."

WHISKEY ISLAND MAGAZINE

Rhodes Tower 1636, Cleveland OH 44115. (216)687-2000. **E-mail:** whiskeyisland@csuohio.edu. **Website:** www.csuohio.edu/class/english/whiskeyisland. "This is a nonprofit literary magazine that has been published (in one form or another) by students of Cleveland State University for over 30 years. Also features the Annual Student Creative Writing Contest."

○ "We accept original poetry, prose, and art submissions from August 15 through May 1 of each year. We accept simultaneous submissions and ask that you identify them as such in your cover letter. No multiple submissions, please, and no previously published work either. Reporting time is about 3 months."

NEEDS No translations. "Please keep fiction submissions to 5,000 words or less."

TIPS "See submissions page. Wait at least a year before submitting again."

◐ WILD VIOLET

P.O. Box 39706, Philadelphia PA 19106. **E-mail:** wildvioletmagazine@yahoo.com. **Website:** www.wildviolet.net. **Contact:** Alyce Wilson, editor. Estab. 2001. *Wild Violet*, published weekly online, aims "to make the arts more accessible, to make a place for the arts in modern life, and to serve as a creative forum for writers and artists. Our audience includes English-speaking readers from all over the world, who are interested in both 'high art' and pop culture."

NEEDS Receives 30 unsolicited mss/month. Accepts 3-5 mss/issue; 135 mss/year. **Publishes 70 new writers/year.** Recently published work by Margaret Karmazin, Nancy S.M. Waldman, David Oates, and

Ron Darian. Also publishes literary essays, literary criticism, poetry. Sometimes comments on rejected mss. "No stories where sexual or violent content is used to shock the reader. No racist writings." Length: 500-6,000 words; average length: 3,000 words.

HOW TO CONTACT Send complete ms. Accepts submissions by e-mail. Include estimated word count and brief bio. Send SASE for return of ms or send a disposable copy of ms and #10 SASE for reply only. Responds in 1 week to queries; 3-6 months to mss. Accepts simultaneous, multiple submissions. Sample copy online. Writer's guidelines by e-mail. Reviews books/chapbooks of poetry in 250 words, single-book format. Query for review consideration.

PAYMENT/TERMS Writers receive bio and links on contributor's page. Sponsors awards/contests.

TIPS "We look for stories that are well-paced and show character and plot development. Even short shorts should do more than simply paint a picture. Mss stand out when the author's voice is fresh and engaging. Avoid muddying your story with too many characters and don't attempt to shock the reader with an ending you have not earned. Experiment with styles and structures but don't resort to experimentation for its own sake."

◑ WILLARD & MAPLE

163 S. Willard St., Freeman 302, Box 34, Burlington VT 05401. (802)860-2700 ext.2462. **E-mail:** willardandmaple@champlain.edu. Estab. 1996. *Willard & Maple*, published annually in spring, is a student-run literary magazine from Champlain College's Professional Writing Program that considers short fiction, essays, reviews, fine art, and poetry by adults, children, and teens. Wants creative work of the highest quality. Does not want any submissions over 10 typed pages in length; all submissions must be in English.

○ Reads submissions September 1-March 31. *Willard & Maple* is 200 pages, digest-sized, digitally printed, perfect-bound. Receives about 500 poems/year, accepts about 20%. Press run is 600 (80 subscribers, 4 libraries); 200 are distributed free to the Champlain College writing community. Single copy: $12. Contact Lulu Press for contributor's copy.

HOW TO CONTACT Send complete mss via e-mail or snail mail. Send SASE for return of ms or send disposable copy of mss and #10 SASE for reply only.

PAYMENT/TERMS Pays 2 contributor's copies.

TIPS "The power of imagination makes us infinite."

WILLOW REVIEW

College of Lake County Publications, College of Lake County, 19351 W. Washington St., Grayslake IL 60030-1198. (847)543-2956. **E-mail:** com426@clcillinois.edu. **Website:** www.clcillinois.edu/community/willowreview.asp. **Contact:** Michael Latza, editor. Estab. 1969. *Willow Review*, published annually, is interested in poetry, creative nonfiction, and fiction of high quality. "We have no preferences as to form, style, or subject, as long as each poem stands on its own as art and communicates ideas."

○ The editors award prizes for best poetry and prose in the issue. Prize awards vary contingent on the current year's budget but normally ranges from $100-400. There is no reading fee or separate application for these prizes. All accepted mss are eligible. *Willow Review* is 88-96 pages, digest-sized, professionally printed, flat-spined, with a 4-color cover featuring work by an Illinois artist. Press run is 1,000. Subscription: $18 for 3 issues, $30 for 6 issues. Sample: $5 (back issue). International: add $5 per issue. Has published poetry by Lisel Mueller, Lucien Stryk, David Ray, Louis Rodriguez, John Dickson, and Patricia Smith.

NEEDS Accepts short fiction. Considers simultaneous submissions, multiple submissions.

HOW TO CONTACT Send complete ms with cover letter. Include estimated word count, brief bio, list of publications. Send either SASE (or IRC) for return of ms or disposable copy of ms and #10 SASE for reply only.

PAYMENT/TERMS Pays 2 contributors copies.

TIPS "Include SASE. No e-mail submissions, please. *Willow Review* can be found on EBSCOhost databases, assuring a broader targeted audience for our authors' work. *Willow Review* is a nonprofit journal partially supported by a grant from the Illinois Arts Council (a state agency), College of Lake County Publications, private contributions, and sales."

WILLOW SPRINGS

501 N. Riverpoint Blvd., Suite 425, Spokane WA 99202. (509)359-7435. **E-mail:** willowspringsewu@gmail.com. **Website:** willowsprings.ewu.edu. **Contact:** Samuel Ligon, editor. Estab. 1977. *Willow Springs* is a semiannual magazine covering poetry, fiction, literary nonfiction, and interviews of notable writers.

Published twice a year, in spring and fall. Submissions in all genres are closed between June 1 and August 31. **NEEDS** We accept any good piece of literary fiction. Buy a sample copy. Does not want to see genre fiction that does not transcend its subject matter. **HOW TO CONTACT** Send complete ms. **TIPS** "Please submit all mss with a cover letter and a brief bio. While we have no specific length restrictions, we generally publish fiction and nonfiction no longer than 10,000 words and poetry no longer than 120 lines, though those are not strict rules. *Willow Springs* values poems and essays that transcend the merely autobiographical and fiction that conveys a concern for language as well as story."

○ WINDHOVER

A Journal of Christian Literature, P.O. Box 8008, 900 College St., Belton TX 76513. (254)295-4561. **E-mail:** windhover@umhb.edu. **Website:** undergrad.umhb .edu/english/windhover-journal. **Contact:** Dr. Nathaniel Hansen, editor. Estab. 1997. "*Windhover* is devoted to promoting writers and literature with Christian perspectives and with a broad definition of those perspectives. We accept poetry, short fiction, nonfiction, and creative nonfiction."

Magazine: 6×9; white bond paper. **NEEDS** Receives 30 unsolicited mss/month. Recently published work by Walt McDonald, Cleatus Rattan, Greg Garrett, Barbara Crooker. No erotica. Length: 1,500-4,000 words. Average length: 3,000 words. **PAYMENT/TERMS** Pays 1 contributor's copy. **TIPS** "We particularly look for convincing plot and character development."

◑ WISCONSIN REVIEW

University of Wisconsin Oshkosh, 800 Algoma Blvd., Oshkosh WI 54901. (920)424-2267. **E-mail:** wisconsinreview@uwosh.edu. **Website:** www.uwosh.edu/wisconsinreview. Estab. 1966. *Wisconsin Review*, published semiannually, is a "contemporary poetry, prose, and art magazine run by students at the University of Wisconsin Oshkosh."

Wisconsin Review is around 100 pages, digest-sized, perfect-bound, with 4-color glossy cover stock. Receives about 400 poetry submissions/year, accepts about 50; Press run is 1,000. Single copy: $7.50; subscription: $10 plus $3 extra per issue for shipments outside the U.S. **NEEDS** "Standard or experimental styles will be considered, although we look for outstanding char-

acterization and unique themes." Submit via postal mail (include SASE) or online submission manager. Length: up to 15 pages, double-spaced with 12-pt. font. **PAYMENT/TERMS** Pays with 2 contributor copies. **TIPS** "We are open to any poetic form and style, and look for outstanding imagery, new themes, and fresh voices—poetry that induces emotions."

WITCHES AND PAGANS

BBI Media, Inc., P.O. Box 687, Forest Grove OR 97116. (888)724-3966. **E-mail:** editor2@bbimedia.com. **Website:** www.witchesandpagans.com. Estab. 2002. "*Witches and Pagans* is dedicated to witches, wiccans, neo-pagans, and various other earth-based, pre-Christian, shamanic, and magical practitioners. We hope to reach not only those already involved in what we cover, but the curious and completely new as well."

"Devoted exclusively to promoting and covering contemporary Pagan culture, *W&P* features exclusive interviews with the teachers, writers, and activists who create and lead our traditions, visits to the sacred places and people who inspire us, and in-depth discussions of our ever-evolving practices. You'll also find practical daily magic, ideas for solitary ritual and devotion, God/dess-friendly craft projects, Pagan poetry and short fiction, reviews, and much more in every 88-page issue. *W&P* is available in either traditional paper copy sent by postal mail or as a digital PDF-eZine download that is compatible with most computers and readers."

NEEDS Does not want faction (fictionalized retellings of real events). Avoid gratuitous sex, violence, sentimentality, and pagan moralizing. Don't beat our readers with the Rede or the Threefold Law. Length: 1,000-5,000 words. **HOW TO CONTACT** Send complete ms. **TIPS** "Read the magazine, do your research, write the piece, send it in. That's really the only way to get started as a writer; everything else is window dressing."

WOMAN'S WORLD

Bauer Publishing Co., 270 Sylvan Ave., Englewood Cliffs NJ 07632. (201)569-6699. **Fax:** (201)569-3584. **E-mail:** dearww@bauerpublishing.com; dearww@aol .com. **Website:** winit.womansworldmag.com. **Contact:** Stephanie Saible, editor-in-chief. Estab. 1980. Publishes short romances and mini-mysteries for all women, ages 18-68.

Woman's World is not looking for freelancers to take assigments generated by the staff, but it will assign stories to writers who have made a successful pitch.

NEEDS Looking for short story, romance, and mainstream of 800 words and mini-mysteries of 1,000 words. Each story should have a light romantic theme and can be written from either a masculine or feminine point of view. Women characters may be single, married, or divorced. Plots must be fast moving with vivid dialogue and action. The problems and dilemmas inherent in them should be contemporary and realistic, handled with warmth and feeling. The stories must have a positive resolution. Specify *Fiction* on envelope. Always enclose SASE. Responds in 4 months. No phone or fax queries. Pays $1,000 for romances on acceptance for North American serial rights for 6 months. The 1,000 word mini-mysteries may feature either a "whodunnit" or "howdunnit" theme. The mystery may revolve around anything from a theft to murder. Not interested in sordid or grotesque crimes. Emphasis should be on intricacies of plot rather than gratuitous violence. The story must include a resolution that clearly states the villain is getting his or her comeuppance. Submit complete mss. Specify *Mini-Mystery* on envelope. Enclose SASE. No phone queries. Not interested in science fiction, fantasy, historical romance, or foreign locales. No explicit sex, graphic language, or seamy settings. Romances: 800 words; mysteries: 1,000 words.

HOW TO CONTACT Send complete ms.

TIPS The whole story should be sent when submitting fiction. Stories slanted for a particular holiday should be sent at least 6 months in advance. "Familiarize yourself totally with our format and style. Read at least a year's worth of *Woman's World* fiction. Analyze and dissect it. Regarding romances, scrutinize them not only for content but tone, mood and sensibility."

THE WORCESTER REVIEW

1 Ekman St., Worcester MA 01607. (508)797-4770. **E-mail:** twr.diane@gmail.com. **Website:** www .theworcesterreview.org. **Contact:** Diane Mulligan, managing editor. Estab. 1972. *The Worcester Review*, published annually by the Worcester County Poetry Association, encourages "critical work with a New England connection; no geographic limitation on poetry and fiction." Wants "work that is crafted, intuitively honest, and empathetic. We like high-quality, creative poetry, artwork, and fiction. Critical articles should be connected to New England."

Magazine: 6×9; 60 lb. white offset paper; 10 pt. CS1 cover stock; illustrations; photos. Has published poetry by Kurt Brown, Cleopatra Mathis, and Theodore Deppe. *The Worcester Review* is 160 pages, digest-sized, professionally printed in dark type on quality stock, perfect-bound, with matte card cover. Press run is 600. Subscription: $30 (includes membership in WCPA).

NEEDS Recently published work by Robert Pinsky, Marge Piercy, Wes McNair, Ed Hirsch. Length: 1,000-4,000 words. Average length: 2,000 words.

HOW TO CONTACT Send complete ms. "Send only 1 short story—reading editors do not like to read 2 by the same author at the same time. We will use only 1."

PAYMENT/TERMS Pays 2 contributor's copies and honorarium, if possible.

TIPS "We generally look for creative work with a blend of craftsmanship, insight, and empathy. This does not exclude humor. We won't print work that is shoddy in any of these areas."

WORD RIOT

P.O. Box 414, Middletown NJ 07748-3143. (732)706-1272. **Fax:** (732)706-5856. **E-mail:** wr.submissions@gmail.com. **Website:** www.wordriot.org. **Contact:** Jackie Corley, publisher. Estab. 2002. "*Word Riot* publishes the forceful voices of up-and-coming writers and poets. We like edgy. We like challenging. We like unique voices. Each month we provide readers with book reviews, author interviews, and, most important, writing from some of the best and brightest making waves on the literary scene."

Online magazine. Member CLMP.

NEEDS Accepts 20-25 mss/issue; 240-300 mss/year. Publishes ms 1-2 months after acceptance. Agented fiction 5%. Publishes 8-10 new writers/year. "No fantasy, science fiction, romance." Length: 1,000-6,500 words.

HOW TO CONTACT Submit via online submission form at wordriot.submittable.com/submit. Do not send submissions by mail.

TIPS "We're always looking for something edgy or quirky. We like writers who take risks."

WORKERS WRITE!

Blue Cubicle Press, LLC, P.O. Box 250382, Plano TX 75025. **E-mail:** info@workerswritejournal.com. **Web-**

site: www.workerswritejournal.com. **Contact:** David LaBounty, managing editor. Estab. 2005. "*Workers Write!* is an annual print journal published by Blue Cubicle Press, an independent publisher dedicated to giving voice to writers trapped in the daily grind. Each issue focuses on a particular workplace; check website for details. Submit your stories via e-mail or send a hard copy."

NEEDS "We need your stories about the workplace for our Overtime series. Word count: 500-5,000 words. Every 3 months, we'll release a chapbook containing 1 story that centers on work." Length: 500-5,000 words.

HOW TO CONTACT Send complete ms.

PAYMENT/TERMS Payment: $5-$50 (depending on length and rights requested).

THE WRITE PLACE AT THE WRITE TIME

E-mail: submissions@thewriteplaceatthewritetime.org. **Website:** www.thewriteplaceatthewritetime.org. **Contact:** Nicole M. Bouchard, editor-in-chief. Estab. 2008. Online literary magazine, published 3 times/year. Publishes fiction, personal nonfiction, and poetry that "speaks to the heart and mind."

"Our writers range from previously unpublished to having written for *The New York Times*, *Time* magazine, *The Wall Street Journal*, *Glimmer Train*, *Newsweek*, and *Business Week*, and they come from all over the world."

NEEDS No erotica, explicit horror/gore/violence, political. Length: 3,500 words maximum. Average length of stories: 3,000 words. Average length of short shorts: 1,000 words.

HOW TO CONTACT Send complete ms with cover letter by e-mail—no attachments. Include estimated word count and brief bio. Accepts multiple submissions, up to 3 stories at a time. Accepts 90-100 mss/year; receives 500-700 mss/year.

TIPS "Visit the website for details before submitting. Our publication is copyrighted. We send prepublication galleys to authors if the story underwent significant edits. If the material is only slightly edited, then we don't."

WRITER'S BLOC

Texas A&M University—Kingsville, Department of Language and Literature, Fore Hall Rm. 110, Kingsville TX 78363. (361)593-2514. **E-mail:** octavio.quintanilla@tamuk.edu. **Website:** www.tamuk.edu/artsci/langlit/index4.html. **Contact:** Dr. Octavio Quinta-

nilla. *Writer's Bloc*, published annually, prints poetry, short fiction, flash fiction, one-act plays, interviews, and essays. "About half of our pages are devoted to the works of Texas A&M University-Kingsville students and half to the works of writers and artists from all over the world." Wants quality poetry; no restrictions on content or form. *Writer's Bloc* is 96 pages, digest-sized. Press run is 300. Subscription: $7. Sample: $7.

NEEDS Submit via postal mail. Include cover letter with contact info, short bio. Accepts about 6 mss/year. Does not read mss June-January. Publishes short shorts. Also publishes literary essays, poetry. No pornography, genre fiction, or work by children. Length: up to 3,500 words. Average length is 2,500 words.

THE WRITING DISORDER

P.O. Box 93613, Los Angeles CA 90093. (323)336-5822. **E-mail:** submit@thewritingdisorder.com. **Website:** www.thewritingdisorder.com. **Contact:** C.E. Lukather, editor; Paul Garson, managing editor; Julianna Woodhead, poetry editor. Estab. 2009. "*The Writing Disorder* is an online literary magazine devoted to literature, art, and culture. The mission of the magazine is to showcase new and emerging writers—particularly those in writing programs—as well as established ones. The magazine also features original artwork, photography, and comic art. Although it strives to publish original and experimental work, *The Writing Disorder* remains rooted in the classic art of storytelling."

NEEDS Does not want to see romance, religious, or fluff. Length: 7,500 words maximum.

HOW TO CONTACT Query.

PAYMENT/TERMS Pays contributor's copies.

TIPS "We are looking for work from new writers, writers in writing programs, and students and faculty of all ages."

XAVIER REVIEW

Xavier University of Louisiana, 1 Drexel Dr., Box 89, New Orleans LA 70125-1098. **Website:** www.xula.edu/review. **Contact:** Ralph Adamo, editor. Estab. 1980. "*Xavier Review* accepts poetry, fiction, translations, creative nonfiction, and critical essays. Content focuses on African-American, Caribbean, and Southern literature, as well as works that touch on issues of religion and spirituality. We do, however, accept quality work on all themes. (Please note: This is not a religious publication.)"

NEEDS Has published work by Andrei Codrescu, Terrance Hayes, Naton Leslie, and Patricia Smith. Also publishes literary essays and literary criticism.

HOW TO CONTACT Send complete ms. Include 2-3 sentence bio and SASE. "We rarely accept mss over 20 pages."

PAYMENT/TERMS Pays 2 contributor's copies; offers 40% discount on additional copies.

THE YALE REVIEW

Yale University, P.O. Box 208243, New Haven CT 06520-8243. (203)432-0499. **Fax:** (203)432-0510. **Website:** www.yale.edu/yalereview. **Contact:** J.D. Mc-Clatchy, editor. Estab. 1911.

HOW TO CONTACT Submit complete ms with SASE. All submissions should be sent to the editorial office.

PAYMENT/TERMS Pays $400-500.

THE YALOBUSHA REVIEW

University of Mississippi, P.O. Box 1848, Department of English, University MS 38677. (662)915-3175. **E-mail:** yreditors@gmail.com. **Website:** yr.olemiss.edu/. Estab. 1995.

NEEDS Length: up to 10,000 words.

HOW TO CONTACT Submit "1 short story of traditional length (let's say 8-20 pages), or up to 3 pieces of shorter fiction (less than 5 pages each). If submitting 3 shorter works, please include all piece in 1 file." Use online submissions manager.

PAYMENT/TERMS Pays honorarium when funding is available.

⚫⚫ YEMASSEE

University of South Carolina, Department of English, Columbia SC 29208. (803)777-2085. **Fax:** (803)777-9064. **E-mail:** editor@yemasseejournalonline.org. **Website:** yemasseejournalonline.org. **Contact:** Lauren Eyler, editor-in-chief. Estab. 1993. "*Yemassee* is the University of South Carolina's literary journal. Our readers are interested in high-quality fiction, poetry, drama, and creative nonfiction. We have no editorial slant; quality of work is our only concern. We publish in the fall and spring, printing 3-5 stories and 12-15 poems per issue. We tend to solicit reviews, essays, and interviews but welcome unsolicited queries. We do not favor any particular aesthetic or school of writing."

⚫ Stories from *Yemassee* have been published in *New Stories from the South*. As of 2012, only accepts submissions through online submissions manager.

NEEDS "We are open to a variety of subjects and writing styles. We publish primarily fiction and poetry, but we are also interested in one-act plays, brief excerpts of novels, and interviews with literary figures. Our essential consideration for acceptance is the quality of the work. No romance, religious/inspirational, young adult/teen, children's/juvenile, erotica. Wants more experimental work." Length: up to 5,000 words.

HOW TO CONTACT Send complete ms. "Submissions for all genres should include a cover letter that lists the titles of the pieces included, along with your contact information (including author's name, address, e-mail address, and phone number)."

PAYMENT/TERMS Pays in contributor copies.

⚫⚫ ZEEK: A JEWISH JOURNAL OF THOUGHT AND CULTURE

P.O. Box 1342, New York NY 10116. (212)666-1404. **Fax:** (646)843-4737. **E-mail:** zeek@zeek.net. **Website:** www.zeek.net. **Contact:** Erica Brody, editor. Estab. 2001. *Zeek: A Jewish Journal of Thought and Culture* "relaunched in late February 2013 as a hub for the domestic Jewish social justice movement, one that showcases the people, ideas, and conversations driving an inclusive and diverse progressive Jewish community. At the same time, we've reaffirmed our commitment to building on Zeek's reputation for original, ahead-of-the-curve Jewish writing and arts, culture and spirituality content, incubating emerging voices and artists, as well as established ones." *Zeek* seeks "great writing in a variety of styles and voices, original thinking, and accessible content. That means we're interested in hearing your ideas for first-person essays, reflections and commentary, reporting, profiles, Q&As, analysis, infographics, and more. For the near future, *Zeek* will focus on domestic issues. Our discourse will be civil."

NEEDS "Pitches should be sent to zeek@zeek.net, with *submission* or *pitch* in the subject line. And please include a little bit about yourself and why you think your pitch is a good fit for *Zeek*."

ZOETROPE: ALL-STORY

Zoetrope: All-Story, The Sentinel Bldg., 916 Kearny St., San Francisco CA 94133. (415)788-7500. **Website:** www.all-story.com. **Contact:** fiction editor. Estab. 1997. *Zoetrope: All Story* presents a new generation of classic stories.

⚫ Does not accept submissions September 1-December 31 (with the exception of stories entered in the annual Short Fiction Contest, which are considered for publication in the magazine).

NEEDS Length: up to 7,000 words. "Excerpts from larger works, screenplays, treatments, and poetry will be returned unread."

HOW TO CONTACT "Writers should submit only 1 story at a time and no more than 2 stories a year. We do not accept artwork or design submissions. We do not accept unsolicited revisions nor respond to writers who don't include an SASE." Send complete ms.

PAYMENT/TERMS Pays up to $1,000.

TIPS "Before submitting, nonsubscribers should read several issues of the magazine to determine if their works fit with *All-Story*. Electronic versions of the magazine are available to read, in part, at the website, and print versions are available for purchase by single-issue order and subscription."

ZYZZYVA

466 Geary Street, Suite 401, San Francisco CA 94102. (415)440-1510. **E-mail:** editor@zyzzyva.org. **Website:** www.zyzzyva.org. **Contact:** Laura Cogan, editor; Oscar Villalon, managing editor. Estab. 1985. "We feature work by writers currently living on the West Coast or in Alaska and Hawaii only. We are essentially a literary magazine but of wide-ranging interests and a strong commitment to nonfiction."

○ Accepts submissions year-round. Does not accept online submissions.

NEEDS Length: no maximum word count.

HOW TO CONTACT Send complete ms by mail. Include SASE and contact information.

PAYMENT/TERMS Pays $50.

TIPS "We are not currently seeking work about any particular theme or topic; that said, reading recent issues is perhaps the best way to develop a sense for the length and quality we are looking for in submissions."

BOOK PUBLISHERS

In this section, you will find many of the "big name" book publishers. Many of these publishers remain tough markets for new writers or for those whose work might be considered literary or experimental. Indeed, some only accept work from established authors, and then often only through an author's agent. Although having your novel published by one of the big commercial publishers listed in this section is difficult, it is not impossible. The trade magazine *Publishers Weekly* regularly features interviews with writers whose first novels are being released by top publishers. Many editors at large publishing houses find great satisfaction in publishing a writer's first novel.

On page 478, you'll find the publishing industry's "family tree," which maps out each of the large book publishing conglomerates' divisions, subsidiaries, and imprints. Remember, most manuscripts are acquired by imprints, not their parent company, so avoid submitting to the conglomerates themselves. (For example, submit to Dutton or Berkley Books, not their parent Penguin.)

Also listed here are "small presses," which publish four or more titles annually. Included among them are independent presses, university presses, and other nonprofit publishers. Introducing new writers to the reading public has become an increasingly important role of these smaller presses at a time when the large conglomerates are taking fewer chances on unknown writers. Many of the successful small presses listed in this section have built their reputations and their businesses in this way and have become known for publishing prize-winning fiction.

These smaller presses also tend to keep books in print longer than larger houses. And, since small presses publish a smaller number of books, each title is equally important to the publisher and each is promoted in much the same way and with the same commitment.

Editors also stay at small presses longer because they have more of a stake in the business—often they own the business. Many smaller book publishers are writers themselves and know firsthand the importance of a close editor-author or publisher-author relationship.

TYPES OF BOOK PUBLISHERS

Large or small, the publishers in this section publish books "for the trade." That is, unlike textbook, technical, or scholarly publishers, trade publishers publish books to be sold to the general consumer through bookstores, chain stores, or other retail outlets. Within the trade book field, however, there are a number of different types of books.

The easiest way to categorize books is by their physical appearance and the way they are marketed. Hardcover books are the more expensive editions of a book, sold through bookstores and carrying a price tag of around $20 and up. Trade paperbacks are softbound books, also sold mostly in bookstores, but they carry a more modest price tag of usually around $10 to $20. Today a lot of fiction is published in this form because it means a lower financial risk than hardcover.

Mass-market paperbacks are another animal altogether. These are the smaller "pocket-size" books available at bookstores, grocery stores, drugstores, chain retail outlets, etc. Much genre or category fiction is published in this format. This area of the publishing industry is very open to the work of talented new writers who write in specific genres such as science fiction, romance, and mystery.

At one time, publishers could be easily identified and grouped by the type of books they produce. Today, however, the lines between hardcover and paperback books are blurred. Many publishers known for publishing hardcover books also publish trade paperbacks and have paperback imprints. This enables them to offer established authors (and a very few lucky newcomers) hard-soft deals in which their book comes out in both versions. Thanks to the mergers of the past decade, too, the same company may own several hardcover and paperback subsidiaries and imprints, even though their editorial focuses may remain separate.

CHOOSING A BOOK PUBLISHER

In addition to checking the bookstores and libraries for books by publishers that interest you, you may want to refer to the Category Index at the back of this book to find publishers divided by specific subject categories. The subjects listed in the index are general. Read individual listings to find which subcategories interest a publisher. For example, you will find several romance publishers listed, but you should read the listings to find which type of romance is considered: gothic, contemporary, regency, futuristic, and so on.

The icons appearing before the names of the publishers will also help you in selecting a publisher. These codes are especially important in this section, because many of the publishing houses listed here require writers to submit through an agent. The ⓐ symbol indicates that a publisher accepts agented submissions only. A ● icon identifies those that mostly publish established and agented authors, while a ○ points to publishers most open to new writers. See the inside back cover of this book for a complete list and explanations of symbols used in this book.

IN THE LISTINGS

As with other sections in this book, we identify new listings with a ➕ symbol. In this section, most with this symbol are not new publishers, but they are established publishers who were unable to list last year (or decided not to) and are therefore new to this edition.

In addition to the ➕ symbol indicating new listings, we include other symbols to help you narrow your search. English-speaking foreign markets are denoted by a ⮑. The maple leaf symbol ✺ identifies Canadian presses. If you are not a Canadian writer but are interested in a Canadian press, check the listing carefully. Many small presses in Canada receive grants and other funds from their provincial or national government and are, therefore, restricted to publishing Canadian authors.

We also include editorial comments set off by a bullet (○) within listings. This is where we include information about any special requirements or circumstances that will help you know even more about the publisher's needs and policies. The ☺ symbol identifies publishers who have recently received honors or awards for their books. The ☻ denotes publishers who produce comics and graphic novels.

Each listing includes a summary of the house's editorial mission, an overarching principle that ties together what they publish. Under the heading **Contact** we list one or more editors, often with their specific area of expertise.

Book editors asked us again this year to emphasize the importance of paying close attention to the **Needs** and **How to Contact** subheads of listings for book publishers. Unlike magazine editors, who want to see complete manuscripts of short stories, most of the book publishers listed here ask that writers send a query letter with an outline and/or synopsis and several chapters of their novel. "The Business of Fiction Writing," beginning on page 52 of this book, outlines how to prepare work to submit directly to a publisher.

There are no subsidy book publishers listed in *Novel & Short Story Writer's Market*. By subsidy, we mean any arrangement in which the writer is expected to pay all or part of the cost of producing, distributing, and marketing his book. We feel a writer should not be asked to share in any cost of turning his manuscript into a book. All the book publishers listed here told us that they do not charge writers for publishing their work. If any of the publishers listed here ask you to pay any part of publishing or marketing your manuscript, please let us know.

A NOTE ABOUT AGENTS

Some publishers are willing to look at unsolicited submissions, but most feel having an agent is in the writer's best interest. In this section more than any other, you'll find a number of publishers who prefer submissions from agents. That's why we've included a section of agents open to submissions from fiction writers (see page 122). For even more agents, along with a great deal of helpful articles about approaching and working with them, refer to *Guide to Literary Agents*.

If you use the Internet or another resource to find an agent not listed in this book, be wary of any agents who charge large sums of money for reading a manuscript. Reading fees do not guarantee representation. Think of an agent as a potential business partner and feel free to ask tough questions about his or her credentials, experience, and business practices.

⊘ ABBEVILLE FAMILY

Abbeville Press, 137 Varick St., New York NY 10013. (212)366-5585. **Fax:** (212)366-6966. **E-mail:** abbeville@abbeville.com. **Website:** www.abbeville.com. Estab. 1977. "Our list is full for the next several seasons."

🗨 *Not accepting unsolicited book proposals at this time.*

NEEDS Picture books: animal, anthology, concept, contemporary, fantasy, folktales, health, hi-lo, history, humor, multicultural, nature/environment, poetry, science fiction, special needs, sports, suspense. Average word length 300-1,000 words.

HOW TO CONTACT Please refer to website for submission policy.

⊘ HARRY N. ABRAMS, INC.

115 W. 18th St., 6th Floor, New York NY 10011. (212)206-7715. **Fax:** (212)519-1210. **E-mail:** abrams@abramsbooks.com. **Website:** www.abramsbooks.com. **Contact:** Managing Editor. Estab. 1951. Publishes hardcover and a few paperback originals.

🗨 Does not accept unsolicited materials.

IMPRINTS Stewart, Tabori & Chang: Abrams Appleseed; Abrams Books for Young Readers; Abrams Image; STC Craft/Melanie Falick Books; SelfMadeHero; Amulet Books.

NEEDS Publishes hardcover and "a few" paperback originals. Averages 150 total titles/year.

TIPS "We are one of the few publishers who publish almost exclusively illustrated books. We consider ourselves the leading publishers of art books and high-quality artwork in the U.S. Once the author has signed a contract to write a book for our firm, the author must finish the ms to agreed-upon high standards within the schedule agreed upon in the contract."

ABRAMS BOOKS FOR YOUNG READERS

115 W. 18th St., New York NY 10011. **Website:** www.abramsyoungreaders.com.

🗨 Abrams no longer accepts unsolicited mss or queries.

ACADEMY CHICAGO PUBLISHERS

363 W. Erie St., Suite 4W, Chicago IL 60654. (312)751-7300. **Fax:** (312)751-7306. **E-mail:** zhanna@academychicago.com. **Website:** www.academychicago.com. **Contact:** Zhanna Vaynberg, managing editor. Estab. 1975. "We publish quality fiction and nonfiction. Our audience is literate and discriminating. No novelized biography, history, or science fiction." No electronic submissions. Publishes hardcover and some paperback originals and trade paperback reprints. Book catalog available online. Guidelines available online.

NEEDS "We look for quality work, but we do not publish experimental, avant-garde, horror, science fiction, thrillers novels."

HOW TO CONTACT Submit proposal package, synopsis, 3 sample chapters, and short bio.

TERMS Pays 7-10% royalty on wholesale price. Responds in 3 months.

TIPS "At the moment, we are looking for good nonfiction; we certainly want excellent original fiction, but we are swamped. No fax queries, no disks. No electronic submissions. We are always interested in reprinting good out-of-print books."

🅐🅓 ACE SCIENCE FICTION AND FANTASY

Imprint of the Berkley Publishing Group, Penguin Group (USA), Inc., 375 Hudson St., New York NY 10014. (212)366-2000. **Website:** www.us.penguingroup.com. **Contact:** Ginjer Buchanan, editor-in-chief. Estab. 1953. Ace publishes science fiction and fantasy exclusively. Publishes hardcover, paperback, and trade paperback originals and reprints.

🗨 As an imprint of Penguin, Ace is not open to unsolicited submissions.

NEEDS No other genre accepted. No short stories.

HOW TO CONTACT Due to the high volume of mss received, most Penguin Group (USA) Inc., imprints do not normally accept unsolicited mss.

TERMS Pays royalty. Pays advance.

⊘ ALADDIN

Simon & Schuster, 1230 Avenue of the Americas, 4th Floor, New York NY 10020. (212)698-7000. **Website:** www.simonandschuster.com. **Contact:** Acquisitions Editor. Aladdin publishes picture books, beginning readers, chapter books, middle-grade and tween fiction and nonfiction, and graphic novels and nonfiction in hardcover and paperback, with an emphasis on commercial, kid-friendly titles. Publishes hardcover/paperback imprints of Simon & Schuster Children's Publishing Children's Division.

HOW TO CONTACT Simon & Schuster does not review, retain, or return unsolicited materials or artwork. "We suggest prospective authors and illustrators submit their mss through a professional literary agent."

ALONDRA PRESS, LLC

4119 Wildacres Dr., Houston TX 77072. **E-mail:** lark@alondrapress.com. **Website:** www.alondrapress.com. **Contact:** Pennelope Leight, fiction editor; Solomon Tager, nonfiction editor. Estab. 2007. Publishes trade paperback originals and reprints. Guidelines online.

NEEDS "Just send us a few pages in an e-mail attachment, or the entire ms. We will look at it quickly and tell you if it interests us."

TERMS Responds in 1 month to queries/proposals; 3 months to mss.

TIPS "Be sure to read our guidelines before sending a submission. We will not respond to authors who do not observe our simple guidelines. Send your submissions in an e-mail attachment only."

AMERICAN CARRIAGE HOUSE PUBLISHING

P.O. Box 1130, Nevada City CA 95959. (530)432-8860. **Fax:** (530)432-7379. **Website:** www.americancarriage housepublishing.com. **Contact:** Lynn Taylor, editor (parenting, reference, child, women). Estab. 2004. Publishes trade paperback and electronic originals. Catalog free on request.

HOW TO CONTACT Query with SASE.

TERMS Pays outright purchase of $300-3,000. Responds in 3 months.

TIPS "We are looking for proposals, both fiction and nonfiction, preferably wholesome topics."

AMERICAN QUILTER'S SOCIETY

5801 Kentucky Dam Road, Paducah KY 42003. (270)898-7903. **Fax:** (270)898-1173. **E-mail:** editor@aqsquilt.com. **Website:** www.americanquilter.com. **Contact:** Andi Reynolds, executive book editor (primarily how-to and patterns, but other quilting books sometimes published, including quilt-related fiction). Estab. 1984. "American Quilter's Society publishes how-to and pattern books for quilters (beginners through intermediate skill level). We are not the publisher for nonquilters writing about quilts. We now publish quilt-related craft cozy romance and mystery titles, series only. Humor is good. Graphic depictions and curse words are bad." Publishes trade paperbacks. Nonfiction proposal guidelines online. Accepts simultaneous nonfiction submissions. Does not accept simultaneous fiction submissions.

HOW TO CONTACT Submit a synopsis and 2 sample chapters, plus an outline of the next 2 books in the series.

TERMS Pays 5% royalty on retail price for both nonfiction and fiction. Responds in 2 months to proposals.

AMIRA PRESS

2721 N. Rosedale St., Baltimore MD 21216. (704)858-7533. **E-mail:** submissions@amirapress.com. **Website:** www.amirapress.com. **Contact:** Yvette A. Lynn, CEO (any subgenre). Estab. 2007. "We are a small press which publishes sensual and erotic romance. Our slogan is 'Erotic and Sensual Romance. Immerse Yourself.' Our authors and stories are diverse." **Published 30 new writers last year.** Averages 50 fiction titles/year. Member EPIC. Distributes/promotes titles through Amazon, Mobipocket, Fictionwise, Barne sandNoble.com, Target.com, Amirapress.com, All-Romance Ebooks, and Ingrams. Format publishes in paperback originals, e-books, POD printing. Guildelines available online.

HOW TO CONTACT Submit complete ms with cover letter by e-mail. "No snail mail." Include estimated word count, heat level, brief bio, list of publishing credits. Accepts unsolicited mss. Sometimes critiques/comments on rejected mss.

TERMS Pays royalties, 8.5% of cover price (print)—30-40% of cover price (e-books). Responds in 3 months.

TIPS "Please read our submission guidelines thoroughly and follow them when submitting. We do not consider a work until we have all the requested information and the work is presented in the format we outline."

AMULET BOOKS

115 W. 18th St., New York NY 10001. **Website:** www .amuletbooks.com. **Contact:** Susan Van Metre, vice president/publisher; Tamar Brazis, editorial director; Cecily Kaiser, publishing director. Estab. 2004.

Does not accept unsolicited mss or queries.

NEEDS Middle readers: adventure, contemporary, fantasy, history, science fiction, sports. Young adults/teens: adventure, contemporary, fantasy, history, science fiction, sports, suspense.

ANAPHORA LITERARY PRESS

5755 E. River Rd., #2201, Tucson AZ 85750. (520)425-4266. **E-mail:** director@anaphoraliterary.com. **Website:** anaphoraliterary.com. **Contact:** Anna Faktorovich, editor-in-chief. Estab. 2007. "In the winter of

2010, Anaphora began accepting book-length single-author submissions. We are actively seeking single and multiple-author books in fiction (poetry, novels, and short story collections) and nonfiction (academic, legal, business, journals, edited and un-edited dissertations, biographies, and memoirs). E-mail submissions. Profits are split 50/50 with writers. We do not offer any free contributor copies." Publishes in trade paperback originals and reprints; mass-market paperback originals and reprints. Catalog and guidelines available online at website.

NEEDS Short stories can be included in *Pennsylvania Literary Journal*. Two novellas might be published in a single book. "We are actively seeking submissions at this time. The genre is not as important as the quality of work. You should have a completed full-length ms ready to be e-mailed or mailed upon request."

HOW TO CONTACT Looking for single and multiple-author books in fiction (poetry, novels, and short story collections). Query.

TERMS Pays 20-30% royalty on retail price. "Book profits are shared with authors." Responds in 1 week to queries, proposals, and mss.

TIPS "Our audience is academics, college students, and graduates, as well as anybody who loves literature. Proofreading your work is very important. See the website for specific submission requirements."

⦸⦾ ANNICK PRESS, LTD.

15 Patricia Ave., Toronto ON M2M 1H9 Canada. (416)221-4802. **Fax:** (416)221-8400. **E-mail:** annickpress@annickpress.com. **Website:** www.annickpress.com. **Contact:** Rick Wilks, director; Colleen MacMillan, associate publisher; Sheryl Shapiro, creative director. "Annick Press maintains a commitment to high-quality books that entertain and challenge. Our publications share fantasy and stimulate imagination, while encouraging children to trust their judgment and abilities." Publishes 5 picture books/year; 6 young readers/year; 8 middle readers/year; 9 young adult titles/year. Publishes picture books, juvenile, and young adult fiction and nonfiction; specializes in trade books. Book catalog and guidelines available online.

◑ *Does not accept unsolicited mss.*

NEEDS Publisher of children's books. Publishes hardcover and trade paperback originals. Average print order: 9,000. First novel print order: 7,000. Plans 18 first novels this year. Averages 25 total titles/year.

Distributes titles through Firefly Books Ltd. Not accepting picture books at this time.

TERMS Pays authors royalty of 5-12% based on retail price. Offers advances (average amount: $3,000). Pays illustrators royalty of 5% minimum.

◑ ANVIL PRESS

P.O. Box 3008 MPO, Vancouver BC V6B 3X5 Canada. (604)876-8710. **Fax:** (604)879-2667. **E-mail:** info@anvilpress.com. **Website:** www.anvilpress.com. **Contact:** Brian Kaufman. Estab. 1988. "Anvil Press publishes contemporary adult fiction, poetry, and drama, giving voice to up-and-coming Canadian writers, exploring all literary genres, discovering, nurturing, and promoting new Canadian literary talent. Currently emphasizing urban/suburban-themed fiction and poetry; de-emphasizing historical novels." Publishes trade paperback originals. Book catalog for 9×12 SAE with 2 first-class stamps. Guidelines available online.

◑ Canadian authors only. No e-mail submissions.

NEEDS Contemporary, modern literature; no formulaic or genre.

HOW TO CONTACT Query with 20-30 pages and SASE.

TERMS Pays advance. Average advance is $500-2,000, depending on the genre. Responds in 2 months to queries; 6 months to mss.

TIPS "Audience is informed, educated, aware, with an opinion, culturally active (films, books, the performing arts). No U.S. authors. Research the appropriate publisher for your work."

ARCADE PUBLISHING

Skyhorse Publishing, 307 W. 36th St., 11th Floor, New York NY 10018. (212)643-6816. **Fax:** (212)643-6819. **E-mail:** arcadesubmissions@skyhorsepublishing.com. **Website:** www.arcadepub.com. **Contact:** Acquisitions Editor. Estab. 1988. "Arcade prides itself on publishing top-notch literary nonfiction and fiction, with a significant proportion of foreign writers." Publishes hardcover originals, trade paperback reprints. Book catalog and ms guidelines for #10 SASE.

NEEDS No romance, historical, science fiction.

HOW TO CONTACT Submit proposal with brief query, one- to two-page synopsis, chapter outline, market analysis, sample chapter, bio.

TERMS Pays royalty on retail price and 10 author's copies. Pays advance. Responds in 2 months if interested.

☺ ARCHAIA

Imprint of Boom! Studios, 5670 Wilshire Blvd., Suite 450, Los Angeles CA 90036. **Website:** www.archaia .com. **Contact:** Mark Smylie, chief creative officer. Use online submission form.

NEEDS Looking for graphic novel submissions that include finished art. "Archaia is an award-winning graphic novel publisher with more than 75 renowned publishing brands, including such domestic and international hits as *Artesia, Mouse Guard*, and a line of Jim Henson graphic novels including *Fraggle Rock* and *The Dark Crystal*." Publishes creator-shared comic books and graphic novels in the adventure, fantasy, horror, pulp noir, and science fiction genres that contain idiosyncratic and atypical writing and art.

○ Archaia does not generally hire freelancers or arrange for freelance work, so submissions should only be for completed book and series proposals.

○ ARSENAL PULP PRESS

#202-211 East Georgia St., Vancouver BC V6A 1Z6 Canada. (604)687-4233. **Fax:** (604)687-4283. **E-mail:** info@arsenalpulp.com. **Website:** www.arsenalpulp .com. **Contact:** Editorial Board. Estab. 1980. "We are interested in literature that traverses uncharted territories, publishing books that challenge and stimulate and ask probing questions about the world around us. With a staff of five, located in a second-floor office in the historic Vancouver district of Gastown, we publish between 14 and 20 new titles per year, as well as an average of 12 to 15 reprints." Publishes trade paperback originals and trade paperback reprints. Book catalog for 9×12 SAE with IRCs or online. Guidelines available online.

IMPRINTS Tillacum Library, Advance Editions.

NEEDS No children's books or genre fiction, i.e., westerns, romance, horror, mystery, etc.

HOW TO CONTACT Submit proposal package, outline, clips, 2-3 sample chapters.

TERMS Responds in 2 months to queries. Responds in 4 months to proposals and mss.

◑ ARTE PUBLICO PRESS

University of Houston, 4902 Gulf Fwy, Bldg. 19, Room 100, Houston TX 77204-2004. **Fax:** (713)743-2847. **E-mail:** submapp@central.uh.edu. **Website:** artepub licopress.uh.edu/arte-publico-wp. **Contact:** Nicolas Kanellos, editor. Estab. 1979. Publishes hardcover

originals, and trade paperback originals and reprints. Book catalog available free. Guidelines online.

○ Arte Publico Press is the oldest and largest publisher of Hispanic literature for children and adults in the U.S. "We are a showcase for Hispanic literary creativity, arts, and culture. Our endeavor is to provide a national forum for U.S.-Hispanic literature."

IMPRINTS Piñata Books.

NEEDS "Written by U.S.-Hispanics."

HOW TO CONTACT Submissions made through online submission form.

TERMS Pays 10% royalty on wholesale price. Provides 20 author's copies; 40% discount on subsequent copies. Pays $1,000-3,000 advance. Responds in 1 month to queries and proposals. Responds in 4 months to mss.

TIPS "Include cover letter in which you 'sell' your book—why should we publish the book, who will want to read it, why does it matter, etc. Use our ms submission online form. Accepted file formats are: Word, plain/text, rich/text files. Other formats will not be accepted. Ms files cannot be larger than 5MB. Once editors review your ms, you will receive an e-mail with the decision. Revision process could take up to 4 months."

Ⓐ⊘☺ ATHENEUM BOOKS FOR YOUNG READERS

Simon & Schuster, 1230 Avenue of the Americas, New York NY 10020. **Website:** kids.simonandschuster.com. **Contact:** Caitlyn Dlouhy, editorial director; Justin Chanda, vice president/publisher; Namrata Tripathi, executive editor; Anne Zafian, vice president. Estab. 1961. Publishes hardcover originals. Guidelines for #10 SASE.

NEEDS All, in juvenile versions. "We have few specific needs except for books that are fresh, interesting and well written. Fad topics are dangerous, as are works you haven't polished to the best of your ability. We also don't need safety pamphlets, ABC books, coloring books, and board books. In writing picture book texts, avoid the coy and 'cutesy,' such as stories about characters with alliterative names." Agented submissions only. No paperback romance-type fiction.

TIPS "Study our titles."

☺○Ⓢ AUTUMN HOUSE PRESS

87½ Westwood St., Pittsburgh PA 15211. (412)381-4261. **E-mail:** info@autumnhouse.org. **Website:** www .autumnhouse.org. **Contact:** Michael Simms, editor-in-chief (fiction). Estab. 1998. "We are a nonprofit literary press specializing in high-quality poetry, fiction, and nonfiction. Our editions are beautifully designed and printed, and they are distributed nationally. Approximately one-third of our sales are to college literature and creative writing classes." Member CLMP, AWP, Academy of American Poets. "We distribute our own titles. We do extensive national promotion through ads, Web marketing, reading tours, book fairs, and conferences. We are open to all genres. The quality of writing concerns us, not the genre." Learn about our annual Fiction Prize, Poetry Prize, Nonfiction Prize, and Chapbook Award competitions, as well as our online journal, *Coal Hill Review*. (Please note that Autumn House accepts unsolicited mss *only* through these competitions; see below.) Publishes hardcover, trade paperback, and electronic originals. Format: acid-free paper; offset-printing; perfect and casebound (cloth) bound; sometimes contains illustrations. Average print order: 1,000. Debut novel print order: 1,000. Catalog free upon request. Guidelines online at website; free on request; or for #10 SASE.

NEEDS Holds competition/award for short stories, novels, story collections, memoirs, nonfiction. We ask that all submissions from authors new to Autumn House come through one of our annual contests. Annual. Prize: $2,500 and book publication. Entries should be unpublished. Open to all writers over the age of 18. Length: approx 200-300 pages. Deadline June 30 each year Results announced September. Winners notified by mail, phone, and e-mail. Results made available to entrants with SASE, by fax, by e-mail, or on website. Published *New World Order*, by Derek Green (collection of stories) and *Drift and Swerve*, by Samuel Ligon (collection of stories). See website for official guidelines. Responds to queries in 2 days. Accepts mss only through contest. Never critiques/comments on rejected mss. Responds to mss by August.

HOW TO CONTACT "Submit only through our annual contest. See guidelines online. Submit completed ms. Cover letter should include name, address, phone, e-mail, novel/story title. The mss are judged blind, so please include 2 cover pages, one with contact information and one without."

TERMS Pays 7% royalty on wholesale price. Pays $0-2,500 advance. Responds in 1-3 days on queries and proposals; 3 months on mss.

TIPS "The competition to publish with Autumn House is very tough. Submit only your best work."

AVON ROMANCE

HarperCollins Publishers, 10 E. 53 St., New York NY 10022. **E-mail:** info@avonromance.com. **Website:** www.avonromance.com. **Contact:** Erika Tsang; Lucia Macro; May Chen; Tessa Woodward; Amanda Bergeron; Chelsey Emmelhainz; Nicole Fischer. Estab. 1941. "Avon has been publishing award-winning books since 1941. It is recognized for having pioneered the historical romance category and continues to bring the best of commercial literature to the broadest possible audience." Publishes paperback and digital originals and reprints.

HOW TO CONTACT Submit a query and ms via the online submission form at www.avonromance.com/impulse.

TIPS Read the Meet the Editors feature online to learn interests and preferences.

AZRO PRESS

PMB 342, 1704 Llano St. B, Santa Fe NM 87505. (505)989-3272. **Fax:** (505)989-3832. **E-mail:** books@azropress.com; azropress@gmail.com. **Website:** www.azropress.com. **Contact:** Gae Eisenhardt. Estab. 1997. Catalog available for #10 SASE and 3 first-class stamps or online.

"We like to publish illustrated children's books by Southwestern authors and illustrators. We are always looking for books with a Southwestern look or theme."

NEEDS Picture books: animal, history, humor, nature/environment. Young readers: adventure, animal, hi-lo, history, humor. Average word length: picture books—1,200; young readers—2,000-2,500.

TERMS Pays authors royalty of 5-10% based on wholesale price. Pays illustrators by the project ($2,000) or royalty of 5%. Responds to queries/mss in 3-4 months.

TIPS "We are not currently accepting new mss. Please see our website for acceptance date."

BAEN BOOKS

P.O. Box 1188, Wake Forest NC 27588. (919)570-1640. **E-mail:** info@baen.com. **Website:** www.baen.com. Estab. 1983. "We publish only science fiction and fantasy. Writers familiar with what we have published in the past will know what sort of material we are most likely to publish in the future: powerful plots with solid scientific and philosophical underpinnings are the sine qua non for consideration for science fiction submissions. As for fantasy, any magical system must be both rigorously coherent and integral to the plot, and overall the work must at least strive for originality."

NEEDS "Style: Simple is generally better; in our opinion good style, like good breeding, never calls attention to itself. Length: 100,000-130,000 words. Generally we are uncomfortable with mss under 100,000 words, but if your novel is really wonderful send it along regardless of length."

HOW TO CONTACT "Query letters are not necessary. We prefer to see complete mss accompanied by a synopsis. We prefer not to see simultaneous submissions. Electronic submissions are strongly preferred. *We no longer accept submissions by e-mail.* Send ms via the submission form at: ftp.baen.com/Slush/submit.aspx. No disks unless requested. Attach ms as a Rich Text Format (.rtf) file. Any other format will not be considered."

TERMS Responds to mss within 12-18 months.

BAILIWICK PRESS

309 East Mulberry St., Fort Collins CO 80524. (970)672-4878. **Fax:** (970)672-4731. **E-mail:** info@bailiwickpress.com. **Website:** www.bailiwickpress.com. "We're a micropress that produces books and other products that inspire and tell great stories. Our motto is 'books with something to say.' We are now considering submissions, agented and unagented, for children's and young adult fiction. We're looking for smart, funny, and layered writing that kids will clamor for. Authors who already have a following have a leg up. We are only looking for humorous children's fiction. Please do not submit work for adults. Illustrated fiction is desired but not required. (Illustrators are also invited to send samples.) Make us laugh out loud, ooh and aah, and cry, 'Eureka!'"

HOW TO CONTACT "Please read the Aldo Zelnick series to determine if we might be on the same page, then fill out our submission form. Please do not send submissions via snail mail or phone calls. You must complete the online submission form to be considered. If, after completing and submitting the form, you also need to send us an e-mail attachment (such as sample illustrations or excerpts of graphics), you may e-mail them to aldozelnick@gmail.com."

TERMS Responds in 6 months.

BAKER BOOKS

Division of Baker Publishing Group, 6030 East Fulton Rd., Ada MI 49301. (616)676-9185. **Website:** bakerpublishinggroup.com/bakerbooks. Estab. 1939. "We will consider unsolicited work only through one of the following avenues. Materials sent through a literary agent will be considered. In addition, our staff attends various writers' conferences at which prospective authors can develop relationships with those in the publishing industry." Publishes in hardcover and trade paperback originals, and trade paperback reprints. Book catalog for #10 envelope and 3 first-class stamps. Guidelines online.

"Baker Books publishes popular religious non-fiction reference books and professional books for church leaders. Most of our authors and readers are evangelical Christians, and our books are purchased from Christian bookstores, mail-order retailers, and school bookstores. Does not accept unsolicited queries."

TIPS "We are not interested in historical fiction, romances, science fiction, biblical narratives, or spiritual warfare novels. Do not call to 'pass by' your idea."

BALZER & BRAY

HarperCollins Children's Books, 10 E. 53rd St., New York NY 10022. **Website:** www.harpercollinschildrens.com. Estab. 2008. "We publish bold, creative, groundbreaking picture books and novels that appeal directly to kids in a fresh way."

NEEDS Picture Books, Young Readers: adventure, animal, anthology, concept, contemporary, fantasy, history, humor, multicultural, nature/environment, poetry, science fiction, special needs, sports, suspense. Middle readers, young adults/teens: adventure, animal, anthology, contemporary, fantasy, history, humor, multicultural, nature/environment, poetry, science fiction, special needs, sports, suspense.

HOW TO CONTACT Agented submissions only.

TERMS Offers advances. Pays illustrators by the project.

BANCROFT PRESS

P.O. Box 65360, Baltimore MD 21209-9945. (410)358-0658. **Fax:** (410)764-1967. **E-mail:** bruceb@bancroftpress.com. **Website:** www.bancroftpress.com. **Contact:** Bruce Bortz, editor/publisher (health, investments, politics, history, humor, literary novels, mystery/thrillers, chick lit, young adult). "Small independent press publishing literary and commercial fiction." Publishes hardcover and trade paperback originals. Also packages books for other publishers (no fee to authors). Published 5 debut authors within the last 2 years. Sometimes comments on rejected mss. Ms guidelines online. "Bancroft Press is a general trade publisher. We publish young adult fiction and adult fiction, as well as occasional nonfiction. Our only mandate is 'books that enlighten.'" Publishes hardcover and trade paperback originals. Guidelines available online

NEEDS "Our current focuses are young adult fiction, women's fiction, and literary fiction."

HOW TO CONTACT Query with SASE or submit outline, 2 sample chapter(s), synopsis, by mail or e-mail, or submit complete ms. Accepts queries by e-mail, fax. Include brief bio, list of publishing credits. Send SASE for return of ms or send a disposable ms and SASE for reply only. Submit complete ms.

TERMS Pays various royalties on retail price. Average advance: $1,500. Publishes ms up to 3 years after acceptance. Pays 6-8% royalty. Pays various royalties on retail price. Pays $750 advance. Responds in 6-12 months.

TIPS "We advise writers to visit our website and to be familiar with our previous work. Patience is the No 1 attribute contributors must have. It takes us a very long time to get through submitted material, because we are such a small company. Also, we only publish 4-6 books per year, so it may take a long time for your optioned book to be published. We like to be able to market our books to be used in schools and in libraries. We prefer fiction that bucks trends and moves in a new direction. We are especially interested in mysteries and humor (especially humorous mysteries)."

⊘⊘ BANTAM BOOKS

Imprint of Random House, Inc., 1745 Broadway, New York NY 10019. (212)782-9000. **Website:** www.bantam-dell.atrandom.com.

○ *Not seeking mss at this time.*

○ BARBOUR PUBLISHING INC.

1810 Barbour Dr., P.O. Box 719, Urichsville OH 44683. (740)922-6045. **E-mail:** editors@barbourbooks.com; aschrock@barbourbooks.com; fictionsubmit@barbourbooks.com. **Website:** www.barbourbooks.com. **Contact:** Ashley Schrock, creative director. Estab. 1981. "Barbour Books publishes inspirational/devotional material that is nondenominational and evangelical in nature. We're a Christian evangelical pub-

lisher." Publishes hardcover, trade paperback and mass-market paperback originals and reprints. Published 40% debut authors within the last year. Averages 250 total titles/year. All stories must have Christian faith as an underlying basis." Published *The Journey*, by Wanda E. Brunstetter (fiction). From time to time, we do look for specific types of mss. These are usually announced through various writers' organizations including the American Christian Writers'. You can follow a link for a submission form and e-mail address that you can send your questions to. Responds in 6 months to mss. Accepts simultaneous submissions. Book catalog online or for 9×12 SAE with 2 first-class stamps; ms guidelines for #10 SASE or online. Specializes in short, easy-to-read Christian bargain books. "Faithfulness to the Bible and Jesus Christ are the bedrock values behind every book Barbour's staff produces."

○ "Please note that Barbour Publishing now only accepts book proposals via e-mail; paper proposals will not be reviewed by our editors and will ultimately be destroyed. Download the guidelines to ensure that your materials meet our specifications and will receive the proper attention from our editorial staff."

NEEDS historical, contemporary, religious, romance, western, mystery. All submissions must be Christian mss. All stories must have Christian faith as an underlying basis. Common writer's mistakes are a sketchy proposal, an unbelievable story, and a story that doesn't fit our guidelines for inspirational romances."

HOW TO CONTACT Submit 3 sample chapter(s), synopsis by e-mail only. For submission of your mss, please follow the link online to download the appropriate guidelines. Submit clips, 3 sample chapters.

TERMS Pays 8-16% royalty on net price. Average advance: $1,000-8,000. Publishes ms 1-2 years after acceptance. Pays 0-16% royalty on net price or makes outright purchase of $500-6,000. Pays $500-10,000 advance. Purchases one-time rights, according to project. Responds only if interested. Responds in 1 month to queries.

TIPS "Audience is evangelical/Christian conservative, nondenominational, young and old. We're looking for great concepts, not necessarily a big-name author or agent. We want to publish books that will consistently sell large numbers, not just flash-in-the-pan releases. Send us your ideas!"

BEHRMAN HOUSE, INC.

11 Edison Place, Springfield NJ 07081. (973)379-7200. **Fax:** (973)379-7280. **E-mail:** customersupport@behrmanhouse.com. **Website:** www.behrmanhouse.com. Estab. 1921. Publishes books on all aspects of Judaism: history, cultural, textbooks, holidays. "Behrman House publishes quality books of Jewish content—history, Bible, philosophy, holidays, ethics—for children and adults." Book catalog free on request.

HOW TO CONTACT Submit outline/synopsis and sample chapters.

TERMS Pays authors royalty of 3-10% based on retail price or buys ms outright for $1,000-5,000. Offers advance. Pays illustrators by the project (range: $500-5,000). Responds in 1 month to queries; 2 months to mss.

TIPS Looking for "religious school texts" with Judaic themes or general trade Judaica.

⬤ BELLEVUE LITERARY PRESS

New York University School of Medicine, Department of Medicine, NYU School of Medicine, 550 First Avenue, OBV 612, New York NY 10016. (212) 263-7802. **E-mail:** BLPsubmissions@gmail.com. **Website:** blpress.org. **Contact:** Erika Goldman, publisher/editorial director. Estab. 2005. "Publishes literary and authoritative fiction and nonfiction at the nexus of the arts and the sciences, with a special focus on medicine. As our authors explore cultural and historical representations of the human body, illness, and health, they address the impact of scientific and medical practice on the individual and society."

HOW TO CONTACT Submit complete ms.

TIPS "We are a project of New York University's School of Medicine, and while our standards reflect NYU's excellence in scholarship, humanistic medicine, and science, our authors need not be affiliated with NYU. We are not a university press and do not receive any funding from NYU. Our publishing operations are financed exclusively by foundation grants, private donors, and book sales revenue."

⬤⊘ BERKLEY BOOKS

Penguin Group (USA), Inc., 375 Hudson St., New York NY 10014. **Website:** us.penguingroup.com/. **Contact:** Leslie Gelbman, president and publisher. Estab. 1955. The Berkley Publishing Group publishes a variety of general nonfiction and fiction including the traditional categories of romance, mystery, and science fiction. Publishes paperback and mass-market originals and reprints.

○ "Due to the high volume of mss received, most Penguin Group (USA), Inc., imprints do not normally accept unsolicited mss. The preferred and standard method for having mss considered for publication by a major publisher is to submit them through an established literary agent."

IMPRINTS Ace; Berkley; Jove.

NEEDS No occult fiction.

HOW TO CONTACT Prefers agented submissions.

⊘ BETHANY HOUSE PUBLISHERS

Division of Baker Publishing Group, 6030 E. Fulton Rd., Ada MI 49301. (616)676-9185. **Fax:** (616)676-9573. **Website:** bakerpublishinggroup.com/bethanyhouse. Estab. 1956. Bethany House Publishers specializes in books that communicate Biblical truth and assist people in both spiritual and practical areas of life. While we do not accept unsolicited queries or proposals via telephone or e-mail, we will consider one-page queries sent by fax and directed to adult nonfiction, adult fiction, or young adult/children. Publishes hardcover and trade paperback originals, mass-market paperback reprints. Book catalog for 9×12 envelope and 5 first-class stamps. Guidelines available online.

○ *All unsolicited mss returned unopened.*

TERMS Pays royalty on net price. Pays advance. Responds in 3 months to queries.

TIPS "Bethany House Publishers' publishing program relates Biblical truth to all areas of life—whether in the framework of a well-told story, of a challenging book for spiritual growth, or of a Bible reference work. We are seeking high-quality fiction and nonfiction that will inspire and challenge our audience."

BKMK PRESS

University of Missouri-Kansas City, 5101 Rockhill Rd., Kansas City MO 64110-2499. (816)235-2558. **Fax:** (816)235-2611. **E-mail:** bkmk@umkc.edu. **Website:** newletters.org. **Contact:** Ben Furnish, managing editor. Estab. 1971. "BkMk Press publishes fine literature. Reading period January-June." Publishes trade paperback originals. Guidelines online.

HOW TO CONTACT Query with SASE.

TERMS Responds in 4-6 months to queries.

TIPS "We skew toward readers of literature, particularly contemporary writing. Because of our limited number of titles published per year, we discourage apprentice writers or `scattershot' submissions."

BLACK HERON PRESS

P.O. Box 13396, Mill Creek WA 98082. **Website:** www.blackheronpress.com. **Contact:** Jerry Gold, publisher. Estab. 1984. "Black Heron Press publishes primarily literary fiction." Publishes hardcover and trade paperback originals, trade paperback reprints. Catalog available online and for 6×9 SAE with 3 first-class stamps. Guidelines available for #10 SASE.

NEEDS "All of our fiction is character driven. We don't want to see fiction written for the mass market. If it sells to the mass market, fine, but we don't see ourselves as a commercial press."

HOW TO CONTACT Submit proposal package, including cover letter and first 40-50 pages pages of your completed novel.

TERMS Pays 8% royalty on retail price. Responds in 6 months to queries and mss.

TIPS "Our Readers love good fiction—they are scattered among all social classes, ethnic groups, and zip code areas. If you can't read our books, at least check out our titles on our website."

BLACK LAWRENCE PRESS

326 Bigham St., Pittsburgh PA 15211. **E-mail:** editors@blacklawrencepress.com. **Website:** www.blacklawrencepress.com. **Contact:** Diane Goettel, executive editor. Estab. 2003. Black Lawrence press seeks to publish intriguing books of literature—novels, short story collections, poetry collections, chapbooks, anthologies, and creative nonfiction. Will also publish the occasional translation from German. Publishes 15-20 books/year, mostly poetry and fiction. Mss are selected through open submission and competition. Books are 20-400 pages, offset-printed or high-quality POD, perfect-bound, with 4-color cover.

HOW TO CONTACT Submit complete ms.

TERMS Pays royalties. Responds in 6 months to mss.

BLACK MOUNTAIN PRESS

P.O. Box 9907, Asheville NC 28815. (828)273-3332. **E-mail:** jackmoe@theBlackMountainPress.com. **Website:** www.theBlackMountainPress.com. **Contact:** Jack Moe, editor (how-to, poetry); James Robiningski (short story collections, novels). Estab. 1994. Publishes hardcover, trade paperback, and electronic originals. Book catalog and ms guidelines online.

NEEDS "Creative literary fiction and poetry or a collection of short stories are wanted for the next few years."

HOW TO CONTACT Submit complete ms.

TERMS Pays 5-10% royalty on retail price. Pays $100-500 advance. Responds in 4-6 months to mss.

TIPS "Don't be afraid of sending your anti-government, anti-religion, anti-art, anti-literature, experimental, avant-garde efforts here. But don't send your work before it's fully cooked; we do, however, enjoy fresh, natural, and sometimes even raw material, just don't send in anything that is 'glowing' unless it was salvaged from a FoxNews book-burning event."

BLACK VELVET SEDUCTIONS PUBLISHING

1015 C Ave., Vinton IA 52349. (319)241-6556. **E-mail:** lauriesanders@blackvelvetseductions.com. **Website:** www.blackvelvetseductions.com. **Contact:** Laurie Sanders, acquisitions editor. Estab. 2005. "We publish 2 types of material: 1) romance novels and short stories and 2) romantic stories involving spanking between consenting adults. We look for well-crafted stories with a high degree of emotional impact. No first-person point of view. All material must be in third-person point of view." Publishes trade paperback and electronic originals. "We have a high interest in republishing backlist titles in electronic and trade paperback formats once rights have reverted to the author." Accepts only complete mss. Query with SASE. Submit complete ms. Publishes trade paperback and electronic originals and reprints. Catalog free or online. Guidelines online.

IMPRINTS Forbidden Experiences (erotic romance of all types); Tender Destinations (sweet romance of all types); Sensuous Journeys (sensuous romance of all types); Amorous Adventures (romantic suspense); Erotic relationship stories (erotic short stories, usually including spanking, with a romantic relationship at their core).

NEEDS All stories must have a strong romance element. "There are very few sexual taboos in our erotic line. We tend to give our authors the widest latitude. If it is safe, sane, and consensual we will allow our authors latitude to show us the eroticism. However, we will not consider mss with any of the following: bestiality (sex with animals), necrophilia (sex with dead people), pedophillia (sex with children)."

HOW TO CONTACT Only accepts electronic submissions.

TERMS Pays 10% royalty for paperbacks; 50% royalty for electronic books. Responds in 6 months to queries; 8 months to proposals; 8-12 months to mss.

TIPS "We publish romance and erotic romance. We look for books written in very deep point of view. Shallow point of view remains the No. 1 reason we reject mss in which the story line generally works."

◐ JOHN F. BLAIR, PUBLISHER

1406 Plaza Dr., Winston-Salem NC 27103. (336)768-1374. **Fax:** (336)768-9194. **E-mail:** editorial@blairpub.com. **Website:** www.blairpub.com. **Contact:** Carolyn Sakowski, president. Estab. 1954.

NEEDS "We specialize in regional books, with an emphasis on nonfiction categories such as history, travel, folklore, and biography. We publish only 1 or 2 works of fiction each year. Fiction submitted to us should have some connection with the Southeast. We do not publish children's books, poetry, or category fiction such as romances, science fiction, or spy thrillers. We do not publish collections of short stories, essays, or newspaper columns."

HOW TO CONTACT Accepts unsolicited mss. Any fiction submitted should have some connection with the Southeast, either through setting or author's background. Send a cover letter, giving a synopsis of the book. Include the first 2 chapters (at least 50 pages) of the ms. "You may send the entire ms if you wish. If you choose to send only samples, please include the projected word length of your book and estimated completion date in your cover letter. Send a biography of the author, including publishing credits and credentials."

TERMS Pays royalties. Pays negotiable advance. Responds in 3-6 months.

TIPS "We are primarily interested in nonfiction titles. Most of our titles have a tie-in with North Carolina or the southeastern United States, we do not accept short story collections. Please enclose a cover letter and outline with the ms. We prefer to review queries before we are sent complete mss. Queries should include an approximate word count."

◐ BLAZEVOX [BOOKS]

131 Euclid Ave., Kenmore NY 14217. **E-mail:** editor@blazevox.org. **Website:** www.blazevox.org. **Contact:** Geoffrey Gatza, editor/publisher. Estab. 2005. "We are a major publishing presence specializing in innovative fictions and wide-ranging fields of innovative forms of poetry and prose. Our goal is to publish works that are challenging, creative, attractive, and yet affordable to individual readers. Articles of submission depend on many criteria, but overall items submitted must conform to one ethereal trait, your work must not suck. This put plainly, bad art should be punished; we will not promote it. However, all submissions will be reviewed and the author will receive feedback. We are human, too." Guidelines online.

NEEDS Submit complete ms via e-mail.

TERMS Pays 10% royalties on fiction and poetry books, based on net receipts. This amount may be split across multiple contributors. "We do not pay advances."

TIPS "We actively contract and support authors who tour, read, and perform their work, play an active part of the contemporary literary scene, and seek a readership."

◐ BLOOMSBURY CHILDREN'S BOOKS

Imprint of Bloomsbury USA, 1385 Broadway, 5th Floor, New York NY 10008. **Website:** www.bloomsbury.com/us/childrens. **Contact:** Catherine Onder, editorial director; Caroline Abbey, senior director; Mary Kate Castellani, senior director; Donna Mark, art director. Book catalog online. Guidelines online.

◐ No phone calls or e-mails. *Agented submissions only.*

HOW TO CONTACT Agented submissions only.

TERMS Pays royalty. Pays advance. Responds in 6 months.

◐◐ BOA EDITIONS, LTD.

250 N. Goodman St., Suite 306, Rochester NY 14607. (585)546-3410. **Fax:** (585)546-3913. **E-mail:** conners@boaeditions.org; hall@boaeditions.org. **Website:** www.boaeditions.org. **Contact:** Peter Conners, editor. Estab. 1976. "BOA Editions publishes distinguished collections of poetry, fiction, and poetry in translation. Our goal is to publish the finest American contemporary poetry, fiction, and poetry in translation." Publishes hardcover and trade paperback originals. Book catalog online. Guidelines online.

NEEDS "We now publish literary fiction through our American Reader Series. While aesthetic quality is subjective, our fiction will be by authors more concerned with the artfulness of their writing than the twists and turns of plot. Our strongest current interest is in short story collections (and short-short story collections), although we will consider novels. We strongly advise you to read our first published fiction collections." *Temporarily closed to novel/collection submissions.*

TERMS Negotiates royalties. Pays variable advance. Responds in 1 week to queries; 5 months to mss.

BOLD STROKES BOOKS, INC.

P.O. Box 249, Valley Falls NY 12185. (518)677-5127. **Fax:** (518)677-5291. **E-mail:** publisher@boldstrokesbooks.com. **E-mail:** submissions@boldstrokesbooks.com. **Website:** www.boldstrokesbooks.com. **Contact:** Len Barot, president; Lee Ligon, operations manager; Cindy Cresap, senior consulting editor and production manager. Publishes trade paperback originals and reprints; electronic originals and reprints. Catalog free on request. Guidelines online.

IMPRINTS BSB Fiction; Matinee Books Romances; Victory Editions Lesbian Fiction; Liberty Editions Gay Fiction; Soliloquy Young Adult; Heat Stroke Erotica.

NEEDS "Submissions should have a gay, lesbian, transgendered, or bisexual focus and should be positive and life affirming."

HOW TO CONTACT Submit completed ms with bio, cover letter, and synopsis—electronically only.

TERMS Sliding scale based on sales volume and format. Responds in 1 month to queries; 2 months to proposals; 4 months to mss.

TIPS "We are particularly interested in authors who are interested in craft enhancement, technical development, and exploring and expanding traditional genre definitions and boundaries, and are looking for a long-term publishing relationship ."

BOOKOUTURE

StoryFire Ltd., 23 Sussex Rd., Ickenham UB10 8P United Kingdom. **E-mail:** questions@bookouture.com. **E-mail:** pitch@bookouture.com. **Website:** www.bookouture.com. **Contact:** Oliver Rhodes, founder and publisher. Estab. 2012. Publishes mass-market paperback and electronic originals and reprints. Book catalog online.

IMPRINTS Imprint of StoryFire Ltd.

NEEDS "We're looking for entertaining fiction targeted at modern women. That can be anything from steampunk to erotica, historicals to thrillers. A distinctive author voice is more important than a particular genre or ms length."

HOW TO CONTACT Submit complete ms.

TERMS Pays 45% royalty on wholesale price. Responds in 1 month.

TIPS "The most important question that we ask of submissions is why would a reader buy the next book? What's distinctive or different about your storytelling that will mean readers will want to come back for more. We look to acquire global English language rights for e-book and Print on Demand."

BOREALIS PRESS, LTD.

8 Mohawk Crescent, Napean ON K2H 7G6 Canada. (613)829-0150. **Fax:** (613)829-7783. **E-mail:** drt@borealispress.com. **Website:** www.borealispress.com. Estab. 1972. "Our mission is to publish work that will be of lasting interest in the Canadian book market." Currently emphasizing Canadian fiction, nonfiction, drama, poetry. De-emphasizing children's books. Publishes hardcover and paperback originals and reprints. Book catalog online. Guidelines online.

IMPRINTS Tecumseh Press.

NEEDS Only material Canadian in content and dealing with significant aspects of the human situation.

HOW TO CONTACT Query with SASE. Submit clips, 1-2 sample chapters. *No unsolicited mss.*

TERMS Pays 10% royalty on net receipts; plus 3 free author's copies. Responds in 2 months to queries; 4 months to mss.

BRANDEN PUBLISHING CO., INC.

P.O. Box 812094, Wellesley MA 02482. (781)235-3634. **Fax:** (781)235-3634. **E-mail:** branden@brandenbooks.com. **Website:** www.brandenbooks.com. **Contact:** Adolph Caso, editor. Estab. 1909. "Branden publishes books by or about women, children, military, Italian-American, or African-American themes." Publishes hardcover and trade paperback originals, reprints, and software.

IMPRINTS International Pocket Library and Popular Technology; Four Seas and Brashear; Branden Books.

NEEDS Looking for contemporary, fast pace, modern society. No science, mystery, experimental, horror, or pornography. *No unsolicited mss.*

HOW TO CONTACT Query with SASE. Paragraph query only with author bio.

TERMS Responds in 1 month to queries.

BROADWAY BOOKS

The Crown Publishing Group/Random House, 1745 Broadway, New York NY 10019. (212)782-9000. **Fax:** (212)782-9411. **Website:** crownpublishing.com/imprint/broadway-books. **Contact:** William Thomas, editor-in-chief. Estab. 1995. Broadway publishes general interest nonfiction and fiction for adults. Publishes hardcover and trade paperback originals and reprints. Publishes hardcover and trade paperback books.

○ "Broadway publishes high-quality general interest nonfiction and fiction for adults."

IMPRINTS Broadway Books; Broadway Business; Doubleday; Doubleday Image; Doubleday Religious Publishing; Main Street Books; Nan A. Talese.

NEEDS Broadway Books publishes a variety of nonfiction books across several categories, including memoir, health and fitness, inspiration and spirituality, history, current affairs and politics, marriage and relationships, animals, travel and adventure narrative, pop culture, humor, and personal finance. Publishes a limited list of commercial literary fiction. Published *Freedomland*, by Richard Price.

HOW TO CONTACT *Agented submissions only.*

TERMS Pays royalty on retail price. Pays advance.

○ BROKEN JAW PRESS

Box 596, STN A, Fredericton NB E3B 5A6 Canada. (506)454-5127. **E-mail:** editors@brokenjaw.com. **Website:** www.brokenjaw.com. "We publish poetry, fiction, drama, and literary nonfiction, including translations and multilingual books. Publishes almost exclusively Canadian-authored literary trade paperback originals and reprints." Book catalog for 6×9 SAE with 2 first-class Canadian stamps in Canada or download PDF from website. Guidelines available online.

○ *Currently not accepting unsolicited mss and queries.*

IMPRINTS Book Rat; Broken Jaw Press; SpareTime Editions; Dead Sea Physh Products; Maritimes Arts Projects Productions.

TERMS Pays 10% royalty on retail price. Pays $0-500 advance. Responds in 1 year to mss.

TIPS "Unsolicited queries and mss are not welcome at this time."

BRONZE MAN BOOKS

Millikin University, 1184 W. Main, Decatur IL 62522. (217)424-6264. **Website:** www.bronzemanbooks.com. **Contact:** Dr. Randy Brooks, editorial board; Edwin Walker, editorial board. Estab. 2006. Publishes hardcover, trade paperback, and mass-market paperback originals.

NEEDS Subjects include art, graphic design, exhibits, general.

HOW TO CONTACT Submit completed ms.

TERMS Outright purchase based on wholesale value of 10% of a press run. Responds in 1-3 months.

TIPS "The art books are intended for serious collectors and scholars of contemporary art, especially of artists from the Midwestern U.S. These books are published in conjunction with art exhibitions at Millikin University or the Decatur Area Arts Council. The children's books have our broadest audience, and the literary chapbooks are intended for readers of contemporary fiction, drama, and poetry."

○ THE BRUCEDALE PRESS

P.O. Box 2259, Port Elgin ON N0H 2C0 Canada. (519)832-6025. **E-mail:** info@brucedalepress.ca. **Website:** brucedalepress.ca. The Brucedale Press publishes books and other materials of regional interest and merit, as well as literary, historical, and/or pictorial works. Publishes hardcover and trade paperback originals. Book catalog for #10 SASE (Canadian postage or IRC) or online. Guidelines available online.

○ *Accepts works by Canadian authors only. Submissions accepted in September and March ONLY.*

TERMS Pays royalty.

TIPS Our focus is very regional. In reading submissions, I look for quality writing with a strong connection to the Queen's Bush area of Ontario. All authors should visit our website, get a catalog, and read our books before submitting.

⊕ BULLITT PUBLISHING

P.O. Box, Austin TX 78729. **E-mail:** bullittpublishing@yahoo.com. **E-mail:** submissions@bullittpublishing.com. **Website:** bullittpublishing.com. **Contact:** Pat Williams, editor. Estab. 2012. "Bullitt Publishing is a royalty-offering publishing house specializing in smart, contemporary romance. We are proud to provide Print-on-Demand distribution through the world's most comprehensive distribution channel including Amazon.com and BarnesandNoble.com. Whether this is your first novel or your 101st novel, Bullitt Publishing will treat you with the same amount of professionalism and respect. While we expect well-written entertaining mss from all of our authors, we promise to provide high-quality, professional product in return." Publishes trade paperback and electronic originals.

IMPRINTS Includes imprint Tempo Romance.

BY LIGHT UNSEEN MEDIA

P.O. Box 1233, Pepperell MA 01463. (978) 433-8866. **Fax:** (978) 433-8866. **E-mail:** vyrdolak@bylightun seenmedia.com. **Website:** www.bylightunseenmedia .com. **Contact:** Inanna Arthen, owner/editor-in-chief. Estab. 2006. Publishes hardcover, paperback, and electronic originals; trade paperback reprints. Catalog online. Ms guidelines online.

NEEDS "We are a niche small press that *only* publishes fiction relating in some way to vampires. Within that guideline, we're interested in almost any genre that includes a vampire trope, the more creative and innovative, the better. Restrictions are noted in the submission guidelines (no derivative fiction based on other works, such as Dracula, no gore-for-gore's-sake 'splatter' horror, etc.) We do not publish anthologies."

HOW TO CONTACT Submit proposal package including synopsis, 3 sample chapters, brief author bio. *We encourage electronic submissions. All unsolicited mss will be returned unopened.*

TERMS Pays royalty of 20-50% on net as explicitly defined in contract. Payment quarterly. Pays $200 advance. Responds in 3 months.

TIPS "We strongly urge authors to familiarize themselves with the vampire genre and not imagine that they're doing something new and amazingly different just because they're not imitating the current fad."

C&R PRESS

812 Westwood Ave., Chattanooga TN 37405. (423)645-5375. **Website:** www.crpress.org. **Contact:** Chad Prevost, editorial director and publisher; Ryan G. Van Cleave, executive director and publisher. Estab. 2006. Publishes hardcover, trade paperback, mass-market paperback, and electronic originals. Catalog and guidelines available online.

IMPRINTS Illumis Books.

NEEDS "We want dynamic, exciting literary fiction, and we want to work with authors (not merely books) who are engaged socially and driven to promote their work because of their belief in the product, and because it's energizing and exciting to do so and a vital part of the process."

HOW TO CONTACT Submit complete ms via e-mail.

TERMS Responds in up to 1 month on queries and proposals, 1-2 months on mss.

⊘ CALAMARI PRESS

Via Titta Scarpetta #28, Rome 00153 Italy. **E-mail:** derek@calamaripress.net. **Website:** www.calamari

press.com. Calamari Press publishes books of literary text and art. Publishes 1-2 books/year. Mss are selected by invitation. Occasionally has open submission period—check website. "Helps to be published in *SleepingFish* first." Order books through the website, Powell's, or SPD. Publishes paperback originals. Writer's guidelines on website.

HOW TO CONTACT Query with outline/synopsis and 3 sample chapters. Accepts queries by e-mail only. Include brief bio. Send SASE or IRC for return of ms.

TERMS Pays in author's copies. Responds to mss in 2 weeks.

CALKINS CREEK

Boyds Mills Press, 815 Church St., Honesdale PA 18431. **Website:** www.calkinscreekbooks.com. Estab. 2004. "We aim to publish books that are a well-written blend of creative writing and extensive research, which emphasize important events, people, and places in U.S. history." Guidelines online.

HOW TO CONTACT Submit outline/synopsis and 3 sample chapters.

TERMS Pays authors royalty or work purchased outright.

TIPS "Read through our recently published titles and review our catalog. When selecting titles to publish, our emphasis will be on important events, people, and places in U.S. history. Writers are encouraged to submit a detailed bibliography, including secondary and primary sources, and expert reviews with their submissions."

⊘⊘ CANDLEWICK PRESS

99 Dover St., Somerville MA 02144. (617)661-3330. **Fax:** (617)661-0565. **E-mail:** bigbear@candlewick .com. **Website:** www.candlewick.com. Estab. 1991. "Candlewick Press publishes high-quality illustrated children's books for ages infant through young adult. We are a truly child-centered publisher." Publishes hardcover and trade paperback originals, and reprints.

🗩 *Candlewick Press is not accepting queries or unsolicited mss at this time.*

NEEDS Picture books: animal, concept, contemporary, fantasy, history, humor, multicultural, nature/environment, poetry. Middle readers, young adults: contemporary, fantasy, history, humor, multicultural, poetry, science fiction, sports, suspense/mystery.

HOW TO CONTACT "We do not accept editorial queries or submissions online. If you are an author or illustrator and would like us to consider your work, please read our submissions policy (online) to learn more."

TERMS Pays authors royalty of 2½-10% based on retail price. Offers advance.

TIPS *"We no longer accept unsolicited mss. See our* website for further information about us."

CANTERBURY HOUSE PUBLISHING, LTD.

7350 S. Tamiami Trail, Suite 215, Sarasota FL 34231. (941)312-6912. **Website:** www.canterburyhousepub lishing.com. **Contact:** Wendy Dingwall, publisher; Sandra Horton, editor. Estab. 2009. "Our audience is made up of readers looking for wholesome fiction with good southern stories, with elements of mystery, romance, and inspiration. They are also looking for true stories of achievement and triumph over challenging circumstances." Publishes hardcover, trade paperback, and electronic originals. Book catalog online. Guidelines availably online, free on request by e-mail.

  "We are very strict on our submission guidelines due to our small staff and our target market of Southern regional settings. The setting needs to be a strong component in the stories. Authors need to be willing to actively promote their books in the beginning 9 months of publication via signing events and social media."

HOW TO CONTACT Query with SASE and through website.

TERMS Pays 10-15% royalty on wholesale price. Responds in 1 month to queries; 3 months to mss.

TIPS "Because of our limited staff, we prefer authors who have good writing credentials and submit edited mss. We also look at authors who are business and marketing savvy and willing to help promote their books."

CAROLINA WREN PRESS

120 Morris St., Durham NC 27701. (919)560-2738. **E-mail:** carolinawrenpress@earthlink.net. **Website:** www.carolinawrenpress.org. **Contact:** Andrea Selch, president. Estab. 1976. "We publish poetry, fiction, and memoirs by, and/or about, people of color, women, gay/lesbian issues. We publish work by writers from, living in, or writing about the U.S. South." Guidelines online.

  Accepts simultaneous submissions, but "let us know if work has been accepted elsewhere."

NEEDS "We are no longer publishing children's literature of any topic." Books: 6×9 paper, typeset, various bindings, illustrations. **Published 1 debut author within the last year.** Distributes titles through Amazon.com, Barnes & Noble, Baker & Taylor, and on their website. "We very rarely accept any unsolicited mss, but we accept submissions for the Doris Bakwin Award for Writing by a Woman in January-March of even-numbered years." Starting in 2013, the Lee Smith Novel Prize contest will accept submissions in summer and fall of odd-numbered years for a novel by an author from, living in, or writing about the U.S. South.

HOW TO CONTACT Query by mail. "We will accept e-mailed queries—a letter in the body of the e-mail describing your project—but please do not send large attachments."

TERMS Responds in 3 months to queries; 6 months to mss.

TIPS "Best way to get read is to submit to a contest."

CARTWHEEL BOOKS

Imprint of Scholastic Trade Division, 557 Broadway, New York NY 10012. (212)343-6100. **Website:** www .scholastic.com. Estab. 1991. Cartwheel Books publishes innovative books for children, up to age 8. "We are looking for 'novelties' that are books first, play objects second. Even without its gimmick, a Cartwheel Book should stand alone as a valid piece of children's literature." Publishes novelty books, easy readers, board books, hardcover and trade paperback originals. Guidelines available free.

NEEDS "The subject should have mass-market appeal for very young children. Humor can be helpful, but not necessary. Mistakes writers make are a reading level that is too difficult, a topic of no interest or too narrow, or mss that are too long."

HOW TO CONTACT *Accepts mss from agents only.*

TIPS "Audience is young children, ages 0-8. Know what types of books the publisher produces. Some mss that don't work for 1 house may be perfect for another. Check out bookstores or catalogs to see where your writing would 'fit' best."

CAVE HOLLOW PRESS

P.O. Drawer J, Warrensburg MO 64093. **E-mail:** gb crump@cavehollowpress.com. **Website:** www.cave hollowpress.com. **Contact:** G.B. Crump, editor. Estab. 2001. Publishes trade paperback originals. Book catalog for #10 SASE. Guidelines available free.

NEEDS "Our website is updated frequently to reflect the current type of fiction Cave Hollow Press is seeking."

HOW TO CONTACT Query with SASE.

TERMS Pays 7-12% royalty on wholesale price. Pays negotiable amount in advance. Responds in 1-2 months to queries and proposals; 3-6 months to mss.

TIPS "Our audience varies based on the type of book we are publishing. We specialize in Missouri and Midwest regional fiction. We are interested in talented writers from Missouri and the surrounding Midwest. Check our submission guidelines on the website for what type of fiction we are interested in currently."

CEDAR FORT, INC.

2373 W. 700 S, Springville UT 84663. (801)489-4084. **Fax:** (801)489-1097. **Website:** www.cedarfort.com. **Contact:** Shersta Gatica, acquisitions editor. Estab. 1986. "Each year we publish well over 100 books, and many of those are by first-time authors. At the same time, we love to see books from established authors. As one of the largest book publishers in Utah, we have the capability and enthusiasm to make your book a success, whether you are a new author or a returning one. We want to publish uplifting and edifying books that help people think about what is important in life, books people enjoy reading to relax and feel better about themselves, and books to help improve lives. Although we do put out several children's books each year, we are extremely selective. Our children's books must have strong religious or moral values, and must contain outstanding writing and an excellent story line." Publishes hardcover, trade paperback originals and reprints, mass-market paperback and electronic reprints. Catalog and guidelines available online at website.

IMPRINTS Council Press, Sweetwater Books, Bonneville Books, Front Table Books, Hobble Creek Press, CFI.

HOW TO CONTACT Submit completed ms.

TERMS Pays 10-12% royalty on wholesale price. Pays $2,000-50,000 advance. Responds in 1 month on queries; 2 months on proposals; 4 months on mss.

TIPS "Our audience is rural, conservative, mainstream. The first page of your ms is very important because we start reading every submission, but good-writing and plot keep us reading."

CHARLESBRIDGE PUBLISHING

85 Main St., Watertown MA 02472. (617)926-0329. **Fax:** (617)926-5720. **E-mail:** tradeart@charlesbridge .com. **Website:** www.charlesbridge.com. Estab. 1980. "Charlesbridge publishes high-quality books for children, with a goal of creating lifelong readers and lifelong learners. Our books encourage reading and discovery in the classroom, library, and home. We believe that books for children should offer accurate information, promote a positive worldview, and embrace a child's innate sense of wonder and fun. To this end, we continually strive to seek new voices, new visions, and new directions in children's literature." Publishes hardcover and trade paperback nonfiction and fiction, children's books for the trade and library markets. Guidelines available online.

"We're always interested in innovative approaches to a difficult genre, the nonfiction picture book."

IMPRINTS Charlesbridge, Imagine Publishing.

NEEDS Strong stories with enduring themes. Charlesbridge publishes both picture books and transitional bridge books (books ranging from early readers to middle-grade chapter books). Our fiction titles include lively, plot-driven stories with strong, engaging characters. No alphabet books, board books, coloring books, activity books, or books with audiotapes or CD-ROMs.

HOW TO CONTACT *Exclusive submissions only.* "Charlesbridge accepts unsolicited mss submitted exclusively to us for a period of 3 months. 'Exclusive Submission' should be written on all envelopes and cover letters." Please submit only 1 or 2 mss at a time. For picture books and shorter bridge books, please send a complete ms. For fiction books longer than 30 ms pages, please send a detailed plot synopsis, a chapter outline, and 3 chapters of text. Mss should be typed and double-spaced. Please do not submit material by e-mail, by fax, or on a computer disk. Illustrations are not necessary. Please make a copy of your ms, as we cannot be responsible for submissions lost in the mail. Include your name and address on the first page of your ms and in your cover letter. Be sure to list any previously published work or relevant writing experience.

TERMS Pays royalty. Pays advance. Responds in 3 months.

TIPS "To become acquainted with our publishing program, we encourage you to review our books and visit our website, where you will find our catalog."

⊘ CHILDREN'S BRAINS ARE YUMMY (CBAY) BOOKS

P.O. Box 92411, Austin TX 78709. (512)789-1004. **Fax:** (512)473-7710. **E-mail:** submissions@cbaybooks.com. **Website:** www.cbaybooks.com. **Contact:** Madeline Smoot, publisher. Estab. 2008. "CBAY Books currently focuses on quality fantasy and science fiction books for the middle-grade and teen markets." Brochure and guidelines online.

    "We are not currently accepting unsolicited submissions."

TERMS Pays authors royalty 10-15% based on wholesale price. Offers advances against royalties. Average amount $500.

●⊘ CHILD'S PLAY (INTERNATIONAL), LTD.

Children's Play International, Ashworth Rd. Bridgemead, Swindon, Wiltshire SN5 7YD United Kingdom. **E-mail:** allday@childs-play.com; neil@childs-play.com; office@childs-play.com. **Website:** www.childs-play.com. **Contact:** Sue Baker, Neil Burden, ms acquisitions. Estab. 1972. Specializes in nonfiction, fiction, educational material, multicultural material. Produces 30 picture books/year; 10 young readers/year; 2 middle readers/year. "A child's early years are more important than any other. This is when children learn most about the world around them and the language they need to survive and grow. Child's Play aims to create exactly the right material for this all-important time."

    "Due to a backlog of submissions, Child's Play is currently no longer able to accept anymore mss."

NEEDS Picture books: adventure, animal, concept, contemporary, folktales, multicultural, nature/environment. Young readers: adventure, animal, anthology, concept, contemporary, folktales, humor, multicultural, nature/environment, poetry. Average word length: picture books—1,500; young readers—2,000.

TIPS "Look at our website to see the kind of work we do before sending. Do not send cartoons. We do not publish novels. We do publish lots of books with pictures of babies/toddlers."

● CHRISTIAN BOOKS TODAY LTD

136 Main St., Buckshaw Village Chorley, Lancashire PR7 7BZ United Kingdom. **E-mail:** editme@christianbookstoday.com. **Website:** www.christianbook stoday.com. **Contact:** Jason Richardson, MD (nonfiction); Lynda McIntosh, editor (fiction). Estab. 2009. Publishes trade paperback originals/reprints and electronic originals/reprints. Catalog and guidelines available online.

NEEDS "Please send us your Christian or 'clean read' fiction. Nondenominational Christian romance, suspense, mystery, and contemporary fiction are always welcome."

HOW TO CONTACT Submit query with synopsis and writing sample.

TERMS Pays 10% royalty on Amazon retail price; 15% e-book; 5% wholesale trade. Responds in 1 month to queries; 2 months to proposals and mss.

TIPS "We appeal to a general Christian readership. We are interested in 'clean read' mss only. No profanity, sexual content, gambling, substance abuse, or graphic violence. Please do not send us conspiracy-type stories."

● CHRISTIAN FOCUS PUBLICATIONS

Geanies House, Fearn, Tain Ross-shire Scotland IV20 1TW United Kingdom. 44 (0) 1862 871 011. **Fax:** 44 (0) 1862 871 699. **E-mail:** info@christianfocus.com. **Website:** www.christianfocus.com. **Contact:** Catherine Mackenzie, publisher. Estab. 1975. Specializes in Christian material, nonfiction, fiction, educational material.

NEEDS Picture books, young readers, adventure, history, religion. Middle readers: adventure, problem novels, religion. Young adult/teens: adventure, history, problem novels, religion. Average word length: young readers—5,000; middle readers—maximum 10,000; young adult/teen—maximum 20,000.

HOW TO CONTACT Query or submit outline/synopsis and 3 sample chapters. Will consider electronic submissions and previously published work.

TERMS Responds to queries in 2 weeks; mss in 3 months.

TIPS "Be aware of the international market in regards to writing style/topics, as well as illustration styles. Our company sells rights to European as well as Asian countries. Fiction sales are not as good as they once were. Christian fiction for youngsters is not performing well compared to nonfiction such as Christian biography/Bible stories/church history, etc."

CHRONICLE BOOKS

680 Second St., San Francisco CA 94107. **E-mail:** submissions@chroniclebooks.com. **Website:** www

.chroniclebooks.com. "We publish an exciting range of books, stationery, kits, calendars, and novelty formats. Our list includes children's books and interactive formats; young adult books; cookbooks; fine art, design, and photography; pop culture; craft, fashion, beauty, and home decor; relationships, mind-body-spirit; innovative formats such as interactive journals, kits, decks, and stationery; and much, much more." Book catalog for 9×12 SAE and 8 first-class stamps. Ms guidelines for #10 SASE.

NEEDS Only interested in fiction for children and young adults. No adult fiction.

HOW TO CONTACT Submit complete ms (picture books); submit outline/synopsis and 3 sample chapters (for older readers). Will not respond to submissions unless interested. Will not consider submissions by fax, e-mail or disk. Do not include SASE; do not send original materials. No submissions will be returned.

TERMS Generally pays authors in royalties based on retail price, "though we do occasionally work on a flat fee basis." Advance varies. Illustrators paid royalty based on retail price or flat fee. Responds to queries in 1 month.

CHRONICLE BOOKS FOR CHILDREN

680 Second St., San Francisco CA 94107. (415)537-4200. **Fax:** (415)537-4460. **E-mail:** submissions@chroniclebooks.com. **Website:** www.chroniclekids.com. "Chronicle Books for Children publishes an eclectic mixture of traditional and innovative children's books. Our aim is to publish books that inspire young readers to learn and grow creatively while helping them discover the joy of reading. We're looking for quirky, bold artwork and subject matter. Currently emphasizing picture books. De-emphasizing young adult." Publishes hardcover and trade paperback originals. Book catalog for 9×12 envelope and 3 first-class stamps. Guidelines available online.

NEEDS Does not accept proposals by fax, via e-mail, or on disk. When submitting artwork, either as a part of a project or as samples for review, do not send original art.

TERMS Pays 8% royalty. Pays variable advance. Responds in 2-4 weeks to queries; 6 months to mss.

TIPS "We are interested in projects that have a unique bent to them—be it in subject matter, writing style, or illustrative technique. As a small list, we are looking for books that will lend our list a distinctive flavor.

Primarily we are interested in fiction and nonfiction picture books for children up to 8 years, and nonfiction books for children up to 12 years. We publish board, pop-up, and other novelty formats as well as picture books. We are also interested in early chapter books, middle-grade fiction, and young adult projects."

CLARION BOOKS

Houghton Mifflin Co., 215 Park Ave. S., New York NY 10003. **Website:** www.houghtonmifflinbooks.com; www.hmco.com. **Contact:** Dinah Stevenson, vice president and publisher; Jennifer B. Greene, senior editor (contemporary fiction, picture books for all ages, nonfiction); Jennifer Wingertzahn, editor (fiction, picture books); Lynne Polvino, editor (fiction, nonfiction, picture books); Christine Kettner, art director. Estab. 1965. "Clarion Books publishes picture books, nonfiction, and fiction for infants and children through grade 12. Avoid telling your stories in verse unless you are a professional poet." Publishes hardcover originals for children. Guidelines for #10 SASE or online.

"We are no longer responding to your unsolicited submission unless we are interested in publishing it. Please do not include an SASE. Submissions will be recycled, and you will not hear from us regarding the status of your submission unless we are interested. We regret that we cannot respond personally to each submission, but we do consider each and every submission we receive."

NEEDS "Clarion is highly selective in the areas of historical fiction, fantasy, and science fiction. A novel must be superlatively written in order to find a place on the list. Mss that arrive without an SASE of adequate size will *not* be responded to or returned. Accepts fiction translations."

HOW TO CONTACT Submit complete ms. No queries, please. Send to only *1* Clarion editor.

TERMS Pays 5-10% royalty on retail price. Pays minimum of $4,000 advance. Responds in 2 months to queries.

TIPS "Looks for freshness, enthusiasm—in short, life."

CLEIS PRESS

Cleis Press & Viva Editions, 2246 Sixth St., Berkeley CA 94710. (510)845-8000 or (800)780-2279. **Fax:** (510)845-8001. **E-mail:** cleis@cleispress.com. **E-mail:** bknight@cleispress.com. **Website:** www.cleispress

.com and www.vivaeditions.com. **Contact:** Brenda Knight, publisher. Estab. 1980. Cleis Press publishes provocative, intelligent books in the areas of sexuality, gay and lesbian studies, erotica, fiction, gender studies, and human rights. Publishes books that inform, enlighten, and entertain. Areas of interest include gift, inspiration, health, family and child care, self-help, women's issues, reference, cooking. "We do our best to bring readers quality books that celebrate life, inspire the mind, revive the spirit, and enhance lives all around. Our authors are practical visionaries; people who offer deep wisdom in a hopeful and helpful manner."

IMPRINTS Viva Editions

NEEDS "We are looking for high-quality fiction and nonfiction."

HOW TO CONTACT Submit complete ms. Include brief bio, list of publishing credits. Send SASE for return of ms or send a disposable ms and SASE for reply only.

TERMS Pays royalty on retail price. Responds in 2 month to queries.

TIPS "Be familiar with publishers' catalogs; be absolutely aware of your audience; research potential markets; present fresh new ways of looking at your topic; avoid `PR' language and include publishing history in query letter."

⟳ COACH HOUSE BOOKS

80 bpNichol Lane, Toronto ON M5S 3J4 Canada. (416)979-2217. **Fax:** (416)977-1158. **E-mail:** editor@ chbooks.com. **Website:** www.chbooks.com. **Contact:** Alana Wilcox, editorial director. Publishes trade paperback originals by Canadian authors. Guidelines available online.

HOW TO CONTACT "Electronic submissions are welcome. Please send your complete ms, along with an introductory letter that describes your work and compares it to at least 2 current Coach House titles, explaining how your book would fit our list, and a literary CV listing your previous publications and relevant experience. If you would like your ms back, please enclose a large enough SASE with adequate postage. If you don't want your ms back, a small stamped envelope or e-mail address is fine. We prefer electronic submissions. Please e-mail PDF files to editor@ch-books.com and include the cover letter and CV as a part of the ms. Please send your ms only once. Revised and updated versions will not be read, so make sure

you're happy with your text before sending. You can also mail your ms. Please do not send it by Express-Post or Canada Post courier—regular Canada Post mail is much more likely to arrive here. Be patient. We try to respond promptly, but we do receive hundreds of submissions, so it may take us several months to get back to you. Please do not call or e-mail to check on the status of your submission. We will answer you as promptly as possible."

TERMS Pays 10% royalty on retail price. Responds in 6 months to queries.

TIPS "We are not a general publisher, and publish only Canadian poetry, fiction, artist books, and drama. We are interested primarily in innovative or experimental writing."

◑◔ ◠◡ COFFEE HOUSE PRESS

79 13th NE, Suite 110, Minneapolis MN 55413. (612)338-0125. **Fax:** (612)338-4004. **E-mail:** info@ coffeehousepress.org. **Website:** www.coffeehouse press.org. **Contact:** Anitra Budd, managing editor. Estab. 1984. This successful nonprofit small press has received numerous grants from various organizations including the NEA, the McKnight Foundation, and Target. Books published by Coffee House Press have won numerous honors and awards. Example: *The Book of Medicines* by Linda Hogan won the Colorado Book Award for Poetry and the Lannan Foundation Literary Fellowship. Publishes hardcover and trade paperback originals. Book catalog and ms guidelines online.

NEEDS Seeks literary novels, short story collections, and poetry.

HOW TO CONTACT Query first with outline and samples (20-30 pages) during annual reading periods (March 1-April 30 and September 1-October 31).

TERMS Responds in 4-6 weeks to queries; up to 6 months to mss.

TIPS "Look for our books at stores and libraries to get a feel for what we like to publish. No phone calls, e-mails, or faxes."

◭ ◠ CONSTABLE & ROBINSON, LTD.

55-56 Russell Square, London WC1B 4HP United Kingdom. 0208-741-3663. **Fax:** 0208-748-7562. **E-mail:** reader@constablerobinson.com. **Website:** constablerobinson.co.uk. **Contact:** Krystyna Green, editorial director (crime fiction). Publishes hardcover and trade paperback originals. Book catalog available free.

IMPRINTS Corsair; Constable Hardback; Robinson Paperback.

NEEDS Publishes "crime fiction (mysteries) and historical crime fiction." Length 80,000 words minimum; 130,000 words maximum.

HOW TO CONTACT *Agented submissions only.*

TERMS Pays royalty. Pays advance. Responds in 1 month to queries and proposals; 3 months to mss.

TIPS Constable & Robinson, Ltd., is looking for "crime novels with good, strong identities. Think about what it is that makes your book(s) stand out from the others. We do not publish thrillers."

☺ COTEAU BOOKS

Thunder Creek Publishing Co-operative Ltd., 2517 Victoria Ave., Regina SK S4P 0T2 Canada. (306)777-0170. **Fax:** (306)522-5152. **E-mail:** coteau@coteaubooks.com. **Website:** www.coteaubooks.com. **Contact:** Geoffrey Ursell, publisher. Estab. 1975. "Our mission is to publish the finest in Canadian fiction, nonfiction, poetry, drama, and children's literature, with an emphasis on Saskatchewan and prairie writers. De-emphasizing science fiction, picture books." Publishes trade paperback originals and reprints. Book catalog available free. Guidelines online.

NEEDS *Canadian authors only.* No science fiction. No children's picture books.

HOW TO CONTACT Submit hard copy query, bio, complete ms, SASE.

TERMS Pays 10% royalty on retail price. Responds in 3 months.

TIPS "Look at past publications to get an idea of our editorial program. We do not publish romance, horror, or picture books but are interested in juvenile and teen fiction from Canadian authors. Submissions, even queries, must be made in hard copy only. We do not accept simultaneous/multiple submissions. Check our website for new submission timing guidelines."

COVENANT COMMUNICATIONS, INC.

920 E. State Rd., American Fork UT 84003. (801)756-9966. **Fax:** (801)756-1049. **E-mail:** submissionsdesk@covenant-lds.com. **Website:** www.covenant-lds.com. **Contact:** Kathryn Jenkins, managing editor. Estab. 1958. "Currently emphasizing inspirational, doctrinal, historical, biography. Our fiction is also expanding, and we are looking for new approaches to Latter-Day Saints (LDS), or 'Mormon,' literature and storytelling." Guidelines available online.

NEEDS "We publish exclusively to the 'Mormon' (The Church of Jesus Christ of Latter-Day Saints) market. Fiction must feature characters who are members of that church, grappling with issues relevant to that religion."

HOW TO CONTACT Submit complete ms.

TERMS Pays 6½-15% royalty on retail price. Responds in 1 month on queries and proposals; 4 months on mss.

TIPS "Our audience is exclusively LDS. We do not accept mss that do not have a strong LDS theme or feature strong LDS characters."

CRAIGMORE CREATIONS

2900 SE Stark St., Suite 1A, Portland OR 97124. (503)477-9562. **E-mail:** info@craigmorecreations.com. **Website:** www.craigmorecreations.com. Estab. 2009.

HOW TO CONTACT Submit proposal package. See website for detailed submission guidelines.

☺ CRESCENT MOON PUBLISHING

P.O. Box 393, Maidstone Kent ME14 5XU United Kingdom. (44)(162)272-9593. **E-mail:** cresmopub@yahoo.co.uk. **Website:** www.crescentmoon.org.uk. **Contact:** Jeremy Robinson, director (arts, media, cinema, literature); Cassidy Hushes (visual arts). Estab. 1988. "Our mission is to publish the best in contemporary work, in poetry, fiction, and critical studies, and selections from the great writers. Currently emphasizing nonfiction (media, film, music, painting). De-emphasizing children's books." Publishes hardcover and trade paperback originals. Book catalog and ms guidelines free.

IMPRINTS *Joe's Press, Pagan America Magazine, Passion Magazine.*

NEEDS "We do not publish much fiction at present but will consider high-quality new work."

HOW TO CONTACT Query with SASE. Submit outline, clips, 2 sample chapters, bio.

TERMS Pays royalty. Pays negotiable advance. Responds in 2 months to queries; 4 months to proposals and mss.

TIPS "Our audience is interested in new contemporary writing."

☺ CRICKET BOOKS

Imprint of Carus Publishing, 70 E. Lake St., Suite 300, Chicago IL 60601. (603)924-7209. **Fax:** (603)924-7380. **Website:** www.cricketmag.com. **Contact:** Submissions Editor. Estab. 1999. Cricket Books publishes picture books, chapter books, and middle-grade novels. Publishes hardcover originals.

○ *Currently not accepting queries or mss. Check website for submissions details and updates.*

TERMS Pays up to 10% royalty on retail price. Average advance: $1,500 and up.

TIPS "Take a look at the recent titles to see what sort of materials we're interested in, especially for nonfiction. Please note that we aren't doing the sort of strictly educational nonfiction that other publishers specialize in."

CRIMSON ROMANCE

Adams Media, a division of F+W Media, Inc., 57 Littlefield St., Avon MA 02322. (508)427-7100. **E-mail:** editorcrimson@gmail.com. **Website:** crimsonromance.com. **Contact:** Tara Gelsomino, editor. "Direct to e-book imprint of Adams Media." Publishes electronic originals.

NEEDS "We're open to romance submissions in 5 popular subgenres: romantic suspense, contemporary, paranormal, historical, and erotic romance. Within those subgenres, we are flexible about what happens. It's romance, so there must be a happily-ever-after, but we're open to how your characters get there. You won't come up against preconceived ideas about what can or can't happen in romance or what kind of characters you can or can't have. Our only rule is everyone has to be a consenting adult. Other than that, we're looking for smart, savvy heroines; fresh voices; and new takes on old favorite themes. We're looking for full-length novels, and while we prefer to work on the shorter end of the spectrum (50,000 words, give or take), we're not going to rule you out because you go shorter or longer."

HOW TO CONTACT Submit brief description of work—please, no attachments.

○○ CROWN PUBLISHING GROUP

Random House, Inc., 1745 Broadway, New York NY 10019. (212)782-9000. **E-mail:** CrownBiz@randomhouse.com. **Website:** www.randomhouse.com/crown. Estab. 1933. Publishes popular fiction and nonfiction hardcover originals.

○ *Agented submissions only.* See website for more details.

IMPRINTS Amphoto Books; Back Stage Books; Billboard Books; Broadway Books; Clarkson Potter; Crown; Crown Archetype; Crown Business; Crown Forum; Doubleday Religion; Harmony Books; Image Books; Potter Craft; Potter Style; Ten Speed Press; Three Rivers Press; Waterbrook Multnomah; Watson-Guptill.

HOW TO CONTACT *Agented submissions only.*

CRYSTAL SPIRIT PUBLISHING, INC.

P.O. Box 12506, Durham NC 27709. **E-mail:** crystalspiritinc@gmail.com. **Website:** www.crystalspiritinc.com. **Contact:** Vanessa S. O'Neal, senior editor; Elise L. Lattier, editor. Estab. 2004. "Our readers are lovers of high-quality books that are sold in book- and gift stores, and placed in libraries and schools. They support independent authors and they expect works that will provide them with entertainment, inspiration, romance, and education. Our audience loves to read and will embrace niche authors that love to write." Publishes hardcover, trade paperback, mass-market paperback, and electronic originals. Book catalog and ms guidelines available online at website.

HOW TO CONTACT Submit cover letter, synopsis, and 30 pages (or 30 chapters) **by USPS mail ONLY.**

TERMS Pays 20-45% royalty on retail price. Responds in 3-6 months to mss.

TIPS "Submissions are accepted for publication throughout the year, but the decisions for publishing considerations are made in March, June, September, and December. Works should be positive and non-threatening. Typed pages only. Non-typed entries will not be reviewed or returned. Ensure that all contact information is correct, abide by the submission guidelines, and do not send follow-up e-mails or calls."

CUP OF TEA BOOKS

PageSpring Publishing, P.O. Box 21133, Columbus OH 43221. **E-mail:** weditor@pagespringpublishing.com. **Website:** www.cupofteabooks.com. Estab. 2012. "Cup of Tea Books publishes novel-length women's fiction. We are interested in finely drawn characters, a compelling story, and deft writing. We accept e-mail queries only; see our website for details." Publishes trade paperback and electronic originals. Guidelines online.

HOW TO CONTACT Submit proposal package via e-mail. Include synopsis and the first 30 pages.

TERMS Pays royalty. Responds in 1 month to queries and mss.

DAW BOOKS, INC.

Penguin Group (USA), 375 Hudson St., New York NY 10014-3658. (212)366-2096. **Fax:** (212)366-2090. **Website:** www.dawbooks.com. **Contact:** Peter Stampfel, submissions editor. Estab. 1971. DAW Books publishes science fiction and fantasy. Publishes hardcover and paperback originals and reprints. Guidelines online.

HOW TO CONTACT Submit entire ms, cover letter, SASE. Do not submit your only copy of anything. The average length of the novels we publish varies but is almost never less than 80,000 words.

TERMS Pays in royalties with an advance negotiable on a book-by-book basis. Responds in 3 months.

⬤⬤ DELACORTE PRESS

Imprint of Random House Publishing Group, 1745 Broadway, New York NY 10019. (212)782-9000. **Website:** www.randomhouse.com. Publishes middle-grade and young adult fiction in hard cover, trade paperback, mass-market, and digest formats.

⬤ All other query letters or ms submissions must be submitted through an agent or at the request of an editor. No e-mail queries.

⬤⬤ DEL REY BOOKS

Imprint of Random House Publishing Group, 1745 Broadway, 18th Floor, New York NY 10019. (212)782-9000. **E-mail:** delrey@randomhouse.com. **Website:** www.randomhouse.com. Estab. 1977. "We are a long-established imprint with an eclectic frontlist. We're seeking interesting new voices to add to our best-selling backlist. Publishes hardcover, trade paperback, and mass-market originals and mass-market paperback reprints. Averages 120 total titles, 80 fiction titles/year. Del Rey publishes top-level fantasy, alternate history, and science fiction.

IMPRINTS Del Rey/Manga, Del Rey/Lucas Books.

NEEDS fantasy (should have the practice of magic as an essential element of the plot), science fiction (well-plotted novels with good characterizations and interesting extrapolations), alternate history. Published *Gentlemen of the Road*, by Michael Chabon; *Kraken*, by China Miéville; *His Majesty's Dragon*, by Naomi Novik; *The Man with the Iron Heart*, by Harry Turtledove; and *Star Wars: Order 66*, by Karen Traviss.

HOW TO CONTACT Does not accept unsolicited mss. *Agented submissions only.*

TERMS Pays royalty on retail price. Average advance: competitive. Publishes ms 1 year after acceptance. Ms guidelines online.

TIPS "Del Rey is a reader's house. Pay particular attention to plotting, strong characters, and dramatic, satisfactory conclusions. It must be/feel believable. That's what the readers like. In terms of mass market,

we basically created the field of fantasy bestsellers. Not that it didn't exist before, but we put the mass into mass market."

DEMONTREVILLE PRESS, INC.

P.O. Box 835, Lake Elmo MN 55042. **E-mail:** publisher@demontrevillepress.com. **Website:** www.demontrevillepress.com. **Contact:** Kevin Clemens, publisher (automotive fiction and nonfiction). Estab. 2006. Publishes trade paperback originals and reprints. Book catalog available online. Guidelines available online.

NEEDS "We want novel-length automotive or motorcycle historicals and/or adventures."

HOW TO CONTACT Submit proposal package, 3 sample chapters, clips, bio.

TERMS Pays 20% royalty on sale price. Responds in 3 months to queries; 4 months to proposals; 6 months to mss.

TIPS "Environmental, energy, and transportation nonfiction works are now being accepted. Automotive and motorcycle enthusiasts, adventurers, environmentalists, and history buffs make up our audience."

⬤ DIAL BOOKS FOR YOUNG READERS

Imprint of Penguin Group USA, 375 Hudson St., New York NY 10014. (212)366-2000. **Website:** www.penguin.com/youngreaders. **Contact:** Lauri Hornik, president/publisher; Kathy Dawson, associate publisher; Kate Harrison, senior editor; Liz Waniewski, editor; Alisha Niehaus, editor; Jessica Garrison, editor; Lily Malcom, art director. Estab. 1961. "Dial Books for Young Readers publishes quality picture books for ages 18 months-6 years; lively, believable novels for middle readers and young adults; and occasional nonfiction for middle readers and young adults." Publishes hardcover originals. Book catalog for 9 ×12 envelope and 4 first-class stamps.

NEEDS Wants "lively and well-written novels for middle-grade and young adult children with a convincing plot and believable characters. The subject matter or theme should not already be overworked in previously published books. The approach must not be demeaning to any minority group, nor should the roles of female characters (or others) be stereotyped, though we don't think books should be didactic, or in any way message-y." No topics inappropriate for the juvenile, young adult, and middle-grade audiences. No plays.

HOW TO CONTACT Accepts unsolicited queries and up to 10 pages for longer works and unsolicited mss for picture books.

TERMS Pays royalty. Pays varies advance. Responds in 4-6 months to queries.

TIPS "Our readers are anywhere from preschool age to teenage. Picture books must have strong plots, lots of action, unusual premises, or universal themes treated with freshness and originality. Humor works well in these books. A very well-thought-out and intelligently presented book has the best chance of being taken on. Genre isn't as much of a factor as presentation."

DIVERSION PRESS

P.O. Box 3930, Clarksville TN 37043. **E-mail:** diversionpress@yahoo.com. **Website:** www.diversionpress.com. Estab. 2008. Publishes hardcover, trade and mass-market paperback originals. Guidelines available online.

NEEDS "We will happily consider any children's or young adult books if they are illustrated. If your story has potential to become a series, please address that in your proposal. Fiction short stories and poetry will be considered for our anthology series. See website for details on how to submit your ms."

TERMS Pays 10% royalty on wholesale price. Responds in 2 weeks to queries. Responds in 1 month to proposals.

TIPS "Read our website and blog prior to submitting. We like short, concise queries. Tell us why your book is different, not like other books. Give us a realistic idea of what you will do to market your book. We will ask for more information if we are interested."

DIVERTIR

P.O. Box 232, North Salem NH 03073. **E-mail:** info@divertirpublishing.com; query@divertirpublishing.com. **Website:** www.divertirpublishing.com. **Contact:** Kenneth Tupper, publisher. Estab. 2009. Publishes trade paperback and electronic originals. Catalog online. Guidelines online.

NEEDS "We are particularly interested in the following: science fiction, fantasy, historical, alternate history, contemporary mythology, mystery and suspense, paranormal, and urban fantasy."

HOW TO CONTACT Electronically submit proposal package, including synopsis and query letter with author's bio.

TERMS Pays 10-15% royalty on wholesale price (for novels and nonfiction). Responds in 1-2 months on queries; 3-4 months on proposals and mss.

TIPS "Please see our Author Info page (online) for more information."

DNA PRESS & NARTEA PUBLISHING

DNA Press, P.O. Box 9311, Glendale CA 91226. **E-mail:** editors@dnapress.com. **Website:** www.dnapress.com. Estab. 1998. Book publisher for young adults, children, and adults. Publishes hardcover and trade paperback originals. Book catalog and ms guidelines free.

NEEDS All books should be oriented to explaining science even if they do not fall 100% under the category of science fiction.

HOW TO CONTACT Submit complete ms.

TERMS Pays 10-15% royalty. Responds in 6 weeks to mss.

TIPS Quick response, great relationships, high commission/royalty.

DOWN EAST BOOKS

Imprint of Down East Enterprise, Inc., P.O. Box 679, Camden ME 04843. (207)594-9544, 800-766-1670. **Fax:** (207)594-7215. **E-mail:** editorial@downeast.com. **E-mail:** submissions@downeast.com. **Website:** www.downeast.com. **Contact:** Paul Doiron, editor-in-chief. Estab. 1967. Down East Books publishes books that capture and illuminate the unique beauty and character of New England's history, culture, and wild places. Publishes hardcover and trade paperback originals, trade paperback reprints. Send SASE for ms guidelines. Send 9×12 SASE for guidelines, plus recent catalog.

NEEDS We publish 2-4 juvenile titles/year (fiction and nonfiction), and 0-1 adult fiction titles/year.

HOW TO CONTACT Query with SASE.

TERMS Pays $500 average advance. Responds in 3 months to queries.

DOWN THE SHORE PUBLISHING

Box 100, West Creek NJ 08092. **Fax:** (609)597-0422. **E-mail:** info@down-the-shore.com; dtsbooks@comcast.net. **Website:** www.down-the-shore.com. "Bear in mind that our market is regional-New Jersey, the Jersey Shore, the mid-Atlantic, and seashore and coastal subjects." Publishes hardcover and trade paperback originals and reprints. Book catalog for 8×10 SAE with 2 first-class stamps or on website. Guidelines available online.

HOW TO CONTACT Query with SASE. Submit proposal package, clips, 1-2 sample chapters.

TERMS Pays royalty on wholesale or retail price, or makes outright purchase. Responds in 3 months to queries.

TIPS "Carefully consider whether your proposal is a good fit for our established market."

DUFOUR EDITIONS

P.O. Box 7, 124 Byers Road, Chester Springs PA 19425. (610)458-5005 or (800)869-5677. **Fax:** (610)458-7103. **Website:** www.dufoureditions.com. Estab. 1948. "We publish literary fiction by good writers which is well received and achieves modest sales. De-emphsazing poetry and nonfiction." Publishes hardcover originals, trade paperback originals and reprints. Book catalog available free.

NEEDS "We like books that are slightly offbeat, different, and well written."

HOW TO CONTACT Query with SASE.

TERMS Pays $100-500 advance. Responds in 3 months to queries and proposals; 6 months to mss.

TIPS Audience is sophisticated, literate readers especially interested in foreign literature and translations, and a strong Irish-Celtic focus, as well as work from U.S. writers. Consider whether the publisher is really a good match for your subject matter.

Ⓐ⊘ THOMAS DUNNE BOOKS

Imprint of St. Martin's Press, 175 Fifth Ave., New York NY 10010. (212)674-5151. **Website:** www.thomasdunnebooks.com. Estab. 1986. "Thomas Dunne Books publishes popular trade fiction and nonfiction. With an output of approximately 175 titles each year, his group covers a range of genres including commercial and literary fiction, thrillers, biography, politics, sports, popular science, and more. The list is intentionally eclectic and includes a wide range of fiction and nonfiction, from first books to international bestsellers." Publishes hardcover and trade paperback originals, and reprints. Book catalog and ms guidelines free.

○ *Accepts agented submissions only.*

HOW TO CONTACT Agents submit query.

Ⓐ⊘ DUTTON ADULT TRADE

Imprint of Penguin Group (USA), Inc., 375 Hudson St., New York NY 10014. (212)366-2000. **Website:** us.penguingroup.com. Estab. 1852. "Dutton currently publishes 45 hardcovers a year, roughly half fiction and half nonfiction." Publishes hardcover originals. Book catalog for #10 SASE.

○ *Does not accept unsolicited ms. Agented submissions only.*

HOW TO CONTACT Agented submissions only. *No unsolicited mss.*

TERMS Pays royalty. Pays negotiable advance.

TIPS "Write the complete ms and submit it to an agent or agents. They will know exactly which editor will be interested in a project."

DUTTON CHILDREN'S BOOKS

Penguin Group (USA), Inc., 375 Hudson St., New York NY 10014. **E-mail:** duttonpublicity@ us.penguingroup.com. **Website:** www.penguin.com. **Contact:** Sara Reynolds, art director. Estab. 1852. Dutton Children's Books publishes high-quality fiction and nonfiction for readers ranging from pre-schoolers to young adults on a variety of subjects. Currently emphasizing middle-grade and young adult novels that offer a fresh perspective. De-emphasizing photographic nonfiction and picture books that teach a lesson. Approximately 80 new hardcover titles are published every year, fiction and nonfiction for babies through young adults. Publishes hardcover originals as well as novelty formats.

○ "Cultivating the creative talents of authors and illustrators and publishing books with purpose and heart continue to be the mission and joy at Dutton."

NEEDS Dutton Children's Books has a diverse, general-interest list that includes picture books; easy-to-read books; and fiction for all ages, from first chapter books to young adult readers.

HOW TO CONTACT Query. Responds only if interested.

TERMS Pays royalty on retail price. Pays advance.

EAKIN PRESS

P.O. Box 331779, Fort Worth TX 76163. **Phone/Fax:** (817)344-7036. **Website:** www.eakinpress.com. **Contact:** Kris Gholson, associate publisher. Estab. 1978. "Our top priority is to cover the history and culture of the Southwest, especially Texas and Oklahoma. We also have successfully published titles related to ethnic studies. We publish very little fiction, other than for children." Publishes hardcover and paperback originals and reprints. Book catalog for $1.25. Guidelines available online.

○ No electronic submissions.

NEEDS Juvenile fiction for grades K-12, preferably relating to Texas and the Southwest or contemporary. No adult fiction.

HOW TO CONTACT Query or submit outline/synopsis

TERMS Responds in up to 1 year to queries.

⚠⊘ THE ECCO PRESS

10 E. 53rd St., New York NY 10022. (212)207-7000. **Fax:** (212)702-2460. **Website:** www.harpercollins .com. **Contact:** Daniel Halpern, editor-in-chief. Estab. 1970. Publishes hardcover and trade paperback originals and reprints.

NEEDS Literary, short story collections. "We can publish possibly 1 or 2 original novels a year." Published *Blonde*, by Joyce Carrol Oates; *Pitching Around Fidel*, by S.L. Price.

HOW TO CONTACT *Does not accept unsolicited mss.*

TERMS Pays royalty. Pays negotiable advance.

TIPS "We are always interested in first novels and feel it's important that they be brought to the attention of the reading public."

◎ EDGE SCIENCE FICTION AND FANTASY PUBLISHING/TESSERACT BOOKS

Hades Publications, Box 1714, Calgary AB T2P 2L7 Canada. (403)254-0160. **Fax:** (403)254-0456. **E-mail:** publisher@hadespublications.com. **Website:** www .edgewebsite.com. **Contact:** Editorial Manager. Estab. 1996. "We are an independent publisher of science fiction and fantasy novels in hardcover or trade paperback format. We produce high-quality books with lots of attention to detail and lots of marketing effort. We want to encourage, produce, and promote thought-provoking and fun-to-read science fiction and fantasy literature by 'bringing the magic alive: one world at a time' (as our motto says) with each new book released." Publishes hardcover and trade paperback originals. Books: natural offset paper; offset/web printing; HC/ perfect binding; b&w illustration only. Average print order: 2,000-3,000. Plans 20 first novels this year. Averages 16-20 total titles/year. Member of Book Publishers Association of Alberta (BPAA), Independent Publishers Association of Canada (IPAC), Publisher's Marketing Association (PMA), Small Press Center. Ms guidelines online.

NEEDS "We are looking for all types of fantasy and science fiction, horror (except juvenile/young adult), erotica, religious fiction, short stories, dark/gruesome fantasy, or poetry." Length: 75,000-100,000/words.

HOW TO CONTACT Submit first 3 chapters and synopsis. Check website for guidelines. Include estimated word count.

TERMS Pays 10% royalty on wholesale price. Negotiable advance. Responds in 4-5 months to mss.

TIPS "Send us your best, polished, completed ms. Use proper ms format. Take the time before you submit to get a critique from people who can offer you useful advice. When in doubt, visit our website for helpful resources, FAQs, and other tips."

◎ EERDMANS BOOKS FOR YOUNG READERS

2140 Oak Industrial Dr. NE, Grand Rapids MI 49505. **E-mail:** youngreaders@eerdmans.com. **Website:** www.eerdmans.com/youngreaders. **Contact:** Acquisitions Editor. "We are seeking books that encourage independent thinking, problem solving, creativity, acceptance, kindness. Books that encourage moral values without being didactic or preachy. Board books, picture books, middle reader fiction, young adult fiction, nonfiction, illustrated storybooks. A submission stands out when it's obvious that someone put time into it—the publisher's name and address are spelled correctly, the package is neat, and all of our submission requirements have been followed precisely. We look for short, concise cover letters that explain why the ms fits with our list, and/or how the ms fills an important need in the world of children's literature. Send exclusive ms submissions to acquisitions editor. We regret that due to the volume of material we receive, we cannot comment on ms we are unable to accept."

○ "We seek to engage young minds with words and pictures that inform and delight, inspire and entertain. From board books for babies to picture books, nonfiction, and novels for children and young adults, our goal is to produce quality literature for a new generation of readers. We believe in books!"

NEEDS Picture books: animal, contemporary, folktales, history, humor, multicultural, nature/environment, poetry, religion, special needs, social issues, sports, suspense. Young readers: animal, contemporary, fantasy, folktales, history, humor, multicultural, poetry, religion, special needs, social issues, sports, suspense. Middle readers: adventure, contemporary, fantasy, history, humor, multicultural, nature/

environment, problem novels, religion, social issues, sports, suspense. Young adults/teens: adventure, contemporary, fantasy, folktales, history, humor, multicultural, nature/environment, problem novels, religion, sports, suspense. Average word length: picture books—1,000; middle readers—15,000; young adult—45,000. "Right now we are not acquiring books that revolve around a holiday. (No Christmas, Thanksgiving, Easter, Halloween, Fourth of July, Hanukkah books.) We do not publish retold or original fairy tales, nor do we publish books about witches or ghosts, or vampires."

HOW TO CONTACT Send exclusive ms submissions (marked so on outside of envelope) to acquisitions editor.

TERMS Pays 5-7% royalty on retail. Responds to mss in 3-4 months.

TIPS "Find out who Eerdmans is before submitting a ms. Look at our website, request a catalog, and check out our books."

WILLIAM B. EERDMANS PUBLISHING CO.

2140 Oak Industrial Dr. NE, Grand Rapids MI 49505. (616)459-4591. **Fax:** (616)459-6540. **E-mail:** info@eerdmans.com. **Website:** www.eerdmans.com. **Contact:** Jon Pott, editor-in-chief. Estab. 1911. "The majority of our adult publications are religious and most of these are academic or semi-academic in character (as opposed to inspirational or celebrity books), though we also publish general trade books on the Christian life. Our nonreligious titles, most of them in regional history or on social issues, aim, similarly, at an educated audience." Publishes hardcover and paperback originals and reprints. Book catalog and ms guidelines free.

○   Will not respond to or accept mss, proposals, or queries sent by e-mail or fax.

IMPRINTS Eerdmans Books for Young Readers.

HOW TO CONTACT Query with SASE.

TERMS Responds in 4 weeks to queries, possibly longer for mss. Please include e-mail and/or SASE.

○○ EGMONT USA

443 Park Ave. S, New York NY 10016. (212)685-0102. **Website:** www.egmontusa.com. **Contact:** Elizabeth Law, vice president/publisher; Regina Griffin, executive editor; Greg Ferguson, senior editor; Alison Weiss, assistant editor. Estab. 2008. Specializes in trade books. Publishes 1 picture book/year; 2 young readers/year; 20 middle readers/year; 20 young adult/

year. "Egmont USA publishes quality commercial fiction. We are committed to editorial excellence and to providing first-rate care for our authors. Our motto is that we turn writers into authors and children into passionate readers."

○   *"Unfortunately, Egmont USA is not currently able to accept unsolicited submissions; we only accept submissions from literary agents."*

NEEDS Young readers: adventure, animal, contemporary, humor, multicultural. Middle readers: adventure, animal, contemporary, fantasy, humor, multicultural, problem novels, science fiction, special needs. Young adults/teens: adventure, animal, contemporary, fantasy, humor, multicultural, paranormal, problem novels, religion, science fiction, special needs.

HOW TO CONTACT Query or submit completed ms.

TERMS Pays authors royalties based on retail price. Responds to queries in 4 weeks; mss in 6 weeks.

ELLORA'S CAVE PUBLISHING, INC.

1056 Home Ave., Akron OH 44310. **E-mail:** submissions@ellorascave.com. **Website:** www.ellorascave.com. Estab. 2000. Publishes electronic originals and reprints; print books. Guidelines available online. "Read and follow detailed submission instructions."

NEEDS Erotic romance and erotica fiction of every subgenre, including gay/lesbian, ménage and more, and BDSM. All must have abundant, explicit, and graphic erotic content.

HOW TO CONTACT Submit electronically only; cover e-mail as defined in our submission guidelines plus 1 attached .docx file containing full synopsis, first 3 chapters, and last chapter.

TERMS Pays 45% royalty on amount received. Responds in 2-4 months to mss. No queries.

TIPS "Our audience is romance readers who want explicit sexual detail. They come to us because we offer sex with romance, plot, emotion. In addition to erotic romance with happy-ever-after endings, we also publish pure erotica detailing sexual adventure and experimentation."

ENETE ENTERPRISES

3600 Mission #10, San Diego CA 92109. **E-mail:** EneteEnterprises@gmail.com. **Website:** www.EneteEnterprises.com. **Contact:** Shannon Enete, editor. Estab. 2011. Publishes trade paperback originals, mass-market paperback originals, electronic originals. Guidelines available on website.

HOW TO CONTACT Submit query, proposal, or ms by e-mail according to guidelines (do not forget a marketing plan).

TERMS Pays royalties of 1-15%. Responds to queries/proposals in 1 month; mss in 1-3 months.

TIPS "Send me your best work. Do not rush a draft."

ENGLISH TEA ROSE PRESS

The Wild Rose Press, P.O. Box 708, Adams Basin NY 14410. (585)752-8770. **E-mail:** queryus@thewildrosepress.com. **Website:** www.thewildrosepress.com. **Contact:** Nicole D'Arienzo, editor. Estab. 2006. Member: EPIC, Romance Writers of America. Distributes/promotes titles through major distribution chains, including iTunes, Kobo, Sony, Amazon.com, Kindle, as well as smaller and online distributors. Publishes paperback originals, reprints, and e-books in a POD format. Guidelines available on website.

○ *Does not accept unsolicited mss.* Agented fiction less than 1%. Always comments on rejected mss. Sends prepublication galleys to author.

NEEDS "In the English Tea Rose line, we have conquering heroes, high seas adventure, and scandalous gossip. The love stories that will take you back in time. From the windswept moors of Scotland to the Emerald Isle to the elegant ballrooms of Regency England, the men and women of this time are larger than life and willing to risk it all for the love of a lifetime. English Tea Rose stories encompass historical romances set before 1900 and not on American soil. Send us your medieval knights, Vikings, Scottish highlanders, marauding pirates, and ladies and gentlemen of the Ton. English Tea Rose romances should have strong conflict and should be emotionally driven; and, whether the story is medieval, Regency, set during the renaissance, or any other pre-1900 time, they must stay true to their period in historical accuracy and flavor. English Tea Roses can range from sweet to spicy, but should not contain overly explicit language."

HOW TO CONTACT Send query letter with outline and a list of publishing credits. Include estimated word count, brief bio, and list of publishing credits.

TERMS Pays royalty of 7% minimum; 35% maximum. Responds in 4 weeks to queries; 3 months to mss.

TIPS "Polish your ms, make it as error-free as possible, and follow our submission guidelines."

○○ EOS

Imprint of HarperCollins General Books Group, 10 E. 53rd St., New York NY 10022. (212)207-7000. **Website:** www.eosbooks.com. Estab. 1998. Eos publishes quality science fiction/fantasy with broad appeal. Publishes hardcover originals, trade and mass-market paperback originals, and reprints. Guidelines for #10 SASE.

NEEDS No horror or juvenile.

HOW TO CONTACT Agented submissions only. *All unsolicited mss returned.*

TERMS Pays royalty on retail price. Pays variable advance.

○ FABER & FABER, LTD.

Bloomsbury House, 74-77 Great Russell St., London WC1B 3DA United Kingdom. (020)7465-0045. **Fax:** (020)7465-0034. **Website:** www.faber.co.uk. **Contact:** Lee Brackstone, Hannah Griffiths, Angus Cargill, (fiction); Walter Donohue, (film); Dinah Wood, (plays); Julian Loose, Neil Belton, (nonfiction); Paul Keegan, (poetry); Belinda Matthews, (music); Suzy Jenvy, Julia Wells, (children's). Estab. 1925. Faber & Faber have rejuvenated their nonfiction, music and children's titles in recent years and the film and drama lists remain market leaders. Publishes hardcover and paperback originals and reprints. Book catalog available online.

○ Faber & Faber will consider unsolicited proposals for poetry only.

HOW TO CONTACT *No unsolicited fiction submissions.*

TERMS Pays royalty. Pays varying advances with each project. Responds in 3 months to mss.

TIPS "Explore the website and downloadable book catalogs thoroughly to get a feel for the lists in all categories and genres."

FANTAGRAPHICS BOOKS, INC.

7563 Lake City Way, NE, Seattle WA 98115. (206)524-1967. **Fax:** (206)524-2104. **E-mail:** fbicomix@fantagraphics.com. **Website:** www.fantagraphics.com. **Contact:** Submissions Editor. Estab. 1976. Publishes comics for thinking readers. Does not want mainstream genres of superhero, vigilante, horror, fantasy, or science fiction. Publishes original trade paperbacks. Book catalog online. Guidelines online.

NEEDS "Fantagraphics is an independent company with a modus operandi different from larger, factory-like corporate comics publishers. If your talents are limited to a specific area of expertise (i.e., inking, writing, etc.), then you will need to develop your own team before submitting a project to us. We want to see an idea that is fully fleshed out in your mind, at least, if not on paper. Submit a minimum of 5 fully inked pages of art, a synopsis, SASE, and a brief note stating approximately how many issues you have in mind."

TERMS Responds in 2-3 months to queries.

TIPS "Take note of the originality and diversity of the themes and approaches to drawing in such Fantagraphics titles as *Love & Rockets* (stories of life in Latin America and Chicano L.A.), *Palestine* (journalistic autobiography in the Middle East), *Eightball* (surrealism mixed with kitsch culture in stories alternately humorous and painfully personal), and *Naughty Bits* (feminist humor and short stories which both attack and commiserate). Try to develop your own, equally individual voice; originality, aesthetic maturity, and graphic storytelling skills are the signs by which Fantagraphics judges whether or not your submission is ripe for publication."

FANTASTIC BOOKS PUBLISHING

Lilac Tree Farm, Honeypots Ln., Elstronwick East Yorkshire HU12 9BP United Kingdom. +44 (07415)388882. **E-mail:** fantasticbookspublishing@gmail.com. **Website:** www.fantasticbookspublishing.com. **Contact:** Daniel Grubb, CEO/COO. Estab. 2012. Publishes trade paperback, electronic originals, and audiobooks. Catalog and guidelines available online at website.

◯   50% author-subsidy published.

HOW TO CONTACT Submit proposal package, including synopsis, 3 sample chapters, and 5GBP submission fee to cover admin and reader report production. "All we ask is that you review our submission guidelines and follow them closely for your submission. Every submission to Fantastic Books Publishing will be returned with a readers report from our editorial team. This may be an offer of publication, suggestions for tightening the ms, or simply a rejection. Even in the case of rejections, we usually suggest alternative routes to publication."

TERMS Pays 40-100% on wholesale price. No advance. Responds in 1 week to queries; 1 month to proposals; 3 months to mss.

TIPS "Be yourself. Don't try to come across as anything different. We work very closely with our clients, and it is our intention to get to know you and to welcome you into our publishing family. This helps us market and promote your book to your target audience. It also helps the reputation of the publishing industry which, in these times of constant change, is

what we intend to do by being honest, transparent, and above all, sincere with our clients."

⑤ FARRAR, STRAUS & GIROUX

18 W. 18th St., New York NY 10011. (646)307-5151. **E-mail:** fsg.editorial@fsgbooks.com. **Website:** us.macmillan.com. **Contact:** Editorial Department. Estab. 1946. "We publish original and well-written material for all ages." Publishes hardcover originals and trade paperback reprints. Catalog available by request. Guidelines online.

IMPRINTS Frances Foster Books.

NEEDS Do not query picture books; just send ms. Do not fax or e-mail queries or mss.

HOW TO CONTACT Send cover letter describing submission with first 50 pages.

TERMS Pays 2-6% royalty on retail price for paperbacks, 3-10% for hardcovers. Pays $3,000-25,000 advance. Responds in 2 months to queries; 3 months to mss

FARRAR, STRAUS & GIROUX FOR YOUNG READERS

18 W. 18th St., New York NY 10011. (212)741-6900. **Fax:** (212)633-2427. **E-mail:** childrens-editorial@fsgbooks.com. **Website:** www.fsgkidsbooks.com. **Contact:** Margaret Ferguson, editorial director; Wesley Adams, executive editor; Janine O'Malley, senior editor; Frances Foster, Frances Foster Books; Robbin Gourley, art director. Estab. 1946. Book catalog available by request. Ms guidelines online.

NEEDS All levels: all categories. "Original and well-written material for all ages."

HOW TO CONTACT Submit cover letter, first 50 pages by mail only.

TIPS "Study our catalog before submitting. We will see illustrators' portfolios by appointment. Don't ask for criticism and/or advice—due to the volume of submissions we receive, it's just not possible. Never send originals. Always enclose SASE."

FENCE BOOKS

Science Library 320, University of Albany, 1400 Washington Ave., Albany NY 12222. (518)591-8162. **E-mail:** fencesubmissions@gmail.com. **E-mail:** peter.n.fence@gmail.com. **Website:** www.fenceportal.org. **Contact:** Submissions Manager. Closed to submissions until June 15. Check website for details. Publishes hardcover originals. Guidelines online.

HOW TO CONTACT Submit via contests and occasional open reading periods.

◑ DAVID FICKLING BOOKS

31 Beamont St., Oxford En OX1 2NP United Kingdom. (018)65-339000. **Fax:** (018)65-339009. **E-mail:** submissions@davidficklingbooks.com. **Website:** www.davidficklingbooks.co.uk. Guidelines online.

NEEDS Considers all categories.

HOW TO CONTACT Submit cover letter and 3 sample chapters as PDF attachment saved in format "Author Name_Full Title."

TERMS Responds to mss in 3 months.

TIPS "We adore stories for all ages, in both text and pictures. Quality is our watchword."

◐ FIRST EDITION DESIGN PUBLISHING

P.O. Box 20217, Sarasota FL 34276. (941)921-2607. **Fax:** (617)866-7510. **E-mail:** support@firstedition design.com; submission@firsteditiondesign.com. **Website:** www.firsteditiondesignpublishing.com. **Contact:** Deborah E. Gordon, executive editor; Tom Gahan, marketing director. Estab. 1985. Guidelines available free on request or online at website.

HOW TO CONTACT Submit complete ms electronically.

TERMS Pays royalty 30-70% on retail price.

TIPS "Follow our FAQs listed on our website."

FIVE STAR PUBLICATIONS, INC.

P.O. Box 6698, Chandler AZ 85246. (480)940-8182. **Fax:** (480)940-8787. **E-mail:** info@fivestarpublica tions.com. **Website:** www.fivestarpublications.com. **Contact:** Linda F. Radke, president. Estab. 1985. "Helps produce and market award-winning books."

◯   "Five Star Publications publishes and promotes award-winning fiction, nonfiction, cookbooks, children's literature, and professional guides. More information about Five Star Publications, Inc., a 25-year leader in the book publishing/book marketing industry, is available online at our website."

TIPS "Not only do we want to recognize and honor accomplished authors in the field of children's literature, but we also want to highlight and reward up-and-coming newly published authors, as well as younger published writers."

◑⊘ FLUX

Llewellyn Worldwide, Ltd., Llewellyn Worldwide, Ltd., 2143 Wooddale Dr., Woodbury, MN 55125. (651)312-8613. **Fax:** (651)291-1908. **Website:** www.fluxnow.com; fluxnow.blogspot.com. **Contact:** Brian Farrey, acquisitions editor. Estab. 2005. "Flux seeks to publish authors who see young adult as a point of view, not a reading level. We look for books that try to capture a slice of teenage experience, whether in real or imagined worlds." Book catalog and guidelines available on website.

◯   *Does not accept unsolicited mss.*

NEEDS Young adults: adventure, contemporary, fantasy, history, humor, problem novels, religion, science fiction, sports, suspense. Average word length: 50,000.

HOW TO CONTACT Accepts agented submissions only.

TERMS Pays royalties of 10-15% based on wholesale price.

TIPS "Read contemporary teen books. Be aware of what else is out there. If you don't read teen books, you probably shouldn't write them. Know your audience. Write incredibly well. Do not condescend."

FOLDED WORD

79 Tracy Way, Meredith NH 03253. **E-mail:** editors@foldedword.com. **Website:** www.foldedword.com. Estab. 2008. "Folded Word is an independent literary press. Our focus? Connecting new voices to readers. Our goal? To make poetry and fiction accessible for the widest audience possible both on and off the page."

TIPS "We are seeking nonformulaic narratives that have a strong sense of place and/or time, especially the exploration of unfamiliar place/time."

FORWARD MOVEMENT

412 Sycamore St., Cincinnati OH 45202. (513)721-6659; (800)543-1813. **Fax:** (513)721-0729. **E-mail:** rthompson@forwardmovement.org. **Website:** www.forwardmovement.org. **Contact:** Richelle Thompson, managing editor. Estab. 1934. "Forward Movement was established to help reinvigorate the life of the church. Many titles focus on the life of prayer, where our relationship with God is centered, death, marriage, baptism, recovery, joy, the Episcopal Church and more. Currently emphasizing prayer/spirituality." Book catalog and ms guidelines free. Guidelines available online.

◯   "Forward Movement is an official agency of the Episcopal Church. In addition to Forward Day by Day, our daily devotional guide, we publish other books and tracts related to the life and concerns of the Christian church, especially within the Anglican Communion. These typically include material introducing the Episcopal Church, meditations and spiritual readings, prayers, liturgical resources, biblical reflections, and material on stewardship, church history, issues before the church, and Christian healing."

TERMS Responds in 1 month.

TIPS "Audience is primarily Episcopalians and other Christians."

FOUR WAY BOOKS

Box 535, Village Station, New York NY 10014. **E-mail:** editors@fourwaybooks.com. **Website:** www.fourwaybooks.com. **Contact:** Martha Rhodes, director. Estab. 1993. "Four Way Books is a not-for-profit literary press dedicated to publishing poetry and short fiction by emerging and established writers. Each year, Four Way Books publishes the winners of its national poetry competitions, as well as collections accepted through general submission, panel selection, and solicitation by the editors."

NEEDS Open reading period: June 1-30. Book-length story collections and novellas. Submission guidelines will be posted online at end of May. Does not want novels or translations.

FRANCES LINCOLN CHILDREN'S BOOKS

Frances Lincoln, 74-77 White Lion St., Islington, London N1 9PF United Kingdom. 00442072844009. **E-mail:** fl@franceslincoln.com. **Website:** www.franceslincoln.com. Estab. 1977. "Our company was founded by Frances Lincoln in 1977. We published our first books 2 years later, and we have been creating illustrated books of the highest quality ever since, with special emphasis on gardening, walking and the outdoors, art, architecture, design and landscape. In 1983, we started to publish illustrated books for children. Since then we have won many awards and prizes with both fiction and nonfiction children's books."

NEEDS Average word length: picture books—1,000; young readers—9,788; middle readers—20,653; young adults— 35,407.

HOW TO CONTACT Query by e-mail.

TERMS Responds in 6 weeks to mss.

FREE SPIRIT PUBLISHING, INC.

217 Fifth Ave. N., Suite 200, Minneapolis MN 55401-1299. (612)338-2068. **Fax:** (612)337-5050. **E-mail:** acquisitions@freespirit.com. **Website:** www.freespirit.com. Estab. 1983. "We believe passionately in empowering kids to learn to think for themselves and make

their own good choices." Publishes trade paperback originals and reprints. Book catalog and ms guidelines online.

Free Spirit does not accept general fiction, poetry, or storybook submissions.

NEEDS "We will consider fiction that relates directly to select areas of focus. Please review catalog and author guidelines (both available online) for details before submitting proposal. If you'd like material returned, enclose an SASE with sufficient postage."

HOW TO CONTACT Accepts queries only—not submissions—by e-mail.

TERMS Pays advance. Responds to proposals in 4-6 months.

TIPS "Our books are issue oriented, jargon-free, and solution focused. Our audience is children, teens, teachers, parents, and youth counselors. We are especially concerned with kids' social and emotional well-being and look for books with ready-to-use strategies for coping with today's issues at home or in school—written in everyday language. We are not looking for academic or religious materials, or books that analyze problems with the nation's school systems. Instead, we want books that offer practical, positive advice so kids can help themselves, and parents and teachers can help kids succeed."

FREESTONE/PEACHTREE, JR.

1700 Chattahoochee Ave., Atlanta GA 30318. (404)876-8761. **Fax:** (404)875-2578. **E-mail:** hello@peachtree-online.com. **Website:** www.peachtree-online.com. **Contact:** Helen Harriss, acquisitions; Loraine Joyner, art director; Melanie McMahon Ives, production manager. Estab. 1977.

Freestone and Peachtree, Jr., are imprints of Peachtree Publishers. See the listing for Peachtree for submission information. No e-mail or fax queries or submissions, please.

NEEDS Middle readers: adventure, animal, history, nature/environment, sports. Young adults: fiction, history, biography, mystery, adventure. Does not want to see science fiction, religion, or romance.

HOW TO CONTACT Submit 3 sample chapters by postal mail only. No query necessary.

TERMS Responds in 6 months-1 year.

FUTURECYCLE PRESS

Website: www.futurecycle.org. **Contact:** Diane Kistner, director/editor-in-chief. Estab. 2007. Guidelines available online at website.

NEEDS Flash fiction.

HOW TO CONTACT Submit complete ms.

TERMS Pays 10% royalty and 25 author's copies. Responds to mss in 3 months.

GIVAL PRESS

Gival Press, LLC, P.O. Box 3812, Arlington VA 22203. (703)351-0079. **E-mail:** givalpress@yahoo.com. **Website:** www.givalpress.com. **Contact:** Robert L. Giron, editor-in-chief (area of interest: literary). Estab. 1998. Publishes trade paperback, electronic originals, and reprints. Book catalog online. Guidelines online.

HOW TO CONTACT Always query first via e-mail; provide description, author's bio, and supportive material.

TERMS Pays royalty. Responds in 1 month to queries, 3 months to proposals and mss.

TIPS "Our audience is those who read literary works with depth to the work. Visit our website—there is much to be read/learned from the numerous pages."

THE GLENCANNON PRESS

P.O. Box 1428, El Cerrito CA 94530. (510)528-4216. **Fax:** (510)528-3194. **E-mail:** merships@yahoo.com. **Website:** www.glencannon.com. **Contact:** Bill Harris (maritime, maritime children's). Estab. 1993. "We publish quality books about ships and the sea." Average print order: 1,000. Member PMA, BAIPA. Distributes titles through Baker & Taylor. Promotes titles through direct mail, magazine advertising, and word-of-mouth. Accepts unsolicited mss. Often comments on rejected mss. Publishes hardcover and paperback originals and hardcover reprints.

IMPRINTS Smyth.

HOW TO CONTACT Submit complete ms. Include brief bio, list of publishing credits. Send SASE for return of ms or send a disposable ms and SASE for reply only.

TERMS Pays 10-20% royalty. Responds in 1 month to queries; 2 months to mss.

TIPS "Write a good story in a compelling style."

DAVID R. GODINE, PUBLISHER

15 Court Square, Suite 320, Boston MA 02108. (617)451-9600. **Fax:** (617)350-0250. **E-mail:** info@godine.com. **Website:** www.godine.com. Estab. 1970. "We publish books that matter for people who care."

This publisher is no longer considering unsolicited mss of any type. Only interested in agented material.

GOLDEN BOOKS FOR YOUNG READERS GROUP

1745 Broadway, New York NY 10019. **Website:** www.randomhouse.com. Estab. 1935. "Random House Books aims to create books that nurture the hearts and minds of children, providing and promoting quality books and a rich variety of media that entertain and educate readers from 6 months to 12 years." Book catalog free on request.

Random House-Golden Books does not accept unsolicited mss, only agented material. They reserve the right not to return unsolicited material.

TERMS Pays authors in royalties; sometimes buys mss outright.

GOOSE LANE EDITIONS

500 Beaverbrook Ct., Suite 330, Fredericton NB E3B 5X4 Canada. (506)450-4251. **Fax:** (506)459-4991. **E-mail:** submissions@gooselane.com. **Website:** www.gooselane.com. **Contact:** Angela Williams, publishing assistant. Estab. 1954. "Goose Lane publishes literary fiction and nonfiction from well-read and highly skilled Canadian authors." Publishes hardcover and paperback originals and occasional reprints.

NEEDS Our needs in fiction never change: Substantial, character-centered literary fiction. No children's, young adult, mainstream, mass-market, genre, mystery, thriller, confessional, or science fiction.

HOW TO CONTACT Query with SAE with Canadian stamps or IRCs. No U.S. stamps.

TERMS Pays 8-10% royalty on retail price. Pays $500-3,000, negotiable advance. Responds in 6 months to queries.

TIPS "Writers should send us outlines and samples of books that show a very well-read author with highly developed literary skills. Our books are almost all by Canadians living in Canada. We consider submissions from outside Canada only when the author is Canadian and the book is of extraordinary interest to Canadian readers. We do not publish books for children or for the young adult market."

GRAYWOLF PRESS

250 Third Ave., N., Suite 600, Minneapolis MN 55401. **E-mail:** wolves@graywolfpress.org. **Website:** www.graywolfpress.org. **Contact:** Katie Dublinski, editorial manager (nonfiction, fiction). Estab. 1974. "Graywolf Press is an independent, nonprofit publisher dedicated to the creation and promotion of thoughtful

and imaginative contemporary literature essential to a vital and diverse culture." Publishes trade cloth and paperback originals. Book catalog free. Guidelines online.

NEEDS "Familiarize yourself with our list." No genre books (romance, western, science fiction, suspense).

HOW TO CONTACT Agented submissions only.

TERMS Pays royalty on retail price. Pays $1,000-25,000 advance. Responds in 3 months to queries.

Ⓐ⊘ GREENWILLOW BOOKS

HarperCollins Publishers, 10 E. 53rd St., New York NY 10022. (212)207-7000. **Website:** www.greenwillowblog.com. **Contact:** Virginia Duncan, vice president/publisher; Paul Zakris, art director. Estab. 1974. Publishes hardcover originals, paperbacks, e-books, and reprints.

Does not accept unsolicited mss. "Unsolicited mail will not be opened and will not be returned."

TERMS Pays 10% royalty on wholesale price for first-time authors. Offers variable advance.

GREY GECKO PRESS

565 S. Mason Rd., Suite 154, Katy TX 77450. (866)535-6078. **Fax:** (866)535-6078. **E-mail:** info@greygeckopress.com. **E-mail:** submissions@greygeckopress.com. **Website:** www.greygeckopress.com. **Contact:** Hilary Comfort, editor-in-chief; Jason Aydelotte, executive director. Estab. 2011. Publishes hardcover, trade paperback, and electronic originals. Book catalog and ms guidelines for #10 SASE, by e-mail or online.

NEEDS "We do not publish extreme horror, erotica, or religious fiction. New and interesting stories by unpublished authors will always get our attention. Innovation is a core value of our company. We prefer electronic submissions but will accept query with SASE. Submit proposal package including outline, detailed, synopsis, and 3 sample chapters."

TERMS Pays 50-80% royalties on wholesale price. Responds in 1-3 months.

TIPS "Be willing to be a part of the Grey Gecko family. Publishing with us is a partnership, not indentured servitude."

GROSSET & DUNLAP PUBLISHERS

Penguin Putnam, Inc., 375 Hudson St., New York NY 10014. **Website:** www.penguingroup.com. **Contact:** Francesco Sedita, vice president/publisher. Estab. 1898. Grosset & Dunlap publishes children's books that show children that reading is fun, with books that speak to their interests and that are affordable so that children can build a home library of their own. "Grosset & Dunlap publishes high-interest, affordable books for children ages 0-10 years. We focus on original series, licensed properties, readers, and novelty books." Publishes hardcover (few) and mass-market paperback originals.

HOW TO CONTACT All book formats except for picture books. Submit a summary and the first chapter or 2 for longer works.

TERMS Pays royalty. Pays advance.

TIPS "Nonfiction that is particularly topical or of wide interest in the mass market; new concepts for novelty format for preschoolers; and very well-written easy readers on topics that appeal to primary graders have the best chance of selling to our firm."

☺ GROUNDWOOD BOOKS

110 Spadina Ave. Suite 801, Toronto ON M5V 2K4 Canada. (416)363-4343. **Fax:** (416)363-1017. **E-mail:** ssutherland@groundwoodbooks.com. **Website:** www.houseofanansi.com. Publishes 13 picture books/year; 3 young readers/year; 5 middle readers/year; 5 young adult titles/year, approximately 2 nonfiction titles/year. Visit website for guidelines: www.houseofanansi.com/Groundwoodsubmissions.aspx.

NEEDS Recently published: *Lily and Taylor*, by Elise Moser; *The Servant*, by Fatima Sharafeddine; *Black Flame*, by Gerelchimeg Blackcrane; *The Spotted Dog Last Seen*, by Jessica Scott Kerrin.

HOW TO CONTACT Submit synopsis and sample chapters.

TERMS Offers advances. Responds to mss in 6-8 months.

⊘☺ GUERNICA EDITIONS

P.O. Box 76080, Abbey Market, Oakville ON L6M 3H5 Canada. (514)712-5304. **Fax:** (416)981-7606. **E-mail:** michaelmirolla@guernicaeditions.com. **Website:** www.guernicaeditions.com. **Contact:** Michael Mirolla, editor/publisher (poetry, nonfiction, short stories, novels). Estab. 1978. Guernica Editions is a literary press that produces works of poetry, fiction, and nonfiction often by writers who are ignored by the mainstream. Publishes trade paperback originals and reprints. Book catalog available online.

NEEDS "We wish to open up into the fiction world and focus less on poetry. We specialize in European, especially Italian, translations."

HOW TO CONTACT E-mail queries only.

TERMS Pays 8-10% royalty on retail price, or makes outright purchase of $200-5,000. Pays $450-750 advance. Responds in 1 month to queries. Responds in 6 months to proposals. Responds in 1 year to mss

HACHAI PUBLISHING

527 Empire Blvd., Brooklyn NY 11225. (718)633-0100. **Fax:** (718)633-0103. **Website:** www.hachai.com. **Contact:** Devorah Leah Rosenfeld, editor. Estab. 1988. Hachai is dedicated to producing high-quality Jewish children's literature, ages 2-10. Story should promote universal values such as sharing, kindness, etc. Publishes hardcover originals. Book catalog available free. Guidelines available online.

- "All books have spiritual/religious themes, specifically traditional Jewish content. We're seeking books about morals and values; the Jewish experience in current and Biblical times; and Jewish observance, Sabbath, and holidays."

NEEDS Picture books and young readers: contemporary, historical fiction, religion. Middle readers: adventure, contemporary, problem novels, religion. Does not want to see fantasy, animal stories, romance, problem novels depicting drug use or violence.

HOW TO CONTACT Submit complete ms.

TERMS Work purchased outright from authors for $800-1,000. Responds in 2 months to mss.

TIPS "We are looking for books that convey the traditional Jewish experience in modern times or long ago; traditional Jewish observance such as Sabbath and holidays and mitzvos such as mezuzah, blessings etc.; positive character traits (middos) such as honesty, charity, respect, sharing, etc. We are also interested in historical fiction for young readers (7-10) written with a traditional Jewish perspective and highlighting the relevance of Torah in making important choices. Please, no animal stories, romance, violence, preachy sermonizing. Write a story that incorporates a moral, not a preachy morality tale. Originality is the key. We feel Hachai publications will appeal to a wider readership as parents become more interested in positive values for their children."

HADLEY RILLE BOOKS

P.O. Box 25466, Overland Park KS 66225. **E-mail:** subs@hadleyrillebooks.com. **Website:** www.hrbpress .com. **Contact:** Eric T. Reynolds, editor/publisher. Estab. 2005.

- Currently closed to submissions. Check website for future reading periods.

TIPS "We aim to produce books that are aligned with current interest in the genres. Anthology markets are somewhat rare in science fiction these days, we feel there aren't enough good anthologies being published each year and part of our goal is to present the best that we can. We like stories that fit well within the guidelines of the particular anthology for which we are soliciting mss. Aside from that, we want stories with strong characters (not necessarily characters with strong personalities, flawed characters are welcome). We want to feel a sense of wonder and awe. We want to feel the world around the character, so scene description is important (however, this doesn't always require a lot of text, just set the scene well so we don't wonder where the character is). We strongly recommend workshopping the story or having it critiqued in some way by readers familiar with the genre. We prefer clichés be kept to a bare minimum in the prose and that writers avoid reworking old story lines."

HAMPTON ROADS PUBLISHING CO., INC.

665 Third St., Suite 400, San Francisco CA 94107. **E-mail:** submissions@rwwbooks.com. **Website:** www .redwheelweiser.com. **Contact:** Ms. Pat Bryce, acquisitions editor. Estab. 1989. "Our reason for being is to impact, uplift, and contribute to positive change in the world. We publish books that will enrich and empower the evolving consciousness of mankind. Though we are not necessarily limited in scope, we are most interested in mss on the following subjects: body/mind/spirit, health and healing, self-help. Please be advised that at the moment we are not accepting fiction or novelized material that does not pertain to body/mind/spirit, channeled writing." Publishes and distributes hardcover and trade paperback originals on subjects including metaphysics, health, complementary medicine, visionary fiction, and other related topics. Guidelines online.

- "Please know that we only publish a handful of books every year and that we pass on many well-written, important works, simply because we cannot publish them all. We review each and every proposal very carefully. However, due to the volume of inquiries, we cannot respond to them all individually. Please give us

30 days to review your proposal. If you do not hear back from us within that time, this means we have decided to pursue other book ideas that we feel fit better within our plan."

NEEDS Fiction should have 1 or more of the following themes: spiritual, inspirational, metaphysical, i.e., past-life recall, out-of-body experiences, near-death experience, paranormal.

HOW TO CONTACT Query with SASE. Submit outline, 2 sample chapters, clips. Submit complete ms.

TERMS Pays royalty. Pays $1,000-50,000 advance. Responds in 2-4 months to queries; 1 month to proposals; 6-12 months to mss.

ⓐⓞ HARCOURT, INC., TRADE DIVISION

Imprint of Houghton Mifflin Harcourt Book Group, 215 Park Ave. S., New York NY 10003. **Website:** www .harcourtbooks.com. Publishes hardcover and trade paperback originals and trade paperback reprints. Book catalog for 9×12 envelope and first-class stamps. Guidelines available online.

HOW TO CONTACT Agented submissions only.

TERMS Pays 6-15% royalty on retail price. Pays $2,000 minimum advance.

ⓞⓒ HARPERCOLLINS CANADA, LTD.

2 Bloor St. E., 20th Floor, Toronto ON M4W 1A8 Canada. (416)975-9334. **Fax:** (416)975-5223. **Website:** www.harpercollins.ca. Estab. 1989.

　　HarperCollins Canada is not accepting unsolicited material at this time.

IMPRINTS HarperCollinsPublishers; HarperPerennialCanada (trade paperbacks); HarperTrophyCanada (children's); Phyllis Bruce Books.

HARPERCOLLINS CHILDREN'S BOOKS/ HARPERCOLLINS PUBLISHERS

10 E. 53rd, New York NY 10022. (212)207-7000. **E-mail:** Dana.fritts@Harpercollins.com; Kate.eng bring@Harpercollins.com. **Website:** www.harper collins.com. **Contact:** Kate Engbring, designer; Dana Fritts, picture book art supervisor. HarperCollins, one of the largest English language publishers in the world, is a broad-based publisher with strengths in academic, business and professional, children's, educational, general interest, and religious and spiritual books, as well as multimedia titles. Publishes hardcover and paperback originals and paperback reprints. Catalog available online.

IMPRINTS HarperCollins Australia/New Zealand: Angus & Robertson, Fourth Estate, HarperBusiness, HarperCollins, HarperPerenniel, HarperReligious, HarperSports, Voyager; **HarperCollins Canada:** HarperFlamingoCanada, PerennialCanada; **HarperCollins Children's Books Group:** Amistad, Julie Andrews Collection, Avon, Joanna Cotler Books, Eos, Laura Geringer Books, Greenwillow Books, HarperAudio, HarperCollins Children's Books, HarperFestival, HarperTempest, HarperTrophy, Rayo, Katherine Tegen Books; **HarperCollins General Books Group:** Access, Amistad, Avon, Caedmon, Ecco, Eos, Fourth Estate, HarperAudio, HarperBusiness, HarperCollins, HarperEntertainment, HarperLargePrint, HarperResource, HarperSanFrancisco, HarperTorch, Harper Design International, Perennial, PerfectBound, Quill, Rayo, ReganBooks, William Morrow, William Morrow Cookbooks; **HarperCollins U.K.:** Collins Bartholomew, Collins, HarperCollins Crime & Thrillers, Collins Freedom to Teach, HarperCollins Children's Books, Thorsons/Element, Voyager Books; **Zondervan:** Inspirio, Vida, Zonderkidz, Zondervan.

NEEDS "We look for a strong story line and exceptional literary talent."

HOW TO CONTACT Agented submissions only. *All unsolicited mss returned.*

TERMS Negotiates payment upon acceptance. Responds in 1 month, will contact only if interested. Does not accept any unsolicited texts.

TIPS "We do not accept any unsolicited material."

ⓐ HARPERTEEN

10 E. 53rd St., New York NY 10022. (212)207-7000. **Fax:** (212)702-2583. **E-mail:** Jennifer.Deason@ HARPERCOLLINS.com. **Website:** www.harpercol lins.com. HarperTeen is a teen imprint that publishes hardcovers, paperback reprints, and paperback originals.

　　HarperCollins Children's Books is not accepting unsolicited and/or unagented mss or queries. Unfortunately the volume of these submissions is so large that they cannot receive the attention they deserve. Such submissions will not be reviewed or returned.

⊕ HARRINGTON & HARRINGTON PRESS

3400 Yosemite St., San Diego CA 92109. **E-mail:** press@harringtonandharrington.com. **E-mail:** sub missions@harringtonandharrington.com. **Website:** www.harringtonandharrington.com. **Contact:** Laurie Champion, general manager and editor-in-chief; Stacy Bodus, acquisitions editor. Estab. 2013. Publishes trade paperback originals. Catalog available for SASE. Guidelines available for SASE.

NEEDS Specializes in literary fiction.

HOW TO CONTACT Query with SASE.

TERMS Pays 10-15% royalties on retail price. Offers an advance between $100-1,000.

⚫⊘ HARVEST HOUSE PUBLISHERS

990 Owen Loop N, Eugene OR 97402. (541)343-0123. **Fax:** (541)302-0731. **Website:** www.harvesthousepublishers.com. Estab. 1974. Publishes hardcover, trade paperback, and mass-market paperback originals and reprints.

NEEDS *No unsolicited mss, proposals, or artwork.*

HOW TO CONTACT Agented submissions only.

TERMS Pays royalty.

TIPS "For first time/nonpublished authors we suggest building their literary résumé by submitting to magazines or perhaps accruing book contributions."

HENDRICK-LONG PUBLISHING CO., INC.

10635 Tower Oaks, Suite D, Houston TX 77070. (832)912-READ. **Fax:** (832)912-7353. **E-mail:** hendrick-long@att.net. **Website:** hendricklongpublishing.com. **Contact:** Vilma Long. Estab. 1969. "Hendrick-Long publishes historical fiction and nonfiction about Texas and the Southwest for children and young adults." Publishes hardcover and trade paperback originals and hardcover reprints. Book catalog for 8½×11 or 9×12 SASE with 4 first-class stamps. Guidelines available online.

HOW TO CONTACT Query with SASE. Submit outline, clips, 2 sample chapters.

TERMS Pays royalty on selling price. Pays advance. Responds in 3 months to queries.

HIGHLAND PRESS PUBLISHING

P.O. Box 2292, High Springs FL 32655. (386) 454-3927. **Fax:** (386) 454-3927. **E-mail:** the.highland.press@gmail.com; submissions.hp@gmail.com. **Website:** www.highlandpress.org. **Contact:** Leanne Burroughs, CEO (fiction); she will forward all mss to appropriate editor. Estab. 2005. "With our focus on historical romances, Highland Press Publishing is known as your 'Passport to Romance.' We focus on historical romances and our award-winning anthologies. Our short stories/novellas are heartwarming. As for our historicals, we publish historical novels like many of us grew up with and loved. History is a big part of the story and is tactfully woven throughout the romance." We have recently opened our submissions to all genres, with the exception of erotica. Our newest lines are inspirational, regency, and young adult. Publishes paperback originals. Catalog and guidelines available online.

HOW TO CONTACT Query with outline/synopsis and sample chapters. Accepts queries by snail mail, e-mail. Include estimated word count, target market.

TERMS Pays royalties 7.5-8%. Responds in 8 weeks to queries; 3-12 months to mss.

TIPS "I don't publish based on industry trends. We buy what we like and what we believe readers are looking for. However, often this proves to be the genres and time periods larger publishers are not currently interested in. Be professional at all times. Present your ms in the best possible light. Be sure you have run spell-checker and that the ms has been vetted by at least 1 critique partner, preferably more. Many times we receive mss that have wonderful stories involved but would take far too much time to edit to make it marketable."

⊕ HIPSO MEDIA

8151 E. 29th Ave., Denver CO 80238. **E-mail:** rob@hipsomedia.com. **Website:** www.hipsomedia.com. **Contact:** Rob Simon; Dan Cohen. Estab. 2012. Publishes trade and mass-market paperback and electronic originals. Catalog available online. Guidelines available online.

HOW TO CONTACT Query with SASE.

TERMS Authors receive between 15-30% on royalty. Responds in 1 month.

TIPS Describes ideal audience as "hip readers of e-books. We are going digital first, so tell us why someone would want to read your book."

HOLIDAY HOUSE, INC.

425 Madison Ave., New York NY 10017. (212)688-0085. **Fax:** (212)421-6134. **E-mail:** info@holidayhouse.com. **Website:** holidayhouse.com. **Contact:** Mary Cash, editor-in-chief. Estab. 1935. "Holiday House publishes children's and young adult books for the school and library markets. We have a commitment to publishing first-time authors and illustrators. We specialize in quality hardcovers from picture books to young adult, both fiction and nonfiction, primarily for the school and library market." Publishes hardcover originals and paperback reprints. Guidelines for #10 SASE.

NEEDS Children's books only.

HOW TO CONTACT Query with SASE. No phone calls, please.

TERMS Pays royalty on list price, range varies. Agent's royalty. Responds in 4 months.

TIPS "We need mss with strong stories and writing."

⚠⚠ HENRY HOLT

175 Fifth Avenue, New York NY 10011. **Website:** www .henryholt.com. Publishes hardcover and paperback originals and reprints.

Agented submissions only.

HOW TO CONTACT Closed to submissions.

⚠⚠⚠⚠ HOPEWELL PUBLICATIONS

P.O. Box 11, Titusville NJ 08560. **Website:** www .hopepubs.com. **Contact:** E. Martin, publisher. Estab. 2002. "Hopewell Publications specializes in classic reprints—books with proven sales records that have gone out of print—and the occasional new title of interest. Our catalog spans from 1-60 years of publication history. We print fiction and nonfiction, and we accept agented and unagented materials. Submissions are accepted online only." Format publishes in hardcover, trade paperback, and electronic originals; trade paperback and electronic reprints. Catalog online. Guidelines online.

IMPRINTS Egress Books, Legacy Classics.

HOW TO CONTACT Query online using our online guidelines.

TERMS Pays royalty on retail price. Responds in 3 months to queries; 6 months to proposals; 9 months to mss.

HOUGHTON MIFFLIN HARCOURT BOOKS FOR CHILDREN

Imprint of Houghton Mifflin Trade & Reference Division, 222 Berkeley St., Boston MA 02116. (617)351-5000. **Fax:** (617)351-1111. **E-mail:** children's_books@ hmco.com. **Website:** www.houghtonmifflinbooks .com. **Contact:** Erica Zappy, associate editor; Kate O'Sullivan, senior editor; Anne Rider, executive editor; Margaret Raymo, editorial director. Houghton Mifflin Harcourt gives shape to ideas that educate, inform, and above all, delight. Query with SASE. Submit sample chapters, synopsis. Faxed or e-mailed mss and proposals are not considered. Complete submission guidelines available on website. Publishes hardcover originals and trade paperback originals and reprints. Guidelines available online.

Does not respond to or return mss unless interested.

IMPRINTS Sandpiper Paperback Books; Graphia.

HOW TO CONTACT Submit complete ms.

TERMS Pays 5-10% royalty on retail price. Pays variable advance. Responds in 4-6 months to queries.

TIPS Faxed or e-mailed mss and proposals are not considered.

⚠⚠ HOUGHTON MIFFLIN HARCOURT CO.

222 Berkeley St., Boston MA 02116. (617)351-5000. **Website:** www.hmhco.com; www.hmhbooks.com. Estab. 1832. Publishes hardcover originals and trade paperback originals and reprints.

"Houghton Mifflin Harcourt gives shape to ideas that educate, inform, and delight. In a new era of publishing, our legacy of quality thrives as we combine imagination with technology, bringing you new ways to know."

IMPRINTS American Heritage Dictionaries; Clarion Books; Great Source Education Group; Houghton Mifflin; Houghton Mifflin Books for Children; Houghton Mifflin Paperbacks; Mariner Books; McDougal Littell; Peterson Field Guides; Riverside Publishing; Sunburst Technology; Taylor's Gardening Guides; Edusoft, Promissor; Walter Lorraine Books; Kingfisher.

⚠⚠ HOUSE OF ANANSI PRESS

110 Spadina Ave., Suite 801, Toronto ON M5V 2K4 Canada. (416)363-4343. **Fax:** (416)363-1017. **Website:** www.anansi.ca. Estab. 1967.

NEEDS Publishes literary fiction that has a unique flair, memorable characters, and a strong narrative voice.

HOW TO CONTACT Query with SASE.

TERMS Pays 8-10% royalties. Pays $750 advance and 10 author's copies.

HQN BOOKS

Imprint of Harlequin, 233 Broadway, Suite 1001, New York NY 10279. **Website:** harlequin.com. **Contact:** Tara Parsons, senior editor. Publishes hardcover, trade paperback, and mass-market paperback originals.

"HQN publishes romance in all subgenres—historical, contemporary, romantic suspense, paranormal—as long as the story's central focus is romance. Prospective authors can familiarize themselves with the wide range of books we publish by reading work by some of our current authors. The imprint is looking for a wide range of authors from known romance stars to first-time authors. At the moment, we are accepting only agented submissions—unagented authors may send a query letter to determine if their project suits our needs. Please send your projects to our New York Editorial Office."

HOW TO CONTACT Accepts unagented material. Length: 90,000 words.

TERMS Pays royalty. Pays advance.

IDEALS CHILDREN'S BOOKS AND CANDYCANE PRESS

2630 Elm Hill Pike, Suite 100, Nashville TN 37214. **Website:** www.idealsbooks.com. **Contact:** Submissions. Estab. 1944.

NEEDS Picture books: animal, concept, history, religion. Board books: animal, history, nature/environment, religion. Ideals publishes for ages 4-8, no longer than 800 words; CandyCane publishes for ages 2-5, no longer than 500 words.

HOW TO CONTACT Submit complete ms.

IDW PUBLISHING

5080 Santa Fe, San Diego CA 92109. **E-mail:** letters@idwpublishing.com. **Website:** www.idwpublishing.com. Estab. 1999. IDW Publishing currently publishes a wide range of comic books and graphic novels including titles based on *Angel*, *Doctor Who*, *GI Joe*, *Star Trek*, *Terminator: Salvation*, and *Transformers*. Creator-driven titles include *Fallen Angel*, by Peter David and JK Woodward; *Locke & Key*, by Joe Hill and Gabriel Rodriguez; and a variety of titles by writer Steve Niles including *Wake the Dead*, *Epilogue*, and *Dead, She Said*. Publishes hardcover, mass-market, and trade paperback originals.

ILIUM PRESS

2407 S. Sonora Dr., Spokane WA 99037. (509)928-7950. **E-mail:** contact@iliumpress.com; submissions@iliumpress.com. **Website:** www.iliumpress.com. **Contact:** John Lemon, owner/editor (literature, epic poetry, how-to). Estab. 2010. Publishes trade paperback originals and reprints, electronic originals and reprints. Guidelines available on website www.iliumpress.com.

NEEDS "See website for guidelines and preferred styles."

HOW TO CONTACT Query with SASE or submit proposal package with outline, first 20 pages, and SASE.

TERMS Pays 20-50% royalties on receipts. Responds in 6 months to queries/proposals/mss.

TIPS "Read submission guidelines and literary preferences on the website: www.iliumpress.com."

ILLUMINATION ARTS

P.O. Box 1865, Bellevue WA 98009. **Website:** www.illumin.com. **Contact:** Ruth Thompson, editorial director. Estab. 1987.

"Note that our submission review process is on hold until otherwise posted on our website, so submissions are not currently being reviewed." Normal requirements include no electronic or CD submissions for text or art. Considers simultaneous submissions.

NEEDS Word length: Prefers under 1,000 but will consider up to 1,500 words.

TERMS Pays authors and illustrators royalty based on wholesale price. Book fliers available for SASE.

TIPS "Read our books or visit website to see what our books are like. Follow submission guidelines found on website. Be patient. We are unable to track unsolicited submissions."

IMAGE COMICS

2001 Center St., 6th Floor, Berkeley CA 94704. **E-mail:** submissions@imagecomics.com. **Website:** www.imagecomics.com. **Contact:** Eric Stephenson, publisher. Estab. 1992. Publishes creator-owned comic books, graphic novels. See this company's website for detailed guidelines.

Does not accept writing samples without art.

HOW TO CONTACT Query with one-page synopsis and 5 pages or more of samples. "We do not accept writing (that is plots, scripts, whatever) samples! If you're an established pro, we might be able to find somebody willing to work with you but it would be nearly impossible for us to read through every script that might find its way our direction. Do not send your script or your plot unaccompanied by art—it will be discarded, unread."

TIPS "We are not looking for any specific genre or type of comic book. We are looking for comics that are well written and well drawn, by people who are dedicated and can meet deadlines."

IMAGES SI, INC

109 Woods of Arden Rd., Staten Island NY 10312. (718)966-3964. **Fax:** (718)966-3695. **Website:** www.imagesco.com. Estab. 1990.

TERMS Pays 10-20% royalty on wholesale price.

IMMEDIUM

P.O. Box 31846, San Francisco CA 94131. (415)452-8546. **Fax:** (360)937-6272. **E-mail:** submissions@immedium.com. **Website:** www.immedium.com. **Contact:** Amy Ma, acquisitions editor. Estab. 2005. *"Immedium* focuses on publishing eye-catching children's picture books, Asian-American topics, and contemporary arts, popular culture, and multicultural issues." Publishes hardcover and trade paperback originals. Catalog available online. Guidelines available online.

HOW TO CONTACT Submit complete ms.

TERMS Pays 5% royalty on wholesale price. Pays on publication. Responds in 1 month to queries; 2 months to proposals; 3 months to mss.

TIPS "Our audience is children and parents. Please visit our site."

INNOVATIVE PUBLISHERS INC.

44 Highland St., Boston MA 02119. (617)963-0886. **Fax:** (617)861-8533. **E-mail:** pub@innovative-publishers.com. **Website:** www.innovative-publishers.com. Estab. 2000. Publishes hardcover, trade paperback, mass-market, and electronic originals; trade paperback and mass-market reprints. Book catalog for 9×12 SASE with 7 first-class stamps. Guidelines for #10 SASE.

NEEDS "Primarily seeking artists that are immersed in their topic. If you live, eat, and sleep your topic, it will show. Our focus is a wide demographic."

HOW TO CONTACT Query with SASE.

TERMS Pays 5-17% royalty on retail price. Offers $1,500-125,000 advance. Responds in 3 months to queries; 4-6 months to mss and proposals.

INSOMNIAC PRESS

520 Princess Ave., London ON N6B 2B8 Canada. (416)504-6270. **E-mail:** mike@insomniacpress.com. **Website:** www.insomniacpress.com. **Contact:** Mike O'Connor, publisher. Estab. 1992. Publishes trade paperback originals and reprints, mass-market paperback originals, and electronic originals and reprints. Guidelines available online.

NEEDS "We publish a mix of commercial (mysteries) and literary fiction."

HOW TO CONTACT Query via e-mail, submit proposal.

TERMS Pays 10-15% royalty on retail price. Pays $500-1,000 advance.

TIPS "We envision a mixed readership that appreciates up-and-coming literary fiction and poetry as well as solidly researched and provocative nonfiction. Peruse our website and familiarize yourself with what we've published in the past."

INTERLINK PUBLISHING GROUP, INC.

46 Crosby St., Northampton MA 01060. (413)582-7054. **Fax:** (413)582-7057. **E-mail:** info@interlinkbooks.com; editor@interlinkbooks.com. **Website:** www.interlinkbooks.com. **Contact:** Michel Moushabeck, publisher; Pam Thompson, editor. Estab. 1987. Interlink is an independent publisher of general trade adult fiction and nonfiction with an emphasis on books that have a wide appeal while also meeting high intellectual and literary standards. Publishes hardcover and trade paperback originals Book catalog and guidelines online.

IMPRINTS Crocodile Books, USA; Codagan Guides, USA; Interlink Books; Olive Branch Press; Clockroot Books.

NEEDS "We are looking for translated works relating to the Middle East, Africa, or Latin America." No science fiction, romance, plays, erotica, fantasy, horror.

HOW TO CONTACT Query with SASE. Submit outline, sample chapters.

TERMS Pays 6-8% royalty on retail price. Pays small advance. Responds in 3-6 months to queries.

TIPS "Any submissions that fit well in our publishing program will receive careful attention. A visit to our website, your local bookstore, or library to look at some of our books before you send in your submission is recommended."

ITALICA PRESS

595 Main St., Suite 605, New York NY 10044-0047. (917)371-0563. **E-mail:** inquiries@italicapress.com. **Website:** www.italicapress.com. **Contact:** Ronald G. Musto and Eileen Gardiner, publishers. Estab. 1985. "Italica Press publishes English translations of modern Italian fiction and medieval and Renaissance nonfiction." Publishes trade paperback originals. Book catalog and guidelines available online.

NEEDS "First-time translators published. We would like to see translations of Italian writers who are well-known in Italy who are not yet translated for an American audience."

HOW TO CONTACT Query with SASE.

TERMS Pays 7-15% royalty on wholesale price; author's copies. Responds in 1 month to queries; 4 months to mss.

TIPS "We are interested in considering a wide variety of medieval and Renaissance topics (not historical fiction). For modern works, we are only interested in translations from Italian fiction by well-known Italian authors." *Only* fiction that has been previously published in Italian. "A *brief* call saves a lot of postage. 90% of proposals we receive are completely off base—but we are very interested in things that are right on target. Please send return postage if you want your ms returned."

JEWISH LIGHTS PUBLISHING

LongHill Partners, Inc., Sunset Farm Offices, Rt. 4, P.O. Box 237, Woodstock VT 05091. (802)457-4000. **Fax:** (802)457-4004. **E-mail:** editorial@jewishlights.com; sales@jewishlights.com. **Website:** www.jewishlights.com. **Contact:** Tim Holtz, art acquisitions. Estab. 1990. "Jewish Lights publishes books for people of all faiths and all backgrounds who yearn for books that attract, engage, educate, and spiritually inspire. Our authors are at the forefront of spiritual thought and deal with the quest for the self and for meaning in life by drawing on the Jewish wisdom tradition. Our books cover topics including history, spirituality, life cycle, children, self-help, recovery, theology, and philosophy. We do not publish autobiography, biography, fiction, haggadot, poetry, or cookbooks. At this point, we plan to do only 2 books for children annually, and 1 will be for younger children (ages 4-10)." Publishes hardcover and trade paperback originals, trade paperback reprints. Book catalog and ms guidelines online.

NEEDS Picture books, young readers, middle readers: spirituality. "We are not interested in anything other than spirituality."

HOW TO CONTACT Query with outline/synopsis and 2 sample chapters; submit complete ms for picture books.

TERMS Pays authors royalty of 10% of revenue received; 15% royalty for subsequent printings. Responds in 3 months to queries.

TIPS "We publish books for all faiths and backgrounds that also reflect the Jewish wisdom tradition. Explain in your cover letter why you're submitting your project to us in particular. Make sure you know what we publish."

JOURNEYFORTH

Imprint of BJU Press, 1700 Wade Hampton Blvd., Greenville SC 29614. (864)242-5100, ext. 4350. **Fax:** (864)298-0268. **E-mail:** jb@bju.edu. **Website:** www.journeyforth.com. **Contact:** Nancy Lohr. Estab. 1974. "Small independent publisher of trustworthy novels and biographies for readers preschool through high school from a conservative Christian perspective, Christian living books, and Bible studies for adults." Publishes paperback originals. Book catalog available free. Guidelines online.

NEEDS "All of our fiction is based on a moral and Christian worldview." Does not want short stories.

HOW TO CONTACT Submit 5 sample chapters, synopsis, SASE.

TERMS Pays royalty. Responds in 1 month to queries. Responds in 3 months to mss.

TIPS "Study the publisher's guidelines. No picture books and no submissions by e-mail."

JUPITER GARDENS PRESS

Jupiter Gardens, LLC, P.O. Box 191, Grimes IA 50111. **E-mail:** submissions@jupitergardens.com. **Website:** www.jupitergardens.com. **Contact:** Mary Wilson, publisher (romance, science fiction/fantasy, new age). Estab. 2007. Format publishes in trade paperback originals and reprints; electronic originals and reprints. Catalog available online at website. Guidelines available online at website.

NEEDS "We only publish romance (all subgenres), science fiction and fantasy, and metaphysical fiction. Our science fiction and fantasy covers a wide variety of topics, such as feminist fantasy and hard science fiction and fantasy, which looks at the human condition. Our young adult imprint, Jupiter Storm, with thought-provoking reads that explore the full range of speculative fiction, includes science fiction or fantasy and metaphysical fiction. These readers enjoy edgy contemporary works. Our romance readers love seeing a couple, no matter the gender, overcome obstacles and grow in order to find true love. Like our readers, we believe that love can come in many forms."

HOW TO CONTACT Via e-mail, submit cover letter detailing writing experience (if any) and attach a 2- to 4-page synopsis and the first 3 chapters in .doc or .rtf format, .

TERMS Pays 40% royalty on retail price. Responds in 1 month to proposals, 2 months to mss.

TIPS "Know your genre and your readership. We publish a diverse catalog, and we're passionate about our main focus. We want romance that takes your breath away and leaves you with that warm feeling that love does conquer all. Our science fiction takes place in wild and alien worlds, and our fantasy transports readers to mythical realms and finds strange worlds within our own. And our metaphysical nonfiction will help readers gain new skills and awareness for the coming age. We want authors who engage with their readers and who aren't afraid to use social media to connect. Read and follow our submission guidelines."

🄲 KAEDEN BOOKS

P.O. Box 16190, Rocky River OH 44116. **Website:** www.kaeden.com. **Contact:** Lisa Stenger, editor. Estab. 1986. "Children's book publisher for education K-3 market: reading stories, fiction/nonfiction, chapter books, science, and social studies materials." Publishes paperback originals. Book catalog and guidelines available online.

NEEDS "We are looking for stories with humor, surprise endings, and interesting characters that will appeal to children in kindergarten through third grade." No sentence fragments. Please do not submit: queries, ms summaries, or résumés, mss that stereotype or demean individuals or groups, mss that present violence as acceptable behavior.

HOW TO CONTACT Submit complete ms. "Can be as minimal as 25 words for the earliest reader or as much as 2,000 words for the fluent reader. Beginning chapter books are welcome. Our readers are in kindergarten to third grade, so vocabulary and sentence structure must be appropriate for young readers. Make sure that all language used in the story is of an appropriate level for the students to read independently. Sentences should be complete and grammatically correct."

TERMS Work purchased outright from authors. Pays royalties to previous authors. Responds only if interested.

TIPS "We are an educational publisher. We are particularly interested in humorous stories with surprise endings and beginning chapter books."

KAMEHAMEHA PUBLISHING

567 S. King St., Honolulu HI 96813. **Website:** www.kamehamehapublishing.org. Estab. 1933. "Kamehameha Schools Press publishes in the areas of Hawaiian history, Hawaiian culture, Hawaiian language and Hawaiian studies." Call or write for book catalog.

NEEDS Young reader, middle readers, young adults: biography, history, multicultural, Hawaiian folklore.

TERMS Work purchased outright from authors or by royalty agreement. Responds in 3 months.

TIPS "Writers and illustrators must be knowledgeable in Hawaiian history/culture and be able to show credentials to validate their proficiency. Greatly prefer to work with writers/illustrators available in the Honolulu area."

🄰🄼🄾🅂 KANE/MILLER BOOK PUBLISHERS

Kane/Miller: A Division of EDC Publishing, 4901 Morena Blvd., Suite 213, San Diego CA 92117. (858)456-0540. **Fax:** (858)456-9641. **E-mail:** submissions@kanemiller.com. **Website:** www.kanemiller.com. **Contact:** Editorial Department. Estab. 1985. "Kane/Miller Book Publishers is a division of EDC Publishing, specializing in award-winning children's books from around the world. Our books bring the children of the world closer to each other, sharing stories and ideas, while exploring cultural differences and similarities. Although we continue to look for books from other countries, we are now actively seeking works that convey cultures and communities within the U.S. We are looking for picture book fiction and nonfiction on those subjects that may be defined as particularly American: sports such as baseball, historical events, American biographies, American folktales, etc. We are committed to expanding our early and middle-grade fiction list. We're interested in great stories with engaging characters in all genres (mystery, fantasy, adventure, historical, etc.) and, as with picture books, especially those with particularly American subjects. All submissions sent via USPS should be sent to: Editorial Department. Please do not send anything requiring a signature. Work submitted for consideration may also be sent via e-mail. Please send either the complete picture book ms, the published book (with a summary and outline in English, if that is not the language of origin) or a synopsis of the work and 2 sample chapters. Do not send originals. Illustrators may send color copies, tear sheets, or other nonreturnable illustration samples. If you have a website with additional samples of your work, please include the Web address. Please do not send original artwork, or samples on CD. A SASE must be included if you send your submission via USPS; otherwise, you will not receive a reply. If we wish to follow up, we will notify you."

○ "We like to think that a child reading a Kane/Miller book will see parallels between his own life and what might be the unfamiliar setting and characters of the story. And that by seeing how a character who is somehow or in some way dissimilar—an outsider—finds a way to fit comfortably into a culture or community or situation while maintaining a healthy sense of self and self-dignity, she might be empowered to do the same."

NEEDS Picture books: concept, contemporary, health, humor, multicultural. Young readers: contemporary, multicultural, suspense. Middle readers: contemporary, humor, multicultural, suspense.

TERMS Responds in 90 days to queries.

○ KAR-BEN PUBLISHING

Lerner Publishing Group, 241 First Ave., N, Minneapolis MN 55401. (612)215-6229. **Fax:** 612-332-7615. **E-mail:** Editorial@Karben.com. **Website:** www.karben.com. Estab. 1974. Publishes hardcover, trade paperback and electronic originals. Book catalog available online; free upon request. Guidelines available online.

NEEDS "We seek picture book mss of about 1,000 words on Jewish-themed topics for children." Picture books: adventure, concept, folktales, history, humor, multicultural, religion, special needs; must be on a Jewish theme. Average word length: picture books—1,000. Recently published titles: *The Count's Hanukkah Countdown, Sammy Spider's First Book of Jewish Holidays, The Cats of Ben Yehuda Street.*

HOW TO CONTACT Submit full ms. Picture books only.

TERMS Pays 5% royalty on net sale. Pays $500-2,500 advance. Responds in 6 weeks.

TIPS "Authors: Do a literature search to make sure a similar title doesn't already exist. Illustrators: Look at our online catalog for a sense of what we like—bright colors and lively composition."

KELLY POINT PUBLISHING, LLC

Martin Sisters Publishing, LLC, P.O. Box 1154, Barbourville KY 40906. **E-mail:** publisher@kellypoint publishing.com; submissions@kellypointpub lishing.com. **Website:** www.kellypointpublish ing.com. **Contact:** Melissa Newman, publisher. Estab. 2012. Subsidiary of Martin Sisters Publishing, LLC.

Publishes trade paperback, mass-market, and electronic originals. Book catalog available online at website. Guidelines available online or by e-mail.

○ *All unsolicited mss returned unopened.*

IMPRINTS Kelly Point Books, KP Mystery, KP Romance.

NEEDS "Please visit our website and read the submissions guidelines for aspiring authors before submitting your query."

HOW TO CONTACT Query with SASE.

TERMS Pays 7.5% royalty on retail price. Responds in 1 month to queries; 2 months to proposals; 4 months to mss.

TIPS "Write a good query letter with a hook and follow the submissions guidelines on our website."

○ KIDS CAN PRESS

25 Dockside Dr., Toronto ON M5A 0B5 Canada. (416)479-7000. **Fax:** (416)960-5437. **E-mail:** info@kidscan.com; kkalmar@kidscan.com. **Website:** www.kidscanpress.com. **Contact:** Corus Quay, acquisitions. Estab. 1973.

○ *Kids Can Press is currently accepting unsolicited mss from Canadian adult authors only.*

NEEDS Picture books, young readers: concepts. "We do not accept young adult fiction or fantasy novels for any age." Adventure, animal, contemporary, folktales, history, humor, multicultural, nature/environment, special needs, sports, suspense/mystery. Average word length: picture books—1,000-2,000; young readers—750-1,500; middle readers—10,000-15,000; young adults—over 15,000.

HOW TO CONTACT Submit outline/synopsis and 2-3 sample chapters. For picture books submit complete ms.

TERMS Responds in 6 months only if interesed.

○ ALFRED A. KNOPF

Imprint of Random House, 1745 Broadway, New York NY 10019. **Website:** knopfdoubleday.com/imprint/knopf. **Contact:** The Editors. Estab. 1915. Publishes hardcover and paperback originals.

NEEDS Publishes book-length fiction of literary merit by known or unknown writers. Length: 40,000-150,000 words.

HOW TO CONTACT Usually only accepts mss submitted by agents. However, writers may submit sample 25-50 pages with SASE.

TERMS Royalties vary. Offers advance. Responds in 2-6 months to queries.

KNOPF PUBLISHING GROUP

Imprint of Random House, 1745 Broadway, New York NY 10019. (212)751-2600. **Website:** knopfdoubleday.com/imprint/knopf. **Contact:** The Editors. Estab. 1915. Publishes hardcover and paperback originals.

○ Knopf is a general publisher of quality nonfiction and fiction. "We usually only accept work through an agent, but you may still send a query to our slush pile."

IMPRINTS Alfred A. Knopf; Everyman's Library; Pantheon Books; Schocken Books; Vintage Anchor Publishing (Vintage Books, Anchor Books); Doubleday; Black Lizard; Nan A. Talese.

NEEDS Publishes book-length fiction of literary merit by known or unknown writers. Length: 40,000-150,000 words.

HOW TO CONTACT Usually only accepts mss submitted by agents. However, writers may submit sample 25-50 pages with SASE.

KNOX ROBINSON PUBLISHING

244 Fifth Ave., Suite 1861, New York NY 10001. **E-mail:** subs@knoxrobinsonpublishing.com. **Website:** www.knoxrobinsonpublishing.com. **Contact:** Dana Celeste Robinson, managing director (historical fiction, historical romance, fantasy). Estab. 2010. Knox Robinson Publishing is an international, independent, specialist publisher of historical fiction, historical romance and fantasy. Guidelines free on request.

○ "KRP publishes historical fiction and historical romance; any story set in an era prior to 1960 is acceptable. We also publish medieval fantasy. We do not publish science fiction. We do not publish fantasy with children and/or animal protagonists. We do not publish novels that involve any aspects of time travel. We welcome the submission of a well-written, detailed synopsis and the first 3 chapters of completed mss directly from authors."

NEEDS "We are seeking historical fiction featuring obscure historical figures."

HOW TO CONTACT Submit first 3 chapters and author questionnaire found on website.

TERMS Pays royalty. Responds in 2 months to submissions of first 3 chapters. "We do not accept proposals."

⊘ KREGEL PUBLICATIONS

Kregel, Inc., P.O. Box 2607, Grand Rapids MI 49501. (616)451-4775. **Fax:** (616)451-9330. **E-mail:** kregel books@kregel.com. **Website:** www.kregelpublications.com. **Contact:** Dennis R. Hillman, publisher. Estab. 1949. "Our mission as an evangelical Christian publisher is to provide—with integrity and excellence—trusted, Biblically based resources that challenge and encourage individuals in their Christian lives. Works in theology and Biblical studies should reflect the historic, orthodox Protestant tradition." Publishes hardcover and trade paperback originals and reprints. Guidelines online.

○ Finds works through The Writer's Edge and Christian Ms Submissions ms screening services.

IMPRINTS Editorial Portavoz (Spanish-language works); Kregel Academic & Professional; Kregel Kidzone.

NEEDS Fiction should be geared toward the evangelical Christian market. Wants books with fast-paced, contemporary story lines presenting a strong Christian message in an engaging, entertaining style.

TERMS Pays royalty on wholesale price. Pays negotiable advance.

TIPS "Our audience consists of conservative, evangelical Christians, including pastors and ministry students."

⊘⊘ LAUREL-LEAF

Imprint of Random House Children's Books/Random House, Inc., 1745 Broadway, New York NY 10019. (212)782-9000. **Website:** www.randomhouse.com/teens.

○ Quality reprint paperback imprint for young adult paperback books. *Does not accept unsolicited mss.*

⊕ LEDGE HILL PUBLISHING

P.O. Box 337, Alton NH 03809. **E-mail:** info@ledgehillpublishing.com. **Website:** www.ledgehillpublishing.com. **Contact:** Amanda Eason. Estab. 2011. Publishes hardcover, trade paperback, and mass-market paperback originals. Book catalog available online at website. Guidelines free on request by e-mail or online at website.

HOW TO CONTACT Submit proposal package, including syopsis and 4 sample chapters, or submit complete ms.

TERMS Pays 2-15% royalty. Responds in 1 month to queries and proposals; 2 months to mss.

◐ LEE & LOW BOOKS

95 Madison Ave., #1205, New York NY 10016. (212)779-4400. **E-mail:** general@leeandlow.com. **Website:** www.leeandlow.com. **Contact:** Louise May, editor-in-chief (multicultural children's fiction/nonfiction). Estab. 1991. "Our goals are to meet a growing need for books that address children of color and to present literature that all children can identify with. We only consider multicultural children's books. Currently emphasizing material for 5- to 12-year-olds. Sponsors a yearly New Voices Award for first-time picture book authors of color. Contest rules online at website or for SASE." Publishes hardcover originals and trade paperback reprints. Book catalog available online. Guidelines available online or by written request with SASE.

NEEDS Picture books, young readers: anthology, contemporary, history, multicultural, poetry. Picture book, middle reader: contemporary, history, multicultural, nature/environment, poetry, sports. Average word length: picture books—1,000-1,500 words. "We do not publish folklore or animal stories."

HOW TO CONTACT Submit complete ms.

TERMS Pays net royalty. Pays authors advances against royalty. Pays illustrators advance against royalty. Photographers paid advance against royalty. Responds in 6 months to mss if interested.

TIPS "Check our website to see the kinds of books we publish. Do not send mss that don't fit our mission."

⊘ LERNER PUBLISHING GROUP

1251 Washington Ave., N., Minneapolis MN 55401. (800)452-7236; (612)332-3344. **Fax:** (612)337-7615. **E-mail:** editorial@karben.com; photoresearch@lernerbooks.com. **Website:** www.karben.com; www.lernerbooks.com. **Contact:** Director of Photo Research. Estab. 1957. Primarily publishes books for children ages pre-K-18. List includes titles in geography, natural and physical science, current events, ancient and modern history, high interest, sports, world cultures, and numerous biography series. Kar-Ben publishes 10-12 new titles each year. All are books on Jewish themes for children and families. "We are happy to review unsolicited mss and artists' samples. If you wish a response, you MUST include an SASE. Please allow 3-5 weeks for a reply. **Illustrators:** Please submit samples that show skill in children's book illustration. Color photocopies and tear sheets are preferred. Please do not send original art. **Writers:** We consider fiction and nonfiction for preschool through high school, including holiday books, life-cycle stories, Bible tales, folktales, board books, and activity books. In particular, we are looking for stories that reflect the ethnic and cultural diversity of today's Jewish family. We do not publish games, textbooks, or books in Hebrew. Your story should be concise; have interesting, believable characters; and provide action that holds the readers' attention. Good prose is far better than tortured verse."

◐   Starting in 2007, Lerner Publishing Group no longer accepts submissions in any of their imprints except for Kar-Ben Publishing.

HOW TO CONTACT "We will continue to seek targeted solicitations at specific reading levels and in specific subject areas. The company will list these targeted solicitations on our website and in national newsletters, such as the SCBWI *Bulletin*."

LES FIGUES PRESS

P.O. Box 7736, Los Angeles CA 90007. **E-mail:** info@lesfigues.com. **Website:** www.lesfigues.com. **Contact:** Teresa Carmody and Vanessa Place, co-directors. Les Figues Press is an independent, nonprofit publisher of poetry, prose, visual art, conceptual writing, and translation. With a mission is to create aesthetic conversations between readers, writers, and artists, Les Figues Press favors projects which push the boundaries of genre, form, and general acceptability. Submissions are only reviewed through its annual NOS Book Contest.

LETHE PRESS

118 Heritage Ave., Maple Shade NJ 08052. (609)410-7391. **E-mail:** editor@lethepressbooks.com. **Website:** www.lethepressbooks.com. **Contact:** Steve Berman, publisher. Estab. 2001. "Welcomes submissions from authors of any sexual or gender identity." Guidelines online.

NEEDS "Named after the Greek river of memory and forgetfulness (and pronounced Lee-Thee), Lethe Press is a small press devoted to ideas that are often neglected or forgotten by mainstream, profit-oriented publishers." Distributes/promotes titles. Lethe Books are distributed by Ingram Publications and Bookazine, and are available at all major bookstores, as well as the major online retailers.

HOW TO CONTACT Query via e-mail.

ARTHUR A. LEVINE BOOKS

Scholastic, Inc., 557 Broadway, New York NY 10012. (212)343-4436. **Fax:** (212)343-6143. **E-mail:** arthur alevinebooks@scholastic.com. **Website:** www .arthuralevinebooks.com. **Contact:** Arthur A. Levine, VP/publisher; Cheryl Klein, executive editor; Emily Clement, assistant editor. Estab. 1996. Imprint of Scholastic, Inc. Publishes hardcover, paperback, and e-book editions. Guidelines online.

NEEDS "Arthur A. Levine is looking for distinctive literature, for children and young adults, for whatever's extraordinary." Averages 18-20 total titles/year.

HOW TO CONTACT Query.

TERMS Responds in 1 month to queries; 5 months to mss.

LILLENAS PUBLISHING CO.

Imprint of Lillenas Drama Resources, P.O. Box 419527, Kansas City MO 64109. (816)931-1900. **Fax:** (816)412-8390. **E-mail:** drama@lillenas.com. **Website:** www .lillenasdrama.com. "We purchase only original, previously unpublished materials. Also, we require that all scripts be performed at least once before it is submitted for consideration. We do not accept scripts that are sent via fax or e-mail. Direct all mss to the Drama Resources Editor." Publishes mass-market paperback and electronic originals. Guidelines online.

NEEDS "Looking for sketch and monologue collections for all ages—adults, children and youth. For these collections, we request 12-15 scripts to be submitted at 1 time. Unique treatments of spiritual themes, relevant issues, and biblical messages are of interest. Contemporary full-length and one-act plays that have conflict, characterization, and a spiritual context that is neither a sermon nor an apologetic for youth and adults. We also need wholesome so-called secular full-length scripts for dinner theaters and schools." No musicals.

TERMS Pays royalty on net price. Makes outright purchase. Responds in 4-6 months to material.

TIPS "We never receive too many mss."

R.C. LINNELL PUBLISHING

2100 Tyler Ln., Louisville KY 40205. **E-mail:** info@ LinnellPublishing.com. **Website:** www.linnellpub lishing.com. **Contact:** Cheri Powell, owner. Estab. 2010. "We are currently very small and have published a limited number of books. We would review books on other subjects on a case-by-case basis. If a book is well-written and has an audience we would consider

it." Publishes Print-on-Demand paperbacks. Book catalog and guidelines online.

HOW TO CONTACT Submit complete ms.

TERMS Pays 10-40% royalty on retail price. Responds in 1 month to mss.

TIPS "Visit our website to understand the business model and our relationship with authors. All sales are through the Internet. Author should have a marketing plan in mind. We can help expand the plan but we do not market books. Author should be comfortable with using the Internet and should know their intended readers. We offer translation services for English to Spanish and Spanish to English. We are especially interested in books that inspire, motivate, amuse, and challenge readers."

LIQUID SILVER BOOKS

10509 Sedgegrass Dr., Indianapolis IN 46235. **E-mail:** acquisitions@liquidsilverbooks.com. **Website:** www .lsbooks.com. **Contact:** Tracey West, acquisitions editor; Terri Schaefer, editorial director. Estab. 1999. Liquid Silver Books is an imprint of Atlantic Bridge Publishing, a royalty paying, full-service e-publisher. Atlantic Bridge has been in business since June 1999. Liquid Silver Books is dedicated to bringing high-quality erotic romance to our readers.

"We are foremost an e-publisher. We believe the market will continue to grow for e-books. It is our prime focus. At this time our print publishing is on hiatus. We will update the submission guidelines if we reinstate this aspect of our publishing."

NEEDS Needs contemporary, gay and lesbian, paranormal, supernatural, science fiction, fantasy, historical, suspense, and western romances. "We do not accept literary erotica submissions."

HOW TO CONTACT E-mail entire ms as an attachment in .rtf file in Arial 12 pt. "Include in the body of the e-mail: author bio, your thoughts on e-publishing, a blurb of your book, including title and series title if applicable. Ms must include pen name, real name, snail mail and e-mail contact information on the first page, top left corner."

TERMS Responds to mss in 4-6 weeks.

LITTLE, BROWN AND CO. ADULT TRADE BOOKS

237 Park Ave., New York NY 10017. **E-mail:** public-ity@littlebrown.com. **Website:** www.hachettebook-group.com. **Contact:** Michael Pietsch, publisher. Es-

tab. 1837. "The general editorial philosophy for all divisions continues to be broad and flexible, with high quality and the promise of commercial success always the first considerations." Publishes hardcover originals and paperback originals and reprints. Guidelines online.

HOW TO CONTACT *Agented submissions only.*

TERMS Pays royalty. Offer advance.

ⒶⓄ LITTLE, BROWN AND CO. BOOKS FOR YOUNG READERS

Hachette Book Group USA, 237 Park Ave., New York NY 10017. (212)364-1100. **Fax:** (212)364-0925. **E-mail:** pamela.gruber@hbgusa.com. **Website:** www.lb-kids.com; www.lb-teens.com. Estab. 1837. "Little, Brown and Co. Children's Publishing publishes all formats including board books, picture books, middle-grade fiction, and nonfiction young adult titles. We are looking for strong writing and presentation, but no predetermined topics." *Only interested in solicited agented material.*

NEEDS Picture books: humor, adventure, animal, contemporary, history, multicultural, folktales. Young adults: contemporary, humor, multicultural, suspense/mystery, chick lit. Multicultural needs include "any material by, for, and about minorities." Average word length: picture books—1,000; young readers—6,000; middle readers—15,000-50,000; young adults—50,000 and up.

HOW TO CONTACT *Agented submissions only.*

TERMS Pays authors royalties based on retail price. Pays illustrators and photographers by the project or royalty based on retail price. Sends galleys to authors; dummies to illustrators. Pays negotiable advance. Responds in 1 month to queries; 2 months to proposals and mss.

TIPS "In order to break into the field, authors and illustrators should research their competition and try to come up with something outstandingly different."

⦿ LITTLE TIGER PRESS

1 The Coda Centre, 189 Munster Rd., London En SW6 6AW United Kingdom. (44)20-7385 6333. **E-mail:** info@littletiger.co.uk; malperin@littletiger.co.uk. **Website:** www.littletigerpress.com.

NEEDS Picture books: animal, concept, contemporary, humor. Average word length: picture books—750 words or less.

TIPS "We take every reasonable care of the mss and samples we receive, but we cannot accept responsibility for any loss or damage. Try to read or look at as many books on the Little Tiger Press list before sending your material. Refer to our website for further details."

⦿ LIVINGSTON PRESS

University of West Alabama, Station 22, Livingston AL 35470. **E-mail:** jwt@uwa.edu. **Website:** www.livingstonpress.uwa.edu. **Contact:** Joe Taylor, director. Estab. 1974. "Livingston Press, as do all literary presses, looks for authorial excellence in style. Currently emphasizing novels." No open reading period. Check back for details. Publishes hardcover and trade paperback originals. Book catalog for SASE. Guidelines online.

IMPRINTS Swallow's Tale Press.

NEEDS "We are interested in form and, of course, style."

TERMS Pays 150 contributor's copies, after sales of 1,500, standard royalty. Responds in 1 month to queries; 6-12 months to mss.

TIPS "Our readers are interested in literature, often quirky literature that emphasizes form and style. Please visit our website for current needs."

ⓄⓈ LOOSE ID

P.O. Box 425690, San Francisco CA 94142-5960. **E-mail:** submissions@loose-id.com. **Website:** www.loose-id.com. **Contact:** Treva Harte, editor-in-chief. Estab. 2004. "*Loose Id* is love unleashed. We're taking romance to the edge." Publishes e-books and some print books. Distributes/promotes titles. "The company promotes itself through web and print advertising wherever readers of erotic romance may be found. We are currently pursuing licensing agreements for foreign translations and have a print program of 2 to 5 titles per month." Guidelines online.

💬 "Loose Id is actively acquiring stories from both aspiring and established authors."

NEEDS Wants nontraditional erotic romance stories, including gay, lesbian, heroes and heroines, multiculturalism, cross-genre, fantasy, and science fiction, straight contemporary, or historical romances.

HOW TO CONTACT Query with outline/synopsis and 3 sample chapters. Accepts queries by e-mail. Include estimated word count, list of publishing credits, and why your submission is love unleashed. "Before submitting a query or proposal, please read the guidelines on our website. Please don't hesitate to contact us by e-mail for any information you don't see there."

TERMS Pays e-book royalties of 40%. Responds to queries in 1 month.

◐ LOST HORSE PRESS

105 Lost Horse Lane, Sandpoint ID 83864. (208)255-4410. **E-mail:** losthorsepress@mindspring.com. **Website:** www.losthorsepress.org. **Contact:** Christine Holbert, publisher; Carolyne Wright, editor; Christi Kramer, editor. Estab. 1998. Distributed by University of Washington Press. Publishes hardcover and paperback originals.

○ *"Does not accept unsolicited mss.* However, we welcome submissions for the *Idaho Prize for Poetry*, a national competition offering $1,000 prize money plus publication for a book length ms. Please check the submission guidelines for the *Idaho Prize for Poetry* online."

LOUISIANA STATE UNIVERSITY PRESS

3990 W. Lakeshore Dr., Baton Rouge LA 70808. (225)578-6294. **Fax:** (225)578-6461. **E-mail:** mkc@lsu.edu. **Website:** www.lsupress.org. **Contact:** MK Callaway, director. Estab. 1935. Publishes in the fall and spring. Publishes hardcover and paperback originals, and reprints. Publishes 8 poetry titles per year and 2 works of original fiction as part of the Yellow Shoe Fiction series. Book catalog and ms guidelines free and online.

HOW TO CONTACT Query with SASE. Submit proposal package, sample chapters, résumé, clips, and cover letter.

TERMS Pays royalty. Responds in 1 month to queries.

LUCKY MARBLE BOOKS

PageSpring Publishing, P.O. Box 21133, Columbus OH 43221. **E-mail:** yaeditor@pagespringpublishing.com. **Website:** www.luckymarblebooks.com. Estab. 2012. "Lucky Marble Books publishes novel-length young adult and middle-grade fiction. We are looking for engaging characters and well-crafted plots that keep our readers turning the page. We accept e-mail queries only; see our website for details." Publishes trade paperback and electronic originals. Guidelines online.

HOW TO CONTACT Submit proposal package via e-mail. Include synopsis and 3 sample chapters.

TERMS Pays royalty. Responds in 3 months to queries and mss.

TIPS "We love books that jump right into the story and sweep us along!"

MAGINATION PRESS

750 First St. NE, Washington DC 20002. (202)336-5618. **Fax:** (202)336-5624. **E-mail:** rteeter@apa.org. **Website:** www.apa.org. **Contact:** Kristine Enderle, managing editor. Estab. 1988. Magination Press is an imprint of the American Psychological Association. "We publish books dealing with the psycho/therapeutic resolution of children's problems and psychological issues with a strong self-help component." Submit complete ms. Materials returned only with SASE.

NEEDS All levels: psychological and social issues, self-help, health, parenting concerns, and special needs. Picture books, middle-school readers.

TERMS Responds to queries in 1-2 months; mss in 2-6 months.

MAIN STREET RAG PUBLISHING COMPANY

P.O. Box 690100, Charlotte NC 28227. (704)573-2516. **E-mail:** editor@mainstreetrag.com. **Website:** www.mainstreetrag.com. **Contact:** M. Scott Douglass, publisher, editor. Estab. 1996. "There are 4 ways to get a book of poetry published: 1) self-publish using our imprint; 2) Enter one of our contests; 3) Be invited; 4) Be recommended."

○ Main Street Rag (our poetry label); Mint Hill Books (fiction label); Pure Heart Press (self-publishing label).

NEEDS "See current themes online. Address to Short Fiction Anthology for consideration for our anthology. We are not open to unsolicited submissions of full-length mss of short fiction."

HOW TO CONTACT Query with SASE. Submit 2 short stories.

TERMS Responds in 3-6 weeks to queries.

TIPS "You can request a free electronic newsletter which is a reference for writers, readers, and publishers by providing limited information and directing them to links and e-mails. Current features include: Call for Submissions; Contests; and New Releases. (No e-mail submissions unless overseas, reviews, images, subscribers to *The Mainstreet Rag*.) In all cases, query prior to submitting for instructions."

MANDALA PUBLISHING

Mandala Publishing and Earth Aware Editions, 10 Paul Dr., San Rafael CA 94903. **E-mail:** info@mandalapublishing.com. **Website:** www.mandalapublishing.com. Estab. 1989. "In the traditions of the East, wisdom, truth, and beauty go hand-in-hand.

This is reflected in the great arts, music, yoga, and philosophy of India. Mandala Publishing strives to bring to its readers authentic and accessible renderings of thousands of years of wisdom and philosophy from these unique, culture-timeless treasures that are our inspirations and guides. At Mandala, we believe that the arts, health, ecology, and spirituality of the great Vedic traditions are as relevant today as they were in sacred India thousands of years ago. As a distinguished publisher in the world of Vedic literature, lifestyle, and interests today, Mandala strives to provide accessible and meaningful works for the modern reader." Publishes hardcover, trade paperback, and electronic originals. Book catalog online.

HOW TO CONTACT Query with SASE.

TERMS Pays 3-15% royalty on retail price. Responds in 6 months.

MANOR HOUSE PUBLISHING, INC.

452 Cottingham Crescent, Ancaster ON L9G 3V6 Canada. **E-mail:** mbdavie@manor-house.biz. **Website:** www.manor-house.biz. **Contact:** Mike Davie, president (novels, poetry, and nonfiction). Estab. 1998. Publishes hardcover, trade paperback, and mass-market paperback originals reprints. Book catalog available online. Guidelines available via e-mail.

NEEDS Stories should have Canadian settings and characters should be Canadian, but content should have universal appeal to wide audience.

HOW TO CONTACT Query via e-mail. Submit proposal package, clips, bio, 3 sample chapters. Submit complete ms.

TERMS Pays 10% royalty on retail price. Queries and mss to be sent by e-mail only. "We will respond in 30 days if interested. If not, there is no response. Do not follow up unless asked to do so."

TIPS "Our audience includes everyone—the general public/mass audience. Self-edit your work first, and make sure it is well written with strong Canadian content."

MARINE TECHNIQUES PUBLISHING

126 Western Ave., Suite 266, Augusta ME 04330. (207)622-7984. **E-mail:** info@marinetechpub lishing.com. **Website:** www.marinetechpublish ing.com. **Contact:** James L. Pelletier, president/owner (commercial maritime); Maritime Associates Globally (commercial maritime). Estab. 1983. "Publishes only books related to the commercial marine/maritime industry." Trade paperback originals and re-

prints. Book catalog available online, by e-mail, and for #10 SASE for $5. Guidelines available by e-mail, and for #10 SASE for $5.

NEEDS Must be commercial maritime/marine related.

HOW TO CONTACT Submit proposal package, including all sample chapters. Submit complete ms.

TERMS Pays 25-55% royalty on wholesale or retail price. Makes outright purchase. Responds in 2 months.

TIPS "Audience consists of commercial marine/maritime firms, persons employed in all aspects of the marine/maritime commercial water transportation–related industries and recreational fresh and salt water fields, persons interested in seeking employment in the commercial marine industry; firms seeking to sell their products and services to vessel owners, operators, and managers; shipyards, vessel repair yards, recreational and yacht boat building, and national and international ports and terminals involved with the commercial marine industry globally worldwide, etc."

MARTIN SISTERS PUBLISHING, LLC

P.O. Box 1749, Barbourville KY 40906-1499. **E-mail:** submissions@martinsisterspublishing.com. **Website:** www.martinsisterspublishing.com. **Contact:** Denise Melton, publisher/editor (fiction/nonfiction); Melissa Newman, publisher/editor (fiction/nonfiction). Estab. 2011. Firm/imprint publishes trade and mass-market paperback originals; electronic originals. Catalog and guidelines available online.

IMPRINTS Ivy House Books—literary/mainstream fiction; rainshower books—christian fiction and nonfiction; Skyvine Books—science fiction/fantasy/paranormal; romance; Martin Sisters Books—nonfiction/short story collections/coffee table books/cookbooks; Barefoot Books—young adult. Query Ms. Newman or Ms. Melton for all imprints listed.

HOW TO CONTACT Send query letter only.

TERMS Pays 7.5% royalty/maximum on retail price. No advance offered. Responds in 1 month on queries, 2 months on proposals, 3-6 months on mss.

MARVEL COMICS

10 E. 40th St., New York NY 10016. **Website:** www .marvel.com. Publishes hardcover originals and reprints, trade paperback reprints, mass-market comic book originals, electronic reprints. Guidelines available online.

NEEDS Our shared universe needs new heroes and villains; books for younger readers and teens needed.

HOW TO CONTACT Submit inquiry letter, idea submission form (download from website), SASE.

TERMS Pays on a per-page, work-for-hire basis or creator owned, which is then contracted. Pays negotiable advance. Responds in 3-5 weeks to queries.

MAVERICK MUSICALS AND PLAYS

89 Bergann Rd., Maleny QLD 4552 Australia. **Phone/Fax:** (61)(7)5494-4007. **E-mail:** gail@mavmuse.com. **Website:** www.mavmuse.com. Estab. 1978. Guidelines available online.

NEEDS "Looking for two-act musicals and one- and two-act plays. See website for more details."

MCBOOKS PRESS

ID Booth Building, 520 N. Meadow St., Ithaca NY 14850. (607)272-2114. **Fax:** (607)273-6068. **E-mail:** mcbooks@mcbooks.com. **Website:** www.mcbooks.com. **Contact:** Alexander G. Skutt, publisher. Estab. 1979. Publishes trade paperback and hardcover originals and reprints. Guidelines available online.

"Currently not accepting submissions or queries for fiction or nonfiction."

NEEDS Publishes Julian Stockwin, John Biggins, Colin Sargent, and Douglas W. Jacobson. Distributes titles through Independent Publishers Group.

TIPS "We are currently only publishing authors with whom we have a pre-existing relationship. If this policy changes, we will announce the change on our website."

THE MCDONALD & WOODWARD PUBLISHING CO.

431 E. College St., Granville OH 43023. (740)321-1140. **Fax:** (740)321-1141. **E-mail:** mwpubco@mwpubco.com. **Website:** www.mwpubco.com. **Contact:** Jerry N. McDonald, publisher. Estab. 1986. McDonald & Woodward publishes books in natural history, cultural history, and natural resources. Currently emphasizing travel, natural and cultural history, and natural resource conservation. Publishes hardcover and trade paperback originals. Book catalog online. Guidelines free on request; by e-mail.

HOW TO CONTACT Query with SASE.

TERMS Pays 10% royalty. Responds in less than 1 month.

TIPS "Our books are meant for the curious and educated elements of the general population."

MARGARET K. MCELDERRY BOOKS

Imprint of Simon & Schuster Children's Publishing Division, 1230 Sixth Ave., New York NY 10020. (212)698-7200. **Website:** www.simonsayskids.com. **Contact:** Justin Chanda, vice president; Karen Wojtyla, editorial director; Gretchen Hirsch, associate editor; Emily Fabre, assistant editor; Ann Bobco, executive art director. Estab. 1971. "Margaret K. McElderry Books publishes hardcover and paperback trade books for children from preschool age through young adult. This list includes picture books, middle-grade and teen fiction, poetry, and fantasy. The style and subject matter of the books we publish are almost unlimited. We do not publish textbooks, coloring and activity books, greeting cards, magazines, pamphlets, or religious publications." Guidelines for #10 SASE.

NEEDS We will consider any category. Results depend on the quality of the imagination, the artwork, and the writing. Average word length: picture books—500; young readers—2,000; middle readers—10,000-20,000; young adults—45,000-50,000. *No unsolicited mss.*

HOW TO CONTACT Send query letter with SASE.

TERMS Pays author royalty based on retail price. Pays illustrator royalty by the project. Pays photographers by the project. Original artwork returned at job's completion. Offers $5,000-8,000 advance for new authors.

TIPS "Read! The children's book field is competitive. See what's been done and what's out there before submitting. We look for high quality: an originality of ideas, clarity, and felicity of expression, a well-organized plot, and strong character-driven stories. We're looking for strong original fiction, especially mysteries and middle-grade humor. We are always interested in picture books for the youngest age reader. Study our titles."

MEDALLION MEDIA GROUP

100 S. River St., Aurora IL 60506. (630)513-8316. **E-mail:** emily@medallionmediagroup.com. **E-mail:** submissions@medallionmediagroup.com. **Website:** medallionmediagroup.com. **Contact:** Emily Steele, editorial director. Estab. 2003. "We are an independent, innovative publisher looking for compelling, memorable stories told in distinctive voices." Publishes trade paperback, hardcover, e-book originals, book apps, and TREEbook.™ Guidelines online.

NEEDS Word count: 40,000-90,000 for young adult; 60,000-120,000 for all others. No short stories, anthologies, erotica.

HOW TO CONTACT Submit first 3 consecutive chapters and a synopsis through our online submission form.

TERMS Offers advance. Responds in 2-3 months to mss.

TIPS "We are not affected by trends. We are simply looking for well-crafted, original, compelling works of fiction and nonfiction. Please visit our website for the most current guidelines prior to submitting anything to us."

⊕ MELANGE BOOKS, LLC

White Bear Lake MN 55110-5538. **E-mail:** melange books@melange-books.com. **E-mail:** submissions@ melange-books.com. **Website:** www.melange-books .com. **Contact:** Nancy Schumacher, publisher and acquiring editor for Melange and Satin Romance; Caroline Andrus, acquiring editor for Fire and Ice for Young Adult. Estab. 2011. Melange is a royalty-paying company publishing e-books and print books. Publishes trade paperback originals and electronic originals. Send SASE for book catalog. Send SASE for mss guidelines or review them online.

IMPRINTS Imprints include Fire and Ice for Young and New Adults and Satin Romance.

NEEDS Submit a clean mss by following guidelines on website.

HOW TO CONTACT Query electronically by clicking on *Submissions* on website. Include a synopsis and 4 chapters.

TERMS Authors receive a minimum of 20% royalty on print sales, 40% on electronic book sales. Does not offer an advance. Responds in 1 month on queries, 2 months on proposals, and 4-6 months on mss.

MERIWETHER PUBLISHING LTD.

885 Elkton Dr., Colorado Springs CO 80907. (719)594-9916. **Fax:** (719)594-4422. **E-mail:** editor@meriweth er.com. **Website:** www.meriwether.com. **Contact:** Ted Zapel; Rhonda Wray. Estab. 1969. "Our niche is drama. Our books cover a wide variety of theater-subjects from play anthologies to theater craft. We publish books of monologues, duologues, short one-act plays, scenes for students, acting textbooks, how-to speech and theater textbooks, improvisation and theater games. We also publish anthologies of Chris-

tian sketches. We do not publish works of fiction or devotionals."

NEEDS Middle readers, young adults: anthology, contemporary, humor, religion. "We publish plays, not prose fiction. Our emphasis is comedy plays instead of educational themes."

TERMS Pays authors royalty of 10% based on retail or wholesale price. Responds to queries in 3 weeks, mss in 2 months or less.

TIPS "We are currently interested in finding unique treatments for theater arts subjects: scene books, how-to books, musical comedy scripts, monologues and short comedy plays for teens."

MERRIAM PRESS

133 Elm St., Suite 3R, Bennington VT 05201. (802)447-0313. **E-mail:** ray@merriam-press.com. **Website:** www.merriam-press.com. Estab. 1988. "Merriam Press specializes in military history, particularly World War II history. We are also branching out into other genres." Publishes hardcover and softcover trade paperback originals and reprints Book catalog available for $5 or visit website to view all available titles and access writer's guidelines and info.

NEEDS Especially but not limited to military, war, World War II.

HOW TO CONTACT Query with SASE or by e-mail first.

TERMS Pays 10% royalty on actual selling price. Responds quickly (e-mail preferred) to queries.

TIPS "Our military history books are geared for military historians, collectors, model-kit builders, war gamers, veterans, general enthusiasts. We now publish some historical fiction and poetry and will consider well-written books on a variety of non-military topics."

MESSIANIC JEWISH PUBLISHERS

6120 Day Long Lane, Clarksville MD 21029. (410)531-6644. **E-mail:** website@messianicjewish.net. **Website:** www.messianicjewish.net. **Contact:** Janet Chaier, managing editor. Publishes hardcover and trade paperback originals and reprints. Guidelines available via e-mail.

IMPRINTS Lederer Books.

NEEDS "We publish very little fiction. Jewish or Biblical themes are a must. Text must demonstrate keen awareness of Jewish culture and thought."

HOW TO CONTACT Query with SASE. Unsolicited mss are not return

TERMS Pays 7-15% royalty on wholesale price.

◉ MILKWEED EDITIONS

1011 Washington Ave. S., Suite 300, Minneapolis MN 55415. (612)332-3192. **Fax:** (612)215-2550. **E-mail:** submissions@milkweed.org. **Website:** www.milkweed.org. Estab. 1979. "Milkweed Editions publishes with the intention of making a humane impact on society, in the belief that literature is a transformative art uniquely able to convey the essential experiences of the human heart and spirit. To that end, Milkweed Editions publishes distinctive voices of literary merit in handsomely designed, visually dynamic books, exploring the ethical, cultural, and esthetic issues that free societies need continually to address." Publishes hardcover, trade paperback, and electronic originals; trade paperback and electronic reprints. Book catalog online. Guidelines online.

NEEDS Novels for adults and for readers ages 8-13. High literary quality. For adult readers: literary fiction, nonfiction, poetry, essays. Middle readers: adventure, contemporary, fantasy, multicultural, nature/environment, suspense/mystery. Average length: middle readers—90-200 pages. No romance, mysteries, science fiction.

HOW TO CONTACT Query with SASE, submit completed ms.

TERMS Pays authors variable royalty based on retail price. Offers advance against royalties. Pays varied advance from $500-10,000. Responds in 6 months.

TIPS "We are looking for excellent writing with the intent of making a humane impact on society. Please read submission guidelines before submitting, and acquaint yourself with our books in terms of style and quality before submitting. Many factors influence our selection process, so don't get discouraged. Nonfiction is focused on literary writing about the natural world, including living well in urban environments."

MILKWEED FOR YOUNG READERS

Milkweed Editions, Open Book Building, 1011 Washington Ave. S., Suite 300, Minneapolis MN 55415. (612)332-3192. **Fax:** (612)215-2550. **E-mail:** submissions@milkweed.org. **Website:** www.milkweed.org. Estab. 1984. "We are looking first of all for high-quality literary writing. We publish books with the intention of making a humane impact on society." Publishes hardcover and trade paperback originals. Book catalog for $1.50. Guidelines for #10 SASE or on the website.

HOW TO CONTACT Query with SASE. "Milkweed Editions now accepts mss online through our Submission Manager. If you're a first-time submitter, you'll need to fill in a simple form and then follow the instructions for selecting and uploading your ms. Please make sure that your ms follows the submission guidelines."

TERMS Pays 7% royalty on retail price. Pays variable advance. Responds in 6 months to queries.

◉⑤ MONDIAL

203 W. 107th St., Suite 6C, New York NY 10025. (212)851-3252. **Fax:** (208)361-2863. **E-mail:** contact@mondialbooks.com. **Website:** www.mondialbooks.com; www.librejo.com. **Contact:** Andrew Moore, editor. Estab. 1996. Publishes hard cover, trade paperback originals and reprints. Guidelines available online.

HOW TO CONTACT Query through online submission form.

TERMS Pays 10% royalty on wholesale price. Responds to queries in 3 months. Responds only if interested.

◉⊘ MOODY PUBLISHERS

Moody Bible Institute, 820 N. LaSalle Blvd., Chicago IL 60610. (800)678-8812. **Fax:** (312)329-4157. **E-mail:** authors@moody.edu. **Website:** www.moodypublishers.org. Estab. 1894. "The mission of Moody Publishers is to educate and edify the Christian and to evangelize the non-Christian by ethically publishing conservative, evangelical Christian literature and other media for all ages around the world, and to help provide resources for Moody Bible Institute in its training of future Christian leaders." Publishes hardcover, trade, and mass-market paperback originals. Book catalog for 9×12 envelope and 4 first-class stamps. Guidelines for SASE and on website.

IMPRINTS Northfield Publishing; Lift Every Voice (African-American interest).

HOW TO CONTACT Agented submissions only.

TERMS Royalty varies. Responds in 2-3 months to queries.

TIPS "In our fiction list, we're looking for Christian storytellers rather than teachers trying to present a message. Your motivation should be to delight the reader. Using your skills to create beautiful works is glorifying to God."

THE NAUTICAL & AVIATION PUBLISHING CO.

845 A Low Country Blvd., Mt. Pleasant SC 29464. (843)856-0561. **Fax:** (843)856-3164. **Website:** www.nauticalaviation.bizland.com. **Contact:** Denise K. James. Estab. 1979. Publishes hardcover and trade paperback originals and reprints. Book catalog and guidelines available free.

HOW TO CONTACT Submit complete ms with cover letter and brief synopsis.

TERMS Pays royalty.

TIPS "We are primarily a nonfiction publisher, but we will review historical fiction of military interest with strong literary merit."

NBM PUBLISHING

160 Broadway, Suite 700, East Bldg., New York NY 10038. **E-mail:** nbmgn@nbmpub.com. **Website:** nbmpub.com. **Contact:** Terry Nantier, editor/art director. Estab. 1976. "One of the best-regarded quality graphic novel publishers. Our catalog is determined by what will appeal to a wide audience of readers." Publishes hardcover originals, paperback originals. Format: offset printing; perfect binding, e-books. Average print order: 3,000-4,000; average debut writer's print order: 2,000. Publishes 1 debut writers/year. Publishes 20 titles/year. Member: PMA, CBC. Distributed/promoted by IPG. Imprints: ComicsLit (literary comics), Eurotica (erotic comics). Publishes graphic novels for an audience of young adults/adults. Types of books include fiction, mystery, and social parodies.

NEEDS literary fiction mostly, children's/juvenile (especially fairy tales, classics), creative nonfiction (especially true crime), erotica, ethnic/multicultural, humor (satire), manga, mystery/suspense, translations, young adult/teen. Does not want superhero or overly violent comics.

HOW TO CONTACT Prefers submissions from writer-artists, creative teams. Send a one-page synopsis of story along with a few pages of comics (copies, NOT originals) and an SASE, or submit by e-mail. Attends San Diego Comicon. Agented submissions: 2%. Responds to queries in 1 week; to ms/art packages in 3-4 weeks. Sometimes comments on rejected mss.

TERMS Royalties and advance negotiable. Publishes ms 6 months to 1 year after acceptance. Writer's guidelines on website. Artist's guidelines on website. Book catalog free upon request.

NEW ISSUES POETRY & PROSE

Western Michigan University, 1903 W. Michigan Ave., Kalamazoo MI 49008-5463. (269)387-8185. **Fax:** (269)387-2562. **E-mail:** new-issues@wmich.edu. **Website:** wmich.edu/newissues. **Contact:** Managing Editor. Estab. 1996. Guidelines online.

HOW TO CONTACT Only considers submissions to book contests.

NEW LIBRI PRESS

4230 95th Ave. SE, Mercer Island WA 98040. **E-mail:** query@newlibri.com. **Website:** www.newlibri.com. **Contact:** Michael Muller, editor; Stanislav Fritz, editor. Estab. 2011. Publishes trade paperback, electronic original, electronic reprints. Catalog online. Guidelines online.

NEEDS "Open to most ideas right now; this will change as we mature as a press. As a new press, we are more open than most and time will probably shape the direction. That said, trite as it is, we want good writing that is fun to read. While we currently are not looking for some subgenres, if it is well written and a bit off the beaten path, submit to us. We are e-book focused. We may not create a paper version if the e-book does not sell, which means some fiction may be less likely to currently sell (e.g., picture books would work only on an iPad or Color Nook as of this writing)."

HOW TO CONTACT Submit proposal package, including synopsis. Prefers complete ms.

TERMS Pays 20-35% royalty on wholesale price. No advance. Responds in 1 month to mss.

TIPS "Our audience is people who are comfortable reading an e-book or people who are tired of the recycled authors of mainstream publishing, but who still want a good, relatively fast reading experience. The industry is changing. While we accept submissions for the traditional model, we are searching for writers who are interested in sharing the risk and controlling their own destiny. We embrace writers with no agent."

NEW VICTORIA PUBLISHERS

2455 W. Warner Ave., Chicago IL 60613. (773)793-2244. **E-mail:** newvictoriapub@att.net. **Website:** www.newvictoria.com. **Contact:** Patricia Feuerhaken, president. Estab. 1976. "Publishes mostly lesbian fiction—strong female protagonists. Best known for Stoner McTavish mystery series." Distributes titles through Amazon Books, Bella books, Bulldog Books (Sydney, Australia), and Women and Children First Books (Chicago). Promotes titles "mostly through lesbian feminist media." Publishes trade paperback originals. Catalog free on request; for #10 SASE or online. Guidelines free on request; for #10 SASE or online.

NEEDS Lesbian, feminist fiction including adventure, erotica, fantasy, historical, humor, mystery (amateur sleuth), or science fiction.

HOW TO CONTACT Accepts unsolicited mss but prefers query first. Submit outline, synopsis, and sample chapters (50 pages). No queries by e-mail or fax; please send SASE or IRC. No simultaneous submissions.

TERMS Pays 10% royalty.

TIPS "We are especially interested in lesbian or feminist novels, ideally with a character or characters who can evolve through a series of books. Stories should involve a complex plot, accurate details, and protagonists with full emotional lives. Pay attention to plot and character development. Read guidelines carefully. We advise you to look through our catalog or to visit our website to see our past editorial decisions as well as what we are currently marketing. Our books average 80,000-100,000 words, or 200-220 single-spaced pages."

NORTH ATLANTIC BOOKS

2526 MLK Jr. Way, Berkeley CA 94704. **Website:** www.northatlanticbooks.com. **Contact:** Douglas Reil, associate publisher; Erin Wiegand, senior acquisitions editor. Estab. 1974. Publishes hardcover, trade paperback, and electronic originals; trade paperback and electronic reprints. Book catalog free on request (if available). Guidelines online.

IMPRINTS Evolver Editions, Blue Snake Books.

NEEDS "We only publish fiction on rare occasions."

HOW TO CONTACT Submit proposal package including an outline, 3-4 sample chapters, and "a 75-word statement about the book, your qualifications as an author, marketing plan/audience for the book, and comparable titles."

TERMS Pays royalty percentage on wholesale price. Responds in 3-6 months.

NORTIA PRESS

Santa Ana CA **E-mail:** acquisitions@nortiapress.com. **Website:** www.nortiapress.com. Estab. 2009. Publishes trade paperback and electronic originals.

NEEDS "We focus mainly on nonfiction as well as literary and historical fiction but are open to other genres. No vampire stories, science fiction, or erotica, please."

HOW TO CONTACT Submit a brief e-mail query. Please include a short bio, approximate word count of book, and expected date of completion (fiction titles should be completed before sending a query and should contain a sample chapter in the body of the e-mail). All unsolicited snail mail or attachments will be discarded without review.

TERMS Pays negotiable royalties on wholesale price. Responds in 1 month to queries and proposals.

TIPS "We specialize in working with experienced authors who seek a more collaborative and fulfilling relationship with their publisher. As such, we are less likely to accept pitches form first-time authors, no matter how good the idea. As with any pitch, please make your e-mail very brief and to the point, so the reader is not forced to skim it. Always include some biographic information. Your life is interesting."

W.W. NORTON & COMPANY, INC.

500 Fifth Ave., New York NY 10110. (212)354-5500. **Fax:** (212)869-0856. **Website:** www.wwnorton.com. **Contact:** Trish Marks. Estab. 1923. "W.W. Norton & Company, the oldest and largest publishing house owned wholly by its employees, strives to carry out the imperative of its founder to 'publish books not for a single season, but for the years.' Fiction, nonfiction, poetry, college textbooks, cookbooks, art books and professional books."

"Due to the workload of our editorial staff and the large volume of materials we receive, *Norton is no longer able to accept unsolicited submissions.* If you are seeking publication, we suggest working with a literary agent who will represent you to the house."

OAK TREE PRESS

1820 W. Lacy Blvd., #220, Hanford CA 93230. **E-mail:** query@oaktreebooks.com. **Website:** www.oaktreebooks.com. **Contact:** Billie Johnson, publisher (mysteries, romance, nonfiction); Sarah Wasson, acquisitions editor (all); Barbara Hoffman, senior editor (children's, young adult, educational). Estab. 1998. "Oak Tree Press is an independent publisher that celebrates writers and is dedicated to the many great unknowns who are just waiting for the opportunity to break into print. We're looking for mainstream fiction, genre fiction, narrative nonfiction, how-to. Sponsors 3 contests annually: Dark Oak Mystery, Timeless Love Romance, and CopTales for true crime and other stories of law enforcement professionals." Publishes trade paperback and hardcover books. Catalog and guidelines online.

"I am always on the lookout for good mysteries, ones that engage quickly. I definitely want to add to our Timeless Love list. I am also looking at a lot of nonfiction, especially in the 'how-to' category. We are one of a few publishers who will consider memoirs, especially memoirs of folks who are not famous, and this is because I enjoy reading them myself. In addition, plans are in progress to launch a political/current affairs imprint, and I am actively looking for titles to build this list. Then, of course, there is always that 'special something' book that you can't quite describe, but you know it when you see it."

NEEDS Emphasis on mystery and romance novels. "No science fiction or fantasy novels, or stories set far into the future. Novels that are substantially longer than our stated word count are not considered, regardless of genre. We look for mss of 70,000-90,000 words. If the story really charms us, we will bend some on either end of the range. No right-wing political or racist agenda, gratuitous sex or violence, especially against women or depicting the harm of animals."

HOW TO CONTACT Does not accept or return unsolicited mss. Query with SASE. Accepts queries by e-mail. Include estimated word count, brief bio, list of publishing credits, brief description of ms.

TERMS Royalties based on sales. No advance. Responds in 4-6 weeks.

TIPS "Perhaps my most extreme pet peeve is receiving queries for projects which we've clearly advertised we don't want: science fiction, fantasy, epic tomes, bigoted diatribes, and so on. Second to that is a practice I call 'over-taping,' or the use of yards and yards of tape to seal your package, or worse yet, using the filament tape so that it takes forever to open the package. Finding story pitches on my voice mail is also annoying."

OCEANVIEW PUBLISHING

595 Bay Isles Rd., Suite 120-G, Longboat Key FL 34228. **E-mail:** submissions@oceanviewpub.com. **Website:** www.oceanviewpub.com. **Contact:** Robert Gussin, CEO. Estab. 2006. "Independent publisher of nonfiction and fiction, with primary interests in original mystery, thriller, and suspense titles. Accepts new and established writers." Publishes hard-

cover and electronic originals. Catalog and guidelines available online.

NEEDS Accepting adult mss with a primary interest in the mystery, thriller, and suspense genres—from new and established writers. No children's or young adult literature, poetry, cookbooks, technical manuals or short stories.

HOW TO CONTACT Within body of e-mail only, include author's name and brief bio (indicate whether this is an agented submission); ms title and word count; author's mailing address, phone number, and e-mail address. Attached to the e-mail should be the following: A synopsis of 750 words or fewer. The first 30 pages of the ms. Please note that we accept only Word documents as attachments to the submission e-mail. Do not send query letters or proposals.

TERMS Responds in 3 months on mss.

OLD HARBOUR PRESS

1723 Forest Hill Dr., Greenville NC 27858. **E-mail:** editor@oldharbourpress.com. **E-mail:** editor@oldharbourpress.com. **Website:** www.oldharbourpress.com. **Contact:** Paul Morin, editor. Estab. 2013. Old Harbour Press is a small, independent publisher located in Greenville, North Carolina, that aims to deliver quality, contemporary travel and cross-cultural literature, both fiction and nonfiction. Publishes hardcover originals, trade paperback originals and reprints, and electronic originals and reprints. Send SAE for catalog. Send SAE for ms guidelines.

NEEDS "We're generally not interested in genre fiction; otherwise, we'll look at anything with a good story. We're especially interested in travel fiction and fiction featuring other cultures."

HOW TO CONTACT Query with SASE.

TERMS Authors are paid between 5-50% on wholesale price. Responds in 1 month to queries and 2 months to proposals.

TIPS "Writers are welcome to query by e-mail with a brief description of the book. (No attachments, please.) We're a newer company, and so we're more open than most to fiction and nonfiction that doesn't fit into any neat category."

ONSTAGE PUBLISHING

190 Lime Quarry Rd., Suite 106-J, Madison AL 35758-8962. (256)461-0661. **E-mail:** onstage123@knology.net. **Website:** www.onstagepublishing.com. **Contact:** Dianne Hamilton, senior editor. Estab. 1999. "At this time, we only produce fiction books for ages 8-18. We

are adding an e-book only side of the house for mysteries for grades 6-12. See our website for more information. We will not publish anthologies of any kind. Query first for nonfiction projects as nonfiction projects must spark our interest."

○ "To everyone who has submitted a ms, we are currently about 6 months behind. We should get back on track eventually. Please feel free to submit your ms to other houses. OnStage Publishing understands that authors work very hard to produce the finished ms and we do not have to have exclusive submission rights. Please let us know if you sell your ms. Meanwhile, keep writing and we'll keep reading for our next acquisitions."

NEEDS Middle readers: adventure, contemporary, fantasy, history, nature/environment, science fiction, suspense/mystery. Young adults: adventure, contemporary, fantasy, history, humor, science fiction, suspense/mystery. Average word length: chapter books—4,000-6,000 words; middle readers—5,000 words and up; young adults—25,000 and up. Recently published *China Clipper* by Jamie Dodson (an adventure for boys ages 12+); *Huntsville, 1892: Clara*, by Wanda Vaughn (a chapter book for grades 3-5). "We do not produce picture books."

HOW TO CONTACT Now accepting e-mail queries and submissions. For submissions: "Put the first 3 chapters in the body of the e-mail. Do not use attachments! We will no longer return any mss. Only an SASE is needed. Send complete ms if under 20,000 words, otherwise send synopsis and first 3 chapters."

TERMS Pays authors/illustrators/photographers advance plus royalties.

TIPS "Study our titles and get a sense of the kind of books we publish, so that you know whether your project is likely to be right for us."

OOLIGAN PRESS

369 Neuberger Hall, 724 SW Harrison St., Portland OR 97201. (503)725-9410. **E-mail:** acquisitions@ooliganpress.pdx.edu. **Website:** www.ooliganpress.pdx.edu. Estab. 2001. Publishes trade paperback, and electronic originals and reprints. Book catalog available online. Guidelines available online.

NEEDS "Ooligan Press is a general trade press at Portland State University. As a teaching press, Ooligan makes as little distinction as possible between the press and the classroom. Under the direction of professional faculty and staff, the work of the press is done by students enrolled in the Book Publishing graduate program at PSU. We are especially interested in works with social, literary, or educational value. Though we place special value on local authors, we are open to all submissions, including translated works and writings by children and young adults. We do not currently publish picture books, board books, easy readers, pop-up books, or middle-grade readers."

HOW TO CONTACT Query with SASE. *"At this time we cannot accept science fiction or fantasy submissions."*

TERMS Pays negotiable royalty on retail price.

TIPS "For children's books, our audience will be middle grades and young adult, with marketing to general trade, libraries, and schools. Good marketing ideas increase the chances of a ms succeeding."

○○ ORCA BOOK PUBLISHERS

P.O. Box 5626, Stn. B, Victoria BC V8R 6S4 Canada. **Fax:** (877)408-1551. **E-mail:** orca@orcabook.com. **Website:** www.orcabook.com. **Contact:** Amy Collins, editor (picture books); Sarah Harvey, editor (young readers); Andrew Wooldridge, editor (juvenile and teen fiction); Bob Tyrrell, publisher (young adult, teen). Estab. 1984. Publishes hardcover and trade paperback originals, and mass-market paperback originals and reprints. Book catalog for 8½×11 SASE. Guidelines available online.

○ Only publishes Canadian authors.

NEEDS Picture books: animals, contemporary, history, nature/environment. Middle readers: contemporary, history, fantasy, nature/environment, problem novels, graphic novels. Young adults: adventure, contemporary, hi-lo (Orca Soundings), history, multicultural, nature/environment, problem novels, suspense/mystery, graphic novels. Average word length: picture books—500-1,500; middle readers—20,000-35,000; young adult—25,000-45,000; Orca Soundings—13,000-15,000; Orca Currents—13,000-15,000. No romance, science fiction.

HOW TO CONTACT Query with SASE. Submit proposal package, outline, clips, 2-5 sample chapters, SASE.

TERMS Pays 10% royalty. Responds in 1 month to queries; 2 months to proposals and mss.

TIPS "Our audience is students in grades K-12. Know our books, and know the market."

ⒶⓄ ORCHARD BOOKS

557 Broadway, New York NY 10012. **E-mail:** mcro land@scholastic.com. **Website:** www.scholastic.com. **Contact:** Ken Geist, vice president/editorial director; David Saylor, vice president/creative director.

🔘 *Orchard is not accepting unsolicited mss.*

NEEDS Picture books, early readers, and novelty: animal, contemporary, history, humor, multicultural, poetry.

TERMS Most commonly offers an advance against list royalties.

TIPS "Read some of our books to determine first whether your ms is suited to our list."

ⒶⓄ THE OVERLOOK PRESS

141 Wooster St., New York NY 10012. (212)673-2210. **Fax:** (212)673-2296. **E-mail:** sales@overlookny.com. **Website:** www.overlookpress.com. Estab. 1971. "Overlook Press publishes fiction, children's books, and nonfiction." Publishes hardcover and trade paperback originals and hardcover reprints. Book catalog available free.

HOW TO CONTACT Agented submissions only.

Ⓒ RICHARD C. OWEN PUBLISHERS, INC.

P.O. Box 585, Katonah NY 10536. (914)232-3903; (800)262-0787. **E-mail:** richardowen@rcowen.com. **Website:** www.rcowen.com. **Contact:** Richard Owen, publisher. Estab. 1982. "We publish child-focused books, with inherent instructional value, about characters and situations with which 5-, 6-, and 7-year-old children can identify—books that can be read for meaning, entertainment, enjoyment, and information. We include multicultural stories that present minorities in a positive and natural way. Our stories show the diversity in America." Not interested in lesson plans or books of activities for literature studies or other content areas. Submit complete ms and cover letter. Book catalog available with SASE. Ms guidelines with SASE or online.

🔘 "Due to high volume and long production time, we are currently limiting to nonfiction submissions only."

TERMS Pays authors royalty of 5% based on net price or outright purchase (range: $25-500). Offers no advances. Pays illustrators by the project (range: $100-2,000) or per photo (range: $100-150). Responds to mss in 1 year.

TIPS "We don't respond to queries or e-mails. Please do not fax or e-mail us. Because our books are so brief,

it is better to send an entire ms. We publish storybooks with inherent educational value for young readers—books they can read with enjoyment and success. We believe students become enthusiastic, independent, lifelong learners when supported and guided by skillful teachers using good books. The professional development work we do and the books we publish support these beliefs."

🔘 PETER OWEN PUBLISHERS

20 Holland Park Ave., London W11 3 QU United Kingdom. (44)(208)350-1775. **Fax:** (44)(208)340-9488. **E-mail:** admin@peterowen.com. **Website:** www.peterowen.com. **Contact:** Antonia Owen, editorial director. "We are far more interested in proposals for nonfiction than fiction at the moment. No poetry or short stories." Publishes hardcover originals and trade paperback originals and reprints. Book catalog for SASE, SAE with IRC, or on website.

NEEDS "No first novels. Authors should be aware that we publish very little new fiction these days."

HOW TO CONTACT Query with synopsis, sample chapters.

TERMS Pays 7½-10% royalty. Pays negotiable advance. Responds in 2 months to queries; 3 months to proposals and mss.

PACIFIC PRESS PUBLISHING ASSOCIATION

Trade Book Division, 1350 N. Kings Rd., Nampa ID 83687. (208)465-2500. **Fax:** (208)465-2531. **E-mail:** booksubmissions@pacificpress.com. **Website:** www.pacificpress.com. **Contact:** Scott Cady, acquisitions editor (children's stories, biography, Christian living, spiritual growth); David Jarnes, book editor (theology, doctrine, inspiration). Estab. 1874. "We publish books that fit Seventh-Day Adventist beliefs only. All titles are Christian and religious. For guidance, see www.adventist.org/beliefs/index.html. Our books fit into the categories of this retail site: www.adventistbookcenter.com." Publishes hardcover and trade paperback originals and reprints. Guidelines online.

NEEDS "Pacific Press rarely publishes fiction, but we're interested in developing a line of Seventh-Day Adventist fiction in the future. Only proposals accepted; no full mss."

TERMS Pays 8-16% royalty on wholesale price. Responds in 3 months to queries.

TIPS "Our primary audience is members of the Seventh-Day Adventist denomination. Almost all are written by Seventh-Day Adventists. Books that do well for us relate the Biblical message to practical human concerns and focus more on the experiential rather than theoretical aspects of Christianity. We are assigning more titles, using less unsolicited material—although we still publish mss from freelance submissions and proposals."

PAGESPRING PUBLISHING

P.O. Box 2113, Columbus OH 43221. **E-mail:** ps@pagespringpublishing.com. **E-mail:** yaeditor@pagespringpublishing.com; weditor@pagespringpublishing.com. **Website:** www.pagespringpublishing.com. Estab. 2012. "PageSpring Publishing publishes young adult and middle-grade titles under the Lucky Marble Books imprint and women's fiction under the Cup of Tea imprint. See imprint websites for submission details." Publishes trade paperback and electronic originals. Guidelines online.

IMPRINTS Lucky Marble Books, Cup of Tea Books.

HOW TO CONTACT Submit proposal package including synopsis and 3 sample chapters.

TERMS Pays royalty on wholesale price. Responds to queries in 1 month.

PALARI PUBLISHING

107 S. West St., PMB 778, Alexandria VA 22314. (866)570-6724. **Fax:** (866)570-6724. **E-mail:** dave@palaribooks.com. **Website:** www.palaribooks.com. **Contact:** David Smitherman, publisher/editor. Estab. 1998. "Palari provides authoritative, well-written nonfiction that addresses topical consumer needs and fiction with an emphasis on intelligence and quality. We accept solicited and unsolicited mss, however, we prefer a query letter describing the project briefly and concisely and an SASE. This letter should include a complete address and telephone number. Palari Publishing accepts queries or any other submissions by e-mail, but prefers queries submitted by U.S. mail. All queries must be submitted by mail according to our guidelines. Promotes titles through book signings, direct mail, and the Internet." Publishes hardcover and trade paperback originals. Guidelines online.

Member of Publishers Marketing Association.

NEEDS "Tell why your idea is unique or interesting. Make sure we are interested in your genre before submitting."

HOW TO CONTACT Query with SASE. Submit bio, estimated word count, list of publishing credits. Accepts queries via e-mail (prefer U.S. Mail), fax.

TERMS Pays royalty. Responds in 1 month to queries; 2-3 months to mss.

TIPS "Send a good bio. I'm interested in a writer's experience and unique outlook on life."

PANTHEON BOOKS

Random House, Inc., 1745 Broadway, 3rd Floor, New York NY 10019. **E-mail:** pantheonpublicity@randomhouse.com. **Website:** www.pantheonbooks.com. Estab. 1942. Publishes hardcover and trade paperback originals and trade paperback reprints.

Pantheon Books publishes both Western and non-Western authors of literary fiction and important nonfiction. "We only accept mss submitted by an agent."

HOW TO CONTACT *Does not accept unsolicited mss.* Agented submissions only.

PARADISE CAY PUBLICATIONS

P.O. Box 29, Arcata CA 95518-0029. (800)736-4509. **Fax:** (707)822-9163. **E-mail:** info@paracay.com; james@paracay.com. **Website:** www.paracay.com. **Contact:** Matt Morehouse, publisher. "Paradise Cay Publications, Inc., is a small independent publisher specializing in nautical books, videos, and art prints. Our primary interest is in mss that deal with the instructional and technical aspects of ocean sailing. We also publish and will consider fiction if it has a strong nautical theme." Publishes hardcover and trade paperback originals and reprints. Book catalog and ms guidelines free on request or online.

IMPRINTS Pardey Books.

NEEDS All fiction must have a nautical theme.

HOW TO CONTACT Query with SASE. Submit proposal package, clips, 2-3 sample chapters.

TERMS Pays 10-15% royalty on wholesale price. Makes outright purchase of $1,000-10,000. Does not normally pay advances to first-time or little-known authors. Responds in 1 month to queries/proposals; 2 months to mss.

PAUL DRY BOOKS

1700 Sansom St., Suite 700, Philadelphia PA 19103. (215)231-9939. **Fax:** (215)231-9942. **E-mail:** pdry@pauldrybooks.com; editor@pauldrybooks.com. **Website:** pauldrybooks.com. "We publish fiction, both novels and short stories, and nonfiction, biography, memoirs, history, and essays, covering subjects from Homer to Chekhov, bird-watching to jazz music, New York City to shogunate Japan." Hardcover and trade paperback originals, trade paperback reprints. Book catalog available online. Guidelines available online.

○ "Take a few minutes to familiarize yourself with the books we publish. Then if you think your book would be a good fit in our line, we invite you to submit the following: A one- or two-page summary of the work. Be sure to tell us how many pages or words the full book will be; a sample of 20-30 pages; your bio. A brief description of how you think the book (and you, the author) could be marketed."

HOW TO CONTACT Submit sample chapters, clips, bio.

TIPS "Our aim is to publish lively books 'to awaken, delight, and educate'—to spark conversation. We publish fiction, nonfiction, and essays."

○ PAYCOCK PRESS

3819 N. 13th St., Arlington VA 22201. (703)525-9296. **E-mail:** gargoyle@gargoylemagazine.com. **Website:** www.gargoylemagazine.com. **Contact:** Richard Peabody. Estab. 1976. "Too academic for the underground, too outlaw for the academic world. We tend to be edgy and look for ultra-literary work." Publishes paperback originals. Books: POD printing. Average print order: 500. Averages 1 total title/year. Member CLMP. Distributes through Amazon and website.

NEEDS Wants: experimental, literary, short story or poetry collections.

HOW TO CONTACT Accepts unsolicited mss. Accepts queries by e-mail. Include brief bio. Send SASE for return of ms or send a disposable ms and SASE for reply only.

TERMS Responds to queries in 1 month; mss in 4 months.

TIPS "Check out our website. Two of our favorite writers are Paul Bowles and Jeanette Winterson."

○○ PEACE HILL PRESS

Affiliate of W.W. Norton, 18021 The Glebe Ln., Charles City VA 23030. (804)829-5043. **Fax:** (804)829-5704. **E-mail:** info@peacehillpress.com. **Website:** www.peacehillpress.com. **Contact:** Peter Buffington, acquisitions editor. Estab. 2001. Publishes hardcover and trade paperback originals.

HOW TO CONTACT Does not take submissions.

TERMS Pays 6-10% royalty on retail price. Pays $500-1,000 advance.

○ PEACHTREE CHILDREN'S BOOKS

Peachtree Publishers, Ltd., 1700 Chattahoochee Ave., Atlanta GA 30318-2112. (404)876-8761. **Fax:** (404)875-2578. **E-mail:** hello@peachtree-online.com. **Website:** www.peachtree-online.com. **Contact:** Helen Harriss, submissions editor. "We publish a broad range of subjects and perspectives, with emphasis on innovative plots and strong writing." Publishes hardcover and trade paperback originals. Book catalog for 6 first-class stamps. Guidelines available online.

IMPRINTS Freestone; Peachtree Jr.

NEEDS Looking for very well-written middle-grade and young adult novels. No adult fiction. No collections of poetry or short stories; no romance or science fiction.

HOW TO CONTACT Submit complete ms with SASE.

TERMS Pays royalty on retail price. Responds in 6 months and mss.

PEACHTREE PUBLISHERS, LTD.

1700 Chattahoochee Ave., Atlanta GA 30318. (404)876-8761. **Fax:** (404)875-2578. **E-mail:** hello@peachtree-online.com; jackson@peachtree-online.com. **Website:** www.peachtree-online.com. **Contact:** Helen Harriss, acquisitions editor; Loraine Joyner, art director; Melanie McMahon Ives, production manager. Estab. 1977.

NEEDS Picture books, young readers: adventure, animal, concept, history, nature/environment. Middle readers: adventure, animal, history, nature/environment, sports. Young adults: fiction, mystery, adventure. Does not want to see science fiction, romance.

HOW TO CONTACT Submit complete ms or 3 sample chapters by postal mail only.

TERMS Responds in 6-7 months.

○○ PEDLAR PRESS

113 Bond St., St. John's NL A16 1T6 Canada. (709)738-6702. **E-mail:** feralgrl@interlog.com. **Website:** www.pedlarpress.com. **Contact:** Beth Follett, owner/editor. Distributes in Canada through LitDistCo.

NEEDS Experimental, feminist, gay/lesbian, literary, short story collections. Canadian writers only.

HOW TO CONTACT Query with SASE, sample chapter(s), synopsis.

TERMS Pays 10% royalty on retail price. Average advance: $200-400.

TIPS "I select mss according to my taste, which fluctuates. Be familiar with some, if not most, of Pedlar's recent titles."

PELICAN PUBLISHING COMPANY

1000 Burmaster St., Gretna LA 70053. (504)368-1175. **Fax:** (504)368-1195. **E-mail:** editorial@pelicanpub.com. **Website:** www.pelicanpub.com. **Contact:** Nina Kooij, editor-in-chief. Estab. 1926. "We believe ideas have consequences. One of the consequences is that they lead to a best-selling book. We publish books to improve and uplift the reader. Currently emphasizing business and history titles." Publishes 20 young readers/year; 1 middle reader/year. "Our children's books (illustrated and otherwise) include history, biography, holiday, and regional. Pelican's mission is to publish books of quality and permanence that enrich the lives of those who read them." Publishes hardcover, trade paperback and mass-market paperback originals and reprints. Book catalog and ms guidelines online.

NEEDS We publish no adult fiction. Young readers: history, holiday, science, multicultural and regional. Middle readers: Louisiana history. Multicultural needs include stories about African-Americans, Irish-Americans, Jews, Asian-Americans, and Hispanics. Does not want animal stories, general Christmas stories, "day at school" or "accept yourself" stories. Maximum word length: young readers—1,100; middle readers—40,000. No young adult, romance, science fiction, fantasy, gothic, mystery, erotica, confession, horror, sex, or violence. Also no psychological novels.

HOW TO CONTACT Query with SASE. Submit outline, clips, 2 sample chapters, SASE.

TERMS Pays authors in royalties; buys ms outright "rarely." Illustrators paid by "various arrangements." Advance considered. Responds in 1 month to queries; 3 months to mss.

TIPS "We do extremely well with cookbooks, popular histories, and business. We will continue to build in these areas. The writer must have a clear sense of the market and knowledge of the competition. A query letter should describe the project briefly, give the author's writing and professional credentials, and promotional ideas."

PENGUIN GROUP USA

375 Hudson St., New York NY 10014. (212)366-2000. **Website:** www.penguin.com. **Contact:** Peter Stampfel, submission editor (DAW Books). General interest publisher of both fiction and nonfiction. Guidelines online.

No unsolicited mss. Submit work through a literary agent. Exceptions are DAW Books and Penguin Young Readers Group.

IMPRINTS Penguin Adult Division: Ace Books, Alpha Books, Avery, Berkley Books, Dutton, Gotham Books, HPBooks, Hudson Street Press, Jove, New American Library, Penguin, The Penguin Press, Perigee, Plume, Portfolio, G.P. Putnam's Sons, Riverhead, Sentinel, Jeremy P. Tarcher, Viking; **Penguin Children's Division**: Dial Books for Young Readers, Dutton Children's Books, Firebird, Grosset & Dunlap, Philomel, Price Stern Sloan, Puffin Books, G.P. Putnam's Sons, Speak, Viking Children's Books, Frederick Warne.

PENNY-FARTHING PRESS INC.

One Sugar Creek Center Blvd., Suite 820, Sugar Land TX 77478. (713)780-0300 or (800)926-2669. **Fax:** (713)780-4004. **E-mail:** submissions@pfpress.com; corp@pfpress.com. **Website:** www.pfpress.com. **Contact:** Ken White, publisher; Marlaine Maddox, editor-in-chief. Estab. 1998. "Penny-Farthing Press officially opened its doors in 1998 with a small staff and a plan to create comic books and children's books that exemplified quality storytelling, artwork, and printing. Starting with only 1 book, *The Victorian*, Penny-Farthing Press has expanded but keeps its yearly output small enough to maintain the highest quality. This 'boutique approach' to publishing has won the recognition of the comics and fine arts industries, and PFP has won numerous awards including the Gutenberg D'Argent Medal and several Spectrum Awards." Guidelines online.

HOW TO CONTACT "Please make sure all submissions include a synopsis that is brief and to the point. Remember, the synopsis is the 'first impression' of your submission, and you know what they say about first impressions. If you are submitting just 1 single-issue story (standard 32 pp.), you may send the full script with your submission. If you are submitting a story for any kind of series or graphic novel, please send only the first chapter of the series. If we like what we see, we will contact you to see more. If you are submitting a completed work (script, artwork and lettering) copies of this may be sent instead."

PERENNIAL

HarperCollins Publishers, 10 E. 53rd St., New York NY 10022. (212)207-7000. **Website:** www.harpercollins.com. **Contact:** Acquisitions Editor. Estab.

1963. Perennial publishes a broad range of adult literary fiction and nonfiction paperbacks that create a record of our culture. Publishes trade paperback originals and reprints. Book catalog available free.

○ "With the exception of Avon romance, HarperCollins does not accept unsolicited submissions or query letters. Please refer to your local bookstore, the library, or a book entitled *Literary Marketplace* on how to find the appropriate agent for you."

HOW TO CONTACT Agented submissions only.

TIPS "See our website for a list of titles or write to us for a free catalog."

◐ THE PERMANENT PRESS

Attn: Judith Shepard, 4170 Noyac Rd., Sag Harbor NY 11963. (631)725-1101. **Fax:** (631)725-8215. **E-mail:** judith@thepermanentpress.com; shepard@thepermanentpress.com. **Website:** www.thepermanentpress.com. **Contact:** Judith and Martin Shepard, acquisitions/co-publishers. Estab. 1978. Midsize, independent publisher of literary fiction. "We keep titles in print and are active in selling subsidiary rights." Average print order: 1,000-2,500. Averages 16 total titles. Accepts unsolicited mss. Pays 10-15% royalty on wholesale price. Offers $1,000 advance. Publishes hardcover originals.

○ *Will NOT accept simultaneous submissions.*

NEEDS Promotes titles through reviews. Literary, mainstream/contemporary, mystery. Especially looking for high-line literary fiction, "artful, original and arresting." Accepts any fiction category as long as it is a "well-written, original full-length novel."

TERMS Pays 10-15% royalty on wholesale price. Offers $1,000 advance. Responds in weeks or months to queries and submissions.

TIPS "We are looking for good books—be they 10th novels or first ones, it makes little difference. The fiction is more important than the track record. Send us the first 25 pages; it's impossible to judge something that begins on page 302. Also, no outlines—let the writing present itself."

PERSEA BOOKS

277 Broadway, Suite 708, New York NY 10007. (212)260-9256. **Fax:** (212)267-3165. **E-mail:** info@perseabooks.com. **Website:** www.perseabooks.com. Estab. 1975. The aim of Persea is to publish works that endure by meeting high standards of literary merit and relevance. "We have often taken on important

books other publishers have overlooked, and we have also made significant discoveries and rediscoveries, whether of a single work or writer's entire oeuvre. Our books cover a wide range of themes, styles, and genres. We have published poetry, fiction, essays, memoir, biography, titles of Jewish and Middle Eastern interest, women's studies, American Indian folklore, and revived classics, as well as a notable selection of works in translation." Guidelines online.

HOW TO CONTACT Queries should include a cover letter, author background and publication history, a detailed synopsis of the proposed work, and a sample chapter. Please indicate if the work is simultaneously submitted.

TERMS Responds in 8 weeks to proposals; 10 weeks to mss.

◐◐ PHILOMEL BOOKS

Imprint of Penguin Group (USA), Inc., 375 Hudson St., New York NY 10014. (212)414-3610. **Website:** www.us.penguingroup.com. **Contact:** Michael Green, president/publisher; Annie Ericsson, junior designer. Estab. 1980. "We look for beautifully written, engaging mss for children and young adults." Publishes hardcover originals. Book catalog for 9×12 envelope and 4 first-class stamps. Guidelines for #10 SASE.

NEEDS All levels: adventure, animal, boys, contemporary, fantasy, folktales, historical fiction, humor, sports, multicultural. Middle readers, young adults: problem novels, science fiction, suspense/mystery. No concept picture books, mass-market "character" books, or series. Average word length: picture books—1,000; young readers—1,500; middle readers—14,000; young adult—20,000. No series or activity books. No generic, mass-market fiction.

HOW TO CONTACT *No unsolicited mss.*

TERMS Pays authors in royalties. Average advance payment "varies." Illustrators paid by advance and in royalties. Pays negotiable advance.

TIPS Wants "unique fiction or nonfiction with a strong voice and lasting quality. Discover your own voice and own story and persevere." Looks for "something unusual, original, well written. Fine art or illustrative art that feels unique. The genre (fantasy, contemporary, or historical fiction) is not so important as the story itself and the spirited life the story allows its main character."

PIANO PRESS

P.O. Box 85, Del Mar CA 92014. (619)884-1401. **Fax:** (858)755-1104. **E-mail:** pianopress@pianopress.com. **Website:** www.pianopress.com. **Contact:** Elizabeth C. Axford, editor. Estab. 1998. "We publish music-related books, either fiction or nonfiction, coloring books, songbooks, and poetry." Book catalog available for #10 SASE and 2 first-class stamps.

NEEDS Picture books, young readers, middle readers, young adults: folktales, multicultural, poetry, music. Average word length: picture books—1,500-2,000.

TERMS Pays authors, illustrators, and photographers royalty of 5-10% based on retail price. Responds to queries in 3 months; mss in 6 months.

TIPS "We are looking for music-related material only for any juvenile market. Please do not send non-music-related materials. Query first before submitting anything."

PIATKUS BOOKS

Little, Brown Book Group, 100 Victoria Embankment, London WA EC4Y 0DY United Kingdom. 0207 911 8000. **Fax:** 0207 911 8100. **E-mail:** info@littlebrown.co.uk. **Website:** piatkus.co.uk. **Contact:** Emma Beswetherick, senior editor. Estab. 1979. "Until 2007, Piatkus operated as an independent publishing house. Now it exists as a commercial imprint of Hachette-owned Little, Brown Book Group." Publishes hardcover originals, paperback originals, and paperback reprints. Guidelines available online.

Piatkus no longer accepts fiction proposals.

NEEDS Quality family saga, historical, literary.

HOW TO CONTACT Agented submissions only.

TERMS Responds in 3 months to mss.

PICADOR USA

MacMillan, 175 Fifth Ave., New York NY 10010. (212)674-5151. **E-mail:** david.saint@picadorusa.com; pressinquiries@macmillanusa.com. **Website:** www.picadorusa.com. **Contact:** Frances Coady, publisher (literary fiction). Estab. 1994. Picador publishes high-quality literary fiction and nonfiction. "We are open to a broad range of subjects, well written by authoritative authors." Publishes hardcover and trade paperback originals and reprints. Titles distributed through Von Holtzbrinck Publishers. Titles promoted through national print advertising and bookstore co-op. Book catalog for 9×12 SASE and $2.60 postage. Ms guidelines for #10 SASE or online.

Does not accept unsolicited mss. *Agented submissions only.*

TERMS Pays 7-15% on royalty. Advance varies. Responds to queries in 2 months.

PICCADILLY PRESS

5 Castle Rd., London NW1 8PR United Kingdom. (44)(207)267-4492. **Fax:** (44)(207)267-4493. **E-mail:** books@piccadillypress.co.uk. **Website:** www.piccadillypress.co.uk. "Piccadilly Press is the perfect choice for a variety of reading for everyone aged 2-16! We're an independent publisher, celebrating 26 years of specializing in teen fiction and nonfiction, childrens' fiction, picture books, and parenting books by highly acclaimed authors and illustrators and fresh new talents too."

NEEDS Picture books: animal, contemporary, fantasy, nature/environment. Young adults: contemporary, humor, problem novels. Average word length: picture books—500-1,000; young adults—25,000-35,000.

HOW TO CONTACT Submit complete ms for picture books or submit outline/synopsis and 2 sample chapters for young adult. Enclose a brief cover letter and SASE for reply.

TERMS Responds to mss in 6 weeks.

TIPS "Take a look in bookshops to see if there are many other books of a similar nature to yours—this is what your book will be competing against, so make sure there is something truly unique about your story. Looking at what else is available will give you ideas as to what topics are popular, but reading a little of them will also give you a sense of the right styles, language, and length appropriate for the age group."

PIÑATA BOOKS

Imprint of Arte Publico Press, University of Houston, 4902 Gulf Fwy., Bldg. 19, Room 100, Houston TX 77204-2004. (713)743-2845. **Fax:** (713)743-3080. **E-mail:** submapp@mail.uh.edu. **Website:** www.latinoteca.com/arte-publico-press. **Contact:** Nicolas Kanellos, director. Estab. 1994. "Piñata Books is dedicated to the publication of children's and young adult literature focusing on U.S. Hispanic culture by U.S. Hispanic authors. Arte Publico's mission is the publication, promotion, and dissemination of Latino literature for a variety of national and regional audiences, from early childhood to adult, through the complete gamut of delivery systems, including personal performance as well as print and electronic media." Publishes hardcover and trade paperback originals. Book catalog and ms guidelines available via website or with #10 SASE.

○ Accepts material from U.S./Hispanic authors only (living abroad OK). Mss, queries, synopses, etc., are accepted in either English or Spanish.

HOW TO CONTACT Submissions made through online submission form.

TERMS Pays 10% royalty on wholesale price. Pays $1,000-3,000 advance. Responds in 2-3 months to queries; 4-6 months to mss.

TIPS "Include cover letter with submission explaining why your ms is unique and important, why we should publish it, who will buy it, etc."

◑ PINEAPPLE PRESS, INC.

P.O. Box 3889, Sarasota FL 34230. (941)739-2219. **Fax:** (941)739-2296. **E-mail:** info@pineapplepress.com. **Website:** www.pineapplepress.com. **Contact:** June Cussen, executive editor. Estab. 1982. "We are seeking quality nonfiction on diverse topics for the library and book trade markets. Our mission is to publish good books about Florida." Publishes hardcover and trade paperback originals. Book catalog for 9×12 SAE with $1.25 postage. Guidelines available online.

NEEDS Picture books, young readers, middle readers, young adults: animal, folktales, history, nature/environment.

HOW TO CONTACT Query or submit outline/synopsis and 3 sample chapters.

TERMS Pays authors royalty of 10-15%. Responds to queries/samples/mss in 2 months.

TIPS "Quality first novels will be published, though we usually only do 1 or 2 novels per year and they must be set in Florida. We regard the author/editor relationship as a trusting relationship with communication open both ways. Learn all you can about the publishing process and about how to promote your book once it is published. A query on a novel without a brief sample seems useless."

⊘ PLAN B PRESS

P.O. Box 4067, Alexandria VA 22303. (215)732-2663. **E-mail:** planbpress@gmail.com. **Website:** www.planbpress.com. **Contact:** Steven Allen May, president. Estab. 1999. Plan B Press is a "small publishing company with an international feel. Our intention is to have Plan B Press be part of the conversation about the direction and depth of literary movements and genres. Plan B Press's new direction is to seek out authors rarely-to-never published, sharing new voices that might not otherwise be heard. Plan B Press is determined to merge text with image, writing with art." Publishes poetry and short fiction. Wants "experimental poetry, concrete/visual work." Has published poetry by Lamont B. Steptoe, Michele Belluomini, Jim Mancinelli, Lyn Lifshin, Robert Miltner, and Steven Allen May. Publishes 1 poetry book/year and 5-10 chapbooks/year. Mss are selected through open submission and through competition (see below). Books/chapbooks are 24-48 pages, with covers with art/graphics.

TERMS Pays author's copies. Responds to queries in 1 month; mss in 3 months.

PLEXUS PUBLISHING, INC.

143 Old Marlton Pike, Medford NJ 08055. (609)654-6500. **Fax:** (609)654-4309. **E-mail:** jbryans@plexuspublishing.com. **Website:** www.plexuspublishing.com. **Contact:** John B. Bryans, editor-in-chief/publisher. Estab. 1977. Plexus publishes regional-interest (southern New Jersey and the greater Philadelphia area) fiction and nonfiction including mysteries, field guides, nature, travel, and history. Also a limited number of titles in health/medicine, biology, ecology, botany, astronomy. Publishes hardcover and paperback originals. Book catalog and book proposal guidelines for 10×13 SASE.

NEEDS Mysteries and literary novels with a strong regional (southern New Jersey) angle.

HOW TO CONTACT Query with SASE.

TERMS Pays $500-1,000 advance. Responds in 3 months to proposals.

▲⊘ POCKET BOOKS

Simon & Schuster, 1230 Avenue of the Americas, New York NY 10020. (212)698-7000. **Website:** www.simonandschuster.com. **Contact:** Jennifer Bergstrom, editor-in-chief. Estab. 1939. Pocket Books publishes commercial fiction and genre fiction (WWE, Downtown Press, Star Trek). Publishes paperback originals and reprints, mass-market and trade paperbacks. Book catalog available free. Guidelines online.

HOW TO CONTACT *Agented submissions only.*

○ POCOL PRESS

P.O. Box 411, Clifton VA 20124. (703)830-5862. **Website:** www.pocolpress.com. **Contact:** J. Thomas Hetrick, editor. Estab. 1999. "Pocol Press is dedicated to producing high-quality print books and e-books from first-time, nonagented authors. However, all submissions are welcome. We're dedicated to good storytellers and to the written word, specializing in short fiction and baseball. Several of our books have been used as literary texts at universities and in book group discussions around the nation. Pocol Press does not publish children's books, romance novels, or graphic novels." Publishes trade paperback originals. Book catalog and guidelines available online.

○ "Our authors are comprised of veteran writers and emerging talents."

NEEDS "We specialize in thematic short fiction collections by a single author and baseball fiction. Expert storytellers welcome." Horror (psychological, supernatural), literary, mainstream/contemporary, short story collections, baseball.

HOW TO CONTACT Does not accept or return unsolicited mss. Query with SASE or submit 1 sample chapter(s).

TERMS Pays 10-12% royalty on wholesale price. Responds in 1 month to queries; 2 months to mss.

TIPS "Our audience is aged 18 and over. Pocol Press is unique; we publish good writing and great storytelling. Write the best stories you can. Read them to you friends/peers. Note their reaction. Publishes some of the finest fiction by a small press."

THE POISONED PENCIL

Poisoned Pen Press, 6962 E. 1st Ave., Suite 103, Scottsdale AZ 85251. (480)945-3375. **Fax:** (480)949-1707. **E-mail:** info@thepoisonedpencil.com. **E-mail:** www.thepoisonedpencil.submittable.com/submit. **Website:** www.thepoisonedpencil.com. **Contact:** Ellen Larson, editor. Estab. 2012. Publishes trade paperback and electronic originals. Guidelines online.

○ *Accepts young adult mysteries only.*

NEEDS "We publish only young adult mystery novels, 45,000 to 90,000 words in length. For our purposes, a young adult book is a book with a protagonist between the ages of 13 and 18. We are looking for both traditional and cross-genre young adult mysteries. We encourage offbeat approaches and narrative choices that reflect the complexity and ambiguity of today's world. Submissions from teens are very welcome. Avoid serial killers, excessive gore, and vampires (and other heavy supernatural themes). We only consider authors who live in the U.S. or Canada, due to practicalities of marketing promotion. Avoid coincidence in plotting. Avoid having your sleuth leap to conclusions rather than discover and deduce. Pay at-

tention to the resonance between character and plot; between plot and theme; between theme and character. We are looking for clean style, fluid storytelling, and solid structure. Unrealistic dialogue is a real turnoff."

HOW TO CONTACT Submit proposal package including synopsis, complete ms, and cover letter.

TERMS Pays 9-15% for trade paperback; 25-35% for e-books. Pays advance of $1,000. Responds in 6 weeks to mss.

TIPS "Our audience is young adults and adults who love YA mysteries."

○○ POISONED PEN PRESS

6962 E. 1st Ave., Suite 103, Scottsdale AZ 85251. (480)945-3375. **Fax:** (480)949-1707. **E-mail:** submissions@poisonedpenpress.com. **Website:** www.poisonedpenpress.com. **Contact:** Jessica Tribble, publisher; Barbara Peters, editor-in-chief. Estab. 1996. "Our publishing goal is to offer well-written mystery novels of crime and/or detection where the puzzle and its resolution are the main forces that move the story forward." Publishes hardcover originals, and hardcover and trade paperback reprints. Book catalog and guidelines online.

○ *Not currently accepting submissions. Check website.*

IMPRINTS The Poisoned Pencil.

NEEDS Mss should generally be longer than 65,000 words and shorter than 100,000 words. Member Publishers Marketing Associations, Arizona Book Publishers Associations, Publishers Association of West. Distributes through Ingram, Baker & Taylor, Brodart. Does not want novels centered on serial killers, spousal or child abuse, drugs, or extremist groups, although we do not entirely rule such works out.

HOW TO CONTACT Accepts unsolicited mss. Electronic queries only. "Query with SASE. Submit clips, first 3 pages. We must receive both the synopsis and ms pages electronically as separate attachments to an e-mail message or on a disk or CD, which we will not return."

TERMS Pays 9-15% royalty on retail price. Responds in 2-3 months to queries and proposals; 6 months to mss.

TIPS "Audience is adult readers of mystery fiction."

POSSIBILITY PRESS

1 Oakglade Circle, Hummelstown PA 17036. **E-mail:** info@possibilitypress.com. **Website:** www.possibili

typress.com. **Contact:** Mike Markowski, publisher. Estab. 1981. "Our mission is to help the people of the world grow and become the best they can be, through the written and spoken word." Publishes trade paperback originals. Catalog available online. Guidelines available online.

IMPRINTS Aeronautical Publishers; Possibility Press; Markowski International Publishers.

NEEDS Parables that teach lessons about life and success.

TERMS Royalties vary. Responds in 1 month to queries.

TIPS "Our focus is on co-authoring and publishing short (15,000-40,000 words) bestsellers. We're looking for kind and compassionate authors who are passionate about making a difference in the world and will champion their mission to do so, especially by public speaking. Our dream author writes well, knows how to promote, will champion their mission, speaks for a living, has a following and a platform, is cooperative and understanding, humbly handles critique and direction, and is grateful, intelligent, and has a good sense of humor."

⊕ PRESS 53

P.O. Box 30314, Winston-Salem NC 27101. **E-mail:** kevin@press53.com. **Website:** www.press53.com. **Contact:** Kevin Morgan Watson, publisher. "Press 53 was founded in October 2005 and quickly began earning a reputation as a quality publishing house of short story and poetry collections." Open submission period in November each year. Guidelines online.

NEEDS "We publish roughly 8 short story collections each year by writers who are active and earning recognition through publication and awards." Collections should include 10-15 short stories with 70% or more of those stories previously published. Does not want novels.

HOW TO CONTACT November submission period. Submit via Submittable. Include a letter of introduction (information about yourself and your collection), where the stories have been published, a few ideas for marketing your book, and the complete ms.

TERMS Responds in 6 months to mss.

TIPS "We are looking for writers who are actively involved in the writing community, writers who are submitting their work to journals, magazines, and contests, and those who are getting published and earning a reputation for their work."

PRUFROCK PRESS, INC.

P.O. Box 8813, Waco TX 76714. (800)988-2208. **Fax:** (800)240-0333. **E-mail:** info@prufrock.com. **Website:** www.prufrock.com. **Contact:** Joel McIntosh, publisher and marketing director. "Prufrock Press offers award-winning products focused on gifted education, gifted children, advanced learning, and special needs learners. For more than 20 years, Prufrock has supported gifted children and their education and development. The company publishes more than 300 products that enhance the lives of gifted children and the teachers and parents who support them." Book catalog for 10×12 envelope and 2 first-class stamps. Guidelines online.

○ Accepts simultaneous submissions, but must be notified about it.

NEEDS No picture books.

HOW TO CONTACT "Prufrock Press does not consider unsolicited mss."

◑ PUFFIN BOOKS

Imprint of Penguin Group (USA), Inc., 375 Hudson St., New York NY 10014. (212)366-2000. **Website:** www.penguinputnam.com. **Contact:** Kristin Gilson, editorial director. "Puffin Books publishes high-end trade paperbacks and paperback reprints for preschool children, beginning and middle readers, and young adults." Publishes trade paperback originals and reprints. Book catalog for 9×12 SAE with 7 first-class stamps.

IMPRINTS Speak, Firebird, Sleuth.

HOW TO CONTACT *No unsolicited mss.* Agented submissions only.

TERMS Royalty varies. Pays varies advance. Responds in 5 months.

TIPS "Our audience ranges from little children 'first books' to young adult (ages 14-16). An original idea has the best luck."

◭ PUSH

Scholastic, 557 Broadway, New York NY 10012. **E-mail:** dlevithan@scholastic.com. **Website:** www.thisispush.com. Estab. 2002. PUSH publishes new voices in teen literature.

○ PUSH does not accept unsolicited mss or queries, only agented or referred fiction/memoir.

HOW TO CONTACT *Does not accept unsolicited mss.*

TIPS "We only publish first-time writers (and then their subsequent books), so authors who have published previously should not consider PUSH. Also, for young writers in grades 7-12, we run the PUSH Novel Contest with the Scholastic Art & Writing Awards. Every year it begins in October and ends in March. Rules can be found on our website."

⚫⊘ G.P. PUTNAM'S SONS HARDCOVER

Imprint of Penguin Group (USA), Inc., 375 Hudson, New York NY 10014. (212)366-2000. **Fax:** (212)366-2664. **Website:** www.penguinputnam.com. Publishes hardcover originals. Request book catalog through mail-order department.

NEEDS Agented submissions only.

TERMS Pays variable royalties on retail price. Pays varies advance.

⭕ QUIXOTE PRESS

3544 Blakslee St., Wever IA 52658. (800)571-2665. **Fax:** (319)372-7485. **Website:** www.heartsntummies .com. **Contact:** Bruce Carlson. Publishes trade paperback originals and reprints.

HOW TO CONTACT Query with SASE.

TERMS Pays 10% royalty on wholesale price.

TIPS "Carefully consider marketing considerations. Audience is women in gift shops, on farm sites, direct-retail outlets, wineries, outdoor sport shops, etc. Contact us at *your idea* stage, not complete ms stage. Be receptive to design input."

⊘⭕ RAINCOAST BOOK DISTRIBUTION, LTD.

2440 Viking Way, Richmond BC V6V 1N2 Canada. (604)448-7100. **Fax:** (604)270-7161. **E-mail:** info@ raincoast.com. **Website:** www.raincoast.com. Publishes hardcover and trade paperback originals and reprints. Book catalog for #10 SASE.

IMPRINTS Raincoast Books; Polestar Books (fiction, poetry, literary nonfiction).

NEEDS *No unsolicited mss.*

TERMS Pays 8-12% royalty on retail price. Pays $1,000-6,000 advance.

RAIN TOWN PRESS

1111 E. Burnside St. #309, Portland OR 97214. (503)962-9612. **E-mail:** submissions@raintownpress .com. **Website:** www.raintownpress.com. **Contact:** Misty V'Marie, acquisitions editor; Ellery Harvey, art director. Estab. 2009. Catalog online. Guidelines online.

◖ "We are Portland, Oregon's first independent press dedicated to publishing literature for middle-grade and young adult readers. We hope to give rise to their voice, speaking directly to the spirit they embody through our books and other endeavors. The gray days we endure in the Pacific Northwest are custom-made for reading a good book—or in our case, making one. The rain inspires, challenges, and motivates us. To that end, we say: Let it drizzle. We will soon publish picture books."

IMPRINTS Raintown Kids.

NEEDS Middle readers/young adult/teens: Wants adventure, animal, contemporary, fantasy, folktales, graphic novels, health, hi-lo, history, humor, multicultural, nature/environment, problem novels, science fiction, special needs, sports. Catalog available on website.

HOW TO CONTACT Query. Submit complete ms.

TERMS Pays 8-15% royalty on net sales. Does not pay advance. Responds in 1-6 months.

TIPS "The middle-grade and young adult markets have sometimes very stringent conventions for subject matter, theme, etc. It's most helpful if an author knows his/her genre inside and out. Read, read, read books that have successfully been published for your genre. This will ultimately make your writing more marketable. Also, follow a publisher's submission guidelines to a tee. We try to set writers up for success. Send us what we're looking for."

⚫⊘ RANDOM HOUSE CHILDREN'S BOOKS

1745 Broadway, New York NY 10019. (212)782-9000. **Website:** www.randomhouse.com. Estab. 1925. "Producing books for preschool children through young adult readers, in all formats from board to activity books to picture books and novels, Random House Children's Books brings together world-famous franchise characters, multimillion-copy series, and top-flight award-winning authors and illustrators."

◖ Submit mss through a literary agent.

IMPRINTS BooksReportsNow.com, GoldenBooks .com, Junie B. Jones, Kids@Random, Seusville, Teachers@Random, Teens@Random; **Knopf/Delacorte/ Dell Young Readers Group:** Bantam, Crown, David Fickling Books, Delacorte Press, Dell Dragonfly, Dell Laurel-Leaf, Dell Yearling, Doubleday, Alfred A. Knopf, Wendy Lamb Books; **Random House Young Readers Group:** Akiko, Arthur, Barbie, Beginner Books, The Berenstain Bears, Bob the Builder, Disney, Dragon Tales, First Time Books, Golden Books,

Landmark Books, Little Golden Books, Lucas Books, Mercer Mayer, Nickelodeon, Nick, Jr., Pat the Bunny, Picturebacks, Precious Moments, Richard Scarry, Sesame Street Books, Step Into Reading, Stepping Stones, Star Wars, Thomas the Tank Engine and Friends.

NEEDS "Random House publishes a select list of first chapter books and novels, with an emphasis on fantasy and historical fiction." Chapter books, middle-grade readers, young adult.

HOW TO CONTACT *Does not accept unsolicited mss.*

TIPS "We look for original, unique stories. Do something that hasn't been done before."

◎◯ RANSOM PUBLISHING

Radley House, 8 St. Cross Road, Winchester Hampshire SO23 9HX United Kingdom. +44 (0) 01962 862307. **Fax:** +44 (0) 05601 148881. **E-mail:** ransom@ ransom.co.uk. **Website:** www.ransom.co.uk. **Contact:** Jenny Ertle, editor. Estab. 1995. Independent U.K. publisher with distribution in English-speaking markets throughout the world. Specializes in books for reluctant and struggling readers. "Our high-quality, visually stimulating, age-appropriate material has achieved wide acclaim for its ability to engage and motivate those who either can't or won't read." One of the few English-language publishers to publish books with very high interest age and very low reading age. Has a developing list of children's books for home and school use. Specializes in phonics and general reading programs. Publishes paperback originals. Ms guidelines by e-mail.

NEEDS Easy reading for young adults. Books for reluctant and struggling readers.

HOW TO CONTACT Accepts unsolicited mss. Query with SASE or submit outline/proposal. Prefers queries by e-mail. Include estimated word count, brief bio, list of publishing credits.

TERMS Pays 10% royalty on net receipts. Responds to mss in 3-4 weeks.

RAZORBILL

Penguin Group, 375 Hudson St., New York NY 10014. (212)414-3448. **Fax:** (212)414-3343. **E-mail:** laura .schechter@us.penguingroup.com; ben.schrank@ us.penguingroup.com. **Website:** www.razorbillbooks .com. **Contact:** Gillian Levinson, assistant edtor; Jessica Rothenberg, editor; Brianne Mulligan, editor. Estab. 2003. "This division of Penguin Young Readers is looking for the best and the most original of commercial contemporary fiction titles for middle-grade and

young adult readers. A select quantity of nonfiction titles will also be considered."

NEEDS Middle readers: adventure, contemporary, graphic novels, fantasy, humor, problem novels. Young adults/teens: adventure, contemporary, fantasy, graphic novels, humor, multicultural, suspense, paranormal, science fiction, dystopian, literary, romance. Average word length: middle readers—40,000; young adult—60,000.

HOW TO CONTACT Submit cover letter with up to 30 sample pages.

TERMS Offers advance against royalties. Responds in 1-3 months.

TIPS "New writers will have the best chance of acceptance and publication with original, contemporary material that boasts a distinctive voice and well-articulated world. Check out www.razorbillbooks. com to get a better idea of what we're looking for."

◎◯ REALITY STREET

63 All Saints St., Hastings, E. Sussex TN34 3BN United Kingdom. +44(0)1424 431271. **E-mail:** info@realit ystreet.co.uk. **Website:** www.realitystreet.co.uk. **Contact:** Ken Edwards, editor and publisher. Estab. 1993. Reality Street is based in Hastings, U.K., publishing new and innovative writing in English and in translation from other languages. Reality Street has published Nicole Brossard, Allen Fisher, Barbara Guest, Fanny Howe, Denise Riley, Peter Riley, and Maurice Scully. Publishes trade paperback originals. Book catalog available online.

○ *Does not accept unsolicited submissions.*

◎◯◯ RED DEER PRESS

195 Allstate Pkwy., Markham ON L3R 4TB Canada. (905)477-9700. **Fax:** (905)477-9179. **E-mail:** rdp@ reddeerpress.com; dionne@reddeerpress.com; val@ reddeerpress.com. **Website:** www.reddeerpress.com. **Contact:** Richard Dionne, publisher. Estab. 1975. Book catalog for 9×12 SASE.

○ Red Deer Press has received numerous honors and awards from the Book Publishers Association of Alberta, Canadian Children's Book Centre, the Governor General of Canada and the Writers Guild of Alberta.

NEEDS Publishes young adult, adult science fiction, fantasy, and paperback originals "focusing on books by, about, or of interest to Canadians." Books: offset paper; offset printing; hardcover/perfect-bound. Average print order: 5,000. First novel print order:

2,500. Distributes titles in Canada and the U.S., the U.K., Australia and New Zealand. Young adult (juvenile and early reader), contemporary. No romance or horror.

HOW TO CONTACT Accepts unsolicited mss. Query with SASE. No submissions on disk.

TERMS Pays 8-10% royalty. Responds to queries in 6 months.

TIPS "We're very interested in young adult and children's fiction from Canadian writers with a proven track record (either published books or widely published in established magazines or journals) and for mss with regional themes and/or a distinctive voice. We publish Canadian authors exclusively."

RED HEN PRESS

P.O. Box 3537, Granada Hills CA 91394. (818)831-0649. **Fax:** (818)831-6659. **E-mail:** redhenpressbooks.com. **Website:** www.redhen.org. **Contact:** Mark E. Cull, publisher/editor (fiction). Estab. 1993. "At this time, the best opportunity to be published by Red Hen is by entering one of our contests. Please find more information in our online award submission guidelines." Publishes trade paperback originals. Book catalog available free. Guidelines available online.

HOW TO CONTACT Query with synopsis and either 20-30 sample pages or complete ms using online submission manager.

TERMS Responds in 1 month to queries; 2 months to proposals and mss.

TIPS "Audience reads poetry, literary fiction, intelligent nonfiction. If you have an agent, we may be too small since we don't pay advances. Write well. Send queries first. Be willing to help promote your own book."

RED SAGE PUBLISHING, INC.

P.O. Box 4844, Seminole FL 33775. (727)391-3847. **E-mail:** submissions@eredsage.com. **Website:** www.eredsage.com. **Contact:** Alexandria Kendall, publisher; Theresa Stevens, managing editor. Estab. 1995. Publishes books of romance fiction, written for the adventurous woman. Guidelines online.

HOW TO CONTACT Read guidelines.

TERMS Pays advance.

☯◉ RED TUQUE BOOKS, INC.

477 Martin St., Unit #6, Penticton BC V2A 5L2 Canada. (778)476-5750. **Fax:** (778)476-5651. **E-mail:** dave@redtuquebooks.ca. **Website:** www.redtuquebooks.ca. **Contact:** David Korinetz, executive editor.

HOW TO CONTACT Submit a query letter and first 5 pages. Include total word count. A one-page synopsis is optional. Accepts queries by e-mail and mail. SASE for reply only.

TERMS Pays 5-7% royalties on net sales. Pays $250 advance. Responds in 3 weeks.

TIPS "Well-plotted, character-driven stories, preferably with happy endings, will have the best chance of being accepted. Keep in mind that authors who like to begin sentences with *and*, *or*, and *but* are less likely to be considered. Don't send anything gruesome or overly explicit; tell us a good story, but think PG."

ROBERT D. REED PUBLISHERS

P.O. Box 1992, Bandon OR 97411. (541)347-9882. **Fax:** (541)347-9883. **Website:** www.rdrpublishers.com. **Contact:** Cleone L. Reed. Estab. 1991. Publishes hardcover and trade paperback originals. Catalog and guidelines online.

NEEDS "We look for high-quality work from authors who will work hard to display their work and travel, selling books."

HOW TO CONTACT Query with SASE or via e-mail.

TERMS Pays 12-17% royalty on wholesale price. Responds in 1 month.

TIPS "Target trade sales and sales to corporations, organizations, and groups. Read over our website and see what we have done."

RENAISSANCE HOUSE

465 Westview Ave., Englewood NJ 07631. (201)408-4048. **E-mail:** info@renaissancehouse.net. **Website:** www.renaissancehouse.net. Publishes biographies, folktales, coffee table books, instructional, textbooks, adventure, picture books, juvenile, and young adult. Specializes in multicultural and bilingual titles, Spanish-English. Submit ms; e-mail submissions. Children's, educational, multicultural, and textbooks. Represents 80 illustrators. 95% of artwork handled is children's book illustration. Currently open to illustrators seeking representation. Open to both new and established illustrators.

NEEDS Picture books: animal, folktales, multicultural. Young readers: animal, anthology, folktales, multicultural. Middle readers, young adult/teens: anthology, folktales, multicultural, nature/environment.

TERMS Responds to queries/mss in 2 weeks.

RING OF FIRE PUBLISHING LLC

6523 California Ave. SW #409, Seattle WA 98136. **E-mail:** contact@ringoffirebooks.com. **E-mail:** submis sions@ringoffirebooks.com. **Website:** www.ringoffirebooks.com. Estab. 2011. "Our audience is comprised of well-read fiction enthusiasts. Let us tell your story." Book catalog and ms guidelines available online.

IMPRINTS Publishes trade paperback and electronic originals.

HOW TO CONTACT Query online. Submit synopsis and 3 sample chapters.

TERMS Pays royalties. Responds in 1 month to queries; 2 months to mss.

⊕ RIPPLE GROVE PRESS

P.O. Box 491, Hubbardston MA 01452. **E-mail:** submit@ripplegrovepress.com. **Website:** www.ripplegrovepress.com. Estab. 2013. Ripple Grove Press is a family-owned children's picture book publishing company started in 2013. "Our mission is to create picture books that come from life experiences, elegant imagination, and the deep passion in our hearts. We want each book to enlighten a child's mind with fun and wonder. Ripple Grove Press searches for a powerful 'timeless' feel in each book we publish. Our stories will make you laugh, think, or keep you guessing and dreaming." Publishes hardcover originals. Guidelines available online.

NEEDS "Our focus is picture books for children aged 2-6. We want something unique, sweet, funny, touching, offbeat, colorful, surprising, charming, different, and creative."

HOW TO CONTACT Submit completed ms. Accepts submissions by mail and e-mail. Please submit a cover letter including a summary of your story, the age range of the story, a brief biography of yourself, and contact information.

TERMS Authors receive between 10-12% royalty on net receipt. Responds to queries within 3 months.

TIPS Also targeting the adults reading to the children. "We create books that children and adults want to read over and over again. Our books showcase art as well as stories and tie them together to create a unique and creative product."

◑ ◐ RIVER CITY PUBLISHING

1719 Mulberry St., Montgomery AL 36106. **E-mail:** fnorris@rivercitypublishing.com. **Website:** www.rivercitypublishing.com. **Contact:** Fran Norris, editor. Estab. 1989. Midsize independent publisher (8-10 books per year). River City primarily publishes narrative nonfiction that reflects the South. "We are looking mainly for narrative histories, sociological accounts, and travel. Only biographies and memoirs from noted persons will be considered; we are closed to all personal memoir submissions." Publishes hardcover and trade paperback originals.

NEEDS No poetry, memoir, or children's books.

HOW TO CONTACT Send appropriate-sized SASE or IRC, "otherwise, the material will be recycled." Also accepts queries by e-mail at: jgilbert@rivercitypublishing.com. "Please include your electronic query letter as in-line text and not an as attachment; we do not open unsolicited attachments of any kind. Please do not include sample chapters or your entire ms as in-line text. We do not field or accept queries by telephone. Please wait at least 3 months before contacting us about your submission." No multiple submissions. Rarely comments on rejected mss.

TERMS Pays 10-15% royalty on retail price. Pays $500-5,000 advance. Responds to mss in 9 months.

TIPS "Only send your best work after you have received outside opinions. From approximately 1,000 submissions each year, we publish no more than 8 books and few of those come from unsolicited material. Competition is fierce, so follow the guidelines exactly. All first-time novelists should submit their work to the Fred Bonnie Award contest."

◉ ◎ RIVERHEAD BOOKS

Penguin Putnam, 375 Hudson St., Office #4079, New York NY 10014. **E-mail:** ecommerce@us.penguingroup.com. **E-mail:** riverhead.web@us.penguingroup.com. **Website:** www.riverheadbooks.com. **Contact:** Megan Lynch, senior editor.

HOW TO CONTACT *Submit through agent only. No unsolicited mss.*

◉ ◎ ROARING BROOK PRESS

175 Fifth Ave., New York NY 10010. (646)307-5151. **E-mail:** david.langva@roaringbrookpress.com. **E-mail:** press.inquiries@macmillanusa.com. **Website:** us.macmillan.com/RoaringBrook.aspx. **Contact:** David Langva. Estab. 2000. Roaring Brook Press is an imprint of MacMillan, a group of companies that includes Henry Holt and Farrar, Straus & Giroux. Roaring Brook is not accepting unsolicited mss.

NEEDS Picture books, young readers, middle readers, young adults: adventure, animal, contemporary, fantasy, history, humor, multicultural, nature/environment, poetry, religion, science fiction, sports, suspense/mystery.

HOW TO CONTACT *Not accepting unsolicited mss or queries.*

TERMS Pays authors royalty based on retail price.

TIPS "You should find a reputable agent and have him/her submit your work."

☼ RONSDALE PRESS

3350 W. 21st Ave., Vancouver BC V6S 1G7 Canada. (604)738-4688. **Fax:** (604)731-4548. **E-mail:** rons dale@shaw.ca. **Website:** ronsdalepress.com. **Contact:** Ronald B. Hatch (fiction, poetry, nonfiction, social commentary); Veronica Hatch (young adult novels and short stories). Estab. 1988. "Ronsdale Press is a Canadian literary publishing house that publishes 12 books each year, 4 of which are young adult titles. Of particular interest are books involving children exploring and discovering new aspects of Canadian history." Publishes trade paperback originals. Book catalog for #10 SASE. Guidelines available online.

NEEDS Young adults: Canadian novels. Average word length: middle readers and young adults—50,000. Recently published *Turn from Troy*, by Patrick Bowman (ages 10-14); *Hannah & The Salish Sea*, by Carol Anne Shaw (ages 10-14); *Dark Times*, edited by Ann Walsh (anthology of short stories, ages 10 and up); *Outlaw in India*, by Philip Roy; *Freedom Bound*, by Jean Rae Baxter (ages 10-14).

HOW TO CONTACT Submit complete ms.

TERMS Pays 10% royalty on retail price. Responds to queries in 2 weeks; mss in 2 months.

TIPS "Ronsdale Press is a literary publishing house, based in Vancouver and dedicated to publishing books from across Canada, books that give Canadians new insights into themselves and their country. We aim to publish the best Canadian writers."

ROSE ALLEY PRESS

4203 Brooklyn Ave. NE, #103A, Seattle WA 98105. (206)633-2725. **E-mail:** rosealleypress@juno.com. **Website:** www.rosealleypress.com. **Contact:** David D. Horowitz. Estab. 1995. "Rose Alley Press primarily publishes books featuring rhymed metrical poetry and an annually updated booklet about writing and publication. We do not read or consider unsolicited mss."

☯☿ ST. MARTIN'S PRESS, LLC

Holtzbrinck Publishers, 175 Fifth Ave., New York NY 10010. (212)674-5151. **Fax:** (212)420-9314. **Website:** www.stmartins.com. Estab. 1952. General-interest publisher of both fiction and nonfiction. Publishes hardcover, trade paperback, and mass-market originals.

IMPRINTS Minotaur; Thomas Dunne Books; Griffin; Palgrave MacMillan (division); Priddy Books; St. Martin's Press Paperback & Reference Group; St. Martin's Press Trade Division; Truman Talley Books.

HOW TO CONTACT Agented submissions only. *No unsolicited mss.*

TERMS Pays royalty. Pays advance.

SAINT MARY'S PRESS

702 Terrace Heights, Winona MN 55987. (800)533-8095. **Fax:** (800)344-9225. **E-mail:** submissions@smp .org. **Website:** www.smp.org. Ms guidelines online or by e-mail.

TIPS "Request product catalog and/or do research online of Saint Mary Press book lists before submitting proposal."

☯ SAKURA PUBLISHING & TECHNOLOGIES

P.O. Box 1681, Hermitage PA 16148. (330)360-5131. **E-mail:** skpublishing124@gmail.com. **Website:** www .sakura-publishing.com. **Contact:** Derek Vasconi, talent finder and CEO. Estab. 2007. Mss that don't follow guidelines will not be considered. Publishes hardcover, trade paperback, mass-market paperback and electronic originals and reprints. Book catalog available for #10 SASE. Guidelines available online.

HOW TO CONTACT Follow guidelines online.

TERMS Pays royalty of 20-60% on wholesale price or retail price. Responds in 1 month to queries, mss, proposals.

TIPS "Sakura Publishing is looking to publish primarily authors who have a marketing plan in place for their books and a strong support network behind them. Also Sakura Publishing has a preference for fiction/nonfiction books specializing in Asian culture."

⊘ SALVO PRESS

E-mail: info@salvopress.com. **E-mail:** submissions@ start-media.com. **Website:** www.salvopress.com. **Contact:** Scott Schmidt, publisher. Estab. 1998. Book catalog and ms guidelines online.

NEEDS "We are a small press specializing in mystery, suspense, espionage, and thriller fiction. Our press publishes in trade paperback and most e-book formats." Publishes hardcover, trade paperback originals, and e-books in most formats. **Published 6 debut authors within the last year.** "Our needs change, check our website."

HOW TO CONTACT Query by e-mail.

TERMS Pays 10% royalty. Responds in 5 minutes to 1 month to queries; 2 months to mss.

SAMHAIN PUBLISHING, LTD

11821 Mason Montgomery Rd., Cincinnati OH 45249. (478)314-5144. **Fax:** (478)314-5148. **E-mail:** editor@samhainpublishing.com. **Website:** www.samhainpublishing.com. **Contact:** Heather Osborn, editorial director. Estab. 2005. "A small, independent publisher, Samhain's motto is 'It's all about the story.' We look for fresh, unique voices who have a story to share with the world. We encourage our authors to let their muse have its way and to create tales that don't always adhere to current trends. One never knows what the next hot genre will be or when it will start, so write what's in your soul. These are the books that, whether the story is based on formula or is an original, when written from the heart will earn you a lifetime readership." Publishes e-books and paperback originals. POD/offset printing; line illustrations. Guidelines available online.

NEEDS Needs erotica and all genres and all heat levels of romance (contemporary, futuristic/time travel, gothic, historical, paranormal, regency period, romantic suspense, fantasy, action/adventure, etc.), as well as fantasy, urban fantasy, or science fiction with strong romantic elements, with word counts between 12,000 and 120,000 words. "Samhain is now accepting submissions for our line of horror novels. We are actively seeking talented writers who can tell an exciting, dramatic, and frightening story, and who are eager to promote their work and build their community of readers. We are looking for novels either supernatural or not, contemporary or historical, that are original and compelling. Authors can be previously unpublished or established, agented or un-agented. Content can range from subtle and unsettling to gory and shocking. The writing is what counts."

HOW TO CONTACT Accepts unsolicited mss. Query with outline/synopsis and either 3 sample chapters or the full ms. Accepts queries by e-mail only. Include estimated word count, brief bio, list of publishing credits, and "how the author is working to improve craft: association, critique groups, etc."

TERMS Pays royalties 30-40% for e-books, average of 8% for trade paper, and author's copies (quantity varies). Responds in 4 months.

TIPS "Because we are an e-publisher first, we do not have to be as concerned with industry trends and can publish less popular genres of fiction if we believe the story and voice are good and will appeal to our customers. Please follow submission guidelines located on our website, include all requested information and proof your query/ms for errors prior to submission."

SARABANDE BOOKS, INC.

2234 Dundee Rd., Suite 200, Louisville KY 40205. (502)458-4028. **Fax:** (502)458-4065. **E-mail:** info@sarabandebooks.org. **Website:** www.sarabandebooks.org. **Contact:** Sarah Gorham, editor-in-chief. Estab. 1994. "Sarabande Books was founded to publish poetry, short fiction, and creative nonfiction. We look for works of lasting literary value. Please see our titles to get an idea of our taste. Accepts submissions through contests and open submissions." Publishes trade paperback originals. Book catalog available free. Contest guidelines for #10 SASE or on website.

Charges $10 handling fee with alternative option of purchase of book from website (e-mail confirmation of sale must be included with submission).

NEEDS "We consider novels and nonfiction in a wide variety of genres and subject matters with a special emphasis on mysteries and crime fiction. We do not consider science fiction, fantasy, or horror. Our target length is 70,000-90,000 words."

HOW TO CONTACT Queries can be sent via e-mail, fax, or regular post.

TERMS Pays royalty. 10% on actual income received. Also pays in author's copies. Pays $500-1,000 advance.

TIPS "Sarabande publishes for a general literary audience. Know your market. Read—and buy—books of literature. Sponsors contests for poetry and fiction. Make sure you're not writing in a vacuum, that you've read and are conscious of contemporary literature. Have someone read your ms, checking it for ordering, coherence. Better a lean, consistently strong ms than one that is long and uneven. We like a story to have good narrative, and we like to be engaged by language."

SASQUATCH BOOKS

1904 Third Ave., Suite 710, Seattle WA 98101. (206)467-4300. **Fax:** (206)467-4301. **E-mail:** ttabor@sasquatchbooks.com. **Website:** www.sasquatchbooks.com. **Contact:** Gary Luke, editorial director; Terence Maikels, acquisitions editor; Heidi Lenze, acquisitions editor. Estab. 1986. "Sasquatch Books publishes books for and from the Pacific Northwest, Alaska, and California and is the nation's premier regional press. Sasquatch Books' publishing program is a veritable celebration of regionally written words. Undeterred by political or geographical borders, Sasquatch defines its region as the magnificent area that stretches from the Brooks Range to the Gulf of California and from the Rocky Mountains to the Pacific Ocean. Our top-selling Best Places® travel guides serve the most popular destinations and locations of the West. We also publish widely in the areas of food and wine, gardening, nature, photography, children's books, and regional history, all facets of the literature of place. With more than 200 books brimming with insider information on the West, we offer an energetic eye on the lifestyle, landscape, and worldview of our region. Considers queries and proposals from authors and agents for new projects that fit into our West Coast regional publishing program. We can evaluate query letters, proposals, and complete mss." Publishes regional hardcover and trade paperback originals. Book catalog for 9×12 envelope and 2 first-class stamps. Guidelines available online.

○   "When you submit to Sasquatch Books, please remember that the editors want to know about you *and* your project, along with a sense of who will want to read your book."

NEEDS Young readers: adventure, animal, concept, contemporary, humor, nature/environment.

TERMS Pays royalty on cover price. Pays wide range advance. Responds to queries in 3 months.

TIPS "We sell books through a range of channels in addition to the book trade. Our primary audience consists of active, literate residents of the West Coast."

⊕ SCARLETTA PRESS

10 S. 5th St., Suite 1105, Minneapolis MN 55402. (612)455-0252. **Website:** www.scarlettapress.com. Estab. 2005. Guidelines online.

○   "We accept submissions only during our reading period, September 1-June 1."

NEEDS Does not publish plays, screenplays, short story collections, or poetry.

HOW TO CONTACT Submit cover letter with synopsis, 1-2 sample chapters.

TERMS Pays 10-20% royalty.

TIPS "Read our submission guidelines carefully before submitting."

Ⓐ SCHOLASTIC PRESS

Imprint of Scholastic, Inc., 557 Broadway, New York NY 10012. (212)343-6100. **Fax:** (212)343-4713. **Website:** www.scholastic.com. **Contact:** David Saylor, editorial director, Scholastic Press, creative director and associate publisher for all Scholastic hardcover imprints. Scholastic Press publishes fresh, literary picture book fiction and nonfiction; fresh, literary nonseries or nongenre-oriented middle-grade and young adult fiction. Currently emphasizing subtly handled treatments of key relationships in children's lives; unusual approaches to commonly dry subjects, such as biography, math, history, or science. De-emphasizing fairy tales (or retellings), board books, genre, or series fiction (mystery, fantasy, etc.). Publishes hardcover originals.

NEEDS Looking for strong picture books, young chapter books, appealing middle-grade novels (ages 8-11) and interesting and well-written young adult novels. Wants fresh, exciting picture books and novels—inspiring, new talent.

TERMS Pays royalty on retail price. Pays variable advance. Responds in 3 months to queries; 6-8 months to mss.

TIPS "Read *currently* published children's books. Revise, rewrite, rework, and find your own voice, style, and subject. We are looking for authors with a strong and unique voice who can tell a great story and have the ability to evoke genuine emotion. Children's publishers are becoming more selective, looking for irresistible talent and fairly broad appeal, yet still very willing to take risks, just to keep the game interesting."

◑ SCRIBE PUBLICATIONS

18-20 Edward St., Brunswick VIC 3056 Australia. (61)(3)9388-8780. **Fax:** (61)(3)9388-8787. **E-mail:** info@scribepub.com.au. **Website:** www.scribepublications.com.au. Estab. 1976. Submission guidelines available on website under About Us.

HOW TO CONTACT Submit synopsis, sample chapters, CV.

SEAL PRESS

1700 4th St., Berkeley CA 94710. (510)595-3664. **E-mail:** seal.press@perseusbooks.com. **E-mail:** seal acquisitions@avalonpub.com. **Website:** www.sealpress.com. Estab. 1976. "Seal Press is an imprint of Avalon Publishing Group, feminist book publisher interested in original, lively, radical, empowering, and culturally diverse nonfiction by women addressing contemporary issues from a feminist perspective or speaking positively to the experience of being female. Currently emphasizing women outdoor adventurists, young feminists, political issues for women, health issues, and surviving abuse. *Not accepting fiction at this time.*" Publishes trade paperback originals. Book catalog and ms guidelines for SASE or online.

NEEDS Ethnic, feminist, gay/lesbian, literary, multicultural. "We are interested in alternative voices."

HOW TO CONTACT *Does not accept fiction at present.* Query with SASE or submit outline, 2 sample chapters, synopsis.

TERMS Pays 7-10% royalty on retail price. Pays variable royalty on retail price. Pays $3,000-10,000 advance. Pays variable advance. Responds in 2 months to queries.

TIPS "Our audience is generally composed of women interested in reading about women's issues addressed from a feminist perspective."

◯ SECOND STORY PRESS

20 Maud St., Suite 401, Toronto ON M5V 2M5 Canada. (416)537-7850. **Fax:** (416)537-0588. **E-mail:** info@secondstorypress.ca; marketing@secondstorypress.com. **Website:** www.secondstorypress.ca.

NEEDS Considers nonsexist, nonracist, and nonviolent stories, as well as historical fiction, chapter books, picture books.

SEEDLING CONTINENTAL PRESS

520 E. Bainbridge St., Elizabethtown PA 17022. **E-mail:** bspencer@continentalpress.com. **Website:** www.continentalpress.com. **Contact:** Megan Bergonzi. Publishes books for classroom use only for the beginning reader in English. "Natural language and predictable text are requisite. Patterned text is acceptable but must have a unique story line. Poetry, books in rhyme and full-length picture books are not being accepted. Illustrations are not necessary."

NEEDS Young readers: adventure, animal, folktales, humor, multicultural, nature/environment. Does not accept texts longer than 12 pages or over 300 words. Average word length: young readers—100.

HOW TO CONTACT Submit complete ms.

TERMS Work purchased outright from authors. Responds to mss in 6 months.

TIPS "See our website. Follow writers' guidelines carefully and test your story with children and educators."

SERIOUSLY GOOD BOOKS

999 Vanderbilt Beach Rd., Naples FL 34119. **E-mail:** seriouslygoodbks@aol.com. **Website:** www.seriouslygoodbks.net. Estab. 2010. Publishes historial fiction only. Publishes trade paperback and electronic originals. Book catalog and guidelines online.

HOW TO CONTACT Query by e-mail.

TERMS Pays 15% minimum royalties. Respons in 1 month to queries.

TIPS "Looking for historial fiction with substance. We seek well-researched historical fiction in the vein of Mary Renault, Maggie Anton, Robert Harris, etc. Please don't query with historical fiction mixed with other genres (romance, time travel, vampires, etc.)."

SEVEN STORIES PRESS

140 Watts St., New York NY 10013. (212)226-8760. **Fax:** (212)226-1411. **E-mail:** info@sevenstories.com. **Website:** www.sevenstories.com. **Contact:** Daniel Simon; Anna Lui. Estab. 1995. Founded in 1995 in New York City, and named for the 7 authors who committed to a home with a fiercely independent spirit, Seven Stories Press publishes works of the imagination and political titles by voices of conscience. While most widely known for its books on politics, human rights, and social and economic justice, Seven Stories continues to champion literature, with a list encompassing both innovative debut novels and National Book Award–winning poetry collections, as well as prose and poetry translations from the French, Spanish, German, Swedish, Italian, Greek, Polish, Korean, Vietnamese, Russian, and Arabic. Publishes hardcover and trade paperback originals. Book catalog and ms guidelines free.

HOW TO CONTACT Submit cover letter with 2 sample chapters.

TERMS Pays 7-15% royalty on retail price. Pays advance. Responds in 1 month to queries and mss.

TIPS "Each year we also publish an annual compilation of censored news stories by Project Censored. Features of this series include the Top 25 Censored News Stories of the year—which has a history of identifying important neglected news stories and which is widely disseminated in the alternative press—as well as the 'Junk Food News' chapter and chapters on hot-button topics for the year. Seven Stories also maintains a publishing partnership with Human Rights Watch through the yearly publication of the World Report, a preeminent account of human rights abuse around the world—a report card on the progress of the world's nations towards the protection of human rights for people everywhere."

ⒶⒼⓈⓄ SEVERN HOUSE PUBLISHERS

Salatin House, 19 Cedar St., Sutton, Surrey SM2 5DA United Kingdom. (44)(208)770-3930. **Fax:** (44)(208)770-3850. **Website:** www.severnhouse.com. **Contact:** Amanda Stewart, editorial director. Severn House is currently emphasizing suspense, romance, mystery. Large print imprint from existing authors. Publishes hardcover and trade paperback originals and reprints. Book catalog available free.

IMPRINTS Creme de la Crime.

HOW TO CONTACT *Agented submissions only.*

TERMS Pays 7½-15% royalty on retail price. Pays $750-5,000 advance. Responds in 3 months to proposals.

SHAMBHALA PUBLICATIONS, INC.

300 Massachusetts Ave., Boston MA 02115. (617)424-0030. **Fax:** (617)236-1563. **E-mail:** editors@shambhala.com. **Website:** www.shambhala.com. Estab. 1969. Publishes hardcover and trade paperback originals and reprints. Book catalog and ms guidelines free.

IMPRINTS Roost Books.

HOW TO CONTACT Submit proposal package, outline, résumé, 2 sample chapters, TOC.

TERMS Pays 8% royalty on retail price. Responds in 4 months to queries, proposals, and mss.

⊕Ⓞ SHIPWRECKT BOOKS PUBLISHING COMPANY LLC

115(B) Parkway Ave., P.O. Box 20, Lanesboro MN 55949. (507)458-8190. **E-mail:** publisher@shipwrecktbooks.com. **E-mail:** contact@shipwrecktbooks.com. **Website:** www.shipwrecktbooks.com. **Contact:** Tom Driscoll, managing editor. Publishes trade paperback originals, mass-market paperback originals, and electronic originals. Send SASE for book catalog. Send SASE for ms guidelines.

IMPRINTS Rocket Science Press (literary); Up On Big Rock Poetry Series; Lost Lake Folk Art (fee-based publishing).

HOW TO CONTACT E-mail query. All unsolicited mss returned unopened.

TERMS Authors receive a maximum of 50% royalties. Responds to queries within a month.

TIPS Quality writing to be considered for royalty contract. Offers full-time editorial services for new and unpublished writers.

ⓐ SILVER LEAF BOOKS, LLC

P.O. Box 6460, Holliston MA 01746. **E-mail:** editor@silverleafbooks.com. **Website:** www.silverleafbooks.com. **Contact:** Brett Fried, editor. "Silver Leaf Books is a small press featuring primarily new and up-coming talent in the fantasy, science fiction, mystery, thrillers, suspense, and horror genres. Our editors work closely with our authors to establish a lasting and mutually beneficial relationship, helping both the authors and company continue to grow and thrive." Average print order: 3,000. Debut novel print order: 3,000. Distributes/promotes titles through Baker & Taylor Books and Ingram. Guidelines online.

Ⓠ Publishes hardcover originals, trade paperback originals, paperback originals, electronic/digital books.

HOW TO CONTACT Query with outline/synopsis and 3 sample chapters. Accepts queries by snail mail. Include estimated word count, brief bio and marketing plan. Send SASE or IRC for return of ms or disposable copy of ms and SASE/IRC for reply only.

TERMS Pays royalties, and provides author's copies. Responds to queries in 6 months; mss in 4 months.

TIPS "Follow the online guidelines, be thorough and professional."

ⒶⓄ SIMON & SCHUSTER

1230 Avenue of the Americas, New York NY 10020. (212)698-7000. **Website:** www.simonandschuster.com.

Ⓠ *Accepts agented submissions only.*

ⒶⓄ SIMON & SCHUSTER ADULT PUBLISHING GROUP

1230 Avenue of the Americas, New York NY 10020. **E-mail:** ssonline@simonsays.com; Lydia.Frost@simonandschuster.com. **Website:** www.simonandschuster.com. Estab. 1924. The Simon & Schuster Adult Publishing Group includes a number of publishing units that offer books in several formats. Each unit has its own publisher, editorial group, and publicity department. Common sales and business departments support all the units. The managing editorial, art, production, marketing, and subsidiary rights departments have staff members dedicated to the individual imprints.

HOW TO CONTACT *Agented submissions only.*

⊘⊘ SIMON & SCHUSTER BOOKS FOR YOUNG READERS

Imprint of Simon & Schuster Children's Publishing, 1230 Avenue of the Americas, New York NY 10020. (212)698-7000. **Fax:** (212)698-2796. **Website:** www .simonsayskids.com. "Simon and Schuster Books For Young Readers (BFYR) is the Flagship imprint of the S&S Children's Division. We are committed to publishing a wide range of contemporary, commercial, award-winning fiction and nonfiction that spans every age of children's publishing. BFYR is constantly looking to the future, supporting our foundation authors and franchises, but always with an eye for breaking new ground with every publication. We publish high-quality fiction and nonfiction for a variety of age groups and a variety of markets. Above all, we strive to publish books that we are passionate about." Publishes hardcover originals. Guidelines online.

○ *No unsolicited mss.* All unsolicited mss returned unopened.

IMPRINTS Paula Wiseman Books.

HOW TO CONTACT Agented submissions only.

TERMS Pays variable royalty on retail price.

TIPS "We're looking for picture books centered on a strong, fully developed protagonist who grows or changes during the course of the story; young adult novels that are challenging and psychologically complex; also imaginative and humorous middle-grade fiction. And we want nonfiction that is as engaging as fiction. Our imprint's slogan is 'Reading You'll Remember.' We aim to publish books that are fresh, accessible, and family oriented; we want them to have an impact on the reader."

SKINNER HOUSE BOOKS

The Unitarian Universalist Association, 25 Beacon St., Boston MA 02108. (617)742-2100 ext. 603. **Fax:** (617)742-7025. **E-mail:** bookproposals@uua.org. **Website:** www.uua.org/publications/skinnerhouse. **Contact:** Betsy Martin. Estab. 1975. "We publish titles in Unitarian Universalist faith, liberal religion, history, biography, worship, and issues of social justice. Most of our children's titles are intended for religious education or worship use. They reflect Unitarian Universalist values. We also publish inspirational titles of poetic prose and meditations. Writers should know that Unitarian Universalism is a liberal religious denomination committed to progressive ideals. Currently emphasizing social justice concerns." Pub-

lishes trade paperback originals and reprints. Book catalog for 6×9 SAE with 3 first-class stamps. Guidelines online.

NEEDS Anthology, multicultural, nature/environment, religion.

HOW TO CONTACT Query or submit proposal with cover letter, TOC, 2 sample chapters.

TERMS Responds to queries in 3 weeks.

TIPS "From outside our denomination, we are interested in mss that will be of help or interest to liberal churches, Sunday School classes, parents, ministers, and volunteers. Inspirational/spiritual and children's titles must reflect liberal Unitarian Universalist values."

⊘ SLEEPING BEAR PRESS

315 East Eisenhower Pkwy, Suite 200, Ann Arbor MI 48108. (800)487-2323. **Fax:** (734)794-0004. **E-mail:** customerservice@sleepingbearpress.com. **Website:** www.sleepingbearpress.com. **Contact:** Heather Hughes. Estab. 1998. Book catalog available via e-mail.

○ *Currently not accepting ms submissions or queries at this time.* "Please check back for further updates."

NEEDS Picture books: adventure, animal, concept, folktales, history, multicultural, nature/environment, religion, sports. Young readers: adventure, animal, concept, folktales, history, humor, multicultural, nature/environment, religion, sports. Average word length: picture books—1,800.

⊘⊘ SMALL BEER PRESS

150 Pleasant St., #306, Easthampton MA 01027. (413)203-1636. **Fax:** (413)203-1636. **E-mail:** info@ smallbeerpress.com. **Website:** www.smallbeerpress .com. **Contact:** Gavin J. Grant, acquisitions. Estab. 2000.

○ Small Beer Press also publishes the zine *Lady Churchill's Rosebud Wristlet.* "SBP's books have recently received the Tiptree and Crawford Awards."

HOW TO CONTACT Does not accept unsolicited novel or short story collection mss. Send queries with an SASE by mail.

TIPS "Please be familiar with our books first to avoid wasting your time and ours, thank you."

SOFT SKULL PRESS INC.

Counterpoint, 1919 Fifth St., Berkeley CA 94710. (510)704-0230. **Fax:** (510)704-0268. **E-mail:** info@

softskull.com. **Website:** www.softskull.com. "Here at Soft Skull we love books that are new, fun, smart, revelatory, quirky, groundbreaking, cage-rattling, and/or otherwise unusual." Publishes hardcover and trade paperback originals. Book catalog and guidelines on website.

NEEDS Does not consider poetry.

HOW TO CONTACT Soft Skull Press no longer accepts digital submissions. Send a cover letter describing your project in detail and a completed ms. For graphic novels, send a minimum of 5 fully inked pages of art, along with a synopsis of your story line. "Please do not send original material, as it will not be returned."

TERMS Pays 7-10% royalty. Average advance: $100-15,000. Responds in 2 months to proposals; 3 months to mss.

TIPS "See our website for updated submission guidelines."

SOHO PRESS, INC.

853 Broadway, New York NY 10003. **E-mail:** soho@sohopress.com **Website:** www.sohopress.com. **Contact:** Bronwen Hruska, publisher; Katie Herman, editor. Estab. 1986. Soho Press publishes primarily fiction, as well as some narrative literary nonfiction and mysteries set abroad. No electronic submissions, only queries by e-mail. Publishes hardcover and trade paperback originals; trade paperback reprints. Guidelines available online.

IMPRINTS Soho Press; Soho Crime; Soho Teen.

NEEDS Adventure, ethnic, feminist, historical, literary, mainstream/contemporary, mystery (police procedural), suspense, multicultural.

HOW TO CONTACT Submit 3 sample chapters and cover letter with synopsis, author bio, SASE. *No e-mailed submissions.*

TERMS Pays 10-15% royalty on retail price (varies under certain circumstances). Responds in 3 months.

TIPS "Soho Press publishes discerning authors for discriminating readers, finding the strongest possible writers and publishing them. Before submitting, look at our website for an idea of the types of books we publish, and read our submission guidelines."

⊕ SOURCEBOOKS CASABLANCA

Sourcebooks, Inc., 1935 Brookdale Rd., Naperville IL 60564. **E-mail:** romance@sourcebooks.com. **Website:** www.sourcebooks.com. **Contact:** Deb Werksman, Mary Altman, Cat Clyne. "Our romance imprint, Sourcebooks Casablanca, publishes single title romance in all subgenres." Guidelines online and by e-mail (deb.werksman@sourcebooks.com). "Please allow 21 days for a response."

○ "We are actively acquiring single-title and single-title series romance fiction (90,000-100,000 words) for our Casablanca imprint. We are looking for strong writers who are excited about marketing their books and building their community of readers, and whose books have something fresh to offer in the genre of romance."

NEEDS "Our editorial criteria call for: a heroine the reader can relate to, a hero she can fall in love with, a world that the reader can escape into, and a hook that we can sell within 2-3 sentences. We want an author who wants to build a career with us."

TERMS Responds in 2-3 months.

SOURCEBOOKS LANDMARK

Sourcebooks, Inc., 232 Madison Ave., Suite 1100, New York NY 10016. **E-mail:** editorialsubmissions@sourcebooks.com. **Website:** www.sourcebooks.com. **Contact:** Shana Drehs, Stephanie Bowen, Deb Werksman, Anna Klenke. "Our fiction imprint, Sourcebooks Landmark, publishes a variety of commercial fiction, including specialties in historical fiction and Austenalia. We are interested first and foremost in books that have a story to tell."

NEEDS "We are actively acquiring contemporary, book club, and historical fiction for our Landmark imprint. We are looking for strong writers who are excited about marketing their books and building their community of readers."

HOW TO CONTACT Submit synopsis and full ms preferred. Receipt of e-mail submissions acknowledged within 3 weeks of e-mail.

TERMS Responds in 2-3 months.

STARCHERONE BOOKS

Dzanc Books, P.O. Box 303, Buffalo NY 14201. (716)885-2726. **E-mail:** starcherone@gmail.com; publisher@starcherone.com. **Website:** www.starcherone.com. **Contact:** Ted Pelton, publisher; Carra Stratton, acquisitions editor. Estab. 2000. Nonprofit publisher of literary and experimental fiction. Publishes paperback originals and reprints. Books: acid-free paper; perfect-bound; occasional illustrations. Average print order: 1,000. Average first novel print order: 1,000. **Published 2 debut authors within the**

last year. Member CLMP. Titles distributed through website, Small Press Distribution, Amazon, independent bookstores. Catalog and guidelines online.

HOW TO CONTACT Accepts queries by mail or e-mail during August and September of each year. Submissions of unsolicited mss will risk being returned or discarded, unread. Include brief bio, list of publishing credits. Always query before sending ms.

TERMS Pays 10-12.5% royalty. Responds in 2 months to queries; 6-10 months to mss.

TIPS "During the late summer/early fall each year, after our contest has concluded, we have an open consideration period of approximately 6 weeks. During this time, we read queries from authors who already have established their credentials in some way, generally through prior publication, awards, and the like. We ask for queries from writers describing their projects and their writing credentials. From these, we invite submissions. Our next period for receiving queries will be in the late summer/early fall."

STONE BRIDGE PRESS

P.O. Box 8208, Berkeley CA 94707. **E-mail:** sbp@stonebridge.com. **Website:** www.stonebridge.com. **Contact:** Peter Goodman, publisher. Estab. 1989. "Independent press focusing on books about Japan and Asia in English (business, language, culture, literature, animation)." Publishes hardcover and trade paperback originals. Books: 60-70 lb. offset paper; web and sheet paper; perfect-bound; some illustrations. Distributes titles through Consortium. Promotes titles through Internet announcements, special-interest magazines, and niche tie-ins to associations. Book catalog for 2 first-class stamps and SASE. Ms guidelines online.

NEEDS Experimental, gay/lesbian, literary, Japan-themed. "Primarily looking at material relating to Japan. Translations only."

HOW TO CONTACT Does not accept unsolicited mss. Query with SASE. Accepts queries by e-mail, fax.

TERMS Pays royalty on wholesale price. Responds to queries in 4 months; mss in 8 months.

TIPS "Fiction translations only for the time being. No poetry."

STONESLIDE BOOKS

Stoneslide Media LLC, P.O. Box 8331, New Haven CT 06530. **E-mail:** editors@stoneslidecorrective.com. **E-mail:** submissions@stoneslidecorrective.com. **Website:** www.stoneslidecorrective.com. **Contact:** Jona-

than Weisberg, editor; Christopher Wachlin, editor. Estab. 2012. Publishes trade paperback and electronic originals. Book catalog and guidelines online.

NEEDS "We will look at any genre. The important factor for us is that the story use plot, characters, emotions, and other elements of storytelling to think and move the mind forward."

HOW TO CONTACT Submit proposal package via e-mail including: synopsis and 3 sample chapters.

TERMS Pays 20-80% royalty. Responds in 1-2 months.

TIPS "Read the Stoneslide Corrective to see if your work fits with our approach."

SUBITO PRESS

University of Colorado at Boulder, Department of English, 226 UCB, Boulder CO 80309-0226. **E-mail:** subitopressucb@gmail.com. **Website:** www.subitopress.org. Subito Press is a nonprofit publisher of literary works. Each year Subito publishes 1 work of fiction and 1 work of poetry through its contest. Publishes trade paperback originals. Guidelines online.

HOW TO CONTACT Submit complete ms to contest.

TIPS "We publish 2 books of innovative writing a year through our poetry and fiction contests. All entries are also considered for publication with the press."

SUNBURY PRESS, INC.

P.O. Box 548, Boiling Springs PA 17007. **E-mail:** info@sunburypress.com. **E-mail:** proposals@sunburypress.com. **Website:** www.sunburypress.com. Estab. 2004. Publishes trade paperback originals and reprints; electronic originals and reprints. Catalog and guidelines online.

○ "Please use our online submission form."

NEEDS "We are especially seeking historical fiction regarding the Civil War and books of regional interest."

TERMS Pays 10% royalty on wholesale price. Responds in 2 months.

TIPS "Our books appeal to very diverse audiences. We are building our list in many categories, focusing on many demographics. We are not like traditional publishers—we are digitally adept and very creative. Don't be surprised if we move quicker than you are accustomed to!"

SWAN ISLE PRESS

P.O. Box 408790, Chicago IL 60640. (773)728-3780. **E-mail:** info@swanislepress.com. **Website:** www.swanislepress.com. Estab. 1999. Publishes hardcover and trade paperback originals. Book catalog online. Guidelines online.

○   *"We do not accept unsolicited mss."*

HOW TO CONTACT Query with SASE. Submit complete mss.

TERMS Pays 7½-10% royalty on wholesale price. Responds in 6 months to queries; 12 months to mss.

SYLVAN DELL PUBLISHING

612 Johnnie Dodds, Suite A2, Mt. Pleasant SC 29464. (843)971-6722. **Fax:** (843)216-3804. **E-mail:** katie hall@sylvanpublishing.com. **E-mail:** donnagerman@ sylvandellpublishing.com. **Website:** www.sylvandell publishing.com. **Contact:** Donna German and Katie Hall, editors. Estab. 2004. "'The picture books we publish are usually, but not always, fictional stories that relate to animals, nature, the environment, math, and science. All books should subtly convey an educational theme through a warm story that is fun to read and that will grab a child's attention. Each book has a 3-5 page '*For Creative Minds*' section to reinforce the educational component. This section will have a craft and/ or game as well as 'fun facts' to be shared by the parent, teacher, or other adult. Authors do not need to supply this information. Mss. should be less than 1,500 words and meet all of the following 4 criteria: fun to read—mostly fiction with nonfiction facts woven into the story; national or regional in scope; must tie into early elementary school curriculum; must be marketable through a niche market such as a zoo, aquarium, or museum gift shop." Publishes hardcover, trade paperback, and electronic originals. Book catalog and guidelines available online.

NEEDS Picture books: animal, folktales, nature/environment, math-related. Word length: picture books— no more than 1,500.

HOW TO CONTACT Accepts electronic submissions only. Snail mail submissions are discarded without being opened.

TERMS Pays 6-8% royalty on wholesale price. Pays small advance. Acknowledges receipt of ms submission within 1 week.

TIPS "Please make sure that you have looked at our website to read our complete submission guidelines and to see if we are looking for a particular subject. Mss must meet all 4 of our stated criteria. We look for fairly realistic, bright and colorful art—no cartoons. We want the children excited about the books.

We envision the books being used at home and in the classroom."

SYNERGEBOOKS

948 New Highway 7, Columbia TN 38401. (863)956-3015. **Fax:** (863)588-2198. **E-mail:** synergebooks@ aol.com. **Website:** www.synergebooks.com. **Contact:** Debra Staples, publisher/acquisitions editor. Estab. 1999. "SynergEbooks is first and foremost a digital publisher, so most of our marketing budget goes to those formats. Authors are required to direct-sell a minimum of 100 digital copies of a title before it's accepted for print." Publishes trade paperback and electronic originals. Book catalog and guidelines online.

NEEDS SynergEbooks publishes at least 40 new titles a year, and only 1-5 of those are put into print in any given year. "SynergEbooks is first and foremost a digital publisher, so most of our marketing budget goes to those formats."

HOW TO CONTACT Submit proposal package, including synopsis, 1-3 sample chapters, and marketing plans.

TERMS Pays 15-40% royalty; makes outright purchase.

TIPS "At SynergEbooks, we work with the authors to promote their work."

⊚   TAFELBERG PUBLISHERS

Imprint of NB Publishers, P.O. Box 879, Cape Town 8000 South Africa. (27)(21)406-3033. **Fax:** (27) (21)406-3812. **E-mail:** kristin@nb.co.za. **Website:** www.tafelberg.com. **Contact:** Danita van Romburgh, editorial secretary; Louise Steyn, publisher. General publisher best known for Afrikaans fiction, authoritative political works, children's/youth literature, and a variety of illustrated and nonillustrated nonfiction.

NEEDS Picture books, young readers: animal, anthology, contemporary, fantasy, folktales, hi-lo, humor, multicultural, nature/environment, science fiction, special needs. Middle readers, young adults: animal (middle reader only), contemporary, fantasy, hi-lo, humor, multicultural, nature/environment, problem novels, science fiction, special needs, sports, suspense/mystery. Average word length: picture books—1,500-7,500; young readers—25,000; middle readers—15,000; young adults—40,000.

HOW TO CONTACT Submit complete ms.

TERMS Pays authors royalty of 15-18% based on wholesale price. Responds to queries in 2 weeks; mss in 6 months.

TIPS "Writers: Story needs to have a South African or African style. Illustrators: I'd like to look, but the chances of getting commissioned are slim. The market is small and difficult. Do not expect huge advances. Editorial staff attended or plans to attend the following conferences: IBBY, Frankfurt, SCBWI Bologna."

◑ ⊘ NAN A. TALESE

Imprint of Doubleday, Random House, Inc., 1745 Broadway, New York NY 10019. (212)782-8918. **Fax:** (212)782-8448. **Website:** www.nanatalese.com. **Contact:** Nan A. Talese, publisher and editorial director; Ronit Feldman, assistant editor. Nan A. Talese publishes nonfiction with a powerful guiding narrative and relevance to larger cultural interests, and literary fiction of the highest quality. Publishes hardcover originals

NEEDS Well-written narratives with a compelling story line, good characterization and use of language. We like stories with an edge.

HOW TO CONTACT Agented submissions only.

TERMS Pays variable royalty on retail price. Pays varying advance.

TIPS "Audience is highly literate people interested in story, information, and insight. We want well-written material submitted by agents only. See our website."

⊘ TANGLEWOOD BOOKS

P.O. Box 3009, Terre Haute IN 47803. **E-mail:** ptier ney@tanglewoodbooks.com. **Website:** www.tangle woodbooks.com. **Contact:** Kairi Hamlin, acquisitions editor; Peggy Tierney, publisher. Estab. 2003. "Tanglewood Press strives to publish entertaining, kid-centric books." Guidelines online.

NEEDS Picture books: adventure, animal, concept, contemporary, fantasy, humor. Average word length: picture books—800.

HOW TO CONTACT Not currently accepting submissions.

TERMS Responds to mss in up to 18 months.

TIPS "Please see lengthy Submissions page on our website."

⊕ TANTOR MEDIA

2 Business Park Road, Old Saybrook CT 06475. (860)395-1155. **Fax:** (860)395-1154. **E-mail:** rightse mail@tantor.com. **Website:** www.tantor.com. **Contact:** Ron Formica, director of acquisitions. Estab. 2001. Tantor is a leading indepedent audiobook publisher, producing more than 50 new titles every month.

Publishes hardcover, trade paperback, mass-market paperback, and electronic originals and reprints. Also publishes audiobooks. Catalog available online.

HOW TO CONTACT Query with SASE, or submit proposal package including synopsis and 3 sample chapters.

TERMS Pays 5-15% royalty on wholesale price. Responds in 2 months to queries, proposals, and mss.

TEXAS TECH UNIVERSITY PRESS

P.O. Box 41037, 3003 15th St., Suite 901, Lubbock TX 79409. (806)834-5821. **Fax:** (806)742-2979. **E-mail:** joanna.conrad@ttu.edu. **Website:** www.ttupress.org. **Contact:** Joanna Conrad, editor-in-chief. Estab. 1971. Texas Tech University Press, the book publishing office of the university since 1971 and an AAUP member since 1986, publishes nonfiction titles in the areas of natural history and the natural sciences; 18th century and Joseph Conrad studies; studies of modern Southeast Asia, particularly the Vietnam War; costume and textile history; Latin American literature and culture; and all aspects of the Great Plains and the American West, especially history, biography, memoir, sports history, and travel. In addition, the Press publishes several scholarly journals, acclaimed series for young readers, an annual invited poetry collection, and literary fiction of Texas and the West. Guidelines online.

NEEDS Fiction rooted in the American West and Southwest, Jewish literature, Latin American and Latino fiction (in translation or English).

☺ THISTLEDOWN PRESS LTD.

401 2nd Ave., Saskatoon SK S7K 2C3 Canada. (306)244-1722. **Fax:** (306)244-1762. **E-mail:** edito rial@thistledownpress.com. **Website:** www.thistle downpress.com. **Contact:** Allan Forrie, publisher. Book catalog free on request. Guidelines available for #10 envelope and IRC.

◖ "Thistledown originates books by Canadian authors only, although we have co-published titles by authors outside Canada. We do not publish children's picture books."

NEEDS Middle readers, young adults: adventure, anthology, contemporary, fantasy, humor, poetry, romance, science fiction, suspense/mystery, short stories. Average word length: young adults—40,000.

HOW TO CONTACT Submit outline/synopsis and sample chapters. *Does not accept mss.* Do not query by e-mail.

TERMS Pays authors royalty of 10-12% based on net dollar sales. Pays illustrators and photographers by the project (range: $250-750). Responds to queries in 4 months.

TIPS "Send cover letter including publishing history and SASE."

⊙⊘ TIGHTROPE BOOKS

602 Markham St., Toronto ON M6G 2L8 Canada. (647)348-4460. **E-mail:** tightropeasst@gmail.com. **E-mail:** info@tightropebooks.com. **Website:** www.tightropebooks.com. **Contact:** Shirarose Wilensky, editor. Estab. 2005. Publishes hardcover and trade paperback originals. Catalog and guidelines online.

○ Accepting submissions for new mystery imprint, Mysterio.

TERMS Pays 5-15% royalty on retail price. Pays advance of $200-300. Responds if interested.

TIPS "Audience is young, urban, literary, educated, unconventional."

⊙⊙ TIN HOUSE BOOKS

2617 NW Thurman St., Portland OR 97210. (503)473-8663. **Fax:** (503)473-8957. **E-mail:** meg@tinhouse.com. **Website:** www.tinhouse.com. **Contact:** Meg Storey, editor; Tony Perez, editor; Masie Cochran, associate editor. "We are a small independent publisher dedicated to nurturing new, promising talent as well as showcasing the work of established writers. Our Tin House New Voice series features work by authors who have not previously published a book." Distributes/promotes titles through Publishers Group West. Publishes hardcover originals, paperback originals, paperback reprints. Guidelines available on website.

HOW TO CONTACT *Agented mss only.* We no longer read unsolicited submissions by authors with no representation. We will continue to accept submissions from agents.

TERMS Responds to queries in 2-3 weeks; mss in 2-3 months.

⊙ TITAN PRESS

PMB 17897, Encino CA 91416. **E-mail:** titan91416@yahoo.com. **Website:** www.calwriterssfv.com. **Contact:** Stefanya Wilson, editor. Estab. 1981. Publishes hardcover and paperback originals. Ms guidelines for #10 SASE.

NEEDS Literary, mainstream/contemporary, short story collections. Published *Orange Messiahs*, by Scott Sonders (fiction).

HOW TO CONTACT Does not accept unsolicited mss. Query with SASE. Include brief bio, social security number, list of publishing credits.

TERMS Pays 20-40% royalty. Responds to queries in 3 months.

TIPS "Look, act, sound, and *be* professional."

⊘ TOP COW PRODUCTIONS, INC.

3812 Dunn Dr., Culver City CA 90232. **Website:** www.topcow.com.

HOW TO CONTACT *No unsolicited submissions.* Prefers submissions from artists. See website for details and advice on how to break into the market.

TOP PUBLICATIONS, LTD.

12221 Merit Dr., Suite 950, Dallas TX 75251. (972)628-6414. **Fax:** (972)233-0713. **E-mail:** info@toppub.com. **E-mail:** submissions@toppub.com. **Website:** www.toppub.com. Estab. 1999. Primarily a mainstream fiction publisher. Publishes hardcover and paperback originals. Guidelines online.

○ "It is imperative that our authors realize they will be required to promote their book extensively for it to be a success. Unless they are willing to make this commitment, they shouldn't submit to TOP."

TERMS Pays 15% royalty on wholesale price. Pays $250-1,000 advance. Acknowledges receipt of queries but only responds if interested in seeing ms. Responds in 6 months to mss.

TIPS "We recommend that our authors write books that appeal to a large mainstream audience to make marketing easier and increase the chances of success. We only publish a few titles a year so the odds at getting published at TOP are slim. If we don't offer you a contract, it doesn't mean we didn't like your submission. We have to pass on a lot of good material each year due to the limitations of our time and budget."

⊘ TOR BOOKS

175 Fifth Ave., New York NY 10010. **Website:** www.tor-forge.com. **Contact:** Juliet Pederson, publishing coordinator. Book catalog available for 9×12 SAE and 3 first-class stamps. See website for latest submission guidelines.

○ Tor Books is the "world's largest publisher of science fiction and fantasy, with strong category publishing in historical fiction, mystery, western/Americana, thriller, young adult."

IMPRINTS Forge, Orb, Starscape, Tor Teen.

NEEDS Average word length: middle readers—30,000; young adults—60,000-100,000.

HOW TO CONTACT "We do not accept queries."

TERMS Pays author royalty. Pays illustrators by the project.

TIPS "Know the house you are submitting to, familiarize yourself with the types of books they are publishing. Get an agent. Allow him/her to direct you to publishers who are most appropriate. It saves time and effort."

TORQUERE PRESS

1380 Rio Rancho Blvd., #1319, Rio Rancho NM 87124. **E-mail:** editor@torquerepress.com. **E-mail:** submissions@torquerepress.com. **Website:** www.torquerepress.com. **Contact:** Shawn Clements, submissions editor (homoerotica, suspense, gay/lesbian); Lorna Hinson, senior editor (gay/lesbian romance, historicals). Estab. 2003. "We are a gay and lesbian press focusing on romance and genres of romance. We particularly like paranormal and western romance." Publishes trade paperback originals and electronic originals and reprints. Book catalog online. Guidelines online.

IMPRINTS Top Shelf (Shawn Clements, editor); Single Shots (Kil Kenny, editor); Screwdrivers (M. Rode, editor); High Balls (Vincent Diamond, editor).

NEEDS All categories gay and lesbian themed.

HOW TO CONTACT Submit proposal package, 3 sample chapters, clips.

TERMS Pays 8-40% royalty. Pays $35-75 for anthology stories. Responds in 1 month to queries and proposals; 2-4 months to mss.

TIPS "Our audience is primarily people looking for a familiar romance setting featuring gay or lesbian protagonists. Please read guidelines carefully and familiarize yourself with our lines."

TORREY HOUSE PRESS, LLC

2806 Melony Dr., Salt Lake City UT 84124. (801)810-9THP. **E-mail:** mark@torreyhouse.com. **Website:** torreyhouse.com. **Contact:** Mark Bailey, publisher. Estab. 2010. "Torrey House Press (THP) publishes literary fiction and creative nonfiction about the world environment with a tilt toward the American West. Want submissions from experienced and agented authors only." Publishes hardcover, trade paperback, and electronic originals. Catalog online. Guidelines online.

NEEDS Literary fiction and creative nonfiction about the world environment and the American West.

HOW TO CONTACT Submit proposal package including: synopsis, complete ms, bio.

TERMS Pays 5-15% royalty on retail price. Responds in 3 months.

TIPS "Include writing experience (none okay)."

TOUCHWOOD EDITIONS

The Heritage Group, 103-1075 Pendergast St., Victoria BC V8V 0A1 Canada. (250)360-0829. **Fax:** (250)386-0829. **E-mail:** edit@touchwoodeditions.com. **Website:** www.touchwoodeditions.com. Publishes trade paperback originals and reprints. Book catalog and submission guidelines online.

HOW TO CONTACT Submit TOC, outline, word count.

TERMS Pays 15% royalty on net price. Responds in 3 months to queries.

TIPS "Our area of interest is Western Canada. We would like more creative nonfiction and books about people of note in Canada's history."

TRADEWIND BOOKS

202-1807 Maritime Mews, Granville Island, Vancouver BC V6H 3W7 Canada. (604)662-4405. **E-mail:** tradewindbooks@mail.lycos.com. **Website:** www.tradewindbooks.com. **Contact:** Michael Katz, publisher; Carol Frank, art director; R. David Stephens, senior editor. "Tradewind Books publishes juvenile picture books and young adult novels. Requires that submissions include evidence that author has read at least 3 titles published by Tradewind Books." Publishes hardcover and trade paperback originals. Book catalog and ms guidelines online.

NEEDS Picture books: adventure, multicultural, folktales. Average word length: 900 words.

HOW TO CONTACT Send complete ms for picture books. *Young adult novels by Canadian authors only. Chapter books by U.S. authors considered.*

TERMS Pays 7% royalty on retail price. Pays variable advance. Responds to mss in 2 months.

TRISTAN PUBLISHING

2355 Louisiana Ave. N, Golden Valley MO 55427. (763)545-1383. **Fax:** (763)545-1387. **E-mail:** info@tristanpublishing.com; manuscripts@tristanpublishing.com. **Website:** www.tristanpublishing.com. **Contact:** Brett Waldman, publisher. Estab. 2002. Publishes hardcover originals. Catalog and guidelines online.

IMPRINTS Tristan Publishing; Waldman House Press; Tristan Outdoors.

HOW TO CONTACT Query with SASE; submit completed mss.

TERMS Pays royalty on wholesale or retail price; outright purchase. Responds in 3 months.

TIPS "Our audience is adults and children."

TUPELO PRESS

P.O. Box 1767, North Adams MA 01247. (413)664-9611. **E-mail:** publisher@tupelopress.org. **E-mail:** www.tupelopress.org/submissions. **Website:** www.tupelopress.org. **Contact:** Jeffrey Levine, publisher/editor-in-chief; Elyse Newhouse, associate publisher; Jim Schley, managing editor. Estab. 2001. "We're an independent nonprofit literary press. We accept book-length poetry, poetry collections (48+ pages), short story collections, novellas, literary nonfiction/memoirs and up to 80 pages of a novel." Guidelines online.

NEEDS "For novels—submit no more than 100 pages along with a summary of the entire book. If we're interested we'll ask you to send the rest. We accept very few works of prose (1 or 2 per year)."

HOW TO CONTACT Submit complete ms. **Charges a $45 reading fee.**

☉①☉ TURNSTONE PRESS

206-100 Arthur St., Winnipeg MB R3B 1H3 Canada. (204)947-1555. **Fax:** (204)942-1555. **E-mail:** info@turnstonepress.com. **E-mail:** editor@turnstonepress.com. **Website:** www.turnstonepress.com. Estab. 1976. "Turnstone Press is a literary publisher, not a general publisher, and therefore we are only interested in literary fiction, literary nonfiction—including literary criticism—and poetry. We do publish literary mysteries, thrillers, and noir under our Ravenstone imprint. We publish only Canadian authors or landed immigrants, we strive to publish a significant number of new writers, to publish in a variety of genres, and to have 50% of each year's list be Manitoba writers and/or books with Manitoba content." Guidelines online.

HOW TO CONTACT "Samples must be 40 to 60 pages, typed/printed in a minimum 12-pt. serif typeface such as Times, Book Antiqua, or Garamond."

TERMS Responds in 4-7 months.

TIPS "As a Canadian literary press, we have a mandate to publish Canadian writers only. Do some homework before submitting works to make sure your subject matter/genre/writing style falls within the publishers area of interest."

TURN THE PAGE PUBLISHING LLC

P.O. Box 3179, Upper Montclair NJ 07043. **E-mail:** rlentin@turnthepagepublishing.com. **E-mail:** inquiry@turnthepagepublishing.com. **Website:** www.turnthepagepublishing.com. **Contact:** Roseann Lentin, editor-in-chief; Ann Kolakowski, editor. Estab. 2009. Publishes hardcover, trade paperback, electronic originals and trade paperback, electronic reprints. Book catalog online. Guidelines by e-mail.

NEEDS "We like new, fresh voices who are not afraid to 'step outside the box,' with unique ideas and storylines. We prefer edgy rather than typical."

HOW TO CONTACT Submit proposal package including synopsis and 3 sample chapters.

TERMS Pays 8-15% royalty on retail price. Responds in 2-3 months.

TIPS "Our audience is made up of intelligent, sophisticated, forward-thinking, progressive readers, who are not afraid to consider reading something different to Turn the Page of their lives. We're an independent publisher, we're avant-garde, so if you're looking for run-of-the-mill, don't submit here."

① TWILIGHT TIMES BOOKS

P.O. Box 3340, Kingsport TN 37664. **E-mail:** publisher@twilighttimesbooks.com. **Website:** www.twilighttimesbooks.com. **Contact:** Andy M. Scott, managing editor. Estab. 1999. "We publish compelling literary fiction by authors with a distinctive voice." Published 5 debut authors within the last year. Averages 120 total titles; 15 fiction titles/year. Member: AAP, PAS, SPAN, SLF. Guidelines online.

HOW TO CONTACT Accepts unsolicited mss. Do not send complete mss. Queries via e-mail only. Include estimated word count, brief bio, list of publishing credits, marketing plan.

TERMS Pays 8-15% royalty. Responds in 4 weeks to queries; 2 months to mss.

TIPS "The only requirement for consideration at Twilight Times Books is that your novel must be entertaining and professionally written."

☉∅ TYNDALE HOUSE PUBLISHERS, INC.

351 Executive Dr., Carol Stream IL 60188. (800)323-9400. **Fax:** (800)684-0247. **Website:** www.tyndale.com. **Contact:** Katara Washington Patton, acquisitions; Talinda Iverson, art acquisitions. Estab. 1962. "Tyndale House publishes practical, user-friendly Christian books for the home and family." Publishes

hardcover and trade paperback originals and mass-market reprints. Guidelines online.

NEEDS "Christian truths must be woven into the story organically. No short story collections. Youth books: characte-building stories with Christian perspective. Especially interested in ages 10-14. We primarily publish Christian historical romances, with occasional contemporary, suspense, or stand-alones."

HOW TO CONTACT Agented submissions only. No unsolicited mss.

TERMS Pays negotiable royalty. Pays negotiable advance.

TIPS "All accepted mss will appeal to Evangelical Christian children and parents."

⊕ TYRUS BOOKS

F+W Media, 1213 N. Sherman Ave., #306, Madison WI 53704. (508)427-7100. **Fax:** (508)427-6790. **E-mail:** submissions@tyrusbooks.com. **Website:** tyrus books.com. **Contact:** Ashley Myers, editor. "We publish crime and literary fiction. We believe in the life-changing power of the written word."

HOW TO CONTACT Submit query, synposis, and up to 20 sample pages.

○ UNBRIDLED BOOKS

200 N. Ninth St., Suite A, Columbia MO 65201. **E-mail:** michalsong@unbridledbooks.com. **Website:** unbridledbooks.com. **Contact:** Greg Michalson. Estab. 2004. "Unbridled Books is a premier publisher of works of rich literary quality that appeal to a broad audience."

HOW TO CONTACT Please query first by e-mail. Due to the heavy volume of submissions, we regret that at this time we are not able to consider uninvited mss.

UNITY HOUSE

1901 N.W. Blue Pkwy., Unity Village MO 64065-0001. (816)524-3550. **Fax:** (816)347-5518. **E-mail:** unity@unityonline.org. **E-mail:** sartinson@unityonline.org. **Website:** www.unityonline.org. **Contact:** Sharon Sartin, executive assistant. Estab. 1889. Unity House publishes metaphysical Christian books based on Unity principles, as well as inspirational books on metaphysics and practical spirituality. All mss must reflect a spiritual foundation and express the Unity philosophy, practical Christianity, universal principles, and/or metaphysics. Publishes hardcover, trade paperback, and electronic originals. Catalog and guidelines online.

NEEDS "We are a bridge between traditional Christianity and New Age spirituality. Unity is based on metaphysical Christian principles, spiritual values, and the healing power of prayer as a resource for daily living."

HOW TO CONTACT Submit complete mss (3 copies).

TERMS Pays 10-15% royalty on retail price. Pays advance. Responds in 6-8 months.

TIPS "We target an audience of spiritual seekers."

UNIVERSITY OF GEORGIA PRESS

Main Library, 3rd Floor, 320 S. Jackson St., Athens GA 30602. (706)369-6130. **Fax:** (706)369-6131. **E-mail:** books@ugapress.uga.edu. **Website:** www.uga press.org. Estab. 1938. University of Georgia Press is a midsized press that publishes fiction only through the Flannery O'Connor Award for Short Fiction competition. Publishes hardcover originals, trade paperback originals, and reprints. Book catalog and ms guidelines for #10 SASE or online.

NEEDS Short story collections published in Flannery O'Connor Award Competition.

HOW TO CONTACT Mss for Flannery O'Connor Award for Short Fiction accepted in April and May.

TERMS Pays 7-10% royalty on net receipts. Pays rare, varying advance. Responds in 2 months to queries.

TIPS "Please visit our website to view our book catalogs and for all ms submission guidelines."

UNIVERSITY OF IOWA PRESS

100 Kuhl House, 119 W. Park Rd., Iowa City IA 52242. (319)335-2000. **Fax:** (319)335-2055. **E-mail:** uipress@uiowa.edu. **Website:** www.uiowapress.org. **Contact:** Holly Carver, director; Joseph Parsons, acquisitions editor. Estab. 1969. "We publish authoritative, original nonfiction that we market mostly by direct mail to groups with special interests in our titles, and by advertising in trade and scholarly publications." Publishes hardcover and paperback originals. Book catalog available free. Guidelines available online.

NEEDS Currently publishes the Iowa Short Fiction Award selections.

TERMS Pays 7-10% royalty on net receipts.

UNIVERSITY OF MICHIGAN PRESS

839 Greene St., Ann Arbor MI 48106. **Website:** www.press.umich.edu. 839 Greene St., Ann Arbor MI 48106. (734) 764-4388. **Fax:** (734) 615-1540. **E-mail:** ump.fiction@umich.edu. **Website:** www.press.umich.edu. **Contact:** Chris Hebert, editor (fiction). Midsize

university press. Publishes hardcover originals. Member AAUP.

NEEDS Literary, short story collections, novels.

HOW TO CONTACT Accepts unsolicited mss. Query with SASE or submit outline, 3 sample chapter(s). Accepts queries by mail. Include brief bio, list of publishing credits. Responds in 4-6 weeks to queries; 6-8 weeks to mss. Accepts simultaneous submissions. No electronic submissions, submissions on disk. Sometimes comments on rejected mss.

TERMS Ms guidelines online.

TIPS "Aside from work published through the Michigan Literary Fiction Awards, we seek only fiction set in the Great Lakes region."

UNIVERSITY OF NEBRASKA PRESS

1111 Lincoln Mall, Lincoln NE 68588. (800)755-1105. **Fax:** (402)472-6214. **E-mail:** pressmail@unl.edu. **E-mail:** arold1@unl.edu. **Website:** nebraskapress.unl.edu. **Contact:** Heather Lundine, editor-in-chief; Alison Rold, production manager. "We primarily publish nonfiction books and scholarly journals, along with a few titles per season in contemporary and regional prose and poetry. On occasion, we reprint previously published fiction of established reputation, and we have several programs to publish literary works in translation." Publishes hardcover and trade paperback originals and trade paperback reprints. Book catalog available free. Guidelines online.

IMPRINTS Bison Books (paperback reprints of classic books).

NEEDS Series and translation only. Occasionally reprints fiction of established reputation.

UNIVERSITY OF NEVADA PRESS

Morrill Hall, Mail Stop 0166, Reno NV 89557. (775)784-6573. **Fax:** (775)784-6200. **Website:** www.unpress.nevada.edu. **Contact:** Joanne O'Hare, director. Estab. 1961. "Small university press. Publishes fiction that primarily focuses on the American West." Member: AAUP Publishes hardcover and paperback originals and reprints. Guidelines online.

NEEDS "We publish in Basque Studies, Gambling Studies, Western literature, Western history, Natural science, Environmental Studies, Travel and Outdoor books, Archeology, Anthropology, and Political Studies, all focusing on the West." The Press also publishes creative nonfiction and books on regional topics for a general audience.

HOW TO CONTACT Submit proposal package, outline, clips, 2-4 sample chapters. Include estimated word count, brief bio, list of publishing credits. Send SASE or IRC. No e-mail submissions.

TERMS Responds in 2 months.

UNIVERSITY OF NORTH TEXAS PRESS

1155 Union Circle, #311336, Denton TX 76203. (940)565-2142. **Fax:** (940)565-4590. **E-mail:** ronald.chrisman@unt.edu; karen.devinney@unt.edu. **Website:** untpress.unt.edu. **Contact:** Ronald Chrisman, director; Paula Oates, assistant editor; Lori Belew, administrative assistant. Estab. 1987. "We are dedicated to producing the highest-quality scholarly, academic, and general-interest books. We are committed to serving all peoples by publishing stories of their cultures and experiences, especially those who have been overlooked. Currently emphasizing military history, Texas history and literature, music, Mexican-American studies." Publishes hardcover and trade paperback originals and reprints. Book catalog for 8½×11 SASE. Guidelines online.

NEEDS "The only fiction we publish is the winner of the Katherine Anne Porter Prize in Short Fiction, an annual, national competition with a $1,000 prize and publication of the winning ms each fall."

TERMS Responds in 1 month to queries.

TIPS "We publish the following series: War and the Southwest; Texas Folklore Society Publications; the Western Life Series; Practical Guide Series; Al-Filo: Mexican-American studies; North Texas Crime and Criminal Justice; Katherine Anne Porter Prize in Short Fiction; and the North Texas Lives of Musicians Series."

UNIVERSITY OF TAMPA PRESS

University of Tampa, 401 W. Kennedy Blvd., Box 19F, Tampa FL 33606-1490. (813)253-6266. **Fax:** (813)258-7593. **E-mail:** utpress@ut.edu. **Website:** www.utpress.ut.edu. **Contact:** Richard Mathews, editor. Publishes hardcover originals and reprints; trade paperback originals and reprints. Book catalog available online.

TERMS Responds in 3-4 months to queries.

TIPS "We only consider book-length poetry submitted through the annual Tampa Review Prize for Poetry, and rarely publish excerpts. No e-mail or handwritten submissions. Submit between September 1 and December 31."

UNIVERSITY OF WISCONSIN PRESS

1930 Monroe St., 3rd Floor, Madison WI 53711. (608)263-1110. **Fax:** (608)263-1132. **E-mail:** gcwalker@uwpress.wisc.edu. **E-mail:** kadushin@wisc.edu. **Website:** uwpress.wisc.edu. **Contact:** Raphael Kadushin, senior acquisitions editor; Gwen Walker, acquisitions editor. Estab. 1937. Publishes hardcover originals, paperback originals, and paperback reprints. Guidelines online.

Check online guidelines for latest submission guidelines.

HOW TO CONTACT Query with SASE or submit outline, 1-2 sample chapter(s), synopsis.

TERMS Pays royalty. Responds in 2 weeks to queries; 8 weeks to mss. Rarely comments on rejected mss.

TIPS "Make sure the query letter and sample text are well written, and read guidelines carefully to make sure we accept the genre you are submitting."

USBORNE PUBLISHING

83-85 Saffron Hill, London En EC1N 8RT United Kingdom. (44)207430-2800. **Fax:** (44)207430-1562. **E-mail:** mail@usborne.co.uk. **Website:** www.usborne.com. "Usborne Publishing is a multiple-award-winning, worldwide children's publishing company publishing almost every type of children's book for every age from baby to young adult."

NEEDS Young readers, middle readers: adventure, contemporary, fantasy, history, humor, multicultural, nature/environment, science fiction, suspense/mystery, strong concept-based or character-led series. Average word length: young readers—5,000-10,000; middle readers—25,000-50,000; young adult—50,000-100,000.

TERMS Pays authors royalty.

TIPS "Do not send any original work and, sorry, but we cannot guarantee a reply."

VÉHICULE PRESS

P.O. 42094 BP Roy, Montreal QC H2W 2T3 Canada. (514)844-6073. **Fax:** (514)844-7543. **E-mail:** vp@vehiculepress.com. **E-mail:** esplanade@vehiculepress.com. **Website:** www.vehiculepress.com. **Contact:** Simon Dardick, president/publisher. Estab. 1973. "Montreal's Véhicule Press has published the best of Canadian and Quebec literature-fiction, poetry, essays, translations, and social history." Publishes trade paperback originals by Canadian authors mostly. Book catalog for 9×12 SAE with IRCs.

IMPRINTS Signal Editions (poetry); Dossier Quebec (history, memoirs); Esplanade Editions (fiction).

NEEDS No romance or formula writing.

HOW TO CONTACT Query with SASE.

TERMS Pays 10-15% royalty on retail price. Pays $200-500 advance. Responds in 4 months to queries.

TIPS "Quality in almost any style is acceptable. We believe in the editing process."

VERTIGO

DC Universe, Vertigo-DC Comics, 1700 Broadway, New York NY 10019. **Website:** www.dccomics.com.

NEEDS "The DC TALENT SEARCH program is designed to offer aspiring artists the chance to present artwork samples directly to the DC editors and art directors. The process is simple: During your convention visit, drop off photocopied samples of your work and enjoy the show! No lines, no waiting. If the DC folks like what they see, a time is scheduled for you the following day to meet a DC representative personally and to discuss your artistic interests and portfolio. At this time, DC Comics does not accept unsolicited writing submissions by mail. See submission guidelines online. "We're seeking artists for all of our imprints, including the DC Universe, Vertigo, WildStorm, Mad magazine, Minx, kids comics, and more!"

VIKING

Imprint of Penguin Group (USA), Inc., 375 Hudson St., New York NY 10014. (212)366-2000. **Website:** us.penguingroup.com/static/pages/publishers/adult/viking.html. Estab. 1925. Viking publishes a mix of academic and popular fiction and nonfiction. Publishes hardcover and originals.

HOW TO CONTACT Agented submissions only.

TERMS Pays 10-15% royalty on retail price.

VIKING CHILDREN'S BOOKS

375 Hudson St., New York NY 10014. **E-mail:** averystudiopublicity@us.penguingroup.com. **Website:** www.penguingroup.com. **Contact:** Catherine Frank, executive editor. "Viking Children's Books is known for humorous, quirky picture books, in addition to more traditional fiction. We publish the highest-quality fiction, nonfiction, and picture books for preschoolers through young adults." Publishes hardcover originals.

Does not accept unsolicited submissions.

NEEDS Adventure, animal, contemporary, fantasy, history, humor, multicultural, nature/environment, poetry, problem novels, romance, science fiction, sports, suspense/mystery.

HOW TO CONTACT *Accepts agented mss only.*

TERMS Pays 2-10% royalty on retail price or flat fee. Pays negotiable advance. Responds in 6 months.

TIPS "No 'cartoony' or mass-market submissions for picture books."

Ⓐ⊘ VILLARD BOOKS

Imprint of Random House Publishing Group, 1745 Broadway, New York NY 10019. (212)572-2600. **Website:** www.atrandom.com. Estab. 1983. "Villard Books is the publisher of savvy and sometimes quirky, best-selling hardcovers and trade paperbacks."

NEEDS Commercial fiction.

HOW TO CONTACT Agented submissions only.

TERMS Pays negotiable royalty. Pays negotiable advance.

Ⓐ⊘ VINTAGE ANCHOR PUBLISHING

Imprint of Random House, 1745 Broadway, New York NY 10019. **Website:** www.randomhouse.com. **Contact:** Furaha Norton, editor.

NEEDS Literary, mainstream/contemporary, short story collections.

HOW TO CONTACT *Agented submissions only.*

TERMS Pays 4-8% royalty on retail price. Average advance: $2,500 and up.

VIVISPHERE PUBLISHING

675 Dutchess Turnpike, Poughkeepsie NY 12603. (845)463-1100, ext. 314. **Fax:** (845)463-0018. **E-mail:** cs@vivisphere.com. **Website:** www.vivisphere.com. **Contact:** Submissions. Estab. 1995. Vivisphere Publishing is now considering new submissions from any genre as follows: game of bridge (cards), nonfiction, history, military, New Age, fiction, feminist/gay/lesbian, horror, contemporary, self-help, science fiction and cookbooks. Publishes trade paperback originals and reprints and e-books. Book catalog and ms guidelines online.

Ｏ "Cookbooks should have a particular slant or appeal to a certain niche. Also publish out-of-print books."

HOW TO CONTACT Query with SASE.

TERMS Pays royalty. Responds in 6-12 months.

☺ VIZ MEDIA LLC

P.O. Box 77010, San Francisco CA 94107. (415)546-7073. **Website:** www.viz.com. "VIZ Media, LLC, is one of the most comprehensive and innovative companies in the field of manga (graphic novel) publishing, animation, and entertainment licensing of Japanese content. Owned by 3 of Japan's largest creators and licensors of manga and animation, Shueisha Inc., Shogakukan Inc., and Shogakukan-Shueisha Productions, Co., Ltd., VIZ Media is a leader in the publishing and distribution of Japanese manga for English-speaking audiences in North America, the United Kingdom, Ireland, and South Africa, and is a global ex-Asia licensor of Japanese manga and animation. The company offers an integrated product line including magazines such as *Shonen Jump* and *Shojo Beat*, graphic novels, and DVDs. It also develops, markets, licenses, and distributes animated entertainment for audiences and consumers of all ages."

HOW TO CONTACT VIZ Media is currently accepting submissions and pitches for original comics. Keep in mind that all submissions must be accompanied by a signed release form.

WALKER AND CO.

Walker Publishing Co., 175 Fifth Ave., 7th Floor, New York NY 10010. (212)727-8300. **Fax:** (212)727-0984. **E-mail:** rebecca.mancini@bloomsburyusa.com. **Website:** bloomsbury.com/us/childrens. **Contact:** Emily Easton, publisher (picture books, middle-grade, and young adult novels); Stacy Cantor, associate editor (picture books, middle-grade, and young adult novels); Mary Kate Castellani, assistant editor (picture books, middle-grade, and young adult novels). Estab. 1959. "Walker publishes general nonfiction on a variety of subjects, as well as children's books." Publishes hardcover trade originals. Book catalog for 9×12 envelope and 3 first-class stamps.

NEEDS Accepts unsolicited mss. Query with SASE. Include "a concise description of the story line, including its outcome, word length of story, writing experience, publishing credits, particular expertise on this subject and in this genre. Common mistakes: not researching our publishing program and forgetting SASE."

HOW TO CONTACT Query with SASE. Send complete ms for picture books.

TERMS Pays 5-10% royalty.

Ⓞ⑤ WASHINGTON WRITERS' PUBLISHING HOUSE

P.O. Box 15271, Washington DC 20003. **E-mail:** wwphpress@gmail.com. **Website:** www.washingtonwriters.org. **Contact:** Patrick Pepper, president. Estab. 1975. Guidelines for SASE or on website.

NEEDS Washington Writers' Publishing House considers book-length mss for publication by fiction writers living within 75 driving miles of the U.S. Capitol, Baltimore area included, through competition only. Has published fiction books by Andrew Wingfield, David Taylor, Elizabeth Bruce, Phil Kurata, Gretchen Roberts, Denis Collins, Elisavietta Ritchie, Laura Brylawski-Miller, Hilary Tham, Catherine Kimrey. Offers $1,000 and 50 copies of published book, plus additional copies for publicity use. Mss may include previously published stories and excerpts. "Author should indicate where they heard about WWPH." **Entry fee:** $25. **Deadline:** July 1-November 1 (postmark). Order sample fiction books on website or by sending $16, plus $3 shipping.

HOW TO CONTACT Submit an electronic copy by e-mail (use .pdf, .doc, or .rtf) or 2 hard copies by snail mail of a short story collection or novel (no more than 350 pages, double- or 1½"-spaced; author's name should not appear on any ms pages). Include separate page of publication acknowledgments plus 2 cover sheets: one with ms title, author's name, address, telephone number, and e-mail address, the other with ms title only. Include SASE for results only; mss will not be returned (will be recycled).

⊘⊘ WATERBROOK MULTNOMAH PUBLISHING GROUP

Random House, 12265 Oracle Blvd., Suite 200, Colorado Springs CO 80921. (719)590-4999. **Fax:** (719)590-8977. **Website:** www.waterbrookmultnomah.com. Estab. 1996. Publishes hardcover and trade paperback originals. Book catalog online.

HOW TO CONTACT Agented submissions only.

TERMS Pays royalty. Responds in 2-3 months.

WESTERN PSYCHOLOGICAL SERVICES

625 Alaska Ave., Torrance CA 90503. (424)201-8800 or (800)648-8857. **Fax:** (424)201-6950. **E-mail:** review@wpspublish.com. **Website:** www.wpspublish.com; www.creativetherapystore.com. Estab. 1948. "Western Psychological Services publishes psychological and educational assessments that practitioners trust. Our products allow helping professionals to accurately screen, diagnose, and treat people in need. WPS publishes practical books and games used by therapists, counselors, social workers, and others in the helping professionals who work with children and adults." Publishes psychological and educational assessments and some trade paperback originals. Book catalog available free. Guidelines online.

NEEDS Children's books dealing with feelings, anger, social skills, autism, family problems, etc.

HOW TO CONTACT Submit complete ms.

TERMS Pays 5-10% royalty on wholesale price. Responds in 2 months to queries.

WHITAKER HOUSE

1030 Hunt Valley Circle, New Kensington PA 15068. **E-mail:** publisher@whitakerhouse.com. **Website:** www.whitakerhouse.com. **Contact:** Editorial Department. Estab. 1970. Publishes hardcover, trade paperback, and mass-market originals. Book catalog available online. Guidelines online.

NEEDS All fiction must have a Christian perspective.

HOW TO CONTACT Query with SASE.

TERMS Pays 5-15% royalty on wholesale price. Responds in 3 months.

TIPS "Audience includes those seeking uplifting and inspirational fiction and nonfiction."

☺ WHITECAP BOOKS, LTD.

210-314 W. Cordova St., Vancouver BC V6B 1 E8 Canada. (604)681-6181. **Fax:** (905)477-9179. **E-mail:** jeffreyb@whitecap.ca. **Website:** www.whitecap.ca. "Whitecap Books is a general trade publisher with a focus on food and wine titles. Although we are interested in reviewing unsolicited ms submissions, please note that we only accept submissions that meet the needs of our current publishing program. Please see some of most recent releases to get an idea of the kinds of titles we are interested in." Publishes hardcover and trade paperback originals. Catalog and guidelines available online at website.

NEEDS No children's picture books or adult fiction.

HOW TO CONTACT See guidelines.

TERMS Pays royalty. Pays negotiated advance. Responds in 2-3 months to proposals.

TIPS "We want well-written, well-researched material that presents a fresh approach to a particular topic."

WHITE MANE KIDS

73 W. Burd St., P.O. Box 708, Shippensburg PA 17257. (717)532-2237. **Fax:** (717)532-6110. **E-mail:** marketing@whitemane.com. **Website:** www.whitemane.com. **Contact:** Harold Collier, acquisitions editor. Estab. 1987. Book catalog and writer's guidelines available for SASE.

IMPRINTS White Mane Books, Burd Street Press, White Mane Kids, Ragged Edge Press.

NEEDS Middle readers, young adults: history (primarily American Civil War). Average word length: middle readers—30,000. Does not publish picture books.

HOW TO CONTACT Query.

TERMS Pays authors royalty of 7-10%. Pays illustrators and photographers by the project. Responds to queries in 1 month, mss in 3 months.

TIPS "Make your work historically accurate. We are interested in historically accurate fiction for middle and young adult readers. We do *not* publish picture books. Our primary focus is the American Civil War and some America Revolution topics."

WILD CHILD PUBLISHING

P.O. Box 4897, Culver City CA 90231. (310) 721-4461. **E-mail:** admin@wildchildpublishing.com. **Website:** www.wildchildpublishing.com. **Contact:** Marci Baun, editor-in-chief (genres not covered by other editors); Faith Bicknell-Brown, managing editor (horror and romance); S.R. Howen, editor (science fiction and nonfiction). Estab. 1999. Wild Child Publishing is a small, independent press that started out as a magazine in September 1999. We are known for working with newer/unpublished authors and editing to the standards of NYC publishers. Publishes paperback originals, e-books. Format: POD printing; perfectbound. Average print order: 50-200. Member EPIC. Distributes/promotes titles through Ingrams and own website, Mobipocket, Kindle, Amazon, and soon with Fictionwise. Freya's Bower already distributes through Fictionwise. Book catalogs on website.

NEEDS Adventure, children's/juvenile, erotica for Freya's Bower only, ethnic/multicultural, experimental, fantasy, feminist, gay, historical, horror, humor/satire, lesbian, literary, mainstream, military/war, mystery/suspense, New Age/mystic, psychic/supernatural, romance, science fiction, short story collections, thriller/espionage, western, young adult/teen (fantasy/science fiction). Multiple anthologies planned.

HOW TO CONTACT Query with outline/synopsis and 1 sample chapter. Accepts queries by e-mail only. Include estimated word count, brief bio. Often critiques/comments on rejected mss.

TERMS Pays royalties 10-40%. Responds in 1 month to queries and mss.

TIPS "Read our submission guidelines thoroughly. Send in entertaining, well-written stories. Be easy to work with and upbeat."

THE WILD ROSE PRESS

P.O. Box 708, Adams Basin NY 14410. (585) 752-8770. **E-mail:** queryus@thewildrosepress.com; rpenders@thewildrosepress.com. **Website:** www.thewildrose press.com. **Contact:** Nicole D'Arienzo, editor. Estab. 2006. Publishes paperback originals, reprints, and e-books in a POD format. Guidelines available on website.

"The American Rose line publishes stories about the French and Indian wars; Colonial America; the Revolutionary War; the war of 1812; the War Between the States; the Reconstruction era; the dawn of the new century. These are the struggles at the heart of the American Rose story. The central romantic relationship is the key driving force, set against historically accurate backdrop. These stories are for those who long for the courageous heroes and heroines who fought for their freedom and settled the new world; for gentle southern belles with spines of steel and the gallant gentlemen who sweep them away. This line is wide open for writers with a love of American history."

NEEDS Please do not submit women's fiction, poetry, science fiction, fan fiction, or any type of nonfiction.

HOW TO CONTACT *Does not accept unsolicited mss.* Send query letter with outline and synopsis of up to 5 pages. Accepts all queries by e-mail. Include estimated word count, brief bio, and list of publishing credits. Agented fiction less than 1%. Always comments on rejected mss. Sends prepublication galleys to author. Only books meeting our length requirement (over 65,000 words) will go to print.

TERMS Pays royalty of 7% minimum; 35% maximum. Responds in 1 month to queries; 3 months to mss.

TIPS "Polish your ms, make it as error-free as possible, and follow our submission guidelines."

WILDSTORM

DC Universe, 1700 Broadway, New York NY 10019. **Website:** www.dccomics.com/wildstorm.

Does not accept unsolicited mss.

WILLIAM MORROW

HarperCollins, 10 E. 53rd St., New York NY 10022. (212)207-7000. **Fax:** (212)207-7145. **Website:** www.harpercollins.com. Estab. 1926. "William Morrow publishes a wide range of titles that receive much recognition and prestige—a most selective house." Book catalog available free.

NEEDS Publishes adult fiction. Morrow accepts only the highest-quality submissions in adult fiction. *No unsolicited mss or proposals.*

HOW TO CONTACT Agented submissions only.

TERMS Pays standard royalty on retail price. Pays varying advance.

WILSHIRE BOOK CO

9731 Variel Ave., Chatsworth CA 91311. (818)700-1522. **Fax:** (818)700-1527. **E-mail:** mpowers@mpowers.com. **Website:** www.mpowers.com. **Contact:** Rights Department. Estab. 1947. Publishes trade paperback originals and reprints. Ms guidelines online.

NEEDS "You are not only what you are today, but also what you choose to become tomorrow." Looking for adult fables that teach principles of psychological growth. Distributes titles through wholesalers, bookstores and mail order. Promotes titles through author interviews on radio and television.Wants adult allegories that teach principles of psychological growth or offer guidance in living. Minimum 30,000 words. No standard fiction.

HOW TO CONTACT Submit 3 sample chapters. Submit complete ms. Include outline, author bio, analysis of book's, competition and SASE.

TERMS Pays standard royalty. Pays advance. Responds in 2 months.

TIPS "We are vitally interested in all new material we receive. Just as you are hopeful when submitting your ms for publication, we are hopeful as we read each one submitted, searching for those we believe could be successful in the marketplace. Writing and publishing must be a team effort. We need you to write what we can sell. We suggest you read the successful books similar to the one you want to write. Analyze them to discover what elements make them winners. Duplicate those elements in your own style, using a creative new approach and fresh material, and you will have written a book we can catapult onto the bestseller list. You are welcome to telephone or e-mail us for immediate feedback on any book concept you may have. To learn more about us and what we publish, and for complete ms guidelines, visit our website."

WINDRIVER PUBLISHING, INC.

3280 Madison Ave., Ogden UT 84403. (801)689-7440. **E-mail:** info@windriverpublishing.com. **Website:** www.windriverpublishing.com. **Contact:** E. Keith Howick, Jr., president; Gail Howick, vice president/editor-in-chief. Estab. 2003. "Authors who wish to submit book proposals for review must do so according to our submissions guidelines, which can be found on our website, along with an online submission form, which is our preferred submission method. *We do not accept submissions of any kind by e-mail.*" Publishes hardcover originals and reprints, trade paperback originals, and mass-market originals. Book catalog online. Guidelines online.

HOW TO CONTACT Not accepting submissions at this time.

TERMS Responds in 1-2 months to queries; 4-6 months to proposals/mss.

TIPS "We do not accept mss containing graphic or gratuitous profanity, sex, or violence. See online instructions for details."

WISDOM PUBLICATIONS

199 Elm St., Somerville MA 02144. (617)776-7416, ext. 28. **Fax:** (617)776-7841. **E-mail:** editors@wisdompubs.org. **Website:** www.wisdompubs.org. **Contact:** David Kittlestrom, senior editor. Estab. 1976. "Wisdom Publications is dedicated to making available authentic Buddhist works for the benefit of all. We publish translations, commentaries, and teachings of past and contemporary Buddhist masters and original works by leading Buddhist scholars. Currently emphasizing popular applied Buddhism, scholarly titles." Publishes hardcover originals and trade paperback originals and reprints. Book catalog and ms guidelines online.

TERMS Pays 4-8% royalty on wholesale price. Pays advance.

TIPS "We are basically a publisher of Buddhist books—all schools and traditions of Buddhism. Please see our catalog or our website before you send anything to us to get a sense of what we publish."

WOODBINE HOUSE

6510 Bells Mill Rd., Bethesda MD 20817. (301)897-3570. **Fax:** (301)897-5838. **E-mail:** info@woodbinehouse.com. **Website:** www.woodbinehouse.com. **Contact:** Nancy Gray Paul, acquisitions editor. Estab. 1985. Woodbine House publishes books for or about individuals with disabilities to help those individuals and their families live fulfilling and satisfying lives in their homes, schools, and communities. Publishes trade paperback originals. Book catalog for 6×9 SAE with 3 first-class stamps. No metered mail or IRCs please. Guidelines online.

NEEDS Receptive to stories about developmental and intellectual disabilities, e.g., autism and cerebral palsy.

HOW TO CONTACT Submit complete ms with SASE.

TERMS Pays 10-12% royalty. Responds in 3 months to queries.

TIPS "Do not send us a proposal on the basis of this description. Examine our catalog or website and a couple of our books to make sure you are on the right track. Put some thought into how your book could be marketed (aside from in bookstores). Keep cover letters concise and to the point; if it's a subject that interests us, we'll ask to see more."

WORDSONG

815 Church St., Honesdale PA 18431. **Fax:** (570)253-0179. **E-mail:** submissions@boydsmillspress.com; eagarrow@boydsmillspress.com. **Website:** www.wordsongpoetry.com. Estab. 1990. "We publish fresh voices in contemporary poetry."

NEEDS Submit complete ms or submit through agent. Label package "Ms Submission" and include SASE. "Please send a book-length collection of your own poems. Do not send an initial query."

TERMS Pays authors royalty or work purchased outright. Responds to mss in 3 months.

TIPS "Collections of original poetry, not anthologies, are our biggest need at this time. Keep in mind that the strongest collections demonstrate a facility with multiple poetic forms and offer fresh images and insights. Check to see what's already on the market and on our website before submitting."

✚ WRITELIFE PUBLISHING, LLC

2323 S. 171st St., Suite 202, Omaha NE 68130. (402)934-1412. **Fax:** (402)519-2173. **E-mail:** info@writelife.com. **E-mail:** queries@writelife.com. **Website:** www.writelife.com. **Contact:** Cindy Grady, publisher; Erin Reel, senior editor/in-house agent. Estab. 2008. WriteLife, LLC, is an independent publisher offering a uniquely collaborative approach to publishing, marketing, and supporting writers serious about their work. Publishes hardcover originals, trade paperback originals, mass-market paperback originals, and electronic originals. Book catalog available for SASE or online. Ms guidelines available for SASE or online.

NEEDS Open to receiving queries from writers who have yet to publish their first book, but wewould like to see evidence of previously published work in literary journals, newspapers, websites, anthologies, etc., included in the book proposal.

HOW TO CONTACT Submit proposal package with synopsis and 3 sample chapters.

TERMS Authors are paid 50% of net royalties on wholesale and retail price.

TIPS "Please describe the audience you envision for your books. We know from talking with our readers that they have just as eclectic tastes in books as we have. When it comes to fiction, our readers love vivid, authentic, and memorable characters and engaging plots. In nonfiction, our readers want books that will help them gain perspective, learn something new, make them feel good, help them to heal and improve their lives, and show them real-life characters who have made, or are making, a difference in the world."

○ YELLOW SHOE FICTION SERIES

P.O. Box 25053, Baton Rouge LA 70894. **Website:** www.lsu.edu/lsupress. **Contact:** Michael Griffith, editor. Estab. 2004.

○ "Looking first and foremost for literary excellence, especially good mss that have fallen through the cracks at the big commercial presses. I'll cast a wide net."

HOW TO CONTACT Does not accept unsolicited mss. Accepts queries by mail, Attn: Rand Dotson. No electronic submissions.

TERMS Pays royalty. Offers advance.

YMAA PUBLICATION CENTER

P.O. Box 480, Wolfeboro NH 03894. (603)569-7988. **Fax:** (603)569-1889. **E-mail:** info@ymaa.com. **Contact:** David Ripianzi, director. Estab. 1982. YMAA publishes books on Chinese Chi Kung (Qigong), Taijiquan, (Tai Chi) and Asian martial arts. We are expanding our focus to include books on healing, wellness, meditation, and subjects related to Asian culture and Asian medicine. De-emphasizing fitness books. Publishes trade paperback originals and reprints. Book catalog available online. Guidelines available free.

NEEDS "We are excited to announce a new category: **martial arts fiction**. We are seeking mss that bring the venerated tradition of true Asian martial arts to readers. Your novel length ms should be a thrilling story that conveys insights into true martial techniques and philosophies."

TERMS Responds in 3 months to proposals.

TIPS "If you are submitting health-related material, please refer to an Asian tradition. Learn about author publicity options, as your participation is mandatory."

ZEBRA BOOKS

Kensington, 119 W. 40th St., New York NY 10018. (212)407-1500. **E-mail:** mrecords@kensingtonbooks .com. **Website:** www.kensingtonbooks.com. **Contact:** Megan Records, associate editor. Zebra Books is dedicated to women's fiction, which includes, but is not limited to romance. Publishes hardcover originals, trade paperback, and mass-market paperback originals and reprints. Book catalog available online.
NEEDS Mostly historical romance. Some contemporary romance, westerns, horror, and humor.
HOW TO CONTACT Send cover letter, first 3 chapters, and synopsis (no more than 5 pages). Note that we do not publish science fiction or fantasy.

ZONDERVAN

Division of HarperCollins Publishers, 3900 Sparks Dr., Grand Rapids MI 49546. (616)698-6900. **Fax:** (616)698-3454. **E-mail:** submissions@zondervan .com. **Website:** www.zondervan.com. Estab. 1931. "Our mission is to be the leading Christian communications company meeting the needs of people with resources that glorify Jesus Christ and promote biblical principles." Publishes hardcover and trade paperback originals and reprints. Guidelines online.
IMPRINTS Zondervan, Zonderkidz, Youth Specialties, Editorial Vida.
NEEDS Will not consider collections of short stories or poetry.
HOW TO CONTACT Submit TOC, CV, chapter outline, intended audience.
TERMS Pays 14% royalty on net amount received on sales of cloth and softcover trade editions; 12% royalty on net amount received on sales of mass-market paperbacks. Pays variable advance. Responds in 2 months to queries; 3 months to proposals; 4 months to mss.

ZUMAYA PUBLICATIONS, LLC

3209 S. Interstate 35, Austin TX 78741. **E-mail:** business@zumayapublications.com; acquisitions@ zumayapublications.com. **Website:** www.zumaya-publications.com. **Contact:** Adrienne Rose, acquisitions editor. Estab. 1999. Publishes trade paperback and electronic originals and reprints. Guidelines online.

> "We accept only electronic queries; all others will be discarded unread. A working knowledge of computers and relevant software is a necessity, as our production process is completely digital."

IMPRINTS Zumaya Arcane (New Age, inspirational fiction, and nonfiction), Zumaya Boundless (GLBT); Zumaya Embraces (romance/women's fiction); Zumaya Enigma (mystery/suspense/thriller); Zumaya Thresholds (young adult/middle-grade); Zumaya Otherworlds (science fiction, fantasy, horror), Zumaya Yesterdays (memoirs, historical fiction, fiction, western fiction); Zumaya Fabled Ink (graphic and illustrated novels).
NEEDS "We are currently oversupplied with speculative fiction and are reviewing submissions in science fiction, fantasy, and paranormal suspense by invitation only. We are much in need of GLBT and young adult/middle-grade, historical and western, New Age/inspirational (no overtly Christian materials, please), noncategory romance, thrillers. As with nonfiction, we encourage people to review what we've already published so as to avoid sending us more of the same, at least, insofar as the plot is concerned. While we're always looking for good specific mysteries, we want original concepts rather than slightly altered versions of what we've already published."
TERMS Responds in 6 months to queries and proposals; 9 months to mss.
TIPS "We're catering to readers who may have loved last year's bestseller but not enough to want to read 10 more just like it. Have something different. If it does not fit standard pigeonholes, that's a plus. On the other hand, it has to have an audience. And if you're not prepared to work with us on promotion and marketing, particularly via social media, it would be better to look elsewhere."

CONTESTS & AWARDS

///

In addition to honors and, quite often, cash prizes, contests and awards programs offer writers the opportunity to be judged on the basis of quality alone, without the outside factors that sometimes influence publishing decisions. New writers who win contests may be published for the first time, while more experienced writers may gain public recognition for an entire body of work.

Listed here are contests for almost every type of fiction writing. Some focus on form, such as short stories, novels, or novellas, while others feature writing on particular themes or topics. Still others are prestigious prizes or awards for work that must be nominated. Chances are, no matter what type of fiction you write, there is a contest or award program that may interest you.

SELECTING AND SUBMITTING TO A CONTEST

Use the same care in submitting to contests as you would sending your manuscript to a publication or book publisher. Deadlines are very important, and where possible, we've included this information. For some contests, deadlines were only approximate at our press deadline, so be sure to write, call, or look online for complete information.

Follow the rules to the letter. If, for instance, contest rules require your name on a cover sheet only, you will be disqualified if you ignore this and put your name on every page. Find out how many copies to send. If you don't send the correct amount, by the time you are contacted to send more, it may be past the submission deadline. An increasing number of contests invite writers to query by e-mail, and many post contest information on their websites. Check listings for e-mail and website addresses.

One note of caution: Beware of contests that charge entry fees that are disproportionate to the amount of the prize. Contests offering a $10 prize and charging $7 in entry fees are a waste of your time and money.

If you are interested in a contest or award that requires your publisher to nominate your work, it's acceptable to make your interest known. Be sure to leave the publisher plenty of time, however, to make the nomination deadline.

24-HOUR SHORT STORY CONTEST

WritersWeekly.com, 5726 Cortez Rd. W., #349, Bradenton FL 34210. **E-mail:** writersweekly@writersweekly.com. **Website:** www.writersweekly.com/misc/contest.php. **Contact:** Angela Hoy. Quarterly contest in which registered entrants receive a topic at start time (usually noon Central Time) and have 24 hours to write a story on that topic. All submissions must be returned via e-mail. Each contest is limited to 500 people. Upon entry, entrant will receive guidelines and details on competition, including submission process. Deadline: Quarterly—see website for dates. Prize: 1st Place: $300; 2nd Place: $250; 3rd Place: $200. There are also 20 honorable mentions and 60 door prizes (randomly drawn from all participants). The top 3 winners' entries are posted on WritersWeekly.com (nonexclusive electronic rights only) and receive a Freelance Income Kit. Writers retain all rights to their work. See website for full details on prizes. Judged by Angela Hoy (publisher of WritersWeekly.com and Booklocker.com).

🜚 AEON AWARD

Albedo One/Aeon Press, Aeon Award, Albedo One, 2 Post Road, Lusk, Dublin Ireland. +353 1 8730177. **E-mail:** fraslaw@yahoo.co.uk. **Website:** www.albedo1.com. **Contact:** Frank Ludlow, event coordinator. Estab. 2004. Prestigious fiction-writing competition for short stories in any speculative fiction genre, such as fantasy, science fiction, horror, or anything in between. Deadline: November 30. Contest begins January 1. Prize: Grand Prize: €1,000; 2nd Prize: €200; and 3rd Prize: €100. The top 3 stories are guaranteed publication in *Albedo One*.

🜚 AESTHETICA CREATIVE WORKS COMPETITION

P.O. Box 371, York YO23 1WL United Kingdom. **E-mail:** cherie@aestheticamagazine.com; info@aestheticamagazine.com. **E-mail:** submissions@aestheticamagazine.com. **Website:** www.aestheticamagazine.com. The Aesthetica Creative Works Competition represents the scope of creative activity today and provides an opportunity for both new and established artists to nurture their reputations on an international scale. There are 3 categories: Short Film Festival, Art Prize, and Creative Writing. Art Prize has 4 subcategories, Creative writing has 2. See website for guidelines and more details. The Aesthetica Creative Works Competition is looking to discover talented artists and writers. The editor of *Aesthetica* is a Fellow of the Royal Society of Arts. See guidelines online. Deadline: August 31. Prize: £500-1,000, Each winner will receive an additional prize from our competition partners. Winners will be published in the *Aesthetica Creative Works Annual*. Winners will receive a complimentary copy of the *Aesthetica Creative Works Annual* and publication of the work in their creative section (3 winners).

🜚 AHWA FLASH & SHORT STORY COMPETITION

AHWA (Australian Horror Writers Association), **E-mail:** ahwacomps@australianhorror.com; ahwa@australianhorror.com. **Website:** australianhorror.com. **Contact:** David Carroll, competitions officer. Competition/award for short stories and flash fiction. Looking for horror stories, tales that frighten, yarns that unsettle readers in their comfortable homes. All themes in this genre will be accepted, from the well-used (zombies, vampires, ghosts, etc.) to the highly original, so long as the story is professional and well written. Deadline: May 31. Prize: The authors of the winning Flash Fiction and Short Story entries will each receive paid publication in *Midnight Echo; The Magazine of the AHWA* and an engraved plaque. Judged by Paul Mannering, Talie Helene, and Zena Shapter.

AKC GAZETTE ANNUAL FICTION CONTEST

260 Madison Ave., New York NY 10016. (212)696-8333. The *Gazette* sponsors an annual fiction contest for short short stories under 2,000 words on some subject relating to purebred or mixed-breed dogs. Fiction for magazine needs a slant toward the serious fancier with real insight into the human/dog bond and breed-specific purebred behavior. Deadline: January 31. Prize: 1st Place: $500; 2nd Place: $250; 3rd Place: $100. AKC retains the right to publish the 3 prize-winning entries. Judges by panel selected by AKC Publications. Winner will be chose based on style, content, originality, and the appeal of the story.

ALABAMA STATE COUNCIL ON THE ARTS INDIVIDUAL ARTIST FELLOWSHIP

201 Monroe St., Montgomery AL 36130. (334)242-4076, ext. 236. **Fax:** (334)240-3269. **E-mail:** anne.kimzey@arts.alabama.gov. **Website:** www.arts.state.al.us. **Contact:** Anne Kimzey, literature program manager. Recognizes the achievements and poten-

tial of Alabama writers. Deadline: March 1. Applications must be submitted online by eGRANTs. Judged by independent peer panel. Winners notified by mail and announced on website in June.

ALLIGATOR JUNIPER AWARD

Alligator Juniper/Prescott College, 220 Grove Ave., Prescott AZ 86301. (928)350-2012. **Fax:** (928)776-5102. **E-mail:** alligatorjuniper@prescott.edu. **Website:** www.prescott.edu/alligatorjuniper/national-contest/index.html. **Contact:** Skye Anicca, managing editor. Annual contest for unpublished fiction, creative nonfiction, and poetry. Open to all age levels. Each entrant receives a personal letter from staff regarding the status of their submission, as well as minor feedback on the piece. Deadline: October 1. Prize: $1,000 plus publication in all 3 categories. Finalists in each genre are recognized as such, published, and paid in copies. Judged by the distinguished writers in each genre and Prescott College writing students enrolled in the Literary Journal Practicum course.

◑ AMERICAN ASSOCIATION OF UNIVERSITY WOMEN AWARD IN JUVENILE LITERATURE

4610 Mail Service Center, Raleigh NC 27699-4610. (919)807-7290. **E-mail:** michael.hill@ncdcr.gov. **Contact:** Michael Hill, awards coordinator. Annual award. Book must be published during the year ending June 30. Submissions made by author, author's agent, or publisher. SASE for contest rules. Recognizes the year's best work of juvenile literature by a North Carolina resident. Deadline: July 15. Prize: Awards a cup to the winner and winner's name inscribed on a plaque displayed within the North Carolina Office of Archives and History. Judged by three-judge panel.

◒ Competition receives 10-15 submissions per category.

THE AMERICAN GEM LITERARY FESTIVAL

FilmMakers Magazine/Write Brothers, **E-mail:** info@filmmakers.com. **Website:** www.filmmakers.com/contests/short/. **Contact:** Jennifer Brooks. Estab. 2004. Worldwide contest to recognize excellent short screenplays and short stories. Deadlines: November 30 (early bird), January 30 (regular), March 15 (late), April 30 (final). Prize: Short Script: 1st Place: $1,000, pitches script to producers, free admission pass to the Great American Pitch Fest, and more; 2nd Place: $250; 3rd Place: $150; 4th Place: $100; 5th Place: $50. Top 3 winner receive screenwriting software from

Write Brothers. Top 25 scripts receive a certificate of achievement award. Short Story: 1st Place: $250. Top 3 winners receive screenwriting software from Write Brothers.

AMERICAN LITERARY REVIEW CONTESTS

American Literary Review, P.O. Box 311307, University of North Texas, Denton TX 76203-1307. (940)565-2755. **E-mail:** americanliteraryreview@gmail.com. **Website:** english.unt.edu/alr. Contest to award excellence in short fiction, creative nonfiction, and poetry. Multiple entries are acceptable, but each entry must be accompanied with a reading fee. Do not put any identifying information in the file itself; include the author's name, title(s), address, e-mail address, and phone number in the boxes provided in the online submissions manager. Short fiction: Limit 8,000 words per work. Creative nonfiction: Limit 6,500 words per work. Deadline: October 1. Submission period begins June 1. Prize: $1,000 prize for each category, along with publication in the spring online issue of the *American Literary Review*.

○ AMERICAN MARKETS NEWSLETTER SHORT STORY COMPETITION

1974 46th Ave., San Francisco CA 94116. **E-mail:** sheila.oconnor@juno.com. Award is to give short story writers more exposure. Contest offered biannually. Open to any writer. All kinds of fiction are considered. Especially looking for women's pieces—romance, with a twist in the tale—but all will be considered. Results announced within 3 months of deadlines. Winners notified by mail if they include SASE. Deadline: June 30 and December 31. Prize: 1st Place: $300; 2nd Place: $100; 3rd Place: $50. Judged by a panel of independent judges.

AMERICAN-SCANDINAVIAN FOUNDATION TRANSLATION PRIZE

The American-Scandinavian Foundation, 58 Park Ave., New York NY 10016. (212)779-3587. **E-mail:** grants@amscan.org. **Website:** www.amscan.org. **Contact:** Matthew Walters, director of fellowships and grants. The annual ASF translation competition is awarded to the most outstanding translations of poetry, fiction, drama, or literary prose written by a Scandinavian author born after 1800. Deadline: June 1. Prize: The Nadia Christensen Prize includes a $2,000 award, publication of an excerpt in Scandinavian Review, and a commemorative bronze medallion; The Leif and Inger Sjöberg Award, given to an individual whose literature translations have not previously been published, includes a $1,000 award, publication of an excerpt in *Scandinavian Review*, and a commemorative bronze medallion.

A MIDSUMMER TALE

E-mail: editors@toasted-cheese.com. **Website:** www.toasted-cheese.com. **Contact:** Theryn Fleming, editor. A Midsummer Tale is open to nongenre fiction and creative nonfiction. There is a different theme each year. Entries must be unpublished. Accepts inquiries by e-mail. Deadline: June 21. Results announced on July 31. Winners notified by e-mail. List of winners on website. Prize: Amazon gift certificates and publication in *Toasted Cheese*. Entries are blind judged.

○ THE SHERWOOD ANDERSON FOUNDATION FICTION AWARD

12330 Ashton Mill Terrace, Glen Allen VA 23059. **E-mail:** sherwoodandersonfoundation@gmail.com. **Website:** sherwoodandersonfoundation.org. **Contact:** Anna McKean, foundation president. Estab. 1988. Contest is to honor, preserve, and celebrate the memory and literary work of Sherwood Anderson, American realist for the first half of the 20th century. Annual award supports developing writers of short stories and novels. Deadline: April 1. Prize: $20,000 grant award.

SHERWOOD ANDERSON SHORT FICTION AWARD

Mid-American Review, Department of English, Box WM, BGSU, Bowling Green OH 43403. (419)372-2725. **Fax:** (419)372-4642. **E-mail:** mar@bgsu.edu. **Website:** www.bgsu.edu/midamericanreview. **Contact:** Katrin Tschirgi, managing editor. Offered annually for unpublished mss (6,000 word limit). Contest is open to all writers not associated with a judge or *Mid-American Review*. Deadline: November 1. Prize: $1,000, plus publication in the spring issue of *Mid-American Review*. Four Finalists: Notation, possible publication. Judged by editors and a well-known writer, i.e., Aimee Bender or Anthony Doerr.

ART AFFAIR SHORT STORY AND WESTERN SHORT STORY CONTESTS

Art Affair Contest, P.O. Box 54302, Oklahoma City OK 73154. **E-mail:** artaffair@aol.com. **Website:** www.shadetreecreations.com. The annual Art Affair Writing Contests include (General) Short Story and Western Short Story categories. Open to any writer. All short stories must be unpublished. Multiple entries accepted in both categories with separate entry fees for each. Submit original stories on any subject and timeframe for general Short Story category, and submit original western stories for Western Short Story—word limit for all entries is 5,000 words. Guidelines available on website. Deadline: October 1. Prize (in both categories): 1st Place: $50; 2nd Place: $25; 3rd Place: $15.

○ ☺ ARTIST TRUST FELLOWSHIP AWARD

1835 12th Ave., Seattle WA 98122. (209)467-8734 ext. 11. **Fax:** (866)218-7878. **E-mail:** info@artisttrust.org. **Website:** www.artisttrust.org. **Contact:** Miguel Guillen, program manager. Fellowships award $7,500 to practicing professional artists of exceptional talent and demonstrated ability. The fellowship is a merit-based, not a project-based award. Recipients present a Meet the Artist Event to a community in Washington State that has little or no access to the artist and their work. Awards 14 fellowships of $7,500 and 2 residencies with $1,000 stipends at the Millay Colony. Deadline: January 13. Applications available December 3. Prize: $7,500.

○ THE ATHENAEUM LITERARY AWARD

The Athenaeum of Philadelphia, 219 S. 6th St., Philadelphia PA 19106-3794. (215)925-2688. **Fax:** (215)925-3755. **E-mail:** jilly@PhilaAthenaeum.org. **Website:** www.PhilaAthenaeum.org. **Contact:** Jill Lee, Circulation Librarian. Estab. 1950. The Athenaeum Literary Award was established in 1950 to recognize and encourage literary achievement among authors who are bona fide residents of Philadelphia or Pennsylvania living within a radius of 30 miles of City Hall at the time their book was written or published. Any volume of general literature is eligible; technical, scientific, and juvenile books are not included. Nominated works are reviewed on the basis of their significance and importance to the general public, as well as for literary excellence. Deadline: December 31.

○ ATLANTIC WRITING COMPETITION FOR UNPUBLISHED MANUSCRIPTS

Writers' Federation of Nova Scotia, 1113 Marginal Rd., Halifax NS B3H 4P7. (902)423-8116. **Fax:** (902)422-0881. **E-mail:** programs@writers.ns.ca. **Website:** www.writers.ns.ca. **Contact:** Hillary Titley. Estab. 1975. Annual program designed to honor work by unpublished writers in all 4 Atlantic Provinces. Entry is open to writers unpublished in the category of writing they wish to enter. Prizes are presented in the fall of each year. Categories include: adult novel, writing for children, poetry, short story, juvenile/young adult novel, creative nonfiction, and play. Judges return written comments when competition is concluded. Deadline: February 3. Prizes vary based on categories. See website for details.

AUTUMN HOUSE FICTION PRIZE

Autumn House Press, 87½ Westwood St., Pittsburgh PA 15211. **E-mail:** info@autumnhouse.org. **Website:** autumnhouse.org. Fiction submissions should be approximately 200-300 pages. All fiction subgenres (short stories, short shorts, novellas, or novels), or any combination of subgenres, are eligible. All finalists will be considered for publication. Deadline: June 30. Prize: Winners will receive book publication, $1,000 advance against royalties, and a $1,500 travel grant to promote his/her work.

ⓞⓢ AUTUMN HOUSE POETRY, FICTION, AND NONFICTION PRIZES

P.O. Box 60100, Pittsburgh PA 15211. (412)381-4261. **E-mail:** gcerto@autumhouse.org; info@autumn house.org. **E-mail:** autumnh420@gmail.com. **Website:** autumnhouse.org. **Contact:** Giuliana Certo, managing editor. Estab. 1999. Offers annual prize and publication of book-length ms with national promotion. Submission must be unpublished as a collection, but individual poems, stories, and essays may have been previously published elsewhere. Considers simultaneous submissions. "Autumn House is a nonprofit corporation with the mission of publishing and promoting poetry and other fine literature. We have published books by Gerald Stern, Ruth L. Schwartz, Ed Ochester, Andrea Hollander Budy, George Bilgere, Jo McDougall, and others." Deadline: June 30. Prize: The winner (in each of 3 categories) will receive book publication, $1,000 advance against royalties, and a $1,500 travel/publicity grant to promote his or her book.

ⓞ AWP AWARD SERIES

Association of Writers & Writing Programs, George Mason University, 4400 University Drive, MSN 1E3, Fairfax VA 22030. **E-mail:** supriya@awpwriter.org. **Website:** www.awpwriter.org. **Contact:** Supriya Bhatnagar, director of publications. AWP sponsors the Award Series, an annual competition for the publication of excellent new book-length works. The competition is open to all authors writing in English regardless of nationality or residence, and is available to published and unpublished authors alike. Offered annually to foster new literary talent. Deadline: Postmarked between January 1 and February 28. Prize: AWP Prize for the Novel: $2,500 and publication by New Issues Press; Donald Hall Prize for Poetry: $5,500 and publication by the University of Pittsburgh Press; Grace Paley Prize in Short Fiction: $5,500 and publication by the University of Massachusetts Press; and AWP Prize for Creative Nonfiction: $2,500 and publication by the University of Georgia Press.

⊕ BALCONES FICTION PRIZE

Austin Commmunity College, Department of Creative Writing, 1212 Rio Grande St., Austin TX 78701. (512)584-5045. **E-mail:** joconne@austincc.edu. **Website:** www.austincc.edu/crw/html/balconescenter .html. **Contact:** Joe O'Connell. Awarded to the best book of literary fiction published the previous year. Books of prose may be submitted by publisher or author. Send 3 copies. Deadline: January 31. Prize: $1,500, winner flown to Austin for a campus reading.

ⓞⓢ THE BALTIMORE REVIEW CONTESTS

The Baltimore Review, 6514 Maplewood Rd., Baltimore MD 21212. **Website:** www.baltimorereview .org. **Contact:** Barbara Westwood Diehl, senior editor. Each summer and winter issue includes a contest theme (see submissions guidelines for theme). Prizes are awarded for 1st, 2nd, and 3rd Place among all categories: poetry, short stories, and creative nonfiction. All entries are considered for publication. Deadline: May 31 and November 30. Prize: 1st Place: $500; 2nd Place: $200; 3rd Place: $100. Most winning works are published. Judged by the editors of *The Baltimore Review*.

BARD FICTION PRIZE

Bard College, P.O. Box 5000, Annandale-on-Hudson NY 12504-5000. (845)758-7087. **E-mail:** bfp@bard .edu. **Website:** www.bard.edu/bfp. **Contact:** Irene Zedlacher. Estab. 2001. The Bard Fiction Prize is intended to encourage and support young writers of fiction to pursue their creative goals and to provide an opportunity to work in a fertile and intellectual environment. Prize: $30,000 cash award and appointment as writer-in-residence at Bard College for 1 semester. Judged by committee of 5 judges (authors associated with Bard College). No entry fee. Cover letter should include name, address, phone, e-mail, and name of publisher where book was previously published. Guidelines available by SASE, fax, phone, e-mail, or on website. Deadline: July 15. Entries must be previously published. Open to U.S. citizens aged 39 and below. Results announced by October 15. Winners notified by phone. For contest results, e-mail, or visit website. Open to younger American writers.

◐ MILDRED L. BATCHELDER AWARD

50 E. Huron St., Chicago IL 60611-2795. **Website:** www.ala.org/alsc/awardsgrants/bookmedia/batchel deraward. **Contact:** Jean Hatfield, Chair. Estab. 1966. The Batchelder Award is given to the most outstanding children's book originally published in a language other than English in a country other than the United States, and subsequently translated into English for publication in the U.S. The purpose of the award, a citation to an American publisher, is to encourage international exchange of quality children's books by recognizing U.S. publishers of such books in translation. Deadline: December 31.

BELLEVUE LITERARY REVIEW GOLDENBERG PRIZE FOR FICTION

Bellevue Literary Review, NYU Department of Medicine, 550 First Ave., OBV-A612, New York NY 10016. (212)263-3973. **E-mail:** info@blreview.org; stacy@blreview.org. **Website:** www.blreview.org. **Contact:** Stacy Bodziak, managing editor. The BLR prizes award outstanding writing related to themes of health, healing, illness, the mind, and the body. Annual competition/award for short stories. Receives about 200-300 entries per category. Send credit card information or make checks payable to Bellevue Literary Review. Guidelines available in February. Accepts inquiries by e-mail, phone, mail. Submissions open in February. Results announced in December and made available to entrants with SASE, by e-mail, on website. Winners notified by mail, by e-mail. Deadline: July 1. Prize: $1,000 and publication in *The Bellevue Literary Review*. BLR editors select semifinalists to be read by an independent judge who chooses the winner. Previous judges include Amy Hempel, Rick Moody, Rosellen Brown, and Andre Dubus III.

◯ GEORGE BENNETT FELLOWSHIP

Phillips Exeter Academy, 20 Main St., Exeter NH 03833. **E-mail:** teaching_opportunities@exeter.edu. **Website:** www.exeter.edu/fellowships. Annual award for fellow and family to provide time and freedom from material considerations to a person seriously contemplating or pursuing a career as a writer. Applicants should have a ms in progress which they intend to complete during the fellowship period. Ms should be fiction, nonfiction, novel, short stories, or poetry. Duties: To be in residency at the Academy for the academic year; to make oneself available informally to students interested in writing. Committee favors writers who have not yet published a book with a major publisher. Deadline for application: December 2. A choice will be made, and all entrants notified in mid-April. Cash stipend (currently $14,626), room and board. Judged by committee of the English department.

BEST LESBIAN EROTICA

BLE 2013, 31-64 21st St., #319, Long Island City NY 11106. **E-mail:** kwarnockble@gmail.com. **Website:** www.kathleenwarnock.com/best-lesbian-erotica .html. **Contact:** Kathleen Warnock, series editor. Call for submissions for *Best Lesbian Erotica*, an annual collection. Categories include: novel excerpts, short stories; poetry will be considered but is not encouraged. Accepts both previously published and unpublished material; will accept submissions that have appeared in other themed anthologies. Open to any writer. All submissions must include an e-mail address for response. No mss will be returned, so please do not include SASE. Deadline: April 1. Prize: $100 for each published story, plus 2 copies of the anthology.

◯ BINGHAMTON UNIVERSITY JOHN GARDNER FICTION BOOK AWARD

Creative Writing Program, Binghamton University, Binghamton University, Department of English, General Literature, and Rhetoric, Library North Room 1149, P.O. Box 6000, Binghamton NY 13902-6000. (607)777-2713. **E-mail:** cwpro@binghamton.edu. **Website:** binghamton.edu/english/creative-writing/. **Contact:** Maria Mazziotti Gillan, director. Estab. 2001. Contest offered annually for a novel or collection of fiction published in previous year in a press run of 500 copies or more. Each book submitted must be accompanied by an application form. Publisher may submit more than 1 book for prize consideration. Send 3 copies of each book. Guidelines available on website. Deadline: March 1. Prize: $1,000. Judged by a professional writer not on Binghamton University faculty.

◐◯ JAMES TAIT BLACK MEMORIAL PRIZES

University of Edinburgh, David Hume Tower, George, Edinburgh EH8 9JX Scotland. **Website:** www.ed.ac

.uk/news/events/tait-black/introduction. Open to any writer. Entries must be previously published. Winners notified by phone, via publisher. Contact department of English Literature for list of winners or check website. Accepts inquiries by fax, e-mail, phone. Deadline: December 1. Prize: Two prizes each of £10,000 are awarded: 1 for the best work of fiction, 1 for the best biography or work of that nature, published during the calendar year January 1 to December 31. Judged by professors of English Literature with the assistance of teams of postgraduate readers.

◐⑤ THE BLACK RIVER CHAPBOOK COMPETITION

Black Lawrence Press, 326 Bingham St., Pittsburgh PA 15211. **E-mail:** editors@blacklawrencepress.com. **Website:** www.blacklawrencepress.com. Contest for unpublished chapbook of poems or short fiction between 18-36 pages in length. Submit via online form. Spring deadline: May 31. Fall deadline: October 31. Prize: $500, publication, and 25 copies.

✎○ THE BOARDMAN TASKER AWARD FOR MOUNTAIN LITERATURE

The Boardman Tasker Charitable Trust, 8 Bank View Rd., Darley Abbey Derby DE22 1EJ U.K. 01332 342246. **E-mail:** steve@people-matter.co.uk. **Website:** www.boardmantasker.com. **Contact:** Steve Dean. Offered annually to reward a work with a mountain theme, whether fiction, nonfiction, drama, or poetry, written in the English language (initially or in translation). Subject must be concerned with a mountain environment. Previous winners have been books on expeditions, climbing experiences, a biography of a mountaineer, novels. Guidelines available in January by e-mail or on website. Entries must be previously published. Open to any writer. The award is to honor Peter Boardman and Joe Tasker, who disappeared on Everest in 1982. Deadline: August 1. Prize: £3,000 Judged by a panel of 3 judges elected by trustees.

BOSTON GLOBE-HORN BOOK AWARDS

The Boston Globe, Horn Book, Inc., 56 Roland St., Suite 200, Boston MA 02129. (617)628-0225. **Fax:** (617)628-0882. **E-mail:** info@hbook.com; khedeen@hbook.com. **Website:** hbook.com/bghb/. **Contact:** Katrina Hedeen. Estab. 1967. Offered annually for excellence in literature for children and young adults (published June 1-May 31). Categories: picture book, fiction and poetry, nonfiction. Judges may also name up to 2 honor books in each category. Books must

be published in the U.S., but may be written or illustrated by citizens of any country. *The Horn Book Magazine* publishes speeches given at awards ceremonies. Guidelines for SASE or online. Deadline: May 15. Prize: $500 and an engraved silver bowl; honor book recipients receive an engraved silver plate. Judged by a panel of 3 judges selected each year.

BOULEVARD SHORT FICTION CONTEST FOR EMERGING WRITERS

Boulevard Magazine, 6614 Clayton Rd., PMB #325, Richmond Heights MO 63117. (314)862-2643. **Website:** www.richardburgin.net/boulevard. **Contact:** Jessica Rogen, managing editor. Offered annually for unpublished short fiction to a writer who has not yet published a book of fiction, poetry, or creative nonfiction with a nationally distributed press. Holds first North American rights on anything not previously published. Open to any writer with no previous publication by a nationally known press. Guidelines for SASE or on website. Deadline: December 31. Prize: $1,500 and publication in 1 of the next year's issues.

○☺ THE BRIAR CLIFF REVIEW FICTION, POETRY, AND CREATIVE NONFICTION COMPETITION

The Briar Cliff Review, Briar Cliff University, 3303 Rebecca St., Sioux City IA 51104-0100. **E-mail:** tricia.currans-sheehan@briarcliff.edu (editor); jeanne.emmons@briarcliff.edu (poetry). **Website:** www.briarcliff.edu/bcreview. **Contact:** Tricia Currans-Sheehan, editor. Guidelines available in August for SASE. Inquiries accepted by e-mail. Deadline: Submissions between August 1 and November 1. No mss returned. Entries must be unpublished. Length: 6,000 words maximum. Open to any writer. Results announced in December or January. Winners notified by phone or letter around December 20. "Send us your best. We want stories with a plot." For contest results, send SASE with submission. *The Briar Cliff Review* sponsors an annual contest offering $1,000 and publication to each 1st-Prize winner in fiction, poetry, and creative nonfiction. Previous year's winner and former students of editors ineligible. Winning pieces accepted for publication on the basis of first-time rights. Considers simultaneous submissions, "but notify us immediately upon acceptance elsewhere. We guarantee a considerate reading." No mss returned. Award to reward good writers and showcase quality writing. Deadline: Varies per category.

◉◯ THE BRIDPORT PRIZE

P.O. Box 6910, Dorset DT6 9QB United Kingdom. **E-mail:** info@bridportprize.org.uk. **Website:** www .bridportprize.org.uk. **Contact:** Frances Everitt, administrator. Award to promote literary excellence, discover new talent. Categories: Short stories, poetry, flash fiction. 2010 introduced a new category for flash fiction: £1,000 sterling 1st Prize for the best short-short story of under 250 words. Deadline: May 31. Prize: £5,000 sterling; £1,000 sterling; £500 sterling; various runners-up prizes and publication of approximately 13 best stories and 13 best poems in anthology; plus 6 best flash-fiction stories. Judged by 1 judge for short stories (in 2014, Andrew Miller), 1 judge for poetry (in 2014, Liz Lochhead) and 1 judge for flash fiction (in 2014, Tania Hershman).

◉ BRITISH CZECH AND SLOVAK ASSOCIATION WRITING COMPETITION

24 Ferndale, Tunbridge Wells Kent TN2 3NS England. **E-mail:** prize@bcsa.co.uk. **Website:** www.bcsa .co.uk/specials.html. Estab. 2002. Annual contest for original writing (1,500-2,000 words) in English on the links between Britain and the Czech/Slovak Republics, or describing society in transition in the Republics since 1989. Entries can be fact or fiction. Topics can include history, politics, the sciences, economics, the arts, or literature. Deadline: June 30. Winners announced in November. Prizes: 1st Place—£300; 2nd Place—100.

◉ BURNABY WRITERS' SOCIETY CONTEST

E-mail: info@bws.bc.ca. **Website:** www.bws.bc.ca; www.burnabywritersnews.blogspot.com. **Contact:** Eileen Kernaghan. Offered annually for unpublished work. Open to all residents of British Columbia. Categories vary from year to year. Send SASE for current rules. For complete guidelines see website or burn abywritersnews.blogspot.com. Purpose is to encourage talented writers in all genres. Deadline: May 31. 1st Place: $200; 2nd Place: $100; 3rd Place: $50; and public reading.

◉◯ THE CAINE PRIZE FOR AFRICAN WRITING

51 Southwark St., London SE1 1RU United Kingdom. **E-mail:** info@caineprize.com. **Website:** www.caine prize.com. **Contact:** Lizzy Attree. Estab. 2000. Entries must have appeared for the first time in the 5 years prior to the closing date for submissions, which is January 31 each year. Publishers should submit 6 copies of the published original with a brief cover note (no pro forma application). "Please indicate nationality or passport held." The Caine Prize is open to writers from anywhere in Africa for work published in English. Its focus is on the short story, reflecting the contemporary development of the African storytelling tradition. Deadline: January 31. Prize: £10,000.

CALIFORNIA BOOK AWARDS

Commonwealth Club of California, 595 Market St., San Francisco CA 94105. (415)597-6700. **Fax:** (415)597-6729. **E-mail:** bookawards@common wealthclub.org. **Website:** www.commonwealthclub .org/bookawards. Estab. 1931. Offered annually to recognize California's best writers and illuminate the wealth and diversity of California-based literature. Award is for published submissions appearing in print during the previous calendar year. Can be nominated by publisher or author. Open to California residents (or residents at time of publication). Deadline: December 31. Prize: Medals and cash prizes to be awarded at publicized event. Judged by 12-15 California professionals with a diverse range of views, backgrounds, and literary experience.

◉ JOHN W. CAMPBELL MEMORIAL AWARD FOR BEST SCIENCE FICTION NOVEL OF THE YEAR

English Department, University of Kansas, Lawrence KS 66045. (785)864-3380. **Fax:** (785)864-1159. **E-mail:** cmckit@ku.edu. **Website:** www.sfcenter .ku.edu/campbell.htm. **Contact:** Chris McKitterick. Estab. 1973. Honors the best science fiction novel of the year. Deadline: Check website. Prize: Campbell Award trophy. Winners receive an expense-paid trip to the university to receive their award. Their names are also engraved on a permanent trophy. Judged by a jury.

◉ CANADIAN AUTHORS ASSOCIATION AWARD FOR FICTION

6 West St. N., Suite 203, Orilla ON L3X 5B8 Canada. **Website:** www.canadianauthors.org. **Contact:** Anita Purcell. Estab. 1975. Award for full-length, English language literature for adults by a Canadian author. Deadline: January15. Prize: $2,000 and a silver medal.

THE ALEXANDER PATTERSON CAPPON FICTION AWARD

New Letters, University of Missouri-Kansas City, 5101 Rockhill Rd., Kansas City MO 64110-2499. (816)235-1168. **Fax:** (816)235-2611. **E-mail:** newletters@umkc

.edu. **Website:** www.newletters.org. **Contact:** Ashley Kaine. Offered annually for the best short story to discover and reward new and upcoming writers. Buys first North American serial rights. Open to any writer. Deadline: May 18. Prize: 1st Place: $1,500 and publication in a volume of *New Letters*. All entries will be given consideration for publication in future issues of *New Letters*.

⊕ CASCADE WRITING CONTEST & AWARDS

Oregon Christian Writers, 1075 Willow Lake Road N., Keizer Oregon 97303. **E-mail:** cascade@oregon christianwriters.org. **Website:** oregonchristianwriters.org/ocw-cascade-writing-contest/. **Contact:** Marilyn Rhoads and Julie McDonald Zander. The Cascade Awards are presented at the annual Oregon Christian Writers Summer Conference (held at the Red Lion on the River in Portland, Oregon, each August) attended by national editors, agents, and professional authors. Award given for each of the following categories: Published Fiction Book, Unpublished Fiction Book, Nonfiction/Memoir, Poetry, Devotional Books, Young Adult Novels, Middle-Grade Fiction Book and Middle-Grade Nonfiction Book, Children's Fiction and Nonfiction Book, and Short Entries, including: Articles, Stories, and Published Blog. Two additional special Cascade Awards are presented each year: the Trailblazer Award to a writer who has distinguished him/herself in the field of Christian writing and a Writer of Promise Award for a writer who demonstrates unusual promise in the field of Christian writing. For a full list of categories, entry rules, and scoring elements, visit website. Annual multigenre competition to encourage both published and emerging writers in the field of Christian writing. Deadline: February 14-March 31. Prize: Award certificate presented at the Cascade Awards ceremony during the Oregon Christian Writers Annual Summer Conference. Finalists are listed in the conference notebook and winners are listed online. Cascade Trophies are awarded to the recipients of the Trailblazer and Writer of Promise Awards. Judged by published authors, editors, librarians, and retail bookstore owners and employees. Final judging by editors, agents, and published authors from the Christian publishing industry.

JAMIE CAT CALLAN HUMOR PRIZE

Category in the Soul-Making Keats Literary Competition, The Webhallow House, 1544 Sweetwood Dr., Broadmoor Village CA 94015-2029. **E-mail:** SoulKeats@mail.com. **Website:** www.soulmaking contest.us. **Contact:** Eileen Malone. Deadline: November 30. Prize: 1st Place: $100; 2nd Place: $50; 3rd Place: $25. Judged by Jamie Cat Callan.

KAY CATTARULLA AWARD FOR BEST SHORT STORY

Texas Institute of Letters, P.O. Box 609, Round Rock TX 78680. **E-mail:** tilsecretary@yahoo.com. **Website:** texasinstituteofletters.org. Offered annually for work published January 1-December 31 of previous year to recognize the best short story. The story submitted must have appeared in print for the first time to be eligible. Writers must have been born in Texas or must have lived in Texas for at least 2 consecutive years, or the subject matter of the work must be associated with Texas. See website for guidelines. Deadline: January 10. Prize: $1,000.

⊕🌐○ PEGGY CHAPMAN-ANDREWS FIRST NOVEL AWARD

P.O. Box 6910, Dorset DT6 9QB United Kingdom. **E-mail:** info@bridportprize.org.uk. **Website:** www.bridportprize.org.uk. **Contact:** Frances Everitt, administrator. Award to promote literary excellence and new writers. Enter first chapters of novel, up to 8,000 words plus 300-word synopsis. Deadline: May 31. Prize: 1st Prize: £1,000 plus mentoring and possible publication. Judged by Alison Moore, The Literary Consultancy and A.M. Heath Literary Agents.

🌐 THE CHARITON REVIEW SHORT FICTION PRIZE

Truman State University Press, 100 East Normal Ave., Kirksville MO 63501-4221. **Website:** tsup.truman.edu. An annual award for the best unpublished short fiction on any theme up to 5,000 words in English. Deadline: September 30. Prize: $1,000 and publication in *The Chariton Review* for the winner. Three finalists will also be published in the spring issue. The final judge will be announced after the finalists have been selected in January.

⊕ CHRISTIAN ADVENTURE/ROMANCE FICTION CONTEST

P.O. Box 1001, Reynoldsburg OH 43068. **E-mail:** dianaperry@DianaPerryBooks.com. **Website:** diana perrybooks.com. **Contact:** Diana Perry. Estab. 2014. "Tell an exciting story in action-adventure genre while weaving a passionate romantic subplot to show that

Christians can wait for marriage and yet be very passionate and loving." Rules on website. Length: up to 20 pages or 5,000 words. Purpose: "To give exposure to beginning writers trying to break in to the business and get noticed." Deadline: November 31. 1st Place: $300, trophy, mention on website, t-shirt, press releases in your local newspapers; 2nd Place: $200, trophy, mention on website, T-shirt, press releases in your local newspapers; 3rd Place: $100, trophy, mention on website, T-shirt, press releases in your local newspapers; 4th/5th places: $50/$25, plaque, mention on website, T-shirt, press releases in your local newspapers. "We also list names of next 25 honorable mentions on website. Contest guidelines and entry form on website. Check website for guest judges. Mail entry form, your story, and a $15 money order only to Christian Adventure/Romance Fiction Contest at above address postmarked no later than November 31. Winners announced both on website and via snail mail January 1. Prizes mailed within 10 days of announcement. Judged by Diana Perry and guest judge.

THE CITY OF VANCOUVER BOOK AWARD

Cultural Services Department, Woodward's Heritage Building, 111 W. Hastings St., Suite 501, Vancouver BC V6B 1H4 Canada. (604) 829-2007. **Fax:** (604)871-6005. **E-mail:** marnie.rice@vancouver.ca. **Website:** https://vancouver.ca/people-programs/city-of-vancouver-book-award.aspx. Estab. 1989. The annual City of Vancouver Book Award recognizes authors of excellence of any genre who contribute to the appreciation and understanding of Vancouver's history, unique character, or the achievements of its residents. Deadline: May 15. Prize: $2,000. Judged by an independent jury.

COLORADO BOOK AWARDS

Colorado Humanities & Center for the Book, 7935 E. Prentice Ave., Suite 450, Greenwood Village CO 80111. (303)894-7951, ext. 21. **Fax:** (303)864-9361. **E-mail:** abu-baker@coloradohumanities.org. **Website:** www.coloradohumanities.org. **Contact:** Reem Abu-Baker. An annual program that celebrates the accomplishments of Colorado's outstanding authors, editors, illustrators, and photographers. Awards are presented in at least 10 categories including anthology/collection, biography, children's, creative nonfiction, fiction, history, nonfiction, pictorial, poetry, and young adult. Celebrates books and their creators and promotes them to readers.

COPTALES CONTEST

Sponsored by Oak Tree Press, 140 E. Palmer St., Taylorville IL 62568. **E-mail:** publisher@oaktreebooks.com. **E-mail:** CT-ContestAdmin@oaktreebooks.com. **Website:** www.oaktreebooks.com. **Contact:** Billie Johnson, publisher. Open to novels and true stories that feature a law-enforcement main character. Word count should range from 60,000-80,000 words. The goal of the CopTales Contest is to discover and publish new authors, or authors shifting to a new genre. This annual contest is open to writers who have not published in the mystery genre in the past 3 years, as well as completely unpublished authors. Deadline: September 1. Prize: Publishing contract, book published in trade paperback and e-book formats with a professionally designed, 4-color cover. See website for details. Judged by a select panel of editors and professional crime writers.

CRAZYHORSE PRIZES IN FICTION, NONFICTION, & POETRY

College of Charleston, Department of English, 66 George St., Charleston SC 29424. (843)953-4470. **Fax:** (843)953-3180. **E-mail:** crazyhorse@cofc.edu. **Website:** crazyhorse.cofc.edu. From January 1 to January 31, *Crazyhorse* will accept entries for prizes in fiction, nonfiction, and poetry. Submit short stories and essays of up to 25 pages or up to 3 poems through website. All mss entered will be be considered for publication. For more information, or to see a list of judges, please visit website. Deadline: January 31. Prize: $2,000 and publication in *Crazyhorse*. Judged by anonymous writer whose identity is disclosed when the winners are announced in April.

CRITIQUE MY NOVEL WRITING CONTEST

Critique My Novel, 2408 W. 8th, Amarillo TX 79106. **E-mail:** contest@critiquemynovel.com. **Website:** critiquemynovel.com/2014_writing_contest. **Contact:** Catherine York, contest/award director. Annual contest for new and emerging writers. Send the first 10,000 words of a novel (must be unpublished, self-published, or published through a vanity/independent press). The main purpose is to help new writers. The focus is on feedback on all entries and prizes for the best. Deadline: March 1-April 30 (early bird), May 1-June 30 (regular deadline). Prize: Personal feedback from 4 judges for every entrant; cash prize, set of writing resources for top 4 novels; final 3 novels also receive a voucher and are sent to agents for feedback and consideration; 10 round-2 novels and author websites listed on Critique My Novel. Judges listed online. Includes guest judges from literary agencies who help in the final deliberations.

THE CRUCIBLE POETRY AND FICTION COMPETITION

Crucible, Barton College, College Station, Wilson NC 27893. (800)345-4973 x6450. **E-mail:** crucible@barton.edu. **Website:** www.barton.edu/SchoolofArts&Sciences/English/Crucible.htm. **Contact:** Terrence L. Grimes, editor. Open annually to all writers. Entries must be completely original, never published, and in ms form. Does not accept simultaneous submissions. Fiction is limited to 8,000 words; poetry is limited to 5 poems. Guidelines online or by e-mail or for SASE. All submissions should be electronic. Deadline: May 1. Prize (for both poetry and fiction): 1st Place: $150; 2nd Place: $100. Winners are also published in *Crucible*. Judged by in-house editorial board.

DANA AWARDS IN THE NOVEL, SHORT FICTION, AND POETRY

www.danaawards.com, 200 Fosseway Dr., Greensboro NC 27445. (336)644-8028. **E-mail:** danaawards@gmail.com. **E-mail:** danaawards@gmail.com. **Website:** www.danaawards.com. **Contact:** Mary Elizabeth Parker, chair. Three awards offered annually for unpublished work written in English. Works previously published online are not eligible. Purpose is monetary award for work that has not been previously published or received monetary award, but will accept work published simply for friends and family. Deadline: October 31 (postmarked). Prizes: $1,000 for each of the 3 awards.

DARK OAK MYSTERY CONTEST

Oak Tree Press, 140 E. Palmer St., Taylorville IL 62568. (217)824-6500. **E-mail:** oaktreepub@aol.com. **E-mail:** DO-ContestAdmin@oaktreebooks.com. **Website:** www.oaktreebooks.com. Offered annually for an unpublished mystery ms (up to 80,000 words) of any sort from police procedurals to amateur-sleuth novels. Acquires first North American, audio and film rights to winning entry. Open to authors not published in the past 3 years. Deadline: September 1. Prize: Publishing Agreement, and launch of the title. Judged by a select panel of editors and professional mystery writers.

O DEAD OF WINTER

E-mail: editors@toasted-cheese.com. **Website:** www.toasted-cheese.com. **Contact:** Stephanie Lenz, editor. The contest is a winter-themed horror fiction contest with a new topic each year. Topic and word limit announced October 1. The topic is usually geared toward a supernatural theme. Deadline: December 21. Results announced January 31. Winners notified by e-mail. List of winners on website. Prize: Amazon gift certificates and publication in *Toasted Cheese*. Also offers honorable mention. Judged by 2 *Toasted Cheese* editors who blind judge each contest. Each judge uses her own criteria to rate entries.

○①⑤ THE DEBUT DAGGER

Crime Writers' Association, New Writing Competition, P.O. Box 3408, Norwich NR3 3WE England. **E-mail:** director@thecwa.co.uk. **Website:** www.thecwa.co.uk. **Contact:** Mary Andrea Clarke. Annual competition for unpublished crime writers. Submit the opening 3,000 words of a crime novel, plus a 500- to 1,000-word synopsis of its continuance. Open to any writer who has not had a novel commercially published in any genre. Deadline: January 31. Submission period begins November 1. Prize: 1st Prize: £700. All short-listed entrants will receive a professional assessment of their entries, and their entries are sent to publishers and agents. Judged by a panel of top crime editors and agents, and.

DELAWARE DIVISION OF THE ARTS

820 N. French St., Wilmington DE 19801. (302)577-8278. **Fax:** (302)577-6561. **E-mail:** kristin.pleasanton@state.de.us. **Website:** www.artsdel.org. **Contact:** Kristin Pleasanton, coordinator. Award to help further careers of emerging and established professional artists. For Delaware residents only. Guidelines available after May 1 on website. Accepts inquiries by e-mail, phone. Results announced in December. Winners notified by mail. Results available on website. Deadline: August 1. Prize: $10,000 for masters; $6,000 for established professionals; $3,000 for emerging professionals. Judged by out-of-state, nationally recognized professionals in each artistic discipline.

Ⓞ   Expects to receive 25 fiction entries.

◑ DIAGRAM/NEW MICHIGAN PRESS CHAPBOOK CONTEST

Department of English, P.O. Box 210067, University of Arizona, Tucson AZ 85721-0067. **E-mail:** nmp@thediagram.com. **Website:** thediagram.com/contest.html. **Contact:** Ander Monson, editor. Estab. 1999. The annual *DIAGRAM*/New Michigan Press Chapbook Contest offers $1,000, plus publication and author's copies, with discount on additional copies. Also publishes 2-4 finalist chapbooks each year. Deadline: April 1. Prize: $1,000, plus publication.

DOBIE PAISANO WRITER'S FELLOWSHIP

The Graduate School, The University of Texas at Austin, Attn: Dobie Paisano Program, 110 Inner Campus Drive Stop G0400, Austin TX 78712-0531. (512)232-3609. **Fax:** (512)471-7620. **E-mail:** gbarton@austin.utexas.edu. **Website:** www.utexas.edu/ogs/Paisano. **Contact:** Gwen Barton. Sponsored by the Graduate School at The University of Texas at Austin and the Texas Institute of Letters, the Dobie Paisano Fellowship Program provides solitude, time, and a comfortable place for Texas writers or writers who have written significantly about Texas. Deadline: January 15. The Ralph A. Johnston memorial Fellowship is for a period of 4 months with a stipend of $5,000 per month. It is aimed at writers who have already demonstrated some publishing and critical success. The Jesse H. Jones Writing Fellowship is for a period of approximately 6 months with a stipend of $3,000 per month. It is aimed at, but not limited to, writers who are early in their careers.

◎ JACK DYER FICTION PRIZE

Crab Orchard Review, Department of English, Mail Code 4503, Faner Hall 2380, Southern Illinois University at Carbondale, 1000 Faner Drive, Carbondale IL 62901. **E-mail:** jtribble@siu.edu. **Website:** www.craborchardreview.siu.edu. **Contact:** Jon C. Tribble, man. editor. Offered annually for unpublished short fiction. *Crab Orchard Review* acquires first North American serial rights to all submitted work. One winner and at least 2 finalists will be chosen. Deadline: April 21. Submissions period begins February 21. Prize: $2,000, publication and one-year subscription to *Crab Orchard Review*. Finalists are offered $500 and publication. Judged by editorial staff (prescreening); winner chosen by genre editor.

MARY KENNEDY EASTHAM FLASH FICTION PRIZE

Category in the Soul-Making Keats Literary Competition, The Webhallow House, 1544 Sweetwood Dr., Broadmoor Village CA 94015-2029. **E-mail:** EileenMalone@comcast.net. **Website:** www.soulmakingcontest.us. **Contact:** Eileen Malone. Keep each story under 500 words. Three stories per entry. One story per page, typed, double-spaced, and unidentified. Deadline: November 30. Prizes: 1st Place: $100; 2nd Place: $50; 3rd Place: $25.

EATON LITERARY AGENCY'S ANNUAL AWARDS PROGRAM

Eaton Literary Agency, P.O. Box 49795, Sarasota FL 34230-6795. (941)366-6589. **Fax:** (941)365-4679. **E-mail:** eatonlit@aol.com. **Website:** www.eatonliterary.com. **Contact:** Richard Lawrence, vice president. Offered biannually for unpublished mss. Prize: $2,500 (over 10,000 words); $500 (under 10,000 words). Judged by an independent agency in conjunction with some members of Eaton's staff. No entry fee. Guidelines available for SASE, by fax, e-mail, or on website. Accepts inquiries by fax, phone, and e-mail. Deadline: **March 31** (mss under 10,000 words); **August 31** (mss over 10,000 words). Entries must be unpublished. Open to any writer. Results announced in April and September. Winners notified by mail. For contest results, send SASE, fax, e-mail, or visit website. Offered biannually for unpublished mss. Open to any writer.

THE EMILY CONTEST

18207 Heaton Dr., Houston TX 77084. **E-mail:** emily.contest@whrwa.com. **Website:** www.whrwa.com. Annual award to promote publication of previously unpublished writers of romance. Open to any writer who has not published in a given category within the past 3 years. The mission of The Emily is to professionally support writers and guide them toward a path to publication. Deadline: October 7. Submission period begins September 1. Final judging done by an editor and an agent.

◉ FABLERS MONTHLY CONTEST

818 Los Arboles Lane, Santa Fe NM 87501. **Website:** www.fablers.net. **Contact:** W.B. Scott. Monthly contest for previously unpublished writers to help develop amateur writers. Guidelines posted online. No entry fee. Open to any writer. Deadline: 14th of each month. Prize: $100. Judged by members of website.

⊕ FAIRY TALE FICTION CONTEST

P.O. Box 1001, Reynoldsburg OH 43068. **E-mail:** di anaperry@DianaPerryBooks.com. **Website:** diana perrybooks.com. **Contact:** Diana Perry. Estab. 2014. "Write a classic fairy tale befitting Grimm, Hans Christian Anderson, or the bedtime stories you came to love as a child, suitable for emergent readers up to age 8, or for adults reading to smaller children." Rules on website. Length: up to 12 pages or 1,500 words. Purpose: "To give exposure to beginning writers trying to break in to the business and get noticed." Deadline: July 31. 1st Place: $200, trophy, mention on website, T-shirt, press releases in your local newspapers; 2nd Place: $150, trophy, mention on website, T-shirt, press releases in your local newspapers; 3rd Place: $100, trophy, mention on website, T-shirt, press releases in your local newspapers; 4th/5th places: $50/$25, plaque, mention on website, T-shirt, press releases in your local newspapers. "We also list names of next 25 honorable mentions on website. Contest guidelines and entry form on website. Check website for guest judges. Mail entry form, your story, and a $15 money order only to Fairy Tale Fiction Contest at above address postmarked no later than July 31. Winners announced both on website and via snail mail September 1. Prizes mailed within 10 days of announcement. Judged by Diana Perry and guest judge.

◯ THE FAR HORIZONS AWARD FOR SHORT FICTION

The Malahat Review, University of Victoria, P.O. Box 1700, Stn CSC, Victoria BC V8W 2Y2 Canada. (250)721-8524. **Fax:** (250)472-5051. **E-mail:** mala hat@uvic.ca. **E-mail:** horizons@uvic.ca. **Website:** www.malahatreview.ca. **Contact:** John Barton, editor. Open to "emerging short fiction writers from Canada, the U.S., and elsewhere," who have not yet published their fiction in a full-length book (48 pages or more). 2011 winner: Zoey Peterson; 2013 winner: Kerry-Lee Powell. Deadline: May 1 (odd-numbered years). Prize: $1,000 CAD, publication in fall issue of *The Malahat Review* (see separate listing in Magazines/Journals). Announced in fall on website, Facebook page, and in quarterly e-newsletter, *Malahat Lite*.

THE VIRGINIA FAULKNER AWARD FOR EXCELLENCE IN WRITING

Prairie Schooner, 123 Andrews Hall, University of Nebraska-Lincoln, Lincoln NE 68588-0334. (402)472-0911. **Fax:** (402)472-1817. **E-mail:** PrairieSchooner@ unl.edu. **Website:** www.prairieschooner.unl.edu. **Contact:** Kwame Dawes. Offered annually for work published in *Prairie Schooner* in the previous year. Categories: short stories, essays, novel excerpts, and translations. Guidelines for SASE or on website. Prize: $1,000. Judged by editorial board.

FINELINE COMPETITION FOR PROSE POEMS, SHORT SHORTS, AND ANYTHING IN BETWEEN

Mid-American Review, Department of English, Bowling Green State University, Bowling Green OH 43403. (419)372-2725. **E-mail:** marsubmissions@bgsu.edu. **Website:** www.bgsu.edu/midamericanreview. **Contact:** Abigail Cloud, editor-in-chief. Offered annually for previously unpublished submissions. Contest open to all writers not associated with current judge or *Mid-American Review*. Deadline: June 1. Prize: $1,000, plus publication in fall issue of *Mid-American Review*; 10 finalists receive notation plus possible publication.

⊕ FIRST NOVEL CONTEST

Harrington & Harrington Press, 3400 Yosemite, San Diego CA 92109. **E-mail:** press@harringtonandhar rington.com. **Website:** www.harringtonandhar rington.com. **Contact:** Laurie Champion, contest/award director. Annual contest for any writer who has not previously published a novel. Entries may be self-published. Accepts full-length works in literary fiction, creative nonfiction, memoir, genre fiction, and short story collections. No poetry. Guidelines available online. Harrington & Harrington Press aims to support writers, and the First Novel Contest will provide many ways to promote authors through networks and connections with writers, artists, and those involved in the technical production of art. Deadline: August 15. Prize: $500 advance royalty and publication by Harrington & Harrington Press. Judged by the Harrington & Harrington staff for the preliminary round. A respected author with numerous publications will act as the final judge.

FIRSTWRITER.COM INTERNATIONAL SHORT STORY CONTEST

firstwriter.com, United Kingdom. **Website:** www .firstwriter.com. **Contact:** J. Paul Dyson, managing editor. Accepts short stories up to 3,000 words on any subject and in any style. Deadline: April 1. Prize: Totals about $300. Ten special commendations will also be awarded and all the winners will be published in *firstwriter* magazine and receive a $36 subscription voucher, allowing an annual subscription to be taken out for free. All submissions are automatically considered for publication in *firstwriter* magazine and may be published there online. Judged by *firstwriter* magazine editors.

🌐◯ FISH PUBLISHING FLASH FICTION COMPETITION

County Cork, Ireland. **E-mail:** info@fishpublishing .com. **Website:** www.fishpublishing.com. Estab. 2004. Annual prize awarding flash fiction. "This is an opportunity to attempt what is 1 of the most difficult and rewarding tasks—to create, in a tiny fragment, a completely resolved and compelling story in 300 words or less." Deadline: February 28. First Prize: €1,000 ($1,200). The 10 published authors will receive 5 copies of the anthology and will be invited to read at the launch during the West Cork Literary Festival in July.

🌐◯ FISH SHORT STORY PRIZE

Cork, Ireland. **E-mail:** info@fishpublishing.com. **Website:** www.fishpublishing.com. Estab. 1994. Annual worldwide competition to recognize the best short stories. Deadline: November 30. Prize: Overall prize fund: €5,000. 1st Prize: €3,000. 2nd Prize: 1 week at Anam Cara Writers Retreat in West Cork and €300. 3rd Prize: €300. Closing date November 30. The best 10 will be published in the Fish Anthology, launched in July at the West Cork Literary Festival. Winners announced March 17.

FOREWORD MAGAZINE BOOK OF THE YEAR AWARDS

ForeWord Magazine, 425 Boardman Ave., Traverse City MI 49684. (231)933-3699. **Fax:** (231)933-3899. **Website:** www.forewordreviews.com. Awards offered annually. In order to be eligible, books must have a current year copyright. *ForeWord*'s Book of the Year Award was established to bring increased attention from librarians and booksellers to the literary achievements of independent publishers and their authors. Deadline: January 15. Prize: $1,500 cash will be awarded to a Best Fiction and Best Nonfiction choice, as determined by the editors of *ForeWord Magazine*. Judged by a jury of librarians, booksellers, and reviewers who are selected to judge the categories for entry and select winners and finalists in 61 categories based on editorial excellence and professional production as well as the originality of the narrative and the value the book adds to its genre.

H.E. FRANCIS SHORT STORY COMPETITION

Ruth Hindman Foundation, University of Alabama in Huntsville, Department of English, Morton Hall Room 222, Huntsville AL 35899. **Website:** www.he franciscompetition.com. Offered annually for unpublished work, not to exceed 5,000 words. Acquires first-time publication rights. Deadline: December 31. Prize: $2,000. Judged by a panel of nationally recognized, award-winning authors, directors of creative writing programs, and editors of literary journals.

SOEURETTE DIEHL FRASER AWARD FOR BEST TRANSLATION OF A BOOK

P.O. Box 609, Round Rock TX 78680. **E-mail:** tilsecre tary@yahoo.com. **Website:** texasinstituteofletters.org. Offered every 2 years to recognize the best translation of a literary book into English. Translator must have been born in Texas or have lived in the state for at least 2 consecutive years at some time. Deadline: January 10. Prize: $1,000.

◯ FREEFALL SHORT PROSE AND POETRY CONTEST

Freefall Literary Society of Calgary, 922 9th Ave. SE, Calgary AB T2G 0S4 Canada. **E-mail:** freefall magazine@yahoo.ca; editors@freefallmagazine.ca. **Website:** www.freefallmagazine.ca. **Contact:** Lynn C. Fraser, managing editor. Offered annually for unpublished work in the categories of poetry (5 poems/ entry) and prose (3,000 words or less). Recognizes writers and offers publication credits in a literary magazine format. Contest rules and entry form online. Acquires first Canadian serial rights; ownership reverts to author after one-time publication. Deadline: December 31. Prize: 1st Place: $600 (CAD); 2nd Place: $150 (CAD); 3rd Place: $75; Honorable Mention: $25. All prizes include publication in the spring edition of *FreeFall Magazine*. Winners will also be invited to read at the launch of that issue, if such a launch takes place. Honorable mentions in each category will be published and may be asked to read. Travel expenses not included. Judged by current guest editor for issue (who are also published authors in Canada).

THE FRENCH-AMERICAN AND THE FLORENCE GOULD FOUNDATIONS TRANSLATION PRIZES

28 W. 44th St., Suite 1420, New York NY 10036. (646)588-6786. **E-mail:** ebriet@frenchamerican.org. **Website:** www.frenchamerican.org. **Contact:** Eug-

enie Briet. Annual contest to promote French literature in the U.S. by extending its reach beyond the first language and giving translators and their craft greater visibility among publishers and readers alike. The prize also seeks to increase the visibility of the publishers who bring these important French works of literature, in translation of exceptional quality, to the American market by publicizing the titles and giving more visibility to the books they publish. Deadline: December 31. Prize: $10,000 award. Jury committee made up of translators, writers, and scholars in French literature and culture.

GEORGETOWN REVIEW

Georgetown Review, 400 East College St., Box 227, Georgetown KY 40324. (502) 863-8308. **Fax:** (502) 863-8888. **E-mail:** gtownreview@georgetowncollege.edu. **Website:** georgetowncolleged.edu/georgetown review. **Contact:** Steve Carter, editor. "Our magazine is a collaboration between English faculty at Georgetown College and undergrads who learn the editing business as they go and who always amaze their elders with their dedication and first-rate work." Deadline: October 15. Prize: $1,000 and publication; runners-up receive publication.

GIVAL PRESS NOVEL AWARD

Gival Press, LLC, P.O. Box 3812, Arlington VA 22203. (703)351-0079. **E-mail:** givalpress@yahoo.com. **Website:** www.givalpress.com. **Contact:** Robert L. Giron. Offered annually for a previously unpublished original novel (not a translation). Guidelines by phone, on website, via e-mail, or by mail with SASE. Results announced late fall of same year. Winners notified by phone. Results made available to entrants with SASE, by e-mail, on website. "To award the best literary novel." Deadline: May 30. Prize: $3,000, plus publication of book with a standard contract and author's copies. Final judge is announced after winner is chosen. Entries read anonymously.

GIVAL PRESS SHORT STORY AWARD

Gival Press, P.O. Box 3812, Arlington VA 22203. (703)351-0079. **E-mail:** givalpress@yahoo.com. **Website:** www.givalpress.com. **Contact:** Robert L. Giron, publisher. Annual literary short story contest. Entries must be unpublished. Open to anyone who writes original short stories that are not a chapter of a novel, in English. Receives about 100-150 entries per category. Guidelines available online, via e-mail, or by mail. Results announced in the fall of the same year. Win-

ners notified by phone. Results available with SASE, by e-mail, and on website. Recognizes the best literary short story. Deadline: August 8. Prize: $1,000 and publication on website. Judged anonymously.

GLIMMER TRAIN'S FAMILY MATTERS CONTEST

Glimmer Train, 4763 SW Maplewood Rd., P.O. Box 80430, Portland OR 97280. (503)221-0836. **Fax:** (503)221-0837. **E-mail:** eds@glimmertrain.org. **Website:** www.glimmertrain.org. **Contact:** Susan Burmeister-Brown. This contest is now held twice a year, during the months of April and October. Winners are contacted 2 months after the close of each contest and results officially announced 1 week later. Submit online. Deadline: April 30 and October 31. Prize: 1st Place: $1,500, publication in *Glimmer Train Stories*, and 20 copies of that issue; 2nd Place: $500 and consideration for publication; 3rd Place: $300 and consideration for publication.

Represented in recent editions of *The Pushcart Prize, New Stories from the Midwest, The PEN/O. Henry Prize Stories, New Stories from the South, Best of the West,* and *Best American Short Stories Anthologies.*

GLIMMER TRAIN'S FICTION OPEN

Glimmer Train, Inc., Glimmer Train Press, Inc., 4763 SW Maplewood Rd., P.O. Box 80430, Portland OR 97280. (503)221-0836. **Fax:** (503)221-0837. **E-mail:** eds@glimmertrain.org. **Website:** www.glimmertrain.org. **Contact:** Linda Swanson-Davies. Submissions to this category generally range from 2,000-8,000 words, but up to 20,000 is fine. Held twice a year. Submit online. Winners will be called 2 months after the close of the contest. Deadline: June 30 and December 31. Prize: 1st Place $2,500, publication in *Glimmer Train Stories*, and 20 copies of that issue; 2nd Place $1,000 and consideration for publication; 3rd Place: $600 and consideration for publication.

Represented in recent editions of *The Pushcart Prize, New Stories from the Midwest, The PEN/O. Henry Prize Stories, New Stories from the South, Best of the West,* and *Best American Short Stories Anthologies.*

GLIMMER TRAIN'S SHORT-STORY AWARD FOR NEW WRITERS

Glimmer Train Press, Inc., 4763 SW Maplewood Rd., P.O. Box 80430, Portland OR 97280. (503)221-0836. **Fax:** (503)221-0837. **E-mail:** eds@glimmertrain.org.

Website: www.glimmertrain.org. **Contact:** Linda Swanson-Davies. Offered for any writer whose fiction hasn't appeared in a nationally distributed print publication with a circulation over 5,000. Submissions to this category generally range from 1,500-6,000 words, but up to 12,000 is fine. Held quarterly. Submit online. Winners will be called 2 months after the close of the contest. Deadline: February 28, May 31, August 31, and November 30. Prize: 1st Place: $1,500, publication in *Glimmer Train Stories*, and 20 copies of that issue; 2nd Place: $500 and consideration for publication; 3rd Place: $300 and consideration for publication.

○ Represented in recent editions of *The Pushcart Prize*, *New Stories from the Midwest*, *The PEN/O. Henry Prize Stories*, *New Stories from the South*, *Best of the West*, and *Best American Short Stories Anthologies*.

GLIMMER TRAIN'S VERY SHORT FICTION CONTEST

Glimmer Train Press, Inc., 4763 SW Maplewood Rd., P.O. Box 80430, Portland OR 97280. (503)221-0836. **Fax:** (503)221-0837. **E-mail:** eds@glimmertrain.org. **Website:** www.glimmertrain.org. **Contact:** Susan Burmeister-Brown. Offered to encourage the art of the very short story. Word count: 3,000 maximum. Held quarterly. Submit online. Results announced 2 months after the close of the contest. Deadline: January 31, April 30, July 31, and October 31. Prize: 1st Place: $1,500, publication in *Glimmer Train Stories*, and 20 copies of that issue; 2nd Place: $500 and consideration for publication; 3rd Place: $300 and consideration for publication.

○ Represented in recent editions of *The Pushcart Prize*, *New Stories from the Midwest*, *The PEN/O. Henry Prize Stories*, *New Stories from the South*, *Best of the West*, and *Best American Short Stories Anthologies*.

○ GOVERNOR GENERAL'S LITERARY AWARD FOR FICTION

Canada Council for the Arts, 150 Elgin St., P.O. Box 1047, Ottawa ON K1P 5V8 Canada. (613)566-4414, ext. 5573. **Fax:** (613)566-4410. **Website:** www.canadacouncil.ca/prizes/ggla. Offered annually for the best English-language and the best French-language work of fiction by a Canadian. Publishers submit titles for consideration. Deadline: Depends on the book's publication date. Books in English: March 15, June 1, or August 7. Books in French: March 15 or July 15. Prize:

Each laureate receives $25,000; nonwinning finalists receive $1,000.

⊕ THE GOVER PRIZE

Best New Writing, P.O. Box 11, Titusville NJ 08530. **Fax:** (609)968-1718. **E-mail:** submissions@bestnewwriting.com. **Website:** www.bestnewwriting.com/BNWgover.html. **Contact:** Christopher Klim, senior editor. The Gover Prize, named after groundbreaking author Robert Gover, awards an annual prize and publication in *Best New Writing* for the best short fiction and creative nonfiction. Deadline: September 15-January 10. Prize: $250 grand prize; publication in *Best New Writing* for finalists (approximately 12), holds 6-month world exclusive rights. Judged by *Best New Writing* editorial staff.

◐ GREAT LAKES COLLEGES ASSOCIATION NEW WRITERS AWARD

535 W. William, Suite 301, Ann Arbor MI 48103. (734)661-2350. **Fax:** (734)661-2349. **E-mail:** wegner@glca.org. **Website:** www.glca.org. **Contact:** Gregory R. Wegner. Annual award for a first published volume of poetry, fiction, and creative nonfiction. Deadline: July 25. Prize: Honorarium of at least $500. Each award winner has the opportunity to tour the 13 colleges and will give readings, meet with students and faculty, and lead discussions or classes. Judged by professors of literature and writers in residence at GLCA colleges.

THE GRUB STREET NATIONAL BOOK PRIZE

Grub Street, 162 Boylston Street, 5th Floor, Boston MA 02116. (617) 695-0075. **Fax:** (617) 695-0075. **E-mail:** info@grubstreet.org. **Website:** grubstreet.org. **Contact:** Christopher Castellani, artistic director. The Grub Street National Book Prize is awarded once annually to an American writer outside New England publishing his or her second, third, fourth (or beyond...) book. First books are not eligible. Writers whose primary residence is Massachusetts, Vermont, Maine, New Hampshire, Connecticut, or Rhode Island are also not eligible. Genre of the prize rotates from year to year, between fiction, nonfiction, and poetry. Deadline: October 15. Prize: $5,000.

◑ LYNDALL HADOW/DONALD STUART SHORT STORY COMPETITION

Fellowship of Australian Writers (WA), P.O. Box 6180, Swanbourne WA 6910 Australia. (61)(8)9384-4771. **Fax:** (61)(8)9384-4854. **E-mail:** admin@fawwa.org

.au. **Website:** www.fawwa.org.au. Annual contest for unpublished short stories (maximum 3,000 words). Reserves the right to publish entries in a FAWWA publication or on website. Guidelines online or for SASE. Deadline: June 1. Prize: 1st Place: $400; 2nd Place; $100; Highly Commended: $50.

HAMMETT PRIZE

International Association of Crime Writers, North American Branch, 328 Eighth Ave., #114, New York NY 10001. **E-mail:** mfrisque@igc.org. **Website:** www .crimewritersna.org. **Contact:** Mary A. Frisque, executive director, North American Branch. Award for crime novels, story collections, nonfiction by 1 author. "Our reading committee seeks suggestions from publishers and they also ask the membership for recommendations." Nominations announced in January; winners announced in fall. Winners notified by e-mail or mail and recognized at awards ceremony. For contest results, send SASE or e-mail. Award established to honor a work of literary excellence in the field of crime writing by a U.S. or Canadian author. Deadline: December 1. Prize: Trophy. Judged by a committee of members of the organization. The committee chooses 5 nominated books, which are then sent to 3 outside judges for a final selection. Judges are outside the crime-writing field.

➕ ROSE HAROOTIAN SHORT STORY CONTEST

327 Lowell St., Reading MA 01867. **E-mail:** pat tiannah@gmail.com. **Website:** www.pattianna .com/#!rose-harootian-literary-journal/c6b3. **Contact:** Pattianna Harootian. Annual contest to honor short stories. *The Rose Harootian Literary Journal* is made up of the entries submitted to the competition. Entries can be fiction or nonfiction but must be based on at least 1 character that overcomes adversity to achieve a goal or fulfill a dream, and conclusions must be hopeful, encouraging, and inspiring. Deadline: March 31. Prize: 1st Place: $500; 2nd Place: $200; 3rd Place: $50.

WILDA HEARNE FLASH FICTION CONTEST

Big Muddy: A Journal of the Mississippi River Valley, WHFF Contest, Southeast Missouri State University Press, One University Plaza, MS 2650, Cape Girardeau MO 63701. **E-mail:** sswartwout@semo.edu. **Website:** www6.semo.edu. **Contact:** Susan Swartwout, publisher. Annual competition for flash fiction, held by Southeast Missouri State University Press.

Deadline: October 1. Prize: $500 and publication in Big *Muddy: A Journal of the Mississippi River Valley*. Semifinalists will be chosen by a regional team of published writers. The final ms will be chosen by Susan Swartwout, publisher of the Southeast Missouri State University Press.

DRUE HEINZ LITERATURE PRIZE

University of Pittsburgh Press, 3400 Forbes Ave., Eureka Bldg., 5th Floor, Pittsburgh PA 15260. (412)383-2492. **Fax:** (412)383-2466. **Website:** www.upress.pitt. edu. Estab. 1981. Offered annually to writers who have published a book-length collection of fiction or a minimum of 3 short stories or novellas in commercial magazines or literary journals of national distribution. Does not return mss. Submit May 1- June 30 only. Prize: $15,000. Judged by anonymous nationally known writers such as Robert Penn Warren, Joyce Carol Oates, and Margaret Atwood.

LORIAN HEMINGWAY SHORT STORY COMPETITION

Hemingway Days Festival, P.O. Box 993, Key West FL 33041. **E-mail:** shortstorykw@gmail.com. **Website:** www.shortstorycompetition.com. **Contact:** Eva Eliot, editorial assistant. Estab. 1981. Offered annually for unpublished short stories up to 3,500 words. Guidelines available via mail, e-mail, or online. Award to encourage literary excellence and the efforts of writers whose voices have yet to be heard. Deadline: May 15. Prizes: 1st Place: $1,500, plus publication of his or her winning story in *Cutthroat: A Journal of the Arts*; 2nd-3rd Place: $500; honorable mentions will also be awarded. Judged by a panel of writers, editors, and literary scholars selected by author Lorian Hemingway. (Lorian Hemingway is the competition's final judge.)

TONY HILLERMAN PRIZE

Wordharvest, 1063 Willow Way, Santa Fe NM 87507. (505)471-1565. **E-mail:** wordharvest@wordhar vest.com. **Website:** www.wordharvest.com. **Contact:** Anne Hillerman and Jean Schaumberg, co-organizers. Estab. 2006. Awarded annually for the best first mystery set in the Southwest. Murder or another serious crime or crimes must be at the heart of the story, with the emphasis on the solution rather than the details of the crime. Honors the contributions made by Tony Hillerman to the art and craft of the mystery. Deadline: June 1. Prize: $10,000 advance and publication by St. Martin's Press. Nominees will be selected by judges chosen by the editorial staff of

St. Martin's Press, with the assistance of independent judges selected by organizers of the Tony Hillerman Writers Conference (Wordharvest), and the winner will be chosen by St. Martin's editors.

◐ THE HODDER FELLOWSHIP

Lewis Center for the Arts, 185 Nassau St., Princeton NJ 08544. (609)258-1500. **E-mail:** anikolop@princeton.edu. **Website:** www.princeton.edu/arts/lewis_center/society_of_fellows. **Contact:** Angelo Nikolopoulos, program assistant, Creative Writing. The Hodder Fellowship will be given to writers of exceptional promise to pursue independent projects at Princeton University during the current academic year. Typically the fellows are poets, playwrights, novelists, creative nonfiction writers, and translators who have published 1 highly acclaimed work and are undertaking a significant new project that might not be possible without the "studious leisure" afforded by the fellowship. Deadline: October 1. Prize: $75,000 stipend.

◐ TOM HOWARD/JOHN H. REID FICTION & ESSAY CONTEST

c/o Winning Writers, 351 Pleasant St., PMB 222, Northampton MA 01060-3961. (866)946-9748. **Fax:** (413)280-0539. **E-mail:** adam@winningwriters.com. **Website:** www.winningwriters.com. **Contact:** Adam Cohen, president. Estab. 1993. Now in its 22nd year. Open to all writers. Submit any type of short story, essay, or other work of prose. Both published and unpublished works are welcome. In the case of published work, the contestant must own the online publication rights. Submit online. Contest sponsored by Winning Writers. Deadline: April 30. Prizes: Two 1st Prizes of $1,000 will be awarded, plus 10 honorable mentions of $100 each. Judged by Arthur Powers.

THE JULIA WARD HOWE/BOSTON AUTHORS AWARD

The Boston Authors Club, 15 Claremont St., Newton MA 02458-1925. (617)244-0646. **E-mail:** bostonauthors@aol.com; leev@bc.edu. **Website:** www.bostonauthorsclub.org. **Contact:** Vera Lee. Estab. 1900. This annual award honors Julia Ward Howe and her literary friends who founded the Boston Authors Club in 1900. It also honors the membership over 110 years, consisting of novelists, biographers, historians, governors, senators, philosophers, poets, playwrights, and other luminaries. There are 2 categories: trade books

and books for young readers (beginning with chapter books through young adult books).

◐ HENRY HOYNS & POE/FAULKNER FELLOWSHIPS

Creative Writing Program, 219 Bryan Hall, P.O. Box 400121, University of Virginia, Charlottesville VA 22904-4121. (434)924-6675. **Fax:** (434)924-1478. **E-mail:** creativewriting@virginia.edu. **Website:** www.creativewriting.virginia.edu. **Contact:** Jeb Livingood, associate director. Two-year MFA program in poetry and fiction; all students receive fellowships and teaching stipends that total $16,000 in both years of study. Sample poems/prose required with application. Deadline: December 15.

○ L. RON HUBBARD'S WRITERS OF THE FUTURE CONTEST

P.O. Box 1630, Los Angeles CA 90078. (323)466-3310. **Fax:** (323)466-6474. **E-mail:** contests@authorservicesinc.com. **Website:** www.writersofthefuture.com. **Contact:** Joni Labaqui, contest director. Estab. 1983. Foremost competition for new and amateur writers of unpublished science fiction or fantasy short stories or novelettes. Offered to find, reward, and publicize new speculative fiction writers so they may more easily attain professional writing careers. Open to writers who have not professionally published a novel or short novel, more than 1 novelette, or more than 3 short stories. Entries must be unpublished. Limit 1 entry per quarter. Open to any writer. Results announced quarterly in e-newsletter. Winners notified by phone. Contest has 4 quarters. There shall be 3 cash prizes in each quarter. In addition, at the end of the year, the four 1st-Place, quarterly winners will have their entries rejudged, and a grand prize winner shall be determined. Deadline: December 31, March 31, June 30, September 30. Prizes (awards quarterly): 1st Place: $1,000; 2nd Place: $750; and 3rd Place: $500. Annual grand prize: $5,000. Judged by Dave Wolverton (initial judge), then by a panel of 4 professional authors.

CAROL OTIS HURST CHILDREN'S BOOK PRIZE

Westfield Athenaeum, 6 Elm St., Westfield MA 01085. (413)568-7833. **Website:** www.westath.org. Estab. 2007. The Carol Otis Hurst Children's Book Prize honors outstanding works of fiction and nonfiction written for children and young adults through the age of 18. For a work to be considered, the writer must either be a native or a current resident of New England.

While the prize is presented annually to an author whose work best exemplifies the highest standards of writing for this age group regardless of genre or topic or geographical setting, the prize committee is especially interested in those books that depict life in the region. Further, entries will be judged on how well they succeed in portraying 1 or more of the following elements: childhood, adolescence, family life, schooling, social and political developments, fine and performing artistic expression, domestic arts, environmental issues, transportation and communication, changing technology, military experience at home and abroad, business and manufacturing, workers and the labor movement, agriculture and its transformation, racial and ethnic diversity, religious life and institutions, immigration and adjustment, sports at all levels, and the evolution of popular entertainment. Prize: $500.

INDEPENDENT PUBLISHER BOOK AWARDS

Jenkins Group/Independent Publisher Online, 1129 Woodmere Ave., Ste. B, Traverse City MI 49686. (231)933-4954, ext. 1011. **Fax:** (231)933-0448. **E-mail:** jimb@bookpublishing.com. **Website:** www.independentpublisher.com. **Contact:** Jim Barnes. Honors the year's best independently published titles from around the world. The IPPY Awards reward those who exhibit the courage, innovation, and creativity to bring about change in the world of publishing. Independent spirit and expertise comes from publishers of all areas and budgets, and we judge books with that in mind. Entries will be accepted in over 70 categories, visit website to see details. Open to any published writer. Deadline: March 16. Price of submission rises after January 25. Prize: Gold, silver, and bronze medals for each category; foil seals available to all. Judged by a panel of experts representing the fields of design, writing, bookselling, library, and reviewing.

INDIANA REVIEW K (SHORT-SHORT/ PROSE-POEM) PRIZE

Indiana Review, Ballantine Hall 465, 1020 E. Kirkwood Ave., Indiana University, Bloomington IN 47405-7103. (812)855-3439. **Fax:** (812)855-9535. **E-mail:** inreview@indiana.edu. **Website:** indianareview.org. **Contact:** Katie Moulton, editor. Offered annually for unpublished work. Maximum story/poem length is 500 words. Guidelines available in March for SASE, by phone, e-mail, on website, or in publi-

cation. Deadline: May 31. Submission period begins August 1. Prize: $1,000, plus publication, contributor's copies, and a year's subscription to *Indiana Review*.

INDIANA REVIEW FICTION CONTEST

Ballantine Hall 465, Indiana University, 1020 E. Kirkwood Ave., Bloomington IN 47405-7103. (812)855-3439. **Fax:** (812)855-4253. **E-mail:** inreview@indiana.edu. **Website:** indianareview.org. **Contact:** Katie Moulton, editor. Contest for fiction in any style and on any subject. Open to any writer. Deadline: October 31. Submission period begins September 1. Prize: $1,000, publication in the *Indiana Review* and contributor's copies. Judged by guest judges.

INDIVIDUAL EXCELLENCE AWARDS

Ohio Arts Council, 727 E. Main St., Columbus OH 43205-1796. (614)466-2613. **E-mail:** ken.emerick@oac.state.oh.us; olgahelpdesk@oac.state.oh.us. **Website:** www.oac.state.oh.us. **Contact:** Ken Emerick. The Individual Excellence Awards program recognizes outstanding accomplishments by artists in a variety of disciplines. The awards give the artists who receive them the time and resources to experiment, explore, and reflect as they develop their skills and advance their art form. They also provide affirmation and acknowledgment of the excellent work of Ohio artists. Deadline: September 1. Prize: $5,000 or $10,000, determined by review panel. Judged by 3-person panel of out-of-state panelists, anonymous review.

INTERNATIONAL 3-DAY NOVEL CONTEST

Box 2106 Station Terminal, Vancouver BC V6B 3T5 Canada. **E-mail:** info@3daynovel.com. **Website:** www.3daynovel.com. **Contact:** Melissa Edwards, managing editor. Estab. 1977. "Can you produce a masterwork of fiction in 3 short days? The 3-Day Novel Contest is your chance to find out. For more than 30 years, hundreds of writers step up to the challenge each Labor Day weekend, fuelled by nothing but adrenaline and the desire for spontaneous literary nirvana. It's a thrill, a grind, a 72-hour kick in the pants, and an awesome creative experience. How many crazed plotlines, coffee-stained pages, pangs of doubt and moments of genius will next year's contest bring forth? And what will you think up under pressure?" Entrants write in whatever setting they wish, in whatever genre they wish, anywhere in the world. Entrants may start writing as of midnight on Friday night and must stop by midnight on Monday night.

Then they print entry and mail it in to the contest for judging. Deadline: Friday before Labor Day weekend. Prize: 1st Place receives publication; 2nd Place receives $500; 3rd Place receives $100.

INTERNATIONAL READING ASSOCIATION CHILDREN'S AND YOUNG ADULTS BOOK AWARDS

P.O. Box 8139, 800 Barksdale Rd., Newark DE 19714-8139. (302)731-1600, ext. 221. **E-mail:** exec@reading.org. **E-mail:** committees@reading.org. **Website:** reading.org. **Contact:** Kathy Baughman. Children's and Young Adults Book Awards is intended for newly published authors who show unusual promise in the children's and young adults' book field. Awards are given for fiction and nonfiction in each of 3 categories: primary, intermediate, and young adult. Books from all countries and published in English for the first time during the previous calendar year will be considered. Deadline: November 1. Prize: $1,000.

◐ THE IOWA REVIEW AWARD IN POETRY, FICTION, AND NONFICTION

308 EPB, University of Iowa, Iowa City IA 52242. **E-mail:** iowa-review@uiowa.edu. **Website:** www.iowareview.org. *The Iowa Review* Award in Poetry, Fiction, and Nonfiction presents $1,500 to each winner in each genre, $750 to runners-up. Winners and runners-up published in *The Iowa Review*. Submit January 1-31 (postmark).

THE IOWA SHORT FICTION AWARD

Iowa Writers' Workshop, 507 N. Clinton St., 102 Dey House, Iowa City IA 52242-1000. **Website:** www.uiowapress.org. **Contact:** Jim McCoy, director. Annual award to give exposure to promising writers who have not yet published a book of prose. Open to any writer. Current University of Iowa students are not eligible. No application forms are necessary. Announcement of winners made early in year following competition. Winners notified by phone. Do not send original ms. Include SASE for return of ms. Deadline: September 30. Submission period: August 1-September 30. Packages must be postmarked by September 30. Prize: Publication by University of Iowa Press Judged by senior Iowa Writers' Workshop members who screen mss; a published fiction author of note makes final selections.

❸ TILIA KLEBENOV JACOBS RELIGIOUS ESSAY PRIZE CATEGORY

Soul Making Keats Literary Competition, The Webhallow House, 1544 Sweetwood Dr., Broadmoor Village CA 94015-2029. **E-mail:** SoulKeats@mail.com. **Website:** www.soulmakingcontest.us. **Contact:** Eileen Malone. Estab. 2012. Call for thoughtful writings of up to 3,000 words. "No preaching, no proselytizing." Open annually to any writer. Deadline: November 30. Prize: 1st Place: $100; 2nd Place $50; 3rd Place $25.

JERRY JAZZ MUSICIAN NEW SHORT FICTION AWARD

Jerry Jazz Musician, 2207 NE Broadway, Portland OR 97232. **E-mail:** jm@jerryjazz.com. **Website:** www.jerryjazz.com. Three times a year, *Jerry Jazz Musician* awards a writer who submits the best original, previously unpublished work of approximately 3,000-5,000 words. The winner will be announced via a mailing of the *Jerry Jazz* newsletter. Publishers, artists, musicians, and interested readers are among those who subscribe to the newsletter. Additionally the work will be published on the home page of *Jerry Jazz Musician* and featured there for at least 4 weeks. The *Jerry Jazz Musician* reader tends to have interests in music, history, literature, art, film, and theater—particularly that of the counterculture of mid-20th century America. Guidelines available online. Deadline: September, January, and May. See website for specific dates. Prize: $100. Judged by the editors of *Jerry Jazz Musician*.

JESSE H. JONES AWARD FOR BEST WORK OF FICTION

P.O. Box 609, Round Rock TX 78680. **E-mail:** tilsecretary@yahoo.com. **Website:** texasinstituteofletters.org. Offered annually by Texas Institute of Letters for work published January 1-December 31 of year before award is given to recognize the writer of the best book of fiction entered in the competition. Writers must have been born in Texas, have lived in the state for at least 2 consecutive years at some time, or the subject matter of the work should be associated with Texas. Deadline: January 10. Prize: $6,000.

JAMES JONES FIRST NOVEL FELLOWSHIP

Wilkes University, Creative Writing Department, Wilkes University, 84 West South Street, Wilkes-Barre PA 18766. (570)408-4547. **Fax:** (570)408-3333. **E-mail:** Jamesjonesfirstnovel@wilkes.edu. **Website:** www.wilkes.edu/pages/1159.asp. Offered annually for unpublished novels, novellas, and closely linked short stories (all works in progress). This competition is open to all American writers who have not previously published novels. The award is intended to honor the spirit of unblinking honesty, determination, and insight into modern culture exemplified by the late James Jones. Deadline: March 1. Submission period begins October 1. Prize: $10,000; 2 runners-up get $1,000 honorarium.

⊕ JUVENILE ADVENTURE FICTION CONTEST

P.O. Box 1001, Reynoldsburg OH 43068. **E-mail:** dianaperry@DianaPerryBooks.com. **Website:** dianaperrybooks.com. **Contact:** Diana Perry. Estab. 2014. "Tell an adventurous tale with an 8-year-old to 12-year-old protagonist; refer to Robert Louis Stevenson or Mark Twain stories. Nothing too dangerous, but very exciting, bigger than life. Must be suitable for juvenile readers." Rules on website. Length: up to 20 pages or 5,000 words. Purpose: "To give exposure to beginning writers trying to break in to the business and get noticed." Deadline: May 31. 1st Place: $300, trophy, mention on website, T-shirt, press releases in your local newspapers; 2nd Place: $200, trophy, mention on website, T-shirt, press releases in your local newspapers; 3rd Place: $100, trophy, mention on website, T-shirt, press releases in your local newspapers; 4th/5th places: $50/$25, plaque, mention on website, T-shirt, press releases in your local newspapers. "We also list names of next 25 honorable mentions on website. Contest guidelines and entry form on website. Check website for guest judges. Mail entry form, your story, and a $15 money order only to Juvenile Adventure Fiction Contest at above address postmarked no later than May 31. Winners announced both on website and via snail mail July 1. Prizes mailed within 10 days of announcement. Judged by Diana Perry and guest judge.

○ E.M. KOEPPEL SHORT FICTION AWARD

P.O. Box 140310, Gainesville FL 32614-0310. **Website:** www.writecorner.com. **Contact:** Mary Sue Koeppel, editor. Annual awards for unpublished fiction in any style and any theme. Send 2 title pages: 1 with title only and 1 with title, name, address, phone, e-mail, short bio. Place no other identification of the author on the ms that will be used in the judging. Guidelines available for SASE or on website. Accepts inquiries by e-mail and phone. Winning stories published on website. Winners notified by mail and phone in July (or earlier). For results, send SASE or see website. Deadline: April 30. Submission period begins October 1.

Prize: 1st Place: $1,100. Editors' Choice: $100 each. Judged by award-winning fiction writers.

LAWRENCE FOUNDATION PRIZE

Michigan Quarterly Review, 0576 Rackham Bldg., 915 E. Washington Street, Ann Arbor MI 48109-1070. (734)764-9265. **E-mail:** mqr@umich.edu. **Website:** michiganquarterlyreview.com. **Contact:** Vicki Lawrence, Managing Editor. Estab. 1978. This annual prize is awarded by the *Michigan Quarterly Review* editorial board to the author of the best short story published in *MQR* that year. The prize is sponsored by University of Michigan alumnus and fiction writer Leonard S. Bernstein, a trustee of the Lawrence Foundation of New York. Approximately 20 short stories are published in *MQR* each year. Prize: $1,000. Judged by editorial board.

LEAGUE OF UTAH WRITERS CONTEST

The League of Utah Writers, (435)755-7609. **E-mail:** luwcontest@gmail.com. **Website:** www.luwriters.org. **Contact:** Tim Keller, Contest Chair. Open to any writer, the LUW Contest provides authors an opportunity to get their work read and critiqued. Multiple categories are offered; see web page for details. Entries must be the original and unpublished work of the author. Winners are announced at the Annual Writers Round-Up in September. Those not present will be notified by e-mail. Submission Period: March 15-June 15. Prize: Cash prizes are awarded. Judged by professional authors and editors from outside the League.

⊕ LES FIGUES PRESS NOS BOOK CONTEST

P.O. Box 7736, Los Angeles CA 90007. **E-mail:** info@lesfigues.com. **Website:** www.lesfigues.com. **Contact:** Teresa Carmody and Vanessa Place, co-directors. Les Figues Press creates aesthetic conversations between writers/artists and readers, especially those interested in innovative/experimental/avant-garde work. The Press intends in the most premeditated fashion to champion the trinity of Beauty, Belief, and Bawdry. Annual NOS (not otherwise specific) book prize given for best ms of poetry, prose, or writing in between. Electronic submissions only. See website for contest guidelines. Deadline: September 30. Prize: $1,000, plus publication by Les Figues Press. Each entry receives LFP book.

LET'S WRITE LITERARY CONTEST

The Gulf Coast Writers Association, P.O. Box 10294, Gulfport MS 39505. **E-mail:** writerpllevin@gmail

.com. **Website:** www.gcwriters.org. **Contact:** Philip Levin. The Gulf Coast Writers Association sponsors this nationally recognized contest, which accepts unpublished poems and short stories from authors all around the U.S. This is an annual event which has been held for over 20 years. Deadline: April 15. Prize: 1st Prize: $100; 2nd Prize: $60; 3rd Prize: $25.

⊖ FENIA AND YAAKOV LEVIANT MEMORIAL PRIZE IN YIDDISH STUDIES

Modern Language Association of America, 26 Broadway, 3rd Floor, New York NY 10004-1789. (646)576-5141. **Fax:** (646)458-0030. **E-mail:** awards@mla.org. **Website:** www.mla.org. **Contact:** Coordinator of Book Prizes. Offered in even-numbered years for an outstanding English translation of a Yiddish literary work. Cultural studies, critical biographies, or edited works in the field of Yiddish folklore or linguistic studies are eligible to compete. Deadline: May 1. Prize: A cash prize and a certificate to be presented at the Modern Language Association's annual convention in January.

LITERAL LATTÉ FICTION AWARD

Literal Latté, 200 E. 10th St., Suite 240, New York NY 10003. (212)260-5532. **E-mail:** litlatte@aol.com. **Website:** www.literal-latte.com. **Contact:** Edward Estlin, contributing editor. Award to provide talented writers with 3 essential tools for continued success: money, publication, and recognition. Offered annually for unpublished fiction (maximum 10,000 words). Guidelines online. Open to any writer. Deadline: January 15. Prize: 1st Place: $1,000 and publication in *Literal Latté*; 2nd Place: $300; 3rd Place: $200; also up to 7 honorable mentions.

LITERAL LATTE SHORT SHORTS CONTEST

Literal Latte, 200 E. 10th St., Suite 240, New York NY 10003. (212)260-5532. **E-mail:** litlatte@aol.com. **Website:** www.literal-latte.com. **Contact:** Jenine Gordon Bockman, editor. Annual contest. Send unpublished shorts. 2,000 words max. All styles welcome. Name, address, phone number, e-mail address (optional) on cover page only. Include SASE or e-mail address for reply. All entries considered for publication. Deadline: June 30. Prize: $500. Judged by the editors.

THE MARY MACKEY SHORT STORY PRIZE CATEGORY

Soul-Making Keats Literary Competition, The Webhallow House, 1544 Sweetwood Dr., Broadmoor Vil-

lage CA 94015. **E-mail:** SoulKeats@mail.com. **Website:** www.soulmakingcontest.us. **Contact:** Eileen Malone. Open annually to any writer. Deadline: November 30. Prize: Cash prizes.

⊙⊙ THE MALAHAT REVIEW NOVELLA PRIZE

The Malahat Review, University of Victoria, P.O. Box 1700 STN CSC, Victoria BC V8W 2Y2 Canada. (250)721-8524. **E-mail:** malahat@uvic.ca. **E-mail:** novella@uvic.ca. **Website:** malahatreview.ca. **Contact:** John Barton, editor. Held in alternate years with the Long Poem Prize. Offered to promote unpublished novellas. Obtains first world rights. After publication, rights revert to the author. Open to any writer. Deadline: February 1 (even years). Prize: $1,500 CAD and 1 year's subscription. Winner published in summer issue of *The Malahat Review* and announced on website, Facebook page, and in quarterly e-newsletter, *Malahat Lite*.

MARY MCCARTHY PRIZE IN SHORT FICTION

Sarabande Books, P.O. Box 4456, Louisville KY 40204. (502)458-4028. **Fax:** (502)458-4065. **E-mail:** info@sarabandebooks.org. **Website:** www.sarabandebooks.org. **Contact:** Kirby Gann, managing editor. Offered annually to publish an outstanding collection of stories, novellas, or a short novel (less than 250 pages). All finalists considered for publication. Submissions accepted January 1-February 14. Prize: $2,000 and publication (standard royalty contract).

⊘ THE MCGINNIS-RITCHIE MEMORIAL AWARD

Southwest Review, P.O. Box 750374, Dallas TX 75275-0374. (214)768-1037. **Fax:** (214)768-1408. **E-mail:** swr@mail.smu.edu. **Website:** www.smu.edu/southwestreview. **Contact:** Jennifer Cranfill, senior editor, and Willard Spiegelman, editor-in-chief. The McGinnis-Ritchie Memorial Award is given annually to the best works of fiction and nonfiction that appeared in the magazine in the previous year. Mss are submitted for publication, not for the prizes themselves. Guidelines for SASE or online. Prize: $500. Judged by Jennifer Cranfill and Willard Spiegelman.

MEMPHIS MAGAZINE FICTION CONTEST

Memphis Magazine, co-sponsored by booksellers of Laurelwood and Burke's Book Store, 460 Tennessee St., Memphis TN 38103. (901)521-9000. **Fax:** (901)521-

0129. **E-mail:** sadler@memphismagazine.com. **Website:** www.memphismagazine.com. **Contact:** Marilyn Sadler. Deadline: February 15. Prize: $1,000 grand prize, along with being published in the annual Cultural Issue; 2 honorable-mention awards of $500 each will be given if the quality of entries warrants.

DAVID NATHAN MEYERSON PRIZE FOR FICTION

Southwest Review, P.O. Box 750374, Dallas TX 75275-0374. (214) 768-1037. **Fax:** (214) 768-1408. **E-mail:** swr@smu.edu. **Website:** www.smu.edu/southwest review. **Contact:** Jennifer Cranfill, senior editor. Annual award given to a writer who has not published a first book of fiction; i.e., a novel or collection of stories. All contest entrants will receive a copy of the issue in which the winning piece appears. Deadline: May 1 (postmarked). Prize: $1,000 and publication in the *Southwest Review*.

THE MILTON CENTER POSTGRADUATE FELLOWSHIP

3307 Third Ave. W., Seattle WA 98119. **Website:** www.imagejournal.org/milton. **Contact:** Tyler McCabe, director of programs. Award to bring emerging writers of Christian commitment to the Center, where their primary goal is to complete their first book-length ms in fiction, poetry, or creative nonfiction. Guidelines on website. Open to any writer. Deadline: March 15. Prize: $16,000 stipend.

Ⓓ MISSISSIPPI REVIEW PRIZE

Mississippi Review, 118 College Dr., #5144, Hattiesburg MS 39406-0001. (601)266-4321. **Fax:** (601)266-5757. **E-mail:** msreview@usm.edu; rief@mississippireview.com. **Website:** www.mississippireview.com. Annual contest starting April 2. Winners and finalists will make up next winter's print issue of the national literary magazine *Mississippi Review*. Each entrant will receive a copy of the prize issue. Deadline: October 1. Prize: $1,000 in fiction and poetry.

NATIONAL OUTDOOR BOOK AWARDS

921 S. 8th Ave., Stop 8128, Pocatello ID 83209. (208)282-3912. **E-mail:** wattron@isu.edu. **Website:** www.noba-web.org. **Contact:** Ron Watters. Nine categories: History/biography, outdoor literature, instructional texts, outdoor adventure guides, nature guides, children's books, design/artistic merit, natural history literature, and nature and the environment. Additionally, a special award, the Outdoor Classic Award, is given annually to books which, over a period of time, have proven to be exceptionally valuable works in the outdoor field. Application forms and eligibilty requirements are available online. Applications for the Awards program become available in early June. Deadline: September 1. Prize: Winning books are promoted nationally and are entitled to display the National Outdoor Book Award (NOBA) medallion.

Ⓞ NATIONAL WRITERS ASSOCIATION NOVEL WRITING CONTEST

The National Writers Association, 10940 S. Parker Rd. #508, Parker CO 80134. (303)841-0246. **E-mail:** natlwritersassn@hotmail.com. **Website:** www.nationalwriters.com. **Contact:** Sandy Whelchel, director. Open to any genre or category. Contest begins December 1. Open to any writer. Annual contest to help develop creative skills, to recognize and reward outstanding ability, and to increase the opportunity for the marketing and subsequent publication of novel mss. Deadline: April 1. Prize: 1st Place: $500; 2nd Place: $250; 3rd Place: $150. Judged by editors and agents.

NATIONAL WRITERS ASSOCIATION SHORT STORY CONTEST

10940 S. Parker Rd., #508, Parker CO 80134. (303)841-0246. **E-mail:** natlwritersassn@hotmail.com. **Website:** www.nationalwriters.com. Estab. 1971. Opens April 1. The purpose of the National Writers Association Short Story Contest is to encourage the development of creative skills, and recognize and reward outstanding ability in the area of short story writing. Prize: 1st - 5th Place awards will be presented at the NWAF Conference. 1st Prize: $250; 2nd Prize: $100; 3rd Prize: $50; 4th through 10th Places will receive a book. 1st- through 3rd-Place winners may be asked to grant one-time rights for publication in *Authorship* magazine. Honorable Mentions receive a certificate. Judging will be based on originality, marketability, research, and reader interest. Copies of the judges evaluation sheets will be sent to entrants furnishing an SASE with their entry.

THE NELLIGAN PRIZE FOR SHORT FICTION

Colorado Review/Center for Literary Publishing, 9105 Campus Delivery, Department of English, Colorado State University, Ft. Collins CO 80523-9105. (970)491-5449. **E-mail:** creview@colostate.edu. **Website:** nelliganprize.colostate.edu. **Contact:** Stephanie

G'Schwind, editor. Annual competition/award for short stories. Receives approximately 900 stories. All entries are read blind by Colorado Review's editorial staff. 10-15 entries are selected to be sent on to a final judge. "The Nelligan Prize for Short Fiction was established in memory of Liza Nelligan, a writer, editor, and friend of many in Colorado State University's English department, where she received her master's degree in literature in 1992. By giving an award to the author of an outstanding short story each year, we hope to honor Liza Nelligan's life, her passion for writing, and her love of fiction." Deadline: March 12. Prize: $2,000 and publication of story in *Colorado Review*.

THE NEUTRINO SHORT-SHORT CONTEST

Passages North, Department of English, Northern Michigan University, 1401 Presque Isle Ave., Marquette MI 49855. (906)227-1203. **Fax:** (906)227-1096. **E-mail:** passages@nmu.edu. **Website:** www.passages north.com. **Contact:** Jennifer Howard. Offered every 2 years to publish new voices in literary fiction, nonfiction, hybrid-essays and prose poems (maximum 1,000 words). Guidelines available for SASE or online. Deadline: March 15. Submission period begins January 15. Prize: $1,000 and publication for the winner; 2 honorable mentions also published; all entrants receive a copy of *Passages North*.

○ NEW LETTERS LITERARY AWARDS

New Letters, UMKC, University House, Room 105, 5101 Rockhill Rd., Kansas City MO 64110-2499. (816)235-1168. **Fax:** (816)235-2611. **Website:** www .newletters.org. Award has 3 categories (fiction, poetry, and creative nonfiction) with 1 winner in each. Offered annually for previously unpublished work. For guidelines, send an SASE to *New Letters*, or visit www.newletters.org. Deadline: May 18. 1st Place: $1,500, plus publication; 1st runners-up: a copy of a recent book of poetry or fiction courtesy of our affiliate BkMk Press. Judged by regional writers of prominence and experience. Final judging by someone of national repute. Previous judges include Maxine Kumin, Albert Goldbarth, Charles Simic, and Janet Burroway.

NORTH CAROLINA ARTS COUNCIL REGIONAL ARTIST PROJECT GRANTS

North Carolina Arts Council, Department of Cultural Resources, MSC #4632, Raleigh NC 27699-4634. (919)807-6500. **Fax:** (919)807-6532. **E-mail:** david.po torti@ncdcr.gov. **Website:** www.ncarts.org. **Contact:** David Potorti, literature director. See website for contact information for the local arts councils that distribute these grants. Deadline: Late summer/early fall. Prize: $500-3,000 awarded to writers to pursue projects that further their artistic development.

FRANK O'CONNOR AWARD FOR SHORT FICTION

descant, Texas Christian University's literary journal, TCU Box 298300, Fort Worth TX 76129. (817)257-5907. **Fax:** (817)257-6239. **E-mail:** descant@tcu.edu. **Website:** www.descant.tcu.edu. **Contact:** Dan Williams and Alex Lemon, editors. Offered annually for unpublished short stories. Publication retains copyright but will transfer it to the author upon request. Submission period: September-March. Prize: $500.

THE FLANNERY O'CONNOR AWARD FOR SHORT FICTION

The University of Georgia Press, Main Library, 3rd Floor, 320 S. Jackson St., Athens GA 30602. (706)369-6130, **Fax:** (706)369-6131. **Website:** www.ugapress.org. Estab. 1981. This competition welcomes short story or novella collections. Stories may have been published singly but should not have appeared in a book-length collection of the author's own work. Length: 40,000-75,000 words. Submission period: April 1-May 31. Prize: 2 winners receive $1,000 and book contracts from the University of Georgia Press.

OHIOANA BOOK AWARDS

Ohioana Library Association, 274 E. First Ave., Suite 300, Columbus OH 43201-3673. (614)466-3831. **Fax:** (614)728-6974. **E-mail:** ohioana@ohioana.org. **Website:** www.ohioana.org. **Contact:** David Weaver, executive director. Offered annually to bring national attention to Ohio authors and their books, published in the last year. (Books can be considered only once.) Categories: Fiction, nonfiction, juvenile, poetry, and books about Ohio or an Ohioan. Deadline: December 31. Prize: Certificate and glass sculpture. Judged by a jury selected by librarians, book reviewers, writers and other knowledgeable people.

OHIOANA WALTER RUMSEY MARVIN GRANT

Ohioana Library Association, 274 E. First Ave., Suite 300, Columbus OH 43201. (614)466-3831. **Fax:** (614)728-6974. **E-mail:** ohioana@ohioana.org. **Website:** www.ohioana.org. **Contact:** David Weaver, executive director. Award to encourage young, unpublished writers 30 years of age or younger. Competition for short stories or novels in progress. Deadline: January 31. Prize: $1,000.

◐ ⊖ ON THE PREMISES CONTEST

On the Premises, LLC, 4323 Gingham Court, Alexandria VA 22310. (202) 262-2168. **E-mail:** questions@onthepremises.com. **Website:** www.onthepremises.com. **Contact:** Tarl Roger Kudrick or Bethany Granger, copublishers. *On the Premises* aims to promote newer and/or relatively unknown writers who can write creative, compelling stories told in effective, uncluttered and evocative prose. Each contest challenges writers to produce a great story based on a broad premise that the editors supply as part of the contest. Deadline: Contests held every 4 months, check website for exact dates. Prize: 1st Prize: $180; 2nd Prize: $140; 3rd Prize: $100; honorable mentions receive $40. All prize winners are published in *On the Premises* magazine in HTML and PDF format. Judged by a panel of judges with professional editing and writing experience.

☺ OPEN SEASON AWARDS

The Malahat Review, University of Victoria, P.O. Box 1700, Stn CSC, Victoria BC V8V 2Y2 Canada. **Fax:** (250)472-5051. **E-mail:** malahat@uvic.ca. **Website:** www.malahatreview.ca. **Contact:** John Barton, editor. The Open Season Awards accepts entries of poetry, fiction, and creative nonfiction. Winners published in spring issue of *Malahat Review* announced in winter on website, facebook page, and in quarterly e-newsletter, *Malahat lite*. Deadline: November 1. Prize: $1,000 CAD and publication in *The Malahat Review* in each category.

○ OREGON LITERARY FELLOWSHIPS

925 S.W. Washington, Portland OR 97205. (503)227-2583. **E-mail:** susan@literary-arts.org. **Website:** www.literary-arts.org. **Contact:** Susan Denning, director of programs and events. Annual fellowships for writers of fiction, poetry, literary nonfiction, young readers, and drama. Deadline: Last Friday in June. Prize: $2,500 minimum award, for approximately 10 writers and 2 publishers. Judged by out-of-state writers.

✚ ⊖ KENNETH PATCHEN AWARD FOR THE INNOVATIVE NOVEL

Eckhard Gerdes Publishing, 12 Simpson Street, Apt. D, Geneva IL 60134. **E-mail:** egerdes@experimental fiction.com. **Website:** www.experimentalfiction.com. **Contact:** Eckhard Gerdes. This award will honor the most innovative novel submitted during the previous calendar year. Kenneth Patchen is celebrated for being among the greatest innovators of American fiction, incorporating strategies of concretism, asemic writing, digression, and verbal juxtaposition into his writing long before such strategies were popularized during the height of American postmodernist experimentation in the 1970s. Deadline: All submissions must be postmarked between January 1 and July 31. Prize: $1,000, 20 complimentary copies. Judged by novelist James Chapman.

THE PATERSON FICTION PRIZE

The Poetry Center at Passaic Community College, 1 College Blvd., Paterson NJ 07505. (973)684-6555. **Fax:** (973)523-6085. **E-mail:** mgillan@pccc.edu. **Website:** www.pccc.edu/poetry. **Contact:** Maria Mazziotti Gillan, executive director. Offered annually for a novel or collection of short fiction published the previous calendar year. For more information, visit the website or send SASE. Deadline: April 1. Prize: $1,000.

○ PEARL SHORT STORY PRIZE

3030 E. Second St., Long Beach CA 90803. (562)434-4523. **E-mail:** Pearlmag@aol.com. **Website:** www.pearlmag.com. **Contact:** Marilyn Johnson, fiction editor. Award to provide a larger forum and help widen publishing opportunities for fiction writers in the small press and to help support the continuing publication of *Pearl*. Submission period: April 1-May 31. Prize: $250, publication in *Pearl* and 10 copies of the journal. Judged by the editors of *Pearl*: Marilyn Johnson and Joan Jobe Smith.

○ JUDITH SIEGEL PEARSON AWARD

Judith Siegel Pearson Award, c/o Department of English, Wayne State University, Attn: Royanne Smith, 5057 Woodward Ave, Suite 9408, Detroit MI 48202. (313)577-2450. **Fax:** (313)577-8618. **E-mail:** ad2073@wayne.edu. Offers an annual award for the best creative or scholarly work on a subject concerning women. The type of work accepted rotates each year: drama in 2012; poetry in 2013; nonfiction in 2014; fiction in 2015. Open to all interested writers and scholars. Only submit the appropriate genre in each year. Deadline: February 21.

PNWA LITERARY CONTEST

Pacifc Northwest Writers Association, PMB 2717, 1420 NW Gilman Blvd., Suite 2, Issaquah WA 98027. (452)673-2665. **E-mail:** pnwa@pnwa.org. **Website:**

www.pnwa.org. Annual literary contest with 12 different categories. See website for details and specific guidelines. Each entry receives 2 critiques. Winners announced at the PNWA Summer Conference, held annually in mid-July. Deadline: February 21. Prize: 1st Place: $700; 2nd Place: $300. Judged by an agent or editor attending the conference.

⊙ POCKETS FICTION-WRITING CONTEST

P.O. Box 340004, Nashville TN 37203-0004. (615)340-7333. **Fax:** (615)340-7267. **E-mail:** pockets@upperroom.org. **Website:** www.pockets.upperroom.org. **Contact:** Lynn W. Gilliam, senior editor. Designed for 6- to 12-year-olds, *Pockets* magazine offers wholesome devotional readings that teach about God's love and presence in life. The content includes fiction, scripture stories, puzzles and games, poems, recipes, colorful pictures, activities, and scripture readings. Freelance submissions of stories, poems, recipes, puzzles and games, and activities are welcome. The primary purpose of *Pockets* is to help children grow in their relationship with God and to claim the good news of the gospel of Jesus Christ by applying it to their daily lives. *Pockets* espouses respect for all human beings and for God's creation. It regards a child's faith journey as an integral part of all of life and sees prayer as undergirding that journey. Deadline: Entries are received beginning March 1 and must be postmarked no later than August 15. Prize: $500 and publication in magazine.

◑ EDGAR ALLAN POE AWARD

1140 Broadway, Suite 1507, New York NY 10001. (212)888-8171. **Fax:** (212)888-8107. **E-mail:** mwa@mysterywriters.org. **Website:** www.mysterywriters.org. Estab. 1945. Mystery Writers of America is the leading association for professional crime writers in the U.S. Members of MWA include most major writers of crime fiction and nonfiction, as well as screenwriters, dramatists, editors, publishers, and other professionals in the field. Purpose of the award: to honor authors of distinguished works in the mystery field. Previously published submissions only. Submissions made by the author, author's agent; "normally by the publisher." Work must be published/produced the year of the contest. Deadline: November 30. Prize: Awards ceramic bust of "Edgar" for winner; scrolls for all nominees. Judged by professional members of Mystery Writers of America (writers).

THE KATHERINE ANNE PORTER PRIZE FOR FICTION

Nimrod International Journal, The University of Tulsa, 800 S. Tucker Dr., Tulsa OK 74104. (918)631-3080. **Fax:** (918)631-3033. **E-mail:** nimrod@utulsa.edu. **Website:** www.utulsa.edu/nimrod. **Contact:** Eilis O'Neal. Deadline: April 30. Prizes: 1st Place: $2,000 and publication; 2nd Place: $1,000 and publication. Judged by the *Nimrod* editors, who select the finalists and a recognized author, who selects the winners.

⊕ PRESS 53 AWARD FOR SHORT FICTION

Press 53, 411 W. Fourth St., Suite 101A, Winston-Salem NC 27101. **E-mail:** kevin@press53.com. **Website:** www.press53.com. **Contact:** Kevin Morgan Watson, publisher. Awarded to an outstanding, unpublished collection of short stories. Deadline: December 31. Submission period begins September 1. Finalists announced March 1. Winner announced on May 3. Publication in October. Prize: Publication of winning short story collection; $1,000 cash advance; travel expenses and lodging for a special reading and book signing in Winston-Salem, NC; attendance as special guest to the Press 53/*Prime Number Magazine* Gathering of Writers; and 10 copies of the book. Judged by publisher Kevin Morgan and fiction editor Christine Norris.

⊕ PRIME NUMBER MAGAZINE AWARDS

Press 53, 411 W. Fourth St., Suite 101A, Winston-Salem NC 27101. **E-mail:** kevin@press53.com. **Website:** www.press53.com. **Contact:** Kevin Morgan Watson, publisher. Awards over $2,000 and publication for winning entries in poetry, flash fiction, short story, flash nonfiction, and creative nonfiction. Deadline: March 30. Submission period begins January 1. Finalists announced June 1. Winner announced August 1. Prize: 1st Prize in each category: $250 cash; 2nd Prize: $100; Honorable Mention: $50. All winners receive publication in *Prime Number Magazine* online and in the *Prime Number Magazine, Editors' Selections* print annual. Judged by industry professionals to be named when the contest begins.

◐ PRISM INTERNATIONAL ANNUAL SHORT FICTION, POETRY, AND CREATIVE NONFICTION CONTESTS

Prism International, Creative Writing Program, University of British Columbia, Buch. E462, 1866 Main Mall, Vancouver BC V6T 1Z1 Canada. **E-mail:**

prismwritingcontest@gmail.com. **Website:** www
.prismmagazine.ca/contests/. Offered annually for unpublished work to award the best in contemporary
fiction, poetry, drama, translation, and nonfiction.
Works of translation are eligible. Guidelines are available on website. Acquires first North American serial
rights upon publication and limited web rights for
pieces selected for website. Open to any writer except
students and faculty in the creative writing department at University of British Columbia, or people who
have taken a creative writing course at University of
British Columbia within 2 years of the contest deadline. Entry includes subscription. Deadline: January
23 (poetry, short fiction); November 28 (nonfiction)
Prize: 1st Place: $1,000-2,000; runners-up (3): $200-
300 each (depends on contest); winners are published.

PRISM INTERNATIONAL ANNUAL SHORT FICTION CONTEST

Creative Writing Program, UBC, Buch. E462-1866
Main Mall, Vancouver BC V6T 1Z1 Canada. (604)822-
2514. **Fax:** (604)822-3616. **Website:** prismmagazine
.ca/contests. **Contact:** Cara Woodruff, fiction editor.
Offered annually for unpublished work to award the
best in contemporary fiction. Works of translation are
eligible. Guidelines for SASE, by e-mail, or on website.
Acquires first North American serial rights upon publication, and limited web rights for pieces selected for
website. Open to any writer except students and faculty in the creative writing department at University
of British Columbia, or people who have taken a creative writing course at University of British Columbia
with the 2 years prior to the contest deadline. Deadline: January 31. Prize: 1st Place: $2,000; 1st Runner-
up: $300; 2nd Runner-up: $200; winner is published.

PURPLE DRAGONFLY BOOK AWARDS

4696 W. Tyson St., Chandler AZ 85226-2903.
(480)940-8182. **Fax:** (480)940-8787. **E-mail:** cris-
ty@fivestarpublications.com. **Website:** www.purple
dragonflybookawards.com; www.fivestarpublica
tions.com; www.fivestarbookawards.com. **Contact:**
Cristy Bertini, contest coordinator. Five Star Publications presents the Purple Dragonfly Book Awards,
which were conceived and designed with children in
mind. "Not only do we want to recognize and honor
accomplished authors in the field of children's literature, but we also want to highlight and reward up-
and-coming, newly published authors and younger published writers." The Purple Dragonfly Book

Awards are divided into 3 distinct subject categories,
ranging from books on the environment and cooking to sports and family issues. (Click on the "Categories" tab on the website for a complete list.) The
Purple Dragonfly Book Awards are geared toward
stories that appeal to children of all ages. Looking
for stories that inspire, inform, teach or entertain. "A
Purple Dragonfly seal on your book's cover tells parents, grandparents, educators, and caregivers they are
giving children the very best in reading excellence."
Being honored with a Purple Dragonfly Award con-
fers credibility upon the winner, as well as provides
positive publicity to further their success. The goal
of these awards is to give published authors the recognition they deserve and provide a helping hand to
further their careers. Deadline: May 1 (postmarked).
Submissions postmarked March 1 or earlier that meet
all submission requirements are eligible for the Early
Bird reward: A free copy of *The Economical Guide to
Self-Publishing* or *Promote Like a Pro: Small Budget,
Big Show.* Prize: Grand Prize winner will receive a
$300 cash prize, 100 foil award seals (more can be or-
dered for an extra charge), 1 hour of marketing consultation from Five Star Publications, and $100 worth
of Five Star Publications' titles, as well as publicity
on Five Star Publications' websites and inclusion in a
winners' news release sent to a comprehensive list of
media outlets. The Grand Prize winner will also be
placed in the Five Star Dragonfly Book Awards virtual
bookstore with a thumbnail of the book's cover, price,
1-sentence description and link to Amazon.com for
purchasing purposes, if applicable. 1st Place: All 1st-
Place winners of categories will be put into a drawing
for a $100 prize. In addition, each 1st-Place winner
in each category receives a certificate commemorat-
ing their accomplishment, 25 foil award seals (more
can be ordered for an extra charge), and mention on
Five Star Publications' websites. Judged by industry
experts with specific knowledge about the categories
over which they preside.

THOMAS H. RADDALL ATLANTIC FICTION AWARD

Writers' Federation of Nova Scotia, 1113 Marginal
Rd., Halifax NS B3H 4P7 Canada. (902)423-8116. **Fax:**
(902)422-0881. **E-mail:** director@writers.ns.ca. **Website:** www.writers.ns.ca. **Contact:** Nate Crawford, executive director. Estab. 1990. The Thomas Head Raddall Atlantic Fiction Award is awarded for a novel or

a book of short fiction by a full-time resident of Atlantic Canada. Deadline: First Friday in December. Prize: Valued at $25,000 for winning title.

DAVID RAFFELOCK AWARD FOR PUBLISHING EXCELLENCE

National Writers Association, 10940 S. Parker Rd., #508, Parker CO 80134. (303)841-0246. **E-mail:** natl writersassn@hotmail.com. **Website:** www.national writers.com. **Contact:** Sandy Whelchel. Contest is offered annually for books published the previous year. Published works only. Open to any writer. Guidelines for SASE, by e-mail, or on website. Winners announced in June at the NWAF conference and notified by mail or phone. List of winners available for SASE or visit website. Purpose is to assist published authors in marketing their works and to reward outstanding published works. Deadline: May 15. Prize: Publicity tour, including airfare, valued at $5,000.

RANDOM HOUSE FOUNDATION, INC. CREATIVE WRITING COMPETITION

1 Scholarship Way, P.O. Box 297, St. Peter MN 56082. (212)782-0316. **Fax:** (212)940-7590. **E-mail:** creative-writing@randomhouse.com. **Website:** www.ran-domhouse.com/creativewriting. **Contact:** Melanie Fallon Hauska, director. Offered annually for unpublished work to New York City public high school seniors. 72 awards given in literary and nonliterary categories. Four categories: poetry, fiction/drama, personal essay and graphic novel. Applicants must be seniors (under age 21) at a New York City high school. No college essays or class assignments will be accepted. Deadline: February 10 for all categories. Prize: Awards range from $500-10,000. The program usually awards just under $100,000 in scholarships.

☺ THE RBC BRONWEN WALLACE AWARD FOR EMERGING WRITERS

The Writers' Trust of Canada, 460 Richmond St. W., Suite 600, Toronto ON M5C 1P1 Canada. (416)504-8222. **Fax:** (416)504-9090. **E-mail:** info@writerstrust .com. **Website:** www.writerstrust.com. **Contact:** Amanda Hopkins. Presented annually to a Canadian writer under the age of 35 who is not yet published in book form. The award, which alternates each year between poetry and short fiction, was established in memory of poet Bronwen Wallace. Deadline: March 7. Prize: $5,000 and $1,000 to 2 finalists.

☺ THE ROGERS WRITERS' TRUST FICTION PRIZE

The Writers' Trust of Canada, 460 Richmond St. W., Suite 600, Toronto ON M5V 1Y1 Canada. (416)504-8222. **Fax:** (416)504-9090. **E-mail:** info@writerstrust .com. **Website:** www.writerstrust.com/Awards/Rog ers-Writers--Trust-Fiction-Prize.aspx. **Contact:** Amanda Hopkins. Awarded annually for a distinguished work of fiction—either a novel or short story collection—published within the previous year. Presented at the Writers' Trust Awards event held in Toronto each fall. Open to Canadian citizens and permanent residents only. Deadline: varies depending on publication date of submission; see online guidelines. Prize: $25,000 and $2,500 to 4 finalists.

☺ LOIS ROTH AWARD

Modern Language Association, 26 Broadway, 3rd Floor, New York NY 10004. (646)576-5141. **Fax:** (646)458-0030. **E-mail:** awards@mla.org. **Website:** www.mla.org. Offered in odd-numbered years for an outstanding translation into English of a book-length literary work. Translators need not be members of the MLA. Deadline: April 1. Prize: A cash award and a certificate to be presented at the Modern Language Association's annual convention in January.

ROYAL DRAGONFLY BOOK AWARDS

4696 W. Tyson St., Chandler AZ 85226. (480)940-8182. **Fax:** (480)940-8787. **E-mail:** cristy@fivestarpublica tions.com. **Website:** www.fivestarpublications.com; www.fivestarbookawards.com; www.royaldragon flybookawards.com. **Contact:** Cristy Bertini. Offered annually for any previously published work to honor authors for writing excellence of all types of literature—fiction and nonfiction—in 52 categories, appealing to a wide range of ages and comprehensive list of genres. Open to any title published in English. Entry forms are downloadable at www.royaldragonfly bookawards.com. Prize: Grand Prize winner receives $300, while another entrant will be the lucky winner of a $100 drawing. All 1st-Place winners receive foil award seals and are included in a publicity campaign announcing winners. All 1st- and 2nd-Place winners and honorable mentions receive certificates.

○ ERNEST SANDEEN PRIZE IN POETRY AND THE RICHARD SULLIVAN PRIZE IN SHORT FICTION

University of Notre Dame, Department of English, 356 O'Shaughnessy Hall, Notre Dame IN 46556-5639.

(574)631-7526. **Fax:** (574)631-4795. **E-mail:** creative writing@nd.edu. **Website:** english.nd.edu/creative-writing/publications/sandeen-sullivan-prizes. **Contact:** Director of Creative Writing. Estab. 1994. The Sandeen/Sullivan Prize in Poetry and Short Fiction is awarded to the author who has published at least 1 volume of short fiction or 1 volume of poetry. Awarded biannually but judged quadrennially. Submission period: May 1-September 1. Prize: $1,000, a $500 award and a $500 advance against royalties from the Notre Dame Press.

ALDO AND JEANNE SCAGLIONE PRIZE FOR A TRANSLATION OF A LITERARY WORK

Modern Language Association, 26 Broadway, 3rd Floor, New York NY 10004-1789. (646)576-5141. **Fax:** (646)458-0030. **E-mail:** awards@mla.org. **Website:** www.mla.org. **Contact:** Coordinator of Book Prizes. Offered in even-numbered years for an outstanding translation into English of a book-length literary work. Deadline: April 1. Prize: A cash award and a certificate to be presented at the Modern Language Association's annual convention in January.

⭕ THE SCARS EDITOR'S CHOICE AWARDS

829 Brian Court, Gurnee IL 60031-3155. **E-mail:** editor@scars.tv. **Website:** scars.tv. **Contact:** Janet Kuypers, editor/publisher. Award to showcase good writing in an annual book. Prize: Publication of story/essay and 1 copy of the book. Reading fee: $19/short story. Make reading fee checks payable to Janet Kuypers.

THE MONA SCHREIBER PRIZE FOR HUMOROUS FICTION & NONFICTION

3940 Laurel Canyon Blvd., #566, Studio City CA 91604. **E-mail:** brad.schreiber@att.net. **Website:** www.bradschreiber.com. **Contact:** Brad Schreiber. Estab. 2000. The purpose of the contest is to award the most creative humor writing, in any form less than 750 words, in either fiction or nonfiction, including but not limited to stories, articles, essays, speeches, shopping lists, diary entries, and anything else writers dream up. Complete rules and previous winning entries on website. Deadline: December 1. Prize: 1st Place: $500; 2nd Place: $250; 3rd Place: $100. Judged by Brad Schreiber, author, journalist, consultant, and instructor.

JOANNA CATHERINE SCOTT NOVEL EXCERPT PRIZE CATEGORY

Soul-Making Keats Literary Competition Category, The Webhallow House, 1544 Sweetwood Dr., Broadmoor Village CA 94015-2029. **E-mail:** soulkeats@mail.com. **Website:** www.soulmakingcontest.us. **Contact:** Eileen Malone. Open annually to any writer. Deadline: November 30. 1st Place: $100; 2nd Place: $50; 3rd Place: $25.

⊕ SCREAMINMAMAS MAGICAL FICTION CONTEST

1911 Cleveland St., Hollywood FL 33020. **E-mail:** screaminmamas@gmail.com. **Website:** www.scream inmamas.com/contests. **Contact:** Darlene Pistocchi, editor/managing director. "The contest celebrates moms and the magical spirit of the holidays. If you had an opportunity to be anything you wanted to be, what would you be? Transport yourself! Become that character and write a short story around that character. Can be any genre." Length: 800-3,000 words. Open only to moms. Deadline: June 30. Prize: $40, publication.

⊕ SCREAMINMAMAS MAGICAL FICTION CONTEST

1911 Cleveland St., Hollywood FL 33020. **E-mail:** screaminmamas@gmail.com. **Website:** www.scream inmamas.com/contests. **Contact:** Darlene Pistocchi, editor/managing director. "Looking for light romantic comedy. Can be historical or contemporary—something to lift the spirits and celebrate the gift of innocent romance that might be found in the everyday life of a busy mom." Length: 800-2,000 words. Open only to moms. Deadline: June 30. Prize: $40, publication.

SCRIPTAPALOOZA TELEVISION WRITING COMPETITION

7775 Sunset Blvd., Suite #200, Hollywood CA 90046. (310)801-5366. **E-mail:** info@scriptapalooza.com. **Website:** www.scriptapaloozatv.com. Biannual competition accepting entries in 4 categories: Reality shows, sitcoms, original pilots, and 1-hour dramas. There are more than 25 producers, agents, and managers reading the winning scripts. Two past winners won Emmys because of Scriptapalooza and 1 past entrant now writes for Comedy Central. Winners announced February 15 and August 30. For contest results, visit website. Deadline: October 1 and April 15. Prize: 1st Place: $500; 2nd Place: $200; 3rd Place:

$100 (in each category); production company consideration.

MICHAEL SHAARA AWARD FOR EXCELLENCE IN CIVIL WAR FICTION

Civil War Institute at Gettysburg College, 300 N. Washington St., Campus Box 435, Gettysburg PA 17325. (717)337-6574. **Fax:** (717)337-6596. **E-mail:** civilwar@gettysburg.edu. **Website:** www.gettysburg.edu/cwi. **Contact:** Diane Brennan, administrative assistant. Estab. 1997. Offered annually for fiction published for the first time in January 1-December 31 of the year of the award, to encourage examination of the Civil War from unique perspectives or by taking an unusual approach. All Civil War novels are eligible. To nominate a novel, send 4 copies of the novel to the address above with a cover letter. Nominations should be made by publishers, but authors and critics can nominate as well. Any novel about the Civil War published (for the first time) in the current calendar year to "encourage fresh approaches to Civil War fiction" is eligible. Self-published books are not eligible. This includes books printed and bound by a company hired and paid by the author to publish his/her work in book form. Deadline: December 31. Prize: $5,000.

⊙ SKIPPING STONES HONOR (BOOK) AWARDS

P.O. Box 3939, Eugene OR 97403. (541)342-4956. **Fax:** (541)342-4956. **E-mail:** editor@skippingstones.org. **Website:** www.skippingstones.org. **Contact:** Arun N. Toké. Estab. 1994. *Skipping Stones* is a respected, multicultural literary magazine now in its 26th year. Annual award to promote multicultural and/or nature awareness through creative writings for children and teens and their educators. Seeks authentic, exceptional, child/youth friendly books that promote intercultural, international, intergenerational harmony, and understanding through creative ways. Deadline: February 1. Prize: Honor certificates; gold seals; reviews; press release/publicity. Judged by a multicultural committee of teachers, librarians, parents, students, and editors.

⊙ SKIPPING STONES YOUTH AWARDS

P.O. Box 3939, Eugene OR 97403-0939. (541)342-4956. **Fax:** (541)342-4956. **E-mail:** editor@skippingstones.org. **Website:** www.skippingstones.org. **Contact:** Arun N. Toké. Deadline: May 25. Prize: Publication in the autumn issue of *Skipping Stones*, honor certificate, subscription to magazine, plus 5 multicultural and/or nature books.

THE BERNICE SLOTE AWARD

Prairie Schooner, 123 Andrews Hall, P.O. Box 880334, Lincoln NE 68588-0334. (402)472-0911. **Fax:** (402)472-1817. **E-mail:** PrairieSchooner@unl.edu. **Website:** www.prairieschooner.unl.edu. **Contact:** Kwame Dawes. Offered annually for the best work by a beginning writer published in *Prairie Schooner* in the previous year. Prize: $500. Judged by editorial staff of *Prairie Schooner*.

BYRON CALDWELL SMITH BOOK AWARD

The University of Kansas, Hall Center for the Humanities, 900 Sunnyside Ave., Lawrence KS 66045. (785)864-4798. **E-mail:** vbailey@ku.edu. **Website:** www.hallcenter.ku.edu. **Contact:** Victor Bailey, director. Offered in odd years. To qualify, applicants must live or be employed in Kansas and have written an outstanding book published within the previous 2 calendar years. Translations are eligible. Guidelines for SASE or online. Deadline: March 1. Prize: $1,500.

JEFFREY E. SMITH EDITORS' PRIZE IN FICTION, ESSAY, AND POETRY

The Missouri Review, 357 McReynolds Hall, UMC, Columbia MO 65211. (573)882-4474. **Fax:** (573)884-4671. **E-mail:** contest_question@moreview.com. **Website:** www.missourireview.com. **Contact:** Editor. Offered annually for unpublished work in 3 categories: fiction, essay, and poetry. Guidelines online or for SASE. Deadline: October 1. Prize: $5,000 and publication for each category winner.

◑ KAY SNOW WRITING CONTEST

Willamette Writers, 2108 Buck St., West Linn OR 97068. (503)305-6729. **Fax:** (503)344-6174. **E-mail:** wilwrite@willamettewriters.com. **Website:** www.willamettewriters.com. **Contact:** Lizzy Shannon, contest director. Willamette Writers is the largest writers' organization in Oregon and 1 of the largest writers' organizations in the United States. It is a nonprofit, tax-exempt Oregon corporation led by volunteers. Elected officials and directors administer an active program of monthly meetings, special seminars, workshops, and annual writing conference. Continuing with established programs and starting new ones is only made possible by strong volunteer support. The purpose of this annual writing contest, named in honor of Willamette Writer's founder, Kay Snow, is to help writers reach professional goals in writing in a broad array of categories and to encourage student writers. Deadline: April 23. Prize: One 1st-Place prize of $300, one 2nd-Place prize of $150, and one 3rd-Place prize of $50 per winning entry in each of the 6 categories.

SOCIETY OF MIDLAND AUTHORS AWARD

Society of Midland Authors, P.O. Box 10419, Chicago IL 60610-0419. **E-mail:** loerzel@comcast.net. **Website:** www.midlandauthors.com. **Contact:** Meg Tebo, president. Since 1957, the Society has presented annual awards for the best books written by Midwestern authors. The Society of Midland Authors (SMA) Award is presented to 1 title in each of 6 categories: adult nonfiction, adult fiction, adult biography and memoir, children's nonfiction, children's fiction, and poetry. Deadline: February 1. Prize: Cash prize of $500 and a plaque that is awarded at the SMA banquet in May in Chicago.

⊘⊘ SUBTERRAIN MAGAZINE'S ANNUAL LITERARY AWARDS COMPETITION: THE LUSH TRIUMPHANT

P.O. Box 3008 MPO, Vancouver BC V6B 3X5 Canada. (604)876-8710. **Fax:** (604)879-2667. **E-mail:** subter@portal.ca. **Website:** www.subterrain.ca. Entrants may submit as many entries in as many categories as they like. Fiction: Maximum of 3,000 words. Poetry: A suite of 5 related poems (maximum of 15 pages). Creative Nonfiction (based on fact, adorned with fiction): Max of 4,000 words. Deadline: May 15. Prize: Winners in each category will receive $750 cash (plus payment for publication) and publication in the winter issue. First runner-up in each category will receive a $250 cash prize and publication in the spring issue of *subTerrain*.

⊕ TEEN MYSTERY FICTION CONTEST

P.O. Box 1001, Reynoldsburg OH 43068. **E-mail:** di anaperry@DianaPerryBooks.com. **Website:** diana perrybooks.com. **Contact:** Diana Perry. Estab. 2014. "Hit the ground running with an exciting, fast-paced mystery with lots of action. Cast of 6-8 teens ages 13-18." Rules on website. Length: up to 20 pages or 5,000 words. Purpose: "To give exposure to beginning writers trying to break in to the business and get noticed." Deadline: January 31. 1st Place: $300, trophy, mention on website, T-shirt, press releases in your local newspapers; 2nd Place: $200, trophy, mention on website, T-shirt, press releases in your local newspapers; 3rd Place: $100, trophy, mention on website, T-shirt,

press releases in your local newspapers; 4th/5th places: $50/$25, plaque, mention on website, T-shirt, press releases in your local newspapers. "We also list names of next 25 honorable mentions on website. Contest guidelines and entry form on website. Check website for guest judges. Mail entry form, your story, and a $15 money order to Teen Mystery Fiction Contest at above address postmarked no later than January 31. Winners announced both on website and via snail mail March 1. Prizes mailed within 10 days of announcement. Judged by Diana Perry and guest judge.

⊘ THREE CHEERS AND A TIGER

E-mail: editors@toasted-cheese.com. **Website:** www.toasted-cheese.com. **Contact:** Stephanie Lenz, editor. Contestants are to write a short story (following a specific theme) within 48 hours. Contests are held first weekend in spring (mystery) and first weekend in fall (science fiction/fantasy). Word limit announced at the start of the contest. Contest-specific information is announced 48 hours before the contest submission deadline. Results announced in April and October. Winners notified by e-mail. List of winners on website. Prize: Amazon gift certificates and publication. Blind judged by 2 *Toasted Cheese* editors. Each judge uses his or her own criteria to choose entries.

⊕ THRILLER FICTION CONTEST

P.O. Box 1001, Reynoldsburg OH 43068. **E-mail:** di anaperry@DianaPerryBooks.com. **Website:** diana-perrybooks.com. **Contact:** Diana Perry. Estab. 2014. "Tell a suspenseful story in the thriller genre; can be viral/disease thriller, legal thriller, espionage thriller, adventure thriller, suspense thriller, technical thriller." Rules on website. Length: up to 20 pages or 5,000 words. Purpose: "To give exposure to beginning writers trying to break in to the business and get noticed." Deadline: March 31. 1st Place: $300, trophy, mention on website, T-shirt, press releases in your local newspapers; 2nd Place: $200, trophy, mention on website, T-shirt, press releases in your local newspapers; 3rd Place: $100, trophy, mention on website, T-shirt, press releases in your local newspapers; 4th/5th places: $50/$25, plaque, mention on website, T-shirt, press releases in your local newspapers. "We also list names of next 25 honorable mentions on website. Contest guidelines and entry form on website." Check website for guest judges. Mail entry form, your story, and a $15 money order to Thriller Fiction Contest at above address postmarked no later than March 31. Winners announced both on website and via snail mail May 1. Prizes mailed within 10 days of announcement. Judged by Diana Perry and guest judge.

◎ TORONTO BOOK AWARDS

City of Toronto c/o Toronto Protocol, 100 Queen St. W., City Clerk's Office, 2nd floor, West Tower, Toronto ON M5H 2N2 Canada. **E-mail:** protocol@toronto.ca. **Website:** www.toronto.ca/book_awards. Estab. 1974. The Toronto Book Awards honor authors of books of literary or artistic merit that are evocative of Toronto. Deadline: March 28. Prize: Each finalist receives $1,000, and the winning author receives the remaining prize money ($15,000 total in prize money available).

⊕ UNDISCOVERED WORLD FICTION CONTEST

P.O. Box 1001, Reynoldsburg OH 43068. **E-mail:** dianaperry@DianaPerryBooks.com. **Website:** dianaperrybooks.com. **Contact:** Diana Perry. Estab. 2014. "Create an undiscovered world here on Earth (no science fiction)." Rules on website. Length: up to 20 pages or 5,000 words. Purpose: "To give exposure to beginning writers trying to break in to the business and get noticed." Deadline: September 30. 1st Place: $300, trophy, mention on website, T-shirt, press releases in your local newspapers; 2nd Place: $200, trophy, mention on website, T-shirt, press releases in your local newspapers; 3rd Place: $100, trophy, mention on website, T-shirt, press releases in your local newspapers; 4th/5th places: $50/$25, plaque, mention on website, T-shirt, press releases in your local newspapers. "We also list names of next 25 honorable mentions on website. Contest guidelines and entry form on website. Check website for guest judges. Mail entry form, your story, and a $15 money order to Undiscovered World Fiction Contest at above address postmarked no later than September 30. Winners announced both on website and via snail mail November 1. Prizes mailed within 10 days of announcement. Judged by Diana Perry and guest judge.

THE WASHINGTON WRITERS' PUBLISHING HOUSE FICTION PRIZE

Washington Writers' Publishing House, P.O. Box 15271, Washington DC 20003. **E-mail:** wwphpress@gmail.com. **Website:** www.washingtonwriters.org. Writers living within 75 miles of the Capitol are invited to submit a ms of either a novel or a collection of short stories. Ms should be 50-70 pages, single-spaced.

Deadline: November 1. Submission period begins July 1. Prize: $1,000 and 50 copies of the book.

WASSNODE SHORT FICTION PRIZE

Passages North, Department of English, Northern Michigan University, 1401 Presque Isle Ave., Marquette MI 49855. (906)227-1203. **Fax:** (906)227-1096. **E-mail:** passages@nmu.edu. **Website:** www.passagesnorth.com. **Contact:** Jennifer Howard. Offered every 2 years to publish new voices in literary fiction (maximum 7,500 words). Guidelines for SASE or online. Submissions accepted online. Deadline: February 15. Submission period begins January 15. Prize: $1,000 and publication for winner; 2 honorable mentions are also published; all entrants receive a copy of *Passages North*.

WESTERN WRITERS OF AMERICA

271CR 219, Encampment WY 82325. (307)329-8942. **Fax:** (307)327-5465 (call first). **E-mail:** wwa.moulton@gmail.com. **Website:** www.westernwriters.org. **Contact:** Candy Moulton, executive director. Estab. 1953. 17 Spur Award categories in various aspects of the American West. The nonprofit Western Writers of America has promoted and honored the best in Western literature with the annual Spur Awards, selected by panels of judges. Awards, for material published last year, are given for works whose inspirations, image, and literary excellence best represent the reality and spirit of the American West.

WILLA LITERARY AWARD

Women Writing the West, 8547 East Arapaho Rd., #J-541, Greenwood Village CO 80112-1436. **E-mail:** pamtartaglio@yahoo.com. **Website:** www.womenwritingthewest.org. **Contact:** Pam Tartaglio. The WILLA Literary Award honors the best in literature featuring women's or girls' stories set in the West published each year. Women Writing the West (WWW), a nonprofit association of writers and other professionals writing and promoting the Women's West, underwrites and presents the nationally recognized award annually (for work published between January 1 and December 31). The award is named in honor of Pulitzer Prize winner Willa Cather, one of the country's foremost novelists. The award is given in 7 categories: Historical fiction, contemporary fiction, original softcover fiction, creative nonfiction, scholarly nonfiction, poetry, and children's/young adult fiction/nonfiction. Submission period: November 1-February 1. Prize: $100 and a trophy. Finalist receives a plaque.

Both receive digital and sticker award emblems for book covers. Winning and finalist titles mailed to more than 4,000 booksellers, libraries, and others. Award announcement is in early August, and awards are presented to the winners and finalists at the annual WWW Fall Conference. Judged by professional librarians not affiliated with WWW.

GARY WILSON SHORT FICTION AWARD

descant, Texas Christian University, Box 298300, Fort Worth TX 76129. (817)257-5907. **Fax:** (817)257-6239. **E-mail:** descant@tcu.edu. **Website:** www.descant.tcu. edu. **Contact:** Dan Williams and Alex Lemon, editors. Estab. 1999. Offered annually for an outstanding story in an issue. Prize: $250.

○ WISCONSIN INSTITUTE FOR CREATIVE WRITING FELLOWSHIP

6195B H.C. White Hall, 600 N. Park St., Madison WI 53706. **E-mail:** rfkuka@wisc.edu. **Website:** www .wisc.edu/english/cw. **Contact:** Sean Bishop, graduate coordinator. Fellowship provides time, space, and an intellectual community for writers working on first books. Receives approximately 300 applicants a year for each genre. Judged by English department faculty and current fellows. Candidates can have up to 1 published book in the genre for which they are applying. Open to any writer with either an M.F.A. or Ph.D. in creative writing. Please enclose a SASE for notification of results. Results announced on website by May 1. Deadline: Last day of February. Prize: $27,000 for a 9-month appointment.

TOBIAS WOLFF AWARD IN FICTION

Bellingham Review, Mail Stop 9053, Western Washington University, Bellingham WA 98225. (360)650-4863. **E-mail:** bhreview@wwu.edu. **Website:** www .bhreview.org. **Contact:** Brenda Miller. Offered annually for unpublished work. Guidelines available on website; online submissions only. Categories: novel excerpts and short stories. Submission period: December 1-March 15. Prize: $1,000, plus publication and subscription.

WORLD FANTASY AWARDS

P.O. Box 43, Mukilteo WA 98275. **E-mail:** sfexecsec@ gmail.com. **Website:** www.worldfantasy.org. **Contact:** Peter Dennis Pautz, president. Offered annually for previously published work in several categories, including life achievement, novel, novella, short story, anthology, collection, artist, special award (pro) and special award (nonpro). Works are recommended by attendees of current and previous 2 years' conventions and a panel of judges. Awards to recognize excellence in fantasy literature worldwide. Deadline: June 1. Prize: Bust of H.P. Lovecraft. Judged by panel.

WORLD'S BEST SHORT-SHORT STORY FICTION CONTEST, NARRATIVE NONFICTION CONTEST & SOUTHEAST REVIEW POETRY CONTEST

English Department, Florida State University, Tallahassee FL 32306. **E-mail:** southeastreview@gmail .com. **Website:** www.southeastreview.org. **Contact:** Brandi George, editor. Estab. 1979. Annual award for unpublished short-short stories (500 words or less), poetry, and narrative nonfiction (6,000 words or less). Deadline: March 15. Prize: $500 per category. Winners and finalists will be published in *The Southeast Review.*

WOW! WOMEN ON WRITING QUARTERLY FLASH FICTION CONTEST

WOW! Women on Writing, P.O. Box 41104, Long Beach CA 90853. **E-mail:** contestinfo@wow-wome nonwriting.com. **Website:** www.wow-womenonwrit ing.com/contest.php. **Contact:** Angela Mackintosh, editor. Contest offered quarterly. "We are open to all themes and genres, although we do encourage writers to take a close look at our literary agent guest judge for the season if you are serious about winning." Entries must be 250-750 words. Deadline: August 31, November 30, February 28, May 31. Prize: 1st Place: $350 cash prize, $25 Amazon gift certificate, book from sponsor, story published on WOW! Women On Writing, interview on blog; 2nd Place: $250 cash prize, $25 Amazon gift certificate, book our sponsor, story published on WOW! Women On Writing, interview on blog; 3rd Place: $150 cash prize, $25 Amazon gift certificate, book from sponsor, story published on WOW! Women On Writing, interview on blog; 7 runners-up: $25 Amazon gift certificate, book from sponsor, story published on WOW! Women on Writing, interview on blog; 10 honorable mentions: $20 gift certificate from Amazon, book from sponsor, story title and name published on WOW!Women On Writing.

WRITER'S DIGEST ANNUAL WRITING COMPETITION

Writer's Digest, a publication of F+W Media, Inc., 10151 Carver Rd., Suite 200, Cincinnati OH 45242. (715)445-4612, ext. 13430. **E-mail:** writing-competition@fwmedia.com; nicole.howard@fwmedia.com. **Website:** www.writersdigest.com. **Contact:** Nicki Howard. Writing contest with 10 categories: Inspirational Writing (spiritual/religious, maximum 2,500 words); Memoir/Personal Essay (maximum 2,000 words); Magazine Feature Article (maximum 2,000 words); Short Story (genre, maximum 4,000 words); Short Story (mainstream/literary, maximum 4,000 words); Rhyming Poetry (maximum 32 lines); Non-rhyming Poetry (maximum 32 lines); Stage Play (first 15 pages and one-page synopsis); TV/Movie Script (first 15 pages and one-page synopsis). Entries must be original, in English, unpublished/unproduced (except for Magazine Feature Articles), and not accepted by another publisher/producer at the time of submission. *Writer's Digest* retains one-time publication rights to the winning entries in each category. Deadline: May. Grand Prize: $3,000 and a trip to the Writer's Digest Conference to meet with editors and agents; 1st Place: $1,000 and $100 of Writer's Digest Books; 2nd Place: $500 and $100 of Writer's Digest Books; 3rd Place: $250 and $100 of Writer's Digest Books; 4th Place: $100 and $50 of *Writer's Digest* Books; 5th Place: $50 and $50 of *Writer's Digest* Books; 6th-10th Place $25.

○ WRITER'S DIGEST POPULAR FICTION AWARDS

Writer's Digest, 10151 Carver Road, Suite 200, Blue Ash OH 45242. (715)445-4612 ext 13430. **E-mail:** WritersDigestWritingCompetition@fwmedia.com. **Contact:** Nicole Howard, contest administrator. Annual competition/award for short stories. Categories include romance, crime, science fiction, thriller, horror, and young adult. Length: 4,000 words or fewer. Top Award Winners will be notified by mail by December 31. Winners will be listed in the May/June issue of Writer's Digest, and on writersdigest.com after the issue is published. Early-Bird Deadline: September 16; Final Deadline: October 15. Prizes: Grand Prize: $2,500, a trip to the Writer's Digest Conference, $100 off a purchase at writersdigest. com, and the latest edition of *Novel & Short Story Writer's Market*; 1st Place (1 for each of 6 categories): $500 cash, $100 off a purchase at writersdigest.com, and the latest edition of *Novel & Short Story Writer's Market*; honorable mentions (4 in each of 6 categories): receive promotion at writersdigest.com and the latest edition of *Novel & Short Story Writer's Market*.

WRITER'S DIGEST SELF-PUBLISHED BOOK AWARDS

Writer's Digest, 10151 Carver Road, Suite 200, Blue Ash OH 45242. (715)445-4612, ext. 13430. **E-mail:** WritersDigestSelfPublishingCompetition@fwmedia .com. **Website:** www.writersdigest.com. **Contact:** Nicole Howard. Estab. 1992. Contest open to all English-language, self-published books for which the authors have paid the full cost of publication, or the cost of printing has been paid for by a grant or as part of a prize. Categories include: Mainstream/Literary Fiction, Genre Fiction, Nonfiction, Inspirational (spiritual/New Age), Life Stories (biographies/autobiographies/family histories/memoirs), Children's Books, Reference Books (directories/encyclopedias/guide books), Poetry, and Middle-Grade/Young Adult Books. Judges reserve the right to re-categorize entries. Judges reserve the right to withhold prizes in any category. All winners will be notified by October 17. Early bird deadline: April 1; Deadline: May 1. Prizes: Grand Prize: $3,000, a trip to the Writer's Digest Conference, promotion in *Writer's Digest* and *Publisher's Weekly*, and 10 copies of the book will be sent to major review houses with a guaranteed review in *Midwest Book Review*; 1st Place (9 winners): $1,000 and promotion in *Writer's Digest*; honorable mentions: $50 worth of Writer's Digest Books and promotion on writersdigest.com. All entrants will receive a brief commentary from 1 of the judges.

WRITER'S DIGEST SHORT SHORT STORY COMPETITION

Writer's Digest, 10151 Carver Road, Suite 200, Blue Ash OH 45242. (715)445-4612; ext. 13430. **E-mail:** WritersDigestShortShortStoryCompetition@fwmedia.com. **Website:** www.writersdigest.com. **Contact:** Nicole Howard. Looking for fiction that's bold, brilliant, and brief. Send your best in 1,500 words or fewer. All entries must be original, unpublished, and not submitted elsewhere at the time of submission. *Writer's Digest* reserves one-time publication rights to the first 25 winning entries. Winners will be notified by Feb. 28. Early bird deadline: November 17. Extended deadline: December 15. Prize: 1st Place: $3,000 and a trip to Writer's Digest Conference; 2nd Place: $1,500; 3rd Place: $500; 4th-10th Place: $100; 11th-25th Place: $50 gift certificate for Writer's Digest Books.

WRITERS-EDITORS NETWORK ANNUAL INTERNATIONAL WRITING COMPETITION

CNW Publishing, P.O. Box A, North Stratford NH 03590-0167. **E-mail:** contest@writers-editors.com. **E-mail:** info@writers-editors.com. **Website:** www.writers-editors.com. **Contact:** Dana K. Cassell, executive director. Annual award to recognize publishable talent. Categories: Nonfiction (previously published article/essay/column/nonfiction book chapter; unpublished or self-published article/essay/column/nonfiction book chapter); fiction (unpublished or self-published short story or novel chapter); children's literature (unpublished or self-published short story/nonfiction article/book chapter/poem); poetry (unpublished or self-published free verse/traditional). Guidelines available online. Deadline: March 15. Prize: 1st Place: $100; 2nd Place: $75; 3rd Place: $50.

All winners and honorable mentions will receive certificates as warranted. Judged by editors, librarians, and writers.

WRITERS' LEAGUE OF TEXAS BOOK AWARDS

Writers' League of Texas, 611 S. Congress Ave., Suite 505, Austin TX 78704. (512)499-8914. **Fax:** (512)499-0441. **E-mail:** wlt@writersleague.org. **E-mail:** sara@writersleague.org. **Website:** www.writersleague.org. Open to Texas authors of books published the previous 2 years. Authors are required to show proof of Texas residency but are not required to be members of the Writers' League of Texas. Deadline: Open to submissions from January 1 to April 30. Prize: $750, a commemorative award, and an appearance at a WLT Third Thursday panel at BookPeople in Austin, TX.

CONFERENCES & WORKSHOPS

Why are conferences so popular? Writers and conference directors alike tell us it's because writing can be such a lonely business—at conferences writers have the opportunity to meet (and commiserate) with fellow writers, as well as meet and network with publishers, editors, and agents. Conferences and workshops provide some of the best opportunities for writers to make publishing contacts and pick up valuable information on the business, as well as the craft, of writing.

The bulk of the listings in this section are for conferences. Most conferences last from one day to one week and offer a combination of workshop-type writing sessions, panel discussions, and a variety of guest speakers. Topics may include all aspects of writing from fiction to poetry to scriptwriting, or they may focus on a specific type of writing, such as those conferences sponsored by the Romance Writers of America (RWA) for writers of romance or by the Society of Children's Book Writers and Illustrators (SCBWI) for writers of children's books.

Workshops, however, tend to run longer—usually one to two weeks. Designed to operate like writing classes, most require writers to be prepared to work on and discuss their fiction while attending. An important benefit of workshops is the opportunity they provide writers for an intensive critique of their work, often by professional writing teachers and established writers.

Each of the listings here includes information on the specific focus of an event as well as planned panels, guest speakers, and workshop topics. It is important to note, however, some conference directors were still in the planning stages for 2015 when we contacted them. If it was not possible to include 2015 dates, fees, or topics, we provided the most up-to-date information available so you can get an idea of what to expect. For the most current information, it's best to check the conference website or send a self-addressed, stamped envelope to the director in question about three months before the date(s) listed.

FINDING A CONFERENCE

Many writers try to make it to at least one conference a year, but cost and location count as much as subject matter or other considerations when determining which conference to attend. There are conferences in almost every state and province, and even some in Europe open to North Americans.

To make it easier for you to find a conference close to home—or to find one in an exotic locale to fit into your vacation plans—we've divided this section into geographic regions. The conferences appear in alphabetical order under the appropriate regional heading.

Note that conferences appear under the regional heading according to where they will be held, which is sometimes different from the address given as the place to register or send for information. The regions are as follows:

Northeast (page 460): Connecticut, Maine, Massachusetts, New Hampshire, New York, Rhode Island, Vermont

Midatlantic (page 462): Washington DC, Delaware, Maryland, New Jersey, Pennsylvania

Midsouth (page 464): North Carolina, South Carolina, Tennessee, Virginia, West Virginia

Southeast (page 465): Alabama, Arkansas, Florida, Georgia, Louisiana, Mississippi, Puerto Rico

Midwest (page 466): Illinois, Indiana, Kentucky, Michigan, Ohio

North Central (page 468): Iowa, Minnesota, Nebraska, North Dakota, South Dakota, Wisconsin

South Central (page 469): Colorado, Kansas, Missouri, New Mexico, Oklahoma, Texas

West (page 472): Arizona, California, Hawaii, Nevada, Utah

Northwest (page 474): Alaska, Idaho, Montana, Oregon, Washington, Wyoming

Canada (page 476)

International (page 476)

LEARNING AND NETWORKING

Besides learning from workshop leaders and panelists in formal sessions, writers at conferences also benefit from conversations with other attendees. Writers on all levels enjoy sharing insights. A conversation over lunch can reveal a new market for your work or let you know which editors are most receptive to the work of new writers. You can find out about recent editor changes and about specific agents. A casual chat could lead to a new contact or resource in your area.

Many editors and agents make visiting conferences a part of their regular search for new writers. A cover letter or query that starts with "I met you at the Green Mountain Writers Conference," or "I found your talk on your company's new romance line at the Moonlight and Magnolias Writers Conference most interesting ..." may give you a small leg up on the competition.

While a few writers have been successful in selling their manuscripts at a conference, the availability of editors and agents does not usually mean these folks will have the time to read your novel or six best short stories (unless, of course, you've scheduled an individual meeting with them in advance). While editors and agents are glad to meet writers and discuss work in general terms, usually they don't have the time (or energy) to give an extensive critique during a conference. In other words, use the conference as a way to make a first, brief contact.

SELECTING A CONFERENCE

Besides the obvious considerations of time, place, and cost, choose your conference based on your writing goals. If, for example, your goal is to improve the quality of your writing, it will be more helpful to choose a hands-on craft workshop rather than a conference offering a series of panels on marketing and promotion. If, on the other hand, you are a science fiction novelist who would like to meet your fans, try one of the many science fiction conferences or "cons" held throughout the country and the world.

Look for panelists and workshop instructors whose work you admire and who seem to be writing in your general area. Check for specific panels or discussions of topics relevant to what you are writing now. Think about the size—would you feel more comfortable with a small workshop of eight people or a large group of one hundred or more attendees?

If your funds are limited, start by looking for conferences close to home, but you may want to explore those that offer contests with cash prizes—and a chance to recoup your expenses. A few conferences and workshops also offer scholarships, but the competition is stiff and writers interested in these should seek out the requirements early. Finally, students may want to look for conferences and workshops that offer college credit. You will find these options included in the listings here. Again, check the conference website or send a self-addressed, stamped envelope for the most current details.

NORTHEAST

⊕◎ BREAD LOAF ORION ENVIRONMENTAL WRITERS' CONFERENCE

Middlebury College, Middlebury VT 05753. (802)443-5286. **Fax:** (802)443-2087. **E-mail:** ncargill@middlebury.edu; BLORION@middlebury.edu. **Website:** www.middlebury.edu/blwc/BLOrion. **Contact:** Michael Collier, director. Estab. 2014. "This week-long conference of workshops, classes, lectures, readings, and discussions is for writers who want to improve their writing about the environment; for writers who seek to become better advocates for the environment through their writing; for poets who are drawn to writing about the natural world; for teachers and scholars who wish to write for a more general readership; and for environmental professionals who want to bring better writing skills to bear on their work. For those who are interested in learning more about environmental and nature writing but who do not wish to workshop their writing, there is also an auditing option available."

COSTS General contributor: $1,995; Auditor (attending conference without ms): $1,695. Cost includes tuition, room and board.

ACCOMMODATIONS Mountain campus of Middlebury College.

BREAD LOAF WRITERS' CONFERENCE

Middlebury College, Middlebury College, Middlebury VT 05753. (802)443-5286. **Fax:** (802)443-2087. **E-mail:** ncargill@middlebury.edu. **E-mail:** blwc@middlebury.edu. **Website:** www.middlebury.edu/blwc. **Contact:** Michael Collier, director. Estab. 1926. "The Bread Loaf Writers' Conference is one of America's most valuable literary institutions. The workshops, lectures, and classes, held in the shadow of the Green Mountains, have introduced generations of participants to rigorous practical and theoretical approaches to the craft of writing, and given America itself proven models of literary instruction." Average attendance: 230.

COSTS General contributor: $2,935; Auditor: $2,810 Cost includes tuition, housing.

ACCOMMODATIONS Bread Loaf Campus in Ripton, Vermont.

ADDITIONAL INFORMATION Information for 2015 conference available in December.

THE BUSINESS OF PET WRITING CONFERENCE

The Pet Socialite, Prince Street Station, P.O. Box 398, New York NY 10012. (212)631-3648. **E-mail:** info@petwritingconference.com. **Website:** www.petwritingconference.com. **Contact:** Charlotte Reed, director. Estab. 2008.

ADDITIONAL INFORMATION Brochures and guidelines available on website.

CAPE COD WRITERS CENTER ANNUAL CONFERENCE

P.O. Box 408, Osterville MA 02655. **E-mail:** writers@capecodwriterscenter.org. **Website:** www.capecodwriterscenter.org. **Contact:** Nancy Rubin Stuart, executive director. "Under the leadership of founder Marion Vuilleumier, the Cape Cod Writers Center Conference evolved from a regional writers' retreat into one commanding national attention. Today over 300 aspiring and published authors are members of the Cape Cod Writers Center. The annual summer conference remains its largest event, but the Center hosts various literary activities throughout the year."

COSTS Vary, depending on the number of courses selected. Three-day courses: $120/course. Two-day courses: $90/course. One-day courses: $60/course. One-day intensives: $90. Non-members pay $60 registration fee.

GREEN MOUNTAIN WRITERS CONFERENCE

47 Hazel St., Rutland VT 05701. (802)236-6133. **E-mail:** ydaley@sbcglobal.net. **E-mail:** yvonnedaley@me.com. **Website:** vermontwriters.com. **Contact:** Yvonne Daley, director. Estab. 1999.

COSTS For 2014 conference (July 28-August 1, 2014): $550 before June 1; $575 before July 1; $600 before July 20. Partial scholarships are available.

ACCOMMODATIONS Dramatically reduced rates at The Mountain Top Inn and Resort for attendees. Close to other area hotels, bed-and-breakfasts in Rutland County, Vermont.

ADDITIONAL INFORMATION Participants' mss can be read and commented on at a cost. Sponsors contests. Conference publishes a literary magazine featuring work of participants. Brochures available on website or e-mail. "We offer the opportunity to learn from some of the nation's best writers at a small, supportive conference in a lakeside setting that allows one-to-one feedback. Participants often continue to correspond and share work after conferences."

JOURNEY INTO THE IMAGINATION: A FIVE-DAY WRITING RETREAT

995 Chapman Rd., Yorktown NY 10598. (914)962-4432. **E-mail:** emily@emilyhanlon.com. **Website:** www.thefictionwritersjourney.com/Spring_Writing_Retreat.html. **Contact:** Emily Hanlon. Estab. 2004.

Retreat is for writers of all levels.

COSTS 2014 rates: 5 nights—$1,150 if you register before March 1; $1,250 after March 1. All rooms are private with shared bath.

KINDLING WORDS EAST

Website: www.kindlingwords.org. "Kindling Words East is a four-day (three-night) retreat held at the charming Essex, Vermont's Culinary Resort and Spa." **COST** 2014 rate: $245. Check website for 2015 rate.

THE MACDOWELL COLONY

100 High St., Peterborough NH 03458. (603)924-3886. **Fax:** (603)924-9142. **E-mail:** admissions@macdowellcolony.org. **Website:** www.macdowellcolony.org. Estab. 1907. "The mission of The MacDowell Colony is to nurture the arts by offering creative individuals of the highest talent an inspiring environment in which they can produce enduring works of the imagination. We welcome artists engaging in the broadest spectrum of artistic practice who are investigating an unlimited array of inquiries and concerns. We apply the same egalitarian standards for all those who serve MacDowell either in a staff, volunteer, or representative capacity."

COSTS Travel reimbursement and stipends are available for participants of the residency, based on need. There are no residency fees.

⊙ ODYSSEY FANTASY WRITING WORKSHOP

P.O. Box 75, Mont Vernon NH 03057. **E-mail:** jcavelos@sff.net. **Website:** www.odysseyworkshop.org. Estab. 1996.

COSTS 2014 rate: $1,965 tuition, $812 housing (double room), $1,624 (single room); $35 application fee, $450-600 food (approximate), $550 processing fee to receive college credit.

ADDITIONAL INFORMATION Students must apply and include a writing sample. Application deadline April 8. Students' works are critiqued throughout the 6 weeks. Workshop information available in

October. For brochure/guidelines, send SASE, e-mail, visit website, or call. Accepts inquiries by SASE, e-mail, phone.

RT BOOKLOVERS CONVENTION

55 Bergen St., Brooklyn NY 11201. (718)237-1097 or (800)989-8816, ext. 12. **Fax:** (718)624-2526. **E-mail:** jocarol@rtconvention.com; nancy@rtbookreviews.com. **Website:** rtconvention.com.

COSTS See website for pricing and other information.

ACCOMMODATIONS Rooms available nearby.

⊙ SOCIETY OF CHILDREN'S BOOK WRITERS & ILLUSTRATORS WINTER CONFERENCE ON WRITING AND ILLUSTRATING FOR CHILDREN

New York City NY. **E-mail:** scbwi@scbwi.org. **Website:** www.scbwi.org. **Contact:** Stephen Mooser. Estab. 2000. 2015 conference is January 30-February 1, 2015.

COSTS See website for current cost and conference information.

ADDITIONAL Information SCBWI also holds an annual summer conference in August in Los Angeles. See the listing in the West section or visit website for details.

THRILLERFEST

P.O. Box 311, Eureka CA 95502. **E-mail:** infocentral@thrillerwriters.org. **Website:** www.thrillerfest.com. **Contact:** Kimberley Howe, executive director. Estab. 2006.

COSTS Price will vary from $300-1,100, depending on which events are selected. Various package deals are available offering savings, and early bird pricing is offered beginning September of each year.

ACCOMMODATIONS Grand Hyatt in New York City.

⊕ UNICORN WRITERS CONFERENCE

P.O. Box 176, Redding CT 06876. (203)938-7405. **E-mail:** bookings@unicornwritersconference.com; unicornwritersconference@gmail.com. **E-mail:** bookings@unicornwritersconference.com; unicornwritersconference@gmail.com. **Website:** www.unicornwritersconference.com.

ACCOMMODATIONS Held at Saint Clements Castle in Connecticut. Directions available on event website.

WRITER'S DIGEST CONFERENCES

F+W Media, Inc., 10151 Carver Road, Suite 200, Blue Ash OH 45242. **E-mail:** jill.ruesch@fwmedia.com.

E-mail: phil.sexton@fwmedia.com. **Website:** www
.writersdigestconference.com. Estab. 1995.

COSTS Cost varies by location and year. There are
typically different pricing options for those who wish
to stay for the entire event vs. daylong passes.

ACCOMMODATIONS A block of rooms at the event
hotel is reserved for guests.

YADDO

The Corporation of Yaddo Residencies, P.O. Box 395,
312 Union Ave., Saratoga Springs NY 12866-0395.
(518)584-0746. **Fax:** (518)584-1312. **E-mail:** chwait@
yaddo.org; lleduc@yaddo.org. **Website:** www.yaddo
.org. **Contact:** Candace Wait, program director. Estab. 1900. Two seasons: large season is May-August;
small season is October-May (stays from 2 weeks to
2 months; average stay is 5 weeks). Accepts 230 art-
ists/year. Accommodates approximately 35 artists in
large season. Those qualified for invitations to Yaddo
are highly qualified writers, visual artists (including
photographers), composers, choreographers, performance artists, and film and video artists who are
working at the professional level in their fields. Artists
who wish to work collaboratively are encouraged to
apply. An abiding principle at Yaddo is that applications for residencies are judged on the quality of the
artists' work and professional promise. Site includes
4 small lakes, a rose garden, woodland, swimming
pool, tennis courts. Yaddo's nonrefundable application fee is $30, to which is added a fee for media up-
loads ranging from $5-10 depending on the discipline.
Application fees must be paid by credit card. Two letters of recommendation are requested. Applications
are considered by the admissions committee and invitations are issued by March 15 (deadline: January
1) and October 1 (deadline: August 1). Information
available on website.

COSTS No fee is charged; residency includes room,
board, and studio space. Limited travel expenses are
available to artists accepted for residencies at Yaddo.

ACCOMMODATIONS No stipends are offered.

MIDATLANTIC

ALGONKIAN FIVE DAY NOVEL CAMP

2020 Pennsylvania Ave. NW, Suite 443, Washington
DC 20006. **E-mail:** algonkian@webdelsol.com. **Website:** fwwriters.algonkianconferences.com.

BALTIMORE COMIC-CON

Baltimore Convention Center, One West Pratt St.,
Baltimore MD 21201. (410)526-7410. **E-mail:** gen
eral@baltimorecomiccon.com. **Website:** www.balti
morecomiccon.com. **Contact:** Marc Nathan. Estab.
1999.

ACCOMMODATIONS Does not offer overnight accommodations. Provides list of area hotels or lodging options.

ADDITIONAL INFORMATION For brochure, visit
website.

BALTIMORE WRITERS' CONFERENCE

English Department, Liberal Arts Building, Towson University, 8000 York Rd., Towson MD 21252.
(410)704-3695. **E-mail:** prwr@towson.edu. **Website:**
baltimorewritersconference.org. Estab. 1994.

◯   This conference has sold out in the past.

COSTS Regular (nonstudent) rate before November 1:
$75; regular (nonstudent) rate after November 1: $95;
student rate before November 1: $35; student rate after
November 1: $50.

ACCOMMODATIONS Hotels are close by, if required.

ADDITIONAL INFORMATION Writers may register
through the BWA website. Send inquiries via e-mail.

BAY TO OCEAN WRITERS' CONFERENCE

P.O. Box 544, St. Michaels MD 21663. (443)786-4536.
E-mail: info@baytoocean.com. **Website:** www.bay
toocean.com. Estab. 1998. (443)786-4536. **E-mail:**
info@baytoocean.com. **Website:** www.baytoocean
.com. Annual. Conference held last Saturday in February. Average attendance: 150. Approximately 25
speakers conduct workshops on publishing; agents;
editing; marketing; craft; the Internet; writing for
television and movies; poetry, fiction, nonfiction and
freelance writing. Site: Chesapeake College, Rt. 213
and Rt. 50, Wye Mills, on Maryland's historic Eastern Shore. Accessible to individuals with disabilities.

COSTS Adults $115, students $55. A paid ms review
is also available—details on website. Includes continental breakfast and networking lunch.

ADDITIONAL INFORMATION Mail-in registration
form available on website in December prior to the
conference. Preregistration is required, no registration at door. Conference usually sells out 1 month in
advance. Conference is for all levels of writers.

MONTROSE CHRISTIAN WRITERS' CONFERENCE

218 Locust St., Montrose PA 18801. (570)278-1001 or (800)598-5030. **Fax:** (570)278-3061. **E-mail:** mbc@ montrosebible.org. **Website:** montrosebible.org. Estab. 1990.

○ "New and experienced writers will be spiritually renewed as they sharpen their word-smithing skills and learn about Christian publishing at this annual conference."

COSTS Tuition is $180. Early bird rates available. Add-ons include professional critiques and private tutorials.

ACCOMMODATIONS Will meet planes in Binghamton, NY and Scranton, PA. On-site accommodations: room and board $325-370/conference; $75-80/ day including food (2014 rates). RV court available.

ADDITIONAL INFORMATION "Writers can send work ahead of time and have it critiqued for a small fee." The attendees are usually church related. The writing has a Christian emphasis. Conference information available in April. For brochure, visit website, e-mail, or call. Accepts inquiries by phone or e-mail.

JENNY McKEAN MOORE COMMUNITY WORKSHOPS

English Department, George Washingtion University, 801 22nd St. NW, Rome Hall, Suite 760, Washington DC 20052. (202) 994-6180. **Fax:** (202) 994-7915. **E-mail:** lpageinc@aol.com. **Website:** www.gwu .edu/~english/creative_jennymckeanmoore.html. **Contact:** Lisa Page, acting director of creative writing. Estab. 1976.

ADDITIONAL INFORMATION Admission is competitive and by ms.

MUSE AND THE MARKETPLACE

Grub Street, 160 Boylston St., 4th Floor, Boston MA 02116. (617)695.0075. **E-mail:** info@grubstreet.org. **Website:** grubstreet.org.

○ The Muse and the Marketplace is a 3-day literary conference designed to give aspiring writers a better understanding about the craft of writing fiction and nonfiction, to prepare them for the changing world of publishing and promotion, and to create opportunities for meaningful networking. On all 3 days, prominent and nationally recognized established and emerging authors lead sessions on the craft of writing—the "muse" side of things—while edi-

tors, literary agents, publicists, and other industry professionals lead sessions on the business side—the "marketplace."

COSTS Varies, depending on if you're a member or nonmember (includes 6 workshop sessions and 2 Hour of Power sessions with options for the Manuscript Mart and a Five-Star lunch with authors, editors and agents). Other passes are available for Saturday-only and Sunday-only guests.

⊕ NEW JERSEY ROMANCE WRITERS PUT YOUR HEART IN A BOOK CONFERENCE

P.O. Box 513, Plainsboro NJ 08536. **E-mail:** dmcom fort@aol.com. **Website:** www.njromancewriters.org. Estab. 1984.

COST Early bird registration: $215 (members) and $240 (nonmembers); late registration: $240 (members) and $265 (nonmembers). Preconference workshop: $45. Annual conference in October.

ACCOMMODATIONS Special rate available for conference attendees at the Sheraton at Renaissance Woodbridge Hotel in Iselin, New Jersey.

ADDITIONAL INFORMATION Conference brochures, guidelines, and membership information are available for SASE. Massive book fair is open to the public with authors signing copies of their books.

PENNWRITERS CONFERENCE

RR #2, Box 241, Middlebury Center PA 16935. **Website:** www.pennwriters.org. Estab. 1987.

○ As the official writing organization of Pennsylvania, Pennwriters is made up of 8 different smaller writing groups that meet in different areas of Pennsylvania. Each of these groups sometimes has their own, smaller event during the year in addition to the annual writing conference.

COST 2014 rates: Full conference: $289 (members), $324 (nonmembers). Rates also available for Friday or Saturday only, and for preconference workshops.

ACCOMMODATIONS See website for current information.

ADDITIONAL INFORMATION Sponsors contest. Published authors judge fiction in various categories. Agent/editor appointments are available on a first come, first serve basis.

PHILADELPHIA WRITERS' CONFERENCE

P.O. Box 7171, Elkins Park PA 19027-0171. (215) 619-7422. **E-mail:** info@pwcwriters.org. **E-mail:** info@ pwcwriters.org. **Website:** pwcwriters.org. Estab. 1949.

○ "A 3-day conference, traditionally held in early June, offers 14 workshops, usually 4 seminars, several 'ms rap' sessions, a Friday Roundtable Forum Buffet with speaker, and the Saturday Annual Awards Banquet with speaker. The 150 to 200 conferees may submit mss in advance for criticism by the workshop leaders, and they are eligible to submit entries in about a dozen contest categories. Cash prizes and certificates are given to 1st- and 2nd-Place winners, plus full tuition for the following year's conference to 1st-Place winners."

COST 2014 rates: $220 (members), $240 (nonmembers).

ACCOMMODATIONS Wyndham Hotel (formerly the Holiday Inn), Independence Mall, Fourth and Arch Streets, Philadelphia, PA 19106-2170. "Hotel offers discount for early registration."

ADDITIONAL INFORMATION Accepts inquiries by e-mail. Agents and editors attend conference. Visit us on the Web for further agent and speaker details. Many questions are answered online.

MIDSOUTH

AMERICAN CHRISTIAN WRITERS CONFERENCES

P.O. Box 110390, Nashville TN 37222-0390. (800)219-7483. **Fax:** (615)834-7736. **E-mail:** acwriters@aol.com. **Website:** www.acwriters.com. **Contact:** Reg Forder, director. Estab. 1981.

COSTS Costs vary based on conference. Prices also depend on whether it is a conference or a mentoring retreat.

ACCOMMODATIONS Special rates are available at the host hotel (usually a major chain like Holiday Inn).

ADDITIONAL INFORMATION Send a SASE for conference brochures/guidelines.

BLUE RIDGE CHRISTIAN "AUTUMN IN THE MOUNTAINS" NOVELISTS RETREAT

1-800-588-7222. **E-mail:** ylehman@bellsouth.net. **Website:** http://ridgecrestconferencecenter.org/event/blueridgechristiannovelistretreat#.U34Vu1h dWis. **Contact:** Yvonne Lehman, director. Estab. 2007. October retreat in the mountains of western North Carolina. Ms critiques and contests offered.

COSTS Before June 1 tuition: on campus $275/off campus $300. After June 1: on campus $325/off campus $350. Lodging $69-$89 per night. Call or go to website to register.

CELEBRATION OF SOUTHERN LITERATURE

Southern Lit Alliance, 3069 S. Broad St., Suite 2, Chattanooga, TN 37408-3056. (423)267-1218. **Fax:** (866)483-6831. **E-mail:** srobinson@southernlitalliance.org. **Website:** www.southernlitalliance.org. **Contact:** Susan Robinson.

○ This event happens every other year in odd-numbered years.

ADDITIONAL INFORMATION Schedule and participating writers for 2015 conference will be announced in the fall.

⊕ HAMPTON ROADS WRITERS CONFERENCE

P.O. Box 56228, Virginia Beach VA 23456. **E-mail:** hrwriters@cox.net. **Website:** hamptonroadswriters.org. Workshops cover fiction, nonfiction, memoir, poetry, and the business of getting published. A book shop, book signings, and many networking opportunities are available.

COSTS Up to $275. Costs vary. There are discounts for members, for early bird registration, for students, and more.

JAMES RIVER WRITERS CONFERENCE

ArtWorks Studios 136, 320 Hull St., #136, Richmond VA 23224. (804)433-3790. **Fax:** (804)291-1466. **E-mail:** info@jamesriverwriters.com; fallconference@jamesriverwriters.com. **Website:** www.jamesriverwriters.com. **Contact:** Katharine Herndon, executive director. Estab. 2003. Annual. "The James River Writers Conference has attracted prize-winning authors and highly regarded editors and agents from around the country to share their wisdom about writing and publishing. More than 300 people attend this multi-day event, known for its inspiring, collegial atmosphere and Southern hospitality." Past years' conference guests have included Sheri Reynolds, Sharyn McCrumb, Claudia Emerson, Eric VanLustbader, Mark Bowden, Rosalind Miles, Dennis McFarland, David L. Robbins, Dean King, James Campbell, and Hampton Sides.

COSTS Two-day conference: $200 (members); $250 (nonmembers); one-day conference (Saturday or Sunday only): $170 (members); $185 (nonmembers). Discount rate available for students.

ACCOMMODATIONS Richmond is easily accessibly by air and train. Provides list of area hotels or lodging options. "Each year we arrange for special conference rates at an area hotel."

ADDITIONAL INFORMATION Workshop material is not required, however, we have offered an option for submissions: the first pages critique session in which submissions are read before a panel of agents and editors who are seeing them for the first time and are asked to react on the spot. No additional fee. No guarantee that a particular submission will be read. Details posted on the website, www.jamesriverwriters.com. Information available in June. For brochure, visit website. Agents participate in conference. Editors participate in conference. Both meet with writers to take pitches. Previous agents in attendance include April Eberhardt, Deborah Grosvenor, Victoria Skurnick, and Paige Wheeler.

◎ KILLER NASHVILLE

P.O. Box 680759, Franklin TN 37068-0686. (615)599-4032. **E-mail:** contact@killernashville.com. **Website:** www.killernashville.com. **Contact:** Clay Stafford, founder. Estab. 2006.

COSTS Early Bird Registration: $210 (February 15); Advanced Registration: $220 (April 30); $230 for 3-day full registration.

ACCOMMODATIONS The Hutton Hotel has all rooms available for the Killer Nashville Writers' Conference.

ADDITIONAL INFORMATION Additional information about registration is provided online.

NORTH CAROLINA WRITERS' NETWORK FALL CONFERENCE

P.O. Box 21591, Winston-Salem NC 27120. (336)293-8844. **E-mail:** mail@ncwriters.org. **Website:** www.ncwriters.org. Estab. 1985.

COSTS See website for fall conference rates.

ACCOMMODATIONS Special rates are usually available at the conference hotel, but conferees must make their own reservations.

ADDITIONAL INFORMATION Available at www.ncwriters.org.

SEWANEE WRITERS' CONFERENCE

735 University Ave., 119 Gailor Hall, Stamler Center, Sewanee TN 37383-1000. (931) 598-1654. **E-mail:** allatham@sewanee.edu. **Website:** www.sewaneewriters.org. **Contact:** Adam Latham. Estab. 1990.

COSTS $1,000 for tuition and $800 for room, board, and activity costs.

ACCOMMODATIONS Participants are housed in single rooms in university dormitories. Bathrooms are shared by small groups.

⊕ SOUTH CAROLINA WRITERS WORKSHOP

4840 Forest Drive, Suite 6B: PMB 189, Columbia SC 29206. **E-mail:** scwwliaison@gmail.com; scww2013@gmail.com. **Website:** www.myscww.org/. Estab. 1991.

ACCOMMODATIONS Hilton Myrtle Beach Resort.

WRITE ON THE RIVER

8941 Kelsey Lane, Knoxville TN 37922. **E-mail:** bob@bobmayer.org. **Website:** www.bobmayer.org. **Contact:** Bob Mayer. Estab. 2002.

COSTS Varies; depends on venue. Please see website for any updates.

ADDITIONAL INFORMATION Limited to 4 participants, and focused on their novel and marketability.

THE WRITERS' WORKSHOP

387 Beaucatcher Rd., Asheville NC 28805. (828)254-8111. **E-mail:** writersw@gmail.com. **Website:** www.twwoa.org. Estab. 1984.

COSTS Vary. Financial assistance available to low-income writers. Information on overnight accommodations is made available.

ADDITIONAL INFORMATION We also sponsor these contests, open to all writers: Annual Poetry Contest, prizes from $100-300 (Deadline: Feb. 28); Hard Times Writing Contest, prizes from $100-300, (Deadline: May 30); Fiction Contest, prizes from $150-350 (Deadline: Aug. 30); Annual Memoirs Competition, prizes from $150-350 (Deadline: Nov. 30). Contests for young writers are posted at our website.

SOUTHEAST

⊕ ATLANTA WRITERS CONFERENCE

E-mail: awconference@gmail.com. **E-mail:** gjweinstein@yahoo.com. **Website:** atlantawritersconference.com. **Contact:** George Weinstein.

ACCOMMODATIONS Westin Airport Atlanta Hotel

ADDITIONAL INFORMATION There is a free shuttle that runs between the airport and the hotel.

FLORIDA CHRISTIAN WRITERS CONFERENCE

530 Lake Kathryn Circle, Casselberry FL 32707. (386)295-3902. **E-mail:** FloridaChristianWriter

sConf@gmail.com. **Website:** floridacwc.net. **Contact:** Eva Marie Everson, Mark Hancock. Estab. 1988.

COSTS 2014 rates: Wednesday-Sunday Full Conference: $575-1,350 (depends on accommodations; student rate available); Thursday-Sunday Conference: $475-1,200 (depends on accommodations; student rate available). These rates include lodging and some meals. À la carte and commuter rates available. Check website for 2015 rates.

ACCOMMODATIONS "We provide a shuttle from Orlando International Airport (MCO) ($90) and Sanford-Orlando International (SFB) ($80)."

ADDITIONAL INFORMATION "Each writer may submit 2 works for critique. We have specialists in every area of writing. Brochures/guidelines are available online or for a SASE."

⊕ FUN IN THE SUN

Florida Romance Writers, P.O. Box 550562, Fort Lauderdale FL 33355. **E-mail:** FRWfuninthesun@yahoo.com. **Website:** frwfuninthesunmain.blogspot.com. Estab. 1986. Cruise conference in February 2015.

⬤ For 2015, the keynote speaker will be best-selling romance author Julia Quinn.

COSTS See website for updates, depending on membership status and registration date.

ADDITIONAL INFORMATION Ours is the longest-running conference of any RWA chapter. Brochures/registration are available online, by e-mail, or for a SASE.

HOW TO BE PUBLISHED WORKSHOPS

P.O. Box 100031, Irondale AL 35210-3006. **E-mail:** mike@writing2sell.com. **Website:** www.writing2sell.com. **Contact:** Michael Garrett. Estab. 1986.

COSTS $79-99.

SOUTHEASTERN WRITERS ASSOCIATION— ANNUAL WRITERS WORKSHOP

161 Woodstone, Athens GA 30605. **E-mail:** purple@southeasternwriters.org. **Website:** www.southeasternwriters.com. **Contact:** Amy Munnell and Sheila Hudson, presidents. Estab. 1975.

ACCOMMODATIONS Multiple hotels available in St. Simon's Island, GA.

MIDWEST

ANTIOCH WRITERS' WORKSHOP

c/o Antioch University Midwest, 900 Dayton St., Yellow Springs OH 45387. (937)769-1803. **E-mail:** info@antiochwritersworkshop.com. **Website:** www.antiochwritersworkshop.com. **Contact:** Sharon Short, director. Estab. 1986. Annual one-week conference held in July. Average attendance: 80. Workshop concentration: fiction, poetry, personal essay, memoir. Workshop located at Antioch University Midwest and at various sites in the Village of Yellow Springs. Competitive scholarships are offered. Full Week experience also includes small group lunches with faculty, agent pitch sessions, optional ms critiques. Presented in partnership with Antioch University Midwest. Continuing education and college-level credit options available.

COSTS Registration for all programs is $125: tuition for Saturday Seminar is covered by registration fee; tuition for Full Week experience ranges from $450 for Ohio college/university students and faculty; $550 for alumni and local participants; $610 for nonlocal first-time participants.

ACCOMMODATIONS Accommodations are available at local hotels and bed and breakfasts.

⊕ BOOKS-IN-PROGRESS CONFERENCE

Carnegie Center for Literacy and Learning, 251 West Second Street, Lexington KY 40507. (859)254-4175. **E-mail:** ccll1@carnegiecenterlex.org; lwhitaker@carnegiecenterlex.org. **Website:** http://carnegiecenterlex.org/event/books-progress-conference-2014-3. **Contact:** Laura Whitaker. Estab. 2010. Conference offers craft and business workshops led by top authors. Topics include revising for publication, children's lit, poetry, nonfiction, and fiction.

⬤ Note: One-on-one meetings are only available to full conference participants. Limited slots available. Please choose only 1 agent; only 1 pitching session per participant.

COSTS $175.

ACCOMMODATIONS Several area hotels are nearby.

CAPON SPRINGS WRITERS' WORKSHOP

2836 Westbrook Dr., Cincinnati OH 45211-0627. (513)481-9884. **E-mail:** beckcomm@fuse.net. Estab. 2000.

COSTS Check in 2015.

ACCOMMODATIONS Facility has swimming, hiking, fishing, tennis, badminton, volleyball, basketball, ping-pong, etc. A 9-hole golf course is available for an additional fee.

ADDITIONAL INFORMATION Brochures available for SASE. Inquire via e-mail.

CHICAGO WRITERS CONFERENCE

E-mail: ines@chicagowritersconference.org; mare@chicagowritersconference.org. **Website:** chicagowritersconference.org. **Contact:** Mare Swallow. Estab. 2011. "Chicago Writers Conference is a 501(c)(3) not-for-profit organization dedicated to connecting Chicago area writers and publishing professionals through conferences, workshops and literary events."

ADDITIONAL INFORMATION Check website for updates on admission fees.

DETROIT WORKING WRITERS ANNUAL WRITERS CONFERENCE

Detroit Working Writers, P.O. Box 82395, Rochester MI 48308. **E-mail:** conference@detworkingwriters.org. **Website:** dww-writers-conference.org/. Estab. 1961.

There are 5 writing contests in different categories: young adult/new adult, creative nonfiction, poetry, children's, adult fiction.

COSTS $60-150, depending on early bird registration and membership status within the organization.

FESTIVAL OF FAITH AND WRITING

Department of English, Calvin College, 1795 Knollcrest Circle SE, Grand Rapids MI 49546. (616)526-6770. **E-mail:** ffw@calvin.edu. **Website:** festival.calvin.edu. Estab. 1990.

COSTS 2014 rates: $185 early bird registration; $200 regular; $85 student; $170 group. Check website for 2015 rates.

ACCOMMODATIONS Shuttles are available to and from local hotels. Shuttles are also available for overflow parking lots. A list of hotels with special rates for conference attendees is available on the festival website. High school and college students can arrange on-campus lodging by e-mail.

ADDITIONAL INFORMATION Online registration is open up to approximately 1 month before the event. Accepts inquiries by e-mail and phone.

KENTUCKY WOMEN WRITERS CONFERENCE

University of Kentucky College of Arts & Sciences, 232 E. Maxwell St., Lexington KY 40506. (859)257-2874. **E-mail:** kentuckywomenwriters@gmail.com. **Website:** womenwriters.as.uky.edu/. **Contact:** Julie Wrinn, director. Estab. 1979. "Held in Homer, Alaska, this nationally recognized writing conference features workshops, readings and panel presentations in fiction, poetry, nonfiction, and the business of writing."

COSTS $175 early bird discount before August 1., $195 thereafter; $30 for undergraduates and younger; includes boxed lunch on Friday; $20 for Writers Reception. Other meals and accommodations are not included.

ADDITIONAL INFORMATION Sponsors prizes in poetry ($200), fiction ($200), nonfiction ($200), playwriting ($500), and spoken word ($500). Winners also invited to read during the conference. Preregistration opens May 1.

KENTUCKY WRITERS CONFERENCE

Western Kentucky University and the Southern Kentucky Book Fest, Western Kentucky University Libraries, 1906 College Heights Blvd., Bowling Green KY 42101. (270)745-4502. **E-mail:** kristie.lowry@wku.edu. **Website:** www.sokybookfest.org/KYWritersConf. **Contact:** Kristie Lowry.

Since the event is free, interested attendees are asked to register in advance. Information on how to do so is on the website.

KENYON REVIEW WRITERS WORKSHOP

Kenyon College, Gambier OH 43022. (740)427-5207. **Fax:** (740)427-5417. **E-mail:** kenyonreview@kenyon.edu; writers@kenyonreview.org. **Website:** www.kenyonreview.org. **Contact:** Anna Duke Reach, director. Estab. 1990.

COSTS $1,995; includes tuition, room and board.

ACCOMMODATIONS The workshop operates a shuttle to and from Gambier and the airport in Columbus, Ohio. Offers overnight accommodations. Participants are housed in Kenyon College student housing. The cost is covered in the tuition.

ADDITIONAL INFORMATION Application includes a writing sample. Admission decisions are made on a rolling basis. Workshop information is available online at www.kenyonreview.org/workshops in November. For brochure send e-mail, visit website, call, fax. Accepts inquiries by SASE, e-mail, phone, fax.

MIDWEST WRITERS WORKSHOP

Ball State University, Department of Journalism, Muncie IN 47306. (765)282-1055. **E-mail:** midwestwriters@yahoo.com. **Website:** www.midwestwriters.org. **Contact:** Jama Kehoe Bigger, director.

"The mission of MWW is to give all writers the opportunity to improve their craft, to associate with highly credentialed professionals, and to network with other writers." Keep in touch with the MWW at facebook.com/MidwestWriters and twitter.com/MidwestWriters. **COSTS** Different packages available. Part I: Intensive session (1 day, Thursday only: $150; Part II: Thursday evening-Saturday night: $275; Part I and Part II Package: $375. Most meals included. **ADDITIONAL INFORMATION** Offers scholarships. See website for more information.

☺ SPACE (SMALL PRESS AND ALTERNATIVE COMICS EXPO)

Back Porch Comics, P.O. Box 20550, Columbus OH 43220. **E-mail:** bpc13@earthlink.net. **Website:** www.backporchcomics.com/space.htm. **COSTS** Admission: $5 per day or $8 for weekend. **ADDITIONAL INFORMATION** For brochure, visit website. Editors participate in conference.

WESTERN RESERVE WRITERS & FREELANCE CONFERENCE

7700 Clocktower Dr., Kirtland OH 44094. (440) 525-7812. **E-mail:** deencr@aol.com. **Website:** www.deannaadams.com. **Contact:** Deanna Adams, director/conference coordinator. Estab. 1983. 2014 conference is September 27, 2014. **COSTS** $105-125, depending on when you register. **ADDITIONAL INFORMATION** Brochures for the conferences are available by January (for spring conference) and July (for fall). Also accepts inquiries by e-mail and phone. Check Deanna Adams' website for all updates. Editors and agents often attend the conferences.

WOMEN WRITERS WINTER RETREAT

Homestead House B&B, 38111 West Spaulding, Willoughby OH 44094. (440)946-1902. **E-mail:** deencr@aol.com. **Website:** www.deannaadams.com. Estab. 2007. **COSTS** 2014 rates: Single room: $305; shared room: $225 (includes complete weekend package, with bed-and-breakfast stay and all meals and workshops); weekend commute: $155; Saturday only: $120 (prices include lunch and dinner). Check website for 2015 rates. **ADDITIONAL INFORMATION** Brochures for the writers retreat are available by December. Accepts inquiries and reservations by e-mail or phone. See Deanna's website for additional information and updates.

WRITE-TO-PUBLISH CONFERENCE

WordPro Communication Services, 9118 W. Elmwood Dr., Suite 1G, Niles IL 60714-5820. (847)296-3964. **Fax:** (847)296-0754. **E-mail:** lin@writetopublish.com. **Website:** www.writetopublish.com. **Contact:** Lin Johnson, director. Estab. 1971. **COSTS** 2014 rates: Full conference; $475 (includes conference and banquet); daily fee: $135 (includes all sessions for that day, 1 ms evaluation, and break refreshments). **ACCOMMODATIONS** In campus residence halls. Cost is approximately $300-385. **ADDITIONAL INFORMATION** Optional ms evaluation available. College credit available. Conference information available in January. For details, visit website, or e-mail brochure@writetopublish.com. Accepts inquiries by e-mail, fax, phone.

NORTH CENTRAL

INTERNATIONAL MUSIC CAMP CREATIVE WRITING WORKSHOP

111-11th Ave. SW, Minot ND 58701. (701)838-8472. **Fax:** (701)838-1351. **E-mail:** info@internationalmusiccamp.com. **Website:** www.internationalmusiccamp.com. **Contact:** Christine Baumann and Tim Baumann, camp directors. Estab. 1956. **COSTS** $395, includes tuition, room and board. Early bird registration (postmarked by May 1) $370. **ACCOMMODATIONS** Airline and depot shuttles are available upon request. Housing is included in the fee. **ADDITIONAL INFORMATION** Conference information is available on the website. Welcomes questions via e-mail.

UW-MADISON WRITERS' INSTITUTE

21 North Park St., Room 7331, Madison WI 53715. (608)265-3972. **Fax:** (608)265-2475. **E-mail:** lscheer@dcs.wisc.edu. **Website:** www.uwwritersinstitute.org. **Contact:** Laurie Scheer. Estab. 1989. **COSTS** 2014 rates: $180-280; includes materials, breaks. See website for 2015 rates. **ACCOMMODATIONS** Provides a list of area hotels or lodging options. **ADDITIONAL INFORMATION** Sponsors contest.

WISCONSIN BOOK FESTIVAL

Madison Public Library, 201 W. Mifflin St., Madison WI 53703. (608)266-6300. **E-mail:** bookfest@

mplfoundation.org. **Website:** www.wisconsinbook
festival.org. Estab. 2002.

COSTS All festival events are free.

SOUTH CENTRAL

ASPEN SUMMER WORDS LITERARY FESTIVAL & WRITING RETREAT

Aspen Writers' Foundation, 110 E. Hallam St., #116,
Aspen CO 81611. (970)925-3122. **Fax:** (970)925-5700.
E-mail: info@aspenwriters.org. **Website:** www.as
penwriters.org. **Contact:** Natalie Lacy, programs coordinator. Estab. 1976.

COSTS Check website each year for updates.

ACCOMMODATIONS Discount lodging at the
conference site will be available. 2015 rates to be announced (see website). Free shuttle around town.

CRESTED BUTTE WRITERS CONFERENCE

P.O. Box 1361, Crested Butte CO 81224. **E-mail:** coor
dinator@conf.crestedbuttewriters.org. **Website:** www
.crestedbuttewriters.org/conf.php. **Contact:** Barbara
Crawford or Theresa Rizzo, co-coordinators. Estab.
2006.

COSTS $330 nonmembers; $300 members; $297 Early
Bird; The Sandy Writing Contest Finalist $280; and
groups of 5 or more $280.

ACCOMMODATIONS The conference is held at The
Elevation Hotel, located at the Crested Butte Mountain Resort at the base of the ski mountain (Mt. Crested Butte, CO). The quaint historic town lies nestled
in a stunning mountain valley 3 short miles from the
resort area of Mt. Crested Butte. A free bus runs frequently between the 2 towns. The closest airport is
30 miles away, in Gunnison, CO. Our website lists 3
lodging options besides rooms at the event facility. All
condos, motels, and hotel options offer special conference rates. No special travel arrangements are made
through the conference; however, information for car
rental from Gunnison airport or the Alpine Express
shuttle is listed on the conference FAQ page.

ADDITIONAL INFORMATION "Our conference
workshops address a wide variety of writing craft and
business. Our most popular workshop is Our First
Pages Readings—with a twist. Agents and editors
read opening pages volunteered by attendees—with
a few best-selling authors' openings mixed in. Think
the A/E can identify the bestsellers? Not so much.
Each year one of our attendees has been mistaken for
a bestseller and obviously garnered requests from

some on the panel. Agents attending: Carlie Webber—CK Webber Associates and TBDs. The agents
will be speaking and available for meetings with attendees through our Pitch and Pages system. Editors
attending: Christian Trimmer, senior editor at Disney
Hyperion Books, and Jessica Williams of HarperCollins. Award-winning authors: Mark Coker, CEO of
Smashwords; Kristen Lamb, social media guru, Kim
Killion, book cover designer; Jennifer Jakes; Sandra
Kerns; and Annette Elton. Writers may request additional information by e-mail."

KINDLING WORDS WEST

Website: www.kindlingwords.org. "Annual week
long workshop at Mountain Thunder Lodge, Breck-
enridge, CO."

COST 2014 rate: $415. Check website for 2015 rate.

⊕ MISSOURI WRITERS' GUILD CONFERENCE

St. Louis MO **E-mail:** mwgconferenceinfo@gmail
.com. **Website:** www.missouriwritersguild.org. **Contact:** Tricia Sanders, vice president/conference chair-
man.

ADDITIONAL Information The primary contact individual changes every year, because the conference
chair changes every year. See the website for contact
info.

NATIONAL WRITERS ASSOCIATION FOUNDATION CONFERENCE

10940 S. Parker Rd., #508, Parker CO 80138. (303)841-
0246. **E-mail:** natlwritersassn@hotmail.com. **Website:** www.nationalwriters.com. **Contact:** Sandy
Whelchel, executive director. Estab. 1926.

COSTS Approximately $100.

ADDITIONAL INFORMATION Awards for previous contests will be presented at the conference. Bro-
chures/guidelines are online, or send an SASE.

NETWO WRITERS CONFERENCE

Northeast Texas Writers Organization, P.O. Box 411,
Winfield TX 75493. (469)867-2624 or Paul at (903)573-
6084. **E-mail:** jimcallan@winnsboro.com. **Website:**
www.netwo.org. Estab. 1987.

COSTS $60+ (discount offered for early registration).

ACCOMMODATIONS "We have posted information on lodging—motels and hotels—online. As the
conference has moved to the Mount Pleasant Civic
Center, we no longer have the 'dorm accommodations'
available in 2011 and before. The NETWO Writers

Conference is at the Mount Pleasant Civic Center, in Mt. Pleasant, Texas. Located on U.S. Business 271 just 1 block south of Interstate 30, it is easily accessible from north, south, east, and west. It offers excellent facilities: climate control, large rooms, excellent sound systems, ability to handle Power Point presentations, ample room for the on-site lunch which is part of the conference, improved restroom facilities, and private rooms for the one-on-one interviews with agents, editor and publisher. There is ample parking available. Several motels are within 2 blocks.

ADDITIONAL INFORMATION Conference is co-sponsored by the Texas Commission on the Arts. See website for current updates.

NIMROD ANNUAL WRITERS' WORKSHOP

800 S. Tucker Dr., Tulsa OK 74104. (918)631-3080. **E-mail:** nimrod@utulsa.edu. **Website:** www.utulsa.edu/nimrod. **Contact:** Eilis O'Neal, editor-in-chief. Estab. 1978.

COSTS Approximately $50. Lunch provided. Scholarships available for students.

ADDITIONAL INFORMATION *Nimrod International Journal* sponsors *Nimrod* Literary Awards: The Katherine Anne Porter Prize for fiction and The Pablo Neruda Prize for poetry. Poetry and fiction prizes: $2,000 each and publication (1st prize); $1,000 each and publication (2nd prize). Deadline: must be postmarked no later than April 30.

NORTHERN COLORADO WRITERS CONFERENCE

108 East Monroe Dr., Fort Collins CO 80525. (970)556-0908. **E-mail:** kerrie@northerncoloradowriters.com. **Website:** www.northerncoloradowriters.com. Estab. 2006.

COSTS $295-480, depending on what package the attendee selects and whether the attendee is a member or nonmember.

ACCOMMODATIONS The conference is hosted at the Fort Collins Hilton, where rooms are available at a special rate.

ROCKY MOUNTAIN FICTION WRITERS COLORADO GOLD

Rocky Mountain Fiction Writers, P.O. Box 735, Confier CO 80433. **E-mail:** conference@rmfw.org. **Website:** www.rmfw.org. Estab. 1982. 2014 conference is September 5-7, 2014.

COSTS Through July 31: $315 (members), $345 (nonmembers); through August: $325 (members), $365

(nonmembers); walk-in rate: $350 (members), $395 (nonmembers).

ACCOMMODATIONS Special rates will be available at conference hotel.

ADDITIONAL INFORMATION Editor-conducted workshops are limited to 8 participants for critique, with auditing available. Pitch appointments available at no charge. Friday morning master classes available. Craft workshops include beginner through professional levels. Writers' retreat available immediately following conference; space is limited.

ROMANCE WRITERS OF AMERICA NATIONAL CONFERENCE

14615 Benfer Road, Houston TX 77069. (832)717-5200. **Fax:** (832)717-5201. **E-mail:** info@rwa.org. **Website:** www.rwa.org/conference. Estab. 1981.

"The RWA Conference is *the* place where career-focused romance writers meet, mingle, and get down to the business of being an author."

COSTS $385-610 depending on your membership status as well as when you register.

ADDITIONAL INFORMATION Annual RTA awards are presented for romance authors. Annual Golden Heart awards are presented for unpublished writers. Numerous literary agents are in attendance to meet with writers and hear book pitches.

STORY WEAVERS CONFERENCE

Oklahoma Writer's Federation, (405)682-6000. **E-mail:** president@owfi.org. **Website:** www.OWFI.org. **Contact:** Linda Apple, president.

"The theme of our conference is to create good stories with strong bones. We will be exploring cultural writing and cultural sensitivity in writing. This year we will also be looking at the cutting edge of publishing and the options it is producing."

COSTS Cost is $150 before April. $175 after April. Cost includes awards banquet and famous author banquet. Three extra sessions are available for an extra fee: How to Self-Publish Your Novel on Kindle, Nook, and iPad (and make more money than being published by New York), with Dan Case; When Polar Bear Wishes Came True: Understanding and Creating Meaningful Stories, with Jack Dalton; How to Create Three-Dimensional Characters, with Steven James.

ACCOMMODATIONS The conference is at the Embassy Suite and uses their meeting halls. There are very few stairs and the rooms are close together for easy access.

ADDITIONAL INFORMATION "We have 20 speakers, 5 agents, and 9 publisher/editors. For a full list and bios; please see website."

SUMMER WRITING PROGRAM

Naropa University, 2130 Arapahoe Ave., Boulder CO 80302. (303)245-4862. **Fax:** (303)546-5287. **E-mail:** swpr@naropa.edu. **Website:** www.naropa.edu/swp. **Contact:** Kyle Pivarnik, special projects manager. Estab. 1974.

COSTS 2014 tuition rates: $975 for credit; $500/wekk for no credit. Check website for most current rates.

ACCOMMODATIONS Housing is available at Snow Lion Apartments. Additional info is available on the housing website: naropa.edu/student-life/housing/.

ADDITIONAL INFORMATION Writers can elect to take the Summer Writing Program for noncredit, graduate, or undergraduate credit. The registration procedure varies, so consider whether or not you'll be taking the SWP for academic credit. All participants can elect to take any combination of the first, second, third, and/or fourth weeks. To request a catalog of upcoming program or to find additional information, visit naropa.edu/swp. Naropa University also welcomes participants with disabilities. Contact Andrea Rexilius at (303)546-5296 or arexilius@naropa.edu before May 15 to inquire about accessibility and disability accommodations needed to participate fully in this event.

TAOS SUMMER WRITERS' CONFERENCE

Department of English Language and Literature, MSC 03 2170, 1 University of New Mexico, Albuquerque NM 87131-0001. (505)277-5572. **Fax:** (505)277-2950. **E-mail:** taosconf@unm.edu. **Website:** www .unm.edu/~taosconf. **Contact:** Sharon Oard Warner. Estab. 1999.

COSTS Weeklong workshop registration $650, weekend workshop registration $350, master classes between $1,250 and $1,525.

ACCOMMODATIONS Held at the Sagebrush Inn and Conference Center.

TEXAS CHRISTIAN WRITERS' CONFERENCE

7401 Katy Freeway, Houston TX 77092. (713)686-7209. **E-mail:** dannywoodall@yahoo.com. **Contact:** Danny Woodall. Estab. 1990. First Baptist Church, 6038 Greenmont, Houston TX 77092. (713)686-7209. **E-mail:** marthalrogers@sbcglobal.net. **Contact:** Danny Woodall. Estab. 1990. Annual. Conference held in August. Conference duration: 1 day. Average attendance: 60-65. "Focus on all genres." Site: Held at the First Baptist Church fellowship center and classrooms.

COSTS $65 for members of IWA, $80 nonmembers, discounts for seniors (60+) and couples, meal at noon, continental breakfast and breaks.

ACCOMMODATIONS Offers list of area hotels or lodging options.

ADDITIONAL INFORMATION Open conference for all interested writers. Sponsors a contest for short fiction; categories include articles, devotionals, poetry, short story, book proposals, drama. Fees. $8-15. Agents participate in conference. (For contest information contact patav@aol.com.)

TONY HILLERMAN WRITER'S CONFERENCE

1063 Willow Way, Santa FE NM 87505. (505)471-1565. **E-mail:** wordharvest@wordharvest.com. **Website:** www.wordharvest.com. **Contact:** Jean Schaumberg, co-director. Estab. 2004. 2014 conference is November 6-8.

COSTS Full registration: $635; weekend registration: $445; Thursday only: $190; Friday only: $265; Saturday only: $315.

ACCOMMODATIONS Hilton Santa Fe Historic Plaza offers $119 single or double occupancy. Book online with the hotel.

ADDITIONAL INFORMATION Sponsors a $10,000 first mystery novel contest with St. Martin's Press. Submission deadline for the Hillerman Mystery Competition is June 1. Visit the website for more guidelines.

THE HELENE WURLITZER FOUNDATION

P.O. Box 1891, Taos NM 87571. (575)758-2413. **Fax:** (575)758-2559. **E-mail:** hwf@taosnet.com. **Website:** www.wurlitzerfoundation.org. **Contact:** Michael A. Knight, executive director. Estab. 1953. Residence duration: 3 months.

ACCOMMODATIONS "Provides individual housing in fully furnished studio/houses (casitas), rent and utility free. Artists are responsible for transportation to and from Taos, their meals, and materials for their work. Bicycles are provided upon request."

WEST

BLOCKBUSTER PLOT INTENSIVE WRITING WORKSHOPS (SANTA CRUZ)

Santa Cruz CA **E-mail:** contact@blockbusterplots .com. **Website:** www.blockbusterplots.com. **Contact:** Martha Alderson M.A. (also known as the Plot Whisperer), instructor. Estab. 2000.

COSTS $95 per day.

ACCOMMODATIONS Provides list of area hotels and lodging options.

ADDITIONAL INFORMATION Brochures available by e-mail or on website. Accepts inquiries by e-mail.

CALIFORNIA CRIME WRITERS CONFERENCE

E-mail: sistersincrimela@gmail.com. **Website:** www. ccwconference.org. Estab. 1995. Co-sponsored by Sisters in Crime/Los Angeles and the Southern California Chapter of Mystery Writers of America.

○ This event happens every other year in odd-numbered years.

DESERT DREAMS CONFERENCE: REALIZING THE DREAM

P.O. Box 27407, Tempe AZ 85285. **E-mail:** desert dreams@desertroserwa.org; desertdreamsconfer ence@gmail.com. **Website:** www.desertroserwa.org. **Contact:** Conference coordinator. Estab. 1986.

COSTS Vary each year; approximately $200-235 for full conference.

ACCOMMODATIONS Hotels may vary for each conference; it is always a resort location in the Phoenix area.

ADDITIONAL INFORMATION Sponsors contest as part of conference, open to conference attendees only. For brochure, inquiries, contact by e-mail, phone, fax, mail, or visit website. Agents and editors participate in conference.

LAS VEGAS WRITERS CONFERENCE

Henderson Writers' Group, 614 Mosswood Dr., Henderson NV 89015. (702)564-2488 or, toll-free, (866)869-7842. **E-mail:** marga614@mysticpublishers .com. **Website:** www.lasvegaswritersconference.com.

COSTS 2014 rates: $425 until January 14, 2014; $475 starting January 15, 2014; $500 at door; $300 for 1 day. Check website for 2015 rates.

ADDITIONAL INFORMATION Sponsors contest. Agents and editors participate in conference.

MENDOCINO COAST WRITERS CONFERENCE

1211 Del Mar Dr., Fort Bragg CA 95437; P.O. Box 2087, Fort Bragg CA 95437. (707)485-4032. **E-mail:** info@ mcwc.org. **Website:** www.mcwc.org. Estab. 1988. "Our three-day conference, held at the Mendocino Coast campus of the College of the Redwoods, runs Thursday through Saturday each year. Participants choose from classes taught by experienced faculty, many of whom are highly regarded published authors. Each morning you will attend an in-depth workshop in the field of your choice taught by the same faculty member each day. The afternoon sessions include a variety of lectures and panels to choose from. The conference fee includes breakfasts, lunches, and two evening dinners."

COSTS $525+ (includes panels, meals, 2 socials with guest readers, 4 public events, 3 morning intensive workshops in 1 of 6 subjects, and a variety of afternoon panels and lectures).

ACCOMMODATIONS Information on overnight accommodations is made available.

ADDITIONAL INFORMATION Emphasis is on writers who are also good teachers. Registration opens March 15. Send inquiries via e-mail.

NAPA VALLEY WRITERS' CONFERENCE

Napa Valley College, 1088 College Ave., St. Helena CA 94574. (707)967-2900, x1611. **E-mail:** writecon@napa valley.edu. **Website:** www.napawritersconference.org. **Contact:** John Leggett and Anne Evans, program directors. Estab. 1981.

○ On Twitter as @napawriters and on Facebook as facebook.com/napawriters.

COSTS Total participation fee is $900. More cost info (including financial assistance info) is online.

ADDITIONAL INFORMATION The conference is held at the Upper Valley Campus of Napa Valley College, located in the heart of California's Wine Country. During the conference week, attendees' meals are provided by the Napa Valley Cooking School, which offers high-quality, intensive training for aspiring chefs.

OZARK CREATIVE WRITERS, INC. CONFERENCE

P.O. Box 424, Eureka Springs AR 72632. **E-mail:** ozarkcreativewriters@gmail.com. **Website:** www.ozarkcreativewriters.org. 2014 conference is October 9-11, 2014.

○ A full list of sessions and speakers is online. The conference usually has agents and/or editors in attendance to meet with writers.

COST $90-145; early bird discount available.

PACIFIC COAST CHILDREN'S WRITERS WHOLE-NOVEL WORKSHOP: FOR ADULTS AND TEENS

P.O. Box 244, Aptos CA 95001. (831)684-2042. **Website:** www.childrenswritersworkshop.com. Estab. 2003.

SAN DIEGO STATE UNIVERSITY WRITERS' CONFERENCE

SDSU College of Extended Studies, 5250 Campanile Dr., San Diego State University, San Diego CA 92182-1920. (619)594-2517. **Fax:** (619)594-8566. **E-mail:** sdsuwritersconference@mail.sdsu.edu. **Website:** ces.sdsu.edu/writers. Estab. 1984. 2015 conference is January 23-25, 2015.

○ "Whether you're a beginning writer or a published professional, the San Diego State University Writers' Conference is for you. Now in its 31st year, this writers conference is designed to help every writer at every writing level. Learn how to improve your writing skills, develop your marketing awareness, and meet with writing professionals who can facilitate the next step in your publishing career."

COSTS Approximately $399-500, depending on when you register.

ACCOMMODATIONS Attendees must make their own travel arrangements. A conference rate for attendees is available at the Doubletree Hotel.

SAN FRANCISCO WRITERS CONFERENCE

1029 Jones St., San Francisco CA 94109. (415)673-0939. **Fax:** (415)673-0367. **E-mail:** Barbara@sfwriters.org. **Website:** sfwriters.org. **Contact:** Barbara Santos, marketing director. Estab. 2003. 2015 conference is February 12-15, 2015.

COSTS 2015 rate: $550-795, depending on when you register. Optional "Speed Dating for Agents" event: $50-60.

ACCOMMODATIONS The Intercontinental Mark Hopkins Hotel is a historic landmark at the top of Nob Hill in San Francisco. The hotel is located so that everyone arriving at the Oakland or San Francisco airport can take BART to either the Embarcadero or Powell Street exits, then walk or take a cable car or taxi directly to the hotel.

ADDITIONAL INFORMATION "Present yourself in a professional manner and the contacts you make will be invaluable to your writing career. Brochures and registration are online."

◎ SOCIETY OF CHILDREN'S BOOK WRITERS & ILLUSTRATORS ANNUAL SUMMER CONFERENCE ON WRITING AND ILLUSTRATING FOR CHILDREN

8271 Beverly Blvd., Los Angeles CA 90048-4515. (323)782-1010. **Fax:** (323)782-1892. **E-mail:** scbwi@scbwi.org. **Website:** www.scbwi.org. Estab. 1972. 2014 conference is August 1-4, 2014.

COSTS Approximately $450 (does not include hotel room).

ACCOMMODATIONS Information on overnight accommodations is made available.

ADDITIONAL INFORMATION Ms and illustration critiques are available. Brochure/guidelines are available in June online or for SASE.

SQUAW VALLEY COMMUNITY OF WRITERS

P.O. Box 1416, Nevada City CA 95959-1416. (530)470-8440. **E-mail:** info@squawvalleywriters.org. **Website:** www.squawvalleywriters.org. **Contact:** Brett Hall Jones, executive director. Estab. 1969. Annual conference held in July. Conference duration: 7 days. Average attendance: 124.

○ "Writers workshops in fiction, nonfiction, and memoir assist talented writers by exploring the art and craft as well as the business of writing." Offerings include daily morning workshops led by writer-teachers, editors, or agents of the staff, each limited to 12-13 participants; seminars; panel discussions of editing and publishing; craft colloquies; lectures; and staff readings. Past themes and panels included: "Personal History in Fiction, Narrative Structure, Promise and Premise: Recognizing Subject"; "The Nation of Narrative Prose: Telling the Truth in Memoir and Personal Essay"; and "Anatomy of a Short Story." The workshops are held in a ski lodge at the foot of Squaw Valley. Literary agent speakers have recently included Michael Carlisle, Henry Dunow, Susan Golomb, Joy Harris, B.J. Robbins, Janet Silver, and Peter Steinberg. Agents will be speaking and available for meetings with attendees.

COSTS Tuition is $995, which includes 6 dinners.

ACCOMMODATIONS The Community of Writers rents houses and condominiums in the Valley for participants to live in during the week of the conference. Single room (1 participant): $700/week. Double room (twin beds, room shared by conference participant of the same sex): $465/week. Multiple room (bunk beds, room shared with 2 or more participants of the same sex): $295/week. All rooms subject to availability; early requests are recommended. Can arrange airport shuttle pickups for a fee.

ADDITIONAL INFORMATION Admissions are based on submitted ms (unpublished fiction, 1 or 2 stories or novel chapters); requires $35 reading fee. Submit ms to Brett Hall Jones, Squaw Valley Community of Writers, P.O. Box 1416, Nevada City, CA 95959. Brochures are available online or for a SASE in February. Send inquiries via e-mail. Accepts inquiries by SASE, e-mail, phone. Agents and editors attend/participate in conferences.

TMCC WRITERS' CONFERENCE

Truckee Meadows Community College, 5270 Neil Rd., Reno NV 89502. (775)829-9010. **Fax:** (775)829-9032. **E-mail:** wdce@tmcc.edu. **Website:** wdce.tmcc.edu. Estab. 1991.

COSTS $119 for a full-day seminar; $32 for a 10-minute one-on-one appointment with an agent or editor.

ACCOMMODATIONS Contact the conference manager to learn about accommodation discounts.

ADDITIONAL INFORMATION "The conference is open to all writers, regardless of their level of experience. Brochures are available online and mailed in January. Send inquiries via e-mail."

WRITERS@WORK CONFERENCE

P.O. Box 711191, Salt Lake City UT 84171-1191. (801)996-3313. **E-mail:** jennifer@writersatwork.org. **Website:** www.writersatwork.org. Estab. 1985.

○ There are several pricing levels for this event, depending on lodging and if the attendees wants a private consultation.

COSTS $690-1,005, based on housing type and consultations.

ACCOMMODATIONS On-site housing available. Additional lodging and meal information is on the website.

WRITING AND ILLUSTRATING FOR YOUNG READERS CONFERENCE

1480 East 9400 South, Sandy UT 84093. **E-mail:** staff@wifyr.com. **Website:** www.wifyr.com. Estab. 2000. (801)422-2568. **Fax:** (801)422-0745. **Contact:** Conferences & Workshops. Estab. 2000. Annual. 5-day workshop held in June of each year. The workshop is designed for people who want to write or illustrate for children or teenagers. Participants focus on a single market during daily four-hour morning writing workshops led by published authors or illustrators. Afternoon workshop sessions include a mingle with the authors, editors, and agents. Workshop focuses on fiction for young readers: picture books, book-length fiction, fantasy/science fiction, nonfiction, mystery, illustration, and general writing. Site: Conference Center at Brigham Young University in the foothills of the Wasatch Mountain range.

○ Guidelines and registration are on the website.

COSTS Costs available online.

ACCOMMODATIONS A block of rooms are available at the Best Western Cotton Tree Inn in Sandy, UT at a discounted rate. This rate is good as long as there are available rooms.

NORTHWEST

⊕ ALASKA WRITERS CONFERENCE

Alaska Writers Guild, P.O. Box 670014, Chugiak AK 99567. **E-mail:** bahartman@me.com; alaskawritersguild.awg@gmail.com. **Website:** alaskawritersguild.com. **Contact:** Brooke Hartman.

○ Ms critiques available. Note also that the AWG has many events and meetings each year in addition to the annual conference.

COSTS Up to $290, though discounts for different memberships bring down that number.

ACCOMMODATIONS Crowne Plaza Hotel in Anchorage. Conference room rates available. Several scholarships are available (see the website).

CLARION WEST WRITERS WORKSHOP

P.O. Box 31264, Seattle WA 98103-1264. (206)322-9083. **E-mail:** info@clarionwest.org. **Website:** www

.clarionwest.org. **Contact:** Nelle Graham, workshop director. "Students write their own stories every week while preparing critiques of all the other students' work for classroom sessions. This gives participants a more focused, professional approach to their writing. The core of the workshop remains speculative fiction, and short stories (not novels) are the focus." Conference information available in fall. For brochure/guidelines send SASE, visit website, e-mail or call. Accepts inquiries by e-mail, phone, SASE. Limited scholarships are available, based on financial need.

COSTS $3,600 (for tuition, housing, most meals). Limited scholarships are available based on financial need.

ACCOMMODATIONS Students stay on-site in workshop housing, at one of the University of Washington's sorority houses. Students must submit 20-30 pages of ms with 4-page biography and $40 fee ($30 if received prior to February 10) for applications sent by mail or e-mail to qualify for admission.

ADDITIONAL INFORMATION This is a critique-based workshop. Students are encouraged to write a story every week; the critique of student material produced at the workshop forms the principal activity of the workshop. Students and instructors critique mss as a group. Conference guidelines are available for a SASE. Visit the website for updates and complete details.

FLATHEAD RIVER WRITERS CONFERENCE

P.O. Box 7711, Kalispell MT 59904-7711. (406)881-4066. **E-mail:** answers@authorsoftheflathead.org. **Website:** www.authorsoftheflathead.org/conference. asp. Estab. 1990.

COSTS Check website regularly for updates on rates.

ACCOMMODATIONS Discount rates at hotel are available; check website.

ADDITIONAL INFORMATION Check website for additional speakers and other details. Register early as seating is limited.

HEDGEBROOK

P.O. Box 1231, Freeland WA 98249-9911. (360)321-4786. **Fax:** (360)321-2171. **Website:** www.hedgebrook. org. **Contact:** Vito Zingarelli, residency director. Estab. 1988. "Hedgebrook is a global community of women writers and people who seek extraordinary books, poetry, plays, films, and music by women. A literary nonprofit, our mission is to support visionary women writers whose stories and ideas shape our culture now and for generations to come. We offer writing residencies, master classes, and salons at our 25-year-old retreat on Whidbey Island, and public programs that connect writers with readers and audiences around the world."

This residency program takes applications 6 months in advance. For example, you can apply for a 2015 residency in June 2014.

ADDITIONAL INFORMATION Go online for more information.

KACHEMAK BAY WRITERS CONFERENCE

Kenai Peninsula College, Kachemak Bay Campus, 533 East Pioneer Ave., Homer AK 99603. **E-mail:** iy conf@uaa.alaska.edu. **Website:** writersconference. homer.alaska.edu.

Previous keynote speakers have included Dave Barry, Amy Tan, Jeffrey Eugenides, and Anne Lamott.

COSTS $395 from May 3-June 12; $450 June 13 and after. Some scholarships available; see the website.

ACCOMMODATIONS HOMER is 225 miles south of Anchorage, Alaska, on the southern tip of the Kenai Peninsula and the shores of Kachemak Bay. There are multiple hotels in the area.

OREGON CHRISTIAN WRITERS SUMMER CONFERENCE

Red Lion Hotel on the River, 909 N. Hayden Island Dr., Portland OR 97217-8118. **E-mail:** summerconf@ oregonchristianwriters.org. **Website:** www.oregon christianwriters.org. **Contact:** Lindy Jacobs, OCW summer conference director. Estab. 1989.

COSTS Check website for fall conference rates.

ACCOMMODATIONS Conference is held at the Red Lion on the River Hotel. Conferees wishing to stay at the hotel must make a reservation through the hotel. Some conferees commute. A block of rooms has been reserved at the hotel at a special rate for conferees and held until mid-July. The hotel reservation link will be posted on the website in late spring. Shuttle bus transportation will be provided by the hotel for conferees from Portland Airport (PDX) to the hotel, which is 20 minutes away.

ADDITIONAL INFORMATION Conference details will be posted online beginning in January. All conferees are welcome to attend the Cascade Awards ceremony, which takes place Wednesday evening during the conference. For more information about the Cascade Writing Contest, please check the website.

OUTDOOR WRITERS ASSOCIATION OF AMERICA ANNUAL CONFERENCE

615 Oak St., Suite 201, Missoula MT 59801. (406)728-7434. **E-mail:** info@owaa.org. **Website:** owaa.org. **Contact:** Jessica Pollett, conference and membership coordinator. 2015 conference is June 26-28 in Knoxville, TN. Check website for 2015 information as it becomes available.

PACIFIC NORTHWEST WRITER ASSOCIATION SUMMER WRITER'S CONFERENCE

PMB 2717, 1420 NW Gilman Blvd., Suite 2, Issaquah WA 98027. (425)673-2665. **E-mail:** pnwa@pnwa.org. **Website:** www.pnwa.org.
COST 2014 rates: $425 (members); $525 (nonmembers). Check website for 2015 rates.

SOUTH COAST WRITERS CONFERENCE

Southwestern Oregon Community College, P.O. Box 590, 29392 Ellensburg Ave., Gold Beach OR 97444. (541)247-2741. **Fax:** (541)247-6247. **E-mail:** scwc@socc.edu. **Website:** www.socc.edu/scwriters. Estab. 1996.
ADDITIONAL INFORMATION See website for cost and additional details.

WHIDBEY ISLAND WRITERS' CONFERENCE

P.O. Box 1289, Langley WA 98260. **E-mail:** admin@nila.edu; wiwc@nila.edu. **Website:** www.nila.edu/wiwc. 2014 conference is October 24-26, 2014.

○ Whether you are a beginning writer or a professional, the Whidbey Island Writers Conference is organized to help you further your knowledge in craft, publishing, and marketing. There are ms critiques, pitching sessions, and "Write Night Parties."

COST $300-365, depending on membership and when you register.

WILLAMETTE WRITERS CONFERENCE

2108 Buck St., West Linn OR 97068. (503)305-6729. **Fax:** (503)344-6174. **Website:** www.willamettewriters.com/wwc/3. Estab. 1981. 2014 conference is August 1-3, 2014.

○ Over 50 literary agents and editors, plus Hollywood film managers, agents, and producers, will be on hand in 2013 to listen to your ideas.

"We'll be bringing back some of the most respected and reputable names in the industry."
COSTS Pricing schedule available online.
ACCOMMODATIONS If necessary, arrangements can be made on an individual basis through the conference hotel. Special rates may be available. 2014 location is the Lloyd Center DoubleTree Hotel.
ADDITIONAL INFORMATION Brochure/guidelines are available for a 8½×11 SASE.

CANADA

○ BOOMING GROUND ONLINE WRITERS STUDIO

Buch E-462, 1866 Main Mall, UBC, Vancouver BC V6T 1Z1 Canada. **Fax:** (604)648-8848. **E-mail:** contact@boomingground.com. **Website:** www.boomingground.com. **Contact:** Robin Evans, director.

○ SASKATCHEWAN FESTIVAL OF WORDS

217 Main St. N., Moose Jaw SK S6J 0W1 Canada. **Website:** www.festivalofwords.com. Estab. 1997.
ACCOMMODATIONS Information available at www.templegardens.sk.ca, campgrounds, and bed-and-breakfast establishments. Complete information about festival presenters, events, costs, and schedule also available on website.

○ THE SCHOOL FOR WRITERS FALL WORKSHOP

The Humber School for Writers, Humber Institute of Technology & Advanced Learning, 3199 Lake Shore Blvd. W., Toronto ON M8V 1K8 Canada. (416)675-6622. **E-mail:** antanas.sileika@humber.ca; hilary.higgins@humber.ca. **Website:** www.humber.ca/scapa/programs/school-writers.
COSTS around $850 (in 2014). Some limited scholarships are available.
ADDITIONAL INFORMATION Accepts inquiries by e-mail, phone, and fax.

INTERNATIONAL

○ ART WORKSHOPS IN GUATEMALA

4758 Lyndale Ave. S, Minneapolis MN 55419-5304. (612)825-0747. **E-mail:** info@artguat.org. **Website:** www.artguat.org. **Contact:** Liza Fourre, director. Estab. 1995.
COSTS See website. Includes tuition, lodging, breakfast, ground transportation.

ACCOMMODATIONS All transportation and accommodations included in price of conference.

ADDITIONAL INFORMATION Conference information available now. For brochure/guidelines visit website, e-mail, or call. Accepts inquiries by e-mail, phone.

◉➕◎ BREAD LOAF IN SICILY WRITERS' CONFERENCE

Middlebury College, Middlebury VT 05753. (802)443-5286. **Fax:** (802)443-2087. **E-mail:** ncargill@middlebury.edu; BLSICILY@middlebury.edu. **Website:** www.middlebury.edu/blwc/SICILY. **Contact:** Michael Collier, director. Estab. 2011. "This intensive program will provide a small group of writers with a concentrated and personalized Bread Loaf experience."

COSTS $2,790 includes tuition, housing.

ACCOMMODATIONS Hotel Villa San Giovanni in Erice, Sicily (western coast of the island).

◉ BYRON BAY WRITERS FESTIVAL

Northern Rivers Writers' Centre, P.O. Box 1846, 69 Johnson St., Byron Bay NSW 2481 Australia. 040755-2441. **E-mail:** jeni@nrwc.org.au. **Website:** www.byronbaywritersfestival.com. **Contact:** Jeni Caffin, director. Estab. 1997. "The focus of the program is firmly on Australian writing, with recognition of our physical place in the world through the inclusion of Indonesian and Asian authors. The Byron Bay Writers' Festival enjoys a close relationship with the Ubud Writers and Readers Festival and believes that through words and ideas, bridges are formed that cross cultures and schisms. Fundamentally, the Festival provides a forum for intelligent discussion and guests are invited to address the issues that matter to them as writers and which necessarily concern us all. It is a celebration of the vitality of thought and creativity with a healthy emphasis on fun."

COSTS See costs online under Tickets. Discounts available for early bird registration, NRWC members and students, kids.

➕◉◎ INTERNATIONAL WOMEN'S FICTION FESTIVAL

Via Cappuccini 8E, Matera 75100 Italy. (39)0835-312044. **Fax:** (39)0835-312093. **E-mail:** e.jennings@ womensfictionfestival.com. **Website:** www.womensfictionfestival.com. **Contact:** Elizabeth Jennings. Estab. 2004.

○ Numerous literary agents and editors are in attendance, both from the United States as well as Italy.

COSTS 220 euros.

ACCOMMODATIONS Le Monacelle, a restored 17th-century convent. A paid shuttle is available from the Bari Airport to the hotel in Matera.

➕ SALT CAY WRITERS RETREAT

Salt Cay Bahamas. (732)267-6449. **E-mail:** admin@ saltcaywritersretreat.com. **Website:** www.saltcaywritersretreat.com. **Contact:** Karen Dionne and Christopher Graham. 2014 retreat is October 20-25, 2014.

○ Individualized instruction from best-selling authors, top editors, and literary agents; dolphin swim; built-in scheduled writing time; evening gatherings with student and author readings; closing festivities including authentic Bahamian feast. All sleeping rooms at the retreat hotel are suites—share a room with a friend, or bring your spouse or family. Free or deeply discounted activities for families, including water park, water bikes, kayaks, dolphin and sea lion encounters, snorkeling, scuba diving, and much more. Complimentary guest access to Atlantis Resort and Casino.

COSTS $2,950.

ACCOMMODATIONS Comfort Suites, Paradise Island, Nassau, Bahamas.

◉ WINCHESTER WRITERS' CONFERENCE, FESTIVAL AND BOOKFAIR, AND IN-DEPTH WRITING WORKSHOPS

University of Winchester, Winchester Hampshire WA S022 4NR United Kingdom. 44 (0) 1962 827238. **E-mail:** judith.heneghan@winchester.ac.uk. **Website:** www.writersfestival.co.uk.

PUBLISHERS & THEIR IMPRINTS

The publishing world is in constant transition. With all the buying, selling, reorganizing, consolidating, and dissolving, it's hard to keep publishers and their imprints straight. To help make sense of these changes, here's a breakdown of major publishers (and their divisions)—who owns whom and which imprints are under each company umbrella. Keep in mind that this information changes frequently. The website of each publisher is provided to help you keep an eye on this ever-evolving business.

HACHETTE BOOK GROUP USA

www.hachettebookgroup.com

CENTER STREET

FAITHWORDS

Jericho Books

GRAND CENTRAL PUBLISHING

5 Spot

Business Plus

Forever

Forever Yours

Grand Central Life & Style

Twelve

Vision

HACHETTE DIGITAL MEDIA

HACHETTE AUDIO

HYPERION

LITTLE, BROWN AND COMPANY

Back Bay Books

Mulholland Books

Reagan Arthur Books

LITTLE, BROWN BOOKS FOR YOUNG READERS

LB Kids

Poppy

ORBIT

Redhook

YEN PRESS

HARLEQUIN ENTERPRISES

www.harlequin.com

CARINA PRESS

HARLEQUIN
Harlequin American Romance
Harlequin Blaze
Harlequin Desire
Harlequin Heartwarming
Harlequin Historical
Harlequin Intrigue
Harlequin Kimani Romance
Harlequin KISS
Harlequin Medical Romance
Harlequin Nocturne
Harlequin Presents
Harlequin Romance
Harlequin Romantic Suspense
Harlequin Special Edition
Harlequin Superromance
Love Inspired
Love Inspired Historical
Love Inspired Suspense

HARLEQUIN HQN
Spice

HARLEQUIN KIMANI ARABESQUE

HARLEQUIN KIMANI TRU

HARLEQUIN KIMANI PRESS

HARLEQUIN TEEN

HARLEQUIN LUNA

HARLEQUIN MIRA

SILHOUETTE SPECIAL RELEASES
Silhouette Desire

Silhouette Romantic Suspense
Silhouette Special Edition

WORLDWIDE LIBRARY ROGUE ANGEL

WORLDWIDE LIBRARY WORLDWIDE MYSTERY

HARLEQUIN U.K.
Mills & Boon
Mira Ink

HARPERCOLLINS

www.harpercollins.com

HARPERCOLLINS GENERAL BOOKS GROUP
Amistad
Avon
Avon Impulse
Avon Red
Ecco
Fourth Estate
Harper
Harper Business
Harper Design
Harper Luxe
Harper Paperbacks
Harper Perennial
Harper Perennial Modern Classics
Harper Voyager
HarperAudio
HarperOne
ItBooks
William Morrow
William Morrow Trade Paperbacks

HARPERCOLLINS CHILDREN'S BOOKS
Amistad Press
Balzer & Bray
Collins
Greenwillow Books
HarperChildren's Audio

HarperCollins Children's Books

HarperCollins e-books

HarperFestival

HarperTeen

Katherine Tegen Books

Rayo

TOKYOPOP

Walden Pond Press

HARPERCOLLINS CHRISTIAN PUBLISHING

Zondervan

Thomas Nelson

HARPERCOLLINS U.K.

Avon

Blue Door

Collins Education

Collins Geo

Collins Language

Fourth Estate

Harper

Harper NonFiction

HarperAudio

HarperCollins Children's Books

HarperImpulse

The Friday Project

Voyager

William Collins

HARPERCOLLINS CANADA

Amistad

Avon Impulse

Avon Romance

Broadside Books

Ecco

Greenwillow

Harper Business

Harper Design

Harper Perennial

Harper Voyager

HarperAudio

HarperCollins Children's

HarperOne

It Books

Katherine Tegen Books

Morrow Cookbooks

Walden Pond Press

William Morrow Paperbacks

HARPERCOLLINS AUSTRALIA/NEW ZEALAND

HARPERCOLLINS INDIA

MACMILLAN US (HOLTZBRINCK)

http://us.macmillan.com

FARRAR, STRAUS AND GIROUX

North Point Press

Hill and Wang

Faber and Faber, Inc.

FSG Books for Young Readers

Sarah Crichton Books

FSG Originals

Scientific American

FIRST SECOND

FLATIRON BOOKS

HENRY HOLT & CO.

Henry Holt Books for Young Readers

Holt Paperbacks

Metropolitan Books

Times

MACMILLAN AUDIO

MACMILLAN CHILDREN'S

FSG Books for Young Readers

Feiwel & Friends

Holt Books for Young Readers

Kingfisher

Roaring Brook

Priddy Books

Starscape/Tor Teen

Square Fish

Young Listeners

Macmillan Children's Publishing Group

PICADOR

QUICK AND DIRTY TIPS

ST. MARTIN'S PRESS

Griffin

Minotaur

St. Martin's Press Paperbacks

Let's Go

Thomas Dunne Books

Truman Talley Books

TOR/FORGE BOOKS

Starscape

Tor Teen

PENGUIN GROUP (USA), INC.

www.penguingroup.com

PENGUIN ADULT DIVISION

Ace Books

Alpha Books

Amy Einhorn Books/Putnam

Avery

Berkley Books

Blue Rider Press

C.A. Press

Current

Dutton Books

Gotham Books

G.P. Putnam's Sons

HP Books

Hudson Street Press

Jeremy P. Tarcher

Jove

NAL

Pamela Dorman Books

Penguin

Penguin Press

Perigree

Plume

Portfolio

Prentice Hall Press

Riverhead

Sentinel

The Viking Press

YOUNG READERS DIVISION

Dial Books for Young Readers

Dutton Children's Books

Firebird

Frederick Warne

G.P. Putnam's Sons Books for Young Readers

Grosset & Dunlap

Nancy Paulsen Books

Philomel

Price Stern Sloan

Puffin Books

Razorbill

Speak

Viking Books for Young Readers

RANDOM HOUSE, INC. (BERTELSMANN)

www.randomhouse.com

CROWN PUBLISHING GROUP

Amphoto Books

Back Stage Books

Billboard Books

Broadway Books

Clarkson Potter

Crown

Crown Archetype

Crown Business

Crown Forum

Doubleday Religion

Harmony Books

Image Books

Potter Craft

Potter Style

Ten Speed Press

Three Rivers Press

Waterbrook Multnomah

Watson-Guptill

KNOPF DOUBLEDAY PUBLISHING GROUP

Alfred A. Knopf

Anchor Books

Doubleday

Everyman's Library

Nan A. Talese

Pantheon Books

Schocken Books

Vintage Books

RANDOM HOUSE PUBLISHING GROUP

Ballantine Books

Bantam

Del Rey/Lucas Books

Del Rey/Manga

Delacorte

Dell

The Dial Press

The Modern Library

One World

Presidio Press

Random House Trade Group

Random House Trade Paperbacks

Spectra

Spiegel and Grau

Triumph Books

Villard Books

RANDOM HOUSE CHILDREN'S BOOKS

Kids@Random (RH Children's Books)

Golden Books

Princeton Review

Sylvan Learning

RANDOM HOUSE DIGITAL PUBLISHING GROUP

Books on Tape

Fodor's Travel

Living Language

Listening Library

Random House Audio

RH Large Print

RANDOM HOUSE INTERNATIONAL

Random House Australia

Random House of Canada

The Random House Group (UK)

Random House India

Random House Mondadori (Argentina)

Random House Mondadori (Chile)

Random House Mondadori (Colombia)

Random House Mondadori (Mexico)

Random House Mondadori (Spain)

Random House Mondadori (Uruguay)

Random House Mondadori (Venezuela)

Random House New Zealand

Random House Struik (South Africa)

Transworld Ireland

Verlagsgruppe Random House

SIMON & SCHUSTER

www.simonandschuster.com

SIMON & SCHUSTER ADULT PUBLISHING

Atria Books

Beyond Words

Folger Shakespeare Library

Free Press

Gallery Books

Howard Books

Pocket Books

Scribner

Simon & Schuster

Threshold Editions

Touchstone

SIMON & SCHUSTER CHILDREN'S PUBLISHING

Aladdin

Atheneum Books for Young Readers

Bench Lane Books

Little Simon

Margaret K. McElderry Books

Paula Wiseman Books

Simon & Schuster Books for Young Readers

Simon Pulse

Simon Spotlight

SIMON & SCHUSTER AUDIO

Simon & Schuster Audio

Pimsleur

SIMON & SCHUSTER INTERNATIONAL

Simon & Schuster Australia

Simon & Schuster Canada

Simon & Schuster UK

GLOSSARY

ADVANCE. Payment by a publisher to an author prior to the publication of a book, to be deducted from the author's future royalties.

ADVENTURE STORY. A genre of fiction in which action is the key element, overshadowing characters, theme, and setting. The conflict in an adventure story is often man against nature. A secondary plot that reinforces this kind of conflict is sometimes included.

ALL RIGHTS. The rights contracted to a publisher permitting a manuscript's use anywhere and in any form, including movie and book club sales, without additional payment to the writer.

AMATEUR SLEUTH. The character in a mystery, usually the protagonist, who does the detection but is not a professional private investigator or police detective.

ANTHOLOGY. A collection of selected writings by various authors.

ASSOCIATION OF AUTHORS' REPRESENTATIVES (AAR). An organization for literary agents committed to maintaining excellence in literary representation.

AUCTION. Publishers sometimes bid against each other for the acquisition of a manuscript that has excellent sales prospects.

BACKLIST. A publisher's books not published during the current season but still in print.

BIOGRAPHICAL NOVEL. A life story documented in history and transformed into fiction through the insight and imagination of the writer. This type of novel melds the elements of biographical research and historical truth into the framework of a novel, complete with dialogue, drama, and mood. A biographical novel resembles historical fiction, save for one aspect: Characters in a historical novel may be fabricated and then placed into an authentic setting; characters in a biographical novel have actually lived.

BOOK PRODUCER/PACKAGER. An organization that may develop a book for a publisher based upon the publisher's idea or may plan all elements of a book, from its initial concept to writing and marketing strategies, and then sell the package to a book publisher and/or movie producer.

CLIFFHANGER. Fictional event in which the reader is left in suspense at the end of a chapter or episode, so that interest in the story's outcome will be sustained.

CLIP. Sample, usually from a newspaper or magazine, of a writer's published work.

CLOAK-AND-DAGGER. A melodramatic, romantic type of fiction dealing with espionage and intrigue.

COMMERCIAL. Publishers whose concern is salability, profit, and success with a large readership.

CONTEMPORARY. Material dealing with popular current trends, themes, or topics.

CONTRIBUTOR'S COPY. Copy of an issue of a magazine or published book sent to an author whose work is included.

CO-PUBLISHING. An arrangement in which the author and publisher share costs and profits.

COPYEDITING. Editing a manuscript for writing style, grammar, punctuation and factual accuracy.

COPYRIGHT. The legal right to exclusive publication, sale, or distribution of a literary work.

COVER LETTER. A brief letter sent with a complete manuscript submitted to an editor.

"COZY" (OR "TEACUP") MYSTERY. Mystery usually set in a small British town, in a bygone era, featuring a somewhat genteel, intellectual protagonist.

ELECTRONIC RIGHTS. The right to publish material electronically, either in book or short story form.

ELECTRONIC SUBMISSION. A submission of material by e-mail or on computer disk.

ETHNIC FICTION. Stories whose central characters are black, Native American, Italian-American, Jewish, Appalachian, or members of some other specific cultural group.

EXPERIMENTAL FICTION. Fiction that is innovative in subject matter and style; avant-garde, non-formulaic, usually literary material.

EXPOSITION. The portion of the story line, usually the beginning, where background information about character and setting is related.

E-ZINE. A magazine that is published electronically.

FAIR USE. A provision in the copyright law that says short passages from copyrighted material may be used without infringing on the owner's rights.

FANTASY (TRADITIONAL). Fantasy with an emphasis on magic, using characters with the ability to practice magic, such as wizards, witches, dragons, elves, and unicorns.

FANZINE. A noncommercial, small-circulation magazine usually dealing with fantasy, horror or science-fiction literature and art.

FIRST NORTH AMERICAN SERIAL RIGHTS. The right to publish material in a periodical before it appears in book form, for the first time, in the United States or Canada.

FLASH FICTION. *See* short short stories.

GALLEY PROOF. The first typeset version of a manuscript that has not yet been divided into pages.

GENRE. A formulaic type of fiction such as romance, western, or horror.

GOTHIC. This type of category fiction dates back to the late eighteenth and early nineteenth centuries. Contemporary gothic novels are characterized by atmospheric, historical settings and feature young, beautiful women who win the favor of handsome, brooding heroes—simultaneously dealing successfully with some life-threatening menace, either natural or supernatural. Gothics rely on mystery, peril, romantic relationships, and a sense of foreboding for their strong, emotional effect on the reader. A classic early gothic novel is Emily Brontë's *Wuthering Heights.*

GRAPHIC NOVEL. A book (original or adapted) that takes the form of a long comic strip or heavily illustrated story of forty pages or more, produced in paperback. Though called a novel, these can also be works of nonfiction.

HARD-BOILED DETECTIVE NOVEL. Mystery novel featuring a private eye or police detective as the protagonist; usually involves a murder. The emphasis is on the details of the crime, and the tough, unsentimental protagonist usually takes a matter-of-fact attitude toward violence.

HARD SCIENCE FICTION. Science fiction with an emphasis on science and technology.

HIGH FANTASY. Fantasy with a medieval setting and a heavy emphasis on chivalry and the quest.

HISTORICAL FICTION. A fictional story set in a recognizable period of history. As well as telling the stories of ordinary people's lives, historical fiction may involve political or social events of the time.

HORROR. Howard Phillips (H.P.) Lovecraft, generally acknowledged to be the master of the horror tale in the twentieth century and the most important American writer of this genre since Edgar Allan Poe, distinguishes horror literature from fiction based entirely on physical fear and the merely gruesome. It is that atmosphere—the creation of a particular sensation or emotional level—that, according to Lovecraft, is the most important element in the creation of horror literature. Contemporary writers enjoying considerable success in horror fiction include Stephen King, Robert Bloch, Peter Straub, and Dean Koontz.

HYPERTEXT FICTION. A fictional form, read electronically, which incorporates traditional elements of storytelling with a nonlinear plot line, in which the reader determines the direction of the story by opting for one of many author-supplied links.

IMPRINT. Name applied to a publisher's specific line (e.g. Owl, an imprint of Henry Holt).

INTERACTIVE FICTION. Fiction in book or computer-software format where the reader determines the path the story will take by choosing from several alternatives at the end of each chapter or episode.

INTERNATIONAL REPLY COUPON (IRC). A form purchased at a post office and enclosed with a letter or manuscript to an international publisher, to cover return postage costs.

JUVENILES, WRITING FOR. This includes works intended for an audience usually between the ages of two and eighteen. Categories of children's books are usually divided in this way: (1) picture books and storybooks (ages two to eight); (2) young readers or easy-to-read books (ages five to eight); (3) middle readers or middle grade (ages nine to eleven); (4) young adult books (ages twelve and up).

LIBEL. Written or printed words that defame, malign, or damagingly misrepresent a living person.

LITERARY AGENT. A person who acts for an author in finding a publisher or arranging contract terms on a literary project.

LITERARY FICTION. The general category of fiction that employs more sophisticated technique, driven as much or more by character evolution than action in the plot.

MAINSTREAM FICTION. Fiction that appeals to a more general reading audience, versus literary or genre fiction. Mainstream is more plot-driven than literary fiction and less formulaic than genre fiction.

MALICE DOMESTIC NOVEL. A mystery featuring a murder among family members, such as the murder of a spouse or a parent.

MANUSCRIPT. The author's unpublished copy of a work, usually typewritten, used as the basis for typesetting.

MASS MARKET PAPERBACK. Softcover book on a popular subject, usually around 4" × 7", directed to a general audience and sold in drugstores and groceries as well as in bookstores.

MIDDLE READER. Also called *middle grade*. Juvenile fiction for readers aged nine to eleven.

MS(S). Abbreviation for *manuscript(s)*.

MULTIPLE SUBMISSION. Submission of more than one short story at a time to the same editor. Do not make a multiple submission unless requested.

MYSTERY. A form of narration in which one or more elements remain unknown or unexplained until the end of the story. The modern mystery story contains elements of the mainstream novel: a convincing account of a character's struggle with various physical and psychological obstacles in an effort to achieve his goal, good characterization, and sound motivation.

NARRATION. The account of events in a story's plot as related by the speaker or the voice of the author.

NARRATOR. The person who tells the story, either someone involved in the action or the voice of the writer.

NEW AGE. A term including categories such as astrology, psychic phenomena, spiritual healing, UFOs, mysticism, and other aspects of the occult.

NOIR. A style of mystery involving hard-boiled detectives and bleak settings.

NOM DE PLUME. French for "pen name"; a pseudonym.

NONFICTION NOVEL. A work in which real events and people are written [about] in novel form, but are not camouflaged, as they are in the roman à clef. In the nonfiction novel, reality is presented imaginatively; the writer imposes a novelistic structure on the actual events, keying sections of narrative around moments that are seen (in retrospect) as symbolic. In this way, he creates a coherence that the actual story might not have had. *The Executioner's Song*, by Norman Mailer, and *In Cold Blood*, by Truman Capote, are notable examples of the nonfiction novel.

NOVELLA (ALSO NOVELETTE). A short novel or long story, approximately 20,000–50,000 words.

#10 ENVELOPE. 4" × 9½" envelope, used for queries and other business letters.

OFFPRINT. Copy of a story taken from a magazine before it is bound.

ONETIME RIGHTS. Permission to publish a story in periodical or book form one time only.

OUTLINE. A summary of a book's contents, often in the form of chapter headings with a few sentences outlining the action of the story under each one; sometimes part of a book proposal.

OVER THE TRANSOM. A phrase referring to unsolicited manuscripts, or those that come in "over the transom."

PAYMENT ON ACCEPTANCE. Payment from the magazine or publishing house as soon as the decision to print a manuscript is made.

PAYMENT ON PUBLICATION. Payment from the publisher after a manuscript is printed.

PEN NAME. A pseudonym used to conceal a writer's real name.

PERIODICAL. A magazine or journal published at regular intervals.

PLOT. The carefully devised series of events through which the characters progress in a work of fiction.

POPULAR FICTION. Generally, a synonym for category or genre fiction; i.e., fiction intended to appeal to audiences for certain kinds of novels. Popular, or category, fiction is defined as such primarily for the convenience of publishers, editors, reviewers, and booksellers who must identify novels of different areas of interest for potential readers.

PRINT ON DEMAND (POD). Novels produced digitally one at a time, as ordered. Self-publishing through print on demand technology typically involves some fees for the author. Some authors use POD to create a manuscript in book form to send to prospective traditional publishers.

PROOFREADING. Close reading and correction of a manuscript's typographical errors.

PROOFS. A typeset version of a manuscript used for correcting errors and making changes, often a photocopy of the galleys.

PROPOSAL. An offer to write a specific work, usually consisting of an outline of the work and one or two completed chapters.

PROTAGONIST. The principal or leading character in a literary work.

PSYCHOLOGICAL NOVEL. A narrative that emphasizes the mental and emotional aspects of its characters, focusing on motivations and mental activities rather than on exterior events. The psychological novelist is less concerned about relating what happened than about exploring why it happened. The term is most often used to describe twentieth-century works that employ techniques such as interior monologue and stream of consciousness. Two examples of contemporary psychological novels are Judith Guest's *Ordinary People* and Mary Gordon's *The Company of Women*.

PUBLIC DOMAIN. Material that either was never copyrighted or whose copyright term has expired.

PULP MAGAZINE. A periodical printed on inexpensive paper, usually containing lurid, sensational stories or articles.

QUERY. A letter written to an editor to elicit interest in a story the writer wants to submit.

READER. A person hired by a publisher to read unsolicited manuscripts.

READING FEE. An arbitrary amount of money charged by some agents and publishers to read a submitted manuscript.

REGENCY ROMANCE. A subgenre of romance, usually set in England between 1811 and 1820.

REMAINDERS. Leftover copies of an out-of-print book, sold by the publisher at a reduced price.

REPORTING TIME. The number of weeks or months it takes an editor to report back on an author's query or manuscript.

REPRINT RIGHTS. Permission to print an already published work whose rights have been sold to another magazine or book publisher.

ROMAN À CLEF. French "novel with a key." A novel that represents actual living or historical characters and events in fictionalized form.

ROMANCE NOVEL. A type of category fiction in which the love relationship between a man and a woman pervades the plot. The story is often told from the viewpoint of the heroine, who meets a man (the hero), falls in love with him, encounters a conflict that hinders their relationship, then resolves the conflict. Romance is the overriding element in this kind of story: The couple's relationship determines the plot and tone of the book.

ROYALTIES. A percentage of the retail price paid to an author for each copy of the book that is sold.

SAE. Self-addressed envelope.

SASE. Self-addressed stamped envelope.

SCIENCE FICTION (VS. FANTASY). It is generally accepted that, to be science fiction, a story must have elements of science in either the conflict or setting (usually both). Fantasy, on the other hand, rarely utilizes science, relying instead on magic, mythological and neomythological beings, and devices and outright invention for conflict and setting.

SECOND SERIAL (REPRINT) RIGHTS. Permission for the reprinting of a work in another periodical after its first publication in book or magazine form.

SELF-PUBLISHING. In this arrangement, the author keeps all income derived from the book, but he pays for its manufacturing, production, and marketing.

SERIAL RIGHTS. The rights given by an author to a publisher to print a piece in one or more periodicals.

SERIALIZED NOVEL. A book-length work of fiction published in sequential issues of a periodical.

SETTING. The environment and time period during which the action of a story takes place.

SHORT SHORT STORY. A condensed piece of fiction, usually under 1,000 words.

SIMULTANEOUS SUBMISSION. The practice of sending copies of the same manuscript to several editors or publishers at the same time. Some editors refuse to consider such submissions.

SLANT. A story's particular approach or style, designed to appeal to the readers of a specific magazine.

SLICE OF LIFE. A presentation of characters in a seemingly mundane situation that offers the reader a flash of illumination about the characters or their situation.

SLUSH PILE. A stack of unsolicited manuscripts in the editorial offices of a publisher.

SOCIAL FICTION. Fiction written with the purpose of bringing positive changes in society.

SOFT/SOCIOLOGICAL SCIENCE FICTION. Science fiction with an emphasis on society and culture versus scientific accuracy.

SPACE OPERA. Epic science fiction with an emphasis on good guys versus bad guys.

SPECULATION (OR SPEC). An editor's agreement to look at an author's manuscript with no promise to purchase.

SPECULATIVE FICTION (SPECFIC). The all-inclusive term for science fiction, fantasy, and horror.

SUBSIDIARY. An incorporated branch of a company or conglomerate (e.g. Alfred Knopf, Inc., a subsidiary of Random House, Inc.).

SUBSIDIARY RIGHTS. All rights other than book publishing rights included in a book contract, such as paperback, book club, and movie rights.

SUBSIDY PUBLISHER. A book publisher who charges the author for the cost of typesetting, printing, and promoting a book. Also called a *vanity publisher*.

SUBTERFICIAL FICTION. Innovative, challenging, nonconventional fiction in which what seems to be happening is the result of things not so easily perceived.

SUSPENSE. A genre of fiction where the plot's primary function is to build a feeling of anticipation and fear in the reader over its possible outcome.

SYNOPSIS. A brief summary of a story, novel or play. As part of a book proposal, it is a comprehensive summary condensed in a page or page and a half.

TABLOID. Publication printed on paper about half the size of a regular newspaper page (e.g. the *National Enquirer*).

TEARSHEET. Page from a magazine containing a published story.

THEME. The dominant or central idea in a literary work; its message, moral, or main thread.

THRILLER. A novel intended to arouse feelings of excitement or suspense. Works in this genre are highly sensational, usually focusing on illegal activities, international espionage, sex, and violence. A thriller is often a detective story in which the forces of good are pitted against the forces of evil in a kill-or-be-killed situation.

TRADE PAPERBACK. A softbound volume, usually around 5" × 8", published and designed for the general public, available mainly in bookstores.

UNSOLICITED MANUSCRIPT. A story or novel manuscript that an editor did not specifically ask to see.

URBAN FANTASY. Fantasy that takes magical characters, such as elves, fairies, vampires, or wizards, and places them in modern-day settings, often in the inner city.

VANITY PUBLISHER. See subsidy publisher.

VIEWPOINT. The position or attitude of the first- or third-person narrator or multiple narrators, which determines how a story's action is seen and evaluated.

WESTERN. Genre with a setting in the West, usually between 1860 and 1890, with a formula plot about cowboys or other aspects of frontier life.

WHODUNIT. Genre dealing with murder, suspense, and the detection of criminals.

WORK-FOR-HIRE. Work that another party commissions you to do, generally for a flat fee. The creator does not own the copyright and therefore cannot sell any rights.

YOUNG ADULT (YA). The general classification of books written for readers twelve and up.

ZINE. A small, noncommercial magazine, often one- or two-person operations run from the home of the publisher/editor. Themes tend to be specialized, personal, experimental, and often controversial.

GENRE GLOSSARY

Definitions of Fiction Subcategories

The following were provided courtesy of The Extended Novel Writing Workshop, created by the staff of Writers Online Workshops (www.writersonlineworkshops.com).

MYSTERY SUBCATEGORIES

The major mystery subcategories are listed below, each followed by a brief description and the names of representative authors, so you can sample each type of work. Note that we have loosely classified "suspense/thriller" as a mystery category. While these stories do not necessarily follow a traditional "whodunit" plot pattern, they share many elements with other mystery categories.

AMATEUR DETECTIVE. As the name implies, the detective is not a professional detective (private or otherwise), but is almost always a professional something. This professional association routinely involves the protagonist in criminal cases (in a support capacity), gives him or her a special advantage in a specific case, or provides the contacts and skills necessary to solve a particular crime. (Jonathan Kellerman, Patricia Cornwell, Jan Burke)

CLASSIC MYSTERY (WHODUNIT). A crime (almost always a murder) is solved. The detective is the viewpoint character; the reader never knows any more or less about the crime than the detective, and all the clues to solving the crime are available to the reader.

COURTROOM DRAMA. The action takes place primarily in the courtroom; protagonist is generally a defense attorney out to prove the innocence of his or her client by finding the real culprit.

COZY. A special class of the amateur detective category that frequently features a female protagonist. (Agatha Christie's Miss Marple stories are the classic example.) There is less onstage violence than in other categories, and the plot is often wrapped up in a final scene where the detective identifies the murderer and explains how the crime was solved. In contemporary stories, the protagonist can be anyone from a chronically curious housewife to a mystery-buff clergyman to a college professor, but he or she is usually quirky, even eccentric. (Susan Isaacs, Andrew Greeley, Lillian Jackson Braun)

ESPIONAGE. The international spy novel is less popular since the end of the Cold War, but stories can still revolve around political intrigue in unstable regions. (John le Carré, Ken Follett)

HEISTS AND CAPERS. The crime itself is the focus. Its planning and execution are seen in detail, and the participants are fully drawn characters that may even be portrayed sympathetically. One character is the obvious leader of the group (the "brains"); the other members are often brought together by the leader specifically for this job and may or may not have a previous association. In a heist, no matter how clever or daring the characters are, they are still portrayed as criminals, and the expectation is that they will be caught and punished (but not always). A caper is more lighthearted, even comedic. The participants may have a noble goal (something other than personal gain) and often get away with the crime. (Eric Ambler, Tony Kenrick, Leslie Hollander)

HISTORICAL. May be any category or subcategory of mystery, but with an emphasis on setting, the details of which must be diligently researched. But beyond the historical details (which must never overshadow the story), the plot develops along the lines of its contemporary counterpart. (Candace Robb, Caleb Carr, Anne Perry)

JUVENILE/YOUNG ADULT. Written for the 8–12 age group (middle grade) or the 12 and up age group (young adult), the crime in these stories may or may not be murder, but it is serious. The protagonist is a kid (or group of kids) in the same age range as the targeted reader. There is no graphic violence depicted, but the stories are scary and the villains are realistic. (Mary Downing Hahn, Wendy Corsi Staub, Cameron Dokey, Norma Fox Mazer)

MEDICAL THRILLER. The plot can involve a legitimate medical threat (such as the outbreak of a virulent plague) or the illegal or immoral use of medical technology. In the former scenario, the protagonist is likely to be the doctor (or team) who identifies the virus and procures the antidote; in the latter he or she could be a patient (or the relative of a victim) who uncovers the plot and brings down the villain. (Robin Cook, Michael Palmer, Michael Crichton, Stanley Pottinger)

POLICE PROCEDURALS. The most realistic category, these stories require the most meticulous research. A police procedural may have more than one protagonist since cops rarely work alone. Conflict between partners, or between the detective and his or her superiors, is a common theme. But cops are portrayed positively as a group, even though there may be a couple of bad or ineffective law enforcement characters for contrast and conflict. Jurisdictional disputes are still popular sources of conflict as well. (Lawrence Treat, Joseph Wambaugh, Ridley Pearson, Julie Smith)

PRIVATE DETECTIVE. When described as "hard-boiled," this category takes a tough stance. Violence is more prominent, characters are darker, the detective—while almost always licensed by the state—operates on the fringes of the law, and there is often open resentment between the detective and law enforcement. More "enlightened" male detectives and a crop of contemporary females have brought about new trends in this category. (For female P.I.s: Sue Grafton, Sara Paretsky; for male P.I.s: John D. MacDonald, Lawrence Sanders)

SUSPENSE/THRILLER. Where a classic mystery is always a whodunit, a suspense/thriller novel may deal more with the intricacies of the crime, what motivated it, and how the villain (whose identity may be revealed to the reader early on) is caught and brought to justice. Novels in this category frequently employ multiple points of view and have broader scopes than more traditional murder mysteries. The crime may not even involve murder—it may be a threat to global economy or regional ecology; it may be technology run amok or abused at the hands of an unscrupulous scientist; it may involve innocent citizens victimized for personal or corporate gain. Its perpetrators are kidnappers, stalkers, serial killers, rapists, pedophiles, computer hackers, or just about anyone with an evil intention and the means to carry it out. The protagonist may be a private detective or law enforcement official, but is just as likely to be a doctor, lawyer, military officer, or other individual in a unique position to identify the villain and bring him or her to justice. (James Patterson, John J. Nance)

TECHNO-THRILLER. These are replacing the traditional espionage novel and feature technology as an integral part of not just the setting but the plot as well.

WOMAN IN JEOPARDY. A murder or other crime may be committed, but the focus is on the woman (and/or her children) currently at risk, her struggle to understand the nature of the danger, and her eventual victory over her tormentor. The protagonist makes up for her lack of physical prowess with intellect or special skills and solves the problem on her own or with the help of her family (but she runs the show). Closely related to this category is romantic suspense. But, while the heroine in a romantic suspense is certainly a "woman in jeopardy,'" the mystery or suspense element is subordinate to the romance. (Mary Higgins Clark, Mary Stewart, Jessica Mann)

ROMANCE SUBCATEGORIES

These categories and subcategories of romance fiction have been culled from the *Romance Writer's Sourcebook* (Writer's Digest Books) and Phyllis Taylor Pianka's *How to Write Romances* (Writer's Digest Books). We've arranged the "major" categories below, with the subcategories beneath them, each followed by a brief description and the names of authors who write in each category, so you can sample representative works.

CATEGORY OR SERIES. These are published in "lines" by individual publishing houses (such as Harlequin); each line has its own requirements as to word length, story content, and amount of sex. (Debbie Macomber, Nora Roberts, Glenda Sanders)

CHRISTIAN. With an inspirational Christian message centering on the spiritual dynamic of the romantic relationship and faith in God as the foundation for that relationship; sensuality is played down. (Janelle Burnham, Ann Bell, Linda Chaikin, Catherine Palmer, Dee Henderson, Lisa Tawn Bergen)

GLITZ. So called because they feature generally wealthy characters with high-powered positions in careers that are considered glamorous—high finance, modeling/acting, publishing, fashion—and are set in exciting or exotic (often metropolitan) locales, such as Monte Carlo, Hollywood, London, or New York. (Jackie Collins, Judith Krantz)

HISTORICAL. Can cover just about any historical (or even prehistorical) period. Setting in the historical is especially significant, and details must be thoroughly researched and accurately presented. For a sampling of a variety of historical styles, try Laura Kinsell (*Flowers from the Storm*), Mary Jo Putney (*The Rake and the Reformer*), and Judy Cuevas (*Bliss*). Some currently popular periods/themes in historicals are:

- **GOTHIC:** Historical with a strong element of suspense and a feeling of supernatural events, although these events frequently have a natural explanation. Setting plays an important role in establishing a dark, moody, suspenseful atmosphere. (Phyllis Whitney, Victoria Holt)
- **HISTORICAL FANTASY:** With traditional fantasy elements of magic and magical beings, frequently set in a medieval society. (Amanda Glass, Jayne Ann Krentz, Kathleen Morgan, Jessica Bryan, Taylor Quinn Evans, Carla Simpson, Karyn Monk)
- **EARLY AMERICAN:** Usually Revolution to Civil War, set in New England or the South, but "frontier" stories set in the American West are quite popular as well. (Robin Lee Hatcher, Ann Maxwell, Heather Graham)
- **NATIVE AMERICAN:** Where one or both of the characters are Native Americans; the conflict between cultures is a popular theme. (Carol Finch, Elizabeth Grayson, Karen Kay, Kathleen Harrington, Genell Dellim, Candace McCarthy)
- **REGENCY:** Set in England during the Regency period from 1811 to 1820. (Carol Finch, Elizabeth Elliott, Georgette Heyer, Joan Johnston, Lynn Collum)

MULTICULTURAL. Most currently feature African-American or Hispanic couples, but editors are looking for other ethnic stories as well. Multiculturals can be contemporary or historical and fall into any subcategory. (Rochelle Alers, Monica Jackson, Bette Ford, Sandra Kitt, Brenda Jackson)

PARANORMAL. Containing elements of the supernatural or science fiction/fantasy. There are numerous subcategories (many stories combine elements of more than one) including:

- **TIME TRAVEL:** One or more of the characters travels to another time—usually the past—to find love. (Jude Deveraux, Linda Lael Miller, Diana Gabaldon, Constance O'Day-Flannery)
- **SCIENCE FICTION/FUTURISTIC:** S/F elements are used for the story's setting: imaginary worlds, parallel universes, Earth in the near or distant future. (Marilyn Campbell, Jayne Ann Krentz, J.D. Robb [Nora Roberts], Anne Avery)
- **CONTEMPORARY FANTASY:** From modern ghost and vampire stories to "New Age" themes such as extraterrestrials and reincarnation. (Linda Lael Miller, Anne Stuart, Antoinette Stockenberg, Christine Feehan)

ROMANTIC COMEDY. Has a fairly strong comic premise and/or a comic perspective in the author's voice or the voices of the characters (especially the heroine). (Jennifer Crusie, Susan Elizabeth Phillips)

ROMANTIC SUSPENSE. With a mystery or psychological thriller subplot in addition to the romance plot. (Mary Stewart, Barbara Michaels, Tami Hoag, Nora Roberts, Linda Howard, Catherine Coulter)

SINGLE TITLE. Longer contemporaries that do not necessarily conform to the requirements of a specific romance line and therefore feature more complex plots and nontraditional characters. (Mary Ruth Myers, Nora Roberts, Kathleen Gilles Seidel, Kathleen Korbel)

YOUNG ADULT. Focus is on first love with very little, if any, sex. These can have bittersweet endings, as opposed to the traditional romance happy ending, since first loves are often lost loves. (YA historical: Nancy Covert Smith, Louise Vernon; YA contemporary: Kathryn Makris)

SCIENCE FICTION SUBCATEGORIES

Peter Heck, in his article "Doors to Other Worlds: Trends in Science Fiction and Fantasy," which appears in the 1996 edition of *Science Fiction and Fantasy Writer's Sourcebook* (Writer's Digest Books), identifies some science fiction trends that have distinct enough characteristics to be defined as categories. These distinctions are frequently the result of marketing decisions as much as literary ones, so understanding them is important in deciding where your novel idea belongs. We've supplied a brief description and the names of authors who write in each category. In those instances where the author writes in more than one category, we've included titles of appropriate representative works.

ALTERNATE HISTORY. Fantasy, sometimes with science fiction elements, that changes the accepted account of actual historical events or people to suggest an alternate view of history.

(Ted Mooney, *Traffic and Laughter*; Ward Moore, *Bring the Jubilee*; Philip K. Dick, *The Man in the High Castle*)

CYBERPUNK. Characters in these stories are tough outsiders in a high-tech, generally near-future society where computers have produced major changes in the way society functions. (William Gibson, Bruce Sterling, Pat Cadigan, Wilhelmina Baird)

HARD SCIENCE FICTION. Based on the logical extrapolation of real science to the future. In these stories the scientific background (setting) may be as, or more, important than the characters. (Larry Niven)

MILITARY SCIENCE FICTION. Stories about war that feature traditional military organization and tactics extrapolated into the future. (Jerry Pournelle, David Drake, Elizabeth Moon)

NEW AGE. A category of speculative fiction that deals with subjects such as astrology, psychic phenomena, spiritual healing, UFOs, mysticism, and other aspects of the occult. (Walter Mosley, *Blue Light*; Neil Gaiman)

SCIENCE FANTASY. Blend of traditional fantasy elements with scientific or pseudoscientific support (genetic engineering, for example, to "explain" a traditional fantasy creature like the dragon). These stories are traditionally more character driven than hard science fiction. (Anne McCaffrey, Mercedes Lackey, Marion Zimmer Bradley)

SCIENCE FICTION MYSTERY. A cross-genre blending that can either be a more-or-less traditional science fiction story with a mystery as a key plot element, or a more-or-less traditional whodunit with science fiction elements. (Philip K. Dick, Lynn S. Hightower)

SCIENCE FICTION ROMANCE. Another genre blend that may be a romance with science fiction elements (in which case it is more accurately placed as a subcategory within the romance genre) or a science fiction story with a strong romantic subplot. (Anne McCaffrey, Melanie Rawn, Kate Elliott)

SOCIAL SCIENCE FICTION. The focus is on how the characters react to their environments. This category includes social satire. (George Orwell's *1984* is a classic example.) (Margaret Atwood, *The Handmaid's Tale*; Ursula K. Le Guin, *The Left Hand of Darkness*; Marge Piercy, *Woman on the Edge of Time*)

SPACE OPERA. From the term "horse opera," describing a traditional good-guys-versus-bad-guys western, these stories put the emphasis on sweeping action and larger-than-life characters. The focus on action makes these stories especially appealing for film treatment. (The Star Wars series is one of the best examples; also Samuel R. Delany.)

STEAMPUNK. A specific type of alternate-history science fiction set in Victorian England in which characters have access to 20th-century technology. (William Gibson; Bruce Sterling, *The Difference Engine*)

YOUNG ADULT. Any subcategory of science fiction geared to a YA audience (12–18), but these are usually shorter novels with characters in the central roles who are the same age as (or slightly older than) the targeted reader. (Jane Yolen, Andre Norton)

FANTASY SUBCATEGORIES

Before we take a look at the individual fantasy categories, it should be noted that, for purposes of these supplements, we've treated fantasy as a genre distinct from science fiction. While these two are closely related, there are significant enough differences to warrant their separation for study purposes. We have included here those science fiction categories that have strong fantasy elements, or that have a significant amount of crossover (these categories appear in both the science fiction and the fantasy supplements), but "pure" science fiction categories are not included below. If you're not sure whether your novel is fantasy or science fiction, consider this definition by Orson Scott Card in *How to Write Science Fiction and Fantasy* (Writer's Digest Books): "Here's a good, simple, semi-accurate rule of thumb: If the story is set in a universe that follows the same rules as ours, it's science fiction. If it's set in a universe that doesn't follow our rules, it's fantasy. Or in other words, science fiction is about what could be but isn't; fantasy is about what couldn't be."

But even Card admits this rule is only "semi-accurate." He goes on to say that the real boundary between science fiction and fantasy is defined by how the impossible is achieved: "If you have people do some magic, impossible thing [like time travel] by stroking a talisman or praying to a tree, it's fantasy; if they do the same thing by pressing a button or climbing inside a machine, it's science fiction."

Peter Heck, in his article "Doors to Other Worlds: Trends in Science Fiction and Fantasy," which appears in the 1996 edition of the *Science Fiction and Fantasy Writer's Sourcebook* (Writer's Digest Books), does note some trends that have distinct enough characteristics to be defined as separate categories. These categories are frequently the result of marketing decisions as much as literary ones, so understanding them is important in deciding where your novel idea belongs. We've supplied a brief description and the names of authors who write in each category, so you can sample representative works.

ARTHURIAN. Reworking of the legend of King Arthur and the Knights of the Round Table. (T.H. White, *The Once and Future King*; Marion Zimmer Bradley, *The Mists of Avalon*)

CONTEMPORARY (ALSO CALLED "URBAN") FANTASY. Traditional fantasy elements (such as elves and magic) are incorporated into an otherwise recognizable modern setting. (Emma

Bull, *War for the Oaks*; Mercedes Lackey, *The SERRAted Edge*; Terry Brooks, the Word & Void series)

DARK FANTASY. Closely related to horror but generally not as graphic. Characters in these stories are the "darker" fantasy types: vampires, witches, werewolves, demons, etc. (Anne Rice; Clive Barker, *Weaveworld*, *Imajica*; Fred Chappell)

FANTASTIC ALTERNATE HISTORY. Set in an alternate historical period (in which magic would not have been a common belief) where magic works, these stories frequently feature actual historical figures. (Orson Scott Card, *Alvin Maker*)

GAME-RELATED FANTASY. Plots and characters are similar to high fantasy, but are based on a particular role-playing game. (Dungeons and Dragons; Magic: The Gathering; World of Warcraft)

HEROIC FANTASY. The fantasy equivalent to military science fiction, these are stories of war and its heroes and heroines. (Robert E. Howard, the Conan the Barbarian series; Elizabeth Moon, *Deed of Paksenarrion*; Michael Moorcock, the Elric series)

HIGH FANTASY. Emphasis is on the fate of an entire race or nation, threatened by an ultimate evil. J.R.R. Tolkien's Lord of the Rings trilogy is a classic example. (Terry Brooks, David Eddings, Margaret Weis, Tracy Hickman)

HISTORICAL FANTASY. The setting can be almost any era in which the belief in magic was strong; these are essentially historical novels where magic is a key element of the plot and/or setting. (Susan Schwartz, *Silk Roads and Shadows*; Margaret Ball, *No Earthly Sunne*; Tim Powers, *The Anubis Gates*)

JUVENILE/YOUNG ADULT. Can be any type of fantasy, but geared to a juvenile (8–12) or YA audience (12–18); these are shorter novels with younger characters in central roles. (J.K. Rowling, Christopher Paolini, C.S. Lewis)

SCIENCE FANTASY. A blend of traditional fantasy elements with scientific or pseudoscientific support (genetic engineering, for example, to "explain" a traditional fantasy creature like the dragon). These stories are traditionally more character driven than hard science fiction. (Anne McCaffrey, Mercedes Lackey, Marion Zimmer Bradley)

HORROR SUBCATEGORIES

Subcategories in horror are less well defined than in other genres and are frequently the result of marketing decisions as much as literary ones. But being familiar with the terms used to describe different horror styles can be important in understanding how your own novel might be best presented to an agent or editor. What follows is a brief description of the most commonly used terms, along with names of authors and, where necessary, representative works.

DARK FANTASY. Sometimes used as a euphemistic term for horror in general, but also refers to a specific type of fantasy, usually less graphic than other horror subcategories, that features more "traditional" supernatural or mythical beings (vampires, werewolves, zombies, etc.) in either contemporary or historical settings. (Contemporary: Stephen King, *Salem's Lot*; Thomas Tessier, *The Nightwalker*. Historical: Brian Stableford, *The Empire of Fear* and *Werewolves of London*.)

HAUNTINGS. "Classic" stories of ghosts, poltergeists, and spiritual possessions. The level of violence portrayed varies, but many writers in this category exploit the reader's natural fear of the unknown by hinting at the horror and letting the reader's imagination supply the details. (Peter Straub, *Ghost Story*; Richard Matheson, *Hell House*)

JUVENILE/YOUNG ADULT. Can be any horror style, but with a protagonist who is the same age as, or slightly older than, the targeted reader. Stories for middle grades (8–12 years old) are scary, with monsters and violent acts that might best be described as "gross," but stories for young adults (12–18) may be more graphic. (R.L. Stine, Christopher Pike, Carol Gorman)

PSYCHOLOGICAL HORROR. Features a human monster with horrific, but not necessarily supernatural, aspects. (Thomas Harris, *The Silence of the Lambs*, *Hannibal*; Dean Koontz, *Whispers*)

SPLATTERPUNK. Very graphic depiction of violence—often gratuitous—popularized in the 1980s, especially in film. (*Friday the 13th*, *Halloween*, *Nightmare on Elm Street*, etc.)

SUPERNATURAL/OCCULT. Similar to the dark fantasy, but may be more graphic in its depiction of violence. Stories feature satanic worship, demonic possession, or ultimate evil incarnate in an entity or supernatural being that may or may not have its roots in traditional mythology or folklore. (Ramsey Campbell; Robert McCammon; Ira Levin, *Rosemary's Baby*; William Peter Blatty, *The Exorcist*; Stephen King, *Pet Sematary*)

TECHNOLOGICAL HORROR. "Monsters" in these stories are the result of science run amok or technology turned to purposes of evil. (Dean Koontz, *Watchers*; Michael Crichton, *Jurassic Park*)

PROFESSIONAL ORGANIZATIONS

AGENTS' ORGANIZATIONS

ASSOCIATION OF AUTHORS' AGENTS (AAA) Johnson & Alcock Ltd. Clerkenwell House, 45-47 Clerkenwell Green, London EC1R0HT. (020)7251-0125. **E-mail:** ed@johnsonandalcock.co.uk. **Website:** www.agentsassoc.co.uk.

ASSOCIATION OF AUTHORS' REPRESENTATIVES (AAR) 676-A Ninth Ave., Suite 312, New York, NY 10036. **E-mail:** administrator@aaronline.org. **Website:** www.aar-online.org.

ASSOCIATION OF TALENT AGENTS (ATA) 9255 Sunset Blvd., Suite 930, Los Angeles, CA 90069. (310)274-0628. **Fax:** (310)274-5063. **E-mail:** rnoval@agentassociation.com. **Website:** www.agentassociation.com.

WRITERS' ORGANIZATIONS

ACADEMY OF AMERICAN POETS 75 Maiden Lane, Suite 901, New York, NY 10038. (212)274-0343. **Fax:** (212)274-9427. **E-mail:** academy@poets.org. **Website:** www.poets.org.

AMERICAN CRIME WRITERS LEAGUE (ACWL) 17367 Hilltop Ridge Dr., Eureka, MO 63205. **Email:** shirley@shirleykennett.com. **Website:** www.acwl.org.

AMERICAN MEDICAL WRITERS ASSOCIATION (AMWA) 30 W. Gude Drive, Suite 525, Rockville, MD 20850-4347. (240)238-0940. **Fax:** (301)294-9006. **E-mail:** amwa@amwa.org. **Website:** www.amwa.org.

AMERICAN SCREENWRITERS ASSOCIATION (ASA) **E-mail:** info@americanscreenwriters.com. **Website:** www.americanscreenwriters.com.

AMERICAN TRANSLATORS ASSOCIATION (ATA) 225 Reinekers Lane, Suite 590, Alexandria, VA 22314. (703)683-6100. **Fax:** (703)683-6122. **E-mail:** ata@atanet.org. **Website:** www.atanet.org.

EDUCATION WRITERS ASSOCIATION (EWA) 3516 Connecticut Avenue NW, Washington, DC 20008. (202)452-9830. **Fax:** (202)452-9837. **E-mail:** ewa@ewa.org. **Website:** www.ewa.org.

GARDEN WRITERS ASSOCIATION (GWA) 7809 FM 179, Shallowater, TX 79363. (806)832.1870. **Fax:** (806)832.5244. **E-mail:** info@gardenwriters.org. **Website:** www.gardenwriters.org.

HORROR WRITERS ASSOCIATION (HWA) 244 Fifth Ave., Suite 2767, New York, NY 10001. (917)720-6959. **E-mail:** hwa@horror.org. **Website:** www.horror.org.

THE INTERNATIONAL WOMEN'S WRITING GUILD (IWWG) 317 Madison Avenue, Suite 1704, New York, NY 10017. **Website:** www.iwwg.com.

MYSTERY WRITERS OF AMERICA (MWA) 1140 Broadway, Suite 1507, New York, NY 10001. (212)888-8171. **Fax:** (212)888-8107. **E-mail:** mwa@mysterywriters.org. **Website:** www.mysterywriters.org.

NATIONAL ASSOCIATION OF SCIENCE WRITERS (NASW) P.O. Box 7905, Berkeley, CA 94707. (510)647-9500. **E-mail:** editor@nasw.org. **Website:** www.nasw.org.

ORGANIZATION OF BLACK SCREENWRITERS (OBS) 3010 Wilshire Blvd., #269, Los Angeles, CA 90010. (323)735-2050. **Website:** www.obswriter.com.

OUTDOOR WRITERS ASSOCIATION OF AMERICA (OWAA) 615 Oak St., Ste. 201, Missoula, MT 59801. (406)728-7434. **E-mail:** info@owaa.org. **Website:** www.owaa.org.

POETRY SOCIETY OF AMERICA (PSA) 15 Gramercy Park, New York, NY 10003. (212)254-9628. **Fax:** (212)673-2352. **Website:** www.poetrysociety.org.

POETS & WRITERS 90 Broad St., Suite 2100, New York, NY 10004. (212)226-3586. **Fax:** (212)226-3963. **Website:** www.pw.org.

ROMANCE WRITERS OF AMERICA (RWA) 14615 Benfer Road, Houston, TX 77069. (832)717-5200. **E-mail:** info@rwa.org. **Website:** www.rwa.org.

SCIENCE FICTION AND FANTASY WRITERS OF AMERICA (SFWA) P.O. Box 3238, Enfield, CT 06083-3238. **Website:** www.sfwa.org.

SOCIETY OF AMERICAN BUSINESS EDITORS & WRITERS (SABEW) Walter Cronkite School of Journalism and Mass Communication, Arizona State University, 555 N. Central Ave., Suite 416, Phoenix, AZ 85004-1248 (602)496-7862. **Fax:** (602)496-7041. **E-mail:** sabew@sabew.org. **Website:** www.sabew.org.

SOCIETY OF AMERICAN TRAVEL WRITERS (SATW) 11950 W. Lake Park Drive, Suite 320, Milwaukee, WI 53224-3049. (414)359-1625. **Fax:** (414)359-1671. **E-mail:** info@satw.org. **Website:** www.satw.org.

SOCIETY OF CHILDREN'S BOOK WRITERS & ILLUSTRATORS (SCBWI) 8271 Beverly Blvd., Los Angeles, CA 90048. (323)782-1010. **Fax:** (323)782-1892. **E-mail:** scbwi@scbwi.org. **Website:** www.scbwi.org.

WESTERN WRITERS OF AMERICA (WWA) **E-mail:** wwa.moulton@gmail.com. **Website:** www.westernwriters.org.

INDUSTRY ORGANIZATIONS

AMERICAN BOOKSELLERS ASSOCIATION (ABA)
333 Westchester Avenue, Suite S202, White Plains, NY 10604. (914)406-7500. **Fax:** (914)417-4013. **E-mail:** info@bookweb.org. **Website:** www.bookweb.org.

AMERICAN SOCIETY OF JOURNALISTS & AUTHORS (ASJA) Times Square, 1501 Broadway, Suite 403, New York, NY 10036. (212)997-0947. **Website:** www.asja.org.

ASSOCIATION FOR WOMEN IN COMMUNICATIONS (AWC) 3337 Duke St., Alexandria VA 22314. (703)370-7436. **Fax:** (703)342-4311. **E-mail:** info@womcom.org. **Website:** www.womcom.org.

ASSOCIATION OF AMERICAN PUBLISHERS (AAP) 71 Fifth Ave., 2nd Floor, New York NY 10003. (212)255-0200. **Fax:** (212)255-7007. Or: 455 Massachusetts Ave. NW, Suite 700, Washington, DC 20001. (202)347-3375. **Fax:** (202)347-3690. **Website:** www.publishers.org.

THE ASSOCIATION OF WRITERS & WRITING PROGRAMS (AWP) George Mason University, 4400 University Drive, MSN 1E3, Fairfax, VA 22030. (703)993-4301. **Fax:** (703)993-4302. **E-mail:** awp@awpwriter.org. **Website:** www.awpwriter.org.

THE AUTHORS GUILD, INC., 31 E. Thirty-second St., 7th Floor, New York, NY 10016. (212)563-5904. **Fax:** (212)564-5363. **E-mail:** staff@authorsguild.org. **Website:** www.authorsguild.org.

CANADIAN AUTHORS ASSOCIATION (CAA) 6 W St. N, Suite 203, Orilla, ON L3V 5B8 Canada. (705)325-3926. **E-mail:** admin@canadianauthors.org. **Website:** www.canadianauthors.org.

CHRISTIAN BOOKSELLERS ASSOCIATION (CBA) 9240 Explorer Drive, Suite 200, Colorado Springs, CO 80920. (800)252-1950. **Fax:** (719)272-3508. **E-mail:** info@cbaonline.org. **Website:** www.cbaonline.org.

THE DRAMATISTS GUILD OF AMERICA 1501 Broadway, Suite 701, New York, NY 10036. (212)398-9366. **Fax:** (212)944-0420. **Website:** www.dramatistsguild.com.

NATIONAL LEAGUE OF AMERICAN PEN WOMEN (NLAPW) Pen Arts Building, 1300 17th St. NW, Washington DC 20036-1973. (202)785-1997. **Fax:** (202)452-8868. **E-mail:** contact@nlapw.org. **Website:** www.nlapw.org.

NATIONAL WRITERS ASSOCIATION (NWA) 10940 S. Parker Rd., #508, Parker, CO 80134. (303)841-0246. **E-mail:** natlwritersassn@hotmail.com. **Website:** www.nationalwriters.com

NATIONAL WRITERS UNION (NWU) 256 W. Thirty-eigth St., Suite 703, New York, NY 10018. (212)254-0279. **Fax:** (212)254-0673. **E-mail:** nwu@nwu.org. **Website:** www.nwu.org.

PEN AMERICAN CENTER 588 Broadway, Suite 303, New York, NY 10012-3225. (212)334-1660. **Fax:** (212)334-2181. **E-mail:** info@pen.org. **Website:** www.pen.org.

THE PLAYWRIGHTS GUILD OF CANADA (PGC) 401 Richmond Street W., Suite 350, Toronto, Ontario M5V 3A8 Canada. (416)703-0201. **Fax:** (416)703-0059. **E-mail:** info@play-wrightsguild.ca. **Website:** http://www.play wrightsguild.ca.

VOLUNTEER LAWYERS FOR THE ARTS (VLA) 1 E. Fifty-third St., Sixth Floor, New York, NY 10022. (212)319-2787, ext.1. **Fax:** (212)752-6575. **E-mail:** vlany@vlany.org. **Website:** www.vlany.org.

WOMEN IN FILM (WIF) 6100 Wilshire Blvd., Suite 710, Los Angeles, CA 90048. (323)935-2211. **Fax:** (323)935-2212. **E-mail:** info@wif.org. **Website:** www.wif.org.

WOMEN'S NATIONAL BOOK ASSOCIATION (WNBA) P.O. Box 237, FDR Station, New York NY 10150. (212)208-4629. **Fax:** (212)208-4629. **E-mail:** info@wnba-books.org. **Website:** www.wnba-books.org.

WRITERS GUILD OF ALBERTA (WGA) Percy Page Centre, 11759 Groat Rd., Edmonton AB T5M 3K6 Canada. (780)422-8174. **Fax:** (780)422-2663 (attn: WGA). **E-mail:** mail@ writersguild.ab.ca. **Website:** writersguild. ab.ca.

WRITERS GUILD OF AMERICA-EAST (WGA) 250 Hudson Street, Suite 700, New York, NY 10013. (212)767-7800. **Fax:** (212)582-1909. **E-mail:** gbynoe@wgaeast.org. **Website:** www .wgaeast.org.

WRITERS GUILD OF AMERICA-WEST (WGA) 7000 W. Third St., Los Angeles CA 90048. (323)951-4000. **Fax:** (323)782-4800. **Website:** www.wga.org.

WRITERS UNION OF CANADA (TWUC) 600-400 Richmond St. W., Toronto, ON M5V 1Y1 Canada. (416)703-8982. **Fax:** (416)504-9090. **E-mail:** info@writersunion.ca. **Website:** www.writersunion.ca.

LITERARY AGENTS SPECIALTIES INDEX

FICTION

ACTION

Congdon Associates Inc., Don 134

Fairbank Literary Representation 143

Finch Literary Agency, Diana 144

Jabberwocky Literary Agency 158

JET Literary Associates 159

Klinger, Inc., Harvey 160

Larsen/Elizabeth Pomada, Literary Agents, Michael 163

Levine Literary Agency, Paul S. 165

Lippincott Massie McQuilkin 165

Marshall Agency, The Evan 170

McBride Literary Agency, Margret 170

Mendel Media Group, LLC 171

P.S. Literary Agency 176

Sanders & Associates, Victoria 179

Seymour Agency, The 183

Simmons Literary Agency, Jeffrey 185

Triada U.S. Literary Agency, Inc. 190

Venture Literary 191

Weiner Literary Agency, Cherry 192

ADVENTURE

Alive Communications, Inc. 124

Amsterdam Agency, Marcia 125

Bova Literary Agency, The Barbara 129

Brown, Ltd., Curtis 131

Congdon Associates Inc., Don 134

D4EO Literary Agency 136

Fairbank Literary Representation 143

Finch Literary Agency, Diana 144

Goumen & Smirnova Literary Agency 150

Hamilburg Agency, The Mitchell J. 154

Jabberwocky Literary Agency 158

JET Literary Associates 159

Klinger, Inc., Harvey 160

Lampack Agency, Inc., Peter 162

Larsen/Elizabeth Pomada, Literary Agents, Michael 163

Levine Literary Agency, Paul S. 165

Lippincott Massie McQuilkin 165

Literary Group International, The 166

Marshall Agency, The Evan 170

McBride Literary Agency, Margret 170

Mendel Media Group, LLC 171

Mura Literary, Dee 172

Prentis Literary, Linn 175

P.S. Literary Agency 176
Sanders & Associates, Victoria 179
Sherman & Associates, Ken 184
Simmons Literary Agency, Jeffrey 185
Triada U.S. Literary Agency, Inc. 190
Venture Literary 191
Weiner Literary Agency, Cherry 192

CARTOON
Lippincott Massie McQuilkin 165

COMIC BOOKS
Levine Literary Agency, Paul S. 165
Lippincott Massie McQuilkin 165
Sherman & Associates, Ken 184

COMMERCIAL
Barrett Books, Inc., Loretta 126
Bender Literary Agency, Faye 127
Bent Agency, The 127
Cameron & Associates, Kimberley 132
Castiglia Literary Agency 133
Cheney Literary Associates, LLC, Elyse
    134
Compass Talent 134
Coover Agency, The Doe 135
Dawson Associates, Liza 166
DeChiara Literary Agency, The Jennifer
    137
Dijkstra Literary Agency, Sandra 138
Dunow, Carlson, & Lerner Agency 140
Edelstein Literary Agency, Anne 141
Ellenberg Literary Agency, Ethan 141
Ehrlich Literary Management, LLC,
    Judith 142
FinePrint Literary Management 144
Folio Literary Management, LLC 145
Foreword Literary 145
Foundry Literary + Media 146
Friedman Literary Agency, Rebecca 176
Hawkins & Associates, Inc., John 154
InkWell Management, LLC 157
LA Literary Agency, The 162
Lampack Agency, Inc., Peter 162

Lowenstein Associates Inc. 167
Mann Agency, Carol 169
Martell Agency, The 170
Moveable Type Management 172
Mura Literary, Dee 172
Naggar Literary Agency, Inc. Jean V. 173
Nelson Literary Agency 173
Perkins Agency, L. 175
Rees Literary Agency, Helen 176
RLR Associates, Ltd. 178
Serendipity Literary Agency, LLC 182
Slopen Literary Agency, Beverley 185
Spencerhill Associates 186
Talcott Notch Literary 189
Transatlantic Literary Agency 189
Trident Media Group 190
Unter Agency, The 191

CONFESSION
Brown, Ltd., Curtis 131
Levine Literary Agency, Paul S. 165
Lippincott Massie McQuilkin 165
Sherman & Associates, Ken 184
Simmons Literary Agency, Jeffrey 185

CONTEMPORARY
Alive Communications, Inc. 124
Barer Literary LLC 126
Bykofsky Associates, Inc., Sheree 183
Clark Associates, WM 193
Congdon Associates Inc., Don 134
Jabberwocky Literary Agency 158
Krichevsky Literary Agency, Inc., Stuart
    161
Larsen/Elizabeth Pomada, Literary
    Agents, Michael 163
Literary Group International, The 166
Mendel Media Group, LLC 171
Mura Literary, Dee 172
Sanders & Associates, Victoria 179
Seligman, Literary Agent, Lynn 182
Weiner Literary Agency, Cherry 192

COZIES

BookEnds, LLC 128

CRIME

Alive Communications, Inc. 124

Axelrod Agency, The 126

Barron's Literary Management 127

Bent Agency, The 127

Bova Literary Agency, The Barbara 129

Castiglia Literary Agency 133

Congdon Associates Inc., Don 134

Finch Literary Agency, Diana 144

FinePrint Literary Management 144

Goodman Literary Agency, Irene 150

Greenburger Associates, Inc., Sanford J. 151

Green Literary Agency, LLC, Kathryn 152

Henshaw Group, Richard 155

InkWell Management, LLC 157

Jabberwocky Literary Agency 158

J de S Associates, Inc. 158

JET Literary Associates 159

Klinger, Inc., Harvey 160

Lampack Agency, Inc., Peter 162

Langlie, Literary Agent, Laura 163

Larsen/Elizabeth Pomada, Literary Agents, Michael 163

Levine Literary Agency, Paul S. 165

Maass Literary Agency, Donald 167

MacGregor Literary Inc. 168

McBride Literary Agency, Margret 170

Mendel Media Group, LLC 171

Mura Literary, Dee 172

New Leaf Literary & Media, Inc. 174

Robbins Literary Agency, B.J. 178

Sanders & Associates, Victoria 179

Scribblers House, LLC Literary Agency 181

Simmons Literary Agency, Jeffrey 185

Triada U.S. Literary Agency, Inc. 190

Trident Media Group 190

Venture Literary 191

Weiner Literary Agency, Cherry 192

DETECTIVE

Amsterdam Agency, Marcia 125

Barron's Literary Management 127

BookEnds, LLC 128

Bova Literary Agency, The Barbara 129

Brown, Ltd., Curtis 131

Congdon Associates Inc., Don 134

D4EO Literary Agency 136

Finch Literary Agency, Diana 144

Goodman Literary Agency, Irene 150

Green Literary Agency, LLC, Kathryn 152

Henshaw Group, Richard 155

Jabberwocky Literary Agency 158

J de S Associates, Inc. 158

JET Literary Associates 159

Klinger, Inc., Harvey 160

Lampack Agency, Inc., Peter 162

Langlie, Literary Agent, Laura 163

Larsen/Elizabeth Pomada, Literary Agents, Michael 163

Levine Literary Agency, Paul S. 165

Literary Group International, The 166

Maass Literary Agency, Donald 167

MacGregor Literary Inc. 168

McBride Literary Agency, Margret 170

Mendel Media Group, LLC 171

P.S. Literary Agency 176

Robbins Literary Agency, B.J. 178

Seligman, Literary Agent, Lynn 182

Sherman & Associates, Ken 184

Simmons Literary Agency, Jeffrey 185

Triada U.S. Literary Agency, Inc. 190

Venture Literary 191

Weiner Literary Agency, Cherry 192

EROTICA

Bradford Literary Agency 130

Brown, Ltd., Curtis 131

D4EO Literary Agency 136

Folio Literary Management, LLC 145

JET Literary Associates 159

Levine Literary Agency, Paul S. 165

Marshall Agency, The Evan 170

Mendel Media Group, LLC 171

Mura Literary, Dee 172

Perkins Agency, L. 175

P.S. Literary Agency 176

Sherman & Associates, Ken 184

Spencerhill Associates 186

ETHNIC

Amster Literary Enterprises, Betsy 125

Barer Literary LLC 126

Brown, Ltd., Curtis 131

Clark Associates, WM 193

Crichton & Associates 136

DeFiore & Co. 138

Dunham Literary, Inc. 140

Finch Literary Agency, Diana 144

Freymann Literary Agency, Sarah Jane 147

Golomb Literary Agency, The Susan 149

Jabberwocky Literary Agency 158

JET Literary Associates 159

Langlie, Literary Agent, Laura 163

Larsen/Elizabeth Pomada, Literary Agents, Michael 163

Levine Literary Agency, Paul S. 165

Literary Group International, The 166

Marshall Agency, The Evan 170

Mendel Media Group, LLC 171

Prentis Literary, Linn 175

P.S. Literary Agency 176

Robbins Literary Agency, B.J. 178

Sanders & Associates, Victoria 179

Schiavone Literary Agency, Inc. 180

Seligman, Literary Agent, Lynn 182

Sherman & Associates, Ken 184

Triada U.S. Literary Agency, Inc. 190

EXPERIMENTAL

Brown, Ltd., Curtis 131

Goumen & Smirnova Literary Agency 150

Hamilburg Agency, The Mitchell J. 154

Larsen/Elizabeth Pomada, Literary Agents, Michael 163

Levine Literary Agency, Paul S. 165

Literary Group International, The 166

Scribe Agency, LLC 181

Sherman & Associates, Ken 184

FAMILY SAGA

Alive Communications, Inc. 124

Cheney Literary Associates, LLC, Elyse 134

Goumen & Smirnova Literary Agency 150

Green Literary Agency, LLC, Kathryn 152

Jabberwocky Literary Agency 158

Klinger, Inc., Harvey 160

Lampack Agency, Inc., Peter 162

Larsen/Elizabeth Pomada, Literary Agents, Michael 163

Levine Literary Agency, Paul S. 165

Lippincott Massie McQuilkin 165

Literary Group International, The 166

Mura Literary, Dee 172

P.S. Literary Agency 176

Sanders & Associates, Victoria 179

Schiavone Literary Agency, Inc. 180

Sherman & Associates, Ken 184

Simmons Literary Agency, Jeffrey 185

Weiner Literary Agency, Cherry 192

FANTASY

Azantian Literary Agency, Jennifer 126

Bent Agency, The 127

Brown, Ltd., Curtis 131

Cameron & Associates, Kimberley 132

Darhansoff & Verrill Literary Agents 137

Dawson Associates, Liza 166

Ellenberg Literary Agency, Ethan 141

FinePrint Literary Management 144

Folio Literary Management, LLC 145

Foreword Literary 145

Fox Literary 146

Grayson Literary Agency, Ashley 151

Greenburger Associates, Inc., Sanford J. 151

Grinberg Literary Agency, Jill 153

Henshaw Group, Richard 155

Hurst Literary Management, Andrea 156

Jabberwocky Literary Agency 158

Kidd Agency, Inc., Virginia 159

Literary Group International, The 166

Lowenstein Associates Inc. 167

Maass Literary Agency, Donald 167

McCarthy Agency, LLC, The 171

Mura Literary, Dee 172

Naggar Literary Agency, Inc. Jean V. 173

Nelson Literary Agency 173

New Leaf Literary & Media, Inc. 174

Prentis Literary, Linn 175

Scribe Agency, LLC 181

Seligman, Literary Agent, Lynn 182

Seymour Agency, The 183

Sherman & Associates, Ken 184

Sternig & Byrne Literary Agency 187

Talcott Notch Literary 189

Trident Media Group 190

Weiner Literary Agency, Cherry 192

FEMINIST

Brown, Ltd., Curtis 131

Crichton & Associates 136

Fairbank Literary Representation 143

Hamilburg Agency, The Mitchell J. 154

Langlie, Literary Agent, Laura 163

Larsen/Elizabeth Pomada, Literary Agents, Michael 163

Levine Literary Agency, Paul S. 165

Lippincott Massie McQuilkin 165

Literary Group International, The 166

Mendel Media Group, LLC 171

Sanders & Associates, Victoria 179

Scribe Agency, LLC 181

Seligman, Literary Agent, Lynn 182

Sherman & Associates, Ken 184

FRONTIER

J de S Associates, Inc. 158

Levine Literary Agency, Paul S. 165

Marshall Agency, The Evan 170

Weiner Literary Agency, Cherry 192

GAY

Brown, Ltd., Curtis 131

Fairbank Literary Representation 143

Foreword Literary 145

Jabberwocky Literary Agency 158

JET Literary Associates 159

Larsen/Elizabeth Pomada, Literary Agents, Michael 163

Levine Literary Agency, Paul S. 165

Lippincott Massie McQuilkin 165

Mendel Media Group, LLC 171

Perkins Agency, L. 175

Prentis Literary, Linn 175

Serendipity Literary Agency, LLC 182

Sherman & Associates, Ken 184

GLITZ

Hamilburg Agency, The Mitchell J. 154

Jabberwocky Literary Agency 158

JET Literary Associates 159

Klinger, Inc., Harvey 160

Larsen/Elizabeth Pomada, Literary Agents, Michael 163

Levine Literary Agency, Paul S. 165

Mendel Media Group, LLC 171

Prentis Literary, Linn 175

Sherman & Associates, Ken 184

Teal Literary Agency, Patricia 189

GOTHIC

Seligman, Literary Agent, Lynn 182

Sherman & Associates, Ken 184

HI LO

Sherman & Associates, Ken 184

HISTORICAL

Alive Communications, Inc. 124

Amsterdam Agency, Marcia 125

Barer Literary LLC 126

Barron's Literary Management 127

Bent Agency, The 127

Books & Such Literary Agency 129

Brown, Ltd., Curtis 131

Cameron & Associates, Kimberley 132

Carvainis Agency, Inc., Maria 133

Cheney Literary Associates, LLC, Elyse
134

Clark Associates, WM 193

D4EO Literary Agency 136

Darhansoff & Verrill Literary Agents 137

Dawson Associates, Liza 166

English Literary Agency, The Elaine P.
142

Finch Literary Agency, Diana 144

Foundry Literary + Media 146

Fox Literary 146

Gelfman Schneider Literary Agents, Inc.
149

Golomb Literary Agency, The Susan 149

Goodman Literary Agency, Irene 150

Goumen & Smirnova Literary Agency
150

Greenburger Associates, Inc., Sanford
J. 151

Green Literary Agency, LLC, Kathryn
152

Gross Literary Agency, Laura 153

Hawkins & Associates, Inc., John 154

Henshaw Group, Richard 155

InkWell Management, LLC 157

Jabberwocky Literary Agency 158

J de S Associates, Inc. 158

JET Literary Associates 159

Langlie, Literary Agent, Laura 163

Larsen/Elizabeth Pomada, Literary
Agents, Michael 163

Levine Literary Agency, Paul S. 165

Lippincott Massie McQuilkin 165

Literary Group International, The 166

Maass Literary Agency, Donald 167

MacGregor Literary Inc. 168

Marshall Agency, The Evan 170

McBride Literary Agency, Margret 170

McGill Agency, Inc., The 171

Mendel Media Group, LLC 171

Mura Literary, Dee 172

New Leaf Literary & Media, Inc. 174

Perkins Agency, L. 175

Prentis Literary, Linn 175

P.S. Literary Agency 176

Rees Literary Agency, Helen 176

Schiavone Literary Agency, Inc. 180

Scribblers House, LLC Literary Agency
181

Seligman, Literary Agent, Lynn 182

Serendipity Literary Agency, LLC 182

Sherman & Associates, Ken 184

Talcott Notch Literary 189

Transatlantic Literary Agency 189

Triada U.S. Literary Agency, Inc. 190

Weiner Literary Agency, Cherry 192

HORROR

Amsterdam Agency, Marcia 125

Azantian Literary Agency, Jennifer 126

Barron's Literary Management 127

Bent Agency, The 127

Brown, Ltd., Curtis 131

D4EO Literary Agency 136

Dijkstra Literary Agency, Sandra 138

Folio Literary Management, LLC 145

Foreword Literary 145

Goumen & Smirnova Literary Agency
150

Henshaw Group, Richard 155

Jabberwocky Literary Agency 158

Literary Group International, The 166

Maass Literary Agency, Donald 167

Marshall Agency, The Evan 170

New Leaf Literary & Media, Inc. 174

Perkins Agency, L. 175
Prentis Literary, Linn 175
P.S. Literary Agency 176
Rees Literary Agency, Helen 176
Schiavone Literary Agency, Inc. 180
Scribe Agency, LLC 181
Seligman, Literary Agent, Lynn 182
Sherman & Associates, Ken 184
Sternig & Byrne Literary Agency 187
Talcott Notch Literary 189
Triada U.S. Literary Agency, Inc. 190

HUMOR

Alive Communications, Inc. 124
Brown, Ltd., Curtis 131
D4EO Literary Agency 136
Foundry Literary + Media 146
Golomb Literary Agency, The Susan 149
Green Literary Agency, LLC, Kathryn 152
Hamilburg Agency, The Mitchell J. 154
Jabberwocky Literary Agency 158
JET Literary Associates 159
Langlie, Literary Agent, Laura 163
Larsen/Elizabeth Pomada, Literary Agents, Michael 163
Levine Literary Agency, Paul S. 165
Lippincott Massie McQuilkin 165
Literary Group International, The 166
Marshall Agency, The Evan 170
McBride Literary Agency, Margret 170
Mendel Media Group, LLC 171
Prentis Literary, Linn 175
P.S. Literary Agency 176
Schiavone Literary Agency, Inc. 180
Seligman, Literary Agent, Lynn 182
Serendipity Literary Agency, LLC 182
Sherman & Associates, Ken 184

INSPIRATIONAL

Alive Communications, Inc. 124
Crichton & Associates 136
Hurst Literary Management, Andrea 156

Larsen/Elizabeth Pomada, Literary Agents, Michael 163
Laube Agency, The Steve 164
Levine Literary Agency, Paul S. 165
MacGregor Literary Inc. 168
Marshall Agency, The Evan 170
Mendel Media Group, LLC 171

JUVENILE

Brown, Ltd., Curtis 131
Brown Literary Agency, Inc., Andrea 130
Compass Talent 134
D4EO Literary Agency 136
Dunham Literary, Inc. 140
Flannery Literary 144
Gallt Literary Agency, Nancy 149
Grayson Literary Agency, Ashley 151
Greenhouse Literary Agency, The 152
Green Literary Agency, LLC, Kathryn 152
Grinberg Literary Agency, Jill 153
Heacock Hill Literary Agency, Inc. 155
Hurst Literary Management, Andrea 156
J de S Associates, Inc. 158
Kroll Literary Agency, Inc., Edite 161
Langlie, Literary Agent, Laura 163
Mansion Street Literary Management 169
McCarthy Agency, LLC, The 171
Mendel Media Group, LLC 171
P.S. Literary Agency 176
Schiavone Literary Agency, Inc. 180
Schulman Literary Agency, Susan 180
Transatlantic Literary Agency 189
Triada U.S. Literary Agency, Inc. 190
Trident Media Group 190
Wells Arms Literary 192

LESBIAN

Fairbank Literary Representation 143
Foreword Literary 145
Jabberwocky Literary Agency 158
JET Literary Associates 159

Larsen/Elizabeth Pomada, Literary Agents, Michael 163
Levine Literary Agency, Paul S. 165
Lippincott Massie McQuilkin 165
Mendel Media Group, LLC 171
Perkins Agency, L. 175
Prentis Literary, Linn 175
Sanders & Associates, Victoria 179
Serendipity Literary Agency, LLC 182

LITERARY

Alive Communications, Inc. 124
Amster Literary Enterprises, Betsy 125
Barer Literary LLC 126
Barrett Books, Inc., Loretta 126
Bender Literary Agency, Faye 127
Bent Agency, The 127
Books & Such Literary Agency 129
Brown, Ltd., Curtis 131
Brown Literary Agency, Inc., Andrea 130
Brown Literary Agency, Tracy 132
Bykofsky Associates, Inc., Sheree 183
Cameron & Associates, Kimberley 132
Carvainis Agency, Inc., Maria 133
Castiglia Literary Agency 133
Chelius Literary Agency, Jane 134
Cheney Literary Associates, LLC, Elyse 134
Clark Associates, WM 193
Compass Talent 134
Congdon Associates Inc., Don 134
Coover Agency, The Doe 135
Crichton & Associates 136
D4EO Literary Agency 136
Darhansoff & Verrill Literary Agents 137
Dawson Associates, Liza 166
DeChiara Literary Agency, The Jennifer 137
DeFiore & Co. 138
Delbourgo Associates, Inc., Joelle 137
Dijkstra Literary Agency, Sandra 138
Dunham Literary, Inc. 140

Dunow, Carlson, & Lerner Agency 140
Edelstein Literary Agency, Anne 141
Ehrlich Literary Management, LLC, Judith 142
Ellenberg Literary Agency, Ethan 141
Eth Literary Representation, Felicia 143
Fairbank Literary Representation 143
Finch Literary Agency, Diana 144
Folio Literary Management, LLC 145
Foreword Literary 145
Foundry Literary + Media 146
Fox Literary 146
Freymann Literary Agency, Sarah Jane 147
Friedman and Co., Inc., Frederica 147
Friedman Literary Agency, Rebecca 176
Full Circle Literary, LLC 148
Gelfman Schneider Literary Agents, Inc. 149
Golomb Literary Agency, The Susan 149
Goumen & Smirnova Literary Agency 150
Greenburger Associates, Inc., Sanford J. 151
Green Literary Agency, LLC, Kathryn 152
Grinberg Literary Agency, Jill 153
Grosjean Literary Agency, Jill 153
Gross Literary Agency, Laura 153
Hawkins & Associates, Inc., John 154
Henshaw Group, Richard 155
Hurst Literary Management, Andrea 156
InkWell Management, LLC 157
Jabberwocky Literary Agency 158
J de S Associates, Inc. 158
JET Literary Associates 159
Klinger, Inc., Harvey 160
Kraas Literary Agency 160
Kroll Literary Agency, Inc., Edite 161
LA Literary Agency, The 162
Lampack Agency, Inc., Peter 162

Langlie, Literary Agent, Laura 163

Larsen/Elizabeth Pomada, Literary Agents, Michael 163

Levine Greenberg Literary Agency, Inc. 164

Levine Literary Agency, Paul S. 165

Lippincott Massie McQuilkin 165

Literary Group International, The 166

Lowenstein Associates Inc. 167

Maass Literary Agency, Donald 167

Mann Agency, Carol 169

Marshall Agency, The Evan 170

McBride Literary Agency, Margret 170

Mendel Media Group, LLC 171

Moveable Type Management 172

Mura Literary, Dee 172

Naggar Literary Agency, Inc. Jean V. 173

Nelson Literary Agency 173

New Leaf Literary & Media, Inc. 174

Paton Literary Agency, Kathi J. 174

Prentis Literary, Linn 175

P.S. Literary Agency 176

Rees Literary Agency, Helen 176

Regal Literary Agency 177

Rittenberg Literary Agency, Inc., Ann 178

RLR Associates, Ltd. 178

Robbins Literary Agency, B.J. 178

Rotrosen Agency LLC, Jane 179

Sanders & Associates, Victoria 179

Schiavone Literary Agency, Inc. 180

Schulman Literary Agency, Susan 180

Scribblers House, LLC Literary Agency 181

Scribe Agency, LLC 181

Seligman, Literary Agent, Lynn 182

Serendipity Literary Agency, LLC 182

Sherman & Associates, Ken 184

Simmons Literary Agency, Jeffrey 185

Slopen Literary Agency, Beverley 185

Spencerhill Associates 186

Spieler Agency, The 186

Strothman Agency, LLC, The 188

Sweeney Agency, LLC, Emma 188

Transatlantic Literary Agency 189

Triada U.S. Literary Agency, Inc. 190

Trident Media Group 190

Venture Literary 191

Weingel-Fidel Agency, The 192

Weissman Literary, LLC, Larry 192

Wolf Literary Services 193

Writers' Representatives, LLC 194

Zimmermann Literary Agency, Helen 194

MAINSTREAM

Alive Communications, Inc. 124

Amsterdam Agency, Marcia 125

Barer Literary LLC 126

Barrett Books, Inc., Loretta 126

BookEnds, LLC 128

Books & Such Literary Agency 129

Brown, Ltd., Curtis 131

Bykofsky Associates, Inc., Sheree 183

Carvainis Agency, Inc., Maria 133

Clark Associates, WM 193

Compass Talent 134

Congdon Associates Inc., Don 134

Crichton & Associates 136

D4EO Literary Agency 136

DeFiore & Co. 138

Delbourgo Associates, Inc., Joelle 137

Dunham Literary, Inc. 140

Dunow, Carlson, & Lerner Agency 140

Eth Literary Representation, Felicia 143

Fairbank Literary Representation 143

Finch Literary Agency, Diana 144

Foreword Literary 145

Fox Literary 146

Freymann Literary Agency, Sarah Jane 147

Gelfman Schneider Literary Agents, Inc. 149

Golomb Literary Agency, The Susan 149
Goumen & Smirnova Literary Agency 150
Green Literary Agency, LLC, Kathryn 152
Grinberg Literary Agency, Jill 153
Grosjean Literary Agency, Jill 153
Gross Literary Agency, Laura 153
Henshaw Group, Richard 155
Hurst Literary Management, Andrea 156
Jabberwocky Literary Agency 158
J de S Associates, Inc. 158
JET Literary Associates 159
Klinger, Inc., Harvey 160
Lampack Agency, Inc., Peter 162
Langlie, Literary Agent, Laura 163
Larsen/Elizabeth Pomada, Literary Agents, Michael 163
Levine Greenberg Literary Agency, Inc. 164
Levine Literary Agency, Paul S. 165
Lippincott Massie McQuilkin 165
Maass Literary Agency, Donald 167
MacGregor Literary Inc. 168
Marshall Agency, The Evan 170
McBride Literary Agency, Margret 170
McGill Agency, Inc., The 171
Mendel Media Group, LLC 171
Moveable Type Management 172
Nelson Literary Agency 173
New Leaf Literary & Media, Inc. 174
Prentis Literary, Linn 175
P.S. Literary Agency 176
Rittenberg Literary Agency, Inc., Ann 178
RLR Associates, Ltd. 178
Robbins Literary Agency, B.J. 178
Sanders & Associates, Victoria 179
Schiavone Literary Agency, Inc. 180
Schulman Literary Agency, Susan 180
Scribe Agency, LLC 181

Seligman, Literary Agent, Lynn 182
Sherman Associates, Inc., Wendy 184
Sherman & Associates, Ken 184
Simmons Literary Agency, Jeffrey 185
Spencerhill Associates 186
Sweeney Agency, LLC, Emma 188
Talcott Notch Literary 189
Teal Literary Agency, Patricia 189
Triada U.S. Literary Agency, Inc. 190
Unter Agency, The 191
Venture Literary 191
Weiner Literary Agency, Cherry 192
Weingel-Fidel Agency, The 192
Whimsy Literary Agency, LLC 193

METAPHYSICAL
Barrett Books, Inc., Loretta 126

MIDDLE-GRADE
Azantian Literary Agency, Jennifer 126
Bender Literary Agency, Faye 127
Bradford Literary Agency 130
Brown, Ltd., Curtis 131
Carvainis Agency, Inc., Maria 133
Congdon Associates Inc., Don 134
D4EO Literary Agency 136
DeChiara Literary Agency, The Jennifer 137
DeFiore & Co. 138
Delbourgo Associates, Inc., Joelle 137
Dijkstra Literary Agency, Sandra 138
Dunow, Carlson, & Lerner Agency 140
East/West Literary Agency, LLC 141
FinePrint Literary Management 144
Flannery Literary 144
Folio Literary Management, LLC 145
Foreword Literary 145
Foundry Literary + Media 146
Full Circle Literary, LLC 148
Gallt Literary Agency, Nancy 149
Gelfman Schneider Literary Agents, Inc. 149
Grayson Literary Agency, Ashley 151

Greenburger Associates, Inc., Sanford
J. 151
Greenhouse Literary Agency, The 152
Green Literary Agency, LLC, Kathryn
152
Heacock Hill Literary Agency, Inc. 155
InkWell Management, LLC 157
Jabberwocky Literary Agency 158
KT Literary, LLC 161
Levine Greenberg Literary Agency, Inc.
164
Lowenstein Associates Inc. 167
Mansion Street Literary Management
169
Mura Literary, Dee 172
Naggar Literary Agency, Inc. Jean V. 173
Nelson Literary Agency 173
New Leaf Literary & Media, Inc. 174
Park Literary Group, LLC 174
P.S. Literary Agency 176
Regal Literary Agency 177
RLR Associates, Ltd. 178
Serendipity Literary Agency, LLC 182
Seymour Agency, The 183
Spieler Agency, The 186
Strothman Agency, LLC, The 188
Talcott Notch Literary 189
Transatlantic Literary Agency 189
Trident Media Group 190
Unter Agency, The 191
Upstart Crow Literary 191
Wells Arms Literary 192

MILITARY
Brown, Ltd., Curtis 131
FinePrint Literary Management 144
Hamilburg Agency, The Mitchell J. 154
Sherman & Associates, Ken 184

MULTICULTURAL
Brown, Ltd., Curtis 131
English Literary Agency, The Elaine P.
142

Grayson Literary Agency, Ashley 151
Hawkins & Associates, Inc., John 154
Literary Group International, The 166
Maass Literary Agency, Donald 167
Sherman & Associates, Ken 184

MULTIMEDIA
Brown, Ltd., Curtis 131
Sherman & Associates, Ken 184

MYSTERY
Alive Communications, Inc. 124
Amsterdam Agency, Marcia 125
Axelrod Agency, The 126
Barrett Books, Inc., Loretta 126
Barron's Literary Management 127
Bent Agency, The 127
BookEnds, LLC 128
Bova Literary Agency, The Barbara 129
Bradford Literary Agency 130
Brown, Ltd., Curtis 131
Bykofsky Associates, Inc., Sheree 183
Cameron & Associates, Kimberley 132
Carvainis Agency, Inc., Maria 133
Castiglia Literary Agency 133
Chelius Literary Agency, Jane 134
Congdon Associates Inc., Don 134
Crichton & Associates 136
D4EO Literary Agency 136
Darhansoff & Verrill Literary Agents 137
DeChiara Literary Agency, The Jennifer
137
DeFiore & Co. 138
Dunow, Carlson, & Lerner Agency 140
Ellenberg Literary Agency, Ethan 141
English Literary Agency, The Elaine P.
142
Fairbank Literary Representation 143
FinePrint Literary Management 144
Folio Literary Management, LLC 145
Foreword Literary 145
Gelfman Schneider Literary Agents, Inc.
149

Goodman Literary Agency, Irene 150
Goumen & Smirnova Literary Agency 150
Grayson Literary Agency, Ashley 151
Greenburger Associates, Inc., Sanford J. 151
Green Literary Agency, LLC, Kathryn 152
Grosjean Literary Agency, Jill 153
Gross Literary Agency, Laura 153
Hamilburg Agency, The Mitchell J. 154
Henshaw Group, Richard 155
J de S Associates, Inc. 158
JET Literary Associates 159
Klinger, Inc., Harvey 160
Lampack Agency, Inc., Peter 162
Langlie, Literary Agent, Laura 163
Larsen/Elizabeth Pomada, Literary Agents, Michael 163
Levine Greenberg Literary Agency, Inc. 164
Levine Literary Agency, Paul S. 165
Literary Group International, The 166
Dawson Associates, Liza 166
Maass Literary Agency, Donald 167
MacGregor Literary Inc. 168
Marshall Agency, The Evan 170
Martell Agency, The 170
McBride Literary Agency, Margret 170
McCarthy Agency, LLC, The 171
McGill Agency, Inc., The 171
Mendel Media Group, LLC 171
Mura Literary, Dee 172
New Leaf Literary & Media, Inc. 174
Perkins Agency, L. 175
P.S. Literary Agency 176
Rees Literary Agency, Helen 176
Robbins Literary Agency, B.J. 178
Rotrosen Agency LLC, Jane 179
Sanders & Associates, Victoria 179
Seligman, Literary Agent, Lynn 182

Serendipity Literary Agency, LLC 182
Seymour Agency, The 183
Sherman & Associates, Ken 184
Simmons Literary Agency, Jeffrey 185
Slopen Literary Agency, Beverley 185
Spectrum Literary Agency 186
Spencerhill Associates 186
Sternig & Byrne Literary Agency 187
Sweeney Agency, LLC, Emma 188
Talcott Notch Literary 189
Teal Literary Agency, Patricia 189
Triada U.S. Literary Agency, Inc. 190
Trident Media Group 190
Venture Literary 191
Weiner Literary Agency, Cherry 192

NEW ADULT
Axelrod Agency, The 126
Azantian Literary Agency, Jennifer 126
Books & Such Literary Agency 129
Foreword Literary 145
Mura Literary, Dee 172
Nelson Literary Agency 173
New Leaf Literary & Media, Inc. 174
Perkins Agency, L. 175
P.S. Literary Agency 176
Rees Literary Agency, Helen 176
Rotrosen Agency LLC, Jane 179
Sanders & Associates, Victoria 179
Seymour Agency, The 183
Transatlantic Literary Agency 189

NEW AGE
Brown, Ltd., Curtis 131
Hamilburg Agency, The Mitchell J. 154
J de S Associates, Inc. 158
Sherman & Associates, Ken 184
Spieler Agency, The 186
Talcott Notch Literary 189

OCCULT
Brown, Ltd., Curtis 131
Hamilburg Agency, The Mitchell J. 154
Sherman & Associates, Ken 184

Triada U.S. Literary Agency, Inc. 190

PARANORMAL
Barron's Literary Management 127
Bradford Literary Agency 130
DeFiore & Co. 138
Foreword Literary 145
Maass Literary Agency, Donald 167
Mura Literary, Dee 172
New Leaf Literary & Media, Inc. 174
Perkins Agency, L. 175
Spencerhill Associates 186
Talcott Notch Literary 189
Trident Media Group 190

PICTURE BOOKS
Bent Agency, The 127
Bradford Literary Agency 130
Brown, Ltd., Curtis 131
Brown Literary Agency, Inc., Andrea 130
D4EO Literary Agency 136
DeChiara Literary Agency, The Jennifer 137
Dunham Literary, Inc. 140
Dunow, Carlson, & Lerner Agency 140
East/West Literary Agency, LLC 141
Folio Literary Management, LLC 145
Foreword Literary 145
Full Circle Literary, LLC 148
Gallt Literary Agency, Nancy 149
Greenburger Associates, Inc., Sanford J. 151
Greenhouse Literary Agency, The 152
Heacock Hill Literary Agency, Inc. 155
InkWell Management, LLC 157
Kroll Literary Agency, Inc., Edite 161
Mendel Media Group, LLC 171
Naggar Literary Agency, Inc. Jean V. 173
New Leaf Literary & Media, Inc. 174
P.S. Literary Agency 176
Regal Literary Agency 177
RLR Associates, Ltd. 178
Sanders & Associates, Victoria 179

Sherman & Associates, Ken 184
Spieler Agency, The 186
Transatlantic Literary Agency 189
Unter Agency, The 191
Upstart Crow Literary 191
Wells Arms Literary 192

PLAYS
Sherman & Associates, Ken 184

POETRY
Sherman & Associates, Ken 184

POLICE
Alive Communications, Inc. 124
Barron's Literary Management 127
Bova Literary Agency, The Barbara 129
Congdon Associates Inc., Don 134
Finch Literary Agency, Diana 144
Green Literary Agency, LLC, Kathryn 152
Henshaw Group, Richard 155
Jabberwocky Literary Agency 158
J de S Associates, Inc. 158
JET Literary Associates 159
Klinger, Inc., Harvey 160
Lampack Agency, Inc., Peter 162
Langlie, Literary Agent, Laura 163
Larsen/Elizabeth Pomada, Literary Agents, Michael 163
Levine Literary Agency, Paul S. 165
Maass Literary Agency, Donald 167
MacGregor Literary Inc. 168
McBride Literary Agency, Margret 170
Mendel Media Group, LLC 171
Robbins Literary Agency, B.J. 178
Simmons Literary Agency, Jeffrey 185
Triada U.S. Literary Agency, Inc. 190
Venture Literary 191
Weiner Literary Agency, Cherry 192

PSYCHIC
Hurst Literary Management, Andrea 156
Jabberwocky Literary Agency 158
Literary Group International, The 166

Maass Literary Agency, Donald 167
Sherman & Associates, Ken 184
Weiner Literary Agency, Cherry 192

REGENCY
Seligman, Literary Agent, Lynn 182

REGIONAL
Brown, Ltd., Curtis 131
Dawson Associates, Liza 166
Hamilburg Agency, The Mitchell J. 154
Jabberwocky Literary Agency 158
Levine Literary Agency, Paul S. 165
Lippincott Massie McQuilkin 165
Literary Group International, The 166
Sherman & Associates, Ken 184

RELIGIOUS
Alive Communications, Inc. 124
Books & Such Literary Agency 129
Brown, Ltd., Curtis 131
Crichton & Associates 136
Folio Literary Management, LLC 145
Hamilburg Agency, The Mitchell J. 154
Hurst Literary Management, Andrea 156
Larsen/Elizabeth Pomada, Literary
    Agents, Michael 163
Laube Agency, The Steve 164
Levine Literary Agency, Paul S. 165
MacGregor Literary Inc. 168
Marshall Agency, The Evan 170
Mendel Media Group, LLC 171
Seymour Agency, The 183
Sherman & Associates, Ken 184

ROMANCE
Ahearn Agency, Inc., The 124
Amsterdam Agency, Marcia 125
Axelrod Agency, The 126
Barrett Books, Inc., Loretta 126
Barron's Literary Management 127
Bent Agency, The 127
BookEnds, LLC 128
Books & Such Literary Agency 129
Bradford Literary Agency 130

Brown, Ltd., Curtis 131
Cameron & Associates, Kimberley 132
Crichton & Associates 136
D4EO Literary Agency 136
Dawson Associates, Liza 166
DeFiore & Co. 138
Ellenberg Literary Agency, Ethan 141
FinePrint Literary Management 144
Folio Literary Management, LLC 145
Foreword Literary 145
Fox Literary 146
Friedman Literary Agency, Rebecca 176
Goodman Literary Agency, Irene 150
Goumen & Smirnova Literary Agency
    150
Grayson Literary Agency, Ashley 151
Greenburger Associates, Inc., Sanford
    J. 151
Green Literary Agency, LLC, Kathryn
    152
Grinberg Literary Agency, Jill 153
Hamilburg Agency, The Mitchell J. 154
Hopkins Literary Associates 156
Hurst Literary Management, Andrea 156
InkWell Management, LLC 157
JET Literary Associates 159
Larsen/Elizabeth Pomada, Literary
    Agents, Michael 163
Levine Literary Agency, Paul S. 165
Literary Group International, The 166
Maass Literary Agency, Donald 167
MacGregor Literary Inc. 168
McCarthy Agency, LLC, The 171
McGill Agency, Inc., The 171
Mendel Media Group, LLC 171
Moveable Type Management 172
Mura Literary, Dee 172
Nelson Literary Agency 173
New Leaf Literary & Media, Inc. 174
P.S. Literary Agency 176
Rees Literary Agency, Helen 176

RLR Associates, Ltd. 178
Rosenberg Group, The 179
Rotrosen Agency LLC, Jane 179
Seligman, Literary Agent, Lynn 182
Serendipity Literary Agency, LLC 182
Seymour Agency, The 183
Sherman & Associates, Ken 184
Spencerhill Associates 186
Steele-Perkins Literary Agency 187
Talcott Notch Literary 189
Teal Literary Agency, Patricia 189
Transatlantic Literary Agency 189
Triada U.S. Literary Agency, Inc. 190
Weiner Literary Agency, Cherry 192

SATIRE
Alive Communications, Inc. 124
Golomb Literary Agency, The Susan 149
Green Literary Agency, LLC, Kathryn
  152
Jabberwocky Literary Agency 158
Larsen/Elizabeth Pomada, Literary
  Agents, Michael 163
Levine Literary Agency, Paul S. 165
Lippincott Massie McQuilkin 165
Marshall Agency, The Evan 170
McBride Literary Agency, Margret 170
Mendel Media Group, LLC 171
Mura Literary, Dee 172

SCIENCE FICTION
Amsterdam Agency, Marcia 125
Azantian Literary Agency, Jennifer 126
Bova Literary Agency, The Barbara 129
Cameron & Associates, Kimberley 132
Castiglia Literary Agency 133
Darhansoff & Verrill Literary Agents 137
Dawson Associates, Liza 166
Dijkstra Literary Agency, Sandra 138
Ellenberg Literary Agency, Ethan 141
FinePrint Literary Management 144
Foreword Literary 145
Fox Literary 146

Grayson Literary Agency, Ashley 151
Greenburger Associates, Inc., Sanford
  J. 151
Grinberg Literary Agency, Jill 153
Henshaw Group, Richard 155
Hurst Literary Management, Andrea 156
Jabberwocky Literary Agency 158
Kidd Agency, Inc., Virginia 159
Lowenstein Associates Inc. 167
Maass Literary Agency, Donald 167
Marshall Agency, The Evan 170
Mura Literary, Dee 172
Nelson Literary Agency 173
Rees Literary Agency, Helen 176
Schiavone Literary Agency, Inc. 180
Scribe Agency, LLC 181
Seligman, Literary Agent, Lynn 182
Seymour Agency, The 183
Sherman & Associates, Ken 184
Spectrum Literary Agency 186
Sternig & Byrne Literary Agency 187
Talcott Notch Literary 189
Trident Media Group 190
Weiner Literary Agency, Cherry 192

SHORT STORY COLLECTIONS
Cheney Literary Associates, LLC, Elyse
  134
Congdon Associates Inc., Don 134
DeFiore & Co. 138
InkWell Management, LLC 157
Sherman & Associates, Ken 184

SPIRITUAL
Brown, Ltd., Curtis 131
Sherman & Associates, Ken 184

SPORTS
Brown, Ltd., Curtis 131
D4EO Literary Agency 136
Fairbank Literary Representation 143
Hamilburg Agency, The Mitchell J. 154
Jabberwocky Literary Agency 158
Levine Literary Agency, Paul S. 165

Literary Group International, The 166
Mendel Media Group, LLC 171
P.S. Literary Agency 176
Robbins Literary Agency, B.J. 178
Sherman & Associates, Ken 184
Venture Literary 191

SUPERNATURAL

Henshaw Group, Richard 155
Hurst Literary Management, Andrea 156
Jabberwocky Literary Agency 158
Maass Literary Agency, Donald 167
Weiner Literary Agency, Cherry 192

SUSPENSE

Ahearn Agency, Inc., The 124
Alive Communications, Inc. 124
Barron's Literary Management 127
Bent Agency, The 127
Bova Literary Agency, The Barbara 129
Bykofsky Associates, Inc., Sheree 183
Carvainis Agency, Inc., Maria 133
Chelius Literary Agency, Jane 134
Cheney Literary Associates, LLC, Elyse 134
Congdon Associates Inc., Don 134
Crichton & Associates 136
Darhansoff & Verrill Literary Agents 137
DeChiara Literary Agency, The Jennifer 137
DeFiore & Co. 138
Dijkstra Literary Agency, Sandra 138
Ellenberg Literary Agency, Ethan 141
English Literary Agency, The Elaine P. 142
Fairbank Literary Representation 143
FinePrint Literary Management 144
Foreword Literary 145
Foundry Literary + Media 146
Friedman Literary Agency, Rebecca 176
Gelfman Schneider Literary Agents, Inc. 149
Grayson Literary Agency, Ashley 151

Green Literary Agency, LLC, Kathryn 152
Gross Literary Agency, Laura 153
Hawkins & Associates, Inc., John 154
Henshaw Group, Richard 155
Hurst Literary Management, Andrea 156
InkWell Management, LLC 157
J de S Associates, Inc. 158
JET Literary Associates 159
Klinger, Inc., Harvey 160
Lampack Agency, Inc., Peter 162
Langlie, Literary Agent, Laura 163
Larsen/Elizabeth Pomada, Literary Agents, Michael 163
Levine Literary Agency, Paul S. 165
Dawson Associates, Liza 166
Maass Literary Agency, Donald 167
MacGregor Literary Inc. 168
Marshall Agency, The Evan 170
Martell Agency, The 170
McBride Literary Agency, Margret 170
Mura Literary, Dee 172
Park Literary Group, LLC 174
Rees Literary Agency, Helen 176
Robbins Literary Agency, B.J. 178
Rotrosen Agency LLC, Jane 179
Scribblers House, LLC Literary Agency 181
Seymour Agency, The 183
Simmons Literary Agency, Jeffrey 185
Slopen Literary Agency, Beverley 185
Sternig & Byrne Literary Agency 187
Talcott Notch Literary 189
Teal Literary Agency, Patricia 189
Trident Media Group 190
Venture Literary 191

THRILLER

Ahearn Agency, Inc., The 124
Alive Communications, Inc. 124
Amsterdam Agency, Marcia 125
Barrett Books, Inc., Loretta 126

Barron's Literary Management 127

Bent Agency, The 127

BookEnds, LLC 128

Bova Literary Agency, The Barbara 129

Bradford Literary Agency 130

Brown, Ltd., Curtis 131

Cameron & Associates, Kimberley 132

Carvainis Agency, Inc., Maria 133

Castiglia Literary Agency 133

Congdon Associates Inc., Don 134

D4EO Literary Agency 136

Darhansoff & Verrill Literary Agents 137

Dawson Associates, Liza 166

DeChiara Literary Agency, The Jennifer 137

DeFiore & Co. 138

Dijkstra Literary Agency, Sandra 138

Dunow, Carlson, & Lerner Agency 140

Ellenberg Literary Agency, Ethan 141

English Literary Agency, The Elaine P. 142

Fairbank Literary Representation 143

Finch Literary Agency, Diana 144

FinePrint Literary Management 144

Folio Literary Management, LLC 145

Foreword Literary 145

Foundry Literary + Media 146

Fox Literary 146

Golomb Literary Agency, The Susan 149

Goodman Literary Agency, Irene 150

Goumen & Smirnova Literary Agency 150

Greenburger Associates, Inc., Sanford J. 151

Green Literary Agency, LLC, Kathryn 152

Gross Literary Agency, Laura 153

Hamilburg Agency, The Mitchell J. 154

Hawkins & Associates, Inc., John 154

Henshaw Group, Richard 155

Hurst Literary Management, Andrea 156

InkWell Management, LLC 157

Jabberwocky Literary Agency 158

JET Literary Associates 159

Klinger, Inc., Harvey 160

Kraas Literary Agency 160

Lampack Agency, Inc., Peter 162

Langlie, Literary Agent, Laura 163

Levine Greenberg Literary Agency, Inc. 164

Levine Literary Agency, Paul S. 165

Literary Group International, The 166

Maass Literary Agency, Donald 167

MacGregor Literary Inc. 168

Manus & Associates Literary Agency, Inc. 169

Martell Agency, The 170

McBride Literary Agency, Margret 170

McGill Agency, Inc., The 171

Mendel Media Group, LLC 171

Mura Literary, Dee 172

Naggar Literary Agency, Inc. Jean V. 173

New Leaf Literary & Media, Inc. 174

Park Literary Group, LLC 174

Perkins Agency, L. 175

Prentis Literary, Linn 175

P.S. Literary Agency 176

Rees Literary Agency, Helen 176

Regal Literary Agency 177

Rittenberg Literary Agency, Inc., Ann 178

Robbins Literary Agency, B.J. 178

Rotrosen Agency LLC, Jane 179

Sanders & Associates, Victoria 179

Scribblers House, LLC Literary Agency 181

Scribe Agency, LLC 181

Serendipity Literary Agency, LLC 182

Seymour Agency, The 183

Sherman & Associates, Ken 184

Simmons Literary Agency, Jeffrey 185

Spencerhill Associates 186

Spieler Agency, The 186
Talcott Notch Literary 189
Trident Media Group 190
Venture Literary 191
Weiner Literary Agency, Cherry 192

TRANSLATION
Brown, Ltd., Curtis 131
Sherman & Associates, Ken 184

URBAN FANTASY
Perkins Agency, L. 175
Rees Literary Agency, Helen 176
Talcott Notch Literary 189

WESTERN
J de S Associates, Inc. 158
Levine Literary Agency, Paul S. 165
Maass Literary Agency, Donald 167
Marshall Agency, The Evan 170
Sherman & Associates, Ken 184
Weiner Literary Agency, Cherry 192

WOMEN'S
Ahearn Agency, Inc., The 124
Amster Literary Enterprises, Betsy 125
Axelrod Agency, The 126
Barrett Books, Inc., Loretta 126
Bender Literary Agency, Faye 127
Bent Agency, The 127
BookEnds, LLC 128
Bova Literary Agency, The Barbara 129
Bradford Literary Agency 130
Brown, Ltd., Curtis 131
Brown Literary Agency, Inc., Andrea 130
Cameron & Associates, Kimberley 132
Carvainis Agency, Inc., Maria 133
Chelius Literary Agency, Jane 134
Cheney Literary Associates, LLC, Elyse 134
Congdon Associates Inc., Don 134
Dawson Associates, Liza 166
DeChiara Literary Agency, The Jennifer 137
DeFiore & Co. 138

Dijkstra Literary Agency, Sandra 138
Ellenberg Literary Agency, Ethan 141
English Literary Agency, The Elaine P. 142
Fairbank Literary Representation 143
FinePrint Literary Management 144
Folio Literary Management, LLC 145
Foreword Literary 145
Foundry Literary + Media 146
Full Circle Literary, LLC 148
Friedman Literary Agency, Rebecca 176
Gelfman Schneider Literary Agents, Inc. 149
Golomb Literary Agency, The Susan 149
Goodman Literary Agency, Irene 150
Goumen & Smirnova Literary Agency 150
Grayson Literary Agency, Ashley 151
Greenburger Associates, Inc., Sanford J. 151
Green Literary Agency, LLC, Kathryn 152
Hopkins Literary Associates 156
Hurst Literary Management, Andrea 156
InkWell Management, LLC 157
JET Literary Associates 159
Levine Greenberg Literary Agency, Inc. 164
Lowenstein Associates Inc. 167
Maass Literary Agency, Donald 167
MacGregor Literary Inc. 168
McCarthy Agency, LLC, The 171
Moveable Type Management 172
Mura Literary, Dee 172
Nelson Literary Agency 173
New Leaf Literary & Media, Inc. 174
Park Literary Group, LLC 174
P.S. Literary Agency 176
Rees Literary Agency, Helen 176
Regal Literary Agency 177
RLR Associates, Ltd. 178

Rosenberg Group, The 179
Rotrosen Agency LLC, Jane 179
Schulman Literary Agency, Susan 180
Scribblers House, LLC Literary Agency 181
Serendipity Literary Agency, LLC 182
Steele-Perkins Literary Agency 187
Talcott Notch Literary 189
Teal Literary Agency, Patricia 189
Transatlantic Literary Agency 189
Triada U.S. Literary Agency, Inc. 190
Trident Media Group 190
Upstart Crow Literary 191
Venture Literary 191
Wolf Literary Services 193

YOUNG ADULT

Amsterdam Agency, Marcia 125
Azantian Literary Agency, Jennifer 126
Bender Literary Agency, Faye 127
Bent Agency, The 127
Books & Such Literary Agency 129
Bova Literary Agency, The Barbara 129
Bradford Literary Agency 130
Brown, Ltd., Curtis 131
Brown Literary Agency, Inc., Andrea 130
Cameron & Associates, Kimberley 132
Carvainis Agency, Inc., Maria 133
Castiglia Literary Agency 133
Congdon Associates Inc., Don 134
Darhansoff & Verrill Literary Agents 137
Dawson Associates, Liza 166
DeChiara Literary Agency, The Jennifer 137
DeFiore & Co. 138
Delbourgo Associates, Inc., Joelle 137
Dijkstra Literary Agency, Sandra 138
Dunham Literary, Inc. 140
Dunow, Carlson, & Lerner Agency 140
East/West Literary Agency, LLC 141
Ellenberg Literary Agency, Ethan 141
Finch Literary Agency, Diana 144

FinePrint Literary Management 144
Flannery Literary 144
Folio Literary Management, LLC 145
Foreword Literary 145
Foundry Literary + Media 146
Fox Literary 146
Freymann Literary Agency, Sarah Jane 147
Friedman Literary Agency, Rebecca 176
Full Circle Literary, LLC 148
Gallt Literary Agency, Nancy 149
Gelfman Schneider Literary Agents, Inc. 149
Golomb Literary Agency, The Susan 149
Goodman Literary Agency, Irene 150
Goumen & Smirnova Literary Agency 150
Grayson Literary Agency, Ashley 151
Greenburger Associates, Inc., Sanford J. 151
Greenhouse Literary Agency, The 152
Green Literary Agency, LLC, Kathryn 152
Grinberg Literary Agency, Jill 153
Heacock Hill Literary Agency, Inc. 155
Henshaw Group, Richard 155
Hurst Literary Management, Andrea 156
InkWell Management, LLC 157
Jabberwocky Literary Agency 158
J de S Associates, Inc. 158
JET Literary Associates 159
Kraas Literary Agency 160
Kroll Literary Agency, Inc., Edite 161
KT Literary, LLC 161
Langlie, Literary Agent, Laura 163
Levine Greenberg Literary Agency, Inc. 164
Literary Group International, The 166
Lowenstein Associates Inc. 167
Maass Literary Agency, Donald 167
Mann Agency, Carol 169

Mansion Street Literary Management 169

Mendel Media Group, LLC 171

Moveable Type Management 172

Mura Literary, Dee 172

Naggar Literary Agency, Inc. Jean V. 173

Nelson Literary Agency 173

New Leaf Literary & Media, Inc. 174

Park Literary Group, LLC 174

Perkins Agency, L. 175

P.S. Literary Agency 176

Rees Literary Agency, Helen 176

Regal Literary Agency 177

RLR Associates, Ltd. 178

Sanders & Associates, Victoria 179

Schiavone Literary Agency, Inc. 180

Serendipity Literary Agency, LLC 182

Seymour Agency, The 183

Sherman & Associates, Ken 184

Spieler Agency, The 186

Strothman Agency, LLC, The 188

Talcott Notch Literary 189

Transatlantic Literary Agency 189

Trident Media Group 190

Unter Agency, The 191

Upstart Crow Literary 191

Wells Arms Literary 192

Wolf Literary Services 193

CATEGORY INDEX

BOOK PUBLISHERS

ADVENTURE

Amira Press 334

Calamari Press 345

Cedar Fort, Inc. 347

Clarion Books 349

Covenant Communications, Inc. 351

Dial Books for Young Readers 353

Divertir 354

Frances Lincoln Children's Books 361

Glencannon Press, The 362

HarperCollins Children's Books/
    HarperCollins Publishers 365

Holiday House, Inc. 366

Hopewell Publications 367

JourneyForth 370

Little, Brown and Co. Books for Young
    Readers 376

Martin Sisters Publishing, LLC 378

Mondial 381

New Victoria Publishers 382

Oak Tree Press 383

Piñata Books 391

Salvo Press 399

Seedling Continental Press 402

Severn House Publishers 403

Soho Press, Inc. 405

Sunbury Press, Inc. 406

WaterBrook Multnomah Publishing
    Group 416

Wild Child Publishing 417

WindRiver Publishing, Inc. 418

CHILDREN'S/JUVENILE

Abrams, Harry N., Inc. 333

Candlewick Press 345

Chronicle Books 348

Covenant Communications, Inc. 351

Craigmore Creations 351

Cricket Books 351

Dial Books for Young Readers 353

Dutton Children's Books 355

Eakin Press 355

Farrar, Straus & Giroux 359

Glencannon Press, The 362

HarperCollins Children's Books/
    HarperCollins Publishers 365

Hendrick-Long Publishing Co., Inc. 366

Highland Press Publishing 366

Holiday House, Inc. 366

Lee & Low Books 374

Lerner Publishing Group 374

Levine Books, Arthur A. 375

Little, Brown and Co. Books for Young
    Readers 376

Oak Tree Press 383

Peachtree Children's Books 388

Pelican Publishing Company 389

Piano Press 391

Puffin Books 394

Random House Children's Books 395

Ransom Publishing 396

Scholastic Press 401

Tradewind Books 410

Whitecap Books, Ltd. 416

Wild Child Publishing 417

COMICS/GRAPHIC NOVELS

Archaia 336

Calamari Press 345

Image Comics 368

Insomniac Press 369

NBM Publishing 382

Nortia Press 383

Top Cow Productions, Inc. 409

Vertigo 414

Viz Media LLC 415

Wildstorm 417

EROTICA

Amira Press 334

Black Velvet Seductions Publishing 341

Crescent Moon Publishing 351

Ellora's Cave Publishing, Inc. 357

Guernica Editions 363

Loose Id 376

Mondial 381

New Victoria Publishers 382

Pedlar Press 388

Samhain Publishing, Ltd 400

Wild Child Publishing 417

ETHNIC/MULTICULTURAL

Amira Press 334

Arte Publico Press 336

Bancroft Press 338

Carolina Wren Press 346

Charlesbridge Publishing 347

Chronicle Books for Children 349

Coteau Books 351

Frances Lincoln Children's Books 361

Gival Press 362

Glencannon Press, The 362

Interlink Publishing Group, Inc. 369

Lee & Low Books 374

Little, Brown and Co. Books for Young
    Readers 376

Mondial 381

Nortia Press 383

Oak Tree Press 383

Piano Press 391

Red Hen Press 397

River City Publishing 398

Seal Press 401

Seedling Continental Press 402

Soho Press, Inc. 405

Sunbury Press, Inc. 406

Torch 319

Wild Child Publishing 417

EXPERIMENTAL

Anvil Press 335

Calamari Press 345

Crescent Moon Publishing 351

Hopewell Publications 367

Insomniac Press 369

Livingston Press 376

Paycock Press 388

Pedlar Press 388

Red Hen Press 397

Small Beer Press 404

Soft Skull Press Inc. 404

Starcherone Books 405

Stone Bridge Press 406

Wild Child Publishing 417

FAMILY SAGA

Bancroft Press 338

Highland Press Publishing 366

Piatkus Books 391

FANTASY

Ace Science Fiction and Fantasy 333

Amira Press 334

Archaia 336

Black Velvet Seductions Publishing 341

Cedar Fort, Inc. 347

Clarion Books 349

Coteau Books 351

DAW Books, Inc. 352

Del Rey Books 353

Dial Books for Young Readers 353

Divertir 354

Edge Science Fiction and Fantasy
  Publishing/Tesseract Books 356

Eos 358

Frances Lincoln Children's Books 361

Hadley Rille Books 364

HarperCollins Children's Books/
  HarperCollins Publishers 365

Highland Press Publishing 366

Hopewell Publications 367

Images SI, Inc. 368

Liquid Silver Books 375

Little, Brown and Co. Books for Young
  Readers 376

Loose Id 376

Martin Sisters Publishing, LLC 378

Medallion Media Group 379

New Victoria Publishers 382

Oak Tree Press 383

Renaissance House 397

Samhain Publishing, Ltd 400

Severn House Publishers 403

Silver Leaf Books, LLC 403

Small Beer Press 404

Sunbury Press, Inc. 406

Thirty-Fourth Parallel - 34th Parallel 318

Twilight Times Books 411

Wild Child Publishing 417

WindRiver Publishing, Inc. 418

FEMINIST

Bancroft Press 338

Cleis Press 349

Coteau Books 351

Crescent Moon Publishing 351

Guernica Editions 363

Little, Brown and Co. Books for Young
  Readers 376

New Victoria Publishers 382

Nortia Press 383

Oak Tree Press 383

Pedlar Press 388

Red Hen Press 397

Seal Press 401

Soho Press, Inc. 405

Wild Child Publishing 417

GAY

Bancroft Press 338

Carolina Wren Press 346

Cleis Press 349

Coteau Books 351

Crescent Moon Publishing 351

Ellora's Cave Publishing, Inc. 357

Gival Press 362

Guernica Editions 363

Hopewell Publications 367

Insomniac Press 369

Lethe Press 374

Liquid Silver Books 375

Little, Brown and Co. Books for Young
  Readers 376

Loose Id 376

Mondial 381

Pedlar Press 388

Red Hen Press 397

Samhain Publishing, Ltd 400

Seal Press 401

Starcherone Books 405

Stone Bridge Press 406

Torquere Press 410

University of Wisconsin Press 414

Wild Child Publishing 417

GLITZ

Samhain Publishing, Ltd 400

HISTORICAL

Amira Press 334

Avon Romance 337

Bancroft Press 338

Barbour Publishing, Inc. 339

Calkins Creek 345

Canterbury House Publishing, Ltd. 346

Cedar Fort, Inc. 347

Clarion Books 349

Coteau Books 351

Covenant Communications, Inc. 351

Divertir 354

Eakin Press 355

Frances Lincoln Children's Books 361

Gival Press 362

Glencannon Press, The 362

HarperCollins Children's Books/
    HarperCollins Publishers 365

Highland Press Publishing 366

Holiday House, Inc. 366

Hopewell Publications 367

JourneyForth 370

Liquid Silver Books 375

Little, Brown and Co. Books for Young
    Readers 376

Martin Sisters Publishing, LLC 378

McBooks Press 379

Medallion Media Group 379

Mondial 381

New Victoria Publishers 382

Nortia Press 383

Pelican Publishing Company 389

Piatkus Books 391

Pineapple Press, Inc. 392

Red Hen Press 397

River City Publishing 398

Samhain Publishing, Ltd 400

Seriously Good Books 402

Severn House Publishers 403

Soft Skull Press Inc. 404

Soho Press, Inc. 405

Twilight Times Books 411

University of Wisconsin Press 414

WaterBrook Multnomah Publishing
    Group 416

Wild Child Publishing 417

WindRiver Publishing, Inc. 418

HORROR

Amira Press 334

Archaia 336

Divertir 354

Medallion Media Group 379

Nortia Press 383

Pocol Press 392

Sakura Publishing & Technologies 399

Samhain Publishing, Ltd 400

Severn House Publishers 403

Silver Leaf Books, LLC 403

Wild Child Publishing 417

HUMOR/SATIRE

Amira Press 334

Bancroft Press 338

Cedar Fort, Inc. 347

Clarion Books 349

Coteau Books 351

Covenant Communications, Inc. 351

Divertir 354

Frances Lincoln Children's Books 361

Glencannon Press, The 362

HarperCollins Children's Books/
    HarperCollins Publishers 365

Holiday House, Inc. 366

Hopewell Publications 367

Insomniac Press 369

Little, Brown and Co. Books for Young
    Readers 376

Martin Sisters Publishing, LLC 378

New Victoria Publishers 382

Nortia Press 383

Oak Tree Press 383

Pedlar Press 388

Quixote Press 395

Seedling Continental Press 402

Wild Child Publishing 417

WindRiver Publishing, Inc. 418

LESBIAN

Carolina Wren Press 346

Ellora's Cave Publishing, Inc. 357

Gival Press 362

Insomniac Press 369

Lethe Press 374

Liquid Silver Books 375

Loose Id 376

New Victoria Publishers 382

Samhain Publishing, Ltd 400

Torquere Press 410

University of Wisconsin Press 414

Wild Child Publishing 417

LITERARY

Anvil Press 335

Arcade Publishing 335

Arte Publico Press 336

Avon Romance 337

Bancroft Press 338

Bellevue Literary Press 340

Broadway Books 343

Calamari Press 345

Canterbury House Publishing, Ltd. 346

Carolina Wren Press 346

Cedar Fort, Inc. 347

Cleis Press 349

Coteau Books 351

Covenant Communications, Inc. 351

Crescent Moon Publishing 351

Divertir 354

Dufour Editions 355

Ecco Press, The 356

Gival Press 362

Goose Lane Editions 362

Graywolf Press 362

Guernica Editions 363

Hampton Roads Publishing Co., Inc. 364

HarperCollins Children's Books/
    HarperCollins Publishers 365

Holiday House, Inc. 366

Houghton Mifflin Harcourt Co. 367

Insomniac Press 369

Knopf, Alfred A. 372

Lethe Press 374

Little, Brown and Co. Adult Trade Books
    375

Livingston Press 376

Lost Horse Press 377

Martin Sisters Publishing, LLC 378

Medallion Media Group 379

Milkweed Editions 381

Mondial 381

New Issues Poetry & Prose 382

Nortia Press 383

Orca Book Publishers 385

Paycock Press 388

Pedlar Press 388

Permanent Press, The 390

Persea Books 390

Piatkus Books 391

Picador USA 391

Pineapple Press, Inc. 392

Pocol Press 392

Press 53 394

Red Hen Press 397

River City Publishing 398

Riverhead Books 398

Ronsdale Press 399

Salvo Press 399

Sarabande Books, Inc. 400

Seal Press 401

Seven Stories Press 402

Small Beer Press 404

Soft Skull Press Inc. 404

Soho Press, Inc. 405

Starcherone Books 405

Stone Bridge Press 406

Talese, Nan A. 408

Tin House Books 409

Titan Press 409

Twilight Times Books 411

Tyrus Books 412

Unbridled Books 412

University of Michigan Press 412

Vehicule Press 414

Viking 414

Vintage Anchor Publishing 415

WaterBrook Multnomah Publishing
    Group 416

Wild Child Publishing 417

WindRiver Publishing, Inc. 418

Yellow Shoe Fiction Series 419

MAINSTREAM

Amira Press 334

Arcade Publishing 335

Arte Publico Press 336

Bancroft Press 338

Barbour Publishing, Inc. 339

Canterbury House Publishing, Ltd. 346

Carolina Wren Press 346

Cave Hollow Press 346

Cedar Fort, Inc. 347

Chronicle Books for Children 349

Coteau Books 351

Covenant Communications, Inc. 351

Divertir 354

Glencannon Press, The 362

Highland Press Publishing 366

Holiday House, Inc. 366

Insomniac Press 369

Little, Brown and Co. Adult Trade Books
    375

Medallion Media Group 379

Mondial 381

Oak Tree Press 383

Orca Book Publishers 385

Permanent Press, The 390

Piatkus Books 391

Pineapple Press, Inc. 392

Pocol Press 392

Red Hen Press 397

Riverhead Books 398

Samhain Publishing, Ltd 400

Severn House Publishers 403

Soft Skull Press Inc. 404

Soho Press, Inc. 405

Titan Press 409

Twilight Times Books 411

Viking 414

Villard Books 415

Vintage Anchor Publishing 415

WaterBrook Multnomah Publishing
    Group 416

Wild Child Publishing 417

MILITARY/WAR

Bancroft Press 338

Glencannon Press, The 362

Highland Press Publishing 366

Martin Sisters Publishing, LLC 378

McBooks Press 379

Nortia Press 383

Samhain Publishing, Ltd 400

Twilight Times Books 411

Wild Child Publishing 417

WindRiver Publishing, Inc. 418

MYSTERY/SUSPENSE

Amira Press 334

Archaia 336

Avon Romance 337

Bancroft Press 338

Canterbury House Publishing, Ltd. 346

Clarion Books 349

Coteau Books 351

Covenant Communications, Inc. 351

Glencannon Press, The 362

Highland Press Publishing 366
Hopewell Publications 367
Insomniac Press 369
JourneyForth 370
Liquid Silver Books 375
Little, Brown and Co. Books for Young
    Readers 376
Martin Sisters Publishing, LLC 378
Medallion Media Group 379
Mondial 381
New Victoria Publishers 382
Oak Tree Press 383
Permanent Press, The 390
Piatkus Books 391
Poisoned Pen Press 393
Salvo Press 399
Samhain Publishing, Ltd 400
Severn House Publishers 403
Silver Leaf Books, LLC 403
Soho Press, Inc. 405
Sunbury Press, Inc. 406
Twilight Times Books 411
Tyrus Books 412
University of Wisconsin Press 414
Viking 414
WaterBrook Multnomah Publishing
    Group 416
Wild Child Publishing 417
WindRiver Publishing, Inc. 418

NEW AGE
Bancroft Press 338
Crescent Moon Publishing 351
Divertir 354
Hampton Roads Publishing Co., Inc. 364
Twilight Times Books 411

PSYCHIC/SUPERNATURAL
Amira Press 334
Hampton Roads Publishing Co., Inc. 364
Lethe Press 374
Liquid Silver Books 375
Samhain Publishing, Ltd 400

Twilight Times Books 411
Wild Child Publishing 417
Write Place At the Write Time, The 326

REGIONAL
Canterbury House Publishing, Ltd. 346
Cave Hollow Press 346
Coteau Books 351
Covenant Communications, Inc. 351
Lost Horse Press 377
Nortia Press 383
Piatkus Books 391
Pineapple Press, Inc. 392
Plexus Publishing, Inc. 392
River City Publishing 398
Twilight Times Books 411
University of Wisconsin Press 414
Vehicule Press 414
Write Place At the Write Time, The 326

RELIGIOUS
Barbour Publishing, Inc. 339
Covenant Communications, Inc. 351
Divertir 354
Highland Press Publishing 366
Samhain Publishing, Ltd 400
WaterBrook Multnomah Publishing
    Group 416
WindRiver Publishing, Inc. 418
Write Place At the Write Time, The 326

ROMANCE
Amira Press 334
Avon Romance 337
Barbour Publishing, Inc. 339
Black Velvet Seductions Publishing 341
Canterbury House Publishing, Ltd. 346
Covenant Communications, Inc. 351
Divertir 354
Ellora's Cave Publishing, Inc. 357
English Tea Rose Press 358
Highland Press Publishing 366
Liquid Silver Books 375
Loose Id 376

Medallion Media Group 379

Mondial 381

Oak Tree Press 383

Piatkus Books 391

Samhain Publishing, Ltd 400

Severn House Publishers 403

Sunbury Press, Inc. 406

WaterBrook Multnomah Publishing
Group 416

Wild Child Publishing 417

Wild Rose Press 417

Write Place At the Write Time, The 326

SCIENCE FICTION

Ace Science Fiction and Fantasy 333

Amira Press 334

Archaia 336

Avon Romance 337

Bancroft Press 338

Cedar Fort, Inc. 347

Clarion Books 349

DAW Books, Inc. 352

Del Rey Books 353

Divertir 354

Edge Science Fiction and Fantasy
Publishing/Tesseract Books 356

Eos 358

Hadley Rille Books 364

Images SI, Inc. 368

Lethe Press 374

Liquid Silver Books 375

Little, Brown and Co. Books for Young
Readers 376

Loose Id 376

Medallion Media Group 379

New Victoria Publishers 382

Salvo Press 399

Samhain Publishing, Ltd 400

Silver Leaf Books, LLC 403

Small Beer Press 404

Sunbury Press, Inc. 406

Twilight Times Books 411

WaterBrook Multnomah Publishing
Group 416

Wild Child Publishing 417

WindRiver Publishing, Inc. 418

SHORT STORY COLLECTIONS

Amira Press 334

Anaphora Literary Press 334

Anvil Press 335

Arcade Publishing 335

Black Velvet Seductions Publishing 341

Calamari Press 345

C/Oasis 229

Coteau Books 351

Crescent Moon Publishing 351

Dufour Editions 355

Ecco Press, The 356

Four Way Books 361

Gival Press 362

Goose Lane Editions 362

Graywolf Press 362

Hadley Rille Books 364

Highland Press Publishing 366

Hopewell Publications 367

Livingston Press 376

Lost Horse Press 377

Mondial 381

Paycock Press 388

Pedlar Press 388

Persea Books 390

Pocol Press 392

Press 53 394

Quixote Press 395

Red Hen Press 397

River City Publishing 398

Ronsdale Press 399

Severn House Publishers 403

Small Beer Press 404

Soft Skull Press Inc. 404

Starcherone Books 405

Sunbury Press, Inc. 406

Tin House Books 409

Titan Press 409
University of Georgia Press 412
University of Michigan Press 412
University of Wisconsin Press 414
Vehicule Press 414
Vintage Anchor Publishing 415
Wild Child Publishing 417

THRILLER/ESPIONAGE
Highland Press Publishing 366
Hopewell Publications 367
JourneyForth 370
Little, Brown and Co. Books for Young
    Readers 376
Oak Tree Press 383
Piatkus Books 391
Salvo Press 399
Samhain Publishing, Ltd 400
Severn House Publishers 403
Soho Press, Inc. 405
Viking 414
WaterBrook Multnomah Publishing
    Group 416
Wild Child Publishing 417
WindRiver Publishing, Inc. 418

TRANSLATIONS
Arcade Publishing 335
Bancroft Press 338
Clarion Books 349
Guernica Editions 363
Interlink Publishing Group, Inc. 369
Italica Press 369
Martin Sisters Publishing, LLC 378
Milkweed Editions 381
Mondial 381
Persea Books 390
Stone Bridge Press 406
Tin House Books 409

WESTERN
Amira Press 334
Barbour Publishing, Inc. 339
Black Velvet Seductions Publishing 341

Cedar Fort, Inc. 347
Glencannon Press, The 362
Highland Press Publishing 366
JourneyForth 370
Martin Sisters Publishing, LLC 378
Samhain Publishing, Ltd 400
Sunbury Press, Inc. 406
Wild Child Publishing 417

YOUNG ADULT/TEEN
Abrams, Harry N., Inc. 333
Amira Press 334
Avon Romance 337
Bancroft Press 338
Candlewick Press 345
Cedar Fort, Inc. 347
Chronicle Books 348
Chronicle Books for Children 349
Coteau Books 351
Covenant Communications, Inc. 351
Craigmore Creations 351
Cricket Books 351
Dial Books for Young Readers 353
Divertir 354
Dutton Children's Books 355
Farrar, Straus & Giroux 359
Frances Lincoln Children's Books 361
Glencannon Press, The 362
HarperCollins Children's Books/
    HarperCollins Publishers 365
Hendrick-Long Publishing Co., Inc. 366
Highland Press Publishing 366
Hopewell Publications 367
JourneyForth 370
Lerner Publishing Group 374
Levine Books, Arthur A. 375
Little, Brown and Co. Books for Young
    Readers 376
Martin Sisters Publishing, LLC 378
Medallion Media Group 379
Oak Tree Press 383
Orca Book Publishers 385

Peachtree Children's Books 388

Persea Books 390

Piano Press 391

Piñata Books 391

Puffin Books 394

Ransom Publishing 396

Red Deer Press 396

Samhain Publishing, Ltd 400

Silver Leaf Books, LLC 403

Sunbury Press, Inc. 406

Twilight Times Books 411

Viking Children's Books 414

Wild Child Publishing 417

Wild Rose Press 417

WindRiver Publishing, Inc. 418

MAGAZINES

ADVENTURE

Adirondack Review, The 202

Advocate, PKA's Publication 202

African Voices 202

Allegheny Review, The 205

Anaphora Literary Press 334

Art Times 211

Barbaric Yawp 214

Bear Deluxe Magazine, The 215

Beginnings Publishing Inc. 215

Big Muddy 217

Blackbird 218

Blueline 219

Cadet Quest Magazine 223

CC&D 225

Cicada Magazine 227

Conceit Magazine 230

Cricket 233

Down in the Dirt 237

Foliate Oak Literary Magazine 247

Green Mountains Review 253

GUD Magazine 254

Harpur Palate 257

Highlights for Children 258

Kentucky Monthly 265

London Magazine, The 269

Lullwater Review 271

MacGuffin, The 272

Magazine of Fantasy & Science Fiction, The 272

New Millennium Writings 280

Nite-Writer's International Literary Arts Journal 282

Now & Then 284

On the Premises 285

Paddlefish 287

Pedestal Magazine, The 289

Pink Chameleon, The 292

Pockets 294

ScreaminMamas 305

SHINE brightly 306

Short Stuff 306

Stone Soup 312

Terrain.org 317

Toasted Cheese 319

Witches and Pagans 324

Write Place At the Write Time, The 326

CHILDREN'S/JUVENILE

Advocate, PKA's Publication 202

African Voices 202

Anaphora Literary Press 334

Conceit Magazine 230

Cricket 233

Highlights for Children 258

Ladybug 265

New Millennium Writings 280

Paddlefish 287

SHINE brightly 306

Toasted Cheese 319

COMICS/GRAPHIC NOVELS

5_Trope 201

Albedo One 204

Anaphora Literary Press 334

Blackbird 218

Cadet Quest Magazine 223

Foliate Oak Literary Magazine 247

Grasslimb 253

Midway Journal 275

New Millennium Writings 280

Packingtown Review 287

Paddlefish 287

PMS poemmemoirstory 294

Wild Violet 322

Writer's Bloc 326

EROTICA

African Voices 202

Ascent Aspirations 211

Ducts 237

First Class 244

Gargoyle 250

Gathering of the Tribes, A 203

GUD Magazine 254

Ledge Magazine, The 267

London Magazine, The 269

New Millennium Writings 280

Nite-Writer's International Literary Arts
    Journal 282

Paddlefish 287

Penthouse Variations 290

Quarter After Eight 299

Tales of the Talisman 316

Witches and Pagans 324

ETHNIC/MULTICULTURAL

ACM (Another Chicago Magazine) 201

Advocate, PKA's Publication 202

African Voices 202

Allegheny Review, The 205

Amoskeag, The Journal of Southern New
    Hampshire University 207

Apalachee Review 209

Art Times 211

Big Muddy 217

Binnacle, The 218

Blackbird 218

Black Lace 219

Boston Review 220

Briar Cliff Review, The 221

Brilliant Corners 221

CC&D 225

Cha 225

Chaffin Journal 226

Conceit Magazine 230

Convergence 232

Crab Orchard Review 233

Creative With Words Publications 233

Cricket 233

Crucible 234

Down in the Dirt 237

Ducts 237

Epoch 240

Essays & Fictions 240

Flint Hills Review 245

Foliate Oak Literary Magazine 247

Fourteen Hills 247

Fugue Literary Magazine 249

Gargoyle 250

Gathering of the Tribes, A 203

Georgetown Review 251

Grasslimb 253

Green Hills Literary Lantern 253

GUD Magazine 254

Gulf Coast 255

Hadassah Magazine 256

Harpur Palate 257

Hayden's Ferry Review 257

Highlights for Children 258

Home Planet News 259

Indiana Review 261

Jabberwock Review 262

Jewish Currents 263

Kenyon Review, The 265

Lake Superior Magazine 266

Ledge Magazine, The 267

Left Curve 267

London Magazine, The 269

Long Story, The 270

Louisiana Review, The 271

Lullwater Review 271

MacGuffin, The 272
Midway Journal 275
Missouri Review, The 275
Mobius 276
Na'amat Woman 277
New Letters 279
New Millennium Writings 280
North Dakota Quarterly 283
Now & Then 284
On the Premises 285
Packingtown Review 287
Paddlefish 287
Painted Bride Quarterly 287
Paperplates 287
Passages North 288
Paterson Literary Review 288
Pedestal Magazine, The 289
Persimmon Tree 291
Pisgah Review 292
Pleiades 293
PMS poemmemoirstory 294
Pockets 294
Pointed Circle 295
Puerto del Sol 299
Quarter After Eight 299
Quarterly West 299
Raven Chronicles, The 301
River Styx Magazine 303
Rockford Review, The 303
Salmagundi 304
Saranac Review, The 304
SHINE brightly 306
So to Speak 308
South Dakota Review 308
Southwestern American Literature 310
Stone Soup 312
Straylight 313
Struggle 314
Talking River 316
Terrain.org 317
Toasted Cheese 319

Transition 320
Wild Violet 322
Windhover 324
Witches and Pagans 324
Write Place At the Write Time, The 326
Writer's Bloc 326
Xavier Review 326
Yemassee 327
ZYZZYVA 328

EXPERIMENTAL

5_Trope 201
580 Split 201
ACM (Another Chicago Magazine) 201
Adirondack Review, The 202
Advocate, PKA's Publication 202
African Voices 202
Alaska Quarterly Review 203
Albedo One 204
Allegheny Review, The 205
American Short Fiction 207
Amoskeag, The Journal of Southern New
    Hampshire University 207
Anaphora Literary Press 334
Antioch Review 208
Apalachee Review 209
Ascent Aspirations 211
Barbaric Yawp 214
Berkeley Fiction Review 217
Big Muddy 217
Binnacle, The 218
Blackbird 218
Boston Review 220
Brilliant Corners 221
Cafe Irreal, The 223
Capilano Review, The 224
CC&D 225
Chapman 226
Coal City Review 229
Conceit Magazine 230
Convergence 232
Crucible 234

Diagram 236

Down in the Dirt 237

Epoch 240

Essays & Fictions 240

Fiction 243

Florida Review, The 245

Foliate Oak Literary Magazine 247

Fourteen Hills 247

Fugue Literary Magazine 249

Gargoyle 250

Gathering of the Tribes, A 203

Georgetown Review 251

Gettysburg Review, The 251

Grasslimb 253

Green Hills Literary Lantern 253

Green Mountains Review 253

GUD Magazine 254

Gulf Coast 255

Harpur Palate 257

Hayden's Ferry Review 257

Home Planet News 259

Idaho Review, The 260

Indiana Review 261

Jabberwock Review 262

J Journal 263

Kenyon Review, The 265

Left Curve 267

Literal Latté 269

London Magazine, The 269

Lullwater Review 271

MacGuffin, The 272

Madison Review, The 272

Mid-American Review 275

Midway Journal 275

Mobius 276

New Letters 279

New Millennium Writings 280

North Dakota Quarterly 283

Now & Then 284

On the Premises 285

Outer Art 286

Packingtown Review 287

Paddlefish 287

Painted Bride Quarterly 287

Paumanok Review, The 289

Pedestal Magazine, The 289

Persimmon Tree 291

Philadelphia Stories 291

Pisgah Review 292

Pleiades 293

PMS poemmemoirstory 294

Portland Review 296

Prism International 298

Puerto del Sol 299

Quarter After Eight 299

Quarterly West 299

Red Rock Review 302

River Styx Magazine 303

Rockford Review, The 303

Salmagundi 304

So to Speak 308

Stone Soup 312

storySouth 313

Straylight 313

Struggle 314

Sycamore Review 315

Terrain.org 317

Toad Suck Review 319

Versal 321

Western Humanities Review 322

Wild Violet 322

Windhover 324

Writer's Bloc 326

Xavier Review 326

Yalobusha Review, The 327

Yemassee 327

ZYZZYVA 328

FAMILY SAGA

Adirondack Review, The 202

Allegheny Review, The 205

Beginnings Publishing Inc. 215

Big Muddy 217

Blackbird 218
CC&D 225
Conceit Magazine 230
Foliate Oak Literary Magazine 247
New Millennium Writings 280
On the Premises 285
Paddlefish 287
Pedestal Magazine, The 289
Persimmon Tree 291
Pink Chameleon, The 292
Salmagundi 304
Terrain.org 317
Write Place At the Write Time, The 326
Yalobusha Review, The 327

FANTASY

Advocate, PKA's Publication 202
African Voices 202
Albedo One 204
Allegheny Review, The 205
Allegory 205
Apalachee Review 209
Art Times 211
Ascent Aspirations 211
Barbaric Yawp 214
Blackbird 218
Cafe Irreal, The 223
CC&D 225
Cicada Magazine 227
Conceit Magazine 230
Cricket 233
DargonZine 234
Down in the Dirt 237
Gathering of the Tribes, A 203
GUD Magazine 254
Harpur Palate 257
Highlights for Children 258
Ideomancer 260
Leading Edge 267
Literal Latté 269
London Magazine, The 269
Lullwater Review 271

Magazine of Fantasy & Science Fiction,
    The 272
Mobius 276
New Millennium Writings 280
Now & Then 284
Nth Degree 284
On Spec 285
On the Premises 285
Orson Scott Card's InterGalactic
    Medicine Show 225
Paddlefish 287
Pedestal Magazine, The 289
Pink Chameleon, The 292
Rockford Review, The 303
ScreaminMamas 305
Stone Soup 312
Summerset Review, The 315
Tales of the Talisman 316
Terrain.org 317
Toasted Cheese 319
Wild Violet 322
Windhover 324
Witches and Pagans 324

FEMINIST

ACM (Another Chicago Magazine) 201
Advocate, PKA's Publication 202
Allegheny Review, The 205
Amoskeag, The Journal of Southern New
    Hampshire University 207
Anaphora Literary Press 334
Apalachee Review 209
Art Times 211
Ascent Aspirations 211
Big Muddy 217
Blackbird 218
Briar Cliff Review, The 221
CC&D 225
Conceit Magazine 230
Convergence 232
Crucible 234
Down in the Dirt 237

Essays & Fictions 240
Foliate Oak Literary Magazine 247
Gathering of the Tribes, A 203
Green Hills Literary Lantern 253
Home Planet News 259
Jabberwock Review 262
Jewish Currents 263
Kenyon Review, The 265
Long Story, The 270
Midway Journal 275
Mobius 276
New Millennium Writings 280
North Dakota Quarterly 283
On the Premises 285
Packingtown Review 287
Paddlefish 287
Painted Bride Quarterly 287
Paperplates 287
Pedestal Magazine, The 289
Persimmon Tree 291
Pleiades 293
PMS poemmemoirstory 294
River Styx Magazine 303
So to Speak 308
Southern Humanities Review 309
Still Crazy 312
Struggle 314
Talking River 316
Terrain.org 317
Toasted Cheese 319
Wild Violet 322
Yemassee 327

GAY

ACM (Another Chicago Magazine) 201
Adirondack Review, The 202
African Voices 202
Allegheny Review, The 205
Art Times 211
Blackbird 218
CC&D 225
Conceit Magazine 230

Convergence 232
Down in the Dirt 237
Essays & Fictions 240
Flint Hills Review 245
Foliate Oak Literary Magazine 247
Fourteen Hills 247
Gargoyle 250
Gathering of the Tribes, A 203
Grasslimb 253
Home Planet News 259
Jabberwock Review 262
J Journal 263
Kenyon Review, The 265
Midway Journal 275
Mobius 276
New Millennium Writings 280
Packingtown Review 287
Paddlefish 287
Painted Bride Quarterly 287
Paperplates 287
Pedestal Magazine, The 289
Persimmon Tree 291
Pleiades 293
Quarter After Eight 299
River Styx Magazine 303
Salmagundi 304
Straylight 313
Terrain.org 317
Toasted Cheese 319
Wild Violet 322
Yemassee 327

GLITZ

Blackbird 218
New Millennium Writings 280
Packingtown Review 287
Paddlefish 287
Pedestal Magazine, The 289
Terrain.org 317

HISTORICAL

Adirondack Review, The 202
Advocate, PKA's Publication 202

African Voices 202

Allegheny Review, The 205

Anaphora Literary Press 334

Apalachee Review 209

Appalachian Heritage 209

Art Times 211

Barbaric Yawp 214

Bear Deluxe Magazine, The 215

Big Muddy 217

Blackbird 218

Briar Cliff Review, The 221

CC&D 225

Chaffin Journal 226

Chapman 226

Cicada Magazine 227

Conceit Magazine 230

Cricket 233

Down in the Dirt 237

Essays & Fictions 240

Flint Hills Review 245

Foliate Oak Literary Magazine 247

Gathering of the Tribes, A 203

Gettysburg Review, The 251

Harpur Palate 257

Highlights for Children 258

Home Planet News 259

Horizons 259

Jewish Currents 263

J Journal 263

Kentucky Monthly 265

Kenyon Review, The 265

Lake Superior Magazine 266

Left Curve 267

London Magazine, The 269

Louisiana Review, The 271

Lullwater Review 271

MacGuffin, The 272

Midway Journal 275

Mobius 276

Na'amat Woman 277

Nassau Review 278

New Millennium Writings 280

Nite-Writer's International Literary Arts Journal 282

North Dakota Quarterly 283

Now & Then 284

Nth Degree 284

On the Premises 285

Packingtown Review 287

Paddlefish 287

Paumanok Review, The 289

Pedestal Magazine, The 289

Persimmon Tree 291

Pockets 294

Portland Review 296

Queen's Quarterly 299

Salmagundi 304

Saranac Review, The 304

ScreaminMamas 305

SHINE brightly 306

Short Stuff 306

Stone Soup 312

Struggle 314

Talking River 316

Terrain.org 317

Toasted Cheese 319

Transition 320

Windhover 324

Witches and Pagans 324

Write Place At the Write Time, The 326

Xavier Review 326

Yalobusha Review, The 327

Yemassee 327

HORROR

African Voices 202

Albedo One 204

Allegheny Review, The 205

Allegory 205

Ascent Aspirations 211

Barbaric Yawp 214

Bear Deluxe Magazine, The 215

Blackbird 218

CC&D 225

Conceit Magazine 230

Down in the Dirt 237

Gathering of the Tribes, A 203

GUD Magazine 254

Harpur Palate 257

Ideomancer 260

Magazine of Fantasy & Science Fiction,
    The 272

MicroHorror 274

Mobius 276

New Millennium Writings 280

Nth Degree 284

On Spec 285

On the Premises 285

Orson Scott Card's InterGalactic
    Medicine Show 225

Paddlefish 287

Paumanok Review, The 289

Pedestal Magazine, The 289

Pseudopod 298

Tales of the Talisman 316

Terrain.org 317

Toasted Cheese 319

Wild Violet 322

Witches and Pagans 324

HUMOR/SATIRE

580 Split 201

Advocate, PKA's Publication 202

African Voices 202

Allegheny Review, The 205

Amoskeag, The Journal of Southern New
    Hampshire University 207

Apalachee Review 209

Art Times 211

Bear Deluxe Magazine, The 215

Big Muddy 217

Binnacle, The 218

Blackbird 218

Blueline 219

Briar Cliff Review, The 221

Chaffin Journal 226

Chapman 226

Cicada Magazine 227

Conceit Magazine 230

Creative With Words Publications 233

Cricket 233

Ducts 237

Essays & Fictions 240

Fiction 243

Foliate Oak Literary Magazine 247

Fourteen Hills 247

Fugue Literary Magazine 249

Gathering of the Tribes, A 203

Gettysburg Review, The 251

Green Hills Literary Lantern 253

Green Mountains Review 253

GUD Magazine 254

Harper's Magazine 256

Harpur Palate 257

Hayden's Ferry Review 257

Highlights for Children 258

Horizons 259

Jewish Currents 263

Kenyon Review, The 265

Lake Superior Magazine 266

London Magazine, The 269

Lullwater Review 271

MacGuffin, The 272

Midway Journal 275

Missouri Review, The 275

Mobius 276

Na'amat Woman 277

Nassau Review 278

New Letters 279

New Millennium Writings 280

Nite-Writer's International Literary Arts
    Journal 282

North Dakota Quarterly 283

Now & Then 284

Nth Degree 284

On the Premises 285

Paddlefish 287
Pearl 289
Pedestal Magazine, The 289
Persimmon Tree 291
Pink Chameleon, The 292
Pleiades 293
Portland Review 296
Quarter After Eight 299
Quarterly West 299
Reform Judaism 302
Rockford Review, The 303
ScreaminMamas 305
SHINE brightly 306
Short Stuff 306
Southern Humanities Review 309
Stone Soup 312
Struggle 314
Summerset Review, The 315
Sycamore Review 315
Talking River 316
Terrain.org 317
Texas Review 317
Toasted Cheese 319
Transition 320
Wild Violet 322
Windhover 324
Witches and Pagans 324
Word Riot 325
Write Place At the Write Time, The 326
Yalobusha Review, The 327
Yemassee 327
ZYZZYVA 328

LESBIAN
ACM (Another Chicago Magazine) 201
Allegheny Review, The 205
Art Times 211
Blackbird 218
Black Lace 219
CC&D 225
Conceit Magazine 230
Convergence 232

Down in the Dirt 237
Essays & Fictions 240
Foliate Oak Literary Magazine 247
Fourteen Hills 247
Gargoyle 250
Gathering of the Tribes, A 203
Home Planet News 259
Kenyon Review, The 265
Midway Journal 275
Mobius 276
New Millennium Writings 280
Paddlefish 287
Painted Bride Quarterly 287
Paperplates 287
Pedestal Magazine, The 289
Persimmon Tree 291
Quarter After Eight 299
River Styx Magazine 303
So to Speak 308
Straylight 313
Terrain.org 317
Toasted Cheese 319
Wild Violet 322
Yemassee 327

LITERARY
5_Trope 201
580 Split 201
ACM (Another Chicago Magazine) 201
Advocate, PKA's Publication 202
African Voices 202
Alaska Quarterly Review 203
Albedo One 204
Alembic, The 204
Alimentum, The Literature of Food 204
Allegheny Review, The 205
American Literary Review 206
American Short Fiction 207
Amoskeag, The Journal of Southern New
    Hampshire University 207
Antioch Review 208
Apalachee Review 209

Appalachian Heritage 209
Art Times 211
Ascent Aspirations 211
Barbaric Yawp 214
Beginnings Publishing Inc. 215
Bellevue Literary Review 215
Beloit Fiction Journal 216
Berkeley Fiction Review 217
Big Muddy 217
Blackbird 218
Black Warrior Review 219
Blueline 219
Boston Review 220
Briar Cliff Review, The 221
Brilliant Corners 221
Broadkill Review, The 221
Button 222
CC&D 225
Chaffin Journal 226
Chapman 226
Chicago Quarterly Review 227
Coal City Review 229
C/Oasis 229
Conceit Magazine 230
Contrary 231
Convergence 232
Crab Orchard Review 233
Crucible 234
Dead Mule School of Southern Literature,
    The 235
descant 236
Descant 235
Diagram 236
DISLOCATE 236
Down in the Dirt 237
Ducts 237
Epoch 240
Essays & Fictions 240
Failbetter.com 242
Faultline 242
Fickle Muses 243

Fiction 243
Fiddlehead, The 243
First Class 244
Florida Review, The 245
Flyway 246
Foliate Oak Literary Magazine 247
Fourteen Hills 247
Front & Centre 249
Fugue Literary Magazine 249
Gargoyle 250
Gathering of the Tribes, A 203
Georgetown Review 251
Gettysburg Review, The 251
Glimmer Train Stories 252
Grasslimb 253
Green Hills Literary Lantern 253
Green Mountains Review 253
GUD Magazine 254
Gulf Coast 255
Gulf Stream Magazine 255
Hayden's Ferry Review 257
Home Planet News 259
Idaho Review, The 260
Indiana Review 261
Italian Americana 262
Jabberwock Review 262
J Journal 263
Journal, The 263
Kenyon Review, The 265
Laurel Review, The 266
Ledge Magazine, The 267
Left Curve 267
Listening Eye, The 268
Literal Latté 269
Literary Review, The 269
Long Story, The 270
Louisiana Literature 271
MacGuffin, The 272
Madison Review, The 272
Manoa 273
Michigan Quarterly Review 274

Mid-American Review 275

Midway Journal 275

Missouri Review, The 275

Mobius 276

Na'amat Woman 277

Nassau Review 278

Natural Bridge 278

Nebo 278

New England Review 279

New Letters 279

New Madrid 280

New Millennium Writings 280

New South 281

Nite-Writer's International Literary Arts
    Journal 282

North American Review 283

North Dakota Quarterly 283

Now & Then 284

On the Premises 285

Outer Art 286

Oyez Review 286

Packingtown Review 287

Paddlefish 287

Painted Bride Quarterly 287

Paperplates 287

Paris Review, The 288

Passages North 288

Paterson Literary Review 288

Paumanok Review, The 289

Pearl 289

Pedestal Magazine, The 289

Pennsylvania English 289

Persimmon Tree 291

Philadelphia Stories 291

Pink Chameleon, The 292

Pinyon Poetry 292

Pisgah Review 292

Pleiades 293

PMS poemmemoirstory 294

Pointed Circle 295

Polyphony H.S. 295

POST ROAD 296

Prairie Journal, The 297

Prairie Schooner 297

Prism International 298

Puerto del Sol 299

Quarter After Eight 299

Quarterly West 299

Queen's Quarterly 299

Rattapallax 301

Raven Chronicles, The 301

Reader, The 301

Redivider 302

Red Rock Review 302

River Styx Magazine 303

Rockford Review, The 303

Salmagundi 304

Saranac Review, The 304

ScreaminMamas 305

Seattle Review, The 305

Slow Trains Literary Journal 307

Snreview 307

So to Speak 308

South Carolina Review 308

South Dakota Review 308

Southern Review, The 310

Southwestern American Literature 310

Southwest Review 310

Stirring 312

storySouth 313

Straylight 313

Struggle 314

subTerrain 314

Subtropics 314

Summerset Review, The 315

Sun, The 315

Sycamore Review 315

Talking River 316

Terrain.org 317

Texas Review 317

Third Coast 318

Threepenny Review, The 318

Toad Suck Review 319

Toasted Cheese 319

Transition 320

Versal 321

Western Humanities Review 322

Wild Violet 322

Willow Springs 323

Windhover 324

Wisconsin Review 324

Worcester Review, The 325

Word Riot 325

Write Place At the Write Time, The 326

Writer's Bloc 326

Xavier Review 326

Yalobusha Review, The 327

Yemassee 327

MAINSTREAM

Advocate, PKA's Publication 202

African Voices 202

Alembic, The 204

Allegheny Review, The 205

American Literary Review 206

Apalachee Review 209

Art Times 211

Ascent Aspirations 211

Barbaric Yawp 214

Beginnings Publishing Inc. 215

Beloit Fiction Journal 216

Berkeley Fiction Review 217

Big Muddy 217

Binnacle, The 218

Blackbird 218

Briar Cliff Review, The 221

Brilliant Corners 221

Chaffin Journal 226

Cicada Magazine 227

Conceit Magazine 230

Ducts 237

Epoch 240

Foliate Oak Literary Magazine 247

Fourteen Hills 247

Gargoyle 250

Gathering of the Tribes, A 203

Gettysburg Review, The 251

Green Hills Literary Lantern 253

Green Mountains Review 253

Gulf Stream Magazine 255

Harpur Palate 257

Home Planet News 259

Horizons 259

Indiana Review 261

Jabberwock Review 262

Kentucky Monthly 265

Kenyon Review, The 265

Lake Superior Magazine 266

London Magazine, The 269

Louisiana Literature 271

Lullwater Review 271

MacGuffin, The 272

Manoa 273

Missouri Review, The 275

Mobius 276

Nassau Review 278

Nebo 278

New Letters 279

New Millennium Writings 280

Nite-Writer's International Literary Arts
    Journal 282

Now & Then 284

On the Premises 285

Packingtown Review 287

Paddlefish 287

Paperplates 287

Passages North 288

Paumanok Review, The 289

Pearl 289

Pedestal Magazine, The 289

Pennsylvania English 289

Persimmon Tree 291

Philadelphia Stories 291

Pink Chameleon, The 292

Pisgah Review 292

Pleiades 293

Puerto del Sol 299

Quarter After Eight 299

Quarterly West 299

Queen's Quarterly 299

Red Rock Review 302

River Styx Magazine 303

ScreaminMamas 305

Shenandoah 306

Short Stuff 306

Snreview 307

So to Speak 308

South Carolina Review 308

South Dakota Review 308

Southwestern American Literature 310

St. Anthony Messenger 311

Straylight 313

Sycamore Review 315

Talking River 316

Terrain.org 317

Texas Review 317

Toad Suck Review 319

Toasted Cheese 319

Witches and Pagans 324

Word Riot 325

Write Place At the Write Time, The 326

Xavier Review 326

Yalobusha Review, The 327

ZYZZYVA 328

MILITARY/WAR

Anaphora Literary Press 334

Big Muddy 217

Blackbird 218

Conceit Magazine 230

J Journal 263

New Millennium Writings 280

On the Premises 285

Packingtown Review 287

Paddlefish 287

Pedestal Magazine, The 289

Terrain.org 317

MYSTERY/SUSPENSE

Advocate, PKA's Publication 202

African Voices 202

Allegheny Review, The 205

Anaphora Literary Press 334

Apalachee Review 209

Ascent Aspirations 211

Bear Deluxe Magazine, The 215

Beginnings Publishing Inc. 215

Big Muddy 217

Blackbird 218

CC&D 225

Cicada Magazine 227

Conceit Magazine 230

Creative With Words Publications 233

Cricket 233

Down in the Dirt 237

Ellery Queen's Mystery Magazine 238

Grasslimb 253

Hardboiled 256

Harpur Palate 257

J Journal 263

London Magazine, The 269

Lullwater Review 271

Nassau Review 278

New Millennium Writings 280

On the Premises 285

Paddlefish 287

Paumanok Review, The 289

Pedestal Magazine, The 289

Pink Chameleon, The 292

ScreaminMamas 305

SHINE brightly 306

Short Stuff 306

Stone Soup 312

Terrain.org 317

Toasted Cheese 319

Witches and Pagans 324

Woman's World 324

NEW AGE

Allegheny Review, The 205

Apalachee Review 209

Ascent Aspirations 211

Blackbird 218

CC&D 225

Conceit Magazine 230

Down in the Dirt 237

New Millennium Writings 280

On the Premises 285

Paddlefish 287

Pedestal Magazine, The 289

Terrain.org 317

Toasted Cheese 319

Wild Violet 322

Write Place At the Write Time, The 326

PSYCHIC/SUPERNATURAL

African Voices 202

Allegheny Review, The 205

Ascent Aspirations 211

Barbaric Yawp 214

Blackbird 218

CC&D 225

Conceit Magazine 230

Down in the Dirt 237

Magazine of Fantasy & Science Fiction,
   The 272

New Millennium Writings 280

On the Premises 285

Paddlefish 287

Terrain.org 317

Toasted Cheese 319

Wild Violet 322

Write Place At the Write Time, The 326

REGIONAL

Advocate, PKA's Publication 202

Appalachian Heritage 209

Barbaric Yawp 214

Big Muddy 217

Blackbird 218

Blueline 219

Boston Review 220

Briar Cliff Review, The 221

Chaffin Journal 226

Convergence 232

Creative With Words Publications 233

Crucible 234

Flint Hills Review 245

Gettysburg Review, The 251

Grasslimb 253

Green Hills Literary Lantern 253

Gulf Coast 255

Hayden's Ferry Review 257

Indiana Review 261

Jabberwock Review 262

J Journal 263

Kelsey Review, The 264

Left Curve 267

Louisiana Literature 271

Louisiana Review, The 271

New Millennium Writings 280

North Carolina Literary Review 283

Now & Then 284

On the Premises 285

Packingtown Review 287

Paddlefish 287

Passages North 288

Pedestal Magazine, The 289

Pleiades 293

PMS poemmemoirstory 294

Pointed Circle 295

Portland Review 296

Prairie Journal, The 297

Raven Chronicles, The 301

Rockford Review, The 303

So to Speak 308

South Dakota Review 308

Southern Humanities Review 309

Southwestern American Literature 310

storySouth 313

Straylight 313

Struggle 314

Sycamore Review 315

Talking River 316

Terrain.org 317

Toad Suck Review 319

Transition 320

Write Place At the Write Time, The 326

Writer's Bloc 326

Xavier Review 326

Yemassee 327

RELIGIOUS

African Voices 202

Allegheny Review, The 205

Barbaric Yawp 214

Blackbird 218

Cadet Quest Magazine 223

Conceit Magazine 230

Evangel 241

Liguorian 268

London Magazine, The 269

Lullwater Review 271

New Millennium Writings 280

Nite-Writer's International Literary Arts
     Journal 282

Paddlefish 287

Pink Chameleon, The 292

Pockets 294

Reform Judaism 302

Seek 306

SHINE brightly 306

St. Anthony Messenger 311

Witches and Pagans 324

Write Place At the Write Time, The 326

Xavier Review 326

ROMANCE

Advocate, PKA's Publication 202

African Voices 202

Allegheny Review, The 205

Anaphora Literary Press 334

Beginnings Publishing Inc. 215

Brilliant Corners 221

Cicada Magazine 227

Conceit Magazine 230

Gathering of the Tribes, A 203

London Magazine, The 269

Louisiana Review, The 271

New Millennium Writings 280

Nite-Writer's International Literary Arts
     Journal 282

On the Premises 285

Paddlefish 287

Pedestal Magazine, The 289

Pink Chameleon, The 292

ScreaminMamas 305

SHINE brightly 306

Short Stuff 306

Toasted Cheese 319

Witches and Pagans 324

Woman's World 324

SCIENCE FICTION

Advocate, PKA's Publication 202

African Voices 202

Albedo One 204

Allegheny Review, The 205

Allegory 205

Analog Science Fiction & Fact 207

Art Times 211

Ascent Aspirations 211

Barbaric Yawp 214

Beginnings Publishing Inc. 215

Cafe Irreal, The 223

CC&D 225

Cicada Magazine 227

Conceit Magazine 230

Cricket 233

Down in the Dirt 237

First Class 244

Foliate Oak Literary Magazine 247

Gathering of the Tribes, A 203

GUD Magazine 254

Harpur Palate 257

Home Planet News 259

Ideomancer 260

La Kancerkliniko 265

Leading Edge 267

Left Curve 267
Literal Latté 269
Lullwater Review 271
Magazine of Fantasy & Science Fiction, The 272
Midway Journal 275
Mobius 276
New Millennium Writings 280
Nth Degree 284
On Spec 285
On the Premises 285
Orson Scott Card's InterGalactic Medicine Show 225
Paddlefish 287
Paumanok Review, The 289
Pedestal Magazine, The 289
Pink Chameleon, The 292
Premonitions 297
Rockford Review, The 303
ScreaminMamas 305
Short Stuff 306
Stone Soup 312
Struggle 314
Tales of the Talisman 316
Terrain.org 317
Toasted Cheese 319
Wild Violet 322

THRILLER/ESPIONAGE
Blackbird 218
Conceit Magazine 230
Cricket 233
Grasslimb 253
New Millennium Writings 280
On the Premises 285
Paddlefish 287
Pedestal Magazine, The 289
Pink Chameleon, The 292
Terrain.org 317
Toasted Cheese 319

TRANSLATIONS
580 Split 201

ACM (Another Chicago Magazine) 201
Adirondack Review, The 202
Alaska Quarterly Review 203
American Short Fiction 207
Anaphora Literary Press 334
Antioch Review 208
Apalachee Review 209
Big Muddy 217
Blackbird 218
Boston Review 220
Cafe Irreal, The 223
Conceit Magazine 230
Convergence 232
Crab Orchard Review 233
Faultline 242
Fiction 243
Flint Hills Review 245
Fourteen Hills 247
Gargoyle 250
Gathering of the Tribes, A 203
Grasslimb 253
Green Mountains Review 253
Gulf Coast 255
Indiana Review 261
Jabberwock Review 262
Jewish Currents 263
Kenyon Review, The 265
Left Curve 267
MacGuffin, The 272
Madison Review, The 272
Manoa 273
Mid-American Review 275
Midway Journal 275
New Letters 279
New Millennium Writings 280
Packingtown Review 287
Paddlefish 287
Painted Bride Quarterly 287
Paperplates 287
Pleiades 293
PMS poemmemoirstory 294

Prism International 298
Puerto del Sol 299
Quarter After Eight 299
Quarterly West 299
River Styx Magazine 303
So to Speak 308
storySouth 313
Struggle 314
Sycamore Review 315
Terrain.org 317
Toad Suck Review 319
Willow Springs 323
Writer's Bloc 326
Xavier Review 326

WESTERN
Advocate, PKA's Publication 202
Allegheny Review, The 205
Bear Deluxe Magazine, The 215
Beginnings Publishing Inc. 215
Blackbird 218
Cicada Magazine 227
Conceit Magazine 230
Cricket 233
Lullwater Review 271
New Millennium Writings 280
On the Premises 285

Paddlefish 287
Paumanok Review, The 289
Pedestal Magazine, The 289
Pink Chameleon, The 292
Short Stuff 306
Terrain.org 317
Toasted Cheese 319

YOUNG ADULT/TEEN
African Voices 202
Anaphora Literary Press 334
Blackbird 218
Cicada Magazine 227
Conceit Magazine 230
Creative With Words Publications 233
Liguorian 268
Magazine of Fantasy & Science Fiction, The 272
New Millennium Writings 280
Nite-Writer's International Literary Arts Journal 282
Nth Degree 284
Paddlefish 287
Pink Chameleon, The 292
Struggle 314

GENERAL INDEX

GENERAL

5_Trope 201

24-Hour Short Story Contest 423

580 Split 201

Abbeville Family 333

Able Muse 201

Abrams Books for Young Readers 333

Abrams, Harry N., Inc. 333

Academy Chicago Publishers 333

Ace Science Fiction and Fantasy 333

ACM (Another Chicago Magazine) 201

Adirondack Review, The 202

Advocate, PKA's Publication 202

Aeon Award 423

Aesthetica Creative Works Competition 423

African Voices 202

Agni 203

Ag Weekly 203

Ahearn Agency, Inc., The 124

AHWA Flash & Short Story Competition 423

AKC Gazette Annual Fiction Contest 423

Alabama State Council on the Arts Individual Artist Fellowship 423

Aladdin 333

Alaska Quarterly Review 203

Alaska Writers Conference 474

Albedo One 204

Alembic, The 204

Algonkian Five Day Novel Camp 462

Alimentum, The Literature of Food 204

Alive Communications, Inc. 124

Alive Now 205

All Due Respect 205

Allegheny Review, The 205

Allegory 205

Alligator Juniper 206

Alligator Juniper Award 424

Alondra Press, LLC 334

Ambassador Literary Agency & Speakers Bureau 124

American Association of University Women Award in Juvenile Literature 424

American Carriage House Publishing 334

American Christian Writers Conferences 464

American Gem Literary Festival, The 424

American Literary Review 206

American Literary Review Contests 424

American Markets Newsletter Short Story
Competition 424

American Poetry Review, The 206

American Quilter's Society 334

American-Scandinavian Foundation
Translation Prize 424

American Short Fiction 207

Amira Press 334

Amoskeag, The Journal of Southern New
Hampshire University 207

Amsterdam Agency, Marcia 125

Amster Literary Enterprises, Betsy 125

Amulet Books 334

Analog Science Fiction & Fact 207

Anaphora Literary Press 334

Ancient Paths 208

Anderson Foundation Fiction Award, The
Sherwood 425

Anderson Short Fiction Award, Sherwood
425

Annick Press, Ltd. 335

Antigonish Review, The 208

Antioch Review 208

Antioch Writers' Workshop 466

Anvil Press 335

Apalachee Review 209

Apex Magazine 209

Appalachian Heritage 209

Apple Valley Review 209

Arcade Publishing 335

Archaia 336

Aries 210

Arkansas Review 210

Arsenal Pulp Press 336

Art Affair Short Story and Western Short
Story Contests 425

Arte Publico Press 336

Artful Dodge 210

Artist Trust Fellowship Award 425

Arts & Letters 210

Art Times 211

Art Workshops in Guatemala 476

Ascent Aspirations 211

Asimov's Science Fiction 211

asinine poetry 212

Aspen Summer Words Literary Festival &
Writing Retreat 469

Athenaeum Literary Award, The 425

Atheneum Books for Young Readers 336

Atlanta Writers Conference 465

Atlantic Monthly, The 212

Atlantic Writing Competition for
Unpublished Manuscripts 425

Authorship 212

Autumn House Fiction Prize 426

Autumn House Poetry, Fiction, and
Nonfiction Prizes 426

Autumn House Press 336

Avalon Literary Review, The 212

Avon Romance 337

AWP Award Series 426

Axelrod Agency, The 126

Azantian Literary Agency, Jennifer 126

Azro Press 337

Babel 213

Babybug 213

Baen Books 337

Bailiwick Press 338

Baker Books 338

Balcones Fiction Prize 426

Baltimore Comic-Con 462

Baltimore Review Contests, The 426

Baltimore Review, The 213

Baltimore Writers' Conference 462

Balzer & Bray 338

Bancroft Press 338

Bangalore Review, The 214

Bantam Books 339

Barbaric Yawp 214

Barbour Publishing, Inc. 339

Barcelona Review, The 214

Bard Fiction Prize 426

Barer Literary, LLC 126

Barrett Books, Inc., Loretta 126

Barron's Literary Management 127

Batchelder Award, Mildred L. 427

Bateau 214

Bayou 215

Bay to Ocean Writers' Conference 462

Bear Deluxe Magazine, The 215

Beginnings Publishing Inc. 215

Behrman House Inc. 340

Bellevue Literary Press 340

Bellevue Literary Review 215

Bellevue Literary Review Goldenberg
    Prize for Fiction 427

Bellingham Review 216

Beloit Fiction Journal 216

Bender Literary Agency, Faye 127

Bennett Fellowship, George 427

Berkeley Fiction Review 217

Berkley Books 340

Best Lesbian Erotica 427

Bethany House Publishers 340

Beyond Centauri 217

Big Muddy 217

Bilingual Review 217

Binghamton University John Gardner
    Fiction Book Award 427

Binnacle, The 218

Bitter Oleander, The 218

BkMk Press 340

Blackbird 218

Black Heron Press 341

Black Lace 219

Black Lawrence Press 341

Black Memorial Prizes, James Tait 427

Black Mountain Press 341

Black River Chapbook Competition, The
    428

Black Velvet Seductions Publishing 341

Black Warrior Review 219

Blair, Publisher, John F. 342

BlazeVOX [books] 342

Bleecker Street Associates, Inc. 128

Blockbuster Plot Intensive Writing
    Workshops (Santa Cruz) 472

Blood Lotus 219

Bloomsbury Children's Books 342

Blueline 219

Blue Mesa Review 220

Blue Ridge Christian 464

Bluestem 220

BOA Editions, Ltd. 342

Boardman Tasker Award for Mountain
    Literature, The 428

Bold Strokes Books, Inc. 343

BookEnds, LLC 128

Bookouture 343

Books-in-Progress Conference 466

Books & Such Literary Agency 129

Booming Ground Online Writers Studio
    476

Borealis Press, Ltd. 343

Boston Globe-Horn Book Awards 428

Boston Review 220

Boulevard 220

Boulevard Short Fiction Contest for
    Emerging Writers 428

Bova Literary Agency, The Barbara 129

Bradford Literary Agency 130

Branden Publishing Co., Inc 343

Bread Loaf in Sicily Writers' Conference
    477

Bread Loaf Orion Environmental Writers'
    Conference 460

Bread Loaf Writers' Conference 460

Briar Cliff Review Fiction, Poetry, and
    Creative Nonfiction Competition, The
    428

Briar Cliff Review, The 221

Bridport Prize, The 429

Brilliant Corners 221

British Czech and Slovak Association Writing Competition 429

Broadkill Review, The 221

Broadway Books 343

Broken Jaw Press 344

Bronze Man Books 344

Brown Literary Agency, Inc., Andrea 130

Brown Literary Agency, Tracy 132

Brown, Ltd., Curtis 131

Brucedale Press, The 344

Bryant Literary Review 222

Bullitt Publishing 344

Burnaby Writers' Society Contest 429

Burnside Review 222

Business of Pet Writing Conference, The 460

Button 222

Bykofsky Associates, Inc., Sheree 183

By Light Unseen Media 345

Byron Bay Writers Festival 477

Cadet Quest Magazine 223

Cafe Irreal, The 223

Caine Prize for African Writing, The 429

Caketrain 223

Calamari Press 345

California Book Awards 429

California Crime Writers Conference 472

Calkins Creek 345

Callaloo 223

Calliope 224

Calyx 224

Cameron & Associates, Kimberley 132

Campbell Memorial Award for Best Science Fiction Novel of the Year, John W. 429

Canadian Authors Association Award for Fiction 429

Canadian Writer's Journal 224

Candlewick Press 345

Canterbury House Publishing, Ltd. 346

Cape Cod Writers Center Annual Conference 460

Capilano Review, The 224

Capon Springs Writers' Workshop 466

Cappon Fiction Award, The Alexander Patterson 429

Carolina Wren Press 346

Cartwheel Books 346

Carvainis Agency, Inc., Maria 133

Cascade Writing Contest & Awards 430

Castiglia Literary Agency 133

Cat Callan Humor Prize, Jamie 430

Cattarulla Award for Best Short Story, Kay 430

Cave Hollow Press 346

CC&D 225

Cedar Fort, Inc. 347

Celebration of Southern Literature 464

Cha 225

Chaffin Journal 226

Chapman 226

Chapman-Andrews First Novel Award, Peggy 430

Chariton Review 430

Chariton Review, The 226

Charlesbridge Publishing 347

Chattahoochee Review, The 226

Chautauqua Literary Journal 227

Chelius Literary Agency, Jane 134

Cheney Literary Associates, LLC, Elyse 134

Chicago Quarterly Review 227

Chicago Writers Conference 467

Children's Brains are Yummy (CBAY) Books 348

Child's Play (International) Ltd. 348

Chiron Review 227

Christian Adventure/Romance Fiction Contest 430

Christian Books Today Ltd 348

Christian Focus Publications 348

Chronicle Books 348

Chronicle Books for Children 349

Cicada Magazine 227

Cimarron Review 228

Cincinnati Review, The 228

City of Vancouver Book Award, The 431

Claremont Review, The 228

Clarion Books 349

Clarion West Writers Workshop 474

Clark Associates, WM 193

Clark Street Review 228

Cleis Press 349

Cloud Rodeo 229

Coach House Books 350

Coal City Review 229

C/Oasis 229

Cobblestone 229

Coffe House Press 350

Cold Mountain Review 230

Colorado Book Awards 431

Colorado Review 230

Columbia 230

Common Ground Review 230

Compass Talent 134

Conceit Magazine 230

Concho River Review 231

Confrontation 231

Congdon Associates Inc., Don 134

Constable & Robinson, Ltd. 350

Contrary 231

Convergence 232

Coover Agency, The Doe 135

CopTales Contest 431

Corvisiero Literary Agency 135

Coteau Books 351

Cottonwood 232

Country Dog Review, The 233

Covenant Communications, Inc. 351

Crab Orchard Review 233

Craigmore Creations 351

Crazyhorse 233

Crazyhorse Prizes in Fiction, Nonfiction,
    & Poetry, The 431

Creative With Words Publications 233

Crescent Moon Publishing 351

Crested Butte Writers Conference 469

Crichton & Associates 136

Cricket 233

Cricket Books 351

Crimson Romance 352

Critique My Novel Writing Contest 431

Crown Publishing Group 352

C&R Press 345

Crucible 234

Crucible Poetry and Fiction Competition,
    The 432

Crystal Spirit Publishing, Inc. 352

Cup of Tea Books 352

Current Accounts 234

D4EO Literary Agency 136

Dalhousie Review, The 234

Dana Awards in the Novel, Short Fiction,
    and Poetry 432

Daniel Literary Group 136

DargonZine 234

Darhansoff & Verrill Literary Agents 137

Dark Oak Mystery Contest 432

Dark, The 235

DAW Books, Inc. 352

Dawson Associates, Liza 166

Dead Mule School of Southern Literature,
    The 235

Dead of Winter 432

Debut Dagger, The 432

DeChiara Literary Agency, The Jennifer
    137

DeFiore & Co. 138

Delacorte Press 353

Delaware Division of the Arts 432

Delbourgo Associates, Inc., Joelle 137

Del Rey Books 353

Demontreville Press, Inc. 353

Denver Quarterly 235

descant 236

Descant 235

Desert Dreams Conference 472

Detroit Working Writers Annual Writers Conference 467

Diagram 236

DIAGRAM/New Michigan Press Chapbook Contest 433

Dial Books for Young Readers 353

Dijkstra Literary Agency, Sandra 138

DISLOCATE 236

Diversion Press 354

Divertir 354

DNA Press and Nartea Publishing 354

Dobie Paisano Writer's Fellowship 433

Donovan Literary, Jim 139

Down East Books 354

Down in the Dirt 237

Down the Shore Publishing 354

Doyen Literary Services, Inc. 139

Dramatics Magazine 237

Ducts 237

Dufour Editions 355

Dunham Literary, Inc. 140

Dunne Books, Thomas 355

Dunow, Carlson, & Lerner Agency 140

Dutton Adult Trade 355

Dutton Children's Books 355

Dyer Fiction Prize, Jack 433

Eakin Press 355

Eastham Flash Fiction Prize. Mary Kennedy 433

East/West Literary Agency, LLC 141

Eaton Literary Agency's Annual Awards Program 433

Ecco Press, The 356

Eclectica 238

Ecotone 238

Edelstein Literary Agency, Anne 141

Edge Science Fiction and Fantasy Publishing/Tesseract Books 356

Eerdmans Books for Young Readers 356

Eerdmans Publishing Co., William 357

Egmont USA 357

Ehrlich Literary Management, LLC, Judith 142

Ellenberg Literary Agency, Ethan 141

Ellery Queen's Mystery Magazine 238

Ellipsis Magazine 239

Ellora's Cave Publishing, Inc. 357

Emily Contest, The 433

Enete Enterprises 357

English Literary Agency, The Elaine P. 142

English Tea Rose Press 358

Eos 358

Epiphany epiphmag.com-Where Creativity and Inspiration Evolve! 239

Epoch 240

Esquire 240

Essays & Fictions 240

Eth Literary Representation, Felicia 143

European Judaism 241

Evangel 241

Evansville Review 241

Evening Street Review 241

Faber & Faber Ltd 358

Fablers Monthly Contest 433

FACES Magazine 241

Failbetter.com 242

Fairbank Literary Representation 143

Faircloth Review, The 242

Fairy Tale Fiction Contest 434

Fantagraphics Books, Inc. 358

Fantastic Books Publishing 359

Far Horizons Award for Short Fiction, The 434

Farrar, Straus & Giroux 359

Farrar, Straus & Giroux for Young Readers 359

Faulkner Award for Excellence in Writing, The Virginia 434

Faultline 242

Feldman Poetry Prize, The Jean 453

Feminist Studies 242

Fence Books 359

Festival of Faith and Writing 467

Fickle Muses 243

Fickling Books, David 360

Fiction 243

Fiddlehead, The 243

filling Station 244

Finch Literary Agency, Diana 144

Fineline Competition 434

FinePrint Literary Management 144

First Class 244

First Edition Design Publishing 360

First Line, The 244

First Novel Contest 434

firstwriter.com International Short Story Contest 434

Fish Publishing Flash Fiction Competition 435

Fish Short Story Prize 435

Five Chapters 244

Five Points 245

Five Star Publications, Inc. 360

Flannery Literary 144

Flathead River Writers Conference 475

Flint Hills Review 245

Florida Christian Writers Conference 465

Florida Review, The 245

Floyd County Moonshine 245

Flux 360

Flyway 246

Fogged Clarity 246

Folded Word 360

Foliate Oak Literary Magazine 247

Folio 247

Folio, A Literary Journal at American University 247

Folio Literary Management, LLC 145

Foreword Literary 145

ForeWord Magazine Book of the Year Awards 435

Forward Movement 360

Foundry Literary + Media 146

Fourteen Hills 247

Four Way Books 361

Fox Literary 146

Frances Lincoln Children's Books 361

Francis Short Story Competition, H.E. 435

Franklin Associates, Ltd., Lynn C. 147

Fraser Award For Best Translation of a Book, Soeurette Diehl 435

FreeFall Magazine 248

FreeFall Short Prose and Poetry Contest 435

Free Spirit Publishing, Inc. 361

Freestone/Peachtree, Jr. 361

FreeXpresSion 248

French-American and the Florence Gould Foundations Translation Prizes, The 435

Freymann Literary Agency, Sarah Jane 147

Friedman and Co., Inc., Fredrica 147

Friedman Literary Agency, Rebecca 176

Frogmore Papers, The 248

Front & Centre 249

Fugue Literary Magazine 249

Full Circle Literary, LLC 148

Fun in the Sun 466

Funny Times 249

FutureCycle Press 361

Gallt Literary Agency, Nancy 149

Garbanzo Literary Journal 250

Garbled Transmissions Magazine 250

Gargoyle 250

Gathering of the Tribes, A 203

Gelfman Schneider Literary Agents, Inc. 149

Georgetown Review 251, 436

Georgia Review, The 251

Gettysburg Review, The 251

GHLL 251

Ginosko 252

Gival Press 362

Gival Press Novel Award 436

Gival Press Short Story Award 436

Glencannon Press, The 362

Glimmer Train's Family Matters Contest 436

Glimmer Train's Fiction Open 436

Glimmer Train's Short-Story Award for New Writers 436

Glimmer Train Stories 252

Glimmer Train's Very Short Fiction Contest 437

Godine, Publisher, David R. 362

Golden Books for Young Readers Group 362

Golomb Literary Agency, The Susan 149

Goodman Literary Agency, Irene 150

Goose Lane Editions 362

Gothic City Press 252

Goumen & Smirnova Literary Agency 150

Governor General's Literary Award for Fiction 437

Gover Prize, The 437

Grain 253

Grasslimb 253

Grayson Literary Agency, Ashley 151

Graywolf Press 362

Great Lakes Colleges Association New Writers Award 437

Greenburger Associates, Inc., Sanford J. 151

Green Hills Literary Lantern 253

Greenhouse Literary Agency, The 152

Green Literary Agency, LLC, Kathryn 152

Green Mountains Review 253

Green Mountain Writers Conference 460

Greensboro Review, The 254

Greenwillow Books 363

Grey Gecko Press 363

Griffin, The 254

Grinberg Literary Agency, Jill 153

Grosjean Literary Agency, Jill 153

Grosset & Dunlap Publishers 363

Gross Literary Agency, Laura 153

Groundwood Books 363

Grub Street National Book Prize 437

GUD Magazine 254

Guernica Editions 363

Guernica Magazine 254

Gulf Coast 255

Gulf Stream Magazine 255

G.W. Review, The 255

Hachai Publishing 364

Hadassah Magazine 256

Hadley Rille Books 364

Hadow/Donald Stuart Short Story Competition, Lyndall 437

Haight Ashbury Literary Journal 256

Hamilburg Agency, The Mitchell J. 154

Hammett Prize 438

Hampton Roads Publishing Co., Inc. 364

Hampton Roads Writers Conference 464

Harcourt, Inc., Trade Division 365

Hardboiled 256

Harootian Short Story Contest, Rose 438

HarperCollins Canada, Ltd. 365

HarperCollins Children's Books/ HarperCollins Publishers 365

Harper's Magazine 256

HarperTeen 365

Harpur Palate 257

Harrington & Harrington Press 365

Hartline Literary Agency 154

Harvest House Publishers 366

Hawaii Review 257

Hawkins & Associates, Inc., John 154

Hayden's Ferry Review 257

Heacock Hill Literary Agency, Inc. 155

Hearne Flash Fiction Contest, Wilda 438

Hedgebrook 475

Heinz Literature Prize, Drue 438

Helix, The 257

HelloHorror 258

Hemingway Short Story Competition,
 Lorian 438

Hendrick-Long Publishing Co., Inc. 366

Henshaw Group, Richard 155

Hidden Value Group 156

Highland Press Publishing 366

Highlights for Children 258

Hillerman Prize, Tony 438

Hillerman Writer's Conference, Tony 471

Hipso Media 366

Hodder Fellowship, The 439

Holiday House, Inc. 366

Holt, Henry 367

Home Planet News 259

Hopewell Publications 367

Hopkins Literary Associates 156

Horizons 259

Hotel Amerika 259

Houghton Mifflin Harcourt Books for
 Children 367

Houghton Mifflin Harcourt Co. 367

House of Anansi Press 367

Howard/John H. Reid Fiction & Essay
 Contest, Tom 439

Howe/Boston Authors Award, The Julia
 Ward 439

How to Be Published Workshops 466

Hoyns & Poe/Faulkner Fellowships,
 Henry 439

HQN Books 367

Hubbard's Writers of the Future Contest,

L. Ron 439

Hudson Review, The 260

Hunger Mountain 260

Hurst Children's Book Prize, Carol Otis
 439

Hurst Literary Management, Andrea 156

ICM Partners 158

Idaho Review, The 260

Ideals Children's Books and Candycane
 Press 368

Ideomancer 260

Idiom 23 261

IDW Publishing 368

Ilium Press 368

Illumination Arts 368

Illya's Honey 261

Image Comics 368

Images SI, Inc. 368

Immedium 369

Independent Publisher Book Awards 440

Indiana Review 261

Indiana Review ½ K (Short-Short/Prose-
 Poem) Prize 440

Indiana Review Fiction Contest 440

Individual Excellence Awards 440

InkWell Management, LLC 157

Innovative Publishers Inc. 369

Insomniac Press 369

Interlink Publishing Group, Inc. 369

International 3-Day Novel Contest 440

International Music Camp Creative
 Writing Workshop 468

International Reading Association
 Children's and Young Adults Book
 Awards 441

International Women's Fiction Festival
 477

Interpreter's House 261

Iowa Review Award in Poetry, Fiction,
 and Nonfiction, The 441

Iowa Review, The 261

Iowa Short Fiction Award, The 441

Island 262

Italian Americana 262

Italica Press 369

Jabberwock Review 262

Jabberwocky Literary Agency 158

Jack and Jill 263

Jacobs Religious Essay Prize Category, Tilia Klebenov 441

James River Writers Conference 464

J de S Associates, Inc. 158

Jerry Jazz Musician New Short Fiction Award 441

JET Literary Associates 159

Jewish Currents 263

Jewish Lights Publishing 370

J Journal 263

Jones Award for Best Work of Fiction, Jesse H. 441

Jones First Novel Fellowship, James 441

Journal, The 263

JourneyForth 370

Journey Into the Imagination 461

Jupiter Gardens Press 370

Juvenile Adventure Fiction Contest 442

Kachemak Bay Writers Conference 475

Kaeden Books 371

Kaimana 264

Kaleidoscope 264

Kamehameha Publishing 371

Kane/Miller Book Publishers 371

Kar-Ben Publishing 372

Kelly Point Publishing LLC 372

Kelsey Review, The 264

Kentucky Monthly 265

Kentucky Women Writers Conference 467

Kentucky Writers Conference 467

Kenyon Review, The 265

Kenyon Review Writers Workshop 467

Kidd Literary Agency, Inc., Virginia 159

Kids Can Press 372

Killer Nashville 465

Kindling Words East 461

Klinger, Inc., Harvey 160

Kneerim, Williams & Bloom 160

Knopf, Alfred A. 372

Knopf Publishing Group 373

Knox Robinson Publishing 373

Koeppel Short Fiction Award, E.M. 442

Kraas Literary Agency 160

Kregel Publications 373

Krichevsky Literary Agency, Inc., Stuart 161

Kroll Literary Agency, Inc., Edite 161

KT Literary, LLC 161

Ladybug 265

La Kancerkliniko 265

Lake Effect 265

Lake Superior Magazine 266

LA Literary Agency, The 162

Lampack Agency, Inc., Peter 162

Landfall 266

Langlie, Literary Agent, Laura 163

La Petite Zine 266

Larsen/Elizabeth Pomada, Literary Agents, Michael 163

Las Vegas Writers Conference 472

Laube Agency, The Steve 164

Laurel-Leaf 373

Laurel Review, The 266

Lawrence Foundation Prize 442

Leading Edge 267

League of Utah Writers Contest 442

Ledge Hill Publishing 373

Ledge Magazine, The 267

Lee & Low Books 374

Le Forum 267

Left Curve 267

Lerner Publishing Group 374

Les Figues Press 374

Les Figues Press NOS Book Contest 442

Lethe Press 374

Let's Write Literary Contest 442

Leviant Memorial Prize in Yiddish Studies, Fenia and Yaakov 443

Levine Books, Arthur A. 375

Levine Greenberg Literary Agency, Inc. 164

Levine Literary Agency, Paul S. 165

Liguorian 268

Lilith Magazine 268

Lillenas Publishing Co. 375

Linnell Publishing, R.C. 375

Lippincott Massie McQuilkin 165

Liquid Silver Books 375

Listening Eye, The 268

Literal Latté 269

Literal Latté Fiction Award 443

Literal Latte Short Shorts Contest 443

Literary Group International, The 166

Literary Juice 269

Literary Mama 269

Literary Review, The 269

Little, Brown and Co. Adult Trade Books 375

Little, Brown and Co. Books for Young Readers 376

Little Tiger Press 376

Livingston Press 376

London Magazine, The 269

Long Life 270

Long Story, The 270

Loose Id 376

Lost Horse Press 377

Lost Lake Folk Opera 270

Louisiana Literature 271

Louisiana Review, The 271

Louisiana State University Press 377

Lowenstein Associates Inc. 167

Lucky Marble Books 377

Lullwater Review 271

LUNGFULL!magazine 271

Maass Literary Agency, Donald 167

MacDowell Colony, The 461

MacGregor Literary Inc. 168

MacGuffin, The 272

Mackey Short Story Prize Category, The Mary 443

Madison Review, The 272

Magazine of Fantasy & Science Fiction, The 272

Magination Press 377

Main Street Rag Publishing Company 377

Main Street Rag, The 272

Malahat Review Novella Prize, The 443

Malahat Review, The 273

Mandala Publishing 377

Mann Agency, Carol 169

Manoa 273

Manor House Publishing, Inc. 378

Mansion Street Literary Management 169

Manus & Associates Literary Agency, Inc. 169

Marine Techniques Publishing 378

Marshall Agency, The Evan 170

Martell Agency, The 170

Martin Sisters Publishing, LLC 378

Marvel Comics 378

Massachusetts Review, The 273

Maverick Musicals and Plays 379

McBooks Press 379

McBride Literary Agency, Margret 170

McCarthy Agency, LLC, The 171

McCarthy Prize in Short Fiction, Mary 443

McDonald & Woodward Publishing Co., The 379

McElderry Books, Margaret K. 379

McGill Agency Inc., The 171

McGinnis-Ritchie Memorial Award, The 443

Medallion Media Group 379

Melange Books, LLC 380

Memphis Magazine Fiction Contest 443

Mendel Media Group, LLC 171

Mendocino Coast Writers Conference 472

MensBook Journal 273

Meridian 273

Meriwether Publishing Ltd. 380

Merriam Press 380

Messianic Jewish Publishers 380

Meyerson Prize for Fiction, David Nathan 444

Michigan Quarterly Review 274

MicroHorror 274

Mid-American Review 275

Midsummer Tale, A 425

Midway Journal 275

Midwest Writers Workshop 467

Milkweed Editions 381

Milkweed for Young Readers 381

Milton Center Postgraduate Fellowship, The 444

Mississippi Review 275

Mississippi Review Prize 444

Missouri Review, The 275

Missouri Writers' Guild Conference 469

Mobius 276

Mondial 381

Montrose Christian Writers' Conference 463

Moody Publishers 381

Moore Community Workshops, Jenny McKean 463

Morpheus Tales 276

Moveable Type Management 172

Mslexia 276

Mura Literary, Dee 172

Muse and the Marketplace 463

Mythic Delirium 276

Na'amat Woman 277

Naggar Literary Agency, Inc., Jean V. 173

Napa Valley Writers' Conference 472

Nassau Review 278

National Outdoor Book Awards 444

National Writers Association Foundation Conference 469

National Writers Association Novel Writing Contest 444

National Writers Association Short Story Contest 444

Natural Bridge 278

Nautical & Aviation Publishing Co., The 382

NBM Publishing 382

Nebo 278

Necrology Shorts 278

Nelligan Prize for Short Fiction, The 444

Nelson Literary Agency 173

Neon Magazine 279

NETWO Writers Conference 469

Neutrino Short-Short Contest, The 445

New England Review 279

New Issues Poetry & Prose 382

New Jersey Romance Writers Put Your Heart in a Book Conference 463

New Leaf Literary & Media, Inc. 174

New Letters 279

New Letters Literary Awards 445

New Libri Press 382

New Madrid 280

New Millennium Writings 280

New Ohio Review 280

New Orleans Review 280

New South 281

New Victoria Publishers 382

New Welsh Review 281

new writer, the 281

New Yorker, The 281

Nimrod Annual Writers' Workshop 470

Ninth Letter 281

Nite-Writer's International Literary Arts

Journal 282
non + X 282
Normal School, The 282
North American Review 283
North Atlantic Books 383
North Carolina Arts Council Regional
    Artist Project Grants 445
North Carolina Literary Review 283
North Carolina Writers' Network Fall
    Conference 465
North Dakota Quarterly 283
Northern Colorado Writers Conference
    470
Northwind 283
Nortia Press 383
Norton & Company, Inc., W.W. 383
Notre Dame Review 284
Now & Then 284
Nth Degree 284
nthposition 285
Oak Tree Press 383
Ocean Magazine 285
Oceanview Publishing 384
O'Connor Award for Short Fiction, Frank
    445
O'Connor Award for Short Fiction, The
    Flannery 445
Odyssey Fantasy Writing Workshop 461
Ohioana Book Awards 445
Ohioana Walter Rumsey Marvin Grant
    445
Old Harbour Press 384
On Spec 285
OnStage Publishing 384
On the Premises 285
On The Premises Contest 446
Ooligan Press 385
Open Season Awards 446
Orca Book Publishers 385
Orchard Books 386
Oregon Christian Writers Summer

Conference 475
Oregon Literary Fellowships 446
Orson Scott Card's InterGalactic
    Medicine Show 225
Outdoor Writers Association of America
    Annual Conference 476
Outer Art 286
Overlook Press, The 386
Overtime 286
Owen Publishers, Peter 386
Owen, Richard C., Publishers, Inc. 386
Oxford Magazine 286
Oyez Review 286
Oyster Boy Review 286
Ozark Creative Writers, Inc. Conference
    473
Pacifica Literary Review 287
Pacific Coast Children's Writers Whole-
    Novel Workshop 473
Pacific Northwest Writers Assn. Summer
    Writer's Conference 476
Pacific Press Publishing Association 386
Packingtown Review 287
Paddlefish 287
PageSpring Publishing 387
Painted Bride Quarterly 287
Palari Publishing 387
Pantheon Books 387
Paperplates 287
Paradise Cay Publications 387
Paris Review, The 288
Park Literary Group, LLC 174
Passages North 288
Passion 288
Patchen Award for the Innovative Novel,
    Kenneth 446
Paterson Fiction Prize, The 446
Paterson Literary Review 288
Paton Literary Agency, Kathi J. 174
Paul Dry Books 387
Paumanok Review, The 289

Paycock Press 388

Peace Hill Press 388

Peachtree Children's Books 388

Peachtree Publishers, Ltd. 388

Pearl 289

Pearl Short Story Prize 446

Pearson Award, Judith Siegel 446

Pedestal Magazine, The 289

Pedlar Press 388

Pelican Publishing Company 389

Penguin Group USA 389

Pennsylvania English 289

Pennsylvania Literary Journal 290

Pennwriters Conference 463

Penny-Farthing Press, Inc. 389

Penthouse Variations 290

Peregrine 290

Perennial 389

Perkins Agency, L. 175

Permafrost 290

Permanent Press, The 390

Persea Books 390

Persimmon Tree 291

Philadelphia Stories 291

Philadelphia Writers' Conference 463

Philomel Books 390

Phoebe 291

Piano Press 391

Piatkus Books 391

Picador USA 391

Piccadilly Press 391

Pilgrimage Magazine 291

Piñata Books 391

Pinch, The 292

Pineapple Press, Inc. 392

Pink Chameleon, The 292

Pinyon Poetry 292

Pisgah Review 292

Plan B Press 392

PLANET-The Welsh Internationalist 293

Pleiades 293

Plexus Publishing, Inc. 392

Ploughshares 293

PMS poemmemoirstory 294

PNWA Literary Contest 446

Pocket Books 392

Pockets 294

POCKETS Fiction-Writing Contest 447

Pocol Press 392

Poe Award, Edgar Allan 447

Poetica Magazine, Contemporary Jewish
    Writing 294

Poetry International 295

Pointed Circle 295

POISONED PENCIL, THE 393

Poisoned Pen Press 393

Polyphony H.S. 295

Porter Prize for Fiction, The Katherine
    Anne 447

Portland Monthly 296

Portland Review 296

Possibility Press 393

POST ROAD 296

Potomac Review 296

Prairie Journal, The 297

Prairie Schooner 297

Prairie Winds 297

Premonitions 297

Prentis Literary, Linn 175

Press 53 394

Press 53 Award for Short Fiction 447

Prime Number Magazine Awards 447

Prism International 298

Prism International Annual Short Fiction
    Contest 448

Prism International Annual Short Fiction,
    Poetry, and CreativeNonfiction
    Contests 447

Prufrock Press, Inc. 394

Pseudopod 298

P.S Literary Agency 176

Puerto del Sol 299

Puffin Books 394

Purple Dragonfly Book Awards 448

PUSH 394

Putnam's Sons Hardcover, GP 395

Quarter After Eight 299

Quarterly West 299

Queen's Quarterly 299

Quixote Press 395

Raddall Atlantic Fiction Award, Thomas H. 448

Raffelock Award for Publishing Excellence, David 449

Rag, The 300

Rainbow Rumpus 300

Raincoast Book Distribution, Ltd. 395

Rain Town Press 395

Raleigh Review Literary & Arts Magazine 300

Random House Children's Books 395

Random House Foundation, Inc. Creative Writing Competition 449

Ransom Publishing 396

Rattapallax 301

Raven Chronicles, The 301

Razorbill 396

RBC Bronwen Wallace Memorial Award, The 449

Reader, The 301

Reality Street 396

Redactions 302

Red Deer Press 396

Red Hen Press 397

Redivider 302

Red Rock Review 302

Red Sage Publishing, Inc. 397

Red Tuque Books, Inc. 397

Reed Magazine 302

Reed Publishers, Robert D. 397

Rees Literary Agency, Helen 176

Reform Judaism 302

Regal Literary Agency 177

Renaissance House 397

Review, Echo Ink 238

Rhino 303

Ring of Fire Publishing LLC 397

Ripple Grove Press 398

Rittenberg Literary Agency, Inc., Ann 178

River City Publishing 398

Riverhead Books 398

River Styx Magazine 303

RLR Associates, Ltd. 178

Roaring Brook Press 398

Robbins Literary Agency, B.J. 178

Rockford Review, The 303

Rocky Mountain Fiction Writers Colorado Gold 470

Rogers Writers' Trust Fiction Prize, The 449

Romance Writers of America National Conference 470

Ronsdale Press 399

Rose Alley Press 399

Rosenberg Group, The 179

Roth Award, Lois 449

Rotrosen Agency LLC, Jane 179

Royal Dragonfly Book Awards 449

RT Booklovers Convention 461

Sacred City Productions 303

Saint Martin's Press, LLC 399

Saint Mary's Press 399

Sakura Publishing & Technologies 399

Salmagundi 304

Salt Cay Writers Retreat 477

Salvo Press 399

Samhain Publishing, Ltd 400

Sandeen Prize in Poetry and the Richard Sullivan Prize in Short Fiction, Ernest 449

Sanders & Associates, Victoria 179

San Diego State University Writers' Conference 473

Sandy River Review 304

San Francisco Writers Conference 473

Sarabande Books, Inc. 400

Saranac Review, The 304

Saskatchewan Festival of Words 476

Sasquatch Books 400

Savage Kick Literary Magazine, The 305

Scaglione Prize for a Translation of a Literary Work, Aldo and Jeanne 450

Scarletta Press 401

Scars Editor's Choice Awards, The 450

SCBWI Winter Conference on Writing and Illustrating for Children 461

Schiavone Literary Agency, Inc. 180

Scholastic Press 401

School for Writers Fall Workshop, The 476

Schreiber Prize for Humorous Fiction & Nonfiction, The Mona 450

Schulman Literary Agency, Susan 180

Scott Novel Excerpt Prize Category, Joanna Catherine 450

ScreaminMamas 305

ScreaminMamas Magical Fiction Contest 450

Scribblers House, LLC Literary Agency 181

Scribe Agency, LLC 181

Scribe Publications 401

Scriptapalooza Television Writing Competition 450

Seal Press 401

Seattle Review, The 305

Second Story Press 402

Secret Agent Man 181

Seedling Continental Press 402

Seek 306

Seligman, Literary Agent, Lynn 182

Serendipity Literary Agency, LLC 182

Seriously Good Books 402

Seven Stories Press 402

Severn House Publishers 403

Sewanee Review, The 306

Sewanee Writers' Conference 465

Seymour Agency, The 183

Shaara Award for Excellence in Civil War Fiction, Michael 451

Shambhala Publications, Inc. 403

Shenandoah 306

Sherman Associates, Inc., Wendy 184

Sherman & Associates, Ken 184

SHINE brightly 306

Shipwreckt Books Publishing Company LLC 403

Short Stuff 306

Sierra Nevada Review 307

Silver Leaf Books, LLC 403

Simmons Literary Agency, Jeffrey 185

Simon & Schuster 403

Simon & Schuster Adult Publishing Group 403

Simon & Schuster Books for Young Readers 404

Skinner House Books 404

Skipping Stones Honor (Book) Awards 451

Skipping Stones Youth Awards 451

Sleeping Bear Press 404

Slopen Literary Agency, Beverley 185

Slote Award, The Bernice 451

Slow Trains Literary Journal 307

Small Beer Press 404

Smith Book Award, Byron Caldwell 451

Smith Editors' Prize in Fiction, Essay and Poetry, Jeffrey E. 451

Snow Writing Contest, Kay 451

Snowy Egret 307

Snreview 307

Society of Children's Book Writers & Illustrators Annual Summer Conference on Writing and Illustrating for Children 473

Society of Midland Authors Award 452

Soft Skull Press Inc. 404

Soho Press, Inc. 405

Soldier of Fortune 308

So to Speak 308

Sourcebooks Casablanca 405

Sourcebooks Landmark 405

South Carolina Review 308

South Carolina Writers Workshop 465

South Coast Writers Conference 476

South Dakota Review 308

Southeastern Writers Association--
    Annual Writers Workshop 466

Southeast Review, The 309

Southern Humanities Review 309

Southern Review, The 310

Southwestern American Literature 310

Southwest Review 310

Sou'wester 311

SPACE (Small Press and Alternative
    Comics Expo) 468

Spectrum Literary Agency 186

Speculative Edge, The 311

Spencerhill Associates 186

Spieler Agency, The 186

Spitball 311

Squaw Valley Community of Writers 473

St. Anthony Messenger 311

Starcherone Books 405

Stauffer Associates, Nancy 187

Steele-Perkins Literary Agency 187

Sternig & Byrne Literary Agency 187

Still Crazy 312

Stirring 312

Stone Bridge Press 406

Stoneslide Books 406

Stone Soup 312

Story Bytes 312

storySouth 313

Story Weavers Conference 470

Stray Branch, The 313

Straylight 313

Strothman Agency, LLC, The 188

Struggle 314

Subito Press 406

subTerrain 314

subTERRAIN Magazine's Annual
    Literary Awards Competition 452

Subtropics 314

Summerset Review, The 315

Summer Writing Program 471

Sunbury Press, Inc. 406

Sun, The 315

Suspense Magazine 315

Swan Isle Press 406

Sweeney Agency, LLC, Emma 188

Sycamore Review 315

Sylvan Dell Publishing 407

SynergEbooks 407

Tafelberg Publishers 407

Talcott Notch Literary 189

Talent Drips Erotic Literary EZine 316

Talese, Nan A. 408

Tales of the Talisman 316

Talking River 316

Tanglewood Books 408

Tantor Media 408

Taos Summer Writers' Conference 471

Teal Literary Agency, Patricia 189

Teen Mystery Fiction Contest 452

Telluride Magazine 316

Terrain.org 317

Texas Christian Writers' Conference 471

Texas Review 317

Texas Tech University Press 408

THE BENT AGENCY 127

THEMA 317

Third Coast 318

Thirty-Fourth Parallel - 34th Parallel 318

Thistledown Press Ltd. 408

Three Cheers and a Tiger 452

Threepenny Review, The 318

Thrillerfest 461
Thriller Fiction Contest 452
Tightrope Books 409
Timber Journal 318
Tin House 319
Tin House Books 409
Titan Press 409
TMCC Writers' Conference 474
Toad Suck Review 319
Toasted Cheese 319
Top Cow Productions, Inc. 409
Top Publications, Ltd. 409
Tor Books 409
Torch 319
Toronto Book Awards 453
Torquere Press 410
Torrey House Press, LLC 410
Touchwood Editions 410
Tradewind Books 410
Transatlantic Literary Agency 189
Transition 320
Triada U.S. Literary Agency, Inc. 190
Trident Media Group 190
TriQuarterly 320
Tristan Publishing 410
Tulane Review 320
Tupelo Press 411
Turnstone Press 411
Turn the Page Publishing LLC 411
Twilight Times Books 411
Tyndale House Publishers, Inc. 411
Tyrus Books 412
Unbridled Books 412
Undiscovered World Fiction Contest 453
Unicorn Writers Conference 461
Unity House 412
University of Georgia Press 412
University of Iowa Press 412
University of Michigan Press 412
University of Nebraska Press 413
University of Nevada Press 413

University of North Texas Press 413
University of Tampa Press 413
University of Wisconsin Press 414
Unter Agency, The 191
Upstart Crow Literary 191
Usborne Publishing 414
U.S. Catholic 320
UV-Madison Writers' Institute 468
Vehicule Press 414
Venture Literary 191
Verandah Literary & Art Journal 321
Versal 321
Vertigo 414
Vestal Review 321
Viking 414
Viking Children's Books 414
Villard Books 415
Vintage Anchor Publishing 415
Virginia Quarterly Review, The 322
Vivisphere Publishing 415
Viz Media LLC 415
Walker and Co. 415
Washington Writers' Publishing House 415
Wassnode Short Fiction Prize 453
WaterBrook Multnomah Publishing Group 416
Weiner Literary Agency, Cherry 192
Weingel-Fidel Agency, The 192
Weissman Literary, LLC, Larry 192
Wells Arms Literary 192
West Branch 322
Western Humanities Review 322
Western Psychological Services 416
Western Reserve Writers & Freelance Conference 468
Western Writers of America 453
Whidbey Island Writers' Conference 476
Whimsy Literary Agency, LLC 193
Whiskey Island Magazine 322
Whitaker House 416

Whitecap Books, Ltd. 416

White Mane Kids 416

Wild Child Publishing 417

Wild Rose Press 417

Wildstorm 417

Wild Violet 322

WILLA Literary Award 453

Willamette Writers Conference 476

Willard & Maple 323

William Morrow 417

Willow Review 323

Willow Springs 323

Wilshire Book Co. 418

Wilson Short Fiction Award, Gary 454

Winchester Writer's Conference, Festival
   and Bookfair, and In-Depth Writing
   Workshops 477

Windhover 324

WindRiver Publishing, Inc. 418

Wisconsin Book Festival 468

Wisconsin Institute for Creative Writing
   Fellowship 454

Wisconsin Review 324

Wisdom Publications 418

Witches and Pagans 324

Wolff Award in Fiction, Tobias 454

Wolf Literary Services, LLC 193

Wolfson Literary Agency 194

Woman's World 324

Women Writers Winter Retreat 468

Woodbine House 418

Worcester Review, The 325

Word Riot 325

Wordsong 419

Workers Write! 325

World Fantasy Awards 454

World's Best Short Short Story Fiction
   Contest, Narrative Nonfiction Contest,
   & Southeast Review Poetry Contest
   454

WOW! Women on Writing Quarterly
   Flash Fiction Contest 454

WriteLife Publishing, LLC 419

Write on the River 465

Write Place At the Write Time, The 326

Writer's Bloc 326

Writer's Digest Annual Writing
   Competition 454

Writer's Digest Conferences 461

Writer's Digest Popular Fiction Awards
   455

Writer's Digest Self-Published Book
   Awards 455

Writer's Digest Short Short Story
   Competition 455

Writers-Editors Network Annual
   International Writing Competition
   456

Writers' League of Texas Book Awards 456

Writers' Representatives, LLC 194

Writers@Work Conference 474

Writers' Workshop, The 465

Write-To-Publish Conference 468

Writing and Illustrating for Young Readers
   Conference 474

Writing Disorder, The 326

Wurlitzer, Helene, Foundation, The 471

Xavier Review 326

Yaddo 462

Yale Review, The 327

Yalobusha Review, The 327

Yellow Shoe Fiction Series 419

Yemassee 327

YMAA Publication Center 419

Zebra Books 420

Zeek 327

Zimmermann Literary Agency, Helen 194

Zoetrope 327

Zondervan 420

Zumaya Publications, LLC 420

ZYZZYVA 328